Getting Started is as EASY as 1, 2, 3 . . . 4!

1. Sign Up

Instructors register with myBusinessCourse.com

2. Setup Your Course

Add your class details and additional materials.

3. Invite Your Students

Students register using your unique course code.

4. Manage Your Course

Study, test, and grade assignments. It's simple!

Provide Instruction and Practice 24/7

- Assign homework from your Cambridge Business Publishers textbook and have myBusinessCourse grade it for you automatically.
- With our eLectures, your students can revisit accounting topics as often as they like or until they master the topic.
- Guided Examples show students how to solve select problems.
- Make homework due before class to ensure students enter your classroom prepared.
- Upgrade to include the eBook and you have all the tools needed for an online course.

STUDENT SELF-STUDY OPTION

Not all instructors choose to incorporate **myBusinessCourse** into their course. In such cases, students can access the Self-Study option for MBC. The Self-Study option provides most of the learning tools available in the Instructor-Led courses, including:

- eLectures
- Guided Examples
- Practice Quizzes

The Self-Study option does not include homework assignments from the textbook. Only the Instructor-Led option includes homework assignments.

Want to learn more about myBusinessCourse?

Contact your sales representative or visit www.mybusinesscourse.com.

STUDENTS: Find your access code on the myBusinessCourse insert on the following pages. If you have a used copy of this textbook, you can purchase access online at www.mybusinesscourse.com.

Cambridge Business Publishers Series in Accounting

Financial Accounting

- **Financial Accounting for Undergraduates, 2e** by Ferris, Wallace, and Christensen
- **Financial Accounting, 4e** by Dyckman, Magee, and Pfeiffer
- **Financial Accounting for MBAs, 6e** by Easton, Wild, Halsey, and McAnally
- **Financial Accounting for Executives & MBAs, 3e** by Simko, Ferris, and Wallace
- **Cases in Financial Reporting, 7e** by Engel, Hirst, and McAnally

Managerial Accounting

- **Managerial Accounting, 7e** by Hartgraves & Morse
- **Cases in Managerial and Cost Accounting, 1e** by Allen, Brownlee, Haskins, and Lynch

Combined Financial & Managerial Accounting

- **Financial & Managerial Accounting for Decision Makers, 2e** by Dyckman, Magee, Pfeiffer, Hartgraves, and Morse
- **Financial & Managerial Accounting for MBAs, 4e** by Easton, Halsey, McAnally, Hartgraves, and Morse

Intermediate Accounting

- **Cases in Financial Reporting, 7e** by Engel, Hirst, and McAnally

Cost Accounting

- **Cases in Managerial and Cost Accounting, 1e** by Allen, Brownlee, Haskins, and Lynch

Financial Statement Analysis & Valuation

- **Financial Statement Analysis & Valuation, 4e** by Easton, McAnally, Sommers, and Zhang
- **Corporate Valuation, 1e** by Holthausen & Zmijewski
- **Cases in Financial Reporting, 7e** by Engel, Hirst, and McAnally

Advanced Accounting

- **Advanced Accounting, 2e** by Hamlen, Huefner, and Largay
- **Advanced Accounting, 2e** by Halsey & Hopkins

FASB Codification and eIFRS

- **Skills for Accounting and Auditing Research, 2e** by Collins

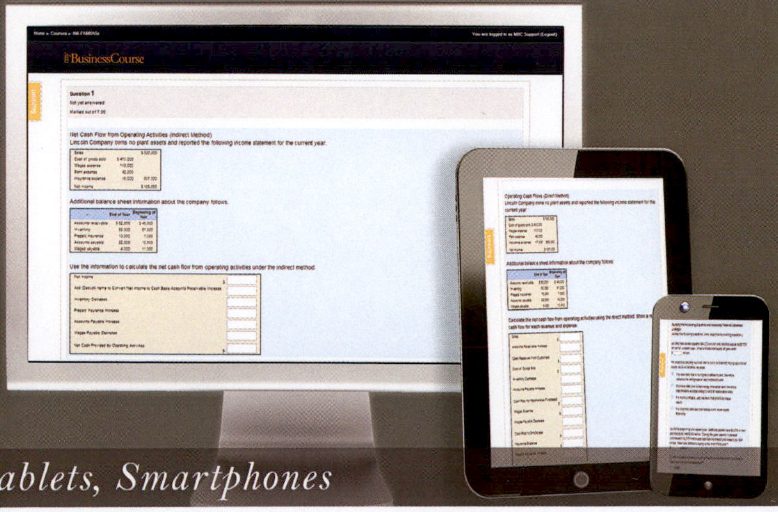

Sixth Edition

Financial Accounting for MBAs

Peter D. Easton

John J. Wild

Robert F. Halsey

Mary Lea McAnally

Cambridge
BUSINESS PUBLISHERS

To my daughters, Joanne and Stacey
—PDE

To my students and my loving family
—JJW

To my wife Ellie and children, Grace and Christian
—RFH

To my husband Brittan and children Loic, Cindy, Maclean, Quinn and Kay
—MLM

Cambridge Business Publishers

FINANCIAL ACCOUNTING FOR MBAs, Sixth Edition, by Peter D. Easton, John J. Wild, Robert F. Halsey, and Mary Lea McAnally.

Student Edition ISBN 978-1-61853-100-1

Bookstores & Faculty: to order this book, call **800-619-6473** or email **customerservice@cambridgepub.com.**

Students: to order this book, please visit the book's Website and order directly online.

Printed in the United States of America.
10 9 8 7 6 5 4 3 2 1

ABOUT THE AUTHORS

The combined skills and expertise of Easton, Wild, Halsey, and McAnally create the ideal team to author the first new financial accounting textbook for MBAs in more than a generation. Their collective experience in award- winning teaching, consulting, and research in the area of financial accounting and analysis provides a powerful foundation for this innovative textbook.

PETER D. EASTON is an expert in accounting and valuation and holds the Notre Dame Alumni Chair in Accountancy in the Mendoza College of Business. Professor Easton's expertise is widely recognized by the academic research community and by the legal community. Professor Easton frequently serves as a consultant on accounting and valuation issues in federal and state courts.

Professor Easton holds undergraduate degrees from the University of Adelaide and the University of South Australia. He holds a graduate degree from the University of New England and a PhD in Business Administration (majoring in accounting and finance) from the University of California, Berkeley.

Professor Easton's research on corporate valuation has been published in the *Journal of Accounting and Economics, Journal of Accounting Research, The Accounting Review, Contemporary Accounting Research, Review of Accounting Studies,* and *Journal of Business Finance and Accounting.* Professor Easton has served as an associate editor for 11 leading accounting journals and he is currently an associate editor for the *Journal of Accounting Research, Journal of Business Finance and Accounting,* and *Journal of Accounting, Auditing, and Finance.* He is an editor of the *Review of Accounting Studies.*

Professor Easton has held appointments at the University of Chicago, the University of California at Berkeley, Ohio State University, Macquarie University, the Australian Graduate School of Management, the University of Melbourne, Tilburg University, National University of Singapore, Seoul National University, and Nyenrode University. He is the recipient of numerous awards for excellence in teaching and in research. Professor Easton regularly teaches accounting analysis and security valuation to MBAs. In addition, Professor Easton has taught managerial accounting at the graduate level.

JOHN J. WILD is a distinguished professor of accounting and business at the University of Wisconsin at Madison. He previously held appointments at Michigan State University and the University of Manchester in England. He received his BBA, MS, and PhD from the University of Wisconsin.

Professor Wild teaches courses in accounting and analysis at both the undergraduate and graduate levels. He has received the Mabel W. Chipman Excellence-in-Teaching Award, the departmental Excellence-in-Teaching Award, and the MBA Teaching Excellence Award (twice) from the EMBA graduation classes at the University of Wisconsin. He also received the Beta Alpha Psi and Salmonson Excellence-in-Teaching Award from Michigan State University. Professor Wild is a past KPMG Peat Marwick National Fellow and is a prior recipient of fellowships from the American Accounting Association and the Ernst & Young Foundation.

Professor Wild is an active member of the American Accounting Association and its sections. He has served on several committees of these organizations, including the Outstanding Accounting Educator Award, Wildman Award, National Program Advisory, Publications, and Research Committees. Professor Wild is author of several best-selling books. His research articles on financial accounting and analysis appear in *The Accounting Review, Journal of Accounting Research, Journal of Accounting and Economics, Contemporary Accounting Research, Journal of Accounting, Auditing & Finance, Journal of Accounting and Public Policy, Journal of Business Finance and Accounting, Auditing: A Journal of Theory and Practice,* and other accounting and business journals. He is past associate editor of *Contemporary Accounting Research* and has served on editorial boards of several respected journals, including *The Accounting Review* and the *Journal of Accounting and Public Policy.*

ROBERT F. HALSEY is Professor of Accounting and Faculty Director of the Master of Science in Accounting program at Babson College. He received his MBA and PhD from the University of Wisconsin. Prior to obtaining his PhD he worked as the chief financial officer (CFO) of a privately held retailing and manufacturing company and as the vice president and manager of the commercial lending division of a large bank.

Professor Halsey teaches courses in financial and managerial accounting at both the graduate and undergraduate levels, including a popular course in financial statement analysis for second year MBA students. He has also taught numerous executive education courses for large multinational companies through Babson's school of Executive Education as well as for a number of stock brokerage firms in the Boston area. He is regarded as an innovative teacher and has been recognized for outstanding teaching at both the University of Wisconsin and Babson College.

Professor Halsey co-authors *Advanced Accounting* published by Cambridge Business Publishers and *Financial Statements: Construction, Analysis and Forecasting*, an undergraduate introductory accounting textbook, to be published in 2014. Professor Halsey's research interests are in the area of financial reporting, including firm valuation, financial statement analysis, and disclosure issues. He has publications in *Advances in Quantitative Analysis of Finance and Accounting, The Journal of the American Taxation Association, Issues in Accounting Education, The Portable MBA in Finance and Accounting,* the *CPA Journal, AICPA Professor/Practitioner Case Development Program*, and in other accounting and analysis journals.

Professor Halsey is an active member of the American Accounting Association and other accounting, analysis, and business organizations. He is widely recognized as an expert in the areas of financial reporting, financial analysis, and business valuation.

MARY LEA McANALLY is the Philip Ljundahl Professor of Accounting and Associate Dean for Graduate Programs at the Mays Business School. She obtained her Ph.D. from Stanford University and B. Comm. from the University of Alberta. She worked as a Chartered Accountant (in Canada) and is a Certified Internal Auditor. Prior to arriving at Texas A&M in 2002, Professor McAnally held positions at University of Texas at Austin, Canadian National Railways, and Dunwoody and Company.

At Texas A&M, Professor McAnally teaches financial reporting, analysis, and valuation in the full-time and Executive MBA programs. Through the Mays Center for Executive Development, she works with corporate clients including Halliburton, AT&T, and Baker Hughes. She has also taught at University of Calgary, IMADEC (in Austria) and at the Indian School of Business, in Hyderabad. She has received numerous faculty-determined and student-initiated teaching awards at the MBA and executive levels. Those awards include the Beazley Award, the Trammell Foundation Award, the MBA Teaching Award, the MBA Association Distinguished Faculty Award, the Award for Outstanding and Memorable Faculty Member, and the Distinguished Achievement Award.

Professor McAnally's research interests include accounting and disclosure in regulated environments, executive compensation, and accounting for risk. She has published articles in the leading academic journals including *Journal of Accounting and Economics, Journal of Accounting Research, The Accounting Review, Review of Accounting Studies,* and *Contemporary Accounting Research*. Professor McAnally received the Mays Business School Research Achievement Award in 2005. She was Associate Editor at *Accounting Horizons* and served on the editorial board of *Contemporary Accounting Research* and was Guest Editor for the MBA-teaching volume of *Issues in Accounting Education* (2012). She is active in the American Accounting Association.

PREFACE

Welcome to the Sixth Edition of *Financial Accounting for MBAs*. Our main goal in writing this book was to satisfy the needs of today's business manager by providing the most contemporary, relevant, engaging, and user-oriented textbook available. This book is the product of extensive market research including focus groups, market surveys, class tests, manuscript reviews, and interviews with faculty from across the country. We are grateful to students and faculty who used the First through Fifth Editions and whose feedback greatly benefited this Sixth Edition.

TARGET AUDIENCE

Financial Accounting for MBAs is intended for use in full-time, part-time, executive, and evening MBA programs that include a financial accounting course as part of the curriculum, and one in which managerial decision making and analysis are emphasized. This book easily accommodates mini-courses lasting several days as well as extended courses lasting a full semester.

INNOVATIVE APPROACH

Financial Accounting for MBAs is managerially oriented and focuses on the most salient aspects of accounting. It helps MBA students learn how to read, analyze, and interpret financial accounting data to make informed business decisions. This textbook makes financial accounting **engaging, relevant,** and **contemporary.** To that end, it consistently incorporates **real company data,** both in the body of each module and throughout assignment material.

FLEXIBLE STRUCTURE

The MBA curricula, instructor preferences, and course lengths vary across colleges. Accordingly and to the extent possible, the 12 modules that make up *Financial Accounting for MBAs* were designed independently of one another. This modular presentation enables each college and instructor to "customize" the book to best fit the needs of their students. Our introduction and discussion of financial statements constitute Modules 1, 2, and 3. Module 4 presents the analysis of financial statements with an emphasis on analysis of operating profitability. Modules 5 through 10 highlight major financial accounting topics including assets, liabilities, equity, and off-balance-sheet financing. Module 11 explains forecasting financial statements and Module 12 introduces simple valuation models. At the end of each module, we present an ongoing analysis project that can be used as a guide for an independent project. Like the rest of the book, the project is independent across the various modules. At the end of the book, we include several useful resources. Appendix A contains compound interest tables and formulas. Appendix B details the process for preparing and analyzing the statement of cash flow. Appendix C is an illustrative case that applies the techniques described in Modules 1 through 12 to an actual company, Kimberly-Clark. Appendix C can be used , in conjunction with the module-end project questions, by students required to prepare a company analysis. Appendix D is a chart of accounts used in the book.

Transaction Analysis and Statement Preparation

Instructors differ in their coverage of accounting mechanics. Some focus on the effects of transactions on financial statements using the balance sheet equation format. Others include coverage of journal entries and T-accounts. We accommodate both teaching styles in this Sixth Edition. Specifically, Module 2 provides an expanded discussion of the effects of transactions using our innovative financial statement effects template. Emphasis is on the analysis of Apple's summary transactions, which concludes with the preparation of its financial statements. Module 3, which is entirely optional, allows an instructor to drill down and focus on accounting mechanics: journal entries and T-accounts. It illustrates accounting for numerous transactions, including those involving accounting adjustments. It concludes with the preparation of a trial balance and the financial statements. This detailed transaction analysis uses the same financial statement effects template, with journal entries and T-accounts highlighted in the margin. Thus, these two modules accommodate the spectrum of teaching styles—instructors can elect to use either or both modules to suit their preferences, and their students are not deprived of any information as a result of that selection.

Flexibility for Courses of Varying Lengths

Many instructors have approached us to ask about suggested class structures based on courses of varying length. To that end, we provide the following table of possible course designs:

	15 Week Semester-Course	10 Week Quarter-Course	6 Week Mini-Course	1 Week Intensive-Course
MODULE 1 FINANCIAL ACCOUNTING FOR MBAS	Week 1	Week 1	Week 1	Day 1 (Module 1 and either Module 2 or Module 3)
MODULE 2 INTRODUCING FINANCIAL STATEMENTS AND TRANSACTION ANALYSIS	Week 2	Week 2	Week 2	
MODULE 3 ACCOUNTING ADJUSTMENTS AND CONSTRUCTING FINANCIAL STATEMENTS	Week 2 (optional)	Week 2 (optional)	Week 2 (optional)	
MODULE 4 ANALYZING AND INTERPRETING FINANCIAL STATEMENTS	Weeks 3 and 4	Week 3	Week 3	Day 2
MODULE 5 REPORTING AND ANALYZING OPERATING INCOME	Week 5	Week 4	Skim	Skim
MODULE 6 REPORTING AND ANALYZING OPERATING ASSETS	Week 6	Week 5	Week 4	Day 3
MODULE 7 REPORTING AND ANALYZING NONOWNER FINANCING	Week 7	Week 6	Week 5	Day 4
MODULE 8 REPORTING AND ANALYZING OWNER FINANCING	Week 8	Week 7	Week 6	Day 5
MODULE 9 REPORTING AND ANALYZING INTERCORPORATE INVESTMENTS	Week 9	Optional	Optional	Optional
MODULE 10 REPORTING AND ANALYZING OFF-BALANCE-SHEET FINANCING	Weeks 10 and 11	Week 8	Optional	Optional
MODULE 11 FORECASTING FINANCIAL STATEMENTS	Weeks 12 and 13	Week 9	Optional	Optional
MODULE 12 ANALYZING AND VALUING EQUITY SECURITIES	Weeks 13 and 14	Week 10	Optional	Optional

MANAGERIAL EMPHASIS

Tomorrow's MBA graduates must be skilled in using financial statements to make business decisions. These skills often require application of ratio analyses, benchmarking, forecasting, valuation, and other aspects of financial statement analysis for decision making. Further, tomorrow's MBA graduates must have the skills to go beyond basic financial statements and to interpret and apply nonfinancial statement disclosures, such as footnotes and supplementary reports. This book, therefore, emphasizes real company data, including detailed footnote and other management disclosures, and shows how to use this information to make managerial inferences and decisions. This approach makes financial accounting interesting and relevant for all MBA students.

As MBA instructors, we recognize that the core MBA financial accounting course is not directed toward accounting majors. *Financial Accounting for MBAs* embraces this reality. This book highlights **financial reporting, analysis, interpretation,** and **decision making.** We incorporate the following **financial statement effects template** to train MBA students in understanding the economic ramifications of transactions and their impact on all key financial statements. This analytical tool is a great resource for MBA students in learning accounting and applying it to their future courses and careers. Each transaction is identified in the "Transaction" column. Then, the dollar amounts (positive or negative) of the financial statement effects are recorded in the appropriate balance sheet or income statement columns. The template also reflects the statement of cash flow effects (via the cash column) and the statement of stockholders' equity effects (via the contributed capital and earned capital columns). The earned capital account is immediately updated to reflect any income or loss arising from each transaction (denoted by the arrow line from net income to earned capital). This template is instructive as it reveals the financial impacts of transactions, and it provides insights into the effects of accounting choices.

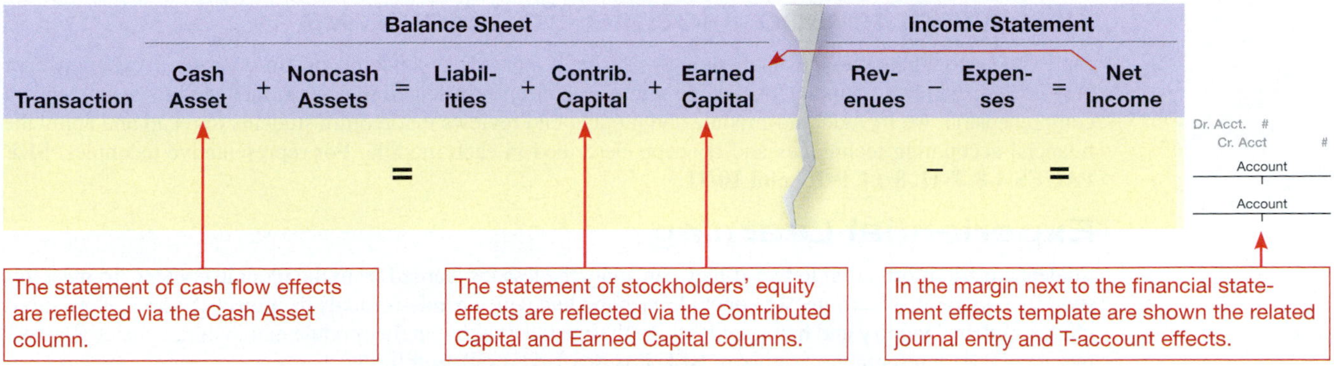

INNOVATIVE PEDAGOGY

Financial Accounting for MBAs includes special features specifically designed for the MBA student.

Focus Companies for Each Module

Each module's content is explained through the accounting and reporting activities of real companies. Each module incorporates a "focus company" for special emphasis and demonstration. The enhanced instructional value of focus companies comes from the way they engage MBA students in real analysis and interpretation. Focus companies were selected based on the industries that MBA students typically enter upon graduation.

MODULE 1	Berkshire Hathaway	**MODULE 8**	IBM
MODULE 2	Apple	**MODULE 9**	Google
MODULE 3	Apple	**MODULE 10**	Southwest Airlines
MODULE 4	Walmart	**MODULE 11**	Procter & Gamble
MODULE 5	Pfizer	**MODULE 12**	Nike
MODULE 6	Cisco	**APPENDIX B**	Starbucks
MODULE 7	Verizon	**APPENDIX C**	Kimberly-Clark

Real Company Data Throughout

Market research and reviewer feedback tell us that one of instructors' greatest frustrations with other MBA textbooks is their lack of real company data. We have gone to great lengths to incorporate real company data throughout each module to reinforce important concepts and engage MBA students. We engage nonaccounting MBA students specializing in finance, taxation, marketing, management, real estate, operations, and so forth, with companies and scenarios that are relevant to them. For representative examples, **SEE PAGES 2-34, 4-7, 5-8, 5-15, 6-10, 7-16, 8-5, 9-26, 10-20, and 11-9.**

Footnotes and Other Management Disclosures

Analyzed on their own, financial statements reveal only part of a corporation's economic story. Information essential for a complete analysis of a company's financial position must be gleaned from the footnotes and other disclosures provided by the company. Consequently, we incorporate footnotes and other disclosures generously throughout the text and assignments. For representative examples, **SEE PAGES 7-7, 7-9, 8-12, 8-27, and 10-6.**

Industry-Level Data

We repeatedly emphasize that financial analysis cannot be performed in a vacuum—appropriate benchmarks are critical to a complete understanding of a company's financial performance and position. To this point, we provide graphics that capture industry-level data including many of the ratios we discuss and compute in the modules. For representative examples, **SEE PAGES 4-15, 4-19, 6-12, and 7-25.**

Decision Making Orientation

One primary goal of a MBA financial accounting course is to teach students the skills needed to apply their accounting knowledge to solving real business problems and making informed business decisions. With that goal in mind, Managerial Decision boxes in each module encourage students to apply the material presented to solving actual business scenarios. For representative examples, **SEE PAGES 2-35, 4-14, 7-23, 8-9, 9-16, and 10-7.**

Mid-Module and Module-End Reviews

Financial accounting can be challenging—especially for MBA students lacking business experience or previous exposure to business courses. To reinforce concepts presented in each module and to ensure student comprehension, we include mid-module and module-end reviews that require students to recall and apply the financial accounting techniques and concepts described in each module. For representative examples, **SEE PAGES 4-8, 7-11, 8-14, 9-16, and 10-11.**

Experiential Learning

Students retain information longer if they can apply the lessons learned from the module content. To meet this need for experiential learning, we conclude each module with a hands-on analysis project. A series of questions guides students' inquiry and helps students synthesize the material in the module and integrate material across modules. For representative examples, **SEE PAGES 1-42, 4-58, and 9-55.**

Excellent, Class-Tested Assignment Materials

Excellent assignment material is a must-have component of any successful textbook (and class). We went to great lengths to create the best assignments possible from contemporary financial statements. In keeping with the rest of the book, we used real company data extensively. We also ensured that assignments reflect our belief that MBA students should be trained in analyzing accounting information to make business decisions, as opposed to working on mechanical bookkeeping tasks. There are six categories of assignments: **Discussion Questions**, **Mini Exercises**, **Exercises**, **Problems**, **IFRS Applications**, and **Management Applications**. For representative examples, **SEE PAGES 4-37, 6-45, and 9-41.**

SIXTH EDITION CHANGES

Based on classroom use and reviewer feedback, a number of substantive changes have been made in the sixth edition to further enhance the MBA students' experiences:

- **Updated Financial Data:** We have updated all Focus Company financial statements and disclosures to reflect each company's latest available filings. We also explain the SEC's EDGAR financial statement retrieval software and how to download excel spreadsheets of financial statements from 10-K filings.
- **Updated Assignments:** We have updated all assignments using real data to reflect each company's latest available filings and have added many new assignments that also utilize real financial data and footnotes. We have expanded the IFRS Applications to include more companies from Canada and Australia.
- **Ongoing Analysis Project:** We have added a project component to each module. See the description above in Experiential Learning.
- **Analyzing Cash Flows:** To help students better understand cash flows, we have included new sections on the analysis of cash flows in Appendix B, including a discussion of the cash flow cycle and interpretation of cash flow patterns.
- **International Financial Reporting Standards (IFRS):** We have updated the IFRS Insight boxes and IFRS Alert boxes on the similarities and differences between U.S. GAAP and IFRS. Each module concludes with a Global Accounting section and an expanded IFRS assignments section, which brings in reports and disclosures from around the globe.
- **New Focus Companies:** We have changed a number of the focus companies: Module 4 now uses Walmart, Module 7 focuses on IBM, Module 10 uses Southwest Airlines, and Module 12 highlights Nike.
- **Accounting Quality:** We augmented the section on accounting quality in Module 5. It describes measures of accounting quality and factors that mitigate accounting quality. We also provide a check list of items in financial statements that should be reviewed when analyzing financial statements.
- **Intercorporate Investments:** Consistent with recent changes in accounting standards, we have revised Module 9 (formerly Module 7) to emphasize investors' control of securities and deemphasize the percentage of ownership as the determining factor in selecting the method used for financial reporting.
- **Credit Ratings:** This edition expands discussion of credit ratings. This includes trends in credit ratings, current credit rating statistics, and rating procedures implemented by companies such as Moody's and Standard and Poor's.
- **Noncontrolling Interest:** We added expanded discussion of noncontrolling interest, how it is reported in financial statements, and the interpretation of its disclosure. The book distinguishes the ROE disaggregation with and without controlling interest and explains how to handle noncontrolling interest for analysis, forecasting, and equity valuation. In Module 9, we also expand our discussion of consolidation to illustrate the allocation of consolidated net income to the noncontrolling interest and to the controlling (parent) interest.
- **Revised Forecasting Module:** We have expanded our discussion of the forecasting of revenues and expenses to distinguish between forecasting using publicly-available databases and forecasting with

proprietary databases. For the latter, we continue to utilize analyst reports and spreadsheets provided to us by Morgan Stanley.

- **Enhanced R&D Analysis:** We have developed a new discussion of R&D costs in Module 5 focusing on the analysis and interpretation of R&D.
- **Expanded analysis of allowance accounts:** We have developed a new appendix to Module 6 to illustrate the accounting for sales returns and analysis. We also present a discussion of the analysis of the allowance accounts in Schedule II (Valuation and Qualifying Accounts) of the 10-K or similar disclosures in other types of annual reports.
- **Pension Accounting:** We have expanded our discussion of analysis of pension disclosures, including the change that many companies now immediately recognize actuarial gains and losses in operating results.
- **New Regulations:** We highlight pending and proposed accounting standards and their likely effects, if passed. These include the proposed standard on Revenue Recognition. This edition also reflects all accounting standards in effect since our last edition, including the new business combination and consolidation standard and goodwill impairment testing.

COMPANION CASEBOOK

Cases in Financial Reporting, 7th edition by Ellen Engel (University of Chicago), D. Eric Hirst (University of Texas – Austin), and Mary Lea McAnally (Texas A&M University). This book comprises 27 cases and is a perfect companion book for faculty interested in exposing students to a wide range of real financial statements. The cases are current and cover companies from Canada, France, Austria, the Netherlands, the UK, India, as well as from the U.S. Many of the U.S. companies are major multinationals. Each case deals with a specific financial accounting topic within the context of one (or more) company's financial statements. Each case contains financial statement information and a set of directed questions pertaining to one or two specific financial accounting issues. This is a separate, saleable casebook (**ISBN 978-1-934319-79-6**). Contact your sales representative to receive a desk copy or email customerservice@cambridgepub.com.

ONLINE INSTRUCTION AND HOMEWORK MANAGEMENT SYSTEM

my BusinessCourse: A web-based learning and assessment program intended to complement your textbook and faculty instruction. This easy-to-use program grades homework automatically and provides students with access to narrated demonstrations and eLecture videos. Assignments with the ✓ in the margin are available in myBusinessCourse. Access is free with new copies of this textbook (look for a page containing the access code near the front of the book). If you buy a used copy of the book, you can purchase access at www.mybusinesscourse.com.

SUPPLEMENT PACKAGE

For Instructors

Solutions Manual: Created by the authors, the *Solutions Manual* contains complete solutions to all the assignments in the textbook.

PowerPoint: Created by the authors, the PowerPoint slides outline key elements of each module.

Test Bank: Written by the authors, the test bank includes multiple-choice items, matching questions, short essay questions, and problems.

Computerized Test Bank: This computerized version of the test bank enables you to add and edit questions; create up to 99 versions of each test; attach graphic files to questions; import and export ASCII files; and select questions based on type or learning objective. It provides password protection for saved tests and question databases and is able to run on a network.

Website: All instructor materials are accessible via the book's Website (password protected) along with other useful links and information. www.cambridgepub.com

For Students

Student Solutions Manual: Created by the authors, the student solutions manual contains all solutions to the even-numbered assignment materials in the textbook. This is a **restricted** item that is only available to students after their instructor has authorized its purchase. ISBN 978-1-61853-120-9

Website: Useful links are available to students free of charge on the book's Website.

ACKNOWLEDGMENTS

All six editions of this book benefited greatly from the valuable feedback of focus group attendees, reviewers, students, and colleagues. We are extremely grateful to them for their help in making this project a success.

Beverley Alleyne, *Belmont University*
Ashiq Ali, *University of Texas—Dallas*
Dan Amiram, *Columbia University*
Steve Baginski, *University of Georgia*
Eli Bartov, *New York University*
Dan Bens, *INSEAD*
Denny Beresford, *University of Georgia*
Mark Bradshaw, *Boston College*
Dennis Bline, *Bryant University*
James Boatsman, *Arizona State University*
John Briginshaw, *Pepperdine University*
Thomas Buchman, *University of Colorado—Boulder*
Mary Ellen Carter, *Boston College*
Judson Caskey, *University of Texas—Austin*
Sandra Cereola, *James Madison University*
Sumantra Chakravarty, *California State University—Fullerton*
Betty Chavis, *California State University—Fullerton*
Agnes Cheng, *Louisiana State University*
Joseph Comprix, *Syracuse University*
Ellen Cook, *University of Louisiana—Lafayette*
Araya Debessay, *University of Delaware*
Roger Debreceny, *University of Hawaii—Manoa*
Carol Dee, *University of Colorado—Denver*
Rosemond Desir, *Colorado State University*
Vicki Dickinson, *University of Mississippi*
Jeffrey Doyle, *University of Utah*
Donald Drake, *Georgia State University*
Joanne Duke, *San Francisco State University*
Cindy Durtschi, *DePaul University*
Thomas Dyckman, *Cornell University*
James Edwards, *University of South Carolina*
John Eichenseher, *University of Wisconsin*
Craig Emby, *Simon Fraser University*
Gerard Engeholm, *Pace University*
Kathryn Epps, *Kennesaw State University*
Mark Finn, *Northwestern University*
Tim Fogarty, *Case Western Reserve University*
Richard Frankel, *Washington University*
Dan Givoly, *Pennsylvania State University*
Andy Garcia, *Bowling Green State University*
Maclean Gaulin, *Rice University*
Julia Grant, *Case Western Reserve University*
Kris Gulick, *University of Iowa*
Karl Hackenbrack, *Vanderbilt University*
Michelle Hanlon, *MIT*
Bob Hartman, *University of Iowa*
David Harvey, *University of Georgia*
Carla Hayn, *University of California—Los Angeles*
Frank Heflin, *Florida State University*
Michele Henney, *University of Oregon*
Elaine Henry, *University of Miami*
Clayton Hock, *Miami University*
Judith Hora, *University of San Diego*
Herbert Hunt, *California State University—Long Beach*
Richard Hurley, *University of Connecticut*
Ross Jennings, *University of Texas—Austin*
Greg Jonas, *Case Western Reserve University*
Sanjay Kallapur, *Indian School of Business*
Greg Kane, *University of Delaware*
Victoria Kaskey, *Ashland University*
Zafar Khan, *Eastern Michigan University*
Saleha Khumawala, *University of Houston*
Marinilka Kimbro, *University of Washington—Tacoma*
Ron King, *Washington University*
Michael Kirschenheiter, *University of Illinois—Chicago*
Krishna Kumar, *George Washington University*
Lisa Kutcher, *University of Oregon*
Brian Leventhal, *University of Illinois—Chicago*
Pierre Liang, *Carnegie Mellon University*
Joshua Livnat, *New York University*
Barbara Lougee, *University of San Diego*
Yvonne Lu, *Lehigh University*
Luann Lynch, *University of Virginia—Darden*
Michael Maier, *University of Alberta*
Ariel Markelevich, *Suffolk University*
Ron Mano, *Westminster College*
Brian McAllister, *University of Colorado at Colorado Springs*
Bruce McClain, *Cleveland State University*
Karen McDougal, *St. Joseph's University*
James McKinney, *University of Maryland*
Greg Miller, *University of Michigan*
Jose Miranda-Lopez, *California State University—Fullerton*
Melanie Mogg, *University of Minnesota*
Steve Monahan, *INSEAD*
John Morris, *Kansas State University*
Dennis Murray, *University of Colorado—Denver*
Sandeep Nabar, *Oklahoma State University*
Suresh Nallareddy, *Columbia University*
Ramesh Narasimhan, *Montclair State University*
Siva Nathan, *Georgia State University*
Doron Nissim, *Columbia University*
Shail Pandit, *University of Illinois—Chicago*
Susan Parker, *Santa Clara University*
William Pasewark, *Texas Tech*
Stephen Penman, *Columbia University*
Mark Penno, *University of Iowa*
Gary Peters, *University of Arkansas*
Kathy Petroni, *Michigan State University*
Christine Petrovits, *New York University*
Kirk Philipich, *University of Michigan—Dearborn*
Morton Pincus, *University of California—Irvine*
Kay Poston, *University of Indianapolis*
Grace Pownall, *Emory University*
David Randolph, *Xavier University*
Laura Rickett, *Kent State University*
Susan Riffe, *Southern Methodist University*
Bruce Samuelson, *Pepperdine University*
Diane Satin, *California State University—East Bay*
Shahrokh Saudagaran, *University of Washington—Tacoma*
Andrew Schmidt, *Columbia University*
Chandra Seethamraju, *Washington University*
Stephen Sefcik, *University of Washington*
Galen Sevcik, *Georgia State University*
Lewis Shaw, *Suffolk University*
Kenneth Shaw, *University of Missouri*
Todd Shawver, *Bloomsburg University*
Evan Shough, *University of North Carolina—Greensboro*
Paul Simko, *University of Virginia—Darden*
Kevin Smith, *University of Kansas*
Pam Smith, *Northern Illinois University*
Rod Smith, *California State University—Long Beach*
Sri Sridharan, *Northwestern University*
Charles Stanley, *Baylor University*
Jens Stephan, *Eastern Michigan University*
Phillip Stocken, *Dartmouth College*
Jerry Strawser, *Texas A&M University*
Sherre Strickland, *University of Massachusetts—Lowell*
Chandra Subramaniam, *University of Texas—Austin*
K.R. Subramanyam, *University of Southern California*
Ziad Syed, *Texas A&M University*
Gary Taylor, *University of Alabama*
Mark Taylor, *Case Western Reserve University*
Suzanne Traylor, *State University of New York Albany*
Sam Tiras, *Louisiana State University*
Brett Trueman, *University of California—Los Angeles*
Jerry Van Os, *Westminster College*
Mark Vargus, *University of Texas—Dallas*
Lisa Victoravich, *University of Denver*
Robert Vigeland, *Texas Christian University*
Marcia Vorholt, *Xavier University*
James Wallace, *Claremont Graduate School*
Charles Wasley, *University of Rochester*
Greg Waymire, *Emory University*
Andrea Weickgenannt, *Xavier University*
Daniel Weimer, *Wayne State University*
Edward Werner, *Drexel University*
Jeffrey Williams, *University of Michigan*
David Wright, *University of Michigan*
Michelle Yetman, *University of California—Davis*
Tzachi Zack, *Ohio State University*
Xiao-Jun Zhang, *University of California—Berkeley*
Yuan Zhang, *Columbia University*
Yuping Zhao, *University of Houston*

In addition, we are extremely grateful to George Werthman, Lorraine Gleeson, Jill Fischer, Marnee Fieldman, Debbie McQuade, Terry McQuade, and the entire team at Cambridge Business Publishers for their encouragement, enthusiasm, and guidance. Their market research, editorial development, and promotional efforts have made this book the best-selling MBA text in the market.

Peter *John* *Bob* *Mary Lea*

February 2014

BRIEF CONTENTS

CONTENTS

MODULE 1

Financial Accounting for MBAs 1-1

MODULE 2

Introducing Financial Statements and Transaction Analysis 2-1

MODULE 3
Accounting Adjustments and Constructing Financial Statements 3-1

MODULE 4
Analyzing and Interpreting Financial Statements 4-1

MODULE 5
Reporting and Analyzing Operating Income 5-1

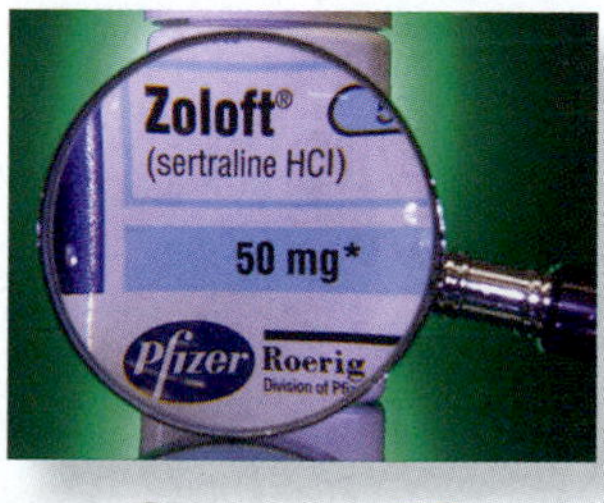

CISCO
TOMORROW starts here.

MODULE 8

Reporting and Analyzing Owner Financing 8-1

MODULE 9

Reporting and Analyzing Intercorporate Investments 9-1

MODULE 10

Reporting and Analyzing Off-Balance-Sheet Financing 10-1

MODULE 11

Forecasting Financial Statements 11-1

MODULE 12

Analyzing and Valuing Equity Securities 12-1

APPENDIX A

Compound Interest Tables A-1

APPENDIX B
Constructing the Statement of Cash Flows B-1

APPENDIX C
Comprehensive Case C-1

APPENDIX D
Chart of Accounts with Acronyms D-1

Module

1

Financial Accounting for MBAs

Learning Objectives

LO1 Identify and discuss the users and suppliers of financial statement information. (p. 1-5)

LO2 Identify and explain the four financial statements, and define the accounting equation. (p. 1-9)

LO3 Explain and apply the basics of profitability analysis. (p. 1-19)

LO4 Describe business analysis within the context of a competitive environment. (p. 1-20)

LO5 Describe the accounting principles and regulations that frame financial statements. (p. 1-26)

Berkshire Hathaway

Berkshire Hathaway owns numerous businesses that pursue diverse activities. The legendary Warren Buffett, the "Sage of Omaha," manages the company. Buffett's investment philosophy is to acquire and hold companies over the long run. His acquisition criteria, taken from Berkshire Hathaway's annual report, follow:

1. Large purchases (and large pretax earnings).
2. Demonstrated consistent earning power (future projections are of *no* interest to us, nor are 'turnaround' situations).
3. Businesses earning good returns on equity while employing little or no debt.
4. Management in place (we can't supply it).
5. Simple businesses (if there's lots of technology, we won't understand it).
6. An offering price (we don't want to waste our time or that of the seller by talking, even preliminarily, about a transaction when price is unknown).

At least three of Buffett's six criteria relate to financial performance. First, he seeks businesses with large and consistent earning power. Buffett is not only looking for consistent earnings, but earnings that are measured according to accounting policies that closely mirror the underlying economic performance of the business.

Second, Buffett focuses on "businesses earning good returns on equity," defined as income divided by average stockholders' equity: "Our preference would be to reach our goal by directly owning a diversified group of businesses that generate cash and consistently earn above-average returns" (Berkshire Hathaway annual report). For management to earn a good return on equity, it must focus on both income (financial performance) and equity (financial condition).

Third, Buffett values companies based on their ability to generate consistent earnings and cash. He focuses on *intrinsic value,* which he defines in each annual report as follows:

> Intrinsic value is an all-important concept that offers the only logical approach to evaluating the relative attractiveness of

Courtesy of Getty Images

> investments and businesses. Intrinsic value can be defined simply: It is the discounted value of the cash that can be taken out of a business during its remaining life.

The discounted value Buffett describes is the present (today's) value of the cash flows the company expects to generate in the future. Cash is generated when companies are well managed and operate profitably and efficiently.

Warren Buffett provides some especially useful investment guidance in his Chairman's letter from a prior period's Berkshire Hathaway annual report:

> Three suggestions for investors: First, beware of companies displaying weak accounting. . . . When managements take the low road in aspects that are visible, it is likely they are following a similar path behind the scenes. There is seldom just one cockroach in the kitchen.
>
> Second, unintelligible footnotes usually indicate untrustworthy management. If you can't understand a footnote or other managerial explanation, it's usually because the CEO doesn't want you to.
>
> Finally, be suspicious of companies that trumpet earnings projections and growth expectations. Businesses seldom operate in a tranquil, no-surprise environment, and earnings simply don't advance smoothly (except, of course, in the offering books of investment bankers).

This book will explain Buffett's references to earnings projections, growth expectations, and return on equity as well as a host of other accounting issues that affect interpretation and valuation of companies' financial performance. We will analyze and interpret the footnotes, which Buffett views as crucial to quality financial reporting and analysis. Our philosophy is simple: we must understand the intricacies and nuances of financial reporting to become critical readers and users of financial reports for company analysis and valuation.

Sources: Berkshire Hathaway *10-K Reports,* Berkshire Hathaway *Annual Reports; The Wall Street Journal,* January 2014.

MODULE ORGANIZATION

Financial Accounting for MBAs

Information Environment
- Reporting on Business Activities
- Demand for Information
- Supply of Information

Financial Statements
- Balance Sheet
- Income Statement
- Statement of Stockholders' Equity
- Statement of Cash Flows

Profitability Analysis
- Measuring Return on Assets
- Disaggregating Return on Assets

Broader Business Environment
- Competitive Analysis
- Business Analysis
- Analyzing Competitive Advantage

Regulatory and Legal Environment
- Financial Accounting Environment
- Audits and Governance
- SEC and the Courts

Financial accounting information serves many purposes. To understand this, imagine that we are a specific user of accounting information. For example, imagine we are a stock investor—how might we use accounting information to identify a stock to buy? Imagine we are a bond trader—how might we use accounting information to assess whether a company is able to repay its debt? Imagine we are a manager—how might we use accounting information to decide whether to acquire another company or divest a current division? Imagine we are an equity or credit analyst—how might we use accounting to assess and communicate an investment appraisal or credit report?

This book explains the concepts, preparation, and application of financial accounting information and, importantly, how decision makers use such information. In general, managers use financial accounting information to make operating, investing, and financing decisions. Investors and analysts use financial accounting information to help decide whether to buy or sell stock. Lenders and rating agencies use accounting information to help decide on a company's creditworthiness and lending terms. Regulators use accounting information to enact social and economic policies and to monitor compliance with laws. Legal institutions use accounting information to assess fines and reparations in litigation. Other decision makers rely on accounting information for purposes ranging from determining demands in labor union negotiations to levying damages for environmental abuses.

This module begins with an overview of the information environment that companies face, and it discusses the demand for and supply of financial information. We then review financial statements and explain what they convey about a company. Profitability is described next and is used as a focus of much of our application of accounting information. We conclude the module with an introduction to business analysis, which is an important part of drawing inferences from financial statements. We include (in the appendix) a discussion of the regulatory environment that defines current financial reporting for companies.

The remainder of the book can be broken into four parts—see figure at top of next page. Part 1 consists of Modules 1, 2, and 3 and offers an introduction of accounting fundamentals and the business environment. Part 2 consists of Module 4, which introduces analysis of financial statements. Although an aim of this book is to help us understand the application of financial statements, it is important that we understand their preparation. Thus, Part 3, which consists of Modules 5 through 10, describes the accounting for assets, liabilities, and equity; Appendix B covers accounting for cash flows. Part 4 consists of Modules 11 and 12, which explain the forecasting of accounting numbers and the valuation of common stock; Appendix C applies many of the analysis tools introduced in this book.

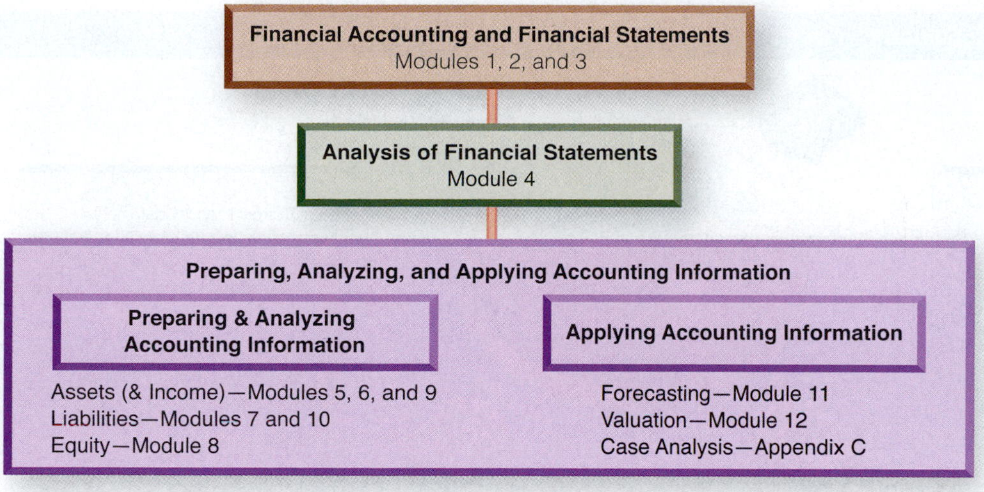

REPORTING ON BUSINESS ACTIVITIES

To effectively manage a company or infer whether it is well managed, we must understand the company's business activities. Financial statements help us understand these business activities. These statements report on a company's performance and financial condition, and reveal executive management's privileged information and insights.

Financial statements satisfy the needs of different users. The functioning of the accounting information system involves application of accounting standards to produce financial statements. Effectively using this information system involves making judgments, assumptions, and estimates based on data contained in the financial reports. The greatest value we derive from this information system as users of financial reports is the insight we gain into the business activities of the company under analysis.

To effectively analyze and use accounting information, we must consider the business context in which the information is created—see Exhibit 1.1. Without exception, all companies *plan* business activities, *finance* those activities, *invest* in those activities, and then engage in *operating* activities. Companies conduct all these activities while confronting *business forces*, including market constraints and competitive pressures. Financial statements provide crucial input for strategic planning. They also provide information about the relative success of those plans, which can be used to take corrective action or make new operating, investing, and financing decisions.

Exhibit 1.1 depicts the business activities for a typical company. The outer (purplish) ring is the planning process that reflects the overarching goals and objectives of the company within which strategic decisions are made. Those strategic decisions involve company financing, asset management, and daily operations. **Apple Inc.**, the focus company in Modules 2 and 3, provides the following description of its business strategy in its annual report:

> **Business Strategy** The Company is committed to bringing the best user experience to its customers through its innovative hardware, software, peripherals, and services. The Company's business strategy leverages its unique ability to design and develop its own operating systems, hardware, application software, and services to provide its customers new products and solutions with superior ease-of-use, seamless integration, and innovative design. The Company believes continual investment in research and development, marketing and advertising is critical to the development and sale of innovative products and technologies. As part of its strategy, the Company continues to expand its platform for the discovery and delivery of third-party digital content and applications through the iTunes Store . . . The Company also supports a community for the development of third-party software and hardware products and digital content that complement the Company's offerings. The Company's strategy also includes expanding its distribution network to effectively reach more customers and provide them with a high-quality sales and post-sales support experience.

EXHIBIT 1.1 Business Activities

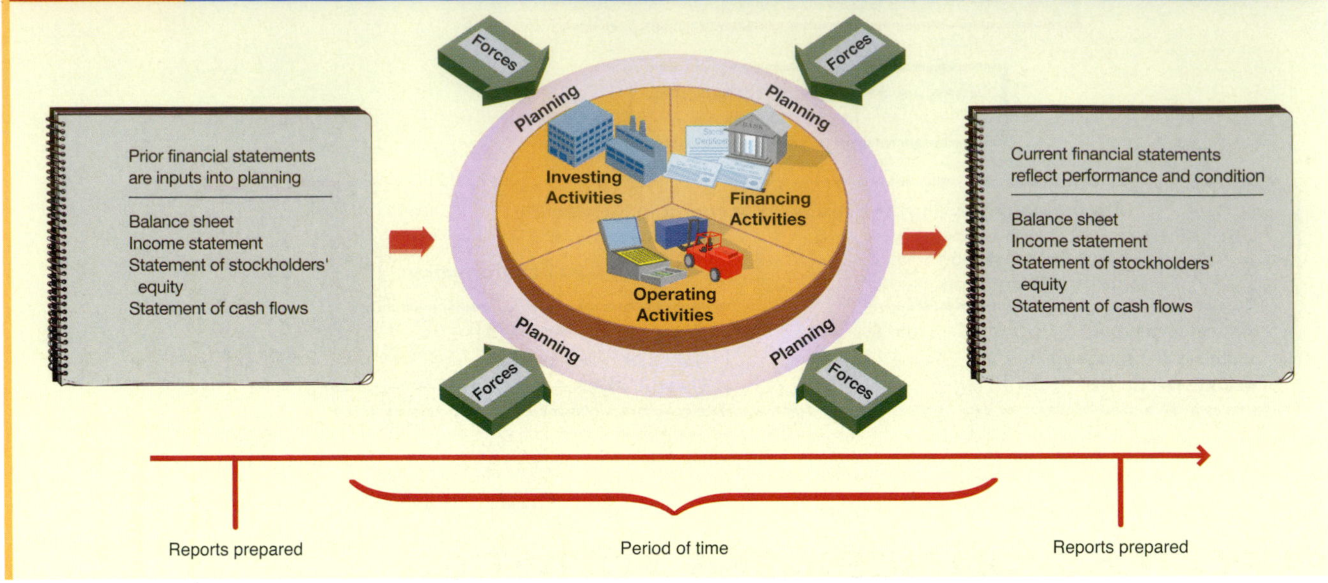

A company's *strategic* (or *business*) *plan* reflects how it plans to achieve its goals and objectives. A plan's success depends on an effective analysis of market demand and supply. Specifically, a company must assess demand for its products and services, and assess the supply of its inputs (both labor and capital). The plan must also include competitive analyses, opportunity assessments, and consideration of business threats.

Historical financial statements provide insight into the success of a company's strategic plan, and are an important input to the planning process. These statements highlight portions of the strategic plan that proved profitable and, thus, warrant additional capital investment. They also reveal areas that are less effective, and provide information to help managers develop remedial action.

Once strategic adjustments are planned and implemented, the resulting financial statements provide input into the planning process for the following year; and this process begins again. Understanding a company's strategic plan helps focus our analysis of financial statements by placing them in proper context.

FINANCIAL STATEMENTS: DEMAND AND SUPPLY

LO1 Identify and discuss the users and suppliers of financial statement information.

Demand for financial statements has existed for centuries as a means to facilitate efficient contracting and risk-sharing. Decision makers and other stakeholders demand information on a company's past and prospective returns and risks. Supply of financial statements is driven by companies' wish to lower their costs of financing and less obvious costs such as political, contracting, and labor. Managers decide how much financial information to supply by weighing the costs of disclosure against the benefits of disclosure. Regulatory agencies intervene in this process with various disclosure requirements that establish a minimum supply of information.

Demand for Information

The following broad classes of users demand financial accounting information:

- Managers and employees
- Investment analysts and information intermediaries
- Creditors and suppliers
- Stockholders and directors
- Customers and strategic partners
- Regulators and tax agencies
- Voters and their representatives

Managers and Employees

For their own well-being and future earnings potential, managers and employees demand accounting information on the financial condition, profitability, and prospects of their companies as well as comparative financial information on competing companies and business opportunities. This permits them to benchmark their company's performance and condition. Managers and employees also demand financial accounting information for use in compensation and bonus contracts that are tied to such numbers. The popularity of employee profit sharing and stock ownership plans has further increased demand for financial information. Other sources of demand include union contracts that link wage negotiations to accounting numbers and pension and benefit plans whose solvency depends on company performance.

Investment Analysts and Information Intermediaries

Investment analysts and other information intermediaries, such as financial press writers and business commentators, are interested in predicting companies' future performance. Expectations about future profitability and the ability to generate cash impact the price of securities and a company's ability to borrow money at favorable terms. Financial reports reflect information about past performance and current resources available to companies. These reports also provide information about claims on those resources, including claims by suppliers, creditors, lenders, and stockholders. This information allows analysts to make informed assessments about future financial performance and condition so they can provide stock recommendations or write commentaries.

Creditors and Suppliers

Banks and other lenders demand financial accounting information to help determine loan terms, loan amounts, interest rates, and required collateral. Loan agreements often include contractual requirements, called **covenants**, that restrict the borrower's behavior in some fashion. For example, loan covenants might require the loan recipient to maintain minimum levels of working capital, retained earnings, interest coverage, and so forth to safeguard lenders. Covenant violations can yield technical default, enabling the creditor to demand early payment or other compensation. Suppliers demand financial information to establish credit terms and to determine their long-term commitment to supply-chain relations. Both creditors and suppliers use financial information to monitor and adjust their contracts and commitments with a company.

Stockholders and Directors

Stockholders and directors demand financial accounting information to assess the profitability and risks of companies. Stockholders and others (such as investment analysts, brokers, and potential investors) search for information useful in their investment decisions. **Fundamental analysis** uses financial information to estimate company value and to form buy-sell stock strategies. Both directors and stockholders use accounting information to evaluate managerial performance. Managers similarly use such information to request an increase in compensation and managerial power from directors. Outside directors are crucial to determining who runs the company, and these directors use accounting information to help make leadership decisions.

Customers and Strategic Partners

Customers (both current and potential) demand accounting information to assess a company's ability to provide products or services as agreed and to assess the company's staying power and reliability. Strategic partners wish to estimate the company's profitability to assess the fairness of returns on mutual transactions and strategic alliances.

Regulators and Tax Agencies

Regulators (such as the SEC, the Federal Trade Commission, and the Federal Reserve Bank) and tax agencies demand accounting information for antitrust assessments, public protection, price setting, import-export analyses, and setting tax policies. Timely and reliable information is crucial to effective regulatory policy, and accounting information is often central to social and economic policy. For example, governments often grant monopoly rights to electric and gas companies serving specific areas in exchange for regulation over prices charged to consumers. These prices are mainly determined from accounting measures.

Voters and Their Representatives

Voters and their representatives to national, state, and local governments demand accounting information for policy decisions. The decisions can involve economic, social, taxation, and other initiatives. Voters and their representatives also use accounting information to monitor government spending. We have all heard of the $1,000 hammer type stories that government watchdog groups uncover while sifting through accounting data. Contributors to nonprofit organizations also demand accounting information to assess the impact of their donations.

IFRS INSIGHT **Development of International Standards**

The accounting standards explained in this book are consistent with generally accepted accounting principles (GAAP) primarily developed by the Financial Accounting Standards Board (FASB). A similar organization, the International Accounting Standards Board (IASB), develops a global set of International Financial Reporting Standards (IFRS) for preparation of financial statements. To increase comparability of financial statements and reduce reporting complexity, the Securities Exchange Commission (SEC), the FASB, and the IASB are committed to a process of convergence to one set of world accounting standards. As we progress through the book, we will provide IFRS Insight boxes like this to identify differences between GAAP and IFRS.

Supply of Information

In general, the quantity and quality of accounting information that companies supply are determined by managers' assessment of the benefits and costs of disclosure. Managers release information provided the benefits of disclosing that information outweigh the costs of doing so. Both *regulation* and *bargaining power* affect disclosure costs and benefits and thus play roles in determining the supply of accounting information. Most areas of the world regulate the minimum levels of accounting disclosures. In the United States, publicly traded firms must file financial accounting information with the Securities and Exchange Commission (SEC). The two main compulsory SEC filings are:

- Form **10-K**: the audited annual report that includes the four financial statements, discussed below, with explanatory notes and the management's discussion and analysis (MD&A) of financial results.
- Form **10-Q**: the unaudited quarterly report that includes summary versions of the four financial statements and limited additional disclosures.

Forms 10-K (which must be filed within 60 [90] days of the year-end for larger [smaller] companies) and 10-Q (which must be filed within 40 [45] days of the quarter-end for larger [smaller] companies, except for the fourth quarter when it is part of the 10-K) are available electronically from the SEC Website (see Appendix 1A). The minimum, regulated level of information is not the standard. Both the quantity and quality of information differ across companies and over time. We need only look at several annual reports to see considerable variance in the amount and type of accounting information supplied. For example, differences abound on disclosures for segment operations, product performance reports, and financing activities. Further, some stakeholders possess ample bargaining power to obtain accounting information for themselves. These typically include private lenders and major suppliers and customers.

Benefits of Disclosure

The benefits of supplying accounting information extend to a company's capital, labor, input, and output markets. Companies must compete in these markets. For example, capital markets provide debt and equity financing; the better a company's prospects, the lower is its cost of capital (as reflected in lower interest rates or higher stock prices). The same holds for a company's recruiting efforts in labor markets and its ability to establish superior supplier-customer relations in the input and output markets.

A company's performance in these markets depends on success with its business activities *and* the market's awareness of that success. Companies reap the benefits of disclosure with good news about their products, processes, management, and so forth. That is, there are real economic incentives for companies to disclose reliable (audited) accounting information enabling them to better compete in capital, labor, input, and output markets.

What inhibits companies from providing false or misleading good news? There are several constraints. An important constraint imposed by stakeholders is that of audit requirements and legal repercussions associated with inaccurate accounting information. Another relates to reputation effects from disclosures as subsequent events either support or refute earlier news.

Costs of Disclosure

The costs of supplying accounting information include its preparation and dissemination, competitive disadvantages, litigation potential, and political costs. Preparation and dissemination costs can be substantial, but companies have often already incurred those costs because managers need similar information for their own business decisions. The potential for information to yield competitive disadvantages is high. Companies are concerned that disclosures of their activities such as product or segment successes, strategic alliances or pursuits, technological or system innovations, and product or process quality improvements will harm their competitive advantages. Also, companies are frequently sued when disclosures create expectations that are not met. Highly visible companies often face political and public pressure, which creates "political costs." These companies often try to appear as if they do not generate excess profits. For example, government defense contractors, large software conglomerates, and oil companies are favorite targets of public scrutiny. Disclosure costs are higher for companies facing political costs.

The SEC adopted Regulation Fair Disclosure (FD), or Reg FD for short, to curb the practice of selective disclosure by public companies (called *issuers* by the SEC) to certain stockholders and financial analysts. In the past, many companies disclosed important information in meetings and conference calls that excluded individual stockholders. The goal of this rule is to even the playing field for all investors. Reg FD reads as follows: "Whenever an issuer discloses any material nonpublic information regarding that issuer, the issuer shall make public disclosure of that information . . . simultaneously, in the case of an intentional disclosure; and . . . promptly, in the case of a non-intentional disclosure." Reg FD increased the cost of voluntary financial disclosure and led some companies to curtail the supply of financial information to all users.

International Accounting Standards and Convergence

IFRS

The International Accounting Standards Board (IASB) oversees the development of accounting standards for a vast number of countries outside the United States. More than 100 countries, including those in the European Union, require use of International Financial Reporting Standards (IFRS) developed by the IASB. For many years, IASB and the FASB operated as independent standard-setting bodies. In the early 2000s, pressure mounted for these two standard-setting organizations to collaborate and create one set of internationally acceptable standards. At a joint meeting in 2002, the FASB and the IASB each acknowledged their commitment to the development of high-quality, compatible accounting standards that could be used for both domestic and cross-border financial reporting.

The original intent of the two boards was to create one set of standards that companies across the globe would adopt. However, resistance from U.S. companies, investors, and legislators thwarted that effort. Instead, a new approach has emerged and has the support of the SEC staff. Under this method, labeled the *endorsement method*, FASB would remain the U.S. standard setter and endorse new IFRS into the U.S. financial reporting system. Additionally, the FASB will consider how to conform current U.S. standards to existing IFRS. During 2013, FASB and IASB made progress on projects concerning revenue recognition, financial instruments, and leases. At present, the two boards have the following projects on their agendas: loan impairment, insurance contracts, and investment entities.

On July 13, 2012, the staff of the SEC's Office of the Chief Accountant published a report on an IFRS Work Plan. The report did not include a final policy decision, or even a recommendation, as to whether or how IFRS should be incorporated into the U.S. financial reporting system. Thus, as of early 2014, there is no formal plan for U.S. companies to transition to IFRS. For now, the endorsement method prevails. Interestingly, foreign companies that are listed on U.S. stock exchanges are permitted to file IFRS financial statements and many do.

Are financial statements prepared under IFRS substantially different from those prepared under U.S. GAAP? At a broad level, the answer is no. Both are prepared using accrual accounting and utilize similar conceptual frameworks. Both require the same set of financial statements: a balance sheet, an income statement, a statement of cash flows, a statement of stockholders' equity, and a set of explanatory footnotes. That does not mean that no differences exist. However, the differences are typically technical in nature, and do not differ on broad principles discussed in this book.

At the end of each module, we summarize key differences between U.S. GAAP and IFRS. Also, there are a variety of sources that provide more detailed and technical analysis of similarities and differences between U.S. GAAP and IFRS. The FASB, the IASB, and each of the "Big 4" accounting firms also maintain Websites devoted to this issue. Search under IFRS and PwC, KPMG, EY and Deloitte. The two standard-setting bodies also provide useful information, see: FASB (www.fasb.org) and IASB (www.iasb.org).

BUSINESS INSIGHT **Accounting Quality**

In the bear market that followed the bursting of the **dot.com** bubble in the early 2000s, and amid a series of corporate scandals such as **Enron**, **Tyco**, and **WorldCom**, Congress passed the ***Sarbanes-Oxley Act,*** often referred to as *SOX*. SOX sought to rectify perceived problems in accounting, including weak audit committees and deficient internal controls. Increased scrutiny of financial reporting and internal controls has had some success. A report by **Glass, Lewis and Co.**, a corporate-governance research firm, shows that the number of financial restatements by publicly traded companies surged to a record 1,295 in 2005—which is one restatement for each 12 public companies, and more than triple the 2002 total, the year SOX passed. The Glass, Lewis and Co. report concluded that "when so many companies produce inaccurate financial statements, it seriously calls into question the quality of information that investors relied upon to make capital-allocation decisions" (CFO.Com). Bottom line: we must be critical readers of financial reports.

FINANCIAL STATEMENTS

LO2 Identify and explain the four financial statements, and define the accounting equation.

Companies use four financial statements to periodically report on business activities. These statements are the: balance sheet, income statement, statement of stockholders' equity, and statement of cash flows. Exhibit 1.2 shows how these statements are linked across time. A balance sheet reports on a company's financial position at a *point in time*. The income statement, statement of stockholders' equity, and the statement of cash flows report on performance over a *period of time*. The three statements in the middle of Exhibit 1.2 (period-of-time statements) link the balance sheet from the beginning to the end of a period.

EXHIBIT 1.2 **Financial Statement Links across Time**

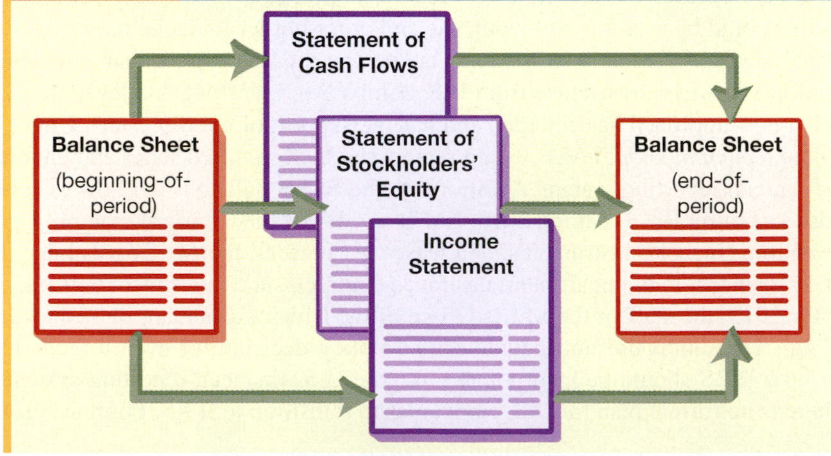

A one-year, or annual, reporting period is common and is called the *accounting*, or *fiscal, year*. Of course, firms prepare financial statements more frequently; semiannual, quarterly, and monthly financial statements are common. *Calendar-year* companies have reporting periods beginning on January 1 and ending on December 31. **Berkshire Hathaway** is a calendar-year company. Some companies choose a fiscal year ending on a date other than December 31, such as when sales and inventory are low. For example, **Target**'s fiscal year ends on the Saturday nearest January 31, after the busy holiday season.

Balance Sheet

A balance sheet reports a company's financial position at a point in time. The balance sheet reports the company's *resources* (*assets*), namely, what the company owns. The balance sheet also reports the *sources* of asset financing. There are two ways a company can finance its assets. It can raise money from stockholders; this is *owner financing*. It can also raise money from banks or other creditors and suppliers; this is *nonowner financing*. This means that both owners and nonowners hold claims on company assets. Owner claims on assets are referred to as *equity* and nonowner claims are referred to as *liabilities* (or debt). Since all financing must be invested in something, we obtain the following basic relation: *investing equals financing*. This equality is called the **accounting equation**, which follows:

Investing = Nonowner Financing + Owner Financing

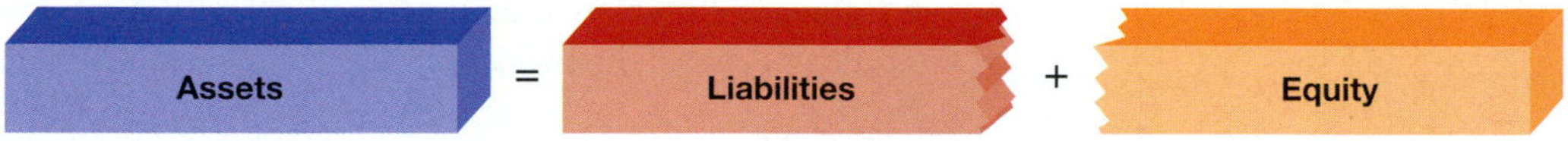

The accounting equation works for all companies at all points in time.

The balance sheet for **Berkshire Hathaway** is in Exhibit 1.3 (condensed). Refer to this balance sheet to verify the following amounts: assets = $427,452 million; liabilities = $235,864 million; and equity = $191,588 million. Assets equal liabilities plus equity, which reflects the accounting equation: investing equals financing.

Investing Activities

Balance sheets are organized like the accounting equation. Investing activities are represented by the company's assets. These assets are financed by a combination of nonowner financing (liabilities) and owner financing (equity).

EXHIBIT 1.3 Balance Sheet ($ millions)

BERKSHIRE HATHAWAY Balance Sheet* December 31, 2012		
Assets		Investing
Cash	$ 46,992	
Noncash assets	380,460	
Total assets	$427,452	Total resources
Liabilities and equity		Financing
Total liabilities	$235,864	Nonowner claim on resources
Equity		
Contributed capital (common stock and paid-in capital)	37,238	
Retained earnings	124,272	
Other equity	26,137	
Berkshire Hathaway equity	187,647	Berkshire Hathaway owners' claim on resources
Noncontrolling interest	3,941	
Total equity	191,588	All owners' claim on resources
Total liabilities and equity†	$427,452	

Callout for the date line: Report amounts at a point in time

* Financial statement titles often begin with the word *consolidated*. This means that the financial statement includes a parent company and one or more subsidiaries, companies that the parent company controls.

† Components of equity are explained as part of Exhibit 1.5. For Berkshire Hathaway, other equity includes accumulated other comprehensive income and treasury stock.

For simplicity, Berkshire Hathaway's balance sheet in Exhibit 1.3 categorizes assets into cash and noncash assets. Noncash assets consist of several asset categories (Module 2 explains the composition of noncash assets). These categories are listed in order of their nearness to cash. For example, companies own a category of assets called inventories. These are goods that the company intends to sell to its customers. Inventories are converted into cash when they are sold, which typically occurs within a short period of time. Hence, they are classified as short-term assets. Companies also report a category of assets called property, plant and equipment. This category includes a company's office buildings or manufacturing facilities. Property, plant and equipment assets will be held for an extended period of time and are, therefore, generally classified as long-term assets.

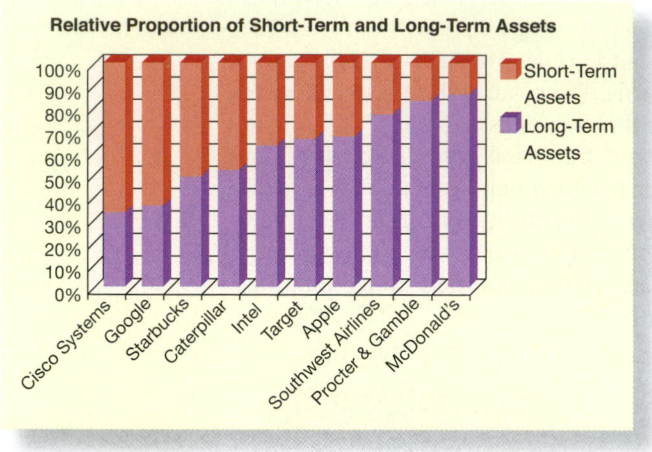

The relative proportion of short-term and long-term assets is largely determined by a company's business model. This is evident in the graph to the side that depicts the relative proportion of short- and long-term assets for several companies that we feature in this book. Companies such as **Cisco** and **Google** require little investment in long-term assets. On the other hand, **Procter & Gamble** and **McDonald's** require a large investment in long-term assets. Although managers can influence the relative amounts and proportion of assets, their flexibility is somewhat limited by the nature of their industries.

Financing Activities

Assets must be paid for, and funding is provided by a combination of owner and nonowner financing. Owner (or equity) financing includes resources contributed to the company by its owners along with any profit retained by the company. Nonowner (creditor or debt) financing is borrowed money. We distinguish between these two financing sources for a reason: borrowed money entails a legal obligation to repay amounts owed, and failure to do so can result in severe consequences for the borrower. Equity financing entails no such legal obligation for repayment.

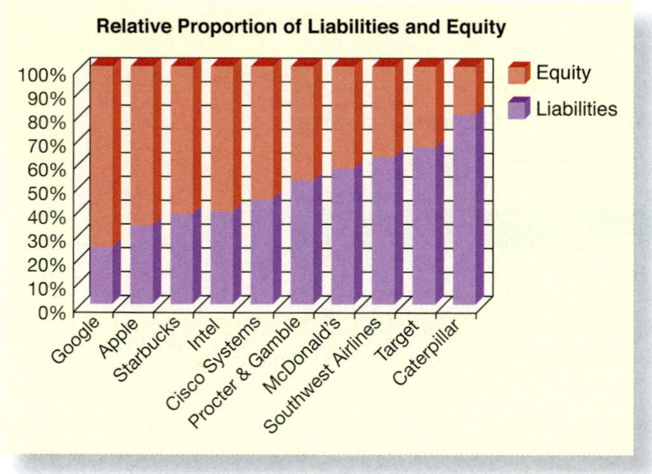

The relative proportion of nonowner (liabilities) and owner (equity) financing is largely determined by a company's business model. This is evident in the graph to the side, again citing many of the companies we feature as focus companies in this book. **Google**'s and **Apple**'s revenues and expenses are more volatile, which means that these companies face greater operating risk than do more established companies that operate in relatively stable markets. On the other hand, **Caterpillar**'s cash flows are relatively stable. They can operate with more nonowner financing.

Our discussion of investing and financing activities uses many terms and concepts that we explain later in the book. Our desire here is to provide a sneak preview into the interplay among financial statements, manager behavior, and economics. Some questions that we might have at this early stage regarding the balance sheet follow:

- Berkshire Hathaway reports $46,992 million of cash on its 2012 balance sheet, which is 11% of total assets. Many investment-type companies such as Berkshire Hathaway and high-tech companies such as Cisco Systems carry high levels of cash. Why is that? Is there a cost to holding too much cash? Is it costly to carry too little cash?
- The relative proportion of short-term and long-term assets is largely dictated by companies' business models. Why is this the case? Why is the composition of assets on balance sheets for companies in the same industry similar? By what degree can a company's asset composition safely deviate from industry norms?

- What are the trade-offs in financing a company by owner versus nonowner financing? If nonowner financing is less costly, why don't we see companies financed entirely with borrowed money?
- How do stockholders influence the strategic direction of a company? How can long-term creditors influence strategic direction?
- Most assets and liabilities are reported on the balance sheet at their acquisition price, called *historical cost*. Would reporting assets and liabilities at fair values be more informative? What problems might fair-value reporting cause?

Review the Berkshire Hathaway balance sheet summarized in Exhibit 1.3 and think about these questions. We provide answers for each of these questions as we progress through the book.

IFRS INSIGHT **Balance Sheet Presentation and IFRS**

Balance sheets prepared under IFRS often classify accounts in reverse order of liquidity (lack of nearness to cash), which is the opposite of what U.S. companies do. For example, intangible assets are typically listed first and cash is listed last among assets. Also, equity is often listed before liabilities, where liabilities are again listed in order of decreasing liquidity. These choices reflect convention and *not* IFRS requirements.

Income Statement

An **income statement** reports on a company's performance over a period of time and lists amounts for revenues (also called sales) and expenses. Revenues less expenses yield the bottom-line net income amount. **Berkshire Hathaway**'s income statement is in Exhibit 1.4. Refer to its income statement to verify the following: revenues = $162,463 million; expenses = $147,151 million; and net income = $15,312 million. Net income reflects the profit (also called earnings) to owners for that specific period.

EXHIBIT 1.4 Income Statement ($ millions)

BERKSHIRE HATHAWAY
Income Statement
For Year Ended December 31, 2012 ← Report amounts over a period of time

Revenues	$162,463 ← Goods or services provided to customers
Expenses	147,151 ← Costs incurred to generate revenues
Net income	$ 15,312
Less: Earnings attributable to noncontrolling interest	488
Net income attributable to Berkshire Hathaway stockholders	$ 14,824

ANALYSIS INSIGHT **Earnings Attributable to Noncontrolling Interest**

The income statement shows net income separated into two parts; one portion *attributable to noncontrolling interest* and a second portion *attributable to Berkshire Hathaway stockholders*. When you buy stock in Berkshire Hathaway, you are a stockholder of that company. Berkshire Hathaway owns stock in other companies, and the companies that Berkshire Hathaway (the *parent*) owns are called *subsidiaries*. Most of Berkshire Hathaway's subsidiaries are owned entirely (100%) by Berkshire Hathaway. These are called "wholly-owned subsidiaries." However, some Berkshire Hathaway subsidiaries are owned jointly by Berkshire Hathaway and other outside stockholders. If Berkshire Hathaway owns more than 50% of the common stock of a given subsidiary, Berkshire has de facto control over the operating, investing, and financing activities of the subsidiary. In this case, Berkshire Hathaway includes *all* of the revenues and *all* of the expenses of such a subsidiary in its own consolidated income statement. Then, Berkshire Hathaway separates the total consolidated net income into the portion that it owns (*income attributable to Berkshire Hathaway stockholders*) and the portion owned by outside stockholders (*income attributable to noncontrolling interest*). The portion is determined by the percent of outstanding common stock that Berkshire Hathaway owns (if Berkshire Hathaway owns 60% of the stock, 60% of the subsidiary's income is attributable to Berkshire Hathaway stockholders and 40% is attributable to the noncontrolling interest). So, which income number should we use in an analysis of Berkshire Hathaway? Because analysis is usually performed from the standpoint of a stockholder of Berkshire Hathaway, we focus on the *net income attributable to Berkshire Hathaway stockholders*.

Manufacturing and merchandising companies typically include an additional expense account, called cost of goods sold (or cost of sales), in the income statement following revenues. It is also common to report a subtotal called gross profit (or gross margin), which is revenues less cost of goods sold. The company's remaining expenses are then reported below gross profit. This income statement layout follows:

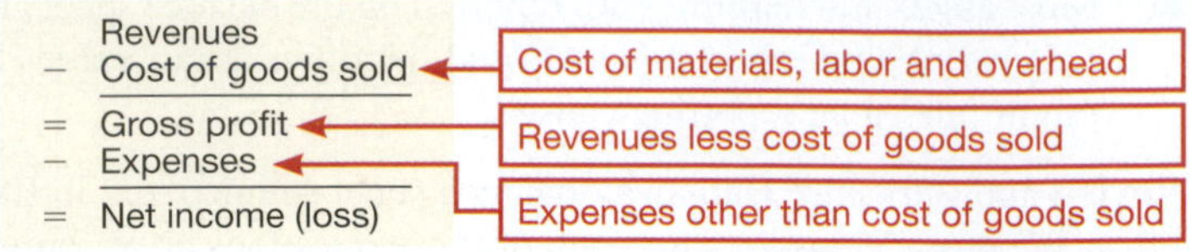

Operating Activities

Operating activities use company resources to produce, promote, and sell its products and services. These activities extend from input markets involving suppliers of materials and labor to a company's output markets involving customers of products and services. Input markets generate most *expenses* (or *costs*) such as inventory, salaries, materials, and logistics. Output markets generate *revenues* (or *sales*) to customers. Output markets also generate some expenses such as marketing and distributing products and services to customers. Net income arises when revenues exceed expenses. A loss occurs when expenses exceed revenues.

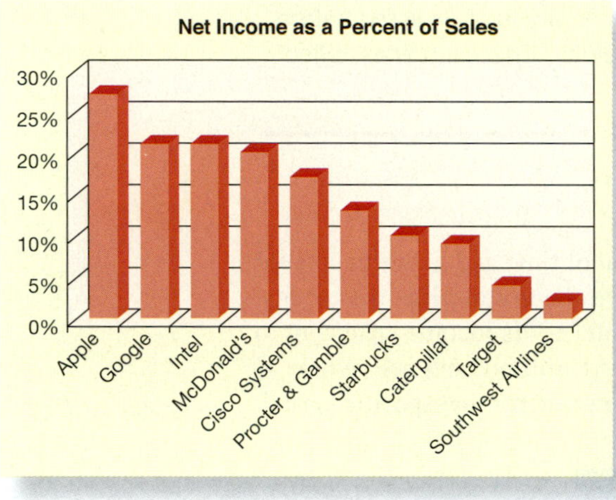

Differences exist in the relative profitability of companies across industries. Although effective management can increase the profitability of a company, business models play a large part in determining company profitability. These differences are illustrated in the graph (to the side) of net income as a percentage of sales for several companies.

Target operates in a mature industry with little ability to differentiate its merchandise from competitors. Hence, its income as a percent of sales is low. **Southwest Airlines** faces a different kind of problem: having competitors that are desperate and trying to survive. Profitability will not return to the transportation industry until weaker competitors are no longer protected by bankruptcy courts. At the other end of the spectrum are **Apple**, **Google**, and **Intel**. All three are dominant in their industries with products protected by patent laws. Their profitability levels are more akin to that of monopolists.

As a sneak preview, we might consider the following questions regarding the income statement:

- Assume that a company sells a product to a customer who promises to pay in 30 days. Should the seller recognize the sale when it is made or when cash is collected?
- When a company purchases a long-term asset such as a building, its cost is reported on the balance sheet as an asset. Should a company, instead, record the cost of that building as an expense when it is acquired? If not, how should a company report the cost of that asset over the course of its useful life?
- Manufacturers and merchandisers report the cost of a product as an expense when the product sale is recorded. How might we measure the costs of a product that is sold by a merchandiser? By a manufacturer?
- If an asset, such as a building, increases in value, that increase in value is not reported as income until the building is sold, if ever. What concerns arise if we record increases in asset values as part of income, when measurement of that increase is based on appraised values?
- Employees commonly earn wages that are yet to be paid at the end of a particular period. Should their wages be recognized as an expense in the period that the work is performed, or when the wages are paid?
- Companies are not allowed to report profit on transactions relating to their own stock. That is, they don't report income when stock is sold, nor do they report an expense when dividends are paid to stockholders. Why is this the case?

Review the Berkshire Hathaway income statement summarized in Exhibit 1.4 and think about these questions. We provide answers for each of these questions as we progress through the book.

BUSINESS INSIGHT **Warren Buffett on Financial Reports**

"When Charlie and I read reports, we have no interest in pictures of personnel, plants or products. References to EBITDA [earnings before interest, taxes, depreciation and amortization] make us shudder—does management think the tooth fairy pays for capital expenditures? We're very suspicious of accounting methodology that is vague or unclear, since too often that means management wishes to hide something. And we don't want to read messages that a public relations department or consultant has turned out. Instead, we expect a company's CEO to explain in his or her own words what's happening." —Berkshire Hathaway Annual Report

Statement of Stockholders' Equity

The **statement of stockholders' equity** reports on changes in key types of equity over a period of time. For each type of equity, the statement reports the beginning balance, a summary of the activity in the account during the year, and the ending balance. **Berkshire Hathaway**'s statement of stockholders' equity is in Exhibit 1.5. During the recent period, its equity changed due to share issuances and income reinvestment. Berkshire Hathaway classifies these changes into four categories:

- *Contributed capital*, the stockholders' net contributions to the company
- *Retained earnings*, net income over the life of the company minus all dividends ever paid
- *Other*, consists of amounts that we explain later in the book
- *Noncontrolling interest*, the equity of outside stockholders

EXHIBIT 1.5 Statement of Equity ($ millions)

BERKSHIRE HATHAWAY
Statement of Stockholders' Equity
For Year Ended December 31, 2012 ← Report amounts over a period of time

	Contributed Capital	Retained Earnings	Other Equity	Noncontrolling Interest	Total
December 31, 2011	$37,815	$109,448	$17,587	$4,111	$168,961 ← Beginning period amounts
Stock issuance (repurchase) . . .	118		(1,296)		(1,178)
Net income		14,824[a]		488[b]	15,312 ← Change in balances over a period
Dividends		(0)			(0)
Other.	(695)		9,846	(658)	8,493
December 31, 2012	$37,238	$124,272	$26,137	$3,941	$191,588 ← Ending period amounts

[a] This is *income attributable to Berkshire Hathaway stockholders*, see Exhibit 1.4
[b] This is *income attributable to noncontrolling interest*, see Exhibit 1.4

Exhibit 1.5 reconciles the activity in each of the equity accounts from the balance sheet in Exhibit 1.3. We briefly discuss each of these accounts here and explain the accounts in depth in Module 8.

- **Contributed capital** represents assets the company received from issuing stock to stockholders (also called shareholders). The balance of this account at the beginning of the year was $37,815 million. During the year, Berkshire Hathaway sold additional shares for $118 million and recorded miscellaneous adjustments of $(695) million to yield a year-end balance of $37,238 million.
- **Retained earnings** (also called *earned capital* or *reinvested capital*) represent the cumulative total amount of income that the company has ever earned and that has been retained in the business; that is, not distributed to stockholders in the form of dividends. The change in retained earnings links consecutive balance sheets via the income statement: Ending retained earnings = Beginning retained earnings + Net income for the period − Dividends for the period. For Berkshire Hathaway, its retained earnings increases from $109,448 million to $124,272 million. This increase of $14,824 million is explained by its net income of $14,824 million as Berkshire Hathaway paid no dividends in 2012.
- **Other equity** for Berkshire Hathaway consists of *accumulated other comprehensive income (AOCI)* and *Treasury stock (TS)*. We defer discussion of AOCI to Module 8. For now, view AOCI

as income that has not been reflected in the income statement and is, therefore, excluded from retained earnings. Treasury stock is the cost of the shares that Berkshire Hathaway has *repurchased* and not *reissued*. It can be seen as the opposite of contributed capital. Treasury stock decreases equity when shares are repurchased (hence, the negative sign).

- **Noncontrolling interest** represents the equity of noncontrolling stockholders who own stock in Berkshire Hathaway's subsidiaries. As with equity for Berkshire Hathaway's stockholders, the equity of noncontrolling interest increases by income attributable to noncontrolling interest and decreases by any dividends paid or losses attributable to the noncontrolling interest (there were none in 2012). We defer discussion of this account to Modules 8 and 9.

RESEARCH INSIGHT **Are Earnings Important?**

A study asked top finance executives of publicly traded companies to *rank the three most important measures to report to outsiders.* The study reports that:

> "[More than 50% of] CFOs state that earnings are the most important financial metric to external constituents . . . this finding could reflect superior informational content in earnings over the other metrics. Alternatively, it could reflect myopic managerial concern about earnings. The emphasis on earnings is noteworthy because cash flows continue to be the measure emphasized in the academic finance literature."

The study also reports that CFOs view year-over-year change in earnings to be of critical importance to outsiders. Why is that? The study provides the following insights.

> "CFOs note that the first item in a press release is often a comparison of current quarter earnings with four quarters lagged quarterly earnings . . . CFOs also mention that while analysts' forecasts can be guided by management, last year's quarterly earnings number is a benchmark that is harder, if not impossible, to manage after the 10-Q has been filed with the SEC . . . Several executives mention that comparison to seasonally lagged earnings numbers provides a measure of earnings momentum and growth, and therefore is a useful gauge of corporate performance."

Thus, are earnings important? To the majority of finance chiefs surveyed, the answer is a resounding yes. (Source: Graham, et al., *Journal of Accounting and Economics,* 2005)

Statement of Cash Flows

The **statement of cash flows** reports the change (either an increase or a decrease) in a company's cash balance over a period of time. The statement reports cash inflows and outflows from operating, investing, and financing activities over a period of time. Berkshire Hathaway's statement of cash flows is in Exhibit 1.6. Its cash balance increased by $9,693 million in the recent period: operating activities generated a $20,950 million cash inflow, investing activities reduced cash by $10,574 million, and financing activities yielded a cash outflow of $683 million.

EXHIBIT 1.6 **Statement of Cash Flows ($ millions)**

Report amounts over a period of time

Net cash inflow from operating

Net cash outflow from investing

Net cash outflow from financing

Cash amounts per balance sheet

BERKSHIRE HATHAWAY Statement of Cash Flows For Year Ended December 31, 2012	
Operating cash flows	$20,950
Investing cash flows	(10,574)
Financing cash flows	(683)*
Net increase in cash	9,693
Cash, December 31, 2011	37,299
Cash, December 31, 2012	$46,992

* Includes $(123) relating to foreign currency exchange rate changes.

Berkshire Hathaway's operating cash flow of $20,950 million does not equal its $14,824 million net income. Generally, a company's net cash flow for a period does *not* equal its net income for the period. This is due to timing differences between when revenue and expense items are recognized on the income statement and when cash is received and paid. (We discuss this concept further in subsequent modules.)

Both cash flow and net income numbers are important for business decisions. Each is used in security valuation models, and both help users of accounting reports understand and assess a company's past, present, and future business activities. As a sneak preview, we might consider the following questions regarding the statement of cash flows:

- What is the usefulness of the statement of cash flows? Do the balance sheet and income statement provide sufficient cash flow information?
- What types of information are disclosed in the statement of cash flows and why are they important?
- What kinds of activities are reported in each of the operating, investing, and financing sections of the statement of cash flows? How is this information useful?
- Is it important for a company to report net cash inflows (positive amounts) relating to operating activities over the longer term? What are the implications if operating cash flows are negative for an extended period of time?
- Why is it important to know the composition of a company's investment activities? What kind of information might we look for? Are positive investing cash flows favorable?
- Is it important to know the sources of a company's financing activities? What questions might that information help us answer?
- How might the composition of operating, investing, and financing cash flows change over a company's life cycle?
- Is the bottom line increase in cash flow the key number? Why or why not?

Review the Berkshire Hathaway statement of cash flows summarized in Exhibit 1.6 and think about these questions. We provide answers for each of these questions as we progress through the book.

Financial Statement Linkages

The four financial statements are linked within and across periods—consider the following:

- The income statement and the balance sheet are linked via retained earnings. For Berkshire Hathaway, the $14,824 million increase in retained earnings (reported on the balance sheet) equals its net income (reported on the income statement) (see Exhibit 1.5). Berkshire Hathaway did not pay dividends in 2012.
- Retained earnings, contributed capital, and other equity balances appear both on the statement of stockholders' equity and the balance sheet.
- The statement of cash flows is linked to the income statement as net income is a component of operating cash flow. The statement of cash flows is also linked to the balance sheet as the change in the balance sheet cash account reflects the net cash inflows and outflows for the period.

Items that impact one financial statement ripple through the others. Linkages among the four financial statements are an important feature of the accounting system.

Information Beyond Financial Statements

Important financial information about a company is communicated to various decision makers through means other than the four financial statements. These include the following:

- Management Discussion and Analysis (MD&A)
- Independent auditor report
- Financial statement footnotes
- Regulatory filings, including proxy statements and other SEC filings

We describe and explain the usefulness of these additional information sources throughout the book.

Choices in Financial Accounting

Some people mistakenly assume that financial accounting is an exact discipline—that is, companies select the one proper accounting method to account for a transaction, and then follow the rules. The reality is that GAAP allows companies choices in preparing financial statements. The choice of methods can yield financial statements that are markedly different from one another in terms of reported income, assets, liabilities, and equity amounts.

People often are surprised that financial statements comprise numerous estimates. For example, companies must estimate the amounts that will eventually be collected from customers, the length of time that buildings and equipment will be productive, the value impairments of assets, the future costs of warranty claims, and the eventual payouts on pension plans. Following are examples of how some managers are alleged to have abused the latitude available in reporting financial results.

Company	Allegations
Adelphia Communications (ADELQ)	Founding Rigas family collected $3.1 billion in off-balance-sheet loans backed by Adelphia; it overstated results by inflating capital expenses and hiding debt.
Time Warner (TWX)	As the ad market faltered and AOL's purchase of Time Warner loomed, AOL inflated sales by booking revenue for barter deals and ads it sold for third parties. These questionable revenues boosted growth rates and sealed the deal. AOL also boosted sales via "round-trip" deals with advertisers and suppliers.
Enron	Created profits and hid debt totaling over $1 billion by improperly using off-the-books partnerships; manipulated the Texas power market; bribed foreign governments to win contracts abroad; manipulated California energy market.
Global Crossing (GLBC)	Engaged in network capacity "swaps" with other carriers to inflate revenue; shredded documents related to accounting practices.
Qwest Communications International (Q)	Inflated revenue using network capacity "swaps" and improper accounting for long-term deals.
Tyco (TYC)	Ex-CEO L. Dennis Kozlowski indicted for tax evasion; Kozlowski and former CFO Mark H. Swartz, convicted of taking unauthorized loans from the company.
WorldCom	Overstated cash flow by booking $11 billion in operating expenses as capital costs; loaned founder Bernard Ebbers $400 million off-the-books.
Autonomy Corp.	Engaged in aggressive revenue recognition ("round-trip transactions") where it bought goods from customers and failed to fully record costs; its overstated results allegedly led Hewlett-Packard to overpay when acquiring Autonomy stock.

Accounting standard setters walk a fine line regarding choice in accounting. On one hand, they are concerned that choice in preparing financial statements will lead to abuse by those seeking to gain by influencing decisions of financial statement users. On the other hand, standard setters are concerned that companies are too diverse for a "one size fits all" financial accounting system.

Enron exemplifies the problems that accompany rigid accounting standards. A set of accounting standards relating to special purpose entities (SPEs) provided preparers with guidelines under which those entities were or were not to be consolidated. Unfortunately, once the SPE guidelines were set, some people worked diligently to structure SPE transactions so as to narrowly avoid the consolidation requirements and achieve *off-balance-sheet* financing. This is just one example of how, with rigid standards, companies can adhere to the letter of the rule, but not its intent. In such situations, the financial statements are not fairly presented.

For most of its existence, the FASB has promulgated standards that were quite complicated and replete with guidelines. This invited abuse of the type embodied by the Enron scandal. In recent years, the pendulum has begun to swing away from such rigidity. Now, once financial statements are prepared, company management is required to step back from the details and make a judgment on whether the statements taken as a whole "fairly present" the financial condition of the company as is asserted in the company's audit report (see below).

Moreover, since the enactment of the **Sarbanes-Oxley Act,** the SEC requires the chief executive officer (CEO) of the company and its chief financial officer (CFO) to personally sign a statement attesting to the accuracy and completeness of the financial statements. This requirement is an important step in restoring confidence in the integrity of financial accounting. The statements signed by both the CEO and CFO contain the following declarations:

- Both the CEO and CFO have personally reviewed the annual report.
- There are no untrue statements of a material fact that would make the statements misleading.
- Financial statements fairly present in all material respects the financial condition of the company.
- All material facts are disclosed to the company's auditors and board of directors.
- No changes to its system of internal controls are made unless properly communicated.

The Sarbanes-Oxley Act (SOX) also imposed fines and potential jail time for executives. Presumably, the prospect of personal losses is designed to make these executives more vigilant in monitoring the financial accounting system. More recently, Congress passed *The Wall Street Reform and Consumer Protection Act* of 2010 (or the Dodd-Frank Act). Among the provisions of the act were rules that strengthened SOX by augmenting "claw-back" provisions for executives' ill-gotten gains.

MANAGERIAL DECISION **You Are the Product Manager**

There is often friction between investors' need for information and a company's desire to safeguard competitive advantages. Assume that you are a key-product manager at your company. Your department has test-marketed a potentially lucrative new product, which it plans to further finance. You are asked for advice on the extent of information to disclose about the new product in the MD&A section of the company's upcoming annual report. What advice do you provide and why? [Answer, p. 1-32]

MID-MODULE REVIEW

The following financial information is from **AXA Equitable Life Insurance Company**, a competitor of Berkshire Hathaway's GEICO Insurance, for the year ended December 31, 2012 ($ millions).

Cash, ending year	$ 3,162
Cash flows from operations	(780)
Revenues	9,160
Net income attributable to AXA stockholders	121
AXA stockholders' equity	15,436
Cash flows from financing	3,407
Total liabilities	158,913
Expenses	8,944
Noncash assets	173,681
Cash flows from investing	(2,692)
Net income	216
Noncontrolling interest (equity)	2,494
Cash, beginning year	3,227

Required

1. Prepare an income statement, balance sheet, and statement of cash flows for AXA at December 31, 2012.
2. Compare the balance sheet and income statement of AXA to those of Berkshire Hathaway in Exhibits 1.3 and 1.4. What differences do we observe?

The solution is on page 1-43.

ANALYSIS OF FINANCIAL STATEMENTS

LO3 Explain and apply the basics of profitability analysis.

This section previews the analysis framework of this book. This framework is used extensively by market professionals who analyze financial reports to evaluate company management and value the company's debt and equity securities. Analysis of financial performance is crucial in assessing prior strategic decisions and evaluating strategic alternatives.

Return on Assets

Suppose we learn that a company reports a profit of $10 million. Does the $10 million profit indicate that the company is performing well? Knowing that a company reports a profit is certainly positive as it indicates that customers value its goods or services and that its revenues exceed expenses. However, we cannot assess how well it is performing without considering the context. To explain, suppose we learn that this company has $500 million in assets. We now assess the $10 million profit as low because relative to the size of its asset investment, the company earned a paltry 2% return, computed as $10 million divided by $500 million. A 2% return on assets is what a much lower-risk investment in government-backed bonds might yield. The important point is that a company's profitability must be assessed with respect to the size of its investment. One common metric is the *return on assets* (ROA)—defined as net income for that period divided by the average assets for that period.

Components of Return on Assets

We can separate return on assets into two components: profitability and productivity. Profitability relates profit to sales. This ratio is called the *profit margin* (PM), and it reflects the net income (profit after tax) earned on each sales dollar. Management wants to earn as much profit as possible from sales.

Productivity relates sales to assets. This component, called *asset turnover* (AT), reflects sales generated by each dollar of assets. Management wants to maximize asset productivity, that is, to achieve the highest possible sales level for a given level of assets (or to achieve a given level of sales with the smallest level of assets).

Exhibit 1.7 depicts the disaggregation of return on assets into these two components. Profitability (PM) and productivity (AT) are multiplied to yield the return on assets (ROA). Average assets are commonly defined as (beginning-year assets + ending-year assets)/2.

EXHIBIT 1.7 Return on Assets Disaggregation

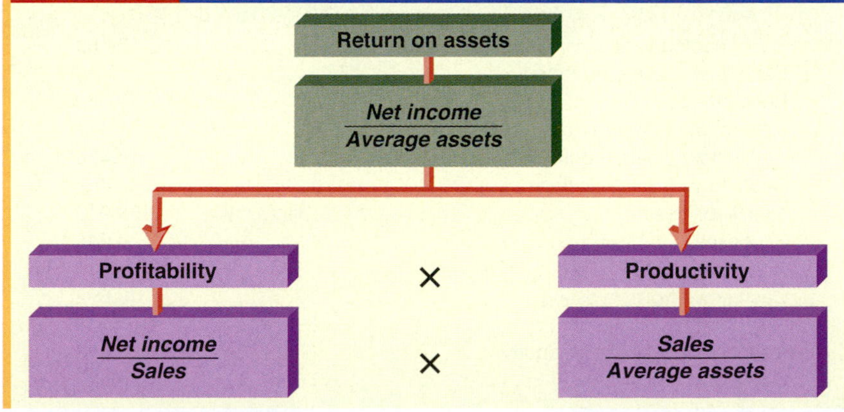

There are an infinite number of combinations of profit margin and asset turnover that yield the same return on assets. To illustrate, Exhibit 1.8 graphs actual combinations of these two components for companies that we highlight in this book (each is identified by its ticker symbol). Retailers, such as **Home Depot** (HD), **Target** (TGT), and **Starbucks** (SBUX) are characterized by relatively low profit margins and a high turnover of their assets. The business models for other companies such as **3M** (MMM), **Johnson & Johnson** (JNJ), and **McDonald's** (MCD) require a larger investment in assets. These companies must earn a higher profit margin to yield an acceptable ROA. We might be surprised to see technology companies such as **Apple** (AAPL), **Google** (GOOG), and **Cisco** (CSCO) in the group with high asset investments. Technology companies typically maintain a high level of cash and short-term investments on their balance sheets, which allows them to respond quickly to opportunities. The solid line represents those profitability and productivity combinations that yield a 10.5% return on assets.

EXHIBIT 1.8 Profitability and Productivity Across Companies

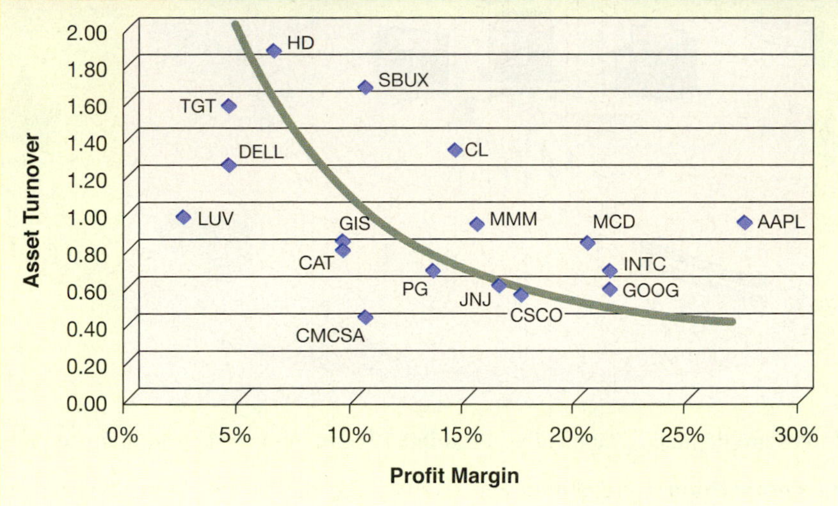

Return on Equity

Another important analysis measure is return on equity (ROE), which is defined as net income attributable to the parent company's stockholders divided by average stockholders' equity, where average equity is commonly defined as (beginning-year equity attributable to the parent company's stockholders + ending-year equity attributable to the parent company's stockholders)/2. In this case, company earnings are compared to the level of stockholder (not total) investment. ROE reflects the return to stockholders, which is different from the return for the entire company (ROA).

MANAGERIAL DECISION You Are the Chief Financial Officer

You are reviewing your company's financial performance for the first six months of the year and are unsatisfied with the results. How can you disaggregate return on assets to identify areas for improvement? [Answer, p. 1-32]

FINANCIAL STATEMENTS AND BUSINESS ANALYSIS

LO4 Describe business analysis within the context of a competitive environment.

Analysis and interpretation of financial statements must consider the broader business context in which a company operates. This section describes how to systematically consider those broader business forces to enhance our analysis and interpretation. This business analysis can sharpen our insights and help us better estimate future performance and company value.

Analyzing the Competitive Environment

Financial statements are influenced by five important forces that confront the company and determine its competitive intensity: (A) industry competition, (B) buyer power, (C) supplier power, (D) product substitutes, and (E) threat of entry (for further discussion, see Porter, *Competitive Strategy: Techniques for Analyzing Industries and Competitors,* 1980 and 1998).

EXHIBIT 1.9 Competitive Forces within the Broader Business Environment

These five forces are depicted graphically in Exhibit 1.9 and are key determinants of profitability.

Ⓐ **Industry competition** Competition and rivalry raise the cost of doing business as companies must hire and train competitive workers, advertise products, research and develop products, and engage in other related activities.

Ⓑ **Bargaining power of buyers** Buyers with strong bargaining power can extract price concessions and demand a higher level of service and delayed payment terms; this force reduces both profits from sales and the operating cash flows to sellers.

Ⓒ **Bargaining power of suppliers** Suppliers with strong bargaining power can demand higher prices and earlier payments, yielding adverse effects on profits and cash flows to buyers.

Ⓓ **Threat of substitution** As the number of product substitutes increases, sellers have less power to raise prices and/or pass on costs to buyers; accordingly, threat of substitution places downward pressure on profits of sellers.

Ⓔ **Threat of entry** New market entrants increase competition; to mitigate that threat, companies expend monies on activities such as new technologies, promotion, and human development to erect *barriers to entry* and to create *economies of scale*.

The broader business environment affects the level of profitability that a company can expect to achieve. Global economic forces and the quality and cost of labor affect the macroeconomy in which the company operates. Government regulation, borrowing agreements exacted by creditors, and internal governance procedures also affect the range of operating activities in which a company can engage. In addition, strategic plans are influenced by the oversight of equity markets, and investors are loathe to allow companies the freedom to manage for the longer term. Each of these external forces affects a company's strategic planning and expected level of profitability.

The relative strength of companies within their industries, and vis-à-vis suppliers and customers, is an important determinant of both their profitability and the structure of their balance sheets. As competition intensifies, profitability likely declines, and the amount of assets companies need to carry on their balance sheet likely increases in an effort to generate more profit. Such changes are revealed in the income statement and the balance sheet.

Applying Competitive Analysis

We apply the competitive analysis framework to help interpret the financial results of McLane Company. McLane is a subsidiary of Berkshire Hathaway and was acquired several years ago. Berkshire describes McLane's business in the following note to the Berkshire Hathaway 2012 annual report:

McLane Company—McLane Company, Inc. ("McLane") provides wholesale distribution and logistics services in all 50 states and internationally in Brazil to customers that include convenience stores, discount retailers, wholesale clubs, drug stores, military bases, quick service restaurants, and casual dining restaurants. Prior to Berkshire's acquisition in 2003, McLane was an integral part of the Wal-Mart Stores, Inc. ("Wal-Mart") distribution network. McLane continues to provide wholesale distribution services to Wal-Mart, which accounts for approximately 28% of McLane's revenues. McLane's business model is based on a high volume of sales, rapid inventory turnover, and tight expense control.

McLane is a wholesaler of food products; it purchases food products in finished and semifinished form from agricultural and food-related businesses and resells them to grocery and convenience food stores. The extensive distribution network required in this business entails considerable investment. Our business analysis of McLane's financial results includes the following observations:

- **Industry competitors** McLane has many competitors with food products that are difficult to differentiate.
- **Bargaining power of buyers** The note above reveals that 28% of McLane's sales are to Wal-Mart, which has considerable buying power that limits seller profits; also, the food industry is characterized by high turnover and low profit margins, which implies that cost control is key to success.
- **Bargaining power of suppliers** McLane is large ($37 billion in annual sales), which implies its suppliers are unlikely to exert forces to increase its cost of sales.
- **Threat of substitution** Grocery items are usually not well differentiated; this means the threat of substitution is high, which inhibits its ability to raise selling prices.
- **Threat of entry** High investment costs, such as warehousing and logistics, are a barrier to entry in McLane's business; this means the threat of entry is relatively low.

Our analysis reveals that McLane is a high-volume, low-margin company. Its ability to control costs is crucial to its financial performance, including its ability to fully utilize its assets. Evaluation of McLane's financial statements should focus on that dimension.

Analyzing the Broader Business Environment

Quality analysis depends on an effective business analysis. Before we analyze a single accounting number, we must ask questions about a company's business environment such as the following:

- *Life cycle* At what stage in its life is this company? Is it a start-up, experiencing growing pains? Is it strong and mature, reaping the benefits of competitive advantages? Is it nearing the end of its life, trying to milk what it can from stagnant product lines?
- *Outputs* What products does it sell? Are its products new, established, or dated? Do its products have substitutes? How complicated are its products to produce?
- *Buyers* Who are its buyers? Are buyers in good financial condition? Do buyers have substantial purchasing power? Can the seller dictate sales terms to buyers?
- *Inputs* Who are its suppliers? Are there many supply sources? Does the company depend on a few supply sources with potential for high input costs?
- *Competition* In what kind of markets does it operate? Are markets open? Is the market competitive? Does the company have competitive advantages? Can it protect itself from new entrants? At what cost? How must it compete to survive?
- *Financing* Must it seek financing from public markets? Is it going public? Is it seeking to use its stock to acquire another company? Is it in danger of defaulting on debt covenants? Are there incentives to tell an overly optimistic story to attract lower-cost financing or to avoid default on debt?
- *Labor* Who are its managers? What are their backgrounds? Can they be trusted? Are they competent? What is the state of employee relations? Is labor unionized?

- *Governance* How effective is its corporate governance? Does it have a strong and independent board of directors? Does a strong audit committee of the board exist, and is it populated with outsiders? Does management have a large portion of its wealth tied to the company's stock?
- *Risk* Is it subject to lawsuits from competitors or stockholders? Is it under investigation by regulators? Has it changed auditors? If so, why? Does it face environmental and/or political risks?

We must assess the broader business context in which a company operates as we read and interpret its financial statements. A review of financial statements, which reflect business activities, cannot be undertaken in a vacuum. It is contextual and can only be effectively undertaken within the framework of a thorough understanding of the broader forces that impact company performance. We should view the above questions as a sneak preview of the types we will ask and answer throughout this book when we read and interpret financial statements.

Analyzing Competitive Advantage

The goal of our analysis is to identify *sustainable operating income and cash flow*. This is true whether our analysis is focused on valuation of equity securities as a current or prospective investor, or on a company's ability to repay its debt as a current or prospective creditor, or on trying to grow company value as part of management. This analysis is much deeper than merely eliminating transitory (nonrecurring) items from financial statements. It is an attempt to answer one of the following two questions:

1. Is the company's competitive advantage sustainable?
2. If the company has no competitive advantage, does its management have a plan to develop a sustainable competitive advantage that can be implemented in an acceptable period of time and with a reasonable amount of investment?

Answers to these questions impact forecasts of the company's future performance.

Companies increase market value when they earn a return on investment that exceeds the usual level of return (we discuss valuation of equity securities in Module 12). It is very difficult, however, to sustain such excess returns given a competitive environment and ever-shortening product life cycles. We already discussed the nature of a competitive environment as advanced by Professor Michael Porter, who also identified *cost leadership* and *differentiation* as potential strategies to achieve sustainable competitive advantage (see Porter, *Competitive Advantage: Creating and Sustaining Superior Performance*, The Free Press, 1985). Our aim is to identify the source of competitive advantage and to investigate the extent to which it is sustainable, that is, whether it can be competed away.

Patents and other protections of intellectual property create *barriers to entry* that allow a company to achieve a comparative advantage and excess returns. These legal barriers typically have a finite life, however, and a company must maintain a pipeline of *innovations* that offer replacements for intellectual property that loses patent protection. The pharmaceutical industry is one example and analysts focus on pending patent expirations and the replacements.

In the absence of legal protection, companies utilize other strategies to achieve sustainable competitive advantage. *Product differentiation* is one strategy, and, if the company is able to effectively differentiate its product so that there are limited or no substitutes, it can charge a premium price to yield excess returns. Typically, differentiation is achieved from technological innovation that produces products and services with attributes valued by customers and not easily replicated by competitors. Differentiation along the dimensions of product design, marketing, distribution, and after-sale customer support are examples. Such differentiation has costs such as research and development, advertising, and other marketing expenses. Our analysis of such strategies focuses on the cost of achieving such differentiation vis-à-vis the price premium extracted from the market. We also focus on the extent competitors can develop an effective response, thus, creating price pressure and reducing returns. Commentary in the Management Discussion and Analysis (MD&A) section of the 10-K can provide useful insights along with financial press articles, actions and plans of competitors, and consumers of the company's products or services.

Another approach to achieve excess returns is to become a *cost leader*. Cost leadership can result from a number of factors, including access to low-cost raw materials or labor (while maintaining quality), manufacturing or service efficiency in the form of cost-efficient processes and manufacturing scale efficiencies, greater bargaining power with suppliers, sophisticated IT systems that permit timely collection of key information, and other avenues. Companies that view themselves as cost leaders frequently highlight the areas in which they excel in the MD&A. Our analysis focuses on the degree such cost efficiencies are likely to persist.

In the absence of a competitive advantage, our analysis focuses on the likelihood that a company develops such an advantage. Management often discusses strategy with stockholders and equity analysts, which are recorded in conference calls that are readily available or reported in the financial press. In the case of a turnaround situation, our focus is on viability of the plan, that is, can it be achieved at an acceptable cost given the current state of the industry. Moreover, our focus is long term. Companies can often achieve short-term gains at long-term cost, such as by selling off profitable segments. Such actions do not create long-term value.

Our increasingly competitive environment has led to an increasing number of failures. Two-thirds of the original Fortune 500 disappeared within three decades and only 71 survive today (see Stangler and Arbesman, *What Does FORTUNE 500 Turnover Mean?* Ewing Marion Kauffman Foundation, 2012). Creating a sustainable competitive advantage that yields excess returns is difficult and we are wary of forecasted excess returns for an extended period. Through a critical and thorough investigation of financial statements, its footnotes, the MD&A, and all publicly available information, we can identify drivers of a company's competitive advantage. We then test the sustainability and validity of those drivers. This is an important step in assessing competitive advantage.

GLOBAL ACCOUNTING

As we discussed earlier, the United States is among only a few economically developed countries (such as India, Singapore, and Taiwan) that do not use IFRS (a list is at **http://www.iasplus.com/en/resources/use-of-ifrs/#totals**). While laws and enforcement mechanisms vary across countries, the demand and supply of accounting information are governed by global economic forces. Thus, it is not surprising that IFRS and U.S. GAAP both prescribe the same set of financial statements. While account titles and note details differ, the underlying principles are the same. That is, U.S. GAAP and IFRS both capture, aggregate, summarize, and report economic activities on an accrual basis.

Given the global economy and liquid transnational capital markets, along with the fact that many non-U.S. companies file IFRS financial statements with the SEC, it is critical that we be conversant with both U.S. GAAP and IFRS. For this purpose, the final section of each module includes a summary of notable differences between these two systems of accounting for topics covered in that module. Also, each module has assignments that examine IFRS companies and their financial statements. By using a wide array of financial information, we will speak the language of accounting in at least two dialects.

MODULE-END REVIEW

Following are selected data from Progressive Corporation's 2012 10-K.

$ millions	2012
Sales	$17,084
Net income	902
Average assets	22,270
Average stockholders' equity	5,907

Required

a. Compute Progressive's return on assets. Disaggregate the ROA into its profitability and productivity components.

b. Compute Progressive's return on equity (ROE).

The solution is on page 1-44.

APPENDIX 1A: Accessing SEC Filings

All publicly traded companies are required to file various reports with the SEC, two of which are the 10-Q (quarterly financial statements) and the 10-K (annual financial statements). Following is a brief tutorial to access these electronic filings. The SEC's Website is **http://www.sec.gov**.

1. Following is the opening screen. Click on **"Company Filings"** (highlighted below).

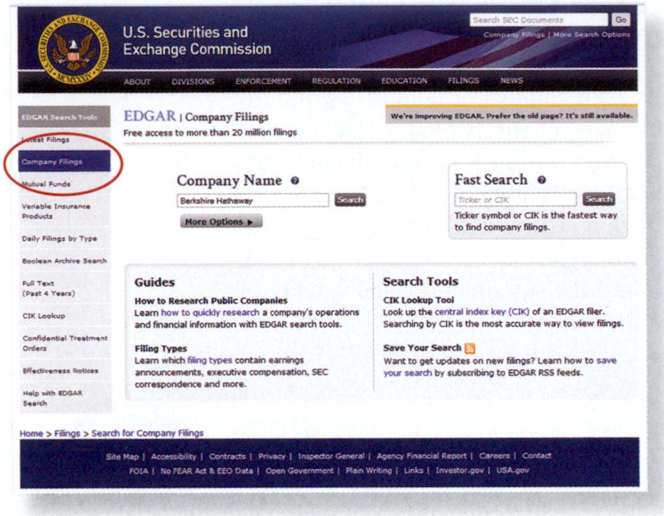

2. In **Company name**, type in the name of the company we are looking for. In this case, we are searching for Berkshire Hathaway. Then click search.

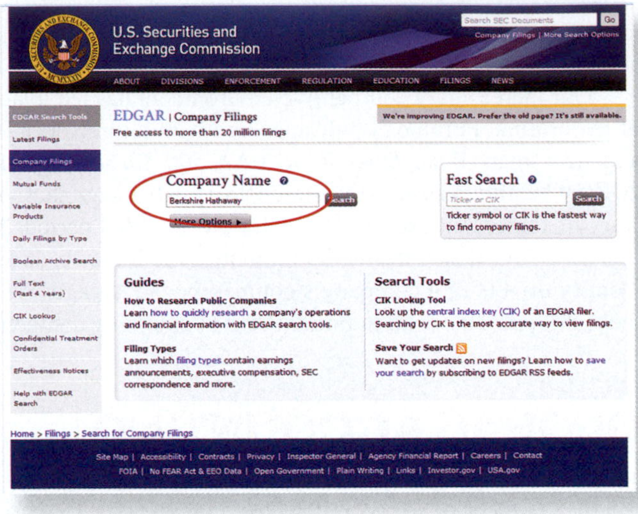

3. Click CIK (Central Index Key), state, country, or SIC (Standard Industrial Classification).

4. Several references to Berkshire appear. Click on the **CIK** (the SEC's numbering system) next to Berkshire Hathaway, Inc.

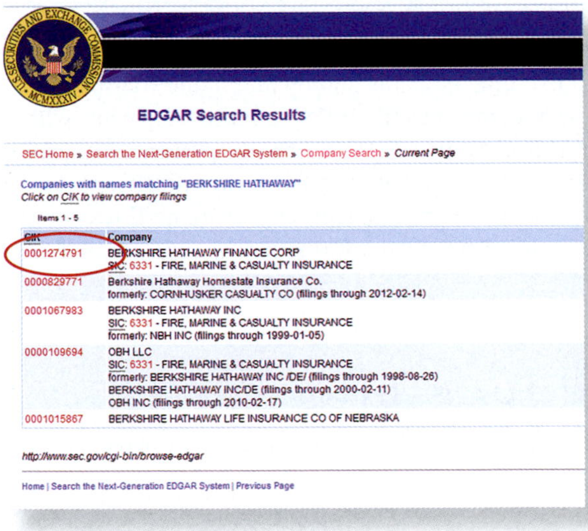

5. Enter the form number under "filing type" that we want to access. Click the Search button. In this case we are looking for the 10-K.

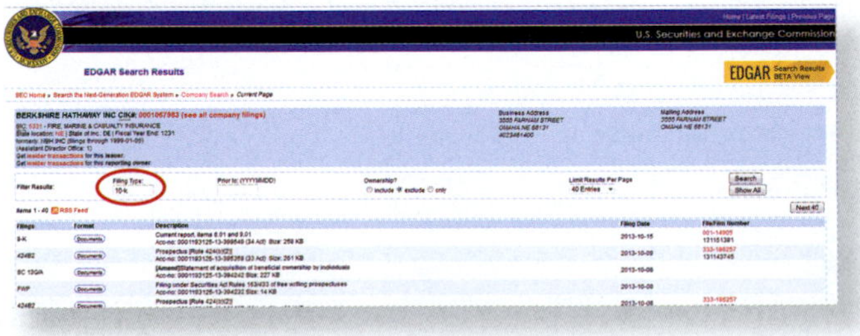

6. Click on the document link for the year that we want to access.

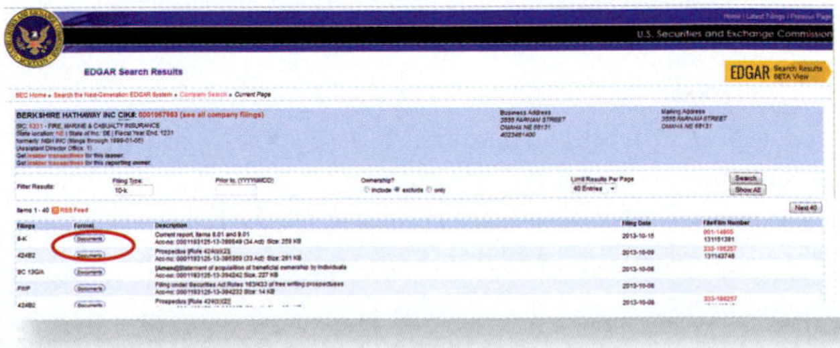

7. Exhibits relating to Berkshire Hathaway's 10-K filing appear; click on the 10-K document.

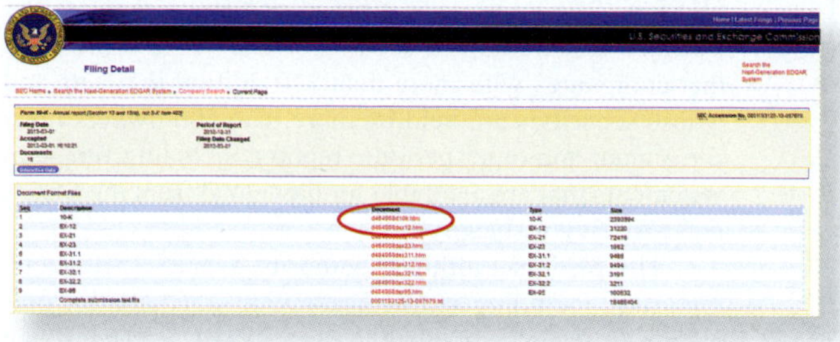

8. The Berkshire Hathaway 10-K will open up; the file is searchable.

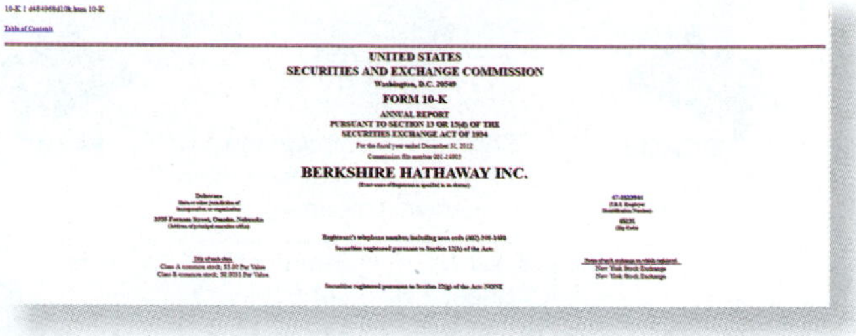

9. Download an Excel file of the financial statement data by clicking on "Interactive Data."

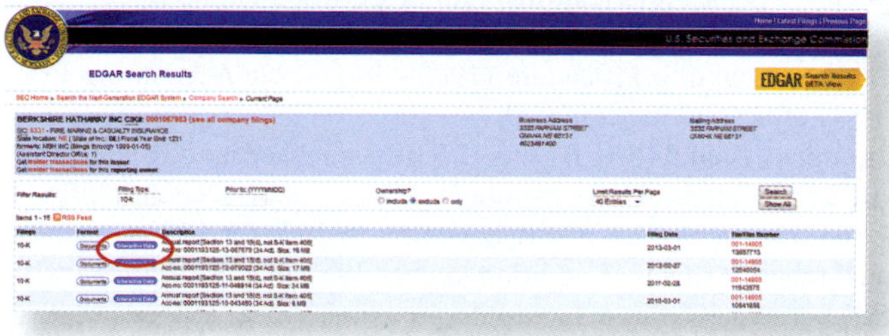

10. Click on "View Excel Document" to view or download as a spreadsheet.

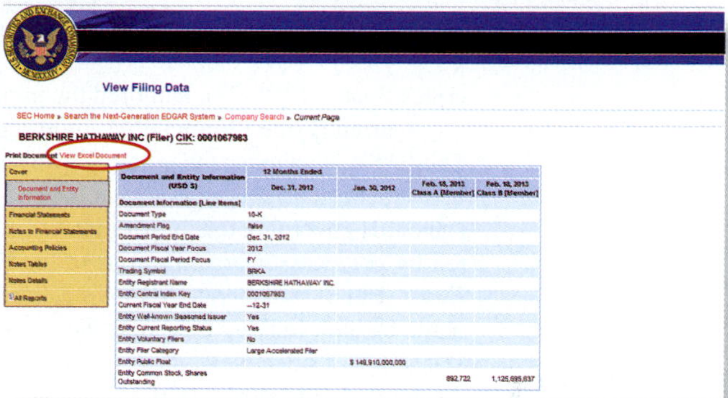

APPENDIX 1B: Accounting Principles and Governance

Financial Accounting Environment

LO5 Describe the accounting principles and regulations that frame financial statements.

Information in financial statements is crucial to valuing a company's debt and equity securities. Financial statement information can affect the price the market is willing to pay for the company's equity securities and interest rates attached to its debt securities.

The importance of financial statements means that their reliability is paramount. This includes the crucial role of ethics. To the extent that financial performance and condition are accurately communicated to business decision makers, debt and equity securities are more accurately priced. When securities are mispriced, resources can be inefficiently allocated both within and across economies. Accurate, reliable financial statements are also important for the effective functioning of many other markets such as labor, input, and output markets.

To illustrate, recall the consequences of a breakdown in the integrity of the financial accounting system at **Enron**. Once it became clear that Enron had not faithfully and accurately reported its financial condition and performance, the market became unwilling to purchase Enron's securities. The value of its debt and equity securities dropped precipitously and the company was unable to obtain cash needed for operating activities. Within months of the disclosure of its financial accounting irregularities, Enron, with revenues of over $100 billion and total company value of over $60 billion, the fifth largest U.S. company, was bankrupt!

Further historical evidence of the importance of financial accounting is provided by the Great Depression of the 20th century. This depression was caused, in part, by the failure of companies to faithfully report their financial condition and performance.

Oversight of Financial Accounting

The stock market crash of 1929 and the ensuing Great Depression led Congress to pass the 1933 Securities Act. This act had two main objectives: (1) to require disclosure of financial and other information about securities being offered for public sale; and (2) to prohibit deceit, misrepresentations, and other fraud in the sale of securities. This act also required that companies register all securities proposed for public sale and disclose information about the securities being offered, including information about company financial condition and performance. This act became and remains a foundation for contemporary financial reporting.

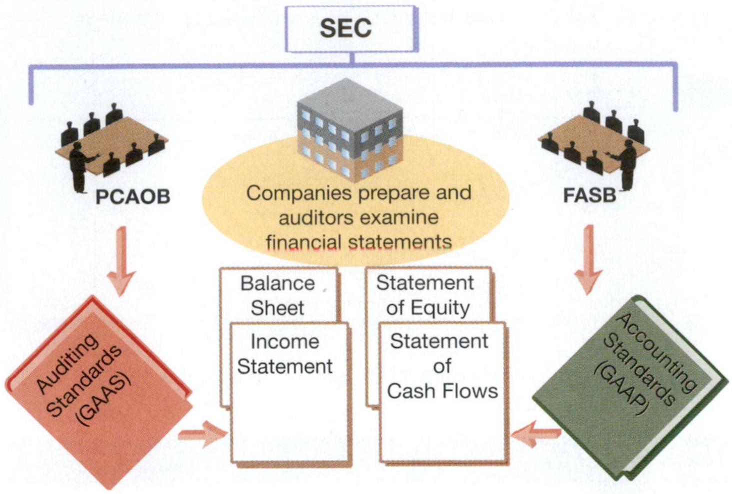

Congress also passed the 1934 Securities Exchange Act, which created the **Securities and Exchange Commission** (SEC) and gave it broad powers to regulate the issuance and trading of securities. The act also provides that companies with more than $10 million in assets and whose securities are held by more than 500 owners must file annual and other periodic reports, including financial statements that are available for download from the SEC's database (**www.sec.gov**).

The SEC has ultimate authority over U.S. financial reporting, including setting accounting standards for preparing financial statements. Since 1939, however, the SEC has looked primarily to the private sector to set accounting standards. One such private sector organization is the American Institute of Certified Public Accountants (AICPA), whose two committees, the Committee on Accounting Procedure (1939–59) and the Accounting Principles Board (1959–73), authored the initial body of accounting standards.

Currently, the **Financial Accounting Standards Board (FASB)** sets U.S. financial accounting standards. The FASB is an independent body overseen by a foundation, whose members include public accounting firms, investment managers, academics, and corporate managers. The FASB has published nearly 170 accounting standards governing the preparation of financial reports. This is in addition to over 40 standards that were written by predecessor organizations to the FASB, numerous bulletins and interpretations, Emerging Issues Task Force (EITF) statements, AICPA statements of position (SOP), and direct SEC guidance, along with speeches made by high-ranking SEC personnel, all of which form the body of accounting standards governing financial statements. Collectively, these pronouncements, rules, and guidance create what is called **Generally Accepted Accounting Principles (GAAP).**

The standard-setting process is arduous, often lasting up to a decade and involving extensive comment by the public, public officials, accountants, academics, investors, analysts, and corporate preparers of financial reports. The reason for this involved process is that amendments to existing standards or the creation of new standards affect the reported financial performance and condition of companies. Consequently, given the widespread impact of financial accounting, there are considerable economic consequences as a result of accounting changes. To influence the standard-setting process, special interest groups often lobby members of Congress to pressure the SEC and, ultimately, the FASB, on issues about which constituents feel strongly.

Audits and Corporate Governance

Even though key executives must personally attest to the completeness and accuracy of company financial statements, markets demand further assurances from outside parties to achieve the level of confidence necessary to warrant investment, credit, and other business decisions. To that end, companies engage external auditors to provide an opinion about financial statements. Further, companies implement a system of checks and balances that monitor managers' actions, which is called *corporate governance*.

Audit Report

Financial statements for each publicly traded company must be audited by an independent audit firm. There are a number of large auditing firms that are authorized by the SEC to provide auditing services for companies that issue securities to the public: **PricewaterhouseCoopers**, **KPMG**, **Ernst & Young**, **Deloitte**, **McGladrey**, **Grant Thornton**, and **BDO**, to name a few. These firms provide opinions about financial statements for the large majority of publicly traded U.S. companies. A company's Board of Directors hires the auditors to review and express an opinion on its financial statements. The audit opinion expressed by Deloitte & Touche, LLP, on the financial statements of **Berkshire Hathaway** is reproduced in Exhibit 1.10.

The basic "clean" audit report is consistent across companies and includes these assertions:

- Financial statements are management's responsibility. Auditor responsibility is to express an *opinion* on those statements.
- Auditing involves a sampling of transactions, not investigation of each transaction.

EXHIBIT 1.10 Audit Report for Berkshire Hathaway

To the Board of Directors and Shareholders of Berkshire Hathaway Inc.

We have audited the accompanying consolidated balance sheets of Berkshire Hathaway Inc. and subsidiaries (the "Company") as of December 31, 2012 and 2011, and the related consolidated statements of earnings, comprehensive income, changes in shareholders' equity, and cash flows for each of the three years in the period ended December 31, 2012. We also have audited the Company's internal control over financial reporting as of December 31, 2012, based on criteria established in Internal Control — Integrated Framework issued by the Committee of Sponsoring Organizations of the Treadway Commission. The Company's management is responsible for these financial statements, for maintaining effective internal control over financial reporting, and for its assessment of the effectiveness of internal control over financial reporting, included in the accompanying Management's Report on Internal Control over Financial Reporting. Our responsibility is to express an opinion on these financial statements and an opinion on the Company's internal control over financial reporting based on our audits.

We conducted our audits in accordance with the standards of the Public Company Accounting Oversight Board (United States). Those standards require that we plan and perform the audit to obtain reasonable assurance about whether the financial statements are free of material misstatement and whether effective internal control over financial reporting was maintained in all material respects. Our audits of the financial statements included examining, on a test basis, evidence supporting the amounts and disclosures in the financial statements, assessing the accounting principles used and significant estimates made by management, and evaluating the overall financial statement presentation. Our audit of internal control over financial reporting included obtaining an understanding of internal control over financial reporting, assessing the risk that a material weakness exists, and testing and evaluating the design and operating effectiveness of internal control based on the assessed risk. Our audits also included performing such other procedures as we considered necessary in the circumstances. We believe that our audits provide a reasonable basis for our opinions.

A company's internal control over financial reporting is a process designed by, or under the supervision of, the company's principal executive and principal financial officers, or persons performing similar functions, and effected by the company's board of directors, management, and other personnel to provide reasonable assurance regarding the reliability of financial reporting and the preparation of financial statements for external purposes in accordance with generally accepted accounting principles. A company's internal control over financial reporting includes those policies and procedures that (1) pertain to the maintenance of records that, in reasonable detail, accurately and fairly reflect the transactions and dispositions of the assets of the company; (2) provide reasonable assurance that transactions are recorded as necessary to permit preparation of financial statements in accordance with generally accepted accounting principles, and that receipts and expenditures of the company are being made only in accordance with authorizations of management and directors of the company; and (3) provide reasonable assurance regarding prevention or timely detection of unauthorized acquisition, use, or disposition of the company's assets that could have a material effect on the financial statements.

Because of the inherent limitations of internal control over financial reporting, including the possibility of collusion or improper management override of controls, material misstatements due to error or fraud may not be prevented or detected on a timely basis. Also, projections of any evaluation of the effectiveness of the internal control over financial reporting to future periods are subject to the risk that the controls may become inadequate because of changes in conditions, or that the degree of compliance with the policies or procedures may deteriorate.

In our opinion, the consolidated financial statements referred to above present fairly, in all material respects, the financial position of Berkshire Hathaway Inc. and subsidiaries as of December 31, 2012 and 2011, and the results of their operations and their cash flows for each of the three years in the period ended December 31, 2012, in conformity with accounting principles generally accepted in the United States of America. Also, in our opinion, the Company maintained, in all material respects, effective internal control over financial reporting as of December 31, 2012, based on the criteria established in Internal Control – Integrated Framework issued by the Committee of Sponsoring Organizations of the Treadway Commission.

DELOITTE & TOUCHE LLP

Omaha, Nebraska
March 1, 2013

- Audit opinion provides *reasonable assurance* that the statements are free of *material* misstatements, not a guarantee.
- Auditors review accounting policies used by management and the estimates used in preparing the statements.
- Financial statements *present fairly, in all material respects* a company's financial condition, in conformity with GAAP.

If the auditor cannot make all of these assertions, the auditor cannot issue a clean opinion. Instead, the auditor issues a "qualified" opinion and states the reasons a clean opinion cannot be issued. Financial report readers should scrutinize with care both the qualified audit opinion and the financial statements themselves.

The audit opinion is not based on a test of each transaction. Instead, auditors usually develop statistical samples to make inferences about the larger set of transactions. The audit report is not a guarantee that no misstatements exist. Auditors only provide reasonable assurance that the statements are free of material misstatements. Their use of the word "reasonable" is deliberate, as they do not want to be held to an absolute standard should problems be subsequently uncovered. The word *material* is used in the sense that an item must be of sufficient magnitude to change the perceptions or decisions of the financial statement user (such as a decision to purchase stock or extend credit).

The requirement of auditor independence is the cornerstone of effective auditing and is subject to debate because the company pays the auditor's fees. Regulators have questioned the perceived lack of independence of auditing firms and the degree to which declining independence compromises the ability of auditing firms to challenge a client's dubious accounting.

The Sarbanes-Oxley Act contained several provisions designed to encourage auditor independence:

1. It established the **Public Company Accounting Oversight Board** (PCAOB) to oversee the development of audit standards and to monitor the effectiveness of auditors,
2. It prohibits auditors from offering certain types of consulting services, and requires audit partners to rotate clients every five years, and
3. It requires audit committees to consist of independent members.

Audit Committee

Law requires each publicly traded company to have a board of directors, where stockholders elect each director. This board represents the company owners and oversees management. The board also hires the company's executive management and regularly reviews company operations.

The board of directors usually establishes several subcommittees to focus on particular governance tasks such as compensation, strategic plans, and financial management. Governance committees are commonplace. One of these, the audit committee, oversees the financial accounting system. Exhibit 1.11 illustrates a typical organization of a company's governance structure.

EXHIBIT 1.11 Business Activities

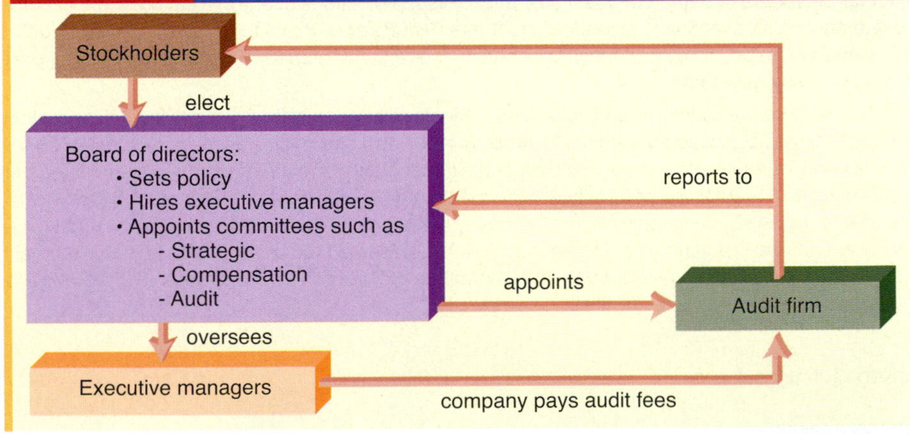

The audit committee must consist solely of outside directors, and cannot include the CEO. As part of its oversight of the financial accounting system, the audit committee focuses on **internal controls**, which are the policies and procedures used to protect assets, ensure reliable accounting, promote efficient operations, and urge adherence to company policies.

Regulatory and Legal Environment

The regulatory and legal environment provides further assurance that financial statements are complete and accurate.

SEC Enforcement Actions

Companies whose securities are issued to the public must file reports with the SEC (see **www.sec.gov**). One of these reports is the 10-K, which includes the annual financial statements (quarterly statements are filed on report 10-Q). The 10-K report provides more information than the company's glossy annual report, which is partly a marketing document (although the basic financial statements are identical). We prefer to use the 10-K because of its additional information.

The SEC critically reviews all of the financial reports that companies submit. If irregularities are found, the SEC has the authority to bring enforcement actions against companies that it feels are misrepresenting their financial condition (remember the phrase in the audit opinion that requires companies to "present fairly, in all material respects, the financial position of . . . "). One such action was brought against **Dell Inc.** and its executives. Following are excerpts from the SEC's complaint:

> The Securities and Exchange Commission today charged Dell Inc. with failing to disclose material information to investors and using fraudulent accounting to make it falsely appear that the company was consistently meeting Wall Street earnings targets and reducing its operating expenses.
>
> The SEC alleges that Dell did not disclose to investors large exclusivity payments the company received from Intel Corporation not to use central processing units (CPUs) manufactured by Intel's main rival. It was these payments rather than the company's management and operations that allowed Dell to meet its earnings targets. After Intel cut these payments, Dell again misled investors by not disclosing the true reason behind the company's decreased profitability . . .
>
> The SEC's complaint, filed in federal district court in Washington, D.C., alleges that Dell Inc., Michael Dell, Rollins, and Schneider misrepresented the basis for the company's ability to consistently meet or exceed consensus analyst EPS estimates from fiscal year 2002 through fiscal year 2006. Without the Intel payments, Dell would have missed the EPS consensus in every quarter during this period . . .
>
> The SEC's complaint further alleges that Dell's most senior former accounting personnel, including Schneider, Dunning, and Jackson engaged in improper accounting by maintaining a series of "cookie jar" reserves that it used to cover shortfalls in operating results from FY 2002 to FY 2005. Dell's fraudulent accounting made it appear that it was consistently meeting Wall Street earnings targets and reducing its operating expenses through the company's management and operations.
>
> According to the SEC's complaint, Intel made exclusivity payments to Dell in order for Dell not to use CPUs manufactured by its rival—Advance Micro Devices, Inc. (AMD). These exclusivity payments grew from 10 percent of Dell's operating income in FY 2003 to 38 percent in FY 2006, and peaked at 76 percent in the first quarter of FY 2007. The SEC alleges that Dell Inc., Michael Dell, Rollins, and Schneider failed to disclose the basis for the company's sharp drop in its operating results in its second quarter of fiscal 2007 as Intel cut its payments after Dell announced its intention to begin using AMD CPUs. In dollar terms, the reduction in Intel exclusivity payments was equivalent to 75 percent of the decline in Dell's operating income. Michael Dell, Rollins, and Schneider had been warned in the past that Intel would cut its funding if Dell added AMD as a vendor. Nevertheless, in Dell's second quarter FY 2007 earnings call, they told investors that the sharp drop in the company's operating results was attributable to Dell pricing too aggressively in the face of slowing demand and to component costs declining less than expected.
>
> The SEC's complaint further alleges that the reserve manipulations allowed Dell to materially misstate its earnings and its operating expenses as a percentage of revenue—an important financial metric that the Company itself highlighted—for over three years. The manipulations also enabled Dell to misstate materially the trend and amount of operating income of its EMEA segment, an important business unit that Dell also highlighted, from the third quarter of FY 2003 through the first quarter of FY 2005.

While not admitting to wrongdoing, Dell agreed to pay a penalty of $100 million to settle the SEC's charges. The SEC's oversight and powers of prosecution are an important check to help insure that companies' reports to investors "present fairly, in all material respects" the companies' financial condition.

BUSINESS INSIGHT **Warren Buffett on Audit Committees**

"Audit committees can't audit. Only a company's outside auditor can determine whether the earnings that a management purports to have made are suspect. Reforms that ignore this reality and that instead focus on the structure and charter of the audit committee will accomplish little. As we've discussed, far too many managers have fudged their company's numbers in recent years, using both accounting and operational techniques that are typically legal but that nevertheless materially mislead investors. Frequently, auditors knew about these deceptions. Too often, however, they remained silent. The key job of the audit committee is simply to get the auditors to divulge what they know. To do this job, the committee must make sure that the auditors worry more about misleading its members than about offending management. In recent years auditors have not felt that way. They have instead generally viewed the CEO, rather than the shareholders or directors, as their client. That has been a natural result of day-to-day working relationships and also of the auditors' understanding that, no matter what the book says, the CEO and CFO pay their fees and determine whether they are retained for both auditing and other work. The rules that have been recently instituted won't materially change this reality. What will break this cozy relationship is audit committees unequivocally putting auditors on the spot, making them understand they will become liable for major monetary penalties if they don't come forth with what they know or suspect."

—Warren Buffett, Berkshire Hathaway Annual Report

Courts

Courts provide remedies to individuals and companies that suffer damages as a result of material misstatements in financial statements. Typical court actions involve stockholders who sue the company and its auditors, alleging that the company disclosed, and the auditors attested to, false and misleading financial statements. Stockholder lawsuits are chronically in the news, although the number of such suits has declined in recent years. Stanford Law School's Securities Class Action Clearinghouse commented that "Two factors are likely responsible for the decline. First, lawsuits arising from the dramatic boom and bust of U.S. equities in the late 1990s and early 2000s are now largely behind us. Second, improved corporate governance in the wake of the **Enron** and **WorldCom** frauds likely reduced the actual incidence of fraud." Nevertheless, courts continue to wield considerable power. For example, the SEC and the New York District Attorney successfully brought suit against **Adelphia Communications Corporation** and its owners on behalf of the U.S. Government and numerous investors, creditors, employees and others affiliated with the company. The press release announcing the settlement read, in part:

> *Washington, D.C., April 25, 2005*—The Securities and Exchange Commission today announced that it and the United States Attorney's Office for the Southern District of New York (USAO) reached an agreement to settle a civil enforcement action and resolve criminal charges against Adelphia Communications Corporation, its founder John J. Rigas, and his three sons, Timothy J. Rigas, Michael J. Rigas and James P. Rigas, in one of the most extensive financial frauds ever to take place at a public company.
>
> In its complaint, the Commission charged that Adelphia, at the direction of the individual defendants: (1) fraudulently excluded billions of dollars in liabilities from its consolidated financial statements by hiding them on the books of off-balance sheet affiliates; (2) falsified operating statistics and inflated earnings to meet Wall Street estimates; and (3) concealed rampant self-dealing by the Rigas family, including the undisclosed use of corporate funds for purchases of Adelphia stock and luxury condominiums.
>
> Mark K. Schonfeld, Director of the SEC's Northeast Regional Office, said, "This settlement agreement presents a strong, coordinated approach by the SEC and the U.S. Attorney's Office to resolving one of the most complicated and egregious financial frauds committed at a public company. The settlement provides an expedient and effective way to provide victims of Adelphia's fraud with a substantial recovery while at the same time enabling Adelphia to emerge from Chapter 11 bankruptcy."

The settlement terms of this action, and related criminal actions against the Rigas family, resulted in the following:

- Rigas family members forfeited in excess of $1.5 billion in assets derived from the fraud; the funds were used, in part, to establish a fund for the fraud victims.
- Rigas family members were barred from acting as officers or directors of a public company.
- John Rigas, the 80-year-old founder of Adelphia Communications, was sentenced to 15 years in prison; he applied for a Presidential pardon in January 2009 but was denied.
- Timothy Rigas, the ex-finance chief, was sentenced to 20 years and is currently serving time at a federal correctional complex in North Carolina.

GUIDANCE ANSWERS

MANAGERIAL DECISION You Are the Product Manager

As a manager, you must balance two conflicting objectives—namely, mandatory disclosure requirements and your company's need to protect its competitive advantages. You must comply with all minimum required disclosure rules. The extent to which you offer additional disclosures depends on the sensitivity of the information; that is, how beneficial it is to your existing and potential competitors. Another consideration is how the information disclosed will impact your existing and potential investors. Disclosures such as this can be beneficial in that they inform investors and others about your company's successful investments. Still, there are many stakeholders impacted by your disclosure decision and each must be given due consideration.

MANAGERIAL DECISION You Are the Chief Financial Officer

Financial performance is often measured by return on assets, which can be disaggregated into the profit margin (profit after tax/sales) and the asset turnover (sales/average assets). This disaggregation might lead you to review factors affecting profitability (gross margins and expense control) and to assess how effectively your company is utilizing its assets (the turnover rates). Finding ways to increase profitability for a given level of investment or to reduce the amount of invested capital while not adversely impacting profitability contributes to improved financial performance.

Superscript $^{A(B)}$ denotes assignments based on Appendix 1A (1B).

DISCUSSION QUESTIONS

Q1-1. A firm's planning activities motivate and shape three types of business activities. List the three activities. Describe how financial statements can provide useful information for each activity. How can subsequent financial statements be used to evaluate the success of each of the activities?

Q1-2. The accounting equation (Assets = Liabilities + Equity) is a fundamental business concept. Explain what this equation reveals about a company's sources and uses of funds and the claims on company resources.

Q1-3. Companies prepare four primary financial statements. What are those financial statements and what information is typically conveyed in each?

Q1-4. Does a balance sheet report on a period of time or at a point in time? Explain the information conveyed in the balance sheet.

Q1-5. Does an income statement report on a period of time or at a point in time? Explain the information conveyed in the income statement.

Q1-6. Does a statement of cash flows report on a period of time or at a point in time? Explain the information and activities conveyed in the statement of cash flows.

Q1-7. Explain how a company's four primary financial statements are linked.

Q1-8. Financial statements are used by several interested stakeholders. List three or more potential external users of financial statements. Explain how each constituent on your list might use financial statement information in their decision making process.

Q1-9. What ethical issues might managers face in dealing with confidential information?

Q1-10.[A] Access the 2012 10-K for **Procter & Gamble** at the SEC's database of financial reports (**www.sec.gov**). Who is P&G's auditor? What specific language does the auditor use in expressing its opinion and what responsibilities does it assume? **Procter & Gamble (PG)**

Q1-11.[B] Business decision makers external to the company increasingly demand more financial information from companies. Discuss the reasons why companies have traditionally opposed the efforts of regulatory agencies like the SEC to require more disclosure.

Q1-12.[B] What are generally accepted accounting principles and what organizations presently establish them?

Q1-13.[B] Corporate governance has received considerable attention since the collapse of **Enron** and other accounting-related scandals. What is meant by corporate governance? What are the primary means by which sound corporate governance is achieved? **Enron**

Q1-14.[B] What is the primary function of the auditor? In your own words, describe what an audit opinion says.

Q1-15. Describe a decision that requires financial statement information, other than a stock investment decision. How is financial statement information useful in making this decision?

Q1-16. Users of financial statement information are vitally concerned with the company's strategic direction. Despite their understanding of this need for information, companies are reluctant to supply it. Why? In particular, what costs are companies concerned about?

Q1-17. One of Warren Buffett's acquisition criteria is to invest in businesses "earning good return on equity." The return on equity (ROE) formula uses both net income and stockholders' equity. Why is it important to relate net income to stockholders' equity? Why isn't it sufficient to merely concentrate on companies with the highest net income?

Q1-18. One of Warren Buffett's acquisition criteria is to invest in businesses "earning good return on equity, while employing little or no debt." Why is Buffett concerned about debt?

Assignments with the ✔ logo in the margin are available in myBusinessCourse. See the Preface of the book for details.

MINI EXERCISES

M1-19. Relating Financing and Investing Activities (LO2)

Dell Inc. (DELL)

In a recent year, the total assets of **Dell Inc.** equal $47,540 million and its equity is $10,701 million. What is the amount of its liabilities? Does Dell receive more financing from its owners or nonowners? What percentage of financing is provided by Dell's owners?

M1-20. Relating Financing and Investing Activities (LO2)

Best Buy (BBY)

In a recent year, the total assets of **Best Buy** equal $16,787 million and its liabilities equal $13,072 million. What is the amount of Best Buy's equity? Does Best Buy receive more financing from its owners or nonowners? What percentage of financing is provided by its owners?

✔ **M1-21. Applying the Accounting Equation and Computing Financing Proportions (LO2)**

Use the accounting equation to compute the missing financial amounts (a), (b), and (c). Which of these companies is more owner-financed? Which of these companies is more nonowner-financed? Discuss why the proportion of owner financing might differ across these three businesses.

Hewlett-Packard (HPQ)
General Mills (GIS)
Target (TGT)

($ millions)	Assets	=	Liabilities	+	Equity
Hewlett-Packard	$108,768	=	$85,935	+	$ (a)
General Mills	$ 22,658	=	$ (b)	+	$ 8,096
Target	$ (c)	=	$31,605	+	$16,558

M1-22.[A] **Identifying Key Numbers from Financial Statements (LO2)**

Starbucks (SBUX)

Access the September 30, 2012, 10-K for **Starbucks Corporation** at the SEC's database for financial reports (www.sec.gov). What did Starbucks report for total assets, liabilities, and equity at September 30, 2012? Confirm that the accounting equation holds. What percent of Starbucks' assets is financed by nonowners?

M1-23.[A] **Verifying Linkages Between Financial Statements (LO2)**

E. I. DuPont de Nemours (DD)

Access the 2012 10-K for **DuPont** at the SEC's database of financial reports (www.sec.gov). Using its December 31, 2012, consolidated statement of stockholders' equity, prepare a table to reconcile the opening and ending balances of its retained (reinvested) earnings for 2012 by showing the activity in the account during the year.

✔ **M1-24. Identifying Financial Statement Line Items and Accounts (LO2)**

Several line items and account titles are listed below. For each, indicate in which of the following financial statement(s) we would likely find the item or account: income statement (IS), balance sheet (BS), statement of stockholders' equity (SE), or statement of cash flows (SCF).

a. Cash asset
b. Expenses
c. Noncash assets
d. Contributed capital
e. Cash outflow for capital expenditures
f. Retained earnings
g. Cash inflow for stock issued
h. Cash outflow for dividends
i. Net income

M1-25. Identifying Ethical Issues and Accounting Choices (LO5)
Assume that you are a technology services provider and you must decide on whether to record revenue from the installation of computer software for one of your clients. Your contract calls for acceptance of the software by the client within six months of installation. According to the contract, you will be paid only when the client "accepts" the installation. Although you have not yet received your client's formal acceptance, you are confident that it is forthcoming. Failure to record these revenues will cause your company to miss Wall Street's earnings estimates. What stakeholders will be affected by your decision and how might they be affected?

M1-26.[B] Understanding Internal Controls and Their Importance (LO5)
The **Sarbanes-Oxley Act** legislation requires companies to report on the effectiveness of their internal controls. The SEC administers the Sarbanes-Oxley Act, and defines internal controls as follows:

> "A process designed by, or under the supervision of, the registrant's principal executive and principal financial officers . . . to provide reasonable assurance regarding the reliability of financial reporting and the preparation of financial statements for external purposes in accordance with generally accepted accounting principles."

Why would Congress believe that internal controls are such an important area to monitor and report on?

EXERCISES

E1-27. Composition of Accounts on the Balance Sheet (LO2)
Answer the following questions about the Target balance sheet.

Target (TGT)

a. Briefly describe the types of assets that Target is likely to include in its inventory.
b. What kinds of assets would Target likely include in its Property and Equipment?
c. Target reports about two-thirds of its total assets as long-term. Given Target's business model, why do we see it report a relatively high proportion of long-term assets?

E1-28. Applying the Accounting Equation and Assessing Financial Statement Linkages (LO2)
Answer the following questions. (*Hint*: Apply the accounting equation.)

a. **Intel** had assets equal to $84,351 million and liabilities equal to $33,148 million for a recent year-end. What was Intel's total equity at year-end? Why would we expect a company like Intel to report a relatively high proportion of equity vis-à-vis liabilities?

Intel (INTC)

b. At the beginning of a recent year, **JetBlue**'s assets were $7,071 million and its equity was $1,757 million. During the year, assets decreased $1 million and liabilities decreased $132 million. What was JetBlue's equity at the end of the year?

JetBlue (JBLU)

c. What balance sheet account provides the link between the balance sheet and the income statement? Briefly describe how this linkage works.

E1-29. Specifying Financial Information Users and Uses (LO1)
Financial statements have a wide audience of interested stakeholders. Identify two or more financial statement users that are external to the company. For each user on your list, specify two questions that could be addressed with financial statement information.

E1-30. Applying Financial Statement Relations to Compute Dividends (LO2)
Colgate-Palmolive reports the following dollar balances in its retained earnings account.

Colgate-Palmolive (CL)

($ millions)	2012	2011
Retained earnings	$16,953	$15,649

During 2012, Colgate-Palmolive reported net income of $2,472 million. What amount of dividends, if any, did Colgate-Palmolive pay to its stockholders in 2012? What percent of its net income did Colgate-Palmolive pay out as dividends in 2012?

Colgate-Palmolive (CL)

E1-31. Computing and Interpreting Financial Statement Ratios (LO3)
Following are selected ratios of Colgate-Palmolive for 2012 and 2011.

Return on Assets (ROA) Component	2012	2011
Profitability (Net income/Sales)	14%	15%
Productivity (Sales/Average net assets)	1.3	1.4

a. Was the company profitable in 2012? What evidence do you have of this?
b. Is the change in productivity (asset turnover) a positive development? Explain.
c. Compute the company's return on assets (ROA) for 2012 (show computations).

Nordstrom, Inc. (JWN)

E1-32. Computing Return on Assets and Applying the Accounting Equation (LO3)
Nordstrom, Inc., reports net income of $735 million for its fiscal year ended February 2013. At the beginning of that fiscal year, Nordstrom had $8,491 million in total assets. By fiscal year-end 2013, total assets had decreased to $8,089 million. What is Nordstrom's return on assets (ROA)?

E1-33. Assessing the Role of Financial Statements in Society (LO1)
Financial statement information plays an important role in modern society and business.

a. Identify two or more external stakeholders that are interested in a company's financial statements and what their particular interests are.
b. What are *generally accepted accounting principles*? What organizations have primary responsibility for the formulation of GAAP?
c. What role does financial statement information play in the allocation of society's financial resources?
d. What are three aspects of the accounting environment that can create ethical pressure on management?

Starbucks (SBUX)

E1-34. Computing Return on Equity (LO3)
Starbucks reports net income for 2012 of $1,383.8 million. Its stockholders' equity is $4,387.3 million and $5,114.5 million for 2011 and 2012, respectively.

a. Compute its return on equity for 2012.
b. Starbucks repurchased over $501 million of its common stock in 2012. How did this repurchase affect Starbucks' ROE?
c. Why do you think a company like Starbucks repurchases its own stock?

PROBLEMS

Wal-Mart Stores, Inc. (WMT)

P1-35. Computing Return on Equity and Return on Assets (LO3)
The following table contains financial statement information for Wal-Mart Stores, Inc.

($ millions)	Total Assets	Net Income	Sales	Equity
2013	$203,105	$16,999	$469,162	$81,738
2012	193,406	15,699	446,950	75,761
2011	180,782	16,389	421,849	71,247

Required

a. Compute the return on equity (ROE) for 2012 and 2013. What trend, if any, is evident? How does Wal-Mart's ROE compare with the approximately 21.5% median ROE for companies in the Dow Jones Industrial average for 2012?
b. Compute the return on assets (ROA) for 2012 and 2013. What trends, if any, are evident? How does Wal-Mart's ROA compare with the approximate 6.7% median ROA for companies in the Dow Jones Industrial average for 2012?
c. What factors might allow a company like Wal-Mart to reap above-average returns?

P1-36. Formulating Financial Statements from Raw Data (LO2, 3)

General Mills, Inc. (GIS)

Following is selected financial information from **General Mills, Inc.**, for its fiscal year ended May 26, 2013 ($ millions).

Revenue	$17,774.1
Cash from operating activities	2,926.0
Cash, beginning year	471.2
Stockholders' equity	8,096.0
Noncash assets	21,916.6
Cash from financing activities*	(1,140.4)
Cost of goods sold	11,350.2
Total expenses (other than cost of goods sold)	4,568.7
Cash, ending year	741.4
Total liabilities	14,562.0
Cash from investing activities	(1,515.4)

* Cash from financing activities includes the effects of foreign exchange rate fluctuations.

Required

a. Prepare the income statement, the balance sheet, and the statement of cash flows for General Mills for the fiscal year ended May 26, 2013.

b. Do the negative amounts for cash from investing activities and cash from financing activities concern us? Explain.

c. Using the statements prepared for part *a*, compute the following ratios (for this part only, use the year-end balance instead of the average for assets and stockholders' equity):

i. Profit margin
ii. Asset turnover
iii. Return on assets
iv. Return on equity

P1-37. Formulating Financial Statements from Raw Data (LO2, 3)

Abercrombie & Fitch (ANF)

Following is selected financial information from **Abercrombie & Fitch** for its fiscal year ended February 2, 2013 ($ millions).

Noncash assets	$2,343
Total expenses (other than cost of goods sold)	2,580
Cash from investing activities	(247)
Cash, ending year	644
Revenue	4,511
Total liabilities	1,169
Cash from operating activities	684
Cash from financing activities*	(377)
Cost of goods sold	1,694
Cash, beginning year	584
Stockholders' equity	1,818

* Cash from financing activities includes the effects of foreign exchange rate fluctuations.

Required

a. Prepare the income statement, the balance sheet, and the statement of cash flows for Abercrombie & Fitch for the fiscal year ended February 2, 2013.

b. Do the negative amounts for cash from investing activities and cash from financing activities concern us? Explain.

c. Using the statements prepared for part *a*, compute the following ratios (for this part only, use the year-end balance instead of the average for assets and stockholders' equity):

i. Profit margin
ii. Asset turnover
iii. Return on assets
iv. Return on equity

Cisco Systems, Inc. (CSCO)

P1-38. Formulating Financial Statements from Raw Data (LO2, 3)

Following is selected financial information from **Cisco Systems, Inc.**, for the year ended July 27, 2013 ($ millions).

Cash, ending year	$ 7,925
Cash from operating activities	12,894
Sales	48,607
Stockholders' equity	59,128
Cost of goods sold	19,167
Cash from financing activities	(3,000)
Total liabilities	42,063
Total expenses (other than cost of goods sold)	19,457
Noncash assets	93,266
Cash from investing activities	(11,768)
Net income	9,983
Cash, beginning year	9,799

Required

a. Prepare the income statement, the balance sheet, and the statement of cash flows for Cisco Systems for the fiscal year ended July 27, 2013.

b. Do the negative amounts for cash from investing activities and cash from financing activities concern us? Explain.

c. Using the statements prepared for part *a*, compute the following ratios (for this part only, use the year-end balance instead of the average for assets and stockholders' equity):

i. Profit margin
ii. Asset turnover
iii. Return on assets
iv. Return on equity

P1-39. Formulating a Statement of Stockholders' Equity from Raw Data (LO2)

Crocker Corporation began calendar-year 2013 with stockholders' equity of $150,000, consisting of contributed capital of $120,000 and retained earnings of $30,000. During 2013, it issued additional stock for total cash proceeds of $30,000. It also reported $50,000 of net income, and paid $25,000 as a cash dividend to stockholders.

Required

Prepare the 2013 statement of stockholders' equity for Crocker Corporation.

Gap, Inc. (GPS)

P1-40. Formulating a Statement of Stockholders' Equity from Raw Data (LO2)

Gap, Inc., reports the following selected information at February 2, 2013 ($ millions).

Contributed capital, February 2, 2013	$ 2,919
Treasury stock, February 2, 2013	(13,465)
Retained earnings, February 2, 2013	13,259
Accumulated other comprehensive income, February 2, 2013	181

During fiscal year 2013, Gap reported the following:

1. Issuance of stock	$ 3
2. Repurchase of stock	705
3. Net income	1,135
4. Cash dividends	240
5. Other comprehensive income (loss)	(48)

Required

Use this information to prepare the statement of stockholders' equity for Gap, Inc., for fiscal year 2013.

P1-41. Computing, Analyzing, and Interpreting Return on Equity and Return on Assets (LO3)
Following are summary financial statement data for Kimberly-Clark for 2010 through 2012.

Kimberly-Clark (KMB)

KIMBERLY-CLARK CORPORATION (KMB)			
($ millions)	2012	2011	2010
Sales	$21,063	$20,846	$19,746
Net income	1,750	1,591	1,843
Total assets	19,873	19,373	19,864
Equity	4,985	5,249	5,917

Required

a. Compute the return on assets and return on equity for 2011 and 2012 (use average assets and average equity), together with the components of ROA (profit margin and asset turnover). What trends do we observe?

b. Which component appears to be driving the change in ROA over this time period?

c. KMB repurchased a large amount of its common shares in recent years at a cost of almost $4.9 billion. How did this repurchase affect its return on equity?

P1-42. Computing, Analyzing, and Interpreting Return on Equity and Return on Assets (LO3)
Following are summary financial statement data for Nordstrom, Inc., for 2011 through 2013.

Nordstrom, Inc. (JWN)

($ millions)	2013	2012	2011
Sales	$11,762	$10,497	$9,310
Net income	735	683	613
Total assets	8,089	8,491	7,462
Equity	1,913	1,956	2,021

Required

a. Compute return on assets and return on equity for each year 2012 and 2013 (use average assets and average equity), together with the components of ROA (profit margin and asset turnover). What trends, if any, do we observe?

b. Which component, if any, appears to be driving the change in ROA over this time period?

P1-43. Computing, Analyzing, and Interpreting Return on Equity (LO3)
Canadian Tire Corporation, Limited operates retail stores in Canada that sell general merchandise, clothing, and sporting goods. Total stockholders' equity for Canadian Tire, (in Canadian dollars), is $4,763.6 in 2012 and $4,409.0 in 2011. In 2012, Canadian Tire reported net income of $499.2 on sales of $11,427.2.

Canadian Tire Corporation, Limited

IFRS

Required

a. What is Canadian Tire's return on equity for 2012?

b. What are total expenses for Canadian Tire for 2012?

c. Canadian Tire used cash to repurchase a large amount of its common stock during the period 2009 through 2012. What motivations might Canadian Tire have for repurchasing its common stock?

P1-44. Comparing Abercrombie & Fitch and TJX Companies (LO3)
Following are selected financial statement data from Abercrombie & Fitch (ANF—upscale clothing retailer) and TJX Companies (TJX—value-priced clothing retailer including TJ Maxx)—both dated 2013.

Abercrombie & Fitch (ANF)
TJX Companies (TJX)

($ millions)	Company	Total Assets	Net Income	Sales
2012	TJX Companies Inc.	$8,282	—	—
2013	TJX Companies Inc.	9,512	$1,907	$25,878
2012	Abercrombie & Fitch	3,117	—	—
2013	Abercrombie & Fitch	2,987	237	4,511

Required

a. Compute the return on assets for both companies for the year ended 2013.

b. Disaggregate the ROAs for both companies into the profit margin and asset turnover.

c. What differences are observed? Evaluate these differences in light of the two companies' business models. Which company has better financial performance?

P1-45. Computing and Interpreting Return on Assets and Its Components (LO3)
McDonald's Corporation (MCD) reported the following balance sheet and income statement data for 2010 through 2012.

($ millions)	Total Assets	Net Income	Sales
2010	$31,975.2	—	—
2011	32,989.9	$5,503.1	$27,006.0
2012	35,386.5	5,464.8	27,567.0

Required

a. What is MCD's return on assets for 2011 and 2012? Disaggregate MCD's ROA into its net profit margin and its asset turnover.

b. What factor is mainly responsible for the change in MCD's ROA over this period?

P1-46. Disaggregating Return on Assets over Multiple Periods (LO3)
Following are selected financial statement data from 3M Company for 2009 through 2012.

($ millions)	Total Assets	Net Income	Sales
2009	$27,250	$3,193	$23,123
2010	30,156	4,085	26,662
2011	31,616	4,283	29,611
2012	33,876	4,444	29,904

Required

a. Compute 3M Company's return on assets for 2010 through 2012. Disaggregate 3M's ROA into the profit margin and asset turnover for 2010 through 2012. What trends do we observe?

b. Which ROA component appears to be driving the trend observed in part *a*? Explain.

P1-47.[A] Reading and Interpreting Audit Opinions (LO5)
Apple Inc.'s 2012 financial statements include the following audit report from Ernst & Young LLP.

Report of Ernst & Young LLP, Independent Registered Public Accounting Firm

The Board of Directors and Shareholders of Apple Inc.

We have audited the accompanying consolidated balance sheets of Apple Inc. as of September 29, 2012 and September 24, 2011, and the related consolidated statements of operations, shareholders' equity and cash flows for each of the three years in the period ended September 29, 2012. These financial statements are the responsibility of the Company's management. Our responsibility is to express an opinion on these financial statements based on our audits.

We conducted our audits in accordance with the standards of the Public Company Accounting Oversight Board (United States). Those standards require that we plan and perform the audit to obtain reasonable assurance about whether the financial statements are free of material misstatement. An audit includes examining, on a test basis, evidence supporting the amounts and disclosures in the financial statements. An audit also includes assessing the accounting principles used and significant estimates made by management, as well as evaluating the overall financial statement presentation. We believe that our audits provide a reasonable basis for our opinion.

In our opinion, the financial statements referred to above present fairly, in all material respects, the consolidated financial position of Apple Inc. at September 29, 2012 and September 24, 2011, and the consolidated results of its operations and its cash flows for each of the three years in the period ended September 29, 2012, in conformity with U.S. generally accepted accounting principles.

We also have audited, in accordance with the standards of the Public Company Accounting Oversight Board (United States), Apple Inc.'s internal control over financial reporting as of September 29, 2012, based on criteria established in *Internal Control—Integrated Framework* issued by the committee of Sponsoring Organizations of the Treadway Commission and our report dated October 31, 2012 expressed an unqualified opinion thereon.

/s/ Ernst & Young LLP

San Jose, California
October 31, 2012

Required

a. To whom is the report addressed? Why?

b. In your own words, briefly describe the audit process. What steps do auditors take to determine whether a company's financial statements are free from material misstatement?

c. What is the nature of Ernst & Young's opinion? What do you believe the word *fairly* means? Is Ernst & Young providing a guarantee to Apple's financial statement users?

d. What other opinion is Ernst & Young rendering? Why is this opinion important?

P1-48. Reading and Interpreting CEO Certifications (LO5)

Following is the CEO Certification required by the Sarbanes-Oxley Act and signed by **Apple** CEO Timothy D. Cook. Apple's Chief Financial Officer signed a similar form.

Apple Inc. (AAPL)

CERTIFICATIONS

I, Timothy D. Cook, certify that:

1. I have reviewed this annual report on Form 10-K of Apple Inc.;
2. Based on my knowledge, this report does not contain any untrue statement of a material fact or omit to state a material fact necessary to make the statements made, in light of the circumstances under which such statements were made, not misleading with respect to the period covered by this report;
3. Based on my knowledge, the financial statements, and other financial information included in this report, fairly present in all material respects the financial condition, results of operations and cash flows of the registrant as of, and for, the periods presented in this report;
4. The registrant's other certifying officer(s) and I are responsible for establishing and maintaining disclosure controls and procedures (as defined in Exchange Act Rules 13a-15(e) and 15d-15(e)) and internal control over financial reporting (as defined in Exchange Act Rules 13a-15(f) and 15d-15(f)) for the registrant and have:

   (a) Designed such disclosure controls and procedures, or caused such disclosure controls and procedures to be designed under our supervision, to ensure that material information relating to the registrant, including its consolidated subsidiaries, is made known to us by others within those entities, particularly during the period in which this report is being prepared;

   (b) Designed such internal control over financial reporting, or caused such internal control over financial reporting to be designed under our supervision, to provide reasonable assurance regarding the reliability of financial reporting and the preparation of financial statements for external purposes in accordance with generally accepted accounting principles;

   (c) Evaluated the effectiveness of the registrant's disclosure controls and procedures and presented in this report our conclusions about the effectiveness of the disclosure controls and procedures, as of the end of the period covered by this report based on such evaluation; and

   (d) Disclosed in this report any change in the registrant's internal control over financial reporting that occurred during the registrant's most recent fiscal quarter (the registrant's fourth fiscal quarter in the case of an annual report) that has materially affected, or is reasonably likely to materially affect, the registrant's internal control over financial reporting; and
5. The registrant's other certifying officer(s) and I have disclosed, based on our most recent evaluation of internal control over financial reporting, to the registrant's auditors and the audit committee of the registrant's board of directors (or persons performing the equivalent functions):

   (a) All significant deficiencies and material weaknesses in the design or operation of internal control over financial reporting which are reasonably likely to adversely affect the registrant's ability to record, process, summarize, and report financial information; and

   (b) Any fraud, whether or not material, that involves management or other employees who have a significant role in the registrant's internal control over financial reporting.

Date: October 31, 2012

By: /s/ TIMOTHY D. COOK
Timothy D. Cook
Chief Executive Officer

Required

a. Summarize the assertions that Timothy D. Cook made in this certification.
b. Why did Congress feel it important that CEOs and CFOs sign such certifications?
c. What potential liability do you believe the CEO and CFO are assuming by signing such certifications?

General Electric (GE)

P1-49. Assessing Corporate Governance and Its Effects (LO5)
Review the corporate governance section of General Electric's Website **http://www.ge.com**. Find and click on: "investor relations"; then, find and click on: "governance" and open the "Governance Principles" PDF.

Required

a. In your words, briefly describe GE's governance structure.
b. What is the main purpose of its governance structure?

IFRS APPLICATIONS

I1-50. Applying the Accounting Equation and Computing Financing Proportions (LO2)
The following table contains fiscal 2012 information for three companies that use IFRS. Apply the accounting equation to compute the missing financial amounts (a), (b), and (c). Which of these companies is more owner-financed? Which of these companies is more nonowner-financed? Discuss why the proportion of owner financing might differ across these three companies.

OMV Group
Ericsson
BAE Systems

(Amounts in millions)	Assets	=	Liabilities	+	Equity
OMV Group (Austria)	€ 13,888		€ 6,034		(a)
Ericsson (Sweden).	SEK 274,996		(b)		SEK 138,483
BAE Systems (UK).	(c)		£18,500		£3,774

AstraZeneca

I1-51. Computing Return on Equity and Return on Assets (LO3)
The following table contains financial statement information for AstraZeneca, which is a global biopharmaceutical company focused on discovery, development, manufacturing and commercialization of medicines and is headquartered in London, UK.

($ millions)	Total Assets	Net Income	Sales	Equity
2010	$56,127	$8,106	$33,269	$23,410
2011	52,830	9,470	33,591	23,472
2012	53,534	6,405	27,973	23,952

Required

a. Compute the return on equity (ROE) for 2011 and 2012. What trend, if any, is evident? How does AstraZeneca's ROE compare with the approximately 21.5% median ROE for companies in the Dow Jones Industrial average for 2012?
b. Compute the return on assets (ROA) for 2011 and 2012. What trends, if any, are evident? How does AstraZeneca's ROA compare with the approximate 6.7% median ROA for companies in the Dow Jones Industrial average for 2012?
c. What factors might allow a company like AstraZeneca to reap above-average returns?

Tesco PLC

I1-52. Computing and Interpreting Return on Assets and Its Components (LO3)
Tesco PLC, which is one of the world's largest retailers and is headquartered in Cheshunt, U.K., reported the following balance sheet and income statement data for 2011 through 2013.

(£ millions)	Total Assets	Net Income	Sales
2011	£12,039	£2,671	£60,455
2012	12,863	2,814	63,916
2013	13,096	120	64,826

Required

a. What is Tesco's return on assets for 2012 and 2013?
b. Disaggregate Tesco's ROA metrics from part *a* into profit margin and asset turnover.
c. What factor is mainly responsible for the change in Tesco's ROA over this period?

MANAGEMENT APPLICATIONS

MA1-53. Strategic Financing (LO2)
You and your management team are working to develop the strategic direction of your company for the next three years. One issue you are discussing is how to finance the projected increases in operating assets. Your options are to rely more heavily on operating creditors, borrow the funds, or to sell additional stock in your company. Discuss the pros and cons of each source of financing.

MA1-54. Statement Analysis (LO3)
You are evaluating your company's recent operating performance and are trying to decide on the relative weights you should put on the income statement, the balance sheet, and the statement of cash flows. Discuss the information each of these statements provides and its role in evaluating operating performance.

MA1-55. Analyst Relations (LO2)
Your investor relations department reports to you that stockholders and financial analysts evaluate the quality of a company's financial reports based on their "transparency," namely the clarity and completeness of the company's financial disclosures. Discuss the trade-offs of providing more or less transparent financial reports.

MA1-56. Ethics and Governance: Management Communications (LO5)
The Business Insight box on page 1-14 quotes Warren Buffett on the use of accounting jargon. Many companies publicly describe their performance using terms such as "EBITDA" or "earnings purged of various expenses" because they believe these terms more effectively reflect their companies' performance than GAAP-defined terms such as net income. What ethical issues might arise from the use of such terms and what challenges does their use present for the governance of the company by stockholders and directors?

MA1-57.[B] Ethics and Governance: Auditor Independence (LO5)
The SEC has been concerned with the "independence" of external auditing firms. It is especially concerned about how large non-audit (such as consulting) fees might impact how aggressively auditing firms pursue accounting issues they uncover in their audits. Congress recently passed legislation that prohibits accounting firms from providing both consulting and auditing services to the same client. How might consulting fees affect auditor independence? What other conflicts of interest might exist for auditors? How do these conflicts impact the governance process?

ONGOING PROJECT

An important part of learning is application. To learn accounting, we must practice the skills taught and apply those skills to real world problems. To that end, we have designed a project to reinforce the lessons in each module and apply that to real companies. The goal of this project is to complete a comprehensive analysis of two (or more) companies in the same industry. We will then create a set of forecasted financial statements and a valuation of the companies' equity. This is essentially what financial analysts and many creditors do. We might not aspire to be an analyst or creditor, but by completing a project of this magnitude, we will have mastered financial reporting at a sufficient level to be able to step into any role in an organization. The goal of Module 1's assignment is to obtain and begin to explore the financial reports for two publicly traded companies that compete with each other.

- Select two publicly traded companies that compete with each other. They must be publicly traded as private company financial statements will not be publicly available. While the two companies do not need to be head-to-head competitors, their main lines of business should broadly overlap.
- Download the annual reports for each company and peruse them. At this stage, choose companies that are profitable (net income is positive) and that have positive retained earnings and stockholders' equity. Select companies whose financial statements are not overly complicated. (Probably avoid the automotive, banking, insurance, and financial services industries. Automotive

companies have recently reported large losses, which complicates the analysis. Banking, insurance, and financial services have operations that differ drastically from the usual industrial companies common in practice. While these companies can be analyzed, they present challenges for the beginning analyst.)

- Use the SEC EDGAR Website to locate the recent Form 10-K (or other annual report such as 20-F or 40-F). Download a spreadsheet version of financial statements. Use Appendix 1A as a guide.
- Use the annual report and the financial statements along with any online sites to assess the companies' business environment. Use Porter's Five Forces or a SWOT analysis to briefly analyze the competitive landscape for the two companies. (Originated by Albert S Humphrey, SWOT Analysis provides a useful way to assess an organization's Strengths, Weaknesses, Opportunities, and Threats.) Our aim is to understand the competitive position of each company so that we can assess their financial statements in a broader business context.
- Explore the financial statements and familiarize yourself with the company basics. The following give an indication of some questions that guide us as we look for answers.
  - What accounting standards are used, U.S. GAAP, IFRS, or other?
  - What is the date of the most recent fiscal year-end?
  - Determine the relative proportion of short-term and long-term assets.
  - Determine the relative proportion of liabilities and equity.
  - Calculate the return on assets (ROA) for the most recent year.
  - Disaggregate ROA into the two component parts as shown in Exhibit 1.7. Compare the numbers/ratios for each company.
  - Find the companies' audit reports. Who are the auditors? Are any concerns raised in the reports?
  - Do the audit reports differ significantly from the one for Berkshire Hathaway in this module?

SOLUTIONS TO REVIEW PROBLEMS

Mid-Module Review

Solution

1.

AXA EQUITABLE LIFE INSURANCE COMPANY Income Statement For Year Ended December 31, 2012	
Revenues	$ 9,160
Expenses	8,944
Net income	216
Net income attributable to noncontrolling interest	95
Net income attributable to AXA stockholders	$ 121

AXA EQUITABLE LIFE INSURANCE COMPANY Balance Sheet December 31, 2012			
Cash	$ 3,162	Liabilities	$158,913
Noncash assets	173,681	Equity	
		AXA stockholders' equity	15,436
		Noncontrolling interest	2,494
		Total stockholders' equity	$ 17,930
Total assets	$176,843	Total liabilities and equity	$176,843

AXA EQUITABLE LIFE INSURANCE COMPANY Statement of Cash Flows For Year Ended December 31, 2012	
Cash flows from operations	$ (780)
Cash flows from investing	(2,692)
Cash flows from financing	3,407
Net increase (decrease) in cash	(65)
Cash, beginning year	3,227
Cash, ending year	$3,162

2. Berkshire Hathaway is a larger company; its total assets are $427,452 million compared to AXA's assets of $176,843 million. The income statements of the two companies are markedly different. Berkshire Hathaway reports nearly eighteen times as much revenue ($162,463 million compared to $9,160 million). The difference in net income attributable to the parent stockholders is also large; Berkshire Hathaway earned $14,824 million whereas AXA reported net income of only $121 million.

Module-End Review

Solution

a. ROA = Net income/Average assets = $902/$22,270 = 4.1%.
The profitability component is Net income/Sales = $902/$17,084 = 5.3%, and the productivity component is Sales/Average assets = $17,084/$22,270 = 0.77. Notice that 5.3% × 0.77 = 4.1%. Thus, the two components, when multiplied, yield ROA.

b. ROE = Net income/Average stockholders' equity = $902/$5,907 = 15.3%.

Module 2

Introducing Financial Statements and Transaction Analysis

Learning Objectives

LO1 Describe information conveyed by the financial statements. (p. 2-3)

LO2 Explain and illustrate linkages among the four financial statements. (p. 2-20)

LO3 Illustrate use of the financial statement effects template to summarize accounting transactions. (p. 2-22)

Apple

The Financial Times reported in August of 1980 that:

> Apple Computer, the fast growing Californian manufacturer of small computers for the consumer, business and educational markets, is planning to go public later this year. [It] is the largest private manufacturer in the U.S. of small computers. Founded about five years ago as a small workshop business, it has become the second largest manufacturer of small computers, after the Radio Shack division of the Tandy company.

On December 12, 1980, **Apple** had its initial public offering at a price of $22. During the next 24 years (through fiscal 2004), Apple reported *cumulative* income of $3.8 billion on $128.5 billion in sales, a 3% net profit margin, and its market capitalization (share price × common shares outstanding) was just over $15 million at the end of fiscal 2004. However, for its *2012 fiscal year alone*, Apple reported income of $41.7 billion on sales of $156.5 billion, which represented a 26.6% net profit margin. In fact, over the past decade, Apple reported cumulative income of $103.2 billion on sales of $482.1 billion, which is a 21.4% profit margin. Its market capitalization at the end of fiscal 2012 was $627 billion, greater than **Google**, **IBM**, **Microsoft**, **Oracle**, **Cisco**, and **Intel**. Apple's meteoric rise over that decade is the result of a number of iconic product introductions: iPod and iTunes in 2001, iPhone in 2007, and iPad in 2010. The rise in the market value of Apple stock has mirrored its product successes. However, 2012 saw a pullback in stock price as cash and other liquid nonproductive assets began to pile up; some saw Apple as a giant ship without a rudder.

Information in financial statements helps us assess a company's financial strength and judge the performance of managers and the company as a whole. This module defines and explains the components of each financial statement: the balance sheet, the income statement, the statement of cash flows, and the statement of stockholders' equity. We begin with a preview of Apple's financial condition and performance through a review of its financial statements.

Apple's balance sheet is quite liquid due to a solid record of generating operating cash flow. Apple ended its 2012 year with $121 billion of cash and marketable investments.

Courtesy of Getty Images

Liquidity is important for companies like Apple that must react quickly to opportunities and changing market conditions. Like other technology companies, much of Apple's production is subcontracted. Consequently, Apple's property, plant and equipment make up only 9% of its assets.

On the financing side of its balance sheet, two-thirds of Apple's resources come from owner financing: from common stock sold to shareholders and from past profits that have been reinvested in the business. Technology companies such as Apple, which have uncertain product life-cycles and highly volatile cash flows, strive to avoid high debt levels that might cause financial problems in a business downturn. Apple's nonowner financing consists of low-cost credit from suppliers (accounts payable) and unpaid overhead expenses (accrued liabilities).

Consider Apple's income statement: driven by the popularity and high profit margins of iPods and iPhones, Apple recently reported over $55 billion of operating income. This is impressive given that Apple spends over $3 billion on research and development and runs expensive advertising campaigns.

Yet, companies cannot live by profits alone. It is cash that pays bills. Profits and cash flow reflect two different concepts, each providing a different perspective on company performance. Apple generated over $50 billion of cash flow from operating activities, and invested most of this cash flow in marketable securities. We review Apple's cash flows in this module.

In March 2012, Apple announced that it would pay a dividend for the first time since 1995 and paid out $2.5 billion in dividends during the year. The company did not sell any additional stock to the public during the year: newly issued common stock relates primarily to executive stock options. These capital transactions are reported in the statement of stockholders' equity.

While it is important to understand what is reported in each of the four financial statements, it is also important to know what is *not* reported. Apple's many intangible assets create a barrier to competition that allows it to earn above-average profits. This represents a valuable resource to Apple, but it is not always reported as an asset on Apple's balance sheet. Consider another example. Apple's software engineers write code and create software that will generate profits for Apple in the future. While this represents a valuable resource to Apple, it is not reported on the balance sheet because Apple expenses the software engineers' salaries when the code is written. We discuss these and other issues relating to asset recognition and measurement in this module.

Sources: Apple 10-K; Apple Annual Report; *Financial Times*, 1980; *Fortune*, 2012.

MODULE ORGANIZATION

Introducing Financial Statements and Transaction Analysis

Financial Statements
- Balance Sheet
- Income Statement
- Statement of Stockholders' Equity
- Statement of Cash Flows

Articulation of Financial Statements
- Retained Earnings Reconciliation
- Financial Statement Linkages

Transaction Analysis
- Recording Transactions
- Accounting Adjustments
- Constructing Financial Statements

This module explains further the details of financial statements and how those statements articulate (relate to each other). Transaction analysis and accounting adjustments conclude the module.

BALANCE SHEET

LO1 Describe information conveyed by the financial statements.

The balance sheet is divided into three sections: assets, liabilities, and stockholders' equity. It provides information about the resources available to management and the claims against those resources by creditors and stockholders. The balance sheet reports the assets, liabilities, and equity at a *point* in time. Balance sheet accounts are called "permanent accounts" in that they carry over from period to period; that is, the ending balance from one period becomes the beginning balance for the next.

Balance Sheet and the Flow of Costs

Companies incur costs to acquire resources that will be used in operations. Every cost creates either an immediate or a future economic benefit. Determining when the company will realize the benefit from a cost is paramount. When a cost creates an immediate benefit, such as gasoline used in delivery vehicles, the company records the cost in the income statement as an expense. When a cost creates a future economic benefit, such as inventory to be resold or equipment to be later used for manufacturing, the company records the cost on the balance sheet as an asset. Indeed, the definition of an asset is "a future economic benefit." An asset remains on the company's balance sheet until it is used up. When an asset is used up, the company realizes the economic benefit from the asset; that is, there is no future economic benefit left so there is no asset left. Then, the asset's cost is transferred from the balance sheet to the income statement where it is labeled an expense. This is why purchased assets are sometimes referred to as future expenses.

Companies expense certain costs, such as advertising, as they are incurred because even though the costs will likely bring future economic benefits, the related asset cannot be reliably measured. Exhibit 2.1 illustrates how costs flow from the balance sheet to the income statement.

EXHIBIT 2.1 Flow of Costs

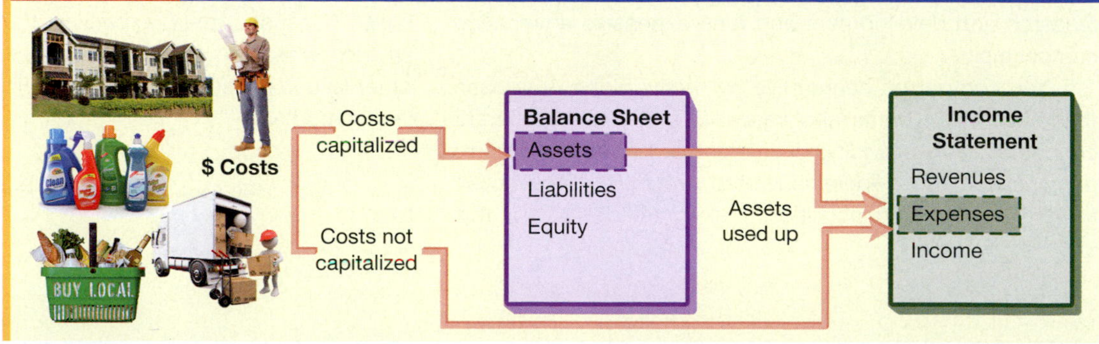

All costs are either held on the balance sheet or are transferred to the income statement. When costs are recorded on the balance sheet (referred to as *capitalized*), assets are reported and expenses are deferred to a later period. Once the company receives benefits from the assets, the related costs are transferred from the balance sheet to the income statement. At that point, assets are reduced and expenses are recorded in the current period. Tracking the flow of costs from the balance sheet to the income statement is an important part of accounting. GAAP allows companies some flexibility in transferring costs. As such, there is potential for abuse, especially when managers confront pressures to achieve income targets.

Corporate scandals involving **WorldCom** and **Enron** regrettably illustrate improper cost transfers designed to achieve higher profit levels. Neither company transferred costs from the balance sheet to the income statement as quickly as they should have. This had the effect of overstating assets on the balance sheet and net income on the income statement. In subsequent litigation, the SEC and the Justice Department contended that these companies intentionally overstated net income to boost stock prices. A number of senior executives from both Enron and WorldCom were sentenced to lengthy jail terms as a result of their criminal actions.

What does GAAP advise about the transfer of costs? Asset costs should transfer to the income statement when the asset no longer has any future economic benefit (which is when it no longer meets the definition of an asset). For example, when inventories are purchased or manufactured, their cost is recorded on the balance sheet as an asset called *inventories*. When inventories are sold, they no longer have an economic benefit to the company and their cost is transferred to the income statement in an expense called *cost of goods sold*. Cost of goods sold represents the cost of inventories sold during that period. This expense is recognized in the same period as the revenue generated from the sale. As another example, consider equipment costs. When a company acquires equipment, the cost of the equipment is recorded on the balance sheet in an asset called *equipment* (often included in the general category of property, plant, and equipment, or PPE). When equipment is used in operations, a portion of the acquisition cost is transferred to the income statement to match against the sales the equipment helped generate. To illustrate, if an asset costs \$100,000, and 10% of it is used up this period in operating activities, then \$10,000 of the asset's cost is transferred from the balance sheet to the income statement. This process is called *depreciation* and the expense related to this transfer of costs is called depreciation expense.

Assets

Companies acquire assets to yield a return for their shareholders. Assets are expected to produce economic benefits in the form of revenues, either directly, such as with inventory, or indirectly, such as with a manufacturing plant that produces inventories for sale. To create stockholder value, assets must yield income that is in excess of the cost of the funds used to acquire the assets.

The asset section of the **Apple** balance sheet is shown in Exhibit 2.2. Apple reports \$176,064 million of total assets as of September 29, 2012, its year-end. Amounts reported on the balance sheet are at a *point in time*—that is, the close of business on the day of the report. An asset must possess two characteristics to be reported on the balance sheet:

1. It must be owned (or controlled) by the company.
2. It must confer expected future economic benefits that result from a past transaction or event.

The first requirement, owning or controlling an asset, implies that a company has legal title to the asset, such as the title to property, or has the unrestricted right to use the asset, such as a lease on the property. The second requirement implies that a company expects to realize a benefit from the asset. Benefits can be cash inflows from the sale of an asset or from sales of products produced by the asset. Benefits also can refer to the receipt of other assets such as an account receivable from a credit sale. Or, benefits can arise from future services the company will receive, such as prepaying for a year-long insurance policy. This requirement also implies that we cannot record an asset such as a brand name without a transaction to acquire it.

Current Assets

The balance sheet lists assets in order of decreasing **liquidity**, which refers to the ease of converting noncash assets into cash. The most liquid assets are called **current assets** and they are listed first. A

EXHIBIT 2.2 Asset Section of Apple's Balance Sheet ($ millions)

Assets used up or converted to cash within one year → Current Assets

Assets used up or converted to cash over more than one year → Long-Term Assets

APPLE INC. Balance Sheet September 29, 2012	
Assets	
Current assets	
Cash and cash equivalents	$ 10,746
Short-term investments	18,383
Accounts receivable, net	10,930
Inventories	791
Other current assets	16,803
Total current assets	57,653
Long-term assets	
Property, plant and equipment, net	15,452
Other long-term assets	102,959*
Total assets	$176,064

*Includes $92,122 million of long-term marketable securities

company expects to convert its current assets into cash or use those assets in operations within the coming fiscal year.[1] Typical examples of current assets follow:

- **Cash**—currency, bank deposits, and investments with an original maturity of 90 days or less (called *cash equivalents*);
- **Short-term investments**—marketable securities and other investments that the company expects to dispose of in the short run;
- **Accounts receivable, net**—amounts due to the company from customers arising from the sale of products and services on credit ("net" refers to the subtraction of uncollectible accounts);
- **Inventories**—goods purchased or produced for sale to customers;
- **Prepaid expenses**—costs paid in advance for rent, insurance, advertising and other services.

Apple reports current assets of $57,653 million in 2012, which is 33% of its total assets. The amount of current assets is an important measure of liquidity, which relates to a company's ability to make short-term payments. Companies require a degree of liquidity to operate effectively, as they must be able to respond to changing market conditions and take advantage of opportunities. However, current assets such as receivables and inventories are expensive to hold (they must be stored, insured, monitored, financed, and so forth)—and they typically generate relatively low returns. As a result, companies seek to maintain only just enough current assets to cover liquidity needs, but not so much to unnecessarily reduce income.

Long-Term Assets

The second section of the balance sheet reports long-term (noncurrent) assets. Long-term assets include the following:

- **Property, plant and equipment (PPE), net**—land, factory buildings, warehouses, office buildings, machinery, motor vehicles, office equipment and other items used in operating activities ("net" refers to the subtraction of accumulated depreciation, the portion of the assets' cost that has been expensed);
- **Long-term investments**—investments that the company does not intend to sell in the near future;
- **Intangible and other assets**—assets without physical substance, including patents, trademarks, franchise rights, goodwill and other costs the company incurred that provide future benefits.

[1] Technically, current assets include those assets expected to be converted into cash within the upcoming fiscal year or the company's operating cycle (the cash-to-cash cycle), whichever is longer. **Beam Inc.** (manufacturer of Jim Beam Whiskey) provides an example of a current asset with a cash conversion cycle of longer than one year. Its inventory footnote reports: In accordance with generally recognized trade practice, maturing spirits inventories are classified as current assets, although the majority of these inventories ordinarily will not be sold within one year, due to the duration of aging processes.

Long-term assets are not expected to be converted into cash for some time and are, therefore, listed after current assets.

Measuring Assets

Most assets are reported at their original acquisition costs, or **historical costs**, and not at their current market values. The concept of historical costs is not without controversy. The controversy arises because of the trade-off between the **relevance** of current market values for many business decisions and the **reliability** of historical cost measures.

To illustrate, imagine we are financial analysts and want to determine the value of a company. The company's value equals the value of its assets less the value of its liabilities. Current market values of company assets (and liabilities) are more informative and relevant to our analysis than are historical costs. But how can we determine market values? For some assets, like marketable securities, values are readily obtained from online quotes or from sources such as *The Wall Street Journal*. For other assets like property, plant, and equipment, their market values are far more subjective and difficult to estimate. It would be easier for us, as analysts, if companies reported credible market values on their balance sheet. However, allowing companies to report estimates of asset market values would introduce potential *bias* into financial reporting. Consequently, companies continue to report historical costs because the loss in reliability from using subjective market values on the balance sheet is considered to be greater than the loss in relevance from using historical costs.

It is important to realize that balance sheets only include items that can be reliably measured. If a company cannot assign a monetary amount to an asset with relative certainty, it does not recognize an asset on the balance sheet. This means that there are, typically, considerable "assets" that are not reflected on a balance sheet. For example, the well-known apple image is absent from Apple's balance sheet. This image is called an "unrecognized intangible asset." Both requirements for an asset are met: Apple owns the brand and it expects to realize future benefits from the logo. The problem is reliably measuring the expected future benefits to be derived from the image. Intangible assets such as the Coke bottle silhouette, the iPod brandname, and the Nike swoosh also are not on their companies' respective balance sheets. Companies only report intangible assets on the balance sheet when the assets are purchased. Any internally created intangible assets are not reported on a balance sheet. A sizable amount of resources is, therefore, potentially omitted from companies' balance sheets.

Excluded intangible assets often relate to *knowledge-based* (intellectual) assets, such as a strong management team, a well-designed supply chain, or superior technology. Although these intangible assets confer a competitive advantage to the company, and yield above-normal income (and clear economic benefits to those companies), they cannot be reliably measured. This is one reason why companies in knowledge-based industries are so difficult to analyze and value.

Presumably, however, companies' market values reflect these excluded intangible assets. This can yield a large difference between the market value and the book (reported) value of a company's equity. This is illustrated in the following ratios of market value to book value (averages from fiscal 2012 year-ends): **Apple** is 5.3 (computed as $626,550/$118,210) and **Target** is 2.4 (computed as [645.294 × $61.15]/$16,558). These market-to-book values (ratios) are greater for companies with large knowledge-based assets that are not reported on the balance sheet, but are reflected in company market value (such as with **Apple**). Companies such as **Target** have fewer of these assets. Hence, their balance sheets usually reflect a greater portion of company value.

Liabilities and Equity

Liabilities and stockholders' equity represent the sources of capital the company uses to finance the acquisition of assets. In general, liabilities represent a company's future economic sacrifices. Liabilities are borrowed funds such as accounts payable and obligations to lenders. They can be interest-bearing or non-interest-bearing.

Equity represents capital that has been invested by the stockholders, either directly via the purchase of stock, or indirectly in the form of *retained earnings* that reflect earnings that are reinvested in the business and not paid out as dividends.

The liabilities and stockholders' equity sections of the **Apple** balance sheet are reproduced in Exhibit 2.3. Apple reports $57,854 million of total liabilities and $118,210 million of stockholders' equity as of its 2012 year-end.

EXHIBIT 2.3 Liabilities and Equity Sections of Apple's Balance Sheet ($ millions)

APPLE INC.
Balance Sheet
September 29, 2012

	Liabilities and Stockholders' Equity		
Liabilities	Current liabilities		
	Accounts payable	$21,175	
	Accrued liabilities	17,367	
	Total current liabilities	38,542	Liabilities requiring payment within one year
	Long-term liabilities	19,312	Liabilities not requiring payment within one year
	Total liabilities	57,854	
Stockholders' Equity	Stockholders' equity		
	Common stock, no par value; 1.8 bil. shares authorized; 939,208,000 shares issued and outstanding	16,422	
	Retained earnings	101,289	
	Other stockholders' equity	499	
	Total stockholders' equity	118,210	
	Total liabilities and stockholders' equity	$176,064	

Why would Apple obtain capital from both borrowed funds and stockholders? Why not just one or the other? The answer lies in their relative costs and the contractual agreements that Apple has with each.

Creditors have the first claim on the assets of the company. As a result, their position is not as risky and, accordingly, their expected return on investment is less than that required by stockholders. Also, interest is tax deductible whereas dividends are not. This makes debt a less expensive source of capital than equity. So, then, why should a company not finance itself entirely with borrowed funds? The reason is that borrowed funds entail contractual obligations to repay the principal and interest on the debt. If a company cannot make these payments when they come due, creditors can force the company into bankruptcy and potentially put the company out of business. Stockholders, in contrast, cannot require repurchase of their stock, or even the payment of dividends. Thus, companies take on a level of debt that they can comfortably repay at reasonable interest costs. The remaining balance required to fund business activities is financed with more costly equity capital.

Current Liabilities

The balance sheet lists liabilities in order of maturity. Obligations that must be settled within one year are called **current liabilities**. Examples of common current liabilities follow:

Accounts payable—amounts owed to suppliers for goods and services purchased on credit.

Accrued liabilities—obligations for expenses that have been incurred but not yet paid; examples are accrued wages payable (wages earned by employees but not yet paid), accrued interest payable (interest that is owing but has not been paid), and accrued income taxes (taxes due).

Unearned revenues—obligations created when the company accepts payment in advance for goods or services it will deliver in the future; also called advances from customers, customer deposits, or deferred revenues.

Short-term notes payable—short-term debt payable to banks or other creditors.

Current maturities of long-term debt—principal portion of long-term debt that is due to be paid within one year.

Apple reports current liabilities of $38,542 million on its 2012 balance sheet.

Accounts payable arise when one company purchases goods or services from another company. Typically, sellers offer credit terms when selling to other companies, rather than expecting cash on delivery. The seller records an account receivable and the buyer records an account payable. Apple reports accounts payable of $21,175 million as of the balance sheet date. Accounts payable are relatively uncomplicated liabilities. A transaction occurs (inventory purchase), a bill is sent, and the amount owed is reported on the balance sheet as a liability.

Apple's accrued liabilities total $17,367 million. Accrued liabilities refer to incomplete transactions. For example, employees work and earn wages, but usually are not paid until later, such as several days after the period-end. Wages must be reported as expense in the period that employees earn them because those wages payable are obligations of the company and a liability (wages payable) must be set up on the balance sheet. This is an *accrual*. Other common accruals include the recording of liabilities such as rent and utilities payable, taxes payable, and interest payable on borrowings. All of these accruals involve recognition of expense in the income statement and a liability on the balance sheet.

Net working capital, or simply working capital, reflects the difference between current assets and current liabilities and is defined as follows:

Net working capital = Current assets − Current liabilities

We usually prefer to see more current assets than current liabilities to ensure that companies are liquid. That is, companies should have sufficient funds to pay their short-term debts as they mature. The net working capital required to conduct business depends on the company's **operating (or cash) cycle**, which is the time between paying cash for goods or employee services and receiving cash from customers—see Exhibit 2.4.

Companies, for example, use cash to purchase or manufacture inventories held for resale. Inventories are usually purchased on credit from suppliers (accounts payable). This financing is called **trade credit**. Inventories are sold, either for cash or on credit (accounts receivable). When receivables are ultimately collected, a portion of the cash received is used to repay accounts payable and the remainder goes to the cash account for the next operating cycle.

EXHIBIT 2.4 Operating Cycle

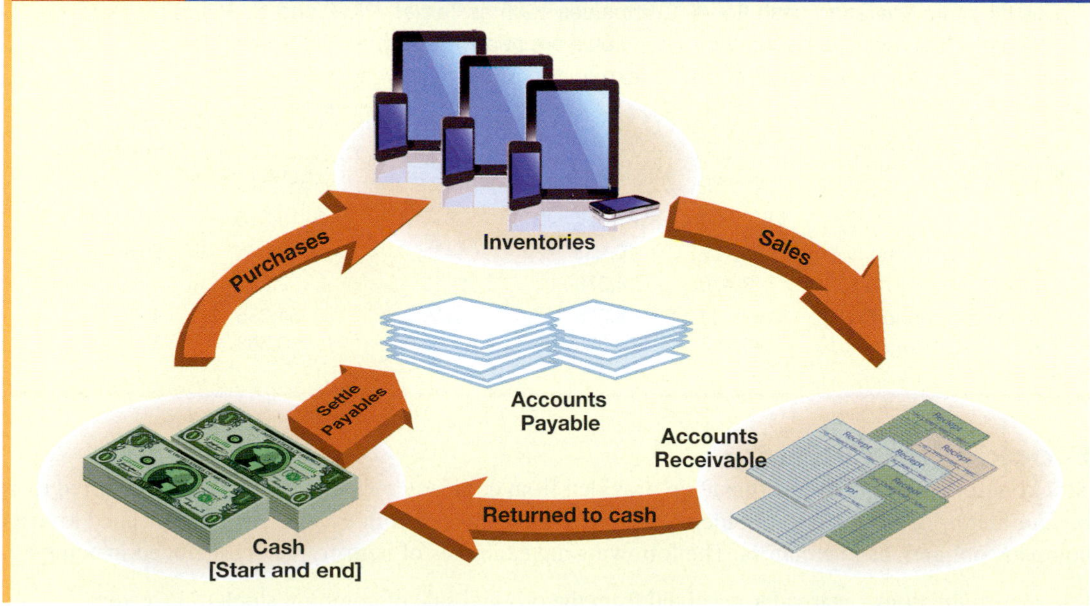

When cash is invested in inventory, the inventory can remain with the company for 30 to 90 days or more. Once inventory is sold, the resulting accounts receivable can remain with the company for another 30 to 90 days. Assets such as inventories and accounts receivable are costly to hold and, consequently, companies strive to reduce operating cycles with various initiatives that aim to:

- Decrease accounts receivable by better collection procedures
- Reduce inventory levels by improved production systems and management
- Increase trade credit to minimize the cash invested in inventories

Analysts often use the "cash conversion cycle" to evaluate company liquidity. The cash conversion cycle is the number of days the company has its cash tied up in receivables and inventories, less the number of days of trade credit provided by company suppliers.

Noncurrent Liabilities

Noncurrent liabilities are obligations due after one year. Examples of noncurrent liabilities follow:

Long-term debt—amounts borrowed from creditors that are scheduled to be repaid more than one year in the future; any portion of long-term debt that is due within one year is reclassified as a current liability called *current maturities of long-term debt*. Long-term debt includes bonds, mortgages, and other long-term loans.

Other long-term liabilities—various obligations, such as pension liabilities and long-term tax liabilities, that will be settled a year or more into the future.

Apple reports $19,312 million of noncurrent liabilities. As is typical of high-tech companies, Apple has no long-term debt. Instead, all of its noncurrent liabilities relate to deferred revenue and deferred taxes. Deferred (unearned) revenue arises when a company receives cash in advance of providing a good or service.

BUSINESS INSIGHT **How Much Debt Is Reasonable?**

Apple reports total assets of $176,064 million, liabilities of $57,854 million, and stockholders' equity of $118,210 million. This reveals that it finances 33% of its assets with borrowed funds and 67% with shareholder investment. This is a lower percentage of nonowner financing than other companies such as Target, Procter & Gamble (P&G), and GAP. Companies must monitor their financing sources and amounts. Too much borrowing is risky as borrowed amounts must be repaid with interest. The level of debt that a company can effectively manage depends on the stability and reliability of its operating cash flows. Companies such as Target, P&G, and GAP can manage relatively high debt levels because their cash flows are relatively stable. Apple operates in an industry that changes rapidly. It cannot afford to take on too much borrowing risk.

($ millions)	Assets	Liabilities	Common Size Liabilities (% of Assets)	Equity	Common Size Equity (% of Assets)
Apple Inc.	$176,064	$57,854	33%	$118,210	67%
Cisco Systems, Inc.	91,759	40,458	44%	51,301	56%
Gap, Inc.	7,470	4,576	61%	2,894	39%
Procter & Gamble Co. . . .	132,244	68,209	52%	64,035	48%
Target Corporation.	48,163	31,605	66%	16,558	34%

Stockholders' Equity

Stockholders' equity reflects financing provided from company owners. Equity is often referred to as *residual interest*. That is, stockholders have a claim on any assets in excess of what is needed to meet company obligations to creditors. The following are examples of items typically included in equity:

Contributed Capital

Common stock—par value received from the original sale of common stock to investors.

Preferred stock—value received from the original sale of preferred stock to investors; preferred stock has fewer ownership rights compared to common stock.

Additional paid-in capital—amounts received from the original sale of stock to investors in excess of the par value of stock.

Treasury stock—amount the company paid to reacquire its common stock from shareholders.

Retained earnings—accumulated net income (profit) that has not been distributed to stockholders as dividends.

Accumulated other comprehensive income or loss—accumulated changes in asset and liability fair values that are not reported in the income statement.

Earned Capital

The equity section of a balance sheet consists of two basic components: contributed capital and earned capital. **Contributed capital** is the net funding that a company received from issuing and reacquiring its equity shares; that is, the funds received from issuing shares less any funds paid to repurchase such shares. Apple reports $118,210 million in total stockholders' equity. Its contributed capital is $16,422 million.

Apple's common stock is "no par" (see Exhibit 2.3). This means that Apple records all of its contributed capital in the common stock account and records no additional paid-in capital. Apple's stockholders (via its board of directors) have authorized it to issue up to 1.8 billion shares of common stock. To date, it has sold (issued) 939,208,000 shares for total proceeds of $16,422 million, or $17.48 per share, on average. Apple has repurchased no shares of stock to date.

Earned capital is the cumulative net income (loss) that has been retained by the company (not paid out to stockholders as dividends). Apple's earned capital (titled Retained Earnings) totals $101,289 million as of its 2012 year-end. Its other equity accounts total $499 million.

ANALYSIS INSIGHT Common Size Balance Sheet

One tool for analyzing a company's balance sheet is the *common size balance sheet*. This is a balance sheet where each item is recast as a percent of total assets. It is called common size because each item is scaled by a common denominator. Common sizing the balance sheet enables us to perform the following types of analyses:

- Compare a company's balance sheets across two or more years. Companies provide side-by-side balance sheets for two years and the Form 10-K often includes an 11-year history of key balance sheet accounts. If the company has grown or shrunk in size over time, comparing dollars (or other currency) masks shifts in relative size of balance sheet items. Percentages reveal a more accurate picture.
- Compare two or more companies' balance sheets. The common sizing eliminates size differences among companies—we can compare a small firm to a large firm because each asset, liability, and equity account is expressed in percentage terms. The other benefit is that common sizing is unit free so we can compare companies that report in different currencies.
- Compare balance sheets to an industry average or some other benchmark. The percentages create a common basis for comparison and this can help assess a particular company's financial position relative to others in the same industry.

Retained Earnings

There is an important relation for retained earnings that reconciles its beginning balance and its ending balance as follows:

	Beginning retained earnings
+	Net income (or − net loss)
−	Dividends
=	Ending retained earnings

This is a useful relation to remember. Apple's retained earnings increases (or decreases) each year by the amount of its reported net income (loss) minus its dividends. (There are other items that can impact retained earnings that we discuss in later modules.) After we explain the income statement, we will revisit this relation and show how retained earnings link the balance sheet and income statement.

Book Value vs Market Value Stockholders' equity is the "value" of the company determined by GAAP and is commonly referred to as the company's **book value**. This value is different from a company's **market value** (market capitalization or *market cap*), which is computed by multiplying the number of outstanding common shares by the company's stock price. We can compute Apple's market cap by multiplying its outstanding shares at September 29, 2012, (939,208,000 shares) by its stock price on that date ($667.10), which equals $626.55 billion. This is considerably larger than its book value of equity on that date of $118.2 billion. Book value and market value can differ for several reasons, mostly related to the following:

- GAAP generally reports assets and liabilities at historical costs, whereas the market attempts to estimate fair market values.
- GAAP excludes resources that cannot be reliably measured (due to the absence of a past transaction or event) such as talented management, employee morale, recent innovations and successful marketing, whereas the market attempts to value these.
- GAAP does not consider market differences in which companies operate, such as competitive conditions and expected changes, whereas the market attempts to factor in these differences in determining value.
- GAAP does not usually report expected future performance, whereas the market attempts to predict and value future performance.

Presently for U.S. companies, book value is, on average, about two-thirds of market value (yielding a 1.5 market-to-book ratio). This means that the market has drawn on information in addition to that provided in the balance sheet and income statement in valuing companies' stock. A major part of this information is in financial statement notes, but not all. It is important to understand that, eventually, all factors determining company market value are reflected in financial statements and book value. Assets are eventually sold and liabilities are settled. Moreover, talented management, employee morale, technological innovations, and successful marketing are eventually recognized in reported profit. The difference between book value and market value is one of timing.

BUSINESS INSIGHT Apple's Market and Book Values

Apple's market value has historically exceeded its book value of equity (see graph below). Much of Apple's market value derives from intangible assets, such as brand equity, that are not fully reflected on its balance sheet, and from favorable expectations of future financial performance (particularly in recent years). Apple has incurred many costs, such as R&D, advertising, and promotion, that will probably yield future economic benefits. However, Apple expensed these costs (did not capitalize them as assets) because their future benefits were uncertain and, therefore, could not be reliably measured. Companies capitalize intangible assets only when those assets are purchased, and not when they are internally developed. Consequently, Apple's balance sheet and the balance sheets of many knowledge-based companies are, arguably, less informative about company value.

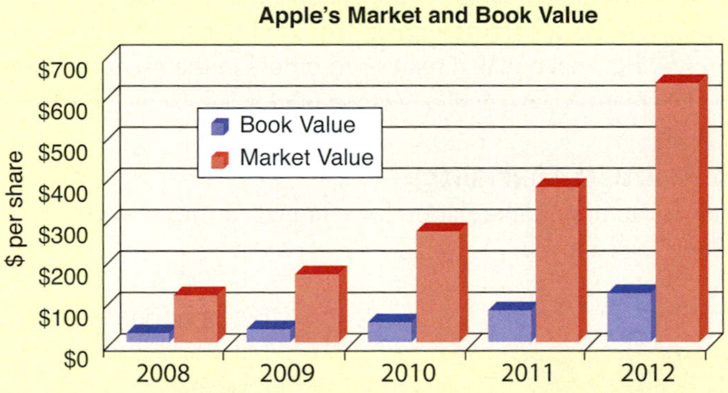

RESEARCH INSIGHT Market-to-Book Ratio

The market-to-book ratio, also called price-to-book, refers to a company's market value divided by its book (equity) value—it is also computed as stock price per share divided by book value per share. Research shows that the market-to-book ratio exhibits considerable variability over time. Specifically, over the past few decades, the median (50th percentile) market-to-book ratio was less than 1.0 during the mid-1970s, over 2.0 during the mid-1990s, and often between 1.0 and 2.0 during the 1960s and 1980s.

INCOME STATEMENT

The income statement reports revenues earned during a period, the expenses incurred to produce those revenues, and the resulting net income or loss. The general structure of the income statement follows:

	Revenues
−	Cost of goods sold
	Gross profit (also titled, Gross margin)
−	Operating expenses
	Operating profit (also titled, Operating income)
−	Nonoperating expenses (+ Nonoperating revenues)
−	Tax expense
	Income from continuing operations
+/−	Nonrecurring items, net of tax
=	Net income
−	Net income attributable to noncontrolling interest
=	Net income attributable to 'parent' stockholders

Apple's income statement from its 2012 10-K is shown in Exhibit 2.5. Apple reports net income of $41,733 million on sales of $156,508 million. This means that about $0.27 of each dollar of sales is brought down to the bottom line, computed as $41,733 million divided by $156,508 million. Apple's net income margin is higher than that of the average publicly-traded company, which reports about $0.06 in profit for each sales dollar. The remaining $0.73 of each sales dollar for Apple (computed as $1 minus $0.27) is consumed by costs incurred to generate sales. These costs include production costs (cost of sales), wages, advertising, research and development, equipment costs (such as depreciation), and taxes.

To analyze an income statement we must understand some terminology. **Revenues** (Sales) are increases in net assets (assets less liabilities) as a result of ordinary operating activities. **Expenses** are decreases in net assets used to generate revenues, including costs of sales, operating costs like wages and advertising (usually titled selling, general, and administrative expenses or SG&A), and nonoperating costs like interest on debt. The difference between revenues and expenses is **net income** when revenues exceed expenses, or **net loss** when expenses exceed revenues. The terms income, profit, and earnings are used interchangeably (as are revenues and sales).

EXHIBIT 2.5 Apple's Income Statement ($ millions)

APPLE INC.
Income Statement
For Year Ended September 29, 2012

Net sales	$156,508
Cost of sales	87,846
Gross margin	68,662
Operating expenses	
Research and development	3,381
Selling, general, and administrative	10,040
Total operating expenses	13,421
Operating income	55,241
Other revenue and expense	
Interest and other income, net	522
Income before provision for income taxes	55,763
Provision for income taxes	14,030
Net income	$41,733

Alert The FASB has released a preliminary draft of a proposal to restructure financial statements to, among other things, better distinguish operating and nonoperating activities.

Operating expenses are the usual and customary costs that a company incurs to support its operating activities. Those include cost of goods sold, selling expenses, depreciation expense, and research and development expense. Not all of these expenses require a cash outlay; for example, depreciation expense is a noncash expense, as are many liabilities such as wages payable, that recognize the expense in advance of cash payment. **Nonoperating expenses** relate to the company's financing and investing activities, and include interest expense, interest or dividend income, and gains and losses from the sale of securities. Business decision makers and analysts usually segregate operating and nonoperating activities as they offer different insights into company performance and condition.

MANAGERIAL DECISION **You Are the Securities Analyst**

You are analyzing the performance of a company that hired a new CEO during the current year. The current year's income statement includes an expense labeled "asset write-offs." Write-offs represent the accelerated transfer of costs from the balance sheet to the income statement. Are you concerned about the legitimacy of these expenses? Why or why not? [Answer, p. 2-35]

Recognition of Revenues and Expenses

An important consideration in preparing the income statement is *when* to recognize revenues and expenses. For many revenues and expenses, the decision is easy. When a customer purchases groceries, pays with a check, and walks out of the store with the groceries, we know that the sale is made and revenue should be recognized. Or, when companies receive and pay an electric bill with a check, they have clearly incurred an expense that should be recognized.

However, should Apple recognize revenue when it sells iPods to a retailer that does not have to pay Apple for 60 days? Should Apple recognize an expense for employees who work this week but will not be paid until the first of next month? The answer to both of these questions is yes.

Two fundamental principles guide recognition of revenues and expenses:

Revenue Recognition Principle—recognize revenues when *earned*.

Expense Recognition (Matching) Principle—recognize expenses when *incurred*.

These two principles are the foundation of **accrual accounting**, which is the accounting system used to prepare all GAAP-based financial statements. The general approach is this: first, recognize revenues in the time period they are earned; then, record all expenses *incurred* to generate those revenues during that same time period (this is called matching expenses to revenues). Net income is then correctly reported for that period.

Recognizing revenues when earned does not necessarily imply the receipt of cash. Revenue is *earned* when the company has done everything that it is supposed to do. This means that a sale of goods on credit would qualify for recognition as long as the revenues are earned. Likewise, companies recognize an expense when it is *incurred*, even if no cash is paid. For example, companies recognize as expenses the wages earned by employees, even though they will not be paid until the next pay period. The company records an expense but pays no cash; instead, it records an accrued liability for the wages payable.

Accrual accounting requires estimates and assumptions. Examples include estimating how much revenue has been earned on a long-term contract, the amount of accounts receivable that will not be collected, the degree to which equipment has been "used up," the cleanup costs that a company must eventually pay for environmental liabilities, and numerous other estimates. All of these estimates and assumptions affect both reported net income and the balance sheet. Judgments affect all financial statements. This is an important by-product of accrual accounting. We discuss these estimates and assumptions, and their effects on financial statements, throughout the book.

ANALYSIS INSIGHT **Common Size Income Statement**

Analysts typically prepare common size income statements as a starting point for their analysis; each income statement item is expressed as a percent of net sales. As with the common size balance sheet, a common size income statement facilitates the same three types of comparisons: one company across years (called time-series analysis), many companies across one year (called cross-sectional analysis), and to a benchmark such as an industry average. Common size analysis is also referred to as "vertical analysis" because the percentages in the column on the income statement add up vertically to 100% of total sales (the top-line number on the income statement). A common size balance sheet adds up vertically to 100% of total assets (the last number on the balance sheet).

MANAGERIAL DECISION **You Are the Operations Manager**

You are the operations manager on a new consumer product that was launched this period with very successful sales. The Chief Financial Officer (CFO) asks you to prepare an estimate of warranty costs to charge against those sales. Why does the CFO desire a warranty cost estimate? What issues must you address in arriving at such an estimate? [Answer, p. 2-35]

Reporting of Transitory Items

To this point, we have only considered income from continuing operations and its components. A more complete income statement format is in Exhibit 2.6. The most noticeable difference involves two additional components of net income located at the bottom of the statement. These two components are specifically segregated from the "income from continuing operations" and are defined as follows:

1. **Discontinued operations** Gains or losses (and net income or loss) from business segments that are being sold or have been sold in the current period.
2. **Extraordinary items** Gains or losses from events that are both *unusual* and *infrequent* and are, therefore, excluded from income from continuing operations.

EXHIBIT 2.6 **General Income Statement Format**

Sales
− Cost of goods sold

Gross profit
− Operating expenses
− Nonoperating expenses (+ Nonoperating revenues)
− Tax expense ← Tax expense applies to income from continuing operations

Income from continuing operations
± Discontinued operations, net of tax
± Extraordinary items, net of tax ← Transitory items are those not expected to recur

Net income

These two components are segregated because they represent **transitory items**, which reflect transactions or events that are unlikely to recur. Many readers of financial statements are interested in *future* company performance. They analyze current-year financial statements to gain clues to better *predict* future performance. (Stock prices, for example, are based on a company's expected profits and cash flows.)

Transitory items, by definition, are unlikely to arise in future periods. Although transitory items can help us analyze past performance, they are largely irrelevant to predicting future performance. This means that investors and other users tend to focus on income from continuing operations because that is the level of profitability that is likely to **persist** (continue) into the future. Likewise, the financial press tends to focus on income from continuing operations when it discloses corporate earnings (often described as *earnings before one-time charges*).

ANALYSIS INSIGHT **Discontinued Operations**

The "discontinued operations" line that we sometimes see on the income statement consists of two parts: (1) the income or loss from the discontinued operation (usually a subsidiary company that is sold) for the portion of the current year prior to sale, and (2) the gain or loss on the sale of the discontinued operation. The latter is computed as the difference between the sales price and the balance sheet value of the discontinued operation at the date it was sold. For example, if a company sells a subsidiary that is reported on the balance sheet at $100 for a sales price of $125, it reports a gain on sale of $25. However, if it was sold at a sales price of $90 a $10 loss on sale is reported. This is just like we would compute the gain or loss on the sale of any asset; a subsidiary company is merely a collection of many assets and liabilities (we discuss gains and losses on the sale of subsidiary companies in Module 7).

How should we treat the income or loss from the discontinued operation and the gain or loss on its sale when we analyze a company? The critical question is whether they represent operating or nonoperating activities. The case for "operating" rests on the assumption that the subsidiary has historically been treated as an operating asset and, therefore, any income, gain, or loss should also be treated as operating. The case for "nonoperating" rests on the assumption that the subsidiary ceases to be part of the company's operations once the decision is made to dispose of it and, therefore, any income, gain, or loss should be treated as nonoperating. Most analysts side with the nonoperating treatment because it is consistent with the motivation for their analyses: to forecast future operating performance for equity and debt valuation. We adopt this view too: our chief aim is to identify core operating income and cash flow *that will persist into the future*. Including results from discontinued operations in the financial analysis could mask core operating income and lead to inaccurate estimates of future operating income and cash flow. The important point is that results from discontinued operations will not recur in the future as those assets are gone and their earning power has ceased. We return to this analysis in Module 4.

STATEMENT OF STOCKHOLDERS' EQUITY

The statement of stockholders' equity reconciles the beginning and ending balances of stockholders' equity accounts. The statement of stockholders' equity for **Apple** is shown in Exhibit 2.7.

EXHIBIT 2.7 **Apple's Statement of Stockholders' Equity**

APPLE INC.
Statement of Stockholders' Equity
For Year Ended September 29, 2012

($ millions)	Contributed Capital	Retained Earnings	Other Equity	Total Equity
Balance at September 24, 2011	$13,331	$62,841	$443	$76,615
Common stock issued	200			200
Net income		41,733		41,733
Dividends		(2,523)		(2,523)
Other	2,891	(762)	56	2,185
Balance at September 29, 2012	$16,422	$101,289	$499	$118,210

Apple's first equity component is common stock. The balance in common stock at the beginning of the year is $13,331 million. During 2012, Apple issued $200 million worth of common stock to employees who exercised stock options and reported other changes to the common stock account in the amount of $2,891 million. At the end of 2012, the common stock account reports a balance of $16,422 million.

Apple's second stockholders' equity component is retained earnings. It totals $62,841 million at the start of fiscal 2012. During the year, it increased by $41,733 million from net income. Apple's retained earnings decreased by $2,523 million representing the payment of dividends; it also reports $(762) million of miscellaneous adjustments. The balance of retained earnings at year-end is $101,289 million.

In sum, total stockholders' equity begins the year at $76,615 million (including $443 million relating to miscellaneous accounts that increase total stockholders' equity) and ends fiscal 2012 with a balance of $118,210 million for a net increase of $41,595 million.

IFRS INSIGHT **Balance Sheet and Income Statement under IFRS**

U.S. GAAP and IFRS require a similar set of financial statements with similar formats. Both standards require current and long-term classifications for assets and liabilities, and both recognize revenues when earned and expenses when incurred. Although differences between U.S. GAAP and IFRS do exist at the "detailed level," there are at least three broader differences worth mention:

- GAAP makes no formal prescription for the balance sheet and the income statement; however, the SEC does prescribe the types of accounts and number of years that should be disclosed per Reg. S-X. Reg. S-X requires three years of comparative income statements whereas IFRS requires only two.
- GAAP requires the reporting of extraordinary items as a separate category of the income statement if they are unusual and infrequent; IFRS has no extraordinary item category.
- For items that are either unusual or infrequent, but not both, GAAP requires separate presentation in the income statement as a component of earnings from continuing operations; IFRS also requires disclosure of these items, but allows for such disclosure in footnotes to financial statements as an alternative to the income statement.

STATEMENT OF CASH FLOWS

The balance sheet and income statement are prepared using accrual accounting, in which revenues are recognized when earned and expenses when incurred. This means that companies can report income even though no cash is received. Cash shortages—due to unexpected cash outlays or when customers refuse to or cannot pay—can create economic hardships for companies and even cause their demise.

To assess cash flows, we must assess a company's cash management. Obligations to employees, creditors, and others are usually settled with cash. Illiquid companies (those lacking cash) are at risk of failure. Given the importance of cash management, companies must report a statement of cash flows in addition to the balance sheet, income statement, and statement of equity.

The income statement provides information about the economic viability of the company's products and services. It tells us whether the company can sell its products and services at prices that cover its costs and provide a reasonable return to lenders and stockholders. On the other hand, the statement of cash flows provides information about the company's ability to generate cash from those same transactions. It tells us from what sources the company has generated its cash (so we can evaluate whether those sources are persistent or transitory) and what it has done with the cash it generated.

Statement Format and Data Sources

The statement of cash flows is formatted to report cash inflows and cash outflows by the three primary business activities:

- *Cash flows from operating activities* Cash flows from the company's transactions and events that relate to its operations.
- *Cash flows from investing activities* Cash flows from acquisitions and divestitures of investments and long-term assets.
- *Cash flows from financing activities* Cash flows from issuances of and payments toward borrowings and equity.

The combined cash flows from these three sections yield the net change in cash for the period. The three sections of the statement of cash flows relate to the income statement and to different parts of the balance sheet. These relations are highlighted in the following table:

Cash flow section	Information from income statement	Information from balance sheet	
Net cash flows from operating activities. . . .	**Revenues** **− Expenses** **= Net income**	**Current operating assets** Long-term operating and all nonoperating assets	**Current operating liabilities** Long-term operating and all nonoperating liabilities Equity
Net cash flows from investing activities	Revenues − Expenses = Net income	Current operating assets **Long-term operating and all nonoperating assets**	Current operating liabilities Long-term operating and all nonoperating liabilities Equity
Net cash flows from financing activities	Revenues − Expenses = Net income	Current operating assets Long-term operating and all nonoperating assets	Current operating liabilities **Long-term operating and all nonoperating liabilities** **Equity**

Specifically, the three sections draw generally on the following information:

- **Net cash flows from operating activities** relate to the income statement and to the current asset and current liabilities sections of the balance sheet.
- **Net cash flows from investing activities** relate to the long-term assets section of the balance sheet.
- **Net cash flows from financing activities** relate to the long-term liabilities and stockholders' equity sections of the balance sheet.

These relations do not hold exactly, but they provide us a useful way to visualize the construction of the statement of cash flows.

In analyzing the statement of cash flows, we should not necessarily conclude that the company is better off if cash increases and worse off if cash decreases. It is not the change in cash as reported on the year-end balance sheet that is most important, but the reasons behind the change. For example, what are the sources of cash inflows? Are these sources transitory? Are these sources mainly from operating activities? To what uses have cash inflows been put? Such questions and answers are key to properly using the statement of cash flows.

Exhibit 2.8 shows **Apple**'s statement of cash flows. Apple reported $50,856 million in net cash inflows from operating activities in 2012. This is substantially greater than its net income of $41,733 million. The operating activities section of the statement of cash flows reconciles the difference between net income and operating cash flow. The difference is due to the add-back of depreciation, a noncash expense in the income statement, and other noncash expenses, together with year-over-year changes in operating assets and liabilities.

Apple reports a net cash outflow of $48,227 million for investing activities, mainly for investments in marketable securities. Apple also used $1,698 million for financing activities, mainly for the payment of dividends.

Overall, Apple's cash flow picture is strong. It is generating cash from operating activities and the sale of stock to employees, and is investing excess cash in marketable securities to ensure future liquidity.

Cash Flow Computations

It is sometimes difficult to understand why certain accounts are added to and subtracted from net income to yield net cash flows from operating activities. It often takes more than one pass through this section to grasp how this part of the cash flow statement is constructed.

A key to understanding these computations is to remember that under accrual accounting, revenues are recognized when earned and expenses when incurred. This recognition policy does not necessarily coincide with the receipt or payment of cash. The top line (net income) of the operating section of the statement of cash flows represents net (accrual) income under GAAP. The bottom line (net cash flows from operating activities) is the *cash profit* the company would have reported had it constructed its income

EXHIBIT 2.8 Apple's Statement of Cash Flows ($ millions)

APPLE INC. Statement of Cash Flows For Year Ended September 29, 2012	
Operating activities	
Net income	$ 41,733
Adjustments to reconcile net income to cash generated by operating activities:	
Depreciation and amortization	3,277
Share-based compensation expense	1,740
Deferred income tax expense	4,405
Changes in operating assets and liabilities:	
Accounts receivable, net	(5,551)
Inventories	(15)
Vendor non-trade receivables	(1,414)
Other current assets and noncurrent assets	(3,162)
Accounts payable	4,467
Deferred revenue	2,824
Other liabilities and noncurrent liabilities	2,552
Cash generated by operating activities	50,856
Investing activities	
Purchases of marketable securities	(151,232)
Proceeds from maturities of marketable securities	13,035
Proceeds from sales of marketable securities	99,770
Payments made in connection with business acquisitions, net of cash acquired	(350)
Payments for acquisition of property, plant and equipment	(8,295)
Payments for acquisition of intangible assets	(1,107)
Other	(48)
Cash used in investing activities	(48,227)
Financing activities	
Proceeds from issuance of common stock	665
Excess tax benefits from equity awards	1,351
Dividends and dividend equivalent rights paid	(2,488)
Taxes paid related to net share settlement of equity awards	(1,226)
Cash used in financing activities	(1,698)
Increase in cash and cash equivalents	931
Cash and cash equivalents, beginning of year	9,815
Cash and cash equivalents, end of the year	$ 10,746

statement on a cash basis rather than an accrual basis. Computing net cash flows from operating activities begins with GAAP profit and adjusts it to compute cash profit using the following general approach:

	Add (+) or Subtract (−) from Net Income
Net income	$ #
Add: depreciation expense	+
Adjust for changes in current assets	
Subtract increases in current assets	−
Add decreases in current assets	+
Adjust for changes in current liabilities	
Add increases in current liabilities	+
Subtract decreases in current liabilities	−
Cash from operating activities	$ #

Typically, net income is first adjusted for noncash expenses such as depreciation, and is then adjusted for changes during the year in current assets and current liabilities to yield cash flow from operating activities, or *cash profit*. The depreciation adjustment merely zeros out (undoes the effect of) depreciation expense, a noncash expense, which is deducted in computing net income. The following table provides brief explanations of adjustments for receivables, inventories, and payables and accruals, which are frequent sources of adjustments in this section:

	Change in account balance...	Means that...	Which requires this adjustment to net income to yield cash profit...
Receivables	Increase	Sales and net income increase, but cash is not yet received	Deduct increase in receivables from net income
	Decrease	More cash is received than is reported in sales and net income	Add decrease in receivables to net income
Inventories	Increase	Cash is paid for inventories that are not yet reflected in cost of goods sold	Deduct increase in inventories from net income
	Decrease	Cost of goods sold includes inventory costs that were paid for in a prior period	Add decrease in inventories to net income
Payables and accruals	Increase	More goods and services are acquired on credit, delaying cash payment	Add increase in payables and accruals to net income
	Decrease	More cash is paid than is reflected in cost of goods sold or operating expenses	Deduct decrease in payables and accruals from net income

BUSINESS INSIGHT **Insights into Apple's Statement of Cash Flows**

The following provides insights into the computation of some amounts in the operating section of Apple's statement of cash flows in Exhibit 2.8 ($ millions).

Statement amount	Explanation of computation
Depreciation and amortization $3,277	When buildings and equipment are acquired, their cost is recorded on the balance sheet as assets. Subsequently, as the assets are used up to generate revenues, a portion of their cost is transferred from the balance sheet to the income statement as an expense, called *depreciation*. Depreciation expense does not involve the payment of cash (that occurs when the asset is purchased). If we want to compute *cash profit*, we must add back depreciation expense to zero it out from income. The $3,277 in the second line of the statement of cash flows merely zeros out (undoes) the depreciation expense that was subtracted when Apple computed GAAP net income. Likewise, the next line (Stock-based compensation expense of $1,740) uses the same concept.
Increase in accounts receivable, $(5,551)	When a company sells goods *on credit*, it records revenue because it is earned, even though cash is not yet received. When Apple sold $(5,551) of goods on credit, its revenues and net income increased by that amount, but no cash was received. Apple's cash profit is, thus, $(5,551) less than net income. The $(5,551) is subtracted from net income in computing net cash inflows from operations.
Increase in inventories, $(15)	When Apple purchases inventories, the purchase cost is reported on its balance sheet as a current asset. When inventories are sold, their cost is removed from the balance sheet and transferred to the income statement as an expense called cost of goods sold. If some inventories acquired are not yet sold, their cost is not yet reported in cost of goods sold and net income. The subtraction of $15 relates to the increase in inventories; it reflects the fact that cost of goods sold does not include all of the cash that was spent on inventories. That is, $15 cash was spent that is not yet reflected in cost of goods sold. Thus, the $15 is deducted from net income to compute *cash profit* for the period.
Increase in accounts payable, $4,497	Apple purchases much of its inventories on credit. The $4,497 increase in accounts payable reflects inventories that have been purchased, but have not yet been paid for in cash. The add-back of this $4,497 to net income reflects the fact that *cash profit* is $4,497 higher because $4,497 of accounts payable are not yet paid.

It is also helpful to use the following decision guide, involving changes in assets, liabilities, and equity, to understand increases and decreases in cash flows.

	Cash flow increases from	Cash flow decreases from
Assets.	Account decreases	Account increases
Liabilities and equity.	Account increases	Account decreases

The preceding table applies to all sections of the statement of cash flows. To determine if a change in each asset and liability account creates a cash inflow or outflow, examine the change and apply the decision rules from the table. For example, in the investing section, cash decreases when PPE assets increase. In the financing section, borrowing from a bank increases cash. Module 3 and Appendix B near the end of the book describe the preparation of the statement of cash flows in detail.

Sometimes the cash flow effect of an item reported in the statement of cash flows does not agree with the difference in the balance sheet accounts that we observe. This can be due to several factors. One common factor is when a company uses its own stock to acquire another entity. There is no cash effect from a stock acquisition and, hence, it is not reported in the statement of cash flows. Yet, the company does increase its assets and liabilities when it adds the acquired company's assets and liabilities to its balance sheet.

Knowledge of how companies record cash inflows and outflows helps us better understand the statement of cash flows. Determining how changes in asset and liability accounts affect cash provides an analytic tool *and* offers greater insight into managing a business. For instance, reducing the levels of receivables and inventories increases cash. Similarly, increasing the levels of accounts payable and accrued liabilities increases cash. Managing cash balances by managing other accounts is called *working capital management*, which is important for all companies.

MID-MODULE REVIEW 1

Following are account balances ($ millions equivalent of Korean Won) for **Samsung Electronics Co. Ltd.** Using these data, prepare Samsung's income statement and statement of cash flows for the fiscal year ended December 31, 2012. Prepare its balance sheet dated December 31, 2012.

Income tax expense	$ 5,667	Receivables	$ 24,904
Other stockholders' equity	(3,554)	Short-term borrowings	7,883
Net cash provided by operating activities	35,452	Cash and cash equivalents, beginning year	31,135
Long-term debt	6,179	Total revenue	187,754
Other long-term assets	23,637	Inventory	16,569
Cash and cash equivalents, ending year	34,962	Accrued expenses	8,865
Retained earnings	112,021	Operating expenses	42,388
Net cash used in investing activities	(29,242)	Other current assets	5,041
Cost of goods sold	118,245	Accounts payable	15,768
Paid in capital	4,949	Other current liabilities	11,302
Net cash provided by financing activities	(2,383)	Net property, plant & equipment	63,939
Nonoperating income	808	Other noncurrent liabilities	5,639

The solution is on page 2-49.

ARTICULATION OF FINANCIAL STATEMENTS

LO2 Explain and illustrate linkages among the four financial statements.

The four financial statements are linked with each other and linked across time. This section demonstrates the linkages (articulation) of financial statements using Apple.

Retained Earnings Reconciliation

The balance sheet and income statement are linked via retained earnings. Recall that retained earnings is updated each period as follows:

	Beginning retained earnings
±	Net income (loss)
−	Dividends
=	Ending retained earnings

Retained earnings reflect cumulative income that has not yet been distributed to shareholders. Exhibit 2.9 shows **Apple**'s retained earnings reconciliation for 2012.

EXHIBIT 2.9 Apple's Retained Earnings Reconciliation

APPLE INC. Retained Earnings Reconciliation ($ millions) For Year Ended September 29, 2012	
Retained earnings, September 24, 2011	$ 62,841
Add: Net income	41,733
Less: Dividends	(2,523)
Other adjustments	(762)
Retained earnings, September 29, 2012	$101,289

This reconciliation of retained earnings links the balance sheet and income statement.

In the absence of transactions with stockholders—such as stock issuances and repurchases, and dividend payments—the change in stockholders' equity equals income or loss for the period. The income statement, thus, measures the change in company value as measured by *GAAP*. This is not necessarily company value as measured by the *market*. Of course, all value-relevant items eventually find their way into the income statement. So, from a long-term perspective, the income statement does measure change in company value. This is why stock prices react to reported income and to analysts' expectations about future income.

Financial Statement Linkages

Linkages of the four financial statements is shown in Exhibit 2.10. Apple begins fiscal 2012 with assets of $116,371 million, consisting of cash of $9,815 million and noncash assets of $106,556 million. These investments are financed with $39,756 million from nonowners and $76,615 million from stockholders. The owner financing consists of contributed capital of $13,331 million, retained earnings of $62,841 million, and other stockholders' equity of $443 million.

Exhibit 2.10 shows balance sheets at the beginning and end of Apple's fiscal year on the left and right columns, respectively. The middle column reflects operating activities for 2012. The statement of cash flows explains how operating, investing, and financing activities increase the cash balance by $931 million from $9,815 million at the beginning of the year to $10,746 million at year-end. The ending balance in cash is reported in the year-end balance sheet on the right.

Apple's $41,733 million net income reported on the income statement is also carried over to the statement of stockholders' equity. Apple's retained earnings increases by the amount of its net income and decreases by dividend payments of $2,523 million (other adjustments reduce retained earnings by $762 million).

MID-MODULE REVIEW 2

Refer to information in Mid-Module Review 1; assume that **Samsung Electronics Co. Ltd.** reports the following balances for the prior year balance sheet and current year income statement ($ in millions). Prepare the articulation of Samsung's financial statements from fiscal years 2011 and 2012 following the format of Exhibit 2.10.

Balance Sheet, December 31, 2011	
Assets	
Cash	$ 31,135
Noncash assets	114,324
Total assets	$145,459
Liabilities and equity	
Total liabilities	$ 50,870
Equity	
Contributed capital	4,949
Retained earnings	91,143
Other stockholders' equity	(1,503)
Liabilities and equity	$145,459

Income Statement, For Year Ended December 31, 2012	
Revenues	$187,754
Expenses	165,492
Net earnings	$ 22,262

The solution is on page 2-50.

EXHIBIT 2.10 Articulation of Apple Financial Statements ($ millions)

Balance Sheet
September 24, 2011

Assets	
Cash	$ 9,815
Noncash assets	106,556
Total assets	$116,371
Liabilities and equity	
Total liabilities	$ 39,756
Equity	
Contributed capital	13,331
Retained earnings	62,841
Other stockholders' equity	443
Liabilities and equity	$116,371

Statement of Cash Flows
For Year Ended September 29, 2012

Operating cash flows	$50,856
Investing cash flows	(48,227)
Financing cash flows	(1,698)
Net change in cash	931
Cash balance, Sept. 24, 2011	9,815
Cash balance, Sept. 29, 2012	$10,746

Income Statement
For Year Ended September 29, 2012

Revenues	$156,508
Expenses	114,775
Net earnings	$ 41,733

Statement of Shareholders' Equity
For Year Ended September 29, 2012

Contributed capital, Sept. 24, 2011	$ 13,331
Stock issuance Sept. 29, 2012	3,091
Contributed capital, Sept. 29, 2012	$ 16,422
Retained earnings, Sept. 24, 2011	$ 62,841
Net income	41,733
Less: dividends	(2,523)
Less: other adjustments	(762)
Retained earnings, Sept. 29, 2012	$101,289
Other stockholders' equity, Sept. 24, 2011	$ 443
Other changes in equity	56
Other stockholders' equity Sept. 29, 2012	$ 499

Balance Sheet
September 29, 2012

Assets	
Cash	$ 10,746
Noncash assets	165,318
Total assets	$176,064
Liabilities and equity	
Total liabilities	$ 57,854
Equity	
Contributed capital	16,422
Retained earnings	101,289
Other stockholders' equity	499
Liabilities and equity	$176,064

Beginning of year — During the year — End of year

TRANSACTION ANALYSIS AND ACCOUNTING

LO3 Illustrate use of the financial statement effects template to summarize accounting transactions.

This section introduces our financial statement effects template, which we use throughout the book to reflect the effects of transactions on financial statements. A more detailed explanation is in Module 3, but that module is not required to understand and apply the template.

Apple reports total assets of $176,064 million, total liabilities of $57,854 million, and equity of $118,210 million. The accounting equation for Apple follows ($ million):

Assets	=	Liabilities	+	Equity
$176,064	=	$57,854	+	$118,210

We often draw on this relation to assess the effects of transactions and events, different accounting methods, and choices that managers make in preparing financial statements. For example, we are interested in knowing the effects of an asset acquisition or sale on the balance sheet, income statement, and cash flow statement. Or, we might want to understand how the failure to recognize a liability would understate liabilities and overstate profits and equity. To perform these sorts of analyses, we employ the following **financial statement effects template**:

Debit #
Credit #

	Balance Sheet									Income Statement				
Transaction	Cash Asset	+	Noncash Assets	=	Liabil-ities	+	Contrib. Capital	+	Earned Capital	Rev-enues	−	Expen-ses	=	Net Income
				=							−		=	

The template captures the transaction and its financial statement effects on the four financial statements: balance sheet, income statement, statement of stockholders' equity, and statement of cash flows. For the balance sheet, we differentiate between cash and noncash assets so as to identify the cash effects of transactions. Likewise, equity is separated into the contributed and earned capital components. Finally, income statement effects are separated into revenues, expenses, and net income (the updating of retained earnings is denoted with an arrow line running from net income to earned capital). This template provides a convenient means to represent relatively complex financial accounting transactions and events in a simple, concise manner for both analysis and interpretation.

In addition to using the template to show the dollar effects of a transaction on the four financial statements, we also include each transaction's *journal entry* and *T-account* representation in the margin. We explain journal entries and T-accounts in Module 3; these are part of the bookkeeping aspects of accounting. The margin entries can be ignored without any loss of insight gained from the template. (Journal entries and T-accounts use acronyms for account titles; a list of acronyms is in Appendix D near the end of the book.)

The process leading up to preparing financial statements involves two steps: (1) recording transactions during the accounting period, and (2) adjusting accounting records to reflect events that have occurred but are not yet evidenced by an external transaction. We provide a brief introduction to these two steps, followed by a comprehensive example that includes preparation of financial statements (a more detailed illustration of this process is in Module 3).

Analyzing and Recording Transactions

All transactions affecting a company are recorded in its accounting records. For example, assume that a company paid $100 cash wages to employees. This is reflected in the following financial statement effects template.

WE 100
Cash 100

WE: 100 (debit)
Cash: 100 (credit)

	Balance Sheet									Income Statement				
Transaction	Cash Asset	+	Noncash Assets	=	Liabil-ities	+	Contrib. Capital	+	Earned Capital	Rev-enues	−	Expen-ses	=	Net Income
Pay $100 cash for wages	−100 Cash			=					−100 Retained Earnings		−	+100 Wages Expense	=	−100

Cash assets are reduced by $100, and wages expense of $100 is reflected in the income statement, which reduces income and retained earnings by that amount. All transactions incurred by the company during the accounting period are recorded similarly. We show several further examples in our comprehensive illustration later in this section.

Adjusting Accounts

We must understand accounting adjustments (commonly called *accruals*) to fully analyze and interpret financial statements. In the transaction above, we record wages expense that has been earned by (and paid to) employees during the period. What if the employees were not paid for wages earned at period-end? Should the expense still be recorded? The answer is yes. All expenses incurred to generate, directly or indirectly, the revenues reported in the period must be recorded. This is the case even if those expenses are still unpaid at period-end. Failure to recognize wages expense would overstate net income for the period because wages have been earned and should be reported as expense in this period. Also, failure to record those wages at period-end would understate liabilities. Thus, neither the income statement nor the balance sheet would be accurate. Adjustments are, therefore, necessary to accurately portray financial condition and performance of a company.

There are four types of adjustments, which are illustrated in the following graphic. The two adjustments on the left relate to the receipt or payment of cash before revenue or expense is recognized. The two on the right relate to the receipt or payment of cash after revenue or expense is recognized.

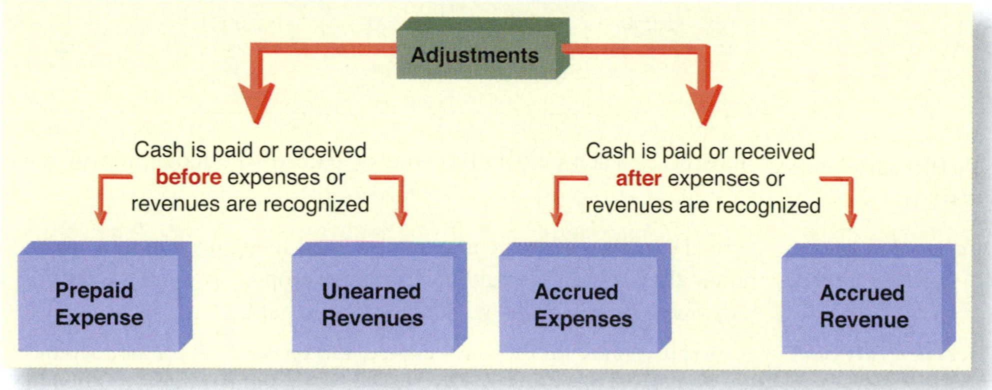

One of two types of accounts arise when cash is received or paid *before* recognition of revenue or expense.

Prepaid expenses Prepaid expenses reflect advance cash payments that will ultimately become expenses; an example is the payment of radio advertising that will not be aired until sometime in the future.

Unearned revenues Unearned revenues reflect cash received from customers before any services or goods are provided; an example is cash received from patrons for tickets to an upcoming concert.

To illustrate the adjustment required with prepaid expenses, assume that Apple pays $3,000 cash at the beginning of this year to rent office space, and that this allows Apple to use the space for the current year and two additional years. When paid, the prepaid rent is an asset for Apple (it now controls the space, which is expected to provide future benefits for its business). At the end of the first year, one-third of the Prepaid Rent asset is used up. Apple, therefore, removes that portion from its balance sheet and recognizes it as an expense in the income statement. The beginning-year payment and year-end expensing of the rental asset are recorded as follows:

	Balance Sheet									Income Statement				
Transaction	Cash Asset	+	Noncash Assets	=	Liabil-ities	+	Contrib. Capital	+	Earned Capital	Rev-enues	−	Expen-ses	=	Net Income
a. Beginning-year $3,000 cash payment in advance for 3-year rent	−3,000 Cash		+3,000 Prepaid Rent	=							−		=	
b. Recognition of 1-year rent expense of $1,000			−1,000 Prepaid Rent	=					−1,000 Retained Earnings		−	+1,000 Rent Expense	=	−1,000

PPRNT 3,000
Cash 3,000

PPRNT: 3,000 (debit)
Cash: 3,000 (credit)

RNTE 1,000
PPRNT 1,000

RNTE: 1,000 (debit)
PPRNT: 1,000 (credit)

To illustrate unearned revenues, assume that Apple receives $5,000 cash in advance of providing services to a client. That amount is initially recorded as a liability for services owed the client. Later, when

Apple provides the services, it can recognize that revenue since it is now earned. The receipt of cash and subsequent recognition of revenue are recorded as follows:

Cash 5,000
UR 5,000

Cash
5,000 |
UR
| 5,000

UR 5,000
REV 5,000

UR
5,000 |
REV
| 5,000

	Balance Sheet									Income Statement				
Transaction	**Cash Asset**	+	**Noncash Assets**	=	**Liabilities**	+	**Contrib. Capital**	+	**Earned Capital**	**Revenues**	−	**Expenses**	=	**Net Income**
a. Receive $5,000 cash in advance for future services	+5,000 Cash			=	+5,000 Unearned Revenue						−		=	
b. Recognition of $5,000 services revenue earned				=	−5,000 Unearned Revenue				+5,000 Retained Earnings	+5,000 Revenue	−		=	+5,000

One of two types of accounts arise when cash is received or paid *after* recognition of revenue or expense.

Accrued expenses Accrued expenses are expenses incurred and recognized on the income statement, even though they are not yet paid in cash; an example is wages owed to employees who performed work but who have not yet been paid.

Accrued revenues Accrued revenues are revenues earned and recognized on the income statement, even though cash is not yet received; examples include accounts receivable and revenue earned under a long-term contract.

To illustrate accrued expenses, assume that $100 of wages earned by Apple employees this period is paid the following period. The period-end adjustment, and subsequent payment the following period, are both reflected in the following template.

WE 100
WP 100

WE
100 |
WP
| 100

WP 100
Cash 100

WP
100 |
Cash
| 100

	Balance Sheet									Income Statement				
Transaction	**Cash Asset**	+	**Noncash Assets**	=	**Liabilities**	+	**Contrib. Capital**	+	**Earned Capital**	**Revenues**	−	**Expenses**	=	**Net Income**
Period 1: Accrue $100 wages expense and liability				=	+100 Wages Payable				−100 Retained Earnings		−	+100 Wages Expense	=	−100
Period 2: Pay $100 cash for wages	−100 Cash			=	−100 Wages Payable						−		=	

Wages expense is recorded in period 1's income statement because it is incurred by the company and earned by employees in that period. Also, a liability is recorded in period 1 reflecting the company's obligation to make payment to employees. In period 2, the wages are paid, which means that both cash and the liability are reduced.

To illustrate the accrual of revenues, assume that Apple is performing work under a long-term contract that allows it to bill the customer periodically as work is performed. At the end of the current period, it determines that it has earned $100,000 per contract. The accrual of this revenue and its subsequent collection are recorded as follows ($ 000s):

Transaction	Balance Sheet: Cash Asset	+ Noncash Assets	= Liabilities	+ Contrib. Capital	+ Earned Capital	Income Statement: Revenues	− Expenses	= Net Income
a. Accrual of $100 of earned revenue		+100 Accounts Receivable			+100 Retained Earnings	+100 Revenue	−	= +100
b. Collection of account receivable	+100 Cash	−100 Accounts Receivable					−	=

AR 100
  REV 100

AR: 100 (debit) | REV: 100 (credit)

Cash 100
  AR 100

Cash: 100 (debit) | AR: 100 (credit)

Companies make these sort of adjustments to more accurately and completely report their financial performance and condition. Each of these adjustments is made by company managers and accountants based on the review of financial statements and information suggesting that adjustments are necessary to properly reflect financial condition and performance.

Constructing Financial Statements

We can prepare each of the four financial statements directly from our financial statement effects template. The balance sheet and income statement accounts, and their respective balances, can be read off the bottom row that totals the transactions and adjustments recorded during the period. The statement of cash flows and statement of stockholders' equity are represented by the cash column and the contributed and earned capital columns, respectively.

Illustration: Recording Transactions, Adjusting Accounts, and Preparing Statements

This section provides a comprehensive illustration that uses the financial statement effects template with a number of transactions related to Apple's 2012 financial statements shown earlier. These summary transactions are described in the far left column of the following template. Each column is summed to arrive at the balance sheet and income statement totals that tie to Apple's statements. Detailed explanations for each transaction are provided after the template. Then, we use the information in the template to construct Apple's financial statements ($ in millions).

Transaction	Balance Sheet: Cash Asset	+ Noncash Assets	= Liabilities	+ Contrib. Capital	+ Earned Capital	Income Statement: Revenues	− Expenses	= Net Income
Bal., Sept. 24, 2011	9,815	106,556	= 39,756	13,331	63,284		−	=
1. Sell common stock for $200	+200 Cash		=	+200 Common Stock			−	=
2. Purchase $8,295 of PPE for cash	−8,295 Cash	+8,295 PPE, net	=				−	=
3. Purchase $87,861 of inventory on credit		+87,861 Inventories	= +87,861 Accounts Payable				−	=

continued

Cash 200
  CS 200

Cash: 200 (debit) | CS: 200 (credit)

PPE 10,952
  Cash 10,952

PPE: 8,295 (debit) | Cash: 8,295 (credit)

INV 87,861
  AP 87,861

INV: 87,861 (debit) | AP: 87,861 (credit)

Journal entry / T-accounts	Transaction	Cash Asset	+ Noncash Assets	= Liabilities	+ Contrib. Capital	+ Earned Capital	Revenues	− Expenses	= Net Income
		Balance Sheet					**Income Statement**		
AR 156,508 Sales 156,508 AR: 156,508 (debit) Sales: 156,508 (credit)	4. Sell inventory costing $87,846 for $156,508 on credit		+156,508 Accounts Receivable			+156,508 Retained Earnings	+156,508 Sales		+156,508
COGS 87,846 INV 87,846 COGS: 87,846 (debit) INV: 87,846 (credit)			−87,846 Inventory			−87,846 Retained Earnings		+87,846 Cost of Goods Sold	−87,846
Cash 69,639 AP 81,318 AR 150,957 Cash: 69,639 (debit) AP: 81,318 (debit) AR: 150,957 (credit)	5. Collect $150,957 of receivables and pay $81,318 of accounts payable and other liabilities	+69,639 Cash	−150,957 Accounts Receivable	−81,318 Accounts Payable					
OE 15,443 Cash 15,443 OE: 15,443 (debit) Cash: 15,443 (credit)	6. Pay operating expenses and taxes (excluding depreciation) of $15,443	−15,443 Cash				−15,443 Retained Earnings		+15,443 Operating Expenses	−15,443
OE 2,167 ACC 2,167 OE: 2,167 (debit) ACC: 2,167 (credit)	7. Accrue expenses of $2,167			+2,167 Accrued Expenses		−2,167 Retained Earnings		+2,167 Operating Expenses	−2,167
Cash 2,824 UR 2,824 Cash: 2,824 (debit) UR: 2,824 (credit)	8. Increase unearned revenue	+2,824 Cash		+2,824 Deferred Revenue					
TE 6,564 DTL 6,564 TE: 6,564 (debit) DTL: 6,564 (credit)	9. Increase other deferred tax liabilities of $6,564			+6,564 Deferred Income Tax Liability		−6,564 Retained Earnings		+6,564 Income Tax Expense	−6,564
MS 43,336 Cash 43,336 MS: 45,993 (debit) Cash: 45,993 (credit)	10. Purchase marketable securities and other assets for $45,993	−45,993 Cash	+45,993 Marketable Securities and other assets						
DE 3,277 PPE, net 3,277 DE: 3,277 (debit) PPE, net: 3,277 (credit)	11. Record depreciation of $3,277		−3,277 PPE, net			−3,277 Retained Earnings		+3,277 Depreciation Expense	−3,277
Cash 522 EI 522 Cash: 522 (debit) EI: 522 (credit)	12. Record net investment income of $522	+522 Cash				+522 Retained Earnings		−522* Investment Income	+522
Noncash asset 2,185 APIC 2,891 AOCI 706 Noncash asset: 2,185 (debit) APIC: 2,891 (credit) AOCI: 706 (debit)	13. Record miscellaneous transactions that affect AOCI		+2,185 Miscel.		+2,891 Miscel.	−706 AOCI			
RE 2,523 Cash 2,523 RE: 2,523 (debit) Cash: 2,523 (credit)	14. Pay dividends of $2,523	−2,523 Cash				−2,523 Retained Earnings			
	Bal., Sept. 29, 2012	10,746	165,318	57,854	16,422	101,788	156,508	114,775	41,733
		176,064		176,064					

* Apple reports investment income as an "addback" to other expenses.

Transaction Explanation Apple begins fiscal year 2012 with $116,371 million in total assets, consisting of $9,815 million of cash and $106,556 million of noncash assets. It also reports $39,756 million of liabilities and $76,615 million of stockholders' equity ($13,331 million of contributed capital and $63,284 million of earned capital, which includes other equity for this exhibit). During the year, fourteen summary transactions occur that are described below.

1. **Owner Financing.** Companies raise funds from two sources: investing from stockholders and borrowing from creditors. Transaction 1 reflects issuance of common stock for $200 million in connection with employee stock options and other incentive compensation plans. Cash is increased by that amount, as is contributed capital. Stock issuance (as well as its repurchase and any dividends paid to stockholders) does not impact income. Companies cannot record profit by trading in their own stock.
2. **Purchase PPE.** Apple acquires $8,295 million of property, plant and equipment (PPE) for cash. Noncash assets increase by the $8,295 million (PPE), and cash decreases by the same amount. PPE is initially reported on the balance sheet at the cost Apple paid to acquire it. When plant and equipment are used, a portion of the purchase cost is transferred from the balance sheet to the income statement as an expense called depreciation. Accounting for depreciation of Apple's PPE is shown in Transaction 11. The purchase of PPE is not an expense. The expense arises as the PPE assets are used.
3. **Purchase inventories on credit.** Companies commonly acquire inventories from suppliers *on credit* (also called *on account*). The phrase "on credit" means that the purchase has not yet been paid for. A purchaser is typically allowed 30 days or more during which to make payment. When acquired in this manner, noncash assets (inventories) increase by the $87,861 million cost of the acquired inventory, and a liability (accounts payable) increases to reflect the amount owed to the supplier.[2] Although inventories (iPods, iPhones, and iPads, for example) normally carry a retail selling price that is higher than cost, this eventual profit is not recognized until inventories are sold.
4. **Sell inventories on credit.** Apple subsequently sells inventories that cost $87,846 million for a retail selling price of $156,508 million *on credit*. The phrase "on credit" means that Apple has not yet received cash for the selling price; cash receipt is expected in the future. (We assume all sales are on credit for simplification; in reality, a portion of sales is for cash.) The sale of inventories is recorded in two parts: the revenue part and the expense part. First, the sale is recorded by an increase in both revenues and noncash assets (accounts receivable). Revenues increase net income which, in turn, increases earned capital (via retained earnings). Second, the cost of inventories sold is removed from the balance sheet (Apple no longer owns those assets), and is transferred to the income statement as an expense, called *cost of goods sold*, which decreases both net income and earned capital by $87,846 (again, via retained earnings).
5. **Collect receivables and settle payables.** Apple receives $150,957 million cash from the collection of its accounts receivable, thus reducing noncash assets (accounts receivable) by that amount. Apple uses these proceeds to pay off $81,318 of its liabilities accounts payable. Collecting accounts receivable does not yield revenue; instead, revenue is recognized when *earned* (see Transaction 4). Thus, recognizing revenue when earned does not necessarily yield immediate cash increase.
6. **Pay cash for operating expenses, including taxes.** Apple pays $15,443 million cash for operating expenses, including taxes. This payment increases expenses, and reduces net income (and earned capital). Expenses are recognized when incurred, regardless of when they are paid. Expenses are paid in this transaction. Transaction 7 is a case where expenses are recognized before being paid.
7. **Accrue expenses.** Accrued expenses, also called *accrued liabilities*, relate to expenses that are incurred but not yet paid. For example, employees often work near the end of a period but are not paid until the next period. The company must record wages expense even though employees have not yet been paid in cash. The rationale is that expenses must be recorded in the period in-

[2] Companies do not report the purchase cost of inventories. We infer the purchases from balance sheet and income statement information using the following formula: Beginning inventory (prior year ending balance sheet amount) + Purchases − Ending inventory (from the current balance sheet) = Cost of goods sold (from the income statement). Using the amounts from Exhibits 2.2 and 2.5, we solve for Purchases (in $ millions): $776 + Purchases − $791 = $87,846, yielding Purchases of $87,861. We discuss this formula and other matters relating to inventories in Module 6.

curred to report the correct income for the period. In this transaction, Apple accrues $2,167 million of expenses, which reduces net income (and earned capital). Apple simultaneously records a $2,167 million increase in liabilities for its obligation to make future payment. This transaction is an accounting adjustment, or accrual.

8. **Increase in unearned revenue.** Revenues are recognized when they are earned, regardless of when cash is received. Apple sometimes receives cash in advance of delivering the product or performing the service. In this example, Apple has received $2,824 million of cash and has not yet provided the product or service. We, therefore, record the increase in cash and also record an increase in a liability called unearned (or deferred) revenue, which represents Apple's obligation to deliver the product or service. When the product or service is ultimately delivered, Apple will reduce the liability and recognize an increase in revenue and income.
9. **Increase in deferred tax liabilities.** Apple accrues another expense in this example. Similar to Transaction 7, Apple calculates that it will incur a future tax liability in the amount of $6,564 million. It increases liabilities by that amount and recognizes a corresponding expense (tax expense in this case), thus reducing net income by that amount.
10. **Purchase noncash assets.** Apple uses $45,993 million of its excess cash to purchase marketable securities and other assets as an investment. Thus, noncash assets increase. This is a common use of excess cash, especially for high-tech companies that desire added liquidity to take advantage of opportunities in a rapidly changing industry.
11. **Record depreciation.** Transaction 11 is another accounting adjustment. In this case, Apple recognizes that a portion of its plant and equipment is "used up" while generating revenues. Thus, it records a portion of the PPE cost as an expense during the period. In this case, $3,277 million of PPE cost is removed from the balance sheet and transferred to the income statement as depreciation expense. Net income (and earned capital) are reduced by $3,277 million.
12. **Record investment income.** Apple recognizes $522 of investment income in Transaction 12. Profit increases by this same amount, resulting in an increase in retained earnings.
13. **Accumulated Other Comprehensive Income (AOCI).** Transaction 13 is a miscellaneous adjustment to noncash assets and an earned capital account called accumulated other comprehensive income (AOCI), which is distinct from retained earnings. We discuss this account in Module 9.
14. **Record payment of dividends.** Apple declared and paid $2,523 million of dividends during the year. This is recognized as a decrease in cash and a decrease in retained earnings. The payment of dividends is not an expense, but rather a distribution of assets to stockholders. It is recognized as a direct reduction of retained earnings and is not reflected in Apple's income statement.

We can use the column totals from the financial statement effects template to prepare Apple's financial statements (in condensed form). We derive Apple's 2012 balance sheet and income statement from the template as follows ($ millions).

APPLE INC. **Condensed Balance Sheet** **September 29, 2012**	
Cash asset	$ 10,746
Noncash assets	165,318
Total assets	$176,064
Liabilities	$ 57,854
Contributed capital	16,422
Earned capital	101,788
Total liabilities and equity	$176,064

APPLE INC. **Condensed Income Statement** **For Year Ended September 29, 2012**	
Revenues	$156,508
Expenses	114,775
Net income	$ 41,733

We can summarize Apple's cash transactions from the cash column of the template. The cash column of the financial effects template reveals that cash increases by $931 million during the year from $9,815 million to $10,746 million; see the following statement. Items that contribute to this net increase are identified by the cash entries in that column (the subtotals for operating, investing, and financing sections are slightly different from actual results because of simplifying assumptions we make for our transactions example).

APPLE INC. Statement of Cash Flows ($ millions) For Year Ended September 29, 2012	
Operating cash flows (+ $69,639 − $15,443 + $2,824 + $522)	$57,542
Investing cash flows (− $10,952 − $43,336)	(54,288)
Financing cash flows (+ $200 − $2,523)	(2,323)
Net change in cash	931
Cash balance, Sept. 24, 2011	9,815
Cash balance, Sept. 29, 2012	$10,746

Apple's statement of stockholders' equity summarizes the transactions relating to its equity accounts. This statement follows and is organized into its contributed capital and earned capital categories of equity.

APPLE INC.
Condensed Statement of Stockholders' Equity
For Year Ended September 29, 2012

($ millions)	Contributed Capital	Earned Capital	Total
Balance, September 24, 2011	$13,331	$ 63,284	$ 76,615
Stock issuance (repurchase)	200		200
Net income (loss)		41,733	41,733
Dividends		(2,523)	(2,523)
Other	2,891	(706)	2,185
Balance, September 29, 2012	$16,422	$101,788	$118,210

Apple's financial statements are abbreviated versions of those reproduced earlier in the module. We describe the preparation of financial statements and other accounting details at greater length in Module 3.

BUSINESS INSIGHT **Controlling vs Noncontrolling Interest**

Financial statements are prepared on a *consolidated* basis. To consolidate a balance sheet, a company includes all assets and liabilities of subsidiaries under its control. When a company controls a subsidiary, it directs all of the subsidiary's operations. However, control does not imply 100% ownership; control can occur when a company owns the majority of a subsidiary's voting stock. For example, **Disney** does not own 100% of the voting stock of **Euro Disney**, a separate legal entity. It does, however, have voting control of Euro Disney, and so, Disney is said to have a **controlling interest**. The ownership interest of the other stockholders of Euro Disney is titled **noncontrolling interest**. To better understand, assume Disney constructs a new attraction at Euro Disney. Disney does not construct only the portion of the attraction that it *controls*. Instead, it constructs the *entire* attraction. Consolidated financial statements reflect this notion of control. Disney's balance sheet includes 100% of Euro Disney's assets and liabilities. Yet, because it owns only a controlling percentage in Euro Disney, Disney reports the interests of the noncontrolling stockholders as "Noncontrolling interest" in the equity section of its balance sheet. The same logic applies to the income statement; that is, 100% of Euro Disney's revenues and expenses are included in the income statement, and then the noncontrolling interest in net income is separated from the net income of the entire company. That is why we see net income apportioned at the bottom of the income statement into that attributable to the parent company (Disney) stockholders and that attributable to the noncontrolling stockholders of the subsidiary companies.

IFRS

GLOBAL ACCOUNTING

Both GAAP and IFRS use accrual accounting to prepare financial statements. Although there are vastly more similarities than differences, we highlight below a few of the more notable differences for financial statements.

Balance Sheet The most visible difference is that many IFRS-based balance sheets are presented in reverse order of liquidity. The least liquid asset, usually goodwill, is listed first and the most liquid asset, cash, is last. The same inverse liquidity order applies to liabilities. There are also several detailed presentation and measurement differences that we explain in other modules. As one example, for GAAP-based balance sheets, bank overdrafts are often netted against cash balances. IFRS does not permit this netting on the balance sheet. However, the IFRS statement of cash flows *does* net the cash balance with any bank overdrafts and, thus, the cash balance on the statement of cash flows might not match the cash amount on the balance sheet.

Income Statement The most visible difference is that GAAP requires three years' data on the income statement whereas IFRS requires only two. Another difference is that GAAP income statements classify expenses by *function* and must separately report cost of goods sold, whereas IFRS permits expense classification by *function* (cost of sales, selling and administrative, etc.) or by *type* (raw materials, labor, depreciation, etc.). This means, for example, that under IFRS, there is no requirement to report a cost of sales figure. Another difference is that no item can be classified as extraordinary under IFRS. Still another is that for items either unusual or infrequent, but not both, GAAP requires separate presentation in the income statement as a component of earnings from continuing operations. IFRS also requires disclosure of these items, but permits disclosure in notes to financial statements.

Statement of Cash Flows One of the more apparent differences between GAAP and IFRS is that a GAAP-based statement of cash flows classifies interest expense, interest revenue, and dividend revenue as operating cash flows, and dividends paid as financing cash flows. IFRS allows firms to choose from between the following two options:

1. Classify interest expense, dividends paid, interest revenue, and dividend revenue as operating cash flows, or
2. Classify interest expense and dividends paid as financing cash flows, and interest revenue and dividend revenue as investing cash flows.

MODULE-END REVIEW

At December 31, 2012, assume that the condensed balance sheet of **LG Display Co., Ltd. (LPL)**, one of Apple's suppliers, shows the following.

Cash	$ 80,000	Liabilities	$200,000
Noncash assets	270,000	Contributed capital	50,000
		Earned capital	100,000
Total assets	$350,000	Total liabilities and equity	$350,000

Assume the following summary transactions occur during 2013.

1. Purchase inventory of $80,000 on credit.
2. Pay employees $10,000 cash for wages earned this year.
3. Sell inventory costing $40,000 for $70,000 on credit.
4. Collect $15,000 cash from the accounts receivable in transaction 3.
5. Pay $35,000 cash toward the accounts payable in transaction 1.
6. Purchase advertising for $25,000 cash that will air next year.
7. Employees earn $5,000 in wages that will not be paid until next year.
8. Record $3,000 depreciation on equipment.

Required

a. Record transactions 1 through 8 using the financial statement effects template.
b. Prepare the income statement and balance sheet for 2013.
c. Show linkage(s) between the income statement and the balance sheet.

The solution is on page 2-50.

APPENDIX 2A: Additional Information Sources

The four financial statements are only a part of the information available to financial statement users. Additional information, from a variety of sources, provides useful insight into company operating activities and future prospects. This section highlights additional information sources.

Form 10-K

Companies with publicly traded securities must file a detailed annual report and discussion of their business activities in their Form 10-K with the SEC (quarterly reports are filed on Form 10-Q). Many of the disclosures in the 10-K are mandated by law and include the following general categories: Item 1, *Business;* Item 1A, *Risk Factors*; Item 2, *Properties*; Item 3, *Legal Proceedings*; Item 4, *Submission of Matters to a Vote of Security Holders*; Item 5, *Market for Registrant's Common Equity and Related Stockholder Matters*; Item 6, *Selected Financial Data*; Item 7, *Management's Discussion and Analysis of Financial Condition and Results of Operations*; Item 7A, *Quantitative and Qualitative Disclosures About Market Risk*; Item 8, *Financial Statements and Supplementary Data;* Item 9, *Changes in and Disagreements With Accountants on Accounting and Financial Disclosure*; Item 9A, *Controls and Procedures*; Item 10, *Directors, Executive Officers and Corporate Governance*; Item 11, *Executive Compensation*; Item 12, *Security Ownership of Certain Beneficial Owners and Management and Related Stockholder Matters*; Item 13, *Certain Relationships and Related Transactions, and Director Independence*; Item 14, *Principal Accountant Fees and Services*.

Description of the Business (Item 1)

Companies must provide a general description of their business, including their principal products and services, the source and availability of required raw materials, all patents, trademarks, licenses, and important related agreements, seasonality of the business, any dependence upon a single customer, competitive conditions, including particular markets in which the company competes, the product offerings in those markets, and the status of its competitive environment. Companies must also provide a description of their overall strategy. **Apple**'s partial disclosure follows:

> The Company is committed to bringing the best user experience to its customers through its innovative hardware, software, peripherals, and services. The Company's business strategy leverages its unique ability to design and develop its own operating systems, hardware, application software, and services to provide its customers new products and solutions with superior ease-of-use, seamless integration, and innovative design. The Company believes continual investment in research and development, marketing and advertising is critical to the development and sale of innovative products and technologies. As part of its strategy, the Company continues to expand its platform for the discovery and delivery of third-party digital content and applications through the iTunes Store . . . The Company's strategy also includes expanding its distribution network to effectively reach more customers and provide them with a high-quality sales and post-sales support experience.

Management's Discussion and Analysis of Financial Condition and Results of Operations (Item 7)

The management discussion and analysis (MD&A) section of the 10-K contains valuable insight into the company's results of operations. In addition to an executive overview of company status and its recent operating results, the MD&A section includes information relating to its critical accounting policies and estimates used in preparing its financial statements, a detailed discussion of its sales activity, year-over-year comparisons of operating activities, analysis of gross margin, operating expenses, taxes, and off-balance-sheet and contractual obligations, assessment of factors that affect future results and financial condition. Item 7A reports quantitative and qualitative disclosures about market risk. For example, Apple makes the following disclosure relating to its Mac operating system and its iPods, iPhones, iPads and other products.

> The markets for the Company's products and services are highly competitive and the Company is confronted by aggressive competition in all areas of its business. These markets are characterized by frequent product introductions and rapid technological advances that have substantially increased the capabilities and use of mobile communication and media devices, personal computers, and other digital electronic devices. The Company's competitors who sell mobile devices and personal computers based on other operating systems have aggressively cut prices and lowered their product margins to gain or maintain market share. The Company's financial condition and operating results can be adversely affected by these and other industry-wide downward pressures on gross margins. Principal competitive factors important to the Company include price, product features, relative price/performance, product quality and reliability, design innovation, a strong third-party software and peripherals ecosystem, marketing and distribution capability, service and support, and corporate reputation.

Schedule II — Valuation and Qualifying Accounts

In addition to the 10-K sections described above, Rule 12-09 of Regulation S-X requires companies to report additional information about certain balance sheet accounts. That information explains reserves and allowances that the company establishes to reflect expected losses or uncollectible amounts. (We discuss these accounts in depth in Module 6.) Many companies comply with this requirement by including the required information in notes to financial statements or as additional information at the end of the Form 10-K. Following is a typical disclosure from **Cisco, Inc.**, in its 2012 10-K:

SCHEDULE II
VALUATION AND QUALIFYING ACCOUNTS

	Allowances For		
(in millions)	Lease Receivables	Loan Receivables	Accounts Receivable
Year ended July 28, 2012			
Balance at beginning of fiscal year	$237	$103	$204
Provisions	22	22	19
Write-offs net of recoveries	(2)	—	(16)
Foreign exchange and other	(10)	(3)	—
Balance at end of fiscal year	$247	$122	$207

Cisco provides information relating to its reserves for anticipated losses on its lease, loan, and accounts receivable. Companies often provide similar analysis on estimated sales returns and deferred tax accounts. Our objective in reviewing these accounts is to determine if they are reasonable in amount and, if not, the extent to which our estimate of core operating income differs from that reported in the company's income statement. We discuss this analysis in Module 6.

Form 20-F and Form 40-F

Non-U.S. companies that are publicly traded in the U.S. also file annual reports with the SEC. These foreign companies must furnish, within four months after the fiscal year end, the same audited financial statements required on Form 10-K. The filing, labeled Form 20-F, requires financial statements prepared according to U.S. GAAP or IFRS. If the company uses accounting standards other than GAAP or IFRS, Form 20-F must discuss major differences between the accounting principles used and GAAP. The company must provide a table that reconciles net income as reported to U.S. GAAP net income. In addition, each balance sheet item and cash flow measure that differs from U.S. GAAP, must be reconciled. Canadian companies file their annual reports, prepared under IFRS, using Form 40-F.

Form 8-K

Another useful report that is required by the SEC and is publicly available is the Form 8-K. This form must be filed within four business days of any of the following events:

- Entry into or termination of a material definitive agreement (including petition for bankruptcy)
- Exit from a line of business or impairment of assets
- Change in the company's certified public accounting firm
- Change in control of the company
- Departure of the company's executive officers
- Changes in the company's articles of incorporation or bylaws

Outsiders typically use Form 8-K to monitor for material adverse changes in the company.

Analyst Reports

Sell-side analysts provide their clients with objective analyses of company operating activities. Frequently, these reports include a discussion of the competitive environment for each of the company's principal product lines, strengths and weaknesses of the company, and an investment recommendation, including financial analysis and a stock price target. For example, Credit Suisse provides the following in its March 2013 report to clients on Apple:

CREDIT SUISSE

08 March 2013
Americas/United States
Equity Research
IT Hardware

Apple Inc (AAPL)

COMMENT

Rating	**OUTPERFORM***
Price(07 Mar 13, US$)	430.40
Target price (US$)	600.00[1]
52-week price range	702.10-420.05
Market cap. (US$ m)	404,170.56

**Stock ratings are relative to the coverage universe in each analyst's or each team's respective sector.*
[1]Target price is for 12 months.

Confident Long Term Outlook

- **Growth drivers remain intact.** We hosted a call with Peter Oppenheimer, and found his tone confident, yet realistic. While the company did not disclose anything material on near term fundamentals, there are several longer term growht drivers that exist for Apple. We believe at current levels the stock is discounting an overly pessimistic scenario for the long term. We relterate out OP rating and $600 PT.
- **iPhone may not be as saturated as you think.** Quoting IDC data the company noted that 45% of smartphones are now above the $400 price point; while growth may be stronger at the low end, the company still believes the hight end of the smartphone market will grow. Management noted Apple's ecosystem and lower churn will help drive iPhone platform growth. This fits with our own thesis initially discussed in *Smartphones – High-end going higher* that the high-end of the smartphone market is growing to unprecedented leveles. Manageement confirmed the ability to add carriers over time, and the reasons for the slower pace of carrier additions last year was the ramp up period of the iPhone 5. From our perspective, Apple canadd an additional 65mn units through carrier expansion alone.
- **Three levers for geographic expansion.** 1) China has grown to $23bn in sales and Apple only has 11 stores in China; with an increased presence in major cities going forward, the company admits it is only "scratching the surface" of this opportunity. 2) As Apple opens its first retail store in Turkey, this year taking its retail presence to 15 countries, it is also increasing its focus on Brazil and Russia as well as India later down the line. 3) New financing terms could make Apple's products more afforadable to consumers. Based on our thesis if Apple addresses EMs from a distribution perspective, it could drive an incremental $90bn in sales and $21 of EPS by 2015.

Quarterly EPS	Q1	Q2	Q3	Q4
2011A	6.43	6.40	7.79	7.05
2012A	13.87	12.30	9.32	8.67
2013E	13.81	10.34	9.32	11.46

Financial and valuation metrics

Year	09/11A	09/12A	09/13E	09/14E
EPS - (Excl. ESO US$)	28.62	45.54	46.29	55.40
EPS (cs adj.) (US$)	27.68	44.16	44.92	54.03
Prev.EPS (CS adj.) (US$)	—	—	—	—
P/E (CS adj., x)	15.6	9.7	9.6	8.0
P/E rel. (CS adj., %)	—	66.0	69.8	64.7
Revenue (US$ m)	108,249.0	156,508.0	180,447.5	206,888.9
EBITDA (US$ m)	35,604.0	58,518.0	60,233.8	69,887.6
Net debt (US$ m)	-25,952	-29,129	-54,137	-100,248
OCFPS (US$)	40.07	53.82	58.41	72.53
P/OCF (x)	9.5	12.4	7.4	5.9

Number of shares (m)	939.03	Price/sales(x)	2.26
BV/share (Next Qtr., US$)	144.0	P/Bvps (x)	3.0
Net debt (Next Qtr., US$ m)	-45,482.2	Dividend (current, US$)	—
Dividend yield (%)	—		

Source: Company data, Credit Suisse estimates.

Credit Services

Several firms including Standard & Poor's (**StandardAndPoors.com**), Moody's Investors Service (**Moodys.com**), and Fitch Ratings (**FitchRatings.com**) provide credit analysis that assists potential lenders, investors, employees, and other users in evaluating a company's creditworthiness and future financial viability. Credit analysis is a specialized field of analysis, quite different from the equity analysis illustrated here. These firms issue credit ratings on publicly issued bonds as well as on firms' commercial paper.

Data Services

A number of companies supply financial statement data in easy-to-download spreadsheet formats. **Thomson Reuters Corporation** (**ThomsonReuters.com**) provides a wealth of information to its database subscribers, including the widely quoted *First Call* summary of analysts' earnings forecasts. Standard & Poor's provides financial data for all publicly traded companies in its *Compustat* database. This database reports a plethora of individual data items for all publicly traded companies or for any specified subset of companies. These data are useful for performing statistical analysis and making comparisons across companies or within industries. Finally, **Capital IQ** (**CapitalIQ.com**), a division of Standard & Poor's, provides "as presented" financial data that conform to published financial statements as well as additional statistical data and analysis.

GUIDANCE ANSWERS

MANAGERIAL DECISION **You Are the Securities Analyst**

Of special concern is the possibility that the new CEO is shifting costs to the current period in lieu of recording them in future periods. Evidence suggests that such behavior occurs when a new management team takes control. The reasoning is that the new management can blame poor current period performance on prior management and, at the same time, rid the balance sheet (and the new management team) of costs that would normally be expensed in future periods.

MANAGERIAL DECISION **You Are the Operations Manager**

The CFO desires a warranty cost estimate that corresponds to the sales generated from the new product. To arrive at such an estimate, you must estimate the expected number and types of deficiencies in your product and the costs to repair each deficiency per the warranty provisions. This is often a difficult task for product engineers because it forces them to focus on product failures and associated costs.

Superscript ^{A} denotes assignments based on Appendix 2A.

DISCUSSION QUESTIONS

Q2-1. The balance sheet consists of assets, liabilities, and equity. Define each category and provide two examples of accounts reported within each category.

Q2-2. Explain how we account for a cost that creates an immediate benefit versus a cost that creates a future benefit.

Q2-3. GAAP is based on the concept of accrual accounting. Define and describe accrual accounting.

Q2-4. Analysts attempt to identify transitory items in an income statement. Define transitory items. What is the purpose of identifying transitory items?

Q2-5. What is the statement of stockholders' equity? What useful information does it contain?

Q2-6. What is the statement of cash flows? What useful information does it contain?

Q2-7. Define and explain the concept of financial statement articulation. What insight comes from understanding articulation?

Q2-8. Describe the flow of costs for the purchase of a machine. At what point do such costs become expenses? Why is it necessary to record the expenses related to the machine in the same period as the revenues it produces?

Q2-9. What are the two essential characteristics of an asset?

Q2-10. What does the concept of liquidity refer to? Explain.

Q2-11. What does the term *current* denote when referring to assets?

Q2-12. Assets are recorded at historical costs even though current market values might, arguably, be more relevant to financial statement readers. Describe the reasoning behind historical cost usage.

Q2-13. Identify three intangible assets that are likely to be *excluded* from the balance sheet because they cannot be reliably measured.

Q2-14. Identify three intangible assets that are recorded on the balance sheet.

Q2-15. What are accrued liabilities? Provide an example.

Q2-16. Define net working capital. Explain how increasing the amount of trade credit can reduce the net working capital for a company.

Q2-17. What is the difference between company *book value* and *market value*? Explain why these two amounts differ.

Q2-18. The financial statement effects template includes an arrow line running from net income to earned capital. What does this arrow line denote?

Assignments with the ✔ logo in the margin are available in myBusinessCourse. See the Preface of the book for details.

MINI EXERCISES

M2-19. Identifying and Classifying Financial Statement Items (LO1)
For each of the following items, indicate whether they would be reported in the balance sheet (B) or income statement (I).

a. Net income	*d.* Accumulated depreciation	*g.* Interest expense
b. Retained earnings	*e.* Wages expense	*h.* Interest payable
c. Depreciation expense	*f.* Wages payable	*i.* Sales

M2-20. Identifying and Classifying Financial Statement Items (LO1)
For each of the following items, indicate whether they would be reported in the balance sheet (B) or income statement (I).

a. Machinery	*e.* Common stock	*i.* Taxes expense
b. Supplies expense	*f.* Factory buildings	*j.* Cost of goods sold
c. Inventories	*g.* Receivables	*k.* Long-term debt
d. Sales	*h.* Taxes payable	*l.* Treasury stock

M2-21. Computing and Comparing Income and Cash Flow Measures (LO1)
Penno Corporation recorded service revenues of $200,000 in 2013, of which $170,000 were on credit and $30,000 were for cash. Moreover, of the $170,000 credit sales for 2013, Penno collected $20,000 cash on those receivables before year-end 2013. The company also paid $25,000 cash for 2013 wages. Its employees also earned another $15,000 in wages for 2013, which were not yet paid at year-end 2013. (a) Compute the company's net income for 2013. (b) How much net cash inflow or outflow did the company generate in 2013? Explain why Penno's net income and net cash flow differ.

M2-22. Assigning Accounts to Sections of the Balance Sheet (LO1)
Identify each of the following accounts as a component of assets (A), liabilities (L), or equity (E).

a. Cash and cash equivalents	_____	*e.* Long-term debt	_____
b. Wages payable	_____	*f.* Retained earnings	_____
c. Common stock	_____	*g.* Additional paid-in capital	_____
d. Equipment	_____	*h.* Taxes payable	_____

M2-23. Determining Missing Information Using the Accounting Equation (LO1)
Use your knowledge of accounting relations to complete the following table for Boatsman Company.

	2012	2013
Beginning retained earnings.	$189,089	$?
Net income (loss)	?	48,192
Dividends	0	15,060
Ending retained earnings	169,634	?

M2-24. Reconciling Retained Earnings (LO1)
Following is financial information from Johnson & Johnson for the year ended December 30, 2012. Prepare the retained earnings reconciliation for Johnson & Johnson for the year ended December 30, 2012 ($ millions).

Johnson & Johnson (JNJ)

Retained earnings, Jan. 1, 2012.	$81,251	Dividends.	$6,614
Net earnings.	10,853	Retained earnings, Dec. 30, 2012. . . .	?
Other retained earnings changes.	502		

M2-25. Analyzing Transactions to Compute Net Income (LO1)
Wasley Corp., a start-up company, provided services that were acceptable to its customers and billed those customers for $350,000 in 2012. However, Wasley collected only $280,000 cash in 2012, and the remaining $70,000 was collected in 2013. Wasley employees earned $225,000 in 2012 wages that were not paid until the first week of 2013. How much net income does Wasley report for 2012? For 2013 (assuming no additional transactions)?

M2-26. Analyzing Transactions Using the Financial Statement Effects Template (LO3)
Report the effects for each of the following transactions using the financial statement effects template.

a. Issue stock for $1,000 cash.
b. Purchase inventory for $500 cash.
c. Sell inventory in transaction *b* for $3,000 on credit.
d. Receive $2,000 cash toward transaction *c* receivable.

EXERCISES

E2-27. Constructing Financial Statements from Account Data (LO1)
Barth Company reports the following year-end account balances at December 31, 2013. Prepare the 2013 income statement and the balance sheet as of December 31, 2013.

Accounts payable	$ 16,000	Inventory	$ 36,000
Accounts receivable	30,000	Land	80,000
Bonds payable, long-term	200,000	Goodwill	8,000
Buildings	151,000	Retained earnings	160,000
Cash	148,000	Sales revenue	500,000
Common stock	150,000	Supplies inventory	3,000
Cost of goods sold	180,000	Supplies expense	6,000
Equipment	70,000	Wages expense	40,000

E2-28. Constructing Financial Statements from Transaction Data (LO1)
Baiman Corporation commences operations at the beginning of January. It provides its services on credit and bills its customers $40,000 for January sales. Its employees also earn January wages of $12,000 that are not paid until the first of February. Complete the following statements for the month-end of January.

Income Statement		Balance Sheet	
Sales	$	Cash	$
Wages expense		Accounts receivable	
Net income (loss)	$	Total assets	$
		Wages payable	$
		Retained earnings	
		Total liabilities and equity	$

E2-29. Analyzing and Reporting Financial Statement Effects of Transactions (LO3)
M.E. Carter launched a professional services firm on March 1. The firm will prepare financial statements at each month-end. In March (its first month), Carter executed the following transactions. Prepare an income statement for Carter Company for the month of March.

a. Carter (owner) invested in the company, $100,000 cash and $20,000 in property and equipment. The company issued common stock to Carter.
b. The company paid $3,200 cash for rent of office furnishings and facilities for March.
c. The company performed services for clients and immediately received $4,000 cash earned.
d. The company performed services for clients and sent a bill for $24,000 with payment due within 60 days.
e. The company compensated an office employee with $4,800 cash as salary for March.
f. The company received $10,000 cash as partial payment on the amount owed from clients in transaction *d*.
g. The company paid $935 cash in dividends to Carter (owner).

E2-30. Analyzing Transactions Using the Financial Statement Effects Template (LO3)
Enter the effects of each of the transactions *a* through *g* from Exercise 2-29 using the financial statement effects template shown in the module.

E2-31. Identifying and Classifying Balance Sheet and Income Statement Accounts (LO1)
Following are selected accounts for **Staples, Inc.**, for the fiscal year ended February 2, 2013.

Staples, Inc. (SPLS)

a. Indicate whether each account appears on the balance sheet (B) or income statement (I).
b. Using the following data, compute total assets and total expenses.
c. Compute net profit margin (net income/sales) and total liabilities-to-equity ratio (total liabilities/ stockholders' equity).

($ millions)	Amount	Classification
Sales	$24,381	
Accumulated depreciation	4,067	
Depreciation expense	408	
Retained earnings	6,694	
Net income	(211)	
Property, plant & equipment, net	6,030	
Selling, general & administrative expense	4,884	
Accounts receivable	1,816	
Total liabilities	6,144	
Stockholders' equity	6,136	

E2-32. Identifying and Classifying Balance Sheet and Income Statement Accounts (LO1)
Following are selected accounts for **Target Corporation**, for the fiscal year ended February 2, 2013.

Target Corporation (TGT)

a. Indicate whether each account appears on the balance sheet (B) or income statement (I).
b. Using the following data, compute total assets and total expenses.
c. Compute net profit margin (net income/sales) and total liabilities-to-equity ratio (total liabilities/ stockholders' equity).

($ millions)	Amount	Classification
Total revenues	$71,960	
Accumulated depreciation	13,311	
Depreciation and amortization expense	2,142	
Retained earnings	13,155	
Net income	2,999	
Property, plant & equipment, net	30,653	
Selling, general & administrative expense	14,914	
Credit card receivables	5,841	
Total liabilities	31,605	
Stockholders' equity	16,558	

E2-33. Comparing Income Statements and Balance Sheets of Competitors (LO1)
Following are selected income statement and balance sheet data from two retailers: **Abercrombie & Fitch** (clothing retailer in the high-end market) and **TJX Companies** (clothing retailer in the value-priced market), for the fiscal year ended February 2, 2013.

Abercrombie & Fitch (ANF)
TJX Companies (TJX)

Income Statement ($ millions)	ANF	TJX
Sales	$4,511	$25,878
Cost of goods sold	1,694	18,521
Gross profit	2,817	7,357
Total expenses	2,580	5,450
Net income	$ 237	$ 1,907

Balance Sheet ($ millions)	ANF	TJX
Current assets	$1,308	$5,712
Long-term assets	1,679	3,800
Total assets	$2,987	$9,512
Current liabilities	$ 691	$3,761
Long-term liabilities	478	2,085
Total liabilities	1,169	5,846
Stockholders' equity	1,818	3,666
Total liabilities and equity	$2,987	$9,512

a. Express each income statement amount as a percentage of sales. Comment on any differences observed between these two companies, especially as they relate to their respective business models.

b. Express each balance sheet amount as a percentage of total assets. Comment on any differences observed between these two companies, especially as they relate to their respective business models.

c. Which company has a higher proportion of stockholders' equity (and a lower proportion of debt)? What do the ratios tell us about relative riskiness of the two companies?

E2-34. Comparing Income Statements and Balance Sheets of Competitors (LO1)

Apple Inc. (AAPL)
Dell (DELL)

Following are selected income statement and balance sheet data from two computer competitors: **Apple** and **Dell**, for the fiscal years ended September 29, 2012 and February 1, 2013, respectively.

Income Statement ($ millions)	Apple	Dell
Sales	$156,508	$56,940
Cost of goods sold	87,846	44,754
Gross profit	68,662	12,186
Total expenses	26,929	9,814
Net income	$ 41,733	$ 2,372

Balance Sheet ($ millions)	Apple	Dell
Current assets	$ 57,653	$27,968
Long-term assets	118,411	19,572
Total assets	$176,064	$47,540
Current liabilities	$ 38,542	$23,439
Long-term liabilities	19,312	13,400
Total liabilities	57,854	36,839
Stockholders' equity	118,210	10,701
Total liabilities and equity	$176,064	$47,540

a. Express each income statement amount as a percentage of sales. Comment on any differences observed between the two companies, especially as they relate to their respective business models. (*Hint:* Apple's gross profit as a percentage of sales is considerably higher than Dell's. What aspect of Apple's business do we believe is driving its profitability?)

b. Express each balance sheet amount as a percentage of total assets. Comment on any differences observed between the two companies. Apple has chosen to structure itself with a higher proportion of equity (and a lower proportion of debt) than Dell. How does this capital structure decision affect our evaluation of the relative riskiness of these two companies?

E2-35. Comparing Income Statements and Balance Sheets of Competitors (LO1)

Comcast (CMCSA)
Verizon (VZ)

Following are selected income statement and balance sheet data for two communications companies: **Comcast** and **Verizon**, for the year ended December 31, 2012.

Income Statement ($ millions)	Comcast	Verizon
Sales	$62,570	$115,846
Operating costs	50,391	102,686
Operating profit	12,179	13,160
Nonoperating expenses	5,976	2,603
Net income	$ 6,203	$ 10,557

Balance Sheet ($ millions)	Comcast	Verizon
Current assets	$ 19,991	$ 21,235
Long-term assets	144,980	203,987
Total assets	$164,971	$225,222
Current liabilities	$ 16,714	$ 26,956
Long-term liabilities	98,461	112,733
Total liabilities	115,175	139,689
Stockholders' equity*	49,796	85,533
Total liabilities and equity	$164,971	$225,222

*Includes noncontrolling interest

a. Express each income statement amount as a percentage of sales. Comment on any differences observed between the two companies.

b. Express each balance sheet amount as a percentage of total assets. Comment on any differences observed between the two companies, especially as they relate to their respective business models.

c. Both Verizon and Comcast have chosen a capital structure with a higher proportion of liabilities than equity. How does this capital structure decision affect our evaluation of the riskiness of these two companies? Take into consideration the large level of capital expenditures that each must make to remain competitive.

E2-36. Comparing Financial Information Across Industries (LO1)

Use the data and computations required in parts *a* and *b* of exercises E2-33 and E2-34 to compare TJX Companies and Apple Inc.

TJX Companies (TJX)
Apple Inc. (AAPL)

a. Compare gross profit and net income as a percentage of sales for these two companies. How might differences in their respective business models explain the differences observed?

b. Compare sales versus total assets. What do observed differences indicate about the relative capital intensity of these two industries?

c. Which company has the higher percentage of total liabilities to stockholders' equity? What do these ratios imply about the relative riskiness of these two companies?

d. Compare the ratio of net income to stockholders' equity for these two companies. Which business model appears to yield higher returns on stockholder investment? Using answers to parts *a* through *c* above, identify the factors that appear to drive the ratio of net income to stockholders' equity.

E2-37. Analyzing Transactions Using the Financial Statement Effects Template (LO3)

Record the effect of each of the following transactions for Hora Company using the financial statement effects template.

a. Wages of $500 are earned by employees but not yet paid.
b. $2,000 of inventory is purchased on credit.
c. Inventory purchased in transaction *b* is sold for $4,000 on credit.
d. Collected $3,000 cash from transaction *c*.
e. Equipment is acquired for $5,000 cash.
f. Recorded $1,000 depreciation expense on equipment from transaction *e*.
g. Paid $10,000 cash toward a note payable that came due.
h. Paid $2,000 cash for interest on borrowings.

PROBLEMS

P2-38. Constructing and Analyzing Balance Sheet Amounts from Incomplete Data (LO1)

Selected balance sheet amounts for 3M Company, a manufacturer of consumer and business products, for three recent years follow.

3M Company (MMM)

$ millions	Current Assets	Long-Term Assets	Total Assets	Current Liabilities	Long-Term Liabilities	Total Liabilities	Stockholders' Equity*
2010	$12,215	$?	$30,156	$?	$ 8,050	$14,139	$16,017
2011	12,240	19,376	?	5,441	10,313	?	15,862
2012	?	20,246	33,876	6,200	9,636	15,836	?

* Includes noncontrolling interest

Required

a. Compute the missing balance sheet amounts for each of the three years shown.
b. What types of accounts would we expect to be included in current assets? In long-term assets?

P2-39. Analyzing Transactions Using the Financial Statement Effects Template (LO3)
Sefcik Company began operations on the first of October. Following are the transactions for its first month of business.

1. S. Sefcik launched Sefcik Company and invested $50,000 into the business in exchange for common stock. The company also borrowed $100,000 from a local bank.
2. Sefcik Co. purchased equipment for $95,000 cash and purchased inventory of $40,000 on credit (the company still owes its suppliers for the inventory at month-end).
3. Sefcik Co. sold inventory costing $30,000 for $50,000 cash.
4. Sefcik Co. paid $12,000 cash for wages owed employees for October work.
5. Sefcik Co. paid interest on the bank loan of $1,000 cash.
6. Sefcik Co. recorded $500 of depreciation expense related to its equipment.
7. Sefcik Co. paid a dividend of $2,000 cash.

Required

a. Record the effects of each transaction using the financial statement effects template.
b. Prepare the income statement and balance sheet at the end of October.

P2-40. Analyzing Transactions Using the Financial Statement Effects Template (LO3)
Following are selected transactions of Mogg Company. Record the effects of each using the financial statement effects template.

1. Shareholders contribute $10,000 cash to the business in exchange for common stock.
2. Employees earn $500 in wages that have not been paid at period-end.
3. Inventory of $3,000 is purchased on credit.
4. The inventory purchased in transaction 3 is sold for $4,500 on credit.
5. The company collected the $4,500 owed to it per transaction 4.
6. Equipment is purchased for $5,000 cash.
7. Depreciation of $1,000 is recorded on the equipment from transaction 6.
8. The Supplies account had a $3,800 balance at the beginning of this period; a physical count at period-end shows that $800 of supplies are still available. No supplies were purchased during this period.
9. The company paid $12,000 cash toward the principal on a note payable; also, $500 cash is paid to cover this note's interest expense for the period.
10. The company received $8,000 cash in advance for services to be delivered next period.

P2-41. Comparing Operating Characteristics Across Industries (LO1)
Following are selected income statement and balance sheet data for companies in different industries.

Target Corp. (TGT)
Nike (NKE)
Harley-Davidson (HOG)
Cisco Systems (CSCO)

($ millions)	Sales	Cost of Goods Sold	Gross Profit	Net Income	Assets	Liabilities	Stockholders' Equity
Target Corp.	$73,301	$50,568	$22,733	$2,999	$ 48,163	$31,605	$16,558
Nike, Inc.	25,313	14,279	11,034	2,485	17,584	6,428	11,156
Harley-Davidson	5,581	3,222	2,359	624	9,171	6,613	2,558
Cisco Systems	48,607	19,167	29,440	9,983	101,191	42,063	59,128

Required

a. Compute the following ratios for each company.
1. Gross profit/Sales
2. Net income/Sales
3. Net income/Stockholders' equity
4. Liabilities/Stockholders' equity

b. Comment on any differences among the companies' gross profit to sales ratios and net income as a percentage of sales. Do differences in the companies' business models explain the differences observed?

c. Which company reports the highest ratio of net income to equity? Suggest one or more reasons for this result.

d. Which company has financed itself with the highest percentage of liabilities to equity? Suggest one or more reasons why this company can take on such debt levels.

P2-42. Comparing Cash Flows Across Retailers (LO1)

Following are selected accounts from the income statement and the statement of cash flows for several retailers, for their fiscal years ended in 2013.

($ millions)	Sales	Net Income (Loss)	Cash Flows from Operating	Investing	Financing
Macy's	$ 27,686	$ 1,335	$ 2,261	$ (863)	$ (2,389)
Home Depot, Inc.	74,754	4,535	6,975	(1,432)	(5,034)
Staples, Inc.	24,381	(211)	1,219	(342)	(812)
Target Corp.	73,301	2,999	5,325	(2,855)	(2,488)
Wal-Mart Stores	469,162	16,999	25,591	(12,611)	(11,972)

Macy's (M)
Home Depot (HD)
Staples (SPLS)
Target (TGT)
Wal-Mart (WMT)

Required

a. Compute the ratio of net income to sales for each company. Rank the companies on the basis of this ratio. Do their respective business models give insight into these differences?

b. Compute net cash flows from operating activities as a percentage of sales. Rank the companies on the basis of this ratio. Does this ranking coincide with the ratio rankings from part *a*? Suggest one or more reasons for any differences you observe.

c. Compute net cash flows from investing activities as a percentage of sales. Rank the companies on the basis of this ratio. Does this ranking coincide with the ratio rankings from part *a*? Suggest one or more reasons for any differences you observe.

d. All of these companies report negative cash flows from financing activities. What does it mean for a company to have net cash *outflow* from financing?

P2-43. Interpreting the Statement of Cash Flows (LO1)

Following is the statement of cash flows for Wal-Mart Stores, Inc.

Wal-Mart (WMT)

WAL-MART STORES, INC.
Statement of Cash Flows
For Year Ended January 31, 2013 ($ millions)

Cash flows from operating activities	
Income from continuing operations	17,756
Adjustments to reconcile income from continuing operations to net cash provided by operating activities:	
Depreciation and amortization	8,501
Deferred income taxes	(133)
Other operating activities	527
Changes in certain assets and liabilities, net of effects of acquisitions:	
Receivables, net	(614)
Inventories	(2,759)
Accounts payable	1,061
Accrued liabilities	271
Accrued income taxes	981
Net cash provided by operating activities	25,591
Cash flows from investing activities	
Payments for property and equipment	(12,898)
Proceeds from the disposal of property and equipment	532
Investments and business acquisitions, net of cash acquired	(316)
Other investing activities	71
Net cash used in investing activities	(12,611)

continued

continued from prior page

Cash flows from financing activities	
Net change in short-term borrowings	2,754
Proceeds from issuance of long-term debt	211
Payments of long-term debt	(1,478)
Dividends paid	(5,361)
Purchase of Company stock	(7,600)
Other financing activities	(498)
Net cash used in financing activities	(11,972)
Effect of exchange rates on cash and cash equivalents	223
Net increase (decrease) in cash and cash equivalents	1,231
Cash and cash equivalents at beginning of year	6,550
Cash and cash equivalents at end of year	$ 7,781

Required

a. Why does Wal-Mart add back depreciation to compute net cash flows from operating activities?

b. Explain why the increase in receivables and inventories is reported as a cash outflow. Why do accounts payable and accrued liabilities provide a source of cash?

c. Wal-Mart reports that it invested $12,898 million in property and equipment. Is this an appropriate type of expenditure for Wal-Mart to make? What relation should expenditures for PPE assets have with depreciation expense?

d. Wal-Mart indicates that it paid $7,600 million to repurchase its common stock in fiscal 2013 and, in addition, paid dividends of $5,361 million. Thus, Wal-Mart paid $12,961 million of cash to its stockholders during the year. How do we evaluate that use of cash relative to other possible uses for Wal-Mart's cash?

e. Provide an overall assessment of Wal-Mart's cash flows for 2013. In the analysis, consider the sources and uses of cash.

P2-44. Interpreting the Statement of Cash Flows (LO1)

Verizon (VZ)

Following is the statement of cash flows for Verizon.

VERIZON Statement of Cash Flows For Year Ended December 31, 2012 ($ millions)	
Cash Flows from Operating Activities	
Net Income	$10,557
Adjustments to reconcile net income to net cash provided by operating activities:	
Depreciation and amortization expense	16,460
Employee retirement benefits	8,198
Deferred income taxes	(952)
Provision for uncollectible accounts	972
Equity in earnings of unconsolidated businesses, net of dividends received	77
Changes in current assets and liabilities, net of effects from acquisition/disposition of businesses	
Accounts receivable	(1,717)
Inventories	(136)
Other assets	306
Accounts payable and accrued liabilities	1,144
Other, net	(3,423)
Net cash provided by operating activities	31,486
Cash Flows from Investing Activities	
Capital expenditures (including capitalized software)	(16,175)
Acquisitions of investments and businesses, net of cash acquired	(913)
Acquisitions of wireless licenses, net	(3,935)
Proceeds from dispositions	—
Net change in short-term investments	27
Other, net	494
Net cash used in investing activities	(20,502)

continued

continued from prior page

Cash Flows from Financing Activities	
Proceeds from long-term borrowings	4,489
Repayments of long-term borrowings and capital lease obligations	(6,403)
Increase (decrease) in short-term obligations, excluding current maturities	(1,437)
Dividends paid	(5,230)
Proceeds from sale of common stock	315
Proceeds from access line spin-off	—
Special distribution to noncontrolling interest	(8,325)
Other, net	(4,662)
Net cash used in financing activities	(21,253)
Increase (decrease) in cash and cash equivalents	(10,269)
Cash and cash equivalents, beginning of period	13,362
Cash and cash equivalents, end of period	$ 3,093

Required

a. Why does Verizon add back depreciation to compute net cash flows from operating activities? What does the size of the depreciation add-back indicate about the relative capital intensity of this industry?

b. Verizon reports that it invested $16,175 million in property and equipment. These expenditures are necessitated by market pressures as the company faces stiff competition from other communications companies, such as Comcast. Where in the 10-K might we find additional information about these capital expenditures to ascertain whether Verizon is addressing the company's most pressing needs? What relation might we expect between the size of these capital expenditures and the amount of depreciation expense reported?

c. Verizon's statement of cash flows indicates that the company paid $6,403 million in debt payments. What problem does Verizon's high debt load pose for its ability to maintain the level of capital expenditures necessary to remain competitive in its industry?

d. During the year, Verizon paid dividends of $5,230 million but did not repay a sizeable portion of its debt. How do dividend payments differ from debt payments? Why would Verizon continue to pay dividends in light of cash demands for needed capital expenditures and debt repayments?

e. Provide an overall assessment of Verizon's cash flows for 2012. In the analysis, consider the sources and uses of cash.

P2-45. Analyzing Transactions Using the Financial Statement Effects Template (LO3)

On March 1, S. Penman (owner) launched AniFoods, Inc., an organic foods retailing company. Following are the transactions for its first month of business.

1. S. Penman (owner) contributed $100,000 cash to the company in return for common stock. Penman also lent the company $55,000. This $55,000 note is due one year hence.
2. The company purchased equipment in the amount of $50,000, paying $10,000 cash and signing a note payable to the equipment manufacturer for the remaining balance.
3. The company purchased inventory for $80,000 cash in March.
4. The company had March sales of $100,000 of which $60,000 was for cash and $40,000 on credit. Total cost of goods sold for its March sales was $70,000.
5. The company purchased future advertising time from a local radio station for $10,000 cash.
6. During March, $7,500 worth of radio spots purchased in transaction 5 are aired. The remaining spots will be aired in April.
7. Employee wages earned and paid during March total $17,000 cash.
8. Prior to disclosing the financial statements, the company recognized that employees had earned an additional $1,000 in wages that will be paid in the next period.
9. The company recorded $2,000 of depreciation for March relating to its equipment.

Required

a. Record the effect of each transaction using the financial statement effects template.

b. Prepare a March income statement and a balance sheet as of the end of March for AniFoods, Inc.

P2-46. Analyzing Transactions Using the Financial Statement Effects Template (LO3)

Hanlon Advertising Company began the current month with the following balance sheet.

Cash	$ 80,000	Liabilities	$ 70,000
Noncash assets	135,000	Contributed capital	110,000
		Earned capital	35,000
Total assets	$215,000	Total liabilities and equity	$215,000

Following are summary transactions that occurred during the current month.

1. The company purchased supplies for $5,000 cash; none were used this month.
2. Services of $2,500 were performed this month on credit.
3. Services were performed for $10,000 cash this month.
4. The company purchased advertising for $8,000 cash; the ads will run next month.
5. The company received $1,200 cash as partial payment on accounts receivable from transaction 2.
6. The company paid $3,400 cash toward the accounts payable balance reported at the beginning of the month.
7. Paid $3,500 cash toward this month's wages expenses.
8. The company declared and paid dividends of $500 cash.

Required

a. Record the effects of each transaction using the financial statement effects template.
b. Prepare the income statement for this month and the balance sheet as of month-end.

P2-47. Reconciling and Computing Operating Cash Flows from Net Income (LO1)
Petroni Company reports the following selected results for its current calendar year.

Net income	$130,000
Depreciation expense	28,000
Accounts receivable increase	10,000
Accounts payable increase	6,000
Prepaid expenses decrease	3,000
Wages payable decrease	4,000

Required

a. Prepare the operating section only of Petroni Company's statement of cash flows for the year.
b. Does the positive sign on depreciation expense indicate that the company is generating cash by recording depreciation? Explain.
c. Explain why the increase in accounts receivable is a use of cash in the statement of cash flows.
d. Explain why the decrease in prepaid expense is a source of cash in the statement of cash flows.

P2-48. Analyzing Transactions Using the Financial Statement Effects Template (LO3)
Werner Realty Company began the month with the following balance sheet.

Cash	$ 30,000	Liabilities	$ 90,000
Noncash assets	225,000	Contributed capital	45,000
		Earned capital	120,000
Total assets	$255,000	Total liabilities and equity	$255,000

Following are summary transactions that occurred during the current month.

1. The company purchased $6,000 of supplies on credit.
2. The company received $8,000 cash from a new customer for services to be performed next month.
3. The company paid $6,000 cash to cover office rent for two months (the current month and the next).
4. The company billed clients for $25,000 of work performed.
5. The company paid employees $6,000 cash for work performed.
6. The company collected $25,000 cash from accounts receivable in transaction 4.
7. The company recorded $4,000 depreciation on its equipment.
8. At month-end, $2,000 of supplies purchased in transaction 1 are still available; no supplies were available when the month began.

Required

a. Record the effects of each transaction using the financial statement effects template.
b. Prepare the income statement for this month and the balance sheet as of month-end.

IFRS APPLICATIONS

I2-49. Comparing Income Statements and Balance Sheets of Competitors (LO1)

Following are selected income statement and balance sheet data from two European grocery chain companies: Tesco PLC (UK) and Ahold (The Netherlands).

Income Statements (for fiscal year ended)	Tesco February 23, 2013 (in £millions)	Ahold December 30, 2012 (in €millions)
Sales	£64,826	€32,841
Cost of goods sold	(60,737)	(24,317)
Gross profit	4,089	8,524
Total expenses	(3,969)	(7,697)
Net income	£ 120	€ 827

Balance Sheet (as of)	Tesco February 23, 2013 (in £millions)	Ahold December 30, 2012 (in €millions)
Current assets	£13,096	€ 4,416
Long-term assets	37,033	10,666
Total assets	£50,129	€15,082
Current liabilities	£18,985	€ 4,427
Long-term liabilities	14,483	4,660
Total liabilities	33,468	9,087
Stockholders' equity	16,661	5,995
Total liabilities and equity	£50,129	€15,082

Required

a. Prepare a common-sized income statement. To do this, express each income statement amount as a percent of sales. Comment on any differences observed between the two companies. Ahold's gross profit percentage of sales is considerably higher than Tesco's. What might explain this difference?

b. Prepare a common-sized balance sheet. To do this, express each balance sheet amount as a percent of total assets. Comment on any differences observed between the two companies.

c. Ahold has chosen to structure itself with a higher proportion of equity (and a lower proportion of debt) than Tesco. How does this capital structure decision affect your assessment of the relative riskiness of these two companies?

I2-50. Interpreting the Statement of Cash Flows (LO1)

Following is the statement of cash flows for AstraZeneca, a multinational pharmaceutical conglomerate, headquartered in London, UK. The company uses IFRS for its financials and provides a conversion to U.S. $ as a convenience to investors.

ASTRAZENECA Consolidated Statement of Cash Flows For Year Ended December 31, 2012 ($ millions)	
Cash flows from operating activities	
Profit before tax	$7,718
Finance income and expense	430
Depreciation, amortisation and impairment	2,518
Decrease in trade and other receivables	755
Increase in inventories	(150)
Decrease in trade and other payables and provisions	(1,311)
Non-cash and other movements	(424)
Cash generated from operations	9,536
Interest paid	(545)
Tax paid	(2,043)
Net cash inflow from operating activities	6,948

continued

continued from prior page

Cash flows from investing activities	
Acquisitions of business operations	$(1,187)
Movement in short-term investments and fixed deposits	3,619
Purchase of property, plant and equipment	(672)
Disposal of property, plant and equipment	199
Purchase of intangible assets	(3,947)
Purchase of noncurrent asset investments	(46)
Disposal of noncurrent asset investments	43
Dividends received	7
Interest received	145
Payments made by subsidiaries to non-controlling interests	(20)
Net cash outflow from investing activities	(1,859)
Net cash inflow before financing activities	5,089
Cash flows from financing activities	
Proceeds from issue of share capital	429
Repurchase of shares	(2,635)
Repayment of obligations under finance leases	(17)
Issue of loans	1,980
Repayment of loans	(1,750)
Dividends paid	(3,665)
Hedge contracts relating to dividend payments	48
Movement in short-term borrowings	687
Net cash outflow from financing activities	(4,923)
Net increase/(decrease) in cash and cash equivalents in the period	$ 166
Cash and cash equivalents at the beginning of the period	7,434
Exchange rate effects	(4)
Cash and cash equivalents at the end of the period	$ 7,596

Required

a. Why does AstraZeneca add back depreciation to compute net cash flows from operating activities?

b. Explain why the decrease in trade and other receivables is reported as a cash inflow and the increase in inventories is reported as a cash outflow. Explain why trade and other payables and provisions are shown as a use of cash.

c. AstraZeneca reports that it invested $672 million in property and equipment. Is this an appropriate type of expenditure for AstraZeneca to make? What relation should expenditures for PPE assets have with depreciation expense?

d. AstraZeneca indicates that it paid dividends of $3,665 million. How do we evaluate that use of cash relative to other possible uses for AstraZeneca's cash?

e. Provide an overall assessment of AstraZeneca's cash flows for 2012. In the analysis, consider the sources and uses of cash.

MANAGEMENT APPLICATIONS

MA2-51. Understanding the Company Operating Cycle and Management Strategy (LO1)
Consider the operating cycle as depicted in Exhibit 2.4, to answer the following questions.

a. Why might a company want to reduce its cash conversion cycle? (*Hint*: Consider the financial statement implications of reducing the cash conversion cycle.)

b. How might a company reduce its cash conversion cycle?

c. Examine and discuss the potential impacts on *customers* and *suppliers* of taking the actions identified in part *b*.

MA2-52. Ethics and Governance: Understanding Revenue Recognition and Expense Recording (LO1)
Revenue should be recognized when it is earned and expense when incurred. Given some lack of specificity in these terms, companies have some latitude when applying GAAP to determine the timing and amount of revenues and expenses. A few companies use this latitude to manage reported earnings. Some have argued that it is not necessarily bad for companies to manage earnings in that, by doing so, management (1) can better provide investors and creditors with reported earnings that are closer to "core" earnings (that is, management purges earnings of components deemed irrelevant or distracting so that share prices better reflect company performance); and (2) can present the company in the best light, which benefits both shareholders and employees—a Machiavellian argument that "the end justifies the means."

a. Is it good that GAAP is written as broadly as it is? Explain. What are the pros and cons of defining accounting terms more strictly?
b. Assess (both pro and con) the Machiavellian argument above that defends managing earnings.

ONGOING PROJECT

(This ongoing project began in Module 1 and continues through most of the book; even if previous segments were not completed, the requirements are still applicable to any business analysis.) The goal of this module's project is to perform vertical analysis of the balance sheet and income statement, assess cash flows, and determine market capitalization.

1. *Balance Sheet Analysis.* Prepare a common size balance sheet. To facilitate this, obtain the balance sheet in a spreadsheet such as Excel. Check with the sec.gov Website as many companies file their financials in spreadsheet form; look for the "Interactive Data" link on the search results page. Compare the two vertical analyses and look for major differences over time and between the companies. Some questions to consider:
   - What are each company's largest assets? Largest liabilities?
   - What proportion of total assets is financed by owners? (Hint: Compare with total equity.)
   - What proportion of total assets is financed by nonowners?
2. *Income Statement Analysis.* Prepare a common size income statement. Express each item on the income statement as a percent of total sales or revenue. Do this for all years on the income statement. Compare the vertical analyses and look for major differences over time and between the companies. Do any patterns emerge? Some questions to consider:
   - What are the companies' major expenses?
   - Are there any unusual or discontinued items? Are they large in magnitude?
   - Which company is more profitable?
   - Was each company more or less profitable when compared to the prior year?
3. *Statement of Cash Flows Analysis.* Determine the size and direction (cash source or use) of cash flows from operations, investing, and financing. One goal is to understand each company's pattern of cash flows and to form an opinion about the general strength of their cash flows. Some questions to consider:
   - What were the companies' cash flows from operations? Were they positive?
   - Were operating cash flows smaller or larger than net income?
   - What are the major differences between operating cash and net income?
   - Did the company purchase new property and equipment ("capital expenditures") during the year?
   - Did the company issue new debt during the year or was debt repaid? (Hint: We must sometimes sum one or more line items on this statement to determine total net debt activity.)
   - Did the company issue new stock?
   - Did the company pay dividends?
4. *Market Capitalization.* Determine the market capitalization at the most recent year-end for each company. We should be able to determine the number of shares outstanding from the balance sheet. Recall that shares outstanding is total shares issued less any treasury shares. We can obtain the year-end stock price from an investment Website such as Seeking Alpha or Yahoo Finance. Compare market cap to the book value (total equity) of the company. Calculate and compare the companies' market-to-book ratios.

SOLUTIONS TO REVIEW PROBLEMS

Mid-Module Review 1

Solution ($ in millions)

SAMSUNG ELECTRONICS CO. LTD.
Income Statement
For Fiscal Year Ended December 31, 2012

Total revenue	$187,754
Cost of goods sold	118,245
Gross profit	69,509
Operating expenses	42,388
Operating income	27,121
Nonoperating income	808
Profit before taxes	27,929
Income tax expense	5,667
Net income	$ 22,262

SAMSUNG ELECTRONICS CO. LTD.
Statement of Cash Flows
For Fiscal Year Ended December 31, 2012

Net cash provided by operating activities	$35,452
Net cash used in investing activities	(29,242)
Net cash provided by financing activities	(2,383)
Net increase in cash and cash equivalents	3,827
Cash and cash equivalents, beginning of year	31,135
Cash and cash equivalents, ending of year	$34,962

SAMSUNG ELECTRONICS CO. LTD.
Balance Sheet
December 31, 2012

Assets		Liabilities	
Current assets		Accounts payable	$ 15,768
Cash and cash equivalents	$ 34,962	Accrued expenses	8,865
Receivables	24,904	Short-term borrowings	7,883
Inventory	16,569	Other current liabilities	11,302
Other current assets	5,041	Total current liabilities	43,818
Total current assets	81,476	Long-term debt	6,179
		Other noncurrent liabilities	5,639
Net property, plant, and equipment	63,939		
Other long-term assets	23,637	Total liabilities	55,636
		Paid-in capital	4,949
		Retained earnings	112,021
		Other stockholders' equity	(3,554)
		Total equity	113,416
Total assets	$169,052	Total liabilities and equity	$169,052

Mid-Module Review 2

Solution ($ in millions)

Balance Sheet December 31, 2011	
Assets	
Cash	$ 31,135
Noncash assets	114,324
Total assets.	$145,459
Liabilities and equity	
Total liabilities	$ 50,870
Equity	
Contributed capital	4,949
Retained earnings.	91,143
Other stockholders' equity.	(1,503)
Liabilities and equity.	$145,459

Statement of Cash Flows For Year Ended December 31, 2012	
Operating cash flows	$35,452
Investing cash flows.	(29,242)
Financing cash flows	(2,383)
Net change in cash.	3,827
Cash balance, Dec. 31, 2011	31,135
Cash balance, Dec. 31, 2012	$34,962

Income Statement For Year Ended December 31, 2012	
Revenues	$187,754
Expenses	165,492
Net earnings	$ 22,262

Statement of Stockholders' Equity For Year Ended December 31, 2012	
Contributed capital, Dec. 31, 2011	$ 4,949
Stock issuance Dec. 31, 2012	0
Contributed capital, Dec. 31, 2012	$ 4,949
Retained earnings, Dec. 31, 2011	$ 91,143
Net income.	22,262
Less: dividends & other	(1,384)
Retained earnings, Dec. 31, 2012	$112,021
Other stockholders' equity, Dec. 31, 2011	$ (1,503)
Other changes in equity	(2,051)
Other stockholders' equity Dec. 31, 2012	$ (3,554)

Balance Sheet December 31, 2012	
Assets	
Cash	$ 34,962
Noncash assets	134,090
Total assets.	$169,052
Liabilities and equity	
Total liabilities	$ 55,636
Equity	
Contributed capital . . .	4,949
Retained earnings. . . .	112,021
Other stockholders' equity.	(3,554)
Liabilities and equity. . . .	$169,052

Beginning of year

During the year

End of year

Module-End Review

Solution

a.

	Balance Sheet									Income Statement				
Transaction	Cash Asset	+	Noncash Assets	=	Liabil-ities	+	Contrib. Capital	+	Earned Capital	Rev-enues	–	Expen-ses	=	Net Income
Beginning balance	+80,000		+270,000	=	+200,000		+50,000		+100,000		–		=	
1. Purchase inventory of $80,000 on credit			+80,000 Inventory	=	+80,000 Accounts Payable						–		=	

continued

continued from prior page

	Balance Sheet										Income Statement				
Transaction	Cash Asset	+	Noncash Assets	=	Liabilities	+	Contrib. Capital	+	Earned Capital		Revenues	−	Expenses	=	Net Income
2. Pay employees $10,000 cash for wages earned this year	−10,000 Cash			=					−10,000 Retained Earnings			−	+10,000 Wages Expense	=	−10,000
3. Sell inventory costing $40,000 for $70,000 on credit			+70,000 Accounts Receivable −40,000 Inventory	=					+70,000 Retained Earnings −40,000 Retained Earning		+70,000 Sales	−	+40,000 Cost of Goods Sold	=	+70,000 −40,000
4. Collect $15,000 cash from the accounts receivable in transaction 3	+15,000 Cash		−15,000 Accounts Receivable	=								−		=	
5. Pay $35,000 cash toward the accounts payable in transaction 1	−35,000 Cash			=	−35,000 Accounts Payable							−		=	
6. Purchase advertising for $25,000 cash that will air next year	−25,000 Cash		+25,000 Prepaid Advertising	=								−		=	
7. Employees earn $5,000 in wages that will not be paid until next year				=	+5,000 Wages Payable				−5,000 Retained Earnings			−	+5,000 Wages Expense	=	−5,000
8. Record $3,000 depreciation on equipment			−3,000 PPE, net	=					−3,000 Retained Earnings			−	+3,000 Depreciation Expense	=	−3,000
Ending balance	+25,000		+387,000	=	+250,000		+50,000		+112,000		+70,000	−	+58,000	=	+12,000

b.

LG DISPLAY CO., LTD. (LPL) Income Statement For Year Ended December 31, 2013	
Revenues	$70,000
Expenses	58,000
Net income	$12,000

LG DISPLAY CO., LTD. (LPL) Balance Sheet December 31, 2013			
Cash	$ 25,000	Liabilities	$250,000
Noncash assets	387,000	Contributed capital	50,000
		Earned capital (retained earnings)	112,000
Total assets	$412,000	Total liabilities and equity	$412,000

c. The linkage between the income statement and the balance sheet is retained earnings. Each period, the retained earnings account is updated for net income less dividends paid. For this period, that updating follows.

LG DISPLAY CO., LTD. (LPL) Retained Earnings Reconciliation For Year Ended December 31, 2013	
Retained earnings, Dec. 31, 2012	$100,000
Add: Net income	12,000
Less: Dividends	(0)
Retained earnings, Dec. 31, 2013	$112,000

Module

3 Accounting Adjustments and Constructing Financial Statements

Learning Objectives

LO1 Analyze and record transactions using the financial statement effects template. (p. 3-4)

LO2 Prepare and explain accounting adjustments and their financial statement effects. (p. 3-8)

LO3 Explain and construct the trial balance. (p. 3-12)

LO4 Construct financial statements from the trial balance. (p. 3-15)

LO5 Describe the closing process. (p. 3-20)

Apple

Apple Inc. launched the iPhone in 2007, arguably one of the most important products in the company's history. The iPhone fundamentally changed the mobile communications industry and launched the era of the smart phone. Marrying the edgy hardware design with the intuitive Apple-like iOS software for navigation, the company had a winning combination. By the end of 2010, Apple was selling 40 million iPhones per year, and its sales exceeded $65 billion. Growth continued into 2012 where Apple sold over 125 million iPhones for over $80 billion, making up more than half of its total sales as shown in the following graphic.

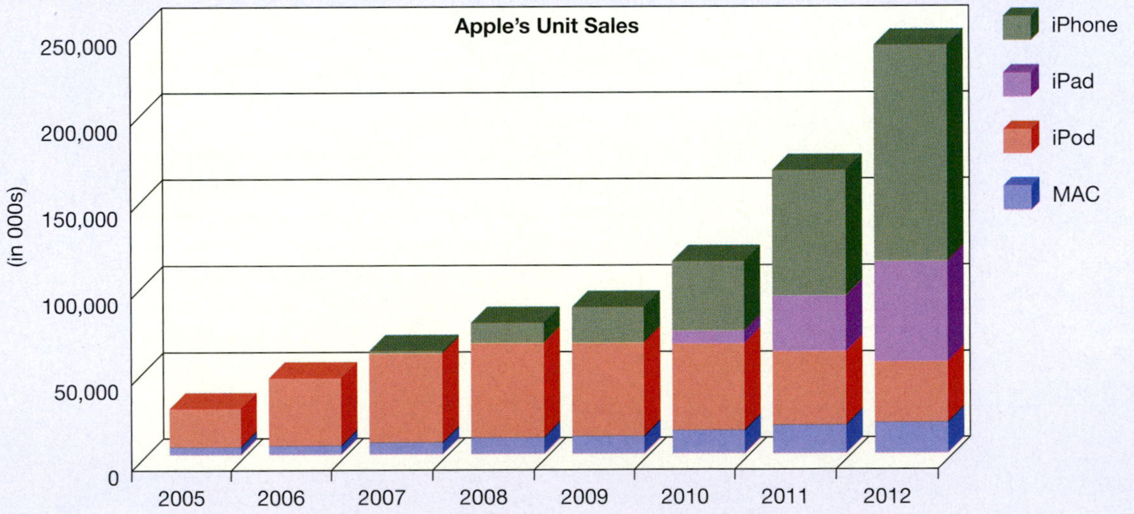

Courtesy of Corbis

To bring each iPhone to market, Apple must purchase component parts, manufacture them, hire sales personnel, pay advertisers, and distribute finished products. Each of these activities involves a transaction that Apple's accounting system must capture and communicate to its stakeholders. The resulting financial statements tell the story of Apple's manufacturing and sales process in financial language. Apple's accounting system must be efficient and effective at delivering timely and relevant information to interested parties.

This module explains how the accounting system captures business transactions, creates financial records, and aggregates the individual records to produce financial reports that we read and interpret in company 10-Ks. The resulting financial statements tell the story of Apple's business activities. We analyze those financial statements for insights into company operations and future performance.

Sources: Apple 10-K and Annual Report; *Fortune*, January 2007 and 2012.

MODULE ORGANIZATION

Accounting Adjustments and Constructing Financial Statements

Accounting for Transactions
- Financial Statement Effects Template
- Capital Investment
- Asset Acquisition
- Revenues and Expenses
- Capital Distribution

Accounting Adjustments
- Prepaid Expenses
- Unearned Revenues
- Accrued Expenses
- Accrued Revenues
- Trial Balance

Financial Statement Preparation
- Income Statement
- Balance Sheet
- Statement of Stockholders' Equity
- Statement of Cash Flows
- Closing Process

Financial statements report on the financial performance of a business using the language of accounting. To prepare these statements, companies translate day-to-day transactions into accounting records (called journals), and then record (post) them to individual accounts. At the end of an accounting period, each of these accounts is totaled, and the resulting balances are used to prepare financial statements. After the financial statements are prepared, the temporary (income statement) accounts are "zeroed out" so that the next period can begin anew—akin to clearing a scoreboard for the next game. Permanent (balance sheet) accounts continue to reflect financial position and carry over from period to period—akin to keeping track of wins and losses even when a particular scoreboard is cleared.

The *accounting cycle* is illustrated in Exhibit 3.1. Transactions are first recorded in the accounting records. Each of these transactions is, generally, the result of an external transaction, such as recording a sale to a customer or the payment of wages to employees. Once all of the transactions have been recorded during the accounting period, the company adjusts the accounting records to recognize a number of events that have occurred, but which have not yet been recorded. These might include the recognition of wage expense and the related wages payable for those employees who have earned wages, but have not yet been paid, or the recognition of depreciation expense for buildings and equipment. These adjustments are made at the end of the accounting period to properly adjust the accounting records before the financial statements are prepared. Once all adjustments are made, financial statements are prepared.

EXHIBIT 3.1 Accounting Cycle

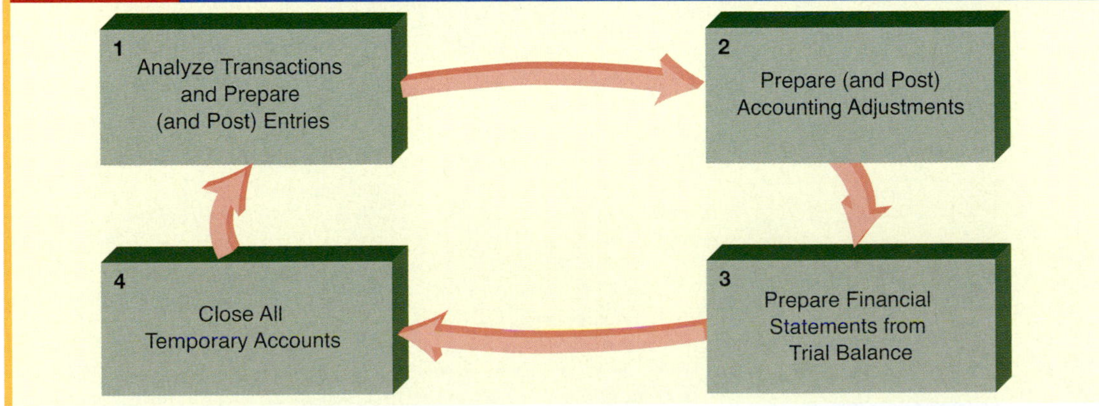

The purpose of Module 3 is to explain further details of the accounting cycle. Our illustration includes journalizing transactions, posting entries to accounts, adjusting those accounts, preparing unadjusted and adjusted trial balances, constructing financial statements, and closing out temporary accounts before beginning the next accounting period. We also show how to construct the statement of cash flows under both the direct and indirect methods. Some topics from Module 2 are repeated here for completeness (the financial statement effects template, accounting adjustments, and basic financial statement preparation, for example). This module provides a more detailed introduction to the accounting recordkeeping process. However, understanding topics in the other modules does not require knowledge of the details in this module.

Understanding the financial statement preparation process requires an understanding of the language used to record business transactions in accounting records. The recording and statement preparation processes are readily understood once we learn that language (of financial statement effects) and its mechanics (entries and posting). Even if we never journalize a transaction or prepare a financial statement, understanding the accounting process aids us in analyzing and interpreting accounting reports. Understanding the accounting language also facilitates our communication with business professionals within a company and with members of the business community outside of a company.

ACCOUNTING FOR TRANSACTIONS

LO1 Analyze and record transactions using the financial statement effects template.

This section explains how we account for and assess business transactions. We describe the financial statement effects template that we use throughout the book. We then illustrate its application to four main categories of business transactions.

Financial Statement Effects Template

Transaction analysis refers to the process of identifying, analyzing, and recording the financial statement effects of transactions. For this purpose, we use the following **financial statement effects template**.

	Balance Sheet									Income Statement				
Transaction	Cash Asset	+	Noncash Assets	=	Liabil-ities	+	Contrib. Capital	+	Earned Capital	Rev-enues	−	Expen-ses	=	Net Income
				=							−		=	

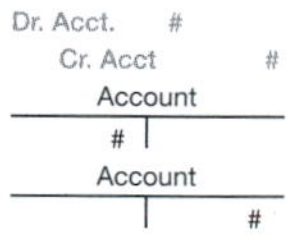

Each transaction is identified in the "Transaction" column. Then, the dollar amounts (positive or negative) of the financial statement effects are recorded in the appropriate balance sheet or income statement columns. The template also reflects the statement of cash flow effects (via the cash column) and the statement of stockholders' equity effects (via the contributed capital and earned capital columns). The retained earnings account, one of the accounts in earned capital, is immediately updated to reflect any income or loss arising from each transaction (denoted by the arrow line from net income to earned capital). This template is instructive as it reveals the financial impacts of transactions, and it provides insights into the effects of accounting choices.

T-Accounts and Journal Entries

The related journal entry and T-account effects are displayed in the margin next to the financial statement effects template. The **T-Accounts**, named for their likeness to a large 'T', are used to reflect increases and decreases to individual accounts. When a transaction occurs, it is recorded (*journalized*); once recorded, the specific accounts affected are updated in the accounting books (*general ledger*) of the company, and the affected accounts are increased or decreased. This process of continuously updating individual account balances is referred to as *posting* transactions to accounts. A T-account provides a simple illustration of the financial effects of each transaction.

Specifically, one side of the T-account is used for increases and the other for decreases. A convenient way to remember which side records increases is to recall the accounting equation: **Assets = Liabilities + Equity.** Assets are on the left side of the equation. So, the left side of an asset T-account records increases in the asset and the right side records decreases. Liabilities and equity are on the right side of the accounting equation. So, the right side of a liability and an equity T-account records increases and the left side records decreases. This relation is represented graphically as follows:

Assets		=	Liabilities		+	Equity	
+ Increases	− Decreases		− Decreases	+ Increases		− Decreases	+ Increases

Journal entries also capture the effects of transactions. Journal entries reflect increases and decreases to accounts using the language of debits and credits. Debits and credits simply refer to the left or right side of a T-account, respectively. We can superimpose the descriptors of debit and credit on a T-account as follows.

Account Title	
Debit (Left side)	Credit (Right side)

The left side of the T-account is the "debit" side and the right side is the "credit" side. This holds for all T-accounts. Thus, to record an increase in an asset, we enter an amount on the left or debit side of the T-account—that is, we *debit the account*. Decreases in assets are recorded with an entry on the opposite (credit) side. To record an increase in a liability or equity account, we enter an amount on the right or credit side of the T-account—we *credit the account*. Decreases in liability or equity accounts are recorded on the left (debit) side.

In the margin of our financial statement effects template, we show the journal entry first, followed by the related T-accounts. In accounting jargon, this sequence relates to *journalizing* the entry and *posting* it to the affected accounts. The T-accounts represent the financial impact of each transaction on the respective asset, liability or equity accounts.

Transaction Analysis

This section uses **Apple Inc.** to illustrate the accounting for selected business transactions. The assumed time frame will be one fiscal quarter, as all public companies are required to prepare financial statements at least quarterly. We select transactions to illustrate four fundamental types of business activities: (1) financing the company, (2) asset acquisition, (3) revenue and expense recognition, and (4) dividend distribution. Next, we record accounting adjustments, prepare the financial statements, and close the books.

Capital Investment

Assume that Apple investors contribute $300 cash to the company in exchange for common stock. Apple's cash and common stock both increase. Recall that common stock is a component of contributed capital. The following financial statement effects template reflects this transaction. If cash financing was obtained from a bank instead of stockholders, the only change would be to increase liabilities by $300, not contributed capital.

Cash 300
CS 300

Cash	
300	

CS	
	300

	Balance Sheet										Income Statement				
Transaction	Cash Asset	+	Noncash Assets	=	Liabilities	+	Contrib. Capital	+	Earned Capital		Revenues	−	Expenses	=	Net Income
Issue stock for $300 cash	+300 Cash			=			+300 Common Stock					−		=	

Journal Entry and T-Account

Although we will not repeatedly refer to journal entries and T-accounts, we will describe them for this first transaction. Specifically, the $300 debit equals the $300 credit in the journal entry: assets ($300 cash) = liabilities ($0) + equity ($300 common stock). This balance in transactions is the basis of *double-entry accounting*. For simplicity, we use acronyms (such as CS for common stock) in journal entries and T-accounts. (A listing of accounts and acronyms is located in Appendix D near the end of the book.) The journal entry for this transaction is

Cash	300	
CS (Common Stock)		300

Convention dictates that debits are listed first, followed by credits—the latter are indented.[1] The total debit(s) must always equal the total credit(s) for each transaction. The T-account representation for this transaction follows:

Cash	
300	

CS	
	300

Cash is an asset; thus, a cash increase is recorded on the left or debit side of the T-account. Common stock is an equity account; thus, a common stock increase is recorded on the right or credit side.

Asset Acquisition

Assume that Apple purchases $2,000 worth of iPods from its supplier (we keep this illustration simple by ignoring Apple's manufacturing activities). When one company buys from another, it is normal to give a period of time in which to pay the obligation due, usually 30 to 60 days, or more. This purchase "on credit" (also called *on account*) means that Apple owes its supplier $2,000 for the purchase. Apple records the cost of the purchased iPods as an asset called inventories, which are goods held for resale. This acquisition of iPods on credit is recorded as follows.

	Balance Sheet									Income Statement				
Transaction	Cash Asset	+	Noncash Assets	=	Liabil-ities	+	Contrib. Capital	+	Earned Capital	Rev-enues	−	Expen-ses	=	Net Income
Purchase iPods for $2,000 on credit			+2,000 Inventory	=	+2,000 Accounts Payable						−		=	

INV 2,000
AP 2,000

INV	
2,000	

AP	
	2,000

Revenue and Expense Recognition

Assume that Apple sells iPods that cost $600 to a retailer for $700 on credit. The sale *on credit* means that the customer has not yet paid and Apple has a $700 account receivable. Can Apple record the $700 sale as revenue even though it has not collected any cash? The answer is yes. This decision reflects an important concept in accounting, called the **revenue recognition principle**. The revenue recognition principle prescribes that a company can recognize revenues provided that two conditions are met:

1. Revenues are *earned*, and
2. Revenues are *realized* or *realizable*.

Earned means that the company has done whatever it is required to do. In this case, it means that Apple has delivered the iPods to its retail customer. **Realized** or **realizable** means that the seller has either received cash or will receive cash at some point in the future. That is, Apple can recognize revenue if it expects to collect the $700 account receivable in the future.

Recording the $700 sale is only half the transaction. Apple must also record the decrease in iPod inventory of $600. When a company purchases inventory, it records the cost on the balance sheet as an asset. When inventory is sold, the "asset" is used up and its cost must be transferred from the balance sheet to the income statement as an expense. In particular, the expense associated with inventory is

---

[1] There can be more than one debit and one credit for a transaction. To illustrate, assume that Apple raises $300 cash, with $200 from investors and $100 borrowed from a bank. The resulting journal entry is:

Cash	300	
CS (common stock)		200
NP (note payable)		100

called cost of goods sold. Thus, the second part of Apple's revenue transaction is to remove the cost of the iPods from the balance sheet and recognize the cost of goods sold (an expense) in its income statement. This will record the cost of the inventory associated with this revenue.

Expenses are recorded as they are **incurred**. Once revenues are recognized (using the revenue recognition principle), we then record all related expenses incurred to generate those revenues *in the same period* that we recognize the revenue. This yields the proper measure of income for the period and is an application of accrual accounting.

The $700 sale of Apple iPods that cost $600 is recorded as follows.

AR 700
Sales 700

AR: 700 (debit)
Sales: 700 (credit)

COGS 600
INV 600

COGS: 600 (debit)
INV: 600 (credit)

	Balance Sheet									Income Statement				
Transaction	Cash Asset	+	Noncash Assets	=	Liabil-ities	+	Contrib. Capital	+	Earned Capital	Rev-enues	−	Expen-ses	=	Net Income
Sell $700 of iPods on credit			+700 Accounts Receivable	=					+700 Retained Earnings	+700 Sales	−		=	+700
Record $600 cost of iPod sale			−600 Inventory	=					−600 Retained Earnings		−	+600 Cost of Goods Sold	=	−600

The first part of this sales transaction records the $700 sale and the $700 increase in accounts receivable. Revenues are earned and therefore recognized even though no cash was received. The sale is reflected in the account receivable that will later be converted to cash. The increase in revenues increases income, which increases retained earnings.[2]

The second part of this sale transaction transfers the $600 in inventory on the balance sheet to the income statement as the cost of iPods sold. This entry increases expenses, and decreases both income and retained earnings. The transaction also reduces assets because Apple no longer owns the inventory; it is "used up."

Capital Distributions

Assume that Apple decides to pay $50 to its stockholders in the form of a cash dividend. Dividends are treated as a return of stockholders' investment. All transactions between the company and its stockholders are considered financing transactions. This includes payment of dividends, the issuance of stock, and any subsequent stock repurchase. Financing transactions affect only the balance sheet; they do not affect the income statement. Dividends are distributions of income. They represent the portion of income that the company chooses to distribute to stockholders—the portion that will no longer be retained. Thus, dividends reduce retained earnings. It is important to distinguish dividends from expenses—dividends are NOT an expense, they do not reduce net income. They are a distribution of net income; they reduce retained earnings. Apple's $50 dividend payment is reflected in the following template. (Companies typically record dividends in a separate dividends account and then later, in the closing process, this account is transferred to retained earnings. The template depicts dividends as a reduction of earned capital; more precisely, it is a reduction of retained earnings, which is part of earned capital. Alternatively, one could record dividends as an immediate reduction to retained earnings; the end result of both approaches is identical.)

DIV 50
Cash 50

DIV: 50 (debit)
Cash: 50 (credit)

	Balance Sheet									Income Statement				
Transaction	Cash Asset	+	Noncash Assets	=	Liabil-ities	+	Contrib. Capital	+	Earned Capital	Rev-enues	−	Expen-ses	=	Net Income
Pay $50 cash for dividends	−50 Cash			=					−50 Dividends		−		=	

[2] The retained earnings account is not automatically updated in most accounting software programs as our financial effects template illustrates. Instead, accountants transfer income to retained earnings using a journal entry as part of the closing process. We briefly explain the closing process near the end of this module and more fully in Appendix 3A.

MID-MODULE REVIEW 1

Assume that Samsung experienced the following six transactions relating to a capital investment, the purchase and sale of inventory, the collection of an account receivable, and the payment of an account payable.

1. Stockholders contribute $3,000 cash to Samsung in exchange for its common shares.
2. Samsung purchases $1,000 of inventory on credit.
3. Samsung sells $300 of inventory for $500 on credit.
4. Samsung collects $300 cash owed by customers.
5. Samsung pays $400 cash toward its accounts payable to suppliers.
6. Samsung pays $20 cash for dividends to its stockholders.

Required

Record each transaction in the financial statement effects template. Include journal entries for each account in the margin and post those entries to T-accounts.

The solution is on page 3-36.

ACCOUNTING ADJUSTMENTS (ACCRUALS)

LO2 Prepare and explain accounting adjustments and their financial statement effects.

Recognizing revenue when earned (even if not received in cash), and recording expenses when incurred (even if not paid in cash), are cornerstones of **accrual accounting**, which is required under GAAP.[3] Understanding accounting adjustments, commonly called *accruals*, is crucial to effectively analyzing and interpreting financial statements. In this module's Apple illustration, we recorded inventory as a purchase even though no cash was paid, and we recognized the sale as revenue even though no cash was received. Both of these transactions reflect accrual accounting. Some accounting adjustments affect the balance sheet alone (as with purchasing inventory on account). Other adjustments affect the balance sheet *and* the income statement (as with selling inventory on account). Accounting adjustments can affect asset, liability or equity accounts, and can either increase or decrease net income.

Companies make adjustments to more accurately report their financial performance and condition. For example, employees might not have been paid for wages earned at the end of an accounting period. Failure to recognize this labor cost would understate the company's total liabilities (because wages payable would be too low), and would overstate net income for the period (because wages expense would be too low). Thus, neither the balance sheet nor the income statement would be accurate.

Accounting adjustments yield a more accurate presentation of the economic results of a company for a period. Despite their generally beneficial effects, adjustments can be misused. Managers can use adjustments to bias reported income, rendering it higher or lower than it really is. Adjustments, if misused, can adversely affect business and investment decisions. Many recent accounting scandals have resulted from improper use of adjustments. Although outsiders cannot directly observe companies' specific accounting entries, their impact can be detected as changes in balance sheet and income statement accounts. Those changes provide signals for financial statement analysis. Consequently, understanding the accrual process will help us know what to look for as we analyze companies' financial reports. Exhibit 3.2 identifies four general types of accounting adjustments, which are briefly described below.

Prepaid expenses Prepaid expenses reflect advance cash payments that will ultimately become expenses. An example is the payment for radio advertising that will not be aired until sometime in the future.

Unearned revenues Unearned revenues reflect cash received from customers before any services or goods are provided. An example is cash received from patrons for tickets to an upcoming concert.

Accrued expenses Accrued expenses are expenses incurred and recognized on the income statement, even though they are not yet paid in cash. An example is wages owed to employees who performed work but who have not yet been paid.

[3] **Cash accounting** recognizes revenues when cash is received and expenses when cash is paid. This is not acceptable accounting under GAAP. However, small businesses that do not prepare financial reports for public investors and creditors sometimes use cash accounting.

Accrued revenues Accrued revenues are revenues earned and recognized on the income statement, even though cash is not yet received. Examples include sales on credit and revenue earned under a long-term contract.

EXHIBIT 3.2 Four Types of Accounting Adjustments

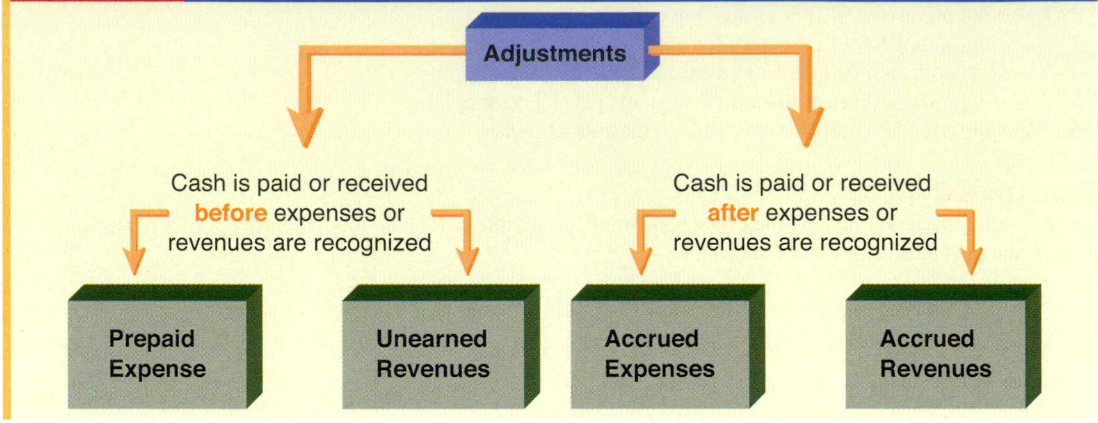

The remainder of this section illustrates how **Apple**'s financial statements would reflect each of these four types of adjustments.

Prepaid Expenses (Assets)

Assume that Apple pays $200 to purchase time on **MTV** for future iPod ads. Apple's cash account decreases by $200. Should the $200 advertising cost be recorded as an expense when Apple pays MTV, when MTV airs the ads, or at some other point? Under accrual accounting, Apple must record an expense when it is incurred. That means Apple should expense the cost of the ads when MTV airs them. When Apple pays for the advertisement, it records an asset; Apple "owns" TV time that will presumably provide future benefits when the ads air. In the interim, the cost of the ads is an asset on the balance sheet. Apple's financial statement effects template follows for this transaction. There is a decrease in cash and an increase in the advertising asset, titled prepaid advertising, when the ad time is paid for. At period-end, $50 of advertisements had aired. At that point, Apple must record an accounting adjustment to reduce the prepaid advertising account by $50 and transfer the cost to the income statement as advertising expense.

PPDA 200
Cash 200
PPDA: 200 |
Cash: | 200

AE 50
PPDA 50
AE: 50 |
PPDA: | 50

	Balance Sheet									Income Statement				
Transaction	Cash Asset	+	Noncash Assets	=	Liabilities	+	Contrib. Capital	+	Earned Capital	Revenues	−	Expenses	=	Net Income
Pay $200 cash in advance for ad time	−200 Cash		+200 Prepaid Advertising	=							−		=	
Record $50 cost of ad air time			−50 Prepaid Advertising	=					−50 Retained Earnings		−	+50 Advertising Expense	=	−50

Unearned Revenues (Liabilities)

Assume that Apple receives $400 cash from a customer as advance payment on a multi-unit iPod sale to be delivered next month. Apple must record cash received on its balance sheet, but cannot recognize revenue from the order until earned, which is generally when iPods are delivered to the customer. Until then, Apple must recognize a liability called unearned or deferred revenue that represents Apple's obligation to fulfill the order at some future point. The financial statement effects template for this transaction follows.

Transaction	Cash Asset	+	Noncash Assets	=	Liabilities	+	Contrib. Capital	+	Earned Capital	Revenues	−	Expenses	=	Net Income
	Balance Sheet									**Income Statement**				
Receive $400 cash in advance for iPod sale	+400 Cash			=	+400 Unearned Revenue						−		=	

Cash 400
UR 400

Cash
400 |

UR
| 400

Assume that Apple delivers the iPods a month later (but still within the fiscal quarter). Apple must recognize the $400 as revenue at delivery because it is now earned. Thus, net income increases by $400. The second part of this transaction is to record the cost of the iPods sold. Assuming the cost is $150, Apple reduces iPod inventory by $150 and records cost of goods sold by the same amount. These effects are reflected in the following template.

Transaction	Cash Asset	+	Noncash Assets	=	Liabilities	+	Contrib. Capital	+	Earned Capital	Revenues	−	Expenses	=	Net Income
	Balance Sheet									**Income Statement**				
Deliver $400 of iPods paid in advance				=	−400 Unearned Revenues				+400 Retained Earnings	+400 Sales	−		=	+400
Record $150 cost of $400 iPod sale			−150 Inventory	=					−150 Retained Earnings		−	+150 Cost of Goods Sold	=	−150

UR 400
Sales 400

UR
400 |

Sales
| 400

COGS 150
INV 150

COGS
150 |

INV
| 150

Accrued Expenses (Liabilities)

Assume that Apple's sales staff earns $100 of sales commissions this period that will not be paid until next period. The sales staff earned the wages as they made the sales. However, because Apple pays its employees twice a month, the related cash payment will not occur until the next pay period. Should Apple record the wages earned by its employees as an expense even though payment has not yet been made? The answer is yes. The expense recognition principle requires Apple to recognize wages expense when it is *incurred*, even if not paid in cash. It must record wages expense incurred as a liability (wages payable). In the next period, when Apple pays the wages, it reduces both cash and wages payable. Net income is not affected by the cash payment; instead, net income decreased in the previous period when Apple accrued the wage expense.

Transaction	Cash Asset	+	Noncash Assets	=	Liabilities	+	Contrib. Capital	+	Earned Capital	Revenues	−	Expenses	=	Net Income
	Balance Sheet									**Income Statement**				
Current period: Incur $100 of wages not yet paid				=	+100 Wages Payable				−100 Retained Earnings		−	+100 Wages Expense	=	−100
Next period: Pay $100 cash for accrued wages	−100 Cash			=	−100 Wages Payable						−		=	

WE 100
WP 100

WE
100 |

WP
| 100

WP 100
Cash 100

WP
100 |

Cash
| 100

As another example of accrued expenses, assume that Apple rents office space and that it owes $25 in rent at period-end. Apple has incurred rent expense in the current period and that expense must be recorded this period. Failing to make this adjustment would mean that Apple's liabilities (rent payable) would be understated and its income would be overstated. The entry to record the accrual of rent expense for office space follows.

RNTE 25
RNTP 25

RNTE
25 |

RNTP
| 25

	Balance Sheet					Income Statement		
Transaction	Cash Asset	+ Noncash Assets	= Liabil-ities	+ Contrib. Capital	+ Earned Capital	Rev-enues	− Expen-ses	= Net Income
Incur $25 of rent not yet paid			= +25 Rent Payable		−25 Retained Earnings		− +25 Rent Expense	= −25

Accrued Revenues (Assets)

Assume that Apple delivers iPods to a customer in Boston who will pay next quarter. The sales price for those units is $500 and the cost is $400. Apple has completed its revenue earning process with this sale and must accrue revenue from the Boston customer even though Apple received no cash. Like all sales transactions, Apple must record two parts, the sales revenue and the cost of sales. The financial effects template for this two-part transaction follows.

AR 500
Sales 500

AR
500 |

Sales
| 500

COGS 400
INV 400

COGS
400 |

INV
| 400

	Balance Sheet					Income Statement		
Transaction	Cash Asset	+ Noncash Assets	= Liabil-ities	+ Contrib. Capital	+ Earned Capital	Rev-enues	− Expen-ses	= Net Income
Sell $500 of iPods on credit		+500 Accounts Receivable	=		+500 Retained Earnings	+500 Sales	−	= +500
Record $400 cost of $500 iPod sale		−400 Inventory	=		−400 Retained Earnings		− +400 Cost of Goods Sold	= −400

Summary of Accounting Adjustments

Adjustments are an important part of the accounting process and are crucial to accurate and informative financial accounting. It is through the accruals process that managers communicate information about future cash flows. For example, from accrual information, we know that Apple paid for a resource (inventories) that it has not yet sold. We know that suppliers have money owed to them (accounts payable) but Apple won't pay them until a future period. We know that revenues have been earned but cash is not yet received (accounts receivable). Those accruals tell us about Apple's past performance and, perhaps more importantly, about Apple's future cash flows. When used properly, accruals convey information about the past and the future that is useful in our evaluation of company financial performance and condition. Thus, we can use accrual information to more precisely value companies' equity and debt securities.

Not all managers are honest; some misuse accounting accruals to improperly recognize revenues and expenses. Abuses include accruing revenue before it is earned; and accruing expenses in the wrong period or in the wrong amount. These actions are fraudulent as they deliberately overstate or understate revenues and expenses and, thus, reported net income is incorrect. Safeguards against this type of managerial behavior include corporate governance systems (internal controls, accounting policies and procedures, routine scrutiny of accounting reports by internal auditors, and audit committees) and external checks and balances (independent auditors, regulatory bodies, and the court system). Collectively, these safeguards aim to protect interests of companies' internal and external stakeholders. When managers abuse accounting systems, tough and swift sanctions remind others that corporate malfeasance is unacceptable. Videos of police officers leading corporate executives to jail in handcuffs (the infamous "perp walk") send that message.

RESEARCH INSIGHT **Accruals: Good or Bad?**

Researchers use accounting accruals to study the effects of earnings management on financial accounting. Earnings management is broadly defined as the use of accounting discretion to distort reported earnings. Managers have incentives to manage earnings in many situations. For example, managers have tendencies to accelerate revenue recognition to increase stock prices prior to equity offerings. In contrast, other research shows that managers decelerate revenue recognition to depress stock prices prior to a management buyout (where management repurchases common stock and takes the company "private"). Research also shows that managers use discretion when reporting special items to either meet or beat analysts' forecasts of earnings and/or to avoid reporting a loss. Not all earnings management occurs for opportunistic reasons. Research shows that managers use accruals to communicate private information about future profitability to outsiders. For example, management might signal future profitability through use of income-decreasing accruals to show investors that it can afford to apply conservative accounting. This "signaling" through accruals is found to precede stock splits and dividend increases. In sum, we must look at reported earnings in conjunction with other earnings quality signals (such as levels of disclosure, degree of corporate governance, and industry performance) to interpret information in accruals.

Trial Balance Preparation and Use

LO3 Explain and construct the trial balance.

After Apple records all of its transactions, it must prepare financial statements so it can assess its financial performance and condition for the quarter. The following template shows a summary of Apple's transactions thus far.

The first step in preparing financial statements is to prepare a **trial balance**, which is a listing of all accounts and their balances at a point in time. Its purpose is to prove the mathematical equality of debits and credits, provide a useful tool to uncover any accounting errors, and help prepare the financial statements. To prepare a trial balance we compile a listing of accounts and their balances, we determine whether that balance is a debit or credit, and then we check to ensure that the total of all debit balances equals the total of all credit balances. (If those totals do not agree, then an accounting error has occurred that must be identified and corrected.) The accounting adjustments at period-end, discussed earlier in this module, are set in dark green font.

	Balance Sheet									Income Statement				
Transaction	**Cash Asset**	+	**Noncash Assets**	=	**Liabil-ities**	+	**Contrib. Capital**	+	**Earned Capital**	**Rev-enues**	−	**Expen-ses**	=	**Net Income**
Issue stock for $300 cash	+300 Cash			=			+300 Common Stock				−		=	
Purchase $2,000 of iPods on credit			+2,000 Inventory	=	+2,000 Accounts Payable						−		=	
Sell $700 of iPods on credit			+700 Accounts Receivable	=					+700 Retained Earnings	+700 Sales	−		=	+700
Record $600 cost of $700 iPod sale			−600 Inventory	=					−600 Retained Earnings		−	+600 Cost of Goods Sold	=	−600
Pay $50 cash for dividends	−50 Cash			=					−50 Dividends		−		=	
Pay $200 cash in advance for ad time	−200 Cash		+200 Prepaid Advertising	=							−		=	
Record $50 cost of ad air time			−50 Prepaid Advertising	=					−50 Retained Earnings		−	+50 Advertising Expense	=	−50
Receive $400 cash in advance for iPod sale	+400 Cash			=	+400 Unearned Revenue						−		=	
Deliver $400 of iPods paid in advance				=	−400 Unearned Revenue				+400 Retained Earnings	+400 Sales	−		=	+400
Record $150 cost of $400 iPod sale			−150 Inventory	=					−150 Retained Earnings		−	+150 Cost of Goods Sold	=	−150
Incur $100 of wages not yet paid				=	+100 Wages Payable				−100 Retained Earnings		−	+100 Wages Expense	=	−100
Incur $25 of rent not yet paid				=	+25 Rent Payable				−25 Retained Earnings		−	+25 Rent Expense	=	−25
Sell $500 of iPods on credit			+500 Accounts Receivable	=					+500 Retained Earnings	+500 Sales	−		=	+500
Record $400 cost of $500 iPod sale			−400 Inventory	=					−400 Retained Earnings		−	+400 Cost of Goods Sold	=	−400
Total	450	+	2,200	=	2,125	+	300	+	225	1,600	−	1,325	=	275

Entries for transactions involving accounting adjustments are set in dark green font.

Cash 300
CS 300
Cash: 300 |
CS: | 300

INV 2,000
AP 2,000
INV: 2,000 |
AP: | 2,000

AR 700
Sales 700
AR: 700 |
Sales: | 700

COGS 600
INV 600
COGS: 600 |
INV: | 600

DIV 50
Cash 50
DIV: 50 |
Cash: | 50

PPDA 200
Cash 200
PPDA: 200 |
Cash: | 200

AE 50
PPDA 50
AE: 50 |
PPDA: | 50

Cash 400
UR 400
Cash: 400 |
UR: | 400

UR 400
Sales 400
UR: 400 |
Sales: | 400

COGS 150
INV 150
COGS: 150 |
INV: | 150

WE 100
WP 100
WE: 100 |
WP: | 100

RNTE 25
RNTP 25
RNTE: 25 |
RNTP: | 25

AR 500
Sales 500
AR: 500 |
Sales: | 500

COGS 400
INV 400
COGS: 400 |
INV: | 400

The trial balance for Apple, which we assume to be as of December 31, 2014, follows.

APPLE Trial Balance December 31, 2014	Debit	Credit
Cash	$ 450	
Accounts receivable	1,200	
Inventory	850	
Prepaid advertising	150	
Accounts payable		$2,000
Wages payable		100
Rent payable		25
Unearned revenues		0
Common stock		300
Dividends	50	
Sales		1,600
Cost of goods sold	1,150	
Wages expense	100	
Advertising expense	50	
Rent expense	25	
Totals	$4,025	$4,025

The trial balance amounts consist of the ending balance for each of the accounts. For the Apple illustration, we total all transactions for each account listed in the template. To illustrate, cash has an ending balance of $450 ($300 − $50 − $200 + $400). Also, because cash is an asset (which is on the left-hand side of the balance sheet), it normally has a debit balance (which is on the left-hand side of the T-accounts). We can confirm the ending cash debit balance by totalling each of the cash T-account entries. Liabilities and equity accounts normally have credit balances (because they are on the right-hand side of the balance sheet), and we can confirm these ending credit balances by referring to individual account balances in the template. (See that Apple's trial balance includes all of the income statement accounts as well as the dividend account, but it does not include the retained earnings account from the financial statement effects template. This is because the template updates retained earnings immediately for each transaction. If we did include both the income statement accounts *and* retained earnings, we would double count all income statement transactions. Most companies' accounting systems do not update retained earnings immediately, which means the retained earnings balance [on the trial balance] is the beginning balance, which for our Apple example is zero.)

The trial balance shows total debits equal $4,025, which equals total credits. Accordingly, we know that all of the template transactions balance. We do not know, however, that all required journal entries have been properly included, or if Apple recorded entries that it should not have.

Precisely speaking, the trial balance above is an **adjusted trial balance**, prepared after all accounting adjustments have been recorded. In practice, we will also encounter an **unadjusted trial balance**, which is a trial balance prepared *before* the accounting adjustments are recorded. For the Apple example here, we show the following spreadsheet that contains the unadjusted and adjusted trial balances, along with middle columns containing the accounting adjustments. Remember that *financial statements are prepared from the adjusted trial balance*.

APPLE Trial Balances December 31, 2014	Unadjusted		Adjustments		Adjusted	
	Debit	Credit	Debit	Credit	Debit	Credit
Cash	$ 450				$ 450	
Accounts receivable	700		$ 500		1,200	
Inventory	1,250			$ 400	850	
Prepaid advertising	200			50	150	
Accounts payable		$2,000				$2,000
Wages payable		0		100		100
Rent payable		0		25		25
Unearned revenues		0				0
Common stock		300				300
Dividends	50				50	
Sales		1,100		500		1,600
Cost of goods sold	750		400		1,150	
Wages expense	0		100		100	
Advertising expense	0		50		50	
Rent expense	0		25		25	
Totals	$3,400	$3,400	$1,075	$1,075	$4,025	$4,025

MID-MODULE REVIEW 2

Refer to the transactions in Mid-Module Review 1. Assume that Samsung has the following two additional transactions (*a* and *b*) and four accounting adjustments (1 through 4).

a. Samsung pays $100 cash for current and future periods' rent of VoIP software.
b. Samsung receives $500 cash in advance from a client for consulting services.

1. As of period-end, Samsung had incurred rent expense of $30; $70 of the prepayment remains for future periods.
2. As of period-end, Samsung had earned $80 of the $500 paid in advance for consulting services.
3. Samsung employees earn $40 in wages that will not be paid until the next period.
4. Samsung provides $150 of services revenue but has not yet billed the client.

Required

Record each of the two accounting transactions and four adjustments using the financial statement effects template. Also record the journal entry for each in the margin and post each entry to T-accounts. Prepare a trial balance spreadsheet that contains columns for the unadjusted and adjusted trial balances and for the accounting adjustments. The unadjusted trial balance should reflect those transactions for Samsung from Mid-Module Review 1 and the two transactions *a* and *b* above.

The solution is on page 3-37.

FINANCIAL STATEMENT PREPARATION

LO4 Construct financial statements from the trial balance.

Financial statement preparation involves working with the accounts in the adjusted trial balance to properly report them in financial statements. There is an order to financial statement preparation. First, a company prepares its income statement using the income statement accounts. It then uses the net income number and dividend information to update the retained earnings account. Second, it prepares the balance sheet using the updated retained earnings account along with the remaining balance sheet accounts from the trial balance. Third, it prepares the statement of stockholders' equity. Fourth, it prepares the statement of cash flows using information from the cash account (and other sources).

Income Statement

Apple's income statement follows. Apple's trial balance reveals four income statement accounts. Those income statement accounts are called *temporary accounts* because they begin each accounting period with a zero balance. Apple's income statement also includes a line for gross profit because that subtotal is important to evaluate manufacturers' performance and profitability. Income for this quarterly period is $275 (we ignore taxes in this illustration).

APPLE Income Statement For Quarter Ended December 31, 2014	
Sales	$1,600
Cost of goods sold	1,150
Gross profit	450
Wages expense	100
Advertising expense	50
Rent expense	25
Net income	$ 275

Retained Earnings Computation

Apple updates its retained earnings balance at period-end using income from the income statement and the dividend information from its trial balance. (For simplicity, we assume retained earnings is zero at the beginning of this period.) This computation follows.

APPLE Retained Earnings Computation For Quarter Ended December 31, 2014	
Retained earnings, beginning of period	$ 0
Add: Net income (loss)	275
Deduct: Dividends	(50)
Retained earnings, end of period	$225

Balance Sheet

Once Apple computes the ending balance in retained earnings, it can prepare its balance sheet, which follows. Balance sheet accounts are called *permanent accounts* because their respective balances carry over from one period to the next. For example, the cash balance at the end of the current accounting period (ended December 31, 2014) is $450, which will be the balance at the beginning of the next accounting period (beginning January 1, 2015).

APPLE Balance Sheet December 31, 2014	
Assets	
Cash	$ 450
Accounts receivable	1,200
Inventory	850
Prepaid advertising	150
Total assets	$2,650
Liabilities and Stockholders' Equity	
Liabilities	
Accounts payable	$2,000
Wages payable	100
Rent payable	25
Total liabilities	2,125
Stockholders' equity	
Common stock	300
Retained earnings	225
Total stockholders' equity	525
Total liabilities and stockholders' equity	$2,650

Statement of Stockholders' Equity

Apple uses the information pertaining to its contributed capital and earned capital categories to prepare the statement of stockholders' equity, as follows.

APPLE Statement of Stockholders' Equity For Quarter Ended December 31, 2014	Contributed Capital	Earned Capital	Total Stockholders' Equity
Beginning balance	**$ 0**	**$ 0**	**$ 0**
Stock issuance	300		300
Net income (loss)		275	275
Dividends		(50)	(50)
Ending balance	**$300**	**$225**	**$525**

Statement of Cash Flows

The statement of cash flows summarizes the cash-based transactions for the period and reports the sources and uses of cash. Each cash transaction represents an operating, investing, or financing activity.

Direct Method Presentation

To prepare the statement, Apple uses the Cash column of the financial statement effects template (see above). The following cash flow statement for Apple is based on the **direct method** for reporting operating cash flows. During the current period, Apple's cash increased by $450. Its increase in cash consists of a $200 net cash inflow from operating activities plus a $250 net cash inflow from financing activities. There were no investing activities during this period.

APPLE Statement of Cash Flows (Direct Method) For Quarter Ended December 31, 2014	
Operating activities	
Receipts from sales contracts	$400
Payments for advertising	(200)
Net cash flows from operating activities	200
Investing activities	
Net cash flows from investing activities	0
Financing activities	
Issuance of common stock	300
Payment of cash dividends	(50)
Net cash flows from financing activities	250
Net change in cash	450
Cash, beginning of period	0
Cash, end of period	$450

In practice, preparing a statement of cash flows is more complicated. Companies can have millions of transactions in the cash account and the task of classifying each transaction as operating, investing or financing would be costly and time-consuming. Instead, companies prepare the statement of cash flows using the current income statement and the balance sheets for the current and prior periods. The basic approach is to adjust net income to arrive at net cash flows from operating activities (the so-called *indirect method*) and then review changes in balance sheet accounts (by comparing the opening and ending balances) to arrive at net cash flows from investing and financing activities.

Indirect Method Presentation

There are two methods to display net cash flows from operating activities: the direct method and the indirect method. Both methods report the same net operating cash flow, the only difference is in presentation. Companies can choose which method to follow. Apple's simplified statement of cash flows above, is an example of the direct method. However, the **indirect method** is, by far, the more widely used method in practice today (over 98% of public companies use it). The indirect method computes operating cash flows *indirectly* by adjusting net income using the following format.

		Add (+) or Subtract (−) from Net Income
	Net income	$ #
Adjustments for noncash revenues, expenses, gains and losses	Add: depreciation expense	+
Adjustments for changes in noncash current operating assets and current operating liabilities	Adjust for changes in current operating assets	
	Subtract increases in current operating assets	−
	Add decreases in current operating assets	+
	Adjust for changes in current operating liabilities	
	Add increases in current operating liabilities	+
	Subtract decreases in current operating liabilities	−
	Net cash flow from operating activities	$ #

Net income is first adjusted for noncash expenses such as depreciation and amortization, and is then adjusted for changes during the year in current operating assets and current operating liabilities to yield cash flow from operating activities, or *cash profit*. The depreciation adjustment merely zeros out (undoes the effect of) depreciation expense, a noncash expense, which is deducted in computing net income. The following table provides brief explanations of adjustments for receivables, inventories, and payables and accruals.

	Change in account balance . . .	Means that . . .	Which requires this adjustment to net income to yield cash profit . . .
Receivables	Increase	Sales and net income increase, but cash is not yet received	Deduct increase in receivables from net income
	Decrease	More cash is received than is reported in sales and net income	Add decrease in receivables to net income
Inventories	Increase	Cash is paid for inventories that are not yet reflected in cost of goods sold	Deduct increase in inventories from net income
	Decrease	Cost of goods sold includes inventory costs that were paid for in a prior period	Add decrease in inventories to net income
Payables and accruals	Increase	More goods and services are acquired on credit, delaying cash payment	Add increase in payables and accruals to net income
	Decrease	More cash is paid than that reflected in cost of goods sold or operating expenses	Deduct decrease in payables and accruals from net income

It is also helpful to use the following decision guide, involving changes in assets, liabilities, and equity, to understand increases and decreases in cash flows.

	Cash flow increases from	Cash flow decreases from
Assets	Account decreases	Account increases
Liabilities and equity	Account increases	Account decreases

Using this decision guide, we can determine the cash flow effects of the income statement and balance sheet information and categorize them into the following table for our Apple illustration.

Financial Element	Change	Source or Use	Cash Flow Effect	Classification on SCF
Current assets				
Accounts receivable	+ $1,200	Use	$(1,200)	Operating
Inventory	+ 850	Use	(850)	Operating
Prepaid advertising	+ 150	Use	(150)	Operating
Noncurrent assets				
PPE	0		0	Investing
Accumulated depreciation		Neither	0*	Operating
Current liabilities				
Accounts payable	+ 2,000	Source	2,000	Operating
Wages payable	+ 100	Source	100	Operating
Rent payable	+ 25	Source	25	Operating
Long-term liabilities	0		0	Financing
Stockholders' equity				
Common stock	+ 300	Source	300	Financing
Retained earnings				
Net income	+ 275	Source	275	Operating
Dividends	+ 50	Use	(50)	Financing
Total (net cash flow)			$ 450	

*Depreciation expense for the period, if present, is added to net income in computing cash flows from operating activities.

Increases in the three current operating assets reflect a use of cash, and are subtracted in the operating section of the statement of cash flows. Increases in noncurrent PPE assets also reflect a use of cash, which are classified as an investing activity. An increase in accumulated depreciation reflects the recording of depreciation expense in the income statement, which is a noncash expense that must be zeroed out (with an addition to net income) to yield cash profit. Increases in the three current operating liabilities reflect sources of cash, and are recorded as positive amounts in the statement of cash flows.

APPLE
Statement of Cash Flows (Indirect Method)
For Quarter Ended December 31, 2014

Operating activities	
Net income	$ 275
Depreciation and other noncash expenses	0
Increase in accounts receivable	(1,200)
Increase in inventories	(850)
Increase in prepaid advertising	(150)
Increase in accounts payable	2,000
Increase in wages payable	100
Increase in rent payable	25
Net cash flows from operating activities	200
Investing activities	
Net cash flows from investing activities	0
Financing activities	
Issuance of common stock	300
Payment of cash dividends	(50)
Net cash flows from financing activities	250
Net change in cash	450
Cash, beginning of period	0
Cash, end of period	$ 450

Issuance of common stock is a source of cash, and the payment of dividends to stockholders is a use of cash. Both of these are reflected in the financing section of the statement of cash flows. The financing section also reflects any increases or decreases in borrowings as sources or uses, respectively. The increase in retained earnings, resulting from net income, is a source of cash, but it is reported as an operating activity. (Components of the change in retained earnings, net income less dividends, are reflected in the statement of cash flows and, consequently, the change in retained earnings is already recognized.)

The sum of these elements yields a net increase in cash of $450. This is the same result we obtained earlier using the direct method. To reiterate, the indirect method represents a different presentation of the operating section only of the statement of cash flows. The investing and financing sections are identical under the direct and indirect approaches. Reporting these elements by operating, investing and financing activities yields the familiar form of the statement of cash flows previously shown.

Closing Process

LO5 Describe the closing process.

The **closing process** refers to "zeroing out" the temporary accounts by transferring their ending balances to retained earnings. Recall, income statement accounts—revenues and expenses—and the dividend account are temporary accounts because their balances are zero at the end of each accounting period; balance sheet accounts carry over from period to period and are called permanent accounts. The closing process is typically carried out via a series of journal entries that successively zero out each revenue and expense account, and the dividend account, transferring those balances to retained earnings. The result is that all income statement accounts and the dividend account begin the next period with zero balances. The balance sheet accounts do not need to be similarly adjusted because their balances carry over from period to period. Recall the scoreboard analogy.

Our financial statement effects template makes the closing process unnecessary because the template updates retained earnings with each revenue and expense entry. The arrow that runs from net income to retained earnings (part of earned capital) highlights the continual updating. To illustrate, recall the following entries that reflect Apple's initial sale of iPods on credit.

	Balance Sheet									Income Statement				
Transaction	Cash Asset	+	Noncash Assets	=	Liabil-ities	+	Contrib. Capital	+	Earned Capital	Rev-enues	−	Expen-ses	=	Net Income
Sell $700 of iPods on credit			+700 Accounts Receivable	=					+700 Retained Earnings	+700 Sales	−		=	+700
Record $600 cost of $700 iPod sale			−600 Inventory	=					−600 Retained Earnings		−	+600 Cost of Goods Sold	=	−600

AR 700
Sales 700

AR: 700 (debit)
Sales: 700 (credit)

COGS 600
INV 600

COGS: 600 (debit)
INV: 600 (credit)

Sales of $700 increase net income by $700, which the template immediately transfers to retained earnings. Likewise, cost of goods sold reduces net income by $600, and this reduction is immediately carried to retained earnings. Consequently, the financial statement effects template always reports an updated retained earnings, making the closing process unnecessary.

It is important to distinguish our financial statement effects template from companies' accounting systems. The financial statement effects template and T-accounts are pedagogical tools that represent transactions' effects on the four financial statements. The template is highly stylized but its simplicity is instructive. In practice, managers use journal entries to record transactions and adjustments. The template captures these in summarized fashion. However, in practice, income statement transactions are not automatically transferred to retained earnings and retained earnings is not continuously updated. All companies perform the closing process—someone or some program must transfer the temporary account balances to retained earnings. Thus, it is important to understand the closing process and why companies "close" the books each period. We describe the mechanical details of the closing process in Appendix 3A.

The entire accounting process, from analysis of basic transactions to financial statement preparation to the closing process, is called the **accounting cycle**. As we discuss at the outset of this module and portray graphically in Exhibit 3.1, there are four basic processes in the accounting cycle.

First, companies analyze transactions and prepare (and post) entries. Second, companies prepare (and post) accounting adjustments. Third, financial statements are prepared from an adjusted trial balance. Fourth, companies perform the closing process. The analysis and posting of transactions is done regularly during each accounting period. However, the preparation of accounting adjustments and financial statements is only done at the end of an accounting period. At this point, we have explained and illustrated all aspects of the accounting cycle.

MANAGERIAL DECISION **You Are the CFO**

Assume that you learn of the leakage of hazardous waste from your company's factory. It is estimated that cleanup could cost $10 million. Part 1: What effect will recording this cost have on your company's balance sheet and its income statement? Part 2: Accounting rules require you to record this cost if it is both probable and can be reliably estimated. Although the cleanup is relatively certain, the cost is a guess at this point. Consequently, you have some discretion whether to record it. Discuss the parties that are likely affected by your decision on whether or not to record the liability and related expense, and the ethical issues involved. [Answer p. 3-23]

GLOBAL ACCOUNTING

The way that accounting data is gathered and recorded does not differ across accounting standards. Thus, the accounting cycle in Exhibit 3.1 applies in countries using IFRS in the same manner as in the United States. The difference is that companies create information systems that conform to the specific accounting rules in that country. For example, the rules for recording research and development (R&D) costs are different in the United States vis-à-vis Germany. Thus, the U.S. and the German company would each tailor their accounting systems to properly record R&D costs so that each company's financial statements comply with their respective countries' accounting standards. The accounting cycle of each company still involves transactions and adjustments and a closing process. The result is that identical R&D expenditures are classified differently and the resulting financial statements diverge.

Large multinational companies often have subsidiaries in different countries. If a U.S. company has a foreign subsidiary, the foreign laws often require a domestic set of financial statements for tax, regulatory, banking, or other purposes. For example, **Apple**'s 2013 Form 10-K reports that it has four major foreign subsidiaries: Apple Sales International, Apple Operations Europe, and Apple Operations International, each of these three are incorporated in Ireland where IFRS is used; and Braeburn Capital, a U.S. company that uses GAAP. The Irish subsidiaries must prepare IFRS financial statements to file with the Irish Revenue Commission (the Irish equivalent of the IRS). During the closing process of the accounting cycle, Apple Inc. (the U.S. parent) must consolidate the four subsidiaries, which means that all assets and liabilities of the four subsidiaries are included on Apple Inc.'s balance sheet. Similarly, all of the revenues and expenses of the four subsidiaries are included on Apple Inc.'s income statement. It would not be appropriate for a simple summing of accounts because of differences between IFRS and U.S. GAAP. Instead, Apple Inc. must convert IFRS financial statements to U.S. GAAP equivalent (as well as convert euros to U.S. dollars). To accomplish this, Apple Inc. might keep two sets of accounting records for subsidiaries, one set in GAAP and the other in IFRS. This is not as complicated as it might seem. Companies like Apple use sophisticated computer accounting systems and enterprise resource planning (ERP) systems that are capable of supporting multiple sets of accounting standards.

MODULE-END REVIEW

Refer to the transactions in Mid-Module Reviews 1 and 2. From those transactions, assume that **Samsung** prepares the following adjusted trial balance. Also assume its transactions are for the year ended December 31, 2014.

SAMSUNG **Adjusted Trial Balance** **December 31, 2014**	**Debit**	**Credit**
Cash	$3,280	
Accounts receivable	350	
Inventory	700	
Prepaid rent	70	
Accounts payable		$ 600
Wages payable		40
Unearned revenues		420
Common stock		3,000
Dividends	20	
Sales		730
Cost of goods sold	300	
Wages expense	40	
Rent expense	30	
Totals	$4,790	$4,790

Required

Prepare **Samsung**'s income statement (including a separate retained earnings computation), statement of stockholders' equity, balance sheet, and statement of cash flows.

The solution is on page 3-38.

APPENDIX 3A: Closing Process Using Journal Entries

The idea of the closing process is to zero out all temporary accounts—all the income statement accounts and any dividend account. The balance in each temporary account is transferred to retained earnings leaving the temporary accounts with zero balances. That way, the temporary accounts are ready to capture transaction data for the next period. The closing process brings the retained earnings account up to date so that it accurately reflects the current period's income statement activity and dividends so that the balance sheet can be prepared. To illustrate, let's return to Apple's income statement.

APPLE **Income Statement** **For Quarter Ended December 31, 2014**	
Sales	$1,600
Cost of goods sold	1,150
Gross profit	450
Wages expense	100
Advertising expense	50
Rent expense	25
Net income	$ 275

The closing process transfers the ending balances for each of these income statement accounts, to retained earnings. The dividend account is a temporary account and therefore, it also must be closed to retained earnings. The journal entries, and the related T-accounts, follow for this three-step process.

1. Close all revenue accounts.

Sales	1,600	
RE		1,600

Sales	
1,600	

RE	
	1,600

2. Close all expense accounts.

RE	1,150	
COGS		1,150

RE		COGS	
1,150			1,150

RE	100	
WE		100

RE		WE	
100			100

RE	50	
AE		50

RE		AE	
50			50

RE	25	
RNTE		25

RE		RNTE	
25			25

3. Close any dividend accounts.

RE	50	
DIV		50

RE		DIV	
50			50

Apple must close one revenue account, four expense accounts, and a dividend account to retained earnings at the end of the period. The first closing entry transfers the $1,600 balance in the sales account to retained earnings. The closing entry debits sales for $1,600 (because the sales account has a $1,600 credit balance at period-end) and credits retained earnings. The second closing entry closes cost of goods sold ($1,150), wages expense ($100), advertising expense ($50), and rent expense ($25). The entry credits each of the expense accounts because their ending balances are debit balances. Third, the $50 dividend account balance is transferred to retained earnings. All the temporary accounts are now *closed.*

Retained earnings, which began the period with a zero balance, now reports a balance of $225, which equals net income for the period less the dividends paid to stockholders. This is the balance Apple reports in the stockholders' equity section of its balance sheet. Further, all of the income statement accounts (sales, cost of goods sold, wages expense, advertising expense, and rent expense) and the dividend account now show zero balances to begin the next period.

GUIDANCE ANSWERS

MANAGERIAL DECISION **You Are the CFO**

Part 1: Liabilities will increase by $10 million for the estimated amount of the cleanup, and an expense in that amount will be recognized in the income statement, thus reducing both income and retained earnings (equity) by $10 million. Part 2: Stakeholders affected by recognition decisions of this type are often much broader than first realized. Management is directly involved in the decision. Recording this cost can affect the market value of the company, its relations with lenders and suppliers, its auditors, and many other stakeholders. Further, if recording this cost is the right accounting decision, failure to do so can foster unethical behavior throughout the company, thus affecting additional company employees.

Superscript A denotes assignments based on Appendix 3A.

DISCUSSION QUESTIONS

Q3-1. What does the term *fiscal year* mean?

Q3-2. What is the purpose of a general journal?

Q3-3. Explain the process of posting.

Q3-4. What four different types of adjustments are frequently necessary before financial statements are prepared at the end of an accounting period? Give at least one example of each type.

Q3-5. On January 1, Prepaid Insurance was debited for $1,896 related to the cost of a two-year premium, with coverage beginning immediately. How should this account be adjusted on January 31 before financial statements are prepared for the current month?

Q3-6. At the beginning of January, the first month of the accounting year, the Supplies account (asset) had a debit balance of $875. During January, purchases of $260 worth of supplies were debited to the account. At the end of January, $630 of supplies were still available. How should this account be adjusted? If no adjustment is made, describe the impact on (a) the income statement for January, and (b) the balance sheet prepared at January 31.

Q3-7. The publisher of *Accounting View*, a monthly magazine, received $9,768 cash on January 1 for new subscriptions covering the next 24 months, with service beginning immediately. (a) Use the financial statement effects template to record the receipt of the $9,768. (b) Use the template to show how the accounts should be adjusted at the end of January before financial statements are prepared for the current month.

Q3-8. Refer to Question Q3-7. Prepare journal entries for the receipt of cash and the delivery of the magazines.

Q3-9. Trombley Travel Agency pays an employee $950 in wages each Friday for the five-day work week ending on Friday. The last Friday of January falls on January 27. How should Trombley Travel Agency adjust wages expense on January 31, its fiscal year-end?

Q3-10. The Basu Company earns interest amounting to $720 per month on its investments. The company receives the interest revenue every six months, on December 31 and June 30. Monthly financial statements are prepared. Which accounts should Basu adjust on January 31?

Q3-11.[A] What types of accounts are closed at the end of the accounting year? What are the three major steps in the closing process?

Assignments with the ✔ logo in the margin are available in myBusinessCourse.
See the Preface of the book for details.

MINI EXERCISES

M3-12. Assessing Financial Statement Effects of Transactions **(LO1)** ✔

DeFond Services, a firm providing art services for advertisers, began business on June 1. The following accounts are needed to record the transactions for June: Cash; Accounts Receivable; Supplies; Office Equipment; Accounts Payable; Common Stock; Dividends; Service Fees Earned; Rent Expense; Utilities Expense; and Wages Expense. Record the following transactions for June using the financial statement effects template.

June	1	M. DeFond invested $12,000 cash to begin the business in exchange for common stock.
	2	Paid $950 cash for June rent.
	3	Purchased $6,400 of office equipment on credit.
	6	Purchased $3,800 of art materials and other supplies; the company paid $1,800 cash with the remainder due within 30 days.
	11	Billed clients $4,700 for services rendered.
	17	Collected $3,250 cash from clients on their accounts billed on June 11.
	19	Paid $5,000 cash toward the account for office equipment (see June 3).
	25	Paid $900 cash for dividends.
	30	Paid $350 cash for June utilities.
	30	Paid $2,500 cash for June wages.

M3-13. Preparing Journal Entries and Posting (LO1)
Refer to the information in M3-12. Prepare a journal entry for each transaction. Create a T-account for each account, and then post the journal entries to the T-accounts (use dates to reference each entry).

M3-14. Assessing Financial Statement Effects of Transactions (LO1)
Verrecchia Company, a cleaning services firm, began business on April 1. The company created the following accounts to record the transactions for April: Cash; Accounts Receivable; Supplies; Prepaid Van Lease; Equipment; Notes Payable; Accounts Payable; Common Stock; Dividends; Cleaning Fees Earned; Wages Expense; Advertising Expense; and Van Fuel Expense. Record the following transactions for April using the financial statement effects template.

April	1	R. Verrecchia invested $9,000 cash to begin the business in exchange for common stock.
	2	Paid $2,850 cash for six months' lease on van for the business.
	3	Borrowed $10,000 cash from bank and signed note payable agreeing to repay it in one year plus 10% interest.
	4	Purchased $5,500 of cleaning equipment; the company paid $2,500 cash with the remainder due within 30 days.
	5	Paid $4,300 cash for cleaning supplies.
	7	Paid $350 cash for advertisements to run in the area newspaper during April.
	21	Billed customers $3,500 for services performed.
	23	Paid $3,000 cash toward the account for cleaning equipment (see April 4).
	28	Collected $2,300 cash from customers on their accounts billed on April 21.
	29	Paid $1,000 cash for dividends.
	30	Paid $2,750 cash for April wages.
	30	Paid $995 cash for gasoline used during April.

M3-15. Preparing Journal Entries and Posting (LO1)
Refer to the information in M3-14. Prepare a journal entry for each transaction. Create a T-account for each account, and then post the journal entries to the T-accounts (use dates to reference each entry).

M3-16. Assessing Financial Statement Effects of Transactions and Adjustments (LO1, 2)
Schrand Services offers janitorial services on both a contract basis and an hourly basis. On January 1, Schrand collected $26,100 cash in advance on a six-month contract for work to be performed evenly during the next six months.

a. Prepare the entry on January 1 to reflect the receipt of $26,100 cash for contract work; use the financial statement effects template.
b. Adjust the appropriate accounts on January 31 for the contract work done during January; use the financial statement effects template.
c. At January 31, a total of 30 hours of hourly rate janitor work was performed but unbilled. The billing rate is $19 per hour. Prepare the accounting adjustment needed on January 31, using the financial statement effects template. (The firm uses the account Fees Receivable to reflect revenue earned but not yet billed.)

M3-17. Preparing Accounting Adjustments (LO1, 2)
Refer to the information in M3-16. Prepare a journal entry for each of parts *a*, *b*, and *c*.

M3-18. Assessing Financial Statement Effects of Transactions and Adjustments (LO2)
Selected accounts of Piotroski Properties, a real estate management firm, are shown below as of January 31, before any accounts have been adjusted.

	Debits	Credits
Prepaid Insurance	$6,660	
Supplies	1,930	
Office Equipment	5,952	
Unearned Rent Revenue		$ 5,250
Salaries Expense	3,100	
Rent Revenue		15,000

Piotroski Properties prepares monthly financial statements. Using the following information, adjust the accounts as necessary on January 31, using the financial statement effects template.
a. Prepaid insurance represents a three-year premium paid on January 1.
b. Supplies of $950 were still available on January 31.
c. Office equipment is expected to last eight years (or 96 months).

d. Earlier this month, on January 1, Piotroski collected $5,250 for six months' rent in advance from a tenant renting space for $875 per month.

e. Salaries of $490 have been earned by employees but not yet recorded as of January 31.

M3-19. Preparing Accounting Adjustments **(LO2)**
Refer to the information in M3-18. Prepare journal entries for each of parts *a* through *e*.

M3-20. Inferring Transactions from Financial Statements **(LO1, 2)**
Foot Locker, Inc., a retailer of athletic footwear and apparel, operates 3,335 stores in the United States, Canada, Europe, Australia, and New Zealand. During its fiscal year ended in 2012, Foot Locker purchased merchandise inventory costing $4,246 ($ millions). Assume that Foot Locker makes all purchases on credit, and that its accounts payable is only used for inventory purchases. The following T-accounts reflect information contained in the company's fiscal 2011 and 2012 balance sheets ($ millions).

Foot Locker, Inc. (FL)

Inventories		
2011 Bal.	1,069	
2012 Bal.	1,167	

Accounts Payable		
	240	2011 Bal.
	298	2012 Bal.

a. Use the financial statement effects template to record Foot Locker's 2012 purchases.

b. What amount did Foot Locker pay in cash to its suppliers during fiscal year 2012? Explain.

c. Use the financial statement effects template to record cost of goods sold for its fiscal year 2012.

M3-21. Preparing Journal Entries **(LO1, 2)**
Refer to the information in M3-20. Prepare journal entries for each of parts *a*, *b* and *c*.

M3-22. Preparing a Statement of Stockholders' Equity **(LO4)**
On December 31, 2012, the accounts of Leuz Architect Services showed credit balances in its Common Stock and Retained Earnings accounts of $30,000 and $18,000, respectively. The company's stock issuances for 2013 totaled $6,000, and it paid $9,700 in cash dividends. During 2013, the company had net income of $27,900. Prepare a 2013 statement of stockholders' equity for Leuz Architect Services.

M3-23.[A] Preparing Closing Journal Entries **(LO5)**
The adjusted trial balance at May 26, 2013, for **General Mills** includes the following selected accounts.

General Mills (GIS)

($ millions)	Debits	Credits
Net sales		$17,774.1
Cost of goods sold	$11,350.2	
Selling, general and administrative expense and other	3,552.3	
Interest expense, net	316.9	
Income tax expense	741.2	
Retained earnings		10,702.6

Assume that the company has not yet closed any accounts to retained earnings. Prepare journal entries to close the temporary accounts above. Set up the needed T-accounts and post the closing entries. After these entries are posted, what is the balance of the Retained Earnings account?

M3-24. Inferring Transactions from Financial Statements **(LO1, 2)**
Lowe's is the second-largest home improvement retailer in the world with 1,754 stores. During its fiscal year ended in 2013, Lowe's purchased merchandise inventory at a cost of $33,439 ($ millions). Assume that all purchases were made on account and that accounts payable is only used for inventory purchases. The following T-accounts reflect information contained in the company's 2013 and 2012 balance sheets.

Lowe's Companies (LOW)

Merchandise Inventories		
2012 Bal.	8,355	
2013 Bal.	8,600	

Accounts Payable		
	4,352	2012 Bal.
	4,657	2013 Bal.

a. Use the financial statement effects template to record Lowe's purchases during fiscal 2013.

b. What amount did Lowe's pay in cash to its suppliers during fiscal-year 2013? Explain.

c. Use the financial statement effects template to record cost of goods sold for its fiscal year ended in 2013.

M3-25.[A] **Closing Journal Entries** **(LO5)**
The adjusted trial balance as of December 31 for Hanlon Consulting contains the following selected accounts.

	Debits	Credits
Service Fees Earned		$80,300
Rent Expense	$20,800	
Salaries Expense	48,700	
Supplies Expense	5,600	
Depreciation Expense	10,200	
Retained Earnings		67,000

Prepare entries to close these accounts in journal entry form. Set up T-accounts for each account and record the adjusted trial balance amount in each account. Then, post the closing entries to the T-accounts. After these entries are posted, what is the balance of the Retained Earnings account?

EXERCISES

E3-26. **Assessing Financial Statement Effects of Adjustments** **(LO2)**
For each of the following separate situations, prepare the necessary accounting adjustments using the financial statement effects template.

a. Unrecorded depreciation on equipment is $610.
b. The Supplies account has an unadjusted balance of $2,990. Supplies still available at the end of the period total $1,100.
c. On the date for preparing financial statements, an estimated utilities expense of $390 has been incurred, but no utility bill has yet been received or paid.
d. On the first day of the current period, rent for four periods was paid and recorded as a $2,800 debit to Prepaid Rent and a $2,800 credit to Cash.
e. Nine months ago, a one-year policy was sold to a customer and recorded the receipt of the premium by crediting Unearned Revenue for $1,248. No accounting adjustments have been prepared during the nine-month period. Allstate's annual financial statements are now being prepared.
f. At the end of the period, employee wages of $965 have been incurred but not paid or recorded.
g. At the end of the period, $300 of interest has been earned but not yet received or recorded.

E3-27. **Preparing Accounting Adjustments** **(LO2)**
Refer to the information in E3-26. Prepare journal entries for each accounting adjustment.

E3-28. **Assessing Financial Statement Effects of Adjustments Across Two Periods** **(LO1, 2)**
Engel Company closes its accounts on December 31 each year. The company works a five-day work week and pays its employees every two weeks. On December 31 Engel accrued $4,700 of salaries payable. On January 9 of the following year the company paid salaries of $15,000 cash to employees. Prepare entries using the financial statement effects template to (a) accrue the salaries payable on December 31; and (b) record the salary payment nine days later on January 9.

E3-29.[A] **Preparing Accounting Adjustments** **(LO1, 2)**
Refer to the information in E3-28. Prepare journal entries to accrue the salaries in December; close salaries expense for the year; and pay the salaries in January of the following year. Assume that there is no change in the pay rate during the year, and no change in the company's work force.

E3-30. **Financial Analysis Using Adjusted Account Data** **(LO2)**
Selected T-account balances for Bloomfield Company are shown below as of January 31, which reflect its accounting adjustments. The firm uses a calendar-year accounting period but prepares *monthly* accounting adjustments.

Supplies		
Jan. 31 Bal.	900	

Supplies Expense		
Jan. 31 Bal.	960	

Prepaid Insurance	
Jan. 31 Bal. 574	

Insurance Expense	
Jan. 31 Bal. 82	

Wages Payable	
	Jan. 31 Bal. 700

Wages Expense	
Jan. 31 Bal. 3,200	

Truck	
Jan. 31 Bal. 8,700	

Accumulated Depreciation-Truck	
	2,610 Bal. Jan. 31

a. If the amount in Supplies Expense represents the January 31 adjustment for the supplies used in January, and $620 worth of supplies were purchased during January, what was the January 1 beginning balance of Supplies?

b. The amount in the Insurance Expense account represents the adjustment made at January 31 for January insurance expense. If the original insurance premium was for one year, what was the amount of the premium and on what date did the insurance policy start?

c. If we assume that no beginning balance existed in either Wages Payable or Wages Expense on January 1, how much cash was paid as wages during January?

d. If the truck has a useful life of five years (or 60 months), what is the monthly amount of depreciation expense and how many months has Bloomfield owned the truck?

E3-31. Assessing Financial Statement Effects of Adjustments (LO2)

T. Lys began Thomas Refinishing Service on July 1. Selected accounts are shown below as of July 31, before any accounting adjustments have been made.

	Debits	Credits
Prepaid Rent	$6,900	
Prepaid Advertising	630	
Supplies	3,000	
Unearned Refinishing Fees		$ 600
Refinishing Fees Revenue		2,500

Using the following information, prepare the accounting adjustments necessary on July 31 using the financial statement effects template.

a. On July 1, the firm paid one year's rent of $6,900 in cash.

b. On July 1, $630 cash was paid to the local newspaper for an advertisement to run daily for the months of July, August, and September.

c. Supplies still available at July 31 total $1,100.

d. At July 31, refinishing services of $800 have been performed but not yet recorded or billed to customers. The firm uses the account Fees Receivable to reflect amounts due but not yet billed.

e. In early July, a customer paid $600 in advance for a refinishing project. At July 31, the project is one-half complete.

E3-32. Preparing Accounting Adjustments and Posting (LO2)

Refer to the information in E3-31. Prepare adjusting journal entries for each transaction. Set up T-accounts for each of the ledger accounts and post the journal entries to them.

E3-33. Inferring Transactions from Financial Statements (LO1)

The Gap, Inc. (GPS)

The GAP is a global clothing retailer for men, women, children, and babies. The following information is taken from The Gap's fiscal 2013 annual report.

Selected Balance Sheet Data	2013	2012
Inventories	$1,758	$1,615
Accounts Payable	1,144	1,066

a. The Gap purchased inventories totalling $8,931 million during fiscal 2013. Use the financial statement effects template to record cost of goods sold for The Gap's fiscal year ended 2013. (Assume that Accounts Payable is used only for recording purchases of inventories and all inventories are purchased on credit.)

b. What amount did the company pay to suppliers during the year? Record this with the financial statement effects template.

The GAP, Inc. (GPS)

E3-34. Inferring Transactions and Preparing Journal Entries (LO1)
Refer to the information in E3-33. Prepare journal entries for each transaction.

The GAP, Inc. (GPS)

E3-35.[A] Preparing Closing Journal Entries (LO5)
The adjusted trial balance of **The GAP, Inc.**, for fiscal 2013, contains the following selected accounts.

($ millions)	Debit	Credit
Net Sales		$15,651
Cost of Goods Sold	$9,480	
Operating Expenses	4,229	
Interest Income, net		6
Income Tax Expense	726	
Retained Earnings (beginning of year)		12,364

Prepare entries to close these accounts in journal entry form. Set up T-accounts for each of the ledger accounts and post the entries to them. After these entries are posted, what is the balance of the Retained Earnings account?

Costco Wholesale Corporation (COST)

E3-36. Inferring Transactions from Financial Statements (LO1, 2)
Costco Wholesale Corporation operates membership warehouses selling food, appliances, consumer electronics, apparel and other household goods at 634 locations across the United States as well as in Canada, the United Kingdom, Japan, Australia, South Korea, Taiwan, Mexico, and Puerto Rico. As of its fiscal year-end 2013, Costco had approximately 71.2 million members. Selected fiscal-year information from the company's balance sheets follows.

Selected Balance Sheet Data ($ millions)	2013	2012
Merchandise inventories	$7,894	$7,096
Deferred membership income (liability)	621	550

a. During fiscal 2013, Costco collected $2,286 million cash for membership fees. Use the financial statement effects template to record the cash collected for membership fees.

b. Costco recorded merchandise costs (that is, cost of goods sold) of $91,948 million in 2013. Record this transaction in the financial statement effects template.

c. Determine the value of merchandise that Costco purchased during 2013. Use the financial statement effects template to record these merchandise purchases. Assume all of Costco's purchases are on credit.

Costco Wholesale Corporation (COST)

E3-37. Inferring Transactions and Preparing Journal Entries (LO1, 2)
Refer to the information in E3-36. Prepare journal entries for transactions in parts *a* through *c*.

E3-38.[A] Preparing Financial Statements and Closing Entries (LO4, 5)
The adjusted trial balance for Beneish Corporation is as follows.

BENEISH CORPORATION Adjusted Trial Balance December 31	Debit	Credit
Cash	$ 8,000	
Accounts receivable	6,500	
Equipment	78,000	
Accumulated depreciation		$ 14,000
Notes payable		10,000
Common stock		43,000
Retained earnings		20,600
Dividends	8,000	
Service fees earned		75,000
Rent expense	18,000	
Salaries expense	37,100	
Depreciation expense	7,000	
Totals	$162,600	$162,600

a. Prepare Beneish Corporation's income statement and statement of stockholders' equity for year-end December 31, and its balance sheet as of December 31. The company paid cash dividends of $8,000 and there were no stock issuances or repurchases during the year.
b. Prepare journal entries to close Beneish's temporary accounts.
c. Set up T-accounts for each account and post the closing entries.

PROBLEMS

P3-39. Assessing Financial Statement Effects of Transactions and Adjustments (LO2)
The following information relates to December 31 accounting adjustments for Koonce Kwik Print Company. The firm's fiscal year ends on December 31.

1. Weekly salaries for a five-day week total $3,600, payable on Fridays. December 31 of the current year is a Tuesday.
2. Koonce Kwik Print has $20,000 of notes payable outstanding at December 31. Interest of $200 has accrued on these notes by December 31, but will not be paid until the notes mature next year.
3. During December, Koonce Kwik Print provided $900 of printing services to clients who will be billed on January 2. The firm uses the account Fees Receivable to reflect amounts earned but not yet billed.
4. Starting December 1, all maintenance work on Koonce Kwik Print's equipment is handled by Richardson Repair Company under an agreement whereby Koonce Kwik Print pays a fixed monthly charge of $400. Koonce Kwik Print paid six months' service charge of $2,400 cash in advance on December 1, and increased its Prepaid Maintenance account by $2,400.
5. The firm paid $900 cash on December 15 for a series of radio commercials to run during December and January. One-third of the commercials have aired by December 31. The $900 payment was recorded in its Prepaid Advertising account.
6. Starting December 16, Koonce Kwik Print rented 800 square feet of storage space from a neighboring business. The monthly rent of $0.80 per square foot is due in advance on the first of each month. Nothing was paid in December, however, because the neighboring business agreed to add the rent for one-half of December to the January 1 payment.
7. Koonce Kwik Print invested $5,000 cash in securities on December 1 and earned interest of $38 on these securities by December 31. No interest will be received until January.
8. Annual depreciation on the firm's equipment is $2,175. No depreciation has been recorded during the year.

Required
Prepare Koonce Kwik Print Company's accounting adjustments required at December 31 using the financial statement effects template.

P3-40. Preparing Accounting Adjustments (LO2)
Refer to the information in P3-39. Prepare adjustments required at December 31 using journal entries.

P3-41. Assessing Financial Statement Effects of Adjustments Across Two Periods (LO1, 2)
The following selected accounts appear in Sloan Company's unadjusted trial balance at December 31, the end of its fiscal year (all accounts have normal balances).

Prepaid Advertising	$ 1,200	Unearned Service Fees	$ 5,400
Wages Expense	43,800	Service Fees Earned	87,000
Prepaid Insurance	3,420	Rental Income	4,900

Required
a. Prepare Sloan Company's accounting adjustments at December 31, using the financial statement effects template and the following additional information.
1. Prepaid advertising at December 31 is $800.
2. Unpaid wages earned by employees in December are $2,600.
3. Prepaid insurance at December 31 is $2,280.
4. Unearned service fees at December 31 are $3,000.
5. Rent revenue of $1,000 owed by a tenant is not recorded at December 31.

b. Prepare entries on January 4, of the following year, using the financial statement effects template to record
1. Payment of $4,800 cash in wages.
2. Cash receipt from the tenant of the $1,000 rent revenue.

P3-42. Preparing Accounting Adjustments (LO1, 2)
Refer to the information in P3-41. Prepare journal entries for parts *a* and *b*.

P3-43. Journalizing and Posting Transactions, and Preparing a Trial Balance and Adjustments (LO1, 2, 3)
D. Roulstone opened Roulstone Roofing Service on April 1. Transactions for April follow.

Apr. 1 Roulstone contributed $11,500 cash to the business in exchange for common stock.
2 Paid $6,100 cash for the purchase of a used truck.
2 Purchased $6,200 of ladders and other equipment; the company paid $1,000 cash, with the balance due in 30 days.
3 Paid $2,880 cash for two-year (or 24-month) premium toward liability insurance.
5 Purchased $1,200 of supplies on credit.
5 Received an advance of $1,800 cash from a customer for roof repairs to be done during April and May.
12 Billed customers $5,500 for roofing services performed.
18 Collected $4,900 cash from customers toward their accounts billed on April 12.
29 Paid $675 cash for truck fuel used in April.
30 Paid $100 cash for April newspaper advertising.
30 Paid $4,500 cash for assistants' wages earned.
30 Billed customers $4,000 for roofing services performed.

Required

a. Set up T-accounts for the following accounts: Cash; Accounts Receivable; Supplies; Prepaid Insurance; Trucks; Accumulated Depreciation–Trucks; Equipment; Accumulated Depreciation–Equipment; Accounts Payable; Unearned Roofing Fees; Common Stock; Roofing Fees Earned; Fuel Expense; Advertising Expense; Wages Expense; Insurance Expense; Supplies Expense; Depreciation Expense–Trucks; and Depreciation Expense–Equipment.
b. Record these transactions for April using journal entries.
c. Post these entries to their T-accounts (reference transactions in T-accounts by date).
d. Prepare an unadjusted trial balance at April 30.
e. Prepare entries to adjust the following accounts: Insurance Expense, Supplies Expense, Depreciation Expense–Trucks, Depreciation Expense–Equipment, and Roofing Fees Earned in journal entry form. Supplies still available on April 30 amount to $200. Depreciation for April was $125 on the truck and $35 on equipment. One-fourth of the roofing fee received on April 5, was earned by April 30.
f. Post adjusting entries to their T-accounts.

P3-44. Assessing Financial Statement Effects of Transactions and Adjustments (LO1, 2)
Refer to the information in P3-43.

Required

a. Use the financial statement effects template to record the transactions for April.
b. Use the financial statement effects template to record the adjustments at the end of April (described in part *e* of P3-43).

P3-45. Preparing an Unadjusted Trial Balance and Accounting Adjustments (LO2, 3)
Pownall Photomake Company, a commercial photography studio, completed its first year of operations on December 31. General ledger account balances before year-end adjustments follow; no adjustments have been made to the accounts at any time during the year. Assume that all balances are normal.

Cash	$ 4,300	Accounts Payable	$ 4,060
Accounts Receivable	3,800	Unearned Photography Fees	2,600
Prepaid Rent	12,600	Common Stock	24,000
Prepaid Insurance	2,970	Photography Fees Earned	34,480
Supplies	4,250	Wages Expense	11,000
Equipment	22,800	Utilities Expense	3,420

An analysis of the firm's records discloses the following (business began on January 1).

1. Photography services of $1,850 have been rendered, but customers have not yet paid or been billed. The company uses the account Fees Receivable to reflect amounts due but not yet billed.

2. Equipment, purchased January 1, has an estimated life of 10 years.
3. Utilities expense for December is estimated to be $400, but the bill will not arrive or be paid until January of next year. (All prior months' utilities bills have been received and paid.)
4. The balance in Prepaid Rent represents the amount paid on January 1, for a 2-year lease on the studio it operates from.
5. In November, customers paid $2,600 cash in advance for photos to be taken for the holiday season. When received, these fees were credited to Unearned Photography Fees. By December 31, all of these fees are earned.
6. A 3-year insurance premium paid on January 1, was debited to Prepaid Insurance.
7. Supplies still available at December 31 are $1,020.
8. At December 31, wages expense of $375 has been incurred but not yet paid or recorded.

Required

a. Prepare Pownall Photomake's unadjusted trial balance at December 31.
b. Prepare its adjusting entries using the financial statement effects template.

P3-46. Recording Adjustments with Journal Entries and T-Accounts (LO2)
Refer to the information in P3-45.

Required

a. Prepare journal entries to record the accounting adjustments.
b. Set up T-accounts for each account and post the journal entries to them.

P3-47. Preparing an Unadjusted Trial Balance and Accounting Adjustments (LO2, 3)
BensEx, a mailing service, has just completed its first year of operations on December 31. Its general ledger account balances before year-end adjustments follow; no adjusting entries have been made to the accounts at any time during the year. Assume that all balances are normal.

Cash	$ 1,700	Accounts Payable	$ 2,700
Accounts Receivable	5,120	Common Stock	9,530
Prepaid Advertising	1,680	Mailing Fees Earned	86,000
Supplies	6,270	Wages Expense	38,800
Equipment	42,240	Rent Expense	6,900
Notes Payable	7,500	Utilities Expense	3,020

An analysis of the firm's records reveals the following (business began on January 1).

1. The balance in Prepaid Advertising represents the amount paid for newspaper advertising for one year. The agreement, which calls for the same amount of space each month, covers the period from February 1 of this first year, to January 31 of the following year. BensEx did not advertise during its first month of operations.
2. Equipment, purchased January 1, has an estimated life of eight years.
3. Utilities expense does not include expense for December, estimated at $325. The bill will not arrive until January of the following year.
4. At year-end, employees have earned $2,400 in wages that will not be paid until January.
5. Supplies available at year-end amount to $1,520.
6. At year-end, unpaid interest of $450 has accrued on the notes payable.
7. The firm's lease calls for rent of $575 per month payable on the first of each month, plus an amount equal to 0.75% of annual mailing fees earned. The rental percentage is payable within 15 days after the end of the year.

Required

a. Prepare its unadjusted trial balance at December 31.
b. Prepare its adjusting entries using the financial statement effects template.

P3-48. Recording Accounting Adjustments with Journal Entries and T-Accounts (LO2, 3)
Refer to information in P3-47.

Required

a. Prepare journal entries to record the accounting adjustments.
b. Set up T-accounts for each account and post the journal entries to them.

P3-49.[A] Preparing Accounting Adjustments (LO2, 4, 5)
Wysocki Wheels began operations on March 1 to provide automotive wheel alignment and balancing services. On March 31 the unadjusted trial balance follows.

WYSOCKI WHEELS Unadjusted Trial Balance March 31	Debit	Credit
Cash	$ 2,900	
Accounts receivable	3,820	
Prepaid rent	4,770	
Supplies	3,700	
Equipment	36,180	
Accounts payable		$ 3,510
Unearned service revenue		1,000
Common stock		38,400
Service revenue		12,360
Wages expense	3,900	
	$55,270	$55,270

The following information is also available.

1. The balance in Prepaid Rent was the amount paid on March 1 to cover the first six months' rent.
2. Supplies available on March 31 amounted to $1,360.
3. Equipment has an estimated life of nine years (or 108 months).
4. Unpaid and unrecorded wages at March 31 were $1,560.
5. Utility services used during March were estimated at $390; a bill is expected early in April.
6. The balance in Unearned Service Revenue was the amount received on March 1 from a car dealer to cover alignment and balancing services on cars sold by the dealer in March and April. Wysocki Wheels agreed to provide the services at a fixed fee of $500 each month.

Required

a. Prepare its accounting adjustments at March 31 in journal entry form.
b. Set up T-accounts and post the accounting adjustments to them.
c. Prepare its income statement for March and its balance sheet at March 31.
d. Prepare entries to close its temporary accounts in journal entry form. Post the closing entries to the T-accounts.

IFRS APPLICATIONS

I3-50.[A] Preparing Closing Journal Entries (LO5)
The adjusted trial balance at June 30, 2013, for Quantas Airlines includes the following selected accounts.

(AUD millions)	Debits	Credits
Total passenger and freight revenue		15,902
Manpower and staff related	3,825	
Fuel	4,154	
Aircraft operating variable	3,066	
Depreciation and amortisation	1,450	
Other expenses	3,203	
Finance costs	187	
Income tax expense	11	
Retained earnings		1,165

Assume that the company has not yet closed any accounts to retained earnings. Prepare journal entries to close the temporary accounts above. Set up the needed T-accounts and post the closing entries. After these entries are posted, what is the balance of the Retained Earnings account?

I3-51. Inferring Transactions from Financial Statements (LO1, 2)

Rio Tinto is a British-Australian multinational metals and mining corporation with headquarters in London and a management office in Melbourne, Australia. Assume that the following amounts have not been recorded.

Sales revenue	50,967
Depreciation expense	4,441
Income taxes paid	5,823

Use the financial statement effects template to record the following transactions for Rio Tinto for fiscal 2012.

a. Sales revenue. Assume that 100% of the company's revenue are credit sales (that is, sales are on accounts receivable).
b. Depreciation expense.
c. Income taxes paid. Assume that this represents the portion of income tax expense paid in cash.

I3-52. Inferring Transactions and Account Balances from Financial Statements (LO1, 2)

Canadian Tire Corporation is a Canadian firm whose core operation is Canadian Tire, a retail and automotive services operation. Its head office is in Toronto, Ontario. The following T-accounts reflect information in the company's 2011 and 2012 balance sheets (in millions of Canadian dollars).

Inventories		
2011 Balance	$1,449	
2012 Balance	$1,503	

Accounts Payable		
	$1,641	2011 Balance
	$1,631	2012 Balance

Required

a. Use the financial statement effects template to record Canadian Tire's purchases during fiscal 2012. Assume Canadian Tire incurred cost of goods sold of $7,594 during 2012.
b. What amount did Canadian Tire pay in cash to its suppliers during fiscal 2012? Explain. Assume all inventory purchases are made on account, and that accounts payable reflects only inventory purchases.
c. Use the financial statement effects template to record cost of goods sold for fiscal 2012.

MANAGEMENT APPLICATIONS

MA3-53. Preparing Accounting Adjustments and Financial Statements (LO1, 2, 4)

Stocken Surf Shop began operations on July 1 with an initial investment of $50,000. During the first three months of operations, the following cash transactions were recorded in the firm's checking account.

Deposits	
Initial investment by owner	$ 50,000
Collected from customers	81,000
Borrowings from bank	10,000
	$141,000
Checks drawn	
Rent	$ 24,000
Fixtures and equipment	25,000
Merchandise inventory	62,000
Salaries	8,000
Other expenses	13,000
	$132,000

Additional information:

1. Most sales were for cash, however, the store accepted a limited amount of credit sales; at September 30, customers owed the store $9,000.

2. Rent was paid on July 1 for six months.
3. Salaries of $4,000 per month were paid on the 1st of each month for salaries earned in the month prior.
4. Inventories were purchased for cash; at September 30, inventory of $28,000 was still available.
5. Fixtures and equipment were expected to last five years (or 60 months) with zero salvage value.
6. The bank charges 12% annual interest (1% per month) on the $10,000 bank loan. Stocken took the loan out July 1.

Required

a. Record all of Stocken's cash transactions and prepare any necessary adjusting entries at September 30. You may either use the financial statement effects template or journal entries combined with T-accounts.

b. Prepare the income statement for the three months ended September 30, and the balance sheet at September 30.

c. Analyze the statements from part *b* and assess the company's performance over its initial three months.

MA3-54. Analyzing Transactions, Impacts on Financial Ratios, and Loan Covenants (LO2)

Kadous Consulting, a firm started three years ago by K. Kadous, offers consulting services for material handling and plant layout. Its balance sheet at the close of the current year follows.

KADOUS CONSULTING
Balance Sheet
December 31

Assets		**Liabilities**	
Cash	$ 3,400	Notes payable	$30,000
Accounts receivable	20,875	Accounts payable	4,200
Supplies	13,200	Unearned consulting fees	11,300
Prepaid insurance	6,500	Wages payable	400
Equipment, gross	68,500	Total liabilities	45,900
Less: Accumulated depreciation	23,975	**Equity**	
		Common stock	8,000
Equipment, net	44,525	Retained earnings	34,600
Total assets	$88,500	Total liabilities and equity	$88,500

Earlier in the year Kadous obtained a bank loan of $30,000 cash for the firm. A provision of the loan is that the year-end debt-to-equity ratio (total liabilities to total equity) cannot exceed 1.0. Based on the above balance sheet, the ratio at December 31 of this year is 1.08. Kadous is concerned about being in violation of the loan agreement and requests assistance in reviewing the situation. Kadous believes that she might have overlooked some items at year-end. Discussions with Kadous reveal the following.

1. On January 1 of this year, the firm paid a $6,500 insurance premium for two years of coverage; the amount in Prepaid Insurance has not yet been adjusted.
2. Depreciation on equipment should be 10% of cost per year; the company inadvertently recorded 15% for this year.
3. Interest on the bank loan has been paid through the end of this year.
4. The firm concluded a major consulting engagement in December, doing a plant layout analysis for a new factory. The $8,000 fee has not been billed or recorded in the accounts.
5. On December 1 of this year, the firm received an $11,300 cash advance payment from Dichev Corp. for consulting services to be rendered over a two-month period. This payment was credited to the Unearned Consulting Fees account. One-half of this fee was earned but unrecorded by December 31 of this year.
6. Supplies costing $4,800 were available on December 31; the company has made no adjustment of its Supplies account.

Required

a. What is the correct debt-to-equity ratio at December 31?

b. Is the firm in violation of its loan agreement? Prepare computations to support the correct total liabilities and total equity figures at December 31.

MA3-55. Ethics, Accounting Adjustments, and Auditors (LO1, 2)

It is the end of the accounting year for Anne Beatty, controller of a medium-sized, publicly held corporation specializing in toxic waste cleanup. Within the corporation, only Beatty and the president know that the firm has been negotiating for several months to land a large contract for waste cleanup in Western Europe. The president has hired another firm with excellent contacts in Western Europe to help with negotiations. The outside firm will charge an hourly fee plus expenses, but has agreed not to submit a bill until the negotiations are in their final stages (expected to occur in another 3 to 4 months). Even if the contract falls through, the outside firm is entitled to receive payment for its services. Based upon her discussion with a member of the outside firm, Beatty knows that its charge for services provided to date will be $150,000. This is a material amount for the company.

Beatty knows that the president wants negotiations to remain as secret as possible so that competitors will not learn of the contract the company is pursuing in Europe. In fact, the president recently stated to her, "This is not the time to reveal our actions in Western Europe to other staff members, our auditors, or the readers of our financial statements; securing this contract is crucial to our future growth." No entry has been made in the accounting records for the cost of contract negotiations. Beatty now faces an uncomfortable situation. The company's outside auditor has just asked her if she knows of any year-end adjustments that have not yet been recorded.

Required

a. What are the ethical considerations that Beatty faces in answering the auditor's question?
b. How should Beatty respond to the auditor's question?

SOLUTIONS TO REVIEW PROBLEMS

Mid-Module Review 1

Solution

	Balance Sheet									Income Statement					
Transaction	Cash Asset	+	Noncash Assets	=	Liabilities	+	Contrib. Capital	+	Earned Capital	Revenues	−	Expenses	=	Net Income	Journal entry / T-accounts
1. Issue stock for $3,000 cash	+3,000 Cash			=			+3,000 Common Stock				−		=		Cash 3,000; CS 3,000. Cash: 3,000 (dr). CS: 3,000 (cr)
2. Purchase $1,000 of inventory on credit			+1,000 Inventory	=	+1,000 Accounts Payable						−		=		INV 1,000; AP 1,000. INV: 1,000 (dr). AP: 1,000 (cr)
3a. Sell inventory for $500 on credit			+500 Accounts Receivable	=					+500 Retained Earnings	+500 Sales	−		=	+500	AR 500; Sales 500. AR: 500 (dr). Sales: 500 (cr)
3b. Record $300 cost of inventory sold			−300 Inventory	=					−300 Retained Earnings		−	+300 Cost of Goods Sold	=	−300	COGS 300; INV 300. COGS: 300 (dr). INV: 300 (cr)
4. Collect $300 cash owed by customers	+300 Cash		−300 Accounts Receivable	=							−		=		Cash 300; AR 300. Cash: 300 (dr). AR: 300 (cr)
5. Pay $400 cash toward accounts payable	−400 Cash			=	−400 Accounts Payable						−		=		AP 400; Cash 400. AP: 400 (dr). Cash: 400 (cr)
6. Pay $20 cash for dividends	−20 Cash			=					−20 Dividends		−		=		DIV 20; Cash 20. DIV: 20 (dr). Cash: 20 (cr)

Mid-Module Review 2

Solution

	Transaction	Cash Asset	+	Noncash Assets	=	Liabilities	+	Contrib. Capital	+	Earned Capital	Revenues	−	Expenses	=	Net Income
		Balance Sheet									**Income Statement**				
PPRNT 100 Cash 100 PPRNT: 100 | Cash: | 100	a. Pay $100 cash for current and future periods' rent	−100 Cash		+100 Prepaid Rent	=							−		=	
Cash 500 UR 500 Cash: 500 | UR: | 500	b. Receive $500 cash advance for future services	+500 Cash			=	+500 Unearned Revenues						−		=	
RE 30 PPRNT 30 RE: 30 | PPRNT: | 30	1. Record $30 of rental fees incurred			−30 Prepaid Rent	=					−30 Retained Earnings		−	+30 Rent Expense	=	−30
UR 80 Sales 80 UR: 80 | Sales: | 80	2. Record $80 of services earned				=	−80 Unearned Revenues				+80 Retained Earnings	+80 Sales	−		=	+80
WE 40 WP 40 WE: 40 | WP: | 40	3. Incur $40 in wages to be paid next period				=	+40 Wages Payable				−40 Retained Earnings		−	+40 Wages Expense	=	−40
AR 150 Sales 150 AR: 150 | Sales: | 150	4. Provide $150 of services not yet billed to client			+150 Accounts Receivable	=					+150 Retained Earnings	+150 Sales	−		=	+150

SAMSUNG
Trial Balances

	Unadjusted		Adjustments		Adjusted	
	Debit	**Credit**	**Debit**	**Credit**	**Debit**	**Credit**
Cash	$3,280				$3,280	
Accounts receivable	200		$150		350	
Inventory	700				700	
Prepaid rent	100			$ 30	70	
Accounts payable		$ 600				$ 600
Wages payable		0		40		40
Unearned revenues		500	80			420
Common stock		3,000				3,000
Dividends	20				20	
Sales		500		230*		730
Cost of goods sold	300				300	
Wages expense	0		40		40	
Rent expense	0		30		30	
Totals	$4,600	$4,600	$300	$300	$4,790	$4,790

*The $230 adjustment is a combination of the $150 and $80 adjustments.

Module-End Review

Solution

SAMSUNG Income Statement For Year Ended December 31, 2014	
Sales	$730
Cost of goods sold	300
Gross profit	430
Wage expense	40
Rent expense	30
Net income	$360

SAMSUNG Retained Earnings Computation For Year Ended December 31, 2014	
Retained earnings, beginning of period	$ 0
Add: Net income (loss)	360
Deduct: Dividends	(20)
Retained earnings, end of period	$340

SAMSUNG Balance Sheet December 31, 2014	
Assets	
Cash	$3,280
Accounts receivable	350
Inventory	700
Prepaid rent	70
Total assets	$4,400
Liabilities and Stockholders' Equity	
Liabilities	
Accounts payable	$ 600
Wages payable	40
Unearned revenues	420
Total liabilities	1,060
Stockholders' equity	
Common stock	3,000
Retained earnings	340
Total stockholders' equity	3,340
Total liabilities and stockholders' equity	$4,400

SAMSUNG
Statement of Stockholders' Equity
For Year Ended December 31, 2014

	Contributed Capital	Earned Capital	Total Stockholders' Equity
Beginning balance	$ 0	$ 0	$ 0
Stock issuance	3,000		3,000
Net income (loss)		360	360
Dividends		(20)	(20)
Ending balance	$3,000	$340	$3,340

SAMSUNG
Statement of Cash Flows
For Year Ended December 31, 2014

Operating activities	
Net income	$ 360
Depreciation and other noncash expenses	0
Increase in accounts receivable	(350)
Increase in inventories	(700)
Increase in prepaid rent	(70)
Increase in accounts payable	600
Increase in wages payable	40
Increase in unearned revenues	420
Net cash flows from operating activities	300
Investing activities	
Net cash flows from investing activities	0
Financing activities	
Issuance of common stock	3,000
Payment of cash dividends	(20)
Net cash flows from financing activities	2,980
Net change in cash	3,280
Cash, beginning of period	0
Cash, end of period	$3,280

Module

4 Analyzing and Interpreting Financial Statements

Learning Objectives

LO1 Compute return on equity (ROE) and disaggregate it into components of operating and nonoperating returns. (p. 4-4)

LO2 Disaggregate operating return (RNOA) into components of profitability and asset turnover. (p. 4-13)

LO3 Explain nonoperating return and compute it from return on equity and the operating return. (p. 4-17)

LO4 Compute and interpret measures of liquidity and solvency. (p. 4-29)

LO5 Describe and illustrate traditional DuPont disaggregation of ROE. (p. 4-33)

Walmart

Walmart employs a number of financial measures to assess its overall performance and financial condition. These measures include ratios related to profitability and asset turnover as well as the return on invested capital. Analysts, too, use a variety of measures to capture different aspects of company performance to answer questions such as: Is it managed efficiently and profitably? Does it use assets effectively? Is performance achieved with a minimum of debt?

One fundamental measure is return on capital, which Warren Buffett, CEO of the investment firm **Berkshire Hathaway**, lists in his acquisition criteria cited in Module 1: "Our preference would be to reach our goal by directly owning a diversified group of businesses that generate cash and consistently earn above-average returns on capital."

All return metrics follow the same basic formula—they divide some measure of profit by some measure of investment. A company's performance is commonly judged by its profitability. Although analysis of profit is important, it is only part of the story. A more meaningful analysis is to compare level of profitability with the amount of capital that has been invested in the business.

The most common return measure is return on equity (ROE), which focuses on shareholder investment as its measure of invested capital. By focusing on the *equity* investment, ROE measures return from the perspective of the common shareholder rather than the company overall. Walmart's ROE for 2013 was 23.02%, up from 22.45% in the prior year.

This module focuses on analysis of return metrics. Beyond ROE, we put special emphasis on the return on net operating assets (RNOA), computed as net operating profit after tax (NOPAT) divided by average net operating assets (NOA). RNOA focuses on operating activities—operating profit relative to investment in net operating assets. It is important to distinguish operating activities from nonoperating activities because the capital markets value each component differently, placing much greater emphasis on operations. Walmart's RNOA improved slightly from 15.03% in 2012 to 15.14% in 2013, but it is less than the 15.63% reported in 2011.

RNOA consists of two components: profitability and asset productivity. Improving either component improves RNOA. These components reflect on the first two questions

Courtesy of Getty Images

we posed above: Is the company managed efficiently and profitably? Does it use assets effectively?

The profitability component of RNOA measures net operating profit after tax for each sales dollar (NOPAT/Sales), and is called the net operating profit margin (NOPM). Walmart's NOPM increased from 3.99% in 2012 to 4.06% in 2013, which is about the same as the 4.08% reported in 2011.

Asset productivity, the second component of RNOA, is reflected in net operating asset turnover (NOAT). NOAT is measured as sales divided by average net operating assets—it captures the notion of how many sales dollars are generated by each dollar of invested assets. Walmart's NOAT declined slightly in 2013, from 3.77 to 3.73 and is less than the 3.83 it reported two years ago. Increasing the turnover for large asset bases is difficult, and NOAT measures tend to fluctuate in a narrow band. When companies are able to make a meaningful improvement in NOAT, however, it usually has a large positive impact on RNOA.

RNOA is an important metric in assessing the performance of company management. We can use the RNOA components, NOPM and NOAT, to assess how effectively and efficiently management uses the company's operating assets to produce a return.

The difference between ROE and RNOA is important for our analysis. Specifically, ROE consists of a return on operating activities (RNOA) *plus* a return on nonoperating activities, where the latter reflects how well the company uses borrowed funds. Companies can increase ROE by borrowing money and effectively using those borrowed funds. However, debt can increase the company's risk—where severe consequences can result if debt is not repaid when due. This is why Warren Buffett focuses on "businesses earning good returns on equity while employing little or no debt." For those companies that do employ debt, our analysis seeks to evaluate their ability to repay the amounts owed when due.

Over the years, analysts, creditors and others have developed hundreds of ratios to measure specific aspects of financial performance. Most of these seek answers to the root question: Can the company achieve a high return on its invested capital and, if so, is that return sustainable?

Sources: *Walmart 10-K and Annual Report*; *Berkshire Hathaway 10-K*.

MODULE ORGANIZATION

Analyzing and Interpreting Financial Statements

Return on Equity (ROE)
- Measuring ROE
- Disaggregating ROE into Operating and Nonoperating Returns
- Distinguishing Operating from Nonoperating Activities

Operating Return (RNOA)
- Operating Revenues and Expenses
- Tax on Operating Profit
- Operating Assets and Liabilities
- Disaggregating RNOA into Margin and Turnover

Nonoperating Return
- Measuring Nonoperating Return
- Leveraging Debt to Increase ROE
- Risks of Debt Financing
- Debt Covenants

Liquidity and Solvency
- Liquidity: Current Ratio and Quick Ratio
- Solvency: Liabilities-to-Equity and Times Interest Earned Ratios
- Limitations of Ratio Analysis

A key aspect of any analysis is identifying the business activities that drive company success. We pursue an answer to the question: Is the company earning an acceptable rate of return on its invested capital? We also want to know the extent to which the company's return on invested capital results from its operating versus its nonoperating activities. The distinction between returns from operating and nonoperating activities is important and plays a key role in our analysis.

Operating activities are the core activities of a company. They consist of those activities required to deliver a company's products or services to its customers. A company engages in operating activities when it conducts research and development, establishes supply chains, assembles administrative support, produces and markets its products, and follows up with after-sale customer services.

The asset side of a company's balance sheet reflects resources devoted to operating activities with accounts such as receivables, inventories, and property, plant and equipment (PPE). Operating activities are reflected in liabilities with accounts such as accounts payable, accrued expenses, and long-term operating liabilities such as pension and health care obligations. The income statement reflects operating activities through accounts such as revenues, costs of goods sold, and operating expenses such as selling, general, and administrative expenses that include wages, advertising, depreciation, occupancy, insurance, and research and development. Operating activities create the most long-lasting (persistent) effects on future profitability and cash flows of the company. Operations provide the primary value drivers for company stakeholders. It is for this reason that operating activities play such a prominent role in assessing profitability.

Nonoperating activities relate to the investing of cash in marketable securities and in other nonoperating investments. Nonoperating activities also relate to borrowings through accounts such as short- and long-term debt. These nonoperating assets and liabilities expand and contract to buffer fluctuations in operating asset and liability levels. When operating assets grow faster than operating liabilities, companies typically increase their nonoperating liabilities to fund the deficit. Later, these nonoperating liabilities decline when operating assets decline. When companies have cash in excess of what is needed for operating activities, they often invest the cash temporarily in marketable securities or other investments to provide some return until those funds are needed for operations.

The income statement reflects nonoperating activities through accounts such as interest and dividend revenue, capital gains or losses relating to sales of investments, and interest expense on borrowed funds. Nonoperating expenses, net of any nonoperating revenues, provide a nonoperating return for a company. Although nonoperating activities are important and must be managed well, they are not the main value drivers for company stakeholders.

We begin this module by explaining the return on equity (ROE). We then discuss in more detail how ROE consists of both an operating return (RNOA) and a nonoperating return. Next, we discuss the two RNOA components that measure profitability and asset turnover. We conclude this module with a discussion of nonoperating return, focusing on the notion that companies can increase ROE through judicious use of debt.

Appendixes 4A and 4B expand our explanation of nonoperating return by exploring how much debt a company can reasonably manage. For this purpose, we examine a number of liquidity and solvency metrics in Appendix 4B. As part of that analysis, we identify ratios that credit analysts typically use to develop credit ratings, which are key determinants of bond prices and the cost of debt financing for public companies.

RETURN ON EQUITY (ROE)

LO1 Compute return on equity (ROE) and disaggregate it into components of operating and nonoperating returns.

Return on equity (ROE) is the principal summary measure of company performance and is broadly defined as follows:

$$\text{ROE} = \frac{\text{Net income}}{\text{Average stockholders' equity}}$$

ROE relates net income to the average investment by stockholders as measured by total stockholders' equity from the balance sheet. Warren Buffett highlights ROE as part of his acquisition criteria: "Businesses earning good returns on equity while employing little or no debt."

BUSINESS INSIGHT Which Net Income and Stockholders' Equity to Use?

Many companies have two sets of stockholders: those that own the common stock of the company whose financial statements we review (called *controlling interest*) and those that own shares in one or more of the parent company's subsidiaries (called *noncontrolling interest*). Current accounting standards require companies to separately identify the stockholders' equity relating to each group of stockholders and, likewise, the net income that is attributable to each. ROE is usually computed from the perspective of the controlling (also called *parent*) stockholders and, thus, the numerator is the net income attributable to the parent stockholders and the denominator is the equity attributable to the parent stockholders. We discuss the concepts of controlling and noncontrolling interest in Appendix 4A.

The ROE formula can be rewritten in a way to better see the point Buffett is making (derivation of this ROE formula is in Appendix 4A):

$$\text{ROE} = \text{Operating return} + \text{Nonoperating return}$$

The equation above shows that ROE consists of two returns: (1) the return from the company's operating activities, linked to revenues and expenses from the company's products or services, and (2) the return from the company's use of debt, net of any return from nonoperating investments. Companies can use debt to increase their return on equity, but this increases risk because the failure to make required debt payments can yield many legal consequences, including bankruptcy. This is one reason why Warren Buffett focuses on companies whose return on equity is derived primarily from operating activities.

BUSINESS INSIGHT Walmart's ROE and RNOA

The following graph shows that **Walmart's** ROE and RNOA have remained fairly constant and at relatively high levels for the past three years. ROE exceeds RNOA in all years, narrowing somewhat in the past two years as the company reduced the nonoperating return component of its ROE.

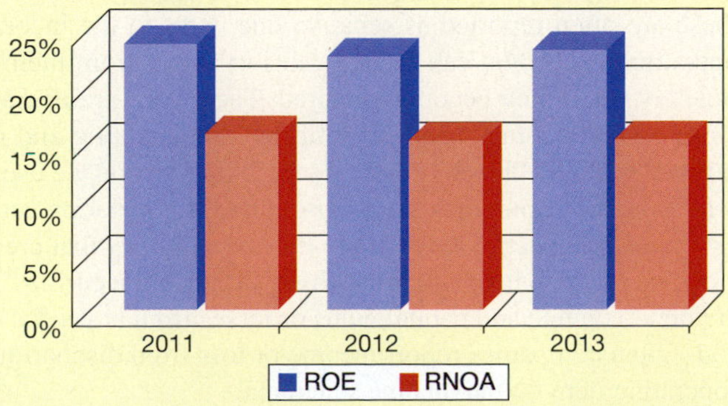

OPERATING RETURN (RNOA)

ALERT The FASB released a preliminary draft of a proposed new format for financial statements to, among other things, better distinguish operating and nonoperating activities. The FASB recognizes the crucial importance of distinguishing between operating and nonoperating activities for analysis purposes.

Operating returns are reflected in the **return on net operating assets (RNOA)**, defined as follows:

$$\text{RNOA} = \frac{\text{Net operating profit after tax (NOPAT)}}{\text{Average net operating assets (NOA)}}$$

To implement this formula, we must first classify the income statement and balance sheet into operating and nonoperating components so that we can assess each separately. We first consider operating activities on the income statement and explain how to compute NOPAT. Second, we consider operating activities on the balance sheet and explain how to compute NOA.

Operating Items in the Income Statement—NOPAT

The income statement reports both operating and nonoperating activities. Exhibit 4.1 shows a typical income statement with the operating activities highlighted.

EXHIBIT 4.1 Operating and Nonoperating Items in the Income Statement

Typical Income Statement Operating Items Highlighted in Red
Revenues
Cost of sales
Gross profit
Operating expenses
Selling, general and administrative
Asset impairment expense
Gains and losses on asset disposal
Total operating expenses
Operating income
Interest expense
Interest and dividend revenue
Investment gains and losses
Total nonoperating expenses
Income from continuing operations before taxes
Tax expense
Income from continuing operations
Income (loss) from discontinued operations, net of tax (see Appendix 4A)
Consolidated net income
Less: consolidated net income attributable to noncontrolling interest (see Appendix 4A)
Consolidated net income attributable to controlling interest (parent company stockholders)

Operating activities are those that relate to bringing a company's products or services to market and any after-sales support. The income statement in Exhibit 4.1 reflects operating activities through revenues, costs of goods sold (COGS), and other expenses. Selling, general, and administrative expense (SG&A) includes wages, advertising, occupancy, insurance, research and development, depreciation, and many other operating expenses the company incurs in the ordinary course of business (some of these are often reported as separate line items in the income statement). Companies also dispose of operating assets, and can realize gains or losses from their disposal, or write them off partially or completely when they become impaired. These, too, are operating activities. Finally, the reported tax expense on the income statement reflects both operating and nonoperating activities, which explains its mix of "red" and "black" colors. Later in this section we use Walmart's income statement to explain how to separately compute tax expense related to operating activities only.

Nonoperating activities relate to borrowed money that creates interest expense. Nonoperating activities also relate to investments such as marketable securities and other investments that yield interest or dividend revenue and capital gains or losses from any sales of nonoperating investments during the period. Often companies report income or loss from discontinued operations; which we consider as a nonoperating item on the income statement.

Following is Walmart's 2011–2013 income statement with the operating items highlighted. Walmart's operating items include sales, cost of sales, SG&A, and depreciation expense. Walmart's pretax operating income is $27,801 million. Its nonoperating activities relate to its borrowed money (interest expense) which yield pretax net nonoperating expense of $2,064 million.

WALMART Income Statement ($ millions) For Year Ended	Jan. 31, 2013	Jan. 31, 2012	Jan. 31, 2011
Revenues			
Net sales	$466,114	$443,854	$418,952
Membership and other Income	3,048	3,096	2,897
Total revenues	469,162	446,950	421,849
Costs and expenses			
Cost of sales	352,488	335,127	314,946
Operating, selling, general & administrative expenses	88,873	85,265	81,361
Operating income	27,801	26,558	25,542
Interest			
Debt	1,977	2,034	1,928
Capital leases	274	288	277
Interest income	(187)	(162)	(201)
Interest, net	2,064	2,160	2,004
Income from continuing operations before income taxes	25,737	24,398	23,538
Provision for income taxes			
Current Income Tax Expense	7,999	6,742	6,703
Deferred Income Tax Expense	(18)	1,202	876
Total provision for income taxes	7,981	7,944	7,579
Income from continuing operations	17,756	16,454	15,959
Loss from discontinued operations, net of income taxes	0	(67)	1,034
Consolidated net income	17,756	16,387	16,993
Less net income attributable to noncontrolling interest	(757)	(688)	(604)
Consolidated net income attributable to Walmart	$ 16,999	$ 15,699	$ 16,389

Computing Tax on Operating Profit

Walmart's income statement reports net operating profit *before* tax (NOPBT) of $27,801 million. But, the numerator of the RNOA formula, defined previously, uses net operating profit *after tax* (NOPAT). Thus, we need to subtract taxes to determine NOPAT.

NOPAT = NOPBT − Tax on operating profit

The tax expense of $7,981 million that Walmart reports on its income statement pertains to both operating *and* nonoperating activities. To compute NOPAT, we need to compute the tax expense relating solely to operating profit as follows:

Tax on operating profit = Tax expense + (Pretax net nonoperating expense × Statutory tax rate)

Tax Shield

The amount in parentheses is called the *tax shield*, which are the taxes that Walmart saved by having tax-deductible nonoperating expenses (see Tax Shield box on the next page for details). By definition, the taxes saved (by the tax shield) do not relate to operating profits; thus, we must add back the tax shield to total tax expense to compute the tax on operating profit. (For companies with nonoperating revenue greater than nonoperating expense, so-called *net nonoperating revenue*, the tax on operating profit is computed as: Tax expense − [Pretax net nonoperating revenue × Statutory tax rate]).

Applying this method to fiscal year 2013, we see that Walmart had a tax shield of $764 million (computed as pretax net nonoperating expense of $2,064 million times its statutory tax rate of 37%) and tax on operating profit of $8,745 million (computed as $7,981 million + $764 million).[1] We subtract the tax on operating profit from the net operating profit before tax to obtain NOPAT. Thus, Walmart's net operating profit after tax is computed as follows ($ millions):

Net operating profit before tax (NOPBT)		$27,801
Less tax on operating profit		
Tax expense (from income statement)	$7,981	
Tax shield ($2,064 × 37%)	+764	(8,745)
Net operating profit after tax (NOPAT)		$19,056

BUSINESS INSIGHT Tax Shield

Persons with home mortgages understand well the beneficial effects of the "interest tax shield." To see how the interest tax shield works, consider two individuals, each with income of $50,000 and each with only one expense: a home. Assume that one person pays $10,000 per year in rent; the other pays $10,000 in interest on a home mortgage. Rent is not deductible for tax purposes, whereas mortgage interest (but not principal) is deductible. Assume that each person pays taxes at 25%, the personal tax rate for this income level. Their tax payments follow.

	Renter	Home owner
Income before interest and taxes	$50,000	$50,000
Less interest deduction	0	(10,000)
Taxable income	$50,000	$40,000
Taxes paid (25% rate)	$12,500	$10,000

The renter reports $50,000 in taxable income and pays $12,500 in taxes. The home owner deducts $10,000 in interest, which lowers taxable income to $40,000 and reduces taxes to $10,000. By deducting mortgage interest, the home owner's tax bill is $2,500 lower. The $2,500 is the *interest tax shield*, and we can compute it directly as the $10,000 interest deduction multiplied by the 25% tax rate.

BUSINESS INSIGHT Tax Rates for Computing NOPAT

In our examples and assignments, we assume the statutory tax rate is 37% as this is the approximate average combined federal and state tax rate for public companies. We can, as an alternative approach, compute a *company-specific* tax rate using the income tax footnote in the 10-K. For example, **Walmart** provides the following table in its 10-K for the year ended January 31, 2013:

Fiscal Years Ended January 31	2013	2012	2011
U.S. statutory tax rate	35.0%	35.0%	35.0%
U.S. state income taxes, net of federal tax benefit	1.7	2.0	1.9
Income tax outside the U.S.	(2.6)	(2.8)	(2.2)
Net impact of repatriated international earnings	(2.5)	(0.3)	(1.5)
Other, net	(0.6)	(1.3)	(1.0)
Effective income tax rate	31.0%	32.6%	32.2%

The federal statutory rate is 35.0%, and **Walmart** pays state taxes amounting to an additional 1.7% (it also reports reductions of 5.7% relating to effects of taxes on income outside the U.S. and "other" items). Thus, **Walmart's** effective tax rate (or average) for *all* of its income is the sum of all its taxes paid less benefits received, or 31.0%. However, the tax shield that we add back in computing NOPAT uses only *federal and state tax rates*. For **Walmart**, the company-specific tax rate that we could use to compute the tax shield is 36.7% (35.0% + 1.7%). It would be incorrect, however, to use **Walmart's** 31.0% company-specific effective tax rate to compute NOPAT, as that rate includes both operating and nonoperating items. We discuss income tax more fully in Module 5.

[1] The statutory federal tax rate for corporations is 35% (per U.S. tax code). Also, most states and some local jurisdictions tax corporate income, and those state taxes are deductible for federal tax purposes. The *net* state tax rate is the statutory rate less the federal tax deduction. The tax rate on operating profit is the sum of the two. On average, the net state tax is about 2%; thus, we use 37% (35% + 2%) as the assumed tax rate on nonoperating expenses and revenues in our examples and assignments at the end of the module.

MID-MODULE REVIEW 1

Following is the income statement of **TJX Companies, Inc.**

TJX COMPANIES, INC. Income Statement ($ thousands) For Fiscal Year Ended February 2, 2013 Amounts in thousands	February 2, 2013 (53 weeks)
Net sales	$25,878,372
Cost of sales, including buying and occupancy costs	18,521,400
Selling, general and administrative expenses	4,250,446
Interest expense, net	29,175
Income from continuing operations before provision for income taxes	3,077,351
Provision for income taxes	1,170,664
Net income	$ 1,906,687

Required

Compute TJX's net operating profit after tax (NOPAT). Assume a statutory rate of 37% applies to nonoperating expenses and revenues.

The solution is on page 4-58.

Operating Items in the Balance Sheet—NOA

RNOA relates NOPAT to the average net operating assets (NOA) of the company. We compute NOA as follows:

Net operating assets = Operating assets − Operating liabilities

To compute NOA we must partition the balance sheet into operating and nonoperating items. Exhibit 4.2 shows a typical balance sheet and highlights the operating items.

EXHIBIT 4.2 Operating and Nonoperating Items in the Balance Sheet

Typical Balance Sheet Operating Items Highlighted in Red	
Current assets	**Current liabilities**
Cash and cash equivalents	Short-term notes and interest payable
Short-term investments	Current maturities of long-term debt
Accounts receivable	Dividends payable
Inventories	**Accounts payable**
Prepaid expenses	**Accrued liabilities**
Deferred income tax assets	**Unearned revenue**
Other current assets	**Deferred income tax liabilities**
Current assets of discontinued operations	Current liabilities of discontinued operations
Loans receivable	
	Long-term liabilities
Long-term assets	Bonds and notes payable
Long-term investments in securities	Capitalized lease obligations
Property, plant and equipment, net	**Pension and other post-employment liabilities**
Capitalized lease assets	**Deferred income tax liabilities**
Natural resources	Long-term liabilities of discontinued operations
Equity method investments	Derivative liabilities
Goodwill and intangible assets	
Deferred income tax assets	**Stockholders' equity**
Other long-term assets	All equity accounts
Long-term assets of discontinued operations	
Derivative assets	Noncontrolling interest

Operating Assets Operating assets are those assets directly linked to operating activities, the company's ongoing (continuing) business operations. They typically include receivables, inventories, prepaid expenses, property, plant and equipment (PPE), and capitalized lease assets. Operating assets are those the company needs to operate normally, and those assets can be purchased outright or leased. Leasing is a way to acquire an asset for use without the upfront cash outlay. If the leased asset is used for operations, then it is an operating asset and we categorize it as such *regardless* of how it was financed.

Operating assets *exclude* short-term and long-term investments in marketable securities. However, companies sometimes purchase equity interests in other companies for strategic purposes (see Module 7). For example, a company might buy the stock of its major supplier or transporter to secure the supply chain. Or a company might take an equity position in another company as a prelude to an acquisition. Such ownership positions usually involve a significant percentage of the outstanding common stock (20% or more). Because such investments are strategic and represent part of the ongoing, ordinary operating activities of a company, we categorize them as *operating* assets.

Intangible assets and goodwill result from mergers with, or acquisitions of, other companies (see Module 7). These deals have the effect of the acquirer buying a collection of operating assets (including operating liabilities). Accordingly, all intangible assets and goodwill are operating assets and we categorize them as such.

Deferred tax assets (and liabilities) are operating items because they relate to future tax deductions (or payments) arising from operating activities (see Module 5). We assume that "other" assets and liabilities, and "other" revenues and expenses, are operating unless information suggests otherwise. For example, details in footnotes might reveal that "other" includes nonoperating items. Or the company might explicitly indicate the "other" is nonoperating by reporting the item after a subtotal for income from operations. In these cases, we would consider the "other" as nonoperating.

Operating Liabilities Operating liabilities are liabilities that arise from operating revenues and expenses. For example, accounts payable and accrued expenses help fund inventories, wages, utilities, and other operating expenses. Unearned revenue is part of operating liabilities because it relates to operating revenue. Similarly, pension and other post-employment obligations relate to long-term obligations for employee retirement and health care, which by definition are operating activities (see Module 10).

Nonoperating Assets Nonoperating assets include cash and cash equivalents (see Business Insight box on next page) and investments in marketable securities, both short- and long-term. These investments can take many forms. Some companies invest in marketable equity securities to earn a return in the form of dividends and price appreciation. Companies might also purchase bonds or other debt instruments issued by other companies and organizations for interest income and price appreciation. These investments represent nonoperating assets. We treat all marketable equity and debt investments like cash and cash equivalents (nonoperating) regardless of whether those non-strategic investments appear on the balance sheet as current or long-term assets.

Sometimes companies make loans to customers, suppliers, or other parties, and we categorize such non-core (receivable) assets as nonoperating. (Note: For financial services companies such as banks and insurance firms, debt and equity securities along with loans and notes to customers, are part of normal operations and are categorized as operating assets; but for non-financial companies such as retailers, manufacturers, and service providers, these items are apart from ordinary operating activities and represent nonoperating assets.) We categorize assets (and liabilities) from discontinued operations as nonoperating as they represent assets and liabilities that have been sold to another party due to a reorganization or spin-off. Similarly, assets and liabilities "held for sale" are categorized as nonoperating because the company has formally decided to sell them to another party (see Special Topics in Appendix 4A for a discussion of how discontinued operations affect our analyses).

Nonoperating Liabilities Nonoperating liabilities include all interest-bearing debt, both short- and long-term. This is the case irrespective of whether the debt relates to the purchase of a specific asset, like a mortgage on a building or a loan on equipment. The purpose of the debt does *not* affect its categorization: interest-bearing debt, whether short-term or long-term, whether tied to an operating asset or not, is always categorized as nonoperating.

Lease liabilities are treated as *nonoperating*. Leases are another form of borrowing where a specific asset is acquired for use in exchange for future lease payments. Simply put, leases are like collateralized loans. Accordingly, lease liabilities are categorized exactly as all loans, as *nonoperating*. Note that lease assets are categorized as operating and lease liabilities are categorized as nonoperating.

Companies use derivatives to hedge (mitigate) risk or to speculate (Module 9 explains derivatives and how we account for them). Derivatives are reported on balance sheets as liabilities or assets, and sometimes both. For analysis purposes, all derivatives are nonoperating items. Admittedly, some derivative positions are operating assets or liabilities; for example, a forward contract on a company's manufacturing feedstock. Other derivatives are clearly nonoperating; for example, an interest rate swap. However, distinguishing between the two is complicated and often impossible for an external analyst. Accordingly, we treat all derivatives as nonoperating, both assets and liabilities.

BUSINESS INSIGHT **Why is Cash a Nonoperating Asset?**

Most analysts consider cash as nonoperating because this account consists almost totally of "cash equivalents," which are short-term investments with a scheduled maturity of 90 days or less. Technically, the amount of cash needed to support routine business transactions is considered as operating and the remainder as a nonoperating short-term investment, similar to investments reported as marketable securities. If we know what portion of the cash balance supports operating activities, we would classify that as operating. Unfortunately, companies do not report that information and most analysts feel that it is probably a small portion. As a result, we, like others, treat the entire cash balance as nonoperating and recognize that we are probably understating net operating assets slightly.

To summarize, operating assets and liabilities relate to the company's core activities, those required to deliver a company's products or services to its customers. Nonoperating assets and liabilities relate to financing, non-core investing, and discontinued operations. (Admittedly, analysts do not all agree on the operating versus nonoperating classification of some assets and liabilities, and we highlight those as we encounter them.) The following are Walmart's balance sheets for 2013 and 2012, with operating assets and operating liabilities highlighted.

WALMART
Balance Sheets

(In millions)	Jan. 31, 2013	Jan. 31, 2012
Assets		
Current assets		
Cash and cash equivalents	$ 7,781	$ 6,550
Receivables, net	6,768	5,937
Inventories	43,803	40,714
Prepaid expenses and other	1,588	1,774
Total current assets	59,940	54,975
Property and equipment		
Property and equipment, gross	165,825	155,002
Less accumulated depreciation	(51,896)	(45,399)
Property and equipment, net	113,929	109,603
Property under capital leases		
Property under capital leases	5,899	5,936
Less accumulated amortization	(3,147)	(3,215)
Property under capital leases, net	2,752	2,721
Goodwill	20,497	20,651
Other assets and deferred charges	5,987	5,456
Total assets	$203,105	$193,406

continued

continued from prior page

Liabilities and equity		
Current liabilities		
Short-term borrowings	$ 6,805	$ 4,047
Accounts payable	**38,080**	**36,608**
Accrued liabilities	**18,808**	**18,180**
Accrued income taxes	**2,211**	**1,164**
Long-term debt due within one year	5,587	1,975
Obligations under capital leases due within one year	327	326
Total current liabilities	71,818	62,300
Long-term debt	38,394	44,070
Long-term obligations under capital leases	3,023	3,009
Deferred income taxes and other	**7,613**	**7,862**
Redeemable noncontrolling interest†	519	404
Equity		
Common stock	332	342
Capital in excess of par value	3,620	3,692
Retained earnings	72,978	68,691
Accumulated other comprehensive income (loss)	(587)	(1,410)
Total Walmart shareholders' equity	76,343	71,315
Noncontrolling interest	5,395	4,446
Total equity	81,738	75,761
Total liabilities and equity	$203,105	$193,406

† *Redeemable noncontrolling interest* is a contractual obligation that Walmart has to repurchase ("redeem") shares owned by noncontrolling shareholders of a Walmart subsidiary (acquired in 2011) if so demanded by those shareholders.

We assume that Walmart's "other" assets and liabilities are operating. We can sometimes make a finer distinction if footnotes to financial statements provide additional information. For now, assume that these "other" items reported in balance sheets pertain to operations.

Using Walmart's highlighted balance sheet above, we compute net operating assets for 2013 and 2012 as follows (recall that Net operating assets (NOA) = Total operating assets − Total operating liabilities).

Walmart ($ millions)	**Jan. 31, 2013**	**Jan. 31, 2012**
Operating assets		
Receivables, net	$ 6,768	$ 5,937
Inventories	43,803	40,714
Prepaid Expense and Other Assets, Current	1,588	1,774
Property and equipment, net	113,929	109,603
Property under capital leases, net	2,752	2,721
Goodwill	20,497	20,651
Other assets and deferred charges	5,987	5,456
Total operating assets	**195,324**	**186,856**
Operating liabilities		
Accounts payable	38,080	36,608
Accrued liabilities	18,808	18,180
Accrued income taxes	2,211	1,164
Deferred income taxes and other	7,613	7,862
Total operating liabilities	**66,712**	**63,814**
Net operating assets (NOA)	$128,612	$123,042

Computing Return on Net Operating Assets (RNOA)

To determine average NOA, we take a simple average of two consecutive years' numbers. Thus, return on net operating assets (RNOA) for Walmart for 2013 is computed as follows ($ millions).

$$\text{RNOA} = \frac{\text{NOPAT}}{\text{Average NOA}} = \frac{\$19{,}056}{(\$128{,}612 + \$123{,}042)/2} = 15.14\%$$

Walmart's 2013 RNOA is 15.14%. By comparison, TJX's (the mid-module review company) RNOA is 80.42% (this computation is shown in Mid-Module Review 2). The average RNOA for publicly traded companies is about 10.5% over the past couple decades, which is apparent from the Research Insight on page 4-18.

Recall that RNOA is related to ROE as follows: ROE = Operating return + Nonoperating return, where RNOA is the operating return. Thus, we can ask how do Walmart's RNOA and ROE compare? To answer this we need Walmart's 2013 ROE, which is computed as follows ($ millions).

$$\text{ROE} = \frac{\textbf{Net income attributable to controlling interest}}{\textbf{Average equity attributable to controlling interest}} = \frac{\$16{,}999}{(\$76{,}343 + \$71{,}315)/2} = 23.02\%$$

In relative terms, Walmart's operating return (RNOA) is 66% (15.14%/23.02%) of its total ROE, which is slightly less than the average publicly traded company's percent of near 71%. Its nonoperating return of 7.88% (23.02% − 15.14%) makes up the remaining 34% of ROE.

Exhibit 4.3 provides a summary of key terms introduced to this point and their definitions.

EXHIBIT 4.3 Key Ratio and Acronym Definitions

Ratio	Definition
ROE: Return on equity	Net income attributable to controlling interest/Average equity attributable to controlling interest
NOPAT: Net operating profit after tax	Operating revenues less operating expenses such as cost of sales, selling, general and administrative expense, and taxes; it excludes nonoperating revenues and expenses such as interest revenue, dividend revenue, interest expense, gains and losses on investments, discontinued operations.
NOA: Net operating assets	Operating assets less operating liabilities; it excludes nonoperating items such as investments in marketable securities and interest-bearing debt.
RNOA: Return on net operating assets	NOPAT/Average NOA
NNE: Net nonoperating expense	NOPAT − Consolidated net income; NNE consists of nonoperating expenses and revenues, net of tax.

ANALYSIS INSIGHT Walmart's Measurement of RNOA

Many companies report RNOA to stockholders and other stakeholders in the MD&A section of their 10-Ks. Because RNOA is, technically, a non-GAAP measure of performance, we see variants of this ratio in practice. Walmart, for example, labels this ratio as Return on Investment (ROI) and offers the following discussion in its 2013 10-K:

> Management believes return on investment ("ROI") is a meaningful metric to share with investors because it helps investors assess how effectively Walmart is deploying its assets . . . We define ROI as adjusted operating income (operating income plus interest income, depreciation and amortization, and rent expense) for the fiscal year divided by average invested capital during that period. We consider average invested capital to be the average of our beginning and ending total assets of continuing operations, plus average accumulated depreciation and average amortization less average accounts payable and average accrued liabilities for that period, plus a rent factor equal to the rent for the fiscal year or trailing twelve months multiplied by a factor of eight . . . Although ROI is a standard financial metric, numerous methods exist for calculating a company's ROI. As a result, the method used by management to calculate our ROI may differ from the methods other companies use to calculate their ROI. We urge you to understand the methods used by other companies to calculate their ROI before comparing our ROI to that of such other companies.

Walmart's ROI is similar to RNOA as defined here in that it focuses on operating income and net operating assets. Because companies generally report metrics that they have adapted for their industries, we agree with the cautionary statement that Walmart includes at the end of its discussion: "We urge you to understand the methods used by other companies to calculate their ROI before comparing our ROI to that of such other companies."

RNOA DISAGGREGATION INTO MARGIN AND TURNOVER

LO2 Disaggregate operating return (RNOA) into components of profitability and asset turnover.

Disaggregating RNOA into its two components, profit margin and asset turnover, yields further insights into a company's performance. This disaggregation follows.

$$\text{RNOA} = \frac{\text{NOPAT}}{\text{Average NOA}} = \underbrace{\frac{\text{NOPAT}}{\text{Sales}}}_{\substack{\text{Net operating profit margin (NOPM)}}} \times \underbrace{\frac{\text{Sales}}{\text{Average NOA}}}_{\substack{\text{Net operating asset turnover (NOAT)}}}$$

Net Operating Profit Margin

Net operating profit margin (NOPM) reveals how much operating profit the company earns from each sales dollar. All things equal, a higher NOPM is preferable. NOPM is affected by the level of gross profit the company earns on its products (revenue minus cost of goods sold), which depends on product prices and manufacturing or purchase costs. NOPM is also affected by the level of operating expenses the company requires to support its products or services. This includes overhead costs such as wages, marketing, occupancy, and research and development. Finally, NOPM is affected by the level of competition (which affects product pricing) and the company's willingness and ability to control costs.

Walmart's net operating profit margin is computed as follows ($ millions).

$$\text{NOPM} = \frac{\text{NOPAT}}{\text{Revenues}} = \frac{\$19{,}056}{\$469{,}162} = 4.06\%$$

This result means that for each dollar of sales at Walmart, the company earns roughly 4.06¢ profit after all operating expenses and taxes. As a reference, the median NOPM for U.S. publicly traded companies with revenues greater than $1 billion in 2012 is about 8¢.

BUSINESS INSIGHT **Walmart's NOPM**

The following chart shows that Walmart's net operating profit margin has decreased slightly from 4.08% to 4.06% of revenues over the past three years. This relatively low absolute level reflects the intense competition that Walmart faces in an industry with largely undifferentiated products and its emphasis on value-pricing.

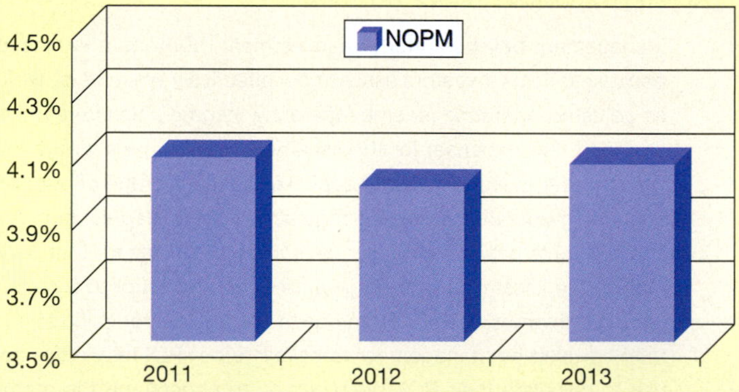

Net Operating Asset Turnover

Net operating asset turnover (NOAT) measures the productivity of the company's net operating assets. This metric reveals the level of sales the company realizes from each dollar invested in net operating assets. All things equal, a higher NOAT is preferable. Walmart's net operating asset turnover ratio follows ($ millions).

$$\text{NOAT} = \frac{\text{Revenues}}{\text{Average NOA}} = \frac{\$469{,}162}{(\$128{,}612 + \$123{,}042)/2} = 3.73$$

This result means that for each dollar of net operating assets, Walmart realizes $3.73 in sales. As a reference, the median for U.S. publicly traded companies with revenues greater than $1 billion in 2012 is about $1.3.

NOAT can be increased by either increasing sales for a given level of investment in operating assets, or by reducing the amount of operating assets necessary to generate a dollar of sales, or both. Reducing operating working capital (current operating assets less current operating liabilities) is usually easier than reducing long-term net operating assets. For example, companies can implement strategies to collect their receivables faster, reduce their inventories, and delay payments to their suppliers. All of these actions reduce operating working capital and, thereby, increase NOAT. These strategies must be managed, however, so as not to negatively impact sales or supplier relations. Working capital management is an important part of managing the company effectively.

It is usually more difficult to reduce the level of long-term net operating assets. The level of PPE required by the company is determined more by the nature of the company's products or services than by management action. For example, telecommunications companies require more capital investment than do retail stores. Still, there are several actions that managers can take to reduce capital investment. Some companies pursue novel approaches, such as corporate alliances, outsourcing, and use of special purpose entities; we discuss some of these approaches in Module 10.

BUSINESS INSIGHT **Walmart's NOAT**

The following chart shows Walmart's net operating asset turnover from 2011 to 2013. Walmart's operating asset turnover has decreased slightly from 3.83 to 3.73 during this period, but it is greater than the median for publicly traded companies. Given Walmart's value-pricing and relatively low operating margins, it must closely manage its operating assets to obtain an acceptable RNOA. Its relatively high NOAT provides evidence of success on this dimension.

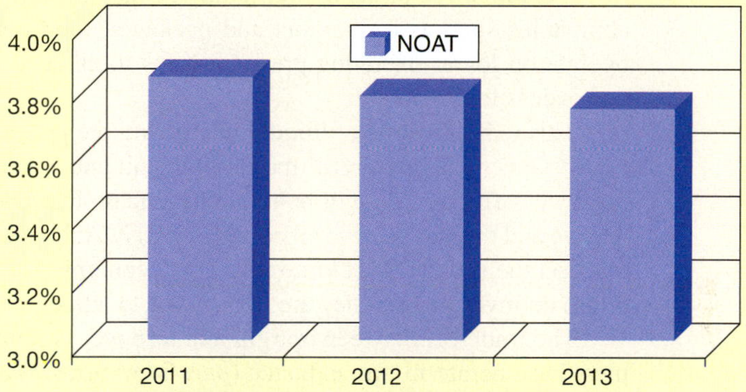

MANAGERIAL DECISION **You Are the CEO**

You are analyzing the performance of your company. Your analysis of RNOA reveals the following (industry benchmarks in parentheses): RNOA is 16% (10%), NOPM is 18% (17%), and NOAT is 0.89 (0.59). What interpretations do you draw that are useful for managing your company? [Answer, p. 4-36]

Trade-Off between Margin and Turnover

Operating profit margin and turnover of net operating assets are largely affected by a company's business model. This is an important concept. Specifically, an infinite number of combinations of net operating profit margin and net operating asset turnover will yield a given RNOA. This relation is depicted in Exhibit 4.4 (where the curved line reflects the median RNOA for all publicly traded companies during 2012).

EXHIBIT 4.4 Profitability and Productivity Across Industries

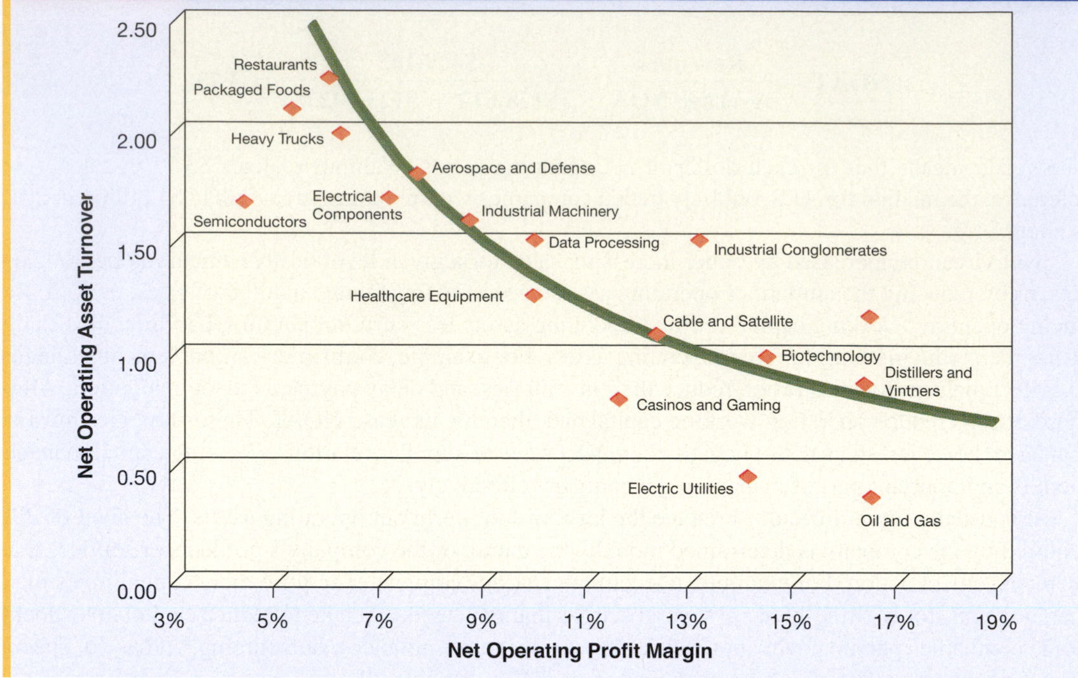

This exhibit reveals that some industries, such as oil and gas and utilities, are capital intensive with relatively low net operating asset turnover. Accordingly, for such industries to achieve a required RNOA (to be competitive in the overall market), they must obtain a higher profit margin. On the other hand, companies such as restaurants and packaged food companies hold fewer assets and, therefore, can operate on lower operating profit margins to achieve a sufficient RNOA. This is because their asset turnover is far greater.

This exhibit warns of blindly comparing the performance of companies across different industries. For instance, a higher profit margin in the oil and gas industry compared with the restaurant industry is not necessarily the result of better management. Instead, the oil and gas industry is extremely capital intensive and thus, to achieve an equivalent RNOA, oil and gas companies must earn a higher profit margin to offset their lower asset turnover. Basic economics suggests that all industries must earn an acceptable return on investment if they are to continue to attract investors and survive.

The trade-off between margin and turnover is relatively straightforward when comparing companies that operate in one industry (*pure-play* firms). Analyzing conglomerates that operate in several industries is more challenging. Conglomerates' margins and turnover rates are a weighted average of the margins and turnover rates for the various industries in which they operate. For example, **Caterpillar, Inc.,** is a blend of a manufacturing company and a financial institution (**Caterpillar Financial Services Corp.**); thus, the margin and turnover benchmarks for Caterpillar on a consolidated basis are a weighted average of those two industries.

To summarize, ROE is the sum of the returns from operating (RNOA) and nonoperating activities. Further, RNOA is the product of NOPM and NOAT.

RESEARCH INSIGHT NOPM and NOAT Explain Stock Prices

Research shows that stock returns are positively associated with earnings—when companies report higher than expected earnings, stock returns rise. Research also reports that the RNOA components (NOPM and NOAT) are more strongly associated with stock returns and future profitability than earnings (or return on assets) alone. This applies to the short-term market response to earnings announcements and long-term stock price changes. Thus, disaggregating earnings and the balance sheet into operating and nonoperating components is a useful analysis tool.

Source: Soliman, Mark T., *Use of DuPont Analysis by Market Participants*, The Accounting Review, May 2008, 83(3): 823-853.

MID-MODULE REVIEW 2

Following is the balance sheet of TJX Companies, Inc.

TJX COMPANIES, INC. Balance Sheets	Fiscal Year Ended	
Amounts in thousands except share amounts	February 2, 2013	January 28, 2012
Assets		
Current assets:		
Cash and cash equivalents	$1,811,957	$1,507,112
Short-term investments	235,853	94,691
Accounts receivable, net	222,788	204,304
Merchandise inventories	3,014,214	2,950,523
Prepaid expenses and other current assets	330,512	270,133
Current deferred income taxes, net	96,219	105,869
Total current assets	5,711,543	5,132,632
Property at cost:		
Land and buildings	607,759	349,778
Leasehold costs and improvements	2,514,998	2,311,813
Furniture, fixtures and equipment	3,771,999	3,426,966
Total property at cost	6,894,756	6,088,557
Less accumulated depreciation and amortization	3,671,514	3,382,180
Net property at cost	3,223,242	2,706,377
Property under capital lease, net of accumulated amortization	—	8,748
Other assets	260,801	253,913
Goodwill and tradename, net of amortization	316,269	179,935
Total assets	$9,511,855	$8,281,605
Liabilities		
Current liabilities:		
Obligation under capital lease due within one year	$ —	$ 2,970
Accounts payable	1,930,568	1,645,324
Accrued expenses and other current liabilities	1,666,216	1,364,705
Federal, foreign and state income taxes payable	163,812	50,424
Total current liabilities	3,760,596	3,063,423
Other long-term liabilities	961,284	861,768
Non-current deferred income taxes, net	349,486	362,501
Obligation under capital lease, less portion due within one year	—	10,147
Long-term debt, exclusive of current installments	774,552	774,476
Shareholders' equity		
Common stock, authorized 1,200,000,000 shares, par value $1, issued and outstanding 723,902,001 and 746,702,028, respectively	723,902	746,702
Additional paid-in capital	—	—
Accumulated other comprehensive income (loss)	(213,392)	(192,575)
Retained earnings	3,155,427	2,655,163
Total shareholders' equity	3,665,937	3,209,290
Total liabilities and shareholders' equity	$9,511,855	$8,281,605

Required

1. Compute TJX's net operating assets for 2013 and 2012.
2. Refer to TJX's income statement and NOPAT from Mid-Module Review 1. Compute TJX's return on net operating assets (RNOA) for 2013.
3. Compute TJX's 2013 ROE. Comment on the reason for the relation between RNOA and ROE.
4. Disaggregate TJX's 2013 RNOA into net operating profit margin (NOPM) and net operating asset turnover (NOAT).
5. Compare and contrast TJX's ROE, RNOA, NOPM, and NOAT with those same measures computed in this module for Walmart. Interpret the results.

The solution is on page 4-59.

Further RNOA Disaggregation

While disaggregation of RNOA into net operating profit margin (NOPM) and net operating asset turnover (NOAT) yields valuable insight into factors driving company performance, analysts and creditors usually disaggregate those components even further. The purpose is to better identify the specific drivers of both profitability and turnover.

To disaggregate NOPM, we examine the gross profit on products sold and the individual expense accounts that affect operating profit as a percentage of sales (such as Gross profit/Sales and SG&A/Sales). These margin ratios aid comparisons across companies of differing sizes and across different time periods for the same company. We further discuss profit margin disaggregation in other modules that focus on operating results.

To disaggregate NOAT, we examine the individual balance sheet accounts that comprise NOA and compare them to the related income statement activity. Specifically, we compute accounts receivable turnover (ART), inventory turnover (INVT), property, plant and equipment turnover (PPET), as well as turnovers for liability accounts such as accounts payable (APT). Analysts and creditors often compute the net operating working capital turnover (NOWCT) to assess a company's working capital management compared to its competitors and recent trends. (Recall that operating working capital is calculated as current operating assets less current operating liabilities.) These turnover rates are further discussed in other modules that focus on operating assets and liabilities. Exhibit 4.5 provides a broad overview of ratios commonly used for component disaggregation and analysis.

EXHIBIT 4.5 ROE Disaggregation

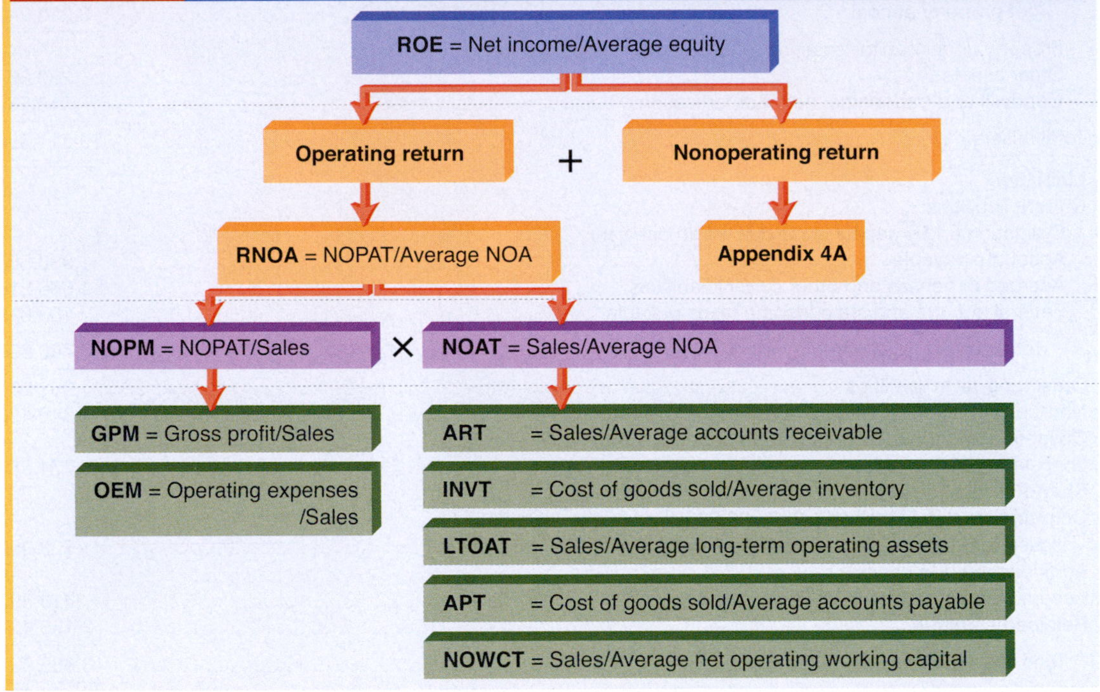

NONOPERATING RETURN

LO3 Explain nonoperating return and compute it from return on equity and the operating return.

This section discusses a company's nonoperating return. In its simplest form, the return on nonoperating activities measures the extent to which a company is using debt to increase its return on equity.

Equity Only Financing

The following example provides the intuition for nonoperating return. Assume that a company has $1,000 in net operating assets for the current year in which it earns a 20% RNOA. It finances those assets entirely with equity investment (no debt). To simplify this example, we assume that taxes are 0%; later, we explain the impact of taxes. Its ROE is computed as follows:

$$\begin{aligned} \textbf{ROE} &= \textbf{Operating return} + \textbf{Nonoperating return} \\ &= \quad \textbf{20\%} \quad + \quad \textbf{0\%} \\ &= \quad \textbf{20\%} \end{aligned}$$

Equity and Debt Financing

Next, assume that this company borrows $500 at 7% interest and uses those funds to acquire additional operating assets yielding the same 20% operating return as above. Its net operating assets for the year now total $1,500, and its profit is $265, computed as follows:

Profit from assets financed with equity ($1,000 × 20%)		$200
Profit from assets financed with debt ($500 × 20%).	$100	
Less interest expense from debt ($500 × 7%)	(35)	65
Net profit.		$265

We see that this company has increased its profit to $265 (up from $200) with the addition of debt, and its ROE is now 26.5% ($265/$1,000). The reason for the increased ROE is that the company borrowed $500 at 7% (and paid $35 of interest expense) and invested those funds in assets earning 20% (which generated $100 of profits). That difference of 13% ($65 profit, computed as [20% − 7%] × $500) accrues to stockholders. Stated differently, the company's ROE now consists of the following.

$$\begin{aligned} \textbf{ROE} &= \textbf{Operating return} + \textbf{Nonoperating return} \\ &= \quad \textbf{20\%} \quad + \quad \textbf{6.5\%} \\ &= \quad \textbf{26.5\%} \end{aligned}$$

The company has made effective use of debt to increase its ROE. Here, we infer the nonoperating return as the difference between ROE and RNOA. This return can be computed directly, and we provide an expanded discussion of this computation in Appendix 4A.

Advantages and Disadvantages of Equity versus Debt Financing

We might further ask: If a higher ROE is desirable, why don't companies use the maximum possible debt? The answer is that creditors, such as banks and bondholders, charge successively higher interest rates for

RESEARCH INSIGHT **Ratio Behavior over Time**

How do RNOA and ROE behave over time? Following is a graph of these ratios (on average for a large set of firms) over the past decade. We see there is considerable variability in these ratios over time. The proportion of RNOA to ROE is greater for some periods of time than for others. Yet, in all periods for this large sample of firms, ROE exceeds RNOA. This is evidence of a positive effect, on average, for ROE from financial leverage.

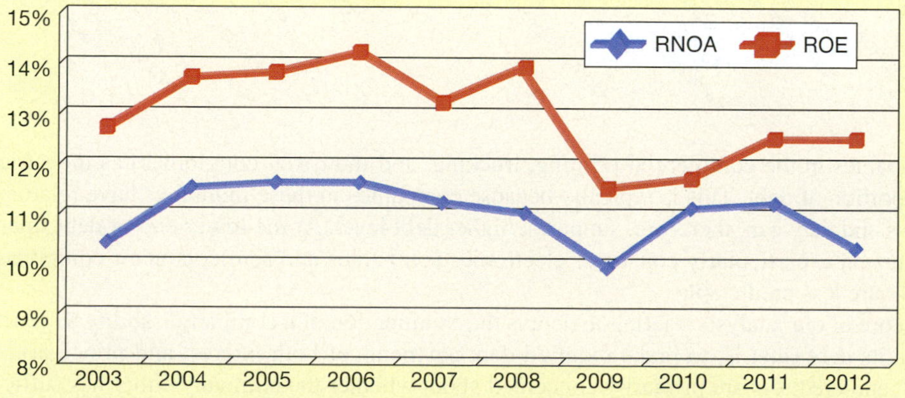

increasing levels of debt relative to the amount of equity investment (see Module 8). At some point, the cost of the additional debt exceeds the return on the additional assets acquired from the debt financing. Thereafter, further debt financing does not make economic sense. The market, in essence, places a limit on the level of debt that a company can effectively acquire. In sum, stockholders benefit from increased use of debt provided that the assets financed with the debt earn a return that exceeds the cost of the debt.

Creditors usually require a company to execute a loan agreement that places varying restrictions on the company's operating activities. These restrictions, called *covenants*, help safeguard debtholders in the face of increased risk. Covenants exist because debtholders do not have a voice on the board of directors like stockholders do. These debt covenants impose a "cost" on the company beyond that of the interest rate, and these covenants are more stringent as a company increases its reliance on debt financing.

FINANCIAL LEVERAGE ACROSS INDUSTRIES

As we have seen, companies can effectively use debt to increase ROE with returns from nonoperating activities. The advantage of debt is that it typically is a less costly source of financing due to the relatively less risky position of debt holders and the tax deductibility of interest expense; over the past few decades, the cost of debt is about 4% versus a cost of equity of about 12%, on average. Although it reduces financing costs, debt does carry default risk: the risk that the company will be unable to repay debt when it comes due. Creditors have several legal remedies when companies default, including forcing a company into bankruptcy and possibly liquidating its assets.

In 2012, the median ratio of total liabilities to stockholders' equity, which measures the relative use of debt versus equity in a company's capital structure, is about 1.5 for U.S. publicly traded companies with sales over $1 billion. This means that the average company is financed with about $1.50 of liabilities for each dollar of stockholders' equity. However, the relative use of debt varies considerably across industries as illustrated in Exhibit 4.6.

EXHIBIT 4.6 Median Ratio of Liabilities to Equity for Selected Industries

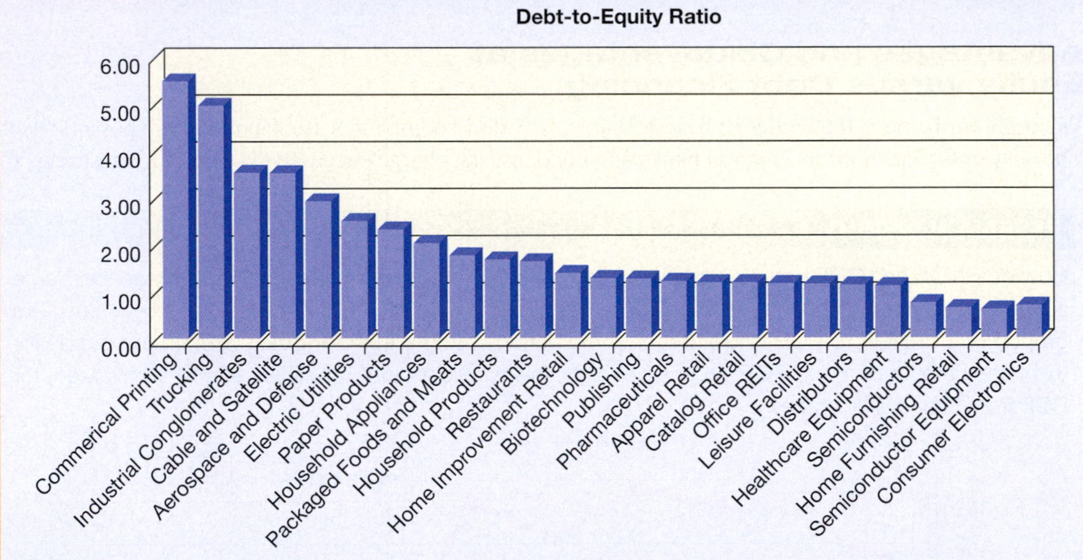

Companies in the commercial printing, trucking, and industrial conglomerates industries have a large proportion of debt. This is typically because companies in these industries have relatively stable cash flows and they can, therefore, support a higher debt level. At the lower end of debt financing are retail companies, particularly consumer electronics companies and semiconductor equipment, whose cash flows are less predictable.

The core of our analysis relating to debt is the examination of a company's ability to generate cash to *service* its debt (that is, to make required debt payments of both interest and principal). Analysts, investors, and creditors are primarily concerned about whether the company either has sufficient cash available or whether it is able to generate the required cash in the future to cover its debt obligations.

The analysis of available cash and a company's ability to service its debt in the short run is called *liquidity analysis*. The analysis of the company's ability to generate sufficient cash in the long run is called *solvency analysis* (so named because a bankrupt company is said to be "insolvent").

Limitations of Ratio Analysis

The quality of financial statement analysis depends on the quality of financial information. We ought not blindly analyze numbers; doing so can lead to faulty conclusions and suboptimal decisions. Instead, we need to acknowledge that current accounting rules (GAAP) have limitations, and be fully aware of the company's environment, its competitive pressures, and any structural and strategic changes. This section discusses some of the factors that limit the usefulness of financial accounting information for ratio analysis.

GAAP Limitations Several limitations in GAAP can distort financial ratios. Limitations include:

1. **Measurability**. Financial statements reflect what can be reliably measured. This results in nonrecognition of certain assets, often internally developed assets, the very assets that are most likely to confer a competitive advantage and create value. Examples are brand name, a superior management team, employee skills, and a reliable supply chain.
2. **Non-capitalized costs**. Related to the concept of measurability is the expensing of costs relating to "assets" that cannot be identified with enough precision to warrant capitalization. Examples are brand equity costs from advertising and other promotional activities, and research and development costs relating to future products.
3. **Historical costs**. Assets and liabilities are usually recorded at original acquisition or issuance costs. Subsequent increases in value are not recorded until realized, and declines in value are only recognized if deemed permanent.

Thus, GAAP balance sheets omit important and valuable assets. Our analysis of ROE and our assessment of liquidity and solvency, must consider that assets can be underreported and that ratios can be distorted. We discuss many of these limitations in more detail in later modules.

Company Changes Many companies regularly undertake mergers, acquire new companies, and divest subsidiaries. Such major operational changes can impair the comparability of company ratios across time. Companies also change strategies, such as product pricing, R&D, and financing. We must understand the effects of such changes on ratios and exercise caution when we compare ratios from one period to the next. Companies also behave differently at different points in their life cycles. For instance, growth companies possess a different profile than do mature companies. Seasonal effects also markedly impact analysis of financial statements at different times of the year. Thus, we must consider life cycle and seasonality when we compare ratios across companies and over time.

Conglomerate Effects Few companies are a pure-play; instead, most companies operate in several businesses or industries. Most publicly traded companies consist of a parent company and multiple subsidiaries, often pursuing different lines of business. Most heavy equipment manufacturers, for example, have finance subsidiaries (**Ford Credit Corporation** and **Caterpillar Financial Services Corporation** are subsidiaries of **Ford** and **Caterpillar** respectively). Financial statements of such conglomerates are consolidated and include the financial statements of the parent and its subsidiaries. Consequently, such consolidated statements are challenging to analyze. Typically, analysts break the financials apart into their component businesses and separately analyze each component. Fortunately, companies must report financial information (albeit limited) for major business segments in their 10-Ks.

Fuzzy View Ratios reduce, to a single number, the myriad complexities of a company's operations. No scalar can accurately capture all qualitative aspects of a company. Ratios cannot meaningfully convey a company's marketing and management philosophies, its human resource activities, its financing activities, its strategic initiatives, and its product management. In our analysis we must learn to look through the numbers and ratios to better understand the operational factors that drive financial results. Successful analysis seeks to gain insight into what a company is really about and what the future portends. Our overriding purpose in analysis is to understand the past and present to better predict the future. Computing and examining ratios is one step in that process.

ANALYSIS INSIGHT Analyzing Gains and Losses on Asset Sales

Gains and losses on asset sales, whether from an individual asset such as a truck or from an entire subsidiary company, are computed as: Gain (loss) = Sale proceeds − Net book value of asset(s) when sold. In the year of sale, the computed gain or loss is a *transitory item*, meaning that it occurs in only one year and will not be repeated. This *transitory* gain or loss complicates our analysis in two ways:

1. The gain (loss) will increase (decrease) income in the year of sale, and
2. The gain or loss reflects estimation error (not errors in GAAP) in prior period financial statements.

Point one is straightforward, however, point two requires additional explanation. Consider a truck purchase which is reported on the balance sheet at cost. The truck is depreciated over its estimated useful life. Each year, as depreciation expense is reported on the income statement, the balance sheet value of the truck decreases by that same amount. If in each year, the depreciation expense perfectly tracks the decline in the truck's economic value, then the value of the truck reported on the balance sheet (its net book value) matches the truck's market value. If and when the truck is sold, its net book value and its market value are equal and there is no gain or loss on the sale. But accounting depreciation expense rarely matches the decline in market value and, consequently, most asset sales create a gain or loss. One can argue that a gain or loss on the sale of the truck indicates that the company misestimated the truck's useful life or the depreciation pattern (in hindsight). A gain suggests that too much depreciation was recorded over the truck's life and that income reported in prior financial statements was too low. A loss suggests the opposite. There are at least two ways to handle these sorts of gains and losses in our analysis:

1. Do nothing. Accept that prior period income statements (and balance sheets) are likely overestimated or underestimated due to these gains and losses.
2. Adjust prior periods' reports by allocating the gain or loss over the time period of the misestimated depreciation and income.

For example, if a company reports a $1,000 gain on sale from an asset that had been in use over the prior five years, counting the current year, we could estimate that reported pretax income was understated by $200 each year (meaning that annual depreciation was overstated by $1,000/5 years). That is, the gain on sale suggests that depreciation was accelerated, which reduced its reported book value below what it should have been and resulted in a gain on sale. Accordingly, we could decrease depreciation by $200 per year and increase pretax income by the same $200. Assuming a 37% tax rate, the full set of adjustments follow:

	2010	2011	2012	2013	2014 (current year)*
Income statement adjustments	−$200 depreciation +$74 tax expense +$126 net income	−$200 depreciation +$74 tax expense +$126 net income	−$200 depreciation +$74 tax expense +$126 net income	−$200 depreciation +$74 tax expense +$126 net income	−$200 depreciation +$74 tax expense +$126 net income −$1,000 gain on sale −$370 tax expense −$630 net income
Balance sheet adjustments	−$200 accumulated depreciation +$74 deferred tax liability +$126 retained earnings	−$400 accumulated depreciation +$148 deferred tax liability +$252 retained earnings	−$600 accumulated depreciation +$222 deferred tax liability +$378 retained earnings	−$800 accumulated depreciation +$296 deferred tax liability +$504 retained earnings	No adjustment required at current year-end (as the year-end balance sheet reflects all prior and current year cost allocations)

*Computed from elimination of $1,000 gain less $200 depreciation; the computation assumes that the sale occurs near year-end (assuming a mid-year sale would mean the current year numbers are cut by one-half).

Whether due to complexity, lack of understanding, lack of data, or other reason, the everyday analyst does not make such adjustments. Notice, however, it is only necessary to adjust prior year statements to the extent we use them for analysis and forecasting purposes. For example, if only the current and two prior years data are used for forecasting income, then there is no need to adjust prior years' statements beyond those periods. Also notice that the basic accounting relation, that assets equal liabilities plus equity, is always maintained.

GLOBAL ACCOUNTING

An important aim of this module is to distinguish between operating and nonoperating items for the balance sheet and income statement. U.S. GAAP and IFRS generally account for items similarly, but there are certain disclosure differences worth noting.

The IFRS balance sheet is similar to its U.S. GAAP counterpart, with the visible exception for the frequent, but not mandatory, reverse ordering of assets and liabilities. However, one notable difference is that IFRS companies routinely report "financial assets" or "financial liabilities" on the balance sheet. We must assess these items. IFRS defines financial assets to include receivables (operating item), loans to affiliates or associates (can be operating or nonoperating depending on the nature of the transactions), securities held as investments (nonoperating), and derivatives (nonoperating). IFRS notes to financial statements, which tend to be more detailed than U.S. GAAP notes, usually detail what financial assets and liabilities consist of. This helps us accurately determine NOA and net nonoperating obligations (NNO).

The IFRS income statement usually reports fewer line items than U.S. GAAP income statements and, further, there is no definition of "operating activities" under IFRS. This means we must devote attention to classify operating versus nonoperating income components. Following is a table that shows common U.S. GAAP income statement items and their classification as operating (O) or nonoperating (N). This table also indicates which items are required for IFRS income statements.

Income Statement Line Items	Operating (O) or Nonoperating (N)	Required on IFRS Income Statement
Net sales	O	YES
Cost of sales	O	—
Selling, general and administrative (SG&A) expense	O	—
Provisions for doubtful accounts	O	—
Nonoperating income	N	—
Interest revenue and interest expense	N	YES
Nonoperating expenses	N	—
Income before income taxes	O and N	—
Income tax expense	O and N	YES
Earnings on equity investments (associates and joint ventures)	O	YES
Income from continuing operations	O	—
Discontinued operations	N	YES
Income before extraordinary items	O and N	—
Extraordinary items, net of income tax	O or N	—
Net income	O and N	YES
Net income attributable to noncontrolling interest	N	YES
Net income attributable to controlling interest	O and N	YES
Earnings per share (Basic EPS and Diluted EPS)	O and N	YES

There is no requirement to report income from operations, yet many IFRS companies do so. However, items that are considered operating such as gains and losses on disposals of operating assets, or income from equity method investments, are often reported below the operating income line. We must examine IFRS income statements and their notes to make an independent assessment of what is operating. IFRS income statements usually report separately the other nonoperating revenues and expenses even though this is not required. We can better assess the nature of these items by reading the accompanying notes.

MODULE-END REVIEW

Refer to the income statement and balance sheet of **TJX Companies, Inc.**, from Mid-Module Reviews 1 and 2 earlier in this module.

Required

1. Compute TJX's nonoperating return for 2013. Explain what the nonoperating return means and interpret the number you calculate.
2. Compute Walmart's nonoperating return for 2013 from the information reported in this module. Compare and contrast the nonoperating return for TJX and Walmart. Interpret the results.
3. Compute TJX's liabilities-to-equity ratio for 2013.
4. Compute Walmart's liabilities-to-equity ratio for 2013 from the balance sheet in this module. Compare and contrast the ratio to TJX's liabilities-to-equity ratio. Interpret the results.

The solution is on page 4-60.

APPENDIX 4A: Nonoperating Return Component of ROE

In this appendix, we consider the nonoperating return component of ROE in more detail. We also provide a derivation of that nonoperating return and discuss several special topics pertaining to it. We begin by considering three special cases of capital structure financing.

Nonoperating Return Framework

In the module, we infer the nonoperating return as the difference between ROE and RNOA. The nonoperating return can also be computed directly as FLEV × Spread, where FLEV is the degree of financial leverage and Spread is the difference between the assets' after-tax operating return (RNOA) and the after-tax cost of debt.

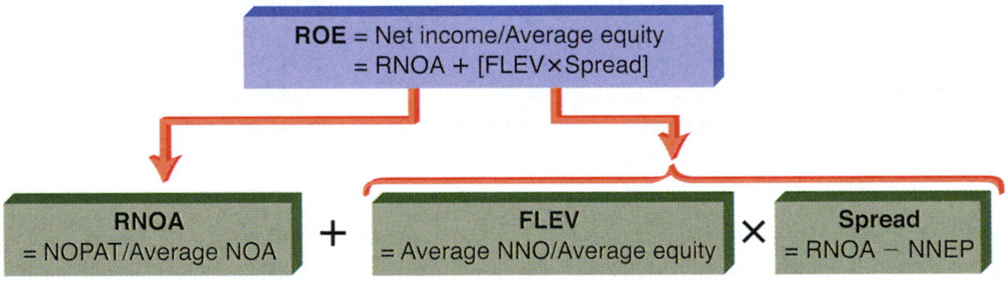

Exhibit 4A.1 provides definitions for each of the terms required in this computation.

EXHIBIT 4A.1 Nonoperating Return Definitions

NNO: Net nonoperating obligations	Nonoperating liabilities less nonoperating assets
FLEV: Financial leverage	Average NNO/Average total stockholders' equity
NNE: Net nonoperating expense	NOPAT – Consolidated net income; NNE consists of nonoperating expenses and revenues, net of tax.
NNEP: Net nonoperating expense percent	NNE/Average NNO
Spread	RNOA – NNEP

Nonoperating Return—With Debt Financing, but Without Nonoperating Assets

To illustrate computation of the nonoperating return when the company has debt and equity financing (without nonoperating assets), let's refer to our example in this module of the company that increases its ROE through use of debt. (For this first illustration, view FLEV as the relative use of debt in the capital structure, and Spread as the difference between RNOA and the net nonoperating expense percent.) Again, assume that this company has \$1,000 of equity, \$500 of 7% debt, total assets of \$1,500 that earn a 20% return, and a tax rate of 0%. The net income of this firm is \$265, computed as follows:

Profit from assets financed with equity (\$1,000 × 20%)		\$200
Profit from assets financed with debt (\$500 × 20%).	\$100	
Less interest expense from debt (\$500 × 7%)	(35)	65
Net profit.		\$265

This company's ROE is 26.5%, computed as \$265/\$1,000 (assuming income received at year-end for simplicity and average equity is \$1,000). Its RNOA is 20%, FLEV is 0.50 (computed as \$500 of average net nonoperating obligations divided by \$1,000 average equity), and its Spread is 13% (computed as 20% less 7%). This company's ROE, shown with the nonoperating return being directly computed, is as follows:

$$\begin{aligned} \textbf{ROE} &= \textbf{RNOA} + [\,\textbf{FLEV} \times \textbf{Spread}\,] \\ &= \textbf{20\%} \quad + [\;\textbf{0.50} \times \textbf{13\%}\;] \\ &= \textbf{26.5\%} \end{aligned}$$

We see that when a company's nonoperating activities relate solely to the borrowing of money (without nonoperating assets), FLEV collapses to the ratio of debt to equity, called the debt-to-equity ratio.

Nonoperating Return—With Debt Financing and Nonoperating Assets

Most companies report both debt and investments on their balance sheets. If that debt markedly exceeds the investment balance, their ROE will look more like our first example (with debt only). Instead, if investments predominate, their ROE will look more like Intel's below. It is important to remember that both the average NNO (and FLEV) and NNE can be either positive (debt) or negative (investments), and it is not always the case that ROE exceeds RNOA. We compute nonoperating return for **Target**, a company with both debt and investments. Later in this Appendix, we calculate the nonoperating return for Walmart whose balance sheet is a bit more complicated because it includes noncontrolling interest.

In Exhibit 4A.1, we define net nonoperating expense (NNE) as NOPAT − Net income. The table below shows data from Target's 2013 financial statements. With these numbers, we can compute NNE as NOPAT of \$3,497 million less net income of \$2,999 million, which yields \$480 million. More generally, NNE can include a number of nonoperating items such as interest expense, interest revenue, dividend income, investment gains and losses, and income (loss) on discontinued operations; all net of tax. (Recall that the simple illustration at the beginning of this appendix *ignored taxes*, which meant NNE was equal to the \$35 interest paid.)

	2013	2012
BALANCE SHEET DATA		
Operating assets	\$41,538	\$45,836
Operating liabilities.	13,957	13,326
Net operating assets (NOA)	27,581	32,510
Nonoperating liabilities.	17,648	17,483
Nonoperating assets	6,625	794
Net nonoperating obligations (NNO)	11,023	16,689
Equity (EQ)	\$16,558	\$15,821
INCOME STATEMENT DATA		
Net income.	\$2,999	
Net operating profit after tax (NOPAT)	\$3,479	

To compute operating return (RNOA) we divided NOPAT from the income statement, by NOA from the balance sheet. Similarly, to compute the net nonoperating expense percent (NNEP), we divide NNE from the income statement by net nonoperating obligations from the balance sheet (NNO). Exhibit 4A.2 shows how a balance sheet can be reorganized into operating and nonoperating items.

EXHIBIT 4A.2 Simplified Balance Sheet

	Assets	**Liabilities**
Net operating assets (NOA)	Current operating assets	Current operating liabilities
(assets – liabilities)	+ Long-term operating assets	+ Long-term operating liabilities
	= Total operating assets	= Total operating liabilities
Net nonoperating obligations (NNO).......	Current nonoperating assets	Current nonoperating liabilities
(liabilities – assets)	+ Long-term nonoperating assets	+ Long-term nonoperating liabilities
	= Total nonoperating assets	= Total nonoperating liabilities
		Equity
Equity (NOA – NNO)		Stockholders' equity (EQ)
	Total assets	Total liabilities and equity

Net nonoperating obligations are total nonoperating liabilities less total nonoperating assets. The accounting equation stipulates that Assets = Liabilities + Equity, so we can adjust it to yield the following key identity:

$$\textbf{Net operating assets (NOA)} = \textbf{Net nonoperating obligations (NNO)} + \textbf{Stockholders' equity (EQ)}$$

Accordingly (drawing on NNE from the income statement and NNO from the balance sheet), we compute the net nonoperating expense percent (NNEP) as follows:

$$\textbf{Net nonoperating expense percent (NNEP)} = \frac{\textbf{Net nonoperating expense (NNE)}}{\textbf{Average net nonoperating obligations (NNO)}}$$

The net nonoperating expense percent (NNEP) measures the average cost of net nonoperating obligations. The denominator uses the average NNO similar to the return calculations (such as ROE and RNOA).

In the simple illustration from earlier in this appendix, net nonoperating expense percent is 7%, computed as $35/$500, which is exactly equal to the interest rate on the loan. With real financial statements, NNEP is more complicated because NNE often includes both interest on borrowed money and nonoperating income, and NNO is the net of operating liabilities less nonoperating assets. Thus NNEP reflects an average return on nonoperating activities. For Target, its 2013 NNEP is 3.46%, computed as $480 million/[($16,689 million + $11,023 million)/2].

Target's 2013 RNOA is 11.58%, computed as: $3,479 million/[($32,510 million + $27,581 million)/2], which means that net operating assets generate more return than the 3.46% cost of net nonoperating obligations. That is, Target earns a Spread of 8.12%, the difference between RNOA (11.58%) and NNEP (3.46%), on each asset financed with borrowed funds. By borrowing funds, Target creates leverage, which can be measured relative to stockholders' equity; that ratio is called financial leverage (FLEV). In sum, total nonoperating return is computed by the following formula:

$$\textbf{Nonoperating return} = \underbrace{\frac{\textbf{Average net nonoperating obligations (NNO)}}{\textbf{Average stockholders' equity (EQ)}}}_{\text{FLEV}} \times \underbrace{(\textbf{RNOA} - \textbf{NNEP})}_{\text{Spread}}$$

Two points are immediately clear from this equation. First, ROE increases with the Spread between RNOA and NNEP. The more profitable the return on operating assets, the higher the return to stockholders. Second, the higher the debt relative to equity, the higher the ROE (assuming, of course, a positive Spread).

Target's 2013 Spread between RNOA and NNEP is 8.12%. It has average NNO of $13,856 million [($16,689 million + $11,023 million)/2] and average equity of $16,190 million [($15,821 million + $16,558 million)/2]. Thus, Target's ROE is as follows:

$$\begin{aligned}
\textbf{ROE} &= \textbf{Operating return} + \textbf{Nonoperating return}\\
&= \textbf{11.58\%} + [\$13{,}856/\$16{,}190] \times [11.58\% - 3.46\%]\\
&= \textbf{11.58\%} + [0.8558] \times [8.12\%]\\
&= \textbf{18.53\%}
\end{aligned}$$

Most companies report both debt and investments on their balance sheets. If that debt markedly exceeds the investment balance, their ROE will look more like our Target example (with net debt). Instead, if investments predominate, their ROE will look more like Intel's (with net investments). It is important to remember that both the average NNO (and FLEV) and NNE can be either positive (debt) or negative (investments), and it is not always the case that ROE exceeds RNOA.

Nonoperating Return—Without Debt Financing, but With Nonoperating Assets

Some companies, such as many high-tech firms, have no debt, and maintain large portfolios of marketable securities. They hold these highly liquid assets so that they can respond quickly to new opportunities or react to competitive pressures. With high levels of nonoperating assets and no nonoperating liabilities, the net nonoperating obligations (NNO) has a negative sign (NNO = Nonoperating liabilities − Nonoperating assets). Likewise, FLEV is negative: Average NNO (−)/Average equity (+). Further, net nonoperating expense (NNE = NOPAT − Net income) is negative because investment *income* is a negative nonoperating expense. However, the net nonoperating expense percent (NNEP) is positive because the negative NNE is divided by the negative NNO. *This causes ROE to be less than RNOA* (see computations below). We use the 2012 10-K of **Intel** to illustrate this curious result (Intel reports no noncontrolling interest).

Intel ($ millions, except percentages)	2012	2011	Average	Computation
NOA	$42,065	$37,843	$39,954	—
NNO	$ (9,138)	$ (8,068)	$ (8,603)	—
Stockholders' equity	$51,203	$45,911	$48,557	—
Net income	$11,005	—	—	—
NOPAT	$10,857	—	—	$14,638 − ($3,868 − [$141 + $94] × 0.37)
NNE (NOPAT − Net income)	$ (148)	—	—	$10,857 − $11,005
FLEV	(0.177)	—	—	$(8,603)/$48,557
RNOA	27.17%	—	—	$10,857/$39,954
NNEP	1.72%	—	—	$(148)/$(8,603)
Spread	25.45%	—	—	27.17% − 1.72%
ROE	22.66%	—	—	$11,005/$48,557

Intel's NNO is negative because its investment in marketable securities exceeds its debt. Intel's ROE is 22.66%, and it consists of the following:

$$
\begin{aligned}
\textbf{ROE} &= \textbf{RNOA} + [\ \textbf{FLEV} \times \textbf{Spread}\ ] \\
&= 27.17\% + [\ -0.177 \times 25.45\%\ ] \\
&= 27.17\% + [-4.50\%] \\
&= 22.67\%\ (0.01\%\ \text{rounding error})
\end{aligned}
$$

Intel's ROE is lower than its RNOA because of its large investment in marketable securities. That is, its excessive liquidity is penalizing its return on equity. The rationale for this seemingly incongruous result is this: Intel's ROE derives from operating and nonoperating assets. Intel's operating assets are providing an outstanding return (27.17%), much higher than the return on its marketable securities (1.72%). Holding liquid assets that are less productive means that Intel's stockholders are funding a sizeable level of liquidity, and sacrificing returns in the process. Why? Many companies in high-tech industries feel the need to maintain excessive liquidity to gain flexibility—the flexibility to take advantage of opportunities and to react quickly to competitor maneuvers. Intel's management, evidently, feels that the investment of costly equity capital in this manner will reap future rewards for its stockholders. Its 22.66% ROE provides some evidence that this strategy is not necessarily misguided.

Nonoperating Return—With Debt Financing, Nonoperating Assets, and Noncontrolling Interest

When a company acquires controlling interest of the outstanding voting stock of another company, the parent company must consolidate the new subsidiary in its balance sheet and income statement (see Module 7). This means that the parent company must include 100% of the subsidiary's assets, liabilities, revenues, and expenses. If the parent acquires less than 100% of the subsidiary's voting stock, the remaining claim of noncontrolling stockholders is reported on the balance sheet as a component of stockholders' equity called noncontrolling interest, and net income is separated into income attributable to company stockholders and that attributable to noncontrolling interests. *The ROE computation, then, should use the net income attributable to company stockholders divided by the average stockholders' equity attributable to controlling interest (CI), which excludes noncontrolling interest.* For firms with noncontrolling interests, we compute RNOA as usual because NOPAT is operating income before any noncontrolling interest on the income statement, and NOA is unaffected by noncontrolling interest on the balance sheet. Similarly, we compute Spread and FLEV as usual. However, we must modify the ROE = RNOA + [FLEV × Spread] formula slightly. Recall that a company's operating and nonoperating activities generate returns to both the controlling interest (labeled CI, which is the parent company's stockholders' equity) and the noncontrolling stockholders (labeled NCI). To account for this, we must multiply the ROE equation, RNOA + [FLEV × Spread] from page 4-24, by a ratio that captures the relative income statement and balance sheet effects of the noncontrolling interest. This ratio is called the *noncontrolling interest ratio*, and is computed as follows:

$$\textbf{Noncontrolling interest ratio} = \left[\frac{\left(\dfrac{\textbf{Net income attributable to controlling interest } (\textbf{NI}_{\textbf{CI}})}{\textbf{Net income } (\textbf{NI})}\right)}{\left(\dfrac{\textbf{Average equity attributable to controlling interest } (\textbf{CI})}{\textbf{Average total equity } (\textbf{EQ})}\right)}\right]$$

Hence, for companies with a noncontrolling interest (NCI), the disaggregated return on equity is expressed as:

$$\textbf{ROE} = [\textbf{RNOA} + (\textbf{FLEV} \times \textbf{Spread})] \times \textbf{NCI ratio}$$

To illustrate the calculation of ROE, FLEV, and Spread in the presence of noncontrolling interest, we consider the balance sheet and income statement items from **Walmart** ($ millions).

Walmart	2013	2012	Average
Balance sheet items			
Net operating assets (NOA)	$128,612	$123,042	$125,827
Net nonoperating obligations (NNO)	$ 46,874	$ 47,281	$ 47,078
Noncontrolling interest (NCI)	5,395	4,446	4,921
Walmart parent stockholders' equity (CI)	76,343	71,315	73,829
Total equity (NCI + CI)	81,738	75,761	78,750
Total net nonoperating obligations and Total equity	$128,612	$123,042	$125,827
Income statement items			
Net operating profit after tax (NOPAT)	$ 19,056		
Net nonoperating expense (NNE)	(1,300)		
Net income	17,756		
Net income attributable to noncontrolling interest (NI_{NCI})	(757)		
Net income attributable to Walmart shareholders (NI_{CI})	$ 16,999		

We compute Walmart's ROE for 2013 using the formula above, as follows:

RNOA = NOPAT/Average NOA	15.14%	($19,056/$125,827)
ROE = NI_{CI}/Average CI	23.02%	($16,999/$73,829)
FLEV = Average NNO/Average EQ	0.5978	($47,078/$78,750)
NNEP = NNE/Average NNO	2.76%	($1,300/$47,078)
Spread = RNOA − NNEP	12.38%	(0.1514 − 0.0276)
Noncontrolling interest (NCI) ratio	1.0212	$\left(\frac{16,999}{17,756} / \frac{73,829}{78,750}\right)$
ROE [RNOA + (FLEV × Spread)] × NCI ratio	23.02%	[0.1514 + (0.5978 × 0.1238)] × 1.0212

Derivation of Nonoperating Return Formula

Following is the algebraic derivation of the nonoperating return formula, where NI is net income, EQ is average stockholders' equity, and all other terms are as defined in Exhibits 4.3 and 4A.1.

$$
\begin{aligned}
\text{ROE} &= \frac{\text{NI}}{\text{EQ}} \\
&= \frac{\text{NOPAT} - \text{NNE}}{\text{EQ}} \\
&= \frac{\text{NOPAT}}{\text{EQ}} - \frac{\text{NNE}}{\text{EQ}} \\
&= \left(\frac{\text{NOA}}{\text{EQ}} \times \text{RNOA}\right) - \left(\frac{\text{NNO}}{\text{EQ}} \times \text{NNEP}\right) \\
&= \left(\frac{(\text{EQ} + \text{NNO})}{\text{EQ}} \times \text{RNOA}\right) - \left(\frac{\text{NNO}}{\text{EQ}} \times \text{NNEP}\right) \\
&= \left[\text{RNOA} \times \left(1 + \frac{\text{NNO}}{\text{EQ}}\right)\right] - \left(\frac{\text{NNO}}{\text{EQ}} \times \text{NNEP}\right) \\
&= \text{RNOA} + \left(\frac{\text{NNO}}{\text{EQ}} \times \text{RNOA}\right) - \left(\frac{\text{NNO}}{\text{EQ}} \times \text{NNEP}\right) \\
&= \text{RNOA} + \left(\frac{\text{NNO}}{\text{EQ}}\right)(\text{RNOA} - \text{NNEP}) \\
&= \text{RNOA} + (\text{FLEV} \times \text{Spread})
\end{aligned}
$$

Special Topics

The return on equity (ROE) computation becomes a bit more complicated in the presence of discontinued operations and preferred stock. The first of these apportions ROE between operating and nonoperating returns, and the other affects the dollar amount included in the denominator (average equity) of the ROE computation. Recall that ROE measures the return on investment for common stockholders. *The ROE numerator should include only the income available to pay common dividends and the ROE denominator should include common equity only, not preferred equity.*

Discontinued Operations Discontinued operations are subsidiaries or business segments that the board of directors has formally decided to divest. Companies must report discontinued operations on a separate line, below income from continuing operations. The separate line item includes the net income or loss from discontinued operations along with any gains or losses on the disposal of discontinued net assets (see Module 5 for details). Although not required, many companies disclose the net assets of discontinued operations on the balance sheet to distinguish them from continuing net assets. If the net assets are not separated on the balance sheet, the footnotes provide details to facilitate a disaggregated analysis. These net assets of discontinued operations should be treated as nonoperating (they represent a nonoperating "investment" once they have been classified as discontinued) and their after-tax profit (loss) should be treated as nonoperating as well. Although the ROE computation is unaffected, the nonoperating portion of the ROE for the year will include the contribution of discontinued operations.

Preferred Stock The ROE formula takes the perspective of the common stockholder in that it relates the income available to pay common dividends to the average common stockholder. As such, preferred stock should not be included in average stockholders' equity in the denominator of the ROE formula. Similarly, any dividends paid on preferred stock should be subtracted from net income to yield the profit available to pay common dividends. (Dividends are not an expense in computing net income; thus, net income is available to both preferred and common stockholders. To determine net income available to common stockholders, we must subtract preferred dividends.) Thus, the presence of preferred stock requires two adjustments to the ROE formula.

1. Preferred dividends must be subtracted from net income in the numerator.
2. Preferred stock must be subtracted from stockholders' equity in the denominator.

This modified return on equity formula is more accurately labeled return on common equity (ROCE).

$$
\text{ROCE} = \frac{\text{Net income} - \text{Preferred dividends}}{\text{Average stockholders' equity} - \text{Average preferred equity}}
$$

APPENDIX 4B: Tools of Liquidity and Solvency Analysis

Liquidity Analysis

LO4 Compute and interpret measures of liquidity and solvency.

Liquidity refers to cash availability: how much cash a company has, and how much it can raise on short notice. Two of the most common ratios used to assess the degree of liquidity are the current ratio and the quick ratio. Both of these ratios link required near-term payments to cash available in the near-term.

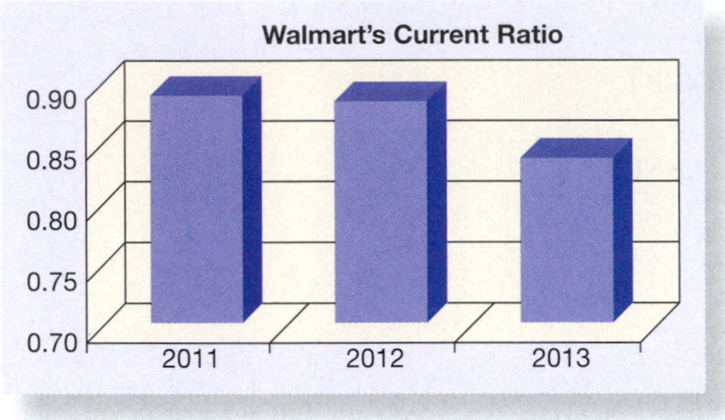

Current Ratio

Current assets are assets that a company expects to convert into cash within the next operating cycle, which is typically a year. *Current liabilities* are liabilities that come due within the next year. An excess of current assets over current liabilities (Current assets − Current liabilities), is known as *net working capital* or simply *working capital*.[2] Positive working capital implies that cash generated by "liquidating" current assets would be sufficient to pay current liabilities. The current ratio expresses working capital as a ratio and is computed as follows:

$$\text{Current ratio} = \frac{\text{Current assets}}{\text{Current liabilities}}$$

A current ratio greater than 1.0 implies positive working capital. Both working capital and the current ratio consider existing balance sheet data only and ignore cash inflows from future sales or other sources. The current ratio is more commonly used than working capital because ratios allow comparisons across companies of different size. Generally, companies prefer a higher current ratio; however, an excessively high current ratio indicates inefficient asset use. Furthermore, a current ratio less than 1.0 is not always bad for at least two reasons:

1. A cash-and-carry company with comparatively fewer accounts receivable (like Walmart) can have potentially few current assets (and a low current ratio), but consistently large operating cash inflows ensure the company will be sufficiently liquid.
2. A company can efficiently manage its working capital by minimizing receivables and inventories and maximizing payables. **Walmart**, for example, uses its buying power to exact extended credit terms from suppliers. Consequently, because it is essentially a cash-and-carry company, its current ratio is less than 1.0 and is sufficiently liquid.

The aim of current ratio analysis is to discern if a company is having, or is likely to have, difficulty meeting its short-term obligations. **Walmart**'s current ratio for 2013 is 0.835 ($59,940 million/$71,818 million). Its current ratio has remained relatively constant for the past three years.

Quick Ratio

The quick ratio is a variant of the current ratio. It focuses on quick assets, which are assets likely to be converted to cash within a relatively short period of time. Specifically, quick assets include cash, marketable securities, and accounts receivable; they exclude inventories, prepaid assets, and other current assets. The quick ratio is defined as follows:

$$\text{Quick ratio} = \frac{\text{Cash} + \text{Marketable securities} + \text{Accounts receivable}}{\text{Current liabilities}}$$

[2] Both operating assets and operating liabilities can be either current or long-term. "Current" means that the asset is expected to be used, or the liability paid, within the next operating cycle or one year, whichever is longer, which for most companies means a year. Using the current versus long-term nature of operating assets and liabilities we derive two types of net operating assets: net operating working capital (NOWC), and net long-term operating assets. Net operating working capital is defined as:

$$\text{Net operating working capital (NOWC)} = \text{Current operating assets} - \text{Current operating liabilities}$$

For Walmart, NOWC is $(6,940) million for 2013 ($6,768 million + $43,803 million + $1,588 million − $38,080 million − $18,808 million − $2,211 million).

The quick ratio reflects on a company's ability to meet its current liabilities without liquidating inventories. It is a more stringent test of liquidity than the current ratio.

Walmart's 2013 quick ratio is 0.203 ($7,781 million + $6,768 million)/$71,818 million). Like the current ratio, Walmart's quick ratio has remained fairly constant over the past three years—see margin graph. It is not uncommon for a company's quick ratio to be less than 1.0. Although liquidity is not a major concern for Walmart, the decline in the quick ratio is something financial statement users would want to monitor.

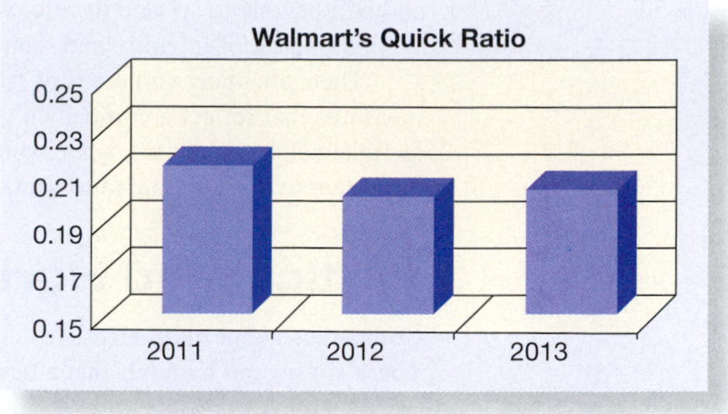

Solvency Analysis

Solvency refers to a company's ability to meet its debt obligations, including both periodic interest payments and the repayment of the principal amount borrowed. Solvency is crucial because an insolvent company is a failed company. There are two general approaches to measuring solvency. The first approach uses balance sheet data and assesses the proportion of capital raised from creditors. The second approach uses income statement data and assesses the profit generated relative to debt payment obligations. We discuss each approach in turn.

Liabilities-to-Equity

The liabilities-to-equity ratio is a useful tool for the first type of solvency analysis. It is defined as follows:

$$\textbf{Liabilities-to-equity ratio} = \frac{\textbf{Total liabilities}}{\textbf{Stockholders' equity}}$$

This ratio conveys how reliant a company is on creditor financing compared with equity financing. A higher ratio indicates less solvency, and more risk. Walmart's 2013 liabilities-to-equity ratio is 1.48 ($71,818 million + $38,394 million + $3,023 million + $7,613 million + $519 million)/$81,738 million. This ratio has declined somewhat over the past three years—see margin graph. Also, its ratio is about 1.5, the median for publicly traded companies. (Because the numerator of this ratio includes the consolidated liabilities of the company, the denominator must use the company's total equity, which includes any noncontrolling interest reported on the balance sheet.)

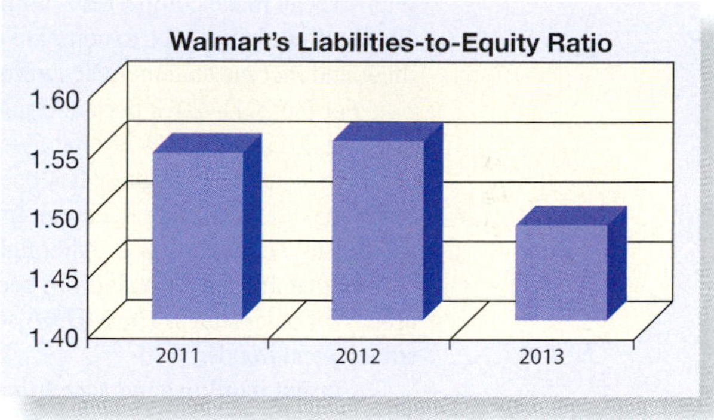

A variant of this ratio considers a company's long-term debt divided by equity. This approach assumes that current liabilities are repaid from current assets (so-called self-liquidating). Thus, it assumes that creditors and stockholders need only focus on the relative proportion of long-term capital.

Times Interest Earned

The second type of solvency analysis compares profits to liabilities. This approach assesses how much operating profit is available to cover debt obligations. A common measure for this type of solvency analysis is the times interest earned ratio, defined as follows:

$$\textbf{Times interest earned} = \frac{\textbf{Earnings before interest and taxes}}{\textbf{Interest expense}}$$

The times interest earned ratio reflects the operating income available to pay interest expense. The underlying assumption is that only interest needs to be paid because the principal will be refinanced. This ratio is sometimes abbreviated as EBIT/I. The numerator is similar to net operating profits after tax (NOPAT), but it is *pretax* instead of after tax. We use earnings before net interest expense, that is, net of any other nonoperating income or expenses.

Management wants this ratio to be sufficiently high so that there is little risk of default. Walmart's 2013 times interest earned is a healthy 13.47, computed as ($25,737 million + $2,064 million)/$2,064 million. This ratio has increased over the past three years—see margin graph. This result implies that Walmart could suffer a large decline in profitability

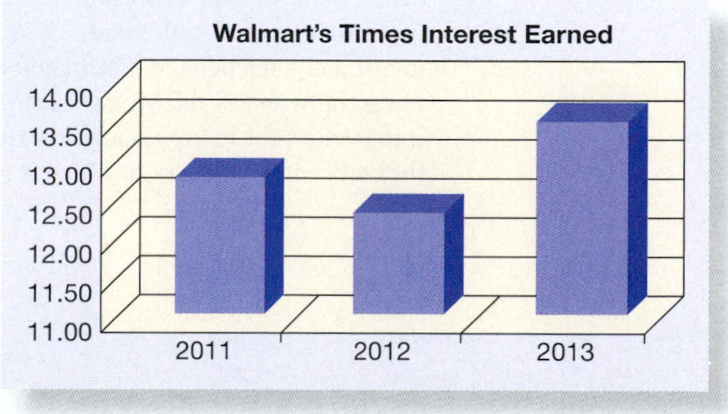

and still be able to service its interest payments when due. Any solvency concerns we might have had relating to Walmart's lack of liquidity and relatively high debt load are mitigated by its earning power.

There are many variations of solvency and liquidity analysis and the ratios used. The basic idea is to construct measures that reflect a company's credit risk exposure. There is not one "best" financial leverage ratio. Instead, as financial statement users, we want to use measures that capture the risk we are most concerned with. It is also important to compute the ratios ourselves to ensure we know what is included and excluded from each ratio.

Vertical and Horizontal Analysis

Companies come in all sizes, which presents difficulties when making comparisons among firms or over time. There are several methods that attempt to overcome this obstacle.

Vertical analysis expresses financial statements in ratio form. Specifically, it is routine to express income statement items as a percent of net sales, and balance sheet items as a percent of total assets. Such *common-size financial statements* facilitate comparisons *across companies* of different sizes and comparisons of accounts within a set of financial statements.

Horizontal analysis is the scrutiny of financial data *across time*. Comparing data across two or more consecutive periods assists in analyzing trends in company performance and in predicting future performance.

Exhibits 4B.1 and 4B.2 present **Walmart**'s common-size balance sheet and common-size income statement. We also present data for horizontal analysis by showing three years of common-size statements.

Walmart's total assets (in dollars) have increased by 12.3% since 2011 to over $200 billion. The sheer size of Walmart can make comparisons with other companies difficult. A common-size analysis such as shown in Exhibits 4B.1 and 4B.2 allows us to compare companies of different sizes by focusing on the relative proportions of balance sheet and income statement accounts.

For the 2011–2013 period, liquidity has generally increased as current assets have grown from 28.77% of total assets in 2011 to 29.51% of total assets in 2013. Cash has remained fairly constant at 3.83% of total assets. Over the past two years, the company has been able to reduce the relative proportion of its total assets invested in PPE and assets that it leases (capital leases). Investment in long-term tangible assets has decreased from 59.68% of total assets in 2011 to 57.44% in 2013. Although we generally prefer less investment in long-term tangible assets, we need to be sure that this reduction has not been achieved by ignoring or postponing needed investment in new stores and the upkeep of older stores. The MD&A section of the 10-K might provide management's insight on its capital investment strategy and trends.

Current liabilities increased sharply in 2013 to 35.36% of total liabilities and equity, up from 32.42% in 2011. That increase is the result of an increase in short-term debt, from 0.57% of total liabilities and equity in 2011 to 3.35% in 2013. Although short-term debt is often cheaper than the interest rates charged on long-term borrowings, the short maturity is generally of concern. Walmart's profitability and cash flow are strong, however, thus mitigating concerns we might have in this area. Corresponding with the increase in short-term debt, has been a decrease in long-term borrowings from 22.51% of total liabilities and equity in 2011 to 18.9% in 2013. Overall, however, Walmart's financial leverage (as measured by the relative proportions of liabilities and equity) has decreased, as Walmart shareholders' equity has increased as a percentage of total liabilities and equity from 39.41% in 2011 to 40.24% in 2013. Overall, Walmart's balance sheet presents sufficient liquidity and lower financial leverage such that we would have little concern about its liquidity and solvency.

On the income side, Walmart's cost of goods sold has increased from 74.66% of total revenues in 2011 to 75.13% in 2013. This increase of 0.47 percentage points is significant for a company that operates on relatively thin gross margins (gross profit percentage), and generally indicates an increasingly competitive environment. Since Walmart's net profit margin (net income/revenues) is lower than that which we generally see for other less competitive industries, the company must match this increase in COGS with a corresponding decrease in SG&A expense as a percentage of total revenues. Indeed, SG&A expense as a percentage of total revenues has decreased from 19.29% in 2011 to 18.94% in 2013. Although it is comforting that the 0.47 percentage point increase in COGS has been largely offset with a 0.35 percentage point decline in SG&A as a percentage of total revenues, we need to better understand the reasons behind both trends. SG&A percentage reduction resulting from wage concessions can lead to employee unrest and reductions in advertising and other marketing expenses can result in a loss of market position. We need to carefully review the MD&A section of the 10-K and trade publications to better understand these trends and their implications for future financial performance. Overall, Walmart's relatively low net profit margin of 3.62% reflects the competitive industry in which it operates. Expense control is crucial in such a competitive environment.

EXHIBIT 4B.1 Common-Size Balance Sheets

WALMART
Common-Size Balance Sheets

	Amounts ($ millions)			Percentages*		
As of January 31	**2013**	**2012**	**2011**	**2013**	**2012**	**2011**
Assets						
Cash and cash equivalents	$ 7,781	$ 6,550	$ 7,395	3.83%	3.39%	4.09%
Receivables, net	6,768	5,937	5,089	3.33	3.07	2.81
Inventories	43,803	40,714	36,437	21.57	21.05	20.16
Prepaid expense and other assets, current	1,588	1,774	2,960	0.78	0.92	1.64
Current assets of discontinued operations	—	—	131	0.00	0.00	0.07
Total current assets	59,940	54,975	52,012	29.51	28.42	28.77
Property and equipment						
Property, plant and equipment, gross	165,825	155,002	148,584	81.64	80.14	82.19
Less accumulated depreciation	(51,896)	(45,399)	(43,486)	(25.55)	(23.47)	(24.05)
Property and equipment, net	113,929	109,603	105,098	56.09	56.67	58.14
Property under capital leases						
Property under capital leases	5,899	5,936	5,905	2.90	3.07	3.27
Less accumulated amortization	(3,147)	(3,215)	(3,125)	(1.55)	(1.66)	(1.73)
Property under capital leases, net	2,752	2,721	2,780	1.35	1.41	1.54
Goodwill	20,497	20,651	16,763	10.09	10.68	9.27
Other assets and deferred charges	5,987	5,456	4,129	2.95	2.82	2.28
Total assets	$203,105	$193,406	$180,782	100.00%	100.00%	100.00%
Current liabilities						
Short-term borrowings	$ 6,805	$ 4,047	$ 1,031	3.35%	2.09%	0.57%
Accounts payable	38,080	36,608	33,676	18.75	18.93	18.63
Accrued liabilities	18,808	18,180	18,701	9.26	9.40	10.34
Accrued income taxes	2,211	1,164	157	1.09	0.60	0.09
Long-term debt due within one year	5,587	1,975	4,655	2.75	1.02	2.57
Obligations under capital leases due within one year	327	326	336	0.16	0.17	0.19
Current liabilities of discontinued operations	—	—	47	0.00	0.00	0.03
Total current liabilities	71,818	62,300	58,603	35.36	32.21	32.42
Long-term debt	38,394	44,070	40,692	18.90	22.79	22.51
Long-term obligations under capital leases	3,023	3,009	3,150	1.49	1.56	1.74
Deferred income taxes and other	7,613	7,862	6,682	3.75	4.07	3.70
Redeemable noncontrolling interest	519	404	408	0.26	0.21	0.23
Liabilities and equity						
Common stock	332	342	352	0.16	0.18	0.19
Capital in excess of par value	3,620	3,692	3,577	1.78	1.91	1.98
Retained earnings	72,978	68,691	63,967	35.93	35.52	35.38
Accumulated other comprehensive income (loss)	(587)	(1,410)	646	(0.29)	(0.73)	0.36
Total Walmart shareholders' equity	76,343	71,315	68,542	37.59	36.87	37.91
Noncontrolling interest	5,395	4,446	2,705	2.66	2.30	1.50
Total equity	81,738	75,761	71,247	40.24	39.17	39.41
Total liabilities and equity	$203,105	$193,406	$180,782	100.00%	100.00%	100.00%

*Percentages are rounded to two decimals and, thus, might not exactly sum to totals and subtotals.

EXHIBIT 4B.2 Common-Size Income Statements

WALMART
Common-Size Income Statements

	Amounts ($ millions)			Percentages*		
For year ended January 31	**2013**	**2012**	**2011**	**2013**	**2012**	**2011**
Revenues						
Net sales	$466,114	$443,854	$418,952	99.35%	99.31%	99.31%
Membership and other Income	3,048	3,096	2,897	0.65	0.69	0.69
Total revenues	469,162	446,950	421,849	100.00	100.00	100.00
Costs and expenses						
Cost of sales	352,488	335,127	314,946	75.13	74.98	74.66
Operating, selling, general and administrative expenses	88,873	85,265	81,361	18.94	19.08	19.29
Operating income	27,801	26,558	25,542	5.93	5.94	6.05
Interest						
Debt	1,977	2,034	1,928	0.42	0.46	0.46
Capital leases	274	288	277	0.06	0.06	0.07
Interest income	(187)	(162)	(201)	(0.04)	(0.04)	(0.05)
Interest, net	2,064	2,160	2,004	0.44	0.48	0.48
Income from continuing operations before income taxes	25,737	24,398	23,538	5.49	5.46	5.58
Provision for income taxes						
Current income tax expense	7,999	6,742	6,703	1.70	1.51	1.59
Deferred income tax expense	(18)	1,202	876	0.00	0.27	0.21
Total provision for income taxes	7,981	7,944	7,579	1.70	1.78	1.80
Income from continuing operations	17,756	16,454	15,959	3.78	3.68	3.78
Income (loss) from discontinued operations, net of income taxes	0	(67)	1,034	0.00	(0.01)	0.25
Consolidated net income	17,756	16,387	16,993	3.78	3.67	4.03
Less consolidated net income attributable to noncontrolling interest	(757)	(688)	(604)	(0.16)	(0.15)	(0.14)
Consolidated net income attributable to Walmart	$ 16,999	$ 15,699	$ 16,389	3.62%	3.51%	3.89%

*Percentages are rounded to two decimals and, thus, might not exactly sum to totals and subtotals.

APPENDIX 4C: DuPont Disaggregation Analysis

LO5 Describe and illustrate traditional DuPont disaggregation of ROE.

Disaggregation of return on equity (ROE) into three components (profitability, turnover, and financial leverage) was initially introduced by the **E.I. DuPont de Nemours and Company** to aid its managers in performance evaluation. DuPont realized that management's focus on profit alone was insufficient because profit can be simply increased by additional investment in low-yielding, but safe, assets. Further, DuPont wanted managers to think like investors and to manage their portfolio of activities using investment principles that allocate scarce investment capital to competing projects in descending order of return on investment (the *capital budgeting approach*). The DuPont model incorporates this investment perspective into performance measurement by disaggregating ROE into the following three components:

1. Profitability
2. Turnover (asset utilization)
3. Financial leverage

Each of these measures is generally positive, in which case an increase in any one would increase ROE. A focus on these measures encourages managers to focus on *both* the balance sheet and the income statement. Such an analysis typically examines each of these components over time. Managers then seek to reverse adverse trends and to sustain positive trends.

Basic DuPont Model

The basic DuPont model disaggregates ROE as follows:

$$\text{ROE} = \frac{\text{Net income}}{\text{Average stockholders' equity}} = \frac{\text{Net income}}{\text{Sales}} \times \frac{\text{Sales}}{\text{Average total assets}} \times \frac{\text{Average total assets}}{\text{Average stockholders' equity}}$$

Profit Margin (PM) | Asset Turnover (AT) | Financial Leverage (FL)

These three components are described as follows:

- **Profit margin** is the amount of profit that the company earns from each dollar of sales. A company can increase its net profit margin by increasing its gross profit margin (Gross profit/Sales) and/or by reducing its expenses (other than cost of sales) as a percentage of sales.
- **Asset turnover** is a productivity measure that reflects the volume of sales that a company generates from each dollar invested in assets. A company can increase its asset turnover by increasing sales volume with no increase in assets and/or by reducing asset investment without reducing sales.
- **Financial leverage** measures the degree to which the company finances its assets with debt rather than equity. Increasing the percentage of debt relative to equity increases the financial leverage. Although financial leverage increases ROE (when performance is positive), debt must be used with care as it increases the company's relative riskiness (see our following discussion of financial leverage).

Return on Assets

The first two terms in the DuPont model, profit margin and asset turnover, relate to company operations and combine to yield return on assets (ROA) as follows:

$$\text{ROA} = \frac{\text{Net income}}{\text{Average total assets}} = \frac{\text{Net income}}{\text{Sales}} \times \frac{\text{Sales}}{\text{Average total assets}}$$

Profit Margin | Asset Turnover

Return on assets (ROA)

Return on assets combines the first two terms in the ROE disaggregation, profit margin and turnover. It measures the return on investment for the company without regard to how it is financed (the relative proportion of debt and equity in its capital structure). Operating managers of a company typically grasp the income statement. They readily understand the pricing of products, the management of production costs, and the importance of controlling overhead costs. However, many managers do not appreciate the importance of managing the balance sheet. The ROA approach to performance measurement encourages managers to also focus on the returns that they achieve from the invested capital under their control. Those returns are maximized by a joint focus on both profitability and productivity.

Profitability

Profitability is measured by the profit margin (Net income/Sales). Analysis of profitability typically examines performance over time relative to benchmarks (such as competitors' or industry performance), which highlights trends and abnormalities. When abnormal performance is discovered, managers either correct suboptimal performance or protect superior performance. There are two general areas of profitability analysis: gross profit margin analysis and expense management.

Gross Profit Margin The gross profit margin (Gross profit/Sales) is crucial. It measures the gross profit (sales less cost of goods sold) for each sales dollar. Gross profit margin is affected by both the selling prices of products and their manufacturing cost. When markets are more competitive (or when products lose their competitive advantage), a company must reduce product prices to maintain market share and any increases in manufacturing costs cannot be directly passed on to customers; this suggests that managers must focus on reducing costs. This might result in outsourcing of activities to lower labor costs and/or finding lower-cost raw materials. Such measures can yield a loss of product quality if not managed properly, which could further deteriorate the product's market position. Another strategy is to reduce product features not valued by the market. Focus groups of consumers can often identify these non-value-added product features that can be eliminated to save costs without affecting the product's value to consumers.

Expense Management Managers can focus on reducing manufacturing and/or administrative (*overhead*) expenses to increase profitability. *Manufacturing overhead* refers to all production expenses other than manufacturing labor and materials. These expenses include utilities, depreciation, and administrative costs related to manufacturing the product. *Administrative overhead* refers to all expenses not in cost of goods sold such as administrative salaries and benefits, marketing, legal, accounting, research and development. These overhead costs must be managed carefully as they can represent investments. Reductions in spending on advertising and research yield short-run, positive impacts on profitability, but can yield long-run deterioration in the company's market position. Likewise, requiring employees to work harder and longer can delay increases in wage-related costs, but the likely decline in employee morale can create long-run negative consequences.

Productivity

Productivity in the DuPont model refers to the volume of dollar sales resulting from each dollar invested in assets. When a decline in productivity is observed, managers have two avenues of attack:

1. Increase sales volume from the existing asset base, and/or
2. Decrease the investment in assets without reducing sales volume.

The first approach focuses on capacity utilization. Increasing throughput lowers per unit manufacturing costs as fixed costs are spread over a larger sales base. The second approach focuses on elimination of excess assets. That reduction increases cash and also reduces carrying costs associated with the eliminated assets.

Manager efforts to reduce assets often initially focus on working capital (current assets and liabilities). Receivables can be reduced by better credit-granting policies and better monitoring of outstanding receivables. Inventories can be reduced through just-in-time delivery of raw materials, elimination of bottlenecks in production to reduce work-in-process inventories, and producing to order rather than to estimated demand to reduce finished goods inventories. Companies can also delay payment of accounts payable to generate needed cash. Payables management is more art than science, and reductions must be managed with care so as not to threaten valuable supply channels.

Manager efforts to reduce long-term assets are more difficult. Recent years have witnessed an increase in use of corporate alliances, joint ventures, and activities that seek joint ownership of assets such as manufacturing, distribution, service facilities, and information technology (IT). Another strategy is to outsource production to reduce manufacturing assets. Outsourcing is effective provided the benefits from eliminating manufacturing assets more than offset the increased costs of purchasing goods from outsourced producers.

Financial Leverage

The third term in the DuPont model is financial leverage, the relative proportion of debt versus equity in the company's capital structure. Financial leverage in the DuPont model is measured by the ratio of average total assets to average stockholders' equity. An increase in this ratio implies an increase in the relative use of debt. This is evident from the accounting equation: assets = liabilities + equity. For example, assume that assets are financed equally with debt and equity. The accounting equation, expressed in percentage terms, follows: 100% = 50% + 50%, and the financial leverage of the company is 2.0 (100%/50%). If we increase the proportion of debt to 75% (decrease the proportion of equity to 25%), the financial leverage increases to 4.0 (100%/25%). The measure of financial leverage is important because debt is a contractual obligation (dividends are not), and a company's failure to make required debt payments can result in legal repercussions and even bankruptcy. As financial leverage increases, so do the required debt payments, along with the probability that the company is unable to meet its debt obligations in a business downturn.

ROA Adjustment in the Basic DuPont Model

The basic DuPont model is not entirely accurate, and adjusting the return on assets for the effect of interest addresses the inaccuracy.

Return on assets typically focuses on the operating side of the business (profit margin and asset turnover). Further, ROA is typically under the control of operating managers while the capital structure decision (the relative proportion of debt and equity) is not. Accordingly, an adjustment is often made to the numerator of ROA, and sometimes to the denominator. The numerator adjustment adds back the after-tax net interest expense (net of any other nonoperating revenues or expenses) and is computed as follows:

$$\text{ROA} = \frac{\textbf{Net income} + [\textbf{Interest expense} \times (\textbf{1} - \textbf{Statutory tax rate})]}{\textbf{Average total assets}}$$

This adjusted numerator better reflects the company's operating profit as it measures return on assets exclusive of financing costs (independent of the capital structure decision). This adjusted ROA is typically reported by data collection services such as **Compustat** and **Capital IQ**, while the unadjusted is not. ("Statutory tax rate" in the ROA formula is the federal statutory tax rate *plus* the state tax rate net of any federal tax benefits; we use the assumed 37% federal and state tax rates as explained in the NOPAT computation earlier in this module.)

The denominator adjustment is less common. That adjustment removes non-interest-bearing short-term liabilities (accounts payable and accrued liabilities) from total assets. The adjusted assets in the denominator are considered to better approximate the net assets that must be financed by long-term creditors and stockholders. In sum, adjustments to ROA move the numerator closer to net operating profit after-tax (NOPAT) and move the denominator closer to net operating assets (NOA). The resulting ROA ratio is then closer to the return on net operating assets (RNOA).

Illustration of DuPont Disaggregation

To illustrate DuPont disaggregation analysis, we use Walmart's income statement and balance sheet reported earlier in this module. Exhibit 4C.1 shows the computation for each component of the DuPont disaggregation analysis applied to Walmart.

EXHIBIT 4C.1 Computation of DuPont Disaggregation Analysis for Walmart

Ratio Component	Definition	Computation
Profit margin (PM).	$\frac{\text{Net income}}{\text{Sales}}$	$\frac{\$16,999}{\$469,162} = 3.62\%$
Asset turnover (AT)	$\frac{\text{Sales}}{\text{Average total assets}}$	$\frac{\$469,162}{[(\$203,105 + \$193,406)/2]} = 2.37$
Financial leverage (FL)	$\frac{\text{Average total assets}}{\text{Average total equity attributable to controlling interest}}$	$\frac{[(\$203,105 + \$193,406)/2]}{[(\$76,343 + \$71,315)/2]} = 2.69$
Return on equity (ROE).	$\frac{\text{Net income attributable to controlling interest}}{\text{Average total equity attributable to controlling interest}}$ or PM × AT × FL	$\frac{\$16,999}{[(\$76,343 + \$71,315)/2]} = 23.02\%$ or 3.62% × 2.37 × 2.69 = 23.08 (0.06 rounding difference)
Return on assets (Adjusted)	$\frac{\text{Net income} + \text{Interest expense} \times (1 - \text{Statutory tax rate})}{\text{Average total assets}}$	$\frac{[\$16,999 + \$2,064\ (1 - 0.37)]}{[(\$203,105 + \$193,406)/2]} = 9.23\%$

GUIDANCE ANSWERS

MANAGERIAL DECISION You Are the CEO

Your company is performing substantially better than its competitors. Namely, your RNOA of 16% is markedly superior to competitors' RNOA of 10%. However, RNOA disaggregation shows that this is mainly attributed to your NOAT of 0.89 versus competitors' NOAT of 0.59. Your NOPM of 18% is essentially identical to competitors' NOPM of 17%. Accordingly, you will want to maintain your NOAT as further improvements are probably difficult to achieve. Importantly, you are likely to achieve the greatest benefit with efforts at improving your NOPM of 18%, which is only marginally better than the industry norm of 17%.

Superscript A(B, C) denotes assignments based on Appendix 4A (4B, 4C).

DISCUSSION QUESTIONS

Q4-1. Explain in general terms the concept of return on investment. Why is this concept important in the analysis of financial performance?

Q4-2.[A] (a) Explain how an increase in financial leverage can increase a company's ROE. (b) Given the potentially positive relation between financial leverage and ROE, why don't we see companies with 100% financial leverage (entirely nonowner financed)?

Q4-3. Gross profit margin (Gross profit/Sales) is an important determinant of NOPAT. Identify two factors that can cause gross profit margin to decline. Is a reduction in the gross profit margin always bad news? Explain.

Q4-4. When might a reduction in operating expenses as a percentage of sales denote a short-term gain at the cost of long-term performance?

Q4-5. Describe the concept of asset turnover. What does the concept mean and why is it so important to understanding and interpreting financial performance?

Q4-6. Explain what it means when a company's ROE exceeds its RNOA.

Q4-7.[A] Discontinued operations are typically viewed as a nonoperating activity in the analysis of the balance sheet and the income statement. What is the rationale for this treatment?

Q4-8. Describe what is meant by the "tax shield."

Q4-9. What is meant by the term "net" in net operating assets (NOA)?

Q4-10. Why is it important to disaggregate RNOA into operating profit margin (NOPM) and net operating assets turnover (NOAT)?

Q4-11. What insights do we gain from the graphical relation between profit margin and asset turnover?

Q4-12. Explain the concept of liquidity and why it is crucial to company survival.

Q4-13. Identify at least two factors that limit the usefulness of ratio analysis.

Q4-14.[A] Define (1) net nonoperating obligations and (2) net nonoperating expense.

Assignments with the ✔ logo in the margin are available in myBusinessCourse.
See the Preface of the book for details.

MINI EXERCISES

M4-15. Identify and Compute Net Operating Assets (LO1)

Home Depot, Inc. (HD)

Following is the balance sheet for **Home Depot, Inc.** Identify and compute fiscal year-end 2013 net operating assets.

(amounts in millions, except share and per share data)	February 3, 2013	January 29, 2012
Assets		
Current Assets		
Cash and cash equivalents	$ 2,494	$ 1,987
Receivables, net	1,395	1,245
Merchandise inventories	10,710	10,325
Other current assets	773	963
Total current assets	15,372	14,520

continued

Property and equipment, at cost	38,491	38,975
Less accumulated depreciation and amortization	14,422	14,527
Net property and equipment	24,069	24,448
Notes receivable	140	135
Goodwill	1,170	1,120
Other assets	333	295
Total assets	$41,084	$40,518
Liabilities and stockholders' equity		
Current liabilities		
Accounts payable	$ 5,376	$ 4,856
Accrued salaries and related expenses	1,414	1,372
Sales taxes payable	472	391
Deferred revenue	1,270	1,147
Income taxes payable	22	23
Current installments of long-term debt	1,321	30
Other accrued expenses	1,587	1,557
Total current liabilities	11,462	9,376
Long-term debt, excluding current installments	9,475	10,758
Other long-term liabilities	2,051	2,146
Deferred income taxes	319	340
Total liabilities	23,307	22,620
Stockholders' equity		
Common stock, par value $0.05; authorized: 10 billion shares; issued: 1.754 billion shares at February 3, 2013 and 1.733 billion shares at January 29, 2012; outstanding: 1.484 billion shares at February 3, 2013 and 1.537 billion shares at January 29, 2012	88	87
Paid-in capital	7,948	6,966
Retained earnings	20,038	17,246
Accumulated other comprehensive income	397	293
Treasury stock, at cost, 270 million shares at February 3, 2013 and 196 million shares at January 29, 2012	(10,694)	(6,694)
Total stockholders' equity	17,777	17,898
Total liabilities and stockholders' equity	$41,084	$40,518

M4-16. Identify and Compute NOPAT (LO1)

Home Depot, Inc. (HD)

Following is the income statement for **Home Depot, Inc.** (1) Compute NOPBT, which is net operating profit *before* tax. (*Hint:* Treat Home Depot's "other" income as nonoperating since the company classifies it as such in its income statement.) (2) Compute NOPAT for 2013 using a combined federal and state statutory tax rate of 37%.

For Fiscal Year Ended (amounts in millions)	February 3, 2013
Net sales	$74,754
Cost of sales	48,912
Gross profit	25,842
Operating expenses	
Selling, general and administrative	16,508
Depreciation and amortization	1,568
Total operating expenses	18,076
Operating income	7,766
Interest and other (income) expense	
Interest and investment income	(20)
Interest expense	632
Other	(67)
Interest and other, net	545
Earnings before provision for income taxes	7,221
Provision for income taxes	2,686
Net earnings	$ 4,535

Nordstrom, Inc. (JWN)

M4-17. Compute RNOA, Net Operating Profit Margin, and NOA Turnover (LO2)
Selected balance sheet and income statement information for **Nordstrom, Inc.**, a department store retailer, follows.

Company ($ millions)	Ticker	2013 Revenues	2013 NOPAT	2013 Net Operating Assets	2012 Net Operating Assets
Nordstrom, Inc.	JWN	$11,762	$836	$3,759	$3,726

a. Compute its 2013 return on net operating assets (RNOA).
b. Disaggregate RNOA into net operating profit margin (NOPM) and net operating asset turnover (NOAT). Confirm that RNOA = NOPM × NOAT.

Lowe's Companies, Inc. (LOW)

M4-18. Identify and Compute Net Operating Assets (LO2)
Following is the balance sheet for **Lowe's Companies, Inc.** Identify and compute its 2013 net operating assets (NOA).

LOWE'S COMPANIES, INC. ($ millions, except par value)	Feb. 01, 2013	Feb. 03, 2012
Current assets		
Cash and cash equivalents	$ 541	$ 1,014
Short-term investments	125	286
Merchandise inventory—net	8,600	8,355
Deferred income taxes—net	217	183
Other current assets	301	234
Total current assets	9,784	10,072
Property, less accumulated depreciation	21,477	21,970
Long-term investments	271	504
Other assets	1,134	1,013
Total assets	$32,666	$33,559
Current liabilities		
Current maturities of long-term debt	$ 47	$ 592
Accounts payable	4,657	4,352
Accrued compensation and employee benefits	670	613
Deferred revenue	824	801
Other current liabilities	1,510	1,533
Total current liabilities	7,708	7,891

continued

Long-term debt, excluding current maturities	9,030	7,035
Deferred income taxes—net	455	531
Deferred revenue—extended protection plans	715	704
Other liabilities	901	865
Total liabilities	18,809	17,026
Shareholders' equity		
Preferred stock—$5 par value, none issued	0	0
Common stock—$0.50 par value; shares issued and outstanding 1,110 at February 1, 2013 and 1,241 at February 3, 2012, respectively	555	621
Capital in excess of par value	26	14
Retained earnings	13,224	15,852
Accumulated other comprehensive income	52	46
Total shareholders' equity	13,857	16,533
Total liabilities and shareholders' equity	$32,666	$33,559

M4-19. Identify and Compute NOPAT (LO2)

Following is the income statement for **Lowe's Companies, Inc.** Compute its 2013 net operating profit after tax (NOPAT) assuming a 37% total statutory tax rate.

Lowe's Companies, Inc. (LOW)

LOWE'S COMPANIES, INC. For Twelve Months Ended (In millions)	Feb. 01, 2013	Feb. 03, 2012	Jan. 28, 2011
Net sales	$50,521	$50,208	$48,815
Cost of sales	33,194	32,858	31,663
Gross margin	17,327	17,350	17,152
Expenses			
Selling, general and administrative	12,244	12,593	12,006
Depreciation	1,523	1,480	1,586
Interest—net	423	371	332
Total expenses	14,190	14,444	13,924
Pre-tax earnings	3,137	2,906	3,228
Income tax provision	1,178	1,067	1,218
Net earnings	$ 1,959	$ 1,839	$ 2,010

M4-20.[C] Compute and Interpret Disaggregation of DuPont Analysis Ratios (LO5)

Selected balance sheet and income statement information for **Macy's, Inc.**, a retailer, follows.

Macy's, Inc. (M)

Company ($ millions)	Ticker	2013 Sales	2013 Net Income	2013 Assets	2012 Assets	2013 Stockholders' Equity	2012 Stockholders' Equity
Macy's	M	$27,686	$1,335	$20,991	$22,095	$6,051	$5,933

a. Compute Macy's 2013 return on equity (ROE).

b. Disaggregate ROE into profit margin, asset turnover, and financial leverage. Confirm that ROE = PM × AT × FL.

M4-21. Compute RNOA, Net Operating Profit Margin, and NOA Turnover for Competitors (LO2)

Selected balance sheet and income statement information from **Abercrombie & Fitch Co.** and **TJX Companies, Inc.**, clothing retailers in the high-end and value-priced segments, respectively, follows.

Abercrombie & Fitch Co. (ANF)

TJX Companies, Inc. (TJX)

Company ($ millions)	Ticker	2013 Sales	2013 NOPAT	2013 Net Operating Assets	2012 Net Operating Assets
Abercrombie & Fitch	ANF	$ 4,511	$ 242	$1,446	$1,545
TJX Companies	TJX	25,878	1,925	2,393	2,395

a. Compute the 2013 return on net operating assets (RNOA) for both companies.
b. Disaggregate RNOA into net operating profit margin (NOPM) and net operating asset turnover (NOAT) for each company. Confirm that RNOA = NOPM × NOAT.
c. Discuss differences observed with respect to NOPM and NOAT and interpret those differences in light of each company's business model.

Verizon Communications, Inc. (VZ)

M4-22.[B] Compute and Interpret Liquidity and Solvency Ratios (LO4)
Selected balance sheet and income statement information from Verizon Communications, Inc. follows.

($ millions)	2012	2011
Current assets	$ 21,235	$ 30,939
Current liabilities	26,956	30,761
Total liabilities	139,689	144,553
Equity	85,533	85,908
Earnings before interest and taxes	12,468	13,310
Interest expense	2,571	2,827
Net cash flow from operating activities	31,486	29,780

a. Compute the current ratio for each year and discuss any trend in liquidity. What additional information about the numbers used to calculate this ratio might be useful in helping us assess liquidity? Explain.
b. Compute times interest earned and the liabilities-to-equity for each year and discuss any noticeable change. (The average liabilities-to-equity ratio for the telecommunications industry is 1.7.) Do you have any concerns about Verizon's financial leverage and the company's ability to meet interest obligations? Explain.
c. Verizon's capital expenditures are expected to increase substantially as it seeks to respond to competitive pressures to upgrade the quality of its communication infrastructure. Assess Verizon's liquidity and solvency in light of this strategic direction.

Home Depot, Inc. (HD)
Lowe's Companies, Inc. (LOW)

M4-23. Compute Tax Rate on Operating Profit and NOPAT (LO2)
Selected income statement information for 2013 is presented below for Home Depot, Inc. and Lowe's Companies, Inc.

Company ($ millions)	Ticker	Net Operating Profit Before Tax	Pretax Net Nonoperating Expense	Tax Expense	Statutory Tax Rate	Sales
Home Depot	HD	$7,766	$545	$2,686	37%	$74,754
Lowe's	LOW	3,560	423	1,178	37%	50,521

a. Compute NOPAT for each company.
b. Compute NOPAT as a percent of sales for each company.

3M Company (MMM)

M4-24.[C] Compute and Interpret Measures for DuPont Disaggregation Analysis (LO5)
Refer to the 2012 fiscal year financial data of 3M Company from Problem 4-36 to answer the following requirements (perform these computations from the perspective of a 3M shareholder).

a. Compute the DuPont model component measures for profit margin, asset turnover, and financial leverage. Then, compute ROA.
b. Compute ROE. Confirm that ROE equals ROE computed using the component measures from part *a* (ROE = PM × AT × FL).
c. Compute adjusted ROA (assume a tax rate of 37% and pretax net interest expense of $132).

EXERCISES

CVS Caremark Corp (CVS)
Walgreen Co. (WAG)

E4-25. Compute and Interpret RNOA, Profit Margin, and Asset Turnover of Competitors (LO2)
Selected balance sheet and income statement information for drug store retailers CVS Caremark Corp. and Walgreen Co. follows.

Company ($ millions)	Ticker	2012 Sales	2012 NOPAT	2012 Net Operating Assets	2011 Net Operating Assets
CVS Caremark	CVS	$123,133	$4,452	$46,152	$46,677
Walgreen Co.	WAG	71,633	2,182	21,465	15,700

a. Compute the 2012 return on net operating assets (RNOA) for each company.
b. Disaggregate RNOA into net operating profit margin (NOPM) and net operating asset turnover (NOAT) for each company.
c. Discuss any differences in these ratios for each company.

E4-26. Compute, Disaggregate, and Interpret RNOA of Competitors (LO2)
Selected balance sheet and income statement information for the clothing retailers, **Abercrombie & Fitch Co.** and **The GAP, Inc.**, follows.

Abercrombie & Fitch Co. (ANF)
The GAP, Inc. (GPS)

Company ($ millions)	Ticker	2013 Sales	2013 NOPAT	2013 Net Operating Assets	2012 Net Operating Assets
Abercrombie & Fitch. . .	ANF	$ 4,511	$ 242	$1,446	$1,545
The GAP.	GPS	15,651	1,186	2,630	2,535

a. Compute the 2013 return on net operating assets (RNOA) for each company.
b. Disaggregate RNOA into net operating profit margin (NOPM) and net operating asset turnover (NOAT) for each company.
c. Discuss any differences in these ratios for each company.

E4-27. Compute, Disaggregate, and Interpret RNOA of Competitors (LO2)
Selected balance sheet and income statement information for the clothing retailers **Nordstrom Inc.** and **Limited Brands Inc.** follows.

Nordstrom Inc. (JWN)
Limited Brands Inc. (LTD)

Company ($ millions)	Ticker	2013 Sales	2013 NOPAT	2013 Net Operating Assets	2012 Net Operating Assets
Nordstrom	JWN	$11,762	$836	$3,759	$3,726
Limited Brands	LTD	10,459	937	2,690	2,741

a. Compute the 2013 return on net operating assets (RNOA) for each company.
b. Disaggregate RNOA into net operating profit margin (NOPM) and net operating asset turnover (NOAT) for each company.
c. Discuss any differences in these ratios for each company. Identify the factor(s) that drives the differences in RNOA observed from your analyses in parts *a* and *b*.

E4-28. Compute, Disaggregate, and Interpret ROE and RNOA (LO1, 2)
Selected fiscal year balance sheet and income statement information for the computer chip maker, **Intel Corp.**, follows ($ millions).

Intel Corp. (INTC)

Company	Ticker	2012 Sales	2012 Net Income	2012 Net Operating Profit After Tax	2012 Net Operating Assets	2011 Net Operating Assets	2012 Stockholders' Equity	2011 Stockholders' Equity
Intel.	INTC	$53,341	$11,005	$10,857	$42,065	$37,843	$51,203	$45,911

a. Compute the 2012 return on equity (ROE) and the 2012 return on net operating assets (RNOA).
b. Disaggregate RNOA into net operating profit margin (NOPM) and net operating asset turnover (NOAT). What observations can we make about the company's NOPM and NOAT?
c. Compute the percentage of RNOA to ROE, and compute the company's nonoperating return for 2012.

Macy's Inc. (M)

E4-29. Compute, Disaggregate and Interpret ROE and RNOA (LO1, 2)
Selected balance sheet and income statement information from Macy's Inc. follows ($ millions).

Company	Ticker	2013 Sales	2013 Net Income	2013 Net Operating Profit After Tax	2013 Net Operating Assets	2012 Net Operating Assets	2013 Stockholders' Equity	2012 Stockholders' Equity
Macy's	M	$27,686	$1,335	$1,687	$11,145	$10,864	$6,051	$5,933

a. Compute the 2013 return on equity (ROE) and 2013 return on net operating assets (RNOA).
b. Disaggregate RNOA into net operating profit margin (NOPM) and net operating asset turnover (NOAT). What observations can we make about Macy's NOPM and NOAT?
c. Compute the percentage of RNOA to ROE, and compute Macy's nonoperating return for 2013.

Cisco Systems, Inc. (CSCO)

E4-30. Compute, Disaggregate and Interpret ROE and RNOA (LO1, 2)
Selected balance sheet and income statement information from the software company, Cisco Systems, Inc., follows ($ millions).

Company	Ticker	2013 Sales	2013 Net Income	2013 Net Operating Profit After Tax	2013 Net Operating Assets	2012 Net Operating Assets	2013 Stockholders' Equity	2012 Stockholders' Equity
Cisco Systems	CSCO	$48,607	$9,983	$9,963	$24,729	$18,913	$59,120	$51,286

a. Compute the 2013 return on equity (ROE) and 2013 return on net operating assets (RNOA).
b. Disaggregate the RNOA from part *a* into net operating profit margin (NOPM) and net operating asset turnover (NOAT).
c. Compute the percentage of RNOA to ROE. Explain the relation we observe between ROE and RNOA, and Cisco's use of equity capital.

Comcast Corporation (CMCSA)

E4-31.[B] Compute and Interpret Liquidity and Solvency Ratios (LO4)
Selected balance sheet and income statement information from Comcast Corporation for 2012 and 2011 follows ($ millions).

	Total Current Assets	Total Current Liabilities	Pretax Income	Interest Expense	Total Liabilities*	Stockholders' Equity
2012	$19,991	$16,714	$11,609	$2,521	$115,175	$49,796
2011	8,573	13,241	8,207	2,505	110,163	47,655

*Includes redeemable noncontrolling interests

a. Compute the current ratio for each year and discuss any trend in liquidity. Do you believe the company is sufficiently liquid? Explain. What additional information about the accounting numbers comprising this ratio might be useful in helping you assess liquidity? Explain.
b. Compute times interest earned and the liabilities-to-equity ratio for each year and discuss any noticeable change.
c. What is your overall assessment of the company's liquidity and solvency from the analyses in parts *a* and *b*? Explain.

Verizon Communications, Inc. (VZ)

E4-32.[B] Compute and Interpret Liquidity and Solvency Ratios (LO4)
Selected balance sheet and income statement information from Verizon Communications, Inc., for 2012 and 2011 follows ($ millions).

	Total Current Assets	Total Current Liabilities	Pretax Income	Interest Expense	Total Liabilities	Stockholders' Equity
2012	$21,235	$26,956	$ 9,897	$2,571	$139,689	$85,533
2011	30,939	30,761	10,483	2,827	144,553	85,908

a. Compute the current ratio for each year and discuss any trend in liquidity. Do you believe the company is sufficiently liquid? Explain. What additional information about the accounting numbers comprising this ratio might be useful in helping you assess liquidity? Explain.

b. Compute times interest earned and the liabilities-to-equity ratio for each year and discuss any noticeable change.

c. What is your overall assessment of the company's liquidity and solvency from the analyses in parts *a* and *b*? Explain.

E4-33.[B] Compute and Interpret Solvency Ratios for Business Segments (LO4)

General Electric Company (GE)

Selected balance sheet and income statement information from General Electric Company and its two principal business segments (Industrial and Financial) for 2012 follows.

($ millions)	Pretax Income	Interest Expense	Total Liabilities	Stockholders' Equity
Industrial segment	$16,852	$ 1,353	$106,698	$123,803
Financial segment	7,955	11,697	456,626	82,597
Other	(7,401)[1]	(542)[2]	(6,466)[2]	(77,930)
General Electric Consolidated	$17,406	$12,508	$556,858	$128,470[3]

[1] Includes unallocated corporate operating activities.

[2] Includes intercompany loans and related interest expense; these are deducted (eliminated) in preparing consolidated financial statements.

[3] Includes noncontrolling interests.

a. Compute times interest earned and the liabilities-to-equity ratio for 2012 for the two business segments (Industrial and Financial) and the company as a whole.

b. What is your overall assessment of the company's solvency? Explain. What differences do you observe between the two business segments? Do these differences correspond to your prior expectations given each company's business model?

c. Discuss the implications of the analysis of consolidated financial statements and the additional insight that can be gained from a more in-depth analysis of primary business segments.

E4-34.[A] Direct Computation of Nonoperating Return (LO1, 3)

TJX Companies (TJX)

Refer to the income statement for TJX Companies from E4-35, and balance sheet, from page 4-16.

a. Compute the return on equity (ROE), FLEV and Spread for 2013.

b. Use RNOA from the Mid-Module Review, and the FLEV and Spread from part *a*, to compute ROE.

E4-35. Compute NOPAT Using Tax Rates from Tax Footnote (LO1)

TJX Companies (TJX)

The income statement for TJX Companies follows.

TJX COMPANIES Consolidated Statements of Income Fiscal Year Ended ($ thousands)	February 2, 2013
Net sales	$25,878,372
Cost of sales, including buying and occupancy costs	18,521,400
Selling, general and administrative expenses	4,250,446
Provision (credit) for computer intrusion related costs	—
Interest expense, net	29,175
Income from continuing operations before provision for income taxes	3,077,351
Provision for income taxes	1,170,664
Net income	$ 1,906,687

TJX provides the following footnote disclosure relating to its effective tax rate:

	February 2, 2013
U.S. federal statutory income tax rate	35.0%
Effective state income tax rate	4.2
Impact of foreign operations	(0.9)
All other	(0.3)
Worldwide effective income tax rate	38.0%

Compute TJX's NOPAT for 2013 using its income tax footnote disclosure.

PROBLEMS

3M Company (MMM)

P4-36. Analysis and Interpretation of Profitability (LO1, 2)
Balance sheets and income statements for 3M Company follow.

Consolidated Statements of Income			
For Years Ended Dec. 31 ($ millions)	**2012**	**2011**	**2010**
Net sales	**$29,904**	$29,611	$26,662
Operating expenses			
Cost of sales	**15,685**	15,693	13,831
Selling, general and administrative expenses	**6,102**	6,170	5,479
Research, development and related expenses	**1,634**	1,570	1,434
Total operating expenses	**23,421**	23,433	20,744
Operating income	**6,483**	6,178	5,918
Interest expense and income			
Interest expense	**171**	186	201
Interest income	**(39)**	(39)	(38)
Total interest expense—net	**132**	147	163
Income before income taxes	**6,351**	6,031	5,755
Provision for income taxes	**1,840**	1,674	1,592
Net income including noncontrolling interest	**$ 4,511**	$ 4,357	$ 4,163
Less: Net income attributable to noncontrolling interest	**67**	74	78
Net income attributable to 3M	**$ 4,444**	$4,283	$4,085

Consolidated Balance Sheets		
At December 31 ($ millions, except per share amount)	**2012**	**2011**
Assets		
Current assets		
Cash and cash equivalents	**$ 2,883**	$ 2,219
Marketable securities—current	**1,648**	1,461
Accounts receivable—net of allowances of $105 and $108	**4,061**	3,867
Inventories		
Finished goods	**1,754**	1,536
Work in process	**1,186**	1,061
Raw materials and supplies	**897**	819
Total inventories	**3,837**	3,416
Other current assets	**1,201**	1,277
Total current assets	**13,630**	12,240

continued

Marketable securities—noncurrent	**1,162**	896
Investments	**163**	155
Property, plant and equipment	**22,525**	21,166
Less: Accumulated depreciation	**(14,147)**	(13,500)
Property, plant and equipment—net	**8,378**	7,666
Goodwill	**7,385**	7,047
Intangible assets—net	**1,925**	1,916
Prepaid pension benefits	**16**	40
Other assets	**1,217**	1,656
Total assets	**$33,876**	$31,616
Liabilities		
Current liabilities		
Short-term borrowings and current portion of long-term debt	**$ 1,085**	$ 682
Accounts payable	**1,762**	1,643
Accrued payroll	**701**	676
Accrued income taxes	**371**	355
Other current liabilities	**2,281**	2,085
Total current liabilities	**6,200**	5,441
Long-term debt	**4,916**	4,484
Pension and postretirement benefits	**3,086**	3,972
Other liabilities	**1,634**	1,857
Total liabilities	**$15,836**	$15,754
Equity		
3M Company shareholders' equity: Common stock, par value $0.01 per share; Shares outstanding—2012: 687,091,650; Shares outstanding—2011: 694,970,041	**$ 9**	$ 9
Additional paid-in capital	**4,044**	3,767
Retained earnings	**30,679**	28,348
Treasury stock	**(12,407)**	(11,679)
Accumulated other comprehensive income (loss)	**(4,750)**	(5,025)
Total 3M Company shareholders' equity	**17,575**	15,420
Noncontrolling interest	**465**	442
Total equity	**$18,040**	$15,862
Total liabilities and equity	**$33,876**	$31,616

Required

a. Compute net operating profit after tax (NOPAT) for 2012. Assume that the combined federal and state statutory tax rate is 37%.

b. Compute net operating assets (NOA) for 2012 and 2011. Treat noncurrent investments as a nonoperating item.

c. Compute and disaggregate 3M's RNOA into net operating profit margin (NOPM) and net operating asset turnover (NOAT) for 2012. Demonstrate that RNOA = NOPM × NOAT.

d. Compute net nonoperating obligations (NNO) for 2012 and 2011. Confirm the relation: NOA = NNO + Stockholders' equity.

e. Compute return on equity (ROE) for 2012.

f. What is the nonoperating return component of ROE for 2012?

g. Comment on the difference between ROE and RNOA. What inference can we draw from this comparison?

P4-37.[B] Analysis and Interpretation of Liquidity and Solvency (LO4)

Refer to the financial information of **3M Company** in P4-36 to answer the following requirements.

3M Company (MMM)

Required

a. Compute the current ratio and quick ratio for 2012 and 2011. Comment on any observed trends.

b. Compute times interest earned and liabilities-to-equity ratios for 2012 and 2011. Comment on any noticeable changes.

c. Summarize your findings about the company's liquidity and solvency. Do you have any concerns about its ability to meet its debt obligations?

3M Company (MMM)

P4-38.[A] Direct Computation of Nonoperating Return (LO1, 2, 3)
Refer to the financial information of 3M Company in P4-36 to answer the following requirements.

Required

a. Compute its financial leverage (FLEV), Spread, and noncontrolling interest (NCI) ratio for 2012. Recall that NNE = NOPAT − Net income.

b. Assume that its return on equity (ROE) for 2012 is 26.94% and its return on net operating assets (RNOA) is 26.65%. Confirm computations to yield the relation: ROE = [RNOA + (FLEV × Spread)] × NCI ratio.

c. What do your computations of the nonoperating return imply about the company's use of borrowed funds?

Costco Wholesale Corporation (COST)

P4-39. Analysis and Interpretation of Profitability (LO1, 2)
Balance sheets and income statements for Costco Wholesale Corporation follow.

Consolidated Statements of Earnings

For Fiscal Years Ended ($ millions)	September 1, 2013	September 2, 2012	August 28, 2011
Revenue			
Net sales	**$102,870**	$97,062	$87,048
Membership fees	**2,286**	2,075	1,867
Total revenue	**105,156**	99,137	88,915
Operating expenses			
Merchandise costs	**91,948**	86,823	77,739
Selling, general and administrative	**10,104**	9,518	8,691
Preopening expenses	**51**	37	46
Operating income	**3,053**	2,759	2,439
Other income (expense)			
Interest expense	**(99)**	(95)	(116)
Interest income and other, net	**97**	103	60
Income before income taxes	**3,051**	2,767	2,383
Provision for income taxes	**990**	1,000	841
Net income including noncontrolling interests	**2,061**	1,767	1,542
Net income attributable to noncontrolling interests	**(22)**	(58)	(80)
Net income attributable to Costco	**$ 2,039**	$ 1,709	$ 1,462

Consolidated Balance Sheets

($ millions, except par value and share data)	September 1, 2013	September 2, 2012
Assets		
Current assets		
Cash and cash equivalents	**$ 4,644**	$ 3,528
Short-term investments	**1,480**	1,326
Receivables, net	**1,201**	1,026
Merchandise inventories	**7,894**	7,096
Deferred income taxes and other current assets	**621**	550
Total current assets	**15,840**	13,526
Property and equipment		
Land	**4,409**	4,032
Buildings and improvements	**11,556**	10,879
Equipment and fixtures	**4,472**	4,261
Construction in progress	**585**	374
	21,022	19,546
Less accumulated depreciation and amortization	**(7,141)**	(6,585)
Net property and equipment	**13,881**	12,961
Other assets	**562**	653
Total assets	**$30,283**	$27,140

continued

Liabilities and equity		
Current liabilities		
Accounts payable	**$ 7,872**	$ 7,303
Accrued salaries and benefits	**2,037**	1,832
Accrued member rewards	**710**	661
Accrued sales and other taxes	**382**	397
Deferred membership fees	**1,167**	1,101
Other current liabilities	**1,089**	966
Total current liabilities	**13,257**	12,260
Long-term debt, excluding current portion	**4,998**	1,381
Deferred income taxes and other liabilities	**1,016**	981
Total liabilities	**19,271**	14,622
Equity		
Preferred stock, $0.005 par value: 100,000,000 shares authorized; no shares issued and outstanding	**0**	0
Common stock, $0.005 par value: 900,000,000 shares authorized; 436,839,000 and 432,350,000 shares issued and outstanding	**2**	2
Additional paid-in-capital	**4,670**	4,369
Accumulated other comprehensive (loss) income	**(122)**	156
Retained earnings	**6,283**	7,834
Total Costco stockholders' equity	**10,833**	12,361
Noncontrolling interests	**179**	157
Total equity	**11,012**	12,518
Total liabilities and equity	**$30,283**	$27,140

Required

a. Compute net operating profit after tax (NOPAT) for 2013. Assume that the combined federal and state statutory tax rate is 37%.

b. Compute net operating assets (NOA) for 2013 and 2012.

c. Compute and disaggregate Costco's RNOA into net operating profit margin (NOPM) and net operating asset turnover (NOAT) for 2013; confirm that RNOA = NOPM × NOAT. Comment on NOPM and NOAT estimates for Costco in comparison to those for Walmart calculated earlier in this module.

d. Compute net nonoperating obligations (NNO) for 2013 and 2012. Confirm the relation: NOA = NNO + Stockholders' equity.

e. Compute return on equity (ROE) for 2013.

f. Infer the nonoperating return component of ROE for 2013.

g. Comment on the difference between ROE and RNOA. What does this relation suggest about Costco's use of equity capital?

P4-40.[B] Analysis and Interpretation of Liquidity and Solvency **(LO4)**

Refer to the financial information of **Costco Wholesale Corporation (COST)** in P4-39 to answer the following requirements.

Costco Wholesale Corporation (COST)

Required

a. Compute Costco's current ratio and quick ratio for 2013 and 2012. Comment on any observed trends.

b. Compute Costco's times interest earned and its liabilities-to-equity ratios for 2013 and 2012. Comment on any noticeable change.

c. Summarize your findings about the company's liquidity and solvency. Do you have any concerns about Costco's ability to meet its debt obligations?

P4-41.[A] Direct Computation of Nonoperating Return **(LO1, 3)**

Refer to the financial information of **Costco Wholesale Corporation (COST)** in P4-39 to answer the following requirements.

Costco Wholesale Corporation (COST)

Required

a. Compute Costco's financial leverage (FLEV), Spread and noncontrolling interest (NCI) ratio for 2013; recall, NNE = NOPAT − Net income.

b. Assume that Costco's return on equity (ROE) for 2013 is 17.58% and its return on net operating assets (RNOA) is 21.78%. Confirm computations to yield the relation: ROE = [RNOA + (FLEV × Spread)] × NCI ratio.

c. What do your computations of the nonoperating return in parts *a* and *b* imply about the company's use of borrowed funds?

Intel Corporation (INTC)

P4-42. Analysis and Interpretation of Profitability (LO1, 2)

Balance sheets and income statements for **Intel Corporation** follow. Refer to these financial statements to answer the requirements.

INTEL CORPORATION
Consolidated Statements of Income

For Fiscal Years Ended (in millions)	2012	2011	2010
Net revenue	**$53,341**	**$53,999**	**$43,623**
Cost of sales	20,190	20,242	15,132
Gross margin	**33,151**	**33,757**	**28,491**
Research and development	10,148	8,350	6,576
Marketing, general and administrative	8,057	7,670	6,309
Amortization of acquisition-related intangibles	308	260	18
Operating expenses	**18,513**	**16,280**	**12,903**
Operating income	**14,638**	**17,477**	**15,588**
Gains (losses) on equity investments, net	141	112	348
Interest and other, net	94	192	109
Income before taxes	**14,873**	**17,781**	**16,045**
Provision for taxes	3,868	4,839	4,581
Net income	**$11,005**	**$12,942**	**$11,464**

INTEL CORPORATION
Consolidated Balance Sheets

(in millions, except par value)	2012	2011
Assets		
Current assets		
Cash and cash equivalents	$ 8,478	$ 5,065
Short-term investments	3,999	5,181
Trading assets	5,685	4,591
Accounts receivable, net of allowance for doubtful accounts of $38 ($36 in 2011)	3,833	3,650
Inventories	4,734	4,096
Deferred tax assets	2,117	1,700
Other current assets	2,512	1,589
Total current assets	**31,358**	**25,872**
Property, plant and equipment, net	**27,983**	**23,627**
Marketable equity securities	**4,424**	**562**
Other long-term investments	**493**	**889**
Goodwill	**9,710**	**9,254**
Identified intangible assets, net	**6,235**	**6,267**
Other long-term assets	**4,148**	**4,648**
Total assets	**$84,351**	**$71,119**
Liabilities and stockholders' equity		
Current liabilities		
Short-term debt	$ 312	$ 247
Accounts payable	3,023	2,956
Accrued compensation and benefits	2,972	2,948
Accrued advertising	1,015	1,134
Deferred income	1,932	1,929
Other accrued liabilities	3,644	2,814

continued

Total current liabilities	**12,898**	**12,028**
Long-term debt	**13,136**	**7,084**
Long-term deferred tax liabilities	**3,412**	**2,617**
Other long-term liabilities	**3,702**	**3,479**
Stockholders' equity		
Preferred stock, $0.001 par value, 50 shares authorized; none issued	—	—
Common stock, $0.001 par value, 10,000 shares authorized; 4,944 issued and outstanding (5,000 issued and outstanding in 2011) and capital in excess of par value	19,464	17,036
Accumulated other comprehensive income (loss)	(399)	(781)
Retained earnings	32,138	29,656
Total stockholders' equity	**51,203**	**45,911**
Total liabilities and stockholders' equity	**$84,351**	**$71,119**

Required

a. Compute net operating profit after tax (NOPAT) for 2012. Assume that the combined federal and state statutory tax rate is 37%.

b. Compute net operating assets (NOA) for 2012 and 2011. (*Hint:* Assume that trading assets and long-term marketable equity securities are investments in marketable securities and are therefore, nonoperating assets; also, footnotes reveal that the other long-term investments are mainly loan receivables and are, therefore, operating.)

c. Compute RNOA and disaggregate it into net operating profit margin (NOPM) and net operating asset turnover (NOAT) for 2012. Comment on the drivers of RNOA.

d. Compute net nonoperating obligations (NNO) for 2012 and 2011. Confirm the relation: NOA = NNO + Stockholders' equity.

e. Compute return on equity (ROE) for 2012.

f. Infer the nonoperating return component of ROE for 2012.

g. Comment on the difference between ROE and RNOA. What does this relation suggest about Intel's use of equity capital?

P4-43. Analysis and Interpretation of Profitability (LO1, 2)

Balance sheets and income statements for **Nordstrom, Inc.**, follow. Refer to these financial statements to answer the requirements.

Nordstrom, Inc. (JWN)

NORDSTROM, INC.
Consolidated Statements of Earnings

For Fiscal Years Ended ($ millions)	2013	2012	2011
Net sales	$11,762	$10,497	$9,310
Credit card revenues	386	380	390
Total revenues	12,148	10,877	9,700
Cost of sales and related buying and occupancy costs	(7,432)	(6,592)	(5,897)
Selling, general and administrative expenses			
Retail	(3,166)	(2,807)	(2,412)
Credit	(205)	(229)	(273)
Earnings before interest and income taxes	1,345	1,249	1,118
Interest expense, net	(160)	(130)	(127)
Earnings before income taxes	1,185	1,119	991
Income tax expense	(450)	(436)	(378)
Net earnings	$ 735	$ 683	$ 613

NORDSTROM, INC.
Consolidated Balance Sheets

($ millions)	February 2, 2013	January 28, 2012
Assets		
Current assets		
Cash and cash equivalents	$1,285	$1,877
Accounts receivable, net	2,129	2,033
Merchandise inventories	1,360	1,148
Current deferred tax assets, net	227	220
Prepaid expenses and other	80	282
Total current assets	5,081	5,560
Land, buildings and equipment, net	2,579	2,469
Goodwill	175	175
Other assets	254	287
Total assets	$8,089	$8,491
Liabilities and Shareholders' Equity		
Current liabilities		
Accounts payable	$1,011	$917
Accrued salaries, wages and related benefits	404	388
Other current liabilities	804	764
Current portion of long-term debt	7	506
Total current liabilities	2,226	2,575
Long-term debt, net	3,124	3,141
Deferred property incentives, net	485	500
Other liabilities	341	319
Shareholders' equity		
Common stock, no par value: 1,000 shares authorized; 197.0 and 207.6 shares issued and outstanding	1,645	1,484
Retained earnings	315	517
Accumulated other comprehensive loss	(47)	(45)
Total shareholders' equity	1,913	1,956
Total liabilities and shareholders' equity	$8,089	$8,491

Required

a. Compute net operating profit after tax (NOPAT) for 2013. Assume that the combined federal and state statutory tax rate is 37%.

b. Compute net operating assets (NOA) for 2013 and 2012.

c. Compute RNOA and disaggregate it into net operating profit margin (NOPM) and net operating asset turnover (NOAT) for 2013; confirm that RNOA = NOPM × NOAT. Comment on NOPM and NOAT estimates for Nordstrom in comparison to the ratios for Walmart calculated earlier in the module.

d. Compute net nonoperating obligations (NNO) for 2013 and 2012. Confirm the relation: NOA = NNO + Stockholders' equity.

e. Compute return on equity (ROE) for 2013.

f. Infer the nonoperating return component of ROE for 2013.

g. Comment on the difference between ROE and RNOA. What does this relation suggest about Nordstrom's use of equity capital?

Kraft Foods Group, Inc. (KFT)

P4-44. Analysis and Interpretation of Profitability (LO1, 2)
Balance sheets and income statements for **Kraft Foods Group, Inc.**, follow. Refer to these financial statements to answer the following requirements.

KRAFT FOODS GROUP, INC.
Income Statements

For Fiscal Years Ended (In millions)	2012	2011	2010
Net revenues	$18,339	$18,655	$17,797
Cost of sales	12,499	12,813	11,777
Gross profit	5,840	5,842	6,020
Selling, general and administrative expenses	3,029	3,016	3,063
Asset impairment and exit costs	141	(2)	(8)
Operating income	2,670	2,828	2,965
Interest and other expense, net	(258)	(7)	(6)
Royalty income from Mondelez International	41	55	43
Earnings from continuing operations before income taxes	2,453	2,876	3,002
Provision for income taxes	811	1,101	1,112
Earnings from continuing operations	1,642	1,775	1,890
Earnings and gain from discontinued operations, net of income taxes	—	—	1,644
Net earnings	$ 1,642	$ 1,775	$ 3,534

KRAFT FOODS GROUP, INC.
Balance Sheets

(In millions, except share data)	December 29, 2012	December 31, 2011
Assets		
Cash and cash equivalents	$ 1,255	$ —
Receivables (net of allowances of $28 in 2012 and $23 in 2011)	1,089	903
Inventories, net	1,928	1,943
Deferred income taxes	420	232
Other current assets	131	194
Total current assets	4,823	3,272
Property, plant and equipment, net	4,204	4,278
Goodwill	11,346	11,316
Intangible assets, net	2,631	2,630
Other assets	325	43
Total assets	$23,329	$21,539
Liabilities		
Current portion of long-term debt	$ 5	$ 8
Accounts payable	1,556	1,447
Accrued marketing	740	575
Accrued employment costs	194	242
Dividends payable	296	—
Accrued postretirement health care costs	236	—
Other current liabilities	579	300
Total current liabilities	3,606	2,572
Long-term debt	9,966	27
Deferred income taxes	288	1,594
Accrued pension costs	1,990	117
Accrued postretirement health care costs	3,502	—
Other liabilities	405	641
Total liabilities	19,757	4,951

continued

continued from prior page

Equity		
Common Stock, no par value (592,783,696 shares issued in 2012 and 0 in 2011) . . .	—	—
Additional paid-in capital	4,240	—
Parent company investment	—	16,713
Retained earnings/(deficit)	(206)	—
Accumulated other comprehensive losses	(460)	(125)
Treasury stock, at cost	(2)	—
Total equity	3,572	16,588
Total liabilities and equity	$23,329	$21,539

Required

a. Compute net operating profit after tax (NOPAT) for 2012. Assume that the combined federal and state statutory tax rate is 37%.

b. Compute net operating assets (NOA) for 2012 and 2011.

c. Compute RNOA and disaggregate it into net operating profit margin (NOPM) and net operating asset turnover (NOAT) for 2012; confirm that RNOA = NOPM × NOAT. The median NOPM and NOAT for companies in the packaged food industry (see Exhibit 4.4) is 5% and 2.1, respectively, yielding a median RNOA of 10.5%. Comment on NOPM and NOAT estimates for KFT in comparison to industry medians.

d. Compute net nonoperating obligations (NNO) for 2012 and 2011. Confirm the relation: NOA = NNO + Stockholders' equity.

e. Compute return on equity (ROE) for 2012.

f. Infer the nonoperating return component of ROE for 2012.

g. Comment on the difference between ROE and RNOA. What does this relation suggest about Kraft's use of debt?

P4-45.[A] Direct Computation of Nonoperating Return (LO1, 3)

Kraft Foods Group, Inc. (KFT)

Refer to the financial information of **Kraft Foods Group, Inc.**, in P4-44 to answer the following requirements.

Required

a. Assume that 2012 net nonoperating expenses (NNE) are $137 million and that 2012 RNOA is 12.18%. Compute financial leverage (FLEV) and Spread for 2012.

b. Assume that 2012 return on equity (ROE) is 16.29%. Confirm computations to yield the relation: ROE = RNOA + (FLEV × Spread).

c. What do your computations of the nonoperating return in parts *a* and *b* imply about the company's use of borrowed funds?

P4-46. Analysis and Interpretation of Profit Margin, Asset Turnover, and RNOA for Several Companies (LO2)

Abbott Laboratories (ABT)
FedEx Corp. (FDX)
CVS Caremark Corp. (CVS)
Kraft Foods Group, Inc. (KFT)
Walgreen Co. (WAG)
Caterpillar, Inc. (CAT)
Target Corp. (TGT)

Net operating profit margin (NOPM) and net operating asset turnover (NOAT) for several selected companies for the most recent year follow.

	NOPM	NOAT
Abbott Laboratories	17.83%	1.24
FedEx Corp.	3.66%	2.90
CVS Caremark Corp.	3.62%	2.65
Kraft Foods Group, Inc.	9.70%	1.26
Walgreen Co.	3.05%	3.85
Caterpillar, Inc.	8.99%	1.36
Target Corp.	4.75%	2.44

Required

a. Graph NOPM and NOAT for each of these companies. Do you see a pattern that is similar to that shown in this module? Explain. (The graph in the module is based on medians for selected industries; the graph for this problem uses fewer companies than in the module and, thus, will not be as smooth.)

b. Consider the trade-off between profit margin and asset turnover. How can we evaluate companies on the profit margin and asset turnover trade-off? Explain.

P4-47.[C] Compute and Analyze Measures for DuPont Disaggregation Analysis (LO5)

Costco Wholesale Corporation (COST)

Refer to the fiscal 2013 financial data of Costco Wholesale Corporation (COST) in P4-39 to answer the following requirements.

Required

a. Apply the basic DuPont model and compute the component measures for profit margin, asset turnover, and financial leverage.

b. Compute ROE. Confirm that ROE equals ROE computed using the component measures from part *a* (ROE = PM × AT × FL).

c. Compute adjusted ROA (assume a tax rate of 37%).

P4-48.[C] Compute and Analyze Measures for DuPont Disaggregation Analysis (LO5)

Kraft Foods Group, Inc. (KFT)

Refer to the fiscal 2012 financial data of Kraft Foods Group, Inc. in P4-44 to answer the following requirements.

Required

a. Apply the basic DuPont model and compute its component measures for profit margin, asset turnover, and financial leverage.

b. Compute ROE. Confirm that ROE equals ROE computed using the component measures from part *a* (ROE = PM × AT × FL).

c. Compute adjusted ROA (assume a tax rate of 37%). Compare the adjusted and unadjusted ROA ratios and explain why they differ.

IFRS APPLICATIONS

IFRS

I4-49. Compute, Disaggregate, and Interpret RNOA of Competitors (LO2)

Shell Oil Company
Royal Dutch Shell
BP Limited

Shell Oil Company is the U.S.-based subsidiary of Royal Dutch Shell, a multinational oil company headquartered in The Hague, The Netherlands. BP Limited is a multinational oil company headquartered in London U.K. Selected balance sheet and income statement information and assumptions for both Royal Dutch Shell and BP follow.

($ millions)	2012 Sales	2012 NOPAT	2012 Net Operating Assets	2011 Net Operating Assets
Royal Dutch Shell.	$467,153	$24,420	$204,264	$191,394
BP Limited	375,580	11,305	123,017	128,795

a. Compute the 2012 return on net operating assets (RNOA) for each company.

b. Disaggregate RNOA into net operating profit margin (NOPM) and net operating asset turnover (NOAT) for each company.

c. Discuss any differences in these ratios for each company. What drives the differences in RNOA observed in parts *a* and *b*?

I4-50. Compute, Disaggregate, and Interpret ROE and RNOA (LO1, 2)

Husky Energy, Inc.

Headquartered in Calgary, Alberta, Husky Energy Inc. is a publicly traded, integrated energy company, with extensive conventional oil and natural gas assets, substantial heavy oil production and a range of midstream and downstream operations. Operating assets include refineries, upgrading facilities, and pipelines. Selected fiscal year balance sheet and income statement information for Husky Energy follow (Canadian $ millions).

2012 Sales	2012 Net Income	2012 NOPAT	2012 Net Operating Assets	2011 Net Operating Assets	2012 Stockholders' Equity	2011 Stockholders' Equity
$22,435	$2,022	$2,121	$21,054	$19,843	$19,161	$17,773

a. Compute the 2012 return on equity (ROE) and the 2012 return on net operating assets (RNOA).

b. Disaggregate RNOA into net operating profit margin (NOPM) and net operating asset turnover (NOAT).

c. Compute the percentage of RNOA to ROE, and compute Husky's nonoperating return for 2012.

I4-51.[B] **Compute and Interpret Liquidity and Solvency Ratios** **(LO4)**

BHP Billiton

Headquartered in Melbourne, Australia, **BHP Billiton**, is a leading global resources company that operates in diverse commodity and geographic markets. The company is among the world's top producers of iron ore, metallurgical coal, conventional and non-conventional oil and gas, copper, energy coal, aluminum, manganese, uranium, nickel, and silver. BHP Billiton is traded on the Australian Securities Exchange (ASX) and also listed in London, Johannesburg, and New York.

($ millions)	Total Current Assets	Total Current Liabilities	Pretax Income	Interest Expense	Total Liabilities	Stockholders' Equity
2011	$25,280	$19,738	$31,255	$561	$45,165	$57,755
2012	20,451	22,034	23,022	730	62,188	67,085

a. Compute the current ratio for each year and discuss any trend in liquidity. Is the company sufficiently liquid? Explain. What additional information about the accounting numbers comprising this ratio might be useful in helping us assess liquidity? Explain.

b. Compute times interest earned and the liabilities-to-equity ratio for each year and discuss any noticeable change.

c. What is the overall assessment of the company's liquidity and solvency from the analyses in parts *a* and *b*? Explain.

I4-52. **Analysis and Interpretation of Profitability** **(LO1, 2)**

BT Group plc

BT Group is one of the largest telecommunications services companies in the world, headquartered in London, United Kingdom. Balance sheets and income statements for BT Group follow.

BT GROUP
Income Statement

Year Ended 31 March	2012 £m	2011 £m
Revenue	**18,897**	**20,076**
Other operating income	368	373
Operating costs	(16,346)	(17,871)
Operating profit	**2,919**	**2,578**
Finance expense	(2,784)	(3,203)
Finance income	2,300	2,279
Net finance expense	**(484)**	**(924)**
Share of post tax profit of associates and joint ventures	10	21
Profit on disposal of interest in associate	0	42
Profit before taxation	**2,445**	**1,717**
Taxation	(442)	(213)
Profit for the year	**2,003**	**1,504**
Attributable to:		
Equity shareholders of the parent	2,002	1,502
Noncontrolling interests	1	2

BT GROUP
Balance Sheet

At 31 March	2012 £m	2011 £m
Non-current assets		
Intangible assets	3,127	3,389
Property, plant and equipment	14,388	14,623
Derivative financial instruments	886	625
Investments[1]	68	61
Associates and joint ventures	153	164
Trade and other receivables	169	286
Deferred tax assets	626	461
	19,417	**19,609**
Current assets		
Inventories	104	121
Trade and other receivables	3,307	3,332
Current tax receivable	139	—
Derivative financial instruments	137	108
Investments[1]	513	19
Cash and cash equivalents	331	351
	4,531	**3,931**
Current liabilities		
Loans and other borrowings	2,887	485
Derivative financial instruments	89	62
Trade and other payables	5,962	6,114
Current tax liabilities	66	221
Provisions	251	149
	9,255	**7,031**
Total assets less current liabilities	**14,693**	**16,509**
Non-current liabilities		
Loans and other borrowings	7,599	9,371
Derivative financial instruments	757	507
Retirement benefit obligations	2,448	1,830
Other payables	875	831
Deferred tax liabilities	1,100	1,212
Provisions	606	807
	13,385	**14,558**
Equity		
Ordinary shares	408	408
Share premium	62	62
Capital redemption reserve	27	27
Other reserves	711	658
Retained earnings	89	770
Total parent shareholders' equity	**1,297**	**1,925**
Noncontrolling interests	11	26
Total equity	**1,308**	**1,951**
	14,693	**16,509**

[1] Investments are nonoperating assets

Required

a. Compute net operating profit after tax (NOPAT) for 2012. Assume that the company's marginal tax rate is 36%.

b. Compute net operating assets (NOA) for 2012 and 2011.

c. Compute and disaggregate RNOA into net operating profit margin (NOPM) and net operating asset turnover (NOAT) for 2012.

d. Compute net nonoperating obligations (NNO) for 2012 and 2011. Confirm the relation: NOA = NNO + Total equity.
e. Compute return on equity (ROE) for 2012.
f. What is the nonoperating return component of ROE for 2012?
g. Comment on the difference between ROE and RNOA. What inference can we draw from this comparison?

I4-53.[B] Analysis and Interpretation of Liquidity and Solvency (LO4)

BT Group plc

BT Group is one of the largest telecommunications services companies in the world, headquartered in London, United Kingdom. Refer to the financial information for BT Group in I4-53 to answer the following requirements.

Required

a. Compute the current ratio and quick ratio for 2012 and 2011. Comment on any observed trends.
b. Compute times interest earned and liabilities-to-equity ratios for 2012 and 2011. Comment on any noticeable changes.
c. Summarize the findings about the company's liquidity and solvency. Do we have any concerns about its ability to meet its debt obligations?

MANAGEMENT APPLICATIONS

MA4-54. Gross Profit and Strategic Management (LO2)

One way to increase overall profitability is to increase gross profit. This can be accomplished by raising prices and/or by reducing manufacturing costs.

Required

a. Will raising prices and/or reducing manufacturing costs unambiguously increase gross profit? Explain.
b. What strategy might you develop as a manager to (i) increase product prices, or (ii) reduce product manufacturing cost?

MA4-55. Asset Turnover and Strategic Management (LO2)

Increasing net operating asset turnover requires some combination of increasing sales and/or decreasing net operating assets. For the latter, many companies consider ways to reduce their investment in working capital (current assets less current liabilities). This can be accomplished by reducing the level of accounts receivable and inventories, or by increasing the level of accounts payable.

Required

a. Develop a list of suggested actions that you, as a manager, could undertake to achieve these three objectives.
b. Describe the marketing implications of reducing receivables and inventories, and the supplier implications of delaying payment. How can a company reduce working capital without negatively impacting its performance?

MA4-56. Ethics and Governance: Earnings Management (LO1)

Companies are aware that analysts focus on profitability in evaluating financial performance. Managers have historically utilized a number of methods to improve reported profitability that are cosmetic in nature and do not affect "real" operating performance. These methods are subsumed under the general heading of "earnings management." Justification for such actions typically includes the following arguments:

- Increasing stock price by managing earnings benefits stockholders; thus, no one is hurt by these actions.
- Earnings management is a temporary fix; such actions will be curtailed once "real" profitability improves, as managers expect.

Required

a. Identify the affected parties in any scheme to manage profits to prop up stock price.
b. Do the ends (of earnings management) justify the means? Explain.
c. To what extent are the objectives of managers different from those of stockholders?
d. What governance structure can you envision that might inhibit earnings management?

ONGOING PROJECT

(This ongoing project began in Module 1 and continues through most of the book; even if previous segments were not completed, the requirements are still applicable to any business analysis.) Analysis of financial statements commonly includes ROE disaggregation and scrutiny of its components as explained in this module.

1. Compute ROE for all three years reported on the income statement. (*Hint:* Do your companies report noncontrolling interest on the income statement and balance sheet? If so, make certain to use income available to the controlling interest (NI_{CI}) in the numerator and equity of the controlling interest (CI) in the denominator. To compute ROE for three years, we must determine average stockholders' equity for three years, which means we need four balance sheet amounts. Because the balance sheets of each company will report only two years, we must collect prior years' financial statements.)
2. Compute RNOA and its two components (NOPM and NOAT) for all three years reported on the income statement. We must use balance sheet numbers for four years to obtain three averages of net operating assets. Examine the income statements and balance sheets to determine the operating and nonoperating items. (*Hint:* Use an online source to understand any line items not described in the textbook. Use cell references in the spreadsheet to compute NOPAT and NOA and the various ratios.)

Compare ROE and RNOA and identify differences over time and between the companies. Evaluate the companies' returns and answer questions such as the following:

- Which company is more profitable?
- How do the operating and nonoperating portions of ROE compare?
- Compare the ROE and RNOA with the graph in the Research Insight box in the module. If the ratios for the companies under analysis differ from the graph, is there an explanation?
- Is the net operating profit margin similar for the two companies? Given that they are roughly in the same industry, major differences should prompt further exploration.
- Are the companies' net operating asset turnover ratios similar or markedly different?

3. Determine FLEV and Spread and the noncontrolling interest ratio (if applicable). Show that:

   ROE = [RNOA + (FLEV × Spread)] × Noncontrolling interest ratio

   Compare the components of the equation for each company over time and follow up on any differences.
4. Compute the four ratios from Appendix 4B for the recent three years for each company: current ratio, quick ratio, liabilities-to-equity, and times interest earned. Compare the ratios for the companies under analysis and identify differences over time and between companies. Evaluate each company's ability to pay its debts in the short term (liquidity) and the long term (solvency), and in the process address the following:
   - Which company is more liquid? More solvent?
   - Look at the bar chart in Exhibit 4.6. Compare the liabilities-to-equity ratios to the norm. If the ratios differ from the industry norm, is there an explanation(s)?
   - Do the ratios change over time? If yes, does the change make sense given the economic and competitive factors that affect the industry and the companies?

SOLUTIONS TO REVIEW PROBLEMS

Mid-Module Review 1

Solution

TJX's NOPAT is computed as follows (in $ millions):

NOPAT = Operating profit before tax − (Tax expense + [Net interest expense × 37%])
= ($25,878,372 − $18,521,400 − $4,250,446) − ($1,170,664 + [$29,175 × 0.37])
= $1,925,067

Mid-Module Review 2

Solution ($ millions)

1.

	Feb. 2, 2013	Jan. 28, 2012
Operating assets		
Accounts receivable, net	$ 222,788	$ 204,304
Merchandise inventories	3,014,214	2,950,523
Prepaid expenses and other current assets	330,512	270,133
Current deferred income taxes, net	96,219	105,869
Net property at cost	3,223,242	2,706,377
Property under capital lease, net	0	8,748
Other assets	260,801	253,913
Goodwill and tradename, net of amortization	316,269	179,935
Total operating assets	$7,464,045	$6,679,802
Operating liabilities		
Accounts payable	$1,930,568	$1,645,324
Accrued expenses and other current liabilities	1,666,216	1,364,705
Federal, foreign and state income taxes payable	163,812	50,424
Other long-term liabilities	961,284	861,768
Non-current deferred income taxes, net	349,486	362,501
Total operating liabilities	5,071,366	4,284,722
Net operating assets	$2,392,679	$2,395,080

2. $$\text{RNOA} = \frac{\$1{,}925{,}067}{(\$2{,}392{,}679 + \$2{,}395{,}080)/2} = 80.42\%$$

3. $$\text{ROE} = \frac{\$1{,}906{,}687}{(\$3{,}665{,}937 + \$3{,}209{,}290)/2} = 55.47\%$$

ROE is markedly less than RNOA because of the large amount of nonoperating assets, which yield a low return. For further discussion of this type of case see Intel as an example in Appendix 4A.

4. $$\text{NOPM} = \frac{\$1{,}925{,}067}{\$25{,}828{,}372} = 7.44\%$$

$$\text{NOAT} = \frac{\$25{,}828{,}372}{(\$2{,}392{,}679 + \$2{,}395{,}080)/2} = 10.81$$

Note: $7.44\% \times 10.81 = 80.42\%$

5.

	ROE	RNOA	NOPM	NOAT
Walmart	23.02%	15.14%	4.06%	3.73
TJX	55.47%	80.42%	7.44%	10.81

TJX's higher ROE is driven by higher RNOA, which is the result of both a much higher NOPM and significantly greater turnover of operating assets.

Module-End Review

Solution ($ millions)

1. We know: TJX ROE = Operating return (RNOA) + Nonoperating return
   Using solutions from Mid-Module Review 2, and substituting, we get:
   55.47% = 80.42% + Nonoperating return

   Then, solving for the missing value we get: −24.95% = Nonoperating return

   The negative nonoperating return reflects the larger nonoperating assets that TJX owns in the form of marketable securities. The return on these securities is much less than the return on net operating assets, thus reducing ROE. This is similar to the issue we discuss in Appendix 4A with respect to Intel.

2. We know: Walmart's ROE = Operating return (RNOA) + Nonoperating return
   23.02% = 15.14% + Nonoperating return

   Then, solving for the missing value we get: 7.88% = Nonoperating return

   TJX's ROE is much greater than Walmart's, due primarily to a much higher RNOA resulting from both a much greater NOPM and NOAT. Its ROE is even more impressive given the amount of nonoperating assets it carries on its balance sheet in the form of marketable securities that carry a much lower return than do its net operating assets. TJX could markedly increase its ROE by liquidating its marketable securities and using the proceeds to declare a one-time dividend or repurchase its common shares on the open market. TJX, therefore, has considerable up-side potential to increase its ROE without increasing its financial leverage.

3. TJX's liabilities-to-equity ratio = Total liabilities/Total equity
   (We use total [consolidated] equity to be consistent with the consolidated liabilities in the numerator.)
   ($3,760,596 + $961,284 + $349,486 + $774,552)/$3,665,937 = 1.59

4. Walmart's liabilities-to-equity ratio = Total liabilities/Total equity
   ($71,818 + $38,394 + $3,023 + $7,613 + $519)/$81,738 = 1.48

   While the liabilities-to-equity ratios for both companies are higher than for the average retail company (see: Exhibit 4.6), neither company's ratio is markedly out of line with medians for all publicly traded companies over the past decade. Further analysis is necessary to evaluate if the companies' debt exposure is excessive. That additional analysis will examine the amount of projected debt payments (found in the long-term debt footnote) with projected net cash from operating activities. Given both companies' high profitability levels, it is unlikely debt levels are too high.

Module

5 Reporting and Analyzing Operating Income

Learning Objectives

LO1 Explain revenue recognition criteria and identify transactions of special concern. (p. 5-5)

LO2 Describe accounting for operating expenses, including research and development, and restructuring. (p. 5-12)

LO3 Explain and analyze accounting for income taxes. (p. 5-19)

LO4 Explain how foreign currency fluctuations affect the income statement. (p. 5-27)

LO5 Compute earnings per share and explain the effect of dilutive securities. (p. 5-31)

LO6 Explain accounting quality and identify areas for analysis. (p. 5-33)

Pfizer

Pfizer's business is to discover, develop, manufacture and market leading prescription medicines. These endeavors define the company's operating activities and include research and development, manufacturing, advertising, sales, after-sale customer support, and all administrative functions necessary to support Pfizer's various activities.

Accounting for operating activities involves numerous estimates and choices, and GAAP often grants considerable latitude. To illustrate, consider the choice of when to recognize sales revenue. Should Pfizer recognize revenue when it receives a customer order? When it ships the drug order? Or, when the customer pays? GAAP requires that revenues be recognized when *earned*. It is up to the company to decide when that condition is met. This module identifies several revenue-recognition scenarios that are especially troublesome for companies, their auditors, regulators, and outside stakeholders.

Pfizer's key operating activity is its research and development (R&D). To protect its discoveries, Pfizer holds thousands of patents and applies for hundreds more each year. However, patents don't protect Pfizer indefinitely—patents expire or fail legal challenges and, then, Pfizer's drugs face competition from other drug manufacturers. This was particularly important in 2012 as Pfizer's revenues decreased by 10% from \$65 billion to \$59 billion, primarily as a result of the loss of patent protection on its blockbuster drug, Lipitor.

Wall Street continues to be optimistic about Pfizer's ability to replace expiring drugs with new discoveries as its stock price has climbed 150% since 2009—see stock price chart below.

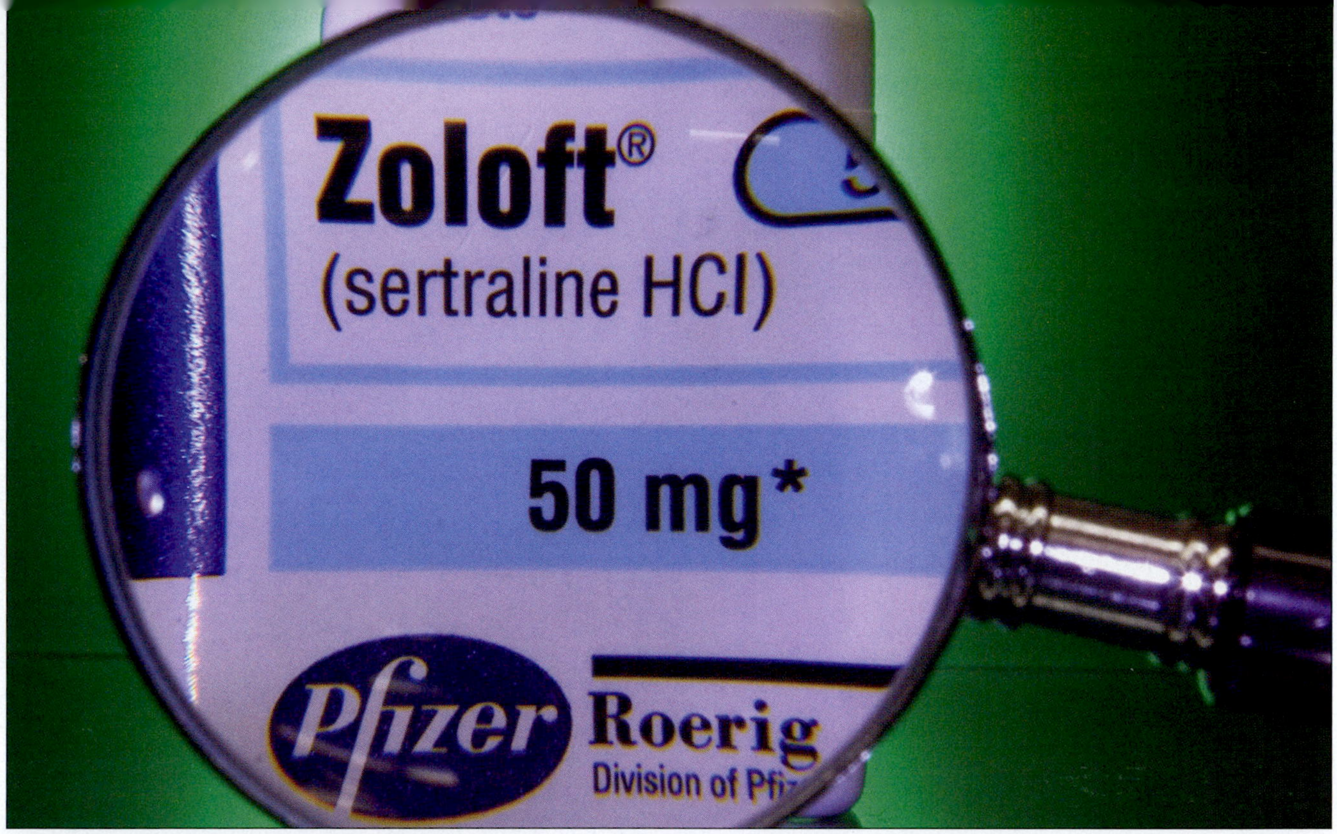

Courtesy of Getty Images

Although R&D activities generally yield future benefits and, thus, meet the criteria to be recorded as an asset, GAAP requires that companies expense most R&D costs. This creates balance sheets with significant "missing" assets. For example, the only asset that Pfizer has on its books specifically related to drugs that it has developed and is currently marketing is the legal cost of filing the patents with the U.S. Patent Office. Clearly this does not capture their full value to Pfizer. This module explains R&D accounting and the resulting financial statement implications.

Pfizer has restructured its business several times in an attempt to maintain operating profit. Restructurings typically involve three types of costs: severance costs relating to employee terminations, asset write-offs, and other costs such as contract termination payments and legal bills.

GAAP grants leeway in how to account for restructuring activities. Should Pfizer expense the severance costs when the board of directors approves the layoffs? Or when the employees are actually paid? Or at some other point? This module discusses accounting for restructurings, including footnote disclosures that can help financial statement readers interpret restructuring activities.

A necessary part of operations is paying income taxes on profits earned. The IRS has its own rules for computing taxes owed. These rules, called the Internal Revenue Code, are different from GAAP. Thus, it is legal (and necessary) for companies to prepare two sets of financial reports, one for shareholders and one for tax authorities. In this module, we will see that tax expense reported on the income statement is not computed as a simple percentage of pretax income. The module also discusses the valuation allowance that is related to deferred tax assets, and explains how the allowance can markedly affect net income.

Earnings per share (EPS) is the most frequently quoted operating number in the financial press. It represents earnings that are available to pay dividends to common shareholders. Companies report two EPS numbers: basic and diluted. The latter represents the lower bound on EPS. It is important that we understand the difference between the two, and this module describes the two EPS computations.

Pfizer does business around the world, transacting in many currencies. Indeed, many of Pfizer's subsidiaries maintain their entire financial records in currencies other than the U.S. dollar. Consequently, to prepare its financial statements in $US, Pfizer must translate its foreign-currency denominated financial records into $US. This module describes the effects of foreign currency translation. When the dollar strengthens and weakens against other world currencies, a company's foreign revenues and expenses decrease or increase in $US value even if unit volumes remain unchanged. Indeed, for 2012, Pfizer reported that its revenues decreased by about $1.5 billion, or 2%, as a result of the strengthening $US. It is important to understand the mechanical relation between foreign exchange rates and income statement items if we are to properly analyze companies with global operations. This module considers these issues.

Sources: Pfizer 2012 10-K, Pfizer 2012 Annual Report.

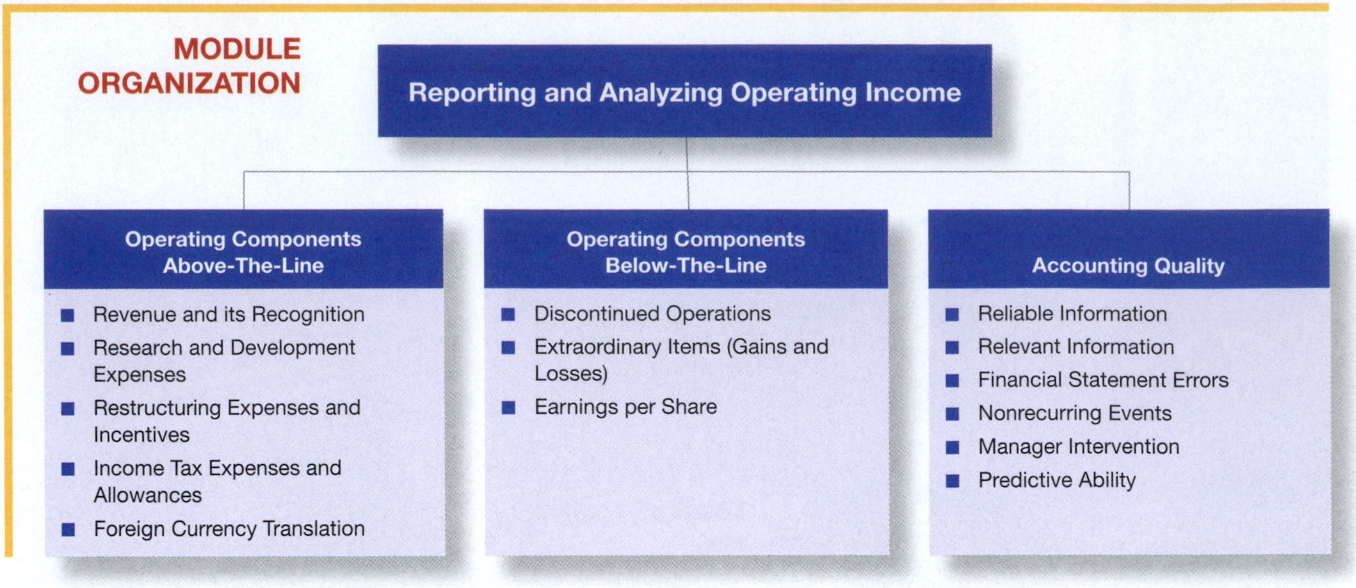

Operating activities refer to a company's primary transactions. These include the purchase of goods from suppliers, the conversion of goods into finished products, the promotion and distribution of goods, the sale of goods to customers, and after-sale customer support. The income statement reports on these operating activities such as sales, cost of goods sold, and selling, general, and administrative expenses. Because they are the lifeblood of any company, operating activities must be executed successfully for a company to consistently succeed.

Nonoperating activities relate to the borrowing of money and the ancillary investment activities of a company. They are not a company's primary activities.[1] These activities are typically reported in the income statement as interest revenues and expenses, dividend revenues, gains and losses on sales of securities, and net income attributable to noncontrolling interest.

Proper identification of operating and nonoperating components is important for valuation of companies' equity (stock) and debt (notes and bonds). It is important, for example, to know whether company profitability results from operating activities, or whether poor operating performance is being masked by income from nonoperating activities. (We know that income from nonoperating activities usually depends on a favorable investment climate, which can be short-lived.)

Exhibit 5.1 classifies common income components as operating or nonoperating.

EXHIBIT 5.1 Distinguishing Operating and Nonoperating Income Components

Operating Activities	Nonoperating Activities
• Sales	• Interest revenues and expenses
• Cost of goods sold	• Dividend revenues
• Selling, general and administrative expenses	• Gains and losses on sales of investments
• Depreciation expense	• Investment write-downs
• Research and development expenses	• Gains and losses on debt retirement
• Restructuring expenses	• Net income from discontinued operations and gains or losses on their disposition
• Income tax expenses	• Gains and losses on derivative activities
• Extraordinary gains and losses	
• Gains and losses on sales of operating assets	
• Foreign currency translation effects	
• Operating asset write-downs	
• Net income or loss from equity investments	
• Other income or expenses	

[1] Exceptions exist; for example, income derived from investments is operating income for financial-services firms such as banks and insurance companies. As another example, the income derived from financing subsidiaries of manufacturing companies, such as Ford Motor Credit and Caterpillar Financial, is part of operating income because these activities can be viewed as extensions of the sales process.

The list of operating activities above includes all the familiar operating items, as well as gains and losses on transactions relating to operating assets and the write-down of operating assets.[2] The list also includes "other" income statement items. We treat these as operating unless the income statement designates them as nonoperating or footnote information indicates that some or all of these "other" items are nonoperating. Footnotes are usually uninformative about "other" income statement items and "other" balance sheet items, and GAAP does not require specific disclosure of such items unless they are deemed *material*.[3]

We build our discussion of operating income around Pfizer's income statement (see Exhibit 5.2), which includes all of the typical operating accounts. We highlight the following topics in this module:

- Revenues
- Research and development expenses
- Restructuring expenses
- Income tax expenses
- Extraordinary gains and losses
- Earnings per share (EPS)
- Foreign currency translation effects

BUSINESS INSIGHT **Ratios Across Industries**

Over time, industries evolve and reach equilibrium levels for operating activities. For example, some industries require a high level of selling, general and administrative (SG&A) expenses, perhaps due to high advertising demands or high occupancy costs. Other industries require intense research and development (R&D) expenditures to remain competitive. To a large extent, these cost structures dictate the prices that firms charge—each industry prices its product or service to yield a sufficient level of gross profit (sales less cost of sales) to cover the operating expenses and allow the industry to remain viable. Review the following table of selected operating margins for companies in various industries (NOPM is net operating profit margin as defined in Module 4).

	Gross profit/Sales	SG&A/Sales	R&D/Sales	NOPM
3M (MMM)	47.5%	20.4%	5.5%	13.7%
Lowes (LOW)	34.3%	24.2%	0.0%	4.4%
Cisco Systems (CSCO)	61.2%	27.5%	11.9%	13.8%
Intel (INTC)	62.1%	15.1%	19.0%	17.3%
Macy's (M)	40.3%	30.6%	0.0%	6.1%
Nike (NKE)	43.4%	30.8%	0.0%	7.9%
Pfizer (PFE)	80.8%	28.2%	13.3%	12.9%
Target (TGT)	31.0%	20.3%	0.0%	4.6%

We see that Cisco, Intel and Pfizer report high gross profit margins. This does not necessarily suggest they are better managed than, for example, Target. Instead, their industries require higher levels of gross profit to cover their high levels of SG&A and R&D. Target, on the other hand, is in a highly price-competitive segment of the retailing industry. To maintain its competitive advantage, Target must control costs. Indeed, Target reports among the lowest SG&A-to-sales ratio of the companies listed.

[2] To explain, a loss on the sale of equipment implies that the company did not depreciate the equipment quickly enough. Had the company recorded the "right" amount of depreciation over the years (that is, the amount of depreciation that perfectly matched the equipment's economic devaluation over time), the equipment's book value would have been exactly the same as its market value and no loss would have been recorded. Thus, we treat the loss on disposal in the same manner as depreciation expense—as operating. The same logic applies to write-downs of operating assets, which occur when the fair value of assets such as property and intangibles has declined below their book value.

[3] *Material* is an accounting term that means the item in question is important enough to make a difference to someone relying on the financial statements when making a business decision. Investors, for example, might find an item material if it is large enough to change their investment decision (whether to buy or sell the stock). This *materiality* judgment is in the eye of the beholder and this subjectivity makes materiality an elusive concept.

OPERATING INCOME COMPONENTS

Pfizer's 2012 income statement in Exhibit 5.2 highlights (in blue) the operating income components we discuss in this module. We defer discussion of cost of goods sold (cost of sales) to Module 6, which focuses on inventories and other operating assets. Modules 2 and 4 discuss items typically included in selling, general and administrative (SG&A) expenses, and Module 9 addresses the accounts related to acquisitions of other companies (such as amortization of intangible assets, merger-related in-process research and development charges, noncontrolling interest, and discontinued operations).

EXHIBIT 5.2 Pfizer Income Statement

Year Ended December 31 (millions, except per share data)	2012
Revenues	$58,986
Costs and expenses	
Cost of sales	11,334
Selling, informational and administrative expenses	16,616
Research and development expenses	7,870
Amortization of intangible assets	5,175
Restructuring charges and acquisition-related costs	1,880
Other deductions—net	4,031
Income from continuing operations before provision for taxes on income	12,080
Provision for taxes on income	2,562
Income from continuing operations	9,518
Discontinued operations	
Income from discontinued operations—net of tax	297
Gain on sale of discontinued operations—net of tax	4,783
Discontinued operations—net of tax	5,080
Net income before allocation to noncontrolling interests	14,598
Less: Net income attributable to noncontrolling interests	28
Net income attributable to Pfizer Inc.	$14,570
Earnings per common share—basic	
Income from continuing operations attributable to Pfizer Inc. common shareholders	$ 1.27
Discontinued operations—net of tax	$ 0.68
Net income attributable to Pfizer Inc. common shareholders	$ 1.96
Earnings per common share—diluted	
Income from continuing operations attributable to Pfizer Inc. common shareholders	$ 1.26
Discontinued operations—net of tax	$ 0.68
Net income attributable to Pfizer Inc. common shareholders	$ 1.94
Weighted-average shares—basic	7,442
Weighted-average shares—diluted	7,508
Cash dividends paid per common share	$ 0.88

We begin by discussing revenue, including the revenue recognition criteria that companies must employ and improper revenue recognition that the SEC has recently challenged. Next, we discuss Pfizer's research and development expenses, restructuring charges, provision for taxes, effects of foreign currency fluctuations, extraordinary items, and earnings per share (EPS).

Revenue and its Recognition

LO1 Explain revenue recognition criteria and identify transactions of special concern.

Pfizer reports $58,986 million in revenue. This revenue represents the culmination of a process that includes the manufacture of the drugs, their promotion, the receipt of orders, delivery to the customer, billing for the sale amount, and collection of the amounts owed. At what point in this process should Pfizer recognize its revenue and the related profit? When the drugs are delivered to the customer? When payment is received? And, how should Pfizer treat sales discounts or rights of return?

IFRS INSIGHT **Income Statement Differences**

IFRS allows companies to classify income statement items by nature (materials, labor, etc.) rather than by function (cost of goods sold, selling expenses, etc.). Based in Austria, **Lenzing AG**'s main business (90% of its sales) is natural textiles and nonwoven cellulose fibers such as Modal, Tencel, and Lyocell. It also produces plastic wrappings used internally to bind fiber bales and for sale to external customers (10% of its sales). Its 2012 IFRS income statement below classifies items by nature. Because Lenzing classifies its income statement items by nature, there is no line item for cost of goods sold. Instead, the manufacturing and inventory costs recognized during the period are reported according to their nature (costs of materials and purchased services, depreciation, amortization, personnel costs, other operating expenses) along with the amount of the net change in inventories for the period. We also see that the operating costs combine product and period costs. For example, personnel costs include the salaries and wages for all staff from the manufacturing employees to the CEO.

Lenzing AG, Consolidated Income Statement For January 1, 2012, to December 31, 2012 (€ thousands)	**2012**
Sales	€2,090,403
Changes in inventories of finished goods and work in progress	8,229
Work performed by the Group and capitalized	57,736
Other operating income	45,401
Cost of material and purchased services	(1,303,180)
Personnel expenses	(307,756)
Amortization of intangibles and depreciation of PP&E.	(107,253)
Other operating expenses	(228,586)
Income from operations (EBIT) before restructuring	254,994
Result from restructuring	(23,486)
Income from operations (EBIT) after restructuring	231,508
Income from investments in associates	5,796
Income from non-current and current financial assets	4,734
Financing costs	(23,309)
Financial result	(12,779)
Allocation of profit or loss to noncontrolling interests	17,314
Income before tax (EBT)	236,043
Income tax expense	(55,119)
Profit for the year	€ 180,924
Attributable to shareholders of Lenzing AG	€ 175,624
Attributable to noncontrolling interests	€ 5,300

GAAP specifies two **revenue recognition criteria** that must both be met for revenue to be recognized on the income statement. Revenue must be (1) **realized or realizable**, and (2) **earned**.[4] (The FASB has proposed a new revenue recognition standard that is scheduled to become effective in 2017; we provide a summary of the new standard in Appendix 5A.) *Realized or realizable* means that the seller's net assets (assets less liabilities) increase. That is, the seller receives an asset, such as cash or accounts receivable, or satisfies a liability, such as deferred revenue, as a result of a transaction. The company does not have to wait to recognize revenue until after it collects the accounts receivable; the increase in the account receivable (asset) means that the revenue is realizable. *Earned* means that the seller has performed its duties under the terms of the sales agreement and that title to the product sold

[4] SEC provides guidance for revenue recognition in *Staff Accounting Bulletin (SAB) 101* (http://www.sec.gov/interps/account/sab101.htm) that states that revenue is realized, or realizable, and earned when *each* of the following criteria are met: (1) there is persuasive evidence that an arrangement exists; (2) delivery has occurred or services have been rendered; (3) the seller's price to the buyer is fixed or determinable; and (4) collectibility is reasonably assured.

has passed to the buyer with no right of return or other contingencies. As long as Pfizer has delivered the drugs ordered by its customers, and its customers are obligated to make payment, Pfizer can recognize revenue. The following conditions would each argue *against* revenue recognition:

- *Rights of return exist,* other than due to routine product defects covered under product warranty.
- *Consignment sales,* where products are held on consignment until ultimately sold by the consignee.
- *Continuing involvement by seller,* such as where the seller has an obligation for future performance like product updates.
- *Contingency sales,* such as when product sales are contingent on product performance or further approvals by the customer.

Revenue is not recognized in these cases until the factors inhibiting revenue recognition are resolved.

Companies are required to report their revenue recognition policies in footnotes to their 10-K reports. Pfizer recognizes its revenues as follows:

> **Revenue Recognition**—We record revenues from product sales when the goods are shipped and title passes to the customer. At the time of sale, we also record estimates for a variety of sales deductions, such as sales rebates, discounts and incentives, and product returns. When we cannot reasonably estimate the amount of future product returns and/or other sales deductions, we record revenues when the risk of product return and/or additional sales deductions has been substantially eliminated.
>
> **Deductions from Revenues**—As is typical in the biopharmaceutical industry, our gross product sales are subject to a variety of deductions that generally are estimated and recorded in the same period that the revenues are recognized and primarily represent rebates and discounts to government agencies, wholesalers, distributors and managed care organizations with respect to our biopharmaceutical products. These deductions represent estimates of the related obligations.

Pfizer recognizes revenues when its products are shipped to customers as those customers have gained "control" over the product inventory at that point. Pfizer does not recognize revenues for the gross selling price. Instead, Pfizer deducts that portion of gross sales that is likely to be refunded to customers through sales rebates, discounts, and incentives (including volume discounts). Pfizer estimates the likely cost of those price reductions and deducts that amount from gross sales. Similarly, Pfizer does not recognize revenues for those products that it estimates will be returned, possibly because the drugs hit their expiration date before they are sold by Pfizer's customers. In sum, Pfizer recognizes revenues for products delivered to customers, and for only the sales price *net* of anticipated discounts and returns. This is why we often see "Revenues, net" on companies' income statements. (We discuss sales returns and allowances more fully in Appendix A to Module 6.)

IFRS INSIGHT **Revenue Recognition and IFRS**

Revenue is recognized under both U.S. GAAP and IFRS when the earning process is complete (when the seller has performed all obligations under the sales arrangement and no performance obligations remain) and benefits are realized or realizable. Further, there is extensive guidance under U.S. GAAP for specific industry transactions. That guidance is not present in IFRS. Moreover, public companies in the U.S. must follow additional guidance set by the SEC. Many believe that companies recognize revenue slightly earlier under IFRS than under GAAP.

BUSINESS INSIGHT **Gross versus Net Revenues**

Groupon, Inc., announced its intentions to offer stock to the public in an initial public offering (IPO) in 2011. The company's original SEC registration statement disclosed that the company recorded revenue at the gross amount it received from selling Groupons (coupons). For example, when Groupon sold a restaurant gift certificate for $20, it would record the full amount of $20 even though a hefty portion (say $9 for example) is owed the restaurant owner. By recording revenues at "gross," Groupon did not comply with GAAP because it held no inventory, did not determine the product or service price, and did not perform the service. The SEC intervened and Groupon restated revenues in an amended SEC filing in September 2011. Groupon now reports revenues at "net," which is the commission on sales, rather than the total value of online coupons. Returning to our restaurant gift certificate example, Groupon's amended revenue would be $11, not $20. Footnote 2 of its latest SEC filing reports the following. Shortly after the amended filing, Groupon's Chief Operating Officer left the company.

Revenues ($ 000s)	2008	2009	2010
As previously reported	$ 94	$30,471	$713,365
Restatement adjustment	(89)	(15,931)	(400,424)
As restated	$ 5	$14,540	$312,941

Percentage-of-Completion Revenue Recognition

Another revenue recognition challenge arises for companies with long-term sales contracts (spanning more than one financial reporting period), such as construction companies, consultants, and defense contractors. For these companies, revenue is often recognized using the percentage-of-completion method, which recognizes revenue by determining the costs incurred under the contract relative to its total expected costs.

To illustrate, assume that Bayer Construction signs a $10 million contract to construct a building. Bayer estimates construction will take two years and will cost $7,500,000. This means the contract yields an expected gross profit of $2,500,000 over two years. The following table summarizes construction costs incurred each year and the revenue Bayer recognizes.

	Construction costs incurred	Percentage complete	Revenue recognized
Year 1	$4,500,000	$\frac{\$4,500,000}{\$7,500,000} = 60\%$	$10,000,000 × 60% = $6,000,000
Year 2	$3,000,000	$\frac{\$3,000,000}{\$7,500,000} = 40\%$	$10,000,000 × 40% = $4,000,000

This table reveals that Bayer would report $6 million in revenue and $1.5 million ($6 million − $4.5 million) in gross profit on the construction project in the first year; it would report $4 million in revenue and $1 million ($4 million − $3 million) in gross profit in the second year.

Next, assume that Bayer's client makes a $1 million deposit at the signing of the contract and that Bayer submits bills to the client based on the percentage of completion. The following table reflects the bills sent to, and the cash received from, the client.

	Revenue recognized	Client billed	Cash received
At signing	$ 0	$ 0	$1,000,000
Year 1	6,000,000	5,000,000	2,000,000
Year 2	4,000,000	4,000,000	7,000,000

At the signing of the contract, Bayer recognizes no revenue because construction has not begun and thus, Bayer has not earned any revenue. By the end of the second year, Bayer has recognized all of the contract revenue and the client has paid all monies owed per the accounts receivable. The following template captures Bayer Construction's transactions over this two-year period (M indicates millions).

		Balance Sheet										Income Statement			
	Transaction	**Cash Asset**	+	**Noncash Assets**	=	**Liabil-ities**	+	**Contrib. Capital**	+	**Earned Capital**		**Rev-enues**	−	**Expen-ses**	=	**Net Income**
Cash 1M UR 1M Cash: 1M (debit) UR: 1M (credit)	Start of year 1: Record $1M deposit received at contract signing	+1M Cash			=	+1M Unearned Revenue							−		=	
COGS 4.5M Cash 4.5M COGS: 4.5M (debit) Cash: 4.5M (credit)	Year 1: Record $4.5M construction costs	−4.5M Cash			=					−4.5M Retained Earnings			−	+4.5M Cost of Sales	=	−4.5M
AR 5M UR 1M REV 6M AR: 5M (debit) UR: 1M (debit) REV: 6M (credit)	Year 1: Recognize $6M revenue on partly completed contract			+5M Accounts Receivable	=	−1M Unearned Revenue				+6M Retained Earnings		+6M Revenue	−		=	+6M
Cash 2M AR 2M Cash: 2M (debit) AR: 2M (credit)	Year 1: Record $2M cash received from client	+2M Cash		−2M Accounts Receivable	=								−		=	
COGS 3M Cash 3M COGS: 3M (debit) Cash: 3M (credit)	Year 2: Record $3M construction costs	−3M Cash			=					−3M Retained Earnings			−	+3M Cost of Sales	=	−3M
AR 4M Rev 4M AR: 4M (debit) Rev: 4M (credit)	Year 2: Recognize $4M revenue for completed contract			+4M Accounts Receivable	=					+4M Retained Earnings		+4M Revenue	−		=	+4M
Cash 7M AR 7M Cash: 7M (debit) AR: 7M (credit)	Year 2: Record $7M cash received from client	+7M Cash		−7M Accounts Receivable	=								−		=	

Revenue recognition policies for these types of contracts are disclosed in a manner typical to the following from the 2012 10-K report footnotes of **Raytheon Company**.

> **Revenue Recognition** We use the percentage-of-completion accounting method to account for our long-term contracts associated with the design, development, manufacture, or modification of complex aerospace or electronic equipment and related services, such as certain cost-plus service contracts. Under this method, revenue is recognized based on the extent of progress towards completion of the long-term contract. . . . The selection of the method by which to measure progress towards completion of a contract requires judgment and is based on the nature of the products or services to be provided. We generally use the cost-to-cost measure of progress for our long-term contracts unless we believe another method more clearly measures progress towards completion of the contract. Under the cost-to-cost measure of progress, the extent of progress towards completion is measured based on the ratio of costs incurred to date to the total estimated costs at completion of the contract.

The percentage-of-completion method of revenue recognition requires an estimate of total costs. This estimate is made at the beginning of the contract and is typically the one used to initially bid the contract. However, estimates are inherently inaccurate. If the estimate changes during the construction period, the percentage-of-completion is computed as the total costs incurred to date divided by the *current* estimate of total anticipated costs (costs incurred to date plus total estimated costs to complete).

If total construction costs are underestimated, the percentage-of-completion is overestimated (the denominator is too low) and revenue and gross profit to date are overstated. The estimation process inherent in this method has the potential for inaccurate or, even, improper revenue recognition. In addition, estimates of remaining costs to complete projects are difficult for the auditors to verify. This uncertainty adds additional risk to financial statement analysis.

BUSINESS INSIGHT Disney's Revenue Recognition

The **Walt Disney Company** uses a method similar to percentage-of-completion to determine the amount of production cost to match against film and television revenues. Following is an excerpt from its 2012 10-K.

> Film and television costs include capitalizable production costs, production overhead, interest, development costs, and acquired production costs... Film and television production, participation and residual costs are expensed over the applicable product life cycle based upon the ratio of the current period's revenues to estimated remaining total revenues (Ultimate Revenues) for each production. For film productions, Ultimate Revenues include revenues from all sources that will be earned within ten years from the date of the initial theatrical release. For television series, Ultimate Revenues include revenues that will be earned within ten years from delivery of the first episode, or if still in production, five years from delivery of the most recent episode, if later. For acquired film libraries, remaining revenues include amounts to be earned for up to twenty years from the date of acquisition.

As Disney pays production costs, it records those costs on the balance sheet as inventory. Then, as film and television revenues are recognized, the company matches a portion of production costs (from inventory) against revenues in computing income. Each period, the costs recognized are equal to the proportion of total revenues recognized in the period to the total revenues expected over the life of the film or television show. Thus, estimates of both costs and income depend on the quality of Disney's revenue estimates, which are, likely, imprecise.

Recognition of Unearned Revenue

In some industries it is common to receive cash before recording revenue. Customers might pay in advance for special orders, make deposits for future services, or buy concert tickets, subscriptions, or gift cards. In those cases, companies must record unearned revenues, a liability, and only record revenue when those products and services are provided. Specifically, deposits or advance payments are not recorded as revenue until the company performs the services owed or delivers the goods. Until then, the company's balance sheet shows the advance payment as a liability (called unearned revenue or deferred revenue) because the company is obligated to deliver those products and services.

Unearned revenue is particularly common among technology companies that sell goods and services as packages. These sales are called "multi-element contracts," which are sales agreements that bundle goods and services that may or may not be delivered simultaneously. When delivery is delayed the company must record unearned revenue. Consider for example, the sale of an Apple iPad. The customer not only purchases the tablet hardware but the software integral to the iPad's function, additional software, and future software upgrades. How should Apple record revenue for such a multi-element contract? The short answer is that the total sales price is allocated among the elements of the contract and revenue is recognized (as it's earned) at different points in time for each element. Allocating the total sales price presents a challenge because elements often do not have stand-alone prices. GAAP allows companies to estimate selling prices for each element if sold separately and then allocate the total selling price ratably among the elements.

More specifically, assume that on September 30, 2012 (the first day of Apple's 2013 fiscal year), Apple sells 60 iPads to a customer and charges the total invoice amount of $36,000 to the customer's credit card (a cash transaction). Apple disclosed the following in its 2012 10-K:

> The Company records deferred revenue when it receives payments in advance of the delivery of products or the performance of services. This includes amounts that have been deferred for unspecified and specified software upgrade rights and non-software services that are attached to hardware and software products. The Company sells gift cards redeemable at its retail and online stores, and also sells gift cards redeemable on the iTunes Store for the purchase of digital content and software. The Company records deferred revenue upon the sale of the card, which is relieved upon redemption of the card by the customer. Revenue from AppleCare service and support contracts is deferred and recognized over the service coverage periods. AppleCare service and support contracts typically include extended phone support, repair services, web-based support resources and diagnostic tools offered under the Company's standard limited warranty.

Assume that, of the $36,000 in cash that Apple receives, it deems that $600 should be allocated to the next 24-month period because it relates to "unspecified and specified software upgrade rights." The $600 for the future software upgrades is unearned at the point of sale. Instead, Apple records a liability (unearned revenue) for this amount. This means that revenue of $35,400 is immediately reported and $600 is reported over the ensuing 24 months. Apple prepares quarterly financial statements and will recognize $75 ($600 × 3/24) of the unearned revenue each quarter for two years. As revenue is earned, the unearned revenue account on the balance sheet is reduced and revenue is recorded in the income statement. The following template reflects the initial sales transaction and the subsequent first quarter accounting adjustment.

	Balance Sheet									Income Statement				
Transaction	Cash Asset	+	Noncash Assets	=	Liabilities	+	Contrib. Capital	+	Earned Capital	Revenues	−	Expenses	=	Net Income
Sep 30: Receive $36,000 cash advance for products	+36,000 Cash			=	+600 Unearned Revenue				+35,400 Retained Earnings	+35,400 Revenue	−		=	+35,400
Dec 30: Recognize three months of unearned revenue				=	−75 Unearned Revenue				+75 Retained Earnings	+75 Revenue	−		=	+75

Cash 36,000
UR 600
Revenue 35,400

Cash: 36,000 |
UR: | 600
Rev

UR 75
Rev 75

UR: 75 |
Rev: | 75

Apple's 2012 balance sheet reports the following liabilities (in millions):

Current liabilities	
Accounts payable	$21,175
Accrued expenses	11,414
Deferred revenue	5,953
Total current liabilities	38,542
Deferred revenue—non-current	2,648
Other non-current liabilities	16,664
Total liabilities	$57,854

The company reports deferred revenue as both current and noncurrent liabilities. These relate to the revenue that will be earned in the coming year ($5,953 million) and in subsequent years ($2,648 million). These are substantial liabilities to Apple because many of its products are sold with guaranteed future services such as software upgrades and long-term service contracts. Each quarter, the deferred revenue account increases by the new sales that are not yet earned, and decreases as revenue is earned.

Research and Development (R&D) Expenses

LO2 Describe accounting for operating expenses, including research and development, and restructuring.

R&D activities are a major expenditure for many companies, especially for those in technology and pharmaceutical industries. Pfizer's R&D costs, for example, make up 13% of revenues ($7,870 million/$58,986 million). These expenses include employment costs for R&D personnel, R&D materials and supplies, R&D related contract services, and R&D fixed-asset costs.

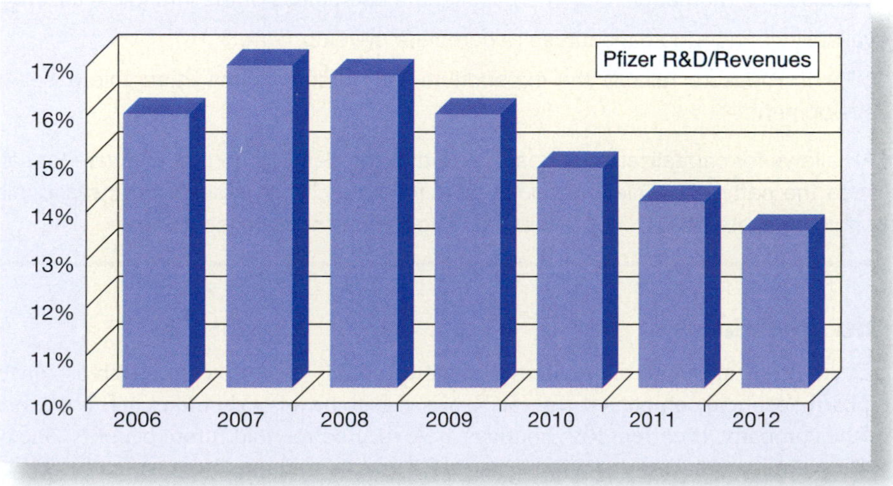

Accounting for R&D

Accounting for R&D is straightforward: R&D costs are expensed as incurred. The key issue is how to classify the expenses for financial reporting purposes. Salaries paid to researchers, and the depreciation and other expenses related to general-purpose research facilities, are accounted for in the usual manner (which is to expense salaries when paid and to capitalize and depreciate general-purpose research facilities). However, these expenses are totaled separately and are classified as R&D in the income statement rather than as SG&A. An exception to this general rule relates to the purchase of R&D assets that are only used for a specific project and then retired when that project is complete. These project-specific assets are expensed when purchased. Consequently, income is reduced in the year of acquisition (but higher in subsequent years) relative to what the company would have reported had the asset been capitalized and depreciated. (Project-specific assets are said to have no "alternate use." One alternate use could be reselling the asset. In that case, the asset is *not* considered project-specific and is accounted for like other long-term assets.)

Following is a footnote excerpt from **Pfizer**'s 2012 annual report related to its research and development expenditures:

> Research and development (R&D) costs are expensed as incurred. These expenses include the costs of our proprietary R&D efforts, as well as costs incurred in connection with certain licensing arrangements. Before a compound receives regulatory approval, we record upfront and milestone payments made by us to third parties under licensing arrangements as expense. Upfront payments are recorded when incurred, and milestone payments are recorded when the specific milestone has been achieved. Once a compound receives regulatory approval, we record any milestone payments in identifiable intangible assets, less accumulated amortization and, unless the asset is determined to have an indefinite life, we amortize the payments on a straight-line basis over the remaining agreement term or the expected product life cycle, whichever is shorter.

Pfizer capitalizes and depreciates general research facilities (those with alternate uses). All other R&D costs are expensed as incurred.

IFRS INSIGHT **Research and Development Expenses and IFRS**

IFRS accounts for research costs and development costs separately. Research costs are always expensed. Development costs must be capitalized if the company can demonstrate all of the following:

- Technical feasibility of completing the intangible asset.
- Intention to complete the intangible asset.
- Ability to use or sell the intangible asset.
- Intangible asset will generate future economic benefits (the company must demonstrate the existence of a market or, if for internal use, the usefulness of the intangible asset).
- Availability of adequate resources to complete development.
- Ability to measure reliably the expenditure attributable to the intangible asset during its development.

U.S. GAAP allows for capitalization of costs related to the development of software for sale to third parties once the software achieves "commercial feasibility," but is silent on the capitalization of other intangible assets—thus, implicitly prescribing expensing of these assets.

Analysis of R&D

When R&D expenses are large and/or growing more quickly than revenue, such as for technology-based and pharmaceutical companies, a question arises as to how we should treat those expenses in our analysis of the company. If current R&D outlays are expected to yield future benefits, one could argue that the R&D spending creates an intangible asset. But GAAP requires expensing of R&D outlays. Arguably then, U.S. companies' balance sheets understate both assets and income. One approach analysts might take to correct for these "errors" in the balance sheet and the income statement would be to undo GAAP by removing R&D expense from the income statement and adding it to the balance sheet as an R&D intangible asset (with a corresponding increase to Retained Earnings to balance the balance sheet). By this treatment, the balance sheet would report the "missing" intangible assets. The R&D intangible asset could be amortized like other intangible assets over its estimated useful life. Under both methods (GAAP or capitalizing and amortizing an R&D asset) *all* of the R&D costs are eventually expensed in the income statement. However, the timing of the expense differs between the two methods.

While this method of analysis might be conceptually appealing, it requires a considerable number of estimates and assumptions about the relation between the R&D cost and the products it produces and the period of time over which future economic benefits from the R&D will occur. For this reason, we do not advise routinely creating pro forma net income and balance sheet numbers by capitalizing and amortizing R&D expenses. (A similar conclusion is drawn in a 2005 study in the *Journal of Applied Finance* by Danielson and Press, "*When Does R&D Expense Distort Profitability Estimates?,*" which concludes that: "unadjusted ROA and adjusted [for R&D costs] ROA typically rank firm profitability in a similar order. Thus, unadjusted ROA is a reasonable proxy for firms' underlying economic profitability in many research applications, and complex adjustment procedures are often unnecessary.")

The capitalization and amortization of the R&D expense is *backward-looking* in that it attempts to evaluate the success of the company's R&D efforts using a historical return on investment analysis. Most financial analysts, however, usually aim to develop *forward-looking* predictions of a company's income and cash flow. In that regard, the historical analysis of R&D may be of limited use. Many analysts develop their forecasts at the product level and, then, aggregate those forecasts to produce the forecasted financial statements that we see in their reports (we discuss this forecasting methodology in our Analysis Insight box below and, again, in Module 11 for Procter & Gamble). The analysis of R&D, then, focuses on monitoring new products in the pipeline and developing estimates of their ultimate commercial feasibility. For example, analysts following pharmaceutical companies frequently prepare schedules of all drugs in development and monitor closely the success of experimental trials. Analysts also monitor the patent expirations of existing products and estimate the impact on sales after a patent expires (see the discussion of Lipitor in the opening vignette and the Analysis Insight box below).

Company managers have a different reason for analyzing R&D—their aim is to maximize return on R&D investments by selecting which projects to fund, along with the level and timing of funding. Managers have a considerable amount of proprietary information about each R&D project, which they can use to make investment decisions. In recent years, companies have developed elaborate return on investment metrics to evaluate the success of R&D investment projects. The goal is to maximize the return on the R&D investment with a strategic investment protocol that focuses on the following areas:

1. **R&D costs** Companies can reduce R&D costs by strategically managing the procurement of raw materials and equipment as they do for other business units, by monitoring closely the investment at each stage of the research process (reducing investment cost in high risk areas and increasing that investment if and when the risk level falls), by outsourcing portions of the research process as they do for other production and business processes, by identifying failed research ventures early and cutting their losses, by partnering with other companies interested in the research to share the investment cost and the risk, and a variety of other measures.
2. **Speed of the research effort** Companies can reduce the period of time over which the research is conducted (and thus the cost of the research) with careful planning and control. Some of the same production and scheduling techniques that companies have applied to their manufacturing processes can be applied to the research units. These include project management techniques, parallel processing, and a number of other techniques discussed in operations courses.
3. **Quality of decisions** Each R&D project requires constant monitoring and numerous decisions relating to a succession of investments and go versus no-go decisions. Failed projects need to be identified early and culled from the research portfolio and managers need to continually analyze the extent to which the research is creating knowledge that will lead to commercially feasible products.

It is important for managers to adopt the mind-set that each R&D project is a separate investment decision similar to other capital-budgeting decisions and one which typically involves a series of related investment decisions. It is only with this degree of discipline that the R&D process will achieve maximum returns on investment.

ANALYSIS INSIGHT **Forecasting Revenues for Pfizer**

Most analysts develop bottom-up revenue forecasts at the product level, assessing market demand and costs of production factors to estimate gross profit for each product. Pharmaceutical companies present particular challenges for analysts who must monitor drugs in the pipeline to estimate the likelihood that they will become commercially feasible products, and to monitor patent expirations and other factors that will affect the demand and pricing of existing drug products. Following is an excerpt from an analyst report for Pfizer by Morgan Stanley in May 2013 ("A" and "E" refer to Actual and Estimated results, respectively). The analyst developed revenue forecasts for each of Pfizer's major drugs and highlighted the expiration dates ("ex") for the relevant patents. Patent expiration inevitably invites competition from generics which depresses revenues, both in quantity of product sold and in the price of those products. The sales estimates below reflect these assumptions and estimates.

Annual Revenues ($M)	2010A	2011A	2012A	2013E	2014E	2015E	2016E	2017E	2018E	2019E	2020E
Total biopharmaceuticals	58,523	57,747	51,214	47,869	43,932	43,052	43,539	45,054	46,799	47,273	48,783
U.S.	25,962	23,705	19,708	18,422	15,761	15,499	16,190	17,337	18,530	18,360	18,853
ex-US	32,561	34,042	31,506	29,447	28,171	27,553	27,350	27,716	28,270	28,913	29,931
Lipitor	10,733	9,577	3,948	1,903	1,469	1,214	1,068	997	937	886	842
U.S.(11/30/11); ACT rev in other biopharma.	5,329	5,003	932	357	232	162	122	97	83	74	71
ex-US (EU Nov-11)	5,404	4,574	3,016	1,547	1,237	1,052	947	899	854	812	771
Caduet	527	538	258	218	173	140	118	106	100	95	90
U.S. (11/30/11)	339	272	33	15	11	7	6	4	4	3	3
ex-US (EU Nov·11)	188	266	225	202	162	133	113	102	97	92	87
Enbrel	3,274	3,666	3,737	3,742	3,817	3,893	3,815	3,625	3.262	2,773	2,218
U.S. (10/23/12)	—	—	—	—	—	—	—	—	—	—	—
ex-US (EU Feb-15; Jap '10)	3,274	3,666	3,737	3,742	3,817	3,893	3,815	3,625	3.262	2,773	2,218
Lyrica	3,063	3,693	4,158	4,568	3,797	3,276	3,064	2,962	2,666	1,111	852
U.S. (12/30/18)	1,424	1,514	1,672	1,817	1,872	1,928	1,986	2,045	1,841	368	184
ex-US (EU Jul 14; Jap Apr-22)	1,639	2,179	2,486	2,751	1,926	1,348	1,078	917	825	742	668
Celebrex	2,374	2,523	2,719	2,799	1,562	683	492	430	386	349	315
U.S. (5/30/14* upside if Dec-15 patent upheld)	1,580	1,597	1,745	1,816	726	182	91	69	61	56	52
ex-US (EU Nov-14)	794	926	974	983	836	502	401	361	325	293	263

BUSINESS INSIGHT **R&D at Pfizer and Its Peers**

The pharmaceutical industry devotes a high percentage of its revenues to R&D. For example, in 2012, Pfizer spent $7.9 billion for R&D compared with its revenues of $59 billion, or about 13.3%. Following is the R&D-expense-to-sales ratio for Pfizer and some of its competitors.

	2010	2011	2012
Pfizer	14.6%	13.9%	13.3%
Bristol-Myers Squibb	18.3	18.1	22.2
Merck	24.2	17.6	17.3
Eli Lilly	21.2	20.7	23.4
Abbott Laboratories	10.6	10.6	10.8

Restructuring Expenses and Incentives

Restructuring expenses are substantial in many income statements. Because of their magnitude, GAAP requires enhanced disclosure, either as a separate line item in the income statement or as a footnote. Restructuring costs typically include three components:

1. Employee severance or relocation costs
2. Asset write-downs
3. Other restructuring costs

The first part, **employee severance or relocation costs**, represents accrued (estimated) costs to terminate or relocate employees as part of a restructuring program. To accrue those expenses, the company must:

- Estimate total costs of terminating or relocating selected employees; these costs might include severance pay (typically a number of weeks of pay based on the employee's tenure with the company), outplacement costs, and relocation or retraining costs for remaining employees.
- Report *total* estimated costs as an expense (and a liability) in the period the restructuring program is announced. Subsequent payments to employees reduce the restructuring accrual (the liability).

The second part of restructuring costs is **asset write-downs**, also called *write-offs* or *charge-offs*. Restructuring activities usually involve closure or relocation of manufacturing or administrative facilities. This can require the write-down of assets whose fair value is less than book value. For example, restructurings can necessitate the write-down of long-term assets (such as plant assets or goodwill) and of inventories. Recall that asset cost is first recorded on the balance sheet and is subsequently transferred from the balance sheet to the income statement as expense when the asset is used. The write-down of an asset accelerates this process for a portion, or all, of the asset cost. Write-downs have no cash flow effects unless the write-down has some potential tax consequences.

The third part of restructuring costs is typically labeled "Other" and includes costs of vacating duplicative facilities, fees to terminate contracts (such as lease agreements and service contracts), and other exit costs (such as legal and asset-appraisal fees). Companies estimate and accrue these costs and reduce the restructuring liability as those costs are paid in cash.

The financial statement effects of restructuring charges can be large and frequent. We must remember that management determines the amount of restructuring costs and when to recognize them. As such, it is not uncommon for a company to time recognition of restructuring costs in a period when its income is already depressed. This behavior is referred to as a **big bath**. Reversals of accruals can be an indicator of excessive accruals in prior years, which is suggestive of a "big bath."

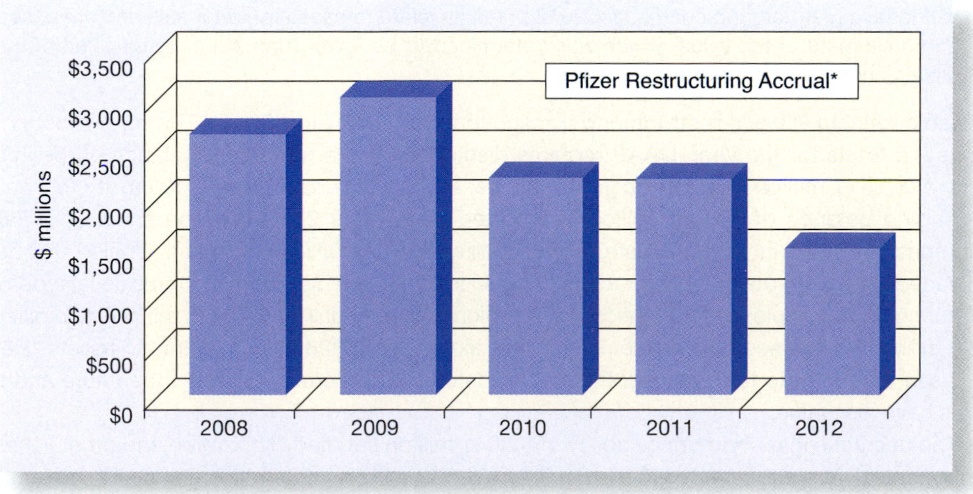

*Represents annual provision to the restructuring liability account.

U.S. GAAP has relatively stringent rules relating to restructuring costs in an effort to mitigate abuses. For example, a company is required to have a formal restructuring plan that is approved by its board of directors before any restructuring charges are accrued. Also, a company must identify the relevant employees and notify them of its plan. In each subsequent year, the company must disclose in its footnotes the original amount of the liability (accrual), how much of that liability is settled in the current period (such as employee payments), how much of the original liability has been reversed because of original cost overestimation, any new accruals for unforeseen costs, and the current balance of the liability. This creates more transparent financial statements, which presumably deters earnings management.

BUSINESS INSIGHT **Pfizer's Restructuring**

Pfizer explains its restructuring efforts as follows in its 2012 10-K:

We incur significant costs in connection with acquiring, integrating and restructuring businesses and in connection with our global cost-reduction and productivity initiatives. For example:

- In connection with acquisition activity, we typically incur costs associated with executing the transactions, integrating the acquired operations, and restructuring the combined company; and
- In connection with our cost-reduction and productivity initiatives, we typically incur costs and charges associated with site closings and other facility rationalization actions, workforce reductions and the expansion of shared services, including the development of global systems.

All of our businesses and functions may be impacted by these actions, including sales and marketing, manufacturing and research and development, as well as groups such as information technology, shared services and corporate operations. The following table provides the components of and changes in our restructuring accruals:

(millions of dollars)	Employee Termination Costs	Asset Impairment Charges	Exit Costs	Accrual
Balance, January 1, 2011	$ 2,149	$ —	$101	$2,250
Provision	1,794	256	125	2,175
Utilization and other	(1,518)	(256)	(134)	(1,908)
Balance, December 31, 2011	2,425	—	92	2,517
Provision	997	328	149	1,474
Utilization and other	(1,629)	(328)	(84)	(2,041)
Balance, December 31, 2012	$ 1,793	$ —	$157	$1,950

Total restructuring charges incurred from the beginning of our cost-reduction and productivity initiatives in 2005 through December 31, 2012 were $15.6 billion. The asset impairment charges included in restructuring charges for 2012 primarily relate to assets held for sale and are based on an estimate of fair value, which was determined to be lower than the carrying value of the assets prior to the impairment charge.

The table reflects Pfizer's restructuring transactions for 2012 (and 2011). The right-most column shows the totals for the year. GAAP requires disclosure of the remaining balance of the initial liability of $2,517 million (labeled Accrual Balance) along with changes in that liability for the year. The ending balance of $1,950 million is reported on Pfizer's 2012 balance sheet as a liability. More specifically, the increase in restructuring liability for 2012 of $1,474 million (labeled "Provision") is included in Pfizer's total 2012 restructuring expense. The table discloses the three usual types of restructuring costs: employee termination ($997 million), asset impairment ($328 million), and exit costs ($149 million). Pfizer records an asset impairment expense of $328 million related to assets "Held for sale" (see the footnote to the table). Pfizer anticipates selling certain assets in the future and those assets have lost value.

The decrease in restructuring liability of $2,041 million (labeled "Utilization and other"), has two components. Pfizer pays cash of $1,713 million ($1,629 million + $84 million) to settle the outstanding restructuring liability related to the employee termination and other exit costs. Some of this cash relates to the 2012 accrual and some of the cash settles prior years' accruals that have not yet been paid. To "settle" the asset impairment, Pfizer does not pay cash. Asset impairments do not involve cash. Instead, the balance sheet value of the assets held for sale is reduced by $328 by increasing the related accumulated depreciation by the same amount.

Financial statement effects of Pfizer's accounting for restructuring costs in 2012 are illustrated in the following template ($ millions).

continued

	Balance Sheet						Income Statement		
Transaction	Cash Asset	+ Noncash Assets	= Liabil-ities	+ Contrib. Capital	+ Earned Capital		Rev-enues	− Expen-ses	= Net Income
Record restructuring expense and liability			+1,474 Restructuring Liability		−1,474 Retained Earnings			+1,474 Restructuring Expense	−1,474
Paid $1,713 toward liability, and record $328 impairment	−1,713 Cash	−328 Accumulated Depreciation	−2,041 Restructuring Liability				−		=

Restructuring costs are typically large and, as such, greatly affect reported profits. Our analysis must consider whether these costs are associated with the accounting period in which they are recognized. Following are some guidelines relating to the components of restructuring costs:

Employee Severance or Relocation Costs* and *Other Costs GAAP permits recognition of costs relating to employee separation or relocation that are *incremental* and that do not benefit future periods. Similarly, other accrued costs must be related to the restructuring and not to expenses that would otherwise have been incurred in the future. Thus, accrual of these costs is treated like other liability accruals. We must, however, be aware of over- or understated costs and their effect on current and future profitability. GAAP requires a reconciliation of this restructuring accrual in future years (see Business Insight on Pfizer's restructuring). A reconciliation reveals either overstatements or understatements: overstatements are followed by a reversal of the restructuring liability, and understatements are followed by further accruals. Should a company develop a reputation for recurring reversals or understatements, its management loses credibility.

Asset Write-downs Asset write-downs accelerate (or catch up) the depreciation process to reflect asset impairment. Impairment implies the loss of cash-generating capability and, likely, occurs over several years. Thus, prior periods' profits are arguably not as high as reported, and the current period's profit is not as low. This measurement error is difficult to estimate and, thus, many analysts do not adjust balance sheets and income statements for write-downs (we discuss an approach that you might use for the analysis of asset sales in the Analysis Insight box on page 4-21; that approach is also applicable to the analysis of asset write-downs). At a minimum, however, we must recognize the qualitative implications of restructuring costs for the profitability of recent prior periods and the current period.

RESEARCH INSIGHT **Restructuring Costs and Managerial Incentives**

Research has investigated the circumstances and effects of restructuring costs. Some research finds that stock prices increase when a company announces a restructuring as if the market appreciates the company's candor. Research also finds that many companies that reduce income through restructuring costs later reverse a portion of those costs, resulting in a substantial income boost for the period of reversal. These reversals often occur when the company would have otherwise reported an earnings decline. Whether or not the market responds favorably to trimming the fat or simply disregards restructuring costs as transitory and, thus, as uninformative, managers have incentives to characterize such income-decreasing items as "one-time" on the income statement and routinely exclude such charges in non-GAAP, pro forma disclosures. These incentives often derive from contracts such as debt covenants and managerial bonus plans.

MANAGERIAL DECISION **You Are the Financial Analyst**

You are analyzing the 10-K of a company that reports a large restructuring expense, involving employee severance and asset write-downs. How do you interpret and treat this cost in your analysis of the company's current and future profitability? [Answer, p. 5-42]

MID-MODULE REVIEW 1

Merck & Co., Inc., reports the following income statements for 2010 through 2012.

In Millions	Dec. 31, 2012	Dec. 31, 2011	Dec. 31, 2010
Sales	$47,267	$48,047	$45,987
Costs, expenses and other			
Materials and production	16,446	16,871	18,396
Marketing and administrative	12,776	13,733	13,125
Research and development	8,168	8,467	11,111
Restructuring costs	664	1,306	985
Equity income from affiliates	(642)	(610)	(587)
Other (income) expense, net	1,116	946	1,304
Total costs, expenses and other	38,528	40,713	44,334
Income before taxes	8,739	7,334	1,653
Taxes on income	(2,440)	(942)	(671)
Net income	6,299	6,392	982
Less: Net income attributable to noncontrolling interests	131	120	121
Net income attributable to Merck & Co., Inc.	$ 6,168	$ 6,272	$ 861

Required

1. Merck's revenue recognition policy, as outlined in footnotes to its 10-K, includes the following: "Revenues from sales of products are recognized at the time of delivery when title and risk of loss passes to the customer." Evaluate Merck's revenue recognition policy.
2. Merck's research and development (R&D) efforts often require specialized equipment and facilities that cannot be used for any other purpose. How does Merck account for costs related to this specialized equipment and facilities? Would Merck account for these costs differently if they had alternate uses? Explain.
3. Merck reports restructuring expense each year. What are the general categories of restructuring expenses? How do accrual accounting and disclosure requirements prevent companies from intentionally overstating restructuring expenses in one year (referred to as taking a "big bath") and reversing the unused expenses in a future year?

The solution is on page 5-68.

Income Tax Expenses and Allowances

LO3 Explain and analyze accounting for income taxes.

Companies prepare financial statements for stockholders using GAAP. When these companies file their income tax returns, they prepare financial statements using the *Internal Revenue Code (IRC)*. These two different sets of accounting rules recognize revenues and expenses differently in many cases and, as a result, can yield markedly different levels of income. In general, companies desire to report lower income to taxing authorities than they do to their stockholders so that they can reduce their tax liability and increase after-tax cash flow. This practice is acceptable so long as the financial statements are prepared in conformity with GAAP and tax returns are filed in accordance with the IRC.

As an example, consider the depreciation of long-term assets. For financial reports, companies typically depreciate long-term assets using straight-line depreciation (meaning the same amount of depreciation expense is reported each year over the useful life of the asset). However, for reports sent to tax authorities, companies use an *accelerated* method of depreciation (meaning more depreciation is taken in the early years of the asset's life and less depreciation in later years). When a company depreciates assets at an accelerated rate for tax purposes, the depreciation deduction for tax purposes is higher and taxable income is lower in the early years of the assets' lives. As a result, tax payments are reduced and after-tax cash flow is increased. That excess cash can then be reinvested in the business to increase its returns to stockholders.

To illustrate, assume that Pfizer purchases an asset with a five-year life. It depreciates that asset using the straight-line method (equal expense per year) when reporting to stockholders and depreciates the asset at a faster rate (accelerated depreciation) for tax purposes. Annual (full year) depreciation expense under these two methods is depicted in Exhibit 5.3.

EXHIBIT 5.3 Straight-Line vs Accelerated Depreciation

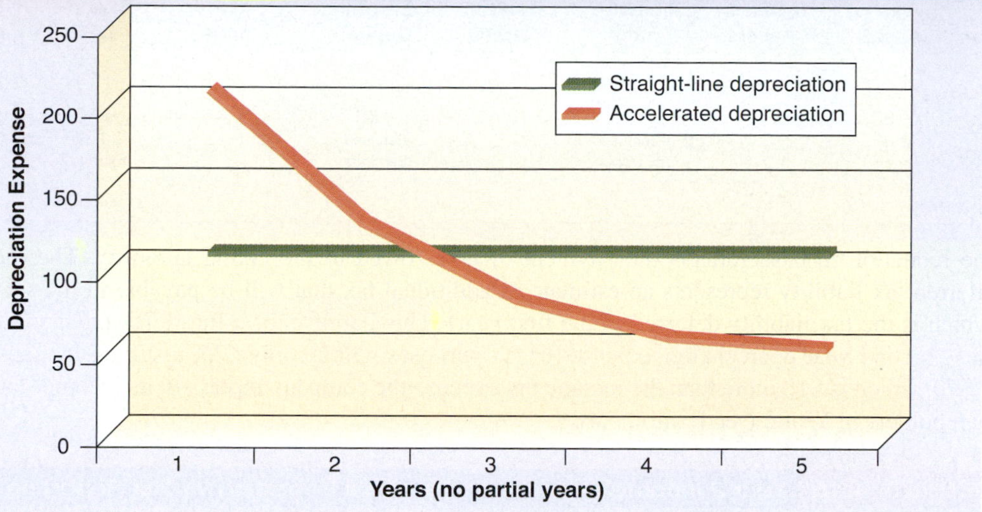

During the first 2.5 years in this example, depreciation is higher in the company's tax returns than it is in its GAAP financial statements. In the last 2.5 years, this is reversed, with lower depreciation expense for tax purposes. Taxable income and tax payments are, therefore, higher during the last 2.5 years. The same total amount of depreciation is recognized under both methods over the five-year life of the asset. Only the timing of the recognition of the expense differs.[5]

We use this timing concept to illustrate the accounting for a **deferred tax liability**. Assume that a company purchases a depreciable asset with a cost of $100 and a two-year useful life. For financial reporting purposes (for GAAP-based reports), it depreciates the asset using the straight-line method, which yields depreciation expense of $50 per year. For tax reporting (when filing income tax returns), it depreciates the asset on an accelerated basis, which yields depreciation deduction of $75 in the first year and $25 in the second year (the same total amount of depreciation is reported under the two depreciation methods; only the amount of depreciation reported per year differs). Assume that this company reports income before depreciation and taxes of $200 and that its tax rate is 40%. Its income statements, for both financial reporting and tax reporting, for the asset's first year are in Exhibit 5.4A.

EXHIBIT 5.4A Year 1 Income Statements: Financial Reporting vs Tax Reporting

Year 1	Financial Reporting	Tax Reporting
Income before depreciation	$200	$200
Depreciation	50	75
Income before tax	150	125
Income tax (40%)	60 [expense]	50 [cash paid]
Net income	$ 90	$ 75

[5] The Modified Accelerated Cost Recovery System (MACRS) is the current method of accelerated asset depreciation required by the United States income tax code. Under MACRS, all assets are divided into classes that dictate the number of years over which an asset's cost is "recovered" and the percentage of the asset cost that can be depreciated per year is fixed by regulation. For a five-year asset, such as in our example, the MACRS depreciation percentages per year are 20%, 32%, 19.2%, 11.52%, 11.52%, and 5.76%. MACRS assumes that assets are acquired in the middle of the year, hence a half-year depreciation in Year 1 and a half-year depreciation in Year 6. The point after which straight-line depreciation exceeds MACRS depreciation is after about 2.5 years as assumed in the example.

This company records income tax expense and a related deferred tax liability for the first year as reflected in the following financial statement effects template:

TE 60
DTL 10
Cash 50

TE: 60 |
DTL: | 10
Cash: | 50

Year 1 Transaction	Balance Sheet: Cash Asset	+	Noncash Assets	=	Liabil-ities	+	Contrib. Capital	+	Earned Capital	Income Statement: Rev-enues	−	Expen-ses	=	Net Income
Record tax expense: expense exceeds cash because of deferral of tax	−50 Cash			=	+10 Deferred Tax Liability				−60 Retained Earnings		−	+60 Tax Expense	=	−60

The reduction in cash reflects the payment of taxes owed to the taxing authority. The increase in deferred tax liability represents an estimate of additional tax that will be payable in the second year (which is the tax liability deferred in the first year). This liability for a future tax payment arises because second-year depreciation expense for tax purposes will be only $25, resulting in taxes payable of $70, which is $10 more than the income tax expense the company reports in its income statement to shareholders in Year 2 (see Exhibit 5.4B).

EXHIBIT 5.4B Year 2 Income Statements: Financial Reporting vs Tax Reporting

Year 2	Financial Reporting	Tax Reporting
Income before depreciation	$200	$200
Depreciation	50	25
Income before tax	150	175
Income tax (40%)	60 [expense]	70 [cash paid]
Net income	$ 90	$105

At the end of Year 1, the company knows that this additional tax must be paid in Year 2 because the financial reporting and tax reporting depreciation schedules are set when the asset is placed in service. Given these known amounts, the company accrues the deferred tax liability in Year 1 in the same manner as it would accrue any estimated future liability, say for wages payable, by recognizing a liability and the related expense.

At the end of Year 2, the additional income tax is paid and the company's deferred tax liability is now satisfied. Financial statement effects related to the tax payment and expense in Year 2 are reflected in the following template:

TE 60
DTL 10
Cash 70

TE: 60 |
DTL: 10 |
Cash: | 70

Year 2 Transaction	Balance Sheet: Cash Asset	+	Noncash Assets	=	Liabil-ities	+	Contrib. Capital	+	Earned Capital	Income Statement: Rev-enues	−	Expen-ses	=	Net Income
Record tax expense: cash exceeds expense because deferred taxes are reversed	−70 Cash			=	−10 Deferred Tax Liability				−60 Retained Earnings		−	+60 Tax Expense	=	−60

The income tax expense for financial reporting purposes is $60 each year. However, the cash payment for taxes is $70 in Year 2; the $10 excess reduces the deferred tax liability accrued in Year 1.

This example demonstrates how accelerated depreciation for tax reporting and straight-line for financial reporting creates deferred tax liabilities. Other differences between tax reporting and financial reporting create other types of deferred tax accounts. **Deferred tax assets** arise when the tax payment is *greater* than the tax expense for financial reporting purposes (opposite of the illustration above).

Restructuring accruals are one source of deferred tax assets. In the year in which a company approves a reorganization plan, it will accrue a restructuring liability for estimated employee severance payments and other costs and it will write down assets to their market values (this reduces the net book value of those assets on the balance sheet). However, tax authorities do not recognize these accrual accounting transactions until they are realized. In particular, for tax purposes, restructuring costs are not deductible until paid in the future, and asset write-downs are not deductible until the loss is realized when the asset is sold. As a result, the restructuring accrual is not a liability for tax reporting until the company makes the payment, and the write-down of assets is not a deductible expense for tax purposes until the assets are sold. Both of these differences (the liability and the assets) give rise to a deferred tax asset. The deferred tax asset will be transferred to the income statement in the future as an expense when the company pays the restructuring costs and sells the impaired assets for a loss.

Another common deferred tax asset relates to **tax loss carryforwards**. Specifically, when a company reports a loss for tax purposes, it can carry back that loss for up to two years to recoup previous taxes paid. Any unused losses can be carried forward for up to twenty years to reduce future taxes. This creates a benefit (an "asset") for tax reporting for which there is no corresponding financial reporting asset. Thus, the company records a deferred tax asset but only if the company is "more likely than not" to be able to use the loss to reduce future taxes. This depends on the company's assessment of whether it will have sufficient profits in the future. (Pfizer's tax footnote to its income statement is shown in Exhibit 5.6. It reports deferred tax assets of $3,439 million in 2012 related to net operating loss carryforwards.)

Companies are required to establish a *deferred tax asset valuation allowance* for deferred tax assets when the future realization of their benefits is uncertain. The effect on financial statements of establishing such an allowance is to reduce reported assets, increase tax expense, and reduce equity (this is similar to accounting for the write-down of any asset). During 2012, Pfizer decreased its valuation allowance from $1,201 million to $1,102 million. Decreases in the valuation allowance increase net income on a dollar-for-dollar basis. The reduction in the valuation allowance during 2012, increased net income by $99 million ($1,201 million − $1,102 million). These effects would have been exactly the opposite if the allowance had been increased instead.

Disclosures Relating to Income Taxes

Pfizer's tax footnote to its income statement is shown in Exhibit 5.5. Pfizer's $2,562 million tax expense reported in its income statement (called the provision) consists of the following two components:

1. *Current tax expense*. Current tax expense is determined from the company's tax returns; it is the amount payable (in cash) to tax authorities (some of these taxes have been paid during the year as the company makes installments). Pfizer labels this "Current income taxes" and reports separate amounts for taxes to federal, state, local, and international tax authorities.

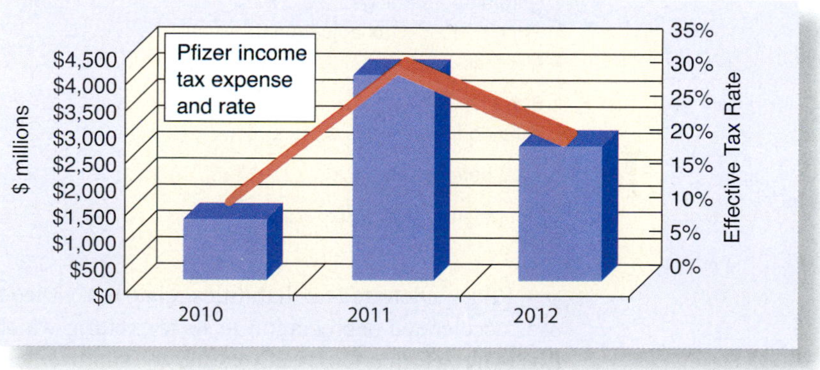

2. *Deferred tax expense*. Deferred tax expense is the effect on tax expense from changes in deferred tax liabilities and deferred tax assets. Pfizer labels this "Deferred income taxes" and reports separate amounts for deferrals related to U.S. and international tax rules.

In financial statement footnotes, companies must disclose the components of deferred tax liabilities and assets. Pfizer's deferred tax footnote to its balance sheet (shown in Exhibit 5.6) reports total deferred tax assets of $15,999 million and total deferred tax liabilities of $33,260 million. On the balance sheet companies report deferred tax assets and liabilities as either current or noncurrent based on when the benefit (payment) is expected to be received (made). Companies are permitted to net some deferred tax assets and liabilities, and also to combine deferred taxes with other accounts on the balance sheet. Thus, for some companies, it is impossible to completely reconcile the tax footnote to the balance sheet. Many of Pfizer's deferred tax assets relate to accrued liabilities or asset write-downs arising from expenses included in financial reporting income, but not yet recognized for tax reporting (such as employee benefits and restructuring accruals). Pfizer has recorded a valuation allowance of $1,102 million. These various items all yield future reductions of the company's tax payments and are, therefore, classified as assets.

EXHIBIT 5.5 Income Tax Expense Footnote for Pfizer

Year Ended December 31 (Millions of dollars)	2012	2011	2010
United States			
Current income taxes			
Federal	$ (752)	$1,349	$(2,790)
State and local	(44)	207	(323)
Deferred income taxes			
Federal	851	364	2,103
State and local	(328)	(240)	8
Total U.S. tax provision (benefit)	(273)	1,680	(1,002)
International			
Current income taxes	2,619	2,046	2,157
Deferred income taxes	216	183	(2)
Total international tax provision	2,835	2,229	2,155
Provision for taxes on income	$2,562	$3,909	$ 1,153

EXHIBIT 5.6 Deferred Taxes Footnote for Pfizer

	2012 Deferred Tax		2011 Deferred Tax	
December 31 (Millions of dollars)	Assets	(Liabilities)	Assets	(Liabilities)
Prepaid/deferred items	$ 1,817	$ (119)	$ 1,659	$ (211)
Inventories	330	(198)	324	(52)
Intangible assets	1,649	(14,187)	1,713	(15,301)
Property, plant and equipment	508	(1,485)	226	(1,311)
Employee benefits	5,042	(391)	4,280	(524)
Restructurings and other charges	784	(334)	553	(95)
Legal and product liability reserves	1,888	—	1,812	—
Net operating loss/credit carryforwards	3,439	—	4,381	—
Unremitted earnings	—	(16,042)	—	(11,699)
State and local tax adjustments	385	—	476	—
All other	1,259	(504)	1,105	(121)
Subtotal	17,101	(33,260)	16,529	(29,314)
Valuation allowances	(1,102)	—	(1,201)	—
Total deferred taxes	$15,999	$(33,260)	$15,328	$(29,314)
Net deferred tax liability		$(17,261)		$(13,986)

Pfizer's deferred tax liabilities relate to a varied assortment of items. As we illustrate above, Pfizer uses accelerated depreciation in its tax return, which results in a deferred tax liability of $1,485 million. The deferred tax asset relating to employee benefits arises from the accrual of pension expense for financial reporting, but has not yet been funded with cash contributions. The deferred tax liability relating to unremitted earnings results from investments that Pfizer has in affiliated companies. Pfizer reports income related to those investments, but the income is not taxable until the companies actually pay dividends to Pfizer. Thus, reported profit is greater than taxable income and a deferred tax liability is recognized (we discuss accounting for intercompany investments in Module 9). Pfizer will pay taxes on the subsidiaries' profits when the subsidiaries pay dividends to the U.S. parent company in the future and then the deferred tax liability will be reduced. Finally, the deferred tax asset of net operating loss carryforwards relates to losses that one or more of Pfizer's subsidiary companies has reported for tax purposes that can be used to reduce future tax liability as explained above.

Pfizer's 2012 income before tax is $12,080 million. Its tax expense of $2,562 million represents an effective tax rate of 21.2%. The *effective tax rate* is defined as tax expense divided by pretax income ($2,562 million/$12,080 million = 21.2%).[6] By comparison, the federal *statutory tax rate* for

[6] This is the effective tax rate for *all* of Pfizer's income. In the previous module we compute the tax rate on operating profit by first deducting the taxes related to nonoperating income (or adding back the tax shield related to nonoperating expenses). The effective tax rate on total income, is a weighted average of the two rates (operating and nonoperating).

corporations (the rate prescribed in tax regulations) is 35%. Companies must provide a schedule that reconciles the effective tax rate (21.2% for Pfizer) with the Federal statutory rate of 35%. Following is the schedule that **Pfizer** reports in its 10-K.

Reconciliation of the U.S. statutory income tax rate to our effective tax rate for income from continuing operations follows:

Year Ended Dec. 31	2012	2011	2010
U.S. statutory income tax rate	35.0%	35.0%	35.0%
Taxation of non-U.S. operations	(3.0)	(3.1)	2.5
Tax settlements and resolution of certain tax positions	(12.0)	(2.8)	(26.3)
U.S. healthcare legislation	1.0	0.7	2.8
U.S. research tax and development tax credit and manufacturing deduction	(0.3)	(0.9)	(2.3)
Certain legal settlements and charges	1.4	—	0.4
Acquired IPR&D	—	—	0.5
Wyeth acquisition-related costs	—	—	0.5
Sales of biopharmaceutical companies	—	0.2	—
All other—net	(0.9)	2.7	(0.9)
Effective tax rate for income from continuing operations	21.2%	31.8%	12.2%

In addition to federal taxes (paid to the IRS), companies also pay taxes to state, local, and foreign jurisdictions where they operate. These tax rates are typically lower than the statutory rate of 35%. (In 2012, the net effect of foreign taxes, reduced Pfizer's overall tax rate by 3.0%.) In 2012, Pfizer's effective tax rate was reduced by 12.0% as a result of favorable rulings in litigation with taxing authorities. Also, several miscellaneous items increased Pfizer's effective tax rate by 1.2%, resulting in a net decrease of 13.8% from the 35.0% statutory tax rate.

In sum, Pfizer's effective tax rate for 2012 is 21.2%, which is 13.8 percentage points below the 35% statutory rate. In 2011, however, the effective tax rate was 31.8% and in 2010 it was 12.2%. Fluctuations, such as these, in the effective tax rate are not uncommon and highlight the difference between income reported under GAAP and that computed using multiple tax codes and tax incentives under which companies operate. Appendix 5B explains accounting for deferred taxes in more detail.

ANALYSIS INSIGHT **Tax Avoidance: Where in the World is Cash?**

Many companies are under scrutiny as governments across the globe seek greater tax revenues. At issue are tax strategies that allow companies to report considerable income to shareholders, but considerably less to the taxing authorities. This is nothing new. Companies have been using tax avoidance strategies for decades. While these strategies comply with tax laws, governments argue that they stretch ethical boundaries. How do these schemes work? One strategy is to establish a subsidiary in a country with lenient tax laws. The Cayman Islands is one such country, as is Ireland. Tax laws define residency (and, thus, the obligation to pay taxes) by considering the management and control of a corporation rather than by where it was formed or incorporated. For Ireland, if the company is not managed and controlled in Ireland, it is not a legal resident of Ireland and, thus, does not pay taxes. Moreover, if the company is not incorporated in the United States, it is not a U.S. tax resident and does not pay taxes there either. To illustrate, assume a foreign company owns the intellectual property (IP) rights (such as software) for an important product sold by a U.S. company. Since most of the value of the product is typically in its IP, the IP owner can charge a large fee to license the IP (to the U.S. company). When the U.S. company sells the product, most of the profit goes to the foreign company by way of the licensing fees. If the foreign company is not a tax resident of any country, most of the profit on the sale is not taxable: the country where the foreign company resides does not use residency for tax purposes and the U.S. only taxes money that is repatriated back to the United States. As long as the cash remains on the foreign company's balance sheet, it is not taxable in the United States. Does that mean that the money must be physically located outside of the United States? No! The foreign company can open accounts in U.S. banks like any customer can. This means the physical cash can be located in the United States but remain on the balance sheet of the foreign company, free from taxation by the IRS. Companies have long used such strategies to move profits into low (or no) tax countries, fueling ongoing battles with taxing authorities and cries of foul from other taxpayers.

Analysis of Income Tax Disclosures

Analysis of deferred taxes can yield useful insights. Some revenue accruals (such as accounts receivable for longer-term contracts) increase deferred tax liabilities as GAAP income exceeds tax income (similar to the effect of using straight-line depreciation for financial reporting purposes and accelerated depreciation for tax returns).

An increase in deferred tax liabilities indicates that a company is reporting higher GAAP income relative to taxable income and can indicate the company is managing earnings upwards. The difference between reported corporate profits and taxable income increased substantially in the late 1990s, just prior to huge asset write-offs. *CFO Magazine* (November 2002) implied that such differences are important for analysis and should be monitored:

> Fueling the sense that something [was] amiss [was] the growing gap between the two sets of numbers. In 1992, there was no significant difference between pretax book income and taxable net income . . . By 1996, according to IRS data, a $92.5 billion gap had appeared. By 1998 [prior to the market decline], the gap was $159 billion—a fourth of the total taxable income reported . . . If people had seen numbers showing very significant differences between book numbers for trading and tax numbers, they would have wondered if those [income] numbers were completely real.

Although an increase in deferred tax liabilities can legitimately result, for example, from an increase in depreciable assets and the use of accelerated depreciation for tax purposes, we must be aware of the possibility that such an increase arises from improper revenue recognition in that the company might not be reporting those revenues to tax authorities.

Adequacy of Deferred Tax Asset Valuation

Analysis of the deferred tax asset valuation account provides us with additional insight. This analysis involves (1) assessing the adequacy of the valuation allowance and (2) determining how and why the valuation account changed during the period and how that change affects net income.

When a company reports a deferred tax asset, the company implies that it will, more likely than not, receive a future tax benefit equal to the deferred tax asset. If the company is uncertain about the future tax benefit, it records an allowance to reduce the asset. How can we gauge the adequacy of a valuation allowance account? We might assess the reasons for the valuation account (typically reported in the tax footnote). We might examine other companies in the industry for similar allowances. We might also review the MD&A for any doubt on company prospects for future profitability.

We can quantify our analysis in at least three ways. First, we can examine the allowance as a percentage of the deferred tax assets. For **Pfizer**, this 2012 percentage is 6.44%; see below. We also want to gather data from other pharmaceutical companies and compare the sizes of their allowance accounts relative to their related deferred tax assets. The important point is that we must be comfortable with the size of the valuation account and remember that management has control over the adequacy and reporting of the allowance account (with audit assurances).

Pfizer ($ millions)	2012	2011
Deferred tax asset	$17,101	$16,529
Valuation allowance	$1,102	$1,201
Valuation allowance as a percent of total deferred tax assets	6.44%	7.27%

Second, we can examine changes in the allowance account. During a year, circumstances change and the company might be more or less assured of receiving the tax benefit. In that case, the company might decrease or increase its allowance account. The valuation allowance in 2012 is smaller than the previous year, both in absolute dollars and as a percent of deferred tax assets. This implies that during the year, Pfizer has revised upward its estimate of the likelihood of realizing the benefits of its deferred tax assets.

ANALYSIS INSIGHT **Historical Trends in Deferred Tax Asset Valuation Allowance**

It is useful to investigate historical trends in the deferred tax assets valuation allowance. Pfizer has increased its valuation allowance from 1.66% of deferred tax assets in 2008 to 6.44% in 2012:

	2012	2011	2010	2009	2008
Deferred tax asset	$17,101	$16,529	$15,921	$16,260	$11,692
Valuation allowance	$ 1,102	$ 1,201	$ 894	$ 353	$ 194
Valuation allowance/Deferred tax asset	6.44%	7.27%	5.62%	2.17%	1.66%

Analysis of components of deferred tax assets reveals the following changes from 2008 to 2012:

Pfizer's deferred tax assets	2012	2008	Chg.
Prepaid/deferred items	$ 1,817	$ 1,000	$ 817
Inventories	330	102	228
Intangible assets	1,649	872	777
Property, plant and equipment	508	205	303
Employee benefits	5,042	3,414	1,628
Restructurings and other charges	784	841	(57)
Legal and product liability reserves	1,888	703	1,185
Net operating loss/credit carryforwards	3,439	3,065	374
State and local tax adjustments	385	585	(200)
All other	1,259	905	354
Total deferred tax assets	$17,101	$11,692	$5,409

The biggest increase in the deferred tax asset relates to the accruals for legal and product liability reserves and to employee benefits. Of the two, the former involves more uncertainty—Pfizer has accrued for potential lawsuit settlements and judgments that may or may not come to fruition. The increase in the valuation allowance from 2008 to 2012, could be due to this uncertainly. Typically, valuation allowances are related to net operating loss (NOL) carryforwards. Thus, the increase of $908 million seems high given the $374 million increase in the NOL. Analysts want to follow up on this seeming anomaly.

Had Pfizer's valuation allowance as a percentage of deferred tax assets remained at 2008 levels, its 2012 allowance would have been $284 million ($17,101 × 1.66%), or $818 million lower than the actual allowance. A higher allowance means Pfizer reported $818 million less in net income over the 2008 to 2012 period. (The increase is after tax, not pre-tax, as, unlike the effects of other allowance accounts, increases in the deferred tax asset valuation allowance are reflected in net income dollar-for-dollar.) Given that Pfizer's ROE has remained constant over this five-year period, and given the significant increase in its stock price, a skeptical analyst might entertain the notion that Pfizer is banking earnings for the future. We look for reversals of the deferred tax asset valuation allowance in future years if this is, indeed, the case.

Third, we can quantify how a change in the valuation allowance affects net income and its effective tax rate. Increases in the valuation allowance affect tax expense in the same direction, dollar for dollar. This in turn, affects net income (in the opposite direction) again, dollar for dollar. Changes in valuation allowances can have (and have had) marked effects on net income for numerous companies. One final note, reductions in the deferred tax asset valuation account can occur as a result of unused loss carryforwards; in that case, a company reduces the deferred tax asset and the related valuation allowance, which is similar in concept to the write-off of an account receivable discussed in Module 6. For our analysis, we must remember, however, that in the absence of expiring loss carryforwards, a company can increase current-period income by deliberately decreasing the valuation allowance. Knowing that such decreases can boost net income, companies might deliberately create too large a valuation allowance in one or more prior years and use it as a *cookie jar reserve* to boost income in future periods. We want to assess the details of the valuation account and changes therein from company footnotes and from the MD&A.

ANALYSIS INSIGHT **Does the Deferred Tax Asset Valuation Allowance Predict Future Earnings?**

When companies report taxable losses, they are allowed to carryback the loss to offset prior years' taxable income and to carry forward any unused carryback to offset future taxable income, thus reducing future tax liability. This tax loss carryforward results in the recognition of a deferred tax asset that is only reported on the balance sheet if it is more likely than not that the benefit will be realized. If not, management must establish a valuation allowance to write down the deferred tax asset as explained in this module. Researchers have examined if the establishment of this valuation allowance conveys information about the future profitability of the company. Using a sample of 20,000 annual reports of companies reporting losses, the researchers found that the failure to establish a valuation allowance in the presence of losses is a credible predictor of positive future earnings for up to three years into the future. Further, for publicly traded companies with low analyst coverage, investors do not appear to recognize this valuation-relevant information, suggesting the possibility of a trading strategy to purchase stock in companies reporting losses and having no substantial additions to the valuation allowance account. Time will tell if this trading strategy bears fruit, but the lesson is clear: understanding the income tax footnote is crucial to a thorough analysis of financial statements.

Source: Dhaliwal, Dan, Steve Kaplan, Rick Laux, and Eric Weisbrod (2013), "The Information Content of Tax Expense for Firms Reporting Losses," Journal of Accounting Research, 51:1, p. 135-164.

MID-MODULE REVIEW 2

Refer to the **Merck & Co., Inc.**, 2012 income statement in Mid-Module Review 1. Merck provides the following additional information in footnotes to its 10-K.

Taxes on income consisted of:

Years Ended December 31 ($ in millions)	2012	2011	2010
Current provision			
Federal	$1,346	$ 859	$ 399
Foreign	651	1,568	1,446
State	(226)	52	(82)
	1,771	2,479	1,763
Deferred provision			
Federal	749	(584)	764
Foreign	(323)	(683)	(1,777)
State	243	(270)	(79)
	669	(1,537)	(1,092)
	$2,440	$ 942	$ 671

Required

1. What is the total income tax expense that Merck reports in its 2012 income statement?
2. What amount of its total tax expense did (or will) Merck pay in cash (that is, what amount is currently payable)?
3. Explain how Merck calculates its income tax expense.

The solution is on page 5-69.

LO4 Explain how foreign currency fluctuations affect the income statement.

Foreign Currency Translation Effects

Many companies conduct international operations and transact business in currencies other than $US. It is common for companies to purchase assets in foreign currencies, borrow money in foreign currencies, and transact business with their customers in foreign currencies. Increasingly many companies have subsidiaries whose balance sheets and income statements are prepared in foreign currencies.

Financial statements prepared according to U.S. GAAP must be reported in $US. This means that the financial statements of any foreign subsidiaries must be translated into $US before consolidation with the U.S. parent company. This translation process can markedly alter both the balance sheet and income statement. We discuss income statement effects of foreign currency translation in this module; we discuss the effects on stockholders' equity in Module 8.

Effects of Foreign Currency Transactions on Income

A change in the strength of the $US vis-à-vis foreign currencies has a direct effect on the $US equivalent for revenues, expenses, and income of the foreign subsidiary because revenues and expenses are translated at the average exchange rate for the period. Exhibit 5.8 shows those financial effects.

EXHIBIT 5.7 Income Statement Effects from Foreign Currency Movements

	Revenues	−	Expenses	=	Net Income (or Loss)
$US Weakens.	Increase		Increase		Increase
$US Strengthens	Decrease		Decrease		Decrease

Specifically, when the foreign currency strengthens (implying $US weakens), the subsidiary's revenues and expenses translate into more $US and, thus, reported income is higher than if the currencies had not fluctuated. On the other hand, when the $US strengthens, the subsidiary's revenues, expenses, and income decrease in $US terms. (The profit effect assumes that revenues exceed expenses; if expenses exceed revenues, a loss occurs, which increases if the $US weakens and decreases if the $US strengthens.)

Pfizer discusses how currency fluctuations affect its income statement in the following excerpt from its MD&A to the company's 2012 10-K.

> Revenues decreased 10% in 2012 to $59.0 billion, compared to $65.3 billion in 2011, which reflects an operational decline of $4.8 billion or 8%, primarily the result of the loss of exclusivity of Lipitor in most major markets, including the U.S. on November 30, 2011, and most of developed Europe in March and May 2012, **and the unfavorable impact of foreign exchange of $1.5 billion, or 2%.** Lipitor and other product losses of exclusivity, as well as the final-year terms of our collaboration agreements in certain markets for Spiriva, negatively impacted revenues by approximately $7.7 billion, or 12%, in 2012 compared to 2011 (emphasis added).

In 2012, the $US strengthened against many foreign currencies in which Pfizer conducts its business. That strengthening of the $US reduces the $US equivalent of transactions denominated in foreign currencies, thus decreasing Pfizer's revenues by $1.5 billion (2%). Even if unit volumes remained unchanged around the world, the resulting revenues (in dollars) would be lower. In 2011, by contrast, the $US weakened against those same currencies, resulting in an increase of Pfizer's reported revenues of $1.9 billion (3%). Fluctuations in the relative exchange value of the $US are common, thus leading to fluctuations in reported revenues, expenses, and income. Pfizer discloses that it utilizes a variety of measures in an attempt to mitigate the income statement impact of these fluctuations:

> **Foreign Exchange Risk** Significant portions of our revenues and earnings are exposed to changes in foreign exchange rates. We seek to manage our foreign exchange risk in part through operational means, including managing same-currency revenues in relation to same-currency costs and same currency assets in relation to same-currency liabilities. Depending on market conditions, foreign exchange risk also is managed through the use of derivative financial instruments and foreign currency debt. As we operate in multiple foreign currencies, including the euro, the Japanese yen, the U.K. pound, the Chinese renminbi, the Canadian dollar and approximately 100 other currencies, changes in those currencies relative to the U.S. dollar will impact our revenues and expenses. If the U.S. dollar weakens against a specific foreign currency, our revenues will increase, having a positive impact, and our overall expenses will increase, having a negative impact, on net income. Likewise, if the U.S. dollar strengthens against a specific foreign currency, our revenues will decrease, having a negative impact, and our overall expenses will decrease, having a positive impact on net income. Therefore, significant changes in foreign exchange rates can impact our results and our financial guidance.

The phrase "operational means" indicates that the company structures its transactions in $US rather than a foreign currency or attempts to match same-currency revenues and expenses (or assets and liabilities) to minimize the effects of currency fluctuations. Foreign currency financial instruments are common and include forward and futures contracts, which lock in future currency values. We explain how these instruments (called derivatives) work in Appendix 7C. In sum, we must be cognizant of the effects of currency fluctuations on reported revenues, expenses, and profits for companies with substantial foreign-currency transactions.

OPERATING COMPONENTS BELOW-THE-LINE

Pfizer's income statement includes a subtotal labeled "income from continuing operations." Historically, this presentation highlighted the nonrecurring (*transitory*) portions of the income statement so that they could be eliminated to facilitate the projection of future profitability. The word "continuing" was meant to imply that income was purged of one-time items, as these were presented "below-the-line," that is, below income from continuing operations. Two categories of items are presented below-the-line:

1. **Discontinued operations** Net income (loss) from business segments that have been or will be sold, and any gains (losses) on net assets related to those segments sold in the current period.
2. **Extraordinary items** Gains or losses from events that are both *unusual* and *infrequent*.

We discuss both of these "below-the-line" items in this section.

Discontinued Operations

Discontinued operations refer to any separately identifiable business unit that the company sells or intends to sell. The income or loss of the discontinued operations (net of tax), and the after-tax gain or loss on sale of the unit, are reported in the income statement below income from continuing operations. Pfizer reports the following in its 2012 10-K:

December 31 (Millions)	2012	2011	2010
Income from continuing operations	$ 9,518	$ 8,395	$8,318
Discontinued operations			
Income (loss) from discontinued operations—net of tax	**297**	**350**	**(19)**
Gain (loss) on sale of discontinued operations—net of tax	**4,783**	**1,304**	**(11)**
Discontinued operations—net of tax	**5,080**	**1,654**	**(30)**
Net income before allocation to noncontrolling interests	14,598	10,049	8,288
Less: Net income attributable to noncontrolling interests	28	40	31
Net income attributable to Pfizer Inc.	$14,570	$10,009	$8,257

Results of the discontinued operations are segregated from those of continuing operations. That is, the revenues and expenses of the discontinued business unit are *not* reported with revenues and expenses from continuing operations. Consolidated revenues and expenses reported on the income statement reflect continuing operations only, and the (persistent) income from continuing operations is reported net of its related tax expense. For 2012, income from continuing operations, net of tax, is $9,518 million. Revenues and expenses from the (transitory) discontinued operations are collapsed into one line item and reported separately, net of related tax. For 2012, discontinued operations generated net income of $297 million. This presentation facilitates the analysis of (persistent) continuing operations, which can be used to predict future operations. Discontinued operations are segregated (reported on one line) in the current year and for the two prior years as presented above.

Details behind Pfizer's transaction underlying its discontinued operations are in its footnotes:

> **Divestitures** On November 30, 2012, we completed the sale of our Nutrition business to Nestlé for $11.85 billion in cash, and recognized a gain of approximately $4.8 billion, net of tax, in *Gain/(loss) on sale of discontinued operations—net of tax*. . . . The operating results of this business are reported as *Income/(loss) from discontinued operations—net of tax* in our consolidated statements of income for all periods presented. In addition, in our consolidated balance sheet as of December 31, 2011, the assets and liabilities associated with this discontinued operation are classified as *Assets of discontinued operations and other assets held for sale* and *Liabilities of discontinued operations*, as appropriate.

Pfizer sold its nutrition business to Nestlé for $11.85 billion. At the time of sale, that subsidiary was reported on Pfizer's balance sheet at $7.05 billion (we discuss the reporting for subsidiaries in Module 9). The sale of an asset (the nutrition business) with a book value of $7.05 billion at a sale price of $11.85 billion resulted in a gain on sale of $4.8 billion, reported below the line. This income statement placement is important: Pfizer will not sell this business again. So, the gain is a *transitory item*. Segregating it in this manner identifies it as such for analysts so that they can consider how the elimination of this business unit affects forecasts of Pfizer's revenues, income and cash flow for 2013 and beyond. For the current and prior years' analysis, we need to understand that the appreciation in the value of the nutrition business did not occur only in the current year. Consequently, in our analysis, we might consider spreading the gain out over the prior years during which the nutrition business was owned by Pfizer.

The footnote also points out that Pfizer segregates the assets and liabilities relating to this business unit on its consolidated balance sheet. Companies do not frequently provide the same segregation of the assets and liabilities of the discontinued operation that they do in the income statement. Typically, information about these assets and liabilities of the discontinued operations are provided in footnotes. GAAP prescribes that this disclosure must be made, but allows for disclosure in the balance sheet or in the footnotes.

An additional note about the discontinued nutrition business: from January 1, 2012, until the date of sale, November 30, 2012, these operations generated an after-tax net income of $297 million. Discontinued operations resulted in net income of $350 million for 2011 and a loss of $19 million for 2010. Some of the prior year results relate to the nutrition business that was discontinued in 2012 so that the income statement columns are comparable. Segregating net income from continuing operations allows analysts to better focus on the income and cash flow that will likely continue into the future.

Extraordinary Items

Extraordinary items refer to events that are both unusual *and* infrequent. Their effects are reported following income from continuing operations. Management determines whether an event is unusual and infrequent (with auditor approval) for financial reporting purposes. Further, management often has incentives to classify unfavorable items as extraordinary because they will be reported separately, after income from continuing operations (*below-the-line*). These incentives derive from managers' beliefs that investors tend to focus more on items included in income from continuing operations and less on nonrecurring items that are not included in continuing operations.

GAAP provides the following guidance in determining whether or not an item is extraordinary:

- *Unusual nature.* The underlying event or transaction must possess a high degree of abnormality and be clearly unrelated to, or only incidentally related to, the ordinary activities of the entity.
- *Infrequency of occurrence.* The underlying event or transaction must be of a type that would not reasonably be expected to recur in the foreseeable future.

The following items are generally **not** reported as extraordinary items:

- Gains and losses on retirement of debt
- Write-down or write-off of operating or nonoperating assets
- Foreign currency gains and losses
- Gains and losses from disposal of specific assets or business segment

- Effects of a strike
- Accrual adjustments related to long-term contracts
- Costs of a takeover defense

Extraordinary items are reported separately (net of tax) and below income from continuing operations on the income statement.

IFRS INSIGHT **Extraordinary Items and IFRS**

IFRS does not permit the reporting of income and expense items as "extraordinary." The IASB justified its position in IAS 1 as follows: "The Board decided that items treated as extraordinary result from the normal business risks faced by an entity and do not warrant presentation in a separate component of the income statement. The nature or function of a transaction or other event, rather than its frequency, should determine its presentation within the income statement. Items currently classified as 'extraordinary' are only a subset of the items of income and expense that may warrant disclosure to assist users in predicting an entity's future performance" (IAS 1).

Earnings Per Share

LO5 Compute earnings per share and explain the effect of dilutive securities.

The income statement reports earnings per share (EPS) numbers. Most firms report two EPS numbers: basic and diluted. The difference between the two measures is shown in Exhibit 5.8.

EXHIBIT 5.8 **Basic and Diluted EPS Computations**

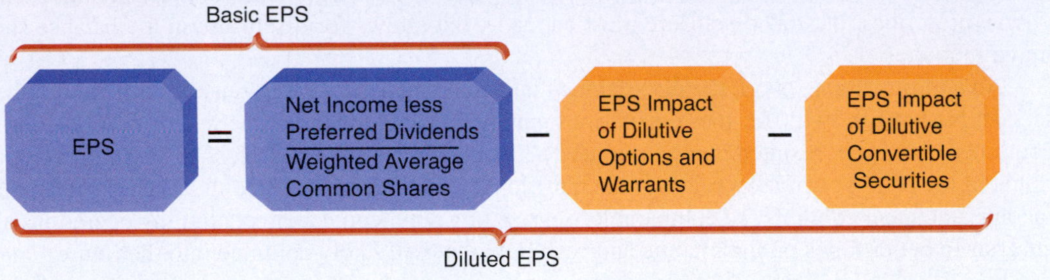

Basic EPS is computed as: (Net income − Dividends on preferred stock)/Weighted average number of common shares outstanding during the year. Subtracting preferred stock dividends yields the income available for dividend payments to common shareholders. Computation of **diluted EPS** reflects the additional shares that would be issued if all stock options, warrants, and convertible securities had been converted into common shares at the beginning of the year or when issued, if issued during the year. Diluted EPS never exceeds basic EPS.

Pfizer reports Basic EPS from continuing operations of $1.27 in 2012 and diluted EPS from continuing operations of $1.26. Given the near identical results for basic and diluted EPS, we know that Pfizer has few dilutive securities. **Virgin Media, Inc.**, however, reports a dilution of 16% in its EPS as evident from its following disclosure:

Fiscal year ended December 31 (in thousands, except per share)	2012	2011	2010
Basic net income per share	£10.40	£0.25	£(0.52)
Diluted net income per share	£ 8.75	£0.24	£(0.52)

Virgin Media, Inc. reports the following dilutive effects on EPS:

Year ended December 31 (in millions)	2012	2011	2010
Numerator for basic income (loss) per common share from continuing operations	£2,852.6	£77.1	£(169.2)
Interest on senior convertible notes, net of tax	41.0	—	—
Numerator for diluted income (loss) per common share from continuing operations	£2,893.6	£77.1	£(169.2)
Weighted average number of shares			
Denominator for basic income (loss) per common share	274.3	310.1	327.1
Effect of dilutive securities			
Share based awards to employees	4.5	6.0	—
Shares issuable under senior convertible notes	52.0	—	—
Denominator for diluted income (loss) per common share	330.8	316.1	327.1

Virgin Media has two potentially dilutive securities. The company granted stock options to its employees that allow those employees to purchase 4.5 million shares in the future at a pre-determined market price. And, Virgin Media has issued convertible notes that allow the holders to surrender their notes in exchange for 52 million shares of common stock instead of cash (at a pre-determined exchange ratio).

Both the numerator and the denominator in the EPS calculation are potentially affected by dilutive securities. If all the convertible notes had been exchanged for stock at the start of the year, the company would have avoided £41 million of annual interest on these notes. Therefore, the after-tax interest of £41 million is added to net income in the numerator.

The denominator in the diluted earnings per share calculation presumes the most-extreme case: at the beginning of the year, all employees exercise their right to purchase common shares and all convertible note holders convert their notes to common shares. The combined effect is to increase the number of shares in the denominator by 56.5 million, thus decreasing the diluted EPS ratio.

Finally, the effects of dilutive securities are only included if they are, in fact, dilutive. Securities that are *antidilutive* are those that would increase EPS, and are, thus, excluded from the computation. An example of an antidilutive security is employee stock options with an exercise price greater than the stock's current market price. These underwater (or out-of-the-money) options are antidilutive and are, therefore, excluded from the EPS computation. Virgin Media provides the following explanation for this exclusion in its footnotes:

The following table sets forth the number of potential common shares excluded from the calculation of the denominator for diluted income (loss) per common shares (in millions):

Year ended December 31	2012	2011	2010
Stock options	2.6	3.4	10.5
Sharesave options	—	0.7	0.5
Restricted stock held in escrow	—	0.6	0.7
Restricted stock units	2.5	2.5	5.2
Warrants	—	—	25.8
Shares issuable under convertible senior notes	—	52.0	52.0

Each of these instruments are excluded from the calculation of diluted net income per common share in periods in which there is a loss, because the inclusion of potential common shares would have an anti-dilutive effect. In the year ended December 31, 2012, certain share based awards to employees have been excluded from the calculation of the diluted weighted average number of shares because their exercise prices exceeded our average share price during the calculation period. In the year ended December 31, 2012, certain restricted stock held in escrow and certain restricted stock units have been excluded from the calculation of the diluted weighted average number of shares because these shares are contingently issuable based on the achievement of performance and/or market conditions that have not been achieved as of December 31, 2012.

Analysts and investors often use EPS figures to compare operating results for companies of different sizes under the assumption that the number of shares outstanding is proportional to the income level (that is, a company twice the size of another will report double the income and will have double the common shares outstanding, leaving EPS approximately equal for the two companies). This assumption is erroneous. Management controls the number of common shares outstanding and there is no relation between firm size and number of shares outstanding. Different companies also have different philosophies regarding share issuance and repurchase. For example, consider that most companies report annual EPS of less than $5, while **Berkshire Hathaway** reported EPS of $8,977 in 2012! This is because Berkshire Hathaway has so few common shares outstanding, not necessarily because it has stellar profits.

ACCOUNTING QUALITY

LO6 Explain accounting quality and identify areas for analysis.

We conclude our coverage of operating income with a discussion of accounting quality. As we saw in earlier modules, there are at least two main uses of financial reports: evaluation and valuation. Financial statement readers use the reported numbers from financial statements along with information in the notes and Management Discussion and Analysis (MD&A), to evaluate company profitability, liquidity, solvency and other financial characteristics. Those users also evaluate its managers and board of directors with a view to assessing the results of past operating, investing and financing decisions. The evaluation of financial reports is also used to value the company, a process that includes forecasting operating, investing and financing results. In a later module we consider more fully the forecasting process. For now, it is important to understand that both uses of financial information (evaluation and valuation) demand high-quality accounting information.

What is high-quality accounting information? Although there is not a single definition of high-quality information, there are factors that enhance information quality.

Reliable High-quality accounting information is **reliable**. In particular, information is reliable when:

- Balance sheet numbers represent economic reality: all included assets will yield future economic benefits and there are no unrecorded assets; all liabilities are recorded and measured at economically appropriate amounts. Assets and liabilities are properly labeled and classified as current or noncurrent. Accounts have not been aggregated so as to obscure their true nature.
- Income statement numbers reflect economic earnings: revenues reflect all sales activity during the period and only those sales for that period; expenses are complete and properly measured. Items are properly labeled and any netting or aggregation of numbers does not obscure their true nature or amount.
- Reported cash flows accurately portray all of the cash that flowed in and out of the company during the period.

Relevant High-quality accounting information is **relevant**. In particular information is relevant when:

- Reported earnings and cash flow numbers can be used to forecast the amount and timing of future earnings and cash flows. This attribute is referred to as "relevance" and we return to it in our forecasting module.
- Footnotes provide additional quantitative and qualitative information that is accurate and complete. Sometimes a balance sheet or income statement number is not the best indicator of current value or is not predictive of future expectations. For example, LIFO inventory is reported on the balance sheet but the footnotes augment relevance by reporting the FIFO value of inventory.

There are several ways that accounting quality is diminished. (For a good discussion of this issue, see Dechow, P., and C. Schrand. "Earnings quality," The Research Foundation of CFA Institute. Charlottesville, VA 2004.)

Unintentional Errors

We must understand that there are errors in financial statements. Two reports signed by external auditors (one concerning adequacy of the company's internal controls and one disclosing the audit opinion) provide some assurance that financial statements are free from material misstatement. However, those reports do not guarantee no errors; instead, they assert that any remaining errors are not large enough to affect the decisions of financial statement readers.

One-time Events and Pro Forma Disclosures

In the ordinary course of business, companies record one-time transactions that are not expected to recur. For example, a lawsuit is settled or commodity prices spike and the company earns a windfall profit. While these nonrecurring events are reliably measured and reported, by definition they cannot be used to predict future periods' events. Those specific line items are not relevant and our expectations about future earnings must not be swayed by such events. The challenge is in determining which items reported on the income statement are truly one-time events. Often companies highlight the existence of one-time items by reporting "pro forma" earnings in company financial statements and press releases. Pro forma income commonly begins with GAAP income from continuing operations (which excludes discontinued operations and extraordinary items), and then adjusts for other one-time items including restructuring charges, large gains and losses, and acquisition expenses (goodwill amortization and other acquisition costs). SEC Regulation G requires that companies reconcile such non-GAAP information to GAAP numbers so that financial statement readers can have a basis for comparison and can determine if the excluded items truly are one-time items. For example, in 2012 Merck & Co., Inc., reported the following "pro forma" (non-GAAP) information in its Form 10-K.

Year Ended December 31 ($ in millions)	2012	2011	2010
Pretax income as reported under GAAP	**$ 8,739**	$ 7,334	$ 1,653
Increase (decrease) for excluded items:			
Acquisition-related costs	**5,344**	5,939	9,403
Restructuring costs	**999**	1,911	1,986
Other items:			
Net charge related to settlement of ENHANCE litigation	**493**	—	—
Arbitration settlement charge	—	500	—
Gain on disposition of interest in JJMCP joint venture	—	(136)	—
Gain on sale of manufacturing facilities and related assets	—	(127)	—
Vioxx liability reserve	—	—	950
Income recognized on AstraZeneca's asset option exercise	—	—	(443)
Other	—	5	—
	15,575	15,426	13,549
Taxes on income as reported under GAAP	**2,440**	942	671
Estimated tax benefit (expense) on excluded items	**1,261**	1,697	1,798
Tax benefit from settlement of federal income tax audit	—	700	—
Tax benefit from foreign and state tax rate changes	—	270	391
Tax charge related to U.S. health care reform legislation	—	—	(147)
	3,701	3,609	2,713
Non-GAAP net income	**11,874**	11,817	10,836
Less: Net income attributable to noncontrolling interests	**131**	120	121
Non-GAAP net income attributable to Merck & Co., Inc.	**$11,743**	$11,697	$10,715

This footnote indicates that Merck considers a number of items to be "one time" including $5,344 million of acquisition-related costs and $999 million of restructuring costs. These one-time charges, if included, portray an inaccurate picture of Merck's performance during the past three years in the opinion of Merck's management.

Deliberate Managerial Intervention

Ideally, all reported numbers are free from deliberate managerial intervention. This implies that the numbers are unbiased because managers have been impartial when choosing accounting policies and when exercising their discretion over reported numbers. However, history is rife with examples where this is not the case: managers can and do "manage" earnings and balance sheet numbers. Sometimes accounting quality is impugned because managers' intervention in the reporting process involves fraud. For example, in 2009, Ramalinga Raju, the CEO of Satyam (an Indian information-technology conglomerate), was arrested for reporting fictitious cash and profits of over $1 billion. However, more frequently, earnings management involves subtle, small increases in net income designed to achieve an outcome such as meeting analysts' forecasts or avoiding losses. While it is more often the case that

RESEARCH INSIGHT **Pro Forma Earnings: Incidence and Outcomes**

In 2010, more than half the companies that comprise the Dow Jones Index reported non-GAAP numbers when reporting quarterly net income. *(See listing at: Larcker, D. and B. Tayan, "Pro Forma Earnings: What's Wrong with GAAP?" August 20, 2010, http://ssrn.com/abstract=1678066.)* Despite the potential for abuse, investors often perceive certain non-GAAP earnings as more permanent than GAAP earnings because pro forma numbers allegedly provide better indication of future earnings power. For this reason, Wall Street analysts' earnings estimates typically use non-GAAP metrics, or "Street" earnings. Recent research reports two results that show how investors' use of pro forma earnings is changing. First, investors appear to pay more attention to pro forma earnings in the post-SOX period (after 2003), which suggests that SOX (abbreviation for Sarbanes-Oxley Act) improved the credibility of non-GAAP disclosures. Second, investors discount earnings announcements in which managers make aggressive exclusions that are potentially misleading and, hence, stock values seem to reflect investors' ability to discern accounting quality. (Black, D., E. Black, T. Christensen, and W. Heninger "Has the Regulation of Pro Forma Reporting in the U.S. Changed Investors' Perceptions of Pro Forma Earnings Disclosures?" *Journal of Business, Finance & Accounting,* 2012, 39:7-8, pp. 876–904.)

"managed" earnings (and assets) are inflated, some managers underreport their true earnings (and assets). The highest quality accounting reports are free from biases in both directions; they are accurate because they are not over- or understated.

Reliable Numbers That Are Not Predictive

Companies can experience changes in economic events that impair the predictive ability of reliable numbers. For example, in June 2011, **Marathon Oil** announced that it was breaking the company into two new companies: **Marathon Oil**, which will engage in upstream oil and gas exploration and development activities, and **Marathon Petroleum**, which will run refineries and distribute products to retail and other customers. The company's 2010 financial statements, while reliable, were no longer relevant because the company's structure was so changed that users could not use its 2010 revenues and expenses to forecast 2011 net income. Expectations about future earnings were markedly altered.

Assessing and Remediating Accounting Quality

There is no tried and true formula for assessing accounting quality or for identifying earnings management. But, at a minimum, we can implement the following analysis and remediation techniques:

- Read both reports from the external auditor and take special note of any deviation from boilerplate language.
- Peruse the footnote on accounting policies (typically footnote 1) and compare the company's policies to its industry peers. Deviations from the norm can signal opportunism.
- Examine changes in accounting policies. What would the company have reported absent the change? Did the new policy help it avoid reporting a loss or violating a debt covenant?
- Compare key ratios over time. Follow up on marked increases or decreases in ratios, read footnotes and the MD&A to see how management explains such changes. Follow up on ratios that do not change when a change is expected. For example, during the tech bubble, **Worldcom, Inc.**, reported an expense-to-revenue ratio (ER ratio) of 42% quarter after quarter, despite the worsening of economic conditions. Later it was discovered that managers had deliberately underreported expenses to maintain the ER ratio. The lesson is that sometimes "no change" signals managerial intervention.
- Review ratios of competitors and consider macro economic conditions and how they have shifted over time. Are the ratios reasonable in light of current conditions? Are changes in the income statement aligning with changes on the balance sheet?

- Identify nonrecurring items and separately assess their impact on company performance and position. Take care when using pro forma numbers reported by the company.
- Recast financial statements as necessary to reflect an accounting policy(ies) that is more in line with competitors or one that better reflects economically relevant numbers. We illustrate recasting at several points in future modules. For example, we can convert LIFO inventory to FIFO and we can capitalize operating leases.

BUSINESS INSIGHT **Meeting or Beating Analysts' Forecasts**

Missing analysts' earnings forecasts can cause stock prices to tumble. Therefore, managers aim to meet or beat the Street's expectation, sometimes resorting to earnings management involving accounting accruals, and other times using real actions (such as channel stuffing). These deliberate manager interventions reduce accounting quality. One way analysts and researchers detect potential earnings management is to identify unusual accruals and reversals (negative accruals) and quantify their effect on earnings. Of particular interest are unusual accruals that move EPS enough to meet or beat analysts' earnings forecasts; such accruals raise suspicion of managerial opportunism. Consider the case of **Green Mountain Coffee**; its consensus EPS forecast was $0.38 for the second quarter of fiscal 2011. When the company reported second-quarter earnings, they beat the consensus forecast by $0.10 per share, a 26% margin! The company's stock price shot up nearly 20% to $75.98. But a closer inspection of Green Mountain Coffee's financial statements reveals that the wide margin by which the company beat earnings forecast was not due to stellar performance but to an accounting anomaly. Its statement of cash flows reveals an unusual (negative) accrual of $22,259 thousand for sales returns for the second quarter of fiscal 2011. GAAP requires that firms report revenues net of anticipated sales returns. Companies use their historical experience with product returns to determine the sales returns expense (a debit on the income statement) with an offsetting entry to a sales-return allowance (a credit balance on the balance sheet). When customers return products, the company reduces the allowance for sales returns on the balance sheet. At the end of the quarter, the company estimates sales returns for the current quarters' sales, records the appropriate expense on the income statement, and updates the sales-return allowance. It is atypical for a company to have a negative expense for sales returns. A negative sales-return expense (a "reversal") increases revenues and earnings. This is what Green Mountain Coffee reported in 2Q 2011. On an after-tax basis, the reversal increased Green Mountain Coffee's net income by $14,468 thousand or about $0.10 per share (147,558,595 shares diluted outstanding at March 26, 2011). A skeptical analyst might conclude that it recorded a negative accrual to beat the Street's expectations. Such behavior hinders the quality of reported earnings.

GLOBAL ACCOUNTING

IFRS

We discussed the reporting of operating income, including revenue measurement and the timing of revenue recognition. However, companies reporting under IFRS are likely to recognize revenues earlier for the following reasons:

1. U.S. GAAP has specific guidance about what constitutes revenue, how revenue is measured, and the timing of its recognition. Also, U.S. GAAP has extensive, industry-specific revenue recognition guidelines. IFRS is not specific about the timing and measurement of revenue recognition and does not provide industry-specific guidance. With less detailed guidance, the general management preference for reporting income earlier will likely prevail.
2. A U.S. GAAP revenue-recognition criterion is that the sales price be fixed or determinable. This means that if a sale involves contingent consideration, no revenue is recognized until the contingency is resolved. IFRS considers the probability that economic benefits will flow to the seller and records such benefits as revenue if they can be reliably measured. This means contingent revenue is recognized earlier under IFRS.
3. For multiple-element contracts, both U.S. GAAP and IFRS allocate revenue based on relative fair values of the elements. However, IFRS requires fair-value estimates that are less restrictive.
4. U.S. GAAP permits the use of completed contract method, which is disallowed under IFRS.

BUSINESS INSIGHT **Pro Forma Income and Managerial Motives**

The purported motive for reporting pro forma income is to eliminate transitory (one-time) items to enhance year-to-year comparability. Although this might be justified on the basis that pro forma income has greater predictive ability, important information is lost in the process. One role for accounting is to report how effective management has been in its stewardship of invested capital. Asset write-downs, liability accruals, and other charges that are eliminated in calculating pro forma income often reflect outcomes of poor management decisions. Our analysis must not blindly eliminate information contained in nonrecurring items by focusing solely on pro forma income. Critics of pro forma income also argue that the items excluded by managers from GAAP income are inconsistent across companies and time. They contend that a major motive for pro forma income is to mislead stakeholders. Legendary investor Warren Buffett puts pro forma in context: ***"When companies or investment professionals use terms such as 'EBITDA' and 'pro forma,' they want you to unthinkingly accept concepts that are dangerously flawed."*** (Berkshire Hathaway, Annual Report)

For these reasons, our analysis of companies reporting under IFRS is likely to find higher revenues (and net income). This front-loading of revenues is likely more pronounced for high revenue-growth companies and for industries with more multiple-element contracts.

We also discussed several expenses in this module, including research and development. There are differences between U.S. GAAP and IFRS for R&D. U.S. GAAP expenses all R&D costs whereas IFRS allows capitalization and subsequent amortization of certain development costs. For some companies and some industries this can create differences for both the balance sheet and income statement. For analysis purposes, we must review the R&D footnote of IFRS companies to determine the development costs capitalized for the period and the amount of amortization of previously capitalized costs. The difference between these two amounts represents the additional pretax expense that would be reported under U.S. GAAP. The IFRS intangible asset footnote reports the unamortized development costs, which represents the net asset that would not appear on a U.S. GAAP balance sheet (with the off-setting entries to deferred taxes and retained earnings).

The module also considered restructuring expenses. There are differences between IFRS and U.S. GAAP on restructuring, but most are minor. The following differences relate to timing:

- Under IFRS, restructuring expense is recognized when there is a plan for the restructuring and if the affected employees expect the plan to be implemented. Under U.S. GAAP, restructuring expense can be recognized earlier because the trigger is managerial approval of a plan.
- Under IFRS, compensation for employees who will be terminated is recognized when employees are deemed redundant. Under U.S. GAAP, restructuring expense can be recognized later, when the employees have been informed.

The following difference relates to the restructuring expense amount:

- Consistent with other accruals under IFRS, a restructuring provision is recorded at its best estimate. This is usually the expected value or, in the case of a range of possible outcomes that are equally likely, the provision is recorded at the midpoint of the range. The U.S. GAAP estimate is at the most-likely outcome; and if there is a range of possible outcomes, the provision is recorded as the minimum amount of the range.

This means that the financial statement differences between IFRS and U.S. GAAP for restructurings cannot be predicted unequivocally. We must review the restructuring footnote; and remember that cumulative expense is the same under both reporting systems.

We also described tax expenses. There are three notable differences: two affect the income statement and one affects the balance sheet. With respect to the income statement:

1. Both U.S. GAAP and IFRS recognize deferred tax assets for timing differences and unused tax losses. However, under U.S. GAAP, a valuation allowance is set up if it is more likely than not (probability > 50%) that some portion of the deferred tax assets will not be utilized. Under IFRS, the deferred tax asset is only recognized to the extent that the future benefit is probable (probability > 50%). That is, there is no deferred tax asset if the company does not expect to earn enough

taxable profit in the future to use the tax credit. This means there are no valuation allowances in IFRS. The net effect on income is identical but our review of an IFRS tax footnote will not involve assessing the adequacy of the allowance or the extent to which changes in the allowance affect net income.

2. Under IFRS, deferred tax assets on employee stock options are computed based on the options' intrinsic value at each reporting date. In contrast, GAAP uses historical value. This results in more volatile tax expense under IFRS.

With respect to the balance sheet, all deferred tax assets and liabilities are classified as long-term under IFRS. This will impact metrics and ratios that involve current assets and liabilities and could affect our comparative assessment of liquidity.

Finally, recall that separate reporting of extraordinary items is not permitted under IFRS. When comparing U.S. GAAP to IFRS, we include any extraordinary items with other expenses, according to their function.

MODULE-END REVIEW

Refer to the Merck & Co., Inc., 2012 income statement in the Mid-Module Review.

Required

1. Assume that during 2012 the $US weakened with respect to the currencies in which Merck conducts its business. How would that weakening affect Merck's income statement?
2. What is the difference between basic and diluted earnings per share?

The solution is on page 5-69.

APPENDIX 5A: Proposed Revenue Recognition Standard

The FASB has proposed a new revenue recognition standard that will become effective in 2017. Under the proposed standard, revenue recognition should occur *when (or as) a good or service is transferred to the customer and the customer obtains control of that good or service*. The recognition of revenue does not need to coincide with the receipt of cash. Companies can receive cash before, concurrent with, or after the recognition of revenue. What is important for the recognition of revenue is that the customer take control over the product or service and, therefore, obtain all of the remaining benefits from the product or service.

For many transactions; the process is straightforward. For example, when Pfizer's customers receive the drugs they have ordered (and are obligated to make payment for their purchases) Pfizer can recognize revenue. However, many transactions are not quite as simple. Following are typical features of transactions that can complicate revenue recognition:

- **Collectibility of amount owed.** When Pfizer sells to its customers on credit, it knows from previous experience that a portion of its receivables will ultimately become uncollectible. Pfizer can still recognize the revenue, as the customer has received (and, therefore, controls) the products ordered, but Pfizer will establish a reserve for estimated uncollectible accounts that reduces the receivables on its balance sheet and records the reduction as an expense. This means that Pfizer records the full amount of the sale along with an estimate of the expense for uncollectible accounts receivable, thus recognizing only that portion of the sales that it expects to collect. (We discuss the allowance for uncollectible accounts in Module 6.) However, if the company expects in advance that collectibility for a *specific* account is in doubt (as opposed to a general expectation about all accounts), a contract with that particular customer may not, in fact, exist and revenue recognition on that sale is unjustified.
- **Rights of return.** Many companies offer a right to return a product. This right can apply to a defective product or to a customer's change-of-mind. Companies offering a right to return will recognize revenue for the amount of the net purchase price that it expects to keep (sales less anticipated product returns) and record a liability for the refund it expects to pay to its customers. (We discuss accounting for rights of return in Module 6.)

- **Consignment sales.** If the seller acts as an agent for another company, say where it might sell another company's product on its Website, it does not recognize the gross amount of the sale as revenue. Instead, it only recognizes its commission from the sale. Indicators that the seller is an agent include: another company is responsible for fulfillment of the contract; the seller does not have the risk of loss of the inventory being sold; the seller does not have full control over product selling price; the seller does not bear the risk of loss for uncollectible accounts receivable; and the seller receives commission or other fee from the sale.
- **Licenses.** Software sales can take the form of licensing arrangements of intellectual property (IP). Revenue recognition depends on whether the arrangement confers a "right" to use the IP (arguing for immediate recognition of revenue) or whether the contract provides a promise to provide access to the company's IP (which would argue for revenue recognition over a period of time).

In these and other transactions, especially those that occur over an extended period of time, the revenue recognition process often requires considerable judgment (see our text box on the revenue recognition process below). The difficulty in determining when revenue should be recognized has led, and will continue to lead, to errors in judgment and outright abuse.

BUSINESS INSIGHT **Proposed Revenue Recognition Process**

To illustrate the complexity in revenue recognition, consider that the revenue recognition standard requires a five-step approach:

Step 1: Identify the contract with the customer

- The contract can be written or oral or implied by the company's customary business practice. Companies need to apply the revenue recognition standard to *each* contract, unless contracts are combined.

Step 2: Identify the separate performance obligations in the contract

- Identifying the separate performance obligations in a contract is essential to applying the revenue recognition model as the satisfaction of those separate performance obligations determines the timing of revenue recognition.
- A promised good or service is a separate performance obligation if the customer can benefit on its own from the good or service and the contract specifies distinct products or services that are not highly dependent upon, or integrated with, other goods or services promised under the contract.
- A company will combine goods or services if they are not individually separable. If the goods or services are provided in a series, the company needs to assess whether the contract is a single performance obligation or whether it contains multiple performance obligations that need to be separately analyzed.

Step 3: Determine the transaction price

- Complications arise when the contract contains payments that are variable or contingent upon other events. If the contract price can be reduced, say by discounts, credits, royalties, etc., the company will recognize revenue as performance obligations are satisfied only up to an amount that is not subject to significant price reversals. Further, the company can only recognize revenues relating to contingencies about which it has relevant previous experience.
- The transaction price should be adjusted for the time value of money when the contract contains a significant financing component, unless the payment stream is one year or less. Companies may have difficulty determining whether a significant financing component exists in contracts that provide for goods or services to be delivered and cash payments received at multiple points in the contract life.

continued

Step 4: Allocate the transaction price to separate performance obligations

- The transaction price will be allocated to separate performance obligations *based on the relative stand-alone selling prices of the goods or services promised*. Management will need to estimate the selling price if a stand-alone selling price is not available. Complications may arise in the presence of discounts or other rebates that should be applied to the price of the contract as companies will need to determine which elements of the contract should be affected.
- This allocation process is critical as it determines the amount of revenue that will be recognized when the performance obligation is satisfied.

Step 5: Recognize revenue when (or as) each performance obligation is satisfied

- An entity will recognize revenue when (or as) a good or service is transferred to the customer and the customer obtains control of that good or service.
- Control of an asset refers to an entity's ability to direct the use of, and obtain substantially all of the remaining benefits from, the asset.
- For performance obligations that are satisfied over time, an entity will recognize revenue over time. This revenue recognition can occur in a variety of ways: the customer receives and consumes the benefits of the entity's performance as the entity performs (i.e., service contracts), the company's performance creates or enhances an asset (work-in-progress) that the customer controls (i.e., most construction contracts), or the company's performance does not create an asset with an alternative use to the company and the customer does not have control over the asset created, but the company has a right to payment for performance completed to date (i.e., highly customized products).
- The revenue recognition standard continues to allow the use of the percentage-of-completion method to the extent that a customer controls the work-in-process. If the customer specifies the design or function of a construction project, which is most often the case, the customer is considered to have control of the work-in-process. If the customer does not control the work-in-process, revenue is recorded at the completion of the project. Companies will be able to use many of the methods currently employed to administer the percentage-of-completion method, including "output methods" that recognize revenue based on units produced or delivered, contract milestones, or surveys of work performed, and "input methods" that recognize revenue based on costs incurred, labor hours expended, time lapsed, or machine hours used.

APPENDIX 5B: Expanded Explanation of Deferred Taxes

The module provided an example of how different depreciation methods for tax and financial reporting create a deferred tax liability. That example showed that total depreciation over the life of the asset is the same under both tax and financial reporting, and that the only difference is the timing of the expense or tax deduction. Because depreciation differs each year, the amount at which the equipment is reported will differ as well for book and tax purposes (cost less accumulated depreciation is called *net book value* for financial reporting purposes and *tax basis* for tax purposes). These book vs tax differences are eliminated at the end of the asset's useful life.

To understand this concept more completely, we modify the example from the module to include a third year. Assume that the company purchases PPE assets at the start of Year 1 for $120. For financial reporting purposes, the company uses straight-line depreciation and records depreciation of $40 each year (with zero salvage). For tax purposes, assume that the company takes tax depreciation deductions of $60, $50, and $10. Exhibit 5B.1 reports the annual depreciation along with the asset's net book value and its tax basis, for each year-end.

EXHIBIT 5B.1 Book and Tax Depreciation and Carrying Value

	Financial Reporting (Net Book Value)	Tax Reporting (Tax Basis)	Book vs Tax Difference	Deferred Tax Liability (Book vs Tax Difference × Tax Rate)	Deferred Tax Expense (Increase or Decrease in Deferred Tax Liability)
At purchase: PPE carrying value	$120	$120	$ 0	$ 0	
Year 1: Depreciation	(40)	(60)			
End of Year 1: PPE carrying value . . .	80	60	$20 ($80 − $60)	$ 8 ($20 × 40%)	$ 8 ($8 − $0)
Year 2: Depreciation	(40)	(50)			
End of Year 2: PPE carrying value . . .	40	10	$30 ($40 − $10)	$12 ($30 × 40%)	$ 4 ($12 − $8)
Year 3: Depreciation	(40)	(10)			
End of Year 3: PPE carrying value . . .	0	0	$ 0 ($0 − $0)	$ 0	$(12) ($0 − $12)

The third column in Exhibit 5B.1 shows the "book-tax" difference, which is the difference between GAAP net book value and the tax basis at the end of each year. The fourth column shows the deferred tax liability at the end of each period, computed as the book-tax differences times the tax rate. We see from the fourth column that when the financial reporting net book value is greater than the tax basis, the company has a deferred tax liability on its balance sheet (as in Years 1 and 2). Companies' footnotes provide information about deferred taxes. For example, **Pfizer**'s footnote reports a deferred tax liability (net) of $977 million for its property, plant and equipment (computed from the liability of $1,485 million less the asset of $508 million), which indicates that tax basis for PPE is less than GAAP net book value, on average, for Pfizer's PPE.

Accounting standards require a company to first compute the taxes it owes (per its tax return), then to compute any changes in deferred tax liabilities and assets, and finally to compute tax expense reported in the income statement (as a residual amount). Thus, tax expense is not computed as pretax income multiplied by the company's tax rate as we might initially expect. Instead, tax expense is computed as follows:

Tax Expense = Taxes Paid − Increase (or + Decrease) in Deferred Tax Assets + Increase (or − Decrease) in Deferred Liabilities

The far-right column in Exhibit 5B.1 shows the deferred tax expense per year, which is the amount added to, or subtracted from, taxes paid, to arrive at tax expense. If we assume this company had $100 of pre-depreciation income, its taxable income and tax expense (assuming a 40% rate) follows:

	Taxes Paid	Deferred Tax Expense	Total Tax Expense
Year 1	$16 ($100 − $60) × 40%	$ 8	$24
Year 2	$20 ($100 − $50) × 40%	$ 4	$24
Year 3	$36 ($100 − $10) × 40%	$(12)	$24

In this example, the timing difference between the financial reporting and tax reporting derives from PPE and creates a deferred tax liability. Other differences between the two sets of books create other types of deferred tax accounts. Exhibit 5B.2 shows the relation between the financial reporting and tax reporting net book values, and the resulting deferred taxes (liability or asset) on the balance sheet.

EXHIBIT 5B.2 Sources of Deferred Tax Assets and Liabilities

For Assets...				
Financial reporting net book value	>	Tax reporting net book value	→	Deferred tax liability on balance sheet
Financial reporting net book value	<	Tax reporting net book value	→	Deferred tax asset on balance sheet
For Liabilities...				
Financial reporting net book value	<	Tax reporting net book value	→	Deferred tax liability on balance sheet
Financial reporting net book value	>	Tax reporting net book value	→	Deferred tax asset on balance sheet

A common deferred tax asset relates to accrued restructuring costs (a liability for financial reporting purposes). Restructuring costs are not deductible for tax purposes until paid in the future and, thus, there is no accrual restructuring liability for tax reporting, which means it has a tax basis of $0. To explain how this timing difference affects tax expense, assume that a company accrues $300 of restructuring costs in Year 1 and settles the liability in Year 2 as follows:

	Financial Reporting (Net Book Value)	Tax Reporting (Tax Basis)	Book vs Tax Difference	Deferred Tax Asset (Book vs Tax Difference × Tax Rate)	Deferred Tax Expense (Change in Deferred Tax Asset)
Year 1: Accrue restructuring costs . . .	$(300)	$ 0			
End of Year 1: Liability book value . . .	$ 300	$ 0	$300 ($300 − $0)	$120 ($300 × 40%)	$(120) ($120 − $0)
Year 2: Pay restructuring costs		$(300)			
End of Year 2: Liability book value . . .	$ 0	0	$ 0 ($0 − $0)	$ 0 ($0 × 40%)	$120 ($120 − $0)

Timing differences created by the restructuring liability yield a deferred tax asset in Year 1. Timing differences disappear in Year 2 when the company pays cash for restructuring costs. To see how tax expense is determined, assume that this company has $500 of pre-restructuring income each year; computations follow:

	Taxes Paid	Deferred Tax Expense	Total Tax Expense
Year 1	$200 ($500 − $0) × 40%	$(120)	$ 80
Year 2	$ 80 ($500 − $300) × 40%	$ 120	$200

Deferred tax accounts derive from timing differences between GAAP expenses and tax deductions. This creates differences between the net book value and the tax basis for many assets and liabilities. Pfizer's deferred tax footnote (see Exhibit 5.6) reports several deferred tax assets and liabilities that explain its book-tax difference and the tax basis. As we saw above, Pfizer's 2012 deferred tax liability associated with PPE is $977 million ($1,485 million liability less $508 million asset). This reflects the cumulative tax savings to Pfizer from accelerated depreciation for its PPE. If we assume a tax rate of 35%, we can compute the book-tax difference for Pfizer's PPE as $2,791 million ($977 million/0.35). Its balance sheet reveals total PPE of $14,461, which implies that the tax basis for these assets is $11,670 million ($14,461 − $2,791).

GUIDANCE ANSWERS

MANAGERIAL DECISION You Are the Financial Analyst

Typically, restructuring charges have three components: asset write-downs (such as inventories, property, plant, and goodwill), severance costs, and other restructuring-related expenses. Write-downs occur when the cash-flow-generating ability of an asset declines, thus reducing its current market value below its book value reported on the balance sheet. Arguably, this decline in cash-flow-generating ability did not occur solely in the current year and, most likely, has developed over several periods. It is not uncommon for companies to delay loss recognition, such as write-downs of assets. Thus, prior period income is, arguably, not as high as reported, and the current period loss is not as great as reported. Turning to severance and other costs, GAAP permits restructuring expense to include only those costs that are *incremental* and will *not* benefit future periods. The accrual of restructuring-related expenses can be viewed like other accruals; that is, it might be over- or understated. In future periods, the required reconciliation of the restructuring accrual will provide insight into the adequacy of the accrual in that earlier period.

Superscript A(B) denotes assignments based on Appendix 5A (5B).

DISCUSSION QUESTIONS

Q5-1. What are the criteria that guide firms in recognition of revenue? What does each of the criteria mean? How are the criteria met for a company like **Abercrombie & Fitch**, a clothing retailer? How are the criteria met for a construction company that builds offices under long-term contracts with developers?

Abercrombie & Fitch (ANF)

Q5-2. Why are extraordinary items reported separately from continuing operations in the income statement?

Q5-3. What are the criteria for categorizing an event as an extraordinary item? Provide an example of an event that would properly be categorized as an extraordinary item and one that would not. How does this accounting treatment differ for IFRS?

Q5-4. What is the difference between basic earnings per share and diluted earnings per share? Are potentially dilutive securities always included in the EPS computation?

Q5-5. What effect, if any, does a weakening $US have on reported sales and net income for companies operating outside the United States?

Q5-6. Identify the three typical categories of restructuring costs and their effects on the balance sheet and the income statement. Explain the concept of a big bath and why restructuring costs are often identified with this event.

Q5-7. What is the current U.S. GAAP accounting treatment for research and development costs? How does this accounting treatment differ for IFRS? Why are R&D costs normally not capitalized under U.S. GAAP?

Q5-8. Under what circumstances will deferred taxes likely result in a cash outflow?

Q5-9. What is the concept of pro forma income and why has this income measure been criticized?

Q5-10. What is unearned revenue? Provide three examples of unearned revenue.

Assignments with the logo in the margin are available in myBusinessCourse. See the Preface of the book for details.

MINI EXERCISES

M5-11. Computing Percentage-of-Completion Revenues (LO1)
Bartov Corporation agreed to build a warehouse for a client at an agreed contract price of $300,500. Expected (and actual) costs for the warehouse follow: 2013, $80,000; 2014, $150,000; and 2015, $40,500. The company completed the warehouse in 2015. Compute revenues, expenses, and income for each year 2013 through 2015 using the percentage-of-completion method. (Round percents to the nearest whole number.)

M5-12. Applying the Financial Statement Effects Template. (LO1)
Refer to the information for Bartov Corporation in M5-11.

a. Use the financial statement effects template to record contract revenues and expenses for each year 2013 through 2015 using the percentage-of-completion method.
b. Prepare journal entries and T-accounts to record contract revenues and expenses for each year 2013 through 2015 using the percentage-of-completion method.

M5-13. Assessing Revenue Recognition of Companies (LO1)
Identify and explain when each of the following companies should recognize revenue.

The GAP (GPS)
Merck & Company (MRK)
Deere & Company (DE)
Bank of America (BAC)
Johnson Controls (JCI)

a. The GAP: The GAP is a retailer of clothing items for all ages.
b. Merck & Company: Merck engages in developing, manufacturing, and marketing pharmaceutical products. It sells its drugs to retailers like CVS and Walgreen.
c. Deere & Company: Deere manufactures heavy equipment. It sells equipment to a network of independent distributors, who in turn sell the equipment to customers. Deere provides financing and insurance services both to distributors and customers.
d. Bank of America: Bank of America is a banking institution. It lends money to individuals and corporations and invests excess funds in marketable securities.
e. Johnson Controls: Johnson Controls manufactures products for the government under long-term contracts.

M5-14. Assessing Risk Exposure to Revenue Recognition (LO1)
BannerAD Corporation manages a Website that sells products on consignment from sellers. It pays these sellers a portion of the sales price, and charges a commission. Identify two potential revenue recognition problems relating to such sales.

M5-15. Estimating Revenue Recognition with Right of Return (LO1)
ModCloth, Inc.
ModCloth, Inc. offers an unconditional return policy. It normally expects 2% of sales at retail selling prices to be returned before the return period expires. Assuming that ModCloth records total sales of $10 million for the current period, what amount of *net* sales should it record for this period?

M5-16. Assessing Research and Development Expenses (LO2)
Abbott Laboratories (ABT)
Abbott Laboratories reports the following (summary) income statement.

Year Ended December 31 ($ millions)	2012
Net sales.	$39,874
Cost of products sold.	(15,120)
Research and development*	(4,610)
Selling, general and administrative	(12,059)
Pretax operating earnings	$ 8,085

* Includes acquired in process research and development.

a. Compute the percent of net sales that Abbott Laboratories spends on research and development (R&D). Compare this level of expenditure with the percentages for other companies that are discussed in the Business Insight box on page 5-15. How would you assess the appropriateness of its R&D expense level?

b. Describe how accounting for R&D expenditures affects Abbott Laboratories' balance sheet and income statement.

M5-17. Interpreting Foreign Currency Translation Disclosure (LO4)

Bristol-Myers Squibb (BMY) reports the following table in its 10-K report relating to the change in sales from 2011 to 2012.

Bristol-Myers Squibb (BMY)

		Analysis of % Change		
Net Sales	Total Change	Volume	Price	Foreign Exchange
United States[(a)]	(26)%	(30)%	4%	—
Europe[(b)]	(4)%	6%	(3)%	(7)%
Rest of the World[(c)]	(1)%	2%	(1)%	(2)%
Total	(17)%	(17)%	2%	(2)%

(a) Includes Puerto Rico.
(b) Includes Russia and Turkey.
(c) Includes Japan, China, Canada, Australia and Brazil, among other countries.
** Change in excess of 100%.

a. Did U.S. net sales increase or decrease during the year? By what percentage? How much of this change is attributable to volume versus price changes?

b. By what percentage did foreign net sales change during the year? How much of this change is attributable to volume versus price changes?

c. Why does the change in total net sales (17%) not equal the sum of the changes in U.S. of (26%), Europe net sales of (4)% and "Rest of the World" net sales of (1)%?

M5-18. Analyzing Income Tax Disclosure (LO3)

Dell Inc. reports the following footnote disclosure to its 2013 10-K report ($ millions).

Dell Inc. (DELL)

The provision for income taxes consisted of the following:

Fiscal Year Ended	February 1, 2013
Federal	
Current	$630
Deferred	(297)
	333
State	
Current	76
Deferred	(23)
	53
Foreign	
Current	191
Deferred	(108)
	83
Total	$469

a. What amount of income tax expense does Dell report in its income statement for 2013?
b. How much of Dell's income tax expense is current (as opposed to deferred)?
c. Why do deferred tax assets and liabilities arise? How do they impact the tax expense that Dell reports in its 2013 income statement?

M5-19. Defining and Computing Earnings per Share (LO5)

Cleantech Solutions International (CLNT)

Cleantech Solutions International reports the following information in footnotes to its 2012 Form 10-K.

Net income available to common shareholders for basic and diluted net income per common share	$4,198,580
Weighted average common shares outstanding—basic	2,538,246
Effect of dilutive securities:	
Series A convertible preferred stock	103,149
Warrants	7,648
Weighted average common shares outstanding—diluted	$2,649,043

a. Explain the concepts of basic and diluted earnings per share.
b. Compute basic and diluted EPS for 2012.
c. What is the effect of dilutive securities on EPS, in percentage terms?

M5-20. Assessing Revenue Recognition for Advance Payments (LO1)

Koonce Company operates a performing arts center. The company sells tickets for its upcoming season of six Broadway musicals and receives $540,000 cash. The performances occur monthly over the next six months.

a. When should Koonce record revenue for the Broadway musical series?
b. Use the financial statement effects template to show the $540,000 cash receipt and recognition of the first month's revenue.

M5-21. Reporting Unearned Revenue (LO1)

Target Corporation (TGT)

Target Corporation sells gift cards that can be used at any of the company's Target or Greatland stores. Target encodes information on the card's magnetic strip about the card's value, and the store where it was purchased. Target gift cards do not have expiration dates.

a. How will Target's balance sheet reflect the gift card? Will the balance sheet amount of these cards be classified as current or noncurrent?
b. When does Target record revenue from the gift card?

EXERCISES

E5-22. Assessing Revenue Recognition Timing (LO1)

Explain when each of the following businesses should recognize revenues:

American Eagle Outfitters, Inc. (AEO)
Boeing Co. (BA)
Supervalu, Inc. (SVU)
MTV
Bank of America Corp. (BAC)
Harley-Davidson Inc. (HOG)
Time-Warner Inc. (TWX)

a. A clothing retailer like **American Eagle Outfitters, Inc.**
b. A contractor like **Boeing Company** that performs work under long-term government contracts.
c. A grocery store like **Supervalu Inc.**
d. A producer of television shows like **MTV** that syndicates its content to television stations.
e. A residential real estate developer that constructs only speculative houses and later sells these houses to buyers.
f. A banking institution like **Bank of America Corp.** that lends money for home mortgages.
g. A manufacturer like **Harley-Davidson Inc.**
h. A publisher of magazines such as **Time-Warner Inc.**

E5-23. Assessing Revenue Recognition Timing and Income Measurement (LO1)

Explain when each of the following businesses should recognize revenue and identify any income measurement issues that could arise.

a. RealMoney.Com, a division of **TheStreet, Inc.**, provides investment advice to customers for an up-front fee. It provides these customers with password-protected access to its Website where customers can download investment reports. RealMoney has an obligation to provide updates on its Website. TheStreet, Inc. (TST)

b. **Oracle Corp.** develops general ledger and other business application software that it sells to its customers. The customer pays an up-front fee for the right to use the software and a monthly fee for support services. Oracle Corp. (ORCL)

c. **Intuit Inc.** develops tax preparation software that it sells to its customers for a flat fee. No further payment is required and the software cannot be returned, only exchanged if defective. Intuit Inc. (INTU)

d. A developer of computer games sells its software with a 10-day right of return period during which the software can be returned for a full refund. After the 10-day period has expired, the software cannot be returned.

E5-24. Constructing and Assessing Income Statements Using Percentage-of-Completion (LO1)

General Electric Company (GE)

Assume that **General Electric Company** agreed in May 2013 to construct a nuclear generator for NSTAR, a utility company serving the Boston area. The contract price of $600 million is to be paid as follows: $200 million at the time of signing; $200 million on December 31, 2013; and $200 million at completion in May 2014. General Electric incurred the following costs in constructing the generator: $200 million in 2013, and $300 million in 2014.

a. Compute the amount of General Electric's revenue, expense, and income for both 2013 and 2014 under the percentage-of-completion revenue recognition method.

b. Discuss whether or not you believe the percentage-of-completion method provides a good measure of General Electric's performance under the contract.

E5-25. Constructing and Assessing Income Statements Using Percentage-of-Completion (LO1) ✔

On March 15, 2014, Frankel Construction contracted to build a shopping center at a contract price of $125 million. The schedule of expected (which equals actual) cash collections and contract costs follows:

Year	Cash Collections	Cost Incurred
2014	$ 30 million	$ 20 million
2015	50 million	45 million
2016	45 million	35 million
Total	$125 million	$100 million

a. Calculate the amount of revenue, expense, and net income for each of the three years 2014 through 2016 using the percentage-of-completion revenue recognition method. (Round percents to the nearest whole number.)

b. Discuss whether or not the percentage-of-completion method provides a good measure of this construction company's performance under the contract.

E5-26. Interpreting the Income Tax Expense Footnote (LO3) ✔

FedEx Corp (FDX)

The income tax footnote to the financial statements of **FedEx Corporation** follows.

The components of the provision for income taxes for the years ended May 31 were as follows:

($ millions)	2013	2012	2011
Current provision (benefit)			
Domestic			
Federal	**$512**	$ (120)	$ 79
State and local	**86**	80	48
Foreign	**170**	181	198
	768	141	325
Deferred provision (benefit)			
Domestic			
Federal	**175**	947	485
State and local	**(7)**	21	12
Foreign	**(42)**	—	(9)
	126	968	488
	$894	$1,109	$813

a. What is the amount of income tax expense reported in FedEx's 2013, 2012, and 2011 income statements?
b. What percentage of total tax expense is currently payable in each year?
c. One possible reason for the $968 million deferred tax expense in 2012 is that deferred tax liabilities increased during that year. Provide an example that gives rise to an increase in the deferred tax liability.

E5-27. Identifying Operating Income Components (LO2)
Following is the income statement information from Apollo Medical Devices. Identify the components that we would consider operating.

($ in thousands)	2013
Net sales	$4,163,770
Cost of sales before special charges	1,382,235
Special inventory obsolescence charge	27,876
Total cost of sales	1,410,111
Gross profit	2,753,659
Selling, general and administrative expense	1,570,667
Research and development expense	531,086
Merger and acquisition costs	46,914
In-process research and development charges	12,244
Litigation settlement	16,500
Operating profit	576,248
Interest expense	(57,372)
Interest income	2,076
Gain on disposal of fixed assets	4,929
Impairment of marketable securities	(5,222)
Other income (expense), net	(2,857)
Earnings before income taxes	517,802
Income tax expense	191,587
Net earnings	$ 326,215

Deere & Company (DE)

E5-28. Identifying Operating Income Components (LO2)
Following is the Deere & Company income statement for 2012.

($ millions)	2012
Net sales and revenues	
Net sales	$33,500.9
Finance and interest income	1,981.3
Other income	674.9
Total	36,157.1

continued

Costs and expenses	
Cost of sales	25,007.8
Research and development expenses	1,433.6
Selling, administrative and general expenses	3,417.0
Interest expense	782.8
Other operating expenses	781.5
Total	31,422.7
Income of consolidated group before income taxes	4,734.4
Provision for income taxes	1,659.4
Income of consolidated group	3,075.0
Equity in income of unconsolidated affiliates	(3.4)
Net income	3,071.6
Less: Net income attributable to noncontrolling interests	6.9
Net income attributable to Deere & Company	$ 3,064.7

Notes:

- Income statement includes John Deere commercial and consumer tractor segment, a finance subsidiary that provides loan and lease financing relating to the sales of those tractors, and a health care segment that provides managed health care services for the company and certain outside customers.
- **Equity in income of unconsolidated affiliates** refers to income John Deere has earned on investments in affiliated (but unconsolidated) companies. These are generally investments made for strategic purposes.

a. Identify the components in its income statement that you would consider operating.

b. Discuss your treatment of the company's finance and interest income that relates to financing of its John Deere lawn and garden, and commercial tractors.

E5-29. Assessing the Income Tax Footnote (LO3)

Colgate-Palmolive reports the following income tax footnote disclosure in its 10-K report.

Colgate-Palmolive (CL)

Deferred Tax Balances at December 31 (In millions)	2012	2011
Deferred tax liabilities		
Goodwill and intangible assets	$ (476)	$(471)
Property, plant and equipment	(365)	(345)
Other	(162)	(104)
	(1,003)	(920)
Deferred tax assets		
Pension and other retiree benefits	544	480
Tax loss and tax credit carryforwards	61	105
Accrued liabilities	208	176
Stock-based compensation	113	115
Other	151	111
	1,077	987
Net deferred income taxes	$ 74	$ 67

a. Colgate reports $365 million of deferred tax liabilities in 2012 relating to "Property." Explain how such liabilities arise.

b. Describe how a deferred tax asset can arise from pension and other retiree benefits.

c. Colgate reports $61 million in deferred tax assets for 2012 relating to tax loss and credit carryforwards. Describe how tax loss carryforwards arise and under what conditions the resulting deferred tax assets will be realized.

d. Colgate's income statement reports income tax expense of $1,243 million. Assume that cash paid for income tax is $1,280 million and that taxes payable decreased by $30 million. Use the financial statement effects template to record tax expense for 2012. (*Hint*: Show the effects of changes in deferred taxes.)

Advanced Micro Devices, Inc. (AMD)

Intel Corp. (INTC)

E5-30. Analyzing and Assessing Research and Development Expenses (LO2)

Advanced Micro Devices, Inc. (AMD) and Intel Corp. (INTC) are competitors in the computer processor industry. Following is a table ($ millions) of sales and R&D expenses for both companies.

AMD	R&D Expense	Sales
2012	$1,354	$5,422
2011	1,453	6,598
2010	1,405	6,494

INTC	R&D Expense	Sales
2012	$10,148	$53,341
2011	8,530	53,999
2010	6,576	43,623

a. What percentage of sales are AMD and INTC spending on research and development?

b. How are AMD and INTC's balance sheets and income statements affected by the accounting for R&D costs?

c. How can one evaluate the effectiveness of R&D spending? Does the difference in R&D as a percentage of sales necessarily imply that one company is more heavily invested in R&D? Why might this not be the case?

Kellogg Co. (K)

E5-31. Analyzing and Interpreting Foreign Currency Translation Effects (LO4)

Kellogg Co. reports the following table and discussion in its 2012 10-K.

The following table provides an analysis of net sales and operating profit performance for 2012 versus 2011 for our reportable segments:

(dollars in millions)	U.S Morning Foods & Kashi	U.S. Snacks	U.S. Specialty	North America Other	Europe	Latin America	Asia Pacific
2012 net sales	**$3,707**	**$3,226**	**$1,121**	**$1,485**	**$2,527**	**$1,121**	**$1,010**
2011 net sales	**$3,611**	**$2,883**	**$1,008**	**$1,371**	**$ 2,334**	**$1,049**	**$ 942**
% change — 2012 vs. 2011:							
Internal business[a]	**2.7%**	**1.9%**	**7.4%**	**7.0%**	**(3.8)%**	**6.7%**	**2.7%**
Acquisitions[b]	—%	10.0%	3.8%	1.8%	16.6%	4.2%	10.9%
Dispositions[c]	—%	—%	—%	—%	—%	—%	(3.4)%
Integration impact[d]	—%	—%	—%	—%	—%	—%	(0.1)%
Foreign currency impact. . . .	—%	—%	—%	(0.5)%	(4.5)%	(4.1)%	(2.8)%
Total change	**2.7%**	**11.9%**	**11.2%**	**8.3%**	**8.3%**	**6.8%**	**7.3%**

(dollars in millions)	U.S Morning Foods & Kashi	U.S. Snacks	U.S. Specialty	North America Other	Europe	Latin America	Asia Pacific
2012 operating profit	**$ 595**	**$ 469**	**$ 241**	**$ 265**	**$ 261**	**$ 167**	**$ 85**
2011 operating profit	**$ 611**	**$ 437**	**$ 231**	**$ 250**	**$ 302**	**$ 176**	**$ 104**
% change — 2012 vs. 2011:							
Internal business[a]	(2.7)%	(0.8)%	(1.2%	5.2%	(15.8)%	(3.7)%	(28.7)%
Acquisitions[b]	—%	12.4%	3.1%	1.7%	12.6%	2.6%	7.6%
Dispositions[c]	—%	—%	—%	—%	—%	—%	9.7%
Integration impact[d]	—%	(4.3)%	—%	—%	(8.0)%	(0.4)%	(4.5)%
Foreign currency impact. . . .	—%	—%	—%	(0.7)%	(2.3)%	(3.5)%	(2.5)%
Total change	**(2.7)%**	**7.3%**	**4.3%**	**6.2%**	**(13.5)%**	**(5.0)%**	**(18.4)%**

[a] Internal net sales and operating profit growth for 2012, exclude the impact of acquisitions, divestitures, integration costs and the impact of currency. Internal net sales and operating profit growth are non-GAAP financial measures which are reconciled to the directly comparable measures in accordance with U.S. GAAP within these tables.

[b] Impact of results for year ended December 29, 2012 from the acquisition of Pringles.

[c] Impact of results for year ended December 29, 2012 from the divestiture of Navigable Foods.

[d] Includes impact of integration costs associated with the Pringles acquisition.

Foreign exchange risk Our Company is exposed to fluctuations in foreign currency cash flows related to third-party purchases, intercompany transactions, and when applicable, nonfunctional currency denominated third-party debt. Our Company is also exposed to fluctuations in the value of foreign currency investments in subsidiaries and cash flows related to repatriation of these investments. Additionally, our Company is exposed to volatility in the translation of foreign currency earnings to U.S. Dollars. Primary exposures include the U.S. Dollar versus the British Pound, Euro, Australian Dollar, Canadian Dollar, and Mexican Peso, and in the case of inter-subsidiary transactions, the British Pound versus the Euro. We assess foreign currency risk based on transactional cash flows and translational volatility and enter into forward contracts, options,

continued

> and currency swaps to reduce fluctuations in net long or short currency positions. Forward contracts and options are generally less than 18 months duration. Currency swap agreements are established in conjunction with the term of underlying debt issuances.

a. Before the effects of foreign currency rates, total consolidated sales increased by 7.6% during 2012. What geographic segment accounted for this overall increase? What other factor explains this significant increase? (*Hint:* see the footnotes to the tables.)
b. How did foreign currency exchange rates affect sales at each of the geographic segments? What can we infer about the strength of the U.S. dollar vis-à-vis the currencies in Kellogg's segments?
c. Operating profit was not uniformly affected, across the board. Which geographic segments exhibited the lowest and which the highest change in profit during the year? Explain.
d. Describe how the accounting for foreign exchange translation affects reported sales and profits.
e. How does Kellogg Co. manage the risk related to its foreign exchange exposure? Describe the financial statement effects of this risk management activity.

E5-32. Interpreting Revenue Recognition for Gift Cards (LO1)
Below are the footnotes to **Barnes & Noble Inc.**'s 2012 annual report and membership information obtained from its Website:

Barnes & Noble Inc. (BKS)

> The Barnes & Noble Member Program offers members greater discounts and other benefits for products and services, as well as exclusive offers and promotions via e-mail or direct mail for an annual fee of $25.00, which is non-refundable after the first 30 days. Revenue is recognized over the twelve-month period based upon historical spending patterns for Barnes & Noble Members. The Barnes & Noble Member Program entitles Members to the following benefits:
>
> - 40% off the list price of the current hardcover Barnes & Noble Store Bestsellers.
> - 10% off the marked Barnes & Noble sale price of other eligible items.
> - Free Express Shipping.
> - Periodic special promotions at Barnes & Noble Stores and at BN.com.

a. Explain in layman's terms how Barnes & Noble accounts for the cash received for its membership program. When does Barnes & Noble record revenue from this program?
b. How does Barnes & Noble's balance sheet reflect those membership fees?
c. Does the 40% discount affect Barnes & Noble's income statement when membership fees are received?

E5-33. Analysis of R&D and Applying it to Forecasting of Revenues and Income (LO2)
Eli Lilly & Co. reports $22,603 million in revenue for 2012 and includes the following risk factor in its MD&A:

Eli Lilly & Co. (LLY)

> We depend on patent-protected products for most of our revenues, cash flows, and earnings, and we will lose effective intellectual property protection for many of them in the next several years. Seven significant patent-protected products, which together composed 68 percent of our worldwide revenue in 2012, recently have lost, or will lose in the next several years, their most significant remaining U.S. patent protection and data-based protection, as well as their intellectual property-based exclusivity in most countries outside the United States:

Product	Worldwide Revenues (2012)	Percent of Total 2012 Revenues	Loss of Relevant U.S. Exclusivity
Cymbalta	$4.99 billion	22	December 2013 (compound patent plus pediatric exclusivity)
Alimta	$2.59 billion	11	2017 (compound patent plus pediatric exclusivity); 2022 (vitamin dosage regimen patent plus pediatric exclusivity)
Humalog	$2.40 billion	11	May 2013
Cialis	$1.93 billion	9	2017
Zyprexa	$1.70 billion	8	2011
Evista	$1.01 billion	4	March 2014
Strattera	$621.4 million	3	2017

Required

a. How is this disclosure important to our analysis of the company?

b. Explain how we incorporate this information into our forecasts of the company's revenue and gross profit.

c. What additional information do we need for predicting revenue and profit (beyond information disclosed above)?

PROBLEMS

P5-34. Analyzing and Interpreting Revenue Recognition Policies and Risks (LO1)

Amazon.com Inc. (AMZN)

Amazon.com, Inc., provides the following explanation of its revenue recognition policies in its 2010 10-K report.

> On January 1, 2010, we prospectively adopted ASU 2009-13, which amends Accounting Standards Codification ("ASC") Topic 605, Revenue Recognition. Under this new standard, we allocate revenue in arrangements with multiple deliverables using estimated selling prices (ESP) if we do not have vendor-specific objective evidence or third-party evidence of the selling prices of the deliverables. Estimated selling prices are management's best estimates of the prices that we would charge our customers if we were to sell the standalone elements separately.
>
> Sales of our Kindle e-reader are considered arrangements with multiple deliverables, consisting of the device, 3G wireless access and delivery for some models, and software upgrades. Under the prior accounting standard, we accounted for sales of the Kindle ratably over the average estimated life of the device. Accordingly, revenue and associated product cost of the device through December 31, 2009, were deferred at the time of sale and recognized on a straight-line basis over the two-year average estimated economic life.
>
> As of January 2010, we account for the sale of the Kindle as multiple deliverables. The revenue related to the device, which is the substantial portion of the total sale price, and related costs are recognized upon delivery. Revenue related to 3G wireless access and delivery and software upgrades is amortized over the average life of the device, which remains estimated at two years.
>
> Because we have adopted ASU 2009-13 prospectively, we are recognizing $508 million throughout 2010 and 2011 for revenue previously deferred under the prior accounting standard.

Required

a. What is a multiple-element contract? What product did Amazon sell that involved a multiple-element contract? Explain.

b. Explain how companies account for multiple-element contracts, in general.

c. Compare the accounting for the Kindle under the old and new accounting standards for revenue recognition. Amazon disclosed that $508 million of previously deferred revenue would now be recognized earlier. Explain.

d. Assume that Amazon sold a Kindle with 3G capabilities for $180 and the company estimated a selling price (ESP) of $20 per unit for 3G access and future software upgrades. Compute the revenue that Amazon would recognize at the point of sale under the old and the new accounting standards.

e. Use the financial statement effects template to record the initial sale of a Kindle and the accounting adjustment required at the end of the first quarter for the new accounting standards.

P5-35. Analyzing and Interpreting Income Tax Disclosures (LO3)

Pfizer Inc. (PFE)

The 2012 income statement for **Pfizer Inc.** is reproduced in this module. Pfizer also reports the following footnote relating to its income taxes in its 2012 10-K report.

Deferred Taxes Deferred taxes arise as a result of basis differentials between financial statement accounting and tax amounts. The tax effect of the major items recorded as deferred tax assets and liabilities, shown before jurisdictional netting, follow:

	2012 Deferred Tax		2011 Deferred Tax	
(Millions of dollars)	**Assets**	**(Liabilities)**	**Assets**	**(Liabilities)**
Prepaid/deferred items	$ 1,817	$ (119)	$ 1,659	$ (211)
Inventories	330	(198)	324	(52)
Intangible assets	1,649	(14,187)	1,713	(15,301)
Property, plant and equipment	508	(1,485)	226	(1,311)
Employee benefits	5,042	(391)	4,280	(524)
Restructurings and other charges	784	(334)	553	(95)
Legal and product liability reserves	1,888	—	1,812	—
Net operating loss/credit carryforwards	3,439	—	4,381	—
Unremitted earnings	—	(16,042)	—	(11,699)
State and local tax adjustments	385	—	476	—
All other	1,259	(504)	1,105	(121)
Subtotal	17,101	(33,260)	16,529	(29,314)
Valuation allowances	(1,102)	—	(1,201)	—
Total deferred taxes	$15,999	(33,260)	$15,328	(29,314)
Net deferred tax liability		$(17,261)		$(13,986)

Required

a. Describe the terms "deferred tax liabilities" and "deferred tax assets." Provide an example of how these accounts can arise.

b. Intangible assets (other than goodwill) acquired in the purchase of a company are depreciated (amortized) similar to buildings and equipment (see Module 9 for a discussion). Describe how the deferred tax liability of $14,187 million relating to intangibles arose.

c. Pfizer has many employee benefit plans, such as a long-term health plan and a pension plan. Some of these are generating deferred tax assets and others are generating deferred tax liabilities. Explain the timing of the recognition of expenses under these plans that would give rise to these different outcomes.

d. Pfizer reports a deferred tax liability labelled "unremitted earnings." This relates to an investment in an affiliated company for which Pfizer is recording income, but has not yet received dividends. Generally, investment income is taxed when received. Explain what information the deferred tax liability for unremitted earnings conveys.

e. Pfizer reports a deferred tax asset relating to net operating loss carryforwards. Explain what loss carryforwards are.

f. Pfizer reports a valuation allowance of $1,102 million in 2012. Explain why Pfizer has established this allowance and its effect on reported profit. Pfizer's valuation allowance was $1,201 million in 2011. Compute the change in its allowance during 2012 and explain how that change affected 2012 tax expense and net income.

P5-36. Analyzing and Interpreting Income Components and Disclosures (LO2)
The income statement for Xerox Corporation follows.

Xerox Corporation (XRX)

Year Ended December 31 (in millions, except per-share data)	2012	2011	2010
Revenues			
Sales	$ 6,578	$ 7,126	$ 7,234
Outsourcing, service and rentals	15,215	14,868	13,739
Finance income	597	632	660
Total Revenues	22,390	22,626	21,633
Costs and expenses			
Cost of sales	4,362	4,697	4,741
Cost of outsourcing, service and rentals	10,802	10,269	9,195
Equipment financing interest	198	231	246
Research, development and engineering expenses	655	721	781
Selling, administrative and general expenses	4,288	4,497	4,594
Restructuring and asset impairment charges	153	33	483
Acquisition-related costs	—	—	77
Amortization of intangible assets	328	398	312
Curtailment gain	—	(107)	—
Other expenses, net	256	322	389
Total costs and expenses	21,042	21,061	20,818
Income before income taxes and equity income	1,348	1,565	815
Income tax expense	277	386	256
Equity in net income of unconsolidated affiliates	152	149	78
Net income	1,223	1,328	637
Less: Net income attributable to noncontrolling interests	28	33	31
Net income attributable to Xerox	$ 1,195	$ 1,295	$ 606
Basic earnings per share	$ 0.90	$ 0.92	$ 0.44
Diluted earnings per share	$ 0.88	$ 0.90	$ 0.43

Notes:

- The income statement includes sales of Xerox copiers and revenue earned by a finance subsidiary that provides loan and lease financing relating to the sales of those copiers.
- **Equity in net income of unconsolidated affiliates** refers to income Xerox has earned on investments in affiliated (but unconsolidated) companies.

Required

a. Xerox reports several sources of income. How should revenue be recognized for each of these business activities? Explain.

b. Compute the relative size of sales revenue (total) and of revenue from outsourcing, service and rentals. *Hint:* Scale each type of revenue by total revenue. What observations can be made about the different sources of revenue?

c. Xerox reports research, development and engineering expenses (R&D) each year. Compare R&D spending over the three years. *Hint:* Scale R&D by total revenue each year.

d. Xerox reports restructuring costs each year. (1) Describe the three typical categories of restructuring costs and the accounting for each. (2) How do you recommend treating these costs for analysis purposes? (3) Should regular recurring restructuring costs be treated differently than isolated occurrences of such costs for analysis purposes? (4) What does a (negative) expense imply about one or more previous year's accruals?

e. Xerox reports $256 million in expenses in 2012 labeled as "Other expenses, net." How can a company use such an account to potentially obscure its actual financial performance?

P5-37.[B] Analyzing and Interpreting Income Tax Footnote (LO3)

Ahold

Ahold, a grocery and retail company located in The Netherlands, reports the following footnote for income taxes in its 2012 annual report.

The following table specifies the current and deferred tax components of income taxes in the income statement:

For year ended (€ million)	2012	2011
Current income taxes		
Domestic taxes—the Netherlands	€ (76)	€(111)
Foreign taxes		
United States	(14)	42
Europe—Other	(22)	(11)
Total current tax expense	(112)	(80)
Deferred income taxes		
Domestic taxes—the Netherlands	(58)	(33)
Foreign taxes		
United States	(39)	(37)
Europe—Other	(2)	10
Total deferred tax expense	(99)	(60)
Total income tax expense	€(211)	€(140)

The significant components of deferred income tax assets and liabilities are as follows, as of:

	2012	2011
Leases and financings	€237	€222
Pensions and other post-employment benefits	—	46
Provisions	114	131
Derivatives and loans	24	7
Interest	57	35
Other	78	52
Total gross deductible temporary differences	510	493
Unrecognised deductible temporary differences	(56)	(20)
Total recognised deductible temporary differences	454	473
Tax losses and credits	179	572
Unrecognised tax losses and credits	(44)	(459)
Total recognised tax losses and credits	135	113
Total net deferred tax asset position	589	586
Pensions and other post-employment benefits	(48)	—
Property, plant and equipment and intangible assets	(364)	(245)
Inventories	(111)	(103)
Other	(5)	(5)
Total deferred tax liabilities	(528)	(353)
Net deferred tax assets	€61	€233

Deferred income tax assets and liabilities are offset on the balance sheet when there is a legally enforceable right to offset current tax assets against current tax liabilities and when the deferred income taxes relate to income taxes levied by the same fiscal authority.

Required

a. What income tax expense does Ahold report in its 2012 income statement? How much of this expense did Ahold pay during the year or anticipate paying in 2013?

b. Ahold reports deferred tax liabilities relating to property, plant and equipment. Describe how these liabilities arise. How likely is it that these liabilities will be paid? Specifically, describe a scenario that will (i) defer these taxes indefinitely, and (ii) result in these liabilities requiring payment within the near future.

c. Ahold reports a deferred tax asset relating to provisions. Footnotes to financial statements indicate that these provisions relate, in part, to self-insurance accruals. When a company self-insures, it does not purchase insurance from a third-party insurance company. Instead, it records an expense and related liability to reflect the probable payment of losses that can occur in the future. Explain why this accrual (provision) results in a deferred tax asset.

d. Ahold reports deferred tax assets relating to tax losses and credits. Explain how these arise and how they will result in a future benefit.

e. The company reports unrecognized temporary differences and unrecognized tax losses and credits. These are the IFRS equivalent of valuation allowances in U.S. GAAP. Why did the company set up these unrecognized portions of deferred tax assets? How did the net decrease in the combined unrecognized amounts from 2011 to 2012 affect net income? How can a company use these accounts to meet its income targets in a particular year?

Under Armour, Inc. (UA)

P5-38.[B] Analyzing and Interpreting Tax Footnote (Financial Statement Effects Template) (LO3)
Under Armour, Inc., reports total tax expense of $74,661 (in thousands) on its income statement for year ended December 31, 2012, and paid cash of $57,739 (in thousands) for taxes. The tax footnote in the company's 10-K filing, reports the following deferred tax assets and liabilities information.

December 31 (In thousands)	2012	2011
Deferred tax assets		
Allowance for doubtful accounts and other reserves	$14,000	$9,576
Stock-based compensation	13,157	11,238
Foreign net operating loss carryforward	12,416	11,078
Deferred rent	6,007	4,611
Inventory obsolescence reserves	4,138	3,789
Tax basis inventory adjustment	3,581	4,317
State tax credits, net of federal tax impact	2,856	—
Foreign tax credits	2,210	1,784
Deferred compensation	1,170	1,448
Other	4,918	3,427
Total deferred tax assets	64,453	51,268
Less: valuation allowance	(3,966)	(1,784)
Total net deferred tax assets	60,487	49,484
Deferred tax liability		
Intangible asset	(610)	(341)
Prepaid expenses	(4,153)	(2,968)
Property, plant and equipment	(10,116)	(13,748)
Total deferred tax liabilities	(14,879)	(17,057)
Total deferred tax assets, net	$45,608	$32,427

Required

a. Under Armour's deferred tax assets increased during the most recent fiscal year. What explains the increase?

b. Did Under Armour's deferred tax liabilities increase or decrease during the most recent fiscal year? Explain how the change arose.

c. The company's valuation allowance relates to foreign net operating tax losses. Explain how tax losses give rise to deferred tax assets. Why does the company record a valuation account? What proportion of these losses, at December 31, 2012, does the company believe will likely expire unused?

d. Explain how the valuation allowance affected 2012 net income.

e. Use the financial statement effects template to record Under Armour's income tax expense for the fiscal year 2012 along with the changes in both deferred tax assets and liabilities. Assume that the amount needed to balance the tax transaction represents the amount payable to tax authorities.

P5-39. Analyzing and Interpreting Restructuring Costs and Effects (LO2)
Hewlett-Packard, Inc., reports the following footnote disclosure (excerpted) in its 2012 10-K relating to its 2012 restructuring program.

Hewlett-Packard, Inc. (HPQ)

Fiscal 2012 Restructuring Plan On May 23, 2012, HP adopted a multi-year restructuring plan (the "2012 Plan") designed to simplify business processes, accelerate innovation and deliver better results for customers, employees and stockholders. HP estimates that it will eliminate approximately 29,000 positions in connection with the 2012 Plan through fiscal year 2014, with a portion of those employees exiting the company as part of voluntary enhanced early retirement ("EER") programs. HP expects to record aggregate charges of approximately $3.7 billion through the end of HP's 2014 fiscal year as accounting recognition criteria are met. Of that amount, HP expects approximately $3.1 billion to relate to the workforce reductions and the EER programs and approximately $0.6 billion to relate to other items, including data center and real estate consolidation. Due to uncertainties associated with attrition and the acceptance rates of future international EER programs, the total expected headcount reductions could vary as much as 15% from our estimates. We could also experience similar variations in the total expense of the 2012 Plan.

HP recorded a charge of approximately $2.1 billion in the fiscal year of 2012 relating to the 2012 Plan. This amount included costs for EER plans in the United States and Canada of $41 million of stock-based compensation expense for accelerated vesting of stock-based awards held by participating EER employees and a special termination benefit ("STB") expense of $126 million. As of October 31, 2012, HP had eliminated approximately 11,700 positions as part of the 2012 Plan. The $2.1 billion charge also includes $105 million for data center and real estate consolidation, of which $56 million related to asset impairments. The cash payments associated with the 2012 Plan are expected to be paid out through fiscal 2015.

Fiscal 2010 Acquisitions In connection with the acquisitions of Palm, Inc. ("Palm") and 3Com Corporation ("3Com") in fiscal 2010, HP's management approved and initiated plans to restructure the operations of the acquired companies, including severance for employees, contract cancellation costs, costs to vacate duplicative facilities and other items. The total expected combined cost of the plans is $101 million, which includes $33 million of additional restructuring costs recorded in the fourth quarter of fiscal 2011 in connection with HP's decision to wind down the webOS device business. The Palm and 3Com plans are now closed with no further restructuring charges anticipated. The unused accrual in the amount of $13 million was credited to restructuring expense in fiscal year 2012.

Fiscal 2010 Enterprise Services Business Restructuring Plan On June 1, 2010, HP's management announced a plan to restructure its ES business, which includes the ITO and ABS business units. The multi-year restructuring program includes plans to consolidate commercial data centers, tools and applications. The total expected cost of the plan that will be recorded as restructuring charges is approximately $1.0 billion, and includes severance costs to eliminate approximately 8,200 positions and infrastructure charges. During the first quarter of fiscal 2012, HP reduced the severance accrual by $100 million and recognized additional infrastructure related charges of $104 million. The majority of the infrastructure charges were paid out during fiscal 2012 with the remaining charges expected to be paid out through the first half of fiscal 2015.

The adjustments to the accrued restructuring expenses related to all of HP's restructuring plans described above for the twelve months ended October 31, 2012, were as follows:

In millions	Balance, October 31, 2011	Fiscal Year 2012 Charges	Cash Payments	Other Adjustments & Non-cash Settlements	Balance, October 31, 2012
Fiscal 2012 Plan					
Severance and EER	$ —	$1,985	$(315)	$(1,073)[(1)]	$ 597
Infrastructure and other	—	105	(26)	(68)	11
Total 2012 Plan	—	2,090	(341)	(1,141)	608
Fiscal 2010 acquisitions	59	(13)	(27)	(9)	10
Fiscal 2010 ES Plan					
Severance	493	(100)	(146)	(20)	227
Infrastructure	3	176	(141)	(37)	1
Total ES Plan	496	76	(287)	(57)	228
Fiscal 2009 Plan	—	7	(9)	2	—

continued

continued from prior page

In millions	Balance, October 31, 2011	Fiscal Year 2012 Charges	Cash Payments	Other Adjustments & Non-cash Settlements	Balance, October 31, 2012
Fiscal 2008 HP/EDS Plan					
Severance	—	5	(5)	—	—
Infrastructure	258	101	(171)	(7)	181
Total HP/EDS Plan	258	106	(176)	(7)	181
Total restructuring plans	$813	$2,266	$(840)	$(1,212)	$1,027

Required

a. Briefly describe the company's 2012 restructuring program. Provide two examples of common noncash charges associated with corporate restructuring activities.

b. Using the financial statement effects template, show the effects on financial statements of the (1) 2012 restructuring charge of $2,266 million, and (2) 2012 cash payment of $840 million.

c. Assume that instead of accurately estimating the anticipated restructuring charge in 2012, the company overestimated them by $30 million. How would this overestimation affect financial statements in (1) 2012, and (2) 2013 when severance costs are paid in cash?

d. The company reports that the total charges will amount to $3.7 billion. What is the effect on the 2012 income statement from this restructuring? Why do investors care to know the total charge if it does not impact current-period earnings?

P5-40. Analyzing and Interpreting Income Tax Footnote (LO3)

E. I. du Pont de Nemours and Co. (DD)

Consider the following income tax footnote information for the E. I. du Pont de Nemours and Company.

Provision for Income Taxes ($ millions)	2012	2011	2010
Current tax expense (benefit) on continuing operations			
U.S. federal	**$121**	$353	$(142)
U.S. state and local	**16**	(20)	(9)
International	**663**	482	401
Total current tax expense on continuing operations	**800**	815	250
Deferred tax expense (benefit) on continuing operations			
U.S. federal	**(103)**	(147)	240
U.S. state and local	**(46)**	(4)	22
International	**(29)**	(38)	3
Total deferred tax (benefit) expense on continuing operations	**(178)**	(189)	265
Provision for income taxes on continuing operations	**$622**	$626	$515

The significant components of deferred tax assets and liabilities at December 31, 2012 and 2011, are as follows:

	2012		2011	
($ millions)	Asset	Liability	Asset	Liability
Depreciation	$ —	$1,696	$ —	$1,781
Accrued employee benefits	5,198	167	5,562	252
Other accrued expenses	1,157	499	1,020	354
Inventories	249	68	199	39
Unrealized exchange gains/losses	—	56	—	35
Tax loss/tax credit carryforwards/backs	2,733	—	2,854	—
Investment in subsidiaries and affiliates	81	92	46	259
Amortization of intangibles	58	1,335	69	1,399
Other	270	287	250	279
Valuation allowance	(1,914)	—	(1,971)	—
	$7,832	$4,200	$8,029	$4,398
Net deferred tax asset	$3,632		$3,631	

continued

An analysis of the company's effective income tax rate (EITR) on continuing operations is as follows:

	2012	2011	2010
Statutory U.S. federal income tax rate	**35.0%**	35.0%	35.0%
Exchange gains/losses	**0.1**	(0.8)	2.2
Domestic operations	**(2.3)**	(3.4)	(3.3)
Lower effective tax rates on international operations-net	**(10.8)**	(11.7)	(16.0)
Tax settlements	**(2.0)**	(0.2)	(2.1)
Sale of a business	**—**	(2.3)	—
	20.0%	16.6%	15.8%

Required

a. What is the total amount of income tax expense that DuPont reports in its 2012 income statement? What portion of this expense did DuPont pay during 2012 or expect to pay in 2013?

b. Explain how the deferred tax liability called "depreciation" arises. Under what circumstances will the company settle this liability? Under what circumstances might this liability be deferred indefinitely?

c. Explain how the deferred tax asset called "accrued employee benefits" arises. Why is it recognized as an asset?

d. Explain how the deferred tax asset called "tax loss/tax credit carryforwards/backs" arises. Under what circumstances will DuPont realize the benefits of this asset?

e. DuPont reports a 2012 valuation allowance of $1,914 million. How does this valuation allowance arise? How did the change in valuation allowance for 2012 affect net income? Valuation allowances typically relate to questions about the realizability of tax loss carryforwards. Under what circumstances might DuPont not realize the benefits of its tax loss carryforwards?

f. DuPont's footnote reports the effective income tax rates (EITR) for the three-year period. What explains the difference between the U.S. statutory rate and the company's EITR?

P5-41. Assessing Revenue Recognition, R&D Expense, EPS, and Income Taxes (LO1, 2, 3, 5)
Following are footnotes (excerpted) from the 10-K of **Intuit, Inc.**

Intuit, Inc. (INTU)

The following table presents the composition of shares used in the computation of basic and diluted net income per share for the periods indicated.

Twelve Months Ended July 31 (In millions, except per share amounts)	2013	2012	2011
Denominator:			
Shares used in basic per share amounts:			
Weighted average common shares outstanding	297	296	307
Shares used in diluted per share amounts:			
Weighted average common shares outstanding	297	296	307
Dilutive common equivalent shares from stock options and restricted stock awards	6	9	10
Dilutive weighted average common shares outstanding	303	305	317

Revenue Recognition We derive revenue from the sale of packaged software products, software subscriptions, hosted services, technical support plans, financial supplies, implementation services, transaction fees, merchant services hardware, and multiple element arrangements that may include a combination of these items. We recognize revenue when all four revenue recognition criteria have been met: persuasive evidence of an arrangement exists, we have delivered the product or performed the service, the fee is fixed or determinable, and collectibility is probable.

Product Revenue We recognize revenue from the sale of our packaged software products, financial supplies such as printed check stock, and merchant services hardware such as retail point-of-sale equipment and credit card readers for mobile phones, when legal title transfers. This

continued

continued from prior page

is generally when our customers download products from the Web, when we ship the products or, in the case of certain agreements, when products are delivered to retailers. We sell some of our QuickBooks, TurboTax and Quicken desktop software products on consignment to certain retailers. We recognize revenue for these consignment transactions only when the end-user sale has occurred. For software products that are sold on a subscription basis and include periodic updates, we recognize revenue ratably over the term of the contract. We record product revenue net of our sales tax obligations.

Service and Other Revenue We recognize revenue from hosted services as the services are performed, provided we have no other remaining obligations to these customers. We generally require customers to remit payroll tax funds to us in advance of the payroll date via electronic funds transfer. We include in total net revenue the interest that we earn on these funds between the time that we collect them from customers and the time that we remit them to outside parties. Service revenue for electronic payment processing services that we provide to merchants is recorded net of interchange fees charged by credit card associations. We offer several QuickBooks technical support plans and recognize support revenue over the life of the plans. Other revenue consists primarily of revenue from revenue-sharing and royalty arrangements with third-party partners. We typically recognize this revenue as earned based upon reporting provided to us by our partners.

Multiple Element Arrangements We enter into multiple element revenue arrangements in which a customer may purchase a combination of software, upgrades, hosted services, technical support, and hardware. For multiple element arrangements that contain only software and software-related elements, we allocate and defer revenue for the undelivered elements based on their vendor-specific objective evidence of fair value (VSOE). VSOE is the price charged when that element is sold separately. In situations where VSOE exists for all elements (delivered and undelivered), we allocate the total revenue to be earned under the arrangement among the various elements, based on their relative fair value. For multiple element arrangements that contain non-software elements such as hosted services or credit card readers for mobile phones, we: (1) determine whether and when each element has been delivered; (2) determine the fair value of each element using the selling price hierarchy of vendor-specific evidence (VSOE) of fair value if available, third-party evidence (TPE) if VSOE is not available, and estimated selling price (ESP) if neither VSOE nor TPE is available; and (3) allocate the total price among the various elements using the relative selling price method. Once we have allocated the total price among the various elements, we recognize revenue when the revenue recognition criteria described above are met for each element.

Income Taxes Differences between income taxes calculated using the federal statutory income tax rate of 35% and the provision for income taxes from continuing operations were as follows for the periods indicated:

Twelve Months Ended July 31 (In millions)	2013	2012	2011
Income from continuing operations before income taxes	$1,210	$1,138	$1,042
Statutory federal income tax	$ 424	$ 398	$ 365
State income tax, net of federal benefit	17	16	36
Federal research and experimentation credits	(24)	(8)	(23)
Domestic production activities deduction	(29)	(27)	(25)
Share-based compensation	7	8	6
Effects of non-U.S. operations	(2)	(5)	(4)
Other, net	(6)	(8)	(1)
Total provision for income taxes from continuing operations	$ 387	$ 374	$ 354

continued

Significant deferred tax assets and liabilities were as follows at the dates indicated:

July 31 (In millions)	2013	2012
Deferred tax assets		
Accruals and reserves not currently deductible	$ 51	$ 46
Deferred rent	11	11
Accrued and deferred compensation	50	48
Loss and tax credit carryforwards	36	41
Property and equipment	12	15
Share-based compensation	97	97
Net basis difference in investments held for sale	41	38
Total deferred tax assets	298	296
Deferred tax liabilities		
Intangible assets	93	92
Other, net	10	11
Total deferred tax liabilities	103	103
Total net deferred tax assets	195	193
Valuation allowance	(25)	(10)
Total net deferred tax assets, net of valuation allowance	$170	$183

We have provided a valuation allowance related to the benefits of federal and state net basis difference in investments held for sale, state capital and operating loss carryforwards, and state tax credit carryforwards that we believe are unlikely to be realized. Changes in the valuation allowance during the twelve months ended July 31, 2013 were primarily related to the federal and state net basis difference in investments held for sale and are reflected in the net gain on disposal of discontinued operations. Changes in the valuation allowance during the twelve months ended July 31, 2012 were not significant.

Required

a. Describe the differences in revenue recognition between product sales and after-sale services. How does the company recognize revenue for consignment sales? For products sold on a subscription basis? How is service revenue recognized?

b. Some of the company's sales involve multiple element arrangements. In general, what are these arrangements? How does the company account for such sales?

c. Intuit reports $685 million of research and development expense, up from $618 million in the prior year.

   i. What kind of research activities would we expect for a company like Intuit?

   ii. Given the kind of research activities described in part i, how does the accounting for Intuit's R&D costs differ from the way that those costs would have been accounted for had Intuit used IFRS for financial reporting?

d. Intuit's earnings per share (EPS) is $2.83 on a diluted basis, compared with its basic EPS of $2.89. What factor(s) accounts for this dilution?

e. Drawing on Intuit's income tax footnote, prepare a table in percentages showing computation of its effective tax rate for each of the three fiscal years. What tax-related items, if any, would we not expect to continue into fiscal year 2014?

f. Intuit reports total net deferred tax assets of $170 million.

   i. Describe how deferred tax assets relating to accruals arise.

   ii. Explain how deferred tax assets relating to loss carryforwards arise.

   iii. Intuit reports an increase of its deferred tax asset valuation allowance of $15 million in 2013. How does this affect Intuit's income?

Costco Wholesale (COST)

P5-42. Analyzing Unearned Revenue Disclosures (LO1, 3)

The following disclosures (excerpted) are from the September 1, 2013, annual report of Costco Wholesale Corporation.

Revenue Recognition We generally recognize sales, net of estimated returns, at the time the member takes possession of merchandise or receives services. When we collect payment from customers prior to the transfer of ownership of merchandise or the performance of services, the amount received is generally recorded as deferred revenue on the consolidated balance sheets until the sale or service is completed. Membership fee revenue represents annual membership fees paid by our members. We account for membership fee revenue, net of estimated refunds, on a deferred basis, whereby revenue is recognized ratably over the one-year membership period.

Revenue ($ millions)	September 1, 2013	September 2, 2012	August 28, 2011
Net sales.	$102,870	$97,062	$87,048
Membership fees	2,286	2,075	1,867
Total revenue.	$105,156	$99,137	$88,915

Current Liabilities ($ millions)	September 1, 2013	September 2, 2012
Accounts payable.	$ 7,872	$ 7,303
Accrued salaries and benefits	2,037	1,832
Accrued member rewards	710	661
Accrued sales and other taxes.	382	397
Deferred membership fees.	1,167	1,101
Other current liabilities	1,089	966
Total current liabilities	$13,257	$12,260

The components of the deferred tax assets (liabilities) are as follows (in $ millions):

	2013	2012
Equity compensation	$ 80	$ 79
Deferred income/membership fees	130	148
Accrued liabilities and reserves	530	461
Other.	42	55
Property and equipment.	(558)	(522)
Merchandise inventories	(190)	(182)
Net deferred tax assets.	$ 34	$ 39

Required

a. Explain in layman's terms how Costco accounts for the cash received for membership fees.

b. Use the balance sheet information on Costco's deferred membership fees liability account and its income statement revenues related to membership fees earned during 2013 to compute the cash that Costco received during 2013 for membership fees.

c. Use the financial statement effects template to show the effect of the cash Costco received during 2013 for membership fees and the recognition of membership fees revenue for 2013.

d. Costco reports a deferred tax asset related to deferred income/membership fees. Explain in layman's terms how this asset arises. When will Costco receive the benefit associated with this asset?

IFRS APPLICATIONS

I5-43. Assessing Research and Development Expenses (LO2)

Bombardier, Inc.

Headquartered in Montreal, Quebec, Canada, **Bombardier, Inc.**, is a multinational aerospace and transportation company, founded in 1941. The company manufactures regional aircraft, business jets, mass transportation equipment, recreational equipment and is a financial services provider. Bombardier is a Fortune Global 500 company and operates two segments: BA (Aerospace) and BT (Transportation).

BOMBARDIER INC.
CONSOLIDATED STATEMENTS OF INCOME
For the fiscal years ended December 31

In millions of U.S. dollars	2012	2011
Revenues	$16,768	$18,347
Cost of sales	14,269	15,444
Gross margin	2,499	2,903
SG&A	1,443	1,439
R&D	299	271
Share of income of associates	(45)	(4)
Other income	(33)	(5)
Special items	140	—
EBIT	695	1,202
Financing expense	596	681
Financing income	(599)	(519)
EBT	698	1,040
Income taxes	100	203
Net income	$ 598	$ 837
Attributable to:		
Equity holders of Bombardier Inc.	$ 588	$ 837
NCI	10	—
	$ 598	$ 837

Bombardier reports the following footnote information (in millions).

R&D expense, net of government assistance, was as follows, for fiscal years:

In millions of U.S. dollars	2012	2011
R&D expenditures	$1,901	$1,351
Less: Development expenditures capitalized to aerospace program tooling	(1,728)	(1,171)
	173	180
Add: Amortization of aerospace program tooling	126	91
	$ 299	$ 271

a. Compute the percent of revenues that Bombardier spends on research and development (R&D) for both years. Determine the year over year growth in R&D expense. Compare this level of expenditure with the percentages for other companies that are discussed in the Business Insight box on page 5-4. How would you assess the appropriateness of its R&D expense level?

b. Describe how Bombardier accounts for R&D expenditures. How does this differ from U.S. GAAP accounting?

c. What would Bombardier have reported for R&D expense for 2012 and 2011 if the company had always used U.S. GAAP? Use these numbers to determine the common-size R&D expense and the year over year growth in R&D expense. How does this compare to your answer in part *a*?

I5-44. Assessing Research and Development Expenses (LO2)

BAE Systems

Headquartered in London in the United Kingdom, **BAE Systems** is a global defense, aerospace and security company employing around 88,200 people worldwide. The company's wide-ranging products and services cover air, land and naval forces, as well as advanced electronics, security, information technology, and support services. BAE Systems is the world's third largest defense and aerospace company based on revenues. The company uses IFRS for its financial statements, which include the following notes:

Research and development The Group undertakes research and development activities either on its own behalf or on behalf of customers.

Group-funded expenditure on research activities is written off as incurred and charged to the income statement.

Group-funded expenditure on development activities applied to a plan or design for the production of new or substantially improved products is capitalised as an internally generated intangible asset if certain conditions are met. The expenditure capitalised includes the cost of materials, direct labour and related overheads. Capitalised development expenditure is stated at cost less accumulated amortisation and impairment losses.

Capitalised development expenditure is amortised over the expected life of the product.

Where the research and development activity is performed for customers, the revenue arising is recognised in accordance with the Group's revenue recognition policy.

Operating costs	2012 £m	2011 £m
Raw materials, subcontracts and other items	£ 6,174	£ 6,947
Change in inventories of finished goods and work-in-progress	23	198
Cost of inventories expensed	6,197	7,145
Staff costs	5,285	5,356
Depreciation, amortisation and impairment	669	695
Loss on disposal of property, plant and equipment, and investment property	5	4
Loss on disposal of businesses	—	29
Other operating charges	3,197	3,249
Operating costs	£15,353	£16,478
Included within the analysis of operating costs are the following expenses:		
Minimum lease and sublease payments	£ 189	£ 178
Research and development expense including amounts funded under contract	1,138	1,149

Required

a. Under IFRS, what six criteria did BAE Systems have to meet in order to capitalize development costs?

b. What was the common-sized research and development expense each year? The company recorded sales revenue of £17,834 and £19,154 in 2012 and 2011 respectively.

c. Assume that during 2012, the company capitalized £432 of additional development expenditures and amortized £229 of previously capitalized costs. Determine what the R&D expense would have been under U.S. GAAP.

I5-45. Assessing Research and Development Expenses (LO2)

Finmeccanica S.p.A.

Headquartered in Rome, Italy, **Finmeccanica S.p.A.** is a multinational conglomerate operating in the defense and aerospace sectors. The company uses IFRS for its financial reports and disclosed the following in its annual report:

Research and development activities for the Energy Sector focused primarily on the following items in 2010:

- Gas turbines: AE94.3A turbine development projects to raise power, efficiency and operational flexibility, while complying with requirements on pollutants in exhaust gas, and projects to retrofit the AE94.2 turbine to increase the power and extend the life of the Class E turbine;
- Steam turbines: international projects investigating the behaviour of special materials (extremely high temperature steels and super alloys) with a view to developing the "ultrasupercritical" turbine (with a power rating in excess of 300 MW);
- Generators: development work on the new air-cooled 400-MVA model intended to complement the large, high-performance gas turbines.

Required

a. How are R&D costs accounted for under IFRS?

b. For each of the three energy sector R&D items described above, determine if the item meets the criteria for capitalization under IFRS.

I5-46. Analyzing Unearned Revenue Transactions and Multiple-Element Arrangements (LO1)

Telstra Corporation Limited

Telstra Corporation Limited is an Australian telecommunications and media company that builds and provides land-based and mobile telecom services along with internet and pay television products. The company is Australia's largest 3G and 4G enabled mobile network covering 99.3% of the Australian population across more than 2.3 million square kilometres (888 thousand square miles). Excerpts from the company's revenue recognition footnote follow.

Revenue Recognition Our categories of sales revenue are recorded after deducting sales returns, trade allowances, discounts, sales incentives, duties and taxes.

Rendering of services Revenue from the provision of our telecommunications services includes telephone calls and other services and facilities provided, such as internet and data. We record revenue earned from:

- telephone calls on completion of the call; and
- other services generally at completion, or on a straight line basis over the period of service provided, unless another method better represents the stage of completion.

Installation and connection fee revenues that are not considered to be separate units of accounting are deferred and recognised over the average estimated customer life. Incremental costs directly related to these revenues are also deferred and amortised over the customer contract life. In relation to basic access installation and connection revenue, we apply management judgement to determine the estimated customer contract life. Based on our reviews of historical information and customer trends, we have determined that our average estimated customer life is 5 years.

Sale of goods Our revenue from the sale of goods includes revenue from the sale of customer equipment and similar goods. This revenue is recorded on delivery of the goods sold. Generally we record the full gross amount of sales proceeds as revenue, however if we are acting as an agent under a sales arrangement, we record the revenue on a net basis, being the gross amount billed less the amount paid to the supplier. We review the facts and circumstances of each sales arrangement to determine if we are an agent or principal under the sale arrangement.

Revenue arrangements with multiple deliverables Where two or more revenue-generating activities or deliverables are sold under a single arrangement, each deliverable that is considered to be a separate unit of accounting is accounted for separately. When the deliverables in a multiple deliverable arrangement are not considered to be separate units of accounting, the arrangement is accounted for as a single unit. We allocate the consideration from the revenue arrangement to its separate units based on the relative selling prices of each unit. If neither vendor specific objective evidence nor third party evidence exists for the selling price, then the item is measured based on the best estimate of the selling price (BESP) of that unit. The revenue allocated to each unit is then recognised in accordance with our revenue recognition policies described above.

Required

a. When Telstra sells a smart phone to a new customer, the sales contract typically comprises three deliverables bundled for one price. What are the three deliverables?

b. Explain in layman's terms how Telstra records revenue from sales of bundled contracts.

c. Telstra sells a number of pre-paid mobile packages for voice, text, and data. Assume a customer pays $100 in cash for a pre-paid plan and Telstra activates service immediately. Explain how and when Telstra recognizes the $100 as revenue.

d. Assume that at the beginning of the fiscal year, a customer makes a volume purchase of 200 iPhones and signs a two-year contract with Telstra for a voice and data package for each phone. The total discounted sales price is $480 per phone and Telstra pays Apple $640 for each iPhone. This contract includes free future software upgrades for two years. Because there is no reliable VSOE, Telstra estimates a BESP of $64 for the future software upgrades. Allocate the consideration received for the 200 units to each respective element in the arrangement, based on its relative selling price (the sale is on account).

e. Use the financial statement effects template to record the original sale in part *d*, above, and the accounting adjustment at the end of the first fiscal year after the sale.

I5-47. Analyzing Income Tax Disclosures (LO3)

Telstra Corporation Limited is an Australian telecommunications and media company that builds and provides land-based and mobile telecom services along with internet and pay television products. The company is Australia's largest 3G and 4G enabled mobile network. The footnote below reports income statement and balance sheet data for the company's income taxes.

	As at 30 June	
($ in millions)	**2012**	**2011**
Major components of income tax expense		
Current tax expense	$1,826	$1,519
Deferred tax resulting from the origination and reversal of temporary differences	(337)	(209)
Under/(over) provision of tax in prior years	21	(3)
	$1,510	$1,307
Notional income tax expense on profit differs from actual income tax expenses recorded as follows:		
Profit before income tax expense	$4,934	$4,557
Notional income tax expense calculated at the Australian tax rate of 30%	$ 1,480	$ 1,367
Which is adjusted by the tax effect of:		
Different rates of tax on overseas income	(15)	(17)
Non-assessable and non-deductible items	63	(16)
Amended assessments	(39)	(24)
Under/(over) provision of tax in prior years	21	(3)
Income tax expense on profit	$1,510	$1,307

Deferred tax (liability) asset		
Property, plant and equipment	$(1,241)	$(1,434)
Intangible assets	(830)	(876)
Borrowings and derivative financial instruments	(59)	(90)
Provision for employee entitlements	292	252
Revenue received in advance	194	52
Provision for workers' compensation	20	21
Allowance for doubtful debts	57	64
Defined benefit liability/asset	98	138
Trade and other payables	111	135
Other provisions	49	52
Income tax losses	39	46
Other	(32)	(29)
	$(1,302)	$(1,669)

Required

a. What income tax expense does Telstra report in its 2012 income statement? How much of this expense was paid during the year or is currently payable?
b. Determine the company's effective tax rate.
c. What is the company's marginal (statutory) tax rate?
d. Telstra reports $1,241 million of deferred tax liabilities in 2012 relating to "Property, plant and equipment." Explain how such liabilities arise.
e. Describe how a $292 million deferred tax asset can arise from "Provision for employee entitlements."

I5-48. Identifying Operating Income Components (LO2)
Refer to the income statement information for Bombardier in I5-43 above. Identify the components that we would consider operating.

I5-49. Identifying Operating Income Components, Analyzing Earnings Per Share (LO1, 2, 5)
Headquartered in Ottawa, Ontario, Canada, **Mitel Networks Corporation** is a high-tech company that provides unified communications solutions for business. The company focuses almost entirely on Voice-over-IP (VoIP) products. Mitel has partners and resellers worldwide and is listed on the NASDAQ; its income statement follows. Mitel (MITL)

MITEL NETWORKS CORPORATION
CONSOLIDATED STATEMENTS OF OPERATIONS

(in U.S. dollars, millions, except per share amounts)	April 30, 2012	April 30, 2011	April 30, 2010
Revenues	$611.8	$589.3	$599.1
Cost of revenues	282.4	281.9	288.6
Gross margin	329.4	307.4	310.5
Expenses:			
Selling, general and administrative	222.9	212.8	203.6
Research and development	58.6	61.3	57.6
Special charges and restructuring costs	17.1	15.5	5.2
Loss (gain) on litigation settlement	1.5	1.0	(5.5)
	300.1	290.6	260.9
Operating income from continuing operations	29.3	16.8	49.6
Interest expense	(18.8)	(20.0)	(29.8)
Debt retirement costs, including write-off of related deferred financing costs	—	(0.6)	(1.0)
Fair value adjustment on derivative instruments	—	1.0	7.4
Other income (expense), net	(0.7)	0.8	0.9
Income (loss) from continuing operations, before income taxes	9.8	(2.0)	27.1
Current income tax recovery (expense)	(8.4)	(8.0)	(3.6)
Deferred income tax recovery (expense)	47.8	96.4	12.6
Net income from continuing operations	49.2	86.4	36.1
Net income from discontinued operations	0.6	1.7	1.1
Net income	$ 49.8	$ 88.1	$ 37.2
Net income (loss) per common share—Basic:			
Net income (loss) per share from continuing operations	$ 0.92	$ 1.63	$ (7.37)
Net income per share from discontinued operations	$ 0.01	$ 0.03	$ 0.07
Net income (loss) per share	$ 0.93	$ 1.66	$ (7.30)
Net income (loss) per common share—Diluted:			
Net income (loss) per share from continuing operations	$ 0.88	$ 1.54	$ (7.37)
Net income per share from discontinued operations	$ 0.01	$ 0.03	$ 0.07
Net income (loss) per share	$ 0.89	$ 1.57	$ (7.30)
Weighted-average number of common shares outstanding:			
Basic	53.5	52.9	14.7
Diluted	56.0	56.0	14.7

Required

a. Identify the components considered operating for each year.
b. Identify the non-recurring items for 2012 and explain how financial analysts would treat each item.

c. What did the company report for basic and diluted earnings per share in 2012?
d. Provide two reasons that basic and diluted earnings per share differ in 2012.

MANAGEMENT APPLICATIONS

MA5-50. Managing Foreign Currency Risk **(LO4)**
Fluctuations in foreign currency exchange rates can result in increased volatility of revenues, expenses, and profits. Companies generally attempt to reduce this volatility.

a. Identify two possible solutions to reduce the volatility effect of foreign exchange rate fluctuations.
b. What costs would arise if you implemented each of your solutions?

MA5-51. Ethics and Governance: Revenue Recognition **(LO1)**
GAAP offers latitude in determining when revenue is earned. Assume that a company that normally required acceptance by its customers prior to recording revenue as earned, delivers a product to a customer near the end of the quarter. The company believes that customer acceptance is assured, but cannot obtain it prior to quarter-end. Recording the revenue would assure "making its numbers" for the quarter. Although formal acceptance is not obtained, the salesperson records the sale, fully intending to obtain written acceptance as soon as possible.

a. What are the revenue recognition requirements in this case?
b. What are the ethical issues relating to this sale?
c. Assume you are on the board of directors of this company. What safeguards can you put in place to provide assurance that the company's revenue recognition policy is followed?

MA5-52. Ethics and Governance: Earnings Management **(LO2)**
Assume that you are CEO of a company. Your company has reported a loss for the current year. Since it cannot carry back the entire loss to recoup taxes paid in prior years, it records a loss carryforward as a deferred tax asset. Your expectation is that future profitability will be sufficient to realize the tax benefits of the carryforward. Your chief financial officer approaches you with an idea to create a deferred tax valuation allowance that will reduce the deferred tax asset, increase tax expense for the year, and increase your reported loss. He reasons that the company's stock price will not be reduced markedly by the additional reported loss since a loss year has already been factored into the current price. Further, this deferred tax valuation allowance will create a reserve that can be used in future years to increase profit (via reversal of the allowance) if needed to meet analyst expectations.

a. What stakeholders are potentially affected by the CFO's proposal?
b. How do you respond to the proposal? Justify your response.

ONGOING PROJECT

(This ongoing project began in Module 1 and continues through most of the book; even if previous segments were not completed, the requirements are still applicable to any business analysis.) Analysis of financial statements commonly includes operating income and its components as explained in this module.

1. *Revenue Recognition* Revenue is the largest item on the income statement and we must assess it on a quantitative and qualitative basis.
   - Use horizontal analysis to identify any time trends
   - Compare the horizontal analyses of the two companies.
   - Consider the current economic environment and the companies' competitive landscape. Given that they operate in the same industry, you might expect similar revenue trends.
   - Read the management's discussion and analysis (MD&A) section of the 10-K to learn how the companies' senior managers explain revenue levels and changes.

   Our goal is to determine whether each company's revenue levels and changes seem appropriate and in line with external factors. *Additional analysis*: (a) If the company distinguishes among types of revenue on the income statement, use horizontal and vertical analysis to identify any changes in the product line mix or where sales are growing most quickly. Find the footnote on segment revenues and profits and identify trends or significant changes. (b) Assess each company's revenue recognition policy by comparing it to the other and to those of some other close competitors. (c) Consider unearned revenue on the balance sheet. How big is it (common size) and is it fluctuating over time? (d) For companies that operate globally, determine the effect of foreign currency fluctuations on revenue. If these are substantial year after year, it might indicate that managers are not effectively hedging and this would warrant additional investigation.

2. *R&D Activities* Do the companies engage in substantial R&D activities?
   - Determine the amount of the expense on the income statement—we might need to look in the footnotes or the MD&A for this information. Is the common-sized amount changing over time? What pattern is detected?
   - Read the footnotes and assess the company's R&D pipeline. What are the major outcomes or innovations during the year? Compare the two companies in terms of outcomes.
   - Does the company acquire the R&D of other companies? Is this a sustained pattern of investment of an occasional event?

   Evaluating the R&D activity of the companies involves a deeper understanding of their operations but the steps above will provide us a broad view and point out major changes or events.

3. *Restructuring Activities* Have the companies restructured operations in the past three years?
   - Determine the amount of the expense on the income statement—we might need to look in the footnotes or the MD&A for this information.
   - Are other close competitors also restructuring during this time period?
   - Read the footnotes and assess the company's restructuring plans. How many years will it take to fully execute the plan? What additional expenditures are required?
   - Find the restructuring liability on the balance sheet (again the notes will help). Does the liability seem reasonable over time?
   - Are there significant reversals of prior accruals? This might indicate income shifting.

4. *Tax Disclosures and Strategies* Examine the income tax expense and deferred tax assets and liabilities.
   - Determine the amount of tax expense on the income statement and distinguish between current and deferred portions.
   - Read the footnotes and assess the company's effective tax rate. Is it a consistent rate? If not, do the fluctuations seem reasonable?
   - Do the deferred tax assets and liabilities seem appropriate given the company's industry?
   - Is there a valuation allowance? If so, how big is it relative to total deferred tax assets? Has the valuation allowance changed markedly during the year? This might indicate income shifting.

5. *Accounting Quality* Evaluating accounting quality is more of an art than a science. The point is to form an overall opinion about the reliability of the numbers in the financial statements.
   - Consider the list in the section titled "Assessing and Remediating Accounting Quality" and use it to assess the quality of the companies' reported numbers.
   - Use an online investment Website to find key ratios for close competitors. Compare to our companies.
   - Find the consensus analysts' EPS forecast for the recent year end. How did our companies fare? Were there any one-time items or unusual changes in any expenses that might have caused the company to just meet or beat the forecast? This could indicate earnings management.
   - Does the company report non-GAAP earnings? What items do they exclude or include? Do the two companies report similar "one-time" items? Do the items seem reasonable or do we detect some self-serving disclosures?

SOLUTIONS TO REVIEW PROBLEMS

Mid-Module Review 1

Solution

1. GAAP specifies that revenue recognition should occur *when (or as) a good or service is transferred to the customer and the customer obtains control of that good or service*. Merck delivers its product before the customer is obligated to make payment. Passage of title typically constitutes delivery. Merck's policy appears to be reasonable given its product and GAAP requirements.
2. All R&D related equipment and/or facilities that have no alternative use must be expensed under GAAP. Assets that have other uses are capitalized and depreciated like other plant assets. R&D costs are aggre-

gated into one line item (research and development expense) on Merck's income statement. Other costs are reported under materials and production and/or marketing and administrative expenses.

3. Restructuring expenses generally fall into three categories: severance costs, asset write-offs, and other costs. Restructuring programs must be approved by the board of directors before they are recognized in financial statements. Further, companies are required to disclose the initial liability (accrual) together with the portion that was subsequently utilized or reversed, if any. Because the restructuring accrual is an estimate, overestimates and subsequent reversals are possible. Should the company develop a reputation for recurring reversals, it will lose credibility with analysts and other stakeholders.

Mid-Module Review 2

Solution

1. Total income tax expense is $2,440 million.
2. $1,771 million is currently payable or has already been paid during 2012.
3. Income tax expense is the sum of current taxes (that is, currently payable as determined from the company's tax returns) plus the change in deferred tax assets and liabilities. It is a calculated figure, not a percentage that is applied to pretax income. For 2012, reported tax expense was *increased* by the deferred provision (a liability) of $669 million.

Module-End Review

Solution

1. Income statement accounts that are denominated in foreign currencies must be translated into $US before the financial statements are publicly disclosed. When the $US weakens, each foreign currency unit is worth more $US. Consequently, each account in Merck's income statement is larger because the dollar weakened. Because Merck reported *positive* earnings (a profit) for 2012, net income also would be larger.
2. Basic earnings per share is equal to net income (less preferred dividends) divided by the weighted average number of common shares outstanding during the period. Diluted EPS considers the effects of dilutive securities. In diluted EPS, the denominator increases by the additional shares that would have been issued assuming exercise of all options and conversion of all convertible securities. The numerator is also adjusted for any preferred dividends and/or interest that would not have been paid upon conversion.

Module

6 Reporting and Analyzing Operating Assets

Learning Objectives

LO1 Describe accounting for accounts receivable and the importance of the allowance for uncollectible accounts in determining profit. (p. 6-3)

LO2 Explain accounting for inventories and assess the effects on the balance sheet and income statement from different inventory costing methods. (p. 6-13)

LO3 Describe accounting for property, plant and equipment and explain the impacts on profit and cash flows from depreciation methods, disposals and impairments. (p. 6-26)

Cisco Systems

Cisco Systems' vision and strategy is to become the most strategic business partner for its customers by delivering intelligent networks, technology and business architectures built on integrated products, services, and software platforms. Nowhere was this more evident than in the role that Cisco played in the 2012 London Olympic Games; the company provided network infrastructure that enabled 1,800 Wi-Fi hot spots and 80,000 data connections and had a capacity four times larger than the network infrastructure of any previous Olympic Games. Cisco technology and solutions helped connect an estimated 10 million spectators, 76,000 volunteers, and 22,000 athletes and coaches in a way never before possible.

Cisco reported 2012 net income of $8 billion on $46 billion in sales, and a return on net operating assets (RNOA) of 42%. In 2001, Cisco reported a *loss* of $1 billion after recording nearly $4 billion of restructuring costs, including costs related to the severance of 6,000 employees and the write-off of obsolete inventory and other assets.

Cisco's turnaround is remarkable. Its return on net operating assets has remained at or above 40% during the past 5 years, which reflects Cisco's effective asset (balance sheet) management. Recall that RNOA comprises both a profitability component and a productivity component (see Module 4). The productivity component (reflected in net operating asset turnover, NOAT) is measured as sales divided by average net operating assets. Effective management of operating assets is crucial to achieving a high RNOA. We focus on three important operating assets in this module: accounts receivable, inventories, and property, plant and equipment (PPE).

As part of their overall marketing efforts, companies extend credit to customers. At Cisco, for example, accounts receivable are an important asset because nearly all sales are on account. While favorable credit terms stimulate sales, the resulting accounts receivable are costly. First, accounts receivable are generally non-interest bearing and tie up a company's working capital in non-earning assets. Second, receivables expose the company to collectibility risk—the risk that some customers won't pay. Third, companies incur the administrative costs associated with billing and collection. These costs must be weighed against the

Courtesy of Shutterstock

costs of other marketing tools, like advertising, sales incentives, and price discounts. Management of receivables is critical to financial success.

Inventories are significant assets at many companies, particularly for manufacturers such as Cisco, where inventories consist of raw materials (the basic product inputs), work in process (the cost of partially completed products), and finished goods (completed products awaiting sale). Inventories are also costly to maintain. The cost of buying and manufacturing the goods must be financed and inventories must be stored, moved, and insured. Consequently, companies prefer lower inventory levels whenever possible. However, companies must be careful to hold enough inventory. If they reduce inventory quantities too far, they risk inventory stock-outs, that is, not having enough inventory to meet demand. Management of inventories is also a critical activity.

Property, plant and equipment (PPE) is often the largest, and usually the most important, asset on the balance sheet. Companies need administrative offices, IT and R&D facilities, regional sales and customer service offices, manufacturing and distribution facilities, vehicles, computers, and a host of other fixed assets. Fixed-asset costs are substantial and are indirectly linked to sales and profits. Consequently, fixed-asset investments are often difficult to justify and, once acquired, fixed assets are often difficult to divest. Effective management of PPE assets usually requires management review of the entire value chain.

John Chambers, CEO of Cisco, recalls a conversation he once had with the legendary Jack Welch, former Chairman of GE. Following Cisco's announced restructuring program in 2001, Welch commented, "John, you'll never have a great company until you go through the really tough times. What builds a company is not just how you handle the successes, but it's the way you handle the real challenges." Cisco survived the tech bubble burst and is now reporting impressive financial results. To ensure future financial performance, however, Cisco must effectively manage both its income statement and its operating assets.

Sources: Cisco Systems 2012 10-K; Cisco Systems 2012 Annual Report; *BusinessWeek,* 2012, 2006 and 2003; *Fortune,* April 2009.

MODULE ORGANIZATION

Reporting and Analyzing Operating Assets

Accounts Receivable
- Allowance for Uncollectible Accounts
- Footnote Disclosures
- Adequacy of Allowance and Income Shifting
- Accounts Receivable Turnover

Inventories
- Inventory Costing Methods
- Footnote Disclosures
- Effects of Inventory Costing
- Gross Profit Analysis
- Inventory Turnover

Property, Plant & Equipment
- Depreciation and Book Value
- Asset Sales and Impairments
- Footnote Disclosures
- Turnover of Property, Plant and Equipment

Managing net operating assets is crucial to creating shareholder value. To manage and assess net operating assets, we need to understand how they are measured and reported. This module describes the reporting and measuring of operating working capital, mainly receivables and inventories, and of long-term operating assets such as property, plant, and equipment. We do not discuss other long-term operating assets, such as equity investments in affiliated companies, investment in intangible assets, and nonoperating investments in marketable securities, as they are covered in other modules.

Receivables are usually a major part of operating working capital. They must be carefully managed as they represent a substantial asset for most companies and are an important marketing tool. GAAP requires companies to report receivables at the amount they expect to collect. This requires estimation of uncollectible accounts. The receivables reported on the balance sheet, and the expenses reported on the income statement, reflect management's estimate of uncollectible amounts. Accordingly, it is important that companies accurately assess uncollectible accounts and timely report them. It is also necessary that readers of financial reports understand management's accounting choices and their effects on reported balance sheets and income statements.

Inventory is another major component of operating working capital. Inventories usually constitute one of the three largest assets (along with receivables and long-term operating assets). Also, cost of goods sold, which flows from inventory, is the largest expense category for retailing and manufacturing companies. GAAP allows several methods for inventory accounting, and inventory-costing choices can markedly impact balance sheets and income statements, especially for companies experiencing relatively high inflation, coupled with slowly turning inventories.

Long-term plant assets are often the largest component of operating assets. Indeed, long-term operating assets are typically the largest asset for manufacturing companies, and their related depreciation expense is typically second only in amount to cost of goods sold in the income statement. GAAP allows different accounting methods for computing depreciation, which can significantly impact the income statement and the balance sheet. When companies dispose of fixed assets, a gain or loss may result. Understanding these gains and losses on asset sales is important as we assess performance. Further, asset write-downs (impairments) not only affect companies' current financial performance, but also future profitability. We must understand these effects when we forecast future income statements. This module considers all of these fixed asset accounting choices and consequences.

LO1 Describe accounting for accounts receivable and the importance of the allowance for uncollectible accounts in determining profit.

ACCOUNTS RECEIVABLE

Our focus on operating assets begins with accounts receivable. To help frame our discussion, we refer to the following graphic as we proceed through the module:

Income Statement
Sales
Cost of goods sold
Selling, general & administrative
Income taxes
Net income

Balance Sheet	
Cash	Current liabilities
Accounts receivable, net	Long-term liabilities
Inventory	
Property, plant, and equipment, net	Stockholders' equity
Investments	

The graphic highlights the balance sheet and income statement effects of accounts receivable. This section explains the accounting, reporting, and analysis of these highlighted items.

Retail companies transact mostly in cash. But other companies, including those that sell to other firms, usually do not expect cash upon delivery. Instead, they offer credit terms and have *credit sales* or *sales on account*.[1] An account receivable on the seller's balance sheet is always matched by a corresponding account payable on the buyer's balance sheet. Accounts receivable are reported on the seller's balance sheet at *net realizable value*, which is the net amount the seller expects to collect.

Sellers do not expect to collect all accounts receivable; they anticipate that some buyers will be unable to pay their accounts when they come due. For example, buyers can suffer business downturns that limit the cash available to meet liabilities. Then, buyers must decide which liabilities to pay. Typically, financially distressed companies decide to pay off liabilities to the IRS, to banks, and to bondholders because those creditors have enforcement powers and can quickly seize assets and disrupt operations, leading to bankruptcy and eventual liquidation. Buyers also try to cover their payroll, as they cannot exist without employees. Then, if there is cash remaining, buyers will pay suppliers to ensure continued flow of goods.

Accounts payable are *unsecured liabilities,* meaning that buyers have not pledged collateral to guarantee payment of amounts owed. As a result, when a company declares bankruptcy, accounts payable are comingled with other unsecured creditors (after the IRS and the secured creditors), and are typically not paid in full. Consequently, there is risk in the collectibility of accounts receivable. This *collectibility risk* is crucial to analysis of accounts receivable.

Cisco reports $4,369 million of accounts receivable in the current asset section of its fiscal year-end 2012 balance sheet.

$ millions	July 28, 2012
Cash and cash equivalents	$ 9,799
Investments	38,917
Accounts receivable, net of allowance for doubtful accounts of $207 at July 28, 2012	4,369
Inventories	1,663
Financing receivables, net	3,661
Deferred tax assets	2,294
Other current assets	1,230
Total current assets	$61,933

Cisco reports its receivables net of allowances for doubtful (uncollectible) accounts of $207 million. This means the total amount owed to Cisco is $4,576 million ($4,369 million + $207 million), but Cisco *estimates* that $207 million are uncollectible and reports on its balance sheet only the amount it expects to collect.

We might ask why buyers would sell to companies from whom they do not expect to collect. The answer is they would not have extended credit *if* they knew beforehand which companies would eventually not pay. For example, Cisco probably cannot identify precisely those companies that constitute the $207 million in uncollectible accounts. Yet, it knows from past experience that a certain portion of its

[1] An example of common credit terms are 2/10, net 30. These terms indicate that the seller offers the buyer an early-pay incentive, in this case a 2% discount off the cost if the buyer pays within 10 days of billing. If the buyer does not take advantage of the discount, it must pay 100% of the invoice cost within 30 days of billing. From the seller's standpoint, offering the discount is often warranted because it speeds up cash collections and then the seller can invest the cash to yield a return greater than the early-payment discount. The buyer often wishes to avail itself of attractive discounts even if it has to borrow money to do so. If the discount is not taken, however, the buyer should withhold payment as long as possible (at least for the full net period) so as to maximize its available cash. Meanwhile, the seller will exert whatever pressure it can to collect the amount due as quickly as possible. Thus, it is normal for there to be some tension between sellers and buyers.

receivables will prove uncollectible. GAAP requires companies to estimate the dollar amount of uncollectible accounts (even if managers cannot identify specific accounts that are uncollectible), and to report accounts receivable at the resulting *net realizable value* (total receivables less an allowance for uncollectible accounts).

Allowance for Uncollectible Accounts

Companies typically use an *aging analysis* to estimate the amount of uncollectible accounts. This requires an analysis of receivables as of the balance sheet date. Specifically, customer accounts are categorized by the number of days that the related invoices have been unpaid (outstanding). Based on prior experience, or on other available statistics, uncollectible percentages are applied to each category, with larger percentages applied to older accounts. The result of this analysis is a dollar amount for the allowance for uncollectible accounts (also called allowance for doubtful accounts) at the balance sheet date.

Aging Analysis

To illustrate, Exhibit 6.1 shows an aging analysis for a seller with $100,000 of gross accounts receivable at period-end. The current accounts are those that are still within their original credit period. As an example, if a seller's credit terms are 2/10, net 30, all invoices that have been outstanding for 30 days or fewer are current. Accounts listed as 1–60 days past due are those 1 to 60 days past their due date. This would include an account that is 45 days outstanding for a net 30-day invoice. This same logic applies to all categories.

EXHIBIT 6.1 Aging of Accounts Receivable

Age of Accounts	Receivable Balance	Estimated Percent Uncollectible	Estimated Uncollectible Accounts
Current	$ 50,000	2%	$1,000
1-60 days past due	30,000	3	900
61-90 days past due	15,000	4	600
Over 90 days past due	5,000	8	400
Total	$100,000		$2,900

Exhibit 6.1 also reflects the seller's experience with uncollectible accounts, which manifests itself in the uncollectible percentages for each aged category. For example, on average, 3% of buyers' accounts that are 1–60 days past due prove uncollectible for this seller. Hence, the company estimates a potential loss of $900 for the $30,000 in receivables 1 to 60 days past due.

Reporting Receivables

The seller represented in Exhibit 6.1 reports its accounts receivable on the balance sheet as follows:

Accounts receivable, net of $2,900 in allowances	$97,100

Assume that, as of the end of the *previous* accounting period, the company had estimated total uncollectible accounts of $2,200 based on an aging analysis of the receivables at that time. Also assume that the company did not write off any accounts receivable during the period. The *reconciliation* of its allowance account for the period follows:

Beginning allowance for uncollectible accounts	$ 2,200
Add: Provision for uncollectible accounts (bad debts expense)	700
Less: Write-offs of accounts receivable	0
Ending allowance for uncollectible accounts	$ 2,900

The aging analysis revealed that the allowance for uncollectible accounts is $700 too low and, therefore, the company increased the allowance accordingly. This adjustment affects the financial statements as follows:

1. Accounts receivable are reduced by an additional $700 on the balance sheet (receivables are reported *net* of the allowance account).

2. A $700 expense, called bad debts expense, is reported in the income statement (usually part of SG&A expense). This reduces pretax profit by the same amount.[2]

The allowance for uncollectible accounts, a contra-asset account, increases with new provisions (additional bad debts expense) and decreases as accounts are written off. Individual accounts are written off when the seller identifies them as uncollectible. (A write-off reduces both accounts receivable and the allowance for uncollectible accounts as described below.) As with all permanent accounts on the balance sheet, the ending balance of the allowance account is the beginning balance for next period.

Writing Off Accounts

To illustrate the write-off of an account receivable, assume that subsequent to the period-end shown above, the seller receives notice that one of its customers, owing $500 at the time, has declared bankruptcy. The seller's attorneys believe that legal costs in attempting to collect this receivable would likely exceed the amount owed. So, the seller decides not to pursue collection and to write off this account. The write-off has the following effects:

1. Gross accounts receivable are reduced from $100,000 to $99,500.
2. Allowance for uncollectible accounts is reduced from $2,900 to $2,400.

After the write-off, the seller's balance sheet appears as follows:

Accounts receivable, net of $2,400 in allowances	$97,100

Exhibit 6.2 shows the effects of this write-off on the individual accounts.

EXHIBIT 6.2 Effects of an Accounts Receivable Write-Off

Account	Before Write-Off	Effects of Write-Off	After Write-Off
Accounts receivable	$100,000	$(500)	$99,500
Less: Allowance for uncollectible accounts	2,900	(500)	2,400
Accounts receivable, net of allowance	$ 97,100		$97,100

The balance of net accounts receivable is the same before and after the write-off. This is always the case. The write-off of an account is a non-event from an accounting point of view. That is, total assets do not change, liabilities stay the same, and equity is unaffected as there is no net income effect. The write-off affects individual asset accounts, but not total assets.

Let's next consider what happens when additional information alters management's expectations of uncollectible accounts. To illustrate, assume that sometime after the write-off above, the seller realizes that it has underestimated uncollectible accounts and that $3,000 (not $2,400) of the remaining $99,500 accounts receivable are uncollectible. The company must increase the allowance for uncollectible accounts by $600. The additional $600 provision has the following financial statement effects:

1. Allowance for uncollectible accounts increases by $600 to the revised estimated balance of $3,000; and accounts receivable (net of the allowance for uncollectible accounts) declines by $600 from $97,100 to $96,500 (or $99,500 − $3,000).
2. A $600 bad debts expense is added to the income statement, which reduces pretax income. Recall that in the prior period, the seller reported $700 of bad debts expense when the allowance account was increased from $2,200 to $2,900.

[2] Companies can also estimate uncollectible accounts using the *percentage of sales* method. The percentage of sales method computes bad debts expense directly, as a percentage of sales and the allowance for uncollectible accounts is estimated indirectly. In contrast, the aging method computes the allowance balance directly and the bad debts expense is the amount required to bring the allowance account up to (or down to) the amount determined by the aging analysis. To illustrate, if the company in Exhibit 6.1 reports sales of $100,000 and estimates the provision at 1% of sales, it would report a bad debts expense of $1,000 and an allowance balance of $3,200 instead of the $700 bad debts expense and the $2,900 allowance as determined using the aging analysis. The two methods nearly always report different values for the allowance, net accounts receivable, and bad debts expense.

Analyzing Receivable Transactions

To summarize, recording bad debts expense increases the allowance for uncollectible accounts, which affects both the *balance sheet* and *income statement*. Importantly, the financial statement effects occur when the allowance is estimated, and not when accounts are written off. In this way, bad debts expense is matched with sales on the income statement, and accounts receivable are reported net of uncollectible accounts on the balance sheet. Exhibit 6.3 illustrates each of the transactions discussed in this section using the financial statement effects template:

AR 100,000
Sales 100,000
AR: 100,000 |
Sales: | 100,000

BDE 700
AU 700
BDE: 700 |
AU: | 700

AU 500
AR 500
AU: 500 |
AR: | 500

BDE 600
AU 600
BDE: 600 |
AU: | 600

EXHIBIT 6.3 Financial Statement Effects of Key Accounts Receivable Transactions

	Balance Sheet					Income Statement		
Transaction	Cash Asset +	Noncash Assets =	Liabilities +	Contrib. Capital +	Earned Capital	Revenues −	Expenses =	Net Income
a. Credit sales of $100,000		+100,000 Accounts Receivable =			+100,000 Retained Earnings	+100,000 Sales −	=	+100,000
b. Increase allowance for uncollectible accounts by $700		−700 Allowance for Uncollectible Accounts =			−700 Retained Earnings	−	+700 Bad Debts Expense =	−700
c. Write off $500 in accounts receivable		−500 Accounts Receivable +500 Allowance for Uncollectible Accounts =				−	=	
d. Increase allowance for uncollectible accounts by $600		−600 Allowance for Uncollectible Accounts =			−600 Retained Earnings	−	+600 Bad Debts Expense =	−600

Footnote and MD&A Disclosures

To illustrate the typical accounts receivable disclosure, consider **Cisco**'s discussion of its allowance for uncollectible accounts (from its MD&A):

Allowances for Receivables

The allowances for receivables were as follows (in millions, except percentages):

	July 28, 2012	July 30, 2011
Allowance for doubtful accounts	$207	$204
Percentage of gross accounts receivable	*4.5%*	*4.2%*
Allowance for credit loss—lease receivables	$247	$237
Percentage of gross lease receivables	*7.2%*	*7.6%*
Allowance for credit loss—loan receivables	$122	$103
Percentage of gross loan receivables	*6.8%*	*7.0%*

The allowance for doubtful accounts is based on our assessment of the collectibility of customer accounts. We regularly review the adequacy of these allowances by considering internal factors

continued

such as historical experience, credit quality and age of the receivable balances as well as external factors such as economic conditions that may affect a customer's ability to pay and expected default frequency rates, which are published by major third-party credit-rating agencies and are generally updated on a quarterly basis. We also consider the concentration of receivables outstanding with a particular customer in assessing the adequacy of our allowances for doubtful accounts. If a major customer's creditworthiness deteriorates, if actual defaults are higher than our historical experience, or if other circumstances arise, our estimates of the recoverability of amounts due to us could be overstated, and additional allowances could be required, which could have an adverse impact on our revenue.

Cisco's allowance for uncollectible accounts increased slightly as a percentage of gross receivables from the prior year, from 4.2% to 4.5%. This percentage is markedly less than the 6.4% Cisco reported in 2009. As the economy emerged from recession in 2010, Cisco estimated that collectibility of its receivables would improve and then reduced its estimate of uncollectible accounts. This reduction increased income because the provision charged to expense was lower. However, Cisco alludes to the level of estimation required and cautions the reader that additional allowances (provisions) could be required under certain circumstances, and that would adversely affect profit.

Cisco provides a footnote reconciliation of its allowance for uncollectible (doubtful) accounts for the past three years as shown in Exhibit 6.4.

EXHIBIT 6.4 **Reconciliation of Cisco's Allowance for Uncollectible Accounts**

$ millions	Allowance for Doubtful Accounts
Year ended July 31, 2010	
Balance at beginning of fiscal year	$216
Provision	44
Write-offs and other	(25)
Balance at end of fiscal year	$235
Year ended July 30, 2011	
Balance at beginning of fiscal year	$235
Provision	7
Write-offs and other	(38)
Balance at end of fiscal year	$204
Year ended July 28, 2012	
Balance at beginning of fiscal year	$204
Provision	19
Write-offs and other	(16)
Balance at end of fiscal year	$207

Reconciling Cisco's allowance account provides insight into the level of the provision (expense) each year relative to the actual write-offs. Over the three-year period ended in 2012, Cisco wrote off $79 million of uncollectible accounts ($25 million + $38 million + $16 million) and increased its allowance by $70 million ($44 million + $7 million + $19 million), resulting in a net decrease of $9 million ($207 million − $216 million). The allowance for uncollectible accounts as a percentage of gross accounts receivable was 4.5% in 2012, 1.9 percentage points less than the level Cisco estimated in 2009, toward the end of the recession. This reduction reflects the company's perception that the credit quality of its receivables portfolio is improving as the economy continues to grow.

Analysis Implications

This section considers analysis of accounts receivable and the allowance for uncollectible accounts.

Adequacy of Allowance Account

A company makes two representations when reporting accounts receivable (net) in the current asset section of its balance sheet:

1. It expects to collect the amount reported on the balance sheet (remember, accounts receivable are reported net of allowance for uncollectible accounts).
2. It expects to collect the amount within the next year (implied by the classification of accounts receivable as a current asset).

From an analysis viewpoint, we scrutinize the adequacy of a company's provision for its uncollectible accounts. If the provision is inadequate, the cash ultimately collected will be less than the net receivables reported on the balance sheet.

How can an outsider assess the adequacy of the allowance account? One answer is to compare the allowance account to gross accounts receivable for the company and for its competitors. For Cisco, the 2012 percentage is 4.5% (see above), a 30% decline from the level it reported in 2009. What does such a decline signify? Perhaps the overall economic environment has improved, rendering write-offs less likely. Perhaps the company has improved its credit underwriting or receivables collection efforts. The MD&A section of the 10-K report is likely to discuss such new initiatives. Or perhaps the company's customer mix has changed and it is now selling to more creditworthy customers (or, it eliminated a risky class of customers).

The important point is that we must be comfortable with the percentage of uncollectible accounts reported by the company. We must remember that management controls the size of the allowance account—albeit with audit assurances.

Income Shifting

We explained how bad debts expense is recognized in the income statement when the allowance is increased and not when the allowance is decreased for the write-off of uncollectible accounts. It is also important to note that management controls the amount and timing of the bad debts expense. Although external auditors assess the reasonableness of the allowance for uncollectible accounts, they do not possess management's inside knowledge and experience. This puts the auditors at an information disadvantage, particularly if any dispute arises.

Studies show that many companies use the allowance for uncollectible accounts to shift income from one year into another. For example, a company can increase current-period income by deliberately underestimating bad debts expense. However, in the future it will become apparent that the bad debts expense was too low when the company's write-offs exceed the balance in the allowance account. Then, the company will need to increase the allowance to make up for the earlier period's underestimate. As an example, consider a company that accurately estimates that it has $1,000 of uncollectible accounts at the end of 2013. Assume that the current balance in the allowance for uncollectible accounts is $200. But instead of recording bad debts expense of $800 as needed to have an adequate ($1,000) allowance, the company records only $100 of bad debts expense and reports an allowance of $300 at the end of 2013. Now if the company's original estimate was accurate, in 2014 it will write off accounts totaling $1,000. The write-offs ($1,000) are greater than the allowance balance ($300) and the company will need to increase the allowance by recording an additional $700 in 2014. The effect of this is that the company borrowed $700 of income from 2014 to report higher income in 2013. This is called "income shifting."

Why would a company want to shift income from a later period into the current period? Perhaps it is a lean year and the company is in danger of missing income targets. For example, internal targets influence manager bonuses and external targets set by the market influence stock prices. Or, perhaps the company is in danger of defaulting on loan agreements tied to income levels. The reality is that income pressures are great and these pressures can cause managers to bend (or even break) the rules.

Companies can just as easily shift income from the current period to one or more future periods by overestimating the current period bad debts expense and allowance for uncollectible accounts. Why would a company want to shift income to one or more future periods? Perhaps the company's current income is high and it wants to "bank" some of that income for future periods, sometimes called a *cookie jar reserve*. It can then draw on that reserve, if necessary, to boost income in one or more future lean years. Another reason for a company to shift income from the current period is that it does not wish to unduly inflate market expectations for future period income. Or perhaps the company is experiencing a very bad year and it feels that overestimating the provision will not drive income materially lower than it is. Thus, it decides to take a *big bath* (a large loss) and create a reserve that can be used in future periods.

Use of the allowance for uncollectible accounts to shift income is a source of concern. This is especially so for banks where the allowance for loan losses is a large component of banks' balance sheets and loan loss expense is a major component of reported income. Our analysis must scrutinize the allowance for uncollectible accounts to identify any changes from past practices or industry norms and, then, to justify those changes before accepting them as valid.

BUSINESS INSIGHT **JP Morgan Loan Loss Allowance**

JP Morgan released its Q1 2012 income statement and reported EPS of $1.31 in April 2012, which beat the Street's expectations by 12%. A closer look at this apparent good news yields some concern. JP Morgan lowered its bad debt expense (called loan loss provision) compared to the prior quarter, and the dollar value of its allowance for doubtful accounts (called allowance for loan losses) dropped over the preceding two years (see graphic). Moreover, the allowance as a percent of accounts receivable (loans) declined more drastically, as the graphic shows. There is no evidence that JP Morgan reduced its bad debt expense and allowance to beat the market's EPS estimate, but interestingly, had bad debt been proportional to that of the prior quarter, JP Morgan would have missed its earnings target by $0.10 per share.

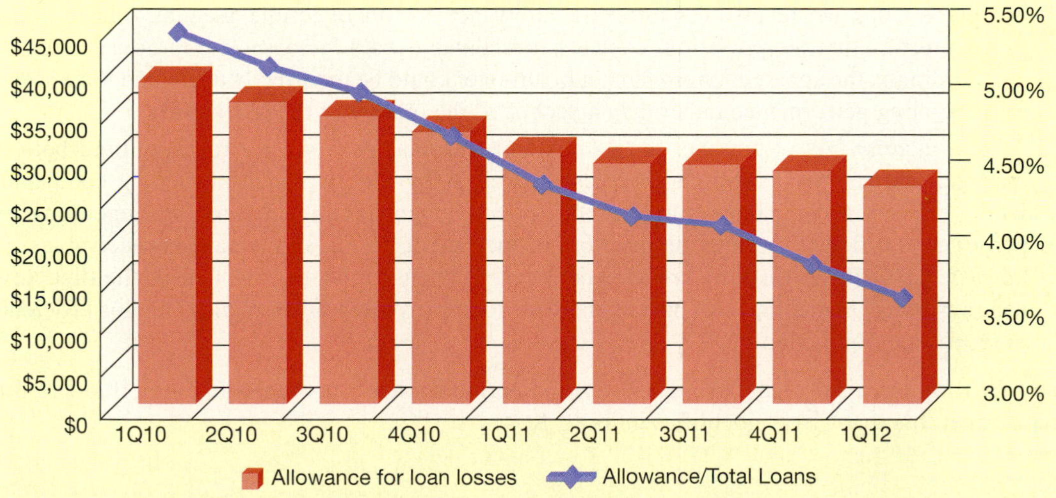

Accounts Receivable Turnover and Average Collection Period

The net operating asset turnover (NOAT) is sales divided by average net operating assets. An important component of this measure is the **accounts receivable turnover (ART)**, which is defined as:[3]

Accounts Receivable Turnover = Sales/Average Accounts Receivable, gross

[3] Technically, the numerator should be net credit sales because receivables arise from credit sales. Including cash sales in the numerator inflates the ratio. Typically, outsiders do not know the level of cash sales and, therefore, must use total sales to calculate the turnover ratio.

Accounts receivable turnover reveals how many times receivables have turned (been collected) during the period. More turns indicate that receivables are being collected more quickly.

A companion measure to accounts receivable turnover is the **average collection period (ACP)** for accounts receivable, also called *days sales outstanding*, which is defined as:

Average Collection Period = Accounts Receivable, gross/Average Daily Sales

where average daily sales equals sales divided by 365 days. The average collection period indicates how long, on average, the receivables are outstanding before being collected.[4]

To illustrate, **Cisco**'s 2012 total net sales (products and services) are \$46,061 million, gross accounts receivable are \$4,576 million at year-end, and \$4,902 million at the prior year-end (average is \$4,739 million). Thus, its accounts receivable turnover is 9.72, computed as \$46,061/\$4,739, and its average collection period (days sales outstanding) is 36 days, computed as \$4,576/(\$46,061/365 days).

The accounts receivable turnover and the average collection period yield valuable insights on at least two dimensions:

1. *Receivables quality* Changes in receivable turnover (and collection period) speak to accounts receivable quality. If turnover slows (collection period lengthens), the reason could be deterioration in collectibility. However, there are at least three alternative explanations:
   a. A seller can extend its credit terms. If the seller is attempting to enter new markets or take market share from competitors, it may extend credit terms to attract buyers.
   b. A seller can take on longer-paying customers. For example, facing increased competition, automobile and other manufacturing companies began leasing their products, thus reducing customers' cash outlays and stimulating sales. Moving away from cash sales and toward leasing reduced receivables turnover and increased the collection period.
   c. The seller can increase the allowance provision. Receivables turnover is sometimes computed using net receivables (after the allowance for uncollectible accounts). In this case, overestimating the provision reduces net receivables and increases the turnover ratio. Accordingly, the apparent improvement in turnover could be incorrectly attributed to improved operating performance rather than a decline in the quality of the receivables.
2. *Asset utilization* Asset turnover is an important financial performance measure used both by managers for internal performance goals, as well as by the market in evaluating companies. High-performing companies must be both effective (controlling margins and operating expenses) and efficient (getting the most out of their asset base). An increase in receivables ties up cash. As well, slower-turning receivables carry increased risk of loss. One of the first "low-hanging fruits" that companies pursue in efforts to improve overall asset utilization is efficiency in receivables collection.

The following chart shows the average collection period for accounts receivable of Cisco and four peer competitors that Cisco indentifies in its 10-K.

[4] The average collection period computation in this module uses *ending* accounts receivable. This focuses the analysis on the most current receivables. Cisco uses a variant of this approach, described in its MD&A section as follows: Accounts receivable/Average annualized 4Q sales (or AR/[(4Q Sales × 4)/365]). Arguably, Cisco's variant focuses even more on the most recent collection period because ending accounts receivable relate more closely to 4Q sales than to reported annual sales. Most analysts use the reported annual sales instead of the annualized 4Q sales because the former are easily accessed in financial statement databases. As an alternative, we could also examine average daily sales in *average* accounts receivable (Average accounts receivable/Average daily sales). The approach we use in the text addresses the average collection period of *current* (ending) accounts receivable, and the latter approach examines the average collection period of *average* accounts receivable. Finally, some analysts use "net" and not "gross" receivables. The concern with using net is that it introduces management's allowance policy as another variable in this analysis. The "correct" ratio depends on the issue we wish to investigate. It is important to choose the formula that best answers the question we are asking.

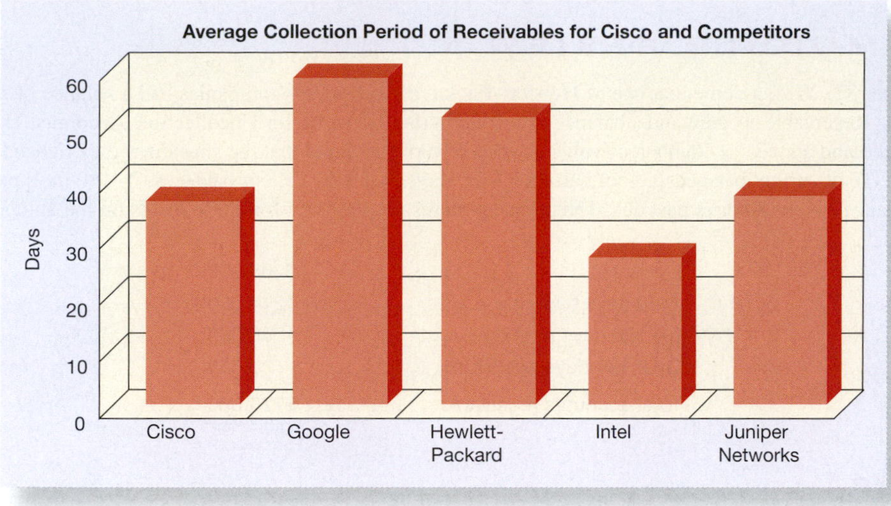

Cisco's average collection period of 36 days compares favorably with its primary competitors. Companies in this industry generally report average collection periods of 40–60 days.

To appreciate differences in average collection periods across industries, let's compare the average collection periods across a number of industries as follows:

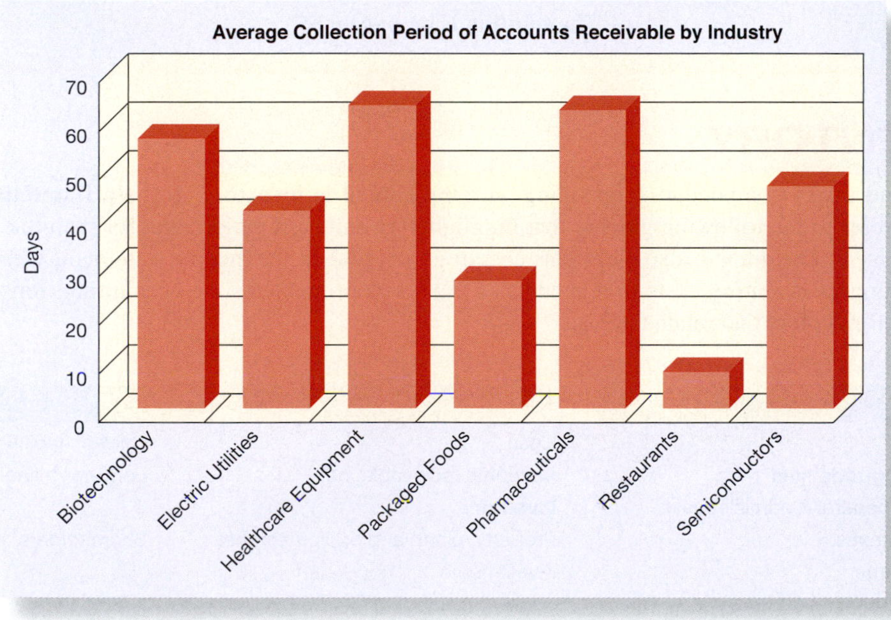

Restaurants have the shortest collection periods. For that industry, receivables are minimal because sales are made mainly via cash, check or credit card. Most of the other industries in the table have collection periods ranging from 40 to 60 days. This corresponds with typical credit terms offered on commercial transactions. Healthcare equipment and pharmaceutical industries have longer collection periods because they often require payment from third-party insurers and government agencies.

MANAGERIAL DECISION **You Are the Receivables Manager**

You are analyzing your receivables turnover report for the period and you are concerned that the average collection period is lengthening. What specific actions can you take to reduce the average collection period? [Answer, p. 6-41]

MID-MODULE REVIEW 1

At December 31, 2014, assume that one of Hewlett-Packard's subsidiary companies had a balance of $770,000 in its Accounts Receivable account and a balance of $7,000 in its Allowance for Uncollectible Accounts. The company then analyzed and aged its accounts receivable as shown below. Assume that the subsidiary experienced past losses as follows: 1% of current balances, 5% of balances 1–60 days past due, 15% of balances 61–180 days past due, and 40% of balances over 180 days past due. The company bases its provision for credit losses on the aging analysis.

Current	$468,000
1–60 days past due	244,000
61–180 days past due	38,000
Over 180 days past due	20,000
Total accounts receivable	$770,000

Required

1. What amount of uncollectible accounts (bad debts) expense will the HP subsidiary report in its 2014 income statement?
2. Show how Accounts Receivable and the Allowance for Uncollectible Accounts appear in its December 31, 2014, balance sheet.
3. Assume that the HP subsidiary's allowance for uncollectible accounts has maintained a historical average of 2% of gross accounts receivable. How do you interpret the current allowance percentage?

The solution is on page 6-59.

INVENTORY

LO2 Explain accounting for inventories and assess the effects on the balance sheet and income statement from different inventory costing methods.

The second major component of operating working capital is inventory. To help frame this discussion, we refer to the following graphic that highlights inventory, a major asset for manufacturers and merchandisers. The graphic also highlights cost of goods sold on the income statement, which reflects the matching of inventory costs to related sales. This section explains the accounting, reporting, and analysis of inventory and related items.

Income Statement	Balance Sheet	
Sales	Cash	Current liabilities
Cost of goods sold	Accounts receivable, net	Long-term liabilities
Selling, general & administrative	**Inventory**	
Income taxes	Property, plant, and equipment, net	Shareholders' equity
Net income	Investments	

Inventory is reported on the balance sheet at its purchase price or the cost to manufacture goods that are internally produced. Inventory costs vary over time with changes in market conditions. Consequently, the cost per unit of the goods available for sale varies from period to period—even if the quantity of goods available remains the same.

When inventory is purchased or produced, it is "capitalized." That is, it is carried on the balance sheet as an asset until it is sold, at which time its cost is transferred from the balance sheet to the income statement as an expense (cost of goods sold). The process by which costs are removed from the balance sheet is important. For example, if higher cost units are transferred from the balance sheet, then cost of goods sold is higher and gross profit (sales less cost of goods sold) is lower. Conversely, if lower cost units are transferred to cost of goods sold, gross profit is higher. The remainder of this section discusses the accounting for inventory including the mechanics, reporting, and analysis of inventory costing.

Capitalization of Inventory Cost

Capitalization means that a cost is recorded on the balance sheet and is not immediately expensed on the income statement. Once costs are capitalized, they remain on the balance sheet as assets until they are used up, at which time they are transferred from the balance sheet to the income statement as expense. If costs are capitalized rather than expensed, then assets, current income, and current equity are all higher.

For purchased inventories (such as merchandise), the amount of cost capitalized is the purchase price. For manufacturers, cost capitalization is more difficult, as **manufacturing costs** consist of three components: cost of direct materials used in the product, cost of direct labor to manufacture the product, and manufacturing overhead. Direct materials cost is relatively easy to compute. Design specifications list the components of each product, and their purchase costs are readily determined. The direct labor cost per unit of inventory is based on how long each unit takes to construct and the rates for each labor class working on that product. Overhead costs are also capitalized into inventory, and include the costs of plant asset depreciation, utilities, supervisory personnel, and other costs that contribute to manufacturing activities—that is, all costs of manufacturing other than direct materials and direct labor. (How these costs are assigned to individual units and across multiple products is a *managerial accounting* topic.)

When inventories are sold, their costs are transferred from the balance sheet to the income statement as cost of goods sold (COGS). COGS is then deducted from sales to yield **gross profit**:

Gross Profit = Sales − Cost of Goods Sold

The manner in which inventory costs are transferred from the balance sheet to the income statement affects both the level of inventories reported on the balance sheet and the amount of gross profit (and net income) reported on the income statement.

BUSINESS INSIGHT **Income Shifting: Inventory Fraud at Beazer Homes**

Companies can potentially shift income between the current period and one or more future periods using cost of goods sold because inventory accounting involves many estimates. This is especially true for manufactured inventory where the company aggregates numerous costs and then allocates those costs to the income statement (via COGS) based on estimates and assumptions. In a 2012 report on corporate criminal activity, the FBI concluded that *income shifting*, or *cookie jar accounting*, was at the heart of fraudulent reporting by **Beazer Homes**, a former Fortune 500 company headquartered in Charlotte, N.C. According to the report, Beazer executives "cut its net income during flush times and smoothed its earnings during the housing crash." The fraud was fairly simple: Beazer Homes bought a large tract of land and subdivided it into individual lots and built a home on each lot. The cost of each home included construction materials, labor, and overhead, which were fairly straightforward to track and measure for each home. The cost of each home also included an allocation of the cost of the land and the related development costs. These were more challenging to track and more subjectively measured for each home. Beazer Homes shifted income to future periods by overestimating the cost of land allocated to the initial lots sold. This overstated the cost of goods sold and thereby understated income (and taxes). In later periods, the company underestimated the cost of goods sold, which had the effect of overstating current earnings (for those later periods). Beazer Homes signed a deferred prosecution agreement acknowledging corporate culpability in the fraud and paid $50 million in restitution. A federal jury convicted Michael Rand, the former chief accounting officer for Beazer Homes, on fraud charges related to the seven-year conspiracy.

Inventory Costing Methods

Exhibit 6.5 shows the computation of cost of goods sold.

EXHIBIT 6.5 Cost of Goods Sold Computation

	Beginning inventory (prior period balance sheet)
+	Inventory purchased and/or produced
	Cost of goods available for sale
−	Ending inventory (current period balance sheet)
	Cost of goods sold (current period income statement)

The cost of inventory available at the beginning of a period is a carryover from the ending inventory balance of the prior period. Current period inventory purchases (or costs of newly manufactured inventories) are added to the beginning inventory balance, yielding the total cost of goods (inventory) available for sale. Then, the goods available are either sold, and end up in cost of goods sold for the period (reported on the income statement), or the goods available remain unsold and are still in inventory at the end of the period (reported on the balance sheet). Exhibit 6.6 shows this cost flow graphically.

EXHIBIT 6.6 Inventory Cost Flows to Financial Statements

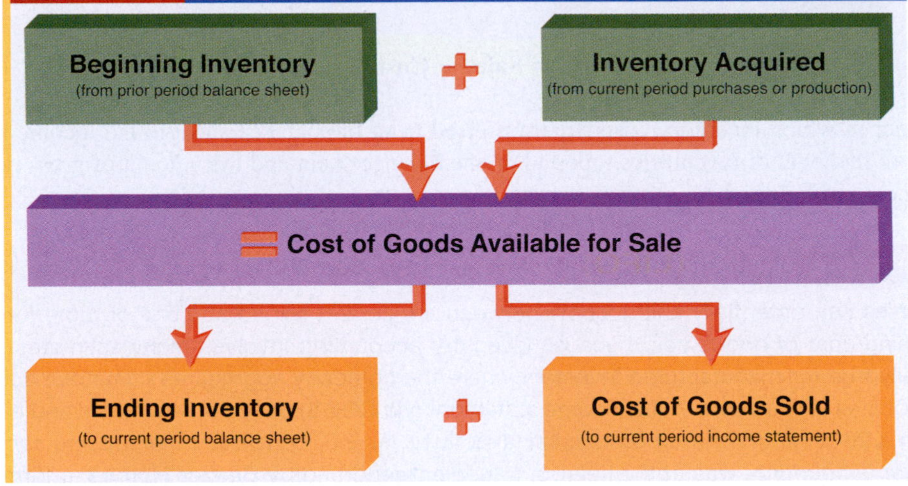

Understanding the flow of inventory costs is important. If all inventory purchased or manufactured during the period is sold, then COGS is equal to the cost of the goods purchased or manufactured. However, when inventory remains at the end of a period, companies must distinguish the cost of the inventories that were sold from the cost of the inventories that remain. GAAP allows for several options.

Exhibit 6.7 illustrates the partial inventory records of a company.

EXHIBIT 6.7 Summary Inventory Records

Inventory on January 1, 2014	500 units	@ $100 per unit	$ 50,000
Inventory purchased in 2014	200 units	@ $150 per unit	30,000
Total cost of goods available for sale in 2014	700 units		$ 80,000
Inventory sold in 2014	450 units	@ $250 per unit	$112,500

This company began the period with 500 units of inventory that were purchased or manufactured for $50,000 ($100 each). During the period the company purchased and/or manufactured an additional 200 units costing $30,000. The total cost of goods available for sale for this period equals $80,000.

The company sold 450 units during 2014 for $250 per unit for total sales of $112,500. Accordingly, the company must remove the cost of the 450 units sold from the inventory account on the balance sheet and match this cost against the revenues generated from the sale. An important question is which costs should management remove from the balance sheet and report as cost of goods sold in the income statement? Three inventory costing methods (FIFO, LIFO and average cost) are common and all are acceptable under GAAP.

First-In, First-Out (FIFO)

The FIFO inventory costing method transfers costs from inventory in the order that they were initially recorded. That is, FIFO assumes that the first costs recorded in inventory (first-in) are the first costs transferred from inventory (first-out). Applying FIFO to the data in Exhibit 6.7 means that the costs of the 450 units sold comes from *beginning* inventory, which consists of 500 units costing $100 each. The company's cost of goods sold and gross profit, using FIFO, is computed as follows:

Sales.	$112,500
COGS (450 @ $100 each).	45,000
Gross profit.	$ 67,500

The cost remaining in inventory and reported on the 2014 year-end balance sheet is $35,000 ($80,000 goods available for sale less $45,000 COGS). The following financial statement effects template captures the transaction.

	Balance Sheet					Income Statement		
Transaction	**Cash Asset** +	**Noncash Assets** =	**Liabil-ities** +	**Contrib. Capital** +	**Earned Capital**	**Rev-enues** −	**Expen-ses** =	**Net Income**
Sold 450 units using FIFO costing (450 @ $100 each)		−45,000 Inventory =			−45,000 Retained Earnings	−	+45,000 Cost of Goods Sold =	−45,000

COGS 45,000
INV 45,000

COGS
45,000 |

INV
| 45,000

Last-In, First-Out (LIFO)

The LIFO inventory costing method transfers the most recent inventory costs from the balance sheet to COGS. That is, the LIFO method assumes that the most recent inventory purchases (last-in) are the first costs transferred from inventory (first-out). The company's cost of goods sold and gross profit, using LIFO, is computed as follows:

Sales.		$112,500
COGS: 200 @ $150 per unit	$30,000	
250 @ $100 per unit	25,000	55,000
Gross profit.		$ 57,500

The cost remaining in inventory and reported on the company's 2014 balance sheet is $25,000 (computed as $80,000 − $55,000). This is reflected in our financial statements effects template as follows.

	Balance Sheet					Income Statement		
Transaction	**Cash Asset** +	**Noncash Assets** =	**Liabil-ities** +	**Contrib. Capital** +	**Earned Capital**	**Rev-enues** −	**Expen-ses** =	**Net Income**
Sold 450 units using LIFO costing (200 @ $150) + (250 @ $100)		−55,000 Inventory =			−55,000 Retained Earnings	−	+55,000 Cost of Goods Sold =	−55,000

COGS 55,000
INV 55,000

COGS
55,000 |

INV
| 55,000

Average Cost (AC)

The average cost method computes the cost of goods sold as an average of the cost to purchase or manufacture all of the inventories that were available for sale during the period. To calculate the average cost of $114.286 per unit the company divides the total cost of goods available for sale by the number of units available for sale ($80,000/700 units). The company's sales, cost of sales, and gross profit follow.

Sales	$112,500
COGS (450 @ $114.286 per unit)	51,429
Gross profit	$ 61,071

The cost remaining in inventory and reported on the company's 2014 balance sheet is $28,571 ($80,000 − $51,429). This is reflected in our financial statements effects template as follows.

COGS 51,429
INV 51,429

COGS
51,429 |
INV
| 51,429

	Balance Sheet									Income Statement				
Transaction	Cash Asset	+	Noncash Assets	=	Liabil-ities	+	Contrib. Capital	+	Earned Capital	Rev-enues	−	Expen-ses	=	Net Income
Sold 450 units using average cost method (450 @ $114.286)			−51,429 Inventory	=					−51,429 Retained Earnings		−	+51,429 Cost of Goods Sold	=	−51,429

It is important to understand that the inventory costing method a company chooses is independent of the actual flow of inventory. The method choice determines COGS and ending inventory but not the actual physical inventory sold. For example, many grocery chains use LIFO inventory but certainly do not sell the freshest products first. (Companies do not frequently change inventory costing methods. Companies can adopt a new inventory costing method if doing so enhances the quality of the company's financial reports. Also, IRS regulations prohibit certain inventory costing method changes.)

Lower of Cost or Market

Companies must write down the carrying amount of inventories (the net book value) on the balance sheet *if* the reported cost (using FIFO, for example) exceeds market value (determined by current replacement cost). This process is called reporting inventories at the **lower of cost or market** and creates the following financial statement effects:

- Inventory book value is written down to current market value (replacement cost), reducing inventory and total assets.
- Inventory write-down is reflected as an expense (part of cost of goods sold) on the income statement, reducing current period gross profit, income, and equity.

To illustrate, assume that a company has inventory on its balance sheet at a cost of $27,000. Management learns that the inventory's replacement cost is $23,000 and writes inventories down to a balance of $23,000. The following financial statement effects template shows the adjustment.

COGS 4,000
INV 4,000

COGS
4,000 |
INV
| 4,000

	Balance Sheet									Income Statement				
Transaction	Cash Asset	+	Noncash Assets	=	Liabil-ities	+	Contrib. Capital	+	Earned Capital	Rev-enues	−	Expen-ses	=	Net Income
Write down inventory from $27,000 to $23,000			−4,000 Inventory	=					−4,000 Retained Earnings		−	+4,000 Cost of Goods Sold	=	−4,000

The inventory write-down (a noncash expense) is reflected in cost of goods sold and reduces gross profit by $4,000. Inventory write-downs are included in cost of goods sold. They are *not* reported in selling, general, and administrative expenses, which is common for other asset write-downs. The most common occurrence of inventory write-downs is in connection with restructuring activities.

The write-down of inventories can potentially shift income from one period to another. If, for example, inventories were written down below current replacement cost, future gross profit would be increased via lower future cost of goods sold. GAAP anticipates this possibility by requiring that inventories not be written down below a floor that is equal to net realizable value less a normal markup. Although this still allows some discretion (and the ability to manage income), the auditors must assess net realizable value and markups.

IFRS INSIGHT **Inventory Measurement under IFRS**

Like GAAP, IFRS measures inventories at the lower of cost or market. The cost of inventory generally is determined using the FIFO (first-in, first-out) or average cost method; use of the LIFO (last-in, first-out) method is prohibited under IFRS.

Footnote Disclosures

Notes to financial statements describe the inventory accounting method a company uses. To illustrate, Cisco reports $1,663 million in inventory on its 2012 balance sheet as a current asset. Cisco includes a general footnote on inventory along with more specific disclosures in other footnotes. Following is an excerpt from Cisco's general footnote on inventories.

> **Inventories** Inventories are stated at the lower of cost or market. Cost is computed using standard cost, which approximates actual cost, on a first-in, first-out basis. The Company provides inventory write-downs based on excess and obsolete inventories determined primarily by future demand forecasts. The write-down is measured as the difference between the cost of the inventory and market based upon assumptions about future demand and charged to the provision for inventory, which is a component of cost of sales. At the point of the loss recognition, a new, lower cost basis for that inventory is established, and subsequent changes in facts and circumstances do not result in the restoration or increase in that newly established cost basis.

This footnote includes at least two items of interest for our analysis of inventory:

1. Cisco uses the FIFO method of inventory costing.
2. Inventories are reported at the lower of cost or market (LCM). For example, if the current value of Cisco's inventories is less than its reported cost, Cisco would set up an "allowance" for inventories, similar to the allowance for uncollectible accounts. The inventory allowance reduces the reported inventory amount to the current (lower) market value.

Cisco also includes a more detailed inventory footnote as follows:

Inventories ($ millions)	July 28, 2012	July 30, 2011
Raw materials	$ 127	$ 219
Work in process	35	52
Finished goods		
Distributor inventory and deferred cost of sales	$ 630	$ 631
Manufacturing finished goods	597	331
Total finished goods	1,227	962
Service-related spares	213	182
Demonstration systems	61	71
Total	$1,663	$1,486

This disclosure separately reports inventory costs by the following stages in the production cycle:

- *Raw materials and supplies* These are costs of direct materials and inputs into the production process including, for example, chemicals in raw state, plastic and steel for manufacturing, and incidental direct materials such as screws and lubricants.
- *Work in process* These are costs of partly finished products (also called work-in-progress).
- *Finished goods* These are the costs of products that are completed and awaiting sale.

Why do companies disclose such details about inventory? First, investment in inventory is typically large—markedly impacting both balance sheets and income statements. Second, risks of inventory losses are often high, due to technical obsolescence and consumer tastes. This is an important issue for a company such as Cisco that operates in a technology-sensitive industry. Indeed, Cisco reported a loss of over $2 billion in 2001 when the tech bubble burst, demand dried up, and the company had to write down unsalable inventories. Third, inventory details can provide insight into future performance—both good and bad. Fourth, high inventory levels result in substantial costs for the company, such as the following:

- Financing costs to hold inventories (when not purchased on credit or when held beyond credit period)
- Storage costs (such as warehousing and related facilities)
- Handling costs (including wages)
- Insurance costs

Consequently, companies seek to minimize inventory levels provided this does not exceed the cost of holding insufficient inventory, called stock-outs. Stock-outs result in lost sales and production delays if machines and employees must be reconfigured to fill order backlogs.

Financial Statement Effects of Inventory Costing

This section describes the financial statement effects of different inventory costing methods.

Income Statement Effects

The three inventory costing methods yield differing levels of gross profit as Exhibit 6.8 shows.

EXHIBIT 6.8 Income Effects from Inventory Costing Methods

	Sales	Cost of Goods Sold	Gross Profit
FIFO	$112,500	$45,000	$67,500
LIFO	112,500	55,000	57,500
Average cost	112,500	51,429	61,071

Recall that inventory costs rose during this period from $100 per unit to $150 per unit. The higher gross profit reported under FIFO arises because FIFO matches older, lower-cost inventory against current selling prices. To generalize: in an inflationary environment, FIFO yields higher gross profit than do LIFO or average cost methods.

In recent years, the gross profit impact from using the FIFO method has been minimal for companies due to lower rates of inflation and increased management focus on reducing inventory quantities through improved manufacturing processes and better inventory controls. The FIFO gross profit effect can still arise, however, with companies subject to high inflation and slow inventory turnover.

Balance Sheet Effects

In our illustration above, the ending inventory using LIFO is less than that reported using FIFO. In periods of rising costs, LIFO inventories are markedly lower than under FIFO. As a result, balance sheets using LIFO do not accurately represent the cost that a company would incur to replace its current investment in inventories.

Caterpillar (CAT), for example, reports 2012 inventories under LIFO costing $15,547 million. As disclosed in the footnotes to its 10-K (see below), if CAT valued these inventories using FIFO, the reported amount would be $2,750 million greater, an 18% increase. This suggests that CAT's balance sheet omits over $2,750 million in inventories.

Cash Flow Effects

Unlike most other accounting method choices, inventory costing methods affect taxable income and, thus, taxes paid. When a company adopts LIFO in its tax filings, the IRS requires it to also use LIFO for financial reporting purposes (in its 10-K). This requirement is known as the *LIFO conformity rule*. In an inflationary economy, using FIFO results in higher taxable income and, consequently, higher taxes payable. Conversely, using LIFO reduces the tax liability.

Caterpillar, Inc., discloses the following inventory information in its 2012 10-K:

> Inventories are stated at the lower of cost or market. Cost is principally determined using the last-in, first-out (LIFO) method. The value of inventories on the LIFO basis represented about 60 percent of total inventories at December 31, 2012, about 65 percent of total inventories at December 31, 2011, and about 70 percent at December 31, 2010. If the FIFO (first-in, first-out) method had been in use, inventories would have been \$2,750 million, \$2,422 million, and \$2,575 million higher than reported at December 31, 2012, 2011, and 2010, respectively.

CAT uses LIFO for most of its inventories.[5] The use of LIFO has reduced the carrying amount of 2012 inventories by \$2,750 million. Had it used FIFO, its inventories would have been reported at \$18,297 million (\$15,547 million + \$2,750 million) rather than the \$15,547 million that is reported on its balance sheet as of 2012. This difference, referred to as the **LIFO reserve**, is the amount that must be added to LIFO inventories to adjust them to their FIFO value.

FIFO Inventory = LIFO Inventory + LIFO Reserve

This relation also impacts cost of goods sold (COGS) as follows:

FIFO COGS = LIFO COGS − Increase in LIFO Reserve (or + Decrease)

Use of LIFO reduced CAT's inventories by \$2,750 million, resulting in a cumulative increase in cost of goods sold and a cumulative decrease in gross profit and pretax profit of that same amount.[6] Because CAT also uses LIFO for tax purposes, the decrease in pretax profits reduced CAT's cumulative tax bill by about \$963 million (\$2,750 million × 35% assumed corporate tax rate). This had real cash flow consequences: CAT's cumulative operating cash flow was \$963 million higher because CAT used LIFO instead of FIFO. The increased cash flow from tax savings is often cited as a compelling reason for management to adopt LIFO.

Because companies use different inventory costing methods, their financial statements are often not comparable. The problem is most serious when companies hold large amounts of inventory and when prices markedly rise or fall. To compare companies using different inventory costing methods, say LIFO and FIFO, we need to adjust the LIFO numbers to their FIFO equivalents or vice versa. For example, one way to compare CAT with another company that uses FIFO, is to add CAT's LIFO reserve to its LIFO inventory. As explained above, this \$2,750 million increase in 2012 inventories would have increased its cumulative pretax profits by \$2,750 million and taxes by \$963 million. Thus, to adjust the 2012 balance sheet we increase inventories by \$2,750 million, tax liabilities by \$963 million (the extra taxes CAT would have had to pay under FIFO), and equity by the difference of \$1,612 million (computed as \$2,750 − \$963).

To adjust CAT's 2012 income statement from LIFO to FIFO, we use the *change* in the LIFO reserve. For CAT, the LIFO reserve increased by \$328 million during 2012 (from \$2,422 million to \$2,750 million). This means that, had the company used FIFO, its COGS would have been \$328 million lower, and 2012 gross profit and pretax income would have been \$328 million higher. In 2012, CAT would have paid \$115 million more in taxes had it used FIFO (\$328 million × 35% assumed tax rate).

---

[5] Neither the IRS nor GAAP requires use of a single inventory costing method. That is, companies are allowed to, and frequently do, use different inventory costing methods for different types of inventory (such as spare parts versus finished goods) or inventory in different geographical locations.

[6] Recall: Cost of Goods Sold = Beginning Inventories + Purchases − Ending Inventories. Thus, as ending inventories decrease, cost of goods sold increases.

RESEARCH INSIGHT **LIFO and Stock Prices**

The value-relevance of inventory disclosures depends at least partly on whether investors rely more on the income statement or the balance sheet to assess future cash flows. Under LIFO, cost of goods sold reflects current costs, whereas FIFO ending inventory reflects current costs. This implies that LIFO enhances the usefulness of the income statement to the detriment of the balance sheet. This trade-off partly motivates the required LIFO reserve disclosure (the adjustment necessary to restate LIFO ending inventory and cost of good sold to FIFO). Research suggests that LIFO-based income statements better reflect stock prices than do FIFO income statements that are restated using the LIFO reserve. Research also shows a negative relation between stock prices and LIFO reserve—meaning that higher magnitudes of LIFO reserve are associated with lower stock prices. This is consistent with the LIFO reserve being viewed as an inflation indicator (for either current or future inventory costs), which the market views as detrimental to company value.

Tools of Inventory Analysis

This section describes several useful tools for analysis of inventory and related accounts.

Gross Profit Analysis

The **gross profit margin (GPM)** is gross profit divided by sales. This important ratio is closely monitored by management and outsiders. Exhibit 6.9 shows the gross profit margin on Cisco's sales for the past three years.

EXHIBIT 6.9 **Gross Profit Margin for Cisco**

Fiscal Year ($ millions)	2012	2011	2010
Product sales	$36,326	$34,526	$32,420
Product cost of goods sold	14,505	13,647	11,620
Gross profit	$21,821	$20,879	$20,800
Gross profit margin	60.1%	60.5%	64.2%

The gross profit margin is commonly used instead of the dollar amount of gross profit as the GPM allows for comparisons across companies and over time. A decline in GPM is usually cause for concern since it indicates that the company has less ability to pass on increased product cost to customers or that the company is not effectively managing product costs. Some possible reasons for a GPM decline follow:

- *Product line is stale.* Perhaps products are out of fashion and the company must resort to markdowns to reduce overstocked inventories. Or, perhaps the product lines have lost their technological edge, yielding reduced demand.
- *New competitors enter the market.* Perhaps substitute products are now available from competitors, yielding increased pressure to reduce selling prices.
- *General decline in economic activity.* Perhaps an economic downturn reduces product demand and places downward pressure on selling prices.
- *Inventory is overstocked.* Perhaps the company overproduced goods and finds itself in an overstock position. This can require reduced selling prices to move inventory.
- *Manufacturing costs have increased.* This could be due to poor planning, production glitches, or unfavorable supply chain reconfiguration.
- *Changes in product mix.* Perhaps the company is selling a higher proportion of low margin goods.

Cisco's gross profit margin on product sales decreased by 0.4 percentage points (60.5% to 60.1%) over the past year. Following is Cisco's discussion of its gross profit taken from its 2012 10-K:

Gross Margin The following table summarizes the key factors that contributed to the change in product gross margin percentage from fiscal 2011 to fiscal 2012:

Product Gross Margin	Percentage
Fiscal 2011	60.5%
Sales discounts, rebates, and product pricing	(2.8)%
Mix of products sold	(0.6)%
Overall manufacturing costs	1.7%
Restructuring and other charges	0.5%
Shipment volume, net of certain variable costs	0.5%
Amortization of purchased intangible assets	0.3%
Fiscal 2012	60.1%

In fiscal 2012, product gross margin decreased by 0.4 percentage points compared with fiscal 2011. The decrease was primarily due to the impact of higher sales discounts, rebates, and unfavorable product pricing, which were driven by normal market factors and by the geographic mix of net product sales . . . Additionally, our product gross margin for fiscal 2012 was negatively impacted by the shift in the mix of products sold, primarily as a result of sales increases in our relatively lower margin Cisco Unified Computing System products and increased sales in other lower margin products. In fiscal 2012, we experienced a positive mix impact from the absence of the lower margin consumer related products due to our exit from the Flip Video camera product line in fiscal 2011. The negative impacts to product gross margin were partially offset by lower overall manufacturing costs, higher shipment volume, lower restructuring charges, the absence of significant impairment charges related to purchased intangible assets, and lower amortization expense in fiscal 2012. The lower overall manufacturing costs were in part due to increased benefits from our value engineering efforts, particularly in certain of our Switching products; favorable component pricing; and continued operational efficiency in manufacturing operations. Value engineering is the process by which production costs are reduced through component redesign, board configuration, test processes, and transformation processes.

Cisco's gross profit margin decreased in 2012 because of higher sales discounts, rebates, unfavorable product pricing, and by an unfavorable shift in the mix of products sold. This decrease was partially offset by lower overall manufacturing costs. There are a number of factors that can adversely affect gross profit margins: changes in product mix, introduction of new products at lower introductory prices to gain market share, increases in production costs, sales discounts, inventory obsolescence and warranty costs, and changes in production volume.

Competitive pressures mean that companies rarely have the opportunity to completely control gross profit with price increases. Improvements in gross profit on existing product lines typically arise from better management of supply chains, production processes, or distribution networks. Companies that succeed do so because of better performance on basic business processes. This is one of Cisco's primary objectives.

Inventory Turnover

Inventory turnover (INVT) reflects the management of inventory and is computed as follows:

Inventory Turnover = Cost of Goods Sold/Average Inventory

Cost of goods sold is in the numerator because inventory is reported at cost. Inventory turnover indicates how many times inventory turns (is sold) during a period. More turns indicate that inventory is being sold more quickly, which decreases the risk of obsolete inventory and increases liquidity.

Average inventory days outstanding (AIDO), also called *days inventory outstanding*, is a companion measure to inventory turnover and is computed as follows:

Average Inventory Days Outstanding = Inventory/Average Daily Cost of Goods Sold

where average daily cost of goods sold equals cost of goods sold divided by 365 days.[7]

For Cisco, cost of products sold, in 2012, is $14,505 million, inventory at year-end is $1,663 million, inventory at prior year-end was $1,486 million (average is $1,574.5 million). Thus, its inventory turnover is 9.2, computed as $14,505 million/$1,574.5 million, which implies that, in 2012, Cisco sold its average inventory 9.2 times. Its 2012 average inventory days outstanding is 42 days, computed as $1,663 million/($14,505 million/365 days), which implies that it takes Cisco 42 days to sell its year-end inventory.

Overall, analysis of inventory turnover and days outstanding is important for at least two reasons:

1. *Inventory quality.* Inventory turnover can be compared over time and across competitors. Higher turnover is viewed favorably, because it implies that products are salable, preferably without undue discounting (we would compare profit margins to assess discounting). Conversely, lower turnover implies that inventory is on the shelves for a longer period of time, perhaps from excessive purchases or production, missed fashion trends or technological advances, increased competition, and so forth. Our conclusions about higher or lower turnover must consider alternative explanations including the following:
   - Product mix can include more (or less) higher margin, slower turning inventories. This can occur from business acquisitions that consolidate different types of inventory.
   - A company can change its promotion policies. Increased, effective advertising is likely to increase inventory turnover. Advertising expense is in SG&A, not COGS. This means the additional advertising cost is in operating expenses, but the benefit is in gross profit and turnover. If the promotion campaign is successful, the positive effects in margin and turnover should more than offset the promotion cost in SG&A.
   - A company can realize improvements in manufacturing efficiency and lower investments in direct materials and work-in-process inventories. Such improvements reduce inventory and, consequently, increase inventory turnover. Although a good sign, it does not yield any information about the desirability of a company's product line.
2. *Asset utilization.* Companies strive to optimize their inventory investment. Carrying too much inventory is expensive, and too little inventory risks stock-outs and lost sales (current and future). Companies can make the following operational changes to reduce inventory.
   - Improved manufacturing processes can eliminate bottlenecks and the consequent buildup of work-in-process inventories.
   - Just-in-time (JIT) deliveries from suppliers, which provide raw materials to the production line when needed, can reduce the level of raw materials and associated holding costs.
   - Demand-pull production, in which raw materials are released into the production process when final goods are demanded by customers instead of producing for estimated demand, can reduce inventory levels. **Harley-Davidson**, for example, does not manufacture a motorcycle until it receives the customer's order; thus, Harley produces for actual, rather than estimated, demand.

Reducing inventories reduces inventory carrying costs, thus improving profitability and increasing cash flows. The reduction in inventory is reflected as an operating cash inflow in the statement of cash flows.

There is normal tension between the sales side of a company that argues for depth and breadth of inventory, and the finance side that monitors inventory carrying costs and seeks to maximize cash flow. Companies, therefore, seek to *optimize* inventory investment, not minimize it.

---

[7] Similar to the average receivables collection period, this formula examines the average daily COGS in *ending* inventories to focus analysis on current inventories. One can also examine average daily COGS in *average* inventories (Average inventories/Average daily COGS). These two approaches address different issues: the first addresses the average days outstanding of *current ending* inventories, and the second examines the average days outstanding of *average* inventories. It is important that we first identify the issue under investigation and then choose the formula that best addresses that issue.

Following is a chart comparing Cisco's average inventory days outstanding with its peer companies.

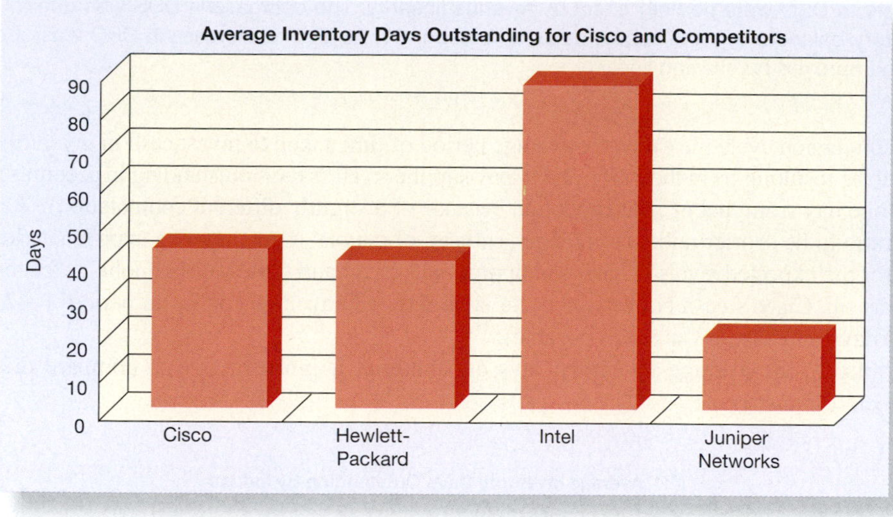

Cisco's average inventory days outstanding of 42 days is higher than that of its peers except for **Intel.** Cisco's 2012 10-K provides the following comments regarding inventory management:

> The inventory increase was due to higher levels of manufactured finished goods in support of current order activity . . . We purchase components from a variety of suppliers and use several contract manufacturers to provide manufacturing services for our products. During the normal course of business, in order to manage manufacturing lead times and help ensure adequate component supply, we enter into agreements with contract manufacturers and suppliers that allow them to procure inventory based upon criteria as defined by us or that establish the parameters defining our requirements and our commitment to securing manufacturing capacity. A significant portion of our reported purchase commitments arising from these agreements are firm, noncancelable, and unconditional commitments. In certain instances, these agreements allow us the option to cancel, reschedule, and adjust our requirements based on our business needs prior to firm orders being placed. Our purchase commitments are for short-term product manufacturing requirements as well as for commitments to suppliers to secure manufacturing capacity . . . Inventory and supply chain management remain areas of focus as we balance the need to maintain supply chain flexibility to help ensure competitive lead times with the risk of inventory obsolescence because of rapidly changing technology and customer requirements. We believe the amount of our inventory and purchase commitments is appropriate for our revenue levels.

The average collection period and the inventory days outstanding metrics can be combined with a third metric, the days payables outstanding (defined as: accounts payable / average cost of goods sold), to yield the cash conversion cycle (defined as: average collection period + inventory days outstanding − days payables outstanding). **Hewlett-Packard** discussed its cash conversion cycle in its 2012 10-K:

Our key working capital metrics are as follows:

October 31	2012	2011	2010
Days of sales outstanding in accounts receivable (DSO)	49	51	50
Days of supply in inventory (DOS)	25	27	23
Days of purchases outstanding in accounts payable (DPO)	(53)	(52)	(52)
Cash conversion cycle	21	26	21

The cash conversion cycle for fiscal 2012 decreased by five days compared to fiscal 2011. The decrease in DSO was due primarily to improved collections, an increase in cash discounts and a decline in extended payment terms. Additionally our DSO benefited from the current-period DSO calculation containing a full quarter of revenue from our Autonomy acquisition versus the approximately one month of revenue that was included in the prior-period DSO calculation. These favorable

continued

continued from prior page

impacts to DSO were partially offset by revenue linearity. The decrease in DOS was due to lower inventory balances in most segments as of October 31, 2012. The increase in DPO was primarily due to improved purchasing linearity.

The cash conversion cycle measures the average period of time taken to invest cash in inventories, collect the receivables resulting from their sale, and to pay suppliers (HP's days outstanding in accounts receivable differs by one day from that of its competition because of a slightly different computation). We generally want this ratio to be shorter rather than longer, subject, of course, to maintaining appropriate levels of inventories for the expected levels of sales and appropriate credit and trade payable policies for the industry. For comparison, Cisco's cash conversion cycle is 56 days (36 average collection period + 42 inventory days − 22 days purchases in accounts payable).

Returning to the average inventory days outstanding, it is instructive to compare this measure across selected industries.

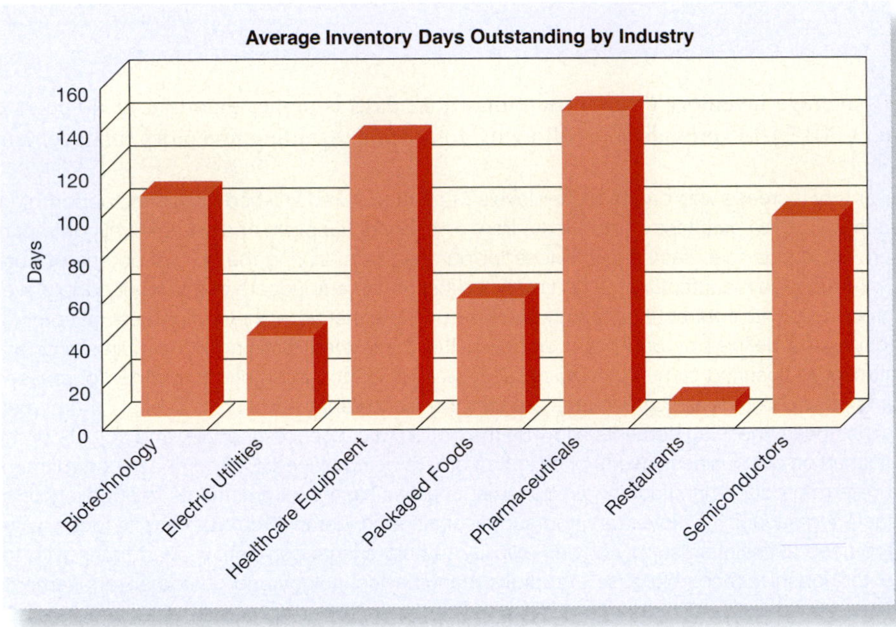

Healthcare equipment and pharmaceutical companies carry over four months' inventory at any point in time. Inventories are low in the restaurant industry because food is prepared and sold daily. On the other hand, manufacturers must carry raw materials, work-in-process and finished goods inventories.

MANAGERIAL DECISION **You Are the Plant Manager**

You are analyzing your inventory turnover report for the month and are concerned that the average inventory days outstanding is lengthening. What actions can you take to reduce average inventory days outstanding? [Answer, p. 6-41]

LIFO Liquidations

When companies acquire inventory at different costs, they are required to account for each cost level as a separate inventory pool or layer (for example, there are the $100 and $150 units in our Exhibit 6.7 illustration). When companies reduce inventory levels, older inventory costs flow to the income statement. These older LIFO costs are often markedly different from current replacement costs. Given the usual inflationary environment, sales of older pools often yield a boost to gross profit as older, lower costs are matched against current selling prices on the income statement.

The increase in gross profit resulting from a reduction of inventory quantities in the presence of rising costs is called **LIFO liquidation**. The effect of LIFO liquidation is evident in the following footnote from Rite Aid's 2013 10-K:

> **Inventory** (in $000s) At March 2, 2013 and March 3, 2012, inventories were $915,241 and $1,063,123, respectively, lower than the amounts that would have been reported using the first-in, first-out ("FIFO") cost flow assumption . . . The Company recorded a LIFO credit for fiscal year 2013 of $147,882 compared to LIFO charges for fiscal years 2012 and 2011 of $188,722 and $44,905, respectively. During fiscal 2013, 2012 and 2011, a reduction in inventories related to working capital initiatives resulted in the liquidation of applicable LIFO inventory quantities carried at lower costs in prior years. This LIFO liquidation resulted in a $4,316, $11,004 and $2,647 cost of sales decrease, with a corresponding reduction to the adjustment to LIFO for fiscal 2013, fiscal 2012 and fiscal 2011, respectively.

Rite Aid Corporation reports that reductions in inventory quantities in 2013 led to the sale (at current selling prices) of products that carried lower costs from prior years. As a result of these inventory reductions, COGS were lower, which increased income by $4.3 million.

MID-MODULE REVIEW 2

At the beginning of the current period, assume that one of Hewlett-Packard's subsidiary companies holds 1,000 units of a certain product with a unit cost of $18. A summary of purchases during the current period follows:

	Units	Unit Cost	Cost
Beginning Inventory	1,000	$18.00	$18,000
Purchases: #1.	1,800	18.25	32,850
#2.	800	18.50	14,800
#3.	1,200	19.00	22,800
Goods available for sale.	4,800		$88,450

During the current period, the HP subsidiary sells 2,800 units.

Required

1. Assume that the HP subsidiary uses the first-in, first-out (FIFO) method for this product. Compute the product's cost of goods sold for the current period and the ending inventory balance.
2. Assume that the HP subsidiary uses the last-in, first-out (LIFO) method for this product. Compute the product's cost of goods sold for the current period and the ending inventory balance.
3. Assume that the HP subsidiary uses the average cost (AC) method for this product. Compute the product's cost of goods sold for the current period and the ending inventory balance.
4. As manager, which of these three inventory costing methods would you choose:
   a. To reflect what is probably the physical flow of goods? Explain.
   b. To minimize income taxes for the period? Explain.
5. Assume that the HP subsidiary utilizes the LIFO method and delays purchasing lot #3 until the next period. Compute cost of goods sold under this scenario and discuss how the LIFO liquidation affects profit.

The solution is on page 6-60.

PROPERTY, PLANT AND EQUIPMENT (PPE)

LO3 Describe accounting for property, plant and equipment and explain the impacts on profit and cash flows from depreciation methods, disposals and impairments.

Many companies' largest operating asset is property, plant, and equipment. To frame our PPE discussion, the following graphic highlights long-term operating assets on the balance sheet, and selling, general and administrative expenses on the income statement. The latter includes depreciation and asset write-downs that match the assets' cost against sales derived from the assets. (Depreciation on manufacturing facilities is included in cost of goods sold.) This section explains the accounting, reporting, and analysis of PPE and related items.

Income Statement
Sales
Cost of goods sold
Selling, general & administrative
Income taxes
Net income

Balance Sheet	
Cash	Current liabilities
Accounts receivable, net	Long-term liabilities
Inventory	
Property, plant, and equipment, net	Shareholders' equity
Investments	

Capitalization of Asset Costs

Companies capitalize costs as an asset on the balance sheet only if that asset possesses both of the following characteristics:

1. The asset is owned or controlled by the company and results from a past transaction.
2. The asset provides future expected benefits.

Owning the asset means the company has title to the asset as provided in a purchase contract. (Assets acquired under leases are also capitalized if certain conditions are met—see Module 10.) Future expected benefits usually refer to future cash inflows. Companies capitalize the full cost to acquire the asset, including the purchase price, transportation, setup, and all other costs necessary to get the asset into service. This is called the asset's acquisition cost.

Companies can only capitalize asset costs that are *directly linked* to future cash inflows, and the costs capitalized as an asset can be no greater than the related expected future cash inflows. This means that if a company reports a $200 asset, we can reasonably expect that it will derive at least $200 in expected cash inflows from the use and ultimate disposal of the asset.

The *directly linked* condition for capitalization of asset cost is important. When a company acquires a machine, it capitalizes the cost because the company expects the machine's output to yield cash inflows from the sale of products associated with the machine and from the cash received when the company eventually disposes of the machine. On the other hand, when it comes to research and development (R&D) activities, it is more difficult to directly link expected cash inflows with the R&D expenditures because R&D activities are often unsuccessful. Further, companies cannot reliably estimate the future cash flows from successful R&D activities. Accordingly, GAAP requires that many R&D expenditures such as R&D-related personnel costs be expensed when paid. Similar arguments are applied to advertising, promotion and wages to justify expensing of those costs. Each of these latter examples relates to items or activities that we generally think will create intangible assets. That is, we reasonably expect R&D efforts and advertising campaigns to produce results. If not, companies would not pursue them.

We generally view employee activities as generating future benefits. Indeed, we often refer to the *human resources* (asset) of a company. However, the link between these items or activities and their outputs is not as direct as GAAP requires for capitalizing such costs. The nonrecognition of these assets is one reason why it is difficult to analyze and value knowledge-based companies and such companies are less suited to traditional ROE disaggregation analysis. Capitalization and non-capitalization of costs can markedly impact financial statements and our analysis inferences and assessment of a company as an investment prospect.

Depreciation

Once the cost of PPE is capitalized on the balance sheet as an asset, it must be systematically transferred from the balance sheet to the income statement as depreciation expense to match the asset's cost to the revenues it generates. The depreciation process requires the following estimates:

1. **Useful life**. Period of time over which the asset is expected to generate cash inflows or other measurable benefits
2. **Salvage value**. Expected disposal proceeds (net of any disposal costs) at the end of the asset's useful life
3. **Depreciation rate**. An estimate of how the asset will be used up over its useful life

Management must determine each of these factors when the asset is acquired. Depreciation commences immediately upon asset acquisition and use. Management also can revise estimates that determine depreciation during the asset's useful life.

The **depreciation base**, also called *nonrecoverable cost*, is the amount to be depreciated. The depreciation base is the acquisition cost less estimated salvage value. This means that at the end of the asset's useful life, only the salvage value remains on the balance sheet.

Depreciation method relates to the manner in which the asset is used up. Companies choose from three methods by determining which of the following assumptions best describes the asset's use:

1. Asset is used up by the same amount each period.
2. Asset is used up more in the early years of its useful life.
3. Asset is used up in proportion to its actual usage.

A company can depreciate different assets using different depreciation methods (and different useful lives). After a depreciation method is chosen, however, the company must generally stick with that method throughout the asset's useful life. This is not to say that companies cannot change depreciation methods, but changes must be justified as providing more useful financial reports.

The using up of an asset generally relates to physical or technological obsolescence. *Physical obsolescence* relates to an asset's diminished capacity to produce output. *Technological obsolescence* relates to an asset's diminished efficiency in producing output in a competitive manner.

All depreciation methods have the following general formula:

Depreciation Expense = Depreciation Base × Depreciation Rate

Remembering this general formula helps us understand the depreciation process. Also, each depreciation method reports the same amount of depreciation expense *over the life of the asset*. The only difference is in the amount of depreciation expense reported *for a given period*. To illustrate, consider a machine with the following details: $100,000 cost, $10,000 salvage value, and a five-year useful life. We look at two of the most common methods of depreciation.

Straight-Line Method

Under the straight-line (SL) method, depreciation expense is recognized evenly over the estimated useful life of the asset as follows:

Depreciation Base	Depreciation Rate
Cost − Salvage value = $100,000 − $10,000 = $90,000	1/Estimated useful life = 1/5 years = 20%

Depreciation expense per year for this asset is $18,000, computed as $90,000 × 20%. For the asset's first full year of usage, $18,000 of depreciation expense is reported in the income statement. (If an asset is purchased midyear, it is typically depreciated only for the portion of the year it is used. For example, had the asset in this illustration been purchased on May 31, the company would report $10,500 of depreciation in the first year, computed as 7/12 × $18,000, assuming the company has a December 31 year-end.) This depreciation is reflected in the company's financial statements as follows:

	Balance Sheet									Income Statement				
Transaction	Cash Asset	+	Noncash Assets	=	Liabilities	+	Contrib. Capital	+	Earned Capital	Revenues	−	Expenses	=	Net Income
Record $18,000 straight-line depreciation			−18,000 Accumulated Depreciation	=					−18,000 Retained Earnings		−	+18,000 Depreciation Expense	=	−18,000

DE 18,000
AD 18,000

DE	
18,000	

AD	
	18,000

The accumulated depreciation (contra asset) account increases by $18,000, thus reducing net PPE by the same amount. Also, $18,000 of the asset cost is transferred from the balance sheet to the income statement as depreciation expense. At the end of the first year the asset is reported on the balance sheet as follows:

	Machine, at cost.	$100,000
	Less accumulated depreciation	18,000
Net book value →	Machine, net (end of Year 1).	$ 82,000

Accumulated depreciation is the sum of all depreciation expense that has been recorded to date. The asset **net book value (NBV)**, or *carrying value*, is cost less accumulated depreciation. Although the word value is used here, it does not refer to market value. Depreciation is a cost allocation concept (transfer of costs from the balance sheet to the income statement), not a valuation concept.

In the second year of usage, another $18,000 of depreciation expense is recorded in the income statement and the net book value of the asset on the balance sheet follows:

	Machine, at cost.	$100,000
	Less accumulated depreciation	36,000
Net book value →	Machine, net (end of Year 2).	$ 64,000

Accumulated depreciation of $36,000 now includes the sum of the first and second years' depreciation, and the net book value of the asset is now reduced to $64,000. After the fifth year, a total of $90,000 of accumulated depreciation will be recorded ($18,000 per year × 5 years), yielding a net book value for the machine of $10,000. The net book value at the end of the machine's useful life is exactly equal to the salvage value that management estimated when the asset was acquired.

Double-Declining-Balance Method

GAAP also allows *accelerated* methods of depreciation, the most common being the double-declining-balance method. This method records more depreciation in the early years of an asset's useful life (hence the term *accelerated*) and less depreciation in later years. At the end of the asset's useful life, the balance sheet will still report a net book value equal to the asset's salvage value. The difference between straight-line and accelerated depreciation methods is not in the total amount of depreciation, but in the rate at which costs are transferred from the balance sheet to the income statement.

For the double-declining-balance (DDB) method, the depreciation base is net book value, which declines over the life of the asset (this is why the method is called "declining balance"). The depreciation rate is twice the straight-line (SL) rate (which explains the word "double"). The depreciation base and rate for the asset in our illustrative example are computed as follows:

Depreciation Base	Depreciation Rate
Net Book Value = Cost − Accumulated Depreciation	2 × SL rate = 2 × 20% = 40%

The depreciation expense for the first year is $40,000, computed as $100,000 × 40%. This depreciation is reflected in the company's financial statements as follows:

DE 40,000
AD 40,000

DE
40,000 |

AD
| 40,000

	Balance Sheet									Income Statement				
Transaction	Cash Asset	+	Noncash Assets	=	Liabil-ities	+	Contrib. Capital	+	Earned Capital	Rev-enues	−	Expen-ses	=	Net Income
Record $40,000 DDB depreciation			−40,000 Accumulated Depreciation	=					−40,000 Retained Earnings		−	+40,000 Depreciation Expense	=	−40,000

The accumulated depreciation (contra asset) account increases by $40,000 which reduces net PPE (compare this to the $18,000 depreciation under straight-line). This means that $40,000 of the asset cost is transferred from the balance sheet to the income statement as depreciation expense. At the end of the first year, the asset is reported on the balance sheet as follows:

Machine, at cost.	$100,000
Less accumulated depreciation	40,000
Machine, net (end of Year 1).	$ 60,000

Net book value → Machine, net (end of Year 1)

In the second year, the net book value of the asset is the new depreciable base, and the company records depreciation of $24,000 ($60,000 × 40%) in the income statement. At the end of the second year, the net book value of the asset on the balance sheet is:

Machine, at cost.	$100,000
Less accumulated depreciation	64,000
Machine, net (end of Year 2).	$ 36,000

Net book value → Machine, net (end of Year 2)

Under the double-declining-balance method, a company continues to record depreciation expense in this manner until the salvage value is reached, at which point the depreciation process is discontinued. This leaves a net book value equal to the salvage value, as with the straight-line method.[8] The DDB depreciation schedule for the life of this asset is in Exhibit 6.10.

EXHIBIT 6.10 Double-Declining-Balance Depreciation Schedule

Year	Book Value at Beginning of Year	Depreciation Expense	Book Value at End of Year
1	$100,000	$40,000	$60,000
2	60,000	24,000	36,000
3	36,000	14,400	21,600
4	21,600	8,640	12,960
5	12,960	2,960*	10,000

*The formula value of $5,184 ($12,960 × 40%) is *not* reported because it would depreciate the asset below salvage value; only the $2,960 needed to reach salvage value is reported.

Exhibit 6.11 shows the depreciation expense and net book value for both the SL and DDB methods. During the first two years, the DDB method yields a higher depreciation expense compared to the SL method. Beginning in the third year, this pattern reverses and the SL method produces higher depreciation expense. Over the asset's life, the same $90,000 of asset cost is transferred to the income statement as depreciation expense, leaving a salvage value of $10,000 on the balance sheet under both methods.

EXHIBIT 6.11 Comparison of Straight-Line and Double-Declining-Balance Depreciation

	Straight-Line		Double-Declining-Balance	
Year	Depreciation Expense	Book Value at End of Year	Depreciation Expense	Book Value at End of Year
1	$18,000	$82,000	$40,000	$60,000
2	18,000	64,000	24,000	36,000
3	18,000	46,000	14,400	21,600
4	18,000	28,000	8,640	12,960
5	18,000	10,000	2,960	10,000
	$90,000		$90,000	

All depreciation methods yield the same salvage value

Total depreciation expense over asset life is identical for all methods

[8] A variant of DDB allows for a change from DDB to SL at the point when SL depreciation exceeds that for DDB.

Companies typically use the SL method for financial reporting purposes and an accelerated depreciation method for tax returns.[9] The reason is that in early years the SL depreciation yields higher income on financial statements, whereas accelerated depreciation yields lower taxable income. Even though this relation reverses in later years, companies prefer to have the tax savings sooner rather than later so that the cash savings can be invested to produce earnings. Further, the reversal may never occur—if depreciable assets are growing at a fast enough rate, the additional first year's depreciation on newly acquired assets more than offsets the lower depreciation expense on older assets, yielding a "permanent" reduction in taxable income and taxes paid.[10]

Asset Sales and Impairments

This section discusses gains and losses from asset sales, and the computation and disclosure of asset impairments.

Gains and Losses on Asset Sales

The gain or loss on the sale (disposition) of a long-term asset is computed as follows.

Gain or Loss on Asset Sale = Proceeds from Sale − Net Book Value of Asset Sold

An asset's net book value is its acquisition cost less accumulated depreciation. When an asset is sold, its acquisition cost and related accumulated depreciation are both removed from the balance sheet and any gain or loss is reported in income from continuing operations.

Gains and losses on asset sales can be large, and analysts must be aware that these gains and losses are usually *transitory operating* income components. Financial statements do not typically report gains and losses from asset sales because, if the gain or loss is small (immaterial), companies include the item in selling, general and administrative expenses. Footnotes can sometimes be informative. To illustrate, **Alcoa** provides the following footnote disclosure relating to the sale of Tapoco Hydroelectric Project ($ millions):

> In November 2012, Alcoa completed the sale of its 351-megawatt Tapoco Hydroelectric Project ("Tapoco") to Brookfield Renewable Energy Partners for $597 in cash. Alcoa recognized a gain of $320 ($173 after-tax) in Other income, net on the accompanying Statement of Consolidated Operations . . . Tapoco is a four-station hydroelectric project located on the Little Tennessee and Cheoah Rivers in eastern Tennessee and western North Carolina. The transaction included four generating stations and dams, 86 miles of transmission lines, and approximately 14,500 acres of land associated with and surrounding Tapoco.

Alcoa sold a hydroelectric project, carried on its balance sheet at a net book value of $277 million (computed as $597 million sale proceeds less $320 million pre-tax gain), for $597 million. The impacts on its financial statements follow:

Cash 597 Mil.
PPE, net 277 Mil.
Gain 320 Mil.

Cash
597 Mil. |

PPE, net
| 277 Mil.

Gain
| 320 Mil.

	Balance Sheet									Income Statement				
Transaction	Cash Asset	+	Noncash Assets	=	Liabilities	+	Contrib. Capital	+	Earned Capital	Revenues	−	Expenses	=	Net Income
Sale of hydroelectric project	+597 Mil. Cash		−277 Mil. Hydroelectric Project (PPE, net)	=					+320 Mil. Retained Earnings	+320 Mil. Gain on Asset Sale	−		=	+320 Mil.

[9] The IRS mandates the use of MACRS (Modified Accelerated Cost Recovery System) for tax purposes. This method specifies the useful life for various classes of assets, assumes no salvage value, and generally uses the double-declining-balance method.

[10] A third, common depreciation method is **units-of-production**, which depreciates assets according to use. Specifically, the depreciation base is cost less salvage value, and the depreciation rate is the units produced and sold during the year compared with the total expected units to be produced and sold. For example, if a truck is driven 10,000 miles out of a total expected 100,000 miles, 10% of its nonrecoverable cost is reflected as depreciation expense. This method is common for extractive industries like timber and coal.

Asset Impairments

Property, plant, and equipment (PPE) assets are reported at their net book values (original cost less accumulated depreciation). This is the case even if the market values of these assets increase subsequent to acquisition. As a result, there can be unrecognized gains hidden within the balance sheet.

On the other hand, if market values of PPE assets subsequently decrease—and the asset value is deemed to be permanently impaired—then companies must write off the impaired cost and recognize losses on those assets. **Impairment** of PPE assets is determined by comparing the asset's net book value to the sum of the asset's *expected* future (undiscounted) cash flows. If the sum of expected cash flow is greater than net book value, there is no impairment. However, if the sum of the expected cash flow is less than net book value, the asset is deemed impaired and it is written down to its current fair value (generally, the present value of those expected cash flows). Exhibit 6.12 depicts this impairment analysis.

EXHIBIT 6.12 Impairment Analysis of Long-Term Assets

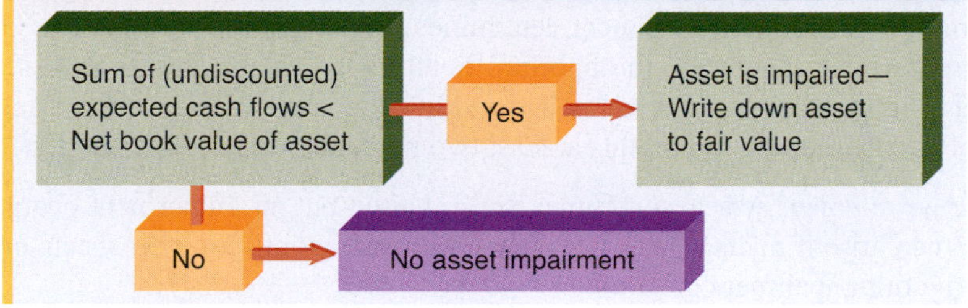

When a company takes an impairment charge, assets are reduced by the amount of the write-down and the loss is recognized in the income statement. To illustrate, a footnote to the 2013 10-K of **Abercrombie & Fitch** reports the following about asset impairments:

> Long-lived assets, primarily comprised of property and equipment, are reviewed whenever events or changes in circumstances indicate that full recoverability of net asset group balances through future cash flows is in question . . . The impairment evaluation is performed as a two-step test. First, the Company utilizes an undiscounted future cash flow model to test the individual asset groups for recoverability. If the net carrying value of the asset group exceeds the undiscounted cash flows, the Company proceeds to step two. Under step two, an impairment loss is recognized for the excess of net book value over the fair value of the assets. Factors used in the evaluation include, but are not limited to, management's plans for future operations, recent operating results and projected cash flows.
>
> In the fourth quarter of Fiscal 2012, as a result of the fiscal year-end review of long-lived store-related assets, the Company incurred store-related asset impairment charges of $7.4 million included in Stores and Distribution Expense on the Consolidated Statement of Operations and Comprehensive Income for Fiscal 2012. The asset impairment charge was primarily related to one Abercrombie & Fitch, three Abercrombie kids, 12 Hollister, and one Gilly Hicks store. In the fourth quarter of Fiscal 2011, as a result of the fiscal year-end review of long-lived store-related assets, the Company incurred store-related asset impairment charges of $68.0 million, included in Stores and Distribution Expense on the Consolidated Statement of Operations and Comprehensive Income for Fiscal 2011. The asset impairment charge was related to 14 Abercrombie & Fitch, 21 Abercrombie kids, 42 Hollister, and two Gilly Hicks stores. In Fiscal 2010, as a result of the review of long-lived store-related assets, the Company incurred store-related asset impairment charges of $50.6 million, included in Stores and Distribution Expense on the Consolidated Statement of Operations and Comprehensive Income for Fiscal 2010. The asset impairment charge was primarily related to 13 Gilly Hicks stores. The charge also included two Abercrombie & Fitch, two Abercrombie kids and nine Hollister stores.

Abercrombie's pretax write-down of impaired assets affected its financial statements as follows:

AIE 7.4 Mil.
PPE, net 7.4 Mil.

AIE
7.4 Mil. |

PPE, net
| 7.4 Mil.

	Balance Sheet					Income Statement		
Transaction	Cash Asset	+ Noncash Assets	= Liabilities	+ Contrib. Capital	+ Earned Capital	Revenues	− Expenses	= Net Income
Write-down long-lived assets by $7.4 Mil.		−7.4 Mil. PPE, net	=		−7.4 Mil. Retained Earnings		− +7.4 Mil. Asset Impairment Expense	= −7.4 Mil.

Abercrombie wrote down the carrying value (net book value) of its long-lived assets by $7.4 million. This write-down accelerated the transfer of the asset's cost from the balance sheet to the income statement. Consequently, Abercrombie recognized a pretax expense of $7.4 million in the current year rather than over time via the depreciation process.

It is important to note that management determines if and when to recognize asset impairments. Thus, there is room for management to opportunistically over- or underestimate asset impairments. Write-downs of long-term assets are often recognized in connection with a restructuring program.

Analysis of asset write-downs presents at least two potential analysis challenges:

1. *Insufficient write-down.* Assets sometimes are impaired but an impairment charge is not recognized. This can arise if management is overly optimistic about future prospects or is reluctant to recognize the full impairment in income.
2. *Aggressive write-down.* This *big bath* scenario can arise if income is already very low in a given year. Management's view is that the market will not penalize the company's stock for an extra write-off when the year was already bad. Taking a larger impairment charge purges the balance sheet of costs that would otherwise hit future years' income.

GAAP does not condone either of these cases. Yet, because management must estimate future cash flows for the impairment test, it has some degree of control over the timing and amount of the asset write-off and can use that discretion to manage reported income.

IFRS INSIGHT **PPE Valuation under IFRS**

Like GAAP, companies reporting under IFRS must periodically assess long-lived assets for possible impairment. Unlike the two-step GAAP approach, IFRS use a one-step approach: firms compare an asset's net book value to its current fair value (estimated as discounted expected future cash flows) to test for impairment and then reduce net book value to that fair value. Under IFRS, impairment losses can be reversed if the PPE subsequently regains its value. The PPE account is increased to the newly estimated recoverable amount, not to exceed the assets' initial cost adjusted for depreciation. GAAP prohibits such reversals. Another IFRS difference is that PPE can be revalued upwards to fair value each period, if fair value can be measured reliably.

Footnote Disclosures

Cisco reports the following PPE asset amounts in its balance sheet:

($ millions)	July 28, 2012	July 30, 2011
Property, plant and equipment, net	$3,402	$3,916

In addition to its balance sheet disclosure, Cisco provides two footnotes that more fully describe its PPE assets:

1. *Summary of Significant Accounting Policies.* This footnote describes Cisco's accounting for PPE assets in general terms:

Depreciation and Amortization Property and equipment are stated at cost, less accumulated depreciation or amortization, whenever applicable. . . Depreciation and amortization are computed using the straight-line method, generally over the following periods.

Buildings.	25 years
Building improvements.	10 years
Furniture and fixtures	5 years
Leasehold improvements.	Shorter of remaining lease term or 5 years
Computer equipment and related software	30 to 36 months
Production, engineering, and other equipment	Up to 5 years
Operating lease assets.	Based on lease term—generally up to 3 years

There are two items of interest in this disclosure: (a) Cisco, like most publicly traded companies, depreciates its PPE assets using the straight-line method (for tax purposes it uses an accelerated method). (b) Cisco provides general disclosures on the useful lives of its assets: 30 months to 25 years. We will discuss a method to more accurately estimate the useful lives in the next section.

2. *Supplemental balance sheet information.* This footnote provides a breakdown of Cisco's PPE assets by category as well as the balance in the accumulated depreciation account:

Property and equipment, net (millions)	July 28, 2012	July 30, 2011
Land, buildings, and building and leasehold improvements	$ 4,363	$ 4,760
Computer equipment and related software	1,469	1,429
Production, engineering, and other equipment	5,364	5,093
Operating lease assets.	300	293
Furniture and fixtures	487	491
	11,983	12,066
Less accumulated depreciation and amortization	(8,581)	(8,150)
Total	$ 3,402	$ 3,916

BUSINESS INSIGHT **Asset Retirement Obligations (ARO)**

At the end of an asset's life, companies often incur substantial costs to retire or dispose of the asset. Examples of such costs include decontaminating the site of a nuclear power plant, removing underground fuel storage tanks at a gas station, environmental cleanup near a fracking site, or demolishing buildings. Under U.S. GAAP and IFRS, companies must provide for costs related to future disposal of assets in the period in which the asset is originally purchased. Companies estimate the future cost of the asset retirement and express this in present value terms. This present value is added to the cost of the asset on the balance sheet and depreciated over the life of the asset. The company also adds the present value to the balance sheet as a liability called asset retirement obligation (ARO). The result is an increase in both assets and liabilities. Inherent in the computation of the ARO are numerous assumptions including the ultimate settlement amounts, future third-party pricing, inflation factors, risk free discount rates, credit risk, timing of settlement and changes in the legal, regulatory, environmental and political environments. Thus, estimating the ARO requires significant judgment as restoration technologies and costs are constantly changing, as are regulatory, political, environmental and safety considerations. In its 2012 annual report, **Husky Energy** reported a large ARO ($2,793 million or 17% of total liabilities) and explained it as follows in its footnotes:

> A liability is recognized for future legal or constructive retirement obligations associated with the Company's assets. The Company has significant obligations to remove tangible assets and restore land after operations cease and the Company retires or relinquishes the asset. The retirement of Upstream and Downstream assets consists primarily of plugging and abandoning wells, removing and disposing of surface and subsea plant and equipment and facilities, and restoring land to a state required by regulation or contract. The amount recognized is the net present value of the estimated future expenditures determined in accordance with local conditions, current technology and current regulatory requirements. . . . The liability is progressively accreted over time as the effect of discounting unwinds, creating an expense recognized in finance expenses. The costs capitalized to the related assets are amortized in a manner consistent with the depletion, depreciation and amortization of the underlying assets. Actual retirement expenditures are charged against the accumulated liability as incurred.

Analysis Implications

This section explains how to measure long-term asset utilization and asset age.

PPE Turnover

A crucial issue in analyzing PPE assets is determining their productivity (utilization). For example, what level of plant assets is necessary to generate a dollar of revenues? How capital intensive are the company and its competitors? To address these and similar questions, we use **PPE turnover**, defined as follows:

PPE Turnover (PPET) = Sales/Average PPE Assets, net

Cisco's 2012 PPE turnover is 12.6 ($46,061 million/[($3,402 million + $3,916 million)/2]). (We use net PPE in the computation above; arguments for using gross PPE are not as compelling as with receivables because managers have less latitude over accumulated depreciation vis-a-vis the allowance for uncollectibles.) This turnover places Cisco somewhat higher than most of its peers (see chart that follows).

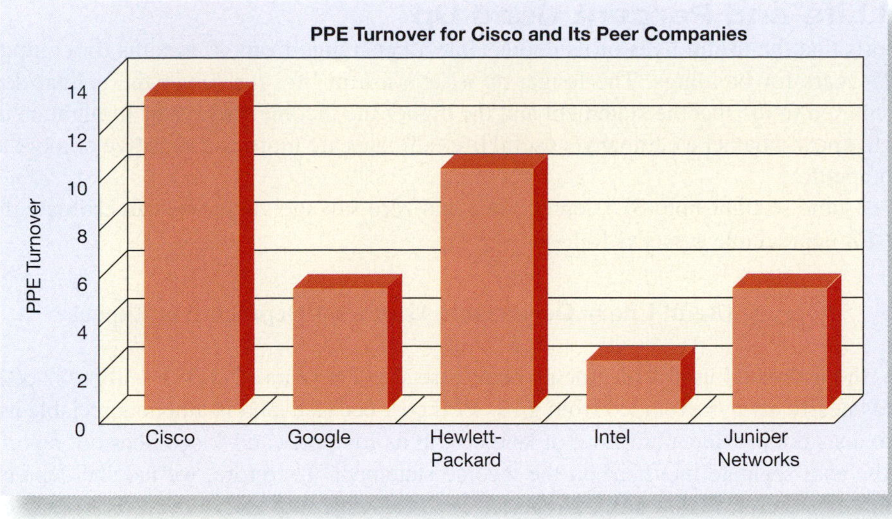

Higher PPE turnover is preferable to lower. A higher PPE turnover implies a lower capital investment for a given level of sales. Higher turnover, therefore, increases profitability because the company avoids asset carrying costs and because the freed-up assets can generate operating cash flow. (PPE turnover that is markedly higher than competitors may hint that the company leases equipment instead of owning it; see Module 10 for explanation.)

PPE turnover is lower for capital-intensive manufacturing companies than it is for companies in service or knowledge-based industries. To this point, consider the following chart of PPE turnover for selected industries.

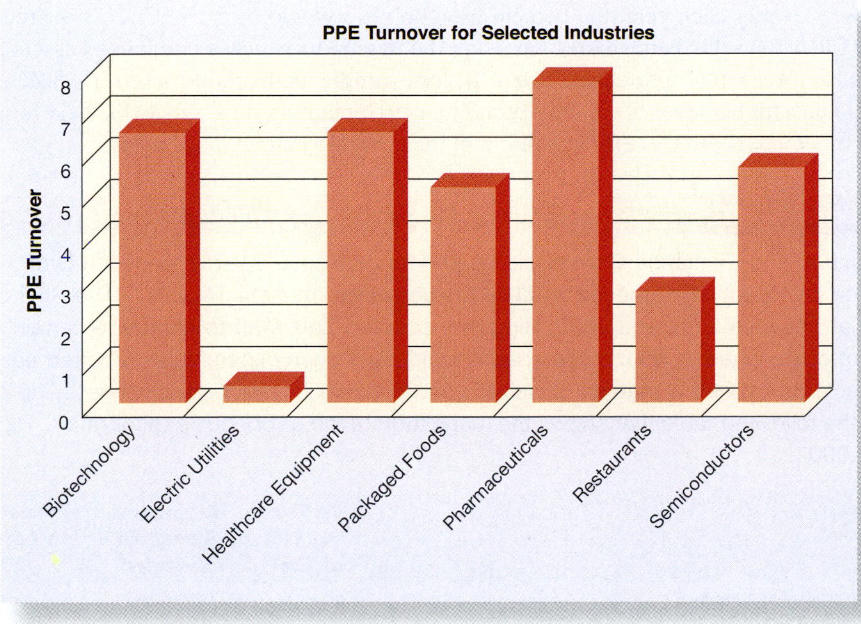

Electric utilities are very capital intensive and this is reflected in the relatively low PPE turnover rate.

MANAGERIAL DECISION **You Are the Division Manager**

You are the manager for a main operating division of your company. You are concerned that a declining PPE turnover is adversely affecting your division's return on net operating assets. What specific actions can you take to increase PPE turnover? [Answer, p. 6-42]

Useful Life and Percent Used Up

Cisco reports that the useful lives of its depreciable assets range from 30 months for computer equipment to 25 years for buildings. The longer an asset's useful life, the lower the annual depreciation expense reported in the income statement and the higher the income each year. It might be of interest, therefore, to know whether a company's useful life estimates are more conservative or more aggressive than its competitors.

If we assume straight-line (SL) depreciation and zero salvage value, we can estimate the average useful life for depreciable assets as follows:

Average Useful Life = Depreciable Asset Cost/Depreciation Expense

For Cisco, the estimated useful life for its plant assets is 4.6 years ($11,983 million/$2,602 million). Land cost is nearly always excluded from gross PPE cost because land is a nondepreciable asset. However, Cisco does not provide a breakout of land cost in its footnotes and Cisco does not report depreciation expense as a separate line item on the income statement. Therefore, we use the depreciation and amortization expense of $2,602 million reported in the statement of cash flows. (For many companies, amortization expense is like depreciation, and often relates, in part, to tangible assets such as leasehold improvements. However, if amortization relates to intangible assets such as patents and copyrights, the amortization should be subtracted from total depreciation and amortization before estimating useful life.)

We can also estimate the proportion of a company's depreciable assets that have already been transferred to the income statement. This ratio reflects the percent of depreciable assets that are no longer productive—as follows:

Percent Used Up = Accumulated Depreciation/Depreciable Asset Cost

Cisco's assets are 72% used up, computed as $8,581 million/$11,983 million. If a company replaced all of its assets evenly each year, the percent used up ratio would be 50%. Cisco's depreciable assets are slightly older than this benchmark. Knowing the degree to which a company's assets are used up is of interest in forecasting future cash flows. If, for example, depreciable assets are 80% used up, we might anticipate a higher level of capital expenditures to replace aging assets in the near future. We also expect that older assets are less efficient and will incur higher maintenance costs.

BUSINESS INSIGHT Zale Corporation and Improper Cost Capitalization

The Securities and Exchange Commission settled a civil case against Rebecca Lynn Higgins, a former vice president of marketing at Zale Corporation, on April 14, 2011. The SEC complaint alleges that between 2004 and 2009, Higgins instructed Zale staff to capitalize certain television advertising costs when, in fact, those costs should have been expensed as incurred each period. Higgins' actions caused a material misstatement to Zale's assets and expenses. The complaint included the following table that shows the magnitude of the erroneous capitalization. Higgins was fined $25,000.

Period	Advertising Error, Net of Tax	Net Income (Loss), As Restated	% Misstated Due to Advertising Error
Nine months ended 4/30/09	$ (9.8)	$ (99.7)	9.9%
Year ended 7/31/08	$ (1.3)	$ 0.6	209.4%
Year ended 7/31/07	$ (1.2)	$ 57.5	(2.1)%
Year ended 7/31/06	$ (4.5)	$ 48.1	(9.5)%
Year ended 7/31/05	$ (0.5)	$106.2	(0.5)%
Cumulative impact on year ended 7/31/04 and prior years	$(11.9)	(Approximately 1.7% of equity)	

GLOBAL ACCOUNTING

Both GAAP and IFRS account similarly for operating assets. Although similarities in accounting dwarf any differences, we highlight some of the more notable differences.

Accounts Receivable Accounts receivable are accounted for identically with one notable exception. Under IFRS, all receivables are treated as *financial* assets. This means that future cash flows from accounts receivable must be discounted and reported at net present value. This measurement applies to both short-term and long-term receivables, assuming the effect of discounting is material. For analysis purposes, we review the notes to determine the discount rate used by the company using IFRS and assess the significance of any discounting. Ratios using accounts receivable (such as turnover ratios and current ratios) can be affected.

Inventory There are three notable differences in accounting for inventory:

1. IFRS does not permit use of the LIFO method; in this module, we discussed the needed adjustments when analyzing a company that uses LIFO.
2. Under U.S. GAAP, inventory is carried at lower of cost or market; under IFRS it is lower of cost or net realizable value. This means that GAAP inventory write-downs are larger than under IFRS because of the floor effect for market value, described earlier in the module. We analyze notes to determine if inventory write-downs are large. If so, GAAP cost of sales can be much higher, which can depress gross profit margins and operating income. This can impact ratios such as inventory turnover, but we cannot determine the direction, which depends on the relative size of the write-down and its impact on cost of sales versus total inventory. (When using LIFO, inventory write-downs are less frequent because the "cost" of LIFO inventory is the oldest costs, which are often low relative to current market replacement values.)
3. IFRS permits companies to reverse inventory write-downs; GAAP does not. This means that if markets recover and inventory previously "impaired" regains some or all of its value, it can be revalued upwards. IFRS notes disclose this revaluation, if material, which permits us to recompute inventory and cost of sales amounts that are comparable to GAAP.

Fixed Assets In accounting for fixed assets, four notable differences deserve mention:

1. GAAP requires the total cost of a fixed asset to be capitalized and depreciated over its useful life. Under IFRS, fixed assets are disaggregated into individual components and then each component is separately depreciated over its useful life. Thus, assets with components with vastly different useful lives, can yield depreciation expense using IFRS that is markedly different from that computed using GAAP. This means that income, and net book values of assets on the balance sheet, can differ for two otherwise identical companies using GAAP versus IFRS. Ratios using plant assets are also impacted. We must review notes regarding depreciation of asset components to make this assessment.
2. Property, plant and equipment can be carried at depreciated cost under U.S. GAAP and IFRS, but can be revalued at fair market value under IFRS. The latter will cause IFRS book values of PPE to be higher. Few companies have opted to revalue assets upwards but in some industries, such as real estate, the practice is common.
3. U.S. GAAP applies a two-step approach for determining impairments. Step 1: compare book value to *undiscounted* expected future cash flows; and Step 2: if book value is higher, measure impairment using *discounted* expected future cash flows. IFRS uses *discounted* expected future cash flows for both steps, which means IFRS uses one step. This results in more asset impairments under IFRS.
4. IFRS fair-value impairments for fixed assets can be reversed; that is, written back up after being written down. The notes to PPE articulate such reversals.

MODULE-END REVIEW

On January 2, assume that one of Hewlett-Packard's subsidiary companies purchases equipment that fabricates a key-product part. The equipment costs $95,000, and its estimated useful life is five years, after which it is expected to be sold for $10,000.

Required

1. Compute depreciation expense for each year of the equipment's useful life for each of the following depreciation methods:
   a. Straight-line
   b. Double-declining-balance
2. Show how the HP subsidiary reports the equipment on its balance sheet at the end of the third year assuming straight-line depreciation.
3. Assume that this is the only depreciable asset the company owns and that it uses straight-line depreciation. Estimate the useful life and the percent used up for this asset at the end of the third year.
4. Assume that the HP subsidiary estimates that, at the end of the third year, the equipment will generate $40,000 in cash flow over its remaining life and that it has a current fair value of $36,000. Is the equipment impaired? If so, what is the effect on the HP subsidiary financial statements?
5. Instead of the facts in part 4, assume that, at the end of the third year, the HP subsidiary sells the equipment for $50,000 cash. What amount of gain or loss does the HP subsidiary report from this sale?

The solution is on page 6-61.

APPENDIX 6A: Sales Returns and Allowances

Levi Strauss & Co. (LS), like most companies, offers its customers the right to return purchases for a refund and it also offers sales discounts and other incentives to encourage increased purchases. Assume that LS sells jeans costing $80 to a customer for $130 on account. LS recognizes the revenue and COGS as we discuss in Module 2, and, at the end of the accounting period, LS will also set up a reserve for uncollectible accounts receivable as we discuss above. Since LS has offered its customers a right of return, and because prior experience leads the company to expect that returns will occur, LS must also set up a reserve for estimated returns. Let's assume that LS expects returns to amount to 3% of sales. In the same period in which LS records the revenue, it also records the estimated returns as follows:

	Balance Sheet									Income Statement				
Transaction	Cash Asset	+	Noncash Assets	=	Liabil-ities	+	Contrib. Capital	+	Earned Capital	Rev-enues	−	Expen-ses	=	Net Income
Establish allowance for sales returns (3% × $130)			−3.90 (Allowance for Sales Returns)	=					−3.90 Retained Earnings	−3.90 (Sales Returns and Allowances)	−		=	−3.90
Adjust COGS ([$80/$130] × $3.90)			2.40 (Inventory adj. for estimated returns)	=					2.40 Retained Earnings		−	−2.40 (COGS adj. for estimated returns)	=	2.40

In the first entry, LS reduces Sales by $3.90 to reflect expected merchandise returns with a corresponding reduction of accounts receivable (similar to the allowance for uncollectible accounts). The second entry reduces COGS by the COGS percentage ($80/$130) and increases inventory for the expected returns. LS income statement through gross profit will, therefore, look like this:

Sales, net ($130 − $3.90)	$126.10
COGS ($80 − $2.40)	77.60
Gross profit	$ 48.50

LS will also report accounts receivable of $126.10 and the estimated product returns of $2.40 will be reported in its inventory account.

Companies are required to provide the details relating to all of their allowance accounts in **Schedule II** (Valuation and Qualifying Accounts) in their 10-K. LS's schedule in its 2013 10-K follows:

LEVI STRAUSS & CO. AND SUBSIDIARIES
Valuation and Qualifying Accounts (Dollars in thousands)

Allowance for Doubtful Accounts	Balance at Beginning of Period	Additions Charged to Expenses	Deductions	Balance at End of Period
November 25, 2012	$22,684	$5,024	$6,970	$20,738
November 27, 2011	$24,617	$4,634	$6,567	$22,684
November 28, 2010	$22,523	$7,536	$5,442	$24,617

Sales Returns	Balance at Beginning of Period	Additions Charged to Net Sales	Deductions	Balance at End of Period
November 25, 2012	$51,023	$161,620	$172,068	$40,575
November 27, 2011	$47,691	$139,068	$135,736	$51,023
November 28, 2010	$33,106	$133,012	$118,427	$47,691

Sales Discounts and Incentives	Balance at Beginning of Period	Additions Charged to Net Sales	Deductions	Balance at End of Period
November 25, 2012	$102,359	$254,556	$254,554	$102,361
November 27, 2011	$ 90,560	$277,016	$265,217	$102,359
November 28, 2010	$ 85,627	$274,903	$269,970	$ 90,560

Valuation Allowance Against Deferred Tax Assets	Balance at Beginning of Period	Charges/ (Releases) to Tax Expense	(Additions)/ Deductions	Balance at End of Period
November 25, 2012	$98,736	$ (1,329)	$22,951	$74,456
November 27, 2011	$97,026	$ (2,421)	$ (4,131)	$98,736
November 28, 2010	$72,986	$28,278	$ 4,238	$97,026

Levi Strauss provides a reconciliation of the beginning and ending balances for the past three years for its four allowance accounts:

1. Doubtful Accounts
2. Sale Returns
3. Sales Discounts and Incentives
4. Deferred Tax assets

This is a typical disclosure, but companies typically do not have all of these accounts. The allowance for doubtful accounts balance of $20,738,000 in 2012 is 4% of the gross balance in accounts receivable of $521,410,000 as of 2012. We would want to compare this percentage with LS's peer group to assess its relative size. The amount by which sales have been reduced by anticipated sales returns in the amount of $161,620,000 represents 3.2% of the gross sales (reported net sales plus sales returns and sales discounts and incentives) of $5,026,369 reported in 2012. Again, we want to measure this with respect to the percentages reported by LS's peer companies to assess its relative magnitude.

Analysis of Allowance Accounts

The account reconciliations report increases and decreases in the allowance accounts from the balance at the beginning of the year to yield the year-end balance. It is important to remember that:

- Increases to the allowance accounts create an expense that is recognized in the income statement. Increases in the allowance for doubtful accounts and the allowance against deferred tax assets are recognized as SG&A and Tax expense, respectively. Increases in Sales Returns and Sales Discounts and

Incentives reduce "Sales, net" in the income statement (the word "net" refers to the reductions resulting from these two contra-sales accounts).

- Decreases to the allowance accounts do not affect the income statement and recognize the write-off of an asset account. There is no net effect on assets or equity since we are writing off a contra-asset account with the asset account to which it relates.

What we are looking for, then, is a divergence of the increases and the decreases. If we notice, for example, that the company is increasing or decreasing the account significantly more than the deductions due to asset write-offs, we need to entertain the possibility that the company is deliberately increasing or depressing reported earnings. An example might be the reversal of $(1,329,000) in the valuation allowance against deferred tax assets in 2012. During 2012, LS significantly reduced the deferred tax asset valuation allowance by $22,951,000. Its footnotes to the 2013 10-K reveal that this decrease "was primarily attributable to expirations of unused net operating loss carryforwards in certain foreign jurisdictions." This is not uncommon. As we discuss in Module 5, tax loss carryforwards have a maximum term over which they can be utilized (20 years in the U.S.) and there are restrictions on their use. So, it is not uncommon for these carryforwards to expire unused. When they do, the company writes off both the deferred tax asset (the loss carryforward) and the allowance. There is no effect on net deferred tax assets as both the asset and the contra-asset are reduced (this is the same principle as the write-off of an account receivable against the allowance for uncollectible accounts).

During 2012, LS also reversed the valuation allowance against deferred tax assets by $1,329,000. Just as an increase in the deferred tax valuation account depresses earnings (via an increase in income tax expense), a reversal of that account increases earnings (via a decrease in income tax expense). Net income, therefore, increased by that amount. The footnotes don't discuss the reason for the reversal as the company may have determined that the amount is not material. One possibility is that the company deems that it is more likely than not that it will be able to utilize the remaining deferred tax assets. Another possibility is that the company is increasing reported net income, say, to meet analysts' earnings forecasts or to avoid default of debt covenants. We want to investigate these possibilities by looking at the relation between LS's reported earnings and the amount forecasted for that year by equity analysts. We would also want to investigate the debt footnote for any mention of debt covenants that might be binding on the company.

All of the allowance accounts work in this manner. Both the asset-related and sales-related contra accounts decrease (increase) reported profit when they are increased (decreased). This is reflected in the "Additions Charged to" column, which also gives the account charged. The "Additions/Deductions" column represents the write-off of an asset (accounts receivable in the case of the allowance for doubtful accounts and for the sales returns and sales discounts, and deferred tax assets in the case of the valuation allowance against deferred tax assets). The asset account is written off against the contra-asset account and, consequently, the write-off does not affect total assets, total liabilities, stockholders' equity or net income.

GUIDANCE ANSWERS

MANAGERIAL DECISION You Are the Receivables Manager

First, we must realize that extending credit is an important tool in the marketing of your products, often as important as advertising and promotion. Given that receivables are necessary, there are certain ways to speed their collection. (1) We can better screen the customers to whom we extend credit. (2) We can negotiate advance or progress payments from customers. (3) We can use bank letters of credit or other automatic drafting procedures that obviate billing. (4) We can make sure products are sent as ordered, to reduce disputes. (5) We can improve administration of past-due accounts to provide for more timely notices of delinquencies and better collection procedures.

MANAGERIAL DECISION You Are the Plant Manager

Companies need inventories to avoid lost sales opportunities; however, there are several ways to minimize inventory needs. (1) We can reduce product costs by improving product design to eliminate costly features that customers don't value. (2) We can use more cost-efficient suppliers; possibly producing in lower wage-rate parts of the world. (3) We can reduce raw material inventories with just-in-time delivery from suppliers. (4) We can eliminate production bottlenecks that increase work-in-process inventories. (5) We can manufacture for orders rather than for estimated demand to reduce finished goods inventories. (6) We can improve warehousing and distribution to reduce duplicate inventories. (7) We can monitor product sales and adjust product mix as demand changes to reduce finished goods inventories.

MANAGERIAL DECISION **You Are the Division Manager**

PPE is a difficult asset to reduce. Because companies need long-term operating assets, managers usually try to maximize throughput to reduce unit costs. Also, many companies form alliances to share administrative, production, logistics, customer service, IT, and other functions. These alliances take many forms (such as joint ventures) and are designed to spread ownership of assets among many users. The goal is to identify underutilized assets and to increase capacity utilization. Another solution might be to reconfigure the value chain from raw material to end user. Examples include the sharing of IT, or manufacturing facilities, outsourcing of production or administration such as customer service centers, and the use of special purpose entities for asset securitization (see Module 10).

DISCUSSION QUESTIONS

Q6-1. Explain how management can shift income from one period into another by its estimation of uncollectible accounts.

Q6-2. Why do relatively stable inventory costs across periods reduce the importance of management's choice of an inventory costing method?

Q6-3. Explain why using the FIFO inventory costing method will increase gross profit during periods of rising inventory costs.

Q6-4. If inventory costs are rising, which inventory costing method—first-in, first-out; last-in, first-out; or average cost—yields the (a) lowest ending inventory? (b) lowest net income? (c) largest ending inventory? (d) largest net income? (e) greatest cash flow, assuming the same method is used for tax purposes?

Q6-5. Even though it may not reflect their physical flow of goods, why might companies adopt last-in, first-out inventory costing in periods when costs are consistently rising?

Q6-6. In a recent annual report, **Kaiser Aluminum Corporation** made the following statement in reference to its inventories: "The Company recorded pretax charges of approximately $19.4 million because of a reduction in the carrying values of its inventories caused principally by prevailing lower prices for alumina, primary aluminum, and fabricated products." What basic accounting principle caused Kaiser Aluminum to record this $19.4 million pretax charge? Briefly describe the rationale for this principle.

Kaiser Aluminum Corporation (KALU)

Q6-7. Why is depreciation expense necessary to properly match revenues and expenses?

Q6-8. How might a company revise its depreciation expense computation due to a change in an asset's estimated useful life or salvage value?

Q6-9. When is a PPE asset considered to be impaired? How is an impairment loss computed?

Q6-10. What is the benefit of accelerated depreciation for income tax purposes when the total depreciation taken over the asset's life is identical under any method of depreciation?

Q6-11. What factors determine the gain or loss on the sale of a PPE asset?

Assignments with the ✔ logo in the margin are available in myBusinessCourse. See the Preface of the book for details.

MINI EXERCISES

M6-12. Estimating Uncollectible Accounts and Reporting Accounts Receivable **(LO1)**

Mohan Company estimates its uncollectible accounts by aging its accounts receivable and applying percentages to various aged categories of accounts. Mohan computes a total of $2,100 in estimated uncollectible accounts as of its current year-end. Its Accounts Receivable has a balance of $86,000, and its Allowance for Uncollectible Accounts has an unused balance of $700 before any year-end adjustments.

a. What amount of bad debts expense will Mohan report in its income statement for the current year?
b. Determine the net amount of accounts receivable reported in current assets at year-end.

M6-13. Interpreting the Allowance Method for Accounts Receivable (LO1)

At a recent board of directors meeting of Bismark Corp., one of the directors expressed concern over the allowance for uncollectible accounts appearing in the company's balance sheet. "I don't understand this account," he said. "Why don't we just show accounts receivable at the amount owed to us and get rid of that allowance?" Respond to the director's question; include in your response (a) an explanation of why the company has an allowance account, (b) what the balance sheet presentation of accounts receivable is intended to show, and (c) how accrual accounting (as opposed to the cash-basis accounting) affects the presentation of accounts receivable.

M6-14. Analyzing the Allowance for Uncollectible Accounts (LO1)

Kraft Foods Group, Inc. (KRFT)

Following is the current asset section from the Kraft Foods Group, Inc., balance sheet.

$ millions	2012	2011
Cash and cash equivalents	$1,255	$ —
Receivables (net of allowances of $28 in 2012 and $23 in 2011)	1,089	903
Inventories, net	1,928	1,943
Deferred income taxes	420	232
Other current assets	131	194
Total current assets	$4,823	$3,272

a. Compute the gross amount of accounts receivable for both 2012 and 2011. Compute the percentage of the allowance for uncollectible accounts relative to the gross amount of accounts receivable for each of those years.

b. Compute the relative size of net accounts receivable to total assets; the latter were $23,329 million and $21,539 million for 2012 and 2011, respectively. Interpret the quality of Kraft's receivables for 2012 compared to 2011. (As additional background, net earnings attributable to the company were $1,642 million and $1,775 million for 2012 and 2011, respectively.)

M6-15. Evaluating Accounts Receivable Turnover for Competitors (LO1)

The Procter & Gamble Company (PG)

Colgate-Palmolive Company (CL)

The Procter & Gamble Company (PG) and Colgate-Palmolive Company (CL) report the following sales and accounts receivable balances ($ millions) for 2012 and 2011.

	Procter & Gamble		Colgate-Palmolive	
$ millions	Sales	Accounts Receivable	Sales	Accounts Receivable
2012	$83,680	$6,068	$17,085	$1,668
2011	81,104	6,275	16,734	1,675

a. Compute the accounts receivable turnover for both companies for 2012.

b. Identify and discuss a potential explanation for the difference between these competitors' accounts receivable turnover.

M6-16. Computing Cost of Goods Sold and Ending Inventory Under FIFO, LIFO, and Average Cost (LO2)

Assume that Gode Company reports the following initial balance and subsequent purchase of inventory.

Inventory balance at beginning of year	1,000 units @ $125 each	$125,000
Inventory purchased during the year	1,500 units @ $150 each	225,000
Cost of goods available for sale during the year	2,500 units	$350,000

Assume that 1,700 units are sold during the year. Compute the cost of goods sold for the year and the inventory on the year-end balance sheet under the following inventory costing methods:

a. FIFO

b. LIFO

c. Average Cost

M6-17. Computing Cost of Goods Sold and Ending Inventory Under FIFO, LIFO, and Average Cost (LO2)
Bartov Corporation reports the following beginning inventory and inventory purchases.

Inventory balance at beginning of year	400 units @ $12 each	$ 4,800
Inventory purchased during the year	700 units @ $14 each	9,800
Cost of goods available for sale during the year	1,100 units	$14,600

Bartov sells 600 of its inventory units during the year. Compute the cost of goods sold for the year and the inventory on the year-end balance sheet under the following inventory costing methods:

a. FIFO
b. LIFO
c. Average Cost

M6-18. Computing and Evaluating Inventory Turnover for Two Companies (LO2)
Abercrombie & Fitch Co. (ANF) and **TJX Companies Inc.** (TJX) report the following information in their respective February 2013 10-K reports relating to their 2012 and 2011 fiscal years.

Abercrombie & Fitch Co. (ANF)
TJX Companies Inc. (TJX)

	Abercrombie & Fitch			TJX Companies		
$ millions	Sales	Cost of Goods Sold	Inventories	Sales	Cost of Goods Sold	Inventories
2012	$4,511	$1,694	$427	$25,878	$18,521	$3,014
2011	4,158	1,608	680	23,191	16,854	2,951

a. Compute the 2012 inventory turnover for each of these two retailers.
b. Discuss any difference you observe in inventory turnover between these two companies. Does the difference confirm your expectations given their respective business models? Explain. (*Hint:* ANF is a higher-end retailer and TJX sells more value-priced clothing.)
c. Describe ways that a retailer can improve its inventory turnover.

M6-19. Computing Depreciation Under Straight-Line and Double-Declining-Balance (LO3)
A delivery van costing $21,000 is expected to have a $1,800 salvage value at the end of its useful life of five years. Assume that the truck was purchased on January 1. Compute the depreciation expense for the first two calendar years under the following depreciation methods:

a. Straight-line
b. Double-declining-balance

M6-20. Computing Depreciation Under Straight-Line and Double-Declining-Balance for Partial Years (LO3)
A company with a calendar year-end, purchases a machine costing $144,000 on July 1, 2013. The machine is expected to be obsolete after three years (36 months) and, thereafter, no longer useful to the company. The estimated salvage value is $6,000. The company's depreciation policy is to record depreciation for the portion of the year that the asset is in service. Compute depreciation expense for both 2013 and 2014 under the following depreciation methods:

a. Straight-line
b. Double-declining-balance

M6-21. Computing and Comparing PPE Turnover for Two Companies (LO3)
Texas Instruments Inc. (TXN) and **Intel Corporation** (INTC) report the following information.

Texas Instruments Inc. (TXN)
Intel Corporation (INTC)

	Intel Corporation		Texas Instruments	
$ millions	Sales	Plant, Property and Equipment, net	Sales	Plant, Property and Equipment, net
2012	$53,341	$27,983	$12,825	$3,912
2011	53,999	23,627	13,735	4,428

a. Compute the 2012 PPE turnover for both companies. Comment on any difference observed.
b. Discuss ways in which high-tech manufacturing companies like these can increase their PPE turnover.

EXERCISES

E6-22. Estimating Uncollectible Accounts and Reporting Accounts Receivable (LO1)
LaFond Company analyzes its accounts receivable at December 31, and arrives at the aged categories below along with the percentages that are estimated as uncollectible.

Age Group	Accounts Receivable	Estimated Loss %
0–30 days past due	$ 80,000	1%
31–60 days past due	20,000	2
61–120 days past due	14,000	5
121–180 days past due	6,000	10
Over 180 days past due	4,000	25
Total accounts receivable	$124,000	

The unused balance of the allowance for uncollectible accounts is $450 on December 31, before any adjustments.

a. What amount of bad debts expense will LaFond report in its income statement for the year?
b. Use the financial statement effects template to record LaFond's bad debts expense for the year.
c. What is the balance of accounts receivable on its December 31 balance sheet?

E6-23. Analyzing and Reporting Receivable Transactions and Uncollectible Accounts (using percentage of sales method) (LO1)
At the beginning of the year, Penman Company had the following account balances.

Accounts receivable	$125,000
Allowance for uncollectible accounts	8,200

During the year, Penman's credit sales were $1,241,000 and collections on accounts receivable were $1,195,000. The following additional transactions occurred during the year.

Feb. 17 Wrote off Nissim's account, $4,100.
May 28 Wrote off Weiss's account, $2,400.
Dec. 15 Wrote off Ohlson's account, $1,100.
Dec. 31 Recorded the bad debts expense assuming that Penman's policy is to record bad debts expense as 0.8% of credit sales. (*Hint*: The allowance account is increased by 0.8% of credit sales regardless of write-offs.)

Compute the ending balances in accounts receivable and the allowance for uncollectible accounts. Show how Penman's December 31 balance sheet reports the two accounts.

E6-24. Interpreting the Accounts Receivable Footnote (LO1)

Hewlett-Packard (HPQ)

Hewlett-Packard Company (HPQ) reports the following in its 2012 10-K report.

October 31 (In millions)	2012	2011
Accounts receivable	$16,407	$18,224

HPQ footnotes to its 10-K provide the following additional information relating to its allowance for doubtful accounts.

For the fiscal years ended October 31 (In millions)	2012	2011	2010
Allowance for doubtful accounts—accounts receivable			
Balance, beginning of period	$470	$525	$629
Increase in allowance from acquisition	—	27	7
Addition of bad debt provision	100	23	80
Deductions, net of recoveries	(106)	(105)	(191)
Balance, end of period	$464	$470	$525

a. What is the gross amount of accounts receivables for HPQ in fiscal 2012 and 2011?
b. What is the percentage of the allowance for doubtful accounts to gross accounts receivable for 2012 and 2011?
c. What amount of bad debts expense did HPQ report each year 2010 through 2012 (ignore increase in allowance from acquisitions)? How does bad debts expense compare with the amounts of its accounts receivable actually written off? (Identify the amounts and explain.)
d. Explain the changes in the allowance for doubtful accounts from 2010 through 2012. Does it appear that HPQ increased or decreased its allowance for doubtful accounts in any particular year beyond what seems reasonable?

E6-25. Estimating Bad Debts Expense and Reporting Receivables (LO1)
At December 31, Sunil Company had a balance of $522,000 in its accounts receivable and an unused balance of $3,700 in its allowance for uncollectible accounts. The company then aged its accounts as follows:

Current	$412,000
1–60 days past due	64,000
61–180 days past due	29,000
Over 180 days past due	17,000
Total accounts receivable	$522,000

The company has experienced losses as follows: 1% of current balances, 5% of balances 1–60 days past due, 15% of balances 61–180 days past due, and 40% of balances over 180 days past due. The company continues to base its allowance for uncollectible accounts on this aging analysis and percentages.

a. What amount of bad debts expense does Sunil report on its income statement for the year?
b. Show how Sunil's December 31 balance sheet will report the accounts receivable and the allowance for uncollectible accounts.

E6-26. Estimating Uncollectible Accounts and Reporting Receivables over Multiple Periods (LO1)
Barth Company, which has been in business for three years, makes all of its sales on credit and does not offer cash discounts. Its credit sales, customer collections, and write-offs of uncollectible accounts for its first three years follow:

Year	Sales	Collections	Accounts Written Off
2011	$642,000	$624,000	$4,200
2012	765,000	755,000	4,700
2013	863,000	829,000	5,400

a. Barth recognizes bad debts expense as 1% of sales. (*Hint:* This means the allowance account is increased by 1% of credit sales regardless of any write-offs and unused balances.) What does Barth's 2013 balance sheet report for accounts receivable and the allowance for uncollectible accounts? What total amount of bad debts expense appears on Barth's income statement for each of the three years?
b. Comment on the appropriateness of the 1% rate used to provide for bad debts based on your analysis in part *a.*

E6-27. Applying and Analyzing Inventory Costing Methods (LO2)
At the beginning of the current period, Chen carried 1,000 units of its product with a unit cost of $21. A summary of purchases during the current period follows:

	Units	Unit Cost	Cost
Beginning Inventory	1,000	$21	$21,000
Purchases: #1	1,800	23	41,400
#2	800	27	21,600
#3	1,200	30	36,000

During the current period, Chen sold 2,800 units.

a. Assume that Chen uses the first-in, first-out method. Compute both cost of goods sold for the current period and the ending inventory balance. Use the financial statement effects template to record cost of goods sold for the period.
b. Assume that Chen uses the last-in, first-out method. Compute both cost of goods sold for the current period and the ending inventory balance.
c. Assume that Chen uses the average cost method. Compute both cost of goods sold for the current period and the ending inventory balance.
d. Which of these three inventory costing methods would you choose to:
1. Reflect what is probably the physical flow of goods? Explain.
2. Minimize income taxes for the period? Explain.
3. Report the largest amount of income for the period? Explain.

E6-28. Analyzing an Inventory Footnote Disclosure (LO2)

General Electric Company (GE)

General Electric Company reports the following footnote in its 10-K report.

December 31 (In millions)	2012	2011
Raw materials and work in process	$ 9,295	$ 8,735
Finished goods.	6,020	4,971
Unbilled shipments.	378	485
	15,693	14,191
Less revaluation to LIFO.	(398)	(450)
	$15,295	$13,741

The company reports its inventories using the LIFO inventory costing method.

a. What is the balance in inventories reported on GE's 2012 balance sheet?
b. What would GE's 2012 balance sheet have reported for inventories had the company used FIFO inventory costing?
c. What cumulative effect has GE's choice of LIFO over FIFO had on its pretax income as of year-end 2012? Explain.
d. Assume GE has a 35% income tax rate. As of the 2012 year-end, how much has GE saved in taxes by choosing LIFO over FIFO method for costing inventory? Has the use of LIFO increased or decreased GE's cumulative taxes paid?
e. What effect has the use of LIFO inventory costing had on GE's pretax income and tax expense for 2012 only (assume a 35% income tax rate)?

E6-29. Computing Cost of Sales and Ending Inventory (LO2)

Stocken Company has the following financial records for the current period.

	Units	Unit Cost
Beginning inventory	150	$50
Purchases: #1.	600	48
#2.	500	46
#3.	250	45

Ending inventory is 350 units. Compute the ending inventory and the cost of goods sold for the current period using (a) first-in, first-out, (b) average cost, and (c) last-in, first-out.

E6-30. Analyzing an Inventory Footnote Disclosure (LO2)

Deere & Co. (DE)

The inventory footnote from Deere & Company's 2012 10-K follows.

Inventories Most inventories owned by Deere & Company and its U.S. equipment subsidiaries are valued at cost, on the "last-in, first-out" (LIFO) basis. Remaining inventories are generally valued at the lower of cost, on the "first-in, first-out" (FIFO) basis, or market. The value of gross inventories on the LIFO basis represented 61 percent and 59 percent of worldwide gross inventories at FIFO value at October 31, 2012 and 2011, respectively. If all inventories had been valued on a FIFO basis, estimated inventories by major classification at October 31 in millions of dollars would have been as follows:

continued

($ millions)	2012	2011
Raw materials and supplies	$1,874	$1,626
Work-in-process.	652	647
Finished goods and parts.	4,065	3,584
Total FIFO value	6,591	5,857
Less adjustment to LIFO value.	1,421	1,486
Inventories	$5,170	$4,371

This footnote reveals that not all of Deere's inventories are reported using the same inventory costing method (companies can use different inventory costing methods for different inventory pools).

a. What amount does Deere report for inventories on its 2012 balance sheet?

b. What would Deere have reported as inventories on its 2012 balance sheet had the company used FIFO inventory costing for all of its inventories?

c. What cumulative effect has the use of LIFO inventory costing had, as of year-end 2012, on Deere's pretax income compared with the pretax income it would have reported had it used FIFO inventory costing for all of its inventories? Explain.

d. Assuming a 35% income tax rate, by what cumulative dollar amount has Deere's tax expense been affected by use of LIFO inventory costing as of year-end 2012? Has the use of LIFO inventory costing increased or decreased Deere's cumulative tax expense?

e. What effect has the use of LIFO inventory costing had on Deere's pretax income and tax expense for 2012 only (assume a 35% income tax rate)?

E6-31. Computing Straight-Line and Double-Declining-Balance Depreciation (LO3)
On January 2, Haskins Company purchases a laser cutting machine for use in fabrication of a part for one of its key products. The machine cost $75,000, and its estimated useful life is five years, after which the expected salvage value is $5,000. For both parts *a* and *b* below: (1) Compute depreciation expense for *each year* of the machine's five-year useful life under that depreciation method. (2) Use the financial statements effects template to show the effect of depreciation for the first year only for that method.

a. Straight-line
b. Double-declining-balance

E6-32. Computing Depreciation, Net Book Value, and Gain or Loss on Asset Sale (LO3)
Sloan Company owns an executive plane that originally cost $920,000. It has recorded straight-line depreciation on the plane for seven full years, calculated assuming an $80,000 expected salvage value at the end of its estimated 10-year useful life. Sloan disposes of the plane at the end of the seventh year.

a. At the disposal date, what is the (1) cumulative depreciation expense and (2) net book value of the plane?

b. How much gain or loss is reported at disposal if the sales price is:
1. A cash amount equal to the plane's net book value.
2. $195,000 cash.
3. $600,000 cash.

E6-33. Computing Straight-Line and Double-Declining-Balance Depreciation (LO3)
On January 2, 2013, Dechow Company purchases a machine that manufactures a part for one of its key products. The machine cost $220,500 and is estimated to have a useful life of six years, with an expected salvage value of $18,600. Compute depreciation expense for 2013 and 2014 for the following depreciation methods. (When equipment is used exclusively in the manufacturing process, the depreciation is more accurately recorded as part of cost of goods sold and not as depreciation expense.)

a. Straight-line.
b. Double-declining-balance.

E6-34. Computing Depreciation, Net Book Value, and Gain or Loss on Asset Sale (LO3)
Palepu Company owns and operates a delivery van that originally cost $28,200. Palepu has recorded straight-line depreciation on the van for four years, calculated assuming a $3,000 expected salvage value at the end of its estimated six-year useful life. Depreciation was last recorded at the end of the fourth year, at which time Palepu disposes of this van.

a. Compute the net book value of the van on the disposal date.
b. Compute the gain or loss on sale of the van if the disposal proceeds are:
1. A cash amount equal to the van's net book value.
2. $13,000 cash.
3. $10,000 cash.

Deere & Co. (DE)

E6-35. Estimating Useful Life and Percent Used Up (LO3)
The property and equipment footnote from the Deere & Company balance sheet follows.

Property and Depreciation A summary of property and equipment at October 31 follows:

Property and Equipment ($ millions)	Useful Lives* (Years)	2012	2011
Land		$ 137	$ 117
Buildings and building equipment	23	2,584	2,430
Machinery and equipment	11	4,393	4,254
Dies, patterns, tools, etc.	8	1,330	1,213
All other	6	819	731
Construction in progress		938	649
Total at cost		10,201	9,394
Less accumulated depreciation		5,250	5,107
Total		$4,951	$4,287

* Weighted averages

Total property and equipment additions in 2012, 2011 and 2010 were $1,376 million, $1,059 million and $802 million and depreciation was $555 million, $516 million and $540 million, respectively.

a. Compute the estimated useful life of Deere's depreciable assets at year-end 2012. (*Hint:* Exclude land and construction in progress.) How does this estimate compare with the useful lives reported in Deere's footnote disclosure?
b. Estimate the percent used up of Deere's depreciable assets at year-end 2012. How do you interpret this figure?

Intel Corp. (INTC)

E6-36. Computing and Evaluating Receivables, Inventory and PPE Turnovers (LO1, 2, 3)
Intel Corporation reports the following financial statement amounts in its 2012 10-K report.

$ millions	Sales	Cost of Goods Sold	Receivables, gross	Inventories	Plant, property and equipment, net
2010	$43,623	$15,132	$2,895	$3,757	$17,899
2011	53,999	20,242	3,686	4,096	23,627
2012	53,341	20,190	3,871	4,734	27,983

a. Compute the receivables, inventory, and PPE turnover ratios for both 2011 and 2012.
b. What changes are evident in the turnover rates of Intel for these years? Discuss ways in which a company such as Intel can improve receivables, inventory, and PPE turnover ratios.

E6-37. Computing and Assessing Plant Asset Impairment (LO3)
On July 1, Zeibart Company purchases equipment for $220,000. The equipment has an estimated useful life of 10 years and expected salvage value of $25,000. The company uses straight-line depreciation. Four years later, economic factors cause the fair value of the equipment to decline to $85,000. On this date, Zeibart examines the equipment for impairment and estimates $115,000 in undiscounted expected cash inflows from this equipment.

a. Compute the annual depreciation expense relating to this equipment.
b. Compute the equipment's net book value at the end of the fourth year.

c. Apply the test of impairment to this equipment as of the end of the fourth year. Is the equipment impaired? Show supporting computations.

d. If the equipment is impaired at the end of the fourth year, compute the impairment loss.

PROBLEMS

P6-38. Evaluating Turnover Rates for Different Companies (LO1, 2, 3)

Following are asset turnover rates for accounts receivable; inventory; and property, plant, and equipment (PPE) for **Best Buy Co., Inc.** (BBY) (retailer), **Caterpillar Inc.** (CAT) (manufacturer of heavy equipment), **Dell Inc.** (DELL) (computers), **Verizon Communications, Inc.** (VZ) (communications), and **Walmart Stores, Inc.** (WMT) (department store).

Best Buy Co., Inc. (BBY)
Caterpillar Inc. (CAT)
Dell Inc. (DELL)
Verizon Communications, Inc. (VZ)
Walmart Stores, Inc. (WMT)

Company	Accounts Receivable Turnover	Inventory Turnover	Plant, Property and Equipment Turnover
Best Buy Co.	18.06	5.60	13.38
Caterpillar Inc	3.57	3.13	4.27
Dell	8.69	32.13	26.80
Verizon	9.51	45.93	1.31
Walmart	73.85	8.34	4.20

Required

a. Interpret and explain difference in receivables turnover for the retailer (Best Buy) vis-à-vis that for the manufacturer (Caterpillar). What reason can you give for a 73.85 turnover for Walmart?

b. Interpret and explain the difference in inventory turnover for Dell versus Caterpillar.

c. Why is the PPE turnover for Verizon low compared with other companies on this list?

d. What are some general observations you might draw regarding the relative levels of these turnover rates across the different industries?

P6-39. Interpreting Accounts Receivable and Related Footnote Disclosure (LO1)

Following is the current asset section from the **W.W. Grainger, Inc.**, balance sheet.

W.W. Grainger, Inc. (GWW)

As of December 31 ($ 000s)	2012	2011	2010
Cash and cash equivalents	$ 452,063	$ 335,491	$ 313,454
Accounts receivable (less allowances for doubtful accounts of $19,449, $18,801, respectively)	940,020	888,697	762,895
Inventories—net	1,301,935	1,268,647	991,577
Prepaid expenses and other assets	110,414	100,081	87,125
Deferred income taxes	55,967	47,410	44,627
Prepaid income taxes	40,241	54,574	38,393
Total current assets	$2,900,640	$2,694,900	$2,238,071

Grainger reports the following footnote relating to its receivables.

Allowance for Doubtful Accounts The following table shows the activity in the allowance for doubtful accounts.

For Years Ended December 31 ($ 000s)	2012	2011	2010
Balance at beginning of period	$18,801	$24,552	$25,850
Provision for uncollectible accounts	9,504	4,761	6,718
Write-off of uncollectible accounts, net of recoveries	(9,100)	(8,138)	(8,302)
Business acquisitions, foreign currency and other	244	(2,374)	286
Balance at end of period	$19,449	$18,801	$24,552

Required

a. What amount do customers owe Grainger at each of the year-ends 2010 through 2012?

b. What percentage of its total accounts receivable does Grainger deem uncollectible? (*Hint:* Percentage of uncollectible accounts = Allowance for uncollectible accounts/Gross accounts receivable)

c. What amount of bad debts expense did Grainger report in its income statement for each of the years 2010 through 2012?

d. Explain the change in the balance of the allowance for uncollectible accounts since 2010. Specifically, did the allowance increase or decrease as a percentage of gross accounts receivable, and why?

e. If Grainger had kept its 2012 allowance for uncollectible accounts at the same percentage of gross accounts receivable as it was in 2010, by what amount would its pretax profit have changed? Explain.

f. Overall, what is your assessment of Grainger's allowance for uncollectible accounts and the related bad debts expense?

Intuit, Inc. (INTU)

P6-40. Analyzing and Interpreting Receivables and Related Ratios (LO1)

Following is the current asset section from **Intuit Inc.**'s balance sheet.

July 31 ($ millions)	2013	2012
Current assets:		
Cash and cash equivalents	$1,009	$ 393
Investments	652	351
Accounts receivable, net of allowance for doubtful accounts of $38 and $46	130	142
Income taxes receivable	62	53
Deferred income taxes	166	183
Prepaid expenses and other current assets	98	65
Current assets of discontinued operations	44	46
Current assets before funds held for customers	2,161	1,233
Funds held for customers	235	290
Total current assets	$2,396	$1,523

Total revenues were $4,171 million ($1,515 million in product sales and $2,656 million in service revenues and other) in 2013.

Required

a. What are Intuit's gross accounts receivable at the end of 2012 and 2013?

b. For both 2013 and 2012, compute the ratio of the allowance for uncollectible accounts to gross receivables. What trend do you observe?

c. Compute the receivables turnover ratio and the average collection period for 2013 based on gross receivables computed in part *a*. Does the collection period (days sales in receivables) appear reasonable given Intuit's lines of business (Intuit's products include QuickBooks, TurboTax and Quicken, which it sells to consumers and small businesses)? Explain.

d. Is the percentage of Intuit's allowance for uncollectible accounts to gross accounts receivable consistent with what you expect for Intuit's line of business? Explain.

e. Intuit discloses the following table related to its allowance for uncollectible accounts from its 10-K. Comment on the change in the allowance account during 2011 through 2013.

(In millions)	Beginning Balance	Additions Charged to Expense/ Revenue	Deductions	Ending Balance
Year ended July 31, 2013				
Allowance for doubtful accounts	$46	$33	$(41)	$38
Year ended July 31, 2012				
Allowance for doubtful accounts	$20	$34	$(8)	$46
Year ended July 31, 2011				
Allowance for doubtful accounts	$22	$18	$(20)	$20

Dow Chemical Co. (DOW)

P6-41. Analyzing and Interpreting Inventories and Related Ratios and Disclosures (LO2)

The current asset section from **The Dow Chemical Company**'s 2012 annual report follows.

December 31 (In millions)	2012	2011
Cash and cash equivalents	$ 4,318	$ 5,444
Marketable securities and interest-bearing deposits	—	2
Accounts and notes receivable		
Trade (net of allowance for doubtful receivables—2012: $121; 2011: $121)	5,074	4,900
Other	4,605	4,726
Inventories	8,476	7,577
Deferred income tax assets—current	877	471
Other current assets	334	302
Total current assets	$23,684	$23,422

The Dow Chemical inventory footnote follows.

The following table provides a breakdown of inventories:

Inventories at December 31 (In millions)	2012	2011
Finished goods	$4,880	$4,327
Work in process	1,910	1,716
Raw materials	866	765
Supplies	820	769
Total inventories	$8,476	$7,577

The reserves reducing inventories from a FIFO basis to a LIFO basis amounted to $842 million at December 31, 2012 and $1,105 million at December 31, 2011. Inventories valued on a LIFO basis, principally hydrocarbon and U.S. chemicals and plastics product inventories, represented 29 percent of the total inventories at December 31, 2012 and 30 percent of total inventories at December 31, 2011.

A reduction of certain inventories resulted in the liquidation of some of the Company's LIFO inventory layers, increasing pretax income $91 million in 2012, $126 million in 2011 and $159 million in 2010.

Required

a. What inventory costing method does Dow Chemical use? As of 2012, what is the effect on cumulative pretax income and cash flow of using this inventory costing method? (Assume a 35% tax rate.) What is the effect on 2012 pretax income and cash flow of using this inventory costing method?

b. Compute inventory turnover and average inventory days outstanding for 2012 (2012 cost of goods sold is $47,792 million). Comment on the level of these two ratios. Is the level what you expect given Dow's industry? Explain.

c. Explain why a reduction of inventory quantities increased income in 2010 through 2012.

P6-42. Estimating Useful Life and Percent Used Up (LO3)

The property and equipment section of the **Abbott Laboratories** 2012 balance sheet follows.

Abbott Laboratories (ABT)

	December 31		
Property and equipment, at cost ($ thousands)	2012	2011	2010
Land	$ 604,462	$ 633,917	$ 648,988
Buildings	4,259,240	4,467,387	4,334,236
Equipment	13,110,833	12,216,388	11,813,618
Construction in progress	954,352	698,873	577,460
	18,928,887	18,016,565	17,374,302
Less: accumulated depreciation and amortization	10,865,840	10,142,610	9,403,346
Net property and equipment	$ 8,063,047	$ 7,873,955	$ 7,970,956

The company also provides the following disclosure relating to the useful lives of its depreciable assets.

Property and Equipment—Depreciation and amortization are provided on a straight-line basis over the estimated useful lives of the assets. The following table shows estimated useful lives of property and equipment:

Classification	Estimated Useful Lives
Buildings.	10 to 50 years (average 27 years)
Equipment	3 to 20 years (average 11 years)

During 2012, the company reported $1,363,673 ($ 000s) for depreciation expense.

Required

a. Compute the estimated useful life of Abbott Laboratories' depreciable assets. How does this compare with its useful lives footnote disclosure above?

b. Compute the estimated percent used up of Abbott Laboratories' depreciable assets. How do you interpret this figure?

Rohm and Haas Company (ROH)

P6-43. Interpreting and Applying Disclosures on Property and Equipment (LO3)

Following are selected disclosures from the Rohm and Haas Company (a specialty chemical company) 2007 10-K.

Land, Building and Equipment, Net

(in millions)	2007	2006
Land	$ 146	$ 142
Buildings and improvements	1,855	1,729
Machinery and equipment	6,155	5,721
Capitalized interest.	352	340
Construction in progress	271	218
Land, buildings, and equipment, gross	8,779	8,150
Less: Accumulated depreciation	5,908	5,481
Total	$2,871	$2,669

The principal lives (in years) used in determining depreciation rates of various assets are: buildings and improvement (10–50); machinery and equipment (5–20); automobiles, trucks and tank cars (3–10); furniture and fixtures, laboratory equipment and other assets (5–10); capitalized software (5–7). The principal life used in determining the depreciation rate for leasehold improvements is the years remaining in the lease term or the useful life (in years) of the asset, whichever is shorter.

Impairment of Long-lived Assets Long-lived assets, other than investments, goodwill and indefinite-lived intangible assets, are depreciated over their estimated useful lives, and are reviewed for impairment whenever changes in circumstances indicate the carrying value of the asset may not be recoverable. Such circumstances would include items such as a significant decrease in the market price of a long-lived asset, a significant adverse change in the manner the asset is being used or planned to be used or in its physical condition or a history of operating or cash flow losses associated with the use of the asset . . . When such events or changes occur, we assess the recoverability of the asset by comparing the carrying value of the asset to the expected future cash flows associated with the asset's planned future use and eventual disposition of the asset, if applicable . . . We utilize marketplace assumptions to calculate the discounted cash flows used in determining the asset's fair value . . . For the year ended December 31, 2007, we recognized approximately $24 million of fixed asset impairment charges.

Required

a. Compute the PPE turnover for 2007 (Sales in 2007 are $8,897 million). Does the level of its PPE turnover suggest that Rohm and Haas is capital intensive? Explain. (*Hint:* The median PPE turnover for all publicly traded companies is approximately 5.03 in 2007.)

b. Rohm and Haas reported depreciation expense of $412 million in 2007. Estimate the useful life, on average, for its depreciable PPE assets.

c. By what percentage are Rohm and Haas' assets "used up" at year-end 2007? What implication does the assets used up computation have for forecasting cash flows?

d. Rohm and Haas reports an asset impairment charge in 2007. How do companies determine if assets are impaired? How do asset impairment charges affect Rohm and Haas' cash flows for 2007? How would we treat these charges for analysis purposes?

IFRS APPLICATIONS

I6-44. Computing and Evaluating Inventory Turnover for Two Companies (LO2)

European car makers, **Volkswagen Group** (headquartered in Wolfsburg, Germany) and **Daimler AG** (headquartered in Stuttgart, Germany) report the following information.

Volkswagen Group
Daimler AG

	Volkswagen			Daimler		
(Euros in millions)	Sales	Cost of Goods Sold	Inventories	Sales	Cost of Goods Sold	Inventories
2011	€159,337	€131,371	€27,551	€106,540	€81,023	€17,081
2012	192,676	157,518	28,674	114,297	88,784	17,720

Required

a. Compute the 2012 inventory turnover and the 2012 gross profit margin (in %) for each of these two companies.

b. Discuss any difference in inventory turnover and gross profit margin between these two companies. Does the difference confirm expectations given their respective business models? Explain.

c. How could the companies improve inventory turnover?

I6-45. Estimating Useful Life and Percent Used Up (LO3)

Husky Energy is one of Canada's largest integrated energy companies. Based in Calgary, Alberta, Husky is publicly traded on the Toronto Stock Exchange. The Company operates in Western and Atlantic Canada, the United States and the Asia Pacific Region with upstream and downstream business segments. The company uses IFRS to prepare its financial statements. During 2012, the company reported depreciation expense of $2,583 million. The property and equipment footnote follows.

Husky Energy (HSE)

Property, Plant and Equipment ($ millions)	Oil and Gas Properties	Processing, Transportation and Storage	Upgrading	Refining	Retail and Other	Total
Cost						
December 31, 2011	$33,640	$ 930	$1,972	$4,916	$2,176	$43,634
Additions	3,971	53	47	349	146	4,566
Aquisitions	16	—	—	—	—	16
Transfers from exploration and evaluation	198	—	—	—	—	198
Changes in asset retirement obligations	1,097	(2)	(13)	(71)	29	1,040
Disposals and derecognition	(76)	—	—	(7)	(127)	(210)
Exchange adjustments	(20)	—	—	(93)	1	(112)
December 31, 2012	$38,826	$ 981	$2,006	$5,094	$2,225	$49,132
Accumulated depletion, depreciation, amortization and impairment						
December 31, 2011	$(15,900)	$(407)	$ (848)	$(1,046)	$(1,154)	$(19,355)
Depletion, depreciation and amortization	(2,101)	(36)	(102)	(241)	(103)	(2,583)
Disposals and derecognition	49	—	—	3	124	176
Exchange adjustments	5	—	—	24	—	29
December 31, 2012	$(17,947)	$(443)	$ (950)	$(1,260)	$(1,133)	$(21,733)
Net book value						
December 31, 2011	$ 17,740	$ 523	$1,124	$3,870	$1,022	$24,279
December 31, 2012	20,879	538	1,056	3,834	1,092	27,399

Required

a. Compute the estimated useful life of Husky Energy's depreciable assets at year-end 2012. Assume that land is 10% of "Refining."

b. Estimate the percent used up of Husky Energy's depreciable assets at year-end 2012. How do we interpret this figure?

c. Husky Energy increased total PPE by $1,097 million for asset retirement obligation related to Oil and Gas Properties. Explain in layman's terms what this represents.

d. Estimate the effect that the asset retirement obligation had on depreciation expense for Oil and Gas Properties for 2012.

Schneider Electric

I6-46. Computing and Evaluating Receivables, Inventory and PPE Turnovers (LO1, 2, 3)

Schneider Electric is a multinational energy company headquartered in Rueil-Malmaison, France. Selected balance sheet and income statement information for 2010 through 2012 follows.

(€ in millions)	Sales	Cost of Goods Sold	Trade Receivables	Inventories	Plant, property, and equipment, net
2010	€19,580	€11,842	€4,441	€3,139	€2,337
2011	22,345	13,958	5,402	3,349	2,573
2012	23,946	14,889	5,289	3,090	2,622

Required

a. Compute the receivables, inventory, and PPE turnover ratios for both 2011 and 2012.

b. What changes are evident in the turnover rates of Schneider Electric for these years?

c. Discuss ways in which a company such as Schneider Electric can improve receivables, inventory, and PPE turnover ratios.

Unilever
Unilever N.V.
Unilever PLC

I6-47. Analyzing and Interpreting Receivables, Inventories, and Related Ratios (LO1, 2)

Unilever is a dual-listed company consisting of Unilever N.V. in Rotterdam, Netherlands and Unilever PLC in London, UK. Both Unilever companies have the same directors and effectively operate as a single business. Following is the current asset section of Unilever's balance sheet.

Current Assets (€ million)	2012	2011
Inventories	€ 4,436	€ 4,601
Trade and other current receivables	4,436	4,513
Current tax assets	217	219
Cash and cash equivalents	2,465	3,484
Other financial assets	401	1,453
Non-current assets held for sale	192	21
Total current assets	€12,147	€14,291

Trade and Other Current Receivables (€ million)	2012	2011
Due within one year		
Trade receivables	€2,793	€2,897
Prepayments and accrued income	549	591
Other receivables	1,094	1,025
	€4,436	€4,513

Aging of Trade Receivables (€ million)	2012	2011
Total trade receivables	€2,916	€3,013
Less impairment provision for trade receivables	(123)	(116)
	€2,793	€2,897
Of which:		
Not overdue	€2,473	€2,505
Past due less than three months	236	300
Past due more than three months but less than six months	80	72
Past due more than six months but less than one year	48	52
Past due more than one year	79	84
Impairment provision for trade receivables	(123)	(116)
	€2,793	€2,897

Required

a. What are Unilever's gross trade and other current receivables at the end of 2011 and of 2012?

b. For both 2011 and 2012, compute the ratio of the allowance for uncollectible accounts to gross receivables. What trend do we observe?

c. The company reported net sales of €51,324 in 2012. Compute the receivables turnover ratio and the average collection period for 2012 based on gross receivables computed in part *a*.

d. The company reported cost of sales of €30,703 in 2012. Compute the inventory turnover and the average inventory days outstanding for 2012.

I6-48. Analyzing and Interpreting Operating Asset Ratios (LO1, 2, 3)

Canadian Tire Corporation, Limited operates retail stores in Canada that sell general merchandise, clothing, and sporting goods. The company offers everyday products and services to Canadians through more than 1,700 retail and gasoline outlets from coast-to-coast. Canadian Tire uses IFRS, and the asset side of the 2012 balance sheet is as follows: Canadian Tire

In Millions of CDN Dollars	2012	2011
Cash and cash equivalents	$ 1,015.5	$ 325.8
Short-term investments	168.9	196.4
Trade and other receivables	750.6	829.3
Loans receivable	4,265.7	4,081.7
Merchandise inventories	1,503.3	1,448.6
Prepaid expenses and deposits	39.1	44.3
Assets classified as held for sale	5.5	30.5
Total current assets	7,748.6	6,956.6
Long-term receivables and other assets	681.2	668.9
Long-term investments	182.7	128.2
Goodwill and intangible assets	1,089.9	1,110.0
Investment property	95.1	72.4
Property and equipment	3,343.5	3,365.9
Deferred income taxes	40.4	36.8
Total assets	$13,181.4	$12,338.8

Required

a. Compute inventory turnover and average inventory days outstanding for 2012 (2012 cost of goods sold is $7,929.3 million). Comment on the level of these two ratios. Is the level what we expect given Canadian Tire's industry? Explain.

b. GAAP allows for FIFO, LIFO, and average cost inventory costing methods. How does IFRS differ?

c. In periods of rising prices, how will net income be affected under the different inventory costing methods?

d. Compute the accounts receivable turnover for 2012. The 2012 sales were C$11,427.2 million and 2011 sales were C$10,387.1 million. Compute the days' sales outstanding for both years. Compare the two and determine which year has better accounts receivable efficiency. (*Hint:* Use trade and other receivables in the ratios.)

e. During 2012, the company recorded depreciation expense of C$335.1 million. Footnotes reported accumulated depreciation on PPE of C$2,118.6 million, and cost of land and construction in progress of C$744.3 million and C$102.3 million respectively. Compute PPE turnover, average useful life, and percent used up for 2012.

I6-49. Analyzing and Interpreting Operating Ratios (LO1, 2, 3)

Headquartered in Bella Vista, NSW, **Woolworths Limited** is the largest retail company in Australia and New Zealand by market capitalization and sales. The company is the largest food retailer, liquor retailer and the largest hotel and gaming poker machine operator in Australia. The company employs over 200,000 people. Woolworths Limited

(AUS$ millions)	2012	2011
Current assets		
Cash	$ 833.4	$1,519.6
Trade and other receivables	869.9	856.1
Inventories	3,698.3	3,736.5
Other financial assets	23.8	120.8
	5,425.4	6,233.0
Assets classified as held for sale	376.7	93.9
Total current assets	$5,802.1	$6,326.9

Trade and Other Receivables (AUS$ millions)	2012	2011
Current		
Trade receivables	$218.0	$196.6
Other receivables	385.3	426.5
Prepayments	266.6	233.0
	$869.9	$856.1

Trade receivables are presented net of impairment allowance. Impairment provision balance as at 24 June 2012 was $13.3 million.

Property, Plant and Equipment (AUS$ millions)	2012	2011
Development properties, Non-current		
At cost	$ 1,415.9	$ 1,576.3
Less: accumulated depreciation	(7.5)	(12.9)
	1,408.4	1,563.4
Freehold land, warehouse, retail and other properties		
At cost	2,839.0	1,638.5
Less: accumulated depreciation	(138.8)	(91.3)
	2,700.2	1,547.2
Leasehold improvements		
At cost	2,270.3	2,080.8
Less: accumulated amortisation	(917.0)	(802.9)
	1,353.3	1,277.9
Plant and equipment		
At cost	10,702.6	10,321.2
Less: accumulated depreciation	(6,575.5)	(6,089.4)
	4,127.1	4,231.8
Total property, plant and equipment—net book value	$ 9,589.0	$ 8,620.3

During 2012, the company reported total revenue from sale of goods of $55,129.8 million and cost of goods sold of $40,792.4 million. Depreciation expense on property, plant and equipment was $894.8 million.

Required

a. What amount does Woolworths expect to collect from its trade customers?

b. What are Woolworths's gross accounts from its trade customers?

c. Determine the number of days it took Woolworths to collect from its trade customers during 2012. Does the figure computed make sense? Why or why not?

d. Compute inventory turnover for 2012. Given the nature of the company's operations, does this ratio make sense?

e. What is the gross amount and total accumulated depreciation and amortization of property, plant and equipment reported on the balance sheet in 2012?

f. Compute PPE turnover for 2012. Explain in layman's terms what this ratio represents.

g. Compute percent used up and useful life of the company's PPE.

MANAGEMENT APPLICATIONS

MA6-50. Managing Operating Asset Reduction **(LO1, 2, 3)**
Return on net operating assets (RNOA = NOPAT/Average NOA, see Module 4) is commonly used to evaluate financial performance. If managers cannot increase NOPAT, they can still increase this return by reducing the amount of net operating assets (NOA). List specific ways that managers could reduce the following assets:

a. Receivables
b. Inventories
c. Plant, property and equipment

MA6-51. Ethics and Governance: Managing the Allowance for Uncollectible Accounts **(LO1)**
Assume that you are the CEO of a publicly traded company. Your chief financial officer (CFO) informs you that your company will not be able to meet earnings per share targets for the current quarter. In that event, your stock price will likely decline. The CFO proposes reducing the quarterly provision for uncollectible accounts (bad debts expense) to increase your EPS to the level analysts expect. This will result in an allowance account that is less than it should be. The CFO explains that outsiders cannot easily detect a reduction in this allowance and that the allowance can be increased next quarter. The benefit is that your shareholders will not experience a decline in stock price.

a. Identify the parties that are likely to be affected by this proposed action.
b. How will reducing the provision for uncollectible accounts affect the income statement and the balance sheet?
c. How will reducing the provision for uncollectible accounts in the current period affect the income statement and the balance sheet in a future period?
d. What argument might the CFO use to convince the company's external auditors that this action is justified?
e. How might an analyst detect this earnings management activity?
f. How might this action affect the moral compass of your company? What repercussions might this action have?

ONGOING PROJECT

(This ongoing project began in Module 1 and continues through most of the book; even if previous segments were not completed, the requirements are still applicable to any business analysis.)

1. *Accounts Receivable* The following provides some guidance for analyzing a company's accounts receivable.
   - Are sales primarily on credit or is a typical sale transacted in cash? Consider the industry and the companies' business model.
   - What is the relative size of accounts receivable? How has this changed over the recent three-year period?
   - How large is the allowance for doubtful accounts? Determine the balance relative to gross accounts receivable.
   - What did the company record for bad debt expense? Compute the common size amount.
   - Compute accounts receivable turnover and days sales outstanding for all three years reported on the income statement. One will need to obtain additional balance sheet information to be able to compute average balances for the denominator. Consider the current economic environment and the companies' competitive landscape. Would one expect collection to have slowed down or sped up during the year?
   - Does the company have any large customers that increase the company's credit risk?

   For each point of analysis, compare across companies and over time. The goal is to determine whether each company's accounts receivable (levels and changes) seems appropriate and to gauge the quality of the receivables.
2. *Inventory* The following provides some guidance for analysis of a company's inventory.
   - What is inventory for the company? Does the company manufacture inventory? What proportion of total inventory is raw materials? Work in process? Finished goods?
   - Compare the two companies' inventory costing methods. Adjust LIFO inventory and cost of goods sold if necessary. Is the LIFO reserve significant? Estimate the tax savings associated with LIFO costing method. (Use the adjusted COGS and inventory figures for all calculations and ratios.)

- What is the relative size of inventory? How has this changed over the recent three-year period?
- Compute inventory turnover and average inventory days for all three years reported on the income statement.
- Compute gross margin in percentage terms. Consider the current economic environment and the companies' competitive landscape. Can we explain any changes in gross profit levels? Have costs for raw materials and labor increased during the year? Have sales volumes softened? What has happened to unit prices? Read the MD&A to determine senior management's take.
- Does the company face any inventory related risk? What has been done to mitigate this risk? Read the MD&A.

For each point of analysis, compare across companies and over time.

3. *Plant Assets* The following provides some guidance to the companies' long-term (fixed) assets.
   - Are fixed assets significant for the companies? What proportion of total assets is held as fixed assets (PPE)? What exactly are the companies' fixed assets? That is, what is their nature?
   - Compare the two companies' depreciation policies. Do they differ markedly?
   - What is the relative size of fixed assets? How has this changed over the three-year period?
   - Did the company increase fixed assets during the year? Was the increase for outright asset purchases or did the company acquire assets via a merger or acquisition?
   - Compute PPE turnover for all three years reported on the income statement.
   - Compute the average age of assets and percentage used up.
   - Are any assets impaired? Is the impairment charge significant? Is the impairment specific to the company or is the industry experiencing a downturn?

   For each point of analysis, compare across companies and over time.

SOLUTIONS TO REVIEW PROBLEMS

Mid-Module Review 1

Solution

1. As of December 31, 2012:

Current	$468,000	×	1%	=	$ 4,680	
1–60 days past due	244,000	×	5%	=	12,200	
61–180 days past due	38,000	×	15%	=	5,700	
Over 180 days past due	20,000	×	40%	=	8,000	
Amount required					30,580	
Unused allowance balance					7,000	
Provision					$ 23,580	2012 bad debts expense

2. Current assets section of balance sheet:

Accounts receivable, net of $30,580 in allowances	$739,420

3. The information here reveals that the HP subsidiary has markedly increased the percentage of the allowance for uncollectible accounts to gross accounts receivable; from the historical 2% to the current 4% ($30,580/$770,000). There are at least two possible interpretations:
   a. The quality of the HP subsidiary's receivables has declined. Possible causes include the following: (1) Sales have stagnated and the company is selling to lower-quality accounts to maintain sales volume; (2) It may have introduced new products for which average credit losses are higher; and (3) Its administration of accounts receivable has become lax.
   b. The company has intentionally increased its allowance account above the level needed for expected future losses so as to reduce current-period income and "bank" that income for future periods (income shifting).

Mid-Module Review 2

Solution

Preliminary computation: Units in ending inventory = 4,800 available − 2,800 sold = 2,000

1. First-in, first-out (FIFO)

Cost of goods sold computation:	Units		Cost		Total
	1,000	@	$18.00	=	$18,000
	1,800	@	$18.25	=	32,850
	2,800				**$50,850**

Cost of goods available for sale	$88,450
Less: Cost of goods sold	50,850
Ending inventory ($22,800 + $14,800)	**$37,600**

2. Last-in, first-out (LIFO)

Cost of goods sold computation:	Units		Cost		Total
	1,200	@	$19.00	=	$22,800
	800	@	$18.50	=	14,800
	800	@	$18.25	=	14,600
	2,800				**$52,200**

Cost of goods available for sale	$88,450
Less: Cost of goods sold	52,200
Ending inventory ($18,000 + [1,000 × $18.25])	**$36,250**

3. Average cost (AC)

Average unit cost	= $88,450/4,800 units	= $18.427
Cost of goods sold	= 2,800 × $18.427	= $51,596
Ending inventory	= 2,000 × $18.427	= $36,854

4. *a.* FIFO is normally the method that most closely reflects physical flow. For example, FIFO would apply to the physical flow of perishable units and to situations where the earlier units acquired are moved out first because of risk of deterioration or obsolescence.

   b. LIFO results in the highest cost of goods sold during periods of rising costs (as in the HP subsidiary case); and, accordingly, LIFO yields the lowest net income and the lowest income taxes.

5. Last-in, first-out with LIFO liquidation

Cost of goods sold computation:	Units		Cost		Total
	800	@	$18.50	=	$14,800
	1,800	@	$18.25	=	32,850
	200	@	$18.00	=	3,600
	2,800				$51,250

Cost of goods available for sale (Beginning inventory + Purchase #1 + Purchase #2)	$65,650
Less: Cost of goods sold	51,250
Ending inventory (800 × $18)	$14,400

The company's LIFO gross profit has increased by $950 ($52,200 − $51,250) because of the LIFO liquidation. The reduction of inventory quantities matched older (lower) cost layers against current selling prices. The company has, in effect, dipped into lower-cost layers to boost current-period profit—all from a simple delay of inventory purchases.

Module-End Review

Solution

1. a. Straight-line depreciation expense = ($95,000 − $10,000)/5 years = $17,000 per year

   b. Double-declining-balance (note: twice straight-line rate = 2 × [100%/5 years] = 40%)

Year	Net Book Value × Rate	Depreciation Expense	Accumulated Depreciation
1	$95,000 × 0.40 =	$38,000	$38,000
2	($95,000 − $38,000) × 0.40 =	22,800	60,800
3	($95,000 − $60,800) × 0.40 =	13,680	74,480
4	($95,000 − $74,480) × 0.40 =	8,208	82,688
5	($95,000 − $82,688) × 0.40 =	2,312*	85,000

*The formula value of $4,925 is not reported for Year 5 because doing so would depreciate the asset below the estimated salvage value; only the $2,312 needed to reach salvage value is depreciated.

2. The HP subsidiary reports the equipment on its balance sheet at its net book value of $44,000.

Equipment, cost	$95,000
Less accumulated depreciation ($17,000 × 3)	51,000
Equipment, net (end of Year 3)	$44,000

3. The estimated useful life is computed as: Depreciable asset cost/Depreciation expense = $95,000/ $17,000 = 5.6 years. Because companies do not usually disclose salvage values (not required disclosure), the useful-life estimate is a bit high for this asset. This estimate is still informative because companies typically only provide a range of useful lives for depreciable assets in the footnotes.

   The percent used up is computed as: Accumulated depreciation/Depreciable asset cost = $51,000/ $95,000 = 53.7%. The equipment is more than one-half used up at the end of the third year. Again, the lack of knowledge of salvage value yields an underestimate of the percent used up. Still, this estimate is useful in that we know that the company's asset is over one-half used up and is likely to require replacement in about two years (estimated as less than one-half of its estimated useful life of 5.6 years). This replacement will require a cash outflow or financing and should be considered in our projections of future cash flows.
4. The equipment is impaired since the undiscounted expected cash flows ($40,000) are less than the net book value of the equipment ($44,000). The HP subsidiary must write down the equipment to its fair value of $36,000. The effect of this write-down is to reduce the net book value of the equipment by $8,000 ($44,000 − $36,000) and recognize a loss in the income statement.
5. The HP subsidiary must report a gain on this sale of $6,000, computed as proceeds of $50,000 less the net book value of the equipment of $44,000 (see part *2*).

Module

7 Reporting and Analyzing Nonowner Financing

Learning Objectives

LO1 Describe the accounting for current operating liabilities, including accounts payable and accrued liabilities. (p. 7-4)

LO2 Describe the accounting for current and long-term nonoperating liabilities. (p. 7-10)

LO3 Explain how credit ratings are determined and identify their effect on the cost of debt. (p. 7-21)

Verizon Communications

Verizon Communications, Inc., began doing business in 2000, when **Bell Atlantic Corporation** merged with **GTE Corporation**. Verizon is one of the world's leading providers of communications services. It is the largest provider of wireline and wireless communications in the U.S., and is the largest of the "Baby Bells" as of 2012 with over $115 billion in revenues and $225 billion in assets.

In the early 2000s, the Internet frenzy had cooled and Verizon's stock price had plunged, falling from an all-time high of $70 in late 1999 to $27 in mid-2002. Since then, the stock has risen to over $50 per share (see chart below).

Verizon survived the Internet and telecom downturn. Now it faces a formidable new challenger: cable. Cable companies spent billions upgrading their infrastructure to

Courtesy of Getty Images

offer customers discounted bundled packages of local voice, high-speed Internet connections, and video. Market analysts estimate that cable companies could capture a quarter of the local voice market over the next decade as they deploy new voice over Internet protocol (VOIP) technology.

While Verizon and the other traditional phone companies see their market positions erode, they also struggle to retain their image as innovators. They face creative pressures from researchers and from companies who continue to develop new wireless technologies.

Competitors are rushing to build networks to deliver TV service and high-speed broadband access and Verizon is spending billions to roll out its FiOS phone, data, and video network to give its customers faster Internet service and an alternative to cable. Indeed, over the past three years, Verizon has spent nearly $50 billion on capital expenditures. The demand for new capital spending is coming at an inopportune time. Verizon is currently saddled with a debt load of over $51 billion as of 2012 (one-third of which matures over the next five years) and employee benefit obligations of over $34 billion. It is also paying over $5 billion in dividends annually.

This module focuses on liabilities; that is, short-term and long-term obligations. Liabilities are one of two financing sources for a company. The other is shareholder financing. Bonds and notes are a major part of most companies' liabilities. In this module, we show how to price liabilities and how the issuance and subsequent payment of the principal and interest affect financial statements. We also discuss the required disclosures that enable us to effectively analyze a company's ability to pay its debts as they come due.

Verizon is now working harder than ever to transform itself in an era of fiber optics and wireless communication. The dilemma now facing Verizon's management is how to allocate available cash flow between strategic investment and debt payments.

Source: *Verizon* 2012 10-K and 2012 Annual Report to Shareholders.

MODULE ORGANIZATION

Reporting and Analyzing Nonowner Financing

Current Liabilities	Long-Term Liabilities	Credit Ratings
■ Accounts Payable	■ Pricing and Issuance	■ Levels of Credit Ratings
■ Accrued Liabilities	■ Interest Expense	■ Criteria Used in Setting Ratings
■ Nonoperating Current Liabilities	■ Gains and Losses on Retirement	

The accounting equation (Assets = Liabilities + Equity) is a useful tool in helping us think about how the balance sheet and income statement are constructed, the linkages among the financial statements, and the effects of transactions on financial statements. The accounting equation is also useful in helping us think about the statements from another perspective, namely, how the business is financed. Consider the following representation of the accounting equation:

Assets	=	Liabilities + Equity
Uses of funds	=	Sources of funds

Assets represent investments (uses of funds) that management has made. It includes current operating assets such as cash, accounts receivable, and inventories. It also includes long-term operating assets such as manufacturing and administrative facilities. Most companies also invest funds in nonoperating assets (marketable securities) that provide the liquidity a company needs to conduct transactions and to react to market opportunities and changes.

Just as asset disclosures provide us with information on where a company invests its funds, its liability and equity disclosures inform us as to how those assets are financed. These are the sources of funds. To be successful, a company must not only invest funds wisely, but must also be astute in the manner in which it raises funds. Companies strive to finance their assets at the lowest possible cost. Current liabilities (such as accounts payable and accrued liabilities) are generally non-interest-bearing. As a result, companies try to maximize the financing of their assets with these sources of funds.

Current liabilities, as the name implies, are short-term in nature, generally requiring payment within the coming year. As a result, they are not a suitable source of funding for long-term assets that generate cash flows over several years. Instead, companies often finance long-term assets with long-term liabilities that require payments over several years. Generally, companies try to link the pattern of the cash outflows of the financing source with the cash inflows of the related asset. As such, long-term financing is usually in the form of bonds, notes, and stock issuances.

When a company acquires assets, and finances them with liabilities, its financial leverage increases. Also, the required liability payments increase proportionally with the level of liabilities, and those larger payments imply a higher probability of default should a downturn in business occur. Greater levels of liabilities, then, make the company riskier to investors who, consequently, demand a higher return. Assessing the appropriate level of liabilities is part of liquidity and solvency analysis.

This module describes and analyzes *on-balance-sheet financing,* namely current and noncurrent liabilities that are reported on financial statements. If companies can find a way to purchase assets and have neither the asset, nor its related financing, appear on the balance sheet, they can report higher levels of asset turnover and appear less risky. This creates off-balance-sheet financing, which is the focus of Module 10.

CURRENT LIABILITIES

LO1 Describe the accounting for current operating liabilities, including accounts payable and accrued liabilities.

Current liabilities consist of both operating and nonoperating liabilities. Most *current operating liabilities* such as those related to inventory (accounts payable) or to utilities, wages, insurance, rent, and taxes (accrued liabilities), impact operating expenses such as cost of goods sold or selling, general and administrative expenses. *Current nonoperating liabilities* comprise short-term bank notes or the current portion of long-term debt. **Verizon**'s balance sheet from its 2012 10-K reports the following current liabilities:

At December 31 ($ millions)	2012	2011
Debt maturing within one year	$ 4,369	$ 4,849
Accounts payable and accrued liabilities	16,182	14,689
Other	6,405	11,223
Total current liabilities	$26,956	$30,761

Verizon reports three categories of current liabilities: (1) long-term debt obligations that are scheduled for payment in the upcoming year, (2) accounts payable and accrued liabilities, and (3) other current liabilities, which consist mainly of customer deposits, dividends payable, and miscellaneous obligations.

Analysis and interpretation of the return on net operating assets (RNOA) requires that we separate current liabilities into operating and nonoperating components. In general, these two components consist of the following:

1. **Current operating liabilities**
   - **Accounts payable** Obligations to others for amounts owed on purchases of goods and services; these are usually non-interest-bearing.
   - **Accrued liabilities** Obligations for which there is no related external transaction in the current period. These include, for example, accruals for employee wages earned but yet unpaid, accruals for taxes (usually quarterly) on payroll and current period profits, and accruals for other liabilities such as rent, utilities, and insurance. Companies make accruals to properly reflect the liabilities owed as of the financial statement date and the expenses incurred for the period. One difference between accounts payable and accrued liabilities is that an invoice has not been received, nor is often expected, for the latter.
   - **Unearned revenue** Obligations to provide goods or services in the coming year; these arise from customers' deposits, subscriptions, or prepayments.
2. **Current nonoperating liabilities**
   - **Short-term interest-bearing debt** Short-term bank borrowings and notes expected to mature in whole or in part during the upcoming year; this item can include any accrued interest payable.
   - **Current maturities of long-term debt** Long-term borrowings that are scheduled to mature in whole or in part during the upcoming year; this current portion of long-term debt includes maturing principal payments only.

The remainder of this section describes, analyzes and interprets current operating liabilities followed by a discussion of current nonoperating liabilities.

Accounts Payable

Accounts payable arise from the purchase of goods and services from others. Accounts payable are normally non-interest-bearing and are, thus, an inexpensive financing source. Verizon does not break out accounts payable on its balance sheet but, instead, reports them with other accruals. It reports $16,182 million in accounts payable and accrued liabilities in 2012, and $14,689 million in 2011. The footnotes reveal that accounts payable represent $4,740 million in 2012, and $4,194 million in 2011, or about 29% of the total each year.

The following financial statement effects template shows the accounting for a typical purchase of goods on credit and the ultimate sale of those goods. A series of four connected transactions illustrate the revenue and cost cycle.

		Balance Sheet						Income Statement				
	Transaction	Cash Asset	+ Noncash Assets	=	Liabilities	+ Contrib. Capital	+ Earned Capital	Revenues	−	Expenses	=	Net Income
INV 100 AP 100 INV 100 AP 100	1. Purchase $100 inventory on credit		+100 Inventory	=	+100 Accounts Payable				−		=	
AR 140 Sales 140 AR 140 Sales 140	2a. Sell inventory on credit for $140		+140 Accounts Receivable	=			+140 Retained Earnings	+140 Sales	−		=	+140
COGS 100 INV 100 COGS 100 INV 100	2b. Record $100 cost of inventory sold in 2a		−100 Inventory	=			−100 Retained Earnings		−	+100 Cost of Goods Sold	=	−100
Cash 140 AR 140 Cash 140 AR 140	3. Collect $140 on accounts receivable	+140 Cash	−140 Accounts Receivable	=					−		=	
AP 100 Cash 100 AP 100 Cash 100	4. Pay $100 cash for accounts payable	−100 Cash		=	−100 Accounts Payable				−		=	

The financial statement effects template reveals several impacts related to the purchase of goods on credit and their ultimate sale.

1. Purchase of inventory is reflected on the balance sheet as an increase in inventory and an increase in accounts payable.

2a. Sale of inventory involves two components—revenue and expense. The revenue part reflects the increase in sales and the increase in accounts receivable (revenue is recognized when earned, even though cash is not yet received).

2b. The expense part of the sales transaction reflects the decrease in inventory and the increase in cost of goods sold (COGS). COGS is reported in the same income statement as the related sale (this expense is recognized because the inventory asset is sold, even though inventory-related payables may not yet be paid).

3. Collection of the receivable reduces accounts receivable and increases cash. It is solely a balance sheet transaction and does not impact the income statement.

4. Cash payment of accounts payable is solely a balance sheet transaction and does not impact income statement accounts (expense relating to inventories is recognized when the inventory is sold or used up, not when the liability is paid).

Accounts Payable Turnover (APT)

Inventories are financed, in large part, by accounts payable (also called *trade credit* or *trade payables*). Such payables usually represent interest-free financing and are, therefore, less expensive than using available cash or borrowed money to finance purchases or inventory production. Accordingly, companies use trade credit whenever possible. This is called *leaning on the trade.*

The **accounts payable turnover** reflects management's success in using trade credit to finance purchases of goods and services. It is computed as:

Accounts Payable Turnover (APT) = Cost of Goods Sold/Average Accounts Payable

Payables reflect the cost of inventory, not its retail value. Thus, to be consistent with the denominator, the ratio uses cost of goods sold (and not sales) in the numerator. Management desires to use trade credit to the greatest extent possible for financing. This means that *a lower accounts payable turnover is preferable*. **Verizon**'s accounts payable turnover rate for 2012 is 10.4 times per year, computed as ($46,275 million/[($4,740 million + $4,194 million)/2]); this compares with 11.3 times the prior year. This decrease in accounts payable turnover indicates that Verizon is paying its obligations more slowly than it did the year before.

A metric analogous to accounts payable turnover is the **accounts payable days outstanding**, which is defined as follows:

Accounts Payable Days Outstanding (APDO) = Accounts Payable/Average Daily Cost of Goods Sold

Because accounts payable are a source of low-cost financing, *management desires to extend the accounts payable days outstanding as long as possible, provided that this action does not harm supply channel relations*. **Verizon**'s accounts payable remain unpaid for 37.4 days in 2012, computed as ($4,740/[$46,275/365 days]), up from 33.4 days the prior year. This ratio confirms that Verizon is paying its suppliers more slowly than it did in 2011.[1]

Accounts payable reflect a source of interest-free financing. Increased payables reduce the amount of net operating working capital as payables (along with other current operating liabilities) are deducted from current operating assets in the computation of net operating working capital. Also, increased payables mean increased cash flow (as increased liabilities increase net cash from operating activities) and increased profitability (as the level of interest-bearing debt that is required to finance operating assets declines). RNOA increases when companies make use of this low-cost financing source.[2] Yet, companies must be careful to avoid excessive "leaning on the trade" as short-term income gains can yield long-term costs such as damaged supply channels.

MID-MODULE REVIEW 1

Verizon's accounts payable turnover (Cost of goods sold/Average accounts payable) decreased from 11.3 in 2011 to 10.4 in 2012.

a. Does this change indicate that accounts payable have increased or decreased relative to cost of goods sold? Explain.
b. What effect does this change have on net cash flows from operating activities?
c. What management concerns, if any, might this change in accounts payable turnover pose?

The solution is on page 7-53.

Accrued Liabilities

Accrued liabilities reflect expenses that have been incurred during the period but not yet paid in cash. Accrued liabilities can also reflect unearned revenue as explained in Module 5. **Verizon** reports details of its accrued liabilities (along with accounts payable) in the following footnote to its 2012 10-K report.

[1] Excessive delays in payment of payables can result in suppliers charging a higher price for their goods or, ultimately, refusing to sell to certain buyers. Although a hidden "financing" cost is not interest, it is still a real cost.

[2] Accounts payable often carry credit terms such as 2/10, net 30. These terms give the buyer 2% off the invoice price of goods purchased if paid within 10 days. Otherwise the entire invoice is payable within 30 days. By failing to take a discount, the buyer is effectively paying a 2% interest charge to keep its funds for an additional 20 days. Because there are approximately 18 such 20-day periods in a year (365/20), this equates to an annual rate of interest of about 36%. Thus, borrowing funds at less than 36% to pay this liability within the discount period would be cost effective.

At December 31 ($ in millions)	2012	2011
Accounts payable	$ 4,740	$ 4,194
Accrued expenses	4,608	3,786
Accrued vacation, salaries and wages	5,006	4,857
Interest payable	632	774
Taxes payable	1,196	1,078
Total accounts payable and accrued liabilities	$16,182	$14,689

Accrued Liabilities

Verizon reports one nonoperating accrual: interest payable. Its other accrued liabilities are operating accruals that include miscellaneous accrued expenses, accrued vacation pay, accrued salaries and wages, and accrued taxes. Verizon's accruals are typical. To record accruals, companies recognize a liability on the balance sheet and a corresponding expense on the income statement. This means that liabilities increase, current income decreases, and equity decreases. When an accrued liability is ultimately paid, both cash and the liability decrease (but no expense is recorded because it was recognized previously).

Accounting for Accrued Liabilities

Accounting for a typical accrued liability such as accrued wages, for two consecutive periods, follows:

	Balance Sheet									Income Statement				
Transaction	Cash Asset	+	Noncash Assets	=	Liabil-ities	+	Contrib. Capital	+	Earned Capital	Rev-enues	−	Expen-ses	=	Net Income
Period 1: Accrued $75 for employee wages earned at period-end				=	+75 Wages Payable				−75 Retained Earnings		−	+75 Wages Expense	=	−75
Period 2: Paid $75 for wages earned in prior period	−75 Cash			=	−75 Wages Payable						−		=	

WE 75
WP 75

WE	
75	

WP	
	75

WP 75
Cash 75

WP	
75	

Cash	
	75

The following financial statement effects result from this accrual of employee wages:

- Employees have worked during a period and have not yet been paid. The effect of this accrual is to increase wages payable on the balance sheet and to recognize wages expense on the income statement. Failure to recognize this liability and associated expense would understate liabilities on the balance sheet and overstate income in the current period and understate income in the subsequent period.
- When the company pays employees in the following period, cash and wages payable both decrease. This payment does not result in expense because the expense was recognized in the prior period when incurred.

The accrued wages illustration relates to events that are fairly certain. We know, for example, when wages are incurred but not paid. Other examples of accruals that are fairly certain are rental costs, insurance premiums, and taxes owed.

Contingent Accrued Liabilities Some accrued liabilities are less certain than others. Consider a company facing a lawsuit. Should it record the possible liability and related expense? The answer depends on the likelihood of occurrence and the ability to estimate the obligation. Specifically, if the obligation is *probable* and the amount *estimable* with reasonable certainty, then a company will recognize this obligation, called a **contingent liability**. If an obligation is only *reasonably possible* (or cannot be reliably estimated), the contingent liability is not reported on the balance sheet and is merely disclosed in the footnotes. All other contingent liabilities that are less than reasonably possible are not disclosed.

Management of Accrued Liabilities Managers have some latitude in determining the amount and timing of accruals. This latitude can lead to misreporting of income and liabilities (unintentional or otherwise). Here's how: If accruals are underestimated, then expenses are underestimated, income is overestimated, and retained earnings are overestimated. In subsequent periods when an understated accrued liability is settled (for more than the "under" estimate), reported income is lower than it should be; this is because prior-period income was higher than it should have been. (The reverse holds for overestimated accruals.) The misreporting of accruals, therefore, shifts income from one period into another. We must be keenly aware of this potential for income shifting as we analyze the financial condition of a company.

Experience tells us that accrued liabilities related to restructuring programs (including severance accruals and accruals for asset write-downs), or to legal and environmental liabilities, or business acquisitions are somewhat problematic. These accruals too often represent early recognition of expenses. Sometimes companies aggressively overestimate one-time accruals and record an even larger expense. This is called taking a *big bath*. The effect of a big bath is to depress current-period income, which relieves future periods of these expenses (thus, shifting income forward in time). Accordingly, we must monitor any change or unusual activity with accrued liabilities and view large one-time charges with skepticism.

IFRS INSIGHT **Accruals and Contingencies under IFRS**

IFRS requires that a "provision" be recognized as a liability if a present obligation exists, if it is probable that an outflow of resources is required, and if the obligation can be reasonably estimated. These provisions are basically the same as accruals under GAAP such as that for wages. However, unlike GAAP, contingent liabilities are not recorded for IFRS such as an accrual for litigation. Contingencies do not meet the IFRS provisions definition because a present obligation does *not* exist as it may or may not be confirmed by uncertain future events. IFRS requires footnote disclosure of such contingent liabilities unless the eventual payment is remote in which case, no disclosure is required.

Estimating Accruals

Some accrued liabilities require more estimation than others. Warranty liabilities are an example of an accrual that requires managerial assumptions and estimates. Warranties are commitments that manufacturers make to their customers to repair or replace defective products within a specified period of time. The expected cost of this commitment can be reasonably estimated at the time of sale based on past experience. As a result, GAAP requires manufacturers to record the expected cost of warranties as a liability, and to record the related expected warranty expense in the income statement in the same period that the sales revenue is reported.

To illustrate, assume that a company estimates that its defective units amount to 2% of sales and that each unit costs \$5 to replace. If sales during the period are \$10,000, the estimated warranty expense is \$1,000 (\$10,000 × 2% × \$5). The entries to accrue this liability and its ultimate payment follow.

	Balance Sheet									Income Statement				
Transaction	Cash Asset	+	Noncash Assets	=	Liabilities	+	Contrib. Capital	+	Earned Capital	Revenues	−	Expenses	=	Net Income
Period 1: Accrued \$1,000 of expected warranty costs on units sold during the period				=	+1,000 Warranty Payable				−1,000 Retained Earnings		−	+1,000 Warranty Expense	=	−1,000
Period 2: Delivered \$1,000 in replacement products to cover warranty claims			−1,000 Inventory	=	−1,000 Warranty Payable						−		=	

WRE 1,000
WRP 1,000

WRE: 1,000 (debit)
WRP: 1,000 (credit)

WRP 1,000
INV 1,000

WRP: 1,000 (debit)
INV: 1,000 (credit)

Accruing warranty liabilities has the same effect on financial statements as accruing wages expense in the previous section. That is, a liability is recorded on the balance sheet and an expense is reported in the income statement. When the defective product is later replaced (or repaired), the liability is reduced together with the cost of the inventory and/or the cash paid for other costs that were necessary to satisfy the claim. (Only a portion of the products estimated to fail does so in the current period; we expect other product failures in future periods. Management monitors this estimate and adjusts it if failure is higher or lower than expected.) As in the accrual of wages, the expense and the liability are reported when incurred and not when paid.

To illustrate, **Harley-Davidson** reports $60,263 thousand of warranty liability on its 2012 balance sheet. Its footnotes reveal the following additional information:

Product Warranty Estimated warranty costs are reserved for motorcycles, motorcycle parts and motorcycle accessories at the time of sale. The warranty reserve is based upon historical Company claim data used in combination with other known factors that may affect future warranty claims. The Company updates its warranty estimates quarterly to ensure that the warranty reserves are based on the most current information available. The Company believes that past claim experience is indicative of future claims; however, the factors affecting actual claims can be volatile. As a result, actual claims experience may differ from estimated which could lead to material changes in the Company's warranty provision and related reserves. . . . The Company currently provides a standard two-year limited warranty on all new motorcycles sold worldwide, except for Japan, where the Company provides a standard three-year limited warranty on all new motorcycles sold. In addition, the Company started offering a one-year warranty for Parts & Accessories (P&A) in 2012. The warranty coverage for the retail customer generally begins when the product is sold to a retail customer. The Company maintains reserves for future warranty claims which are based primarily on historical Company claim information. Additionally, the Company has from time to time initiated certain voluntary safety recall campaigns. The Company reserves for all estimated costs associated with safety recalls in the period that the safety recalls are announced. Changes in the Company's warranty and safety recall liability were as follows (in thousands):

Warranty and Safety Recall Liability (in thousands)	2012	2011	2010
Balance, beginning of period	$54,994	$54,134	$68,044
Warranties issued during the period	54,394	44,092	36,785
Settlements made during the period	(67,247)	(55,386)	(58,067)
Recalls and changes to pre-existing warranty liabilities	18,122	12,154	7,372
Balance, end of period	$60,263	$54,994	$54,134

The liability for safety recall campaigns was $4.6 million, $10.7 million and $3.2 million at December 31, 2012, 2011 and 2010, respectively.

At the beginning of 2012, Harley reported a reserve of $54,994 thousand for estimated product warranty and safety recall costs. During 2012, the company added $72,516 thousand ($54,394 thousand + $18,122 thousand) to the reserve. The company recognized an expense in 2012 of the same amount. Also during 2012, the company paid out $67,247 thousand to settle warranty claims. The settlements are cash paid to customers for refunds, wages paid to employees who repair the motorcycles, and the cost of parts used in repairs. It is important to understand that only the increase in the liability resulting from additional accruals ($72,516 thousand) impacts the income statement, reducing income through additional warranty expense. Payments made to settle warranty claims do not affect current-period income; they merely reduce the preexisting liability.

GAAP requires that the warranty liability reflects the estimated amount of cost that the company expects to incur as a result of warranty claims. This is often a difficult estimate to make and is prone to error. There is also the possibility that a company might underestimate its warranty liability to report higher current income, or overestimate it so as to depress current income and create an additional liability on the balance sheet (*cookie jar reserve*) that can be used to absorb future warranty costs and, thus, to reduce future expenses. The overestimation would shift income from the current-period to one or more future periods. Warranty liabilities must, therefore, be examined closely and compared with sales levels. Any deviations from the historical relation of the warranty liability to sales, or from levels reported by competitors, should be scrutinized.

MID-MODULE REVIEW 2

Assume that Verizon's employees worked during the current month and earned $10,000 in wages that Verizon will not pay until the first of next month. Must Verizon recognize any wages liability and expense for the current month? Explain. Use the financial statement effects template to show the effect of this accrual.

The solution is on page 7-53.

Current Nonoperating Liabilities

LO2 Describe the accounting for current and long-term nonoperating liabilities.

Current nonoperating liabilities include short-term bank loans, accrued interest on those loans, and the current maturities of long-term debt. Companies generally try to structure their financing so that debt service requirements (payments) coincide with the cash inflows from the assets financed. This means that current assets are usually financed with current liabilities, and that long-term assets are financed with long-term liabilities (and equity).

To illustrate, assume that a seasonal company's investment in current assets tends to fluctuate during the year as depicted in the graphic below:

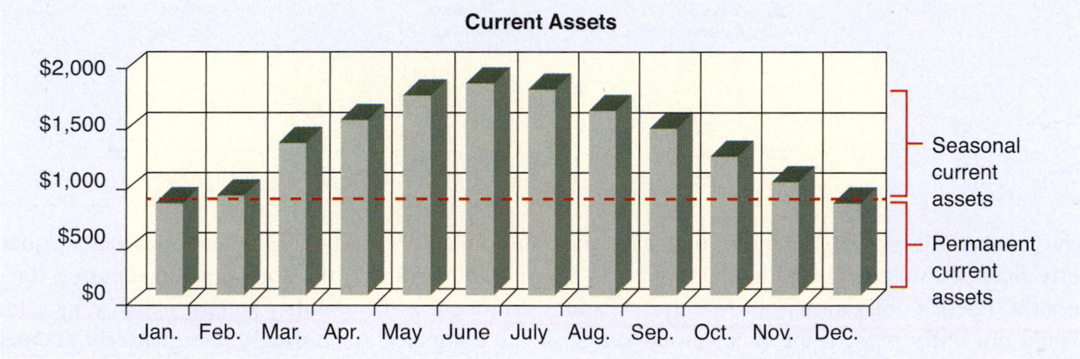

This company does most of its selling in the summer months. More inventory is purchased and manufactured in the early spring than at any other time of the year. High summer sales give rise to accounts receivable that are higher than normal during the fall. The company's working capital peaks at the height of the selling season and is lowest as the business slows in the off-season. There is a permanent level of working capital required for this business (about $750), and a seasonal component (maximum of about $1,000). Different businesses exhibit different patterns in their working capital requirements, but many have both permanent and seasonal components.

The existence of permanent and seasonal current operating assets often requires that financing sources also have permanent and seasonal components. Consider again the company depicted in the graphic above. A portion of the company's assets is in inventories that are financed, in part, with accounts payable and accruals. Thus, we expect that current operating liabilities also exhibit a seasonal component that fluctuates with the level of operations. These payables are generally non-interest-bearing and, thus, provide low-cost financing that should be used to the greatest extent possible. Additional financing needs are covered by short-term interest-bearing debt.

This section focuses on current nonoperating liabilities, which include short-term debt, current maturities of long-term liabilities, and accrued interest expenses.

Short-Term Interest-Bearing Debt

Seasonal swings in working capital are often financed with a bank line of credit (short-term debt). In this case the bank commits to lend up to a maximum amount with the understanding that the amounts borrowed will be repaid in full sometime during the year. An interest-bearing note evidences any such borrowing.

When the company borrows these short-term funds, it reports the cash received on the balance sheet together with an increase in liabilities (notes payable). The note is reported as a current liability because the company expects to repay it within a year. This borrowing has no effect on income or equity. The borrower incurs (and the lender earns) interest on the note as time passes. GAAP requires the borrower to accrue the interest liability and the related interest expense each time financial statements are issued.

To illustrate, assume that **Verizon** borrows $1,000 cash on January 1. The note bears interest at a 12% annual rate, and the interest (3% per quarter) is payable on the first of each subsequent quarter (April 1, July 1, October 1, January 1). Assuming that Verizon issues calendar-quarter financial statements, this borrowing results in the following financial statement effects for January 1 through April 1.

Jan 1 journal entry: Cash 1,000; NP 1,000. T-accounts: Cash 1,000 (debit); NP 1,000 (credit).

Mar 31 journal entry: IE 30; IP 30. T-accounts: IE 30 (debit); IP 30 (credit).

Apr 1 journal entry: IP 30; Cash 30. T-accounts: IP 30 (debit); Cash 30 (credit).

	Balance Sheet									Income Statement				
Transaction	Cash Asset	+	Noncash Assets	=	Liabilities	+	Contrib. Capital	+	Earned Capital	Revenues	−	Expenses	=	Net Income
Jan 1: Borrow $1,000 cash and issue note payable	+1,000 Cash			=	+1,000 Note Payable						−		=	
Mar 31: Accrue quarterly interest on 12%, $1,000 note payable				=	+30 Interest Payable				−30 Retained Earnings		−	+30 Interest Expense	=	−30
Apr 1: Pay $30 cash for interest due	−30 Cash			=	−30 Interest Payable						−		=	

The January 1 borrowing increases both cash and notes payable. On March 31, Verizon issues its quarterly financial statements. Although interest is not paid until April 1, the company has incurred three months' interest obligation as of March 31. Failure to recognize this liability and the expense incurred would not fairly present the financial condition of the company. Accordingly, the quarterly accrued interest payable is computed as follows:

$$\text{Interest Expense} = \text{Principal} \times \text{Annual Rate} \times \text{Portion of Year Outstanding}$$
$$\$30 = \$1{,}000 \times 12\% \times 3/12$$

The subsequent interest payment on April 1 reduces both cash and the interest payable that Verizon accrued on March 31. There is no expense reported on April 1, as it was recorded the previous day (March 31) when Verizon prepared its financial statements. (For fixed-maturity borrowings specified in days, such as a 90-day note, we assume a 365-day year for interest accrual computations, see Mid-Module Review 3.)

Current Maturities of Long-Term Debt

Principal payments that must be made during the upcoming 12 months on long-term debt (such as for a mortgage), or on bonds and notes that mature within the next year, are reported as current liabilities called *current maturities of long-term debt*. All companies must provide a schedule of the maturities of their long-term debt in the footnotes to the financial statements (see the discussion later in this module). To illustrate, Verizon reports $4,369 million in long-term debt due within one year in the current liability section of the balance sheet shown earlier in the module.

MID-MODULE REVIEW 3

Assume that on January 15, **Verizon** borrowed $10,000 on a 90-day, 6% note payable. The bank accrues interest daily based on a 365-day year. Use the financial statement effects template to show the January 31 interest accrual.

The solution is on page 7-54.

LONG-TERM NONOPERATING LIABILITIES

Companies often include long-term nonoperating liabilities in their capital structure to fund long-term assets. Smaller amounts of long-term debt can be readily obtained from banks, private placements with insurance companies, and other credit sources. However, when a large amount of financing is required, the issuance of bonds (and notes) in capital markets is a cost-efficient way to raise funds. The following discussion uses bonds for illustration, but the concepts also apply to long-term notes.

Bonds are structured like any other borrowing. The borrower receives cash and agrees to pay it back with interest. Generally, the entire **face amount** (principal) of the bond is repaid at maturity (at the end of the bond's life) and interest payments are made in the interim (usually semiannually).

Companies that raise funds in the bond market normally work with an underwriter (like **Merrill Lynch**) to set the terms of the bond issue. The underwriter then sells individual bonds (usually in $1,000 denominations) from this general bond issue to its retail clients and professional portfolio managers (like **The Vanguard Group**), and receives a fee for underwriting the bond issue. These bonds are investments for individual investors, other companies, retirement plans and insurance companies.

After they are issued, the bonds can trade in the secondary market just like stocks. Market prices of bonds fluctuate daily despite the fact that the company's obligation for payment of principal and interest normally remains fixed throughout the life of the bond. Then, why do bond prices change? The answer is that the bond's fixed rate of interest can be higher or lower than the interest rates offered on other securities of similar risk. Because bonds compete with other possible investments, bond prices are set relative to the prices of other investments. In a competitive investment market, a particular bond will become more or less desirable depending on the general level of interest rates offered by competing securities. Just as for any item, competitive pressures will cause bond prices to rise and fall.

This section analyzes and interprets the reporting for bonds. We also examine the mechanics of bond pricing and describe the accounting for, and reporting of, bonds.

Pricing of Debt

The following two different interest rates are crucial for pricing debt.

- **Coupon (contract** or **stated) rate** The coupon rate of interest is stated in the bond contract; it is used to compute the dollar amount of interest payments that are paid to bondholders during the life of the bond issue.
- **Market (yield** or **effective) rate** This is the interest rate that investors expect to earn on the investment in this debt security; this rate is used to price the bond.

The coupon (contract) rate is used to compute interest payments and the market (yield) rate is used to price the bond. The coupon rate and the market rate are nearly always different. This is because the coupon rate is fixed prior to issuance of the bond and normally remains fixed throughout its life. Market rates of interest, on the other hand, fluctuate continually with the supply and demand for bonds in the marketplace, general macroeconomic conditions, and the borrower's financial condition.

The bond price, both its initial sales price and the price it trades at in the secondary market subsequent to issuance, equals the present value of the expected cash flows to the bondholder. Specifically, bondholders normally expect to receive two different types of cash flows:

1. **Periodic interest payments** (usually semiannual) during the bond's life; these payments are called an *annuity* because they are equal in amount and made at regular intervals.
2. **Single payment** of the face (principal) amount of the bond at maturity; this is called a *lump-sum* because it occurs only once.

The bond price equals the present value of the periodic interest payments plus the present value of the single payment. If the present value of the two cash flows is equal to the bond's face value, the bond is sold at par. If the present value is less than or greater than the bond's face value, the bond sells at a discount or premium, respectively. We next illustrate the issuance of bonds at three different prices: at par, at a discount, and at a premium.

Bonds Issued at Par

To illustrate a bond issued (also said to be sold) at par, assume that a bond with a face amount of $10 million, has a 6% annual coupon rate payable semiannually (3% semiannual rate), and a maturity of 10 years. Semiannual interest payments are typical for bonds. This means that the issuer pays bondholders two interest payments per year. Each semiannual interest payment is equal to the bond's face value times the annual rate divided by two. Investors purchasing these bonds receive the following cash flows.

	Number of Payments	Dollars per Payment	Total Cash Flows
Semiannual interest payments.	10 years × 2 = 20	$10,000,000 × 3% = $300,000	$ 6,000,000
Principal payment at maturity.	1	$10,000,000	10,000,000
			$16,000,000

Specifically, the bond agreement dictates that the borrower must make 20 semiannual payments of $300,000 each, computed as $10,000,000 × (6%/2). At maturity, the borrower must repay the $10,000,000 face amount. To price bonds, investors identify the *number* of interest payments and use that number when computing the present value of *both* the interest payments and the principal (face) payment at maturity.

The bond price is the present value of the periodic interest payments (the annuity) plus the present value of the principal payment (the lump sum). In our example, assuming that investors desire a 3% semiannual market rate (yield), the bond sells for $10,000,000, which is computed as follows:

Present value factors are from Appendix A

Calculator
N = 20
I/Yr = 3
PMT = −300,000
FV = −10,000,000
PV = 10,000,000

Excel
= PV(rate,nper, pmt,[fv],[type])
= PV(3%, 20, −300000, −10000000, 0)
= 10,000,000

	Payment	Present Value Factor[a]	Present Value
Interest	$ 300,000	14.87747[b]	$ 4,463,200[d]
Principal	$10,000,000	0.55368[c]	5,536,800
			$10,000,000

[a] Mechanics of using tables to compute present values are explained in Appendix 7A; present value factors come from Appendix A near the end of the book.

[b] Present value of an ordinary annuity for 20 periods discounted at 3% per period.

[c] Present value of a single payment in 20 periods discounted at 3% per period.

[d] Rounded.

Because the bond contract pays investors a 3% semiannual rate when investors demand a 3% semiannual market rate, given the borrower's credit rating and the time to maturity, the investors purchase those bonds at the **par (face) value** of $10 million.

Discount Bonds

As a second illustration, assume investors demand a 4% semiannual return for the 3% semiannual coupon bond, while all other details remain the same. The bond now sells for $8,640,999, computed as follows:

Calculator
N = 20
I/Yr = 4
PMT = −300,000
FV = −10,000,000
PV = 8,640,967.37*
*rounding difference

Excel
= PV(rate,nper, pmt,[fv],[type])
= PV(4%, 20, −300000, −10000000, 0)
= 8,640,967.37

	Payment	Present Value Factor	Present Value
Interest	$ 300,000	13.59033[a]	$4,077,099
Principal	$10,000,000	0.45639[b]	4,563,900
			$8,640,999

[a] Present value of an ordinary annuity for 20 periods discounted at 4% per period.

[b] Present value of a single payment in 20 periods discounted at 4% per period.

Because the bond carries a coupon rate *lower* than what investors demand, the bond is less desirable and sells at a **discount**. More generally, bonds sell at a discount whenever the coupon rate is less than the market rate.

Premium Bonds

As a third illustration, assume that investors demand a 2% semiannual return for the 3% semiannual coupon bonds, while all other details remain the same. The bond now sells for $11,635,129, computed as follows:

	Payment	Present Value Factor	Present Value
Interest	$ 300,000	16.35143[a]	$ 4,905,429
Principal	$10,000,000	0.67297[b]	6,729,700
			$11,635,129

[a] Present value of an ordinary annuity for 20 periods discounted at 2% per period.

[b] Present value of a single payment in 20 periods discounted at 2% per period.

Calculator
N = 20
I/Yr = 2
PMT = −300,000
FV = −10,000,000
PV = 11,635,143.33*
*rounding difference

Excel
= PV(rate,nper, pmt,[fv],[type])
= PV(2%, 20, −300000, −10000000,0)
= 11,635,143.33

Because the bond carries a coupon rate *higher* than what investors demand, the bond is more desirable and sells at a **premium**. More generally, bonds sell at a premium whenever the coupon rate is greater than the market rate.[3] Exhibit 7.1 summarizes this relation for bond pricing.

EXHIBIT 7.1 Coupon Rate, Market Rate, and Bond Pricing

Coupon rate > market rate	→	Bond sells at a **premium** (above face amount)
Coupon rate = market rate	→	Bond sells at **par** (at face amount)
Coupon rate < market rate	→	Bond sells at a **discount** (below face amount)

Exhibit 7.2 shows an announcement (called a *tombstone*) of a **Union Pacific Corp** $500 million debt issuance. It has a 4% coupon rate paying 2% semiannual interest, maturing in 2021, with an issue price of 99.525 (sold at a discount). Union Pacific Corp's underwriters took 0.65% in fees ($3.25 million) for underwriting and selling this debt issue.[4]

Effective Cost of Debt

When a bond sells for par, the cost to the issuing company is the cash interest paid. In our first illustration above, the *effective cost* of the bond is the 6% interest paid by the issuer.

When a bond sells at a discount, the issuer must repay more (the face value when the bond matures) than the cash received at issuance (the discounted bond proceeds). This means that the effective cost of a discount bond is greater than if the bond had sold at par. A discount is a cost and, like any other cost, must eventually be transferred from the balance sheet to the income statement as an expense.

When a bond sells at a premium, the borrower received more cash at issuance than it must repay. The difference, the premium, is a benefit that must eventually find its way into the income statement as a *reduction* of interest expense. As a result of the premium, the effective cost of a premium bond is less than if the bond had sold at par.

Bonds are priced to yield the return (market rate) demanded by investors. Consequently, the effective rate of a bond *always* equals the yield (market) rate demanded by investors, regardless of the coupon rate of the bond. This means that companies cannot influence the effective cost of debt by raising or lowering the coupon rate. Doing so will only result in a bond premium or discount. We discuss the factors affecting the yield demanded by investors later in the module.

The effective cost of debt is reflected in the amount of interest expense reported in the issuer's income statement. Because of bond discounts and premiums, interest expense is usually different from

[3] Bond prices are often stated in percent form. For example, a bond sold at par is said to be sold at 100 (that is, 100% of par). The bond sold at $8,640,999 is said to be sold at 86.41 (86.41% of par, computed as $8,640,999/$10,000,000). The bond sold for a premium is said to be sold at 116.35 (116.35% of the bond's face value).

[4] The tombstone makes clear that if we purchase any of these notes (in denominations of $1,000) after the semiannual interest date, we must pay accrued interest in addition to the purchase price. This interest is returned to us in the regular interest payment. (This procedure makes the bookkeeping easier for the issuer/underwriter because all interest payments are equal regardless of when the company actually sold the bond.)

EXHIBIT 7.2 Announcement (Tombstone) of Debt Offering to Public

$500,000,000

Union Pacific Corporation

4.00% Notes due 2021

We will pay interest on the notes each February 1 and August 1, commencing February 1, 2011. The notes will mature on February 1, 2021. We may redeem some or all of the notes at any time and from time to time at the redemption price described in this prospectus supplement. There is no sinking fund for the notes. See "Description of the Notes" for a description of the terms of the notes.

	Price to Public (1)	Underwriting Discount	Proceeds to the Company
Per Note	99.525%	0.650%	98.875%
Total	$497,625,000	$3,250,000	$494,375,000

(1) Plus accrued interest, if any, from August 2, 2010.

Neither the Securities and Exchange Commission nor any state securities commission has approved or disapproved of these securities or determined if this prospectus supplement or the accompanying prospectus is truthful or complete. Any representation to the contrary is a criminal offense. Delivery of the notes, in book-entry form only through The Depository Trust Company, will be made on or about August 2, 2010. The date of this prospectus supplement is July 28, 2010.

Joint Book-Running Managers

BofA Merrill Lynch **J.P. Morgan** **Morgan Stanley**

Senior Co-Managers

BNP PARIBAS **Citi**

Co-Managers

Mitsubishi UFJ Securities **Sun Trust Robinson Humphrey**

US Bancorp **RBS** **Wells Fargo Securities**

the cash interest paid. The next section discusses how management reports, and how we interpret, bonds on the balance sheet and interest expense on the income statement.

REPORTING OF DEBT FINANCING

This section identifies and describes the financial statement effects of bond transactions.

Financial Statement Effects of Debt Issuance

Bonds Issued at Par

When a bond sells at par, the issuing company receives the cash proceeds and accepts an obligation to make payments per the bond contract. Specifically, cash is increased and a long-term liability (bonds payable) is increased by the same amount. There is no revenue or expense at bond issuance. Using the facts from our $10 million bond illustration above, the issuance of bonds at par has the following financial statement effects:

	Balance Sheet									Income Statement				
Transaction	Cash Asset	+	Noncash Assets	=	Liabil-ities	+	Contrib. Capital	+	Earned Capital	Rev-enues	−	Expen-ses	=	Net Income
Issue bonds at par for cash	+10,000,000 Cash			=	+10,000,000 Long-Term Debt						−		=	

Cash 10,000,000
LTD 10,000,000

Cash
10,000,000 |

LTD
| 10,000,000

Discount Bonds

When a bond is sold at a discount, the cash proceeds and net bond liability are recorded at the amount of the proceeds received (not the face amount of the bond). Again, using the facts above from our bond discount illustration, the financial statement effects follow:

	Balance Sheet									Income Statement				
Transaction	Cash Asset	+	Noncash Assets	=	Liabil-ities	+	Contrib. Capital	+	Earned Capital	Rev-enues	−	Expen-ses	=	Net Income
Issue bonds at discount for cash	+$8,640,999 Cash			=	+$8,640,999 Long-Term Debt						−		=	

Cash 8,640,999
LTD 8,640,999

Cash
8,640,999 |

LTD
| 8,640,999

The net bond liability (long-term debt) reported on the balance sheet consists of two components as follows:

Bonds payable, face.	$10,000,000
Less bond discount	(1,359,001)
Bonds payable, net	$ 8,640,999

Bonds are reported on the balance sheet net of any discount. When the bond matures, however, the company is obligated to repay the face amount ($10 million). Accordingly, at maturity, the bonds payable account needs to read $10 million, the amount that is owed. This means that between the bond

BUSINESS INSIGHT **Germany's Zero-Coupon Debt**

Zero-coupon bonds and notes, called *zeros,* do not carry a coupon rate. Pricing of these bonds and notes is done in the same manner as those with coupon rates—the exception is the absence of an interest annuity. This means that the price is the present value of the principal payment at maturity; hence the bond is sold at a *deep discount.* A press release reported the outcome of a zero-coupon bond sale by the German government as follows:

> An offering of a new line of Germany's zero coupon two-year bonds drew strong demand on Wednesday and the country paid record low yield as investors looked for a safe haven amid rising speculation of Greece's exit from the euro area. The country raised EUR 4.555 billion from the sale of its new June 2014 Federal Treasury Notes or Schatz, the Bundesbank said. The auction target was EUR 5 billion. . . . The yield on the zero interest debt was 0.07 percent, which was reportedly the lowest on record for similar securities. Source: http://www.rttnews.com/1892575/germany-zero-coupon-bond-sale-attracts-strong-demand-record-low-yield.aspx

When Germany's central bank, the Bundesbank, issued its zero-coupon convertible notes in May 2012, they had a maturity value of €4.561 billion and were slated to mature in 2014. No interest is paid in the interim. The notes sold for €4.555 billion. The difference between the sales proceeds and the maturity value represents Germany's interest costs, which is the return to the investor. The effective cost of the debt is the interest rate that equates the issue price and maturity value, or approximately 0.07%, a very low rate of interest.

issuance and its maturity, the discount must decline to zero. This reduction of the discount over the life of the bond is called **amortization**. The next section shows how discount amortization results in additional interest expense in the income statement. This amortization causes the effective interest expense to be greater than the periodic cash interest payments.

Premium Bonds

When a bond is sold at a premium, the cash proceeds and net bond liability are recorded at the amount of the proceeds received (not the face amount of the bond). Again, using the facts above from our premium bond illustration, the financial statement effects follow:

Cash 11,635,129
LTD 11,635,129

Cash: 11,635,129 |

LTD: | 11,635,129

	Balance Sheet									Income Statement				
Transaction	Cash Asset	+	Noncash Assets	=	Liabil-ities	+	Contrib. Capital	+	Earned Capital	Rev-enues	−	Expen-ses	=	Net Income
Issue bonds at premium for cash	+$11,635,129 Cash			=	+$11,635,129 Long-Term Debt						−		=	

The bond liability reported on the balance sheet, again, consists of two parts:

Bonds payable, face.	$10,000,000
Add bond premium	1,635,129
Bonds payable, net	$11,635,129

The $10 million must be repaid at maturity, and the premium amortized to zero over the life of the bond. The premium represents a *benefit,* which *reduces* interest expense on the income statement.

Effects of Discount and Premium Amortization

For bonds issued at par, interest expense reported on the income statement equals the cash interest payment. However, for bonds issued at a discount or premium, interest expense reported on the income statement also includes any amortization of the bond discount or premium as follows:

Bonds issued at a discount		Bonds issued at a premium
Cash interest paid		Cash interest paid
+ Amortization of discount	or	− Amortization of premium
Interest expense		Interest expense

Specifically, periodic amortization of a discount is added to the cash interest paid to get interest expense. Amortization of the discount reflects the additional cost the issuer incurs from issuing the bonds at a discount. Over the bond's life, the discount is transferred from the balance sheet to the income statement via amortization, as an increase to interest expense. For a premium bond, the premium is a benefit the issuer receives at issuance. Amortization of the premium reduces interest expense over the bond's life. In both cases, interest expense on the income statement represents the *effective cost* of debt (the *nominal cost* of debt is the cash interest paid).

Calculator
N = 6
I/Yr = 2
PMT = −9,000
FV = −600,000
PV = 583,195.71

Excel
= PV(rate,nper, pmt,[fv],[type])
= PV(2%,6,-9000,-600000,0)
= 583,195.71

Companies amortize discounts and premiums using the effective interest method. To illustrate, assume that **Verizon** issues bonds with a face amount of $600,000, a 3% annual coupon rate payable semiannually (1.5% semiannual rate), a maturity of three years (six semiannual payment periods), and a market (yield) rate of 4% annual (2% semiannual). These facts yield a bond issue price of $583,195.71, which we round to $583,196 for the bond discount amortization table of Exhibit 7.3.

The interest period is denoted in the left-most column. Period 0 is the point at which the bond is issued, and period 1 and following are successive six-month periods (recall, interest is paid semiannually). Column [A] is interest expense, which is reported in the income statement. Interest expense is computed as the bond's net balance sheet value (the carrying amount of the bond) at the beginning of the period (column [E]) multiplied by the 2% semiannual rate used to compute the bond issue price. Column [B] is cash interest paid, which is a constant $9,000 per the bond contract (face amount × coupon rate). Column [C] is discount amortization, which is the difference between interest expense and cash interest paid. Column [D] is the discount balance, which is the previous balance of the discount less the discount amortization in column [C]. Column [E] is the net bond payable, which is the $600,000 face amount less the unamortized discount from column [D].

EXHIBIT 7.3 Bond Discount Amortization Table

Period	[A] ([E] × market%) Interest Expense	[B] (Face × coupon%) Cash Interest Paid	[C] ([A] − [B]) Discount Amortization	[D] (Prior bal − [C]) Discount Balance	[E] (Face − [D]) Bond Payable, Net
0				$16,804	$583,196
1	$11,664	$ 9,000	$2,664	14,140	585,860
2	11,717	9,000	2,717	11,423	588,577
3	11,772	9,000	2,772	8,651	591,349
4	11,827	9,000	2,827	5,824	594,176
5	11,884	9,000	2,884	2,940	597,060
6	11,940	9,000	2,940	0	600,000
	$70,804	$54,000	$16,804		

During the bond life, carrying value is adjusted to par and the discount to zero

Cash paid plus discount amortization equals interest expense

The table shows amounts for the six interest payment periods. The amortization process continues until period 6, at which time the discount balance is 0 and the net bond payable is $600,000 (the maturity value). Each semiannual period, interest expense is recorded at 2%, the market rate of interest at the bond's issuance. This rate does not change over the life of the bond, even if the prevailing market interest rates change. An amortization table reveals the financial statement effects of the bond for its duration. Specifically, we see the income statement effects in column [A], the cash effects in column [B], and the balance sheet effects in columns [D] and [E].

To illustrate amortization of a premium bond, we assume that Verizon issues bonds with a $600,000 face value, a 3% annual coupon rate payable semiannually (1.5% semiannual rate), a maturity of three years (six semiannual interest payments), and a 2% annual (1% semiannual) market interest rate. These facts yield a bond issue price of $617,386.43, which we round to $617,386. Exhibit 7.4 shows the premium amortization table for this bond.

Calculator
N = 6
I/Yr = 1
PMT = −9,000
FV = −600,000
PV = 617,386.43

Excel
= PV(rate,nper, pmt,[fv],[type])
= PV(1%,6,-9000,-600000,0)
= 617,386.43

EXHIBIT 7.4 Bond Premium Amortization Table

Period	[A] ([E] × market%) Interest Expense	[B] (Face × coupon%) Cash Interest Paid	[C] ([B] − [A]) Premium Amortization	[D] (Prior bal − [C]) Premium Balance	[E] (Face + [D]) Bond Payable, Net
0				$17,386	$617,386
1	$ 6,174	$ 9,000	$ 2,826	14,560	614,560
2	6,146	9,000	2,854	11,706	611,706
3	6,117	9,000	2,883	8,823	608,823
4	6,088	9,000	2,912	5,911	605,911
5	6,059	9,000	2,941	2,970	602,970
6	6,030	9,000	2,970	0	600,000
	$36,614	$54,000	$17,386		

During the bond life, carrying value is adjusted to par and the premium to zero

Cash paid less premium amortization equals interest expense

Interest expense is computed using the same process that we used for discount bonds. The difference is that the yield rate is 1% semiannual in the premium case. Also, cash interest paid follows from the bond contract (face amount × coupon rate), and the other columns' computations reflect the premium amortization. After period 6, the premium is fully amortized (equals zero) and the net bond payable balance is $600,000, the amount owed at maturity. Again, an amortization table reveals the financial statement effects of the bond—the income statement effects in column [A], the cash effects in column [B], and the balance sheet effects in columns [D] and [E].

Financial Statement Effects of Bond Repurchase

Companies report bonds payable at *historical (adjusted) cost.* Specifically, net bonds payable amounts follow from the amortization table, as do the related cash flows and income statement numbers. All financial statement relations are set when the bond is issued; they do not subsequently change.

Once issued, however, bonds trade in secondary markets. The yield rate used to compute bond prices for these subsequent transactions is the market interest rate prevailing at the time. These rates change daily based on the level of interest rates in the economy and the perceived creditworthiness of the bond issuer.

Companies can and sometimes do repurchase (or *redeem* or *retire*) their bonds prior to maturity. The bond indenture (contract agreement) can include provisions giving the company the right to repurchase its bonds directly from the bond holders. Or, the company can repurchase bonds in the open market. To illustrate, **Abbott Laboratories** 10-K includes the following footnote relating to its extinguishment of debt in 2012:

> **Net Loss on Extinguishment of Debt** In the fourth quarter of 2012, Abbott extinguished $7.7 billion of long-term debt . . . The loss on the extinguishment of debt . . . consists of the premium paid on the notes and the write off of deferred financing costs totaling $1.83 billion and was partially offset by a gain of $479 million related to the unwinding of interest rate swaps related to a portion of the debt.

When a bond repurchase occurs, a gain or loss usually results, and is computed as follows:

Gain or Loss on Bond Repurchase = Net Bonds Payable − Repurchase Payment

The net bonds payable, also referred to as the *book value,* is the net amount reported on the balance sheet. If the issuer pays more to retire the bonds than the amount carried on its balance sheet, it reports a loss on its income statement, usually called *loss on bond retirement.* The issuer reports a *gain on bond retirement* if the repurchase price is less than the net bonds payable.

GAAP prescribes that gains or losses on bond repurchases be reported as part of ordinary income unless the repurchase meets the criteria for treatment as an extraordinary item (unusual and infrequent, see Module 5). Relatively few debt retirements meet these criteria and, hence, most gains and losses on bond repurchases are reported as part of income from continuing operations.

How should we treat these gains and losses for analysis purposes? That is, do they carry economic effects? The answer is no—the gain or loss on repurchase is exactly offset by the present value of the future cash flow implications of the repurchase (Appendix 7B demonstrates this).

Another analysis issue involves assessing the fair value of bonds and other long-term liabilities. This information is relevant for some investors and creditors in revealing unrealized gains and losses (similar to that reported for marketable securities). GAAP requires companies to provide information about current fair values of their long-term liabilities in footnotes (see Verizon's fair value of debt disclosure in the next section). However, these fair values are *not* reported on the balance sheet and changes in these fair values are not reflected in net income. We must make our own adjustments to the balance sheet and income statement if we want to include changes in fair values of liabilities.

Financial Statement Footnotes

Companies are required to disclose details about their long-term liabilities, including the amounts borrowed under each debt issuance, the interest rates, maturity dates, and other key provisions. Following is **Verizon**'s disclosure for its long-term debt.

Long-Term Debt Outstanding long-term obligations are as follows:

At December 31 ($ millions)	Interest Rates %	Maturities	2012	2011
Verizon Communications—notes payable and other . . .	0.70 – 3.85	2013–2042	$11,198	$ 6,900
	4.35 – 5.50	2013–2041	7,062	7,832
	5.55 – 6.90	2016–2041	11,031	11,043
	7.35 – 8.95	2018–2039	5,017	6,642
	Floating	2014	1,000	1,000
Verizon Wireless—notes payable and other.	5.55 – 8.88	2013–2018	8,635	9,331
Verizon Wireless—Alltel assumed notes	6.50 – 7.88	2013–2032	1,500	2,315
Telephone subsidiaries—debentures	4.75 – 7.00	2013–2033	2,045	4,045
	7.15 – 7.88	2022–2032	1,349	1,449
	8.00 – 8.75	2019–2031	880	880
Other subsidiaries—debentures and other	6.84 – 8.75	2018–2028	1,700	1,700
Capital lease obligations (average rate of 6.3% in 2012 and 2011).			298	352
Unamortized discount, net of premium			(228)	(271)
Total long-term debt, including current maturities			51,487	53,218
Less long-term debt maturing within one year.			3,869	2,915
Total long-term debt.			$47,618	$50,303

Verizon reports a net book value for long-term debt of $51,487 million at year-end 2012. Of this amount, $3,869 million matures in the next year and is classified as a current liability (current maturities of long-term debt). The remainder of $47,618 matures after 2013. Verizon also reports $228 million in unamortized discount (net of premium) on this debt.

In addition to long-term debt amounts, rates, and due dates, and as required under GAAP, Verizon reports aggregate maturities for the five years subsequent to the balance sheet date as follows:

Maturities of Long-Term Debt Maturities of long-term debt outstanding at December 31, 2012, are as follows:

Years	(dollars in millions)
2013	$ 3,869
2014	6,809
2015	2,188
2016	4,146
2017	1,342
Thereafter	33,133

This reveals that Verizon is required to make principal payments that total $18,354 million in the next five years and an additional $33,133 million in principal payments thereafter. Such maturities are important information as a company must either meet its required payments, negotiate a rescheduling of the indebtedness, or refinance the debt to avoid default. Failing to repay debts (defaulting) usually has severe consequences as debt holders have legal remedies available to them that can bankrupt the company. Verizon's debt maturities are well-sequenced with no significant amounts coming due in any of the next five years. Further, Verizon's operating cash flow ($31,486 million) less capital expenditures ($16,175) appears sufficient to provide for repayment of the amounts due should Verizon decide not to refinance the maturing debt with new debt. In sum, Verizon's debt appears well-structured with sufficient free cash flow to manage the required payments.

Verizon's disclosure on the fair value of its total debt follows:

	2012		2011	
At December 31, (dollars in millions)	Carrying Amount	Fair Value	Carrying Amount	Fair Value
Short- and long-term debt, excluding capital leases.	$51,689	$61,552	$54,800	$64,485

As of 2012, indebtedness with a book value of $51,689 million had a fair value of $61,552 million, resulting in an unrecognized liability (which would be realized if Verizon redeemed the debt) of $9,863 million. The increase in fair value is due mainly to a decline in interest rates subsequent to the bonds' issuance (Verizon's credit ratings have not changed in recent years—see next section). The justification for not recognizing unrealized gains and losses on the balance sheet and income statement is that such amounts can reverse with future fluctuations in interest rates. Further, since only the face amount of debt is repaid at maturity, unrealized gains and losses that arise during intervening years do not affect the company's expected cash flows. This is the same logic for nonrecognition of gains and losses on held-to-maturity debt investments (see Module 9).

CREDIT RATINGS AND THE COST OF DEBT

LO3 Explain how credit ratings are determined and identify their effect on the cost of debt.

Earlier in the module we explained that the effective cost of debt to the issuing company is the market (yield) rate of interest used to price the bond, regardless of the bond coupon rate. The market rate of interest is usually defined as the yield on U.S. Government borrowings such as treasury bills, notes, and bonds, called the *risk-free rate,* plus a *risk premium* (also called a *spread*).

Yield Rate = Risk-Free Rate + Risk Premium

Both the treasury yield (the so-called risk-free rate) and the corporate yield vary over time as illustrated in the following graphic.

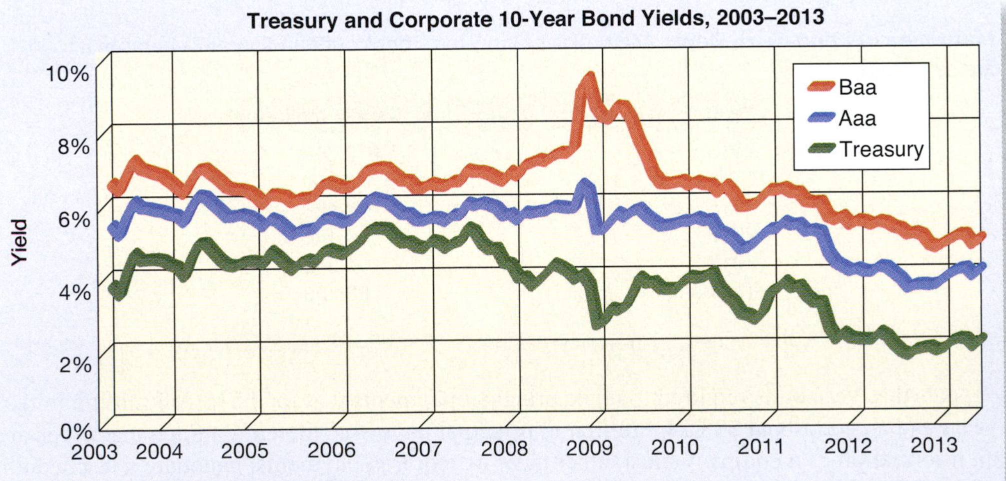

Source: Federal Reserve Bank of St. Louis.

The rate of interest that investors expect for a particular bond is a function of the risk-free rate and the risk premium, where the latter depends on the creditworthiness of the issuing entity.

The yield increases (shifts upward) as debt quality moves from Treasury securities (generally considered to be risk free), which is the highest-quality debt reflected in the lowest line in the graph, to the Aaa (highest) rated corporates and, finally, to the Baa (lower-rated) corporates shown in this graph. That is, higher credit-rated issuers warrant a lower rate than lower credit-rated issuers. This difference is substantial. For example, in May 2013, the average 10-year treasury bond yield was 1.93%, while the Aaa corporate bond yield was 3.89% and the average Baa (the lowest investment grade corporate bond) yield was 4.73%.

RESEARCH INSIGHT **Accounting Conservatism and Cost of Debt**

Research indicates that companies that use more conservative accounting policies incur a lower cost of debt. Research also suggests that while accounting conservatism can lead to lower-quality accounting income (because such income does not fully reflect economic reality), creditors are more confident in the numbers and view them as more credible. Evidence also implies that companies can lower the required return demanded by creditors (the risk premium) by issuing high-quality financial reports that include enhanced footnote disclosures and detailed supplemental reports.

What Are Credit Ratings?

A company's credit rating, also referred to as debt rating, credit quality, or creditworthiness, is related to default risk. **Default** refers to the nonpayment of interest and principal and/or the failure to adhere to the various terms and conditions (covenants) of the bond indenture. Companies that want to obtain bond financing from the capital markets, normally first seek a rating on their proposed debt issuance from one of several rating agencies such as **Standard & Poor's**, **Moody's Investors Service**, or **Fitch Ratings**. The aim of rating agencies is to rate debt so that its default risk is more accurately conveyed to, and priced by, the market. Each rating agency uses its own rating system, as Exhibit 7.5 shows. This exhibit includes the general description for each rating class—for example, AAA is assigned to debt of prime maximum safety (highest in creditworthiness).

EXHIBIT 7.5 **Corporate Debt Ratings and Descriptions**

Moody's	S&P	Fitch	Description
Aaa	AAA	AAA	Prime Maximum Safety
Aa1	AA+	AA+	High Grade, High Quality
Aa2	AA	AA	
Aa3	AA−	AA−	
A1	A+	A+	Upper-Medium Grade
A2	A	A	
A3	A−	A−	
Baa1	BBB+	BBB+	Lower-Medium Grade
Baa2	BBB	BBB	
Baa3	BBB−	BBB−	
Ba1	BB+	BB+	Non-Investment Grade
Ba2	BB	BB	Speculative
Ba3	BB−	BB−	
B1	B+	B+	Highly Speculative
B2	B	B	
B3	B−	B−	
Caa1	CCC+	CCC	Substantial Risk
Caa2	CCC		In Poor Standing
Caa3	CCC−		
Ca	CC		Extremely Speculative
C	C		May be in Default
		DDD	Default
		DD	
	D	D	

MANAGERIAL DECISION **You Are the Vice President of Finance**

Your company is currently rated B1/B+ by the Moody's and S&P credit rating agencies, respectively. You are considering restructuring to increase your company's credit rating. What types of restructurings might you consider? What benefits will your company receive from those restructurings? What costs will your company incur to implement such restructurings? [Answer, p. 7-34]

What Determines Credit Ratings?

Verizon bonds are rated Baa1, BBB+, and A− by Moody's, S&P, and Fitch, respectively, as of 2013, a downgrade from A3, A and A, respectively, as a result of its decision to purchase Vodafone Group PLC's stake in Verizon Wireless for about $130 billion. It is this rating, in conjunction with the maturity of Verizon's bonds, that establishes the market interest rate and the bonds' selling price. There are a number of considerations that affect the rating of a bond. **Standard & Poor's** lists the following factors, categorized by business risk and financial risk, among its credit rating criteria:

Business Risk	Financial Risk
Industry characteristics	Financial characteristics
Competitive position (marketing, technology, efficiency, regulation)	Financial policy
Management	Profitability
	Capital structure
	Cash flow protection
	Financial flexibility

Debt ratings convey information primarily to debt investors who are interested in assessing the probability that the borrower will make interest and principal payments on time. If a company defaults on its debt, debt holders seek legal remedies, including forcing the borrower to liquidate its assets to settle obligations. However, in forced liquidations, debt holders rarely realize the entire amounts owed to them.

It's important to bear in mind that debt ratings are opinions. Rating agencies use several financial ratios to assess default risk. A partial listing of ratios utilized by Moody's, together with median averages for various ratings, is in Exhibit 7.6. In examining the ratios, recall that debt is increasingly more risky as we move from the first row, Aaa, to the last, C.

EXHIBIT 7.6 **Ratio Values for Different Risk Classes of Corporate Debt***

	EBITA/ Avg AT	EBITA Margin	EBITA/ Int Exp	Oper Margin	(FFO + Int Exp)/ Int Exp	FFO/ Debt	RCF/Net Debt	Debt/ EBITDA	Debt/ Book Cap	CAPEX/ Dep Exp	Rev Vol
Aaa	21.1%	25.1%	27.0	21.7%	23.2	109.0%	209.9%	0.6	21.1%	1.3	9.4
Aa	13.5%	19.8%	14.7	16.1%	16.3	45.0%	28.0%	1.5	34.3%	1.3	11.3
A	12.0%	15.4%	9.3	14.3%	10.7	38.8%	30.1%	2.0	40.0%	1.3	10.3
Baa	9.9%	14.6%	5.2	13.0%	6.8	28.4%	26.0%	2.6	45.7%	1.3	13.2
Ba	9.3%	13.8%	3.4	12.4%	4.7	23.1%	22.6%	3.2	51.9%	1.2	16.8
B	7.3%	10.0%	1.6	8.6%	2.6	11.6%	11.8%	4.8	69.9%	1.0	16.5
Caa-C	3.2%	5.0%	0.5	3.7%	1.4	3.5%	3.3%	7.6	100.6%	0.7	15.2

* Table reports 2012 median values; from Moody's Financial Metrics™, Key Ratios by Rating and Industry for Global nonfinancial corporations: December 2012 (reproduced with permission).

Ratio	Definition
EBITA/Average Assets	EBITA/Average of Current and Previous Year Assets
EBITA Margin	EBITA/Net Revenue
EBITA/Interest Expense	EBITA/Interest Expense
Operating Margin	Operating Profit/Net Revenue
(FFO + Interest Exp)/Interest Exp	(Funds From Operations + Interest Expense)/Interest Expense
FFO/Debt	Funds From Operations/(Short-Term Debt + Long-Term Debt)
RCF/Net Debt	(FFO − Preferred Dividends − Common Dividends − Minority Dividends)/(Short-Term Debt + Long-Term Debt)
Debt/EBITDA	(Short-Term Debt + Long-Term Debt)/EBITDA
Debt/Book Capitalization	(Short-Term Debt + Long-Term Debt)/(Short-Term Debt + Long-Term Debt + Deferred Taxes + Minority Interest + Book Equity)
CAPEX/Depreciation Exp	Capital Expenditures/Depreciation Expense
Revenue Volatility	Standard Deviation of Trailing Five Years of Net Revenue Growth

where: EBITA = Earnings from continuing operations before interest, taxes, and amortization
EBITDA = Earnings from continuing operations before interest, taxes, depreciation, and amortization
FFO = Net income from continuing operations plus depreciation, amortization, deferred income taxes, and other noncash items

A review of these ratios indicates that Moody's considers the following factors, grouped by area of emphasis, as relevant in evaluating a company's ability to meet its debt service requirements:

1. Profitability ratios (first four metrics in footnote to Exhibit 7.6)
2. Cash flow ratios (metrics five, six and seven in footnote to Exhibit 7.6)
3. Solvency ratios (metrics eight, nine, ten and eleven in footnote to Exhibit 7.6)

Further, these ratios are variants of many of the ratios we describe in Module 4 and elsewhere in the book. Other relevant debt-rating factors include the following:

- **Collateral** Companies can provide security for debt by pledging certain assets against the bond. This is like mortgages on assets. To the extent debt is secured, the debt holder is in a preferred position vis-à-vis other creditors.
- **Covenants** Debt agreements (indentures) can restrict the behavior of the issuing company so as to protect debt holders. For example, covenants commonly prohibit excessive dividend payment, mergers and acquisitions, further borrowing, and commonly prescribe minimum levels for key liquidity and solvency ratios. These covenants provide debt holders an element of control over the issuer's operations because, unlike equity investors, debt holders have no voting rights.
- **Options** Options are sometimes written into debt contracts. Examples are options to convert debt into stock (so that debt holders have a stake in value creation) and options allowing the issuing company to repurchase its debt before maturity (usually at a premium).

IFRS Alert
Unlike GAAP, IFRS requires that companies treat the conversion feature like an option and revalue it each period using the appropriate market rate. The difference in value each period is recorded as nonoperating revenue or expense.

RESEARCH INSIGHT Valuation of Debt Options

Debt instruments can include features such as conversion options, under which the debt can be converted to common stock. Such conversion features are not accounted for separately under GAAP. Instead, convertible debt is accounted for just like debt with no conversion features (unless the conversion option can be separately traded). However, option-pricing models can be used to estimate the value of such debt features even when no market for those features exists. Empirical results suggest that those debt features represent a substantial part of debt value. These findings contribute to the current debate regarding the separation of compound financial instruments into debt and equity portions for financial statement presentation and analysis.

Any Trends with Credit Ratings?

Companies strive to maintain an "investment-grade" credit rating. This allows them to sell their bonds to institutional investors such as pension, mutual and other investment funds. Many institutional investors will not invest in bonds that are rated below investment-grade rating of Baa3 (Moody's) or BBB- (S&P and Fitch). To achieve a higher credit rating, companies must have lower financial leverage and maintain greater liquidity. This is costly to shareholders. As a result, financial managers face a difficult task in finding the optimal capital structure that maximizes returns to shareholders while reducing the cost of debt capital.

The data suggest that corporate CFOs try to maintain investment-grade bond ratings but do not rely markedly on costly equity capital. Following is a graph of the distribution of companies across bond ratings. Ratings of A+ through BBB− account for half of all corporate issuers, while those issuers in the top ratings categories (AAA through AA−) account for only 3.2% of corporate issuers (source: Compustat).

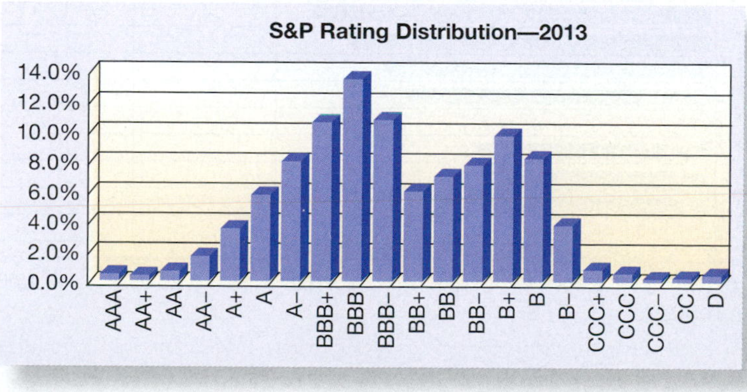

Financial Ratios across Industries

Many of the financial ratios we discuss above vary across industries due to differences in fundamental economic factors. For example, the following graphic reflects differences across industries on financial returns.

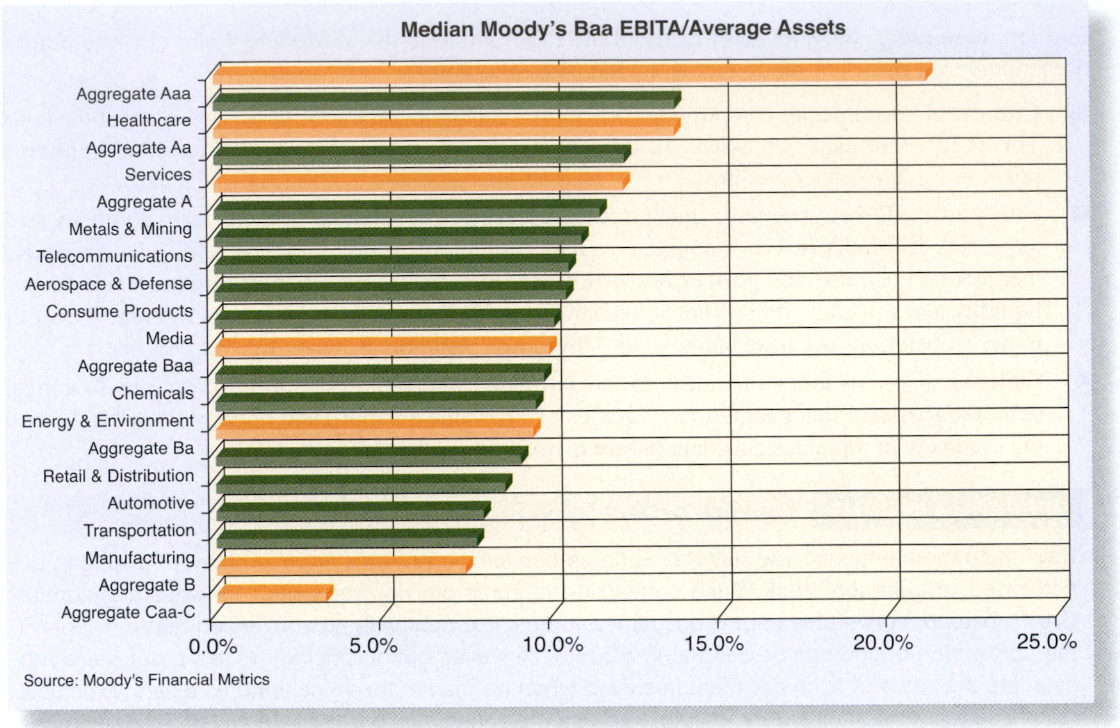

Median EBITA to average assets (a measure of return on assets) for Baa issuers is highest for healthcare, services, metals and mining, and telecommunications industries. The median EBITA margin (EBITA as a percent of revenues) is highest for metals and mining, telecommunications, media and healthcare companies as shown in the following graphic.

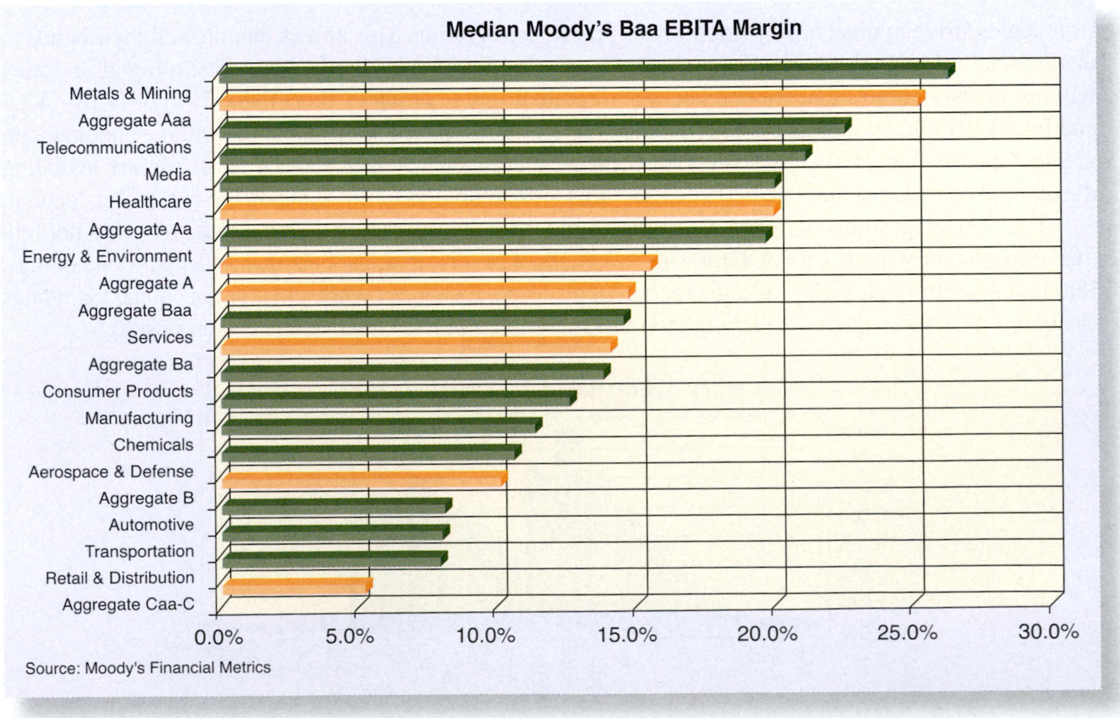

What Financial Ratios Matter?

We cited a number of financial and nonfinancial factors that analysts consider when developing credit ratings. **UBS** (www.UBS.com), a global investment banking and securities firm, measured the correlation between credit ratios, such as those described in this section, and bond ratings. The "t-statistics" from those correlations are in the following chart ("The New World of Credit Ratings," *UBS Investment Bank*, 2004):

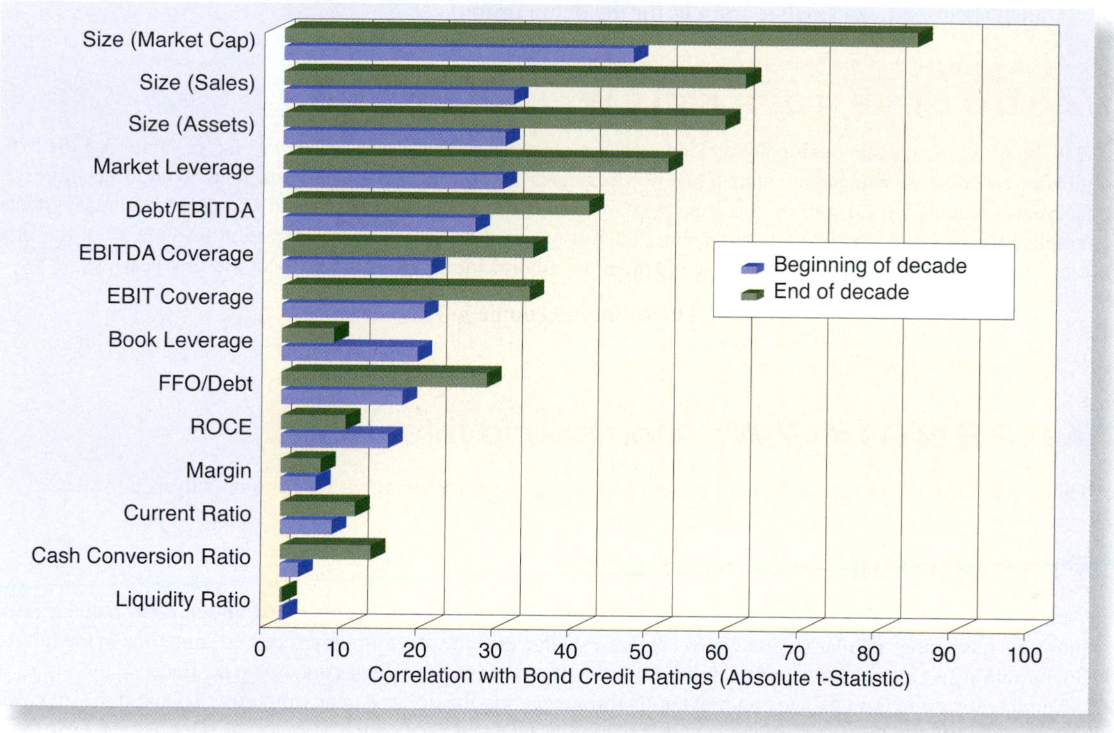

Measures relating to the size of the company, its financial leverage, and its cash flow in relation to its debt payment obligations, are most highly correlated with bond credit ratings (implying a higher "t-statistic"). These findings are consistent with the analysis and focus of this module.

GLOBAL ACCOUNTING

The FASB and the IASB have worked on a number of joint convergence projects and the differences in accounting for liabilities are limited. We list here some differences that we encounter in studying IFRS financial statements and the implications for comparing GAAP and IFRS companies.

- Under U.S. GAAP, if a contingent liability is probable it must be disclosed *and* if it can also be reasonably estimated, it must be accrued. Under IFRS, companies can limit disclosure of contingent liabilities if doing so would severely prejudice the entity's competitive or legal position; for example, disclosing the amount of a potential loss on a lawsuit could sway the legal outcome. Accordingly, IFRS likely yields less disclosure of contingencies.
- Accruals sometimes involve a range of estimates. If all amounts within the range are equally probable, U.S. GAAP requires the company to accrue the lowest number in the range whereas IFRS requires the company to accrue the expected amount. Also, contingencies are discounted under IFRS if the effect of discounting is material whereas U.S. GAAP records contingencies at their nominal value. For both of these reasons, contingent liabilities are likely smaller under U.S. GAAP.
- IFRS offers more disclosure of liabilities and accruals. For each IFRS provision (the term used for accrued liabilities and expenses), the company must reconcile the opening and closing carrying amounts, describe any additional provision for the period, and explain any reversals for the period. Reconciliation is less prevalent under U.S. GAAP (required for example for allowance for doubtful

accounts, warranty accruals, restructuring accruals). Recall that an over-accrual in one period shifts income to a subsequent period when the accrual is reversed. This increased transparency under IFRS might make it easier to spot earnings management.

- U.S. GAAP classifies convertible debt as a liability. Under IFRS, convertible debt is split into two parts: debt and equity (reflecting the option to convert). The amount assigned to each part is based on fair values when the debt is issued. So, for equivalent convertible debt outstanding, IFRS balance sheets show a smaller amount for the debt portion.

MODULE-END REVIEW

On January 1, assume that **Sprint Nextel Corporation** issues $300,000 of 15-year, 10% bonds payable for $351,876, yielding an effective semiannual interest rate of 4%. Interest is payable semiannually on June 30 and December 31. (1) Show computations to confirm the issue price of $351,876, and (2) complete Sprint's financial statement effects template for (a) bond issuance, (b) semiannual interest payment and premium amortization on June 30 of the first year, and (c) semiannual interest payment and premium amortization on December 31 of the first year.

The solution is on page 7-54.

APPENDIX 7A: Compound Interest

This appendix explains the concepts of present and future value, which are useful for our analysis purposes.

Present Value Concepts

Would you rather receive a dollar now or a dollar one year from now? Most people would answer, a dollar now. Intuition tells us that a dollar received now is more valuable than the same amount received sometime in the future. Sound reasons exist for choosing the dollar now, the most obvious of which concerns risk. Because the future is uncertain, any number of events can prevent us from receiving the dollar a year from now. To avoid this risk, we choose the earlier date. Another reason is that the dollar received now could be invested. That is, one year from now, we would have the dollar and the interest earned on that dollar.

Present Value of a Single Amount

Risk and interest factors yield the following generalizations: (1) the right to receive an amount of money now, its **present value**, is worth more than the right to receive the same amount later, its **future value**; (2) the longer we must wait to receive an amount, the less attractive the receipt is; (3) the greater the interest rate the greater the amount we will receive in the future. (Putting 2 and 3 together we see that the difference between the present value of an amount and its future value is a function of both interest rate and time, that is, Principal × Interest Rate × Time); and (4) the more risk associated with any situation, the higher the interest rate.

To illustrate, let's compute the amount we would need to receive today (the present value) that would be equivalent to receiving $100 one year from now if money can be invested at 10%. We recognize intuitively that, with a 10% interest rate, the present value (the equivalent amount today) will be less than $100. The $100 received in the future must include 10% interest earned for the year. Thus, the $100 received in one year (the future value) must be 1.10 times the amount received today (the present value). Dividing $100/1.10, we obtain a present value of $90.91 (rounded). This means that we would do as well to accept $90.91 today as to wait one year and receive $100. To confirm the equality of the $90.91 receipt now to a $100 receipt one year later, we calculate the future value of $90.91 at 10% for one year as follows:

$$\$90.91 \times 1.10 \times 1 \text{ year} = \$100 \text{ (rounded)}$$

To generalize, we compute the present value of a future receipt by *discounting* the future receipt back to the present at an appropriate interest rate (also called the *discount rate*). We present this schematically below:

Present Value $90.91 ← [Discounted for 1 year at 10%] ← Future Value $100

If either the time period or the interest rate were increased, the resulting present value would decrease. If more than one time period is involved, our future receipts include interest on interest. This is called *compounding*.

Time Value of Money Tables

Appendix A near the end of the book includes time value of money tables. Table 1 is a present value table that we can use to compute the present value of future amounts. A present value table provides present value factors (multipliers) for many combinations of time periods and interest rates that determine the present value of $1.

Present value tables are used as follows. First, determine the number of interest compounding periods involved (three years compounded annually are 3 periods, and three years compounded semiannually are 6 periods). The extreme left-hand column indicates the number of periods. It is important to distinguish between years and compounding periods. The table is for compounding periods (years × number of compounding periods per year).

Next, determine the interest rate per compounding period. Interest rates are usually quoted on a *per year* (annual) basis. The rate per compounding period is the annual rate divided by the number of compounding periods per year. For example, an interest rate of 10% *per year* would be 10% per period if compounded annually, and 5% *per period* if compounded semiannually.

Finally, locate the present value factor, which is at the intersection of the row of the appropriate number of compounding periods and the column of the appropriate interest rate per compounding period. Multiply this factor by the dollars that will be paid or received in the future.

All values in Table 1 are less than 1.0 because the present value of $1 received in the future is always smaller than $1. As the interest rate increases (moving from left to right in the table) or the number of periods increases (moving from top to bottom), the present value factors decline. This illustrates two important facts: (1) present values decline as interest rates increase, and (2) present values decline as the time lengthens. Consider the following three cases:

Case 1. Compute the present value of $100 to be received one year from today, discounted at 10% compounded semiannually:

Number of periods (one year, semiannually) = 2
Rate per period (10%/2) = 5%
Multiplier = 0.90703
Present value = $100.00 × 0.90703 = $90.70 (rounded)

Calculator
N = 2
I/Yr = 5
PMT = 0
FV = 100
PV = −90.703

Excel
= PV(rate,nper, pmt,[fv],[type])
= PV(5%,2,0,100,0)
= −90.703

Case 2. Compute the present value of $100 to be received two years from today, discounted at 10% compounded semiannually:

Number of periods (two years, semiannually) = 4
Rate per period (10%/2) = 5%
Multiplier = 0.82270
Present value = $100 × 0.82270 = $82.27 (rounded)

Calculator
N = 4
I/Yr = 5
PMT = 0
FV = 100
PV = −82.270

Excel
= PV(rate,nper, pmt,[fv],[type])
= PV(5%,4,0,100,0)
= −82.270

Case 3. Compute the present value of $100 to be received two years from today, discounted at 12% compounded semiannually:

Number of periods (two years, semiannually) = 4
Rate per period (12%/2) = 6%
Multiplier = 0.79209
Present value = $100 = 0.79209 = $79.21 (rounded)

Calculator
N = 4
I/Yr = 6
PMT = 0
FV = 100
PV = −79.209

Excel
= PV(rate,nper, pmt,[fv],[type])
= PV(6%,4,0,100,0)
= −79.209

In Case 2, the present value of $82.27 is less than for Case 1 ($90.70) because the time increased from two to four compounding periods—the longer we must wait for money, the lower its value to us today. Then in Case 3, the present value of $79.21 was lower than in Case 2 because, while there were still four compounding periods, the interest rate per year was higher (12% annually instead of 10%)—the higher the interest rate the more interest that could have been earned on the money and therefore the lower the value today.

Present Value of an Annuity

In the examples above, we computed the present value of a single amount (also called a lump sum) made or received in the future. Often, future cash flows involve the same amount being paid or received each period. Examples include semiannual interest payments on bonds, quarterly dividend receipts, or monthly insurance premiums. If the payment or the receipt (the cash flow) is equally spaced over time and each cash flow is the same dollar amount, we have an *annuity*. One way to calculate the present value of the annuity would be to calculate the present value of each future cash flow separately. However, there is a more convenient method.

To illustrate, assume $100 is to be received at the end of each of the next three years as an annuity. When annuity amounts occur at the *end of each period*, the annuity is called an *ordinary annuity*. As shown below, the present value of this ordinary annuity can be computed from Table 1 by computing the present value of each of the three individual receipts and summing them (assume a 5% annual rate).

Calculator
N = 3
I/Yr = 5
PMT = 100
FV = 0
PV = −272.32

Excel
= PV(rate,nper, pmt,[fv],[type])
= PV(5%,3,100,0,0)
= −272.32

Future Receipts (ordinary annuity) Year 1	Year 2	Year 3	PV Multiplier (Table 1)		Present Value
$100			× 0.95238	=	$ 95.24
	$100		× 0.90703	=	90.70
		$100	× 0.86384	=	86.38
			2.72325		$272.32

Table 2 in Appendix A provides a single multiplier for computing the present value of an ordinary annuity. Referring to Table 2 in the row for three periods and the column for 5%, we see that the multiplier is 2.72325. When applied to the $100 annuity amount, the multiplier gives a present value of $272.33. As shown above, the same present value (with 1 cent rounding error) is derived by summing the three separate multipliers from Table 1. Considerable computations are avoided by using annuity tables.

Bond Valuation

Recall that a bond agreement specifies a pattern of future cash flows—usually a series of interest payments (cash outflow) and a single payment of the face amount at maturity (cash outflow), and bonds are priced using the prevailing market rate on the day the bond is sold (cash inflow). This is the case for the original bond issuance and for subsequent open-market sales. The market rate on the date of the sale is the rate we use to determine the bond's market value (its price). That rate is the bond's *yield*. The selling price of a bond is determined as follows:

1. Use Table 1 to compute the present value of the future principal payment at the prevailing market rate.
2. Use Table 2 to compute the present value of the future series of interest payments (the annuity) at the prevailing market rate.
3. Add the present values from steps 1 and 2.

We illustrate in Exhibit 7A.1 the price of $100,000, 8%, four-year bonds paying interest semiannually and sold when the prevailing market rate was (1) 8%, (2) 10% or (3) 6%. Note that the price of 8% bonds sold to yield 8%

EXHIBIT 7A.1 Calculation of Bond Price Using Present Value Tables

Future Cash Flows	Multiplier (Table 1)	Multiplier (Table 2)	Present Values at 4% Semiannually
(1) $100,000 of 8%, 4-year bonds with interest payable semiannually priced to yield 8%.			
Principal payment, $100,000 (a single amount received after 8 semiannual periods)	0.73069		$ 73,069
Interest payments, $4,000 at end of each of 8 semiannual periods		6.73274	26,931
Present value (issue price) of bonds			$100,000

Future Cash Flows	Multiplier (Table 1)	Multiplier (Table 2)	Present Values at 5% Semiannually
(2) $100,000 of 8%, 4-year bonds with interest payable semiannually priced to yield 10%.			
Principal payment, $100,000 (a single amount received after 8 semiannual periods)	0.67684		$ 67,684
Interest payments, $4,000 at end of each of 8 semiannual periods		6.46321	25,853
Present value (issue price) of bonds			$ 93,537

Future Cash Flows	Multiplier (Table 1)	Multiplier (Table 2)	Present Values at 3% Semiannually
(3) $100,000 of 8%, 4-year bonds with interest payable semiannually priced to yield 6%.			
Principal repayment, $100,000 (a single amount received after 8 semiannual periods)	0.78941		$ 78,941
Interest payments, $4,000 at end of each of 8 semiannual periods		7.01969	28,079
Present value (issue price) of bonds			$107,020

Calculator
N = 8
I/Yr = 4
PMT = −4,000
FV = −100,000
PV = 100,000

Excel
= PV(rate,nper, pmt,[fv],[type])
= PV(4%,8,-4000,-100000,0)
= 100,000

Calculator
N = 8
I/Yr = 5
PMT = −4,000
FV = −100,000
PV = 93,536.79

Excel
= PV(rate,nper, pmt,[fv],[type])
= PV(5%,8,-4000,-100000,0)
= 93,536.79

Calculator
N = 8
I/Yr = 3
PMT = −4,000
FV = −100,000
PV = 107,019.69

Excel
= PV(rate,nper, pmt,[fv],[type])
= PV(3%,8,-4000,-100000,0)
= 107,019.69

is the face (or par) value of the bonds. A bond issue price of $93,537 (discount bond) yields 10%. A bond issue price of $107,020 (premium bond) yields 6%.

Time Value of Money Computations Using a Calculator

We can use a financial calculator for time value of money computations. There are five important function keys for these calculations. If we know values for four of those five, the calculator will compute the fifth. Those function keys are:

N	Number of compounding (or discounting) periods
I/Yr	Interest (yield) rate per period—entered in % terms, for example, 12% is entered as 12 and not as 0.12. This key is labeled "interest per year" but it can handle any rate per different compounding periods; for example, if we have semiannual interest payments, our compounding periods are semiannual and the interest rate is the semiannual rate.
FV	Future value of the cash flows, this is a lump sum
PMT	Annuity (coupon) per discount period
PV	Present value of the cash flows, this is a lump sum

Calculator inputs follow for the three examples in Exhibit 7A.1. In these examples, the unknown value is the bond price, which is the present value (PV) of the bond's cash flows. (For additional instruction on entering inputs into a specific calculator, or how to do more complicated computations, review the calculator's user manual or review online calculator tutorials.)

A note about positive and negative signs for variables. Financial calculators use a convention to capture the direction of cash flows. This can be understood by thinking about the direction of the cash flows from the company's perspective. Consider the examples in Exhibit 7A.1. The unknown value is the bond proceeds, the present value. From the perspective of the company, the interest payment is a cash outflow. We enter this in the calculator as a negative. Again, from the company's perspective, the cash paid to investors when the bond matures is a cash outflow (negative in the calculator). With both PMT and FV entered as negative numbers, the calculator returns a positive number—this can be understood as a cash inflow to the company. As long as we are consistent in the sign of our variables and we understand the calculator convention, we can interpret the result from the calculator. For example, if we enter PMT and FV as positive numbers, the PV returned is a negative number. (This would be considering cash flows from the investor's perspective.) Yet, be careful, if we enter PMT and FV with opposite signs, the result is nonsensical.

Example (1), Exhibit 7A.1: Bond priced to yield 8%.

N	=	8 (4 years × 2 periods per year = 8 semiannual periods)
I/Yr	=	4 (8% annual yield ÷ 2 periods per year = 4% semiannually)
FV	=	−100,000 (face value, which is the lump sum that must be repaid in the future, a cash outflow)
PMT	=	−4,000 ($100,000 × 4% semiannual coupon rate, a cash outflow)
PV	=	100,000 (output obtained from calculator)

Example (2), Exhibit 7A.1: Bond priced to yield 10%.

N = 8 I/Yr = 5 FV = −100,000 PMT = −4,000 PV = 93,537

Example (3), Exhibit 7A.1: Bond priced to yield 6%.

N = 8 I/Yr = 3 FV = −100,000 PMT = −4,000 PV = 107,020

Time Value of Money Computations Using Excel

We can use Excel or other spreadsheet software, to perform time value of money calculations. There are a number of functions for time value of money, but all of them involve the same six variables, which are:

rate	Interest (yield) rate per period, entered as either a percent (4%) or as a number 0.04. The variable is labeled rate and should be understood to mean per period; if we have semiannual interest payments, our compounding periods are semiannual and the interest rate is the semiannual rate
nper	Number of compounding or discounting periods
pmt	Annuity per discounting or compounding period; if there is no annuity, enter 0
pv	Present value of the cash flow, this is a lump sum
fv	Future value of the cash flow, this is a lump sum
type	Timing of the annuity payment, this is a 0 or 1 variable; if the annuity is paid at the end of each compounding period (as for interest payments), then type =0; if the annuity is paid at the beginning of each compounding period, then type =1 (type = 0 is the default value in Excel)

The Excel functions for present value and future value are as follows:

= PV(rate,nper,pmt,fv,type)

= FV(rate,nper,pmt,pv,type)

Unlike for a calculator, the variables must be entered in the correct order. Yet, once we open the bracket in the function, Excel prompts us for the variables in order. Similar to the calculator, Excel maintains the convention for positive and negative cash flows.

Example (1), Exhibit 7A.1: Bond priced to yield 8%.

rate	=	4% (8%/2 compounding periods = 4% semiannually)
nper	=	8 (4 years × 2 compounding periods = 8 semiannual periods)
pmt	=	−4,000 ($100,000 × 4% semiannual interest rate); this is a cash outflow so we enter a negative value
fv	=	−100,000 face value, which is the lump sum to be repaid in the future; this is a cash outflow so we enter a negative value
type	=	0 because interest is paid at the end of each semiannual period
	=	PV(rate,nper,pmt,fv,type)
	=	PV(4%, 8, −4000, −100000, 0) = 100,000

Example (2), Exhibit 7A.1: Bond priced to yield 10%.

= PV(5%, 8, −4000, −100000, 0) = 93,537

Example (3), Exhibit 7A.1: Bond priced to yield 6%.

= PV(3%, 8, −4000, −100000, 0) = 107,020

Excel is more powerful than a calculator because we can use cell addresses for the variables. For example, consider the three examples in Exhibit 7A.1 that could be defined as follows:

	A	B	C	D	E	F	G	H
1	Example	rate	nper	pmt	fv	type	Bond Price	
2	Yield 8%	4%	8	−4000	−100000	0	= pv(B2,C2,D2,E2,F2)	
3								

The value in cell G2 will be 100,000. By changing cell B2 to 5%, the present value in G2 immediately changes to $93,537 and then when B2 is set to 3%, cell G2 displays $107,020.

Future Value Concepts

Future Value of a Single Amount

The **future value** of a single sum is the amount that a specific investment is worth at a future date if invested at a given rate of compound interest. To illustrate, suppose that we decide to invest $6,000 in a savings account that pays 6% annual interest and we intend to leave the principal and interest in the account for five years. We assume that interest is credited to the account at the end of each year. The balance in the account at the end of five years is determined using Table 3 in Appendix A, which gives the future value of a dollar, as follows:

Principal	× Factor	= Future Value
$6,000	**× 1.33823 =**	**$8,029**

Calculator
N = 5
I/Yr = 6
PMT = 0
PV = −6,000
FV = 8,029.35

Excel
= FV(rate,nper, pmt,[pv],[type])
= FV(6%,5,0,-6000,0)
= 8,029.35

The factor 1.33823 is at the intersection of the row for five periods and the column for 6%.

Next, suppose that the interest is credited to the account semiannually rather than annually. In this situation, there are 10 compounding periods, and we use a 3% semiannual rate (one-half the annual rate because there are two compounding periods per year). The future value calculation follows:

Principal	× Factor	= Future Value
$6,000	**× 1.34392 =**	**$8,064**

Calculator
N = 10
I/Yr = 3
PMT = 0
PV = −6,000
FV = 8,063.50

Excel
= FV(rate,nper, pmt,[pv],[type])
= FV(3%,10,0,-6000,0)
= 8,063.50

Future Value of an Annuity

If, instead of investing a single amount, we invest a specified amount *each period,* then we have an annuity. To illustrate, assume that we decide to invest $2,000 at the end of each year for five years at an 8% annual rate of return. To determine the accumulated amount of principal and interest at the end of five years, we refer to Table 4 in Appendix A, which furnishes the future value of a dollar invested at the end of each period. The factor 5.86660 is in the row for five periods and the column for 8%, and the calculation is as follows:

Periodic Payment	× Factor	= Future Value
$2,000	**× 5.86660 =**	**$11,733**

Calculator
N = 5
I/Yr = 8
PMT = −2,000
PV = 0
FV = 11,733.20

Excel
= FV(rate,nper, pmt,[pv],[type])
= FV(8%,5,-2000,0,0)
= 11,733.20

If we decide to invest $1,000 at the end of each six months for five years at an 8% annual rate of return, we would use the factor for 10 periods at 4%, as follows:

Periodic Payment	× Factor	= Future Value
$1,000	**× 12.00611 =**	**$12,006**

Calculator
N = 10
I/Yr = 4
PMT = −1,000
PV = 0
FV = 12,006.11

Excel
= FV(rate,nper, pmt,[pv],[type])
= FV(4%,10,-1000,0,0)
= 12,006.11

APPENDIX 7B: Economics of Gains and Losses on Bond Repurchases

Is a reported gain or loss on bond repurchases before maturity of economic substance? The short answer is no. To illustrate, assume that on January 1, a company issues $50 million face value bonds with an 8% annual coupon rate. The interest is to be paid semiannually (4% each semiannual period) for a term of five years (10 semiannual periods), at which time the principal will be repaid. If investors demand a 10% annual return (5% semiannually) on their investment, the bond price is computed as follows:

Present value of semiannual interest ($2,000,000 × 7.72173)	=	$15,443,460
Present value of principal ($50,000,000 × 0.61391)	=	30,695,500
Present value of bond	=	$46,138,960

Calculator
N = 10
I/Yr = 5
PMT = −2,000,000
FV = −50,000,000
PV = 46,139,132.54*
*rounding difference

Excel
= PV(rate,nper, pmt,[fv],[type])
= PV(5%,10,-2000000,
-50000000,0)
= 46,139,132.54

This bond's amortization table follows:

EXHIBIT 7B.1 Bond Discount Amortization Table

Period	[A] ([E] × market%) Interest Expense	[B] (Face × coupon%) Cash Interest Paid	[C] ([A] − [B]) Discount Amortization	[D] (Prior bal − [C]) Discount Balance	[E] (Face − [D]) Bond Payable, Net
0				$3,861,040	$46,138,960
1	$2,306,948	$2,000,000	$306,948	3,554,092	46,445,908
2	2,322,295	2,000,000	322,295	3,231,797	46,768,203
3	2,338,410	2,000,000	338,410	2,893,387	47,106,613
4	2,355,331	2,000,000	355,331	2,538,056	47,461,944
5	2,373,097	2,000,000	373,097	2,164,959	47,835,041
6	2,391,752	2,000,000	391,752	1,773,207	48,226,793
7	2,411,340	2,000,000	411,340	1,361,867	48,638,133
8	2,431,907	2,000,000	431,907	929,960	49,070,040
9	2,453,502	2,000,000	453,502	476,458	49,523,542
10	2,476,458	2,000,000	476,458	0	50,000,000

Next, assume we are at period 6 (three years after issuance) and the market rate of interest for this bond has risen from 10% to 12%. The firm decides to retire (redeem) the outstanding bond issue and finances the retirement by issuing new bonds. That is, it issues bonds with a face amount equal to the market value of the old bonds and uses the proceeds to retire the existing (old) bonds. The new bond issue will have a term of two years (four semiannual periods), the remaining life of the existing bond issue.

At the end of the third year, there are four $2,000,000 semiannual interest payments remaining on the old bonds, plus the repayment of the face amount of the bond due at the end of the fourth semiannual period. The present value of this cash flow stream, discounted at the current 12% annual rate (6% semiannual rate) is:

Calculator
N = 4
I/Yr = 6
PMT = −2,000,000
FV = −50,000,000
PV = 46,534,894.39*
*rounding difference

Present value of semiannual interest ($2,000,000 × 3.46511)	=	$ 6,930,220
Present value of principal ($50,000,000 × 0.79209)	=	39,604,500
Present value of bond	=	$46,534,720

Excel
= PV(rate,nper, pmt,[fv],[type])
= PV(6%,4,-2000000, -50000000,0)
= 46,534,894.39

This means the company pays $46,534,720 to redeem a bond that is on its books at a carrying amount of $48,226,793. The difference of $1,692,073 is reported as a gain on repurchase (also called *redemption*). GAAP requires this gain be reported in income from continuing operations unless it meets the tests for treatment as an extraordinary item (the item is both unusual and infrequent).

Although the company reports a gain in its income statement, has it actually realized an economic gain? Consider that this company issues new bonds that carry a coupon rate of 12% (6% semiannually) for $46,534,720. If we assume that those bonds are sold with a coupon rate equal to the market rate, they will sell at par (no discount or premium). The interest expense per six-month period, therefore, equals the interest paid in cash, or $2,792,083 ($46,534,720 × 6%). Total expense for the four-period life of the bond is $11,168,333 ($2,792,083 × 4). That amount, plus the $46,534,720 face amount of bonds due at maturity, results in total bond payments of $57,703,053. Had this company not redeemed the bonds, it would have paid four additional interest payments of $2,000,000 each plus the face amount of $50,000,000 at maturity, for total bond payments of $58,000,000. On the surface, it appears that the firm is able to save $296,947 by redeeming the bonds and, therefore, reports a gain. (Also, total interest expense on the new bond issue is $3,168,333 [$11,168,333 − $8,000,000] more than it would have recorded under the old issue; so, although it is recording a present gain, it also incurs future higher interest costs which are not recognized under GAAP.)

However, this gain is misleading. Specifically, this gain has two components. First, interest payments increase by $792,083 per year ($2,792,083 − $2,000,000). Second, the face amount of the bond that must be repaid in four years decreases by $3,465,280 ($50,000,000 − $46,534,720). To evaluate whether a real gain has been realized, we must consider the present value of these cash outflows and savings. The present value of the increased interest outflow, a four-period annuity of $792,083 discounted at 6% per period, is **$2,744,655** ($792,083 × 3.46511). The present value of the reduced maturity amount, $3,465,280 in four periods, is **$2,744,814** ($3,465,280 × 0.79209)—note: the two amounts differ by $159, which is due to rounding. The conclusion is that the two amounts are the same.

This analysis shows there is no real economic gain from early redemption of debt. The present value of the increased interest payments exactly offsets the present value of the decreased amount due at maturity. Why, then, does GAAP yield a gain? The answer lies in use of historical costing. Bonds are reported at amortized cost, that is, the face amount less any applicable discount or plus any premium. These amounts are a function of the bond issue price and its yield rate at issuance, which are both fixed for the life of the bond. Market prices for bonds, however, vary continually with changes in market interest rates. Companies do not adjust bond liabilities for these changes in market value. As a result, when companies redeem bonds, their carrying amount differs from market value and GAAP reports a gain or loss equal to this difference.

GUIDANCE ANSWERS

MANAGERIAL DECISION **You Are the Vice President of Finance**

You might consider the types of restructuring that would strengthen financial ratios typically used to assess liquidity and solvency by the rating agencies. Such restructuring includes generating cash by reducing inventory, reallocating cash outflows from investing activities (PPE) to debt reduction, and issuing stock for cash and using the proceeds to reduce debt (an equity for debt recapitalization). These actions increase liquidity or reduce financial leverage and, thus, should improve debt rating. An improved debt rating will attract more investors because your current debt rating is below investment grade and is not a suitable investment for many professionally managed portfolios. An improved debt rating will also lower the interest rate on your debt. Offsetting these benefits are costs such as the following: (1) potential loss of sales from inventory stock-outs; (2) potential future cash flow reductions and loss of market power from reduced PPE investments; and (3) costs of equity issuances (equity costs more than debt because investors demand a higher return to compensate for added risk and, unlike interest payments, dividends are not tax deductible for the company), which can yield a net increase in the total cost of capital. All cost and benefits must be assessed before you pursue any restructuring.

Superscript $^{A(B)}$ denotes assignments based on Appendix 7A (7B).

DISCUSSION QUESTIONS

Q7-1. What does the term *current liabilities* mean? What assets are usually used to settle current liabilities?

Q7-2. What is an accrual? How do accruals impact the balance sheet and the income statement?

Q7-3. What is the difference between a bond's coupon rate and its market interest rate (yield)?

Q7-4. Why do companies report a gain or loss when they repurchase their bonds? Is this a real economic gain or loss?

Q7-5. How do credit (debt) ratings affect the cost of borrowing for a company?

Q7-6. How would you interpret a company's reported gain or loss on the repurchase of its bonds?

Assignments with the logo in the margin are available in myBusinessCourse. See the Preface of the book for details.

MINI EXERCISES

M7-7. Interpreting a Contingent Liability Footnote (LO1)

NCI Building Systems reports the following footnote to one of its recent 10-Ks related to its manufacturing of metal coil coatings and metal building components. NCI Building Systems (NCS)

> We have discovered the existence of trichloroethylene in the ground water at our Southlake, Texas facility. Horizontal delineation concentrations in excess of applicable residential assessment levels have not been fully identified. We have filed an application with the Texas Commission of Environmental Quality ("TCEQ") for entry into the voluntary cleanup program. The cost of required remediation, if any, will vary depending on the nature and extent of the contamination. As of October 28, we have accrued $0.1 million to complete site analysis and testing. At this time, we cannot estimate a loss for any potential remediation costs, but we do not believe there will be a material adverse effect on our Consolidated Financial Statements.

a. How has NCI reported this potential liability on its balance sheet?

b. Does the $0.1 million accrual "to complete site analysis and testing" relate to a contingent liability? Explain.

M7-8. Analyzing and Computing Financial Statement Effects of Interest (LO2)
Smithe Inc. signed a 90-day, 6% note payable for $6,900 on December 16. Use the financial statement effects template to illustrate the year-end December 31 accounting adjustment Smithe must make.

M7-9. Analyzing and Determining Liability Amounts (LO1)
For each of the following situations, indicate the liability amount, if any, that is reported on the balance sheet of Heller, Inc., at December 31, 2014.

a. Heller owes $110,000 at year-end 2014 for inventory purchases.
b. Heller agreed to purchase a $28,000 drill press in January 2015.
c. During November and December of 2014, Heller sold products to a customer and warranted them against product failure for 90 days. Estimated costs of honoring this 90-day warranty during 2015 are $2,200.
d. Heller provides a profit-sharing bonus for its executives equal to 5% of reported pretax annual income. The estimated pretax income for 2014 is $600,000. Bonuses are not paid until January of the following year.

M7-10. Interpreting Relations among Bond Price, Coupon, Yield, and Credit Rating (LO2, 3)

Citigroup Inc. (C)

The following appeared in Yahoo! Finance (reports.finance.yahoo.com) regarding outstanding bonds by **Citigroup Inc.**

Price	Coupon (%)	Maturity	Yield to Maturity (%)	Fitch Ratings
123.97	6.625	2028	4.339	A
103.05	4.950	2043	4.758	A

a. Discuss the relation among the coupon rate, price, and yield for the bond maturing in 2028.
b. Compare the yields on the two bonds. Why are the yields different when the credit ratings are the same?

M7-11. Determining Gain or Loss on Bond Redemption (LO2)
On April 30, one year before maturity, Nissim Company retired $100,000 of its 9% bonds payable at the current market price of 101 (101% of the bond face amount, or $100,000 × 1.01= $101,000). The bond book value on April 30 is $98,300, reflecting an unamortized discount of $1,700. Bond interest is currently fully paid and recorded up to the date of retirement. What is the gain or loss on retirement of these bonds? Is this gain or loss a real economic gain or loss? Explain.

M7-12. Interpreting Bond Footnote Disclosures (LO2)

Bristol-Myers Squibb Company (BMY)

Bristol-Myers Squibb Co. reports the following long-term debt as part of its MD&A in its 2012 10-K ($ millions).

	Obligations Expiring by Period						
Maturity Date	Total	2013	2014	2015	2016	2017	Later Years
Long-term debt . . .	$6,631	648	27	—	659	750	$4,547

a. What does this information indicate about Bristol-Myers Squibb's future payment obligations for 2013 through 2015?
b. What implications does this payment schedule have for our evaluation of Bristol-Myers Squibb's liquidity and solvency?

M7-13. Classifying Liability-Related Accounts into Balance Sheet or Income Statement (LO2)
Indicate the proper financial statement classification (balance sheet or income statement) for each of the following liability-related accounts.

a. Gain on Bond Retirement
b. Discount on Bonds Payable
c. Mortgage Notes Payable
d. Bonds Payable
e. Bond Interest Expense
f. Bond Interest Payable (due next period)
g. Premium on Bonds Payable
h. Loss on Bond Retirement

M7-14. Interpreting Bond Footnote Disclosures (LO2)

Comcast Corporation (CMCSA)

Comcast Corporation reports the following information from the Management Discussion and Analysis section of its 2012 10-K.

> We and our Cable Communications subsidiaries that have provided guarantees are subject to the covenants and restrictions set forth in the indentures governing Comcast's public debt securities and in the credit agreements governing Comcast's and Comcast Cable Communications' credit facilities. NBCUniversal is subject to the covenants and restrictions set forth in the indentures governing its public debt securities and in the credit agreement governing its credit facility. We test for compliance with the covenants for each of our credit facilities on an ongoing basis. The only financial covenant in each of our credit facilities pertains to leverage, which is the ratio of debt to operating income before depreciation and amortization. As of December 31, 2012, we and NBCUniversal each met this financial covenant by a significant margin. Neither we nor NBCUniversal expect to have to reduce debt or improve operating results in order to continue to comply with this financial covenant.

a. The financial ratio to which Comcast refers is similar to those discussed in the section on credit ratings and the cost of debt. What effects might these ratios have on the degree of freedom that management has in running Comcast?

b. What pressures might management face if the company's ratios are near covenant limits?

M7-15. Analyzing Financial Statement Effects of Bond Redemption (LO2)

Holthausen Corporation issued $300,000 of 11%, 20-year bonds at 106 on January 1, 2009. Interest is payable semiannually on June 30 and December 31. Through January 1, 2014, Holthausen amortized $5,000 of the bond premium. On January 1, 2014, Holthausen retired the bonds at 103. Use the financial statement effects template to illustrate the bond retirement at January 1, 2014.

M7-16. Analyzing Financial Statement Effects of Bond Redemption (LO2)

Dechow, Inc., issued $225,000 of 8%, 15-year bonds at 96 on July 1, 2009. Interest is payable semiannually on December 31 and June 30. Through June 30, 2014, Dechow amortized $3,000 of the bond discount. On July 1, 2014, Dechow retired the bonds at 101. Use the financial statement effects template to illustrate the bond retirement.

M7-17. Analyzing and Computing Accrued Interest on Notes (LO2)

Compute any interest accrued for each of the following notes payable owed by Penman, Inc., as of December 31, 2014 (assume a 365-day year).

Lender	Issuance Date	Principal	Coupon Rate (%)	Term
Nissim.	11/21/2014	$19,000	12%	120 days
Klein	12/13/2014	11,000	10	90 days
Bildersee. . . .	12/19/2014	15,000	8	60 days

M7-18. Interpreting Credit Ratings (LO3)

Cummins Inc. (CMI)

Cummins Inc. reports the following information in the Management Discussion & Analysis section of its 2012 10-K report.

> **Credit Ratings** A number of our contractual obligations and financing agreements, such as our revolving credit facility, have restrictive covenants and/or pricing modifications that may be triggered in the event of downward revisions to our corporate credit rating. There were no downgrades of our credit ratings in 2012 that have impacted these covenants or pricing modifications. In September 2011, Standard & Poor's Rating Services upgraded our rating to 'A' and changed our outlook to stable. In November 2011, Moody's Investors Service, Inc. raised our rating to 'Baa1' and changed our outlook to positive. In October 2012, Fitch Ratings upgraded our ratings to 'A' and changed our outlook to stable. Our ratings and outlook from each of the credit rating agencies as of the date of filing are shown in the table below.

continued

continued from prior page

Credit Rating Agency	Senior L-T Debt Rating	Outlook
Standard & Poor's Rating Services	A	Stable
Fitch Ratings	A	Stable
Moody's Investors Service, Inc.	Baa1	Positive

a. Cummins has reduced the level of its financial leverage over the past several years. Why does the reduction in financial leverage result in an increase in the credit ratings for Cummins' debt?
b. What effect will a higher credit rating have on Cummins' borrowing costs? Explain.

M7-19. Computing Bond Issue Price (LO2)
Bushman, Inc., issues $600,000 of 9% bonds that pay interest semiannually and mature in 10 years. Compute the bond issue price assuming that the prevailing market rate of interest is:

a. 8% per year compounded semiannually.
b. 10% per year compounded semiannually.

M7-20. Computing Issue Price for Zero Coupon Bonds (LO2)
Abarbanell, Inc., issues $450,000 of zero coupon bonds that mature in 10 years. Compute the bond issue price assuming that the bonds' market rate is:

a. 8% per year compounded semiannually.
b. 10% per year compounded semiannually.

M7-21. Determining the Financial Statement Effects of Accounts Payable Transactions (LO1)
Petroni Company had the following transactions relating to its accounts payable.

a. Purchases $420 of inventory on credit.
b. Sells inventory for $550 on credit.
c. Records $420 cost of sales for transaction *b*.
d. Receives $550 cash toward accounts receivable.
e. Pays $420 cash to settle accounts payable.

Use the financial statement effects template to identify the effects (both amounts and accounts) for these transactions.

M7-22. Computing Bond Issue Price and Preparing an Amortization Table in Excel (LO2)
On January 1, 2014, Bushman, Inc., issues $400,000 of 8% bonds that pay interest semiannually and mature in 10 years (December 31, 2023).

a. Using the Excel PRICE function, compute the issue price assuming that the bonds' market rate is 7% per year compounded semiannually. (Use 100 for the redemption value to get a price as a percentage of the face amount, and use 1 for the basis.)
b. Prepare an amortization table in Excel to demonstrate the amortization of the book (carrying) value to the $400,000 maturity value at the end of the 20th semiannual period.

EXERCISES

E7-23. Analyzing and Computing Accrued Warranty Liability and Expense (LO1)
Waymire Company sells a motor that carries a 60-day unconditional warranty against product failure. From prior years' experience, Waymire estimates that 2% of units sold each period will require repair at an average cost of $125 per unit. During the current period, Waymire sold 70,000 units and repaired 1,000 of those units.

a. How much warranty expense must Waymire report in its current-period income statement?
b. What warranty liability related to current-period sales will Waymire report on its current period-end balance sheet? (*Hint:* Remember that some units were repaired in the current period.)
c. What analysis issues must we consider with respect to reported warranty liabilities?

E7-24. Analyzing Contingent and Other Liabilities (LO1)
The following independent situations represent various types of liabilities. Analyze each situation and indicate which of the following is the proper accounting treatment for the company: (a) record a liability on the balance sheet, (b) disclose the liability in a financial statement footnote, or (c) neither record nor disclose any liability.

1. A stockholder has filed a lawsuit against **Clinch Corporation**. Clinch's attorneys have reviewed the facts of the case. Their review revealed that similar lawsuits have never resulted in a cash award and it is highly unlikely that this lawsuit will either.
2. **Foster Company** signed a 60-day, 10% note when it purchased items from another company.
3. The Environmental Protection Agency notifies **Shevlin Company** that a state where it has a plant is filing a lawsuit for groundwater pollution against Shevlin and another company that has a plant adjacent to Shevlin's plant. Test results have not identified the exact source of the pollution. Shevlin's manufacturing process often produces by-products that can pollute groundwater.
4. **Sloan Company** manufactured and sold products to a retailer that later sold the products to consumers. The Sloan Company will replace the product if it is found to be defective within 90 days of the sale to the consumer. Historically, 1.2% of the products are returned for replacement.

E7-25. Recording and Analyzing Warranty Accrual and Payment (LO1)
Refer to the discussion of and excerpt from the **Harley-Davidson, Inc.** warranty reserve on page 7-9 to answer the following questions.

Harley-Davidson, Inc. (HOG)

a. Using the financial statement effects template, record separately the accrual of warranty liability relating (1) to the "Warranties issued during the period" and (2) "Recalls and changes to preexisting warranty obligations" and (3) to the "Settlements made during the period."
b. Does the level of Harley-Davidson's warranty accrual appear to be reasonable?

E7-26. Analyzing and Computing Accrued Wages Liability and Expense (LO1)
Demski Company pays its employees on the 1st and 15th of each month. It is March 31 and Demski is preparing financial statements for this quarter. Its employees have earned $32,000 since the 15th of March and have not yet been paid. How will Demski's balance sheet and income statement reflect the accrual of wages on March 31? What balance sheet and income statement accounts would be incorrectly reported if Demski failed to make this accrual (for each account indicate whether it would be overstated or understated)?

E7-27. Analyzing and Reporting Financial Statement Effects of Bond Transactions (LO2)
On January 1, Hutton Corp. issued $250,000 of 15-year, 10% bonds payable for $293,230 yielding an effective interest rate of 8%. Interest is payable semiannually on June 30 and December 31.

a. Show computations to confirm the issue price of $293,230.
b. Indicate the financial statement effects using the template for (1) bond issuance, (2) semiannual interest payment and premium amortization on June 30 of the first year, and (3) semiannual interest payment and premium amortization on December 31 of the first year.

E7-28. Analyzing and Reporting Financial Statement Effects of Mortgages (LO2)
On January 1, Piotroski, Inc., borrowed $800,000 on a 12%, 15-year mortgage note payable. The note is to be repaid in equal semiannual installments of $58,119 (payable on June 30 and December 31). Each mortgage payment includes principal and interest. Interest is computed using the effective interest method. Indicate the financial statement effects using the template for (a) issuance of the mortgage note payable, (b) payment of the first installment on June 30, and (c) payment of the second installment on December 31.

E7-29. Assessing the Effects of Bond Credit Rating Changes (LO3)
Ford Motor Co. reports the following information from the Risk Factors and the Management Discussion and Analysis sections of its 2010 10-K report.

Ford Motor Co. (F)

> **Credit Ratings** Our short-term and long-term debt is rated by four credit rating agencies designated as nationally recognized statistical rating organizations ("NRSROs") by the Securities and Exchange Commission:
> - Dominion Bond Rating Service Limited ("DBRS");
> - Fitch, Inc. ("Fitch");
> - Moody's Investors Service, Inc. ("Moody's"); and
> - Standard & Poor's Rating Services, a division of The McGraw-Hill Companies ("S&P").

continued

continued from prior page

Lower credit ratings generally result in higher borrowing costs and reduced access to capital markets. In 2005 and 2006, the credit ratings assigned to Ford Credit were lowered to below investment grade, which increased its unsecured borrowing costs and restricted its access to the unsecured debt markets. In response, Ford Credit increased its use of securitization transactions (including other structured financings) and other sources of funding. In 2010, although Ford Credit experienced several credit rating upgrades and its credit spreads narrowed considerably, its credit ratings are still below investment grade. Ford Credit's higher credit ratings have provided it more economical access to the unsecured debt markets, but it is still utilizing asset-backed securitization transactions for a substantial amount of its funding . . . Over time, and particularly in the event of any credit rating downgrades, market volatility, market disruption, or other factors, Ford Credit may reduce the amount of receivables it purchases or originates because of funding constraints . . . A significant reduction in the amount of receivables Ford Credit purchases or originates would significantly reduce its ongoing profits and could adversely affect its ability to support the sale of Ford vehicles. The following ratings actions have been taken by these NRSROs since the filing of our Quarterly Report on Form 10-Q for the quarter ended September 30, 2010:

Ford

- On January 28, 2011, Moody's affirmed Ford Motor Company's ratings and changed the rating outlook to positive from stable.
- On January 28, 2011, Fitch upgraded Ford's corporate rating to BB from BB- , the senior secured rating to BBB- from BB+, and the senior unsecured rating to BB- from B. Fitch also changed the outlook to positive from stable.
- On February 1, 2011, S&P upgraded Ford's corporate credit rating to BB- from B+, the senior secured debt rating to BB+ from BB and the senior unsecured debt rating to B+ from B. The outlook remains positive.

Ford Credit

- On January 28, 2011, Moody's affirmed Ford Credit's ratings and changed the rating outlook to positive from stable.
- On January 28, 2011, Fitch upgraded Ford Credit's corporate rating to BB from BB-. Fitch also affirmed the senior unsecured rating at BB- and the short-term rating at B. Fitch changed the outlook to positive from stable.
- On February 1, 2011, S&P upgraded Ford Credit's corporate credit rating to BB- from B+ and its senior unsecured debt rating to BB- from B+. The outlook remains positive.

a. What financial ratios do credit rating companies such as the four NRSROs listed above, use to evaluate the relative riskiness of borrowers?
b. Why might an increase in credit ratings result in lower interest costs and increase Ford's access to credit markets?
c. What type of actions can Ford take to improve its credit ratings?

E7-30. Analyzing and Reporting Financial Statement Effects of Bond Transactions (LO2)
Lundholm, Inc., reports financial statements each December 31 and issues $600,000 of 9%, 15-year bonds dated May 1, 2014, with interest payments on October 31 and April 30. Assuming the bonds are sold at par on May 1, 2014, complete the financial statement effects template to reflect the following events: (a) bond issuance, (b) the first semiannual interest payment, and (c) retirement of $350,000 of the bonds at 101 on November 1, 2014.

E7-31. Analyzing and Reporting Financial Statement Effects of Bond Transactions (LO2)
On January 1, 2014, McKeown, Inc., issued $275,000 of 8%, 9-year bonds for $242,854, which implies a market (yield) rate of 10%. Semiannual interest is payable on June 30 and December 31 of each year.

a. Show computations to confirm the bond issue price.
b. Indicate the financial statement effects using the template for (1) bond issuance, (2) semiannual interest payment and discount amortization on June 30, 2014, and (3) semiannual interest payment and discount amortization on December 31, 2014.

E7-32. Analyzing and Reporting Financial Statement Effects of Bond Transactions (LO2)
On January 1, 2014, Shields, Inc., issued $900,000 of 9%, 20-year bonds for $989,067, yielding a market (yield) rate of 8%. Semiannual interest is payable on June 30 and December 31 of each year.

a. Show computations to confirm the bond issue price.
b. Indicate the financial statement effects using the template for (1) bond issuance, (2) semiannual interest payment and premium amortization on June 30, 2014, and (3) semiannual interest payment and premium amortization on December 31, 2014.

E7-33. Determining Bond Prices, Interest Rates, and Financial Statement Effects (LO2)

Deere & Co (DE)

Deere & Company's 2012 10-K reports the following footnote relating to long-term debt for its equipment operations subsidiary. Deere's borrowings include $300 million, 7.125% notes, due in 2031 (highlighted below).

Long-term borrowings at October 31 consisted of the following in millions of dollars:

	2012	2011
Notes and debentures:		
6.95% notes due 2014: ($700 principal)	$ 718	$ 736
4.375% notes due 2019	750	750
8-1/2% debentures due 2022	105	105
2.60% notes due 2022	1,000	
6.55% debentures due 2028	200	200
5.375% notes due 2029	500	500
8.10% debentures due 2030	250	250
7.125% notes due 2031	**300**	**300**
3.90% notes due 2042	1,250	
Other notes	372	326
Total	$5,445	$3,167

A recent price quote (from **Yahoo! Finance Bond Center**) on Deere's 7.125% notes follows.

Type	Issuer	Price	Coupon (%)	Maturity	YTM (%)	Current Yield (%)	Fitch Rating	Callable
Corp	Deere & CO	131.47	7.125	2031	4.488	5.420	A	No

This price quote indicates that Deere's 7.125% notes have a market price of 131.47 (131.47% of face value), resulting in a yield to maturity of 4.488%.

a. Assuming that these notes were originally issued at par value, what does the market price reveal about interest rate changes since Deere issued its notes? (Assume that Deere's credit rating has remained the same.)

b. Does the change in interest rates since the issuance of these notes affect the amount of interest expense that Deere reports in its income statement? Explain.

c. How much cash would Deere have to pay to repurchase the 7.125% notes at the quoted market price of 131.47? (Assume no interest is owed when Deere repurchases the notes.) How would the repurchase affect Deere's current income?

d. Assuming that the notes remain outstanding until their maturity, at what market price will the notes sell on their due date in 2031?

E7-34.[A] Computing Present Values of Single Amounts and Annuities (LO2)

Refer to Tables 1 and 2 in Appendix A near the end of the book to compute the present value for each of the following amounts:

a. $80,000 received 10 years hence if the annual interest rate is:
1. 10% compounded annually.
2. 10% compounded semiannually.

b. $1,000 received at the end of each year for the next eight years discounted at 8% compounded annually.

c. $500 received at the end of each six months for the next 15 years if the interest rate is 10% per year compounded semiannually.

d. $500,000 received 10 years hence discounted at 10% per year compounded annually.

E7-35. Analyzing and Reporting Financial Statement Effects of Bond Transactions (LO2)

On January 1, 2014, Trueman Corporation issued $700,000 of 20-year, 11% bonds for $647,338, yielding a market (yield) rate of 12%. Interest is payable semiannually on June 30 and December 31.

a. Confirm the bond issue price.

b. Indicate the financial statement effects using the template for (1) bond issuance, (2) semiannual interest payment and discount amortization on June 30, 2014, and (3) semiannual interest payment and discount amortization on December 31, 2014.

E7-36. Analyzing and Reporting Financial Statement Effects of Bond Transactions (LO2)
On January 1, 2014, Verrecchia Company issued $450,000 of 5-year, 13% bonds for $502,121, yielding a market (yield) rate of 10%. Interest is payable semiannually on June 30 and December 31.

a. Confirm the bond issue price.
b. Indicate the financial statement effects using the template for (1) bond issuance, (2) semiannual interest payment and premium amortization on June 30, 2014, and (3) semiannual interest payment and premium amortization on December 31, 2014.

PROBLEMS

P7-37. Interpreting Term Structures of Coupon Rates and Yield Rates (LO2, 3)

PepsiCo, Inc. (PEP)

PepsiCo, Inc. reports $26,445 million of long-term debt outstanding as of December 2012 in the following schedule to its 10-K report.

Debt Obligations and Commitments

	2012	2011
Short-term debt obligations		
Current maturities of long-term debt	**$ 2,901**	$ 2,549
Commercial paper (0.1% and 0.1%)	**1,101**	2,973
Other borrowings (7.4% and 7.6%)	**813**	683
	$ 4,815	$ 6,205
Long-term debt obligations		
Notes due 2012 (3.0%)	**$ —**	$ 2,353
Notes due 2013 (2.3%)	**2,891**	2,841
Notes due 2014 (4.4% and 4.6%)	**3,237**	3,335
Notes due 2015 (1.5% and 2.3%)	**3,300**	1,632
Notes due 2016 (3.9%)	**1,878**	1,876
Notes due 2017 (2.0% and 5.0%)	**1,250**	258
Notes due 2018–2042 (4.4% and 4.8%)	**13,781**	10,548
Other, due 2013–2020 (9.3% and 9.9%)	**108**	274
	26,445	23,117
Less: current maturities of long-term debt obligations	**(2,901)**	(2,549)
Total	**$23,544**	$20,568

Long-Term Contractual Commitments

Payments Due by Period ($ millions)	Total	2013	2014–2015	2016–2017	2018 and beyond
Long-term debt obligations	$26,445	$2,901	$6,450	$3,105	$13,989

Our borrowing costs and access to capital and credit markets may be adversely affected by a downgrade or potential downgrade of our credit ratings.
Our objective is to maintain credit ratings that provide us with ready access to global capital and credit markets. Any downgrade of our credit ratings by a credit rating agency, especially any downgrade to below investment grade, could increase our future borrowing costs and impair our ability to access capital and credit markets on terms commercially acceptable to us, or at all. In addition, any downgrade of our current short-term credit ratings could impair our ability to access the commercial paper market with the same flexibility that we have experienced historically, and therefore require us to rely more heavily on more expensive types of debt financing. Our borrowing costs and access to the commercial paper market could also be adversely affected if a credit rating agency announces that our ratings are under review for a potential downgrade.

Moody's Investor Service (www.moodys.com) reported the following regarding PepsiCo:

Rating Action: Moody's downgrades Pepsi to A1; affirms P-1 short-term rating; outlook is stable.
New York, June 25, 2013—Moody's today lowered the long-term ratings of PepsiCo ("Pepsi") and its rated subsidiaries to A1 from Aa3. Pepsi's short-term rating was affirmed at P-1 and the outlook for the company is stable. Today's action concludes Moody's review of Pepsi for downgrade which was initiated on May 30th. Source: Moody's Investor Service (www.moodys.com)

As of December 2013, the price of its $1 billion 5.0% senior notes maturing in 2018 follows (from **Yahoo! Finance, reports.finance.yahoo.com**):

Type	Issuer	Price	Coupon(%)	Maturity	YTM(%)	Fitch Ratings	Callable
Corp	PEPSICO INC	113.79	5.0	01-Jun-2018	1.75	A	No

Required

a. PepsiCo reports current maturities of long-term debt of $2,901 million as part of short-term debt. Why is this amount reported that way? PepsiCo reports $6,450 million of long-term debt due in 2014–2015. What does this mean? Is this amount important to our analysis of PepsiCo? Explain.

b. The $1 billion 5.0% notes maturing in 2018 are priced at 113.79 (113.79% of face value, or $1.1379 billion) as of December 2013, resulting in a yield to maturity of 1.75%. Assuming that the credit rating of PepsiCo has not changed, what does the pricing of this bond imply about interest rate changes since PepsiCo issued the bond?

c. What does the schedule of long-term contractual commitments reveal that might be useful in analyzing PepsiCo's liquidity?

d. Moody's Investors Service lowered the long-term ratings of PepsiCo in 2013. Why might a reduction in credit ratings result in higher interest costs and restrict PepsiCo's access to credit markets?

e. What type of actions can PepsiCo take to improve its credit ratings?

P7-38. Interpreting Debt Footnotes on Interest Rates and Interest Expense (LO2)

CVS Caremark Corporation discloses the following as part of its long-term debt footnote in its 2012 10-K.

CVS Caremark Corporation (CVS)

BORROWING AND CREDIT AGREEMENTS

The following table is a summary of the Company's borrowings as of December 31:

In millions	2012	2011
Commercial paper	$ 690	$ 750
4.875% senior notes due 2014	550	550
3.25% senior notes due 2015	550	550
6.125% senior notes due 2016	421	700
5.75% senior notes due 2017	1,310	1,750
6.6% senior notes due 2019	394	1,000
4.75% senior notes due 2020	450	450
4.125% senior notes due 2021	550	550
6.25% senior notes due 2027	1,000	1,000
Trust Preferred Securities	—	50
6.125% senior notes due 2039	1,500	1,500
5.75% senior notes due 2041	950	950
Enhanced Capital Advantage Preferred Securities due 2062	41	42
2.75% senior notes due 2022	1,250	—
Mortgage notes payable	1	4
Capital lease obligations	171	168
	9,828	10,014
Less:		
Short-term debt (commercial paper)	(690)	(750)
Current portion of long-term debt	(5)	(56)
	$ 9,133	$ 9,208

CVS also discloses the following information.

Interest expense, net—Interest expense, net of capitalized interest, was $561 million, $588 million and $539 million, and interest income was $4 million, $4 million and $3 million in 2012, 2011 and 2010, respectively. Capitalized interest totaled $29 million, $37 million and $47 million in 2012, 2011 and 2010, respectively. Interest paid totaled $581 million, $647 million and $583 million in 2012, 2011 and 2010 respectively.

Maturities of long-term debt—The aggregate maturities of long-term debt for each of the five years subsequent to December 31, 2012 are $5 million in 2013, $555 million in 2014, $556 million in 2015, $427 million in 2016, and $1.3 billion in 2017.

The price of the $1,500 million 6.125% senior note due 2039 as of May 2013 follows (from Yahoo! finance).

Maturity Date	Issuer	Security Type	Coupon	Current Price	Current Yield	Fitch Rating	Callable
2039	CVS Caremark (NYSE: CVS)	Corporate Debentures	6.125	117.49	5.213	BBB	No

Required

a. What is the average coupon rate (interest paid) and the average effective rate (interest expense) on the long-term debt? (*Hint:* Use the disclosure for interest expense.)

b. Does your computation of the coupon rate in part *a* seem reasonable given the footnote disclosure relating to specific bond issues? Explain.

c. Explain how the amount of interest paid can differ from the amount of interest expense recorded in the income statement.

d. On its 2012 balance sheet, CVS reports current maturities of long-term debt of $5 million as part of short-term debt. Why is this amount reported that way? Is this amount important to our analysis of CVS? Explain.

e. The $1,500 million 6.125% senior note due in 2039 is priced at 117.49 (117.49% of face value, or $1,762.35 million) as of 2013, resulting in a yield to maturity of 5.213%. Assuming that the credit rating of CVS has not changed, what does the pricing of this 6.125% coupon bond imply about interest rate changes since CVS issued the bond?

Dell Inc. (DELL)

P7-39. Analyzing Debt Terms, Yields, Prices, and Credit Ratings (LO2, 3)
Reproduced below is the debt footnote from the 2013 10-K report of Dell Inc.

Long-Term Debt (in millions)	February 1, 2013	February 3, 2012
Senior Notes		
$400 million issued on June 10, 2009, at 3.375% due June 2012 ("2012 Notes")	$ —	$ 400
$600 million issued on April 17, 2008, at 4.70% due April 2013 ("2013A Notes")	601	605
$500 million issued on September 7, 2010, at 1.40% due September 2013	500	499
$500 million issued on April 1, 2009, at 5.625% due April 2014[b]	500	500
$300 million issued on March 28, 2011, with a floating rate due April 2014 ("2014B Notes")	300	300
$400 million issued on March 28, 2011, at 2.10% due April 2014	400	400
$700 million issued on September 7, 2010, at 2.30% due September 2015[b]	702	701
$400 million issued on March 28, 2011, at 3.10% due April 2016[b]	402	401
$500 million issued on April 17, 2008, at 5.65% due April 2018[b]	502	501
$600 million issued on June 10, 2009, at 5.875% due June 2019[b]	604	602
$400 million issued on March 28, 2011, at 4.625% due April 2021	398	398
$400 million issued on April 17, 2008, at 6.50% due April 2038	400	400
$300 million issued on September 7, 2010, at 5.40% due September 2040	300	300
Senior Debentures		
$300 million issued on April 3, 1998, at 7.10% due April 2028 ("Senior Debentures")[a]	379	384
Other		
Long-term structured financing debt	872	920
Less: current portion of long-term debt	(1,618)	(924)
Total long-term debt	5,242*	6,387

continued

Long-Term Debt (in millions)	February 1, 2013	February 3, 2012
Short-Term Debt		
Commercial paper	1,807	1,500
Short-term structured financing debt	416	440
Current portion of long-term debt	1,618	924
Other	2	3
Total short-term debt	3,843	2,867
Total debt	$9,085	$9,254

*Reflects carrying value (net book value) of debt.

Aggregate future maturities of long-term debt at face value were as follows at February 1, 2013:

	Maturities by Fiscal Year						
(in millions)	2014	2015	2016	2017	2018	Thereafter	Total
Aggregate future maturities of long-term debt outstanding	$1,617	$1,465	$790	$400	$—	$2,500	$6,772**

**Reflects face value of debt.

Reproduced below is a summary of the market values as of November 2013 of the Dell bonds maturing from 2021 to 2040 (from Morningstar, quicktake.morningstar.com).

Name	Maturity Date	Amount $	Price	Coupon %	Yield to Maturity %
Dell 5.4%	9/10/2040	300	69.50	5.4	8.24
Dell 6.5%	4/15/2038	400	77.30	6.5	8.77
Dell 4.625%	4/1/2021	400	91.50	4.625	6.07

Required

a. What is the amount of long-term debt reported on Dell's February 1, 2013, balance sheet? What are the scheduled maturities for this indebtedness? Why is information relating to a company's scheduled maturities of debt useful in an analysis of its financial condition?

b. Dell reported $270 million in interest expense in the notes to its 2013 income statement. In the note to its statement of cash flows, Dell indicates that the cash portion of this expense is $279 million. What could account for the difference between interest expense and interest paid? Explain.

c. Dell's long-term debt is rated Baa1 by Moody's, BBB+ by S&P, and BBB+ by Fitch. What factors would be important to consider in attempting to quantify the relative riskiness of Dell compared with other borrowers? Explain.

d. Dell's $300 million 5.4% notes traded at 69.5 or 69.5% of par, as of November 2013. What is the market value of these notes on that date? How is the difference between this market value and the $300 million face value reflected in Dell's financial statements? What effect would the repurchase of this entire note issue have on Dell's financial statements? What does the 69.5 price tell you about the general trend in interest rates since Dell sold this bond issue? Explain.

e. Examine the yields to maturity of the three bonds in the table above. What relation do we observe between these yields and the maturities of the bonds? Also, explain why this relation applies in general.

P7-40. Analyzing Notes, Yields, Financial Ratios, and Credit Ratings (LO2, 3)

Comcast Corp. (CMCSA)

Comcast Corporation reports long-term senior notes totaling over $40 billion in its 2012 10-K. Following are selected ratios from Exhibit 7.6 computed for Comcast Corp. utilizing its 2012 data.

EBITA/Average assets	8.57%
EBITA/Interest expense	5.48
EBITA margin	22.10%
Operating margin	13.14%
(Funds from operations + Interest expense)/Interest expense	6.89
Funds from operations/Debt	36.71%
Debt/EBITDA	2.03
Debt/Book capitalization	29.45%

Required

This debt is rated "A3" by Moody's, which is an upper medium grade. Examine the ratios provided above. (*Hint:* Compare Comcast's ratios to the ratio values reported in Exhibit 7.6.) What factors do you believe contribute to Comcast's credit rating being less than stellar?

IFRS APPLICATIONS

I7-41. Interpreting a Contingent Liability Footnote (LO1)

BP p.l.c. (BP)

BP operates off-shore drilling rigs including rigs in the Gulf of Mexico. On April 20, 2010, explosions and fire on the Deepwater Horizon rig led to the death of 11 crew members and a 200-million-gallon oil spill in the Gulf of Mexico. BP's 2010 annual report (prepared under IFRS) included the following concerning estimates of contingent liabilities (provisions):

> In estimating the amount of the provision, BP has determined a range of possible outcomes for Individual and Business Claims, and State and Local Claims. . . . BP has concluded that a reasonable range of possible outcomes for the amount of the provision as at 31 December 2010 is \$6 billion to \$13 billion. BP believes that the provision recorded at 31 December 2010 of \$9.2 billion represents a reliable best estimate from within this range of possible outcomes.

How did BP record the \$9.2 billion estimate in its 2010 financial statements? How would the accounting for this provision differ if BP had prepared its financial statements in accordance with U.S. GAAP?

I7-42. Interpreting Bond Footnote Disclosures (LO2)

Foncière des Régions

In October 2012, French real estate company Foncière des Régions issued bonds with a total face value of €500 million. The bond proceeds were €504.087 million. The 2012 annual report has the following note:

> Foncière des Régions launched a bond issue as described below:

Issue date	19/10/2012
Issue amount (€M)	500
Nominal rate	3.875%
Maturity	16/01/2018

a. Determine the annual interest payments. (*Hint*: Nominal rate of 3.875% is the coupon or face rate of interest.)

b. Assume the bonds are due in 5.25 years (October 2012 till January 2018). Determine the effective interest rate.

c. What amount of interest expense does the company report related to these bonds for the first full year after they are issued?

I7-43. Assessing Liability Footnotes in Financial Statements (LO1, 3)

Deutsche Telekom AG

Deutsche Telekom AG, headquartered in Bonn, Germany, is the largest telecommunications company in Europe. The company uses IFRS to prepare its financial statements. The company's 2012 financial statements report the following:

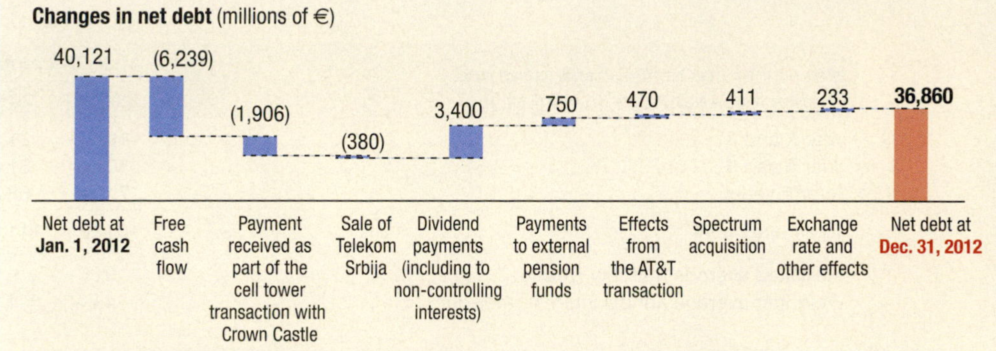

The debt footnotes report details about Deutsche Telekom's financing activities as follows:

At the reporting date, the foreign-currency liabilities for which currency risks were hedged mainly consisted of bonds and medium-term notes in Australian dollars, pound sterling, Japanese yen, Norwegian kroner, Swiss francs, Czech koruna, and U.S. dollars. On account of these hedging activities, Deutsche Telekom was not exposed to any significant currency risks in the area of financing at the reporting date.

Required

a. The graphic shows changes in net debt, which is debt less cash and marketable securities. For each of the changes shown in the graphic, determine if the cash flow was operating, investing, or financing.

b. Explain why the company issues debt in so many currencies.

I7-44. Analyzing Debt Terms, Yields, Prices, and Credit Ratings (LO2, 3)

Statoil ASA (STO)

Statoil ASA, headquartered in Stavanger, Norway, is a fully integrated petroleum company. The company uses IFRS to prepare its financial statements. Reproduced below is the long-term debt note from its 2012 annual report.

	Carrying amount in NOK billion		Fair value in NOK billion	
At 31 December	**2012**	**2011**	**2012**	**2011**
Total financial liabilities	106.7	118.8	126.1	135.5
Less current portion	5.7	7.2	5.9	7.2
Financial liabilities, non-current portion	101.0	111.6	120.2	128.3

	Weighted average interest rates in %		Carrying amount in NOK billion at 31 December		Fair value in NOK billion at 31 December	
Financial liabilities	**2012**	**2011**	**2012**	**2011**	**2012**	**2011**
Unsecured bonds						
US dollar (USD)	4.52	4.92	69.9	65.5	80.2	74.8
Euro (EUR)	4.99	4.99	18.4	19.5	22.8	23.1
Japanese yen (JPY)	—	1.66	—	0.4	—	0.4
Great Britain Pound (GBP)	6.71	6.71	9.2	9.5	13.8	13.2
Total			97.5	94.9	116.8	111.5

continued

continued from prior page

Maturity profile bonds, bank loans and finance lease liabilities (in NOK billion)	At 31 December	
	2012	2011
Year 2 and 3	19.1	21.3
Year 4 and 5	10.8	21.8
After 5 years	71.1	68.5
Total repayment	101.0	111.6
Weighted average maturity (year)	9	9
Weighted average annual interest rate (%)	4.74	4.84

Reproduced below is a summary of the market values, at July 2013, of the Statoil ASA bonds maturing from 2014 to 2040.

Currency	Maturity date	Amount Outstanding	Current price	Coupon	Yield
Statoil Asa USD	08/17/2017	1,250.0	105.8	3.125	1.67
Statoil Asa USD	08/17/2040	750.0	106.6	5.100	4.67
Statoil Asa USD	04/30/2014	500.0	102.6	3.875	0.50

Required

a. What is the amount of total financial liabilities (debt) reported on Statoil's 2012 balance sheet? Of the total financial liabilities, what proportion is due within one year?

b. In what currencies has Statoil issued financial liabilities? Why do companies borrow money in foreign currencies?

c. What are the scheduled maturities for Statoil's indebtedness? Why is information relating to a company's scheduled maturities of debt useful in analyzing financial condition?

d. Statoil's long-term debt is rated AA- by Standard and Poor's and similarly by other credit agencies. What factors would be important to consider in quantifying the relative riskiness of Statoil compared to other borrowers? Explain.

e. Statoil's $1,250 million, 3.125% notes traded at 105.8 or 105.8% of par, as of July 2013. What is the market value of these notes on that date? How is the difference between this market value and the $1,250 million face value reflected on Statoil's financial statements? What does the 105.8 price tell you about the general trend in interest rates since Statoil sold this bond issue? Explain.

f. Examine the yields to maturity of the bonds in the previous table. What relation do we observe between these yields and the maturities of the bonds? Explain why this relation applies in general.

I7-45. Analyzing Contingent Liabilities: Warranty Reserves (LO1)

Bombardier, Inc. (BDRBF)

Headquartered in Montreal, Quebec, Canada, **Bombardier, Inc.**, is a multinational aerospace and transportation company, founded in 1941. The company manufactures regional aircraft, business jets, mass transportation equipment, and recreational equipment and is also a financial services provider. Bombardier is a Fortune Global 500 company and operates two segments: BA (Aerospace) and BT (Transportation). Bombardier's 2012 annual report includes the following details about the company's warranty reserve:

Balance as at December 31, 2011	$1,073
Additions	308
Utilization	(365)
Reversals	(66)
Accretion expense	1
Effect of changes in discount rates	—
Effect of foreign currently exchange	15
Balance as at December 31, 2012	**$ 966**
Of which current	$ 818
Of which non-current	148
	$ 966

Required

a. In common language, explain what is a warranty reserve. When do companies create such reserves?
b. What amount is included on the 2012 balance sheet for warranty reserve?
c. What amount is included on the 2012 income statement related to warranties?
d. What is meant by "Utilization" in the table? What sort of costs does this entail?

I7-46. Analyzing Contingent Liabilities: Restructuring Reserves (LO1)

Headquartered in Brampton Ontario, Canada, **Loblaw Companies** is a supermarket chain with numerous stores across Ontario and Quebec. In western Canada, Loblaw operates as Real Canadian Superstore. The company's 2012 annual report included the following:

Loblaw Companies (L.TO)

Provisions consist primarily of amounts recorded in respect of restructruing, self-insurance, commodity taxes, environmental and decommissioning liabilities and onerous lease arrangements. The following are continuities relating to the Company's provisions:

(millions of Canadian dollars)	2012	2011
Provisions, beginning of year	$ 85	$105
Additions	80	56
Payments	(20)	(50)
Reversals	(8)	(26)
Provisions, end of year	$137	$ 85

(millions of Canadian dollars)	2012	2011
Recorded on the consolidated balance sheets as follows:		
Current portion of provisions	$ 78	$ 35
Non-current portion of provisions	59	50
Total provisions	$137	$ 85

Required

a. In common language, explain what is a restructuring provision. When do companies create such provisions?
b. What amount is included on the 2012 balance sheet for total provisions?
c. What amount is included on the 2012 income statement related to total provisions?
d. What is meant by "Payments" in the table? What sort of costs does this entail?
e. What is a reversal and how do they occur?

I7-47. Analyzing Debt Footnotes (LO2)

Headquartered in Montreal, Canada, **Valeant Pharmaceuticals International, Inc.** is a multinational specialty pharmaceutical company that develops and markets prescription and non-prescription pharmaceuticals, principally in the areas of dermatology and neurology. The company is the largest pharmaceutical company in Canada with a portfolio of more than 500 products and 400 employees involved in R&D activities. The company is listed on both the NYSE and the Toronto Stock Exchange. Its 2012 income statement reported the following line item:

Valeant (VRX)

($000s)	2012	2011	2010
Loss of extinguishment on debt	$(20,080)	$(36,844)	$(32,413)

Required

a. What is a loss on extinguishment of debt? Why does such a loss arise?
b. How does the company calculate the loss on extinguishment of debt?
c. Would we categorize this income statement item as operating or nonoperating?

Potash Corporation of Saskatchewan (POT)

I7-48. Analyzing Debt Footnotes (LO2, 3)

Potash Corporation of Saskatchewan—the world's largest potash producer—is a Canadian corporation based in Saskatoon, Saskatchewan. The company produces nitrogen and phosphate used to produce fertilizer. At the end of 2011, the company controlled 20% of the world's potash production capacity, 2% of nitrogen production capacity and 5% of phosphate supply. Its 2012 financial statements disclose the following as part of its long-term debt footnote.

Short-term debt at December 31 was comprised of:

	2012	2011
Commercial paper	$369	$829

Long-term debt at December 31 was comprised of:

	2012	2011
Senior notes[1]		
4.875% notes due March 1, 2013	$ 250	$ 250
5.250% notes due May 15, 2014	500	500
3.750% notes due September 30, 2015	500	500
3.250% notes due December 1, 2017	500	500
6.500% notes due May 15, 2019	500	500
4.875% notes due March 30, 2020	500	500
5.875% notes due December 1, 2036	500	500
5.625% notes due December 1, 2040	500	500
Other	6	7
	3,756	3,757
Less net unamortized debt costs	(44)	(49)
	3,712	3,708
Less current maturities	(250)	(7)
Add current portion of amortization	4	4
	$3,466	$3,705

[1] Each series of senior notes is unsecured and has no sinking fund requirements prior to maturity. Each series is redeemable, in whole or in part, at the company's option, at any time prior to maturity for a price not less than the principal amount of the notes to be redeemed, plus accrued and unpaid interest. Under certain conditions related to a change in control, the company is required to make an offer to purchase all, or any part, of the senior notes other than those maturing in 2013 at 101 percent of the principal amount of the notes repurchased, plus accrued and unpaid interest.

Long-term debt obligations at December 31, 2012 will mature as follows:

2013	$ 250
2014	500
2015	500
2016	–
2017	506
Subsequent years	2,000
	$3,756

continued

FINANCE COSTS

	2012	2011	2010
Interest expense on			
Short-term debt	$ 5	$ 8	$ 8
Long-term debt.	203	227	217
Unwinding of discount on asset retirement obligations. . . .	12	16	11
Borrowing costs capitalized to property, plant and equipment	(102)	(84)	(107)
Interest income.	(4)	(8)	(8)
	$114	$159	$121

Borrowing costs capitalized to property, plant and equipment during 2012 were calculated by applying an average capitalization rate of 4.6 percent (2011: 4.4 percent, 2010: 5.0 percent) to expenditures on qualifying assets.

	2012	2011	2010
Supplemental cash flow disclosure:			
Interest paid	$209	$233	$212

Reproduced below is a summary of the May 2013 market values of the Potash bonds maturing from 2015 to 2040 (from Morningstar, quicktake.morningstar.com).

Name	Maturity Date	Amount $(Mil)	Credit Quality	Price	Coupon %	Coupon Type (Fixed/ Floating)	Callable	Rule 144A	Yield to Maturity %
Potash Corp Sask 3.75%. . . .	09/30/2015	500.0	High	106.1	3.750	Fixed	No	No	0.96
Potash Corp Sask 3.25%. . . .	12/01/2017	500.0	High	104.7	3.250	Fixed	No	No	2.11
Potash Corp Sask 6.5%.	05/15/2019	500.0	High	120.5	6.500	Fixed	No	No	2.69
Potash Corp Sask 4.875%. . .	03/30/2020	500.0	High	110.4	4.875	Fixed	No	No	3.14
Potash Corp Sask 5.875%. . .	12/01/2036	500.0	High	111.3	5.875	Fixed	No	No	5.05
Potash Corp Sask 5.625%. . .	12/01/2040	500.0	High	112.5	5.625	Fixed	No	No	4.80

a. What is the average coupon rate (interest paid) and the average effective rate (interest expense) on long-term debt? (*Hint:* Use the disclosure for interest expense.)

b. Does the coupon rate computed in part *a* seem reasonable given the footnote disclosure relating to specific bond issues? Explain.

c. Explain how the amount of interest paid in cash can differ from the amount of interest expense recorded in the income statement.

d. On its 2012 balance sheet, Potash reports current maturities of long-term debt of $246 million as part of short-term debt. Why is this amount reported that way? Is this amount important to our analysis of Potash? Explain.

e. The table above shows that the $500 million 5.625% note due in 2040 is priced at 112.5 (112.50% of face value, or $562.5 million) as of 2012, resulting in a yield to maturity of 4.80%. Assuming that the credit rating of Potash has not changed, what does the pricing of this 5.625% coupon bond imply about interest rate changes since Potash issued the bond?

f. Examine the yield to maturity of the bonds in the table above. What relation do we observe between these yields and the maturities of the bonds? Also, explain why this relation applies in general.

Rio Tinto Group

I7-49. Analyzing Debt Footnotes (LO2, 3)

Rio Tinto Group, a British-Australian multinational corporation, is among the world leaders in the production of many commodities, including aluminum, iron ore, copper, uranium, coal, and diamonds. Reproduced below is the debt footnote from its 2012 financial statements.

Borrowings at 31 December	Non-current 2012 US$m	Current 2012 US$m	Total 2012 US$m
USD Commercial Paper	$ —	$ 200	$ 200
Alcan Inc. Global Notes 4.875% due 2012	—	—	—
Alcan Inc. Global Notes 4.50% due 2013	—	498	498
Rio Tinto Finance (USA) Limited Bonds 5.875% 2013	—	595	595
Rio Tinto Finance (USA) Limited Bonds 7.125% 2013	—	100	100
Alcan Inc. Global Notes 5.20% due 2014	498	—	498
Rio Tinto Finance (USA) Limited Bonds 8.95% 2014	1,935	—	1,935
Rio Tinto Finance (USA) plc Bonds 1.125% 2015	498	—	498
Alcan Inc. Global Notes 5.00% due 2015	501	—	501
Rio Tinto Finance (USA) Limited Bonds 1.875% 2015	500	—	500
Rio Tinto Finance (USA) Limited Bonds 2.500% 2016	696	—	696
Rio Tinto Finance (USA) Limited Bonds 2.250% 2016	497	—	497
Rio Tinto Finance (USA) plc Bonds 2.0% 2017	499	—	499
Rio Tinto Finance (USA) plc Bonds 1.625% 2017	1,241	—	1,241
Rio Tinto Finance (USA) Limited Bonds 6.5% 2018	2,059	—	2,059
Rio Tinto Finance (USA) Limited Bonds 9.0% 2019	1,456	—	1,456
Rio Tinto Finance Plc Euro Bonds 2.0% due 2020(c)	971	—	971
Rio Tinto Finance (USA) Limited Bonds 3.5% 2020	994	—	994
Rio Tinto Finance (USA) Limited Bonds 4.125% 2021	997	—	997
Rio Tinto Finance (USA) Limited Bonds 3.750% 2021	1,143	—	1,143
Rio Tinto Finance (USA) plc Bonds 3.5% 2022	992	—	992
Rio Tinto Finance (USA) plc Bonds 2.875% 2022	984	—	984
Rio Tinto Finance Plc Euro Bonds 2.875% due 2024	636	—	636
Rio Tinto Finance (USA) Limited Bonds 7.125% 2028	1,053	—	1,053
Alcan Inc. Debentures 7.25% due 2028	107	—	107
Rio Tinto Finance Plc Sterling Bonds 4.0% due 2029	804	—	804
Alcan Inc. Debentures 7.25% due 2031	432	—	432
Alcan Inc. Global Notes 6.125% due 2033	738	—	738
Alcan Inc. Global Notes 5.75% due 2035	283	—	283
Rio Tinto Finance (USA) Limited Bonds 5.20% 2040	1,146	—	1,146
Rio Tinto Finance (USA) plc Bonds 4.75% 2042	489	—	489
Rio Tinto Finance (USA) plc Bonds 4.125% 2042	725	—	725
Loans from equity accounting units	111	72	183
Other secured loans	918	78	996
Other unsecured loans	519	556	1,075
Finance leases	41	12	53
Bank overdrafts	—	94	94
Total borrowings including overdrafts	24,463	2,205	26,668
Derivative financial instruments	70	23	93
Other financial liabilities	58	—	58
Total other financial liabilities	128	23	151
Total borrowings and other financial liabilities	$24,591	$2,228	$26,819

The table below analyses the Group's financial liabilities by relevant maturity groupings based on the remaining period from the statement of financial position date to the contractual maturity date. As the amounts disclosed in the table are the contractual undiscounted cash flows, these balances will not necessarily agree with the amounts disclosed in the statement of financial position.

continued

At 31 December 2012 (Outflows)/Inflows	Within 1 year or on demand US$m	Between 1 and 2 years US$m	Between 2 and 3 years US$m	Between 3 and 4 years US$m	Between 4 and 5 years US$m	After 5 years US$m	Total US$m
Non-derivative financial liabilities							
Trade and other payables	(7,612)	(147)	—	—	—	—	(7,759)
Borrowings before swaps	(2,199)	(2,627)	(1,798)	(1,342)	(2,054)	(16,328)	(26,348)
Expected future interest payments	(1,072)	(970)	(878)	(847)	(821)	(6,891)	(11,479)
Other financial liabilities	(49)	(90)	(31)	(5)	(5)	—	(180)
Derivative financial liabilities							
Derivatives related to net debt – net settled	—	—	—	—	—	—	—
Derivatives related to net debt – gross settled:							
– gross inflows	80	80	80	80	80	1,359	1,759
– gross outflows	(71)	(71)	(71)	(71)	(71)	(1,297)	(1,652)
Total	(10,923)	(3,825)	(2,698)	(2,185)	(2,871)	(23,157)	(45,659)

a. What is the amount of debt reported on Rio Tinto's, 2012, balance sheet?

b. What are the scheduled maturities for this indebtedness? Why is information relating to a company's scheduled maturities of debt useful in an analysis of its financial condition?

c. Rio Tinto reported $1,005 million in interest expense in the notes to its 2012 financial statements. In its statement of cash flows, Rio Tinto indicates that the cash portion of this expense was $837 million. What could account for the difference between interest expense and interest paid? Explain.

d. Rio Tinto's long-term debt is rated A3 by Moody's and A- by S&P. What factors would be important to consider in attempting to quantify the relative riskiness of Rio Tinto compared with other borrowers? Explain.

e. Assume that the 4.125% Rio Tinto Finance bonds with a face value of $725 million maturing in 2042 were trading at 96.2, or 96.2% of par, as of December 2012. What is the market value of these notes on that date? How is the difference between this market value and the $725 million face value reflected in Rio Tinto's financial statements? If the company had repurchased this entire note issue on December 31, 2012, what would have been the effect on Rio Tinto's financial statements? What does the 96.2 price tell us about the general trend in interest rates since Rio Tinto sold this bond issue? Explain.

MANAGEMENT APPLICATIONS

MA7-50. Coupon Rate versus Effective Rate (LO2)

Assume that you are the CFO of a company that intends to issue bonds to finance a new manufacturing facility. A subordinate suggests lowering the coupon rate on the bond to lower interest expense and to increase the profitability of your company. Is the rationale for this suggestion a good one? Explain.

MA7-51. Ethics and Governance: Bond Covenants (LO2)

Because lenders do not have voting rights like shareholders do, they often reduce their risk by invoking various bond covenants that restrict the company's operating, financing and investing activities. For example, debt covenants often restrict the amount of debt that the company can issue (in relation to its equity) and impose operating restrictions (such as the ability to acquire other companies or to pay dividends). Failure to abide by these restrictions can have serious consequences, including forcing the company into bankruptcy and potential liquidation. Assume that you are on the board of directors of a company that issues bonds with such restrictions. What safeguards can you identify to ensure compliance with those restrictions?

ONGOING PROJECT

(This ongoing project began in Module 1 and continues through most of the book; even if previous segments were not completed, the requirements are still applicable to any business analysis.) Review liabilities that arise from operating and financing transactions, including the type and quantity of both

categories. The goal is to consider how the companies are financed and whether they can repay their obligations as they come due in the short and longer term.

1. *Operating Liabilities.* Operating liabilities arise from ordinary operations and provide a less expensive source of financing. The following questions help direct our analysis.
   - Are operating liabilities large for the companies? Compare common-sized amounts. What proportion of total liabilities are operating?
   - What are the companies' main operating liabilities?
   - Compute accounts payable turnover and compare it over time and between the two companies.
   - Are there substantial contingencies? What gives rise to these? Read the footnote and determine whether the company has recorded a liability on its balance sheet for these contingencies.
2. *Nonoperating Liabilities.* Examine the debt footnote and consider the following questions.
   - What proportion of total liabilities are nonoperating? What is the common-sized debt and how does that compare to published industry averages?
   - What types of debt does the company have? Is it publicly traded? Are there bank loans? Other types of debt?
   - When does the debt mature? Determine if there is a large proportion due in the next year or two. If so, can the company refinance given its current level of debt?
   - What is the average interest rate on debt? Compare it to the coupon rates reported.
   - Read the footnote and the MD&A to see if there are any debt covenants and whether the company is in compliance.
   - If the company has publicly traded debt, determine its current price. Sharp drops in bond prices could indicate a deterioration in the company's credit quality.
3. *Credit Ratings.* Find the companies' credit ratings at two or three ratings agencies' Websites.
   - What are the credit ratings and how do they compare across the agencies? Are the two companies similarly rated?
   - Have the ratings changed during the year? If so, why?
   - Are the companies on a credit watch or a downgrade list?
   - If possible, find a credit report online and read it to gain a better understanding of the companies' creditworthiness.
   - Calculate the ratios in Exhibit 7.6 for your firms. Compare the ratios to those for firms with similar credit ratings. Do the credit ratings for the firms seem reasonable?

SOLUTIONS TO REVIEW PROBLEMS

Mid-Module Review 1

Solution

a. We know that accounts payable turnover is computed as cost of goods sold divided by average accounts payable. Thus, a decrease in accounts payable turnover indicates that accounts payable have increased relative to cost of goods sold (all else being equal).

b. An increase in accounts payable results in an increase in net cash flows from operating activities because Verizon is using cash to pay bills more slowly.

c. Increased accounts payable decreases net operating working capital (all else being equal), with a consequent increase in cash flow. While favorable to cash flow, the less timely payment of accounts payable can strain supplier relations. Analysts must be aware of the costs and benefits of leaning on the trade to a greater or lesser extent.

Mid-Module Review 2

Solution

Yes. Verizon must recognize liabilities and expenses when incurred, regardless of when payment is made. Accruing expenses as incurred will match the expenses to the revenues they helped generate. Failure to recognize the wages owed to employees for the period would understate liabilities and overstate income. Verizon must reflect the wages earned and the related expense in its financial statements as follows:

Transaction	Balance Sheet: Cash Asset	+	Noncash Assets	=	Liabilities	+	Contrib. Capital	+	Earned Capital	Income Statement: Revenues	−	Expenses	=	Net Income
Accrue $10,000 in wages expense				=	+10,000 Wages Payable				−10,000 Retained Earnings		−	+10,000 Wages Expense	=	−10,000

WE 10,000
WP 10,000

WE
10,000 |

WP
| 10,000

Mid-Module Review 3

Solution

Transaction	Balance Sheet: Cash Asset	+	Noncash Assets	=	Liabilities	+	Contrib. Capital	+	Earned Capital	Income Statement: Revenues	−	Expenses	=	Net Income
Jan 31: Accrue $26 interest expense*				=	+26 Interest Payable				−26 Retained Earnings		−	+26 Interest Expense	=	−26

IE 26
IP 26

IE
26 |

IP
| 26

*Accrued interest = $10,000 × 0.06 × 16/365 = $26.

Module-End Review

Solution

1.

Issue price for $300,000, 15-year bonds that pay 10% interest semiannually, discounted at 8%:

Present value of principal payment ($300,000 × 0.30832)	$ 92,496
Present value of semiannual interest payments ($15,000 × 17.29203)	259,380
Issue price of bonds	$351,876

Calculator
N = 30
I/Yr = 4
PMT = −15,000
FV = −300,000
PV = 351,876.10

Excel
= PV(rate,nper, pmt,[fv],[type])
= PV(4%, 30, −15000, −300000, 0)
= 351,876.10

2.

Transaction	Balance Sheet: Cash Asset	+	Noncash Assets	=	Liabilities	+	Contrib. Capital	+	Earned Capital	Income Statement: Revenues	−	Expenses	=	Net Income
January 1: Issue 10% bonds	+351,876 Cash			=	+351,876 Long-Term Debt						−		=	
June 30: Pay interest and amortize bond premium[1]	−15,000 Cash			=	−925 Long-Term Debt				−14,075 Retained Earnings		−	+14,075 Interest Expense	=	−14,075
December 31: Pay interest and amortize bond premium[2]	−15,000 Cash			=	−962 Long-Term Debt				−14,038 Retained Earnings		−	+14,038 Interest Expense	=	−14,038

Cash 351,876
LTD 351,876

Cash
351,876 |

LTD
| 351,876

IE 14,075
LTD 925
Cash 15,000

IE
14,075 |

LTD
925 |

Cash
| 15,000

IE 14,038
LTD 962
Cash 15,000

IE
14,038 |

LTD
962 |

Cash
| 15,000

[1] $300,000 × 0.10 × 6/12 = $15,000 cash payment; 0.04 × $351,876 = $14,075 interest expense; the difference of $925, is the bond premium amortization, which reduces the net bond carrying amount.

[2] 0.04 × ($351,876 − $925) = $14,038 interest expense. The difference between this amount and the $15,000 cash payment ($962) is the premium amortization, which reduces the net bond carrying amount.

Module

8 Reporting and Analyzing Owner Financing

Learning Objectives

LO1 Describe and illustrate accounting for contributed capital, including stock sales and repurchases, and equity-based compensation. (p. 8-4)

LO2 Explain and illustrate accounting for earned capital, including cash dividends, stock dividends, and comprehensive income. (p. 8-15)

LO3 Describe accounting for equity carve-outs and convertible debt. (p. 8-24)

IBM Corporation

IBM creates value for clients and solves business problems through integrated solutions that leverage information technology and deep knowledge of business processes. IBM solutions typically create value by reducing a client's operational costs or by enabling new capabilities that generate revenue. These solutions draw from an industry leading portfolio of consulting, delivery and implementation services, enterprise software, systems and financing. In its transformation from a hardware company to a consulting company, IBM shifted its business mix, exited certain segments and increased its presence in higher-profit lines of business such as services and software. As part of this shift, the company acquired more than 140 companies since 2000, complementing and scaling its portfolio of products and offerings. To capture the opportunities arising from global market trends, IBM is focused on four key growth initiatives: *Smarter Planet*, *Growth Markets*, *Business Analytics*, and *Optimization and Cloud Computing*. Each initiative represents a significant growth opportunity with attractive profit margins for IBM.

The company's business model is built to support two principal goals: (1) helping clients to become more innovative, efficient and competitive through the application of business insight and IT solutions; and (2) providing long-term value to stockholders. The company's global capabilities include services, software, systems, fundamental research and related financing. The company's major operations consist of five business segments: *Global Technology Services* and *Global Business Services*, which the company collectively calls Global Services, and the three remaining being *Software*, *Systems and Technology*, and *Global Financing*.

IBM's R&D operations differentiate the company from its competitors. IBM annually invests over $6 billion for R&D, focusing on high-growth, high-value opportunities. IBM Research works with clients and the company's business units through 12 global labs that focus on near-term and mid-term innovations. It contributes many new technologies to IBM's portfolio every year and helps clients address their most difficult challenges. In 2012, IBM was awarded more U.S. patents than any other company for the 20th consecutive year. IBM's 6,478 patents in 2012 included inventions that will enable fundamental advancements in analytics, big data, cyber security, cloud, mobile, social networking and software defined environments, as well as industry solutions for retail, banking, healthcare and transportation.

Courtesy of Shutterstock

The value IBM creates for its stockholders lies not in plant assets, such as land and buildings, but in the knowledge capital of its employees. This module considers how stockholders' investment is accounted for on a company's financial statements. We consider common stock features, stock options, share issuances, share repurchases, and dividend payments.

IBM has one class of stock (and its price behavior over the recent five years is shown below). Of the 4.7 billion shares that have been authorized for issuance, 2.2 billion have been issued to date. It also has restricted stock units. This stock is awarded to employees as incentive compensation. This module explains and assesses equity-based compensation.

IBM has repurchased over 1.1 billion shares of its stock at a purchase price of over $123 billion. Many companies routinely repurchase their common stock as it is the best use of excess cash when there exist no better outside investment opportunities. Some companies repurchase their stock to offset the dilutive effect of stock-based compensation programs. This module explains and analyzes stock repurchases. The module also discusses a variety of equity transactions under the general heading of equity carve-outs and convertibles. These transactions include several methods by which companies seek to unlock hidden value for the benefit of their stockholders.

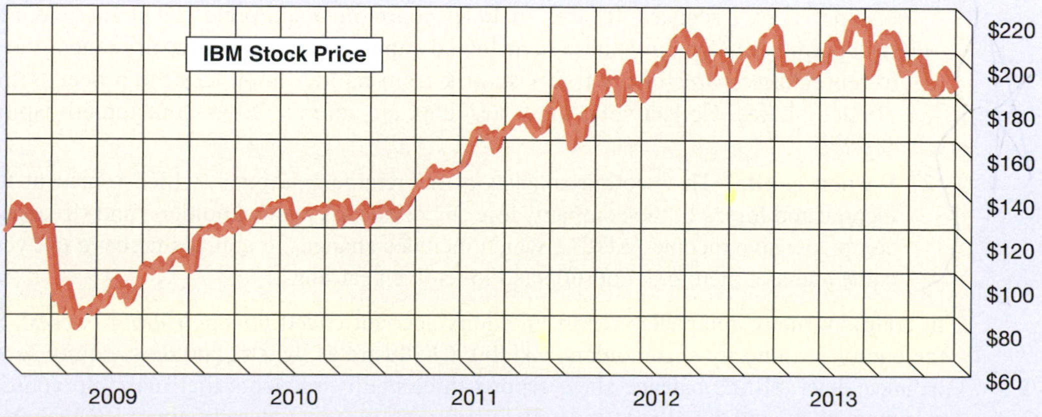

Source: IBM Corporation, Form 2012 10-K and 2012 Annual Report to Stockholders.

MODULE ORGANIZATION

Reporting and Analyzing Owner Financing

Contributed Capital
- Classes of Stock
- Stock Transactions
- Stock-based Compensation

Earned Capital
- Cash Dividends
- Stock Dividends and Splits
- Comprehensive Income
- Foreign Currency Effects
- Noncontrolling Interest

Equity Carve-Outs and Convertibles
- Sell-Offs
- Spin-Offs
- Split-Offs
- Convertible Securities

A company finances its assets through operating cash flows or it taps one or both of the following sources: either it borrows funds or it sells stock to stockholders. On average, companies obtain about half of their external financing from borrowed sources and the other half from stockholders. This module describes the issues relating to stockholders' equity, including the accounting for stock transactions (sales and repurchases of stock, dividends, stock-based compensation, and convertible securities). We also discuss equity carve-outs, a process by which companies can unlock substantial shareholder value via spin-offs and split-offs of business units into separate companies. Finally, we discuss the accumulated other comprehensive income and noncontrolling interest components of stockholders' equity.

When a company issues stock to the public, it records the receipt of cash (or other assets) and an increase in stockholders' equity, representing the stockholders' investment in the company. The increase in cash and equity is equal to the market price of the stock on the issue date multiplied by the number of shares sold.

Like bonds, stockholders' equity is accounted for at *historical cost*. Consequently, the company's financial statements do not reflect fluctuations in the market price of the stock subsequent to its issuance. The company's stock price results from market transactions that involve outside parties and not the company. However, if the company repurchases and/or resells shares of its own stock, the balance sheet will be affected because those transactions involve the company.

There is an important difference between accounting for stockholders' equity and accounting for transactions involving assets and liabilities: *there is never any gain or loss reported on the purchase and sale of a company's own stock or the payment of dividends to its stockholders*. Instead, these "gains and losses" are reflected as increases and decreases in stockholders' equity and do not affect net income (nor earned capital, see below).

The typical balance sheet has two broad categories of stockholders' equity:

1. **Contributed capital** These accounts report the proceeds received by the issuing company from original stock issuances. It often includes common stock, preferred stock, and additional paid-in capital. Netted against these contributed capital accounts is treasury stock, the amounts paid to repurchase shares of the issuer's stock from its investors, less the proceeds from the resale of such shares. Collectively, these accounts are referred to as contributed capital (or *paid-in capital*).
2. **Earned capital** This section consists of (a) retained earnings, which represent the cumulative income and losses of the company, less any dividends to stockholders, and (b) accumulated other comprehensive income (AOCI), which includes changes to equity that have not yet impacted income and are, therefore, not reflected in retained earnings.

In addition, many companies report an equity account called *noncontrolling interest*, which reflects the equity of minority shareholders. Exhibit 8.1 illustrates the stockholders' equity section of **IBM**'s balance sheet. IBM's balance sheet reports three equity accounts that make up contributed capital: common stock, additional paid-in capital, and treasury (repurchased) stock. IBM's balance sheet also reports two earned capital accounts: retained earnings and accumulated other comprehensive income (loss). The final component of IBM's stockholders' equity is the noncontrolling interest account.

EXHIBIT 8.1 Stockholders' Equity from IBM's Balance Sheet

	Stockholders' Equity ($ in millions except per share amounts)	December 31, 2012	December 31, 2011
Contributed Capital	Common stock-par value $.20 per share, and additional paid-in capital Authorized: 4,687,500,000 shares (issued: 2012—2,197,561,159; 2011—2,182,469,838) . . .	$ 50,110	$ 48,129
	Treasury stock at cost (shares: 2012—1,080,193,483; 2011—1,019,287,274).	(123,131)	(110,963)
Earned Capital	Retained earnings.	117,641	104,857
	Accumulated other comprehensive loss	(25,759)	(21,885)
	Total IBM stockholders' equity	18,860	20,138
Noncontrolling Interest	Noncontrolling interests	124	97
	Total equity	$ 18,984	$ 20,236

* We list contributed and earned capital accounts together for learning purposes; in the IBM balance sheet, these accounts are reported in another order.

We discuss contributed capital, earned capital, and noncontrolling interest in order. For each section, we provide a graphic that displays the part of stockholders' equity in the balance sheet impacted by the discussion of that section.

CONTRIBUTED CAPITAL

Contributed capital represents the cumulative cash inflow that the company has received from the sale of various classes of stock, less the net cash that it has paid out to repurchase its stock from the market. The contributed capital of IBM is highlighted in the following graphic.

	Stockholders' Equity ($ in millions except per share amounts)	December 31, 2012	December 31, 2011
Contributed Capital	**Common stock-par value $.20 per share, and additional paid-in capital Authorized: 4,687,500,000 shares (issued: 2012—2,197,561,159; 2011—2,182,469,838)** . . .	**$ 50,110**	**$ 48,129**
	Treasury stock at cost (shares: 2012—1,080,193,483; 2011—1,019,287,274).	**(123,131)**	**(110,963)**
Earned Capital	Retained earnings	117,641	104,857
	Accumulated other comprehensive loss	(25,759)	(21,885)
	Total IBM stockholders' equity.	18,860	20,138
Noncontrolling Interest	Noncontrolling interests	124	97
	Total equity.	$ 18,984	$ 20,236

In 2012, IBM's contributed capital consists of par value and additional paid-in capital for the 2,197,561,159 shares of its common stock that IBM has issued. Its contributed capital is reduced by the cost of treasury stock for the 1,080,193,483 shares that IBM has repurchased.

Classes of Stock

LO1 Describe and illustrate accounting for contributed capital, including stock sales and repurchases, and equity-based compensation.

There are two general classes of stock: preferred and common. The difference between the two lies in the legal rights conferred upon each class.

Preferred Stock

Preferred stock generally has preference, or priority, with respect to common stock. Two usual preferences are:

1. **Dividend preference** Preferred stockholders receive dividends on their shares before common stockholders do. If dividends are not paid in a given year, those dividends are normally forgone. However, some preferred stock contracts include a *cumulative provision* stipulating that any forgone dividends (dividends in *arrears*) must first be paid to preferred stockholders, together with the current year's dividends, before any dividends are paid to common stockholders.
2. **Liquidation preference** If a company fails, its assets are sold (liquidated) and the proceeds are paid to the creditors and stockholders, in that order. Stockholders, therefore, have a greater risk of loss than creditors. Among stockholders, the preferred stockholders receive payment in full before

common stockholders. This liquidation preference makes preferred shares less risky than common shares. Any liquidation payment to preferred shares is normally at par value, although sometimes the liquidation is specified in excess of par; called a *liquidating value*.

To illustrate the typical provisions contained in preferred stock agreements, consider the following stockholders' equity and related footnote disclosure from **Dow Chemical Company** (2012 10-K).

At December 31 (In millions, except share amounts)	2012	2011
Stockholders' equity		
Preferred stock, series A ($1.00 par, $1,000 liquidation preference, 4,000,000 shares)	$ 4,000	$ 4,000
Common stock (authorized 1,500,000,000 shares of $2.50 par value each; issued 2012: 1,203,292,822 shares; 2011: 1,184,562,287 shares)	3,008	2,961
Additional paid-in capital	3,281	2,663
Retained earnings	18,495	19,087
Accumulated other comprehensive loss	(7,516)	(5,996)
Unearned ESOP shares	(391)	(434)
Treasury stock at cost (2012: zero shares; 2011: zero shares)	—	—
The Dow Chemical Company's stockholders' equity	20,877	22,281
Noncontrolling interests	990	1,010
Total equity	21,867	23,291

Cumulative Convertible Perpetual Preferred Stock, Series A Equity securities in the form of Cumulative Convertible Perpetual Preferred Stock, Series A ("preferred series A") were issued on April 1, 2009 to Berkshire Hathaway Inc. in the amount of $3 billion (3 million shares) and the Kuwait Investment Authority in the amount of $1 billion (1 million shares). The Company will pay cumulative dividends on preferred series A at a rate of 8.5 percent per annum in either cash, shares of common stock, or any combination thereof, at the option of the Company. Dividends may be deferred indefinitely, at the Company's option. If deferred, common stock dividends must also be deferred. Any past due and unpaid dividends will accrue additional dividends at a rate of 10 percent per annum, compounded quarterly. If dividends are deferred for any six quarters, the preferred series A shareholders may elect two directors to the Company's Board of Directors until all past due dividends are paid. Ongoing dividends related to preferred series A are $85 million per quarter; no dividends had been deferred at December 31, 2012.

Shareholders of preferred series A may convert all or any portion of their shares, at their option, at any time, into shares of the Company's common stock at an initial conversion rate of 24.2010 shares of common stock for each share of preferred series A. Under certain circumstances, the Company will be required to adjust the conversion rate. On or after the fifth anniversary of the issuance date, if the common stock price exceeds $53.72 per share for any 20 trading days in a consecutive 30-day window, the Company may, at its option, at any time, in whole or in part, convert preferred series A into common stock at the then applicable conversion rate. Upon conversion, accrued and unpaid dividends will be payable, at the option of the Company, in either cash, shares of common stock, or any combination thereof.

Following are several important features of Dow Chemical Company's convertible preferred stock:

- Preferred stock is typically reported before common stock to indicate that these stockholders will receive payments (dividends or payments if the company is liquidated) before common stockholders.
- Holders of convertible preferred stock are entitled to dividends equal to 8.5% of the $1 par value per share; during 2012, the company paid $340 million dividends ($85 million per quarter) on preferred shares.
- Holders of convertible preferred stock have a liquidation preference of $1,000. This means that if Dow Chemical ceases operations and liquidates, preferred stockholders receive $1,000 per share before common stockholders receive a payment.

- Each share of convertible preferred stock is convertible into 24.201 shares of common stock at the discretion of the stockholder. Upon conversion, the preferred stockholder receives 24.201 common shares for each preferred share. Subsequent to conversion, the stockholder no longer receives preferred dividends of $0.085 per share and loses the liquidation preference of $1,000. Instead, the stockholder is able to participate in the wealth creation of the company with unlimited upside potential both for dividends and share price appreciation.
- On or after the fifth anniversary of the issuance date, if the common stock price exceeds $53.72 per share for any 20 trading days in a consecutive 30-day window, Dow Chemical has the option to convert the preferred series A into common stock. This conversion would give preferred stockholders a gain of $300 per share. At a stock price of $53.72, preferred stockholders receive 24.201 shares, which is $1,300 (24.201 × $53.72), a gain of $300 per share over the $1,000 per share purchase price for the preferred stock.

In addition to the sorts of conversion features outlined above, preferred shares sometimes carry a *participation feature* that allows preferred stockholders to share ratably with common stockholders in dividends. The dividend preference over common shares can be a benefit when dividend payments are meager, but a fixed dividend yield limits upside potential if the company performs exceptionally well. A participation feature can overcome this limitation.

IFRS INSIGHT **Preferred Stock Under IFRS**

Under IFRS, preferred stock (called *preference shares*) is classified according to its underlying characteristics. Preference shares are classified as equity if they are not redeemable, or redeemable at the option of the issuer. Preference shares are classified as liabilities if the company must redeem the shares (mandatorily redeemable) or if they are redeemable at the option of the shareholder. Under IFRS, the critical feature that distinguishes a liability is if the company must (or can be required to) deliver cash or some other financial instrument to the liability holder. Accounting for payments to preference shareholders follows from the balance sheet classification: cash paid out is recorded as interest expense or dividends, when the shares are classified as liabilities or equity, respectively. Under US GAAP, preferred stock is classified as equity and cash paid out to preferred shareholders is classified as a dividend.

IFRS

Common Stock

IBM has one class of common stock, Class A, which has the following important characteristics:

- IBM's Class A common stock has a par value of $0.20 per share. **Par value** is an arbitrary amount set by company organizers at the time of company formation and has no relation to, or impact on, the stock's market value. Generally, par value has no substance from a financial reporting perspective (there are some legal implications, which are usually minor). Its main impact is in specifying the allocation of proceeds from stock issuances between the two contributed capital accounts on the balance sheet: common stock and additional paid-in capital, as we describe below.
- IBM has 4,687,500,000 shares of stock that have been **authorized** for issuance. The company cannot issue (sell) more shares than have been authorized. So, if more shares are needed, say for an acquisition or for one of its various stock purchase programs, it must first get additional authorization by its stockholders.
- To date, IBM's management has **issued** (sold) 2,197,561,159 shares of stock. The number of issued shares is a cumulative amount. As of 2011, IBM had issued 2,182,469,838 shares of stock and it issued an additional 15,091,321 (2,197,561,159 − 2,182,469,838) shares in 2012.
- IBM has repurchased 1,080,193,483 shares from its stockholders at a cumulative cost of $123,131 million. These shares are currently held in the company's treasury, hence the name treasury stock. These shares neither have voting rights nor do they receive dividends.
- The number of **outstanding** shares is equal to the issued shares less treasury shares. There were 1,117,367,676 (2,197,561,159 − 1,080,193,483) shares outstanding at the end of 2012.

Accounting for Stock Transactions

We analyze the accounting for stock transactions in this section, including the accounting for stock issuances and repurchases.

Stock Issuance

Companies issue stock to obtain cash and other assets for use in their business. Stock issuances increase assets (cash) by the issue proceeds: the number of shares sold multiplied by the price of the stock on the issue date. Equity increases by the same amount, which is reflected in contributed capital accounts. If the stock has a par value, the common stock account increases by the number of shares sold multiplied by its par value. The additional paid-in capital account increases for the remainder. Stock can also be issued as "no-par" or as "no-par with a stated value." For no-par stock, the common stock account is increased by the entire proceeds of the sale and no amount is assigned to additional paid-in capital. For no-par stock with a stated value, the stated value is treated just like par value, that is, common stock is increased by the number of shares multiplied by the stated value, and the remainder is assigned to the additional paid-in capital account.

To illustrate, assume that IBM issues 100,000 shares of its $0.20 par value common stock at a market price of $43 cash per share. This stock issuance has the following financial statement effects:

	Balance Sheet									Income Statement				
Transaction	Cash Asset	+	Noncash Assets	=	Liabilities	+	Contrib. Capital	+	Earned Capital	Revenues	−	Expenses	=	Net Income
Issue 100,000 common shares with $0.20 par value for $43 cash per share	+4,300,000			=			+20,000 Common Stock +4,280,000 Additional Paid-In Capital				−		=	

Cash 4,300,000
CS 20,000
APIC 4,280,000

Cash
4,300,000 |

CS
| 20,000

APIC
| 4,280,000

Specifically, the stock issuance affects the financial statements as follows:

1. Cash increases by $4,300,000 (100,000 shares × $43 per share)
2. Common stock increases by the par value of shares sold (100,000 shares × $0.20 par value = $20,000)
3. Additional paid-in capital increases by the $4,280,000 difference between the issue proceeds and par value ($4,300,000 − $20,000)

Once shares are issued, they are traded in the open market among investors. The proceeds of those sales and their associated gains and losses, as well as fluctuations in the company's stock price subsequent to issuance, do not affect the issuing company and are not recorded in its accounting records.

Refer again to the following report of common stock on IBM's balance sheet:

(In millions except for share amounts)	2012	2011
Common stock, par value $0.20 per share, and additional paid-in capital	50,110	48,129
Shares authorized: 4,687,500,000		
Shares issued (2012—2,197,561,159; 2011—2,182,469,838)		

IFRS Alert
Stock terminology can differ between IFRS and GAAP. Under IFRS, common stock is called *share capital* and additional paid-in capital (APIC) is called *share premium*. Despite different terminology, the accounting for these items is identical under both systems.

IBM common stock and additional paid-in capital of $50,110 million, equals the number of shares issued multiplied by the market price of the stock at the time of issue. The $50,110 has two components; common stock at par value (the number of shares issued multiplied by the par value of $0.20 per share) and additional paid-in capital account (the remainder). In this case the credit to common stock at par value is $440 million (2,198 million shares issued × $0.20 par value). The remainder of $49,670 million ($50,110 million − $440 million) is credited to the additional paid-in capital account. Total proceeds of $50,110 million imply that common shares were sold, on average, for $22.80 per share ($50,110 million/2,198 million shares). On December 31, 2012, IBM's stock closed at a price of

$191.55 per share, markedly higher than the average selling price per share of $22.80. Stockholders' equity is carried on the balance sheet at historical cost; price appreciation is not captured by GAAP. With 1,117,367,676 shares outstanding at the end of 2012, IBM's **market capitalization** (or *market cap*) was $214,032 million (1,117 million shares × $191.55). This represents the market value of IBM's equity, which is the value of the company to its stockholders.

RESEARCH INSIGHT **Stock Issuance and Stock Returns**

Research shows that, historically, companies issuing equity securities experience unusually low stock returns for several years following those offerings. Evidence suggests that this poor performance is partly due to overly optimistic estimates of long-term growth for these companies by equity analysts. That optimism causes offering prices to be too high. This over-optimism is most pronounced when the analyst is employed by the brokerage firm that underwrites the stock issue. There is also evidence that companies manage earnings upward prior to an equity offering. This means the observed decrease in returns following an issuance likely reflects the market's negative reaction, on average, to lower earnings, especially if the company fails to meet analysts' forecasts.

Stock Repurchase

IBM has repurchased 1,080 million shares of its common stock for a cumulative cost of $123,131 million. One reason a company repurchases shares is because it believes that the market undervalues them. The logic is that the repurchase sends a favorable signal to the market about the company's financial condition that positively impacts its share price and, thus, allows it to resell those shares for a "gain." Any such gain on resale, however, is *never* reflected in the income statement. Instead, any excess of the resale price over the repurchase price is added to additional paid-in capital. GAAP prohibits companies from reporting gains and losses from stock transactions with their own stockholders.

Another reason companies repurchase shares is to offset the dilutive effects of an employee stock option program. When an employee exercises stock options, the number of shares outstanding increases. These additional shares reduce earnings per share and are, therefore, viewed as *dilutive*. In response, many companies repurchase an equivalent number of shares in a desire to keep outstanding shares constant.

A stock repurchase reduces the size of the company (cash declines and, thus, total assets decline). A repurchase has the opposite financial statement effects from a stock issuance. That is, cash is reduced by the price of the shares repurchased (number of shares repurchased multiplied by the purchase price per share), and stockholders' equity is reduced by the same amount. The reduction in equity is achieved by increasing a contra equity (negative equity) account called **treasury stock**, which reduces stockholders' equity. Thus, when the treasury stock contra equity account increases, total equity decreases.

When the company subsequently reissues treasury stock there is no accounting gain or loss. Instead, the difference between the proceeds received and the original purchase price of the treasury stock is reflected as an increase or decrease to additional paid-in capital.

To illustrate, assume that 3,000 common shares of IBM previously issued for $43 are repurchased for $40. This repurchase has the following financial statement effects:

	Balance Sheet									Income Statement				
Transaction	Cash Asset	+	Noncash Assets	=	Liabil-ities	+	Contrib. Capital	+	Earned Capital	Rev-enues	−	Expen-ses	=	Net Income
Repurchase 3,000 common shares for $40 cash per share	−120,000 Cash			=			−120,000 Treasury Stock				−		=	

TS 120,000
Cash 120,000

TS: 120,000 (debit)
Cash: 120,000 (credit)

Assets (cash) and equity both decrease. Treasury stock (a contra equity account) increases by $120,000, which reduces stockholders' equity by that amount.

Assume that these 3,000 shares are subsequently resold for $42 cash per share. This resale of treasury stock has the following financial statement effects:

Cash 126,000
TS 120,000
APIC 6,000

Cash
126,000 |

TS
| 120,000

APIC
| 6,000

	Balance Sheet									Income Statement				
Transaction	Cash Asset	+	Noncash Assets	=	Liabil-ities	+	Contrib. Capital	+	Earned Capital	Rev-enues	−	Expen-ses	=	Net Income
Reissue 3,000 treasury (common) shares for $42 cash per share	+126,000 Cash			=			+120,000 Treasury Stock +6,000 Additional Paid-In Capital				−		=	

IFRS Alert
Accounting for stock repurchases under IFRS is similar to GAAP except that IFRS provides little guidance on how to allocate the treasury stock to equity accounts. Thus, repurchases can be recorded as an increase to treasury stock, or as a decrease to common stock and APIC (share capital and premium), retained earnings (reserves), or some combination.

Cash assets increase by $126,000 (3,000 shares × $42 per share), the treasury stock account is reduced by the $120,000 cost of the treasury shares issued (thus increasing contributed capital), and the $6,000 excess (3,000 shares × $2 per share) is reported as an increase in additional paid-in capital. (If the reissue price is below the repurchase price, then additional paid-in capital is reduced until it reaches a zero balance, after which retained earnings are reduced.) Again, there is no effect on the income statement as companies are prohibited from reporting gains and losses from repurchases and reissuances of their own stock.

The treasury stock section of IBM's balance sheet is reproduced below:

(In millions, except for share amounts)	2012	2011
Treasury stock, at cost (shares: 2012—1,080,193,483; 2011—1,019,287,274). . .	$(123,131)	$(110,963)

IBM repurchased a cumulative total of 1,080 million shares of common stock for $123,131 million, an average repurchase price of about $114 per share. These shares, while legally owned by IBM, have no voting rights and receive no dividends. Treasury shares can be reissued should IBM need to raise capital or acquire another entity. Treasury shares can also be used to compensate employees and executives. Sometimes, companies "retire" treasury stock. In that event, the treasury stock account is reduced by the cost of the treasury shares retired (thus increasing stockholders' equity) and the common stock account is likewise reduced (thus reducing stockholders' equity by the same amount). When treasury shares are retired, total stockholders' equity remains unchanged.

MANAGERIAL DECISION **You Are the Chief Financial Officer**

As CFO, you believe that your company's stock price is lower than its real value. You are considering various alternatives to increase that price, including the repurchase of company stock in the market. What are some factors you should consider before making your decision? [Answer, p. 8-30]

Stock-Based Compensation

Common stock has been an important component of executive compensation for decades. The general idea follows: If the company executives own stock they will have an incentive to increase its value. This aligns the executives' interests with those of other stockholders. Although the strength of this alignment is the subject of much debate, its logic compels boards of directors of most American companies to use stock-based compensation.

Employee Stock Options

One popular incentive plan is to give an employee the right to purchase common stock at a pre-specified price for a given period of time. This is called a *stock option plan*. Options allow employees to purchase a predetermined number of shares at a fixed price (called the *exercise price* or *strike price*) for a specified period of time. Because there is a good chance of future stock price increases, options are valuable to employees when they receive them, even if the exercise price is exactly equal to the stock's market price the day the options are awarded. The intrinsic value of an option is the difference between the current stock price and the option's strike price. When an option is issued with a strike price equal to the current stock price, which is common practice among U.S. companies, the option has a $0 intrinsic value.

Companies use employee stock options (ESO) as a means to compensate employees and to better align the interests of employees and stockholders. The notion is that employees will work harder to increase their company's stock price when they can benefit directly from future price increases. Because an employee with stock options can purchase stock at a fixed price and resell it at the prevailing (expectedly higher) market price, the options create the possibility of a future gain. Unlike cash compensation, options give employees the same incentives as stockholders—to increase stock price.

Over the past 30 years, use of stock options has skyrocketed and, for many companies, options make up the bulk of executive compensation packages. Despite their popularity, stock options have a downside—they can create incentives for employees to increase stock price at any cost and by any means, including misstating earnings and engaging in transactions whose sole purpose is to inflate stock price. Options can also induce managerial myopia—managers want stock price to increase, at least until they can exercise their options and capture their gains.

To illustrate the accounting for stock options, assume that a company grants an employee 100,000 stock options with a strike price of $26, which will vest over a four-year period. The vesting period is the time over which an employee gains ownership of the shares, commonly over three to seven years. Employees usually acquire ownership ratably over time, such as 1/4 each year over four years, or acquire full (100%) vesting after the vesting period ends, called *cliff vesting*. Under current standards, the company recognizes as compensation expense the fair value of the stock options granted over the employees' service period (generally interpreted as the options' vesting period).

A first step, then, is to determine the "fair value" of the option. Accounting standards do not specify the method companies must use to estimate fair value, but most companies use the *Black-Scholes model* to estimate the value of exchange-traded options. This model, developed by professors Fischer Black and Myron Scholes, has six inputs, two of which are observable (the company's current stock price and the option's strike price). Companies must estimate the other four model inputs: option life, risk-free interest rate, stock price volatility, and dividend payout rate. These six inputs yield an estimate of the option's fair value. It is important we recognize that management selects the model inputs and, thus, can exercise some discretion over the reported fair value. The option's value computed using Black-Scholes increases with the estimated option life, risk-free interest rate, and stock price volatility; it decreases with the estimated dividend payout. (Free online Black-Scholes option calculators abound, which simplifies fair value estimation.) For analysis purposes, we can partly assess the quality of the reported fair values by comparing a company's model inputs to industry standards and to historical measures (of stock price volatility, for example).

Some companies have recently switched from the common Black-Scholes model to a more complicated binomial (or lattice-binomial) valuation method. The basic mathematics of the Black-Scholes and binomial methods are identical, but the binomial method allows companies to insert additional assumptions into Black-Scholes and some claim that this provides a more accurate fair value. It also generally provides a lower fair value estimate than the Black-Scholes model, thus reducing the expense related to the options.

Returning to our example, assume that the Black-Scholes fair value of the 100,000 options granted is $1,000,000. Thus, the company records fair value compensation expense of $250,000 each year (fair value of $1,000,000 spread over the four-year vesting period) and its additional paid-in capital increases by $250,000 each year (or $1,000,000 over the four years). Two points are worth noting. First, the company expenses the entire fair value of the options granted ($1,000,000) regardless of whether the employee actually exercises the options. Second, subsequent changes in the options' value are *not* recognized in financial statements. Thus, the stock option expense and the increase to additional paid-in capital reflect the ESO fair value measured at the grant date.

As with any expense, there are tax consequences to stock option expense. That is, net income is affected on an after-tax basis—each dollar of expense is offset by a reduction in tax expense. Granting stock options creates a book-tax timing difference because the expense is recognized in the income statement at the grant date but is deductible for income tax purposes at the exercise date (see Module 5 for more details about book-tax timing differences). The general approach is that a deferred tax asset is recorded at the statutory rate for this timing difference. This difference reverses when the options are exercised. (Most companies grant *nonqualified stock options* (NQSOs), which are taxed like other compensation but *not* until the options are exercised; when NQSOs are exercised, the options' intrinsic value is taxed as ordinary income to the employee and the employer takes a corresponding tax deduction for the intrinsic value.)

Continuing with our example, the company reports a deferred tax asset to recognize the future tax deduction of the compensation payment. Specifically, the company reports a deferred tax benefit of $87,500 ($250,000 × 0.35) in each of the four years of the vesting period to reflect the expected reduction in future tax liability when the options are exercised. Thus, the after-tax stock option compensation expense is $162,500 (computed as $250,000 − $87,500). Each year, the company increases the deferred tax asset account (on the balance sheet) by $87,500. The balance grows until the fourth year when the deferred tax asset balance is $350,000. When the employee exercises the options and the company realizes the tax benefits, the company reduces taxes payable and reverses the deferred tax asset previously set up.[1] The financial statement effects template would record these transactions as follows in each of the four years of the vesting period.

Journal entries and T-accounts	Transaction	Balance Sheet: Cash Asset	+ Noncash Assets	= Liabilities	+ Contrib. Capital	+ Earned Capital	Income Statement: Revenues	− Expenses	= Net Income
WE 250,000 DTA 87,500 TE 87,500 APIC 250,000 WE: 250,000 (Dr) DTA: 87,500 (Dr) TE: 87,500 (Cr) APIC: 250,000 (Cr)	Years 1,2,3,4: Grant 100,000 stock options with fair value of $10 per share, vesting over 4 years		+87,500 Deferred Tax Asset		+250,000 Additional Paid-In Capital	−162,500 Retained Earnings		+250,000 Wages Expense −87,500 Tax Expense	−162,500 Net Income
Cash 2,600,000 APIC 2,600,000 Cash: 2,600,000 (Dr) APIC: 2,600,000 (Cr)	At exercise: 100,000 stock options exercised at a $26 exercise price	+2,600,000 Cash			+2,600,000 Additional Paid-In Capital				
TP 350,000 DTA 350,000 TP: 350,000 (Dr) DTA: 350,000 (Cr)	At exercise: Tax effect of the exercised stock options		−350,000 Deferred Tax Asset	−350,000 Taxes Payable					

IBM's following footnote discloses many details of its stock option activities.

Stock options are awards which allow the employee to purchase shares of the company's stock at a fixed price. Stock options are granted at an exercise price equal to the company's average high and low stock price on the date of grant. These awards, which generally vest 25 percent per year, are fully vested four years from the date of grant and have a contractual term of 10 years. The company estimates the fair value of stock options at the date of grant using the Black-Scholes valuation model. Key inputs and assumptions used to estimate the fair value of stock options include the grant price of the award, the expected option term, volatility of the company's stock, the risk-free rate and the company's dividend yield. Estimates of fair value are not intended to predict actual future events or the value ultimately realized by employees who receive equity awards, and subsequent events are not indicative of the reasonableness of the original estimates of fair value made by the company.

During the years ended December 31, 2012, 2011 and 2010, the company did not grant stock options . . . In lieu of stock options, the company currently grants its employees stock awards. These awards are made in the form of Restricted Stock Units (RSUs), including Retention Restricted Stock Units (RRSUs), or Performance Share Units (PSUs). The following table summarizes option activity under the Plans during the years ended December 31, 2012, 2011 and 2010.

continued

[1] The tax benefit the company receives is based on the options' intrinsic value (current stock price less strike price) on the exercise date. Often, the exercise-date intrinsic value is greater than the grant-date fair value. Recall that deferred taxes are recorded based on grant-date fair value. Thus, the tax benefit received is often larger than the deferred tax asset on the company's balance sheet. In that case, any tax benefit in excess of the deferred tax asset is included in additional paid-in capital and not in net income. The excess tax benefit is classified as cash from financing activities on the statement of cash flows.

	2012		2011		2010	
	Weighted-Average Exercise Price	Number of Shares Under Option	Weighted-Average Exercise Price	Number of Shares Under Option	Weighted-Average Exercise Price	Number of Shares Under Option
Balance at January 1	$90	20,662,322	$ 94	39,197,728	$ 98	73,210,457
Options exercised	86	(9,080,170)	98	(18,144,309)	101	(33,078,316)
Options canceled/expired	75	(192,431)	107	(391,097)	108	(934,413)
Balance at December 31	$94	11,389,721	$ 90	20,662,322	$ 94	39,197,728
Exercisable at December 31	$94	11,389,721	$ 90	20,662,322	$ 94	39,197,728

Exercises of Employee Stock Options The total intrinsic value of options exercised during the years ended December 31, 2012, 2011 and 2010 was $1,005 million, $1,269 million and $1,072 million, respectively. The total cash received from employees as a result of employee stock option exercises for the years ended December 31, 2012, 2011 and 2010 was approximately $785 million, $1,786 million and $3,347 million, respectively. In connection with these exercises, the tax benefits realized by the company for the years ended December 31, 2012, 2011 and 2010 were $341 million, $412 million and $351 million, respectively.

IBM reports that it no longer grants stock options and, instead, compensates employees with Restricted Stock units (described below). During 2012, employees exercised 9,080,170 stock options at an average exercise price of $86. This yielded total cash to IBM of about $781 million. The intrinsic value of $1,005 million is the benefit employees received when they exercised their options. (The average stock price for IBM shares during 2012 was about $200, which compared to the exercise price of $86 meant that employees received a benefit of about $114 per share.) IBM deducted the intrinsic value of $1,005 million on its 2012 tax return and realized a tax benefit of $341 million. The number of outstanding options at the end of 2012 was 11,389,721, all of which were exercisable. (Recall that outstanding options affect the company's diluted EPS calculation, see Module 5.)

Option grants and option exercises both affect the statement of cash flows. At grant, there is no cash inflow or outflow. However, the noncash stock option compensation expense is added back as a reconciling item in the operating section of the statement of cash flows (indirect method). IBM reported an add-back on its 2012 statement of cash flows of $688 million relating to stock-based compensation.

An interesting, often underappreciated, fact is that stock option expense pervades the income statement. Below is a footnote from Cisco System's 2012 10-K that details the allocation of its stock option expense to cost of sales, research and development, sales and marketing expenses, and general and administrative expenses.

The following table presents share-based compensation expense (in millions):

Years Ended	July 28, 2012	July 30, 2011	July 31, 2010
Cost of sales—product	$ 53	$ 61	$ 57
Cost of sales—service	156	177	164
Share-based compensation expense in cost of sales	209	238	221
Research and development	401	481	450
Sales and marketing	588	651	602
General and administrative	203	250	244
Share-based compensation expense in operating expenses	1,192	1,382	1,296
Total share-based compensation expense	$1,401	$1,620	$1,517

Restricted Stock and Restricted Stock Units

Many companies, including IBM, compensate employees with restricted stock instead of with stock options. Increasingly, firms have moved away from stock options in favor of restricted stock, also called nonvested stock, as compensation for several reasons. First, stock options were seen as creating excess compensation during recent stock-market booms. Second, stock options can create incentives for managers to take on excessive firm risk because the value of an option increases with firm risk. Restricted stock does not create such severe risk-taking incentives. Third, there are certain tax advantages to restricted stock vis-á-vis stock options. Under a restricted stock plan, the company transfers shares to the employee, but the shares are restricted in that they cannot be sold until the end of a vesting period.

Restricted stock units differ from restricted stock in two key ways: first, the company does not distribute shares of stock to employees until certain conditions are met; and second, the number of shares ultimately given to employees is typically a function of their performance relative to specified targets. IBM describes its restricted stock unit plan as follows:

Restricted stock unit awards RSUs are stock awards granted to employees that entitle the holder to shares of common stock as the award vests, typically over a one- to five-year period . . . The fair value of RSUs granted during the years ended December 31, 2012, 2011 and 2010 was $486 million, $803 million and $421 million, respectively. The total fair value of RSUs vested and released during the years ended December 31, 2012, 2011 and 2010 was $509 million, $373 million and $503 million, respectively. As of December 31, 2012, 2011 and 2010, there was $938 million, $1,021 million and $865 million, respectively, of unrecognized compensation cost related to nonvested RSUs. The table below summarizes RSU activity under the Plan during the years ended December 31, 2012, 2011 and 2010.

	2012		2011		2010	
	Weighted-Average Grant Price	Number of Units	Weighted-Average Grant Price	Number of Units	Weighted-Average Grant Price	Number of Units
Balance at January 1	$129	12,218,601	$110	11,196,446	$102	13,405,654
RSUs granted.	184	2,635,772	154	5,196,802	122	3,459,303
RSUs released	117	(4,338,787)	106	(3,508,700)	98	(5,102,951)
RSUs canceled/forfeited	139	(674,125)	122	(665,947)	105	(565,560)
Balance at December 31 . . .	$148	9,841,461	$129	12,218,601	$110	11,196,446

The accounting for restricted stock and restricted stock units is similar to that which we describe for stock options. Specifically, compensation expense is recognized at an amount equal to the value of the shares given to employees as those shares are earned. The consequent decline in retained earnings is offset by an increase in paid-in capital. Stockholders' equity is, therefore, unaffected.

Accounting for restricted stock is illustrated in the following template:

DC 2.6 mil.
APIC 2.6 mil.
DC
2.6 mil. |
APIC
| 2.6 mil.

WE 650,000
TP 227,500
DC 650,000
TE 227,500
WE
650,000 |
TP
227,500 |
DC
| 650,000
TE
| 227,500

Transaction	Cash Asset	+	Noncash Assets	=	Liabilities	+	Contrib. Capital	+	Earned Capital	Revenues	−	Expenses	=	Net Income
	Balance Sheet									Income Statement				
Year 1: Company issues 100,000 shares of restricted stock with a market value of $26 per share, vesting ratably over 4 years				=			+2,600,000 Additional Paid-In Capital −2,600,000 Deferred Compensation				−		=	
Years 1,2,3,4: Record compensation expense for year				=	−227,500 Taxes Payable		+650,000 Deferred Compensation		−422,500 Retained Earnings		−	+650,000 Wages Expense −227,500 Tax Expense	=	−422,500 Net Income

The company records the restricted stock grants as a share issuance exactly as if the shares were sold. That is, the common stock account increases by the par value of the shares if any, and additional paid-in capital increases for the remainder of the share value. However, instead of cash received, the company records a deferred compensation (contra equity) account for the value of the shares that have not yet been issued. This reduces equity. Thus, granting restricted shares leaves the total dollar amount of equity unaffected.

Subsequently, the value of shares given to employees is treated as compensation expense and recorded over the vesting period. Each year, the deferred compensation account is reduced by the vested shares and wage expense is recorded, thus reducing retained earnings. Total equity is unaffected by this transaction as the reduction of the deferred compensation contra equity account (thereby increasing stockholders' equity) is exactly offset by the decrease in retained earnings. The remaining deferred compensation account decreases total stockholders' equity until the end of the vesting period when the total restricted stock grant has been recognized as wage expense. Equity is, therefore, never increased when restricted stock is issued.

We see differences when comparing the financial statement effects of the restricted stock example and stock option example from earlier in the module. The first difference is that while the fair value is expensed for each, the numbers differ markedly because the fair value of a share and the fair value of an option were vastly different when each was "granted" to the employee. The company expensed $26 per share for the restricted stock (over the four-year vesting period) but only $10 per share for the stock options. In practice, companies grant fewer restricted shares than they do options. For example, the company might have granted one share of restricted stock in lieu of three stock options, in which case, the accounting outcomes would have been about the same. A second difference concerns the total amount added to stockholders' equity. For restricted stock it is the fair value of the stock at the grant date ($26 per share) but for the option it is $36 per share—the sum of the fair value of the option at grant date ($10) plus the cash received from the employee at exercise ($26). A third difference relates to taxes. For both restricted stock and stock options, the company can claim a deduction for tax purposes as the stock is transferred to the employee (that is, as the restricted stock vests or as the stock options are exercised). In the case above, the restricted stock vests "ratably" over the four-year vesting period. Thus, the tax deduction occurs in the same year as the compensation expense is recorded, so no deferred taxes arise. If, instead, the restricted stock vested entirely in year 4, the company would have recorded a deferred tax asset of $227,500 each year ($2,600,000 × 35% = $910,000 total, recorded over four years). The deferred tax asset would have been removed from the balance sheet in year 4 when the tax deduction occurred.

MID-MODULE REVIEW 1

Part 1 Assume that Accenture (ACN) reported the following transactions relating to its stock accounts in 2012.

Jan 15 Issued 10,000 shares of $5 par value common stock at $17 cash per share.
Mar 31 Purchased 2,000 shares of its own common stock at $15 cash per share.
June 25 Reissued 1,000 shares of its treasury stock at $20 cash per share.

Use the financial statement effects template to identify the effects of these stock transactions.

Part 2 Accenture reports the following table in its 10-K, which is related to its stock compensation plan.

	Number of Options	Weighted Average Exercise Price	Weighted Average Remaining Contractual Term (In Years)	Aggregate Intrinsic Value
Options outstanding as of August 31, 2011...	8,095,463	$23.96	3.1	$242,116
Granted...	—	—		
Exercised ...	(2,218,602)	22.56		
Forfeited ...	(40,199)	24.42		
Options outstanding as of August 31, 2012...	5,836,662	24.49	2.3	216,291
Options exercisable as of August 31, 2012...	5,715,100	24.32	2.2	212,750
Options exercisable as of August 31, 2011...	7,902,845	23.79	3.0	237,690
Options exercisable as of August 31, 2010...	20,386,549	19.42	2.5	351,374

Required

a. Explain the terms "Granted," "Exercised," and "Forfeited." What is the meaning of "Weighted Average Exercise Price"?

b. Explain how the compensation cost related to the options above is recognized in financial statements.

The solution is on page 8-52.

EARNED CAPITAL

LO2 Explain and illustrate accounting for earned capital, including cash dividends, stock dividends, and comprehensive income.

We now turn to the earned capital portion of stockholders' equity. Earned capital represents the cumulative profit that the company has retained. Recall that earned capital increases each period by income earned and decreases by any losses incurred. Earned capital also decreases by dividends paid to shareholders. Not all dividends are paid in the form of cash. Companies can pay dividends in many forms, including property (land, for example) or additional shares of stock. We cover both cash and stock dividends in this section. Earned capital also includes the positive or negative effects of accumulated other comprehensive income (AOCI). The earned capital of IBM is highlighted in the following graphic.

	Stockholders' Equity ($ in millions except per share amounts)	December 31, 2012	December 31, 2011
Contributed Capital	Common stock-par value $.20 per share, and additional paid-in capital Authorized: 4,687,500,000 shares (issued: 2012—2,197,561,159; 2011—2,182,469,838)	$ 50,110	$ 48,129
	Treasury stock at cost (shares: 2012—1,080,193,483; 2011—1,019,287,274)	(123,131)	(110,963)
Earned Capital	**Retained earnings**	**117,641**	**104,857**
	Accumulated other comprehensive loss	**(25,759)**	**(21,885)**
	Total IBM stockholders' equity	18,860	20,138
Noncontrolling Interest	Noncontrolling interests	124	97
	Total equity	$ 18,984	$ 20,236

* We list contributed and earned capital accounts together for learning purposes; in the IBM balance sheet, these accounts are reported in another order.

Cash Dividends

Many companies, but not all, pay dividends. Their reasons for dividend payments are varied. Most dividends are paid in cash on a quarterly basis. IBM makes the following disclosure relating to dividends in its 2012 10-K:

> **Dividend** In 2012, the company continued to focus its cash utilization on returning value to shareholders including $3.8 billion in dividends and $10.5 billion in net stock transactions, including the common stock repurchase program. In the second quarter of 2012, the Board of Directors increased the company's quarterly common stock dividend from $0.75 to $0.85 per share.

Outsiders closely monitor dividend payments. It is generally perceived that the level of dividend payments is related to the company's expected long-term recurring income. Accordingly, dividend increases are usually viewed as positive signals about future performance and are accompanied by stock price increases. By that logic, companies rarely reduce their dividends unless absolutely necessary because dividend reductions are often met with substantial stock price declines.

IFRS Alert The dividend payout ratio is called "dividend cover" in some IFRS countries.

Two common metrics that analysts use to assess a company's dividends are dividend payout and dividend yield. These ratios follow:

$$\textbf{Dividend payout} = \frac{\textbf{Dividends}}{\textbf{Net income attributable to controlling interest}}$$

Dividend payout can be computed with either total dividends and net income or with per share values. This ratio measures the proportion of net income paid out to stockholders or alternatively, provides an idea of how much earnings the company generated to support the normal dividend payments. More mature companies tend to have a higher payout ratio because they have fewer investment opportunities that require retained cash. For IBM, its 2012 dividend payout was 22.72%, computed as \$3,773 million/\$16,604 million.

$$\textbf{Dividend yield} = \frac{\textbf{Dividends per share}}{\textbf{Current share price}}$$

Dividend yield is typically computed with per share values. The ratio measures the cash return to stockholders given the cash investment. Of course, the other way to earn a return is via stock price appreciation, but dividend yield reflects only the one-year cash return. During 2012, dividends per share for IBM were \$0.75 + (3 × \$0.85) = \$3.30 and year-end stock price was \$191.55. Therefore, IBM's 2012 dividend yield was 1.72%, computed as \$3.30/\$191.55.

Financial Effects of Cash Dividends

Cash dividends reduce both cash and retained earnings by the amount of the cash dividends paid. To illustrate, assume that IBM declares and pays cash dividends in the amount of \$10 million. The financial statement effects of this cash dividend payment are as follows:

	Balance Sheet									Income Statement				
Transaction	**Cash Asset**	+	**Noncash Assets**	=	**Liabilities**	+	**Contrib. Capital**	+	**Earned Capital**	**Revenues**	−	**Expenses**	=	**Net Income**
Payment of \$10 million in cash dividends	−10 mil. Cash			=					−10 mil. Retained Earnings		−		=	

RE 10 mil.
Cash 10 mil.

RE	
10 mil.	

Cash	
	10 mil.

Dividend payments do not affect net income. They directly reduce retained earnings and bypass the income statement.

Dividends on preferred stock have priority over those on common stock, including unpaid prior years' preferred dividends (called *dividends in arrears*) when preferred stock is cumulative. To illustrate, assume that a company has 15,000 shares of \$50 par value, 8% preferred stock outstanding; assume that the preferred stock is cumulative, which means that any unpaid dividends cumulate and must be paid before common dividends. The company also has 50,000 shares of \$5 par value common stock outstanding. During its first three years in business, assume that the company declares \$20,000 dividends in the first year, \$260,000 of dividends in the second year, and \$60,000 of dividends in the third year. Cash dividends paid to each class of stock in each of the three years follows:

	Preferred Stock	Common Stock
Year 1—\$20,000 cash dividends paid		
Current-year dividend (15,000 shares × \$50 par × 8%; but only \$20,000 paid, leaving \$40,000 in arrears)	\$20,000	
Balance to common		\$ 0
Year 2—\$260,000 cash dividends paid		
Dividends in arrears from Year 1 ([15,000 shares × \$50 par × 8%] − \$20,000)	40,000	
Current-year dividend (15,000 shares × \$50 par × 8%)	60,000	
Balance to common		160,000
Year 3—\$60,000 cash dividends paid		
Current-year dividend (15,000 shares × \$50 par × 8%)	60,000	
Balance to common		0

MID-MODULE REVIEW 2

Assume that Accenture (ACN) has outstanding 10,000 shares of $100 par value, 5% preferred stock and 50,000 shares of $5 par value common stock. During its first three years in business, assume that Accenture declared no dividends in the first year, $300,000 of cash dividends in the second year, and $80,000 of cash dividends in the third year.

a. If preferred stock is cumulative, determine the dividends paid to each class of stock for each of the three years.

b. If preferred stock is noncumulative, determine the dividends paid to each class of stock for each of the three years.

The solution is on page 8-53.

Stock Dividends and Splits

Dividends need not be paid in cash. Many companies pay dividends in the form of additional shares of stock. Companies can also distribute additional shares to their stockholders with a stock split. We cover both of these distributions in this section.

Stock Dividends

When dividends are paid in the form of the company's stock, retained earnings are reduced and contributed capital is increased. However, the amount by which retained earnings are reduced depends on the proportion of the outstanding shares distributed to the total outstanding shares on the dividend distribution date. Exhibit 8.2 illustrates two possibilities depending on whether stock dividends are classified as small stock dividends or large stock dividends. The break point between small and large is 20–25% of the outstanding shares. When the number of additional shares issued as a stock dividend is so great that it could materially reduce share price, the transaction is akin to a stock split. The 20–25% guideline is used as a rule of thumb to distinguish material stock price effects.

For *small stock dividends,* retained earnings are reduced by the *market* value of the shares distributed (dividend shares × market price per share), and par value and contributed capital together are increased by the same amount. For *large stock dividends,* retained earnings are reduced by the *par* value of the shares distributed (dividend shares × par value per share), and common stock is increased by the same amount (no change to additional paid-in capital).

EXHIBIT 8.2 Analysis of Stock Dividend Effects

Percentage of Outstanding Shares Distributed	Retained Earnings	Contributed Capital
Less than 20-25% *(small stock dividend treated as a dividend)*	Reduce by **market value** of shares distributed	Common stock increased by: Dividend shares × Par value per share; Additional paid-in capital increased for the balance
More than 20-25% *(large stock dividend treated as a stock split)*	Reduce by **par value** of shares distributed	Common stock increased by: Dividend shares × Par value per share

To illustrate the financial statement effects of stock dividends, assume that BearingPoint has 1 million shares of $5 par common stock outstanding. It then declares a small stock dividend of 15% of the outstanding shares (1,000,000 shares × 15% = 150,000 shares) when the market price of the stock is $30 per share. This small stock dividend has the following financial statement effects:

	Balance Sheet									Income Statement				
Transaction	Cash Asset	+	Noncash Assets	=	Liabil-ities	+	Contrib. Capital	+	Earned Capital	Rev-enues	−	Expen-ses	=	Net Income
Distribute 150,000 shares with a market value of $4.5 mil. as a *small* stock dividend				=			+750,000 Common Stock +3,750,000 Additional Paid-In Capital		−4,500,000 Retained Earnings		−		=	

RE 4.5 mil.
CS 0.75 mil.
APIC 3.75 mil.
RE
4.5 mil. |
CS
| 0.75 mil.
APIC
| 3.75 mil.

The company reduces retained earnings by $4,500,000, which equals the market value of the small stock dividend (150,000 shares × $30 market price per share). The increase in contributed capital is split between the par value of $750,000 (150,000 shares × $5 par value) and additional paid-in capital ($3,750,000). Similar to cash dividend payments, stock dividends, whether large or small, never impact income.

Next, assume that instead, **BearingPoint** declares a large stock dividend of 70% of the 1 million outstanding common ($5 par) shares when the market price of the stock is $30 per share. This large stock dividend is treated like a stock split and has the following financial statement effects:

	Balance Sheet									Income Statement				
Transaction	Cash Asset	+	Noncash Assets	=	Liabil-ities	+	Contrib. Capital	+	Earned Capital	Rev-enues	−	Expen-ses	=	Net Income
Distribute 700,000 shares as a *large* stock dividend				=			+3,500,000 Common Stock		−3,500,000 Retained Earnings		−		=	

RE 3.5 mil.
CS 3.5 mil.
RE
3.5 mil. |
CS
| 3.5 mil.

The company's retained earnings declines by $3,500,000, which equals the par value of the large stock dividend (700,000 shares × $5 par value per share). Common stock is increased by the par value of $3,500,000. There is no effect on additional paid-in capital since large stock dividends are reported at par value.

For both large and small stock dividends, companies are required to show comparable shares outstanding for all prior periods for which earnings per share (EPS) is reported in the statements. The reasoning is that a stock dividend has no effect on the ownership percentage of each common stockholder. As such, to show a dilution in reported EPS would erroneously suggest a decline in profitability when it is simply due to an increase in shares outstanding.

Stock Splits

A stock split is a proportionate distribution of shares and, as such, is similar in substance to a large stock dividend. A typical stock split is 2-for-1, which means that the company distributes one additional share for each share owned by a shareholder. Following the distribution, each investor owns twice as many shares, so that their percentage ownership in the company is unchanged.

A stock split is not a monetary transaction and, as such, there are no financial statement effects. However, companies must disclose the new number of shares outstanding for all periods presented in the financial statements. Further, many states require that the par value of shares be proportionately adjusted as well (for example, halved for a 2-for-1 split).

If state law requires that par value not be reduced for a stock dividend, this event should be described as a *stock split effected in the form of a dividend*. The following disclosure from **TJX Companies, Inc.**'s 2013 10-K provides such an example:

Stock Split in Form of Dividend In February 2012, TJX effected a two-for-one stock split of its common stock in the form of a stock dividend resulting in the issuance of 372 million shares of common stock. The balance sheets and statement of shareholders' equity for fiscal 2012 and prior have been adjusted to retroactively reflect the two-for-one stock split. In addition, all historical per share amounts and references to common stock activity, as well as basic and diluted share amounts utilized in the calculation of earnings per share in this report, have been adjusted to reflect this stock split.

MID-MODULE REVIEW 3

Assume that the stockholders' equity of **Arbitron, Inc.** at December 31, 2012, follows.

5% preferred stock, $100 par value, 10,000 shares authorized; 4,000 shares issued and outstanding	$ 400,000
Common stock, $5 par value, 200,000 shares authorized; 50,000 shares issued and outstanding	250,000
Paid-in capital in excess of par value-Preferred stock	40,000
Paid-in capital in excess of par value-Common stock	300,000
Retained earnings	656,000
Total stockholders' equity	$1,646,000

Use the template to identify the financial statement effects for each of the following transactions that occurred during 2013:

Apr. 1 Declared and issued a 100% stock dividend on all outstanding shares of common stock when the market value of the stock was $11 per share.

Dec. 7 Declared and issued a 3% stock dividend on all outstanding shares of common stock when the market value of the stock was $7 per share.

Dec. 31 Declared and paid a cash dividend of $1.20 per share on all outstanding shares.

The solution is on page 8-53.

Accumulated Other Comprehensive Income

Comprehensive income is a more inclusive notion of company performance than net income. It includes all changes in equity (assets less liabilities) that occur during a period except those resulting from contributions by and distributions to owners. It's important to note that comprehensive income includes both net income and other items, which collectively are called *other comprehensive income*.

Specifically, other comprehensive income includes (and net income excludes) foreign currency translation adjustments, unrealized changes in market values of available-for-sale securities, pension liability adjustments, and changes in market values of certain derivative investments. Comprehensive income, therefore, includes the effects of economic events that are often outside of management's control. Accordingly, some assert that net income measures management's performance, while comprehensive income measures company performance. Each period, net income or loss is added to retained earnings so that the balance sheet maintains a running total of the company's cumulative net income and losses (less any dividends paid out). In the same way, each period, comprehensive income items that are not included in net income (that is, all *other comprehensive income* items) are added to a balance sheet account called Accumulated Other Comprehensive Income (or Accumulated Other Comprehensive Loss if the comprehensive items are losses). This account maintains a running balance of the cumulative differences between net income and comprehensive income.

IBM reports the following components of its accumulated other comprehensive income in its 2012 10-K report:

Accumulated Other Comprehensive Income/(Loss) (net of tax)

($ in millions)	Net Unrealized Gains/(Losses) on Cash Flow Hedges	Foreign Currency Translation Adjustments*	Net Change Retirement-Related Benefit Plans	Net Unrealized Gains/(Losses) on Available-For-Sale Securities	Accumulated Other Comprehensive Income/(Loss)
December 31, 2009	$(481)	$1,836	$(20,297)	$113	$(18,830)
Other comprehensive income before reclassifications	251	643	(1,684)	51	(739)
Amount reclassified from accumulated other comprehensive income	134	0	692	0	826
Total change for the period	385	643	(992)	51	87
December 31, 2010	(96)	2,478	(21,289)	164	(18,743)
Other comprehensive income before reclassifications	(162)	(711)	(3,581)	(7)	(4,461)
Amount reclassified from accumulated other comprehensive income	329	0	1,133	(143)	1,319
Total change for the period	167	(711)	(2,448)	(150)	(3,142)
December 31, 2011	71	1,767	(23,737)	13	(21,885)
Other comprehensive income before reclassifications	5	(34)	(5,164)	16	(5,177)
Amount reclassified from accumulated other comprehensive income	(167)	0	1,495	(25)	1,303
Total change for the period	(161) †	(34)	(3,669)	(9)	(3,874)
December 31, 2012	$ (90)	$1,733	$(27,406)	$ 4	$(25,759)

* Foreign currency translation adjustments are presented gross except for any associated hedges which are presented net of tax.
† IBM subtracts $(167) from $5 to get $(161); we assume this reflects rounding in the underlying numbers.

IBM's 2012 accumulated other comprehensive income (AOCI) includes the four following items that affect stockholders' equity but are not reflected in net income:

1. **Net unrealized gains (losses) on cash flow hedges**, $(90) million. Hedging transactions relate to the company's use of financial instruments (derivatives) to hedge exposure to various risks such as fluctuations in foreign currency exchange rates, commodity prices, and interest rates. This $90 million relates to unrealized losses on cash flow hedges, which we discuss in the appendix to Module 9.
2. **Foreign currency translation adjustments**, $1,733 million. This is the cumulative translation adjustment for the net assets of foreign subsidiaries whose balance sheets are denominated in foreign currencies. A gain implies that the $US has weakened relative to foreign currencies; which means that the subsidiaries' assets denominated in foreign currencies translate to more $US at the end of 2012 than when the assets were originally purchased. We discuss the effects of foreign currency translation adjustments on AOCI in more detail below.
3. **Net change retirement-related benefit plans**, $(27,406) million. This amount relates to unrealized losses on pension investments or to changes in pension-plan assumptions that increase the pension liability. We discuss the accounting for pension plans and other postretirement benefit obligations in Module 10.
4. **Net unrealized gains/(losses) on available-for-sale securities**, $4 million. Unrealized gains and losses on available-for sale securities are not reflected in net income. Instead, they are accumulated in AOCI until the securities are sold. We discuss the accounting for these unrealized gains and losses in Module 9.

We discuss accounting for available-for-sale securities and derivatives in Module 9, pensions in Module 10, and the income statement effects of foreign currency translation adjustments in Module 5. In the next section, we discuss the balance sheet effects of foreign currency translation adjustments, specifically their impact on accumulated other comprehensive income. During 2012, IBM reported other comprehensive loss, net of tax, of $(3,874) million, which is the sum of the changes in each of the four components of AOCI, as shown on the statement above. This other comprehensive loss when added to the AOCI balance of $(21,885) million at the beginning of the year yields the AOCI balance of $(25,759) million at year-end.

Foreign Currency Translation Effects on Accumulated Other Comprehensive Income

Many companies have international transactions denominated in foreign currencies. They might purchase assets in foreign currencies, borrow money in foreign currencies, and transact business with their customers and suppliers in foreign currencies. Other companies might have subsidiaries whose entire balance sheets and income statements are stated in foreign currencies. Financial statements prepared according to U.S. GAAP must be reported in $US. This means that financial statements of foreign subsidiaries must be translated into $US before they are consolidated with those of the U.S. parent company. This translation process can markedly alter both the balance sheet and income statement. We discuss the income statement effects of foreign currency translation in Module 5 and the balance sheet effects in this section.

Consider a U.S. company with a foreign subsidiary that conducts its business in Euros. The subsidiary prepares its financial statements in Euros. Assume that the $US weakens vis-à-vis the Euro during the current period—that is, each Euro can now purchase more $US. When the balance sheet is translated into $US, the assets and liabilities are reported at higher $US than before the $US weakened. This result is shown in accounting equation format in Exhibit 8.3.[2]

EXHIBIT 8.3 Balance Sheet Effects of Changes in U.S. Dollar to Euro Exchange Rates

Currency	Assets	=	Liabilities	+	Equity
$US weakens	Increase	=	Increase	+	Increase
$US strengthens.	Decrease	=	Decrease	+	Decrease

The amount reflected as an increase (decrease) in equity is called a **foreign currency translation adjustment**. The *cumulative* foreign currency translation adjustment is included in accumulated other comprehensive income (or loss) as illustrated above for IBM. Foreign currency translation adjustments are direct adjustments to stockholders' equity; they do not impact reported net income. Because assets are greater than liabilities for solvent companies, the cumulative translation adjustment is positive when the $US weakens and negative when the dollar strengthens.

Referring to IBM's AOCI table on the previous page, the cumulative foreign currency translation is a gain of $1,767 million at the beginning of 2012, which shrinks by $(34) million during the year to yield a cumulative year-end gain of $1,733 million. The $34 million reduction in IBM's equity reflects a strengthening of the $US vis-à-vis the foreign currencies in which IBM transacted in 2012. That is, as the $US strengthened, IBM's foreign assets and liabilities translated into fewer $US at year-end. This decreased IBM's equity (because assets are greater than liabilities for solvent companies). In general, unrealized losses (or gains) remain in AOCI as long as the company owns the foreign subsidiaries to which the losses (or gains) relate. The translation adjustment fluctuates between positive and negative amounts as the value of the $US fluctuates. However, when a subsidiary is sold, any remaining foreign currency translation adjustment (positive or negative) that relates to the subsidiary sold is immediately recognized in current income along with other gains or losses arising from sale of the subsidiary.

NONCONTROLLING INTEREST

Noncontrolling interest represents the equity of noncontrolling (minority) shareholders who only have a claim on the net assets of one or more of the subsidiaries in the consolidated entity. As we discuss in Module 9, if a company acquires a controlling interest in a subsidiary, it must consolidate that

[2] We assume that the company translates the subsidiary's financial statements using the more common **current rate method**, which is required for subsidiaries operating independently from the parent. Under the current rate method, most items in the balance sheet are translated using exchange rates in effect at the period-end consolidation date and the income statement is translated using the average exchange rate for the period. An alternative procedure is the *temporal method,* covered in advanced accounting courses, which uses historical exchange rates for some assets and liabilities.

subsidiary when preparing its financial statements, thus reporting all of the subsidiary's assets and liabilities on the consolidated balance sheet and reporting all of the subsidiary's revenues and expenses in the consolidated income statement. If the company acquires less than 100% of the subsidiary, it must still include 100% of the subsidiary's assets, liabilities, revenues and expenses in its consolidated balance sheet and income statement, but now there are two groups of shareholders that have a claim on the net assets and earnings of the subsidiary company: the parent company and the noncontrolling shareholders (those shareholders who continue to own shares of the subsidiary company).

Consolidated stockholders' equity must now report the equity of these two groups of shareholders and consolidated net income must now be apportioned between the two groups. For Walmart, our focus company in Module 4, the consolidated income statement apportions net income as follows:

Walmart Stores Consolidated Statement of Income ($ millions)	2013
Revenues	$469,162
Expenses	451,406
Consolidated net income	17,756
Less consolidated net income attributable to noncontrolling interest	(757)
Consolidated net income attributable to Walmart	$ 16,999

Net income is apportioned between the portion attributable to the noncontrolling interest and the portion attributable to the parent company's shareholders. Although it can be more complicated, in its simplest form, if the noncontrolling shareholders own 20% of a subsidiary, 20% of the subsidary's net income is attributable to that shareholder group and the balance of 80%, is attributable to the parent's shareholders.

The common stock, additional paid-in capital and retained earnings accounts we see on the consolidated balance sheet represent those of the parent's shareholders. The retained earnings attributable to the parent's shareholders is increased (decreased) by the income (loss) attributable to the parent's shareholders and is decreased by the dividends paid to the parent's shareholders in a reconciliation similar to the following for Walmart:

Walmart Retained Earnings Account ($ millions)	2013
Beginning balance of retained earnings	$68,691
Net income attributable to parent	16,999
Dividends	(5,361)
Other adjustments	(7,351)
Ending balance of retained earnings	$72,978

The equity of the *noncontrolling* interest, however, is only represented by one equity account labeled noncontrolling interest. It is updated similarly to the stockholders' equity for the parent's shareholders, that is, it is increased (decreased) by the income (loss) attributable to the noncontrolling shareholders and is decreased by the dividends paid to the noncontrolling shareholders:

Walmart Noncontrolling Interest Equity Account ($ millions)	2013
Beginning balance (fair value at acquisition date)	$4,446
Net income attributable to noncontrolling interest	684*
Dividends declared and paid to noncontrolling shareholders	0
Other adjustments	265
Ending balance	$5,395

* The remaining $73 million of the $757 million of net income attributable to noncontrolling interest was allocated to the "redeemable noncontrolling interest" and updated that account in the same manner.

Again, although it can be more complicated, if the noncontrolling interest owns 20% of a subsidiary company, the balance in the noncontrolling interest equity account will equal 20% of the stockholders' equity of the subsidiary company. (This is not 20% of the consolidated company, only 20% of the subsidiary company.)

Finally, the noncontrolling interest equity account is reported as a separate line in the consolidated stockholders' equity as follows:

Walmart Consolidated Balance Sheet (partial) Stockholders' Equity (In millions)	2013
Equity	
Common stock	$ 332
Capital in excess of par value	3,620
Retained earnings	72,978
Accumulated other comprehensive income (loss)	(587)
Total Walmart shareholders' equity	76,343
Nonredeemable noncontrolling interest	5,395
Total equity	$81,738

Analysis and Interpretation of Noncontrolling Interest

As we discuss more fully in Module 4, the return on equity (ROE) computation is usually performed from the perspective of the parent company's shareholders. Consequently, the numerator is the net income attributable to the parent company shareholders and the denominator includes only the equity of the parent company's shareholders (excluding noncontrolling interest equity). For Walmart and other companies with noncontrolling interest (NCI), we use the following equation for ROE, where NI_{CI} is the net income attributable to Walmart shareholders (controlling interest) and EQ_{CI} is the equity attributable to the controlling interest, which reflects Walmart's stockholders (we use only year-end CI for simplicity because only one year's balance sheet is shown above):

$$\text{ROE} = \frac{NI_{CI}}{EQ_{CI}} = \frac{\$16{,}999}{\$76{,}343} = 22.3\%$$

Noncontrolling interest is reported as a component of stockholders' equity and represents the claim of the noncontrolling interest to their proportionate share of the net assets and net income *of the subsidiary in which they own stock*. These shareholders do not have a claim on the net assets or income of any other subsidiary or of the parent company. Further, their claim is a residual claim, like that of any other shareholder; that is, they are not entitled to a preference in dividends or payouts in liquidation.

Summary of Stockholders' Equity

The statement of shareholders' equity summarizes the transactions that affect stockholders' equity during the period. This statement reconciles the beginning and ending balances of important stockholders' equity accounts. IBM's statement of stockholders' equity is in Exhibit 8.4.

IBM's statement of stockholders' equity reveals the following key activities for 2012:

1. Net income is credited to the retained earnings account, resulting in an increase of $16,604 million.
2. Comprehensive income includes net income of $16,604 million as well as the changes to the AOCI accounts that we discuss above. During 2012, accumulated other comprehensive income accounts decreased by $(3,874) million. Thus, IBM's 2012 comprehensive income is $12,731 million. (IBM's 10-K includes a $1 rounding discrepancy for this item.)
3. IBM paid cash dividends to its stockholders amounting to $3,773 million in 2012. These dividends reduced retained earnings by that amount.
4. Shares issued are recorded as an increase in common stock (for the par value) and additional paid-in capital (for the excess of the value of the shares issued over the par value). IBM combines common stock and additional paid-in capital accounts into one column for total proceeds. Total increase for 2012 is $1,532 million.

EXHIBIT 8.4 IBM's Statement of Stockholders' Equity

	($ in millions)	Common Stock and Additional Paid-in Capital	Retained Earnings	Treasury Stock	Accumulated Other Comprehensive Income/(Loss)	Total IBM Stockholders' Equity	Non-controlling Interests	Total Equity
	Equity, January 1, 2012	$48,129	$104,857	$(110,963)	$(21,885)	$20,138	$ 97	$20,236
	Net income plus other comprehensive income/(loss)							
1	Net income	—	16,604	—	—	16,604	—	16,604
2	Other comprehensive income/(loss)	—	—	—	(3,874)	(3,874)	—	(3,874)
	Total comprehensive income/(loss)	—	—	—	—	$12,731	—	$12,731
3	Cash dividends declared—common stock	—	(3,773)	—	—	(3,773)	—	(3,773)
4	Common stock issued under employee plans (15,091,320 shares)	1,532	—	—	—	1,532	—	1,532
5	Purchases (2,406,007 shares) and sales (2,746,169 shares) of treasury stock under employee plans—net	—	(48)	(160)	—	(208)	—	(208)
6	Other treasury shares purchased, not retired (61,246,371 shares)	—	—	(12,008)	—	(12,008)	—	(12,008)
	Change in other equity	448	—	—	—	448	—	448
	Changes in noncontrolling interests	—	—	—	—	—	27	27
	Equity, December 31, 2012	**$50,110**	**$117,641**	**$(123,131)**	**$(25,759)**	**$18,860**	**$124**	**$18,984**

Amounts may not add due to rounding.

5 This entry includes both purchases and reissuances of treasury stock. The $(48) million reduction of retained earnings arises when treasury stock is reissued at a price that is less than the cost at which it was acquired.

6 The cost of shares repurchased is recorded as an increase to the treasury stock account. During 2012, IBM had net purchases of treasury shares at a total cost of $12,008 million.

One final point: the financial press sometimes refers to a measure called **book value per share**. This is the net book value of the company that is available to common shareholders, defined as: stockholders' equity of the parent's shareholders less preferred stock (and preferred additional paid-in capital) divided by the number of common shares outstanding (issued common shares less treasury shares). IBM's book value per share of its common stock at the end of 2012 is $16.87, computed as: $18,860 million/(2,198 million shares – 1,080 million shares). In contrast, IBM's market price per share ranged from $184.78 to $211.79 in the 4th quarter of 2012. The ratio of the **market price per share** to the book value per share is the market-to-book ratio and for IBM during the 4th quarter of 2012, this ratio is between 11 and 12.

EQUITY CARVE-OUTS AND CONVERTIBLES

LO3 Describe accounting for equity carve-outs and convertible debt.

Corporate divestitures, or **equity carve-outs**, are increasingly common as companies seek to augment shareholder value through partial or total divestiture of operating units. Generally, equity carve-outs are motivated by the notion that consolidated financial statements often obscure the performance of individual business units, thus complicating their evaluation by outsiders. Corporate managers are concerned that this difficulty in assessing the performance of individual business units limits their ability to reach full valuation. Shareholder value is, therefore, not maximized. In response, conglomerates have divested subsidiaries so that the market can individually price them.

Sell-Offs

Equity carve-outs take many forms. The first and simplest form of divestiture is the outright sale of a business unit, called a **sell-off**. In this case, the company sells its equity interest to an unrelated party. The sale is accounted for just like the sale of any other asset. Specifically, any excess (deficit) of cash received over the book value of the business unit sold is recorded as a gain (loss) on the sale.

To illustrate, in 2012, **United Technologies Corporation** sold its **Sundstrand Industrial** businesses for $3.4 billion and recorded a pretax gain on sale of $2.1 billion as disclosed in the following excerpt from its 2012 annual report:

Discontinued Operations In 2012, the UTC Board of Directors approved plans for the divestiture of a number of non-core businesses. . . . On June 29, 2012, management approved a plan for the divestiture of UTC Power. The operating results of Clipper and UTC Power . . . have been reclassified to discontinued operations in our Consolidated Statement of Operations and Consolidated Statement of Cash Flows for all periods presented. The remaining assets and liabilities of these non-core businesses to be sold in the first half of 2013, have been reclassified to Assets held for sale and Liabilities held for sale in our Consolidated Balance Sheet as of December 31, 2012. . . . On December 13, 2012, we completed the sale of the legacy Hamilton Sundstrand Industrial businesses to BC Partners and The Carlyle Group for $3.4 billion. The sale generated a pre-tax gain of approximately $2.1 billion ($0.9 billion after tax) which has been included in discontinued operations in the accompanying Consolidated Statement of Operations.

The financial statement effects of this transaction follow:

- UTC received $3.4 billion in cash, which it reported as cash flows from investing activities in its statement of cash flows.
- The Hamilton Sundstrand Industrial businesses were reported on UTC's balance sheet at $1.3 billion on December 13, 2012, the date of sale.
- UTC's gain on sale equaled the proceeds ($3.4 billion) less the carrying amount of the business sold ($1.3 billion), or $2.1 billion.
- UTC subtracts the gain on sale in computing net cash flows from operating activities to remove the gain from net income; cash proceeds are reported as a cash inflow in the investing section.

Spin-Offs

A **spin-off** is a second form of divestiture. In this case, the parent company distributes the subsidiary shares that it owns as a dividend to its shareholders who, then, own shares in the subsidiary directly rather than through the parent company. In recording this dividend, the parent company reduces retained earnings by the book value of the equity method investment, thereby removing the investment in the subsidiary from the parent's balance sheet.

In 2011, **Beam, Inc.**, formerly known as Fortune Brands, Inc., separated its three business segments. It completed the sale of the golf business (Acushnet Company, maker of Titleist and FootJoy golf products) in July 2011 and the tax-free spin-off of Fortune Brands Home & Security, Inc. (MasterBrand cabinets, Moen faucets, and other companies) in October 2011. As a result of the spin-off, Fortune Brands Home & Security became an independent public company trading under the symbol "FBHS" on the New York Stock Exchange and Beam, Inc., the surviving company, is now a pure play spirits company selling a wide product line of spirits, most notably Jim Beam bourbon. The company trades under the ticker symbol "BEAM." Beam's sale of the FBHS subsidiary is an example of a spin-off, which Beam describes as follows:

In October 2011, Beam completed the Spin-Off of Home & Security by paying a pro rata dividend of one share of common stock, par value $0.01 per share, of Home & Security for each share of common stock, par value $3.125 per share, of the Company outstanding as of 6:00 p.m. New York City time on the record date. The Spin-Off was completed without the payment of any consideration or the exchange of any shares by the Company's stockholders. On October 4, 2011, as a result of the Spin-Off, Home & Security became an independent public company trading under the symbol "FBHS" on the New York Stock Exchange. The Spin-Off was completed pursuant to the Separation and Distribution Agreement between the Company and Home & Security, dated as of September 27, 2011 (the "Separation Agreement"). Under the terms of the Separation Agreement, immediately prior to the effective time of the Spin-Off, Home & Security paid a cash dividend to the Company in the amount of $500 million using the proceeds of a new debt financing arrangement entered into by Home & Security.

Beam treats the distribution of its Fortune Brands Home & Security shares as a dividend, which it reports in the following excerpt from its statement of stockholders' equity.

(In millions)	$2.67 Convertible Preferred Stock	Common Stock	Paid-In Capital	Accumulated Other Comprehensive Income (Loss)	Retained Earnings	Treasury Stock, At Cost	Non-controlling Interests	Total Equity
Balance at December 31, 2010	$4.9	$734.0	$820.2	$(172.0)	$7,499.3	$(3,215.3)	$16.9	$5,688.0
Net income	—	—	—	—	911.4	—	4.1	915.5
Other comprehensive loss	—	—	—	(239.9)	—	—	—	(239.9)
Dividends paid to noncontrolling interests	—	—	—	—	—	—	(0.8)	(0.8)
Dividends	—	—	—	—	(117.8)	—	—	(117.8)
Stock-based compensation	—	—	54.8	—	(3.4)	103.4	—	154.8
Tax benefit on exercise of stock options	—	—	9.2	—	—	—	—	9.2
Conversion of preferred stock	(0.2)	—	(1.8)	—	—	2.0	—	—
Sale of Acushnet Company	—	—	—	—	—	—	(16.6)	(16.6)
Spin-off of Fortune Brands Home & Security, Inc.	—	—	—	107.8	(2,396.9)	—	(3.6)	(2,292.7)
Balance at December 31, 2011	$4.7	$734.0	$882.4	$(304.1)	$5,892.6	$(3,109.9)	$ —	$4,099.7

Prior to the spin-off, Fortune Brands Home & Security subsidiary was reported on Beam's balance sheet as an equity investment with a book value of $2,400.5 million. This amount is removed from Beam's balance sheet when the shares are distributed to Beam's stockholders; $2,396.9 million of that amount is subtracted from Beam's retained earnings for the portion of the dividend relating to its stockholders and $3.6 million is subtracted from noncontrolling interests for the portion relating to the noncontrolling stockholders. Beam also removes all amounts relating to Fortune Brands Home & Security that impacted its accumulated other comprehensive income (a net of $107.8 million, representing a deferred gain). In total, the Fortune Brands Home & Security spin-off reduced Beam's equity by $2,292.7 million.

Split-Offs

The **split-off** is a third form of equity carve-out. In this case, the parent company buys back its own stock using the shares of the subsidiary company instead of cash. After completing this transaction, the subsidiary is an independent publicly traded company.

The parent treats the split-off like any other purchase of treasury stock. As such, the treasury stock account is increased and the equity method investment account is reduced, reflecting the distribution of that asset. The dollar amount recorded for this treasury stock depends on how the distribution is set up. There are two possibilities:

1. **Pro rata distribution**. Shares are distributed to stockholders on a pro rata basis. Namely, a shareholder owning 10% of the outstanding stock of the parent company receives 10% of the shares of the subsidiary. The treasury stock account is increased by the *book value* of the investment in the subsidiary. The accounting is similar to the purchase of treasury stock for cash, except that shares of the subsidiary are paid to shareholders instead of cash.
2. **Non pro rata distribution**. This case is like a tender offer where individual stockholders can accept or reject the distribution. The treasury stock account is recorded at the *market value* of the shares of the subsidiary distributed. Since the investment account can only be reduced by its book value, a gain or loss on distribution is recorded in the income statement for the difference. (The SEC allows companies to record the difference as an adjustment to additional paid-in capital; the usual practice, as might be expected, is for companies to report any gain as part of income.)

Bristol-Myers Squibb's non pro rata split-off of its subsidiary, Mead Johnson, provides an example. This transaction is described in the following excerpt from footnotes to Bristol-Myers' 2009 10-K:

Mead Johnson Nutrition Company Split-off The split-off of the remaining interest in Mead Johnson was completed on December 23, 2009. The split-off was effected through the exchange offer of previously held 170 million shares of Mead Johnson, after converting its Class B common stock to Class A common stock, for 269 million outstanding shares of the Company's stock resulting in a pre-tax gain of $7,275 million, $7,157 million net of taxes. The shares received in connection with the exchange were valued using the closing price on December 23, 2009, of $25.70 and reflected as treasury stock. The gain on the exchange was determined using the sum of the fair value of the shares received plus the net deficit of Mead Johnson attributable to the Company less taxes and other direct expenses related to the transaction, including a tax reserve of $244 million which was established.

From an accounting standpoint, the split-off of Mead Johnson is treated like the purchase of treasury stock, using the stock of Mead Johnson to fund the purchase instead of cash (such as exchanging Mead Johnson stock for Bristol-Myers stock). As a result of the transaction, the treasury stock account on Bristol-Myers' balance sheet increased (became more negative) by $6.9 billion (269 million shares × $25.70 per share), which reduced equity by $6.9 billion. This reduction was offset, however, by the recognition of a gain on the exchange amounting to $7.2 billion after tax. This split-off was affected by a tender offer with Bristol-Myers shareholders. Consequently, it is a non pro rata exchange and is, therefore, valued at market value with a resulting gain. The net effect on equity is minimal, but the income statement reports a substantial gain for that year.

Analysis of Equity Carve-Outs

Sell-offs, spin-offs, and split-offs all involve the divestiture of an operating segment. Although they are one-time occurrences, they can result in substantial gains that can markedly alter the income statement and balance sheet. Consequently, we need to interpret them carefully. This involves learning as many details about the carve-out as possible from the annual report, the Management Discussion and Analysis, and other publicly available information.

Following an equity carve-out, the parent company loses the cash flows (positive or negative) of the divested business unit. As such, the divestiture should be treated like any other discontinued operation. Any recognized gain or loss from divestiture is treated as a nonoperating activity. The sale price of the divested unit reflects the valuation of *future expected* cash flows by the purchaser and is best viewed as a nonoperating activity. Income (and cash flows) of the divested unit up to the date of sale, however, is part of operations, although discontinued operations are typically segregated.

MID-MODULE REVIEW 4

Assume that BearingPoint announced the split-off of its Canadian subsidiary. BearingPoint reported a gain from the split-off. (1) Describe the accounting for a split-off. (2) Why was BearingPoint able to report a gain on this transaction?

The solution is on page 8-54.

Convertible Securities

Convertible securities are debt and equity securities that provide the holder with an option to convert those securities into other securities. In this section, we consider two specific types of convertibles: convertible debt securities, where debt is converted to common stock, and convertible preferred securities, where preferred stock is converted to common stock.

Convertible Debt Securities

Xilinx had convertible debt transactions in 2010, as explained in the following excerpt from footnotes to its 10-K report:

2.625% Senior Convertible Debentures In June 2010, the Company issued $600.0 million principal amount of 2.625% Debentures to qualified institutional investors. The 2.625% Debentures are senior in right of payment to the Company's existing and future unsecured indebtedness... The 2.625% Debentures are initially convertible, subject to certain conditions, into shares of Xilinx common stock at a conversion rate of 33.0164 shares of common stock per $1 thousand principal amount of the 2.625% Debentures, representing an initial effective conversion price of approximately $30.29 per share of common stock.

The convertible debentures are reported as a long-term liability on Xilinx's balance sheet. To see the effects that conversion would have on Xilinx's financial statements, assume that the bonds are reported at their face amount of $600 million and that all of the bonds are subsequently converted into 19,809,840 shares ([$600 million/$1,000] × 33.0164 shares) of common stock with a par value of $0.01 per share. The financial statement effects of the conversion are as follows (Xilinx reports its balance sheet in $000s):

	Balance Sheet												Income Statement				
Transaction	Cash Asset	+	Noncash Assets	=	Liabil-ities	+	Contrib. Capital	+	Earned Capital		Rev-enues	−	Expen-ses	=	Net Income
Conversion of convert-ible debt				=	−600,000 Long-Term Debt		+198 Common Stock +599,802 Additional Paid-In Capital					−		=	

L-T Debt 600,000
CS 198
APIC 599,802

LTD
600,000 |

CS
| 198

APIC
| 599,802

Upon conversion, the debt is removed from the balance sheet at its book value ($600 million assumed in this case) and the common stock is issued for that amount, resulting in an increase in the Common Stock account of $198,000 (assuming 19,809,840 shares issued with a par value of $0.01 per share). Additional Paid-In Capital is increased for the remaining amount. No gain or loss (or cash inflow or outflow) is recognized as a result of the conversion.

Convertible Preferred Stock

Preferred stock can also contain a conversion privilege. Xerox provides an example in its 2012 10-K report:

Series A Convertible Preferred Stock In 2010, in connection with our acquisition of ACS, we issued 300,000 shares of Series A convertible perpetual preferred stock with an aggregate liquidation preference of $300 and an initial fair value of $349. The convertible preferred stock pays quarterly cash dividends at a rate of 8% per year ($24 per year). Each share of convertible preferred stock is convertible at any time, at the option of the holder, into 89.8876 shares of common stock for a total of 26,966 thousand shares (reflecting an initial conversion price of approximately $11.125 per share of common stock), subject to customary anti-dilution adjustments.

Accounting for the conversion of preferred stock is essentially the same as that for convertible debt that we describe above: the preferred stock account is removed from the balance sheet and common stock is issued for the dollar amount of the preferred.

Conversion privileges offer an additional benefit to the holder of a security. That is, debtholders and preferred stockholders carry senior positions as claimants in bankruptcy, and also carry a fixed interest payment or dividend yield. Thus, they are somewhat protected from losses and their annual return is guaranteed. With a conversion privilege, debtholders or preferred stockholders can enjoy the residual benefits of common shareholders should the company perform well.

A conversion option is valuable and yields a higher price for the securities than they would otherwise command. However, conversion privileges impose a cost on common shareholders. That is, the higher market price received for convertible securities is offset by the cost imposed on the subordinate (common) securities.

One final note, diluted earnings per share (EPS) takes into account the potentially dilutive effect of convertible securities. Specifically, the diluted EPS computation assumes conversion at the beginning of the year (or when the security is issued if during the year). The earnings available to common shares in the numerator are increased by any forgone after-tax interest expense or preferred dividends, and the additional shares that would have been issued in the conversion, increase the shares outstanding in the denominator (see Module 5).

IFRS

IFRS INSIGHT **Convertible Securities under IFRS**

Unlike GAAP, convertible securities (called *compound financial instruments* under IFRS) are split into separate debt and equity components. The idea is that the conversion premium is akin to a call option on the company's stock. This embedded option has a value of its own even if it is not legally detachable. Thus, under IFRS, the proceeds from the issuance are allocated between the liability component (at fair value) and an equity component (the residual amount).

IFRS

GLOBAL ACCOUNTING

Under IFRS, accounting for equity is similar to that under U.S. GAAP. Following are a few terminology differences (seen primarily in European balance sheets):

U.S. GAAP	IFRS
Common stock	Share capital *or* Ordinary shares
Preferred shares	Preference shares
Additional paid-in capital	Share premium
Retained earnings	Reserves
Accumulated other comprehensive income	Other equity *or* Other components of equity
—	Revaluation surplus *or* Revaluation reserve*

* In Modules 6 and 9, we noted that certain assets including fixed assets and intangible assets may be revalued upwards (and later, revalued downwards) under IFRS. These revaluations do not affect net income or retained earnings but, instead, are reported in a separate equity account. For comparative purposes our analysis might exclude revaluations from both equity and the asset accounts to which they relate.

U.S. GAAP has a more narrow definition of liabilities than IFRS. Therefore, more items are classified as liabilities under IFRS. For example, some preferred shares are deemed liabilities under IFRS and equity under GAAP. (Both systems classify preferred shares that are mandatorily redeemable or redeemable at the option of the shareholder, as liabilities.) For comparative purposes, we look at classification of preferred shares that are not mandatorily redeemable and make the numbers consistent. To do this we add preference shares classified as liabilities under IFRS to equity.

Treasury stock transactions are sometimes difficult to identify under IFRS because companies are not required to report a separate line item for treasury shares on the balance sheet. Instead treasury share transactions reduce share capital and share premium. We must review the statement of shareholders' equity to assess stock repurchases for IFRS companies.

For example, at March 31, 2013, **BT Group plc** (BT) reports the following in the equity section of its IFRS balance sheet (in £ millions):

Ordinary shares	£ 408
Share premium	62
Own shares	(832)
Other reserves	1,790
Retained (loss) earnings	(1,690)
Total (deficit) equity	**£ (262)**

Its balance sheet reports no treasury stock line item, but footnotes disclose that the Own shares (£832) include the following:

(£ million)	Treasury shares
At 1 April 2012	**£(1,018)**
Net issue of treasury shares	318
At 31 March 2013	**£ (700)**

Share-based compensation gives rise to timing differences and both IFRS and U.S. GAAP require companies to record deferred tax assets. Under IFRS, the deferred tax asset is adjusted each period to reflect fluctuations in the market price of equity. These market-value adjustments impact the income statement via tax expense. U.S. GAAP computes the deferred tax asset using the grant-date fair value and does not adjust for stock price fluctuations. This makes IFRS tax expense more volatile.

MODULE-END REVIEW

Assume that **Express Scripts, Inc.**, has issued the following convertible debentures: each $1,000 bond is convertible into 200 shares of $1 par common. Assume that the bonds were sold at a discount, and that each bond has a current unamortized discount equal to $150. Using the financial statements effect template, illustrate the effects on the financial statements of the conversion of one of these convertible debentures.

The solution is on page 8-54.

GUIDANCE ANSWERS

MANAGERIAL DECISION You Are the Chief Financial Officer

Several points must be considered. (1) Buying stock back reduces the number of shares outstanding, which can prop up earnings per share (EPS). However, foregone earnings from the cash used for repurchases can dampen earnings. The net effect is that EPS is likely to increase because of the reduced shares in the denominator. (2) Another motivation is that, if the shares are sufficiently undervalued (in management's opinion), the stock repurchase and subsequent resale can provide a better return than alternative investments. (3) Stock repurchases send a strong signal to the market that management feels its stock is undervalued. This is more credible than merely making that argument with analysts. On the other hand, company cash is diverted from other investments. This is bothersome if such investments are mutually exclusive either now or in the future.

DISCUSSION QUESTIONS

Q8-1. Define *par value stock.* What is the significance of a stock's par value from an accounting and analysis perspective?

Q8-2. What are the basic differences between preferred stock and common stock? What are the typical features of preferred stock?

Q8-3. What features make preferred stock similar to debt? Similar to common stock?

Q8-4. What is meant by preferred dividends in arrears? If dividends are two years in arrears on $500,000 of 6% preferred stock, and dividends are declared at the end of this year, what amount of total dividends must the company pay to preferred stockholders before paying any dividends to common stockholders?

Q8-5. Distinguish between authorized shares and issued shares. Why might the number of shares issued be more than the number of shares outstanding?

Q8-6. Describe the difference between contributed capital and earned capital. Specifically, how can earned capital be considered as an investment by the company's stockholders?

Q8-7. How does the account "additional paid-in capital" (APIC) arise? Does the amount of APIC reported on the balance sheet relative to the common stock amount provide any information about the financial condition of the company?

Q8-8. Define *stock split*. What are the major reasons for a stock split?

Q8-9. Define *treasury stock*. Why might a corporation acquire treasury stock? How is treasury stock reported in the balance sheet?

Q8-10. If a corporation purchases 600 shares of its own common stock at $10 per share and resells them at $14 per share, where would the $2,400 increase in capital be reported in the financial statements? Why is no gain reported?

Q8-11. A corporation has total stockholders' equity of $4,628,000 and one class of $2 par value common stock. The corporation has 500,000 shares authorized; 300,000 shares issued; and 40,000 shares as treasury stock. What is its book value per share?

Q8-12. What is a stock dividend? How does a common stock dividend distributed to common stockholders affect their respective ownership interests?

Q8-13. What is the difference between the accounting for a small stock dividend and the accounting for a large stock dividend?

Q8-14. Employee stock options potentially dilute earnings per share (EPS). What can companies do to offset these dilutive effects and how might this action affect the balance sheet?

Q8-15. What information is reported in a statement of stockholders' equity?

Q8-16. What items are typically reported under the stockholders' equity category of accumulated other comprehensive income (AOCI)?

Q8-17. What is the difference between a spin-off and a split-off? Under what circumstances can either result in the recognition of a gain in the income statement?

Q8-18. Describe the accounting for a convertible bond. Can the conversion ever result in the recognition of a gain in the income statement?

Assignments with the ✓ logo in the margin are available in myBusinessCourse. See the Preface of the book for details.

MINI EXERCISES

M8-19. Analyzing and Identifying Financial Statement Effects of Stock Issuances (LO1)
During the current year, Beatty Company, (*a*) issues 9,000 shares of $50 par value preferred stock at $72 cash per share and (*b*) issues 14,000 shares of $1 par value common stock at $10 cash per share. Indicate the financial statement effects of these two issuances using the financial statement effects template.

M8-20. Analyzing and Identifying Financial Statement Effects of Stock Issuances (LO1)
During the current year, Magliolo, Inc., (*a*) issues 17,000 shares of $10 par value preferred stock at $39 cash per share and (*b*) issues 120,000 shares of $2 par value common stock at $28 cash per share. Indicate the financial statement effects of these two issuances using the financial statement effects template.

M8-21. Distinguishing Between Common Stock and Additional Paid-in Capital (LO1)
Cisco Systems, Inc. (CSCO)
Following is the 2012 stockholders' equity section from the Cisco Systems, Inc., balance sheet.

Shareholders' Equity (in millions, except par value)	July 2013
Preferred stock, no par value: 5 shares authorized; none issued and outstanding	$ —
Common stock and additional paid-in capital, $0.001 par value: 20,000 shares authorized; 5,389 and 5,298 shares issued and outstanding at July 27, 2013, and July 28, 2012, respectively	42,297
Retained earnings	16,215
Accumulated other comprehensive income	608
Total Cisco shareholders' equity	59,120
Noncontrolling interests	8
Total equity	$59,128

a. For the $42,297 million reported as "common stock and additional paid-in capital," what portion is common stock and what portion is additional paid-in capital?

b. Explain why Cisco does not report the two components described in part *a* separately.

M8-22. Identifying Financial Statement Effects of Stock Issuance and Repurchase (LO1)

On January 1, Bartov Company issues 7,000 shares of $100 par value preferred stock at $250 cash per share. On March 1, the company repurchases 7,000 shares of previously issued $1 par value common stock at $92 cash per share. Use the financial statement effects template to record these two transactions.

M8-23. Assessing the Financial Statement Effects of a Stock Split (LO2)

The Andersons, Inc. (ANDE)

The following is taken from a press release dated December 20, 2013:

> The Board of The Andersons, Inc. has approved a three-for-two stock split of its common stock. This is the first stock split of Andersons since the financial crisis of 2008. Per the stock split, for every two stocks owned by a shareholder an additional share will be given in the form of a dividend, which will be paid on February 18, 2014, to stockholders of record as of January 21, 2014.

What adjustments will Andersons make to its balance sheet as a result of the stock split?

M8-24. Reconciling Common Stock and Treasury Stock Balances (LO1)

Abercrombie & Fitch Co. (ANF)

Following is the stockholders' equity section from the Abercrombie & Fitch Co. balance sheet.

Stockholders' equity ($ thousands, except par value amounts)	February 2, 2013	January 28, 2012
Class A common stock—$0.01 par value: 150,000 shares authorized and 103,300 shares issued at each of February 2, 2013, and January 28, 2012	$ 1,033	$ 1,033
Paid-in capital	403,271	369,171
Retained earnings	2,567,261	2,389,614
Accumulated other comprehensive (loss) income, net of tax	(13,288)	6,291
Treasury stock at average cost: 24,855 and 17,662 shares at February 2, 2013 and January 28, 2012, respectively	(1,140,009)	(834,774)
Total stockholders' equity	$1,818,268	$1,931,335

a. Show the computation to yield the $1,033 balance reported for common stock.

b. How many shares are outstanding at 2013 fiscal year-end?

c. Use the common stock and paid-in capital accounts to determine the average price at which Abercrombie & Fitch issued its common stock.

d. Use the treasury stock account to determine the average price Abercrombie & Fitch paid when it repurchased its common shares.

M8-25. Identifying and Analyzing Financial Statement Effects of Cash Dividends (LO2)

Freid Company has outstanding 7,000 shares of $50 par value, 6% preferred stock, and 30,000 shares of $1 par value common stock. The company has $328,000 of retained earnings. At year-end, the company declares and pays the regular $3 per share cash dividend on preferred stock and a $2.20 per share cash dividend on common stock. Use the financial statement effects template to indicate the effects of these two dividend payments.

M8-26. Identifying and Analyzing Financial Statement Effects of Stock Dividends **(LO2)**
Dutta Corp. has outstanding 60,000 shares of $5 par value common stock. At year-end, the company declares and issues a 4% common stock dividend when the market price of the stock is $23 per share. Use the financial statement effects template to indicate the effects of this stock dividend declaration and payment.

M8-27. Identifying, Analyzing and Explaining the Effects of a Stock Split **(LO2)**
On September 1, Weiss Company has 200,000 shares of $15 par value ($159 market value) common stock that are issued and outstanding. Its balance sheet on that date shows the following account balances relating to its common stock:

Common stock.	$3,000,000
Paid-in capital in excess of par value.	1,750,000

On September 2, Weiss splits its stock 3-for-2 and reduces the par value to $10 per share.

a. How many shares of common stock are issued and outstanding immediately after the stock split?
b. What is the dollar balance of the common stock account immediately after the stock split?
c. What is the likely reason that Weiss Company split its stock?

M8-28. Determining Cash Dividends to Preferred and Common Shareholders **(LO2)**
Dechow Company has outstanding 20,000 shares of $50 par value, 6% cumulative preferred stock and 50,000 shares of $10 par value common stock. The company declares and pays cash dividends amounting to $160,000.

a. If there are no preferred dividends in arrears, how much in total dividends, and in dividends per share, does Dechow pay to each class of stock?
b. If there are one year's dividends in arrears on the preferred stock, how much in total dividends, and in dividends per share, does Dechow pay to each class of stock?

M8-29. Reconciling Retained Earnings **(LO2)**
Use the following data to reconcile the 2014 retained earnings for Bamber Company (that is, explain the change in retained earnings during the year).

Total retained earnings, December 31, 2013	$456,000
Stock dividends declared and paid in 2014.	37,000
Cash dividends declared and paid in 2014	44,000
Net income for 2014.	102,000

M8-30. Interpreting a Spin-Off Disclosure **(LO3)**
NCR Corp. (NCR)
NCR Corporation discloses the following in notes to its 2007 10-K report.

> **Spin-off of Teradata Data Warehousing Business** On September 30, 2007, NCR completed the spin-off of its Teradata Data Warehousing business through the distribution of a tax-free dividend to its stockholders. NCR distributed one share of common stock of Teradata Corporation (Teradata) for each share of NCR common stock to NCR stockholders of record as of the close of business on September 14, 2007. Upon the distribution of Teradata, NCR stockholders received 100% (approximately 181 million shares) of the common stock of Teradata, which is now an independent public company trading under the symbol "TDC" on the New York Stock Exchange.

a. Describe the difference between a spin-off and a split-off.
b. What effects did NCR's spin-off of Teradata have on NCR's balance sheet and income statement?

M8-31. Interpreting a Proposed Split-Off Disclosure **(LO3)**
Viacom Inc. (VIA)
Viacom Inc. reports the following footnote in its 2005 10-K.

> **Discontinued Operations** In 2004, Viacom completed the exchange offer for the split-off of Blockbuster Inc. ("Blockbuster") (NYSE: BBI and BBI.B). Under the terms of the offer, Viacom accepted 27,961,165 shares of Viacom common stock in exchange for the 144 million common shares of Blockbuster that Viacom owned. Each share of Viacom Class A or Class B common stock accepted for exchange by Viacom was exchanged for 5.15 shares of Blockbuster common stock, consisting of 2.575 shares of Blockbuster Class A common stock and 2.575 shares of Blockbuster Class B common stock.

a. Describe the accounting for a split-off.
b. How will the proposed split-off affect the number of Viacom shares outstanding?
c. Under what circumstances will Viacom be able to report a gain for this proposed split-off?

M8-32. Interpreting Disclosure Related to Spin-Off **(LO3)**

Altria Group, Inc. reports the following footnote to its 2008 10-K.

Altria Group, Inc. (MO)

> On March 28, 2008, Altria Group, Inc. distributed all of its interest in Philip Morris International Inc. ("PMI") to Altria Group, Inc. stockholders of record as of the close of business on March 19, 2008, in a tax-free distribution. Altria Group, Inc. distributed one share of PMI common stock for every share of Altria Group, Inc. common stock outstanding as of the PMI Record Date. Following the PMI Distribution Date, Altria Group, Inc. does not own any shares of PMI stock. Altria Group, Inc. has reflected the results of PMI prior to the PMI Distribution Date as discontinued operations on the consolidated statements of earnings and the consolidated statements of cash flows for all periods presented. The assets and liabilities related to PMI were reclassified and reflected as discontinued operations on the consolidated balance sheet at December 31, 2007. The distribution resulted in a net decrease to Altria Group, Inc.'s total stockholders' equity of $14.4 billion on the PMI Distribution Date.

a. Describe the accounting for a spin-off.
b. What effects did this transaction have on Altria's balance sheet and income statement?

M8-33. Analyzing Financial Statement Effects of Convertible Securities **(LO3)**

JetBlue Airways Corporation reports the following footnote to its 2012 10-K.

JetBlue Airways Corporation (JBLU)

> On June 9, 2009, we completed a public offering of $115 million aggregate principal amount of 6.75% Series A convertible debentures due 2039, or the Series A 6.75% Debentures, and $86 million aggregate principal amount of 6.75% Series B convertible debentures due 2039, or the Series B 6.75% Debentures, and collectively with the Series A 6.75% Debentures, the 6.75% Debentures. The net proceeds were approximately $197 million after deducting underwriting fees and other transaction related expenses. Interest on the 6.75% Debentures is payable semi-annually on April 15 and October 15. The first interest payment on the 6.75% Debentures was paid October 15, 2009. Holders of either the Series A or Series B 6.75% Debentures may convert them into shares of our common stock at any time at a conversion rate of 204.6036 shares per $1,000 principal amount of the 6.75% Debentures.

a. Describe the effects on JetBlue's balance sheet if the convertible bonds are converted.
b. Would the conversion affect earnings? Explain.

EXERCISES

E8-34. Identifying and Analyzing Financial Statement Effects of Stock Transactions **(LO1)**

Lipe Company reports the following transactions relating to its stock accounts in the current year.

Feb. 20	Issued 10,000 shares of $1 par value common stock at $20 cash per share.
Feb. 21	Issued 15,000 shares of $100 par value, 8% preferred stock at $250 cash per share.
June 30	Purchased 3,000 shares of its own common stock at $15 cash per share.
Sep. 25	Sold 1,500 shares of its treasury stock at $18 cash per share.

Use the financial statement effects template to indicate the effects from each of these transactions.

E8-35. Identifying and Analyzing Financial Statement Effects of Stock Transactions **(LO1)**

McNichols Corp. reports the following transactions relating to its stock accounts in the current year.

Jan. 15 Issued 40,000 shares of $5 par value common stock at $17 cash per share.
Jan. 20 Issued 9,000 shares of $50 par value, 8% preferred stock at $78 cash per share.
Mar. 31 Purchased 5,000 shares of its own common stock at $20 cash per share.
June 25 Sold 3,000 shares of its treasury stock at $28 cash per share.
July 15 Sold the remaining 2,000 shares of treasury stock at $19 cash per share.

Use the financial statement effects template to indicate the effects from each of these transactions.

Campbell Soup Co. (CPB)

E8-36. Analyzing and Computing Average Issue Price and Treasury Stock Cost (LO1)
Following is the stockholders' equity section from the Campbell Soup Company balance sheet. (*Note:* Campbell's uses *shareowners' equity* in lieu of the more common title of stockholders' equity.)

Shareowners' Equity (millions, except per share amounts)	July 28, 2013	July 29, 2012
Preferred stock: authorized 40 shares; none issued	$ —	$ —
Capital stock, $.0375 par value; authorized 560 shares; issued 323 shares as of July 28, 2013, and 542 as of July 29, 2012	12	20
Additional paid-in capital	362	329
Earnings retained in the business	1,772	9,584
Capital stock in treasury, at cost	(364)	(8,259)
Accumulated other comprehensive loss	(565)	(776)
Total Campbell Soup Company shareowners' equity	1,217	898
Noncontrolling interests	(7)	—
Total equity	1,210	898
Total liabilities and equity	$8,323	$6,530

Campbell Soup Company also reports the following statement of stockholders' equity.

CAMPBELL SOUP COMPANY
Shareowners' Equity

(Millions, except per share amounts)	Capital Stock				Additional Paid-in Capital	Earnings Retained in the Business	Accumulated Other Comprehensive Income (Loss)	Noncontrolling Interests	Total Equity
	Issued		In Treasury						
	Shares	Amount	Shares	Amount					
Balance at July 29, 2012	542	$20	(230)	$(8,259)	$329	$9,584	$(776)	$—	$ 898
Contribution from noncontrolling interests								3	3
Net earnings (loss)						458		(9)	449
Other comprehensive income (loss)							211	(1)	210
Dividends ($1.16 per share)						(371)			(371)
Treasury stock purchased			(4)	(153)					(153)
Treasury stock retired	(219)	(8)	219	7,907		(7,899)			—
Treasury stock issued under management incentive and stock option plans			4	141	33				174
Balance at July 28, 2013	323	$12	(11)	$ (364)	$362	$1,772	$(565)	$ (7)	$1,210

a. Show the computation, using par value and share numbers, to arrive at the $12 million in the common stock account.

b. At what average price were the Campbell Soup shares issued?

c. Reconcile the beginning and ending balances of retained earnings.

d. Campbell Soup retired treasury stock during the year. Explain why a company chooses to retire treasury stock. What effect did the retirement of treasury stock have on the common stock account, treasury stock account and retained earnings this year?

e. Campbell Soup reports an increase in stockholders' equity relating to the exercise of stock options (titled "Treasury stock issued under management incentive and stock option plans"). This transaction involves the purchase of common stock by employees at a preset price. Describe how this set of transactions affects stockholders' equity.

f. Describe the transaction relating to the "Treasury stock purchased" line in the statement of stockholders' equity.

E8-37. Analyzing Cash Dividends on Preferred and Common Stock (LO2)
Moser Company began business on March 1, 2012. At that time, it issued 25,000 shares of $50 par value, 7% cumulative preferred stock and 80,000 shares of $5 par value common stock. Through the end of 2014, there has been no change in the number of preferred and common shares outstanding.

a. Assume that Moser declared and paid cash dividends of $0 in 2012, $192,000 in 2013, and $200,000 in 2014. Compute the total cash dividends and the dividends per share paid to each class of stock in 2012, 2013, and 2014.
b. Assume that Moser declared and paid cash dividends of $0 in 2012, $87,500 in 2013, and $150,000 in 2014. Compute the total cash dividends and the dividends per share paid to each class of stock in 2012, 2013, and 2014.

E8-38. Analyzing Cash Dividends on Preferred and Common Stock (LO2)
Potter Company has outstanding 20,000 shares of $50 par value, 8% preferred stock and 60,000 shares of $5 par value common stock. During its first three years in business, it declared and paid no cash dividends in the first year, $280,000 in the second year, and $80,000 in the third year.

a. If the preferred stock is cumulative, determine the total amount of cash dividends paid to each class of stock in each of the three years.
b. If the preferred stock is noncumulative, determine the total amount of cash dividends paid to each class of stock in each of the three years.

E8-39. Analyzing and Computing Issue Price, Treasury Stock Cost, and Shares Outstanding (LO1)
Following is the stockholders' equity section from **Altria Group, Inc.**'s 2012 balance sheet.

Altria Group, Inc. (MO)

December 31 ($ million)	2012
Common stock, par value $0.33 1/3 per share (2,805,961,317 shares issued)	$ 935
Additional paid-in capital	5,688
Earnings reinvested in the business	24,316
Accumulated other comprehensive losses	(2,040)
Cost of repurchased stock (796,221,021 shares)	(25,731)
Total stockholders' equity attributable to Altria Group, Inc.	3,168
Noncontrolling interests	2
Total stockholders' equity	$ 3,170

a. Show the computation to derive the $935 million for common stock.
b. At what average price has Altria issued its common stock?
c. How many shares of Altria common stock are outstanding as of December 31, 2012?
d. At what average cost has Altria repurchased its treasury stock as of December 31, 2012?
e. Why would a company such as Altria want to repurchase $25,731 million of its common stock?
f. What does the Noncontrolling interests account of $2 million represent?

E8-40. Analyzing Cash Dividends on Preferred and Common Stock (LO2)
Skinner Company began business on June 30, 2012. At that time, it issued 18,000 shares of $50 par value, 8% cumulative preferred stock and 100,000 shares of $10 par value common stock. Through the end of 2014, there has been no change in the number of preferred and common shares outstanding.

a. Assume that Skinner declared and paid cash dividends of $84,000 in 2012, $0 in 2013, and $378,000 in 2014. Compute the total cash dividends and the dividends per share paid to each class of stock in 2012, 2013, and 2014.
b. Assume that Skinner declared and paid cash dividends of $0 in 2012, $144,000 in 2013, and $189,000 in 2014. Compute the total cash dividends and the dividends per share paid to each class of stock in 2012, 2013, and 2014.

E8-41. Identifying and Analyzing Financial Statement Effects of Dividends (LO2)
Chaney Company has outstanding 25,000 shares of $10 par value common stock. It also has $405,000 of retained earnings. Near the current year-end, the company declares and pays a cash dividend of $2.10 per share and declares and issues a 5% stock dividend. The market price of the stock the day the dividends are declared is $30 per share. Use the financial statement effects template to indicate the effects of these two separate dividend transactions.

E8-42. Identifying and Analyzing Financial Statement Effects of Dividends (LO2)
The stockholders' equity of Pagach Company at December 31, 2013, appears below.

Common stock, $10 par value, 200,000 shares authorized; 70,000 shares issued and outstanding	$700,000
Paid-in capital in excess of par value	480,000
Retained earnings	295,000

During 2014, the following transactions occurred:

May 12 Declared and issued a 7% stock dividend; the common stock market value was $18 per share.
Dec. 31 Declared and paid a cash dividend of 75 cents per share.

a. Use the financial statement effects template to indicate the effects of these transactions.
b. Reconcile retained earnings for 2014 assuming that the company reports 2014 net income of $283,000.

✔ **E8-43. Identifying and Analyzing Financial Statement Effects of Dividends (LO2)**
The stockholders' equity of Kinney Company at December 31, 2013, is shown below.

5% preferred stock, $100 par value, 10,000 shares authorized; 5,000 shares issued and outstanding	$ 500,000
Common stock, $5 par value, 200,000 shares authorized; 60,000 shares issued and outstanding	300,000
Paid-in capital in excess of par value—preferred stock	40,000
Paid-in capital in excess of par value—common stock	300,000
Retained earnings	656,000
Total stockholders' equity	$1,796,000

The following transactions, among others, occurred during 2014:

Apr. 1 Declared and issued a 100% stock dividend on all outstanding shares of common stock. The market value of the stock was $11 per share.
Dec. 7 Declared and issued a 4% stock dividend on all outstanding shares of common stock. The market value of the stock was $14 per share.
Dec. 20 Declared and paid (1) the annual cash dividend on the preferred stock and (2) a cash dividend of 80 cents per common share.

a. Use the financial statement effects template to indicate the effects of these separate transactions.
b. Compute retained earnings for 2014 assuming that the company reports 2014 net income of $262,000.

E8-44. Identifying, Analyzing and Explaining the Effects of a Stock Split (LO2)
On March 1 of the current year, Zhang Company has 500,000 shares of $20 par value common stock that are issued and outstanding. Its balance sheet shows the following account balances relating to common stock.

Common stock	$10,000,000
Paid-in capital in excess of par value	5,300,000

On March 2, Zhang Company splits its common stock 2-for-1 and reduces the par value to $10 per share.

a. How many shares of common stock are issued and outstanding immediately after the stock split?
b. What is the dollar balance in the common stock account immediately after the stock split?
c. What is the dollar balance in the paid-in capital in excess of par value account immediately after the stock split?

Caterpillar Inc. (CAT)

E8-45. Analyzing and Computing Issue Price, Treasury Stock Cost, and Shares Outstanding (LO1)
Following is the stockholders' equity section of the 2012 Caterpillar Inc., balance sheet.

Stockholders' Equity ($ millions)	2012	2011	2010
Common stock of $1.00 par; Authorized shares: 2,000,000,000; Issued shares (2012, 2011, and 2010—814,894,624) at paid-in amount	**$ 4,481**	$ 4,273	$ 3,888
Treasury stock (2012: 159,846,131; 2011: 167,361,280 shares; and 2010: 176,071,910 shares) at cost	**(10,074)**	(10,281)	(10,397)
Profit employed in the business	**29,558**	25,219	21,384
Accumulated other comprehensive income (loss)	**(6,433)**	(6,328)	(4,051)
Noncontrolling interests	**50**	46	40
Total stockholders' equity	**$17,582**	$12,929	$10,864

a. How many shares of Caterpillar common stock are outstanding at year-end 2012?
b. What does the phrase "at paid-in amount" in the stockholders' equity section mean?
c. At what average cost has Caterpillar repurchased its stock as of year-end 2012?
d. Why would a company such as Caterpillar want to repurchase its common stock?
e. Explain how CAT's "issued shares" remains constant over the three-year period while the dollar amount of its common stock account increases.

E8-46. Analyzing Equity Changes from Convertible Preferred Stock (LO3)
Xerox Corp. reports the following stockholders' equity information in its 10-K report.

Xerox Corporation (XRX)

Shareholders' Equity (In millions, except share data in thousands)	December 31 2012	December 31 2011
Series A convertible preferred stock	**$ 349**	$ 349
Common stock, $1 par value	**1,239**	1,353
Additional paid-in capital	**5,622**	6,317
Treasury stock, at cost	**(104)**	(124)
Retained earnings	**7,991**	7,046
Accumulated other comprehensive loss	**(3,227)**	(2,716)
Xerox shareholders' equity	**$11,521**	$11,876

(In millions, except share data in thousands)	Common Stock	Additional Paid-in Capital	Treasury Stock	Retained Earnings	Accumulated Other Comprehensive Loss	Xerox Shareholders' Equity	Non-controlling Interests	Total Equity
Balance at December 31, 2011	$1,353	$6,317	$ (124)	$7,046	$(2,716)	$11,876	$149	$12,025
Comprehensive income	—	—	—	1,195	(511)	684	28	712
Cash dividends declared—common stock	—	—	—	(226)	—	(226)	—	(226)
Cash dividends declared—preferred stock	—	—	—	(24)	—	(24)	—	(24)
Contribution of common stock to U.S. pension plan	15	115	—	—	—	130	—	130
Stock option and incentive plans, net	18	115	—	—	—	133	—	133
Payments to acquire treasury stock, including fees	—	—	(1,052)	—	—	(1,052)	—	(1,052)
Cancellation of treasury stock	(147)	(925)	1,072	—	—	—	—	—
Distributions to noncontrolling interests	—	—	—	—	—	—	(34)	(34)
Balance, December 31, 2012	$1,239	$5,622	$ (104)	$7,991	$(3,227)	$11,521	$143	$11,664

Preferred Stock As of December 31, 2012, we had one class of preferred stock outstanding. We are authorized to issue approximately 22 million shares of cumulative preferred stock, $1.00 par value per share.

Series A Convertible Preferred Stock: In 2010, in connection with our acquisition of ACS, we issued 300,000 shares of Series A convertible perpetual preferred stock with an aggregate liquidation preference of $300 and an initial fair value of $349. The convertible preferred stock pays quarterly cash dividends at a rate of 8% per year ($24 per year). Each share of convertible preferred stock is convertible at any time, at the option of the holder, into 89.8876 shares of common stock for a total of 26,966 thousand shares (reflecting an initial conversion price of approximately $11.125 per share of common stock), subject to customary anti-dilution adjustments.

continued

continued from prior page

Common Stock We have 1.75 billion authorized shares of common stock, $1.00 par value per share. At December 31, 2012, 155 million shares were reserved for issuance under our incentive compensation plans, 48 million shares were reserved for debt to equity exchanges, 27 million shares were reserved for conversion of the Series A convertible preferred stock and 2 million shares were reserved for the conversion of convertible debt.

Required

a. At December 31, 2012, Xerox reports $349 million of 8% Series A Convertible Preferred stock. What is the dollar amount of dividends that Xerox must pay on this stock (assume a par value of $100 per share)?

b. Describe the effects that will occur to Xerox's balance sheet and its income statement when the Series A Convertible Preferred stock is converted.

c. What is the benefit, if any, of issuing equity securities with a conversion feature? How are these securities treated in the computation of earnings per share (EPS)?

E8-47. Analyzing and Computing Issue Price, Treasury Stock Cost, and Shares Outstanding (LO1)

Merck & Co., Inc. (MRK)

Following is the stockholders' equity section of the 2012 **Merck & Co., Inc.**, balance sheet.

Stockholders' Equity ($ millions)	2012
Common stock, $0.50 par value; Authorized—6,500,000,000 shares; Issued—3,577,103,522 shares	$ 1,788
Other paid-in capital	40,646
Retained earnings	39,985
Accumulated other comprehensive loss	(4,682)
	77,737
Less treasury stock, at cost: 550,468,221 shares	24,717
Total stockholders' equity	$53,020

a. Show the computation of the $1,788 million in the common stock account.

b. At what average price were the Merck common shares issued?

c. At what average cost was the Merck treasury stock purchased?

d. How many common shares are outstanding as of December 31, 2012?

PROBLEMS

P8-48. Identifying and Analyzing Financial Statement Effects of Stock Transactions (LO1)

The stockholders' equity section of Gupta Company at December 31, 2013, follows:

8% preferred stock, $25 par value, 50,000 shares authorized; 7,200 shares issued and outstanding	$180,000
Common stock, $10 par value, 200,000 shares authorized; 40,000 shares issued and outstanding	400,000
Paid-in capital in excess of par value—preferred stock	68,000
Paid-in capital in excess of par value—common stock	200,000
Retained earnings	280,000

During 2014, the following transactions occurred:

Jan. 10	Issued 28,000 shares of common stock for $16 cash per share.
Jan. 23	Repurchased 8,000 shares of common stock at $18 cash per share.
Mar. 14	Sold one-half of the treasury shares acquired January 23 for $20 cash per share.
July 15	Issued 2,800 shares of preferred stock for $128,000 cash.
Nov. 15	Sold 1,000 of the treasury shares acquired January 23 for $24 cash per share.

Required

a. Use the financial statement effects template to indicate the effects from each of these transactions.

b. Prepare the December 31, 2014, stockholders' equity section of the balance sheet assuming the company reports 2014 net income of $62,000.

P8-49. Identifying and Analyzing Financial Statement Effects of Stock Transactions (LO1, 2)

The stockholders' equity of Sougiannis Company at December 31, 2013, follows:

7% Preferred stock, $100 par value, 20,000 shares authorized; 4,000 shares issued and outstanding.	$ 400,000
Common stock, $15 par value, 100,000 shares authorized; 30,000 shares issued and outstanding.	450,000
Paid-in capital in excess of par value—preferred stock.	36,000
Paid-in capital in excess of par value—common stock.	360,000
Retained earnings	325,000
Total stockholders' equity	$1,571,000

The following transactions, among others, occurred during the following year:

Jan. 12	Announced a 3-for-1 common stock split, reducing the par value of the common stock to $5 per share. The authorized shares were increased to 300,000 shares.
Sept. 1	Repurchased 10,000 shares of common stock at $11 cash per share.
Oct. 12	Sold 1,500 treasury shares acquired September 1 at $13 cash per share.
Nov. 21	Issued 5,000 shares of common stock at $22 cash per share.
Dec. 28	Sold 1,200 treasury shares acquired September 1 at $9 cash per share.

Required

a. Use the financial statement effects template to indicate the effects from each of these transactions.

b. Prepare the December 31, 2014, stockholders' equity section of the balance sheet assuming that the company reports 2014 net income of $83,000.

P8-50. Identifying and Analyzing Financial Statement Effects of Stock Transactions (LO1)

The stockholders' equity of Verrecchia Company at December 31, 2013, follows:

Common stock, $5 par value, 350,000 shares authorized; 250,000 shares issued and outstanding.	$1,250,000
Paid-in capital in excess of par value.	600,000
Retained earnings	346,000

During 2014, the following transactions occurred:

Jan. 5	Issued 10,000 shares of common stock for $12 cash per share.
Jan. 18	Repurchased 4,000 shares of common stock at $15 cash per share.
Mar. 12	Sold one-fourth of the treasury shares acquired January 18 for $18 cash per share.
July 17	Sold 500 shares of treasury stock for $13 cash per share.
Oct. 1	Issued 5,000 shares of 8%, $25 par value preferred stock for $35 cash per share. This is the first issuance of preferred shares from the 50,000 authorized preferred shares.

Required

a. Use the financial statement effects template to indicate the effects of each transaction.

b. Prepare the December 31, 2014, stockholders' equity section of the balance sheet assuming that the company reports net income of $65,800 for the year.

P8-51. Identifying and Analyzing Financial Statement Effects of Stock Transactions (LO1, 2)

Following is the stockholders' equity of Dennis Corporation at December 31, 2013:

8% preferred stock, $50 par value, 10,000 shares authorized; 8,000 shares issued and outstanding.	$ 400,000
Common stock, $20 par value, 50,000 shares authorized; 25,000 shares issued and outstanding.	500,000
Paid-in capital in excess of par value—preferred stock.	70,000
Paid-in capital in excess of par value—common stock.	385,000
Retained earnings	238,000
Total stockholders' equity	$1,593,000

The following transactions, among others, occurred during 2014:

Jan. 15	Issued 1,000 shares of preferred stock for $60 cash per share.
Jan. 20	Issued 4,000 shares of common stock at $34 cash per share.
May 18	Announced a 2-for-1 common stock split, reducing the par value of the common stock to $10 per share. The number of shares authorized was increased to 100,000 shares.
June 1	Issued 2,000 shares of common stock for $56,000 cash.
Sept. 1	Repurchased 2,500 shares of common stock at $16 cash per share.
Oct. 12	Sold 900 treasury shares at $19 cash per share.
Dec. 22	Issued 500 shares of preferred stock for $57 cash per share.

Required

Use the financial statement effects template to indicate the effects of each transaction.

The Procter & Gamble Company (PG)

P8-52. Analyzing and Interpreting Equity Accounts and Comprehensive Income (LO2)

Following is the shareholders' equity section of the 2013 balance sheet for Procter & Gamble Company and its statement of shareholders' equity.

June 30 (In millions, expect per share amounts)	2013
Shareholders' Equity	
Convertible Class A preferred stock, stated value $1 per share (600 shares authorized)	$ 1,137
Non-Voting Class B preferred stock, stated value $1 per share (200 shares authorized)	—
Common stock, stated value $1 per share (10,000 shares authorized; shares issued: 2013—4,009.2)	4,009
Additional paid-in capital	63,538
Reserve for ESOP debt retirement.	(1,352)
Accumulated other comprehensive income/(loss).	(7,499)
Treasury stock, at cost (shares held: 2013—1,266.9)	(71,966)
Retained earnings	80,197
Noncontrolling interest.	645
Total shareholders' equity	$68,709

Consolidated Statement of Shareholders' Equity

Dollars in millions; Shares in thousands	Common Shares Outstanding	Common Stock	Preferred Stock	Additional Paid-in Capital	Reserve for ESOP Debt Retirement	Accumulated Other Comprehensive Income (Loss)	Treasury Stock	Retained Earnings	Non-controlling Interest	Total
Balance June 30, 2012.	2,748,033	$4,008	$1,195	$63,181	$(1,357)	$(9,333)	$(69,604)	$75,349	$596	$64,035
Net earnings.								11,312	90	11,402
Other comprehensive income						1,834				1,834
Dividends to shareholders:										
Common.								(6,275)		(6,275)
Preferred, net of tax benefits								(244)		(244)
Treasury purchases	(84,234)						(5,986)			(5,986)
Employee plan issuances.	70,923	1		352			3,573			3,926
Preferred stock conversions.	7,605		(58)	7			51			—
ESOP debt impacts					5			55		60
Noncontrolling interest, net				(2)					(41)	(43)
Balance June 30, 2013.	2,742,327	$4,009	$1,137	$63,538	$(1,352)	$(7,499)	$(71,966)	$80,197	$645	$68,709

Required

a. What does the term *convertible* (in reference to the company's Class A preferred stock) mean?

b. How many shares of common stock did Procter & Gamble issue when convertible Class A preferred stock was converted during fiscal 2013?

c. Describe the transactions relating to employee plan issuances. At what average price was the common stock issued as of year-end 2013?

d. What is other comprehensive income? What is the accumulated other comprehensive income account? Explain.

e. What cash dividends did Procter & Gamble pay in 2013 for each class of stock?

P8-53. Analyzing and Interpreting Equity Accounts and Accumulated Other Comprehensive Income (LO1, 2)

Beam Inc. (BEAM)

Following is the stockholders' equity section of **Beam Inc.** balance sheet and its statement of stockholders' equity.

December 31 (In millions, except per share amounts)	2012
Stockholders' equity	
$2.67 Convertible preferred stock	$ —
Common stock, par value $3.125 per share (750.0 shares authorized; 234.9 shares issued; 160.1 shares outstanding in 2012 and 155.9 shares outstanding in 2011)	734.0
Paid-in capital	873.7
Accumulated other comprehensive loss	(186.0)
Retained earnings	6,139.7
Treasury stock, at cost	(2,949.3)
Total equity	$4,612.1

(In millions, except per share amounts)	$2.67 Convertible Preferred Stock	Common Stock	Paid-in Capital	Accumulated Other Comprehensive Income (Loss)	Retained Earnings	Treasury Stock At Cost	Total Equity
Balance at December 31, 2011	$4.7	$734.0	$882.4	$(304.1)	$5,892.6	$(3,109.9)	$4,099.7
Net income	—	—	—	—	382.4	—	382.4
Other comprehensive Income	—	—	—	118.1	—	—	118.1
Dividends	—	—	—	—	(130.1)	—	(130.1)
Stock-based compensation	—	—	13.2	—	(3.2)	126.1	136.1
Tax benefit on exercise of stock options	—	—	12.8	—	—	—	12.8
Conversion of preferred stock	(3.4)	—	(31.2)	—	—	34.5	(0.1)
Redemption of preferred stock	(1.3)	—	(0.4)	—	—	—	(1.7)
Spin-off of Fortune Brands Home & Security, Inc.	—	—	(3.1)	—	(2.0)	—	(5.1)
Balance at December 31, 2012	$ —	$734.0	$873.7	$(186.0)	$6,139.7	$(2,949.3)	$4,612.1

(In millions)	2012
Other comprehensive income:	
Foreign currency translation adjustments	
Foreign currency translation gains (losses)	$122.0
Reclassification adjustments included in earnings	—
Tax benefit	2.4
Foreign currency translation adjustments, net	124.4
Derivative instruments	
Derivative instrument losses	(3.4)
Reclassification adjustments included in earnings	3.4
Tax expense	(0.2)
Derivative instruments, net	(0.2)
Pension and other postretirement benefit adjustments	
Current year actuarial loss—pension plans	(28.0)
Current year actuarial loss—other postretirement benefit plans	(0.2)
Reclassification adjustments included in earnings	17.1
Tax benefit	5.0
Pension and other postretirement benefit adjustments, net	(6.1)
Total other comprehensive income	$118.1

Required

a. Explain the "$2.67" component of the convertible preferred stock account title.
b. Show (confirm) the computation that yields the $734.0 million common stock at year-end 2012.
c. At what average price were Beam's common shares issued as of year-end 2012?
d. What is included in Beam's other comprehensive income for 2012? What other items are typically included in other comprehensive income?
e. Explain the $12.8 million tax benefit on exercise of stock options, reported in the statement of stockholders' equity.

P8-54. Interpreting Footnote Disclosure on Convertible Debentures (LO3)

Alloy, Inc. (ALOY)

Alloy, Inc., reports the following footnote related to its convertible debentures in its 2007 10-K ($ thousands).

In August 2003, Alloy completed the issuance of $69,300 of 20-Year 5.375% Senior Convertible Debentures due August 1, 2023. If converted, bondholders would currently receive 29.851 shares of Alloy common for each $1,000 face amount bond. Alloy continues to be responsible for repaying the Convertible Debentures in full if they are not converted into shares of Alloy common stock. If not previously converted to common stock, Alloy may redeem the Convertible Debentures after August 1, 2008 at 103% of their face amount from August 1, 2008 through December 31, 2008 and at declining prices to 100% in January 2011 and thereafter, with accrued interest. From August 30, 2006 through December 7, 2006, holders converted approximately $67,903 face amount of their Debentures, in accordance with their terms, into approximately 2,026,000 shares of Alloy common stock. During fiscal 2006, the Company's additional paid-in capital increased by $67,883 as a result of the conversions. At January 31, 2007, the Company had $1,397 in principal amount of outstanding Convertible Debentures. At January 31, 2007, the fair value of the Convertible Debentures was approximately $1,504, which is estimated based on quoted market prices.

Required

a. How did Alloy initially account for the issuance of the 5.375% debentures, assuming that the conversion option cannot be detached and sold separately?
b. Consider the conversion terms reported in the footnote. At what minimum stock price would it make economic sense for debenture holders to convert to Alloy common stock?
c. Use the financial statement effects template to show how Alloy accounted for the conversion of the 5.375% debentures in 2006. The par value of the company's stock is $0.01.
d. Assume that the conversion feature is valued by investors and, therefore, results in a higher initial issuance price for the bonds. What effect will the conversion feature have on the amount of interest expense and net income that Alloy reports?
e. How are the convertible debentures treated in the computation of basic and diluted earnings per share (EPS)?

P8-55. Interpreting Disclosure on Convertible Preferred Securities (LO3)

Northrop Grumman Corp. (NOC)

The 2008 annual report of **Northrop Grumman Corporation** includes the following disclosure in its shareholders' equity footnote:

Conversion of Preferred Stock On February 20, 2008, the company's board of directors approved the redemption of all of the 3.5 million shares of mandatorily redeemable convertible preferred stock on April 4, 2008. Prior to the redemption date, substantially all of the preferred shares were converted into common stock at the election of shareholders. All remaining unconverted preferred shares were redeemed by the company on the redemption date. As a result of the conversion and redemption, the company issued approximately 6.4 million shares of common stock.

Required

a. Explain what is meant by "mandatorily redeemable" and "convertible" preferred stock.
b. The company's balance sheet reports preferred stock of $350 million at December 31, 2007 (and $0 at December 31, 2008). As is typical, Northrop Grumman originally sold these preferred at par. Confirm that the par value of the preferred stock is $100 per share.
c. Northrop's footnotes report that the fair value of the preferred shares was $146 per share at December 31, 2008. What would explain this large increase in its preferred stock's market price?

d. Use the financial statement effects template to record the conversion of the preferred stock on April 4, 2008. Assume that all 3.5 million shares were converted. The par value of the company's common stock is $1 per share.

P8-56. Identifying and Analyzing Financial Statement Effects of Share-Based Compensation (LO1)
Weaver Industries implements a new share-based compensation plan in 2011. Under the plan, the company's CEO and CFO each will receive non-qualified stock options to purchase 100,000, no par shares. The options vest ratably (1/3 of the options each year) over three years, expire in 10 years, and have an exercise (strike) price of $23 per share. Weaver uses the Black-Scholes model to estimate a fair value per option of $15. The company's tax rate is 35%.

Required

a. Use the financial statement effects template to record the compensation expense related to these options for each year 2011 through 2013. Include the effects of any anticipated deferred tax benefits.

b. In 2014, the company's stock price is $20. If you were the Weaver Industries CEO, would you exercise your options? Explain.

c. In 2016, the company's stock price is $42 and the CEO exercises all of her options. Use the financial statement effects template to record the exercise.

d. What tax benefit will Weaver Industries receive related to the CEO's exercise in part *c*? What will be the tax consequences to the CEO?

P8-57. Interpreting Disclosure on Employee Stock Options (LO1)
Intel Corporation reported the following in its 2012 10-K report.

Intel Corporation (INTC)

Share-Based Compensation Share-based compensation recognized in 2012 was $1.1 billion ($1.1 billion in 2011 and $917 million in 2010). . . .During 2012, the tax benefit that we realized for the tax deduction from share-based awards totaled $510 million ($327 million in 2011 and $266 million in 2010). . . . We use the Black-Scholes option pricing model to estimate the fair value of options granted under our equity incentive plans and rights to acquire stock granted under our stock purchase plan. We based the weighted average estimated value of employee stock option grants and rights granted under the stock purchase plan, as well as the weighted average assumptions used in calculating the fair value, on estimates at the date of grant, as follows:

	Stock Options			Stock Purchase Plan		
	2012	2011	2010	2012	2011	2010
Estimated values	$4.22	$3.91	$4.82	$5.47	$4.69	$4.71
Expected life (in years)	5.3	5.4	4.9	0.5	0.5	0.5
Risk-free interest rate	1.0%	2.2%	2.5%	0.1%	0.2%	0.2%
Volatility	25%	27%	28%	24%	26%	32%
Dividend yield	3.3%	3.4%	2.7%	3.3%	3.6%	3.1%

Additional information with respect to stock option activity is as follows:

(In millions, except per option amounts)	Number of Options	Weighted Average Exercise Price
December 26, 2009	451.3	$25.08
Grants	20.2	$23.25
Exercises	(16.6)	$18.36
Cancellations and forfeitures	(16.1)	$24.76
Expirations	(52.4)	$60.68
December 25, 2010	386.4	$20.45
Grants	14.7	$21.49
Assumed in acquisition	12.0	$15.80
Exercises	(86.3)	$20.06
Cancellations and forfeitures	(8.6)	$20.47
Expirations	(19.9)	$24.85

continued

continued from prior page

(In millions, except per option amounts)	Number of Options	Weighted Average Exercise Price
December 31, 2011	298.3	$20.12
Grants	13.5	$27.01
Exercises	(85.8)	$20.45
Cancellations and forfeitures	(3.9)	$21.17
Expirations	(19.3)	$22.45
December 29, 2012	202.8	$20.20
Options exercisable as of:		
December 25, 2010	263.0	$21.03
December 31, 2011	203.6	$20.44
December 29, 2012	139.8	$19.76

Required

a. What did Intel expense for share-based compensation for 2012? How many options did Intel grant in 2012? Compute the fair value of all options granted during 2012. Why do the fair value of the option grants and the expense differ?

b. Intel used the Black-Scholes formula to estimate fair value of the options granted each year. How did the change in volatility from 2011 to 2012 affect share-based compensation in 2012? What about the change in risk-free rate?

c. How many options were exercised during 2012? Estimate the cash that Intel received from its employees when these options were exercised.

d. What was the intrinsic value per share of the options exercised in 2012? If employees who exercised options in 2012 immediately sold them, what "profit" did they make from the shares? (*Hint:* Assume that Intel grants options at-the-money.)

e. The tax benefit that Intel will receive on the options exercised is computed based on the intrinsic value of the options exercised. Estimate Intel's tax benefit from the 2012 option exercises assuming a tax rate of 37%.

f. What was the average exercise price of the 19.3 million options expired in 2012? Explain what benefit the employees lost by not exercising their options.

Intel Corporation (INTC)

P8-58. Interpreting Disclosure on Share-Based Compensation (LO1)

Intel reported the following information in its 2012 10-K related to its restricted stock plan.

Information with respect to outstanding restricted stock unit (RSU) activity is as follows:

(In Millions, Except Per RSU Amounts)	Number of RSUs	Weighted Average Grant-Date Fair Value
December 26, 2009	105.4	$17.03
Granted	32.4	$22.56
Vested	(34.6)	$17.70
Forfeited	(3.4)	$17.98
December 25, 2010	99.8	$18.56
Granted	43.3	$19.86
Assumed in acquisition	5.8	$20.80
Vested	(37.5)	$18.60
Forfeited	(4.4)	$19.07
December 31, 2011	107.0	$19.18
Granted	49.9	$25.32
Vested	(43.2)	$18.88
Forfeited	(4.4)	$20.93
December 29, 2012	109.3	$22.03
Expected to vest as of December 29, 2012	103.5	$20.21

continued

The aggregate fair value of awards that vested in 2012 was $1.2 billion ($753 million in 2011 and $808 million in 2010), which represents the market value of Intel common stock on the date that the restricted stock units vested. The grant-date fair value of awards that vested in 2012 was $816 million ($697 million in 2011 and $612 million in 2010). The number of restricted stock units vested includes shares that we withheld on behalf of employees to satisfy the minimum statutory tax withholding requirements. Restricted stock units that are expected to vest are net of estimated future forfeitures. As of December 29, 2012, there was $1.5 billion in unrecognized compensation costs related to restricted stock units granted under our equity incentive plans.

Required

a. How do restricted stock and stock options differ? In what respects are they the same?

b. Why do companies impose vesting periods on restricted stock grants?

c. Use the financial statement effects template to record the restricted stock granted to senior executives during 2012. The common stock has a par value of $0.001 per share.

d. Use the financial statement effects template to record the 2012 compensation expense related to Intel's restricted stock awards. (*Hint:* The expense is equal to the grant-date fair value of the RSUs that vested during the year.)

IFRS APPLICATIONS

I8-59. Analyzing Revaluation Reserve (LO2)

WorkCover Queensland offers workers compensation coverage to people in Queensland, Australia. Its 2012 notes (compliant with IFRS) reported the following information on the asset revaluation reserve, which is included in stockholders' equity on the balance sheet.

WorkCover Queensland

(in 000 Australian dollars)	Land	Buildings	Total
Carrying amount at the beginning of the prior year	$6,720	$12,332	$19,052
Movements for the prior year revaluation:			
Revaluation of land and building	—	(898)	(898)
Income tax effect on revaluation of land and building	—	269	269
	—	(629)	(629)
Carrying amount at the end of the prior year	6,720	11,703	18,423
Carrying amount at the beginning of the current year	6,720	11,703	18,423
Movements for the current year revaluation:			
Revaluation of land and building	—	(1,641)	(1,641)
Income tax effect on revaluation of land and building	—	492	492
	—	(1,149)	(1,149)
Carrying amount at the end of the current year	$6,720	$10,554	$17,274

Explain the concept of asset revaluation. What happened to the fair value of land during fiscal 2011 and fiscal 2012? Were the fair values of buildings similarly affected? How was the income statement affected by these revaluations?

I8-60. Analyzing and Computing Average Issue Price and Treasury Stock Cost and Market Cap (LO1, 2)

Ahold is a major international supermarket operator based in Zaandam, Netherlands. Following is information taken from Ahold's financial statements prepared in accordance with IFRS.

Ahold

Shareholders' Equity (€ millions)	December 30, 2012	January 1, 2012
Issued and paid-in share capital	€ 318	€ 330
Additional paid-in capital	8,713	9,094
Legal reserves	(100)	44
Accumulated deficit	(3,763)	(4,608)
Net income	827	1,017
Equity attributable to common shareholders	**€5,995**	**€5,877**

Footnotes to financial statements disclose the following: At December 30, 2012, and January 1, 2012, there were 1,700,000,000 shares authorized, and 1,060,988,000 and 1,100,888 shares issued respectively. During 2012, Ahold repurchased 26,832,085 shares for a total consideration of €277 million, and the company cancelled some of the treasury shares held. At year end 2012, the company had treasury stock of 22,481,000 shares.

Required

a. How many shares are authorized at December 30, 2012?
b. How many shares are issued at December 30, 2012? At what average price were these shares issued December 30, 2012?
c. At what average price did the company repurchase treasury shares during 2012?
d. How many shares are outstanding as of December 30, 2012?
e. At December 30, 2012, the share price for Ahold was €10.14. Compute the company's market capitalization on that date. How does this compare to the net book value of equity?

I8-61. Analyzing and Interpreting Equity Accounts and Comprehensive Income (LO1, 2)

Henkel AG & Co.

Henkel AG & Co. is an international, fast-moving consumer goods (FMCG) company headquartered in Düsseldorf, Germany. Following is its shareholders' equity statement, prepared using IFRS, from its 2012 annual report (in Euros millions).

Statement of changes in equity

In millions euro	Issued capital: Ordinary shares	Issued capital: Preferred shares	Capital reserve	Treasury shares	Retained earnings	Other components: Currency translation	Other components: Hedge reserve per IAS 39	Other components: Available-for-sale reserve	Shareholders of Henkel AG & Co.	Non-controlling Interests	Total
At December 31, 2011/ January 1, 2012	€260	€178	€652	€(93)	€8,494	€(662)	€(278)	€(2)	€8,549	€121	€8,670
Net income	—	—	—	—	1,510	—	—	—	1,510	46	1,556
Other comprehensive income	—	—	—	—	(273)	(144)	79	3	(335)	(1)	(336)
Total comprehensive income for the period	—	—	—	—	*1,237*	*(144)*	*79*	*3*	*1,175*	*45*	*1,220*
Dividends	—	—	—	—	(342)	—	—	—	(342)	(27)	(369)
Sale of treasury shares	—	—	—	2	3	—	—	—	5	—	5
Changes in ownership interest with no change in control	—	—	—	—	(4)	—	—	—	(4)	(6)	(10)
Other changes in equity	—	—	—	—	(7)	—	—	—	(7)	2	(5)
At December 31, 2012	**€260**	**€178**	**€652**	**€(91)**	**€9,381**	**€(806)**	**€(199)**	**€ 1**	**€9,376**	**€135**	**€9,511**

Required

a. Did Henkel issue any additional ordinary or preferred shares during 2012?
b. How much did Henkel pay in dividends during 2012? To whom were these dividends paid?
c. Did the company repurchase any stock during 2012?
d. Did Henkel sell any treasury shares? If so, what did the company receive in exchange for the sale of treasury stock?
e. Consider the currency translation account. Explain how the change of (€144) arose during the year.
f. Henkel reports noncontrolling interest of €135. Why did this account increase during the year?
g. Compute return on equity for 2012. (*Hint:* Use the net income attributable to controlling interest [shareholders of Henkel] and equity attributable to controlling interest.)

I8-62. Analyzing and Computing Average Issue Price and Treasury Stock Transactions (LO1)

Telefónica, S.A. (TEF)

Telefónica, S.A. is a Spanish broadband and telecommunications provider with operations in Europe, Latin America, North America and Asia. The company's statement of changes in equity reported the following:

(In million €)	December 31, 2012	December 31, 2011
Share capital	€ 4,551	€ 4,564
Share premium	460	460
Reserves	(3,215)	(854)
Treasury shares (47,847,810 and 84,209,364 shares)	(788)	(1,782)
Retained earnings	19,453	19,248
Total attributable to equityholders of parent	20,461	21,636
Noncontrolling interests	7,200	5,747
Total equity	**€27,661**	**€27,383**

Notes to the financial statements reveal that the company has net debt of €53.3 billion as at December 31, 2012. On March 26, 2013, *Bloomberg BusinessWeek* reported the following:

> **Telefónica S.A. (TEF)**, taking advantage of an 18 percent increase by its shares in the past month, raised about 975 million euros ($1.3 billion) after selling all of its treasury stock to reduce the Spanish carrier's debt.

Required

a. Consider the treasury shares at December 31, 2012. At what average price did the company repurchase these shares?

b. Use the information above to infer the number of treasury shares sold during fiscal 2012.

c. Use the financial statement effects template to record the sale of treasury shares announced on March 26, 2013.

d. Assume the company uses all the anticipated proceeds to reduce debt. Quantify the effect on the total debt to total equity ratio.

I8-63. Interpreting Disclosure on Share-Based Compensation (LO1)

Research in Motion

Research in Motion is a Canadian telecommunication and wireless equipment company best known as the developer of the BlackBerry brand of smartphones and tablets. The company is headquartered in Waterloo, Ontario, Canada. The company' 2013 10-K reported the following information related to restricted stock.

> ***Restricted Share Unit Plan*** The Company recorded compensation expense with respect to RSUs of approximately $78 million in the year ended March 2, 2013. A summary of RSU activity since March 3, 2012 is shown below:

RSUs Outstanding	Number (000's)	Weighted-Average Grant Date Fair Value	Average Remaining Contractual Life in Years	Aggregate Intrinsic Value (millions)
Balance as at March 3, 2012 . . .	8,595	$31.96		
Granted during the year	11,189	7.94		
Vested during the year	(2,697)	38.96		
Cancelled during the year	(1,902)	25.46		
Balance as at March 2, 2013 . . .	15,185	$13.83	1.59	$201

> The aggregate intrinsic value in the table above represents the total pre-tax intrinsic value (the aggregate closing share price of the Company's common shares on March 2, 2013) that would have been received by RSU holders if all RSUs had been vested on March 2, 2013.

a. How do restricted stock and stock options differ? In what respects are they the same?

b. Why do companies impose vesting periods on restricted stock grants?

c. Use the financial statement effects template to record the restricted stock granted during the fiscal year 2012–2013. Assume RIM common stock has no par value.

d. In your opinion, how effective were the RSUs that vested during the year at creating incentives for Research in Motion employees?

I8-64. Analyzing Stockholders' Equity Accounts and Transactions (LO1 ,2)

Potash Corporation (POT)

Potash Corporation—the world's largest potash producer—is a Canadian corporation based in Saskatoon, Saskatchewan. The following is information taken from its financial statements reported in $US but prepared in accordance with IFRS.

Equity Attributable to Common Shareholders (In millions of US dollars)	Share Capital	Contributed Surplus	Accumulated Other Comprehensive Income: Net unrealized gain on available-for-sale investments	Net loss on derivatives designated as cash flow hedges	Net actuarial loss on defined benefit plans	Other	Total Accumulated Other Comprehensive Income	Retained Earnings	Total Equity
Balance—December 31, 2011	$1,483	$291	$982	$(168)	$—	$2	$816	$5,257	$7,847
Net income	—	—	—	—	—	—	—	2,079	2,079
Other comprehensive income (loss)	—	—	557	30	(62)	(4)	521	—	521
Dividends declared	—	—	—	—	—	—	—	(603)	(603)
Effect of share-based compensation including issuance of common shares	47	8	—	—	—	—	—	—	55
Shares issued for dividend reinvestment plan	13	—	—	—	—	—	—	—	13
Transfer of net actuarial loss on defined benefit plans	—	—	—	—	62	—	62	(62)	—
Balance—December 31, 2012	$1,543	$299	$1,539	$(138)	$—	$(2)	$1,399	$6,671	$9,912

Authorized The company is authorized to issue an unlimited number of common shares without par value and an unlimited number of first preferred shares. The common shares are not redeemable or convertible. The first preferred shares may be issued in one or more series with rights and conditions to be determined by the Board of Directors. No first preferred shares have been issued.

Issued	Number of Common Shares	Consideration
Balance, December 31, 2011	858,702,991	$1,483
Issued under option plans	5,895,730	47
Issued for dividend reinvestment plan	301,792	13
Balance, December 31, 2012	864,900,513	$1,543

a. How many shares are authorized at December 31, 2012?

b. How many shares are issued at December 31, 2012? At what average price were these shares issued as of December 31, 2012?

c. How many shares are issued under option plans at December 31, 2012? At what average price were these shares issued?

d. Does the company have any treasury stock? How do we know?

e. On January 30, 2013, the company's Board of Directors declared a quarterly dividend of $0.28 per share, payable to all shareholders of record on April 11, 2013. Assuming that the number of shares outstanding on April 11, 2013, is the same as on December 31, 2012, what dividends will the company pay?

f. Comprehensive income includes net income plus other comprehensive income. What was the company's comprehensive income for 2012? Why does it differ from net income for 2012?

I8-65. Analyzing Stockholders' Equity Accounts and Transactions (LO1 ,2)

BHP Billiton (BHP)

Headquartered in Melbourne, Australia, **BHP Billiton Group** is a leading global resources company that operates in diverse commodity and geographic markets. Its stock is traded on the Australian Securities Exchange (ASX) and also listed in London, Johannesburg, and New York. Following is information taken from its financial statements prepared in accordance with IFRS.

BHP Billiton Group was formed in June 2001 from the merger of BHP Limited (an Australian listed company) and Billiton Plc (a UK listed company). The merger was effected by way of a dual listed companies (DLC) structure, meaning that although the companies technically continue to be separate legal entities (now renamed BHP Billiton Limited and BHP Billiton Plc) with separate share listings and share registers, they are managed and run as a single economic entity. The companies have a common Board of Directors and management team. Shareholders in BHP Billiton Limited and BHP Billiton Plc have equal economic and voting rights, as if they held shares in a single company.

continued

Shareholders' Equity (US$M)	June 30, 2012	June 30, 2011
Share capital – BHP Billiton Limited	$ 1,186	$ 1,183
Share capital – BHP Billiton Plc	1,069	1,070
Treasury shares	(533)	(623)
Reserves	1,912	2,001
Retained earnings	62,236	53,131
Total to BHP Billiton Group	65,870	56,762
Noncontrolling interests	1,215	993
Total equity	$67,085	$57,755

	BHP Billiton Limited 2012 Shares	BHP Billiton Plc 2012 Shares
Share capital issued		
Ordinary shares fully paid	3,211,691,105	2,136,185,454
Comprising		
Shares held by the public	3,211,448,985	2,111,273,967
Treasury shares	242,120	24,911,487
Special voting share of no par value	1	—
5.5% Preference shares of $1 each	—	50,000
Special voting share of US$0.50 par value	—	1

a. How many total shares has the BHP Billiton Group issued at June 30, 2012?

b. Does BHP Billiton Group have treasury shares? How many? What are possible reasons why a company would buy back its shares?

c. Determine the average amount the Group paid for treasury shares as of June 30, 2012.

d. By what amount did Retained Earnings change during the year? Can we infer that this difference represents net income for the year?

I8-66. Analyzing Stockholders' Equity Accounts and Transactions (LO1 ,2)

Rogers Communications Inc. is a Canadian company headquartered in Toronto, operating primarily in the fields of wireless communication, cable television, telephone, and Internet connectivity. Following is its shareholders' equity statement, prepared using IFRS, from its 2012 annual report.

Rogers Communications Inc. (RCI)

CONSOLIDATED STATEMENTS OF CHANGES IN SHAREHOLDERS' EQUITY

Years ended December 31, 2012 (in millions of Canadian dollars)	Class A Voting Shares Amount	Class A Number of Shares (000s)	Class B Non-Voting Shares Amount	Class B Number of Shares (000s)	Share Premium	Retained Earnings	Available-for-Sale Financial Assets Reserve	Hedging Reserve	Total Shareholders' Equity
Balances, January 1, 2012	$72	112,462	$406	412,395	$243	$2,443	$433	$(25)	$3,572
Net income for the year	—	—	—	—	—	1,700	—	—	1,700
Other comprehensive income (loss):									
Defined benefit pension plans, net of tax	—	—	—	—	—	(180)	—	—	(180)
Available-for-sale investments, net of tax	—	—	—	—	—	—	(190)	—	(190)
Derivative instruments, net of tax	—	—	—	—	—	—	—	35	35
Total other comprehensive loss	—	—	—	—	—	(180)	(190)	35	(335)
Comprehensive income for the year	—	—	—	—	—	1,520	(190)	35	1,365
Transactions with shareholders, recorded directly in equity:									
Repurchase of Class B Non-Voting shares	—	—	(10)	(9,637)	(243)	(97)	—	—	(350)
Dividends declared	—	—	—	—	—	(820)	—	—	(820)
Shares issued on exercise of stock options	—	—	1	30	—	—	—	—	1
Total transactions with shareholders	—	—	(9)	(9,607)	(243)	(917)	—	—	(1,169)
Balances, December 31, 2012	$72	112,462	$397	402,788	$—	$3,046	$243	$10	$3,768

Required

a. Did Rogers Communications issue any additional Class A or Class B shares during 2012?

b. Use the information above to determine how much Rogers Communications paid in dividends during 2012.

c. The company repurchased stock during 2012. Explain how many shares and what Class were repurchased.

d. Did the transaction involving shares issued on exercise of stock options affect net income for the year? Explain.

e. Explain the available-for-sale financial assets reserve. Why did the account balance decrease during the year?

f. Compute return on equity for 2012.

MANAGEMENT APPLICATIONS

MA8-67. Ethics and Governance: Equity Carve-Outs **(LO3)**

Many companies use split-offs as a means to unlock shareholder value. The split-off effectively splits the company into two pieces, each of which can then be valued separately by the stock market. If managers are compensated based on reported profit, how might they strategically structure the split-off? What corporate governance issues does this present?

ONGOING PROJECT

(*This ongoing project began in Module 1 and continues through most of the book; even if previous segments were not completed, the requirements are still applicable to any business analysis.*) Company analysis should include that of stockholders' equity, including how the companies are financed and what transactions were executed with stockholders during the recent year or so.

1. *Contributed Capital.* Use the balance sheet and the statement of stockholders' equity to determine how the company has structured its equity.
   - What proportion of assets are financed with equity?
   - What classes of equity does the company have? What transactions occurred during the year?
   - Does the company have treasury stock? Read the MD&A and the footnotes to determine the main reason for holding treasury stock. Assess the treasury stock transactions during the year. How much was spent and/or received? What did the company do with the proceeds? Compare the average price paid for treasury shares to the current stock price.
   - Does the company use share-based compensation? What types of plans are used? What was the magnitude of the compensation? What is the magnitude of the outstanding (unvested) options and/or shares? To assess this, consider their common size and their effect on diluted earnings per share. Compare the level of treasury shares to outstanding (unvested) options and / or shares.
   - Compute the market capitalization of the firms and compare to the book value of equity. Find an online source for the average market-to-book ratio for the industry and see where the firms fit. Follow up on anything unusual.
2. *Earned Capital.* Recall that the least costly form of financing is internal – that is, plowing earned profits (and cash) into new investments is a low-cost means to grow the company and return even more to stockholders.
   - How profitable were the companies? Compare return on equity for the three-year period and determine causes for major differences over time and between companies.
   - Review accumulated other comprehensive income and determine the main components of that account. How did AOCI change during the year?
   - Did the companies pay cash dividends? Compute the dividend payout and the dividend yield for all three years and compare them.
   - Did the company have any stock splits or pay stock dividends?
3. *Equity Carve-Outs.* Read the footnotes and the MD&A to determine if the company engaged in any equity carve-outs during the year.
   - How was the transaction structured? That is, explain any sell-off, spin-off, or split-off.
   - What consideration was received for the sale? Did this result in a gain or loss on disposal?
   - What did the company do with the proceeds?

4. *Convertible Securities.* Read the debt footnote to determine if the company has any convertible securities.
   - What types of convertible securities are outstanding?
   - Are these securities substantive? To assess this, consider their common size and their effect on diluted earnings per share.
   - Did the company have any convertible transactions during the year? If yes, determine the effect on the balance sheet and income statement.

SOLUTIONS TO REVIEW PROBLEMS

Mid-Module Review 1

Part 1

Solution

	Balance Sheet									Income Statement				
Transaction	Cash Asset	+	Noncash Assets	=	Liabilities	+	Contrib. Capital	+	Earned Capital	Revenues	−	Expenses	=	Net Income
Jan. 15: Issue 10,000 shares, $5 par, common at $17 per share	+170,000 Cash			=			+50,000 Common Stock +120,000 Additional Paid-In Capital				−		=	
Mar. 31: Repurchase 2,000 shares of common at $15 per share	−30,000 Cash			=			−30,000 Treasury Stock				−		=	
June 25: Reissue 1,000 treasury shares at $20 per share	+20,000 Cash			=			+15,000 Treasury Stock +5,000 Additional Paid-In Capital				−		=	

Cash 170,000
CS 50,000
APIC 120,000

Cash: 170,000 (debit)
CS: 50,000 (credit)
APIC: 120,000 (credit)

TS 30,000
Cash 30,000

TS: 30,000 (debit)
Cash: 30,000 (credit)

Cash 20,000
TS 15,000
APIC 5,000

Cash: 20,000 (debit)
TS: 15,000 (credit)
APIC: 5,000 (credit)

Part 2

Solution

a. *Granted* relates to the number of shares under option that have been awarded to employees for the year. *Exercised* refers to the number of shares that employees have purchased that were previously under option. *Forfeited* relates to the number of shares under option that are no longer exercisable because the options were not exercised before they expired. The "Weighted Average Exercise Price" is the average price at which employees can purchase shares of stock that are under option, weighted by the number of shares at each exercise price.

b. Compensation cost is computed as the total value of employee stock options spread over the vesting period. For example, if Accenture grants employees stock options with an estimated value of $1 billion that vest over a four-year period, the expense that is recognized over the subsequent four years is $250 million per year. The "unrecognized compensation cost" is that portion of the total estimated value of the stock options that has not yet been recognized as expense in the income statement.

Mid-Module Review 2

Solution

a.

Cumulative Preferred Stock	Preferred Stock	Common Stock
Year 1—$0 cash dividends paid.	$ 0	$ 0
Year 2—$300,000 cash dividends paid		
Dividends in arrears from Year 1 ($1,000,000 × 5%)	50,000	
Current-year dividend ($1,000,000 × 5%)	50,000	
Balance to common		200,000
Year 3—$80,000 cash dividends paid		
Current-year dividend ($1,000,000 × 5%)	50,000	
Balance to common		30,000

b.

Noncumulative Preferred Stock	Preferred Stock	Common Stock
Year 1—$0 cash dividends paid.	$ 0	$ 0
Year 2—$300,000 cash dividends paid		
Current-year dividend ($1,000,000 × 5%)	50,000	
Balance to common		250,000
Year 3—$80,000 cash dividends paid		
Current-year dividend ($1,000,000 × 5%)	50,000	
Balance to common		30,000

Mid-Module Review 3

Solution

		Balance Sheet									Income Statement				
	Transaction	Cash Asset	+	Noncash Assets	=	Liabilities	+	Contrib. Capital	+	Earned Capital	Revenues	−	Expenses	=	Net Income
RE 250,000 CS 250,000 RE: 250,000 | CS: | 250,000	Apr. 1: Declare and issue 100% stock dividend; stock is $11 per share				=			+250,000 Common Stock		−250,000[1] Retained Earnings		−		=	
RE 21,000 CS 15,000 APIC 6,000 RE: 21,000 | CS: | 15,000 APIC: | 6,000	Dec. 7: Declare and issue 3% stock dividend; stock is $7 per share				=			+15,000 Common Stock +6,000 Additional Paid-In Capital		−21,000[2] Retained Earnings		−		=	
RE 123,600 Cash 123,600 RE: 123,600 | Cash: | 123,600	Dec. 31: Declare and pay cash dividend of $1.20 per share	−123,600 Cash			=					−123,600[3] Retained Earnings		−		=	

[1] This large stock dividend reduces retained earnings at the par value of shares distributed (50,000 shares × 100% × $5 par value = $250,000). Contributed capital (common stock) increases by the same amount.

[2] This small stock dividend reduces retained earnings at the market value of shares distributed (3% × 100,000 shares × $7 per share = $21,000). Contributed capital increases by the same amount ($15,000 to common stock and $6,000 to paid-in capital). Note that the number of common shares outstanding on December 7 was 100,000—the large stock dividend on April 7 doubled the number of common stock outstanding.

[3] At the time of the cash dividend, there are 103,000 shares outstanding. The cash paid is, therefore, 103,000 shares × $1.20 per share = $123,600.

Mid-Module Review 4

Solution

1. A split-off is like a treasury stock transaction, but instead of repurchasing stock with cash, shares of the parent company owned by the shareholders are exchanged for shares of the subsidiary owned by the parent. If the distribution is non pro rata, the parent can report a gain equal to the difference between the fair value of the subsidiary and its book value on the parent's balance sheet.
2. BearingPoint met the conditions for a split-off as described in part 1, which enabled it to report a gain.

Module-End Review

Solution

	Balance Sheet									Income Statement				
Transaction	Cash Asset	+	Noncash Assets	=	Liabilities	+	Contrib. Capital	+	Earned Capital	Revenues	−	Expenses	=	Net Income
Convert a bond with $850 book value into 200 common shares with $1 par value				=	−850 Long-Term Debt		+200 Common Stock +650 Additional Paid-In Capital				−		=	

LTD	850	
CS		200
APIC		650

LTD	
850	

CS	
	200

APIC	
	650

Module

9 Reporting and Analyzing Intercorporate Investments

Learning Objectives

LO1 Describe and illustrate accounting for passive investments. (p. 9-4)

LO2 Explain and illustrate accounting for equity method investments. (p. 9-11)

LO3 Describe and illustrate accounting for consolidations. (p. 9-17)

Google

With a market capitalization of over $250 billion as of mid-2013, **Google** is the third most valuable U.S. publicly-traded company, trailing only **Apple** and **Exxon** and more valuable than **Berkshire Hathaway**, **Walmart**, **GE**, **Microsoft**, and **IBM**. Since its IPO in 2004, Google's (GOOG) stock price has increased more than tenfold making Google one of the fastest growing companies on any stock exchange.

Google's operations generated nearly $17 billion of operating cash flow in 2012, nearly three times the cash generated five years before. By the end of 2012, Google reported over $48 billion in cash and marketable securities on its balance sheet.

Google has considerable investments in government bonds. It holds these investments because it has excess cash awaiting deployment in other business activities. In the interim, the company expects to earn dividends and (potentially) capital gains from these securities. The accounting for these types of marketable securities differs markedly from the accounting for most other assets—Google's balance sheet reports these marketable securities at their current fair (or market) value instead of at their historical cost. As a result, the assets on Google's balance sheet fluctuate with the stock market. This causes stockholders' equity to fluctuate because, as we know from the accounting equation, assets equal liabilities plus equity.

We might wonder why Google would report these assets at fair value when nearly all other assets are reported at historical cost. As well, we might ask how these fluctuations in fair value affect Google's reported profit, if at all. This module answers both questions and explains the accounting for, and analysis of, such "passive" investments in marketable securities.

To expand its business activities beyond its current search-engine and advertising base, Google has strategically invested in the stock of other companies, which is a second category of investments. Through these strategic investments, Google can acquire substantial ownership of the companies such that Google can significantly influence their operations. The nature and purpose of these investments differs from Google's passive investment in marketable securities and, accordingly, the accounting reflects that difference. In particular, if Google owns enough voting stock to exert significant influence over another company, Google uses the *equity method* to account for those investments. Under the equity method, Google carries the investment on its balance sheet at an amount equal to its proportionate share of the investee company's equity. An equity method investment increases and decreases, not with changes in the stock's market value, but with changes in the investee company's stockholders' equity.

An interesting by-product of the equity method is that Google's balance sheet does not reflect the investee company's individual assets and liabilities, but only Google's share of the investee's net assets (its stockholders' equity). This is important because Google could be using the investee's assets and be responsible, to some extent, for the investee's liabilities. Yet, those liabilities are not detailed on Google's balance sheet. This creates what is called *off-balance-sheet financing*, potentially of great concern to accountants, analysts, creditors, and others

Courtesy of iStock

who rely on financial reports. This module describes the equity method of accounting for investments, including the implications of this type of off-balance-sheet financing.

When an investor company acquires a sufficiently large proportion of the voting stock of another company, it can effectively control the other company. At that point, the financial statements of the acquired company must be *consolidated* with those of the investor (or parent) company. Most of the financial statements of public companies are titled "consolidated." Consolidation essentially adds together the financial statements of two or more companies. It is important that we understand what consolidated financial statements tell us and what they do not. This module covers consolidation along with a discussion of its implications for analysis.

There was much consternation among investors when Google's stock price passed $100, then $200, then $600, then $800. At each milestone, investors became increasingly concerned that Google's stock was overvalued. That concern still abounds. But, as Google continues to make strategic investments necessary to broaden its revenue base, its share price will likely increase. Google's management believes that investments are a crucial part of the company's strategic plan. Understanding the accounting for all three types of intercorporate investment is, thus, important to our understanding of Google's (and other companies') ongoing operations.

Sources: *Google Form 10-K*, 2012; *Google Annual Report*, 2012; *BusinessWeek*, 2006; and *Fortune*, 2006 and 2011.

MODULE ORGANIZATION

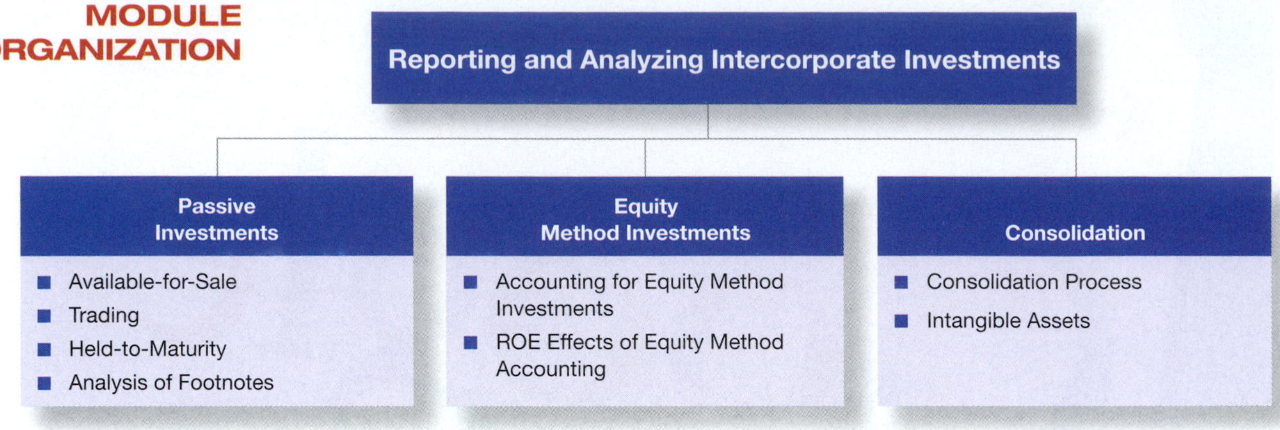

It is common for one company to purchase the voting stock of another. These purchases, called *intercorporate investments,* have the following strategic aims:

- **Short-term investment of excess cash.** Companies might invest excess cash to use during slow times of the year (after receivables are collected and before seasonal production begins) or to maintain liquidity (such as to counter strategic moves by competitors or to quickly respond to acquisition opportunities).
- **Alliances for strategic purposes.** Companies might acquire an equity interest in other companies for strategic purposes, such as gaining access to their research and development activities, to their supply or distribution markets, or to their production and marketing expertise.
- **Market penetration or expansion.** Companies might acquire control of other companies to achieve vertical or horizontal integration in existing markets or to penetrate new and growth markets.

Accounting for intercorporate investments follows one of three different methods, each of which affects the balance sheet and the income statement differently. These differences can be quite substantial. To help assimilate the materials in this module, Exhibit 9.1 graphically depicts the accounting for investments.

EXHIBIT 9.1 Accounting for Investments Based on Corporate Control

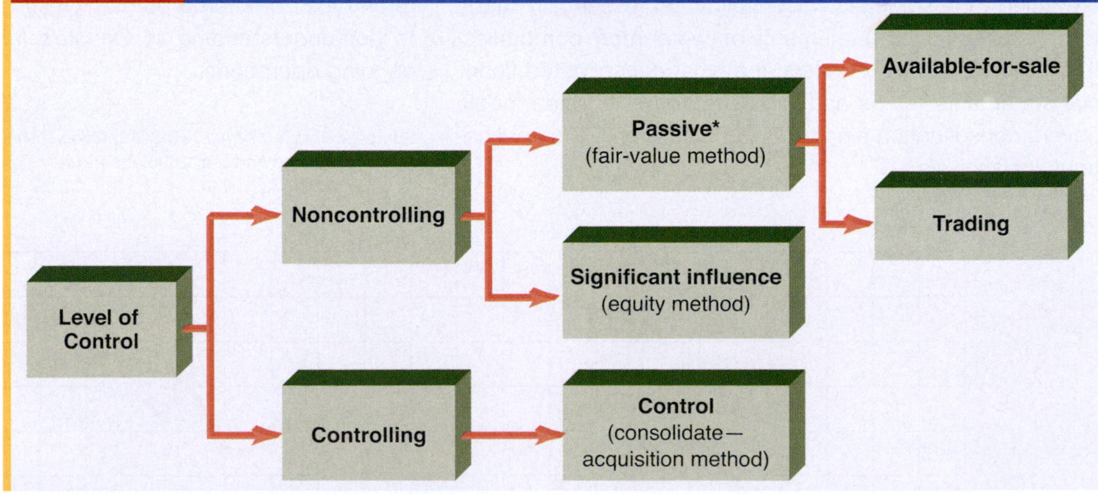

* There is another passive category in which the *cost method* is used for (1) held-to-maturity debt securities, and (2) non-marketable equity (and debt) securities; both applications are explained in this module.

The degree of influence or control that the investor company (purchaser) can exert over the investee company (the company whose securities are being purchased) determines the accounting method. GAAP identifies three levels of influence/control.

1. **Passive.** A passive investment is one where the purchasing company has a relatively small investment and cannot exert influence over the investee company. The investor's goal is to realize dividends and capital gains. Generally, the investment is considered passive if the investor company owns less than 20% of the outstanding voting stock of the investee company.
2. **Significant influence.** A company can sometimes exert significant influence over, but not control, the activities of the investee company. Significant influence can result when the percentage of voting stock owned is greater than a passive, short-term investment. However, an investment can also exhibit "significant influence" if there exist legal agreements between the investor and investee, such as a license to use technology, a formula, or a trade secret like production know-how. Absent other contractual arrangements such as those described above, significant influence is presumed at investment levels between 20% and 50%.
3. **Control.** When a company has control over another, it has the ability to elect a majority of the board of directors and, as a result, the ability to affect the investee company's strategic direction and the hiring of executive management. Control is generally presumed if the investor company owns more than 50% of the outstanding voting stock of the investee company, but can sometimes occur at less than 50% stock ownership by virtue of legal agreements, technology licensing, or other contractual means.

The level of influence/control determines the specific accounting method applied and its financial statement implications as outlined in Exhibit 9.2.

EXHIBIT 9.2 Investment Type, Accounting Treatment, and Financial Statement Effects

	Accounting	Balance Sheet Effects	Income Statement Effects	Cash Flow Effects
Passive	Fair-value method	Investment account is reported at fair value	Dividends and capital gains and losses included in income Interim changes in fair value affect income if the investor actively trades the securities Sale of investment yields capital gain or loss	Dividends and sale proceeds are cash inflows from investing activities Purchases are cash outflows from investing activities
Significant influence	Equity method	Investment account equals percent owned of investee company's equity*	Dividends reduce investment account Investor reports income equal to percent owned of investee income Sale of investment yields capital gain or loss	Dividends and sale proceeds are cash inflows from investing activities Purchases are cash outflows from investing activities
Control	Consolidation	Balance sheets of investor and investee are combined	Income statements of investor and investee are combined Sale of investee yields capital gain or loss	Cash flows of investor and investee are combined and retain original classification (operating, investing, or financing) Sale and purchase of investee are investing cash flows

*Investments are often acquired at purchase prices in excess of book value (the market price of S&P 500 companies was 2.6 times their book value as of November 2013). In this case the investment account exceeds the proportionate ownership of the investee's equity.

There are two basic reporting issues with investments: (1) how investment income should be recognized in the income statement and (2) at what amount (cost or fair value) the investment should be reported on the balance sheet. We next discuss both of these issues as we consider the three investment types.

PASSIVE INVESTMENTS

LO1 Describe and illustrate accounting for passive investments.

Short-term investments of excess cash are typically passive investments. Passive investments can involve equity or debt securities. Equity securities involve an ownership interest such as common stock or preferred stock, whereas debt securities have no ownership interest. A voting stock investment is passive when the investor does not possess sufficient ownership to either influence or control the investee company. The *fair-value method* is used to account for passive investments in both debt and equity securities.

Acquisition and Sale

When a company makes a passive investment, it records the shares acquired on the balance sheet at fair value, that is, the purchase price. This is the same as accounting for the acquisition of other assets such as inventories or plant assets. Subsequent to acquisition, passive investments are carried on the balance sheet as current or long-term assets, depending on management's expectations about their ultimate holding period.

When investments are sold, any recognized gain or loss on sale is equal to the difference between the proceeds received and the book (carrying) value of the investment on the balance sheet as follows:

Gain or Loss on Sale = Proceeds from Sale − Book Value of Investment Sold

To illustrate the acquisition and sale of a passive investment, assume that **Microsoft** purchases 1,000 shares of **Skype** for $20 cash per share (this includes transaction costs such as brokerage fees). Microsoft, subsequently, sells 400 of the 1,000 shares for $23 cash per share. The following financial statement effects template shows how these transactions affect Microsoft.

MS 20,000
Cash 20,000

MS: 20,000 (debit)
Cash: 20,000 (credit)

Cash 9,200
MS 8,000
GN 1,200

Cash: 9,200 (debit)
MS: 8,000 (credit)
GN: 1,200 (credit)

Transaction	Cash Asset	+	Noncash Assets	=	Liabilities	+	Contrib. Capital	+	Earned Capital	Revenues	−	Expenses	=	Net Income
	Balance Sheet									**Income Statement**				
1. Purchase 1,000 shares of Skype common stock for $20 cash per share	−20,000 Cash		+20,000 Marketable Securities	=							−		=	
2. Sell 400 shares of Skype common stock for $23 cash per share	+9,200 Cash		−8,000 Marketable Securities	=					+1,200 Retained Earnings	+1,200 Gain on Sale	−		=	+1,200

Income statements include the gain or loss on sale of marketable securities as a component of *other income*, which is typically reported separately from operating income and often aggregated with interest and dividend revenue. Accounting for the purchase and sale of passive investments is the same as for any other asset. Further, there is no difference in accounting for purchases and sales across the different types of passive investments discussed in this section. However, there are differences in accounting for different types of passive investments between their purchase and their sale. We next address this issue.

Fair Value versus Cost

If a passive investment in equity securities has an active market with published prices, that investment is reported on the balance sheet at fair value. Fair value is specifically defined under GAAP. It is the value a willing party would pay to buy the asset in a well-functioning market. Quoted market prices must be used when available, which are called *Level 1 fair values*. In the absence of quoted market prices, companies can use market prices for similar assets, which are called *Level 2 fair values* or, if market prices for similar assets are not available, an estimate of investment value using financial models, which are *Level 3 fair values* (see the reporting for Google's investments later in this module). For marketable securities, **fair value** is the published price (as listed on a stock exchange) multiplied by the number of shares owned. This is one of few assets that are reported at fair value instead of historical cost.[1] For marketable securities, the current market value is almost always equal to the "fair" value and, thus, the two terms are often used interchangeably. If there exists no active market with published prices for the stock, the investment is reported at its historical cost.

Why are passive investments recorded at current fair value on the balance sheet? The answer lies in understanding the trade-off between the *objectivity* of historical cost and the *relevance* of market

[1] Other assets reported at fair value include (1) derivative securities (such as forward contracts, options, and futures) that are purchased to provide a hedge against price fluctuations or to eliminate other business risks (such as interest or exchange rate fluctuations), and (2) inventories and long-term assets that must be written down to market when their values permanently decline.

value. All things equal, current fair values of assets are more relevant in determining the market value of the company as a whole. However, for most assets, market values cannot be reliably determined. Adding unreliable "market values" to the balance sheet would introduce undue subjectivity into financial reports.

In the case of marketable securities, market prices result from numerous transactions between willing buyers and sellers. Market prices in this case provide an unbiased (objective) estimate of fair value to report on balance sheets. This reliability is the main reason GAAP allows passive investments to be recorded at fair value instead of at historical cost.

This fair-value method of accounting for securities causes asset values (the marketable securities) to fluctuate, with a corresponding change in equity (liabilities are unaffected). This is reflected in the following accounting equation:

Assets ↑ = Liabilities + Equity ↑ or **Assets ↓ = Liabilities + Equity ↓**

An important issue is whether such changes in equity should be reported as income (with a consequent change in retained earnings), or whether they should bypass the income statement and directly impact equity via *accumulated other comprehensive income (AOCI)*. The answer differs depending on the classification of securities, which we explain next.

Investments Marked to Market

For accounting purposes, marketable securities are classified into two types, both of which are reported on the balance sheet at fair value. Remember that for marketable securities, current market value is usually synonymous with fair value, thus we say that marketable securities are *marked to market*.

1. **Available-for-sale (AFS).** These are securities that management intends to hold for capital gains and dividend revenue; although, they might be sold if the price is right.
2. **Trading (T).** These are investments that management intends to actively buy and sell for trading profits as market prices fluctuate.

Management classifies securities depending on the degree of turnover (transaction volume) it expects in the investment portfolio, which reflects management's intent to actively trade the securities or not. Available-for-sale portfolios exhibit less turnover than trading portfolios. (GAAP permits companies to have multiple portfolios, each with a different classification, and management can change portfolio classification provided it adheres to strict disclosure and reporting requirements about its expectations of turnover change.) The classification as either available-for-sale or trading determines the accounting treatment, as Exhibit 9.3 summarizes.

EXHIBIT 9.3 Accounting Treatment for Available-for-Sale and for Trading Investments

Investment Classification	Reporting of Fair-Value Changes	Reporting of Dividends Received and Gains and Losses on Sale
Available-for-Sale (AFS)	Fair-value changes bypass the income statement and are reported in accumulated other comprehensive income (AOCI) as part of equity	Reported as *other income* in income statement
Trading (T)	Fair-value changes are reported in the income statement and impact equity via retained earnings	Reported as *other income* in income statement

The difference between the accounting treatment of available-for-sale and trading investments relates to how fair-value changes affect equity. Changes in the fair value of available-for-sale securities have no income effect; changes in fair value of trading securities have an income effect. The impact on total stockholders' equity is identical for both classifications. The only difference is whether the change is reflected in retained earnings or in the accumulated other comprehensive income (AOCI) component of stockholders' equity. Dividends and any gains or losses on security sales are reported in the other income section of the income statement for both classifications. (GAAP gives companies an option to account for available-for-sale securities like trading securities and report all changes in fair value on the income statement.) When sold, *unrealized* gains (losses) on available-for-sale investments are transferred ("reclassified") from AOCI into income and, thereby, become *realized* gains (losses).

Fair-Value Adjustments

To illustrate the accounting for changes in fair value subsequent to purchase (and before sale), assume that Microsoft's investment in Skype (600 remaining shares purchased for $20 per share) increases in value to $25 per share at year-end. The investment must be marked to market to reflect the $3,000 unrealized gain ($5 per share increase for 600 shares). The financial statement effects depend on whether the investment is classified as available-for-sale or as trading as follows:

MS 3,000
AOCI 3,000
MS: 3,000 (debit)
AOCI: 3,000 (credit)

MS 3,000
UG 3,000
MS: 3,000 (debit)
UG: 3,000 (credit)

	Balance Sheet					Income Statement		
Transaction	Cash Asset +	Noncash Assets =	Liabilities +	Contrib. Capital +	Earned Capital	Revenues −	Expenses =	Net Income
If classified as available-for-sale								
$5 increase in fair value of Skype investment		+3,000 Marketable Securities =			+3,000 AOCI	−		=
If classified as trading								
$5 increase in fair value of Skype investment		+3,000 Marketable Securities =			+3,000 Retained Earnings	+3,000 Unrealized Gain −		= +3,000

Under both classifications, the investment account increases by $3,000 to reflect the increase in the stock's market value. If Microsoft classifies these securities as available-for-sale, the unrealized gain increases the accumulated other comprehensive income (AOCI) account (which analysts typically view as a component of earned capital). However, if Microsoft classifies the securities as trading, the unrealized gain is recorded as income, thus increasing both reported income and retained earnings for the period. (Our illustration uses a portfolio with only one security for simplicity. Portfolios usually consist of multiple securities, and the unrealized gain or loss is computed based on the total cost and total market value of the entire portfolio.)

These fair-value adjustments only apply if market prices are available, that is, for publicly traded securities. Thus, this mark-to-market accounting does not apply to investments in start-up companies or privately held corporations. Investments in nonpublicly traded companies are accounted for at cost as we discuss later in this section.

Financial Statement Disclosures

Companies are required to disclose cost and fair values of their investment portfolios in footnotes to financial statements. **Google** reports the accounting policies for its investments in the following footnote to its 2012 10-K report:

> **Cash, Cash Equivalents, and Marketable Securities** We invest our excess cash primarily in time deposits, money market and other funds, including cash collateral received related to our securities lending program, highly liquid debt instruments of the U.S. government and its agencies, debt instruments issued by foreign governments and municipalities in the U.S., corporate securities, mortgage-backed securities, and asset-backed securities. We classify all highly liquid investments with stated maturities of three months or less from date of purchase as cash equivalents and all highly liquid investments with stated maturities of greater than three months as marketable securities...We have classified and accounted for our marketable securities as available-for-sale... We carry these securities at fair value, and report the unrealized gains and losses, net of taxes, as a component of stockholders' equity, except for unrealized losses determined to be other-than-temporary, which we record as interest and other income, net. We determine any realized gains or losses on the sale of marketable securities on a specific identification method, and we record such gains and losses as a component of interest and other income, net.

Google accounts for its investments in marketable securities at fair value. Because Google classifies those investments as "available-for-sale," unrealized gains and losses flow to the accumulated other comprehensive income component of stockholders' equity. When Google sells the securities, it will record any *realized* gains or losses in income.

Following is the current asset section of Google's 2012 balance sheet reflecting these investments.

December 31 ($ millions)	2011	2012
Cash and cash equivalents	$ 9,983	$14,778
Marketable securities	34,643	33,310
Total cash, cash equivalents, and marketable securities (including securities loaned of $2,778 and $3,160)	44,626	48,088
Accounts receivable, net of allowance of $133 and $581	5,427	7,885
Inventories	35	505
Receivable under reverse repurchase agreements	745	700
Deferred income taxes, net	215	1,144
Prepaid revenue share, expenses and other assets	1,710	2,132
Total current assets	$52,758	$60,454

Google's investments in marketable securities that are expected to mature within 90 days of the balance sheet date are recorded together with cash as cash equivalents. Its remaining investments are reported as marketable securities.

Footnotes to Google's 2012 10-K provide further information about the composition of its investment portfolio.

As of December 31, 2012 ($ millions)	Adjusted Cost	Gross Unrealized Gains	Gross Unrealized Losses	Fair Value	Cash and Cash Equivalents	Marketable Securities
Cash	$ 8,066	$ 0	$ 0	$ 8,066	$ 8,066	$ 0
Level 1:						
Money market and other funds	5,221	0	0	5,221	5,221	0
U.S. government notes	10,853	77	(1)	10,929	0	10,929
Marketable equity securities	12	88	0	100	0	100
	16,086	165	(1)	16,250	5,221	11,029
Level 2:						
Time deposits	984	0	0	984	562	422
Money market and other funds	929	0	0	929	929	0
U.S. government agencies	1,882	20	0	1,902	0	1,902
Foreign government bonds	1,996	81	(3)	2,074	0	2,074
Municipal securities	2,249	23	(6)	2,266	0	2,266
Corporate debt securities	7,200	414	(14)	7,600	0	7,600
Agency residential mortgage-backed securities	7,039	136	(6)	7,169	0	7,169
Asset-backed securities	847	1	0	848	0	848
	23,126	675	(29)	23,772	1,491	22,281
Total	$47,278	$840	$(30)	$48,088	$14,778	$33,310

The majority of Google's 2012 investments are in government debt securities such as bonds and T-bills, with a relatively small portion invested in equity securities. Google accounts for all of these investments as available-for-sale and reports them in the current asset section of the balance sheet because they mature within the coming year or can be readily sold, if necessary.

Google provides additional (required) disclosures in the table above on the costs, fair values, and unrealized gains and losses for its available-for-sale investments. Google's net unrealized gain of $810 million ($840 million − $30 million) is reported net of tax in the accumulated other comprehensive income (AOCI) section of its stockholders' equity as follows ($ millions):

December 31 ($ millions)	2011	2012
Class A and Class B common stock	$20,264	$22,835
Accumulated other comprehensive income	276	538
Retained earnings	37,605	48,342
Total stockholders' equity	58,145	71,715
Total liabilities and stockholders' equity	$72,574	$93,798

Google identifies the components of its 2012 accumulated other comprehensive income of $538 million in the following footnote disclosure:

The components of accumulated other comprehensive income were as follows (in millions):

As of December 31	2011	2012
Foreign currency translation adjustment	$(148)	$ (73)
Net unrealized gains on available-for-sale investments, net of taxes	327	604
Unrealized gains on cash flow hedges, net of taxes	97	7
Accumulated other comprehensive income	$ 276	$538

The majority of this account relates to the unrealized gains on available-for-sale investments (we discuss the foreign currency translation adjustment and unrealized gains on cash flow hedges later in this module and its appendix). The net unrealized gain of $810 million ($840 million − $30 million) reported in the investment footnote is pretax while the $604 million amount (as well as the $(73) million and $7 million amounts) reported in the accumulated other comprehensive income section of stockholders' equity is after-tax.

Investments Reported at Cost

Companies often purchase debt securities, including bonds issued by other companies or by the U.S. government. Such debt securities have maturity dates—dates when the security must be repaid by the borrower. If a company buys debt securities, and *management intends to hold the securities to maturity* (as opposed to selling them early), the securities are classified as **held-to-maturity** (HTM). The cost method applies to held-to-maturity securities. Exhibit 9.4 identifies the reporting of these securities.

EXHIBIT 9.4 Accounting Treatment for Held-to-Maturity Investments

Investment Classification	Reporting of Fair-Value Changes	Reporting Interest Received and the Gains and Losses on Sale
Held-to-Maturity (HTM)	Fair-value changes are *not* reported in either the balance sheet or income statement	Interest reported as *other income* in income statement IF sold before maturity (the exception), any gain or loss on sale is reported in income statement

Changes in fair value of held-to-maturity securities do not affect either the balance sheet or the income statement. The presumption is that these investments will indeed be held to maturity, at which time their market value will be exactly equal to their face value. Fluctuations in fair value, as a result, are less relevant for this investment classification. Finally, any interest received is recorded in current income. (GAAP gives companies an option to report held-to-maturity investments at fair value; if this fair-value option is elected, the accounting for held-to-maturity securities is like that for trading securities.)

Sometimes companies acquire held-to-maturity debt securities for more or less than the security's face value. Because the value of debt securities fluctuates with the prevailing rate of interest, the market value of the security will be greater than its face value if current market interest rates are lower than what the security pays for interest. In that case, the acquirer will pay a premium for the security.

Conversely, if current market interest rates exceed what the security pays in interest, the acquirer will purchase the security at a discount. (We cover premiums and discounts on debt securities in more detail in Module 7.) Either way, the company records the investment at its acquisition cost (like any other asset) and amortizes any discount or premium over the remaining life of the held-to-maturity investment. At any point in time, the acquirer's balance sheet carries the investment at "amortized cost," which is never adjusted for subsequent market value changes.

Companies can acquire equity interests in other companies that are not traded on an organized exchange. These might be start-ups that have never issued stock or established privately held companies. Because there is no market for such securities, they cannot be classified as marketable securities and are carried at historical cost on the balance sheet. **Google** references such investment in its 2012 10-K.

> **Non-Marketable Equity Securities** We have accounted for non-marketable equity securities either under the equity or cost method. Investments through which we exercise significant influence but do not have control over the investee are accounted for under the equity method. Investments through which we are not able to exercise significant influence over the investee are accounted for under the cost method. We periodically review our marketable and non-marketable securities for impairment. If we conclude that any of these investments are impaired, we determine whether such impairment is other-than-temporary. Factors we consider to make such determination include the duration and severity of the impairment, the reason for the decline in value and the potential recovery period and our intent to sell . . . If any impairment is considered other-than-temporary, we will write down the asset to its fair value and record the corresponding charge as interest and other income, net.

Google uses historical cost to account for investments in non-marketable securities (equity investments where Google cannot exert significant influence over the investee company). Google monitors the value of these investments and writes them down to market value if they suffer a permanent decline in value. If such an investee company ever goes public, Google will change its accounting method. If Google's ownership percentage does not allow it to exert significant influence or control, Google will account for this investment following the procedures described above for marketable securities. However, if Google can exert significant influence or control, it will apply different accounting methods that we explain in later sections of this module.

MID-MODULE REVIEW 1

Assume that **Google** had the following four transactions involving investments in marketable securities. Use this information to answer requirements *a* and *b* below.

1. Purchased 1,000 shares of **Yahoo!** common stock for $15 cash per share.
2. Received cash dividend of $2.50 per share on Yahoo! common stock.
3. Year-end market price of Yahoo! common stock is $17 per share.
4. Sold all 1,000 shares of Yahoo! common stock for $17,000 cash in the next period.

Yahoo! reports the following table in the footnotes to its 2012 10-K. Use this information to answer requirements *c* and *d* below.

December 31, 2012 ($ Thousands)	Gross Amortized Costs	Gross Unrealized Gains	Gross Unrealized Losses	Estimated Fair Value
Government and agency securities	$1,312,876	$ 985	$ (45)	$1,313,816
Corporate debt securities, commercial paper, and bank certificates of deposit	2,039,809	1,597	(622)	2,040,784
Corporate equity securities	230	—	(33)	197
Alibaba Group Preference Shares	816,261	—	—	816,261
Total investments in available-for-sale securities	$4,169,176	$2,582	$(700)	$4,171,058

Required

a. Using the financial statement effects template, enter the effects (amount and account) relating to the four transactions assuming the investments are classified as available-for-sale.
b. Using the financial statement effects template enter the effects (amount and account) relating to the four transactions assuming that the investments are classified as trading securities.
c. What amount does Yahoo! report as investments on its balance sheet? What does this balance represent?
d. How did the net unrealized gains affect reported income in 2012?

The solution is on page 9-56.

INVESTMENTS WITH SIGNIFICANT INFLUENCE

LO2 Explain and illustrate accounting for equity method investments.

Many companies make equity investments that yield them significant influence over the investee companies. These intercorporate investments are usually made for strategic reasons such as the following:

- **Prelude to acquisition**. Significant ownership can allow the investor company to gain a seat on the board of directors from which it can learn much about the investee company, its products, and its industry.
- **Strategic alliance**. Strategic alliances permit the investor to gain trade secrets, technical know-how, or access to restricted markets. For example, a company might buy an equity interest in a company that provides inputs for the investor's production process. This relationship is closer than the usual supplier–buyer relationship and will convey benefits to the investor company.
- **Pursuit of research and development**. Many research activities in the pharmaceutical, software, and oil and gas industries are conducted jointly. The common motivation is to reduce the investor's risk or the amount of capital investment. The investment often carries an option to purchase additional shares, which the investor can exercise if the research activities are fruitful.

A crucial feature in each of these investments is that the investor company has a level of ownership that is sufficient for it to exert *significant influence* over the investee company. GAAP requires that such investments be accounted for using the *equity method*.

Significant influence is the ability of the investor to affect the financing, investing and operating policies of the investee. Ownership levels of 20% to 50% of the outstanding common stock of the investee typically convey significant influence. Significant influence can also exist when ownership is less than 20%. Evidence of such influence can be that the investor company is able to gain a seat on the board of directors of the investee by virtue of its equity investment, or the investor controls technical know-how or patents that are used by the investee, or the investor is able to exert significant influence by virtue of legal contracts with the investee. (There is growing pressure from regulators for determining significant influence by the facts and circumstances of the investment instead of a strict ownership percentage rule.)

Accounting for Investments with Significant Influence

GAAP requires that investors use the **equity method** when significant influence exists. The equity method reports the investment on the balance sheet at an amount equal to the percentage of the investee's equity owned by the investor; hence, the name equity method. (This assumes acquisition at book value; acquisition at an amount greater than book value is covered later in this section.) Contrary to passive investments whose carrying amounts increase or decrease with the market value of the investee's stock, equity method investments increase (decrease) with increases (decreases) in the investee's stockholders' equity.

Equity method accounting is summarized as follows:

- Investments are recorded at their purchase cost.
- Dividends received are treated as a recovery of the investment and, thus, reduce the investment balance (dividends are not reported as income).
- The investor reports income equal to its percentage share of the investee's reported net income; the investment account is increased by the percentage share of the investee's income or is decreased by the percentage share of any loss.
- Changes in fair value do not affect the investment's carrying value. (GAAP gives companies an option to report equity method investments at fair value unless those investments relate to consolidated subsidiaries; we discuss consolidation later in the module.)

IFRS Alert
There is no fair-value option for investments accounted for by the equity method under IFRS.

To illustrate the equity method, consider the following scenario: Assume that **Google** acquires a 30% interest in Mitel Networks, a company seeking to develop a new technology. This investment is a strategic alliance for Google. At the acquisition date, Mitel's balance sheet reports $1,000 of stockholders' equity, and Google purchases a 30% stake for $300, giving it the ability to exert significant influence over Mitel. At the first year-end, Mitel reports profits of $100 and pays $20 in cash dividends to its shareholders ($6 to Google). Following are the financial statement effects for Google from this investment using the equity method.

	Balance Sheet						Income Statement			
Transaction	**Cash Asset**	+ **Noncash Assets**	=	**Liabilities**	+ **Contrib. Capital**	+ **Earned Capital**	**Revenues**	− **Expenses**	=	**Net Income**
1. Purchase 30% investment in Mitel for $300 cash	−300 Cash	+300 Investment in Mitel	=					−	=	
2. Mitel reports $100 income; Google's share is $30		+30 Investment in Mitel	=			+30 Retained Earnings	+30 Investment Income	−	=	+30
3. Mitel pays $20 cash dividends; $6 to Google	+6 Cash	−6 Investment in Mitel	=					−	=	
Ending balance of Google's investment account		324								

EMI 300
Cash 300
EMI: 300 |
Cash: | 300

EMI 30
EI 30
EMI: 30 |
EI: | 30

Cash 6
EMI 6
Cash: 6 |
EMI: | 6

The investment is initially reported on Google's balance sheet at its purchase price of $300, representing a 30% interest in Mitel's total stockholders' equity of $1,000. During the year, Mitel's equity increases to $1,080 ($1,000 plus $100 income and less $20 dividends). Likewise, Google's investment increases by $30 to reflect its 30% share of Mitel's $100 income, and decreases by $6, relating to its share of Mitel's dividends. After these transactions, Google's investment in Mitel is reported on Google's balance sheet at 30% of $1,080, or $324.

Google's investment in Mitel is an asset, just like any other asset. As such, it must be tested annually for impairment. If the investment is found to be permanently impaired, Google must reduce the investment amount on the balance sheet and report a loss on the write-down of the investment in its income statement (unlike investments accounted for using the market method, equity method investments are not written up if fair values increase). If and when Google sells Mitel, any gain or loss on the sale is reported in Google's income statement. The gain or loss is computed as the difference between the sales proceeds and the investment's carrying value on the balance sheet. For example, if Google sold Mitel for $500, Google would report a gain on sale of $176 ($500 proceeds − $324 balance sheet value).

Companies often pay more than book value when they make equity investments. For example, if Google paid $400 for its 30% stake in Mitel, Google would initially report its investment at its $400 purchase price. The $400 investment consists of two parts: the $300 equity investment described above and the $100 additional investment. Google is willing to pay the higher purchase price because it believes that Mitel's reported equity is below its current market value. Perhaps some of Mitel's assets are reported at costs that are below market values or Mitel has intangible assets such as a patent or internally generated goodwill that are missing from the balance sheet. The $300 portion of the investment is accounted for as described above. Google's management must decide how to allocate the excess of the amount paid over the book value of the investee company's equity and account for the excess accordingly. For example, if management decides that the $100 relates to depreciable assets, the $100 is depreciated over the assets' estimated useful lives. Or, if it relates to identifiable intangible assets that have a determinable useful life (like patents), it is amortized over the useful lives of the intangible assets. If it relates to goodwill, however, it is not amortized and remains on the balance sheet at $100 unless and until it is deemed to be impaired. (See Appendix 9A for an expanded illustration.)

Two final points about equity method accounting: First, there can be a substantial difference between the book value of an equity method investment and its fair value. An increase in value is not recognized until the investment is sold. If the fair value of the investment has permanently declined, however, the investment is deemed impaired and it is written down to that lower fair value. Second, if the investee company reports income, the investor company reports its share. Recognition of equity income by the investor, however, does not mean that it has received that income in cash. Cash is only received if the investee pays a dividend. To highlight this, the investor's statement of cash flows will include a reconciling item (a deduction from net income in computing operating cash flow) for its percentage share of the investee's net income. This is typically reported net of any cash dividends received.

RESEARCH INSIGHT **Equity Income and Stock Prices**

Under the equity method of accounting, the investor does not recognize as income any dividends received from the investee, nor any changes in the investee's fair value, until the investment is sold. However, research has found a positive relation between investors' and investees' stock prices at the time of investees' earnings and dividend announcements. This suggests that the market includes information regarding investees' earnings and dividends when assessing the stock prices of investor companies, and implies that the market looks beyond the book value of the investment account in determining stock prices of investor companies.

Equity Method Accounting and ROE Effects

The investor company reports equity method investments on the balance sheet at an amount equal to the percentage owned of the investee company's equity when that investment is acquired at book value. To illustrate, consider the case of the **Altria Group, Inc.** equity investment in **SABMiller**. Altria owns an approximate 26.9% economic and voting interest of SABMiller and provides the following disclosure in its 2012 10-K:

Investment in SABMiller At December 31, 2012, Altria Group, Inc. held approximately 26.9% of the economic and voting interest of SABMiller. Altria Group, Inc. accounts for its investment in SABMiller under the equity method of accounting. Pre-tax earnings from Altria Group, Inc.'s equity investment in SABMiller consisted of the following:

For the Years Ended December 31 (in millions)	2012	2011	2010
Equity earnings.	$1,181	$703	$578
Gains resulting from issuances of common stock by SABMiller	43	27	50
	$1,224	$730	$628

continued

Altria Group, Inc.'s equity earnings for the year ended December 31, 2012, included its share of pre-tax non-cash gains of $342 million resulting from SABMiller's strategic alliance transactions with Anadolu Efes and Castel. Summary financial data of SABMiller is as follows:

At December 31 (in millions)	2012	2011
Current assets	$ 5,742	$ 5,967
Long-term assets	51,733	46,438
Current liabilities	8,944	7,591
Long-term liabilities	22,000	22,521
Noncontrolling interests	1,105	1,013

For the Years Ended December 31 (in millions)	2012	2011	2010
Net revenues	$23,449	$20,780	$18,981
Operating profit	5,243	3,603	2,821
Net earnings	4,362	2,596	2,133

The fair value of Altria Group, Inc.'s equity investment in SABMiller is based on unadjusted quoted prices in active markets and is classified in level 1 of the fair value hierarchy. The fair value of Altria Group, Inc.'s equity investment in SABMiller at December 31, 2012 and 2011, was $19.8 billion and $15.2 billion, respectively, as compared with its carrying value of $6.6 billion and $5.5 billion, respectively.

The equity investment in SABMiller is carried on Altria's balance sheet at $6,637 million. Given the stockholders' equity of SABMiller of $25,426 million ($5,742 million + $51,733 million − $8,944 million − $22,000 million − $1,105 million), the investment balance is $203 million less than the $6,840 ($25,426 million × 0.269) we would expect. This difference can arise because of dividends received in excess of equity income or a number of other factors.

In its income statement, Altria reports equity earnings of $1,181 million, slightly more than the $1,173 million ($4,362 million × 0.269) we would compute based on its proportionate share of the net income of SABMiller (the difference may be due to an ownership percentage slightly greater than the 26.9% rounded percentage that it reports in its footnotes). One final point, Altria subtracts the equity earnings (plus gains from stock issuance) of $1,224 million on the statement of cash flows and, then, adds in the $402 million received in dividends from SABMiller. The deduction recognizes the non-cash nature of the equity earnings and the addition recognizes the cash received in the form of dividends. This excess of equity earnings over dividends received is sometimes referred to as *undistributed earnings*.

It is sometimes helpful to visualize the equity investment in relation to the assets and liabilities to which it relates. Following is a summary of the Altria 2012 balance sheet:

	Altria
Cash	$ 2,900
Non-cash assets	25,792
Investment in SABMiller	6,637
Total assets	$35,329

	SABMiller
Total assets	$57,475
Liabilities	$30,944
Noncontrolling interests	1,105
Stockholders' equity	25,426
Liabilities and equity	$57,475

The $6,637 million equity investment on Altria's balance sheet belies an investment in a very large company with assets over $57 billion and liabilities over $30 billion. Although not a serious concern for beer manufacturers, we might want to know more about the investee company if the investment were in a pharmaceutical company with significant potential liabilities or in a venture with highly variable cash flows. The investor company may have no direct legal obligation for the investee's liabilities, but it might need to fund the investee company, via additional investment or advances to maintain the investee's viability, if the company is important to the investor's strategic plan. Further, companies that routinely fund R&D activities through equity investments in other companies, a common practice in the pharmaceutical and software industries, can find themselves supporting underperforming equity-method investments to assure continued external funding. One cannot always assume, therefore, that the investee's liabilities and business fortunes will not adversely affect the investor.

The concern with unreported liabilities becomes particularly problematic when the investee company reports losses that are substantial. In extreme cases, the investee company can become insolvent (when equity is negative) as the growing negative balance in retained earnings more than offsets paid-in capital. Once the equity of the investee company reaches zero, the investor must discontinue accounting for the investment by the equity method. Instead, it accounts for the investment at cost with a zero balance and no further recognition of its proportionate share of investee company losses (until the investee company's equity becomes positive again). In this case, the investor's income statement no longer includes the losses of the investee company and its balance sheet no longer reports the troubled investee company. Unreported liabilities can be especially problematic in this case.

To summarize, under equity method accounting, only the net equity owned is reported on the balance sheet (not the underlying assets and liabilities), and only the net equity in earnings is reported in the income statement (not the investee's sales and expenses). This is simply illustrated as follows using the (assumed) income statement and balance sheet from Mitel, the company in which Google invests $300 for a 30% ownership stake, at the end of the first year.

Mitel Income Statement	
Mitel sales	$300
Mitel expenses	200
Mitel income	$100

Mitel Balance Sheet	
Mitel assets	$2,580
Mitel liabilities	1,500
Mitel equity	$1,080

Google's Income Statement and Balance Sheet (Equity Method Accounting)		
Equity income of Mitel (investee) (Mitel income × 30% owned)	$ 30	
Investment in Mitel (investee)	$324	← × 30% owned (Mitel equity)

From an analysis standpoint, because the assets and liabilities are left off the Google balance sheet, and because the sales and expenses are omitted from the Google income statement, the *components* of ROE are markedly affected as follows:

- **Net operating profit margin (NOPM = NOPAT/Sales).** Most analysts include equity income (sales less expenses) in NOPAT since it relates to operating investments. However, investee's sales are not included in the NOPM denominator. The reported NOPM is, thus, overstated.
- **Net operating asset turnover (NOAT = Sales/Average NOA).** Investee's sales are excluded from the NOAT numerator, and net operating assets in excess of the investment balance are excluded from the denominator. This means the impact on NOAT is *indeterminate*.
- **Financial leverage (FLEV = Net nonoperating obligations/Average equity).** Financial leverage is understated due to the absence of investee liabilities in the numerator.

Although ROE components are affected, ROE is unaffected by equity method accounting because the correct amount of investee net income and equity *is* included in the ROE numerator and denominator, respectively. Still, the evaluation of the quality of ROE is affected. Analysis using reported equity method accounting numbers would use an overstated NOPM and an understated FLEV because the numbers are based on net balance sheet and net income statement numbers. As we discuss in a later module, analysts should adjust reported financial statements for these types of items before conducting analysis. One such adjustment might be to consolidate (for analysis purposes) the equity method investee with the investor company.

IFRS INSIGHT **Equity Method Investments and IFRS**

Like US GAAP, IFRS requires use of the equity method for investments in "associates" where the investor has significant influence. Unlike US GAAP, companies using IFRS cannot cease applying the equity method when the associate is operating under severe long-term restrictions that impair its ability to transfer funds to the investor. Instead, significant influence must be lost before the equity method ceases to apply. US GAAP allows the equity method to cease once the investee's equity reaches zero.

MANAGERIAL DECISION **You Are the Chief Financial Officer**

You are receiving capital expenditure requests for long-term operating asset purchases from various managers. You are concerned that capacity utilization is too low. What potential courses of action can you consider? Explain. [Answer, p. 9-35]

MID-MODULE REVIEW 2

Assume that Google had the following five transactions involving investments in marketable securities accounted for using the equity method. Use this information to answer requirement *a* below.

1. Purchased 5,000 shares of LookSmart common stock at $10 cash per share; these shares reflect 30% ownership of LookSmart.
2. Received a $2 per share cash dividend on LookSmart common stock.
3. Recorded an accounting adjustment to reflect $100,000 income reported by LookSmart.
4. Year-end market price of LookSmart has increased to $12 per common share.
5. Sold all 5,000 shares of LookSmart common stock for $90,000 cash in the next period.

Yahoo! reports a $2,230 million equity investment in Yahoo! Japan related to its 35% ownership interest, and Yahoo!'s footnotes reveal the following financial information about Yahoo! Japan ($ millions). Use this information to answer requirements *b.* and *c.* below.

Twelve Months Ended September 30	2010	2011	2012
Operating data			
Revenues	$3,564	$3,988	$4,266
Gross profit	2,883	3,311	3,595
Income from operations	1,679	1,964	2,189
Net income	976	1,108	1,309

September 30	2011	2012
Balance sheet data		
Current assets	$3,623	$5,753
Long-term assets	2,907	1,838
Current liabilities	1,118	1,168
Long-term liabilities	36	49

Required

a. Use the financial statement effects template to enter the effects (amount and account) for the five Google transactions, above.

b. How much income does Yahoo! report in its 2012 income statement related to this equity investment?

c. Show the computations required to yield the $2,230 million balance in the equity investment account on Yahoo!'s balance sheet.

The solution is on page 9-57.

INVESTMENTS WITH CONTROL

LO3 Describe and illustrate accounting for consolidations.

This section discusses accounting for investments where the investor company "controls" the investee company. For example, in its footnote describing its accounting policies, **Google** reports the following:

> **Basis of Consolidations** The consolidated financial statements include the accounts of Google Inc. and our wholly-owned subsidiaries. All intercompany balances and transactions have been eliminated.

This means that Google's financial statements are an aggregation (an adding up) of those of the parent company, Google, and all its subsidiary companies, less any intercompany activities such as intercompany sales or receivables.

Accounting for Investments with Control

IFRS Alert
Consolidation accounting is generally similar with IFRS; differences exist in technical details, but not with presentation of consolidated financial statements.

Accounting for business combinations (acquiring a controlling interest) goes one step beyond equity method accounting. Under the equity method, the investor's investment balance represents the proportion of the investee's equity owned by the investor, and the investor company's income statement includes its proportionate share of the investee's income. Once "control" over the investee company is achieved, GAAP requires consolidation for financial statements issued to the public (not for the internal financial records of the separate companies). Consolidation accounting includes 100% of the investee's assets and liabilities on the investor's balance sheet and 100% of the investee's sales and expenses on the investor's income statement. Specifically, the consolidated balance sheet includes the gross assets and liabilities of the investee company, and the income statement includes the investee's gross sales and expenses rather than just the investor's share of the investee company's net assets or income. All intercompany sales and expenses, and receivables and payables, are eliminated in the consolidation process to avoid double-counting when, for example, goods are sold from the investee (called a subsidiary) to the investor (called the parent company) for resale to the parent's ultimate customers.

Investments Purchased at Book Value: Subsidiary Wholly-Owned To illustrate, consider the following scenario. Penman Company acquires 100% of the common stock of Nissim Company by exchanging newly issued Penman shares for all of Nissim's common stock. The purchase price is equal to the book value of Nissim's stockholders' equity (contributed capital plus retained earnings). On its balance sheet, Penman accounts for the investment in Nissim using the equity method. This is important. Even if the investor (the parent) owns 100% of the investee (the subsidiary), it can still record the investment on its (parent-company) balance sheet using the equity method described in the previous section. That is, Penman records an initial balance in the equity investment account in the amount of the purchase price, which is equal to Nissim's stockholders' equity. Thereafter, the equity investment account on Penman's balance sheet will increase and decrease with Nissim's stockholders' equity, reflecting profits earned and losses incurred, and decreasing with any payment of dividends.

Because Penman Company owns 100% of the stock of its subsidiary (and, therefore, "controls" the activities of Nissim), GAAP requires consolidation of the balance sheets and income statements of the two companies. That process, shown in Exhibit 9.5, involves summing each balance sheet and income statement account for the two companies, *after eliminating any intercompany transactions* (such as the investment that Penman has in Nissim Company, together with any intercompany sales/purchases and receivables/payables).

The upper part of Exhibit 9.5 shows the balance sheets of Penman and Nissim in the first two columns, the consolidating adjustments in the next column and the consolidated balance sheet in the far right column. The consolidated balance sheet reports total assets of $21,000, total liabilities of $7,000, and equity of $14,000. Because Penman owns 100% of the stock of Nissim, and the purchase

EXHIBIT 9.5 Mechanics of Consolidation Accounting (Wholly-Owned Subsidiary, Purchased at Book Value)

	Penman Company	Nissim Company	Consolidating Adjustments	Consolidated
Balance Sheet				
Current assets	$ 6,000	$ 1,000		$ 7,000
Investment in Nissim	3,000	0	(3,000)	0
PPE, net	10,000	4,000		14,000
Total assets	$19,000	$ 5,000		$21,000
Liabilities	$ 5,000	$ 2,000		$ 7,000
Contributed capital	10,000	2,000	(2,000)	10,000
Retained earnings	4,000	1,000	(1,000)	4,000
Total liabilities and equity	$19,000	$ 5,000		$21,000
Income statement				
Sales	$25,000	$10,000		$35,000
Cost of goods sold	(20,000)	(7,000)		(27,000)
Gross profit	5,000	3,000		8,000
Operating expenses	(3,600)	(2,600)		(6,200)
Equity income from investment	400	—	(400)	0
Net income	$ 1,800	$ 400	(400)	$ 1,800

was made at book value, the equity investment account on Penman's balance sheet equals Nissim's stockholders' equity to which it relates. Both amounts are removed in the consolidation process and each row in the balance sheet is, then, summed to arrive at the consolidated totals. The result of this process is to remove both the equity investment account and Nissim's stockholders' equity from the consolidated balance sheet and to replace the equity investment with the assets and liabilities of Nissim to which it relates. *The consolidated stockholders' equity equals the equity of the parent company—this is always the case when the subsidiary is wholly owned.*

The consolidated income statement is shown in the lower part of Exhibit 9.5. Penman reports equity income in its income statement equal to the net income reported by Nissim Company. The effect of the consolidation process is to remove the equity income account in Penman's income statement and replace it with the sales and expenses of Nissim Company to which it relates. This is accomplished by summing the rows in the income statement and eliminating the equity income account to yield the consolidated income statement. *The consolidated net income equals the net income of the parent company—this is always the case* (because the equity income that the parent reports equals the net income of the subsidiary when the subsidiary is wholly owned).

Investments Purchased at Book Value: Subsidiary Not Wholly-Owned When a subsidiary is not wholly-owned, we must account for the equity interest of noncontrolling shareholders. This will affect both the balance sheet and the income statement. To illustrate, assume that Penman acquires 80% of Nissim instead of 100% as in our previous example. Now, the equity investment account on Penman's balance sheet will reflect only 80% of Nissim's equity; and, the equity income it reports in its income statement will only reflect 80% of Nissim's net income. The remaining 20% of the net assets of the subsidiary and its net income is owned by noncontrolling shareholders. Their equity in the net assets of Nissim is reflected on the consolidated balance sheet in a new account titled **noncontrolling interest**. In addition, we must now apportion Nissim's net income into the 80% attributed to Penman's shareholders and the 20% attributed to noncontrolling shareholders.

We demonstrate the accounting for noncontrolling interests in Exhibit 9.6. Again, the balance sheets of Penman and Nissim are shown in the upper part of Exhibit 9.6 in the first two columns. The consolidating adjustments are shown in the third column and the consolidated balance sheet and income statement in the last column. The claim of noncontrolling shareholders on Nissim's net assets is recognized in consolidated equity, just like that of the majority shareholders. Their equity in the net assets of Nissim is reported in an equity account called noncontrolling interest. The $2,400 equity investment account on Penman's balance sheet reflects its 80% interest in Nissim's equity ([$2,000 + $1,000] × 80%). That equity investment account is eliminated in the consolidation process.

EXHIBIT 9.6 Mechanics of Consolidation Accounting (Subsidiary Not Wholly-Owned, Purchased at Book Value)

	Penman Company	Nissim Company	Consolidating Adjustments	Consolidated
Balance Sheet				
Current assets	$ 6,000	$1,000		$ 7,000
Investment in Nissim	2,400	0	(2,400)	0
PPE, net	10,000	4,000		14,000
Total assets	$18,400	$5,000		$21,000
Liabilities	$ 5,000	$2,000		$ 7,000
Contributed capital	10,000	2,000	(2,000)	10,000
Retained earnings	3,400	1,000	(1,000)	3,400
Noncontrolling interest			600	600
Total liability and equity	$18,400	$5,000		$21,000
Income statement				
Sales	$25,000	$10,000		$35,000
Cost of goods sold	(20,000)	(7,000)		(27,000)
Gross profit	5,000	3,000		8,000
Operating expenses	(3,600)	(2,600)		(6,200)
Equity income from investment	320	—	(320)	0
Net income	$ 1,720	$ 400	(320)	$ 1,800
Net income attributable to noncontrolling interest				80
Net income attributable to Penman shareholders				$ 1,720

The consolidated income statement shows the consolidated revenues, consolidated expenses, and consolidated net income. The $320 equity income account in Penman's income statement reflects 80% of Nissim's net income that it owns ($400 × 80%). This equity income account is eliminated in the consolidation process just like the equity investment account on the balance sheet. When less than 100% of the subsidiary is owned by the parent, the consolidated income statement allocates net income into that portion *attributable to the parent (controlling) shareholders* (80% here) and that portion *attributable to the noncontrolling shareholders* (20% here).

BUSINESS INSIGHT Accounting for Noncontrolling Interests

When a company acquires less than 100% of a subsidiary, it must account for the interests of the noncontrolling shareholders separately from those of its own shareholders. This has two implications for consolidated financial statements:

1. Consolidated net income is first computed for the company as a whole as revenues less expenses. Then, it is allocated to the portion attributable to the parent's shareholders and the noncontrolling shareholders in proportion to their respective ownership interests.
2. The balance of the noncontrolling interests is reported on the balance sheet in the stockholders' equity section. It is increased each year by the net income allocated to noncontrolling interests and is decreased by any dividends paid to those noncontrolling shareholders.

Investments Purchased above Book Value The illustrations above assume that the purchase price of the acquisition equals the book value of the investee company. It is more often the case, however, that the purchase price exceeds the book value. This might arise, for example, if an investor company believes it is acquiring something of value that is not reported on the investee's balance sheet—such as tangible assets whose market values have risen above book value, or unrecorded intangible assets, like patents or corporate synergies. When the acquisition price exceeds book value, all net assets acquired (both tangible and intangible) must be recognized on the consolidated balance sheet.

To illustrate, let's return to the example of Exhibit 9.5 in which Penman acquires 100% interest in Nissim. Let's now assume that Penman paid a premium to Nissim of $1,000 more than the book value of Nissim's stockholders' equity on the acquisition date (see the increase in Penman's contributed capital to $11,000 reflecting the additional $1,000 of stock issued to Nissim's shareholders). Assume that Penman paid the additional $1,000 because Penman expects to realize $1,000 in additional value from corporate synergies, such as increased market presence, ability to consolidate offices, and increased buying power. General "synergies" such as this are recognized on the balance sheet as an intangible asset with an indefinite useful life, called *goodwill*. The $4,000 investment account now reflects two components: the book value acquired of $3,000 (as before) and an additional $1,000 of newly acquired assets (goodwill asset). Exhibit 9.7 shows the balance sheets of the two companies, along with the consolidating adjustments and the consolidated balance sheet, on the date of acquisition.

EXHIBIT 9.7 Mechanics of Consolidation Accounting (Purchase Price above Book Value)

	Penman Company	Nissim Company	Consolidating Adjustments	Consolidated
Current assets	$ 6,000	$1,000		$ 7,000
Investment in Nissim	4,000	0	(4,000)	0
PPE, net	10,000	4,000		14,000
Goodwill			1,000	1,000
Total assets	$20,000	$5,000		$22,000
Liabilities	$ 5,000	$2,000		$ 7,000
Contributed capital	11,000	2,000	(2,000)	11,000
Retained earnings	4,000	1,000	(1,000)	4,000
Total liabilities and equity	$20,000	$5,000		$22,000

The consolidated current assets and liabilities are the sum of those accounts on each company's balance sheet. The investment account, however, includes $1,000 of the newly acquired goodwill asset that must now be reported on the consolidated balance sheet. The consolidation process in this case has two steps. First, the $3,000 equity of Nissim Company is eliminated against the equity investment account as before. Then, the remaining $1,000 of the investment account is eliminated and the newly acquired asset ($1,000 of goodwill, which is not reported on Nissim's balance sheet) is added to the consolidated balance sheet. The goodwill asset is now recognized on the consolidated balance sheet as a separate asset and, like all other assets, that goodwill asset must be tested annually for impairment and written down (or written off entirely) if found to be impaired. (In 2012, for example, Hewlett-Packard wrote off $18 billion of goodwill and other purchased intangible assets relating to its acquisitions of Autonomy and Compaq).

In our example here, we recognized just one intangible asset: goodwill. Often, the excess purchase price is assigned to several intangible assets that have a useful life (such as the value of brands, patents, licensing agreements, and customer relationships; also, see the Kellogg example later in this module). If recognized, the cost of such intangible assets (other than goodwill) are amortized over their useful lives in the same manner that we depreciate a tangible asset. Consolidated net income is reduced by the amortization of those intangible assets; and, the amount by which the equity investment account exceeds the book value of the subsidiary's equity is, then, equal to the unamortized balance of separately identifiable intangible assets plus the goodwill asset, if any.

Consolidation Disclosures To illustrate consolidation mechanics with an actual company, we consider Caterpillar (CAT). The company's Form 10-K reports consolidated financial statements: the parent company financial statements (Machinery and Power Systems) are combined with those of the subsidiary (Financial Products). Exhibit 9.8 (taken from Cat's 10-K) reports the parent and the subsidiary balance sheets separately as well as the adjustments that yield the consolidated financial statements. Following are a few observations relating to Exhibit 9.8.

EXHIBIT 9.8 Caterpillar Consolidated Balance Sheet

At December 31, 2012 (In millions)	Machinery & Power Systems	Financial Products	Consolidating Adjustments	Consolidated
Balance sheet				
Current assets	$26,535	$16,388	❹ $ (399)	$42,524
Noncurrent assets	27,316	20,068	❹ (552)	46,832
Investment in Financial Products subsidiaries	❶ 4,433		❸ (4,433)	0
Total assets	$58,284	$36,456	$(5,384)	$89,356
Current liabilities	$18,172	$11,987	❹ $ (404)	$29,755
Long-term liabilities	22,530	20,036	❹ (547)	42,019
Stockholders' Equity:				
Common stock	4,481	906	(906)	4,481
Treasury stock	(10,074)			(10,074)
Retained earnings	29,558	3,185	(3,185)	29,558
Accumulated other comprehensive income	(6,433)	236	(236)	(6,433)
Noncontrolling interests	50	106	(106)	50
Total stockholders' equity	17,582	❷ 4,433	❸ (4,433)	17,582
Total liabilities and equity	$58,284	$36,456	$(5,384)	$89,356
Income statement				
Revenues	$63,068	$ 3,160	❹ $ (353)	$65,875
Operating expense	(54,954)	(2,419)	❹ 71	(57,302)
Operating profit	8,114	741	(282)	8,573
Other income (expense)	$ (658)	$ 39	282	$ (337)
Income before tax	7,456	780	0	$ 8,236
Income tax expense	$ (2,314)	$ (214)	$ (192)	$ 2,528
Equity in profit of unconsolidated affiliated companies	14			14
Equity in profit of Financial Products subsidiaries	❺ 555		❺ (555)	0
Net income	5,711	566		5,722
Less: profit attributable to noncontrolling interests	30	11		41
Profit attributable to Caterpillar shareholders	$ 5,681	$ 555	$ (555)	$ 5,681

❶ The parent company (Machinery and Power Systems) reports an investment on its balance sheet called Investment in Financial Products subsidiaries with a balance of $4,433 million at 2012. This investment represents the parent's investment in its wholly-owned subsidiaries and it is accounted for using the equity method. On the parent's books, this investment account represents net assets (total assets less total liabilities) of the Financial Products subsidiaries in the same way that Altria represents the percentage that it owns of the net assets of SABMiller on its balance sheet. The parent maintains its separate parent company financial records for taxation and other internal decision making purposes. But for external reporting purposes, CAT must present consolidated financial statements. (CAT controls its Financial Products subsidiaries. Altria does not control SABMiller. That is why CAT must consolidate its Financial Products subsidiaries while Altria reports SAB-Miller as an equity investment.)

❷ The subsidiary balance sheet reports total stockholders' equity in the amount of $4,433 million, the same amount as the equity investment on the parent's balance sheet. That is not a coincidence. As we discuss earlier in this module, if the investment is acquired at book value and the investee company is wholly-owned, the investment account on the parent's balance sheet will always be equal to the stockholders' equity of the subsidiary (investee) company. In this case, CAT formed (not acquired) its financial products subsidiary, which is why the equity investment balance equals the equity of the financial products subsidiary and there are no recorded intangible assets.

❸ The consolidation process eliminates all intercompany investments, including intercompany sales and receivables, which we discuss below. Then, the rows are summed to yield the consolidated totals reported in the 10-K. This first group of eliminations removes the equity investment from total assets ($4,433 million) and the subsidiary's stockholders' equity ($4,433 million). Notice that the equity investment shows a zero balance (and is, therefore not reported) on the consolidated balance sheet. Notice also that consolidated stockholders' equity is equal to parent company stockholders' equity (that will always be the case if the equity investment is purchased at book value).

❹ All intercompany transactions are eliminated in both the income statement and the balance sheet to avoid double counting. These include intercompany sales (and offsetting purchases) and intercompany receivables (and offsetting payables).

❺ Finally, since the subsidiaries are wholly-owned, the parent company reports equity income equal to the net income of its subsidiaries ($555 million). This income statement line is eliminated in the consolidations and is replaced by the revenues and expenses to which it relates. Net income remains unchanged, but the consolidated income statement separately reports the sales and expenses of its Financial Products subsidiaries rather than just the net income.

Following the eliminations of *all intercompany transactions*, the adjusted balance sheets and income statement line items are summed to yield the financial statement reported in CAT's 10-K. In the case that a subsidiary is controlled, but not wholly-owned, the consolidated financial statements will reflect the *noncontrolling interest*, which we discuss above.

ANALYSIS INSIGHT **Foreign Currency Translation Adjustment**

Companies typically own foreign subsidiaries that maintain their accounting records in currencies other than the U.S. dollar. In Module 5, we discussed how the income statement reported the effects of currency fluctuations. Similarly, the balance sheets of these foreign subsidiaries grow (shrink) as the $US weakens (strengthens) vis-à-vis the reporting currencies of the foreign subsidiaries. As assets and liabilities increase in equivalent $US, that increase must be balanced with an increase in stockholders' equity in order to maintain the balance sheet equation (Assets = Liabilities + Equity). That balancing amount is called a cumulative translation adjustment and is reported in stockholders' equity in the accumulated other comprehensive income account. This cumulative translation adjustment represents a deferred gain or loss that will be recognized only when the subsidiary is sold. Until then, the account will increase or decrease as exchange rates fluctuate. From an analysis perspective, this account only becomes relevant if the company intends to sell the foreign subsidiary. Then, the deferred gain or loss will impact reported profit in the year of sale.

Reporting of Acquired Intangible Assets

The market value of a company's equity can differ substantially from its book value because of unrecorded assets. These unrecorded assets typically relate to intangible assets such as market position, brand equity, managerial talent, and internally developed technology. When companies are acquired, however, such unrecorded assets are recognized on the acquirer's balance sheet. The purchase price is allocated to the assets acquired and the liabilities assumed. First tangible assets, like PPE and inventory are identified and valued. Then, intangible assets are identified and valued. All of these assets are recorded on the acquirer's consolidated balance sheet at fair market value just like any other purchased asset. Finally, any excess purchase price is allocated to Goodwill. Common types of intangible assets recognized during acquisitions follow:

- Marketing-related assets like trademarks and Internet domain names
- Customer-related assets like customer lists and customer contracts
- Artistic-related assets like plays, books, and videos
- Contract-based assets like licensing, lease contracts, and franchise and royalty agreements

- Technology-based assets like patents, in-process research and development, software, databases, and trade secrets

To illustrate, **Kellogg Company** reports the following footnote disclosure relating to its purchase of the *Pringles*® business from **Procter & Gamble** for $2.668 billion in the footnotes to its 2012 10-K report.

GOODWILL AND OTHER INTANGIBLE ASSETS

Pringles® acquisition On May 31, 2012, the Company completed its acquisition of the Pringles® business (Pringles) from The Procter & Gamble Company (P&G) for . . . $2.668 billion. The acquisition was accounted for under the purchase method and was financed through a combination of cash on hand, and short-term and long-term debt. The assets and liabilities of Pringles are included in the Consolidated Balance Sheet as of December 29, 2012, and the results of the Pringles operations subsequent to the acquisition date are included in the Consolidated Statement of Income. The acquired assets and assumed liabilities include the following:

(millions)	May 31, 2012
Accounts receivable, net	$ 128
Inventories	103
Other prepaid assets	18
Property	317
Goodwill	1,306
Other intangibles:	
Definite-lived intangible assets	79
Brand	776
Other assets:	
Deferred income taxes	21
Other	16
Notes payable	(3)
Accounts payable	(9)
Other current liabilities	(24)
Other liabilities	(60)
	$2,668

Goodwill is calculated as the excess of the purchase price over the fair value of the net assets recognized. The goodwill recorded as part of the acquisition primarily reflects the value of providing an established platform to leverage the Company's existing brands in the international snacks category, synergies expected to arise from the combined brand portfolios, as well as any intangible assets that do not qualify for separate recognition.

Kellogg allocates over 80% of the purchase price to the following identifiable intangible assets:

- Goodwill ($1,306 million)
- Definite-lived intangible assets ($79 million)
- Brand ($776 million)

Definite-lived intangible assets (those with finite useful lives) will be subsequently amortized similar to depreciation. Kellogg deems the goodwill and brand assets to have indefinite lives and they will not be amortized but will be tested annually for impairment and written down if found to be impaired.

Goodwill Once the purchase price has been allocated to identifiable tangible and intangible assets (net of liabilities assumed), any remaining purchase price is allocated to goodwill. Goodwill, thus, represents the remainder of the purchase price that is not allocated to other assets. Kellogg allocated $1.3 billion (49%) of the Pringles purchase price to goodwill. The SEC scrutinizes companies that assign an excessive proportion of the purchase price to goodwill (companies might do this to avoid the future earnings drag from the amortization expense relating to identifiable intangible assets with useful lives).

BUSINESS INSIGHT **Recognition and Valuation of Intangibles**

Intangible Assets Relating to Customer Relationships An investor can recognize a number of intangible assets relating to customer relationships:

Customer lists—A customer list generally does not arise from contractual or other legal rights. However, customer lists are frequently leased or exchanged. Therefore, a customer list acquired in a business combination normally meets the separability criterion.

Order backlog—An order or production backlog arises from contracts such as purchase or sales orders. An order or production backlog acquired in a business combination meets the contractual-legal criterion even if the purchase or sales orders are cancelable.

Customer relationship—If an entity has relationships with its customers through sales orders, the customer relationships also arise from contractual rights and, therefore, meet the contractual-legal criterion. Customer relationships also may arise through means other than contracts, such as through regular contact by sales or service representatives.

How does a company decide whether to assign fair value to Customer Relationships and, if so, what value to place on that asset? **Novell Inc.**'s CFO, Mr. Dana Russell, focuses on the degree to which customers can be relied upon to generate future cash flows. That reliance is strengthened with the length and stability of the relationship, especially if the relationship is contractual.

> For each acquisition, we retain an outside company, typically an accounting firm other than our auditing firm, who is an expert in the valuation of these intangibles, to advise us in the allocation process. The history of the customer relationship and the presence of ongoing purchase contracts lend support to the conclusion that the cash flows will continue and, therefore, that they should be given greater weight in the valuation process and the allocation of the purchase price. (Mr. Dana Russell, CFO of Novell, Inc.)

IFRS Alert
When a firm purchases in-process research and development in the course of an acquisition, those costs are capitalized as an intangible asset under both IFRS and U.S. GAAP.

BUSINESS INSIGHT **Valuation of Earn-Outs**

Martha Stewart Living Omnimedia agreed to acquire some business units run by celebrity chef Emeril Lagasse for $50 million in cash and stock and a lucrative *earn-out* that could reach $20 million if Lagasse and company met specific profit goals. An earn-out is an incentive offered to key employees of a target company to entice them to remain with the company and increase value. Then, if the target company hits profit goals set by the buyer, the identified key employees earn a share of the profit. Under current GAAP, buyers must determine the estimated fair value of the future earn-out on the day of acquisition and record it as part of the purchase price. One impetus for an earn-out is when the buyer and seller cannot agree on a purchase price; in this way, the buyer is saying "I will pay if you make hay." Finally, any difference between the estimated fair value and the ultimate actual payout is recorded as an expense or gain.

BUSINESS INSIGHT **Restructuring Liabilities**

Many acquisitions are accompanied by restructuring activities that are designed to maximize asset utilization. These restructuring activities typically involve relocation and retraining or termination of employees and the exiting of less profitable product lines resulting in costs from closure of manufacturing, retailing, and administrative facilities and the write-off of assets. Acquirers can recognize restructuring liabilities when they purchase a subsidiary *only* if that subsidiary has previously accrued those liabilities. It also requires the Board of Directors to approve a formal restructuring plan and to communicate that plan to affected employees. Restructuring activities beginning *after* acquisition must be accrued and the expense recognized in post-acquisition consolidated income statements. In its 2012 10-K, **Oracle Corporation** provides the following footnote relating to its accounting for anticipated restructuring activities in connection with an acquisition:

> We account for costs to exit or restructure certain activities of an acquired company separately from the business combination. These costs are accounted for as one-time termination and exit costs pursuant to ASC 420, *Exit or Disposal Cost Obligations.* A liability for a cost associated with an exit or disposal activity is recognized and measured at its fair value in our consolidated statement of operations in the period in which the liability is incurred. When estimating the fair value of facility restructuring activities, assumptions are applied regarding estimated sub-lease payments to be received, which can differ materially from actual results. This may require us to revise our initial estimates which may materially affect our results of operations and financial position in the period the revision is made.

It is not sufficient that the investor *expect* to restructure operations following the acquisition, but that a restructuring plan must be *in place* to record a restructuring liability at acquisition. If not, the liability, and associated expense, is recognized subsequent to acquisition. This is important as recording a restructuring liability at acquisition allows the investor to immediately record a restructuring expense and, as a result, post-acquisition profits are higher.

Reporting of Goodwill

Goodwill is not amortized. Instead, GAAP requires companies to test the goodwill asset annually for impairment just like any other asset. The impairment test is a two-step process:

1. The fair value of the investee company is compared with the book value of the investor's equity investment account.[2]
2. If the fair value is less than the investment balance, the *investment* is deemed impaired. Next, one determines if the *goodwill* portion of the investment is impaired. The investor estimates the goodwill value as if the subsidiary were acquired at current fair value, and determines the imputed balance for goodwill. If this imputed goodwill amount is less than its book value, the company writes goodwill down, resulting in an impairment loss on the consolidated income statement. (If not, no impairment of goodwill exists and no write-down is necessary; which, implies the impairment in this case relates to the investee's tangible assets, such as PPE, that must be tested separately for impairment.)

To illustrate the impairment computation, assume that an investment, currently reported at $1 million on the investor's balance sheet, has a current fair value of $900,000 (we know, therefore, that the investment is impaired); also assume the consolidated balance sheet reports goodwill at $300,000.

---

[2] GAAP allows firms to estimate fair value in three ways: using quoted market prices for identical assets, using quoted prices on similar assets, or using other valuation methods (such as the discounted cash flow model or residual operating income model—see Module 12). The Hewlett-Packard footnote, which follows later in this section, provides an example of the third method of determining fair value: an income approach. A company can avoid the goodwill impairment test if qualitative indicators (see GAAP) suggest a likelihood that the fair value of the reporting unit is greater than its carrying value; if not, then the company must apply the two-step test.

Management's review reveals that the current fair value of the net assets of the investee company (absent goodwill) is $700,000. This indicates that the goodwill component of the investment account is impaired by $100,000, which is computed as follows:

Fair value of investee company	$ 900,000
Fair value of net assets (absent goodwill)	(700,000)
Implied goodwill	200,000
Current goodwill balance	(300,000)
Impairment loss	$(100,000)

This analysis implies that goodwill must be written down by $100,000. The impairment loss is reported in the consolidated income statement. The related footnote disclosure would describe the reasons for the write-down and the computations involved.

Hewlett-Packard provides an example of a goodwill impairment disclosure relating to its acquisitions of **Compaq** and **Autonomy** in its 2012 10-K report:

> HP's goodwill impairment test involves a two-step process. In the first step, HP compares the fair value of each reporting unit to its carrying value. If the fair value of the reporting unit exceeds its carrying value, goodwill is not impaired and no further testing is required. If the fair value of the reporting unit is less than the carrying value, HP must perform the second step of the impairment test to measure the amount of impairment loss, if any. In the second step, the reporting unit's fair value is allocated to all of the assets and liabilities of the reporting unit, including any unrecognized intangible assets, in a hypothetical analysis that calculates the implied fair value of goodwill in the same manner as if the reporting unit was being acquired in a business combination. If the implied fair value of the reporting unit's goodwill is less than the carrying value, the difference is recorded as an impairment loss. In fiscal 2012, we recorded goodwill impairment charges of $8.0 billion and $5.7 billion associated with the Services segment and the acquisition of Autonomy, respectively. In addition, we recorded intangible asset impairment charges of $3.1 billion and $1.2 billion associated with the acquisition of Autonomy and the "Compaq" trade name, respectively.

HP determined that goodwill and other intangible assets, reported on its balance sheet at $18 billion (computed as $8.0 billion + $5.7 billion + $3.1 billion + $1.2 billion), had no current (implied) market value. HP acquired Compaq in 2002 and Autonomy in 2011 and decided that some of the goodwill associated with both had no value. HP's 2012 income statement reflects the magnitude of these write-offs as follows:

In millions	2012
Net revenue:	
Products	$ 77,887
Services	42,008
Financing income	462
Total net revenue	120,357
Costs and expenses:	
Cost of products	59,468
Cost of services	32,600
Financing interest	317
Research and development	3,399
Selling, general and administrative	13,500
Amortization of purchased intangible assets	1,784
Impairment of goodwill and purchased intangible assets	18,035
Restructuring charges	2,266
Acquisition-related charges	45

continued

continued from prior page

In millions	2012
Total operating expenses	131,414
(Loss) earnings from operations	(11,057)
Interest and other, net	(876)
(Loss) earnings before taxes	(11,933)
Provision for taxes	(717)
Net (loss) earnings	$(12,650)

IFRS INSIGHT **Goodwill Impairment and Revaluation**

Similar to GAAP, all long-term assets, including goodwill, must be periodically evaluated for impairment. But, under IFRS, any previous impairment losses must be reversed if the asset subsequently increases in value. However, this does not apply to goodwill; once it is impaired under IFRS, it can not be revalued upwards. This is consistent with GAAP. Impairment losses are typically larger in magnitude under IFRS because IFRS computes the impairment loss as the excess of the carrying amount of the goodwill over its recoverable amount. Under GAAP, the impairment is relative to the implied fair value of the goodwill, which by definition is higher than the recoverable amount. Thus, for identical circumstances, goodwill impairments will be larger under IFRS.

Reporting Subsidiary Stock Issuances

After subsidiaries are acquired, they can, and sometimes do, issue stock. If issued to outside investors, the result is an infusion of cash into the subsidiary and a reduction in the parent's percentage ownership. For example, in February, 2013, **Pfizer**'s wholly-owned subsidiary, **Zoetis**, sold shares of its common stock to outside investors (not to the parent company, Pfizer) as described in the following footnote to Pfizer's 1Q, 2013 report:

> On February 6, 2013, an IPO of the Class A common stock of Zoetis was completed, pursuant to which we sold 99.015 million shares of Class A common stock of Zoetis . . . in exchange for the retirement of approximately $2.5 billion of Pfizer commercial paper issued in 2013. The Class A common stock sold in the IPO represented approximately 19.8% of the total outstanding Zoetis shares. On February 1, 2013, Zoetis shares began trading on the New York Stock Exchange under the symbol "ZTS." The excess of the consideration received over the net book value of our divested interest was approximately $2.3 billion and was recorded in Additional paid-in capital . . . We continue to consolidate Zoetis, as we retain control over Zoetis.

Prior to the IPO, Zoetis was a wholly-owned subsidiary of Pfizer. The IPO resulted in the issuance of 90.015 million shares by Zoetis, representing 19.8% of the outstanding Class A common stock. The IPO increased Pfizer's stockholders' equity by $2.3 billion via increased additional paid-in capital.

BUSINESS INSIGHT **Pitfalls of Acquired Growth**

One of the greatest destructions of shareholder value occurred during the bull market between 1995 and 2001 when market exuberance fueled a tidal wave of corporate takeovers. Companies often overpaid as a result of overestimating the cost-cutting and synergies their planned takeovers would bring. Then, acquirers failed to quickly integrate operations. The result? Subsequent years' market returns of most acquirers fell below those of their peers and were often negative. Indeed, 61% of corporate buyers saw their shareholders' wealth *decrease* after the acquisition. Who won? The sellers; the target-company shareholders who sold their stock within the first week of the takeover and reaped enormous profits at the expense of the acquirers' shareholders.

Reporting the Sale of Subsidiary Companies

Recall that Kellogg Company purchased the *Pringles®* business from Procter & Gamble for $2.7 billion. In this section, we illustrate the transaction from P&G's perspective. Following is the footnote disclosure relating to the sale from P&G's 2012 10-K:

> **DISCONTINUED OPERATIONS** In May 2012, the Company completed the divestiture of our global snacks business to The Kellogg Company (Kellogg) for $2.7 billion of cash. Under the terms of the agreement, Kellogg acquired our branded snacks products, our manufacturing facilities in Belgium and the United States and the majority of the employees working on the snacks business. The Company recorded an after-tax gain on the transaction of $1.4 billion, which is included in net earnings from discontinued operations in the Consolidated Statement of Earnings for the year ended June 30, 2012. . . In accordance with the applicable accounting guidance for the disposal of long-lived assets, the results of the snacks business are presented as discontinued operations and, as such, have been excluded from both continuing operations and segment results for all years presented.

Once P&G decided to sell its snacks business, it accounted for the business unit as a discontinued operation (see Module 5 for a discussion of discontinued operations) with the following financial statement effects:

1. It removed from the consolidated income statement, the revenues and expense relating to the snacks business (for each of the three years presented) and reported only the net profit after tax of the snacks business unit in a separate section below income from continuing operations. This is done to specifically identify the revenues, expenses and profit of the business units that will continue to generate future profit and cash flows.
2. In the year of sale, P&G reported a $1.4 billion gain on the sale of the snacks business unit (sales proceeds of $2.7 billion less book value of the snacks business unit of $1.3 on the date of sale).

P&G combines the two amounts on its 2012 income statement and reports the total below income from continuing operations to identify the $1,587 million as transitory.

Year ended June 30 (amounts in millions)	2012
Net sales	$83,680
Cost of products sold	42,391
Selling, general and administrative expense	26,421
Goodwill and indefinite-lived intangible asset impairment charges	1,576
Operating income	13,292
Interest expense	769
Other non-operating income, net	262
Earnings from continuing operations before income taxes	12,785
Income taxes on continuing operations	3,468
Net earnings from continuing operations	9,317
Net earnings from discontinued operations	1,587
Net earnings	10,904
Less: Net earnings attributable to noncontrolling interests	148
Net earnings attributable to Procter & Gamble	$10,756

Limitations of Consolidation Reporting

Consolidation of financial statements is meant to present a financial picture of the entire set of companies under the control of the parent. Since investors typically purchase stock in the parent company, and not in the subsidiaries, a consolidated view is more relevant than the parent company merely reporting subsidiaries as equity investments in its balance sheet. Still, we must be aware of certain limitations of consolidation:

1. Consolidated income does not imply that the parent company has received any or all of the subsidiaries' net income as cash. The parent can only receive cash from subsidiaries via dividend payments. Conversely, the consolidated cash is not automatically available to the individual subsidiaries. It is quite possible, therefore, for an individual subsidiary to experience cash flow problems even though the consolidated group has strong cash flows. Likewise, unguaranteed debts of a subsidiary are not obligations of the consolidated group. Thus, even if the consolidated balance sheet is strong, creditors of a failing subsidiary are often unable to sue the parent or other subsidiaries to recoup losses.
2. Consolidated balance sheets and income statements are a mix of the various subsidiaries, often from different industries. Comparisons across companies, even if in similar industries, are often complicated by the different mix of subsidiary companies.
3. Consolidated disclosures are highly aggregated, which can preclude effective analysis. Consolidated numbers can mask poorly performing subsidiaries whose losses are offset by the positive performance of others.

IFRS

GLOBAL ACCOUNTING

Both U.S. GAAP and IFRS account similarly for investments by companies in the debt and equity securities of other companies. However, differences exist and we highlight the notable ones here.

Passive Investments Under both U.S. GAAP and IFRS, companies classify financial (passive) instruments as trading, available-for-sale, or held-to-maturity.

- Under IFRS the definition of financial instrument is much broader, including for example accounts receivable and loans to customers or associates. For analysis, such instruments are disclosed in the notes, which will aid our reclassification for comparison purposes.
- Under U.S. GAAP, unlisted securities are not considered "marketable" and are carried at cost. Under IFRS, unlisted securities can be valued at fair value, if it can be reliably measured.
- U.S. GAAP prohibits companies from reclassifying trading securities as available-for-sale or held-to-maturity but, under certain circumstances, requires companies to reclassify securities as trading (for example, if there has been a sale of a held-to-maturity security). Under IFRS, both reclassifications to and from the trading portfolio are prohibited. This provides opportunity for strategic reporting behavior under U.S. GAAP. We should review the notes that report reclassifications to assess such behavior and identify any reporting incentives managers might have.

Equity Method Investment U.S. GAAP allows only the equity method in accounting for joint ventures, whereas IFRS allows the equity method or proportionate consolidation. Under the latter, the company's share of investee's assets and liabilities (and revenues and expenses) are added line-by-line on the balance sheet (and income statement). Proportionate consolidation means that every line on the IFRS financial statement is "grossed up" as compared to GAAP. The net numbers (equity and income) are identical but comparisons of individual line items between an IFRS and a GAAP report are problematic. This is similar to the effect of equity method accounting versus consolidation. There is currently a proposal to prohibit proportionate consolidation. In the interim, as discussed in the module, GAAP notes often disclose total revenue, assets, and liabilities of equity method investees. Thus, it is possible for us to amend certain GAAP accounts for comparative analysis.

Consolidation As part of their convergence effort, the FASB and IASB engaged in a joint project for business combinations (IFRS 3 and SFAS 141). Despite the common goal to develop a consistent and comprehensive standard, a few differences remain.

- The most notable difference is how to measure noncontrolling interests. Under IFRS, companies can measure noncontrolling interests either at fair value (full goodwill approach) or at the proportionate share of the identifiable net assets acquired (purchased goodwill approach). U.S. GAAP permits fair value only. Relative to the proportionate method, the U.S. GAAP balance sheet reports a larger goodwill and a larger noncontrolling interest in equity. This difference is most pronounced when a company acquires significantly less than 100% of the target's stock or when goodwill is a larger proportion of the cost of acquisition. This IFRS-GAAP difference affects ratios based on operating assets, such as RNOA. Because goodwill is not routinely amortized, the difference will have no income statement impact (recall from Module 4 that we exclude noncontrolling interest from our calculation of return on equity).

- Under U.S. GAAP, parent and subsidiaries' accounting policies do not need to conform. Under IFRS, parent and subsidiaries' accounting policies must conform.
- IFRS fair-value impairments for intangible assets, excluding goodwill, can be later reversed (that is, written back up after being written down). Companies must have reliable evidence that the value of the intangible has been restored and the reversal cannot exceed the original impairment. While the original impairment was reported as a charge on the income statement, subsequent reversals do not affect income but, instead, are added to equity through a "reserve" much like that for accumulated other comprehensive income. IFRS notes disclose any reversals of a prior impairment (again, goodwill impairments cannot be reversed).

MODULE-END REVIEW

On January 1 of the current year, assume that **Yahoo!, Inc.**, purchased all of the common shares of **EarthLink** for $600,000 cash—this is $200,000 more than the book value of EarthLink's stockholders' equity. Balance sheets of the two companies immediately after the acquisition follow:

	Yahoo! (Parent)	EarthLink (Subsidiary)	Consolidating Adjustments	Consolidated
Current assets	$1,000,000	$100,000		
Investment in EarthLink	600,000	—		
PPE, net	3,000,000	400,000		
Goodwill	—	—		
Total assets	$4,600,000	$500,000		
Liabilities	$1,000,000	$100,000		
Contributed capital	2,000,000	200,000		
Retained earnings	1,600,000	200,000		
Total liabilities and equity	$4,600,000	$500,000		

During purchase negotiations, EarthLink's PPE was appraised at $500,000, and all of EarthLink's remaining assets and liabilities were appraised at values approximating their book values. Also, Yahoo! concluded that payment of an additional $100,000 was warranted because of anticipated corporate synergies. Prepare the consolidating adjustments and the consolidated balance sheet at acquisition.

The solution is on page 9-57.

APPENDIX 9A: Accounting for Derivatives

Although there is some speculative use of derivatives by U.S. companies (both industrial and financial), most companies use derivatives to shelter their income statements and cash flows from fluctuations in the market prices of currencies, commodities, and financial instruments, as well as for market rates of interest. Companies routinely face risk exposures that can markedly affect their balance sheets, profitability, and cash flows. These exposures can be grouped into two general categories:[3]

[3] Risks relating to changes in the fair value of a recognized asset or liability, or the variation in cash flows relating to a contractual obligation or a forecasted transaction, that results from fluctuations in the exchange value of the $US vis-à-vis other world currencies are particularly troublesome for companies. The use of derivatives to mitigate **foreign-currency risk** can fall into either of the risk categories.

1. Exposure to changes in the **fair value** of an asset (such as accounts receivable, inventory, marketable securities, or a firm contract to sell an asset) or of a liability (such as accounts payable, a firm commitment to purchase an asset, or a fixed-rate liability).
2. Exposure to variation in **cash flows** relating to a forecasted transaction (such as *planned* inventory purchases or anticipated foreign revenues) or cash-flow exposure relating to a variable-rate debt obligation.

Both of these types of risks can be managed (hedged) with a variety of financial instruments, including futures, forward contracts, options, and swap contracts. For an example in the first risk category, consider a company with a fair-value exposure from a receivable denominated in a foreign currency. If the $US strengthens subsequently, the receivable declines in value and the company incurs a foreign-currency loss. To avoid this situation, the company can hedge the receivable with a foreign-currency derivative. Ideally, when the $US strengthens, the derivative will increase in value by an amount that exactly offsets the decrease in the value of the receivable. As a result, the company's net asset position (receivable less derivative) remains unaffected and no gain or loss arises when the $US weakens or strengthens. For accounting purposes, this is called a **fair-value hedge**.

As an example for the second risk category, consider a company that routinely purchases a food commodity used in its manufacturing process. Any price increases during the coming year will flow to cost of goods sold and profit will decrease (unless the company can completely pass the price increase along to its customers, which is rarely the case). To avoid this situation, the company can hedge the forecasted inventory purchases with a commodity derivative contract that locks in a price today. When the price of the commodity increases, the derivative contract will shelter the company and, as a result, the company's cost of goods sold remains unaffected. For accounting purposes, this is called a **cash-flow hedge**.

Accounting for derivatives essentially boils down to this: all derivatives are reported at fair value on the balance sheet. For fair-value hedges, the asset or liability being hedged (the foreign receivable in the example above), is reported on the balance sheet at fair value. If the market value of the hedged asset or liability changes, the value of the derivative changes in the opposite direction if the hedge is effective and, thus, net assets and liabilities are unaffected. Likewise, the related gains and losses are largely offsetting, leaving income unaffected.

For cash-flow hedges, there is no hedged asset or liability on the books. In our example above, it is the anticipated commodity purchases that are being hedged. Thus, the company has no inventory yet and changes in the fair value of the derivative are not met with opposite changes in an asset or liability. For these cash-flow hedges, gains or losses from the fair value of the derivative are not reported on the income statement. Instead they are held in accumulated other comprehensive income (AOCI), as part of shareholders' equity. Later, when the hedged item impacts income (say, when the commodity cost is reflected in cost of goods sold), the derivative gain or loss is reclassified from AOCI to income. If the hedge was effective, the gain or loss on the hedged transaction is offset with the loss or gain on the derivative and income is unaffected.

For both fair-value and cash-flow hedges, income is impacted only to the extent that the hedging activities are ineffective. Naturally, if a company uses derivatives to speculate, gains and losses are not offset and directly flow to income. It is this latter activity, in particular, that prompted regulators to formulate newer, tougher accounting standards for derivatives.

Disclosures for Derivatives

Companies must disclose both qualitative and quantitative information about derivatives in notes to their financial statements and elsewhere (in the Management's Discussion and Analysis section). The aim of these disclosures is to inform outsiders about potential risks associated with derivative use. We present footnotes relating to fair-value hedges and cash-flow hedges below as examples of common transactions relating to use of derivatives to mitigate risk. We discuss the accounting for each and how we should interpret these disclosures in our analysis of the company.

Fair-Value Hedge

Fair-value hedges are used to mitigate risks relating to the change in the fair values of existing assets and liabilities. These fair values can change, for example, with changes in commodity prices, interest rates, or foreign exchange rates. Following is an example from the Kellogg 2012 10-K.

> **Foreign exchange risk** Our company is exposed to fluctuations in foreign currency cash flows related primarily to third-party purchases, intercompany transactions, and when applicable, nonfunctional currency denominated third-party debt . . . Additionally, our company is exposed to volatility in the translation of foreign currency denominated earnings to U.S. dollars. Primary exposures include the U.S. dollar versus the euro, British

continued

pound, Australian dollar, Canadian dollar, and Mexican peso, and in the case of inter-subsidiary transactions, the British pound versus the euro. We assess foreign currency risk based on transactional cash flows and translational volatility and may enter into forward contracts, options, and currency swaps to reduce fluctuations in long or short currency positions. Forward contracts and options are generally less than 18 months duration. Currency swap agreements may be established in conjunction with the term of underlying debt issuances.

To illustrate the accounting for the Kellogg fair-value hedge, assume that the company sells goods for €3.7 million ($5 million equivalent) on account to a customer located in Ireland. The company is concerned about the potential effects of a strengthening or weakening of the $US and enters into a forward contract to hedge that foreign-currency (FX) risk. Before the receivable is collected, the $US weakens vis-à-vis the Euro, and the Euros received (€3.7 million) converts to $5.5 million. The transactions are accounted for as follows:

	Balance Sheet					Income Statement		
Transaction	Cash Asset	+ Noncash Assets	= Liabilities	+ Contrib. Capital	+ Earned Capital	Revenues	− Expenses	= Net Income
1. Credit sale for €3.7 mil. ($5 mil. equivalent)		+5.0 mil. Accounts Receivable	=		+5.0 mil. Retained Earnings	+5.0 mil. Sales	−	= +5.0 mil.
2a. Receive €3.7 mil. ($5.5 mil. equivalent) per transaction *1*	+5.5 mil. Cash	−5.0 mil. Accounts Receivable	=		+0.5 mil. Retained Earnings	+0.5 mil. Gain on Foreign Currency Transaction	−	= +0.5 mil.
2b. Record loss on settlement of foreign exchange contract	−0.5 mil. Cash		=		−0.5 mil. Retained Earnings		− +0.5 mil. Loss on Foreign Exchange Derivative Contract	= −0.5 mil.

AR 5.0M
Sales 5.0M
AR: 5M |
Sales: | 5M

Cash 5.5M
AR 5.0M
GN 0.5M
Cash: 5.5M |
AR: | 5M
Gain on FX: | 0.5M

LS 0.5M
Cash 0.5M
Loss on Contract: 0.5M |
Cash: | 0.5M

In this transaction, the company hedged its foreign exchange exposure via a forward contract. As the $US weakens, the value of the accounts receivable increases by $0.5 million, resulting in a foreign exchange gain, and the fair value of the derivative contract decreases by $0.5 million, resulting in an offsetting loss. The net cash received is the $5.5 million from the receivable less the $0.5 million to settle the forward contract.

Why would the company want to enter into a contract such as this that resulted in a loss? After all, had the company not "hedged" the Euro receivable, the cash collected would have been $5.5 million and the company would have reported a gain. The answer is that a company does not know in advance which way currencies will move. As the Kellogg footnote indicates, sometimes the derivative suffers a loss, and at other times creates a gain. The purpose of the derivative is to lock in the operating profit on the sale and to shield the company from risk in the form of fluctuating foreign-currency exchange rates.

Cash-Flow Hedge

Following is **Tiffany & Co.**'s disclosures from its 2013 10-K report relating to its use of derivatives:

Precious Metal Collars & Forward Contracts The Company periodically hedges a portion of its forecasted purchases of precious metals for use in its internal manufacturing operations in order to minimize the effect of volatility in precious metal prices. The Company may use either a combination of call and put option contracts in net-zero-cost collar arrangements ("precious metal collars") or forward contracts. For precious metal collars, if the price of the precious metal at the time of the expiration of the precious metal collar is within the call and put price, the precious metal collar expires at no cost to the Company. The Company accounts for its precious metal collars and forward contracts as cash flow hedges. The Company assesses hedge effectiveness based on the total changes in the precious metal collars and forward contracts' cash flows. The maximum term over which the Company is hedging its exposure to the variability of future cash flows for all forecasted transactions is 12 months. As of January 31, 2013, there were approximately 13,600 ounces of platinum and 315,000 ounces of silver precious metal derivative instruments outstanding.

Tiffany uses derivatives to hedge against the risk of fluctuations in the market price of precious metals that the company anticipates purchasing in the future.

These derivatives are cash-flow hedges. Thus, unrealized gains and losses on these derivative contracts are added to the Accumulated Other Comprehensive Income (AOCI) (part of stockholders' equity) until the precious metal is purchased. Once that precious metal is purchased, any unrealized gains and losses are removed from AOCI and recognized in current-period income via cost of goods sold. The gain (loss) on the derivative contract offsets the increased (decreased) cost of the precious metal.

Tiffany includes gains and losses from its cash flow hedges in Accumulated Other Comprehensive Income (AOCI) on its balance sheet and provides the following detail for the AOCI account in its footnotes:

The following sets forth the changes in each component of accumulated other comprehensive losses, net of tax:

(in thousands)	Foreign Currency Translation Adjustments	Unrealized (Loss) Gain on Marketable Securities	Deferred Hedging Loss	Net Unrealized Loss on Benefit Plans	Accumulated Other Comprehensive Loss
January 31, 2010	$16,512	$(1,899)	$(2,607)	$ (45,271)	$(33,265)
Period change, before tax	27,167	3,135	2,446	(11,365)	21,383
Income tax (expense) benefit . . .	(2,264)	(1,094)	(1,031)	3,706	(683)
January 31, 2011	41,415	142	(1,192)	(52,930)	(12,565)
Period change, before tax	9,997	(19)	(12,050)	(118,366)	(120,438)
Income tax (expense) benefit . . .	(2,203)	7	4,513	45,556	47,873
January 31, 2012	49,209	130	(8,729)	(125,740)	(85,130)
Period change, before tax	(11,567)	2,646	7,729	(18,171)	(19,363)
Income tax benefit (expense) . . .	6,422	(927)	(2,207)	7,330	10,618
January 31, 2013	$44,064	$ 1,849	$(3,207)	$(136,581)	$(93,875)

The Company expects approximately $11,995,000 of net pre-tax derivative gains included in accumulated other comprehensive income at January 31, 2013, will be reclassified into earnings within the next 12 months. This amount will vary due to fluctuations in foreign currency exchange rates and precious metal prices.

Tiffany reports a net after-tax deferred hedging loss of $(3,207) thousand in its AOCI as of January 2013. This includes both deferred gains and deferred losses. The company expects that $11,995 thousand of net pre-tax deferred hedging gains will be transferred from AOCI to income (to reduce COGS) in the upcoming year. This transfer occurs when Tiffany exercises its option and purchases precious metals (whose prices have increased) at the pre-established (lower) strike price. As that jewelry is sold, Tiffany transfers the deferred hedging gain from AOCI to reduce COGS, thus offsetting the increase in the COGS relating to price increases in the precious metals used in the manufacturing process. Using derivatives to hedge against commodity price increases is a common practice.

Although the market value of derivatives and their related assets or liabilities can be large, the net effect on stockholders' equity is usually minor. This is because companies use derivatives mainly to hedge and not to speculate. The FASB enacted SFAS 133, "Accounting for Derivative Instruments and Hedging Activities," to respond to concerns that speculative activities were not adequately disclosed. However, subsequent to the passage of SFAS 133, the financial effects have been minimal. Either companies were not speculating to the extent suspected, or they have since reduced their level of speculation in response to increased scrutiny from better disclosures.

To illustrate the accounting for cash-flow hedge, assume that Tiffany knows that it must purchase platinum over the coming year. The platinum would cost $1 million at the current market prices but Tiffany anticipates price increases. Simultaneously, Tiffany purchases call options to lock in the $1 million purchase price. (Tiffany would pay an option premium which would be recorded as an asset and amortized over time; to keep the example simple, we ignore this premium.) Delivery of the platinum takes place over the year and the market price of the platinum purchases is $1.686 million. During the year, Tiffany adjusts the option to fair value, the combined mark-to-market adjustments are $0.686 million. Those transactions are accounted for as follows:

	Balance Sheet									Income Statement				
Transaction	Cash Asset	+	Noncash Assets	=	Liabilities	+	Contrib. Capital	+	Earned Capital	Revenues	−	Expenses	=	Net Income
1. Record unrealized fair-value gain on call option			+0.686 mil. Call Option	=					+0.686 mil. AOCI		−		=	
2a. Purchase and use platinum during the year	−1.686 mil. Cash			=					−1.686 mil. Retained Earnings		−	+1.686 mil. COGS	=	−1.686 mil.
2b. Exercise call option as Tiffany purchases platinum	+0.686 mil. Cash		−0.686 mil. Call Option	=							−		=	
2c. Recognize unrealized fair-value gain as Tiffany uses platinum				=					+0.686 mil. Retained Earnings −0.686 mil. AOCI		−	−0.686 mil. COGS	=	+0.686 mil.

1. Call Op 0.686M
AOCI 0.686M
Call Option: 0.686M |
AOCI: | 0.686M

2a. FE 1.686M
Cash 1.686M
Platinum Exp: 1.686M |
Cash: | 1.686M

2b. Cash 0.686M
Call Op 0.686M
Cash: 0.686M |
Call Option: | 0.686M

2c. AOCI 0.686M
FE 0.686M
AOCI: 0.686M |
Platinum Exp: | 0.686M

In this transaction, Tiffany has hedged its platinum purchase via call options. As the price of platinum increases, so does the value of the call option. This unrealized gain on the option is reflected in AOCI until the platinum is consumed. At that time, the unrealized gain is removed from AOCI and expenses are reduced, thereby offsetting the increase in COGS resulting from the higher platinum cost. The net effect is that Tiffany reports $1 million for COGS. The net cash outlay for platinum is also $1 million as a result of the cash inflow related to the call option. The purpose of Tiffany's derivative program is to attempt to lock in the price of platinum. This is an operating activity and the gain on the derivative contract should be included in NOPAT to offset the increased cost of the platinum. Because Tiffany hedged the precious metal purchases, there is no net effect on income.

In both of our illustrations, the derivative contract is perfectly correlated with the asset or cash flow to which it relates. In practice, this is unlikely. As a result, the change in the fair value of the derivatives might not exactly offset the change in the cost of the platinum. Only the effective portion of the hedge is deferred in AOCI. The ineffective portion of the hedge affects current income. Bottom line, some of the risk will impact net income if the company cannot perfectly hedge the risk or chooses not to manage 100% of the risk.

BUSINESS INSIGHT **Counter-Party Risk**

The purpose of derivative financial instruments is to transfer risk from one company to another. For example, a company might be concerned about the possible decline in the $US value of a foreign-currency-denominated account receivable. In order to hedge that risk, the company might execute a forward contract to sell the foreign currency and receive $US. That forward contract only has value, however, if the party on the other side of the transaction (the counter-party) ultimately purchases the foreign currency for $US when the contract matures. If the counter-party fails to honor its part of the agreement, the forward contract is of no value. The risk that the other party might not live up to its part of the bargain is known as *counter-party risk*. The only justification for recognizing a gain in a forward contract to offset the loss in a foreign-currency-denominated receivable is the expectation that the counter-party has the intention and ability to purchase the foreign currency in exchange for $US when the contract matures. Counter-party risk is very real. Many companies require counter-parties to back up their agreement with cash collateral or other acceptable forms of guarantees (like a bank letter of credit, for example). As a result, there is a hidden risk in companies' use of derivatives that is difficult to quantify.

Analysis of Derivatives

In Module 4, we indicated that derivatives can be classified as nonoperating items. With additional contextual information, we could choose to refine our classification. For example, in the **Kellogg** example, the fair value of the foreign exchange contract is grouped with the accounts receivable to which it relates, and the gain (loss) on that derivative is considered an operating item (part of NOPAT). The commodity derivative investments that **Tiffany** uses are treated similarly. In this case, both the balance sheet accounts and income statement effects are treated as operating.

Companies also frequently use a variety of derivative instruments to hedge exposure to interest rates. Companies can, for example, use swap contracts to convert floating-rate debt to fixed-rate debt and vice-versa. In this case, the fair values of the derivatives and their ultimate income statement effects are nonoperating because they relate to interest-bearing debt.

In addition to proper classification of balance sheet and income statement accounts for computation of NOPAT and NOA, we are interested in understanding the extent to which the company is hedged. That is, are there still risks over which the company has no control and that are not hedged? Unfortunately, footnote disclosures do not provide a completely satisfactory answer. We are not privy to the internal risk analysis that the company performs. As a result, we do not know, for example, the precise extent to which the hedges are ineffective, to what degree the company has decided to hedge, and whether the company is facing risks for which a derivative instrument is not available. To gain further insight into these questions, we must often look to other sources of information such as analyst reports, the financial press, and communications from the company.

GUIDANCE ANSWERS

MANAGERIAL DECISION You Are the Chief Financial Officer

Capacity utilization is important. If long-term operating assets are used inefficiently, cost per unit produced is too high. Cost per unit does not relate solely to manufacturing products, but also applies to the cost of providing services and many other operating activities. However, if we purchase assets with little productive slack, our costs of production at peak levels can be excessive. Further, the company may be unable to service peak demand and risks losing customers. In response, the company might explore strategic alliances. These take many forms. Some require a simple contract to use another company's manufacturing, service, or administrative capability for a fee (note: these executory contracts are not recorded under GAAP). Another type of alliance is that of a joint venture to share ownership of manufacturing or IT facilities. In this case, if demand can be coordinated with that of a partner, perhaps operating assets can be more effectively used. Finally, a special purpose entity (SPE) can be formed to acquire the asset for use by the company and its partner—explained in Module 10.

Superscript ^{A} denotes assignments based on Appendix 9A.

DISCUSSION QUESTIONS

Q9-1. What measure (fair value or amortized cost) is on the balance sheet for (a) trading securities, (b) available-for-sale securities, and (c) held-to-maturity securities?

Q9-2. What is an unrealized holding gain (loss)? Explain.

Q9-3. Where are unrealized holding gains and losses related to trading securities reported in the financial statements? Where are unrealized holding gains and losses related to available-for-sale securities reported in the financial statements?

Q9-4. What does significant influence imply regarding intercorporate investments? Describe the accounting procedures used for such investments.

Q9-5. On January 1 of the current year, Yetman Company purchases 40% of the common stock of Livnat Company for $500,000 cash. This 40% ownership allows Yetman to exert significant influence over Livnat. During the year, Livnat reports $160,000 of net income and pays $120,000 in cash dividends. At year-end, what amount should appear in Yetman's balance sheet for its investment in Livnat?

Q9-6. What accounting method is used when a stock investment represents more than 50% of the investee company's voting stock and allows the investor company to "control" the investee company? Explain.

Q9-7. What is the underlying objective of consolidated financial statements?

Q9-8. Finn Company purchases all of the common stock of Murray Company for $375,000 when Murray Company has $150,000 of common stock and $225,000 of retained earnings. If a consolidated balance sheet is prepared immediately after the acquisition, what amounts are eliminated in consolidation? Explain.

Q9-9. Bradshaw Company owns 100% of Dee Company. At year-end, Dee owes Bradshaw $150,000 arising from a loan made during the year. If a consolidated balance sheet is prepared at year-end, how is the $150,000 handled? Explain.

Q9-10. What are some limitations of consolidated financial statements?

Assignments with the ✔ logo in the margin are available in myBusinessCourse.
See the Preface of the book for details.

MINI EXERCISES

M9-11. Interpreting Disclosures of Available-for-Sale Securities (LO1)

Use the following year-end footnote disclosure from **Intel**'s 10-K report to answer parts *a* and *b*. Intel (INTC)

(Millions of Dollars)	2012
Cost of available-for-sale equity securities	$12,927
Gross unrealized gains	1,079
Gross unrealized losses	(5)
Fair value of available-for-sale equity securities	$14,001

a. What amount does Intel report on its balance sheet as available-for-sale equity securities? Explain.

b. How does Intel report the net unrealized gain of $1,074 million ($1,079 million − $5 million) in its financial statements?

M9-12. Accounting for Available-for-Sale and Trading Securities (LO1)

Assume that Wasley Company purchases 12,000 common shares of Pincus Company for $12 cash per share. During the year, Wasley receives a cash dividend of $1.10 per common share from Pincus, and the year-end market price of Pincus common stock is $13 per share. How much income does Wasley report relating to this investment for the year if it accounts for the investment as:

a. Available-for-sale investment

b. Trading investment

M9-13. Interpreting Disclosures of Investment Securities (LO1)

Amgen Inc. reports the following disclosure relating to its December 31, 2012, accumulated other comprehensive income ($ millions). (*a*) How is Amgen accounting for its investment in marketable equity securities? How do you know? (*b*) Explain how its 2012 financial statements are impacted by Amgen's unrealized gains on its investment in marketable equity securities. (*c*) Explain the reclassification adjustments to income of $132 million. Amgen Inc. (AMGN)

	Foreign Currency Translation	Cash-Flow Hedges	Available-for-Sale Securities	Other	AOCI
Balance as of December 31, 2011	$21	$ 43	$120	$(13)	$171
Other comprehensive income:					
Foreign currency translation adjustments	(13)	—	—	—	(13)
Unrealized (losses) gains	—	15	233	(1)	247
Reclassification adjustments to income	—	(134)	(132)	—	(266)
Income taxes	4	41	(38)	—	7
Balance as of December 31, 2012	$12	$(35)	$183	$(14)	$146

M9-14. Analyzing and Interpreting Equity Method Investments (LO2)

Stober Company purchases an investment in Lang Company at a purchase price of $2 million cash, representing 30% of the book value of Lang. During the year, Lang reports net income of $200,000 and pays cash dividends of $80,000. At the end of the year, the market value of Stober's investment is $2.4 million.

a. What amount does Stober report on its balance sheet for its investment in Lang?

b. What amount of income from investments does Stober report? Explain.

c. Stober's $364,000 unrealized gain in the market value of the Lang investment (choose one and explain):

(1) Is not reflected on either its income statement or balance sheet.

(2) Is reported in its current income.

(3) Is reported on its balance sheet only.

(4) Is reported in its accumulated other comprehensive income.

M9-15. Computing Income for Equity Method Investments (LO2)
Kross Company purchases an equity investment in Penno Company at a purchase price of $2.5 million, representing 40% of the book value of Penno. During the current year, Penno reports net income of $300,000 and pays cash dividends of $100,000. At the end of the year, the fair value of Kross's investment is $2.65 million. What amount of income does Kross report relating to this investment in Penno for the year? Explain.

M9-16. Interpreting Disclosures on Investments in Affiliates (LO2)

Merck & Co., Inc. (MRK)

Merck's 10-K report included the following footnote disclosure:

> Investments in affiliates accounted for using the equity method . . . totaled $1.3 billion at December 31, 2012 . . . These amounts are reported in *Other assets*.

a. At what amount are the equity method investments reported on Merck's balance sheet? Does this amount represent Merck's adjusted cost or fair value?
b. How does Merck account for the dividends received on these investments?
c. What sources of income does the company report for these investments?

M9-17. Computing Consolidating Adjustments and Noncontrolling Interest (LO3)
Philipich Company purchases 80% of Hirst Company's common stock for $300,000 cash when Hirst Company has $150,000 of common stock and $225,000 of retained earnings. If a consolidated balance sheet is prepared immediately after the acquisition, what amounts are eliminated when preparing that statement? What amount of noncontrolling interest appears in the consolidated balance sheet?

M9-18. Computing Consolidated Net Income (LO3)
Benartzi Company purchased a 90% interest in Liang Company on January 1 of the current year and the purchase price reflected 90% of Liang's book value of equity. Benartzi Company had $300,000 net income for the current year *before* recognizing its share of Liang Company's net income. If Liang Company had net income of $75,000 for the year, what is the consolidated net income attributable to Benartzi shareholders for the year?

M9-19. Assigning Purchase Price in Acquisitions (LO3)
Weaver Company acquired 80% of Koonce Company at the beginning of the current year. Weaver paid $100,000 more than the book value of Koonce's stockholders' equity and determined that this excess purchase price related to intangible assets. How does the $100,000 appear on the consolidated Weaver Company balance sheet if the intangible assets acquired related to (*a*) patents, or alternatively (*b*) goodwill? How would the consolidated income statement be affected under each scenario?

EXERCISES

E9-20. Assessing Financial Statement Effects of Trading and Available-for-Sale Securities (LO1)
a. Use the financial statement effects template to record the following four transactions involving investments in marketable securities classified as trading.
(1) Purchased 12,000 common shares of Liu, Inc., for $12 cash per share.
(2) Received a cash dividend of $1.10 per common share from Liu.
(3) Year-end market price of Liu common stock was $11.25 per share.
(4) Sold all 12,000 common shares of Liu for $133,800.
b. Using the same transaction information as above, complete the financial statement effects template (with amounts and accounts) assuming the investments in marketable securities are classified as available-for-sale.

E9-21. Assessing Financial Statement Effects of Trading and Available-for-Sale Securities (LO1)
Use the financial statement effects template to record the accounts and amounts for the following four transactions involving investments in marketable securities:
(1) Ohlson Co. purchases 10,000 common shares of Freeman Co. at $16 cash per share.
(2) Ohlson Co. receives a cash dividend of $1.25 per common share from Freeman.
(3) Year-end market price of Freeman common stock is $17.50 per share.
(4) Ohlson Co. sells all 10,000 common shares of Freeman for $172,800 cash.
a. Assume the investments are classified as trading.
b. Assume the investments are classified as available-for-sale.

E9-22. Interpreting Footnotes on Security Investments (LO1)
Cisco Systems, Inc., reports the following in its 10-K report.

Cisco Systems, Inc., (CSCO)

(In millions)	Shares of Common Stock	Common Stock and Additional Paid-In Capital	Retained Earnings	Accumulated Other Comprehensive Income	Total Cisco Shareholders' Equity	Noncontrolling Interests	Total Equity
BALANCE AT JULY 30, 2011	5,435	$38,648	$ 7,284	$1,294	$47,226	$33	$47,259
Net income	—	—	8,041	—	8,041	—	8,041
Change in:							
Unrealized gains and losses on investments, net	—	—	—	(78)	(78)	(18)	(96)
Derivative instruments	—	—	—	(59)	(59)	—	(59)
Cumulative translation adjustment and other	—	—	—	(496)	(496)	—	(496)
Comprehensive income (loss)					7,408	(18)	7,390
Issuance of common stock	137	1,372	—	—	1,372	—	1,372
Repurchase of common stock	(274)	(2,090)	(2,470)	—	(4,560)	—	(4,560)
Cash dividends declared ($0.28 per common share)	—	—	(1,501)	—	(1,501)	—	(1,501)
Tax effects from employee stock incentive plans	—	(66)	—	—	(66)	—	(66)
Share-based compensation expense	—	1,401	—	—	1,401	—	1,401
Purchase acquisitions	—	6	—	—	6	—	6
BALANCE AT JULY 28, 2012	5,298	$39,271	$11,354	$ 661	$51,286	$15	$51,301

Summary of Available-for-Sale Investments
The following table summarizes the Company's available-for-sale investments (in millions):

July 28, 2012	Amortized Cost	Gross Unrealized Gains	Gross Unrealized Losses	Fair Value
Fixed income securities:				
U.S. government securities	$24,201	$ 41	$(1)	$24,241
U.S. government agency securities	5,367	21	—	5,388
Non-U.S. government and agency securities	1,629	9	—	1,638
Corporate debt securities	5,959	74	(3)	6,030
Total fixed income securities	37,156	145	(4)	37,297
Publicly traded equity securities	1,107	524	(11)	1,620
Total	$38,263	$669	$(15)	$38,917

a. At what amount does Cisco report its investment portfolio on its balance sheet? Does that amount include any unrealized gains or losses? Explain.

b. How is Cisco accounting for its investment portfolio—as an available-for-sale or trading portfolio? How do you know?

c. What does the number $(78) represent in the Accumulated Other Comprehensive Income column? Explain.

E9-23. Interpreting Footnote Disclosures for Investments (LO1)
CNA Financial Corporation provides the following footnote to its 2012 10-K report.

CNA Financial Corporation (CNA)

Valuation of investments The company classifies its fixed maturity securities and its equity securities as either available-for-sale or trading, and as which, they are carried at fair value. Changes in fair value of trading securities are reported within Net investment income on the Consolidated Statements of Operations. Changes in fair value related to available-for-sale securities are reported as a component of Other comprehensive income. . . . Losses may be recognized within Net realized investment gains (losses) on the Consolidated Statements of Operations when a decline in value is determined by the Company to be other-than-temporary.

The following table provides a summary of fixed maturity and equity securities.

Summary of Fixed Maturity and Equity Securities December 31, 2012 (In millions)	Cost or Amortized Cost	Gross Unrealized Gains	Gross Unrealized Losses	Estimated Fair Value	Unrealized OTTI Losses (Gains)
Fixed maturity securities available-for-sale					
Corporate and other bonds	$19,530	$2,698	$ 21	$22,207	$ —
States, municipalities and political subdivisions	9,372	1,455	44	10,783	—
Asset-backed:					
Residential mortgage-backed	5,745	246	71	5,920	(28)
Commercial mortgage-backed	1,692	147	17	1,822	(3)
Other asset-backed	929	23	—	952	—
Total asset-backed	8,366	416	88	8,694	(31)
U.S. Treasury and obligations of government sponsored enterprises	172	11	1	182	—
Foreign government	588	25	—	613	—
Redeemable preferred stock	113	13	1	125	—
Total fixed maturity securities available-for-sale	38,141	4,618	155	42,604	(31)
Total fixed maturity securities trading	29	—	—	29	
Equity securities available-for-sale:					
Common stock	38	14	—	52	
Preferred stock	190	7	—	197	
Total equity securities available-for-sale	228	21	—	249	
Total	$38,398	$4,639	$155	$42,882	

a. At what amount does CNA report its investment portfolio on its balance sheet? In your answer identify the portfolio's fair value, cost, and any unrealized gains and losses.

b. How do CNA's balance sheet and income statement reflect any unrealized gains and/or losses on the investment portfolio?

c. How do CNA's balance sheet and income statement reflect gains and losses realized from the sale of available-for-sale securities?

E9-24. Assessing Financial Statement Effects of Equity Method Securities **(LO2)**

Use the financial statement effects template (with amounts and accounts) to record the following transactions involving investments in marketable securities accounted for using the equity method:

a. Purchased 6,000 common shares of Barth Co. at $9 per share; the shares represent 30% ownership in Barth.

b. Received a cash dividend of $1.25 per common share from Barth.

c. Barth reported annual net income of $40,000.

d. Sold all 6,000 common shares of Barth for $60,250.

E9-25. Assessing Financial Statement Effects of Equity Method Securities **(LO2)**

Use the financial statement effects template (with amounts and accounts) to record the following transactions involving investments in marketable securities accounted for using the equity method:

a. Healy Co. purchases 7,500 common shares of Palepu Co. at $8 per share; the shares represent 25% ownership of Palepu.

b. Healy receives a cash dividend of $0.80 per common share from Palepu.

c. Palepu reports annual net income of $60,000.

d. Healy sells all 7,500 common shares of Palepu for $70,000.

E9-26. Assessing Financial Statement Effects of Passive and Equity Method Investments **(LO1, 2)**

On January 1, Ball Corporation purchased shares of Leftwich Company common stock.

a. Assume that the stock acquired by Ball represents 15% of Leftwich's voting stock and that Ball classifies the investment as available-for-sale. Use the financial statement effects template (with amounts and accounts) to record the following transactions:

1. Ball purchased 5,000 common shares of Leftwich at $15 cash per share.
2. Leftwich reported annual net income of $40,000.
3. Ball received a cash dividend of $1.10 per common share from Leftwich.
4. Year-end market price of Leftwich common stock is $19 per share.

b. Assume that the stock acquired by Ball represents 30% of Leftwich's voting stock and that Ball accounts for this investment using the equity method since it is able to exert significant influence. Use the financial statement effects template (with amounts and accounts) to record the following transactions:

1. Ball purchased 5,000 common shares of Leftwich at $15 cash per share.
2. Leftwich reported annual net income of $40,000.
3. Ball received a cash dividend of $1.10 per common share from Leftwich.
4. Year-end market price of Leftwich common stock is $19 per share.

E9-27. Interpreting Equity Method Investment Footnotes (LO2)

Ford Motor Company (F)

Ford Motor Company includes the following table in its 2012 Form 10-K. The table reports the ownership percentages and carrying value of equity method investments (in millions, except percentages):

	Ownership Percentage	Investment Balance	
Automotive Sector	**December 31, 2012**	**December 31, 2012**	**December 31, 2011**
Changan Ford Automobile Corporation, Ltd	50.0%	$ 990	$ —
Changan Ford Mazda Automobile Corporation, Ltd	—	—	468
Jiangling Motors Corporation, Ltd	30.0	419	373
AutoAlliance International, Inc	—	—	372
Ford Otomotiv Sanayi Anonim Sirketi	41.0	394	369
AutoAlliance (Thailand) Co., Ltd.	50.0	391	367
FordSollers Netherlands B.V.	50.0	407	361
Getrag Ford Transmissions GmbH	50.0	242	229
Ford Romania S.A.*	100.0	63	92
Tenedora Nemak, S.A. de C.V.	6.8	73	68
Changan Ford Mazda Engine Company, Ltd.	25.0	50	33
DealerDirect LLC	97.7	25	18
OEConnection LLC	50.0	20	13
Percepta, LLC	45.0	9	7
Blue Diamond Truck, S. de R.L. de C.V.	25.0	11	7
Ford Performance Vehicles Pty Ltd.	49.0	5	6
Blue Diamond Parts, LLC	25.0	4	4
Automotive Fuel Cell Cooperation Corporation	30.0	5	4
Other	Various	4	6
Total Automotive sector		$3,112	$2,797

*Although we manage the day-to-day operations for Ford Romania, through December 31, 2012, the Romanian government contractually maintained the ability to influence key decisions regarding the business, including implementation of the business plan, employment levels, and capital expenditure and investment levels. As a result, we did not consolidate our investment in Ford Romania as of year-end 2012.

a. What does Ford report on its balance sheet at December 31, 2012, for its investment in equity method affiliates? Does this reflect the adjusted cost or fair value of Ford's interest in these companies?

b. What is the total stockholders' equity of the Changan Ford Mazda Engine Company affiliate at the end of 2012? Explain.

c. Ford owns 100% of the voting stock of Ford Romania yet this investment is not consolidated. Explain. How might this accounting for the Romanian investment using the equity method impede our analysis and interpretation?

d. Assume that Jiangling Motors paid no dividends in 2012. Determine Jiangling's net income for the year.

e. Explain why Ford has so many equity-method investments.

E9-28. Analyzing and Interpreting Disclosures on Equity Method Investments (LO2)

Cummins Inc. (CMI)

Cummins Inc. (CMI) reports investments in affiliated companies, consisting mainly of investments in nine manufacturing joint ventures. Cummins reports those investments on its balance sheet at $886 million, and provides the following financial information of its investee companies in a footnote to its 10-K report:

Equity Investee Financial Summary

In millions	As of and for the years ended December 31, 2012	2011	2010
Net sales	$8,296	$8,659	$7,107
Gross margin	1,870	1,948	1,651
Net income	747	788	668
Cummins' share of net income	$ 347	$ 375	$ 321
Royalty and interest income	37	41	30
Total equity, royalty and interest income from investees	$ 384	$ 416	$ 351
Current assets	$2,843	$2,892	
Noncurrent assets	1,588	1,440	
Current liabilities	(2,039)	(2,055)	
Noncurrent liabilities	(431)	(391)	
Net assets	$1,961	$1,886	
Cummins' share of net assets	$ 886	$ 885	

a. What assets and liabilities of unconsolidated affiliates are omitted from Cummins' balance sheet as a result of the equity method of accounting for those investments?

b. Do the liabilities of the unconsolidated affiliates affect Cummins directly? Explain.

c. How does the equity method impact Cummins' ROE and its RNOA components (net operating asset turnover and net operating profit margin)?

E9-29. Reporting and Interpreting Stock Investment Performance (LO1)

Kasznik Company began operations on June 15 of the current calendar year and, by year-end (December 31), had made six stock investments. Year-end information on these stock investments follows.

December 31	Cost or Equity Basis (as appropriate)	Year-End Fair Value	Market Classification
Barth, Inc.	$34,000	$32,650	Trading
Foster, Inc.	81,250	80,000	Trading
McNichols, Inc.	98,500	96,000	Available-for-sale
Patell Company	78,500	77,350	Available-for-sale
Ertimur, Inc.	50,000	51,200	Equity method
Soliman, Inc.	68,000	66,600	Equity method

a. What does Kasznik's balance sheet report for trading stock investments at December 31?

b. What does Kasznik's balance sheet report for available-for-sale investments at December 31?

c. What does Kasznik's balance sheet report for equity method investments at December 31?

d. What total amount of unrealized holding gains or unrealized holding losses related to investments appear in Kasznik's income statement?

e. What total amount of unrealized holding gains or unrealized holding losses related to investments appear in the stockholders' equity section of Kasznik's December 31 balance sheet?

f. What total amount of fair-value adjustment to investments appears in the December 31 balance sheet? Which category of investments does the fair-value adjustment relate to? Does the fair-value adjustment increase or decrease the carrying value of these investments?

E9-30. Interpreting Equity Method Investment Footnotes (LO2)

AT&T Inc. (T)

AT&T reports the following footnote to its 2012 10-K report ($ millions).

Equity Method Investments Investments in partnerships, joint ventures and less than majority-owned subsidiaries in which we have significant influence are accounted for under the equity method . . . The following table is a reconciliation of our investments in equity affiliates as presented on our Consolidated Balance Sheets.

continued

($ in millions)	2012	2011
Beginning of year	$3,718	$4,515
Additional investments	405	35
Equity in net income of affiliates	752	784
Dividends received	(137)	(161)
Dispositions	—	(660)
Currency translation adjustments	95	(515)
América Móvil equity adjustments	(260)	(171)
Other adjustments	8	(109)
End of year	$4,581	$3,718

Undistributed earnings from equity affiliates were $6,375 and $5,760 at December 31, 2012 and 2011.

a. At what amount is the equity investment in affiliates reported on AT&T's balance sheet?
b. Did affiliates pay dividends in 2012? How do you know?
c. How much income did AT&T report in 2012 relating to this investment in affiliates?
d. Interpret the AT&T statement that "undistributed earnings from equity affiliates were $6,375 and $5,760 at December 31, 2012 and 2011."
e. How does use of the equity method impact AT&T's ROE and its RNOA components (net operating asset turnover and net operating profit margin)?
f. AT&T accounts for its investment in affiliates under the equity method. Why?

E9-31. Interpreting Equity Method Investment Footnotes (LO2, 3)

On December 29, 2006, **AT&T** acquired **Bell South**. Prior to the acquisition, AT&T and Bell South jointly owned AT&T Mobility (formerly known as Cingular Wireless) and each accounted for its investment in AT&T Mobility under the equity method. AT&T purchased Bell South for $66,834 million and reported the following allocation of the purchase price in its 2007 10-K:

AT&T (T)
Bell South

Bell South Purchase Price Allocation ($ millions)	As of 12/31/06	Adjustments	As of 12/29/07
Assets acquired			
Current assets	$ 4,875	$ 6	$ 4,881
Property, plant and equipment	18,498	225	18,723
Intangible assets not subject to amortization			
Trademark/name	330	—	330
Licenses	214	100	314
Intangible assets subject to amortization			
Customer lists and relationships	9,230	(25)	9,205
Patents	100	—	100
Trademark/name	211	—	211
Investments in AT&T Mobility	32,759	2,039	34,798
Other investments	2,446	(3)	2,443
Other assets	11,211	(168)	11,043
Goodwill	26,467	(1,554)	24,913
Total assets acquired	106,341	620	106,961
Liabilities assumed			
Current liabilities, excluding current portion of long-term debt	5,288	(427)	4,861
Long-term debt	15,628	(4)	15,624
Deferred income taxes	10,318	(89)	10,229
Postemployment benefit obligation	7,086	163	7,249
Other noncurrent liabilities	1,223	941	2,164
Total liabilities assumed	39,543	584	40,127
Net assets acquired	$ 66,798	$ 36	$ 66,834

a. Describe how AT&T accounts for its investment in AT&T Mobility (formerly Cingular Wireless) following its acquisition of Bell South.

b. AT&T had the following disclosure in its 2007 10-K regarding the reporting of its investment in AT&T Mobility: "We recorded the consolidation of AT&T Mobility as a step acquisition, retaining 60% of AT&T Mobility's prior book value and adjusting the remaining 40% to fair value." Why is AT&T only adjusting 40% of its investment in AT&T Mobility to fair value?

c. AT&T adjusted the purchase price allocation for Bell South subsequent to the acquisition. Most of the allocation relates to an increased value placed on Bell South's equity investment in AT&T Mobility due to "increased value of licenses and customer lists and relationships acquired." Why did the increase in the allocation of the purchase price to Bell South's investment in AT&T Mobility decrease the allocation to goodwill? How will this increase in allocation to the equity investment impact AT&T's income statement?

d. More than half of the purchase price is allocated to intangible assets and goodwill. How is the fair value of customer lists and relationships estimated? How is the fair value of goodwill estimated? Why does it matter whether the allocation of the purchase price for intangible assets relates to "customer lists and relationships" or to goodwill?

✔ **E9-32. Constructing the Consolidated Balance Sheet at Acquisition (LO3)**

On January 1 of the current year, Healy Company purchased all of the common shares of Miller Company for $250,000 cash. Balance sheets of the two firms immediately after the acquisition follow:

	Healy Company	Miller Company	Consolidating Adjustments	Consolidated
Current assets	$ 850,000	$ 60,000		
Investment in Miller	250,000	—		
Plant assets, net	1,500,000	205,000		
Goodwill	—	—		
Total assets	$2,600,000	$265,000		
Liabilities	$ 350,000	$ 45,000		
Contributed capital	1,750,000	200,000		
Retained earnings	500,000	20,000		
Total liabilities and equity	$2,600,000	$265,000		

During purchase negotiations, Miller's plant assets were appraised at $212,500 and all of its remaining assets and liabilities were appraised at values approximating their book values. Healy also concluded that an additional $22,500 (for goodwill) demanded by Miller's shareholders was warranted because Miller's earning power was better than the industry average. Prepare the consolidating adjustments and the consolidated balance sheet at acquisition.

E9-33. Constructing the Consolidated Balance Sheet at Acquisition (LO3)

Rayburn Company purchased all of Kanodia Company's common stock for $300,000 cash on January 1, at which time the separate balance sheets of the two corporations appeared as follows:

	Rayburn Company	Kanodia Company	Consolidating Adjustments	Consolidated
Investment in Kanodia	$ 300,000	—		
Other assets	1,150,000	$350,000		
Goodwill	—	—		
Total assets	$1,450,000	$350,000		
Liabilities	$ 450,000	$ 80,000		
Contributed capital	700,000	150,000		
Retained earnings	300,000	120,000		
Total liabilities and equity	$1,450,000	$350,000		

During purchase negotiations, Rayburn determined that the appraised value of Kanodia's Other Assets was $360,000; and, all of its remaining assets and liabilities were appraised at values approximating their book values. The remaining $20,000 of the purchase price was ascribed to goodwill. Prepare the consolidating adjustments and the consolidated balance sheet at acquisition.

E9-34. Assessing Financial Statement Effects from a Subsidiary Stock Issuance (LO3)

Ryan Company owns 80% of Lev Company. Information reported by Ryan Company and Lev Company as of the current year end follows:

Ryan Company	
Shares owned of Lev	80,000
Book value of investment in Lev	$640,000
Lev Company	
Shares outstanding	100,000
Book value of equity	$800,000
Book value per share	$8

Assume Lev Company issues 60,000 additional shares of previously authorized but unissued common stock solely to outside investors (none to Ryan Company) for $12 cash per share. Indicate the financial statement effects of this stock issuance on Ryan Company using the financial statement effects template.

Ryan Company's Financial Statements

	Balance Sheet									Income Statement				
Transaction	Cash Asset	+	Noncash Assets	=	Liabil-ities	+	Contrib. Capital	+	Earned Capital	Rev-enues	−	Expen-ses	=	Net Income
Lev Co. issues 60,000 shares				=							−		=	

E9-35. Estimating Goodwill Impairment (LO3)

On January 1 of the current year, Engel Company purchases 100% of Ball Company for $8.4 million. At the time of acquisition, the fair value of Ball's tangible net assets (excluding goodwill) is $8.1 million. Engel ascribes the excess of $300,000 to goodwill. Assume that the fair value of Ball declines to $6.25 million and that the fair value of Ball's tangible net assets is estimated at $6.15 million as of December 31.

a. Determine if the goodwill has become impaired and, if so, the amount of the impairment.
b. What impact does the impairment of goodwill have on Engel's financial statements?

E9-36. Allocating Purchase Price (LO3)

Adobe Systems, Inc., reports the following footnote to its 10-K report.

Adobe Systems (ADBE)

During fiscal 2006, we completed the acquisition of Macromedia, a provider of software technologies that enables the development of a wide range of Internet and mobile application solutions . . . The total $3.5 billion purchase price is allocated to the acquired net assets of Macromedia based on their estimated fair values as of December 3, 2005, and the associated estimated useful lives at that date:

(in 000s)	Amount	Estimated Useful Life
Net tangible assets	$ 713,164	N/A
Identifiable intangible assets		
Acquired product rights	365,500	4 years
Customer contracts and relationships	183,800	6 years
Non-competition agreements	500	2 years
Trademarks	130,700	5 years
Goodwill	1,993,898	N/A
Stock-based compensation	150,951	2.18 years
Total purchase price	$3,538,513	

a. Of the total assets acquired, what portion is allocated to net tangible assets?
b. Are the assets (both tangible and intangible) of Macromedia reported on the consolidated balance sheet at the book value or at the fair value on the date of the acquisition? Explain.
c. How are the tangible and intangible assets accounted for subsequent to the acquisition?
d. Describe the accounting for goodwill. Why is an impairment test difficult to apply?

E9-37. Constructing the Consolidated Balance Sheet at Acquisition (LO3)
Easton Company acquires 100 percent of the outstanding voting shares of Harris Company. To obtain these shares, Easton pays $420,000 in cash and issues 5,000 of its $10 par value common stock. On this date, Easton's stock has a fair value of $72 per share, and Harris's book value of stockholders' equity is $560,000. Easton is willing to pay $780,000 for a company with a book value for equity of $560,000 because it believes that (1) Harris's buildings are undervalued by $80,000, and (2) Harris has an unrecorded patent that Easton values at $60,000. Easton considers the remaining balance sheet items to be fairly valued (no book-to-market difference). The remaining $80,000 of the purchase price is ascribed to corporate synergies and other general unidentifiable intangible assets (goodwill). The balance sheets at the acquisition date follow:

	Easton Company	Harris Company	Consolidating Adjustments	Consolidated
Cash	$ 168,000	$ 80,000		
Receivables	320,000	180,000		
Inventory	440,000	260,000		
Investment in Harris	780,000	—		
Land	200,000	120,000		
Buildings, net	800,000	220,000		
Equipment, net	240,000	100,000		
Total assets	$2,948,000	$960,000		
Accounts payable	$ 320,000	$ 60,000		
Long-term liabilities	760,000	340,000		
Common stock	1,000,000	80,000		
Additional paid-in capital	148,000	—		
Retained earnings	720,000	480,000		
Total liabilities & equity	$2,948,000	$960,000		

a. Show the breakdown of the investment into the book value acquired, the excess of fair value over book value, and the portion of the investment representing goodwill.
b. Prepare the consolidating adjustments and the consolidated balance sheet on the date of acquisition.
c. How will the excess of the purchase price over book value acquired be treated in years subsequent to the acquisition?

Johnson & Johnson (JNJ)

E9-38.[A] Reporting and Analyzing Derivatives (LO1)
Johnson & Johnson reports the following schedule of other comprehensive income in its 2011 10-K report ($ millions):

(Dollars in Millions)	Foreign Currency Translation	Gains/ (Losses) on Securities	Employee Benefit Plans	Gains/ (Losses) on Derivatives & Hedges	Total Accumulated Other Comprehensive Income/(Loss)
January 3, 2010	$(508)	$(30)	$(2,665)	$145	$(3,058)
2010 changes					
Unrealized gain (loss)	—	99	—	(333)	
Net amount reclassed to net earnings	—	(45)	—	288	
Net 2010 changes	(461)	54	(21)	(45)	(473)
January 2, 2011	$(969)	$24	$(2,686)	$100	$(3,531)

a. Describe how firms like Johnson & Johnson typically use derivatives.
b. How does Johnson & Johnson report its derivatives designated as cash-flow hedges on its balance sheet?

c. By what amount have the unrealized losses of $(333) million on the cash-flow hedges affected current income? What are the analysis implications?

d. What does the $288 million classified as "Net amount reclassed to net earnings" relate to? How has this affected Johnson & Johnson's profit?

PROBLEMS

P9-39. Analyzing and Interpreting Available-for-Sale Securities Disclosures (LO1)

MetLife, Inc. (MET)

Following is a portion of the investments footnote from MetLife's 2012 10-K report. Investment earnings are a crucial component of the financial performance of insurance companies such as MetLife, and investments comprise a large part of MetLife's assets. MetLife accounts for its fixed maturity (debt security or bond) investments as available-for-sale securities.

December 31, 2011 (In millions)	Cost or Amortized Cost	Gross Unrealized Gain	Gross Unrealized Temporary Loss	Gross Unrealized OTTI* Loss	Estimated Fair Value
Fixed Maturity Securities:					
U.S. corporate securities	$ 98,621	$ 8,544	$1,380	$ —	$105,785
Foreign corporate securities	61,568	3,789	1,338	1	64,018
Foreign government securities	49,840	3,053	357	—	52,536
U.S. Treasury, agency and government guaranteed securities	34,132	5,882	2	—	40,012
RMBS	42,092	2,281	1,033	703	42,637
CMBS	18,565	730	218	8	19,069
ABS	13,018	278	305	12	12,979
State and political subdivision securities	11,975	1,416	156	—	13,235
Total fixed maturity securities	$329,811	$25,973	$4,789	$724	$350,271
Equity Securities:					
Common stock	$ 2,219	$ 83	$ 97	$ —	$ 2,205
Non-redeemable preferred stock	989	31	202	—	818
Total equity securities	$ 3,208	$ 114	$ 299	$ —	$ 3,023

*OTTI refers to "Other-Than-Temporary Impairment" that MetLife does not expect to reverse.

December 31, 2012 (In millions)	Cost or Amortized Cost	Gross Unrealized Gain	Gross Unrealized Temporary Loss	Gross Unrealized OTTI* Loss	Estimated Fair Value
Fixed Maturity Securities:					
U.S. corporate securities	$102,669	$11,887	$430	$ —	$114,126
Foreign corporate securities	61,806	5,654	277	(1)	67,184
Foreign government securities	51,967	5,440	71	—	57,336
U.S. Treasury, agency and government guaranteed securities	41,874	6,104	11	—	47,967
RMBS	35,666	2,477	315	349	37,479
CMBS	18,177	1,009	57	—	19,129
ABS	15,762	404	156	13	15,997
State and political subdivision securities	12,949	2,169	70	—	15,048
Total fixed maturity securities	$340,870	$35,144	$1,387	$361	$374,266
Equity Securities:					
Common stock	$ 2,034	$ 147	$ 19	$ —	$ 2,162
Non-redeemable preferred stock	804	65	140	—	729
Total equity securities	$ 2,838	$ 212	$ 159	$ —	$ 2,891

*OTTI refers to "Other-Than-Temporary Impairment" that MetLife does not expect to reverse.

Required

a. At what amount does MetLife report its fixed maturity securities on its balance sheets for 2012 and 2011?

b. What is the difference between realized and unrealized gains and losses?

c. What are the net unrealized gains (losses) for 2012 and 2011 on its fixed maturity securities? How did these unrealized gains (losses) affect the company's reported income in 2012 and 2011? (*Hint*: see the Google footnote excerpt on page 9-7 for an explanation of how OTTI losses affect income.)

General Mills, Inc. (GIS)

P9-40. Analyzing and Interpreting Disclosures on Equity Method Investments (LO2)

General Mills, Inc. invests in a number of joint ventures to manufacture and distribute its food products as discussed in the following footnote to its fiscal year 2013 10-K report:

INVESTMENTS IN JOINT VENTURES Our investments in companies over which we have the ability to exercise significant influence are stated at cost plus our share of undistributed earnings or losses . . . We make advances to our joint ventures in the form of loans or capital investments. We also sell certain raw materials, semi-finished goods, and finished goods to the joint ventures, generally at market prices.

We have a 50 percent equity interest in Cereal Partners Worldwide (CPW), which manufactures and markets ready-to-eat cereal products in more than 130 countries and republics outside the United States and Canada . . . We also have a 50 percent equity interest in Häagen-Dazs Japan, Inc. (HDJ).

Joint venture related balance sheet activity follows:

(In Millions)	May 26, 2013	May 27, 2012
Cumulative investments	$478.5	$529.0
Goodwill and other intangibles	537.2	522.1
Aggregate advances	291.5	268.1

Joint venture earnings and cash flow activity follows:

Fiscal Year (In Millions)	2013	2012	2011
Sales to joint ventures	$ 12.3	$10.4	$10.2
Net advances (repayments)	36.7	22.2	1.8
Dividends received	115.7	68.0	72.2

Summary combined financial information for the joint ventures on a 100 percent basis follows:

Fiscal Year (In Millions)	2013	2012	2011
Net sales	$2,552.7	$2,581.5	$2,452.2
Gross margin	1,057.3	1,084.1	1,073.6
Earnings before income taxes	260.3	250.3	233.4
Earnings after income taxes	201.6	189.0	164.2

(In Millions)	May 26, 2013	May 27, 2012
Current assets	$ 976.7	$ 934.8
Noncurrent assets	1,088.2	1,078.0
Current liabilities	1,717.4	1,671.0
Noncurrent liabilities	115.1	91.0

Required

a. How does General Mills account for its investments in joint ventures? How are these investments reflected on General Mills' balance sheet, and how, generally, is income recognized on these investments?

b. Does the $187.0 million investment reported on General Mills' balance sheet sufficiently reflect the assets and liabilities required to conduct these operations? Explain.

c. Do you believe that the liabilities of these joint venture entities represent actual obligations of General Mills? Explain.

d. What potential problem(s) does equity method accounting present for analysis purposes?

Snap-on Incorporated (SNA)

P9-41. Analyzing and Interpreting Disclosures on Consolidations (LO3)

Snap-on Incorporated consists of two business units: the manufacturing company (parent corporation) and a wholly-owned finance subsidiary. These two units are consolidated in Snap-on's 10-K report. Following is a supplemental disclosure that Snap-on includes in its 10-K report that shows the separate balance sheets of the parent and the subsidiary. This supplemental disclosure is not mandated under GAAP, but is voluntarily reported by Snap-on as useful information for investors and creditors. Using this disclosure, answer the following requirements:

Required

a. Do the parent and subsidiary companies each maintain their own financial statements? Explain. Why does GAAP require consolidation instead of separate financial statements of individual companies?

b. What is the balance of Investments in Financial Services as of December 31, 2012, on the parent's balance sheet? What is the equity balance of the financial services subsidiary to which this relates as of December 31, 2012? Do you see a relation? Will this relation always exist?

c. Refer to your answer for part *a*. How does the equity method of accounting for the investment in the subsidiary obscure the actual financial condition of the parent company as compared to the consolidated financial statements?

d. Recall that the parent company uses the equity method of accounting for its investment in the subsidiary, and that this account is eliminated in the consolidation process. What is the relation between consolidated net income and the net income of the parent company? Explain.

e. What is the implication for the consolidated balance sheet if the fair value of the Financial Services subsidiary (subsequent to acquisition) is greater than the book value of its stockholders' equity?

	Operations*		Financial Services	
(Amounts in millions)	**2012**	**2011**	**2012**	**2011**
ASSETS				
Current assets				
Cash and cash equivalents	$ 211.2	$ 181.1	$ 3.3	$ 4.5
Intersegment receivables	14.1	10.8	—	—
Trade and other accounts receivable—net	497.5	463.3	0.4	0.2
Finance receivables—net	—	—	323.1	277.2
Contract receivables—net	7.4	6.5	55.3	43.2
Inventories—net	404.2	386.4	—	—
Deferred income tax assets	68.8	90.0	13.0	2.6
Prepaid expenses and other assets	88.3	78.1	1.0	0.9
Total current assets	1,291.5	1,216.2	396.1	328.6
Property and equipment—net	373.2	351.9	2.0	1.0
Investment in Financial Services	165.3	142.0	—	—
Deferred income tax assets	110.2	119.8	0.2	5.4
Long-term finance receivables—net	—	—	494.6	431.8
Long-term contract receivables—net	12.1	9.1	182.3	156.0
Goodwill	807.4	795.8	—	—
Other intangibles—net	187.2	188.3	—	—
Other assets	65.3	83.7	1.1	1.0
Total assets	$3,012.2	$2,906.8	$1,076.3	$ 923.8
LIABILITIES AND SHAREHOLDERS' EQUITY				
Current liabilities				
Notes payable	$ 5.2	$ 16.2	$ —	$ —
Accounts payable	142.1	124.0	0.4	0.6
Intersegment payables	—	—	14.1	10.8
Accrued benefits	50.6	48.8	—	—
Accrued compensation	84.9	87.1	3.4	3.9
Franchisee deposits	54.7	47.3	—	—
Other accrued liabilities	207.8	229.7	46.9	31.1
Total current liabilities	545.3	553.1	64.8	46.4
Long-term debt and intersegment long-term debt	143.2	257.6	827.2	710.3
Deferred income tax liabilities	125.7	108.0	1.4	0.1
Retiree health care benefits	48.4	52.8	—	—
Pension liabilities	260.7	317.7	—	—
Other long-term liabilities	69.9	70.3	17.6	25.0
Total liabilities	1,193.2	1,359.5	911.0	781.8
Total shareholders' equity attributable to Snap-on Inc.	1,802.1	1,530.9	165.3	142.0
Noncontrolling interests	16.9	16.4	—	—
Total shareholders' equity	1,819.0	1,547.3	165.3	142.0
Total liabilities and shareholders' equity	$3,012.2	$2,906.8	$1,076.3	$ 923.8

*Snap-on Incorporated with Financial Services on the equity method.

Verizon Communications Inc. (VZ)

P9-42. Analyzing Reports and Disclosures on Noncontrolling Interests (LO3)
The following four items are reproduced from Verizon Communications' 2012 10-K: its income statement, its balance sheet's stockholders' equity section, its noncontrolling interest section from the statement of changes in stockholders' equity, and its footnotes relating to noncontrolling interests.

Years Ended December 31 (dollars in millions)	2012	2011	2010
Operating revenues	$115,846	$110,875	$106,565
Operating expenses			
Cost of services and sales (exclusive of items shown below)	46,275	45,875	44,149
Selling, general and administrative expense	39,951	35,624	31,366
Depreciation and amortization expense	16,460	16,496	16,405
Total operating expenses	102,686	97,995	91,920
Operating income	13,160	12,880	14,645
Equity in earnings of unconsolidated businesses	324	444	508
Other income and (expense), net	(1,016)	(14)	54
Interest expense	(2,571)	(2,827)	(2,523)
Income before (provision) benefit for income taxes	9,897	10,483	12,684
(Provision) benefit for income taxes	660	(285)	(2,467)
Net Income	$ 10,557	$ 10,198	$ 10,217
Net income attributable to noncontrolling interest	$ 9,682	$ 7,794	$ 7,668
Net income (loss) attributable to Verizon	875	2,404	2,549
Net Income	$ 10,557	$ 10,198	$ 10,217

At December 31 (dollars in millions, except per share amounts)	2012	2011
Equity		
Series preferred stock ($.10 par value; none issued)	$ —	$ —
Common stock ($.10 par value; 2,967,610,119 shares issued in both periods)	297	297
Contributed capital	37,990	37,919
Reinvested earnings (deficit)	(3,734)	1,179
Accumulated other comprehensive income	2,235	1,269
Common stock in treasury, at cost	(4,071)	(5,002)
Deferred compensation—employee stock ownership plans and other	440	308
Noncontrolling interest	52,376	49,938
Total equity	$85,533	$85,908

Years Ended December 31 (dollars in millions)	2012	2011	2010
Noncontrolling Interest			
Balance at beginning of year	$49,938	$48,343	$42,761
Net income attributable to noncontrolling interest	9,682	7,794	7,668
Other comprehensive income (loss)	10	1	(35)
Total comprehensive income	9,692	7,795	7,633
Distributions and other	(7,254)	(6,200)	(2,051)
Balance at end of year	$52,376	$49,938	$48,343

Consolidation The method of accounting applied to investments, whether consolidated, equity or cost, involves an evaluation of all significant terms of the investments that explicitly grant or suggest evidence of control or influence over the operations of the investee. The consolidated financial statements include our controlled subsidiaries. For controlled subsidiaries that are not wholly owned, the noncontrolling interest is included in Net income and Total equity.

continued

Noncontrolling Interest Noncontrolling interests in equity of subsidiaries were as follows:

At December 31 (dollars in millions)	2012	2011
Noncontrolling interests in consolidated subsidiaries:		
Verizon Wireless	$51,492	$49,165
Wireless partnerships	884	773
	$52,376	$49,938

Wireless Joint Venture Our Verizon Wireless segment is primarily comprised of Cellco Partnership doing business as Verizon Wireless. Cellco Partnership is a joint venture formed in April 2000 by the combination of the U.S. wireless operations and interests of Verizon and Vodafone. Verizon owns a controlling 55% interest in Verizon Wireless and Vodafone owns the remaining 45%.

Required

a. What are noncontrolling interests and how are they accounted for?

b. The noncontrolling interests relate primarily to a joint venture between Verizon and Vodafone described in the footnote. Why does Verizon consolidate this joint venture rather than to account for its investment using the equity method? What are the financial reporting implications for the decision to consolidate the joint venture?

c. What does the significant amount of net income allocated to the noncontrolling interests imply about the profitability of the wireless subsidiary relative to other subsidiaries in the consolidated entity?

d. What does the "Distributions and other" line with an amount of $(7,254) million in the noncontrolling interest portion of the statement of changes in stockholders' equity relate to?

e. How should we treat noncontrolling interests in our return on equity (ROE) computation? Compute ROE for both the Verizon shareholders and for the noncontrolling interests.

IFRS APPLICATIONS

I9-43. Interpreting Equity Method Investment Footnotes (LO2)

Carrefour

Carrefour S.A. is a French multinational retailer headquartered near Paris. Second only to Walmart in terms of worldwide retail sales, the company operates in Europe, Central and South America, China, and the middle east. Unlike Walmart, most Carrefour stores are smaller than a typical supermarket. Carrefour means "crossroads" and "public square" in French. The company uses IFRS for its financial reports and reports the following details about its investments in associates, which are accounted for using the equity method:

(in € millions)	
At December 31, 2010	€256
Translation adjustment	(2)
Equity in net income	64
Dividends received	(26)
Other	(13)
At December 31, 2011	280
Translation adjustment	(2)
Equity in net income	72
Dividends received	(27)
Other	61
At December 31, 2012	€384

Required

a. Carrefour holds between 20% and 50% ownership of all its investments in associates. Carrefour uses the equity method to account for these investments. Why?

b. What amount does Carrefour report on its balance sheet for investments in associates at December 31, 2012? Is this a fair value or not?
c. For the fiscal period ended December 31, 2012, were Carrefour's associates profitable, in the aggregate?
d. How do changes in the market value of the associates' stock affect the "Investment in associates" balance sheet account for Carrefour?
e. How does use of the equity method impact Carrefour's ROE and its RNOA components (net operating asset turnover and net operating profit margin) as compared with the assets and liabilities and the sales and expenses that would be recorded with consolidation?

Koninklijke Ahold N.V.

I9-44. Interpreting Equity Method Investment Footnotes (LO2)

Koninklijke Ahold N.V., a food retailer headquartered in the Netherlands, reported in notes to its annual report that it owns 60% of the outstanding common shares in a joint venture, **ICA**. Selected notes to Ahold's annual report (prepared under IFRS) follow:

> The 60% shareholding does not entitle Ahold to unilateral decision-making authority over ICA due to the shareholders' agreement with the joint venture partner, which provides that strategic, financial and operational decisions will be made only on the basis of mutual consent. On the basis of this shareholders' agreement, the Company concluded that it has no control over ICA and, consequently, does not consolidate ICA's financial statements.

Required

a. What is a joint venture?
b. Given that Ahold owns more than 50% of this joint venture, why does the company not consolidate this investment? Does this differ from U.S. GAAP?
c. What method does Ahold use to report the ICA joint venture? Explain how this method works.

Deutsche Telekom AG

I9-45. Allocating Purchase Price Including Intangibles (LO3)

Deutsche Telekom AG, headquartered in Bonn, Germany, is the largest telecommunications company in Europe. The company uses IFRS to prepare its financial statements. Assume that during 2011, Deutsche Telekom acquired a controlling interest in **Hellenic Telecommunications Organization**, S.A. (Hellenic). The table below shows the pre- and post-acquisition values of Hellenic's assets and liabilities.

(millions of €)	Fair Value at Acquisition Date	Carrying Amounts Immediately Prior to Acquisition
Cash and cash equivalents	€ 1,558	€ 1,558
Non-current assets held for sale	195	158
Other assets	1,716	1,716
Current assets	3,469	3,432
Intangible assets	5,348	4,734
Goodwill	2,500	3,835
Property, plant, and equipment	6,965	5,581
Other assets	823	782
Non-current assets	15,636	14,932
Assets	€19,105	€18,364

Required

a. At the acquisition, which measurement does the company use, fair value or carrying value, to record the acquired tangible and intangible assets on its consolidated balance sheet?
b. At the acquisition date, why is fair value of goodwill less than its carrying value?
c. What are some possible reasons why intangible assets increased in value at the acquisition date?
d. Describe accounting for goodwill. Why is an impairment test difficult to apply?
e. What would Deutsche Telekom record if it determined at the end of fiscal 2011 that the goodwill purchased in the Hellenic acquisition had a reliably measured fair value of €2,000? Later, if in 2014 the company determined that the fair value of the Hellenic goodwill was €3,000, how would its balance sheet and income statement be affected?

I9-46. Analyzing and Interpreting Securities Disclosures (LO1)

Energias de Portugal

Energias de Portugal ranks among Europe's major electricity operators, as well as being one of Portugal's largest business groups. The company is headquartered in Lisbon, Portugal. Assume that at December 31, 2012, Energias de Portugal had an available-for-sale portfolio with original cost of €135,948 (in 000s). Its 2012 annual report disclosed the following for available-for-sale investments.

Thousands of Euros	Balance at 1 January	Acquisitions	Disposals	Impairment	Change in Fair Value Reserve	Other Variations	Balance at 31 December
Banco Comercial Português	€ 19,665	€10,031	€ —	€ (5,495)	€5,452	€ —	€ 29,653
REN - Rede Energéticas Nacionais	39,361	—	—	—	(953)	—	38,408
Tejo Energia	29,507	—	—	—	(3,261)	—	26,246
Other	82,780	12,701	(1,126)	(3,833)	1,451	(4,982)	86,991
	€171,313	€22,732	€(1,126)	€(9,328)	€2,689	€(4,982)	€181,298

Required

a. What were total unrealized gains or losses in the available-for-sale portfolio at year end 2012?

b. How would pretax income be affected if Energias de Portugal had instead classified all of its available-for-sale investments as trading?

c. Explain how the impairment of the available-for-sale securities affected the balance sheet amount during 2012. Are impairment reversals permitted under U.S. GAAP?

I9-47. Analyzing and Interpreting Disclosures on Equity Method Investments (LO2)

Rogers Communications Inc.

Maple Leaf Sports & Entertainment Ltd.

Headquartered in Toronto, Rogers Communications Inc. is a diversified public Canadian communications and media company. It operates wireless communications, cable television, telephone, and Internet connectivity with significant additional telecommunications and mass media assets. In August 2012, Rogers acquired a 37.5% equity interest in Maple Leaf Sports & Entertainment Ltd. ("MLSE"). MLSE, one of Canada's largest sports and entertainment companies, owns and operates the Air Canada Centre, the NHL's Toronto Maple Leafs, the NBA's Toronto Raptors, the MLS' Toronto FC, and the AHL's Toronto Marlies. The Company's net cash investment was $540 million and investment in MLSE is accounted for using the equity method. Rogers follows IFRS.

Required

a. How is the MLSE investment reflected on Rogers' balance sheet.

b. How, generally, is income recognized on this sort of investment?

c. Does the $540 million investment reported on Rogers' balance sheet sufficiently reflect the assets and liabilities required to conduct all of MLSE's operations? Explain.

d. Do the liabilities of MLSE's represent actual obligations to Rogers? Explain.

e. What potential problem(s) does equity method accounting present for analysis purposes?

I9-48. Interpreting Equity Method Investment Footnotes (LO2)

Brookfield Office Properties (BPO)

Brookfield Office Properties is a Canadian-American commercial real estate company with headquarters in New York City and Toronto. The company owns, manages and develops office properties in the downtown core of cities in the U.S. (New York City, Washington, Boston, Houston, Los Angeles, Denver, and Minneapolis), Canada (Toronto, Calgary, Ottawa, and Vancouver) as well as Australia (Perth, Sydney, and Melbourne). The company has many investments and reports the following footnote (in IFRS):

Investments in Associates The company exercises significant influence over the following investments which have been accounted for using the equity method:

Name of Investment	Principal Activity	Ownership Interest Dec. 31, 2012	Ownership Interest Dec. 31, 2011
BSREP Australia Trust	Investment properties	41.22%	—
Brookfield LePage Johnson Controls	Facilities management	40.00%	40.00%
Oakridges	Residential development	23.75%	23.75%

continued

continued from prior page

In the fourth quarter of 2012, the company acquired a 41.22% indirect equity interest in BSREP Australia Trust. Summarized financial information in respect of the company's investment in associates is set out below:

(Millions)	2012	2011
Revenue	$553	$520
Expense	(542)	(500)
Net earnings	$ 11	$ 20
Company's share of net earnings	$ 4	$ 7

Required

a. The company uses the equity method to account for its investment in associates. Why is this the appropriate method for the three investments disclosed in the footnotes?

b. The balance in the Investments in Equity account was $13 million at December 31, 2011. During the year, the company received no dividends from its associates. Assume that the company paid $139 million for the BSREP Australia acquisition. Determine the balance in the Investments in Equity account at December 31, 2012.

c. Explain how the use of the equity method impacts Brookfield's ROE and its RNOA components (net operating asset turnover and net operating profit margin) as compared to the case of consolidation.

I9-49. Interpreting Acquisition Transaction with Goodwill (LO3)

The Shoppers Drug Mart Corporation

Headquartered in Toronto, **The Shoppers Drug Mart Corporation** is Canada's largest retail pharmacy chain with more than 1,241 stores across Canada. The company also licenses or owns 60 medical clinic pharmacies as well as six luxury beauty destinations. The company reported the following in its annual report for the year ended December 29, 2012:

BUSINESS ACQUISITIONS (in thousands of Canadian dollars)

Paragon Pharmacies Limited

On August 1, 2012, the Company acquired substantially all of the assets of Paragon Pharmacies Limited ("Paragon") for a cash purchase price of $72,059. The acquisition included 19 retail pharmacies and three central fill pharmacies in British Columbia, Alberta, and Manitoba. . . . The following table summarizes the consideration paid for Paragon, and the amounts recognized for the assets acquired and liabilities assumed at the acquisition date.

Fair value of net assets acquired as at acquisition date	
Cash	$ 43
Accounts receivable (gross amount of $4,751, net of allowance of $430)	4,321
Inventory	7,906
Prepaid expenses	611
Property and equipment	4,929
Prescription files	20,000
Customer relationships	8,000
Accounts payable and accrued liabilities	(1,245)
Net assets acquired	44,565
Goodwill, net of deferred taxes	27,494
Total cash purchase price	72,059
Cash acquired	(43)
Purchase price, net of cash acquired	$72,016

Required

a. Identify the tangible and intangible assets that the company acquired. What proportion of the total price was for intangible assets?

b. Do any of the acquired intangible assets have indefinite lives? Explain.
c. Explain in layman's terms the meaning of goodwill.
d. Why is prescription files an intangible asset? How will Shoppers Drug Mart realize value from this asset?
e. How will the company account for goodwill in 2013 and beyond?
f. How did Shoppers Drug Mart account for the income of Paragon in fiscal 2012?

I9-50. Accounting for Passive Investments (LO1)

Westpac Banking Corporation (WBK)

With assets of $675 billion (AUS), **Westpac Banking Corporation** is one of Australia's largest banks. The company provides a broad range of banking and financial services including retail, business and institutional banking and wealth management services. The company has branches throughout Australia, New Zealand and the Pacific region and employs 34,000 people. The company's September 30, 2012, fiscal year end balance sheet (IFRS) reported the following:

(In $AUS millions)	2012
Assets	
Cash and balances with central banks	$ 12,523
Receivables due from other financial institutions	10,228
Derivative financial instruments	35,489
Trading securities	44,603
Other financial assets designated at fair value	2,664
Available-for-sale securities	24,472
Loans—housing and personal	365,221
Loans—business	149,224
Life insurance assets	8,240
Regulatory deposits with central banks overseas	1,893
Deferred tax assets	2,176
Goodwill and other intangible assets	12,134
Property, plant and equipment	1,137
Other assets	4,961
Total assets	$674,965

Required

a. Westpac reports trading securities of $44,603 million and available-for-sale securities of $24,472 million. Are these substantial assets for the bank?
b. At what amount does Westpac Banking Corporation report its trading securities on its balance sheets for 2012?
c. Assume that the historic cost of the available-for-sale securities was $24,390 at September 30, 2012. Did Westpac have an unrealized gain or loss on these securities?
d. Explain how the unrealized gain or loss on available-for-sale securities affects Westpac's balance sheet and income statement in 2012.
e. Assume that the historic cost of the trading securities was $45,812 at September 30, 2012. Did Westpac have an unrealized gain or loss on these securities?
f. Explain how the unrealized gain or loss on trading securities affects Westpac's balance sheet and income statement in 2012.

MANAGEMENT APPLICATIONS

MA9-51. Determining the Reporting of an Investment (LO1, 2, 3)

Assume that your company acquires 20% of the outstanding common stock of APEX Software as an investment. You also have an option to purchase the remaining 80%. APEX is developing software (its only activity) that it hopes to eventually package and sell to customers. You do not intend to exercise your option unless its software product reaches commercial feasibility. APEX has employed your software engineers to assist in the development efforts and you are integrally involved in its software design. Your ownership interest is significant enough to give you influence over APEX's software design specifications.

Required

a. Describe the financial statement effects of the three possible methods to accounting for this investment (fair-value, equity, or consolidation).

b. What method of accounting is appropriate for this investment (fair-value, equity, or consolidation)? Explain.

MA9-52. Ethics and Governance: Establishing Corporate Governance (LO2, 3)
Effective corporate governance policies are a crucial component of contemporary corporate management.

Required
What provisions do you believe should be incorporated into such a policy? How do such policies impact financial accounting?

ONGOING PROJECT

(*This ongoing project began in Module 1 and continues through most of the book; even if previous segments were not completed, the requirements are still applicable to any business analysis.*) Company analysis should include an assessment of the companies' various investments, transactions during the year, the effect on net income, and the balance sheet results at year end.

1. *Passive Investments.* To analyze nonoperating investments in debt and equity securities, consider the following questions that will help us understand both companies' level of excess cash and how they invest it.
   - What is the magnitude of the passive investments in common-sized terms? Has this changed over time? What proportion is short-term versus long-term?
   - What types of investments does the company hold—trading, available-for-sale, at cost? What are the types of securities—debt, marketable equity securities, private-company equity?
   - Analyze the unrealized gains and losses by gauging their magnitude. What proportion of the reported fair values are level 1, 2 and 3? How reliable are the fair values? (The higher the level the lower the reliability.)
   - What explanation do the companies provide for their level of investments? Does the MD&A section of the Form 10-K discuss plans for expansion or other strategic initiatives that would require cash? Is there cash-flow volatility in the industry that would explain the levels of excess cash?
2. *Investments with Significant Influence.* Our goal is to assess how the companies structure their operations to better understand their strategies.
   - What types of investments does the company have: associates, joint ventures, or other?
   - Remember that companies classify their investments based on intent. Why does the company engage in equity-method investments; what is their intent? Read the MD&A section of the Form 10-K and the financial statement footnotes.
   - What are the main equity-method investments? (IFRS: Does the company have any proportionate consolidation?) How large are these in common-sized terms?
   - Have there been changes during the year in terms of new investments or disposals? The MD&A and footnotes will be instructive.
   - Are the equity method investments profitable? Do they provide cash dividends?
3. *Investments with Control (Consolidations).* Most multinational corporations are consolidated entities that structure their operations to meet many goals including legal requirements, tax planning, and foreign ownership restrictions. Financial statements will not report information to completely comprehend all these intricacies; the goal here is to understand the companies' structure at a very high level.
   - What types of companies does each company control? What are the main subsidiaries?
   - What strategic advantages do these subsidiaries afford? Foreign? Domestic? Supplier or distributors? Read the MD&A section of the Form 10-K and the financial statement footnotes to learn about strategic investment and plans for the future.
   - Have there been new investments during the year? How were these acquisitions financed (debt, equity)? Did these yield intangible assets including goodwill? What proportion of the acquisition price was allocated to intangibles?
   - Were there disposals during the year? Why were these made? Did the transaction cause a gain or loss?

- Gauge the significance of previously acquired intangibles in common-size terms. Have any been impaired during the year?
- If the company reports subsidiary-level profit, which are the most profitable? The least?

SOLUTIONS TO REVIEW PROBLEMS

Mid-Module Review 1

a.

Transaction	Cash Asset	+	Noncash Assets	=	Liabilities	+	Contrib. Capital	+	Earned Capital	Revenues	−	Expenses	=	Net Income
1. Purchased 1,000 shares of Yahoo! common stock for $15 cash per share	−15,000 Cash		+15,000 Marketable Securities	=							−		=	
2. Received cash dividend of $2.50 per share on Yahoo! common stock	+2,500 Cash			=					+2,500 Retained Earnings	+2,500 Dividend Income	−		=	+2,500
3. Year-end market price of Yahoo! common stock is $17 per share			+2,000 Marketable Securities	=					+2,000 AOCI		−		=	
4. Sold 1,000 shares of Yahoo! common stock for $17,000 cash	+17,000 Cash		−17,000 Marketable Securities	=					−2,000 AOCI +2,000 Retained Earnings	+2,000 Gain on Sale	−		=	+2,000

Journal entries and T-accounts (margin):

1. MS 15,000 / Cash 15,000. MS: 15,000 (debit). Cash: 15,000 (credit).
2. Cash 2,500 / DI 2,500. Cash: 2,500 (debit). DI: 2,500 (credit).
3. MS 2,000 / AOCI 2,000. MS: 2,000 (debit). AOCI: 2,000 (credit).
4. Cash 17,000; AOCI 2,000 / MS 17,000; GN 2,000. Cash: 17,000 (debit). AOCI: 2,000 (debit). MS: 17,000 (credit). GN: 2,000 (credit).

b.

Transaction	Cash Asset	+	Noncash Assets	=	Liabilities	+	Contrib. Capital	+	Earned Capital	Revenues	−	Expenses	=	Net Income
1. Purchased 1,000 shares of Yahoo! common stock for $15 cash per share	−15,000 Cash		+15,000 Marketable Securities	=							−		=	
2. Received cash dividend of $2.50 per share on Yahoo! common stock	+2,500 Cash			=					+2,500 Retained Earnings	+2,500 Dividend Income	−		=	+2,500
3. Year-end market price of Yahoo! common stock is $17 per share			+2,000 Marketable Securities	=					+2,000 Retained Earnings	+2,000 Unrealized Gain	−		=	+2,000
4. Sold 1,000 shares of Yahoo! common stock for $17,000 cash	+17,000 Cash		−17,000 Marketable Securities	=							−		=	

Journal entries and T-accounts (margin):

1. MS 15,000 / Cash 15,000. MS: 15,000 (debit). Cash: 15,000 (credit).
2. Cash 2,500 / DI 2,500. Cash: 2,500 (debit). DI: 2,500 (credit).
3. MS 2,000 / UG 2,000. MS: 2,000 (debit). UG: 2,000 (credit).
4. Cash 17,000 / MS 17,000. Cash: 17,000 (debit). MS: 17,000 (credit).

c. Yahoo! reports an investment portfolio of $4,171,058. This represents the portfolio's current market value.

d. Yahoo! classifies these investments as available-for-sale. Consequently, the net unrealized gains of $1,882 thousand (computed as gross unrealized gains of $2,582 thousand less gross unrealized losses of $700 thousand), had no effect on Yahoo!'s reported income. Yahoo! will realize gains and losses only when it sells the investments. Then, Yahoo! will recognize the gains or losses in current-period income.

Mid-Module Review 2

a.

Journal entry / T-accounts	Transaction	Balance Sheet: Cash Asset	+ Noncash Assets	=	Liabilities	+ Contrib. Capital	+ Earned Capital	Income Statement: Revenues	− Expenses	= Net Income
EMI 50,000 Cash 50,000 EMI: 50,000 (debit) Cash: 50,000 (credit)	1. Purchased 5,000 shares of LookSmart common stock at $10 cash per share; these shares reflect 30% ownership	−50,000 Cash	+50,000 Investments	=					−	=
Cash 10,000 EMI 10,000 Cash: 10,000 (debit) EMI: 10,000 (credit)	2. Received a $2 per share cash dividend on LookSmart stock	10,000 Cash	−10,000 Investments	=					−	=
EMI 30,000 EI 30,000 EMI: 30,000 (debit) EI: 30,000 (credit)	3. Record 30% share of the $100,000 income reported by LookSmart		+30,000 Investments	=			+30,000 Retained Earnings	+30,000 Equity Income	−	= +30,000
	4. Market value has increased to $12 per share	NOTHING RECORDED								
Cash 90,000 EMI 70,000 GN 20,000 CASH: 90,000 (debit) EMI: 70,000 (credit) GN: 20,000 (credit)	5. Sold all 5,000 shares of LookSmart stock for $90,000	+90,000 Cash	−70,000 Investments	=			+20,000 Retained Earnings	+20,000 Gain on Sale	−	= +20,000

b. Yahoo! reports $458 million ($1,309 million × 35%) of equity income related to this investment in its 2012 income statement.

c. Yahoo! Japan's stockholders' equity is $6,374 million (computed as $5,753 + $1,838 − $1,168 − $49, in $ millions), and Yahoo!'s investment account equals $2,230 million, computed as $6,374 million × 35%.

Module-End Review

Solution

	Yahoo! (Parent)	EarthLink (Subsidiary)	Consolidating Adjustments	Consolidated
Current assets	$1,000,000	$100,000		$1,100,000
Investment in EarthLink	600,000	—	$(600,000)	
PPE, net	3,000,000	400,000	100,000	3,500,000
Goodwill	—	—	100,000	100,000
Total assets	$4,600,000	$500,000		$4,700,000
Liabilities	$1,000,000	$100,000		$1,100,000
Contributed capital	2,000,000	200,000	(200,000)	2,000,000
Retained earnings	1,600,000	200,000	(200,000)	1,600,000
Total liabilities and equity	$4,600,000	$500,000		$4,700,000

Explanation: The $600,000 investment account is eliminated together with the $400,000 book value of EarthLink's equity to which Yahoo's investment relates. The remaining $200,000 consists of the additional $100,000 in PPE assets and the $100,000 in goodwill from expected corporate synergies. Following these adjustments, the balance sheet items are summed to yield the consolidated balance sheet.

Module 10 Reporting and Analyzing Off-Balance-Sheet Financing

Learning Objectives

LO1 Describe and illustrate the accounting for capitalized leases. (p. 10-4)

LO2 Describe and illustrate the accounting for pensions. (p. 10-12)

LO3 Explain the accounting for special purpose entities (SPEs). (p. 10-25)

Southwest Airlines

Southwest Airlines (LUV) is solvent and profitable, but still must be strategic about its cash flow as it carries a heavy debt load that includes borrowed money and aircraft leases that reduce available cash flow. The magnitude of obligations arising from aircraft leases often surprises those outside the industry. Specifically, many airlines, including Southwest Airlines, do not typically own the planes they fly. Instead, planes are owned by commercial leasing companies like **General Electric Commercial Credit** (GE's financial subsidiary), and are leased by the airlines.

If structured in a specific way, neither the leased planes (the assets) nor the lease obligations (the liabilities) are reported on an airline's balance sheet. That exclusion affects ratios that investors compute and could alter investors' perceptions of the capital investment that airlines such as Southwest need to operate as well as the level of debt the company carries. In this module, we describe an analytical procedure that provides an alternative view of the company's investing and financing activities that reflect leases. The analytical adjustment would increase Southwest Airlines' liabilities. Its lease payment obligations on aircrafts total \$3.4 billion in 2012, which is a staggering amount when compared to the company's net operating assets of \$7.2 billion. We discuss the accounting for leases and explain this analytical adjustment and how to apply it.

Courtesy of Southwest Airlines

Another substantial obligation for many large companies is pensions and long-term health care plans. Until recently, information about pension and health care obligations was only in footnotes. Recent accounting rule changes now require companies to report that information on the balance sheet. In particular, the balance sheet reports the net pension and health care liabilities (the total liability less related investments that fund the liabilities). For example, **FedEx**'s 2012 net pension and health care liability exceeds pension assets by $4.9 billion. That amount represents 16% of FedEx's total liabilities and equity. We explain the accounting for both pensions and health care obligations and examine footnote disclosures that convey a wealth of information relating to assumptions underlying estimates of those obligations.

Methods that companies apply to avoid reporting potential liabilities (and expenses), are commonly referred to as off-balance-sheet financing. Although companies have long practiced off-balance-sheet financing, more recent techniques have become increasingly complex and require careful analysis. We explain one such off-balance-sheet technique, special purpose entities (SPEs), in Appendix 10B.

Sources: Southwest Airlines 2012 10-K and Annual Report and FedEx 2012 10-K and Annual Report.

MODULE ORGANIZATION

Reporting and Analyzing Off-Balance-Sheet Financing

Leases
- Lessee Reporting of Leases
- Lease Footnote Disclosures
- Capitalization of Operating Leases

Pensions
- Reporting of Defined Benefit Plans
- Pension Footnote Disclosures
- Other Post-Employment Benefits

Special Purpose Entities
- Applying SPEs as Financing Tools
- Reporting of Consolidated SPEs

Company stakeholders pay attention to the composition of the balance sheet and its relation to the income statement. This attention extends to their analysis and valuation of both equity and debt securities. Of particular importance in this valuation process is the analysis of return on equity (ROE) and its components: return on net operating assets (RNOA)—including net operating profit margin (NOPM) and net operating asset turnover (NOAT)—and the degree of financial leverage (FLEV). Module 4 and its appendix explain these measures.

To value debt securities such as bonds and notes, one must consider a company's financial leverage (claims against assets) and the level of debt service (interest and principal payments), and compare them with expected cash flows. If analysis reveals that profitability (as measured by ROE and RNOA) and cash flows are inadequate, a company's credit rating could decline. The resulting higher cost of debt capital could limit the number of investment projects that yield a return greater than their financing cost. This restricts the company's growth and profitability.

Financial managers are aware of the importance of how financial markets perceive their companies. They also recognize the market attention directed at the quality of their balance sheets and income statements. This reality can pressure managers to *window dress* financial statements to present the company's financial condition and performance in the best possible light. To increase reported solvency and decrease risk metrics, companies generally wish to present a balance sheet with low levels of debt. Companies that are more liquid and less financially leveraged are viewed as less likely to go bankrupt. As a result, the risk of default on their debt is less, resulting in a better credit rating and a lower interest rate.

Companies also generally wish to present a balance sheet with fewer assets. This is driven by return considerations. ROE has two components: operating return and nonoperating return. The latter is a function of the company's effective use of debt. Investors generally prefer a company's ROE to be derived from operations (RNOA) rather than from its use of debt. So, if a company can maintain a given level of profitability with fewer assets, the related increase in ROE is perceived to be driven by higher RNOA (asset turnover), and not by increased financial leverage.

Off-balance-sheet financing means that assets or liabilities, or both, are not reported on the balance sheet. Even though GAAP requires detailed footnote disclosures, managers generally believe that keeping such assets and liabilities off the balance sheet improves market perception of their operating performance and financial condition. This belief presumes that the market is somewhat inefficient, a notion that persists despite empirical evidence suggesting that analysts adjust balance sheets to include assets and liabilities that managers exclude.

This module explains and illustrates several types of off-balance-sheet financing. Major topics we discuss are leases, pensions, health care liabilities, and special purpose entities (SPEs). This is not an exhaustive list of the techniques that managers employ to achieve off-balance-sheet financing, but it includes the most common methods. We must keep one point in mind: the relevant information to assess off-balance-sheet financing is mainly in footnotes. While GAAP footnote disclosures on such financing are fairly good, we must have the analytic tools to interpret them and to understand the nature and the magnitude of assets and liabilities that managers have moved off of the balance sheet. This module provides those tools.

LEASES

LO1 Describe and illustrate the accounting for capitalized leases.

We begin the discussion of off-balance-sheet financing with leases. The following graphic shows that leasing impacts both sides of the balance sheet (liabilities and assets) and the income statement (leasing expenses are often reported in selling, general and administrative expenses).

Income Statement
Sales
Cost of goods sold
Selling, general and administrative expenses
Income taxes
Net income

Balance Sheet	
Cash	Current liabilities
Accounts receivable	**Long-term liabilities**
Inventory	
Long-term operating assets	Shareholders' equity
Investments	

A lease is a contract between the owner of an asset (the **lessor**) and the party desiring to use that asset (the **lessee**). Since this is a private contract between two willing parties, it is governed only by applicable commercial law, and can include whatever provisions the parties negotiate.

Leases generally provide for the following terms:

- Lessor allows the lessee the unrestricted right to use the asset during the lease term.
- Lessee agrees to make periodic payments to the lessor and to maintain the asset.
- Title to the asset remains with the lessor, who usually takes physical possession of the asset at lease-end unless the lessee negotiates the right to purchase the asset at its market value or other predetermined price.

From the lessor's standpoint, lease payments are set at an amount that yields an acceptable return on investment, commensurate with the lessee's credit rating. The lessor has an investment in the lease asset, and the lessee gains use of the asset.

The lease serves as a financing vehicle, similar to a secured bank loan. However, there are several advantages to leasing over bank financing:

- Leases often require less equity investment by the lessee (borrower) compared with bank financing. Leases usually require the first lease payment be made at the inception of the lease. For a 60-month lease, this amounts to a 1/60 (1.7%) investment by the lessee, compared with a typical bank loan of 70-80% of the asset cost (thus requiring 20-30% equity investment by the borrower).
- Because leases are contracts between two parties, their terms can be structured to meet both parties' needs. For example, a lease can allow variable payments to match the lessee's seasonal cash inflows or have graduated payments for start-up companies.
- A lease can be structured such that neither the lease asset nor the lease liability is reported on the balance sheet. Accordingly, leasing can be a form of off-balance-sheet financing.

Lessee Reporting of Leases

GAAP identifies two different approaches for the reporting of leases by the lessee:

- **Capital lease method**. This method requires that both the lease asset and the lease liability be reported on the balance sheet. The lease asset is depreciated like any other long-term asset. The lease liability is amortized like debt, where lease payments are separated into interest expense and principal repayment.
- **Operating lease method**. Under this method, neither the lease asset nor the lease liability is reported on the balance sheet. Lease payments are recorded as rent expense by the lessee.

The financial statement effects for the lessee of these methods are summarized in Exhibit 10.1.

EXHIBIT 10.1 Financial Statement Effects of Lease Type for the Lessee

Lease Type	Assets	Liabilities	Expenses	Cash Flows
Capital	Lease asset reported	Lease liability reported	Depreciation and interest expense	Payments per lease contract
Operating	Lease asset **not** reported	Lease liability **not** reported	Rent expense	Payments per lease contract

GAAP defines criteria to determine whether a lease is capital or operating.[1] Managers seeking off-balance-sheet financing structure their leases around the GAAP rules so as to fail the "capitalization tests." (A proposal currently under review by the FASB and the IASB would require companies to record the rights and obligations related to *all* leases on their balance sheets. If approved, substantially all leases would be recorded on the balance sheet as an asset and a liability.)

Under the operating method, lease assets and lease liabilities are *not* recorded on the balance sheet. The company merely discloses key details of the transaction in the lease footnote. The income statement reports the lease payment as rent expense. And, the cash outflows (payments to lessor) per the lease contract are included in the operating section of the statement of cash flows.

For capital leases, both the lease asset and lease liability are reported on the balance sheet. In the income statement, depreciation and interest expense are reported instead of rent expense. (Because only depreciation is an operating expense, NOPAT is higher when a lease is classified as a capital lease.) Further, although the cash payments to the lessor are identical whether or not the lease is capitalized on the balance sheet, the cash flows are classified differently for capital leases—that is, each payment is part interest (operating cash flow) and part principal (financing cash flow). Operating cash flows are, therefore, greater when a lease is classified as a capital lease.

Classifying leases as "operating" has four financial reporting consequences for the lessee:

1. The lease asset is not reported on the balance sheet. This means that net operating asset turnover (NOAT) is higher because reported operating assets are lower and revenues are unaffected.
2. The lease liability is not reported on the balance sheet. This means that balance sheet measures of financial leverage (like the total liabilities-to-equity ratio) are improved; many managers believe the reduced financial leverage will result in a better credit rating and, consequently, a lower interest rate on borrowed funds.
3. Without analytical adjustments (see later section on capitalization of operating leases), the portion of ROE derived from operating activities (RNOA) appears higher, which improves the perceived quality of the company's ROE.
4. During the early years of the lease term, rent expense reported for an operating lease is less than the depreciation and interest expense reported for a capital lease.[2] This means that net income is higher in those early years with an operating lease.[3] Further, if the company is growing and continually adding operating lease assets, the level of profits will continue to remain higher during the growth period.

The benefits of applying the operating method for leases are obvious to managers, thus leading some to avoid lease capitalization. Furthermore, the lease accounting standard includes rigid requirements relating to capitalization. Whenever accounting standards are rigidly defined, managers can structure transactions to meet the letter of the standard to achieve a desired accounting result when the essence of the transaction would suggest a different accounting treatment. This is *form over substance*.

[1] Leases must be capitalized when one or more of the following four criteria are met: (1) The lease automatically transfers ownership of the lease asset from the lessor to the lessee at termination of the lease. (2) The lease provides that the lessee can purchase the lease asset for a nominal amount (a bargain purchase) at termination of the lease. (3) The lease term is at least 75% of the economic useful life of the lease asset. (4) The present value of the lease payments is at least 90% of the fair market value of the lease asset at inception of the lease.

[2] This is true even if the company employs straight-line depreciation for the lease asset since interest expense accrues on the outstanding balance of the lease liability, which is higher in the early years of the lease life. Total expense is the same *over the life of the lease*, regardless of whether the lease is capitalized or not. That is: Total rent expense (from operating lease) = Total depreciation expense (from capital lease) + Total interest expense (from capital lease).

[3] However, NOPAT is *lower* for an operating lease because rent expense is an operating expense whereas only depreciation expense (and not interest expense) is an operating expense for a capital lease.

IFRS INSIGHT **Lease Accounting under IFRS**

U.S. GAAP and IFRS both require that leases be capitalized if the lease asset's risks and rewards are transferred to the lessee. The main difference between the two reporting systems is that IFRS are more principles based and GAAP is more rules based (for example, see the criteria details in this module's footnote 1). Given the broader application of principles, IFRS classify more leases as *finance leases* (termed "capital leases" under GAAP). Other small differences exist in the accounting for leases but these will not lead to materially different reporting outcomes in most cases.

Footnote Disclosure of Leases

Disclosures of expected payments for leases are required for both operating and capital leases. Southwest Airlines provides a typical disclosure from its 2012 annual report:

LEASE OBLIGATIONS Total rental expense for operating leases, both aircraft and other, charged to operations in 2012, 2011, and 2010 was $943 million, $847 million, and $631 million, respectively. The majority of the Company's terminal operations space, as well as 187 aircraft, were under operating leases at December 31, 2012. For aircraft operating leases and for terminal operations leases, expense is included in Aircraft rentals and in Landing fees and other rentals, respectively, in the Consolidated Statement of Income. Future minimum lease payments under capital leases and noncancelable operating leases and rentals to be received under subleases with initial or remaining terms in excess of one year at December 31, 2012, were:

(in millions)	Capital Leases	Operating Leases	Subleases	Operating Leases, Net
2013	$ 5	$ 693	$ (5)	$ 688
2014	6	663	(49)	614
2015	6	598	(91)	507
2016	5	497	(105)	392
2017	6	474	(105)	369
Thereafter	18	2,161	(338)	1,823
Total minimum lease payments	46	$5,086	$(693)	$4,393
Less amount representing interest	10			
Present value of minimum lease payments	36			
Less current portion	3			
Long-term portion	$33			

The aircraft leases generally can be renewed for one to five years at rates based on fair market value at the end of the lease term. Most aircraft leases have purchase options at or near the end of the lease term at fair market value, generally limited to a stated percentage of the lessor's defined cost of the aircraft.

Lease disclosures such as this provide information concerning current and future payment obligations. These contractual obligations are similar to debt payments and must be factored into our evaluation of the company's financial condition.

Southwest Airlines' footnote disclosure reports minimum (base) contractual lease payment obligations for each of the next five years and the total lease payment obligations that come due in year six and beyond. This is similar to disclosures of future maturities for long-term debt. The company also must provide separate disclosures for operating leases and capital leases (Southwest Airlines has both operating and capital leases outstanding).

MANAGERIAL DECISION You Are the Division President

You are the president of an operating division. Your CFO recommends operating lease treatment for asset acquisitions to reduce reported assets and liabilities on your balance sheet. To achieve this classification, you must negotiate leases with shorter base terms and lease renewal options that you feel are not advantageous to your company. What is your response? [Answer, p. 10-31]

Capitalization of Operating Leases

U.S. GAAP as of 2013 permits the classification of leases as operating or capital as explained above. As of the publication of this textbook, U.S. standard-setters are deliberating a new accounting standard that would require all leases to be accounted for much like capital leases currently (namely, lease assets and lease liabilities would be capitalized on the balance sheet following the procedures we outline below). However, until passage of the new standard, companies will report only capital leases on their balance sheets, whereas information on their operating leases will be in footnotes such as that shown above for Southwest.

Although not recognized on-balance-sheet, leased properties arguably represent assets (and create liabilities) as defined under GAAP. That is, the company controls the assets and will profit from their future benefits. Also, lease liabilities represent real contractual obligations. Although the financial statements are prepared in conformity with current (2013) GAAP, the failure to capitalize operating lease assets and lease liabilities for analysis purposes distorts ROE analysis—specifically:

- Net operating profit margin (NOPM) is understated. Over the life of the lease, rent expense under operating leases equals depreciation plus interest expense under capital leases; however, only depreciation expense is included in net operating profit (NOPAT) as interest is a nonoperating expense. Operating expense is, therefore, overstated, and NOPM is understated. While cash payments are the same whether the lease is classified as operating or capital, *operating cash flow* is higher with capital leases since depreciation is an add-back, and the reduction of the capital lease obligation is classified as a *financing* outflow. Operating cash flows are, therefore, lower with operating leases than with capital leases.
- Net operating asset turnover (NOAT) is overstated due to nonreporting of lease assets.
- Financial leverage (FLEV) is understated by the omitted lease liabilities—recall that lease liabilities are nonoperating.

Although aggregate ROE is relatively unaffected (assuming that the leases are at their midpoint on average so that rent expense is approximately equal to depreciation plus interest) failure to capitalize an operating lease results in a balance sheet that, arguably, neither reflects all of the assets that are used in the business, nor the nonoperating obligations for which the company is liable. Such noncapitalization of leases makes ROE appear to be of higher quality because it derives from higher RNOA (due to higher NOA turnover) and not from higher financial leverage. This is, of course, the main reason why some managers want to exclude leases from the balance sheet.

Lease disclosures that are required under GAAP allow us to capitalize operating leases for analysis purposes. This capitalization process involves three steps (this is the same basic process that managers will use to capitalize leases under the proposed lease-accounting standard):

1. Determine the discount rate.
2. Compute the present value of future lease payments.
3. Adjust the balance sheet to include the present value from step 2 as both a lease asset and a lease liability. Adjust the income statement to include depreciation and interest in lieu of rent expense.

Step 1. There are at least two approaches to determine the appropriate discount rate for our analysis: (1) If the company discloses capital leases, we can impute (infer) an implicit rate of return: a rate that yields the present value computed by the company given the future capital lease payments (see Business Insight box below). (2) Use the rate that corresponds to the company's credit rating or the rate from any recent borrowings involving intermediate-term secured obligations. Companies typically disclose these details in their long-term debt footnote. To illustrate the capitalization of operating leases, we use the **Southwest Airlines** lease footnote reproduced above. Step 1 estimates the implicit rate for Southwest Airlines' capital leases to be 5.67% (see the following Business Insight box on computing the imputed discount rate for leases).

BUSINESS INSIGHT **Imputed Discount Rate Computation for Leases**

When companies report both operating and capital leases, we can use disclosures in the lease footnote to impute the average interest rate used to discount capital leases. **Southwest Airlines** reports total undiscounted minimum capital lease payments of $46 million and a discounted value for those lease payments of $36 million. Using Excel, we estimate the discount rate that Southwest used for its capital lease computations with the IRR function (= IRR (values,guess)) as shown in the following spreadsheet. The entries in cells B2 through G2 are taken from Southwest's reported schedule of lease maturities in the footnote shown earlier in this section, and those in cells H2 through J2 sum to $18 million, the total lease payments due after 2017 (year 5). We assume that Southwest continues to pay $6 million per year (the same as in 2017) until the $18 is used up (3 years). The spreadsheet estimates that Southwest Airlines implicitly used a discount rate of 5.67% to capitalize leases in its 2012 balance sheet.

IRR spreadsheet.xlsx - Microsoft Excel

File Home Insert Page Layout Formulas Data Review View Acrobat

B3 fx =IRR(B2:J2,0.1)

	A	B	C	D	E	F	G	H	I	J	K
1	N	0	1	2	3	4	5	6	7	8	
2	Amount	-36	5	6	6	5	6	6	6	6	
3	IRR	5.67% *									
4											
5		* Formula for cell B3 is =IRR(B2:J2)							= 18		

Step 2. Compute the present value of future operating lease payments using the 5.67% discount rate that we estimated in Step 1, see Exhibit 10.2. We demonstrate this computation using a spreadsheet (without rounding of numbers); we show those same computations using both a financial calculator and present value tables in Appendix 10C. The spreadsheet (and calculator) method is more exact, but may or may not yield a material difference to the number obtained when using present value tables. Given the widespread use of spreadsheets such as Excel, we use the spreadsheet method hereafter.

EXHIBIT 10.2 **Present Value of Operating Lease Payments ($ millions)**

Year	Operating Lease Payment	Discount Factor (i = 0.0567)	Present Value
1.	$ 688	0.94634	$ 651
2.	614	0.89556	550
3.	507	0.84751	430
4.	392	0.80203	314
5.	369	0.75900	280
>5.	$1,823 ($369 × 4.94 years)	4.20608 × 0.75900	1,178
			$3,403
Remaining life.	$1,823/$369 = 4.94 years		

Spreadsheet Method. The present value of the operating lease payments equals the sum of the present values for each of the lease payments Year 1 through Year 5 and the present value of the lease payments after Year 5. This two-step computation follows:

1. *Present values for Years 1 through 5.* The present value of each forecasted lease payment for Years 1 through 5 is computed as the product of (a) the lease payment for that year and (b) the present value factor for that year using the following formula: $\frac{1}{(1+i)^t}$ where i is the discount factor

and t is the year (1, 2, 3, 4 and 5). To illustrate using Southwest, we enter the discount rate of 5.67% and the year 1, 2, 3, 4 and 5 separately for each year to obtain a present value factor for each year. For example, for Year 1 the present value factor is 0.94634, computed as $\frac{1}{(1.0567)^1}$; and, for Year 2 the present value factor is 0.89556, computed as $\frac{1}{(1.0567)^2}$; and so forth. Thus, the present value ($ in millions) of the Year 1 lease payment equals $651, computed from: $688 $\times \left[\frac{1}{(1.0567)^1}\right]$; the present value of the Year 2 lease payment equals $550, computed from: $614 $\times \left[\frac{1}{(1.0567)^2}\right]$; and so forth. In Excel, for Year 2, the present value factor is entered as: = 1/1.0567^2. The present values for Year 1 through Year 5 are in the far right column of Exhibit 10.2.

2. *Present value for Year 6 and thereafter.* To compute the present value of the lease payments remaining after Year 5, we make an assumption that the company continues to make lease payments at the Year 5 level for the remainder of the lease term. The remaining lease term is, therefore, estimated as: (Total payments for Year 6 and thereafter)/(Year 5 lease payment). This means the remaining payments are an annuity for the remainder of the lease term, the present value of which equals the product of (a) the lease payment for Year 5 and (b) the present value factor for that annuity using the following formula: $\frac{1 - [1/(1 + i)^n]}{i} \times \frac{1}{(1 + i)^5}$, where i is the discount factor and n is the remainder of the lease term. To illustrate using Southwest, we enter the 5.67% discount rate and the 4.94 years estimate of the remaining lease term (computed from $1,823/$369). The present value of the remaining lease payments equals $1,178, computed from:

$$\$369 \text{ million} \times \frac{1 - [1/(1.0567)^{4.94}]}{0.0567} \times \frac{1}{(1.0567)^5}$$

The first term in this computation is the assumed annual payment after Year 5; the second term is the present value factor for the remaining annuity after Year 5; and the third term discounts the second term to the present. In Excel, the second and third terms are entered as = ((1−(1/(1.0567)^4.94))/(0.0567) * (1/1.0567^5). The present value of the lease payments for Year 6 and thereafter is in the sixth row of the far right column of Exhibit 10.2.

We sum the present values of Year 1 through Year 5 payments and the present value of the payments in Year 6 and beyond to obtain the present value of future operating lease payments; for Southwest, this totals $3,403 ($ millions), computed as $651 + $550 + $430 + $314 + $280 + $1,178.

Step 3. Use the computed present value of future operating lease payments to adjust the balance sheet, income statement, and financial ratios as we illustrate below.

Balance Sheet Effects To adjust the balance sheet, add the present value from Step 2 to both operating assets (PPE) and nonoperating liabilities (long-term debt). Exhibit 10.3 shows the adjustments for Southwest Airlines at year-end 2012. The capitalization of operating leases has a marked impact on Southwest's balance sheet. For the airline and retailing industries, in particular, lease assets (airplanes and real estate) comprise a large portion of net operating assets, which are typically accounted for using the operating lease method. Thus, companies in these industries usually have sizeable off-balance-sheet assets and liabilities.

EXHIBIT 10.3 Adjustments to Balance Sheet from Capitalization of Operating Leases

Southwest Airlines ($ millions)	Reported Figures	Adjustments	Adjusted Figures	Percent Increase
Net operating assets	$7,176	$3,403	$10,579	47.4%
Net nonoperating obligations . . .	184	3,403	3,587	1,849.5%
Equity	6,992	—	6,992	0.0%

Income Statement Effects Capitalizing operating leases affects the income statement via depreciation of the leased equipment and interest on the lease liability. Operating lease payments are reported as rent expense, typically included in selling, general and administrative expenses. The income statement adjustments relating to the capitalization of operating leases involve two steps:

1. Remove "rent expense" of $688 million from operating expense.[4]
2. Add depreciation expense from the lease assets to operating expense and add interest expense from the lease obligation as a nonoperating expense. Lease assets are estimated at $3,403 million (see Exhibit 10.3). GAAP requires companies to depreciate capital lease assets over their useful lives or the lease terms, whichever is less. For this example, we assume that the remaining lease term is 9.94 years (five years reported in the lease schedule plus 4.94 years after the fifth year). Using this term and zero salvage value results in estimated straight-line depreciation for lease assets of $342 million ($3,403 million/9.94 years). Interest expense on the $3,403 million lease liability at the 5.67% capitalization rate is $193 million ($3,403 million × 5.67%) for the first year.

Southwest Airlines reports NOPAT of $496 million, nonoperating expense of $75 million, and net income of $421 million. Assuming a tax rate of 37%, the net adjustment to NOPAT is $218 million ([$688 million rent expense − $342 million depreciation expense] × [1 − 0.37]), see Exhibit 10.4. The increase in after-tax nonoperating expense is $122 million ($193 million × [1 − 0.37]), which is the additional after-tax interest expense on the capitalized lease obligation. Exhibit 10.4 summarizes those adjustments to Southwest's profitability measures.

EXHIBIT 10.4 Adjustments to Income Statement from Capitalization of Operating Leases

Southwest Airlines ($ millions)	Reported Figures	Adjustments	Adjusted Figures	Percent Increase
NOPAT	$496	$218	$714	44.0%
Nonoperating expense	75	122	197	162.7%
Net income	$421	$ 96	$517	22.8%

ROE and Disaggregation Effects Adjustments to capitalize operating leases can alter our assessment of ROE components. Using the adjustments we describe in Exhibits 10.3 and 10.4, the impact for ROE and its components (defined in Module 4), is summarized in Exhibit 10.5 for Southwest Airlines.

EXHIBIT 10.5 Ratio Effects of Adjustments from Capitalization of Operating Leases

Southwest Airlines ($ millions)	Reported	Adjusted	Computations for Adjusted Numbers
NOPM	2.9%	4.2%	$714/$17,088
NOAT	2.38	1.62	$17,088/$10,579*
RNOA	6.9%	6.7%	$714/$10,579*
Financial leverage (FLEV = NNO/Equity)	0.03	0.51	$3,587/$6,992
ROE	6.0%	7.4%	$517/$6,992*
Nonoperating return	−0.9%	0.7%	7.4% − 6.7%

* For simplicity, we use year-end values for the denominator in lieu of average values.

Using *year-end* (reported and adjusted) data, and Southwest Airlines' total revenues of $17,088 million, adjusted RNOA is 6.7% (down from 6.9% reported). RNOA decreased because the increase in net operating profit margin (from 2.9% to 4.2%) was more than offset by a much lower net operating asset turnover (from 2.38 to 1.62). After capitalization of its operating leases, Southwest Airlines is more

[4] This approach uses the operating lease payments from Year 1 to approximate the current period rent expense for operating leases. This approach also uses the computed present value of future lease payments (from Step 2) to compute the depreciation and interest expense for capital leases.

Another approach is to set the rent expense in step #1 equal to the depreciation plus interest computed in step #2. Under this approach, the rent expense removed in step #1 would equal $535 million ($342 million + $193 million) instead of $688 million. This approach means that net income is unchanged and only adjusts the allocation of rent expense between depreciation (operating) and interest (nonoperating); it also maintains the equality of the balance sheet equation.

profitable (from an operating standpoint) and more capital intensive than we would infer from a review of its unadjusted income statement and balance sheet.

Southwest's ROE increases by 1.4 percentage points (from 6.0% to 7.4%). The analysis reveals that the nonoperating return component of its ROE increases from (0.9)% using reported figures to an adjusted 0.7%. The adjusted figures reveal the effect of a much greater financial leverage from capitalized lease obligations that is not apparent prior to capitalization. Specifically, financial leverage is 51% of equity using adjusted figures versus 3% of equity using reported figures. Financial leverage is, therefore, revealed to play a greater role in ROE in partially offsetting the lower spread. In sum, Southwest's adjusted figures reveal a company with a lower ROE and with more assets and more financial leverage than was apparent from reported figures.

Adjusted assets and liabilities arguably present a more realistic picture of the invested capital required to operate Southwest Airlines and of the amount of leverage represented by its leases. Similarly, operating profitability is revealed to be higher than reported, since a portion of Southwest's rent payments represents repayment of the lease liability (a nonoperating cash outflow) rather than operating expense.

MID-MODULE REVIEW

Following is the leasing footnote disclosure from **United Parcel Service's (UPS)** 2012 10-K report.

We lease certain aircraft, facilities, land, equipment and vehicles under operating leases, which expire at various dates through 2038. Certain of the leases contain escalation clauses and renewal or purchase options. Rent expense related to our operating leases was $619, $629 and $615 million for 2012, 2011 and 2010, respectively. The following table sets forth the aggregate minimum lease payments under capital and operating leases (in millions).

Year	Capital Leases	Operating Leases
2013	$ 55	$ 342
2014	52	271
2015	50	203
2016	49	145
2017	48	118
After 2017	426	358
Total	680	$1,437
Less: imputed interest	(240)	
Present value of minimum capitalized lease payments	$440	
Less: current portion	(31)	
Long-term capitalized lease obligations	$409	

Required

1. Impute the discount rate that UPS uses, on average, to compute the present value of its capital leases.
2. What adjustments would we make to UPS's balance sheet to capitalize the operating leases at the end of 2012? (*Hint:* The implicit rate on its capital leases is approximately 7%; use this approximation to solve parts 2 and 3 if one cannot solve for the implicit rate.)
3. Assuming the same facts as in part 2, what income statement adjustments might we consider?

The solution is on page 10-53.

PENSIONS

LO2 Describe and illustrate the accounting for pensions.

Companies frequently offer pension plans as a benefit for their employees. There are two general types of pension plans:

1. **Defined contribution plan**. This plan requires the company make periodic contributions to an employee's account (usually with a third-party trustee like a bank), and many plans require an employee matching contribution. Following retirement, the employee makes periodic withdrawals from that account. A tax-advantaged 401(k) account is a typical example. Under a 401(k) plan, the employee makes contributions that are exempt from federal taxes until they are withdrawn after retirement.
2. **Defined benefit plan**. This plan also requires the company make periodic payments to a third party, which then makes payments to an employee after retirement. Payments are usually based on years of service and the employee's salary. The company may or may not set aside sufficient funds to cover these obligations (federal law does set minimum funding requirements). As a result, defined benefit plans can be overfunded or underfunded. All pension investments are retained by the third party until paid to the employee. In the event of bankruptcy, employees have the standing of a general creditor, but usually have additional protection in the form of government pension benefit insurance.

For a defined contribution plan, the company contribution is recorded as an expense in the income statement when the cash is paid or the liability accrued. For a defined benefit plan, it is not so simple. This is because while the company contributes cash or securities to the pension investment account, the pension obligation is not satisfied until the employee receives pension benefits, which may be many years into the future. This section focuses on how a defined benefit plan impacts financial statements, and how we assess company performance and financial condition when such a plan exists.

Reporting of Defined Benefit Pension Plans

There are two accounting issues concerning the reporting of defined benefit pension plans.

1. How are pension plans (assets and liabilities) reported in the balance sheet (if at all)?
2. How is the expense relating to pension plans reported in the income statement?

The following graphic shows where pensions appear on the balance sheet (liabilities and assets) and the income statement (pension expense is reported in the same expense accounts as employee wages; for example, pension expense for manufacturing employees is in cost of goods sold, whereas pension expense for salespeople is in SG&A).

Income Statement
Sales
Cost of goods sold
Selling, general and administrative expenses
Income taxes
Net income

Balance Sheet	
Cash	Current liabilities
Accounts receivable	**Long-term liabilities**
Inventory	
Long-term operating assets	Shareholders' equity
Investments	

Balance Sheet Effects

Pension plan assets are primarily investments in stocks and bonds (mostly of other companies, but it is not uncommon for companies to invest pension funds in their own stock). Pension liabilities (called the **projected benefit obligation** or **PBO**) are the company's obligations to pay current and former employees. The difference between the market value of the pension plan assets and the projected benefit obligation is called the **funded status** of the pension plan. If the PBO exceeds the pension plan assets, the pension is **underfunded**. Conversely, if pension plan assets exceed the PBO, the pension plan is **overfunded**. Under current GAAP, companies are required to record only the funded status on their balance sheets (namely, the *net* amount, not the pension plan assets and PBO separately), either as an asset if the plan is overfunded, or as a liability if it is underfunded.

Pension plan assets consist of stocks and bonds whose value changes each period in three ways. First, the value of the investments increases or decreases as a result of interest, dividends, and gains or losses on the stocks and bonds held. Second, the pension plan assets increase when the company contributes additional cash or stock to the investment account. Third, the pension plan assets decrease by the amount of benefits paid to retirees during the period. These three changes in the pension plan assets are articulated below.

	Pension Plan Assets
	Pension plan assets, beginning balance
+	Actual returns on investments (interest, dividends, gains and losses)
+	Company contributions to pension plan
−	Benefits paid to retirees
=	Pension plan assets, ending balance

The pension liability, or PBO (projected benefit obligation), is computed as the present value of the expected future benefit payments to employees. The present value of these future payments depends on the number of years the employee is expected to work (years of service), the employee's salary level at retirement, and the number of years the employee will receive benefits. Consequently, companies must estimate future wage increases, as well as the number of employees expected to reach retirement age with the company and how long they are likely to receive pension benefits following retirement. Once the future retiree pool is determined, the expected future payments under the plan are discounted to arrive at the present value of the pension obligation. This is the PBO. A reconciliation of the PBO from beginning balance to year-end balance follows.

	Pension Obligation
	Projected benefit obligation, beginning balance
+	Service cost
+	Interest cost
+/−	Actuarial losses (gains)
−	Benefits paid to retirees
=	Projected benefit obligation, ending balance

As this reconciliation shows, the balance in the PBO changes during the period for four reasons.

- First, as employees continue to work for the company, their pension benefits increase. The annual **service cost** represents the additional (future) pension benefits earned by employees during the current year.
- Second, **interest cost** accrues on the outstanding pension liability, just as it would with any other long-term liability (see the accounting for bond liabilities in Module 7). Because there are no scheduled interest payments on the PBO, the interest cost accrues each year, that is, interest is added to the existing liability.
- Third, the PBO can increase (or decrease) due to **actuarial losses (and gains)**, which arise when companies make changes in their pension plans or make *changes in actuarial assumptions* (such as the rate of wage inflation, termination and mortality rates, and the discount rate used to compute the present value of future obligations). For example, if a company increases the discount rate used to compute the present value of future pension plan payments from, say, 8% to 9%, the present value of future benefit payments declines (just like bond prices). Conversely, if the discount rate is reduced to 7%, the present value of the PBO increases. Other actuarial assumptions used to estimate the pension liability (such as the expected wage inflation rate or the expected life span of current and former employees) can also create similar actuarial losses or gains.
- Fourth, pension benefit payments to retirees reduce the PBO (just as the payments reduce the pension plan assets).

Finally, companies are permitted to net the pension plan assets and the PBO and then report this net amount on the balance sheet. This net amount is called the **funded status** and is reported as an asset if pension assets exceed the PBO, and as a liability if the PBO exceeds pension assets.

Net Pension Asset (or Liability)
Pension plan assets (at market value)
− Projected benefit obligation (PBO)
Funded status

If the funded status is positive (assets exceed liabilities such that the plan is overfunded), the overfunded pension plan is reported on the balance sheet as an asset, typically called prepaid pension cost. If the funded status is negative (liabilities exceed assets and the plan is underfunded), it is reported as a liability.[5] During the late 2000s, long-term interest rates declined drastically and many companies lowered their discount rate for computing the present value of future pension payments. Lower discount rates meant higher PBO values. This period also witnessed a bear market and pension plan assets declined in value. The combined effect of the increase in PBO and the decrease in asset values caused many pension funds to become severely underfunded. Of the 1,144 publicly traded companies reporting pension plans in 2012 and with revenues over $500 million, a total of 1,071 (94%) were underfunded (source: **S&P Compustat**).

IFRS INSIGHT **Reporting of Pension Funded Status under IFRS**

Like U.S. GAAP, IFRS requires companies to report the funded status of their defined benefit pension plans on the balance sheet. The IFRS calculation of the unfunded status is slightly different than under GAAP. The IFRS unfunded status is calculated as projected benefit obligation minus the fair value of plan assets; but, unlike GAAP, any actuarial gains are added (losses are subtracted). There are other differences in detailed computations, which means that for pension assets and liabilities it is difficult to reliably compare GAAP and IFRS reports.

Income Statement Effects

A company's net pension expense is computed as follows.

Net Pension Expense
Service cost
+ Interest cost
− *Expected* return on pension plan assets
± Amortization of deferred amounts
Net pension expense

The net pension expense is rarely reported separately on the income statement. Instead, it is included with other forms of compensation expense. However, pension expense is disclosed separately in footnotes.

The net pension expense has four components. The previous PBO section described the first two components: service costs and interest costs. The third component of pension expense relates to the return on pension plan assets, which *reduces* total pension expense. To compute this component, companies use the long-term *expected* rate of return on the pension plan assets, rather than the *actual* return, and multiply that expected rate by the prior year's balance in the pension plan assets account (usually the average balance in the prior year). Use of the expected return rather than actual return is an important distinction. Company CEOs and CFOs dislike income variability because they believe that stockholders react negatively to it, and so company executives intensely (and successfully) lobbied the FASB to use the more stable expected long-term investment return, rather than the actual return, in

[5] Companies typically maintain many pension plans. Some are overfunded and others are underfunded. Current GAAP requires companies to separately group all of the overfunded and all of the underfunded plans, and to present a net asset for the overfunded plans and a net liability for the underfunded plans.

computing pension expense. Thus, the pension plan assets' expected return is deducted to compute net pension expense.[6]

BUSINESS INSIGHT **How Pensions Confound Income Analysis**

Overfunded pension plans and boom markets can inflate income. Specifically, when the stock market is booming, pension investments realize large gains that flow to income (via reduced pension expense). Although pension plan assets do not belong to shareholders (as they are the legal entitlement of current and future retirees), the gains and losses from those plan assets are reported in income. The following graph plots the funded status of **General Electric**'s pension plans together with pension expense (revenue) that GE reported from 1998 through 2012.

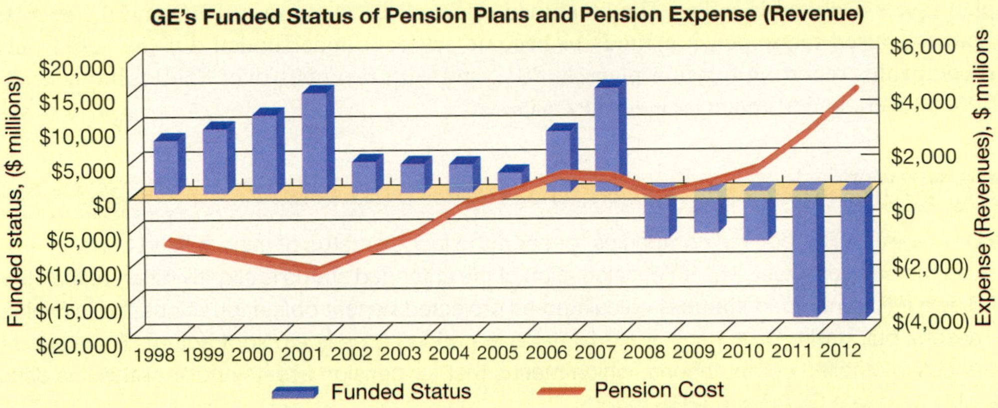

GE's funded status had consistently been positive (indicating an overfunded plan) until the market decline of 2008. The degree of overfunding peaked in 2001 at the height of the stock market, and began to decline during the bear market of the early 2000s. It peaked again in 2007, just prior to the recession and the ensuing bear market. GE reported pension *revenue* (not expense) during 1998–2007. In 2001, GE's reported pension *revenue* was $2,095 million (10.6% of its pretax income). Because of the plan's overfunded status, the expected return and amortization of deferred gains components of pension expense amounted to $5,288 million, far in excess of the service and interest costs of $3,193 million. In the mid to late 2000s, GE recorded pension *expense* (rather than revenue) as the pension plan's overfunding and expected long-term rates of return declined.

Any difference between the expected and the actual return is accumulated, together with other deferred amounts, off-balance-sheet and reported in the footnotes. (Other deferred amounts include changes in PBO resulting from changes in estimates used to compute the PBO and from amendments to the pension plans made by the company.) However, if the deferred amount exceeds certain limits, the excess is recognized on-balance-sheet with a corresponding amount recognized (as amortization of deferred amounts) in

[6] The IASB has amended its standard on accounting for pensions and other postretirement benefits (OPEB), which potentially has important implications for U.S. GAAP. Those amendments took effect for years starting on or after January 1, 2013, and include the following key changes:

- *Elimination of deferred recognition.* The full value of the benefit obligation and plan assets will be reported in the balance sheet with changes arising from actuarial gains and losses recognized in full in other comprehensive income (OCI). Companies will not have an option to recognize those gains and losses in net income, either in the periods in which they occur or through amortization. Prior service cost will be recognized in full in determining net income in the period the plan amendment is made.
- *Disaggregation of benefit cost.* The components of pension and OPEB cost (service cost, finance cost, and remeasurement cost) will be reported separately in the footnotes. Separate or aggregate presentation of service and finance cost components will be permitted in the statement of comprehensive income.
- *Elimination of expected return on plan assets.* The discount rate would be applied to the net funded position to determine the net financing cost, which will include an implied return on assets. A separate expected long-term rate of return on plan assets will no longer be used.

the income statement.[7] This amortization is the fourth component of pension expense and can be either a positive or negative amount depending on the sign of the difference between expected and actual return on plan assets. (We discuss the amortization component of pension expense further in Appendix 10A.)

A final point to consider is the operating or nonoperating nature of the components of pension expense. Most analysts consider the service cost portion of pension expense to be an operating expense, similar to salaries and other benefits. However, the interest cost component is generally viewed as a nonoperating (financing) cost. Similarly, the expected return on plan assets is considered nonoperating.

Footnote Disclosures—Components of Plan Assets and PBO

GAAP requires extensive footnote disclosures for pensions (and other post-employment benefits which we discuss later). These notes provide details relating to the net pension liability reported in the balance sheet and for the components of pension expense on the income statement.

FedEx Corp.'s pension footnote below indicates that the funded status of its pension plan is $(4,853) million on December 31, 2012. This means FedEx's plan is underfunded. Following are the disclosures FedEx makes in its pension footnote, $ millions.

Pension Plans	2012	2011
Changes in projected benefit obligation ("PBO")		
PBO at the beginning of year	$17,372	$14,484
Service cost	593	521
Interest cost	976	900
Actuarial loss	3,789	1,875
Benefits paid	(502)	(468)
Other	(41)	60
PBO at the end of year	$22,187	$17,372
Change in plan assets		
Fair value of plan assets at the beginning of year	$15,841	$13,295
Actual return on plan assets	1,235	2,425
Company contributions	780	557
Benefits paid	(502)	(468)
Other	(20)	32
Fair value of plan assets at the end of year	$17,334	$15,841
Funded status of the plans	$ (4,853)	$ (1,531)

FedEx's PBO began the year with a balance of $17,372 million. The PBO increased by $593 million due to 2012 service cost and $976 million as a result of the accrual of interest on the discounted pension liability. During the year, FedEx also realized an actuarial loss of $3,789 million, which increased the pension liability. The PBO decreased as a result of $502 million in benefits paid to retirees and $41 million for "other" pension liability adjustments, leaving a balance of $22,187 million at year-end.[8]

Pension plan assets began the year with a fair value of $15,841 million, which increased by $1,235 million from investment returns and by $780 million from company contributions. Plan assets decreased by $502 million for the benefit payments made to retirees and by $20 million relating to "other" adjustments. The $502 million benefit payments to retirees reduced both the plan assets and the PBO by the same amount, as discussed above. At year-end, the pension plan assets had a fair value of $17,334 million. The funded status of FedEx's pension plan at year-end was $(4,853) million, computed as $22,187 million − $17,334 million. The negative balance indicates that the FedEx pension plan is underfunded.

[7] To avoid amortization, the deferred amounts must be less than 10% of the PBO or pension investments, whichever is less. The excess, if any, is amortized until no further excess remains. When the excess is eliminated (by investment returns or company contributions, for example), the amortization ceases.

[8] This actuarial loss derives from a decrease in the discount rate, from 5.76% to 4.44% which increased pension liability, yielding the actuarial loss.

We can treat the funded status as an operating item (either asset or liability).

FedEx incurred $524 million of pension expense in 2012. Details of this expense are found in its 2012 pension footnote, which follows ($ millions):

Components of net periodic benefit cost	Pension Plans 2012
Service cost	$ 593
Interest cost	976
Expected return on plan assets	(1,240)
Recognized actuarial losses (gains) and other	195
Net periodic benefit cost	$ 524

The service and interest cost components of pension expense relate to the increase in the PBO of employees working another year for the company (expected benefits typically increase with longevity and salary, and the PBO increases because it is discounted for one less year). This expense is offset by the *expected* return on pension assets. Notice the use of expected returns rather than actual returns. Expected returns do not fluctuate as much as actual returns, and this yields a less volatile year-on-year pension expense and, consequently, less volatility in net income. The use of expected returns is in conformity with GAAP and companies lobbied for its use because of the reduced volatility for pension expense. Finally, because we cannot separate the operating and nonoperating components of a company's funded status and, hence, treat it entirely as operating, we do the same for pension expense and treat it entirely as operating. (We do this for consistency purposes even though we know that expense components related to interest cost, expected returns on plan assets, and many amortizations are nonoperating.)

RESEARCH INSIGHT **Valuation Implications of Pension Footnote Disclosures**

The FASB requires footnote disclosure of the major components of pension cost presumably because it is useful for investors. Pension-related research has examined whether investors assign different valuation multiples to the components of pension cost when assessing company market value. Research finds that the market does, indeed, attach different interpretation to pension components, reflecting differences in information about perceived permanence in earnings.

Footnote Disclosures and Future Cash Flows

Companies use their pension plan assets to pay pension benefits to retirees. When markets are booming, as during the 1990s, pension plan assets can grow rapidly. However, when markets reverse, as in the bear markets of the early and late 2010s, the value of pension plan assets can decline. The company's annual pension plan contribution is an investment decision that is influenced, in part, by market conditions and minimum required contributions specified by law. Companies' cash contributions come from borrowed funds or operating cash flows.

RESEARCH INSIGHT **Why Do Companies Offer Pensions?**

Research examines why companies choose to offer pension benefits. It finds that deferred compensation plans and pensions help align the long-term interests of owners and employees. Research also examines the composition of pension investments. It finds that a large portion of pension fund assets are invested in fixed-income securities, which are of lower risk than other investment securities. This implies that pension assets are less risky than nonpension assets. The FASB has mandated new pension disclosures that require firms (after 2009) to provide more detail about the types of assets held in pension plans. These disclosures presumably help investors better assess the riskiness of pension assets.

FedEx paid $502 million in pension benefits to retirees in 2012, and it contributed $780 million to pension assets that year. Cash contributions to the pension plan assets are the relevant amounts for an analysis of projected cash flows. Benefits paid in relation to the pension liability balance can provide a clue about the need for *future* cash contributions. Companies are required to disclose the expected benefit payments for five years after the statement date and the remaining obligations thereafter. Following is FedEx's benefit disclosure statement:

Benefit payments, which reflect expected future service, are expected to be paid as follows for the years ending May 31:

($ millions)	Pension Plans
2013	$ 640
2014	723
2015	803
2016	861
2017	922
2018–2022	6,289

As of 2012, FedEx pension plan assets account reports a balance of $17,334 million, as discussed above, and during the year, the plan assets generated actual returns of $1,235 million. The pension plan asset account is currently generating investment returns that are more than enough to cover the projected benefit payments that FedEx expects to pay to retirees as outlined in the schedule above. Should future investment returns decline, however, the company will have to use operating cash flow or borrow money to fund the deficit.

One application of the pension footnote is to assess the likelihood that the company will be required to increase its cash contributions to the pension plan. This estimate is made by examining the funded status of the pension plan and the projected payments to retirees. For severely underfunded plans, the projected payments to retirees might not be covered by existing pension assets and projected investment returns. In this case, the company might need to divert operating cash flow from other prospective projects to cover its pension plan. Alternatively, if operating cash flows are not available, it might need to borrow to fund those payments. This can be especially troublesome as the debt service payments include interest, which increase the required pension contribution. The decline in the financial condition and ultimate bankruptcy of General Motors was due in large part to its inability to meet its pension and health care obligations from pension assets. The company was forced to divert much needed operating cash flow and to borrow funds to meet its cash payment obligations.

Footnote Disclosures and Profit Implications

Recall the following earlier breakdown for pension expense:

	Net Pension Expense
	Service cost
+	Interest cost
−	*Expected* return on pension plan assets
±	Amortization of deferred amounts
	Net pension expense

Interest cost is the product of the PBO and the discount rate. This discount rate is set by the company. The expected dollar return on pension assets is the product of the pension plan asset balance and the expected long-run rate of return on the investment portfolio. This rate is also set by the company. Further, PBO is affected by the expected rate of wage inflation, termination and mortality rates, all of which are estimated by the company.

GAAP requires disclosure of several rates used by the company in its estimation of PBO and the related pension expense. FedEx discloses the following in its pension footnote:

	Pension Plans		
Net Periodic Benefit Cost (Year Ended December 31)	**2012**	**2011**	**2010**
Discount rate used to determine benefit obligation.	4.44%	5.76%	6.37%
Discount rate used to determine net periodic benefit cost	5.76	6.37	7.68
Rate of increase in future compensation levels used to determine benefit obligation	4.62	4.58	4.63
Rate of increase in future compensation levels used to determine net periodic benefit cost.	4.58	4.63	4.42
Expected long-term rate of return on assets	8.00	8.00	8.00

During 2012, FedEx decreased its discount rate (used to compute the present value of its pension obligations, or PBO) from 5.76% to 4.44%, a decrease of 1.32 percentage points, while leaving unchanged its estimate of the expected return on plan assets. FedEx also decreased slightly the anticipated increases in compensation costs used to determine the annual expense.

Changes in these assumptions have the following general effects on pension expense and, thus, profitability. This table summarizes the effects of increases in the various rates. Decreases have the exact opposite effects.[9]

Assumption change	Probable effect on pension expense	Reason for effect
Discount rate ↑	↑	While the higher discount rate reduces the PBO, the lower PBO is multiplied by a higher rate when the company computes the interest component of pension expense. The rate effect is larger than the discount effect, resulting in increased pension expense.
Investment return ↑. . .	↓	The dollar amount of expected return on plan assets is the product of the plan assets balance and the expected long-term rate of return. Increasing the return increases the expected return on plan assets, thus reducing pension expense.
Wage inflation ↑	↑	The expected rate of wage inflation affects future wage levels that determine expected pension payments. An increase, thus, increases PBO, which increases both the service and interest cost components of pension expense.

In the case of FedEx, the decrease in both the discount rate and the assumed health care cost trend rate, coupled with no change in the expected return on investments, served to decrease pension costs and increase profitability in that year. It is often the case that companies reduce the expected investment returns with a lag, but increase them without a lag, to favorably impact profitability. We must be aware of the impact of these changes in assumptions in our evaluation of company profitability.

Analysis Implications

There are two important analysis issues relating to pensions:

1. To what extent will the company's pension plans compete with investing and financing needs for the available cash flows?
2. In what ways has the company's choice of estimates affected its profitability?

Regarding the first issue, pension plan assets are the source of funds to pay benefits to retirees, and federal law (Employee Retirement Income Security Act) sets minimum standards for pension

[9] Interest cost is computed as the product of the PBO and the assumed discount rate. As interest rates increase, the PBO decreases as we are discounting future payment obligations at a higher discount rate. We are, therefore, applying a higher interest rate to a lower PBO with opposite effects on interest cost. Generally, the rate effect dominates and the interest cost component of pension expense changes in the direction of the discount rate change. Following is the disclosure by FedEx of the effects on pension expense of a one percentage point change in the discount rate:

Sensitivity (in millions)	Effect on 2013 Pension Expense	Effect on 2012 Pension Expense
One-basis-point change in discount rate.	$2.3	$1.9

contributions. Consequently, if investment returns are insufficient, companies must make up the shortfall with additional contributions. Any such additional contributions compete for available operating cash flows with other investing and financing activities. This can be especially severe in a business downturn when operating cash flows are depressed. As debt payments are contractual, companies can be forced to postpone needed capital investment to make the contributions necessary to ensure funding of their pension plans as required by law or labor agreements. Analysts must be aware of funding requirements when projecting future cash flows.

ANALYSIS INSIGHT **Lower Interest Rates Impact Ford's Pension Contributions**

In its 2012 10-K, **Ford** disclosed that its pension plans "were underfunded by $18.7 billion at December 31, 2012, compared with being underfunded by $15.4 billion at December 31, 2011. The deterioration is more than explained by sharply lower discount rates, with the U.S. weighted-average discount rate declining to 3.84% at the end of 2012 from 4.64% at the end of 2011." As interest rates decline, the present value of pension obligations increases, thus increasing an unfunded status (the amount reported on the balance sheet). Lower interest rates can also affect the amount of cash that Ford is required to contribute to its pension plan to keep it solvent. The reason is that pension investments yield lower cash flow in periods of lower interest rates, and pension investments are the primary source of cash to fund pension obligations; the Ford 10-K reports: "In 2012, we contributed $3.4 billion to our worldwide funded pension plans, an increase of $2.3 billion compared with 2011. During 2013, we expect to contribute . . . about $5 billion to our worldwide funded plans . . . and to make $400 million of benefit payments to participants in unfunded plans, for a total of about $5.4 billion." To address the increasing burden of pension obligations, Ford is taking action on several fronts:

> The key elements of this strategy include:
> - Limiting liability growth in our defined benefit plans by closing participation to new participants;
> - Reducing plan deficits through discretionary cash contributions;
> - Progressively re-balancing assets to more fixed income investments . . . ; and
> - Taking other strategic actions to reduce pension liabilities, such as the voluntary lump sum payout program started in 2012 for U.S. salaried retirees.

As rates *increase*, however, the opposite occurs: pension obligations decrease, as does the negative funded status, and fixed income investments should begin to generate a greater return from which to make payments to retirees. This will enable Ford to spend those billions of dollars on other developments. Bob Shanks, Ford's CFO, said during Ford's second-quarter conference call, according to *Automotive News*, that:

> "We won't have to allocate as much capital to pensions as we have the last couple of years and certainly this year. That will give us the ability to take the cash that we're generating and invest it in other parts of the business that can support further growth."

A thorough reading and understanding of the pension footnote is essential to effective analysis of financial statements. It is only by wading through the detail of the pension disclosures, that we can begin to understand the factors that impact upon the cash demands of pension plans and their claim on the operating cash flows of the company. Ford's diversion of operating cash flow into pension contributions has a real impact on its ability to invest in other areas of strategic importance.

Regarding the second issue, accounting for pensions requires several assumptions, including the expected return on pension investments, the expected rate of wage inflation, the discount rate used to compute the PBO, and other actuarial assumptions that are not reported in footnotes (mortality rates, for example). Each of these assumptions affects reported profit as already explained. Analysts must be aware of changes in these assumptions and their effects on profitability. An increase in reported profit that is due to an increase in the expected return on pension investments, for example, is not related to core operating activities and, further, might not be sustainable. Such changes in estimates must be considered in our evaluation of reported profitability.

BUSINESS INSIGHT **Amortization of Deferred Gains and Losses**

Some companies are changing the way they account for pension plans. In our discussion of pension expense above, we point out that unexpected returns on pension investments and changes in the PBO resulting from changes in the discount rate are recognized in other comprehensive income and are subsequently recognized in current income only to the extent that they exceed certain levels. In practice, a comparatively small proportion of these deferred gains and losses is recognized in the income statement. Recently, some companies are choosing to record changes in pension obligations (PBO) resulting from changes in the discount rate ("actuarial gains and losses") in current income rather than to defer those gains and losses. Following is an excerpt from AT&T's 2010 10-K describing this accounting change:

> **Pension and Other Postretirement Benefits** In January 2011, we announced a change in our method of recognizing actuarial gains and losses for pension and other postretirement benefits for all benefit plans. Historically, we have recognized the actuarial gains and losses as a component of the Stockholders' Equity on our consolidated balance sheets on an annual basis and have amortized them into our operating results over the average future service period of the active employees of these plans, to the extent such gains and losses were outside of a corridor. We have elected to immediately recognize actuarial gains and losses in our operating results, noting that it is generally preferable to accelerate the recognition of deferred gains and losses into income rather than to delay such recognition. This change will improve transparency in our operating results by more quickly recognizing the effects of economic and interest rate conditions on plan obligations, investments and assumptions. These gains and losses are generally only measured annually as of December 31 and accordingly will be recorded during the fourth quarter. Additionally, for purposes of calculating the expected return on plan assets, we will no longer use a permitted averaging technique for the market-related value of plan assets but instead will use actual fair value of plan assets. We have applied these changes retrospectively, adjusting all prior periods. The cumulative effect of the change on retained earnings as of January 1, 2008, was a reduction of $1,533, with an offset to accumulated other comprehensive income (OCI). The annual recognition of actuarial gains and losses, which is reported as "Actuarial loss on pension and postretirement benefit plans" on our consolidated statement of cash flows total $2,521 in 2010, $215 in 2009 and $25,150 in 2008. This change did not have a material impact on cash provided by or used in operations for any period presented.

At the time of this change, AT&T reported accumulated other comprehensive income of $(14,408) million as a component of its 2009 stockholders' equity. After the change, that account increased to $2,678 million. Among other things, the significant difference in the amount of $17,422 million represented a deferred loss relating to its pension plans. The "retrospective" application of the accounting change discussed in the pension footnote above means that this deferred loss was removed from the accumulated other comprehensive income account in stockholders' equity and was recognized in earnings with the following effects on net income and the consequent reduction of retained earnings:

Year	Effect on net income
2009	$ (397) million
2008	(15,492) million
Total	(15,889) million
Adjustment to 1/1/08 retained earnings	(1,533) million
Cumulative adjustment to retained earnings	$(17,422) million

As a result of this change, $17,422 of deferred losses was recognized in income statements for prior years. Moreover, AT&T's accounting for pension cost now reflects changes in actuarial assumptions in current income. In 2012, for example, AT&T reduced the discount rate from 5.8% to 5.3%, thus increasing its PBO and resulting in the recognition of over $5 billion of additional pension cost. Although the change was unfavorable for 2012, interest rates are at historic lows and future increases in the discount rate will result in the recognition in current income of actuarial gains on AT&T's pension plans. These actuarial gains could be substantial.

Other Post-Employment Benefits

In addition to pension benefits, many companies provide health care and insurance benefits to retired employees. These benefits are referred to as **other post-employment benefits (OPEB)**. These benefits present reporting challenges similar to pension accounting. However, companies most often provide these benefits on a "pay-as-you-go" basis and it is rare for companies to make contributions in advance for OPEB. As a result, this liability, known as the **accumulated post-employment benefit obligation (APBO)**, is largely, if not totally, unfunded. GAAP requires that the unfunded APBO liability, net of any unrecognized amounts, be reported in the balance sheet and the annual service costs and interest costs be accrued as expenses each year. This requirement is controversial for two reasons. First, future health care costs are especially difficult to estimate, so the value of the resulting APBO (the present value of the future benefits) is fraught with error. Second, these benefits are provided at the discretion of the employer and can be altered or terminated at any time. Consequently, employers argue that without a legal obligation to pay these benefits, the liability should not be reported in the balance sheet.

These other post-employment benefits can produce large liabilities. For example, **FedEx**'s footnotes report a funded status for the company's health care obligation of $(790) million, consisting of an APBO liability of $790 million less no funds set aside for payment of future benefits. Our analysis of cash flows related to pension obligations can be extended to other post-employment benefit obligations. For example, in addition to its pension payments, FedEx discloses that it is obligated to make health care payments to retirees totaling about $40 million per year. Because health care obligations are rarely funded until payment is required (federal minimum funding standards do not apply to OPEB and there is no tax benefit to pre-funding), there are no investment returns to fund the payments. Our analysis of projected cash flows must consider this potential cash outflow in addition to that relating to pension obligations.

RESEARCH INSIGHT **Valuation of Nonpension Post-Employment Benefits**

The FASB requires employers to accrue the costs of all nonpension post-employment benefits; known as *accumulated post-employment benefit obligation* (APBO). These benefits consist primarily of health care and insurance. This requirement is controversial due to concerns about the reliability of the liability estimate. Research finds that the APBO (alone) is associated with company value. However, when other pension-related variables are included in the research, the APBO liability is no longer useful in explaining company value. Research concludes that the pension-related variables do a better job at conveying value-relevant information than the APBO number alone, which implies that the APBO number is less reliable.

GLOBAL ACCOUNTING

IFRS

We discussed three forms of off-balance-sheet financing. Moreover, there are several differences between U.S. GAAP and IFRS on these items, which we highlight below.

Leases IFRS lease standards currently allow for operating leases, but the standards are such that it is very difficult for a lease agreement to qualify as an operating lease. IFRS standards are more principles based and so for lease accounting, there are no bright-line rules for lease classification. Instead the parties must consider the economic substance of the transaction. In addition, IFRS will classify as capital leases (labeled *financial leases*) various "arrangements" that convey the right to use an asset or compel the company to make specified payments, but that do not take the legal form of a lease. Examples include contracts where the company must make payments regardless of whether they take delivery of the contracted product or service (take-or-pay contracts) and outsourcing contracts. This will result in more capital leases under IFRS. A minor difference is that IFRS requires the separation of land and buildings for leases that involve both.

Pensions For pension accounting, there are several disclosure differences and one notable accounting difference. The accounting difference pertains to actuarial gains and losses. As discussed in Appendix 10A, U.S. GAAP permits deferral of actuarial gains and losses and then amortizes them to net income over time. A notable difference is that IFRS companies can recognize all actuarial gains and losses in comprehensive income in the year they occur. These gains and losses are not deferred, and they are *never* reported on the IFRS income statement. Many IFRS companies select this option. Turning to disclosure, one difference is that pension expense is not reported as a single item under IFRS; various components can be aggregated with other expenses. For example, interest cost can be included with other interest expenses and reported as finance expense under IFRS. A second disclosure difference is that IFRS companies do not disclose the full funded status of their pension plan on the balance sheet as U.S. GAAP requires. However, they must do so in the footnotes. These disclosure differences make it more challenging to analyze IFRS pension costs and balance sheet items. FASB and IASB continue to work toward convergence on pension accounting.

Special Purpose Entities Companies use special purpose entities (SPE) to structure projects or transactions. Under U.S. GAAP, the primary beneficiary (the party with the power to direct SPE activities and with the obligation to absorb SPE losses) is required to consolidate the SPE. At the publication of this book, the IASB has not yet addressed the issue of SPEs. Instead, IFRS focuses on the general concept of "control" to determine if the SPE is consolidated.

MODULE-END REVIEW

Following is the pension disclosure footnote from American Airlines' 10-K report (in millions).

Pension Benefits	2012	2011
Reconciliation of benefit obligation		
Obligation at January 1	$14,568	$12,968
Service cost	341	386
Interest cost	729	757
Actuarial (gain) loss	2,345	1,237
Plan amendments	301	—
Curtailments	(1,841)	—
Benefit payments	(548)	(780)
Obligation at December 31	$15,895	$14,568
Reconciliation of fair value of plan assets		
Fair value of plan assets at January 1	$ 8,132	$ 7,773
Actual return on plan assets	1,204	614
Employer contributions	277	525
Benefit payments	(548)	(780)
Fair value of plan assets at December 31	$ 9,065	$ 8,132
Funded status at December 31	$ (6,830)	$ (6,436)

Following is American Airlines' footnote for its pension cost as reported in its income statement (in millions).

Pension Benefits	2012	2011
Components of net periodic benefit cost		
Defined benefit plans:		
Service cost	$341	$386
Interest cost	729	757
Expected return on assets	(676)	(657)
Curtailments	58	—
Amortization of:		
Prior service cost	10	13
Unrecognized net loss	211	154
Net periodic benefit cost for defined benefit plans	673	653
Defined contribution plans	202	162
	$875	$815

Required

1. In general, what factors impact a company's pension benefit obligation during a period?
2. In general, what factors impact a company's pension plan investments during a period?
3. What amount is reported on the balance sheet relating to the American Airlines pension plan?
4. How does the expected return on plan assets affect pension cost?
5. How does American Airlines' expected return on plan assets compare with its actual return (in $s) for 2012?
6. How much net pension expense is reflected in American Airlines' 2012 income statement?
7. Assess American Airlines' ability to meet payment obligations to retirees.

The solution is on page 10-54.

APPENDIX 10A: Amortization Component of Pension Expense

One of the more difficult aspects of pension accounting relates to the issue of what is recognized on-balance-sheet and what is disclosed in the footnotes off-balance-sheet. This is an important distinction, and the FASB is moving toward more on-balance-sheet recognition and less off-balance-sheet disclosure. The FASB is considering whether to eliminate deferred gains and losses, and to require recognition in the income statement of *all* changes to pension assets and liabilities. Until this standard is enacted, deferred gains and losses will only impact reported pension expense via their amortization (the fourth component of pension expense described earlier in this module).

There are three sources of *unrecognized gains and losses*:

1. The difference between actual and expected return on pension investments.
2. Changes in actuarial assumptions such as expected wage inflation, termination and mortality rates, and the discount rate used to compute the present value of the projected benefit obligation.
3. Amendments to the pension plan to provide employees with additional benefits (called **prior service costs**).

Accounting for gains and losses resulting from these three sources is the same; specifically:

- Balance sheets report the net pension asset (overfunded status) or liability (underfunded status) irrespective of the magnitude of deferred gains and losses; that is, based solely on the relative balances of the pension assets and PBO accounts.
- Cumulative unrecognized gains and losses from all sources are recorded in one account, called deferred gains and losses, which is only disclosed in the footnotes, not on-balance-sheet.
- When the balance in the deferred gains and losses account exceeds prescribed levels, companies transfer a portion of the deferred gain or loss onto the balance sheet, with a matching expense on the income statement. This is the amortization process described in the text.

Recall that a company reports the *estimated* return on pension investments as a component (reduction) of pension expense. The pension assets, however, increase (decrease) by the *actual* return (loss). The difference between the two returns is referred to as a deferred (unrecognized) gain or loss. To illustrate, let's assume that the pension plan is underfunded at the beginning of the year by $200, with pension assets of $800, a PBO of $1,000, and no deferred gains or losses. Now, let's assume that actual returns for the year of $100 exceed the long-term expected return of $70. We can illustrate the accounting for the deferred gain as follows:

	On Financial Statements				Footnotes	
Year 1	Funded Status (Liabilities)	Earned Capital	Accumulated Other Comprehensive Income (AOCI)	Income Statement	Pension Assets	PBO
Balance, Jan. 1.	$200		$ 0	$ 0	$800	$1,000
Return.	(100)	$70 (Retained Earnings) 30 (AOCI)	30	70	100	
Balance, Dec. 31	$100	$70 (Retained Earnings) 30 (AOCI)	$30	$70	$900	$1,000

The balance sheet at the beginning of the year reports the funded status of the pension plan as a $200 liability, reflecting the underfunded status of the pension plan. Neither the $800 pension asset account, nor the $1,000 PBO appear on-balance-sheet. Instead, their balances are only disclosed in a pension footnote.

During the year, pension assets (off-balance-sheet) increase by the actual return of $100 with no change in the PBO, thus decreasing the pension liability (negative funded status) by $100. The pension expense on the income statement, however, only reflects the expected return of $70, and retained earnings increase by that amount. The remaining $30 is recognized in accumulated other comprehensive income (AOCI), a component of earned capital.

These deferred gains and losses do not affect reported profit until they exceed prescribed limits, after which the excess is gradually recognized in income.[10] For example, assume that in the following year, $5 of the $30 deferred gain is amortized (recognized on the income statement as expense, which flows to retained earnings on the balance sheet). This amortization would result in the following effects:

	On Financial Statements				Footnotes	
Year 2	Funded Status (Liabilities)	Earned Capital	Accumulated Other Comprehensive Income (AOCI)	Income Statement	Pension Assets	PBO
Balance, Jan. 1.	$100	$70 (Retained Earnings) 30 (AOCI)	$30	$ 0	$900	$1,000
Amortization		$ 5 (Retained Earnings)	(5)	5		
Balance, Dec. 31 . . .	$100	$75 (Retained Earnings) 25 (AOCI)	$25	$ 5	$900	$1,000

The deferred gain is reduced by $5 and is now recognized in reported income as a reduction of pension expense. (This amortization is the fourth item in the Net Pension Expense computation table from earlier in this module.) This is the only change, as the pension assets still report a balance of $900 and the PBO reports a balance of $1,000, for a funded status of $(100) that is reported as a liability on the balance sheet.

In addition to the difference between actual and expected gains (losses) on pension assets, the deferred gains (losses) account includes increases or decreases in the PBO balance that result from changes in assumptions used to compute it, namely, the expected rate of wage inflation, termination and mortality rates for employees, and changes in the discount rate used to compute the present value of the pension obligations. Some of these can be offsetting, and all accumulate in the same deferred gains (losses) account. Justification for off-balance-sheet treatment of these items was the expectation that their offsetting nature would combine to keep the magnitude of deferred gains (losses) small. It is only in relatively extreme circumstances that this account becomes large enough to warrant amortization and, consequently, on-balance-sheet recognition. Further, the amortization portion of reported pension expense is usually small.

APPENDIX 10B: Special Purpose Entities (SPEs)

LO3 Explain the accounting for special purpose entities (SPEs).

Special purpose entities (SPEs) allow companies to structure projects or transactions with a number of financial advantages. SPEs have long been used and are an integral part of corporate finance. The SPE concept is illustrated by the following graphic that summarizes information taken from **Ford**'s 2012 10-K relating to the SPE structure it uses to securitize the receivables of Ford Credit (its financing subsidiary):

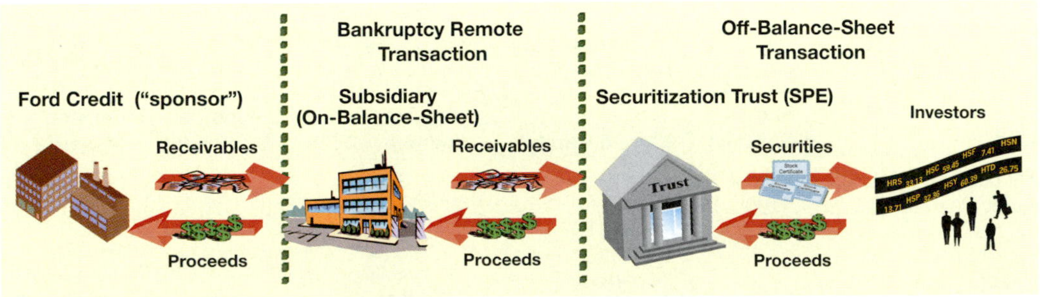

[10] The upper (lower) bound on the deferred gains (losses) account is 10% of the PBO or Plan Asset account balance, whichever is greater, at the beginning of the year. Once this limit is exceeded, the excess is amortized until the account balance is below that threshold, irrespective of whether such reduction results from amortization, or changes in the PBO or Pension Asset accounts (from changes in actuarial assumptions, company contributions, or positive investment returns).

This graphic is typical of many SPEs and has the following characteristics of all SPEs:

- A sponsoring company (here, Ford Credit) forms a subsidiary that is capitalized entirely with equity; this creates a *bankruptcy remote* structure. This means that even if Ford Credit becomes bankrupt, neither it nor its creditors will be able to access the subsidiary's assets; this reduces the risk for subsequent investors.
- The subsidiary purchases assets from the sponsoring company and sells them to a securitization (off-balance-sheet) trust (the SPE), which purchases the assets using borrowed funds (here, the SPE purchases receivables from Ford Credit's subsidiary using cash from investors).
- Cash flows from the acquired assets are used by the SPE to repay its debt (here, the SPE collects receivables and uses the funds to repay any borrowings).

The sponsoring company benefits in two ways. First, SPEs create direct economic benefits by speeding up receipt of the company's operating cash flows and by mitigating certain types of risk. Second, SPEs create indirect economic benefits by providing financial reporting benefits and alternatives. These indirect benefits derive from having assets, and their related debt, moved off-balance-sheet. Also, the SPE owns the sponsoring company's former assets. Thus, the sponsoring company enjoys an improved asset turnover ratio (assets are typically less in the denominator of the turnover ratio) and an improved financial leverage ratio (liabilities are less in the numerator of the liabilities-to-equity ratio).

Applying SPEs as Financing Tools

This section describes two common means of using SPEs as financing tools.

Asset Securitization

Consumer finance companies, retailers, and financial subsidiaries of manufacturing companies commonly use SPEs to securitize (sell) their financial assets. **Ford Credit**, the finance subsidiary of **Ford Motor Company**, provides a common example as illustrated in the MD&A of Ford's 2012 10-K report.

> **Funding** Ford Credit's funding sources include primarily securitization transactions (including other structured financings) and unsecured debt. Ford Credit issues both short- and long-term debt that is held by both institutional and retail investors, with long-term debt having an original maturity of more than 12 months. Ford Credit sponsors a number of securitization programs that can be structured to provide both short- and long-term funding through institutional investors in the United States and international capital markets.

Funding Portfolio. The chart below details the trends in the funding of Ford Credit's managed receivables:

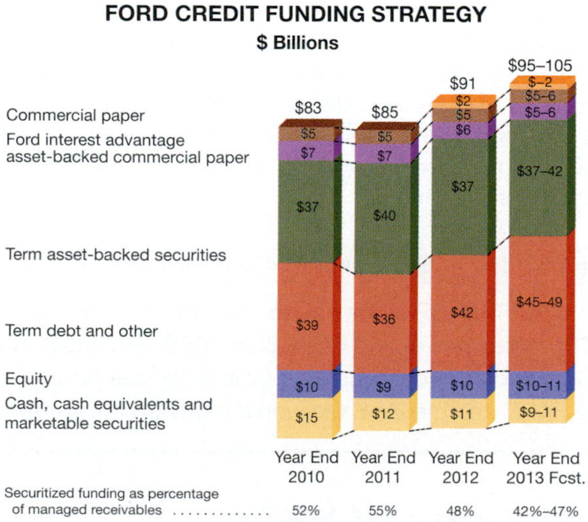

Ford Credit's use of SPEs is typical. As Ford Credit provides financing to customers who purchase autos from Ford Motor Company, it accumulates the receivables on its balance sheet. Periodically, through a subsidiary, it packages certain receivables and sells them to its SPE, which funds the purchase by selling certificates entitling the holder to a portion of the cash receipts from eventual collection of receivables. Ford Credit does not provide any other form of protection to the outside certificate holders (its footnote indicates that the receivables are sold "without recourse," meaning without collection rights against Ford Credit or its parent, Ford Motor Company). As the footnote disclosure presented above illustrates, the phrase asset-backed securities (securitizations) highlighted in green represent a substantial source of Ford's overall funding.

Ford Motor Company's credit ratings have declined in recent years, thus making its unsecured borrowings more costly and limiting its availability to borrow funds. In response, it has increased its use of SPEs as a financing source. This funding mechanism is now an important source of liquidity for the company, as Ford Credit's cost of debt capital is substantially less, and exhibits less volatility, than that for Ford Motor Company. Thus, Ford's use of SPEs as a funding source provides necessary liquidity and also provides capital at a substantially lower interest rate. Due to the SPE's limited scope of operations, and its isolation from the general business risk of the parent company, the SPE's lenders face lower risk of default and can, therefore, charge a comparatively lower rate of interest on money they lend to the SPE.

Project and Real Estate Financing

Another common use of SPEs is to finance construction projects. For example, a sponsoring company desires to construct a manufacturing plant. It establishes an SPE and executes a contract with the SPE to build the plant and to later purchase output from the plant. The SPE uses the contract, and the newly constructed manufacturing plant assets, to collateralize debt that it issues to finance the plant's construction. The sponsoring company obtains the benefits of the plant, but does not recognize either the PPE asset or the related liability on its balance sheet. The sponsoring company has commitments with the SPE, labeled executory contracts, but GAAP currently does not require such contracts be recognized in the balance sheet, nor does it even require footnote disclosure of these contracts.

Clothing retailers such as **The Gap** and **Abercrombie & Fitch** use these types of executory contracts involving outside manufacturers. The manufacturing assets, and related liabilities, are reported on the balance sheet of the SPE and not of the company itself.

A slight variation is to add leasing to this transaction. To illustrate, assume a company desires to construct an office building. It establishes an SPE to construct and finance the building and then leases the building back from the SPE under an operating lease. As we explained earlier in this module, if the lease is structured as an operating lease, neither the lease asset nor the lease obligation is reported on the company's balance sheet. Thus, the company obtains the use and benefit of the building without recording either the building or the related debt on its balance sheet.

Reporting of SPEs Designated as VIEs

Special purpose entities that meet the test to be designated as a Variable Interest Entity (VIE), such as those that Ford uses to securitize its loan and lease assets, must be consolidated by the primary beneficiary, whichever company has the power to direct the activities of the VIE and the right to receive its benefits (or absorb the losses). As we discuss in Module 9, for companies that issue common stock, consolidation means that the balance sheet and income statement of the VIE are reported together with that of the parent company. The consolidation of VIEs is no different and their financial statements must be combined with those of the sponsoring company (Ford Credit in this case).

The effect of consolidation of VIEs is to report both the loan and lease receivables on Ford's consolidated balance sheet as well as the liabilities of the VIE. Similarly, the loan and lease income is reported in Ford's income statement together with the VIE's expenses, including interest expense on borrowed funds. As a result, the securitization process is fully reflected in Ford's financial statements. Further, companies are required to provide extensive disclosures relating to the magnitude of the assets securitized and the effects (and risks) on their liquidity of reliable access to securitization credit markets.

IFRS

IFRS INSIGHT **Consolidation of SPEs under IFRS**

Under both U.S. GAAP and IFRS, SPEs are consolidated based on the transfer of risks and rewards. But unlike GAAP's more rules-based orientation, IFRS requires a more conceptual analysis of risks and rewards. This leads to consolidation of more special purpose entities under IFRS as compared to GAAP. The FASB and the IASB are working toward convergence on this standard.

Analysis Implications of SPEs

Despite that SPEs which have been designated as VIEs are consolidated in the financial statements of the sponsoring company, the securitization process continues to provide a lower-cost financing source to companies by reducing credit risk for the lenders. Accordingly, SPEs will continue to be part of the business landscape. As such, there are at least two analysis implications related to SPEs:

- **Cost of capital**. As discussed, SPEs reduce business risk and bankruptcy risk for their lenders. Consequently, the sponsoring company is able to obtain capital at a lower cost. Ford Motor Company (a manufacturer), for example, has witnessed a reduction in its credit ratings and a consequent increase in its cost of borrowed funds. Ordinarily, its negative credit rating would be ascribed to its subsidiaries as well, including its finance subsidiary. Using SPEs, however, the finance subsidiary, Ford Credit, is able to obtain financing at lower interest rates, which allows it to pass along that lower cost in the form of lower interest rates on auto and other loans to its customers. Without that financing source, Ford Credit would be less competitive in the marketplace vis-à-vis other, financially stronger, financial institutions.
- **Liquidity**. Financial institutions, and finance subsidiaries of manufacturing companies, rely on a business model of generating a high volume of loans, each of which carries a relatively small profit (spread of the interest rate over the cost of the funds). If they were forced to hold all of those loans on their own balance sheets, they would eventually need to raise costly equity capital to balance the increase in debt financing. That would also serve to reduce their competitiveness in the marketplace. These companies must, therefore, be able to package loans for sale, a crucial source of liquidity.

Given the importance of the cash flows contributed by its Ford Credit financing subsidiary to Ford Motor Company, analysts would be concerned about the welfare of the overall entity were there indications that its SPE financing sources would no longer be available (say, if further accounting standards limited Ford's ability to remove these loans from its consolidated balance sheet and record their transfer to the SPE as a sale). Analysts would also be concerned if the credit markets no longer favored this SPE structure as a financing mechanism (say, if the presumed bankruptcy protection of the SPEs was ultimately proven to be false following the bankruptcy of the sponsoring company and the consequent bankruptcy of an SPE that it sponsored). Neither of these events has occurred, and lenders rely on legal opinions that SPEs are "bankruptcy remote." Analysts must always assess these risks when assessing the financial strength of companies that rely on the SPE financial structure.

APPENDIX 10C: Lease Capitalization Using a Calculator and Present Value Tables

This Appendix identifies the keystrokes to compute both the present value of projected operating lease payments and the imputed discount rate using two popular financial calculators: **Hewlett-Packard 10bII** and **Texas Instruments BA II Plus**. It also computes the present value of projected lease payments using present value tables.

Hewlett-Packard 10bII: Present value of projected operating lease payments

Following are the keystrokes to compute the present value of the Southwest Airlines projected lease payments. This approach utilizes the same computational steps as our illustrations.

Enter #	Key[a]	
1	**P/YR**	Enter the number of periods per year
0	**CF_j**	Enter the cash flow in year 0 (current year)
688	**CF_j**	Enter the cash flow in year 1
614	**CF_j**	Enter the cash flow in year 2
507	**CF_j**	Enter the cash flow in year 3
392	**CF_j**	Enter the cash flow in year 4
369	**CF_j**	Enter the cash flow in year 5 (and assumed thereafter)
5	**N_j**	Enter the number of years the year 5 cash flow is paid (including year 5)
347	**CF_j**	Enter the cash flow in final partial year ($369 × 0.94 years)
5.67	**I/YR**	Enter the annual discount rate
	NPV	Press **NPV** button to get present value ($3,403)

[a] To enter a number, type the number and then press the corresponding key; for example, to enter P/YR, type "1" and then press **P/YR**.

Hewlett-Packard 10bII: Imputed discount rate

This example computes the imputed discount rate given the capitalized lease disclosures in the lease footnote; we again use Southwest Airlines.

Enter #	Key[a]	
1	**P/YR**	Enter the number of periods per year
−36[a]	**CF_j**	Enter the cash flow in year 0 (current year)
5	**CF_j**	Enter the cash flow in year 1
6	**CF_j**	Enter the cash flow in year 2
6	**CF_j**	Enter the cash flow in year 3
5	**CF_j**	Enter the cash flow in year 4
6	**CF_j**	Enter the cash flow in year 5 (and assumed thereafter)
4[b]	**N_j**	Enter the number of years the year 5 cash flow is paid (including year 5)
	IRR	Press **IRR** button to get implicit discount rate (5.67%)

[a] To enter a negative number, type in the absolute value of that number and then press +/− button; for example, to enter the initial cash flow in year 0, enter "36", press +/−, and then press **CF_j**.

[b] In this case, the company's payments in year 6 and beyond are an exact multiple of the year 5 payment. If such is not the case, enter the cash flow in the partial year after you enter the number of years. For example, if the payments after year 5 had totalled $20 instead of $18, we would have entered 2 and then CF_j and then entered IRR.

Texas Instruments BA II Plus: Present value of projected operating lease payments

Following are the keystrokes to compute the present value of the Southwest Airlines projected operating lease payments. This approach utilizes the same computational steps as our illustrations.

Key	Enter # [a]	
FORMAT	0	Press the **FORMAT** button and enter decimal places desired
CF	0	Enter the cash flow in year 0 (**CF_0**)
↓	688	Enter the cash flow in year 1 (**CO1**)
↓		Frequency (**FO1**) should be pre-set at "1", so nothing need be entered
↓	614	Enter the cash flow in year 2 (**CO2**)
↓		Frequency (**FO2**) should be pre-set at "1"
↓	507	Enter the cash flow in year 3 (**CO3**)
↓		Frequency (**FO3**) should be pre-set at "1"
↓	392	Enter the cash flow in year 4 (**CO4**)
↓		Frequency (**FO4**) should be pre-set at "1"
↓	369	Enter the cash flow in year 5 (**CO5**) and assumed thereafter
↓	5	Enter the number of years the year 5 cash flow is paid (including year 5) (**FO5**)
↓	347	Enter the cash flow in final partial year (369 × 0.94 years) (**CO6**)
↓		Frequency (**FO6**) should be pre-set at "1"
NPV	5.67	Press **NPV** button, the pre-set discount rate should say "0"; enter "5.67" the discount rate
↓, **CPT**	3,403	Press ↓ button and then press **CPT** to get present value

[a] After entering in a number from this column, press **ENTER**.

Texas Instruments BA II Plus: Imputed discount rate

Following are the keystrokes to compute the imputed discount rate of the Southwest Airlines projected capital lease payments. This approach utilizes the same computational steps as our illustrations.

Key	Enter[a]	
CF	−36[a]	Enter the cash flow in year 0 (CF_0)
↓	5	Enter the cash flow in year 1 (CO1)
↓		Frequency (FO1) should be pre-set at "1"
↓	6	Enter the cash flow in year 2 (CO2)
↓		Frequency (FO2) should be pre-set at "1"
↓	6	Enter the cash flow in year 3 (CO3)
↓		Frequency (FO3) should be pre-set at "1"
↓	5	Enter the cash flow in year 4 (CO4)
↓		Frequency (FO4) should be pre-set at "1"
↓	6	Enter the cash flow in year 5 and assumed thereafter (CO5)
↓	4[b]	Enter the number of years the year 5 cash flow is paid (including year 5) (FO5)
IRR		Press **IRR** button, the pre-set IRR should say "0"
↓, CPT		Press ↓ button and then press **CPT** to get implicit discount rate

[a] After typing in a number from this column, press **ENTER**.

[b] To enter a negative number, type in the absolute value of that number and then press +/− button; for example, to enter the initial cash flow in year 0, press **CF**, enter "36", press +/−, and then press **ENTER**.

Lease Capitalization Using Present Value Tables

Present value tables list the factors for selected interest rates and discount periods (often in whole numbers). To compute the present value of the operating lease payments using those tables (see Appendix A near the end of this book), we must first round the remaining lease term (4.94 for Southwest Airlines) to the nearest whole year (5), and round the discount rate (5.67% for Southwest Airlines) to its nearest whole interest rate (6%). After that, computation of the present value of future operating lease payments is identical to the spreadsheet method and is shown below. We see that the present value of each projected lease payment for Years 1 through 5 is computed using the present value factor for that particular year (taken from tables similar to Appendix A, Table 1, "Present Value of Single Amount") using a discount rate of 6%. To compute the present value of the lease payments remaining after Year 5, we again assume that lease payments continue at the Year 5 amount for the remainder of the lease term. Those payments represent an annuity, $369 for 5 years (4.94 rounded to 5), that is discounted at 6% (taken from tables similar to Appendix A, Table 2, "Present Value of Ordinary Annuity"), which is then discounted back five more years to the present.

Year ($ millions)	Operating Lease Payment	Discount Factor (i = 0.06)	Present Value
1.	$ 688	0.94340	$ 649
2.	614	0.89000	546
3.	507	0.83962	426
4.	392	0.79209	310
5.	369	0.74726	276
>5.	1,823 [$369 for 4.94 years]	4.21236 × 0.74726	1,162
			$3,369
Remaining life.	$1,823 [$369 for 4.94 years, rounded to 5 years].		

Regardless of the method used, the computed amount is the present value of future operating lease payments. That value is $3,403 million using the spreadsheet method, $3,403 million using a calculator, and $3,369 million using present value tables.

GUIDANCE ANSWERS

MANAGERIAL DECISION **You Are the Division President**

Lease terms that are not advantageous to your company but are structured merely to achieve off-balance-sheet financing can destroy shareholder value. Long-term shareholder value is created by managing your operation well, including negotiating leases with acceptable terms. Lease footnote disclosures also provide sufficient information for skilled analysts to undo the operating lease treatment. This means that you can end up with de facto capitalization of a lease with lease terms that are not in the best interests of your company and with few benefits from off-balance-sheet financing. There is also the potential for lost credibility with stakeholders.

Superscript $^{A\,(B,\,C)}$ denotes assignments based on Appendix 10A (B, C).

DISCUSSION QUESTIONS

Q10-1. What are the financial reporting differences between an operating lease and a capital lease? Explain.

Q10-2. Are footnote disclosures sufficient to overcome nonrecognition on the balance sheet of assets and related liabilities for operating leases? Explain.

Q10-3. Is the expense of a lease over its entire life the same whether or not it is capitalized? Explain.

Q10-4. What are the economic and accounting differences between a defined contribution plan and a defined benefit plan?

Q10-5. Under what circumstances will a company report a net pension asset? A net pension liability?

Q10-6. What are the components of pension expense that are reported in the income statement?

Q10-7. What effect does the use of expected returns on pension investments and the deferral of unexpected gains and losses on those investments have on income?

Q10-8. What is a special purpose entity (SPE)? Provide an example of the use of an SPE as a financing vehicle.

Q10-9. What effect does consolidating SPEs have on both accounting for SPEs and the balance sheets of companies that sponsor them?

Assignments with the ✔ in the margin are available in myBusinessCourse.
See the Preface of the book for details.

MINI EXERCISES

M10-10. Analyzing and Interpreting Lease Footnote Disclosures (LO1)

The GAP, Inc. (GPS)

The GAP, Inc., discloses the following schedule to its 2013 10-K report relating to its leasing activities.

The aggregate minimum noncancelable annual lease payments under leases in effect on February 2, 2013, are as follows:

Fiscal Year ($ millions)	
2013	$1,093
2014	1,069
2015	924
2016	753
2017	584
Thereafter	1,709
Total minimum lease commitments	$6,132

a. Compute the present value of GAP's operating leases using a 6% discount rate and round the remaining lease term to the nearest whole year.

b. What types of adjustments might we consider to GAP's balance sheet and income statement for analysis purposes?

M10-11. Analyzing and Capitalizing Operating Lease Payments Disclosed in Footnotes (LO1)
Costco Wholesale Corporation discloses the following in footnotes to its 10-K report relating to its leasing activities.

Costco Wholesale Corp. (COST)

At the end of 2013, future minimum payments . . . under noncancelable leases with terms of at least one year were as follows ($ millions):

2014	$ 189
2015	175
2016	167
2017	160
2018	153
Thereafter	1,753
Total	$2,597

Operating leases are not reflected on-balance-sheet. In our analysis of a company, we often capitalize these operating leases, that is, add the present value of the future operating lease payments to both the reported assets and liabilities.

a. Compute the present value of Costco's operating lease payments assuming a 6% discount rate and round the remaining lease term to the nearest whole year.
b. What effect does capitalization of operating leases have on Costco's total liabilities and total assets (it reported total liabilities and total assets of $19,271 million and $30,283 million, respectively)?

M10-12. Analyzing and Interpreting Pension Disclosures—Expenses and Returns (LO2)
Stanley Black & Decker, Inc. discloses the following pension footnote in its 10-K report.

Stanley Black & Decker, Inc. (SWK)

($ millions)	2012
Service cost	$ 6.6
Interest cost	62.9
Expected return on plan assets	(67.1)
Prior service cost amortization	1.0
Transition obligation amortization	—
Actuarial loss amortization	6.2
Settlement/curtailment loss (gain)	11.3
Net periodic pension expense	$ 20.9

a. How much pension expense does Stanley Black & Decker report in its 2012 income statement?
b. Explain, in general, how expected return on plan assets affects reported pension expense. How did expected return affect Stanley Black & Decker's 2012 pension expense?
c. Explain use of the word "expected" as it relates to pension plan assets.

M10-13. Analyzing and Interpreting Pension Disclosures—PBO and Funded Status (LO2)
YUM! Brands, Inc., discloses the following pension footnote in its 10-K report.

YUM! Brands, Inc. (YUM)

Pension Benefit Obligation ($ millions)	2012	2011
Change in benefit obligation		
Benefit obligation at beginning of year	$1,381	$1,108
Service cost	26	24
Interest cost	66	64
Participant contributions	—	—
Plan amendments	5	—
Curtailments	(10)	(7)
PBO reduction in excess of settlement payments	(74)	—
Special termination benefits	3	5
Exchange rate changes	—	—
Benefits paid	(14)	(11)
Settlement payments	(278)	(29)
Actuarial (gain) loss	185	227
Benefit obligation at end of year	$1,290	$1,381

a. Explain the terms "service cost" and "interest cost."
b. How do actuarial losses arise?
c. The fair value of YUM!'s pension assets is $945 million as of 2012. What is the funded status of the plan, and how will this be reflected on YUM!'s balance sheet?

M10-14. Analyzing and Interpreting Pension Disclosures—Plan Assets and Cash Flow (LO2)

YUM! Brands, Inc. (YUM)

YUM! Brands, Inc., discloses the following pension footnote in its 10-K report.

Pension Plan Assets ($ millions)	2012	2011
Fair value of plan assets at beginning of year	$998	$907
Actual return on plan assets	144	83
Employer contributions	100	53
Participant contributions	—	—
Settlement payments	(278)	(29)
Benefits paid	(14)	(11)
Exchange rate changes	—	—
Administrative expenses	(5)	(5)
Fair value of plan assets at end of year	$945	$998

a. How does the "actual return on plan assets" of $144 million affect YUM!'s reported profits for 2012?
b. What are the cash flow implications of the pension plan for YUM! in 2012?
c. YUM!'s pension plan paid out $14 million in benefits during 2012. Where else is this payment reflected?

M10-15. Analyzing and Interpreting Retirement Benefit Footnote (LO2)

Abercrombie & Fitch Co. (ANF)

Abercrombie & Fitch Co. discloses the following footnote relating to its retirement plans in its 2012 10-K report.

Retirement Benefits The Company maintains the Abercrombie & Fitch Co. Savings & Retirement Plan, a qualified plan. All U.S. associates are eligible to participate in this plan if they are at least 21 years of age and have completed a year of employment with 1,000 or more hours of service. In addition, the Company maintains the Abercrombie & Fitch Co. Nonqualified Savings and Supplemental Retirement, composed of two sub-plans (Plan I and Plan II). Plan I contains contributions made through December 31, 2004, while Plan II contains contributions made on and after January 1, 2005. Participation in these plans is based on service and compensation. The Company's contributions are based on a percentage of associates' eligible annual compensation. The cost of the Company's contributions to these plans was $21.1 million in Fiscal 2012, $16.4 million in Fiscal 2011 and $19.4 million in Fiscal 2010.

a. Does Abercrombie have a defined contribution or defined benefit pension plan? Explain.
b. How does Abercrombie account for its contributions to its retirement plan?
c. How does Abercrombie report its obligation for its retirement plan on the balance sheet?

M10-16. Analyzing and Interpreting Lease Disclosure (LO1)

Dow Chemical Company (DOW)

Dow Chemical Company provided the following footnote in its 2012 10-K report relating to operating leases.

Leased Property The Company routinely leases premises for use as sales and administrative offices, warehouses and tanks for product storage, motor vehicles, railcars, computers, office machines, and equipment under operating leases. In addition, the Company leases aircraft in the United States. At the termination of the leases, the Company has the option to purchase certain leased equipment and buildings based on a fair market value determination. Rental expenses under operating leases, net of sublease rental income, were $476 million in 2012, $437 million in 2011 and $404 million in 2010. Future minimum rental payments under operating leases with remaining noncancelable terms in excess of one year are as follows:

continued

Minimum Operating Lease Commitments (in millions)	December 31, 2012
2013	$ 223
2014	216
2015	177
2016	150
2017	121
2018 and thereafter	1,322
Total	$2,209

Required

a. Dow describes all of its leases as "operating." What is the significance of this designation?

b. How might we treat these operating leases in our analysis of the company?

M10-17. Analyzing and Interpreting Disclosure on Contract Manufacturers (LO3)

Nike, Inc. (NKE)

Nike, Inc. reports the following information relating to its manufacturing activities in footnotes to its 10-K report for the year ended May 31, 2013.

Manufacturing Virtually all of our footwear is manufactured outside of the United States by independent contract manufacturers. In fiscal 2013, contract factories in Vietnam, China and Indonesia manufactured approximately 42%, 30%, and 26% of total NIKE Brand footwear, respectively.

We also have manufacturing agreements with independent factories in Argentina, Brazil, India, and Mexico to manufacture footwear for sale primarily within those countries. The largest single footwear factory with which we have contracted accounted for approximately 6% of total fiscal 2013 NIKE Brand footwear production. Almost all of NIKE Brand apparel is manufactured outside of the United States by independent contract manufacturers located in 28 countries. Most of this apparel production occurred in China, Vietnam, Thailand, Indonesia, Sri Lanka, Pakistan, Malaysia, Turkey, Mexico, and Cambodia. The largest single apparel factory that we have contracted with accounted for approximately 6% of total fiscal 2013 apparel production.

a. What effect does the use of contract manufacturers have on Nike's balance sheet?

b. How does Nike's use of contract manufacturers affect Nike's return on net operating assets (RNOA) and its components, net operating profit margin (NOPM) and net operating asset turnover (NOAT)? Explain.

c. Nike executes agreements with its contract manufacturers to purchase their output. How are such "executory contracts" reported under GAAP? Does your answer suggest a possible motivation for the use of contract manufacturing?

M10-18. Analyzing and Interpreting Pension Plan Benefit Footnotes (LO2)

Lockheed Martin Corp. (LMT)

Lockheed Martin Corporation discloses the following funded status for its defined benefit pension plans in its 10-K report.

Defined Benefit Pension Plans (In millions)	2012	2011
Unfunded status of the plans	$(15,093)	$(13,324)

Lockheed contributed $3,637 million to its pension plan assets in 2012, up from $2,285 million in the prior year. The company also reports that it is obligated for the following expected payments to retirees in the next five years.

(In millions)	Qualified Pension Benefits
2013	$ 1,900
2014	1,970
2015	2,050
2016	2,130
2017	2,220
Years 2018–2020	12,880

a. How is this funded status reported in Lockheed's balance sheet under current GAAP?

b. How should we interpret this funded status in our analysis of the company?

c. What likely effect would a substantial decline in the financial markets have on Lockheed's contribution to its pension plans? Explain.

EXERCISES

Lowe's Companies (LOW)

E10-19. Analyzing and Interpreting Leasing Footnote (LO1)

Lowe's Companies, Inc., reports the following footnote relating to its leased facilities in its fiscal 2012 10-K report for the year ended February 1, 2013.

The Company leases facilities and land for certain facilities under agreements with original terms generally of 20 years. . . . The future minimum rental payments required under operating leases and capitalized lease obligations having initial or remaining noncancelable lease terms in excess of one year are summarized as follows:

(In millions)	Operating Leases	Lease Obligations	Total
2013	$ 420	$ 79	$ 499
2014	412	76	488
2015	409	68	477
2016	406	56	462
2017	395	46	441
Later years	3,478	383	3,861
Total minimum lease payments	$5,520	708	$6,228
Less amount representing interest		(289)	
Present value of minimum lease payments		419	
Less current maturities		(44)	
Present value of minimum lease payments, less current maturities		$375	

a. Using your financial calculator or Excel spreadsheet, confirm that Lowe's capitalized its capital leases using a rate of 9.47%. Lowe's labels its capital leases "Lease Obligations."

b. What effect does the failure to capitalize operating leases have on Lowe's balance sheet? Over the life of the lease, what effect does this classification have on net income?

c. Compute the present value of these operating leases using a discount rate of 9% and round the remaining lease term to the nearest whole year. How might we use this information in our analysis of the company?

E10-20. Analyzing and Interpreting Footnote on Operating and Capital Leases (LO1)

Verizon Communications, Inc. (VZ)

Verizon Communications, Inc., provides the following footnote relating to leasing activities in its 10-K report.

The aggregate minimum rental commitments under noncancelable leases for the periods shown at December 31, 2012, are as follows:

Years (dollars in millions)	Capital Leases	Operating Leases
2013	$ 86	$ 2,038
2014	67	1,840
2015	57	1,572
2016	54	1,280
2017	44	992
Thereafter	99	4,119
Total minimum rental commitments	407	$11,841
Less interest and executory costs	109	
Present value of minimum lease payments	298	
Less current installments	64	
Long-term obligation at December 31, 2012	**$234**	

a. Using your financial calculator or Excel spreadsheet, confirm that Verizon capitalized its capital leases using a rate of 9.44%.

b. What effect does the failure to capitalize operating leases have on Verizon's balance sheet? Over the life of its leases, what effect does this lease classification have on net income?

c. Compute the present value of Verizon's operating leases, assuming a 9.44% discount rate and rounding the remaining lease life to three decimal places. How might we use this additional information in our analysis of the company?

E10-21. Analyzing, Interpreting and Capitalizing Operating Leases (LO1)

Staples, Inc. (SPLS)

Staples, Inc., reports the following footnote relating to its operating leases in its 10-K report for the fiscal year ended February 2013 ($ thousands).

Future minimum lease commitments due for retail, distribution, fulfillment and support facilities (including restructured facilities, commitments related to discontinued operations, and lease commitments for three retail stores not yet opened at February 2, 2013) and equipment leases under noncancelable operating leases are as follows (in thousands):

Fiscal Year	Total
2013	$ 838,677
2014	730,008
2015	617,862
2016	511,859
2017	398,157
Thereafter	1,032,307
	$4,128,870

a. What dollar adjustment(s) might we consider to Staples' balance sheet and income statement given this information and assuming that Staples intermediate-term borrowing rate is 8% and rounding the remaining lease life to the nearest whole year? Explain.

b. Would the adjustment from part *a* make a substantial difference to Staples' total liabilities? (Staples reported total assets of nearly $12 billion and total liabilities of nearly $6 billion for 2013.)

YUM! Brands, Inc. (YUM)

E10-22. Analyzing, Interpreting and Capitalizing Operating Leases (LO1)
YUM! Brands, Inc., reports the following footnote relating to its capital and operating leases in its 2012 10-K report ($ millions).

Future minimum commitments . . . under noncancelable leases are set forth below. At December 29, 2012, and December 31, 2011, the present value of minimum payments under capital leases was $170 million and $279 million, respectively.

Commitments ($ millions)	Capital	Operating
2013	$ 18	$ 678
2014	18	634
2015	19	592
2016	19	556
2017	17	500
Thereafter	189	2,714
	$280	$5,674

a. Confirm that the implicit rate on YUM!'s capital leases is 6.66%. Using a 6.66% discount rate, compute the present value of YUM!'s operating leases and rounding the remaining lease life to three decimal places. Describe the adjustments we might consider to YUM!'s balance sheet and income statement using that information.
b. YUM! reported total liabilities of $6,699 million for 2012. Would the adjustment from part *a* make a substantial difference to YUM!'s total liabilities? Explain.

TJX Companies, Inc. (TJX)

E10-23. Analyzing, Interpreting and Capitalizing Operating Leases (LO1)
TJX Companies, Inc. reports the following footnote relating to its capital and operating leases in its 10-K report.

The following is a schedule of future minimum lease payments for continuing operations as of February 2, 2013:

Fiscal Year ($ 000s)	Operating Leases
2014	$1,185,379
2015	1,104,693
2016	975,405
2017	819,532
2018	667,721
Later years	1,966,484
Total future minimum lease payments	$6,719,214

Required
a. Using a 7% discount rate and rounding the remaining lease life to the nearest whole year, compute the present value of TJX's operating leases. Explain the adjustments we might consider to its balance sheet and income statement using that information.
b. TJX reported total liabilities of nearly $5.85 billion for fiscal 2013. Would the adjustment from part *a* make a substantial difference to the company's total liabilities? Explain.

E10-24. Analyzing and Interpreting Pension Disclosures (LO2)

General Mills, Inc. (GIS)

General Mills, Inc. reports the following pension footnote in its 10-K report.

Defined Benefit Pension Plans (In millions)	Fiscal Year 2013	Fiscal Year 2012
Change in Plan Assets		
Fair value at beginning of year	$4,353.9	$4,264.0
Actual return on assets	698.7	56.3
Employer contributions	223.1	222.1
Plan participant contributions	15.2	20.3
Benefits payments	(222.6)	(203.3)
Foreign currency	(2.2)	(5.5)
Fair value at end of year	$5,066.1	$4,353.9
Change in Projected Benefit Obligation		
Benefit obligation at beginning of year	$4,991.5	$4,458.4
Service cost	124.4	114.3
Interest cost	237.3	237.9
Plan amendment	0.2	(13.4)
Curtailment/other	—	(27.1)
Plan participant contributions	15.2	20.3
Medicare Part D reimbursements	—	—
Actuarial loss (gain)	237.5	405.7
Benefits payments	(222.8)	(203.5)
Foreign currency	(1.9)	(5.9)
Acquisitions	—	4.8
Projected benefit obligation at end of year	$5,381.4	$4,991.5

Estimated benefit payments . . . are expected to be paid from fiscal 2014–2023 as follows:

(in millions)	Defined Benefit Pension Plans
2014	$ 236.3
2015	243.6
2016	251.6
2017	260.6
2018	270.1
2019–2023	1,512.3

a. Describe what is meant by *service cost* and *interest cost.*

b. What is the total amount paid to retirees during fiscal 2013? What is the source of funds to make these payments to retirees?

c. Compute the 2013 funded status for the company's pension plan.

d. What are actuarial gains and losses? What are the plan amendment adjustments, and how do they differ from the actuarial gains and losses?

e. General Mills projects payments to retirees of over $236 million per year. How is the company able to contribute only $223.1 million to its pension plan?

f. What effect would a substantial decline in the financial markets have on General Mills' contribution to its pension plans?

E10-25. Analyzing and Interpreting Pension and Health Care Footnote (LO2)

Xerox Corporation (XRX)

Xerox Corporation reports the following pension and retiree health care ("Other") footnote as part of its 10-K report.

(in millions)	Pension Benefits 2012	Pension Benefits 2011	Retiree Health 2012	Retiree Health 2011
Change in Benefit Obligation				
Benefit obligation, January 1	$10,505	$ 9,731	$1,007	$ 1,006
Service cost	195	186	9	8
Interest cost	552	612	42	47
Plan participants' contributions	9	10	19	33
Actuarial loss	1,017	916	18	26
Currency exchange rate changes	232	(85)	4	(3)
Curtailments	(1)	—	—	—
Benefits paid/settlements	(765)	(870)	(103)	(106)
Other	(3)	5	(7)	(4)
Benefit obligation, December 31	**$11,741**	**$10,505**	**$ 989**	**$ 1,007**
Change in Plan Assets				
Fair value of plan assets, January 1	$ 8,277	$ 7,940	$ —	$ —
Actual return on plan assets	792	694	—	—
Employer contribution	494	556	84	73
Plan participants' contributions	9	10	19	33
Currency exchange rate changes	197	(57)	—	—
Benefits paid/settlements	(765)	(870)	(103)	(106)
Other	—	4	—	—
Fair value of plan assets, December 31	**$ 9,004**	**$ 8,277**	**$ —**	**$ —**
Net funded status at December 31	**$ (2,737)**	**$ (2,228)**	**$ (989)**	**$(1,007)**

(in millions)	Pension Benefits 2012	Pension Benefits 2011	Retiree Health 2012	Retiree Health 2011
Components of Net Periodic Benefit Cost				
Service cost	$195	$186	$ 9	$ 8
Interest cost	552	612	42	47
Expected return on plan assets	(613)	(647)	—	—
Recognized net actuarial loss	106	72	1	—
Amortization of prior service credit	(23)	(23)	(41)	(41)
Recognized settlement loss	83	84		
Recognized curtailment gain	—	(107)		
Defined benefit plans	300	177		
Defined contribution plans	63	66		
Total net periodic cost	**$363**	**$243**	**$11**	**$14**
Other Changes in Plan Assets and Benefit Obligations Recognized in Other Comprehensive Income				
Net actuarial loss	$843	$750	$18	$25
Prior service credit	(3)	(3)	(6)	(3)
Amortization of net actuarial loss	(189)	(167)	(1)	—
Amortization of net prior service credit	23	23	41	41
Curtailment gain	—	107	—	—
Total recognized in other comprehensive income	$674	$710	$52	$63

a. Describe what is meant by *service cost* and *interest cost* (the service and interest costs appear both in the reconciliation of the PBO and in the computation of pension expense).

b. What is the actual return on the pension and the health care ("Other") plan investments in 2012? Was Xerox's profitability impacted by this amount?

c. Provide an example under which an "actuarial loss," such as the $843 million loss in 2012 that Xerox reports, might arise.

d. What is the source of funds to make payments to retirees?

e. How much did Xerox contribute to its pension and health care plans in 2012?

f. How much cash did retirees receive in 2012 from the pension plan and the health care plan? How much cash did Xerox pay these retirees in 2012?

g. Show the computation of the 2012 funded status for the pension and health care plans.

h.[A] The company reports $843 million "Net actuarial loss" in the table relating to other comprehensive income, a credit of $3 million relating to "Prior service credit," a loss of $(189) million relating to "Amortization of net actuarial loss," and a credit of $23 million relating to "Amortization of prior service credit" in the net periodic benefit cost table. Describe the process by which these amounts are transferred from other comprehensive income to pension expense in the income statement.

E10-26. Analyzing and Interpreting Pension and Health Care Disclosures (LO2)

Verizon Communications Inc. reports the following pension and health care benefits footnote as part of its 10-K report.

Verizon Communications Inc. (VZ)

	Pension		Healthcare	
At December 31 (dollars in millions)	**2012**	**2011**	**2012**	**2011**
Change in Benefit Obligations				
Beginning of year	**$30,582**	$29,217	**$ 27,369**	$ 25,718
Service cost	**358**	307	**359**	299
Interest cost	**1,449**	1,590	**1,284**	1,421
Plan amendments	**183**	(485)	**(1,826)**	—
Actuarial loss, net	**6,074**	3,360	**1,402**	1,687
Benefits paid	**(2,735)**	(2,564)	**(1,744)**	(1,756)
Annuity purchase	**(8,352)**	—	**—**	—
Settlements paid	**(786)**	(843)	**—**	—
End of year	**$26,773**	$30,582	**$ 26,844**	$ 27,369
Change in Plan Assets				
Beginning of year	**$24,110**	$25,814	**$ 2,628**	$ 2,945
Actual return on plan assets	**2,326**	1,191	**312**	63
Company contributions	**3,719**	512	**1,461**	1,376
Benefits paid	**(2,735)**	(2,564)	**(1,744)**	(1,756)
Settlements paid	**(786)**	(843)	**—**	—
Annuity purchase	**(8,352)**	—	**—**	—
End of year	**$18,282**	$24,110	**$ 2,657**	$ 2,628
Funded Status				
End of year	**$ (8,491)**	$ (6,472)	**$(24,187)**	$(24,741)

Years Ended December 31 (dollars in millions)	Pension			Healthcare		
	2012	**2011**	**2010**	**2012**	**2011**	**2010**
Service cost	**$ 358**	$ 307	$ 353	**$ 359**	$ 299	$ 305
Amortization of prior service cost (credit)	**(1)**	72	109	**(89)**	(57)	375
Subtotal	**357**	379	462	**270**	242	680
Expected return on plan assets	**(1,795)**	(1,976)	(2,176)	**(171)**	(163)	(252)
Interest cost	**1,449**	1,590	1,797	**1,284**	1,421	1,639
Subtotal	**11**	(7)	83	**1,383**	1,500	2,067
Remeasurement (gain) loss, net	**5,542**	4,146	(166)	**1,262**	1,787	758
Net periodic benefit (income) cost	**5,553**	4,139	(83)	**2,645**	3,287	2,825
Curtailment and termination benefits	**—**	—	860	**—**	—	386
Total	**$5,553**	$4,139	$ 777	**$2,645**	$3,287	$3,211

a. Describe what is meant by *service cost* and *interest cost*.
b. What payments did retirees receive during fiscal 2012 from the pension and health care plans? What is the source of funds to make payments to retirees?
c. Show the computation of Verizon's 2012 funded status for both the pension and health care plans.
d. What expense does Verizon's income statement report for both its pension and health care plans?

E10-27.[B] Analyzing and Interpreting Disclosure on Off-Balance-Sheet Financing (LO3)

Harley-Davidson, Inc. provides the following footnote in its 2012 10-K report relating to the securitization of receivables by its finance subsidiary, Harley-Davidson Financial Services (HDFS).

Harley-Davidson, Inc. (HOG)

Term Asset-Backed Securitization VIEs The Company transfers U.S. retail motorcycle finance receivables to SPEs which in turn issue secured notes to investors, with various maturities and interest rates, secured by future collections of the purchased U.S. retail motorcycle finance receivables. Each term asset-backed securitization SPE is a separate legal entity and the U.S. retail motorcycle finance receivables included in the term asset-backed securitizations are only available for payment of the secured debt and other obligations arising from the term asset-backed securitization transactions and are not available to pay other obligations or claims of the Company's creditors until the associated secured debt and other obligations are satisfied. Cash and cash equivalent balances held by the SPEs are used only to support the securitizations.

In 2012 and 2011, HDFS transferred $715.7 million and $1.21 billion, respectively, of U.S. retail motorcycle finance receivables to three separate SPEs. The SPEs in turn issued $675.3 million and $1.09 billion, respectively, of secured notes. At December 31, 2012, the Company's consolidated balance sheet included outstanding balances related to the following secured notes with the related maturity dates and interest rates (in thousands):

Issue Date	Principal Amount at Date of Issuance	Weighted-Average Rate at Date of Issuance	Contractual Maturity Date
July 2012	$675,306	0.59%	August 2013–June 2018
November 2011 . . .	513,300	0.88	November 2012–February 2018
August 2011	573,380	0.76	September 2012–August 2017
November 2010 . . .	600,000	1.05	December 2011–April 2018
December 2009 . . .	562,499	1.55	December 2010–June 2017

a. Describe in your own words, the securitization process employed by HDFS.
b. What benefits does Harley-Davidson derive by securitizing receivables in this manner?
c. Current accounting standards require consolidation of the VIEs. What effect does this have on Harley-Davidson? Is there still a benefit to securitization? Explain.

PROBLEMS

Aeropostale, Inc. (ARO)

P10-28. Analyzing, Interpreting and Capitalizing Operating Leases (LO1)
The **Aeropostale, Inc.** 10-K report contains the following footnote relating to leasing activities. This is the only information it discloses relating to its leasing activity.

We are committed under noncancelable leases for our entire store, distribution centers and office space locations . . . Certain leases also require contingent rent based on sales. The aggregate minimum annual real estate rent commitments as of February 2, 2013, are as follows (in thousands):

Due in Fiscal Year	Total
2013	$143,978
2014	133,456
2015	120,403
2016	105,480
2017	94,011
Thereafter	351,452
Total	$948,780

Required

a. What lease assets and lease liabilities does Aeropostale report on its balance sheet? How do we know?
b. What effect does the lease classification have on Aeropostale's balance sheet? Over the life of the lease, what effect does this classification have on the company's net income?
c. Using a 6% discount rate and rounding the remaining lease life to the nearest whole year, estimate the assets and liabilities that Aeropostale fails to report as a result of its off-balance-sheet lease financing.
d. What adjustments would we consider to Aeropostale's income statement corresponding to the adjustments we would make to its balance sheet in part *c*?
e. Indicate the direction (increase or decrease) of the effect that capitalizing these leases would have on the following financial items and ratios for Aeropostale: return on equity (ROE), net operating

profit after tax (NOPAT), net operating assets (NOA), net operating profit margin (NOPM), net operating asset turnover (NOAT), and measures of financial leverage.

P10-29. Analyzing, Interpreting and Capitalizing Operating Leases (LO1)
The **Best Buy Co., Inc.** 10-K report has the following footnote related to leasing activities.

Best Buy Co., Inc. (BBY)

The future minimum lease payments under our capital and operating leases by fiscal year (not including contingent rentals) at February 2, 2013, were as follows:

Fiscal Year ($ millions)	Capital Leases	Operating Leases
2014	$27	$1,238
2015	25	1,156
2016	17	1,034
2017	5	888
2018	3	703
Thereafter	20	1,994
Subtotal	97	$7,013
Less: imputed interest	(17)	
Present value	$80	

Required

a. What is the balance of the lease liabilities reported on Best Buy's balance sheet?

b. What effect has the operating lease classification had on its balance sheet? Over the life of the lease, what effect does this classification have on the company's net income?

c. Confirm that the implicit discount rate used by Best Buy for its capital leases is 6.09%. Use this discount rate to estimate the assets and liabilities that Best Buy fails to report as a result of its off-balance-sheet lease financing. Round the remaining lease life to two decimals.

d. What adjustments would we make to Best Buy's income statement corresponding to the adjustments we made to its balance sheet in part *c*?

e. Indicate the direction (increase or decrease) of the effect that capitalizing the operating leases would have on the following financial items and ratios for Best Buy: return on equity (ROE), net operating profit after tax (NOPAT), net operating assets (NOA), net operating profit margin (NOPM), net operating asset turnover (NOAT), and measures of financial leverage.

P10-30. Analyzing, Interpreting and Capitalizing Operating Leases (LO1)
FedEx Corp. reports total assets of $24,902 and total liabilities of $11,091 for 2013 ($ millions). Its 10-K report has the following footnote related to leasing activities.

FedEx Corp. (FDX)

A summary of future minimum lease payments under noncancelable operating leases with an initial or remaining term in excess of one year at May 31, 2013, is as follows (in millions):

	Operating Leases		
	Aircraft and Related Equipment	Facilities and Other	Total Operating Leases
2014	$ 462	$ 1,474	$ 1,936
2015	448	1,386	1,834
2016	453	1,183	1,636
2017	391	1,298	1,689
2018	326	904	1,230
Thereafter	824	5,826	6,650
Total	$2,904	$12,071	$14,975

Property and equipment recorded under capital leases and future minimum lease payments under capital leases were immaterial at May 31, 2013. Capital lease obligations were reported as part of FedEx's long-term debt to be $11 million at May 31, 2013.

Required

a. What is the balance of lease assets and lease liabilities reported on FedEx's balance sheet? Explain.

b. Assume FedEx uses a rate of 4.8% to discount its capital leases. Use this discount rate and round the remaining lease life to two decimals to estimate the amount of assets and liabilities that FedEx fails to report as a result of its off-balance-sheet lease financing.

c. What adjustments would we make to FedEx's income statement corresponding to the adjustments we make to its balance sheet in part *b*?

d. Indicate the direction (increase or decrease) of the effect that capitalizing the operating leases would have on the following financial items and ratios for FedEx: return on equity (ROE), net operating profit after tax (NOPAT), net operating assets (NOA), net operating profit margin (NOPM), net operating asset turnover (NOAT), and measures of financial leverage.

e. What portion of total lease liabilities did FedEx report on-balance-sheet and what portion is off-balance-sheet?

f. Based on your analysis, do you believe that FedEx's balance sheet adequately reports its aircraft and facilities assets and related obligations? Explain.

E. I. Du Pont De Nemours and Co. (DD)

P10-31. Analyzing and Interpreting Pension Disclosures (LO2)

E. I. Du Pont De Nemours and Co.'s 10-K report has the following disclosures related to its retirement plans ($ millions).

Obligations and Funded Status December 31 ($ millions)	Pension Benefits 2012	2011
Change in benefit obligation		
Benefit obligation at beginning of year	**$27,083**	$23,924
Service cost	**277**	249
Interest cost	**1,165**	1,253
Plan participants' contributions	**24**	21
Actuarial loss	**2,245**	3,062
Benefits paid	**(1,593)**	(1,610)
Amendments	**(22)**	2
Net effects of acquisitions/divestitures	**—**	182
Benefit obligation at end of year	**$29,179**	$27,083
Change in plan assets		
Fair value of plan assets at beginning of year	**$17,794**	$18,403
Actual gain on plan assets	**2,326**	471
Employer contributions	**848**	341
Plan participants' contributions	**24**	21
Benefits paid	**(1,593)**	(1,610)
Net effects of acquisitions/divestitures	**—**	168
Fair value of plan assets at end of year	**$19,399**	$17,794
Funded status		
U.S. plans with plan assets	**$ (6,625)**	$ (6,894)
Non-U.S. plans with plan assets	**(1,443)**	(901)
All other plans	**(1,712)**	(1,494)
Total	**$ (9,780)**	$ (9,289)
Amounts recognized in the Consolidated Balance Sheets consist of:		
Other assets	**$ 5**	$ 4
Other accrued liabilities	**(110)**	(107)
Other liabilities	**(9,303)**	(9,186)
Liabilities related to assets held for saie	**(372)**	—
Net amount recognized	**$ (9,780)**	$ (9,289)

Components of net periodic benefit cost (credit) and amounts recognized in other comprehensive income	Pension Benefits (In millions)		
	2012	2011	2010
Net periodic benefit cost			
Service cost	**$ 277**	$ 249	$ 207
Interest cost	**1,165**	1,253	1,262
Expected return on plan assets	**(1,517)**	(1,475)	(1,435)
Amortization of loss	**887**	613	507
Amortization of prior service cost	**13**	16	16
Curtailment/settlement loss	**7**	—	—
Net periodic benefit cost	**$ 832**	$656	$ 557
Changes in plan assets and benefit obligations recognized in other comprehensive income			
Net loss	**1,433**	$4,069	$ 635
Amortization of loss	**(887)**	(613)	(507)
Prior service (benefit) cost	**(22)**	2	—
Amortization of prior service cost	**(13)**	(16)	(16)
Curtailment/settlement loss	**(7)**	—	—
Total loss recognized in other comprehensive income	**504**	3,442	112
Noncontrolling interest	**(1)**	(11)	(1)
Accumulated other comprehensive income assumed from purchase of noncontrolling interest	**25**	—	—
Total loss recognized in other comprehensive income, attributable to DuPont	**$ 528**	$3,431	$ 111
Total recognized in net periodic benefit cost and other comprehensive income	**$1,360**	$4,087	$ 668

Weighted-average assumptions used to determine net periodic benefit cost for years ended December 31	Pension Benefits		
	2012	2011	2010
Discount rate	**4.32%**	5.32%	5.80%
Expected return on plan assets	**8.61%**	8.73%	8.64%
Rate of compensation increase	**4.18%**	4.24%	4.24%

The following benefit payments, which reflect future service, as appropriate, are expected to be paid:

($ millions)	Pension Benefits
2013	$1,629
2014	1,604
2015	1,629
2016	1,637
2017	1,667
Years 2018–2022	8,678

Required

a. How much pension expense (revenue) does DuPont report in its 2012 income statement?

b. DuPont reports a $1,517 million expected return on pension plan assets as an offset to 2012 pension expense. Approximately, how is this amount computed (estimate from the numbers reported)? What is DuPont's actual gain or loss realized on its 2012 pension plan assets? What is the purpose of using this expected return instead of the actual gain or loss (return)?

c. What main factors (and dollar amounts) affected DuPont's pension liability during 2012? What main factors (and dollar amounts) affected its pension plan assets during 2012?

d. What does the term *funded status* mean? What is the funded status of the 2012 DuPont pension plans?

e. DuPont decreased its discount rate from 5.32% to 4.32% in 2012. What effect(s) does this decrease have on its balance sheet and its income statement?

f. How did DuPont's pension plan affect the company's cash flow in 2012? (Identify any inflows and outflows, including amounts.)

g. Explain how the returns on pension assets affect the amount of cash that DuPont must contribute to fund the pension plan.

P10-32. Analyzing and Interpreting Pension Disclosures (LO2)

Johnson & Johnson (JNJ)

Johnson & Johnson provides the following footnote disclosures in its 10-K report relating to its defined benefit pension plans and its other post-retirement benefits.

	Retirement Plans		Other Benefit Plans	
($ in millions)	**2012**	**2011**	**2012**	**2011**
Change in Benefit Obligation				
Projected benefit obligation—beginning of year	$17,424	$14,993	$ 3,790	$ 3,572
Service cost	722	638	175	149
Interest cost	878	853	165	188
Plan participant contributions	35	54	—	—
Amendments	12	(24)	—	—
Actuarial losses	2,662	1,698	459	213
Divestitures & acquisitions	629	14	—	—
Curtailments & settlements & restructuring	(6)	(6)	—	—
Benefits paid from plan	(697)	(659)	(432)	(320)
Effect of exchange rates	170	(137)	2	(12)
Projected benefit obligation—end of year	$21,829	$17,424	$ 4,159	$ 3,790
Change in Plan Assets				
Plan assets at fair value—beginning of year	$13,736	$13,433	$ 8	$ 14
Actual return (loss) on plan assets	1,926	(102)	3	(1)
Company contributions	1,838	1,135	543	315
Plan participant contributions	35	54	—	—
Settlements	(2)	(2)	—	—
Divestitures & acquisitions	593	(2)	—	—
Benefits paid from plan assets	(697)	(659)	(432)	(320)
Effect of exchange rates	107	(121)	—	—
Plan assets at fair value—end of year	$17,536	$13,736	$ 122	$ 8
Funded status—end of year	$ (4,293)	$ (3,688)	$(4,037)	$(3,782)

	Retirement Plans			Other Benefit Plans		
($ in millions)	**2012**	**2011**	**2010**	**2012**	**2011**	**2010**
Service cost	$ 722	$ 638	$ 550	$175	$149	$134
Interest cost	878	853	791	165	188	202
Expected return on plan assets	(1,236)	(1,108)	(1,005)	(4)	(1)	(1)
Amortization of prior service cost (credit)	6	9	10	(3)	(3)	(4)
Amortization of net transition obligation	1	1	1	—	—	—
Recognized actuarial losses	494	388	236	76	45	48
Curtailments and settlements	—	—	1	—	—	—
Net periodic benefit cost	$ 865	$ 781	$ 584	$409	$378	$379

	Retirement Plans			Other Benefit Plans		
	2012	**2011**	**2010**	**2012**	**2011**	**2010**
Worldwide Benefit Plans						
Discount rate	4.25%	5.13%	5.71%	4.55%	5.25%	6.00%
Expected long-term rate of return on plan assets	8.45	8.62	8.68			
Rate of increase in compensation levels	4.08	4.19	4.19	4.28	4.28	4.29

Required

a. How much pension expense does Johnson & Johnson report in its 2012 income statement?

b. The company reports a $1,236 million expected return on pension plan assets as an offset to 2012 pension expense. Approximately, how is this amount computed? What is the actual gain or loss realized on its 2012 pension plan assets? What is the purpose of using this expected return instead of the actual gain or loss?

c. What factors affected the company's pension liability during 2012? What factors affected the pension plan assets during 2012?

d. What does the term *funded status* mean? What is the funded status of the 2012 pension plans and postretirement benefit plans?

e. The company decreased its discount rate from 5.13% to 4.25% in 2012. What effect(s) does this decrease have on its balance sheet and its income statement?

f. How did Johnson & Johnson's pension plan affect the company's cash flow in 2012?

IFRS APPLICATIONS

IFRS

I10-33. Analyzing and Capitalizing Operating Lease Payments Disclosed in Footnotes (LO1)

GlaxoSmithKline plc, headquartered in London, United Kingdom, is the world's third largest pharmaceutical company. The company's 2012 balance sheet reported total assets of £41,475 million and total liabilities of £34,728 million. The footnotes disclosed the following information related to leasing activities.

Commitments under noncancelllable operating leases are disclosed below. £343 million (2011 – £62 million) of these commitments are provided against on the Group's balance sheet.

Commitments under noncancelable operating leases	2012 £m	2011 £m
Rental payments due within one year	£146	£113
Rental payments due between one and two years	98	65
Rental payments due between two and three years	77	46
Rental payments due between three and four years	61	30
Rental payments due between four and five years	54	17
Rental payments due after five years	413	83
Total commitments under noncancelable operating leases	£849	£354

Operating leases are not reflected on-balance-sheet. In our analysis of a company, we often capitalize operating leases, that is, add the present value of the future operating lease payments to both the reported assets and liabilities.

a. Compute the present value of GlaxoSmithKline's operating payments assuming a 6% discount rate and round the remaining lease life to three decimals.

b. What effect would capitalization of operating leases have on GlaxoSmithKline's total liabilities and total assets?

I10-34. Analyzing, Interpreting and Capitalizing Operating Leases (LO1)

Total S.A. is a French multinational oil company and one of the six "supermajor" oil companies in the world. The company is headquartered in Courbevoie, France, and uses IFRS to prepare its financial statements. Total S.A. reports the following footnote relating to its finance and operating leases in its 2012 20-F report (€ millions).

The Group leases real estate, retail stations, ships, and other equipment. The future minimum lease payments on operating and finance leases to which the Group is committed are shown as follows:

continued

continued from prior page

For year ended December 31, 2012 (€ million)	Operating leases	Finance leases
2013	€ 781	€ 55
2014	569	54
2015	514	53
2016	441	51
2017	337	19
2018 and beyond	971	236
Total minimum payments	€3,613	€468

On December 31, 2012, the present value of minimum lease payments under finance leases was €360 million.

a. Confirm that the implicit rate of Total's finance leases is 4%.

b. Use 4% as the discount rate and round the remaining lease term to three decimals to compute the present value of Total's operating leases.

c. Describe the adjustments we might consider to Total's balance sheet and income statement using the information from part *b*.

d. Total reported total liabilities of €97,636 million for 2012. Are these finance leases substantial? Would capitalizing the operating leases make a difference to our assessment of Total's liquidity or solvency?

I10-35. Analyzing, Interpreting and Capitalizing Operating Leases (LO1)

Air Canada is the largest Canadian airline and is the world's ninth largest passenger airline by number of destinations. The company is headquartered in Montreal, Quebec. Air Canada used Canadian GAAP to prepare its 2012 financial statements. Its footnotes include the following:

Operating Lease Commitments The table below presents the future minimum lease payments under existing operating leases of aircraft and other property as at December 31, 2012.

CDN$ millions	2013	2014	2015	2016	2017	Thereafter	Total
Aircraft	$318	$253	$207	$174	$152	$333	$1,437
Other property	57	46	43	33	30	142	351
	$375	$299	$250	$207	$182	$475	$1,788

MATURITY ANALYSIS Principal and interest repayment requirements as at December 31, 2012 on long-term debt and lease obligations are as follows:

Principal	2013	2014	2015	2016	2017	Thereafter	Total
Long-term debt obligations	$446	$268	$1,383	$473	$555	$519	$3,644
Finance lease obligations	60	56	50	25	25	147	363
	$506	$324	$1,433	$498	$580	$666	$4,007

Interest	2013	2014	2015	2016	2017	Thereafter	Total
Long-term debt obligations	$220	$201	$140	$49	$68	$31	$709
Finance lease obligations	34	28	22	18	15	49	166
	$254	$229	$162	$67	$83	$80	$875

The following table reflects Air Canada's adjusted net debt balances as at December 31, 2012 and as at December 31, 2011.

continued

(Canadian dollars in millions)	December 31, 2012	December 31, 2011	Change $
Total long-term debt and finance leases	$3,449	$3,906	$(457)
Current portion of long-term debt and finance leases	506	424	82
Total long-term debt and finance leases, including current portion	3,955	4,330	(375)
Less cash, cash equivalents and short-term investments	(2,026)	(2,099)	73
Net debt	1,929	2,231	(302)
Capitalized operating leases[1]	2,352	2,345	7
Adjusted net debt	$4,281	$4,576	$(295)

[1] Adjusted net debt is a non-GAAP financial measure used by Air Canada and may not be comparable to measures presented by other public companies. Adjusted net debt is a key component of the capital managed by Air Canada and provides management with a measure of its net indebtedness. Air Canada includes capitalized operating leases which is a measure commonly used in the industry to ascribe a value to obligations under operating leases. Common industry practice is to multiply annualized aircraft rent expense by 7.0. This definition of capitalized operating leases is used by Air Canada and may not be comparable to similar measures presented by other public companies. Aircraft rent was $336 million for the twelve months ended December 31, 2012 and $335 million for the twelve months ended December 31, 2011.

Required

a. Combine the principal and interest payments for the company's finance lease obligations reported in the "Maturity Analysis" footnote to determine the total annual finance lease payments. Confirm that the implicit rate that Air Canada used to capitalize these leases was 9.4%.

b. The company explains its "adjusted net debt" in its footnotes. Why is this a metric that airline industry analysts might want to use?

c. Recompute the "capitalized operating leases" of $2,352 million reported in the last footnote shown above using the method described in the note (1) below the table.

d. Use the reported Operating Lease Commitments footnote to determine an independent estimate of the amount that would be capitalized if the company's operating leases were classified as finance leases under IFRS. Use a discount rate of 9.4%.

e. Compare the amounts we obtained in parts *c* and *d* above. Why might the two be different?

f. Indicate the direction (increase or decrease) of the effect that capitalizing the operating leases would have on the following financial items and ratios for Air Canada: return on equity (ROE), net operating profit after tax (NOPAT), net operating assets (NOA), and measures of financial leverage.

I10-36. Analyzing, Interpreting and Capitalizing Operating Leases (LO1)

LM Ericsson, one of Sweden's largest companies, is a provider of telecommunication and data communication systems. The company reports total assets of SEK 180,100 and total liabilities of SEK 102,075 for 2012 (in millions). Its annual report has the following footnote related to leasing activities.

As of December 31, 2012, future minimum lease payment obligations for leases were distributed as follows:

In SEK millions	Finance Leases	Operating Leases
2013	150	2,847
2014	229	1,794
2015	127	1,388
2016	85	1,105
2017	76	777
2018 and later	795	2,472
Total	1,462	10,383
Future finance charges	(398)	n/a
Present value of finance lease liabilities	1,064	10,383

Required

a. What is reported on Ericsson's balance sheet as lease liabilities?

b. Confirm that the implicit rate that Ericsson uses to discount its capital leases is 5.03%. Use this discount rate and round the remaining years to 3 decimals to estimate the amount of assets and liabilities that Ericsson fails to report as a result of its off-balance-sheet lease financing.

c. What adjustments would we make to Ericsson's income statement corresponding to the balance sheet adjustments implied in part *b*?

d. What portion of total lease liabilities did Ericsson report on-balance-sheet and what portion is off-balance-sheet?

e. Indicate the direction (increase or decrease) of the effect that capitalizing the operating leases would have on the following financial items and ratios for Ericsson: return on equity (ROE), net operating profit after tax (NOPAT), net operating assets (NOA), net operating profit margin (NOPM), net operating asset turnover (NOAT), and measures of financial leverage.

f. Based on your analysis, do you believe that Ericsson's balance sheet adequately reports its facilities assets and related obligations? Explain.

Potash Corporation of Saskatchewan (POT.TO)

I10-37. Analyzing and Interpreting Pension Disclosures (LO2)

Potash Corporation of Saskatchewan, the world's largest potash producer, is a Canadian corporation based in Saskatoon, Saskatchewan. The company produces nitrogen and phosphate used to produce fertilizer. At the end of 2011, the company controlled 20% of the world's potash production capacity, 2% of nitrogen production capacity and 5% of phosphate supply.

Defined Benefit Plans

The components of total expense recognized in the consolidated statements of income for the company's defined benefit pension and other post-retirement benefit plans, computed actuarially, were as follows:

	Pension			Other			Total		
	2012	2011	2010	2012	2011	2010	2012	2011	2010
Current service cost for benefits earned during the year	$30	$24	$20	$11	$ 8	$ 7	$41	$32	$27
Interest cost on benefit obligations	49	49	47	17	16	16	66	65	63
Expected return on plan assets	(57)	(53)	(47)	—	—	—	(57)	(53)	(47)
Prior service costs	—	4	—	(2)	(1)	(1)	(2)	3	(1)
Plan settlements	—	—	(1)	—	—	—	—	—	(1)
Total expense recognized in net income	$22	$24	$19	$26	$23	$22	$48	$47	$41

Of the total expense recognized in net income, $38 (2011—$38, 2010—$33) was included in cost of goods sold and $10 (2011—$9, 2010—$8) in selling and administrative expenses.

The change in benefit obligations and the change in plan assets for the above defined benefit pension and other post-retirement benefit plans were as follows at December 31:

	Pension		Other		Total	
	2012	2011	2012	2011	2012	2011
Change in benefit obligations						
Balance, beginning of year	$1,051	$893	$366	$298	$1,417	$1,191
Current service cost	30	24	11	8	41	32
Interest cost	49	49	17	16	66	65
Actuarial loss (gain)	130	116	(2)	53	128	169
Foreign exchange rate changes	3	1	1	(1)	4	—
Contributions by plan participants	—	—	5	4	5	4
Benefits paid	(42)	(38)	(10)	(12)	(52)	(50)
Prior service costs	3	6	—	—	3	6
Balance, end of year	$1,224	$1,051	$388	$366	$1,612	$1,417

continued

Change in plan assets						
Fair value, beginning of year	$ 887	$ 753	$ —	$ —	$ 887	$ 753
Expected return on plan assets	57	53	—	—	57	53
Actuarial gain (loss)	35	(42)	—	—	35	(42)
Foreign exchange rate changes	1	2	—	—	1	2
Contributions by plan participants	—	—	5	4	5	4
Employer contributions	114	159	5	8	119	167
Benefits paid	(42)	(38)	(10)	(12)	(52)	(50)
Fair value, end of year	$1,052	$ 887	$ —	$ —	$1,052	$ 887
Funded status	$ (172)	$ (164)	$(388)	$ (366)	$ (560)	$(530)

The assumptions used to determine the benefit obligation and expense for the company's significant plans were as follows as of December 31:

	Pension			Other		
	2012	2011	2010	2012	2011	2010
Discount rate—obligation, %	3.85	4.60	5.45	3.85	4.60	5.45
Discount rate—expense, %	4.60[1]	5.45[2]	5.85	4.60[1]	5.45[2]	5.85
Long-term rate of return on assets, %	6.50	7.00	7.00	n/a	n/a	n/a
Rate of increase in compensation levels, %	4.00	4.00	4.00	n/a	n/a	n/a
Medical cost trend rate—assumed, %	n/a	n/a	n/a	7.00-4.50[3]	6.00	6.00
Medical cost trend rate—year reaches ultimate trend rate	n/a	n/a	n/a	2027	2011	2010

[1] Discount rate changed to 4.05 percent effective June 30, 2012, as a result of significant market fluctuations that had occurred since the prior year-end.

[2] Discount rate changed to 4.75 percent effective October 1, 2011, as a result of significant market fluctuations that had occurred since the prior year-end.

[3] The Company has assumed a graded medical cost trend rate starting at 7.00 percent in 2013 moving to 4.50 percent by 2027.

n/a = not applicable

Required

a. How much pension expense does Potash Corporation report in its 2012 income statement?

b. The company reports a $57 million expected return on pension plan assets as an offset to 2012 pension expense. In general terms, how is this amount computed? What is the purpose of using this expected return instead of the actual gain or loss?

c. What factors affected the company's pension liability during 2012? What factors affected the pension plan assets during 2012?

d. What does the term *funded status* mean? What is the funded status of the 2012 pension plans and postretirement benefit plans?

e. The company decreased its discount rate on the pension obligation from 4.60% to 3.85% in 2012. What effect(s) does this decrease have on the company's balance sheet and income statement?

f. How did Potash Corporation's pension plan affect the company's cash flow in 2012?

I10-38. Analyzing and Interpreting Pension Disclosures (LO2)

Qantas Airways Limited (QAN)

Qantas Airways Limited is the flagship carrier of Australia. It provides the following footnote disclosures in its annual report relating to its defined pension plans and its other post-retirement benefits (amounts in millions of U.S. dollars):

EXPENSE RECOGNISED IN THE CONSOLIDATED INCOME STATEMENT	Qantas Group 2012 $M	2011 $M
Current service cost	$154	$152
Past service cost	–	(3)
Interest cost	106	102
Contributions by plan participants	(27)	(23)
Expected return on plan assets	(151)	(144)
Actuarial losses	20	26
Total included in manpower and staff related expenditure	$102	$110

ACTUAL RETURN (LOSS)/GAIN ON PLAN ASSETS	$M	$M
Actual return (loss)/gain on plan assets	$ (27)	$137

MAJOR CATEGORIES OF PLAN ASSETS AS A PERCENTAGE OF TOTAL PLAN ASSETS	%	%
Equity instruments (Australian and overseas)	50	50
Fixed interest, cash and indexed bonds (Australian and overseas)	30	30
Property	5	5
Alternative assets	15	15

RECONCILIATION TO THE CONSOLIDATED BALANCE SHEET	$M	$M
Fair value of plan assets	$2,082	$2,101
Present value of defined benefit obligation	2,561	2,274
Deficit	(479)	(173)
Less: unrecognized actuarial losses	(772)	(431)
Recognized prepayments in the Consolidated Balance Sheet (refer to Note 14)	$ 293	$ 258

CHANGES IN THE PRESENT VALUE OF DEFINED BENEFIT OBLIGATION	$M	$M
Opening defined benefit obligation	$2,274	$2,210
Current service cost	154	152
Past service cost	–	(3)
Interest cost	106	102
Actuarial losses/(gains)	183	(41)
Exchange differences on foreign plans	3	(18)
Benefits paid	(159)	(128)
Closing defined benefit obligation	$2,561	$2,274

CHANGES IN THE FAIR VALUE OF PLAN ASSETS	$M	$M
Opening fair value of plan assets	$2,101	$1,964
Expected return	151	144
Actuarial losses	(178)	(7)
Exchange differences on foreign plans	2	(15)
Contributions by employer	138	120
Contributions by plan participants	27	23
Benefits paid	(159)	(128)
Closing fair value of plan assets	$2,082	$2,101

continued

PRINCIPAL ACTUARIAL ASSUMPTIONS (EXPRESSED AS WEIGHTED AVERAGES PER ANNUM)	2012 %	2011 %
Discount rate	4.4	5.3
Expected return on plan assets	6.8	7.2
Future salary increases	3.0	3.0

a. How much pension expense does Qantas report in its 2012 income statement?

b. The company reports a $151 million expected return on pension plan assets as an offset to 2012 pension expense. In general terms, how is this amount computed? What is the purpose of using this expected return instead of the actual gain or loss?

c. What factors affected the company's pension liability during 2012? What factors affected the pension plan assets during 2012?

d. What does the term *funded status* mean? What is the funded status of the 2012 pension plans and postretirement benefit plans?

e. The company decreased its discount rate from 5.3% to 4.4% in 2012. What effect(s) does this decrease have on its balance sheet and its income statement?

f. How did Qantas's pension plan affect the company's cash flow in 2012?

ONGOING PROJECT

(This ongoing project began in Module 1 and continues through most of the book; even if previous segments were not completed, the requirements are still applicable to any business analysis.) Your project should include a discussion of leases (capital and operating) as well as defined benefit obligations. The objective is to quantify any off-balance-sheet obligations and approximate the economic impact of the exclusion on key performance and leverage ratios.

1. *Capital and Operating Leases.* Read the debt and lease footnotes to determine whether the company uses leases.
   - Does the company use leases? What types of assets are leased?
   - What proportion of leases are capital (finance) versus operating?
   - Are leases a substantial component of overall financing?
   - Determine the discount rate implicit in the company's capital leases.
   - Use the rate from above to approximate the amount that would have been included in the balance sheet had the operating leases been capitalized. Is the missing amount economically important?
   - Quantify the effect that capitalizing the operating leases would have on the following financial items and ratios for each company: return on equity (ROE), net operating profit after tax (NOPAT), net operating assets (NOA), and measures of financial leverage, liquidity, and solvency.
2. *Pensions.* Read the pension footnote to determine whether the company has defined benefit obligations.
   - What is the funded status of the pension and other benefits plans? Is the underfunded or overfunded obligation substantial? Compare between the companies.
   - Are the plans substantial to the company?
   - How much pension expense does each company report in its 2012 income statement? Is this a substantial amount?
   - Determine the factors that affect the pension liability and plan assets for the year.
   - Compare the cash paid into the plan assets to the amounts paid to retirees. Assess the cash flow implications of the company's future payment obligations. The point is to determine whether the company will be able to meet its obligations as they come due.

SOLUTIONS TO REVIEW PROBLEMS

Mid-Module Review

Solution

1. The interest rate that **UPS** uses in the computation of its capital lease balance is imputed to be 6.60%; this rate is determined as follows (using a spreadsheet).

UPS IRR spreadsheet.xlsx - Microsoft Excel

	A	B	C	D	E	F	G	H	I	J	K	L	M	N	O	P
1	N	0	1	2	3	4	5	6	7	8	9	10	11	12	13	14
2	Amount	-440	55	52	50	49	48	48	48	48	48	48	48	48	48	42
3	IRR	6.60% *														
4																
5			* Formula for cell B3 is =IRR(B2:P2)									= 426				

2. We present the present value computations below for both the actual implicit rate of 6.6% and the rounded 7%.

Excel Year	Operating Lease Payment	Discount Factor (i = 0.066)	Present Value
1	$342	0.93809	$ 321
2	271	0.88001	238
3	203	0.82552	168
4	145	0.77441	112
5	118	0.72646	86
>5	358	2.67076	229**
Remaining life.	3.034*		$1,154

*$358/$118 = 3.034 years
**The annuity factor for 3.034 years at 6.6% is 2.67076.
$118 × 2.67076 × 0.72646 = $229

Tables Year ($ millions)	Operating Lease Payment	Discount Factor (i = 0.070)	Present Value
1	$342	0.93458	$ 320
2	271	0.87344	237
3	203	0.81630	166
4	145	0.76290	111
5	118	0.71299	84
>5	358	2.62432	221*
Remaining life.	3.034		$1,139
Round life to.	3.0		
Round rate to	7.0%		

*The annuity factor for 3 years at 7% is 2.62432.
$118 × 2.62432 × 0.71299 = $221

These amounts should be added to the balance sheet for analysis purposes.

3. Income statement adjustments relating to capitalization of operating leases involve two steps:
   a. Remove rent expense of $342 million from operating expense.
   b. Add depreciation expense from lease assets to operating expense and also reflect interest expense on the lease obligation as a nonoperating expense. Using the spreadsheet computations above, we assume that the remaining lease term is 8.034 years (five years reported in the lease schedule plus 3.034 years after Year 5). Applying this lease term and zero salvage value, we get an estimated straight-line depreciation for lease assets of $144 million ($1,154/8.034 years). Interest expense on the $1,154 million lease liability at the 6.6% capitalization rate is $76 million ($1,154 million × 6.6%). The net adjustment to NOPAT, reflecting the elimination of rent expense and the addition of depreciation expense, is $125 million (($342 million rent expense − $144 million depreciation) × (1 − 0.37)).

Module-End Review

Solution

1. A pension benefit obligation increases primarily by service cost, interest cost, and actuarial losses (which are increases in the pension liability as a result of changes in actuarial assumptions). It is decreased by the payment of benefits to retirees and by any actuarial gains.
2. Pension assets increase by positive investment returns for the period and cash contributions made by the company. Assets decrease by benefits paid to retirees and by investment losses.
3. American Airlines' funded status is $(6,830) million ($15,895 million PBO − $9,065 million Pension Assets) as of 2012. The negative amount indicates that the plan is underfunded. Consequently, this amount is reflected as a liability on American's balance sheet.
4. Expected return on plan assets acts as an offset to service cost and interest cost in computing net pension cost. As the expected return increases, net pension cost decreases.
5. American Airlines' expected return of $676 million is less than its actual return of $1,204 million in 2012.
6. American Airlines reports a net pension expense of $875 million in its 2012 income statement. Of this, $673 million pertained to the company's defined benefit plans, and $202 million to defined contribution plans.
7. American Airlines' funded status is negative, indicating an underfunded plan. In 2012, the company contributed $277 million to the pension plan, down from $525 million in the prior year. It is likely that the company will need to increase its future funding levels to cover the plan's requirements. This might have negative repercussions for its ability to fund other operating needs, and could eventually damage its competitive position.

Module 11 Forecasting Financial Statements

Learning Objectives

LO1 Explain the process of forecasting financial statements. (p. 11-3)

LO2 Forecast revenues and the income statement. (p. 11-7)

LO3 Forecast the balance sheet. (p. 11-24)

LO4 Forecast the statement of cash flows. (p. 11-34)

LO5 Prepare multiyear forecasts of financial statements. (p. 11-35)

LO6 Implement a parsimonious method for multiyear forecasting of net operating profit and net operating assets. (p. 11-39)

Procter & Gamble (P&G)

A.G Lafley came out of retirement in 2013 to assume the position as Chairman and CEO of Procter & Gamble (P&G), a position that he held for the first decade of the 2000s. In his 2013 Chairman's letter to shareholders, his focus was clear:

> We have to win at the first moment of truth, when the consumer chooses our product at the store shelf, and the second moment of truth, when the consumer uses the product at home and decides whether to buy it again. We also have to win at the "zero moment of truth," when the consumer discovers information about our brands and products before they shop. When P&G products win the consumer value equation versus competitors, consumers reward us—and our shareholders—with their hard-earned money. . . We'll measure our business performance through operating total shareholder return. This goal is important because it's an integrated measure of value creation at the business unit level. Strong operating TSR requires sales growth, progress on gross and operating margins, and strong cash flow productivity. Business units will be guided by disciplined strategies and operating plans that focus on the most important choices for creating value.

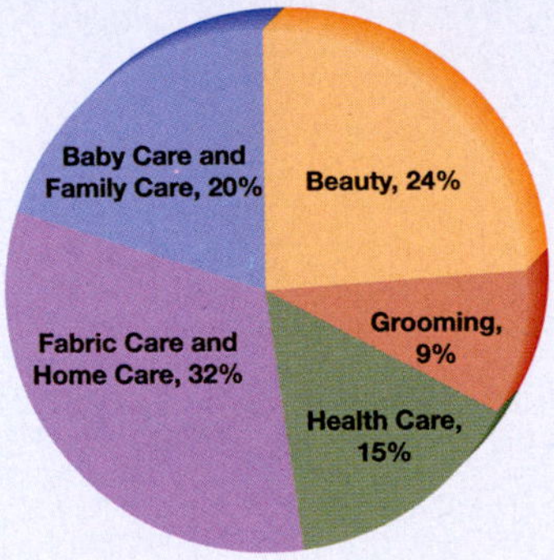

Lafley certainly has an impressive stable of products with which to work. It consists of numerous well-recognized household brands. Total sales of Procter & Gamble products are distributed across its five business segments as illustrated in the chart to the side. A partial listing of its billion-dollar brands follows:

- **Beauty.** Head & Shoulders, Olay, Pantene, SK-II, Wella
- **Grooming.** Fusion, Gillette, Mach3, Prestobarba
- **Health Care.** Always, Crest, Oral-B, Vicks
- **Fabric Care and Home Care.** Ace, Ariel, Dawn, Downy, Duracell, Febreze, Gain, Iams, Tide
- **Baby Care and Family Care.** Bounty, Charmin, Pampers

Courtesy of Getty Images

As the chart below demonstrates, P&G's stock price languished following Lafley's departure as CEO in 2009 through his return in June of 2013. The question facing analysts upon his return is the extent to which PG will be able to capture more value for its shareholders from its market-dominating brands. That will only happen if PG is successful in growing sales, reducing costs, and managing its balance sheet in order to increase operating cash flow. It is this expectation, the *forecast* of financial performance, that drives stock price. Historical financial statements are relevant to the extent that they provide information useful to forecast financial performance and analysts typically utilize a combination of financial and nonfinancial data in developing those forecasts.

This module explains the forecasting process, including the forecasting of the income statement, the balance sheet, and the statement of cash flows. From all accounts, the rebound in P&G's stock price following Lafley's return as CEO in 2013 reflects optimism about its future financial performance and condition.

Sources: *Procter & Gamble* 2013 10-K and Annual Report.

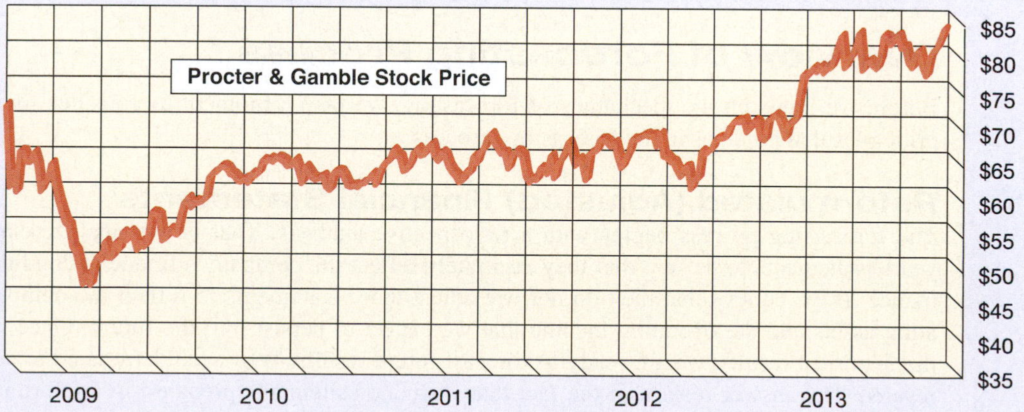

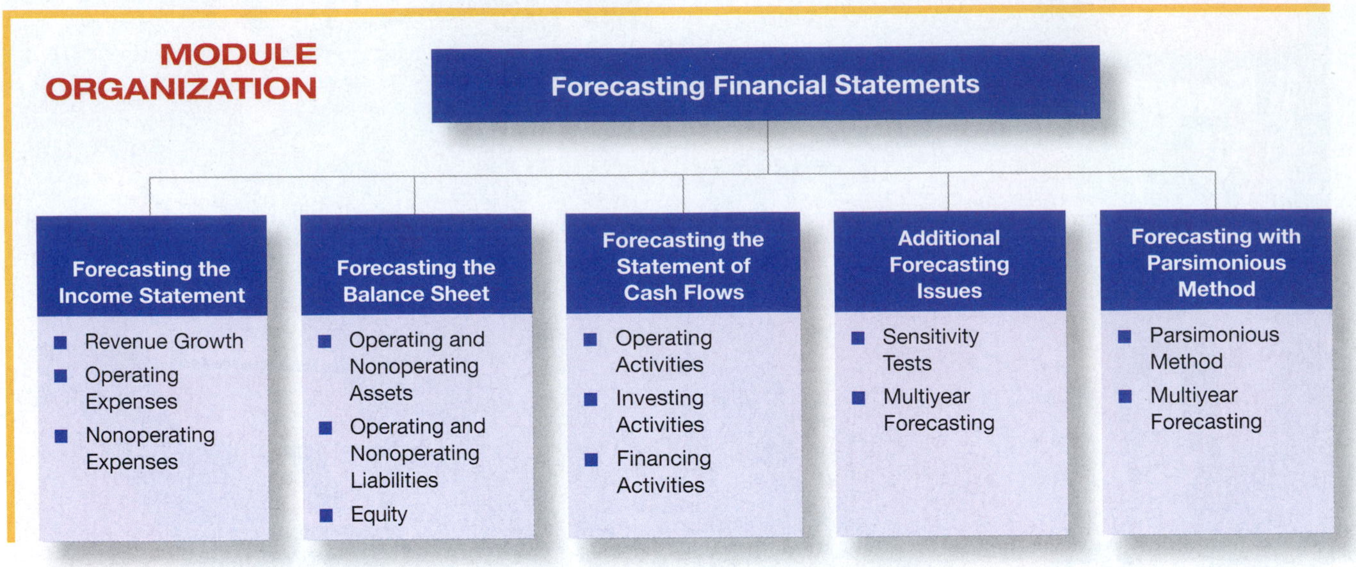

Forecasting financial performance is integral to a variety of business decisions ranging from investing to managing a company effectively. We might, for example, wish to value a company's common stock before purchasing its shares. To that end, we might use one of the valuation models we discuss in Module 12 that rely on financial statement forecasts as a crucial input. Or, we might be interested in evaluating the creditworthiness of a prospective borrower. In that case, we forecast the borrower's cash flows to estimate its ability to repay its obligations. We might also be interested in evaluating alternative strategic investment decisions. In this case, we can use our forecasts to evaluate the shareholder value that the strategic investment alternatives will create. All of these decisions require accurate financial forecasts. In this module, we illustrate the most common method to forecast the income statement, balance sheet, and statement of cash flows.

FORECASTING PROCESS

LO1 Explain the process of forecasting financial statements.

The forecasting process estimates future income statements, balance sheets, and statements of cash flows, in that order. The reason for this ordering is that each statement uses information from the preceding statement(s). For example, we update retained earnings on the balance sheet to reflect our forecast of the company's net income. And, the forecasted income statement and balance sheets are used in preparing forecasts for the statement of cash flows, which follows the same process described in Modules 2 and 3 for preparing the historical statement of cash flows.

Overview of Forecasting Process

Before we focus on the mechanics of forecasting, we take a moment to consider some overarching principles that guide us in the forecasting process.

Reformulated (Adjusted) Financial Statements

The forecasting process begins with a retrospective analysis. That is, we analyze current and prior years' statements to be sure that they accurately reflect the company's financial condition and performance. If we believe that they do not, we adjust those statements to reflect the company's net operating assets and the operating income that we expect to persist into the future. Once we've adjusted the historical results, we are ready to forecast future results. Why would we need to adjust historical results? The answer resides in the fact that financial statements prepared in conformity with GAAP do not always accurately reflect the "true" financial condition and performance of the company. This *adjusting process*, also referred to as recasting or reformulating (or *scrubbing the numbers*), is not "black and white." It requires judgment and estimation. Repeatedly in Modules 5 through 10, we have explained estimation, accounting choice, deliberate managerial intervention in reporting, and transitory versus persistent items. These concepts are integral to adjustments we make to financial statements. It is important to distinguish between the purposes of GAAP-based financial statements and the adjusting process for purposes of forecasting. Specifically, GAAP-based statements provide more than just information for forecasting. For example, financial statements are key inputs into contracts among business parties. This means that historical results, including any transitory activities, must be reported to meet management's fiduciary responsibilities. On the other hand, to forecast future performance, we need to create a set of financial statements that focus on those items that we expect to persist, with a special emphasis on persistent operating activities.

Garbage-In, Garbage-Out

All forecasts are based on a set of forecasting assumptions. For example, to forecast the income statement, we must make assumptions about revenue growth and other assumptions about how expenses will change in relation to changes in revenues. Then, to forecast the balance sheet, we make assumptions about the relation between balance sheet accounts and changes in revenues. Consequently, before we make business decisions based on forecasted financial statements, we must understand and agree with the underlying assumptions used to produce them. The old adage, "garbage-in, garbage-out," is apt. That is, the quality of our decision is only as good as the quality of the information on which it is based. We must be sure that our forecasting assumptions are consistent with our beliefs and predictions for future growth and key financial relations.

Optimism vs Conservatism

Many people believe that it is appropriate to be overly conservative in their financial forecasts so as to minimize the likelihood of making a bad decision. "Let's be conservative in our forecasts so that we are certain our forecast will be met" is a frequent prelude to the forecasting process. Although this approach might appear reasonable, being too conservative can result in missed valuable opportunities that, in the end, can be very costly. Instead, our objective is not to be overly optimistic or overly conservative. The objective for forecasting is accuracy.

Level of Precision

Computing forecasts out to the "nth decimal place" is easy using spreadsheets. This increased precision makes the resulting forecasts appear more "professional," but not necessarily more accurate. As we discuss in this module, our financial statement forecasts are highly dependent on our revenues forecast. Whether revenues are expected to grow by 4% or 5% can markedly impact profitability and other forecasts. Estimating cost of goods sold and other items to the nth decimal place is meaningless if we have imprecise revenue forecasts. Consequently, borderline decisions that depend on a high level of forecasting precision are probably ill-advised.

Smell Test

At the end of the forecasting process, we must step back and make sure that the numbers we predict pass the *smell test*. That is, we need to assess whether our forecasts are reasonable—do they make economic sense, do they fit with the underlying relations that drive financial forecasts? For example, if our forecasts are dependent on increasing selling prices, it is wise to explore the likely consequences of a price increase. Companies cannot raise prices without a consequent loss of demand unless the product in question is protected in some way from competitive attacks. Our forecasts must appear reasonable and consistent with basic business economics.

Internal Consistency

The forecasted income statement, balance sheet, and statement of cash flows are linked in the same way that historical financial statements are. That is, they must articulate (link together within and across time) as we explain in Module 2. Preparing a forecasted statement of cash flows, although tedious, is often a useful way to uncover forecasting assumptions that are inconsistently applied across financial statements (examples are capital expenditures [CAPEX], depreciation, debt payments, and dividends). If the forecasted cash balance on the balance sheet agrees with that on the statement of cash flows, it is likely that our income statement and balance sheet articulate properly. We also must ensure that our forecast assumptions are internally consistent. It is nonsense to forecast an increased gross profit margin during an economic recession unless we can make compelling arguments based on economics.

Crucial Forecasting Assumptions

Analysts commonly perform sensitivity analyses following preparation of their forecasts. This entails increasing and decreasing the forecast assumptions to identify those assumptions that have the greatest impact. By "impact," we mean large enough to alter business decisions. Assumptions that are identified as crucial to a decision must be investigated thoroughly to ensure that forecast assumptions are as accurate as possible.

Summary of Forecasting Process

Some professionals assert that forecasting is more art than science. Whatever it is, it must begin with a business analysis, including an assessment of general economic activity and the competitive forces within the broader business environment that we discuss in Module 1. Ideally, forecasts should be developed at an individual-product level and consider competitive advantage, trends in manufacturing costs, logistical requirements, necessary marketing support, after-sale customer service, and so forth. The narrower the focus, the more we can focus on the business environment in which the company operates and the more informed our forecasts are. Unfortunately, as external users of financial statements, we only have access to general-purpose financial statements, which we adjust as we see fit, given publicly available information and our own assessments. Then, we formulate forecast assumptions that are reasonable and consistent with the economic realities defining that company.

All-Important Revenues Forecast

The revenues (sales) forecast is, arguably, the most crucial and difficult estimate in the forecasting process. It is a crucial estimate because other income statement and balance sheet accounts derive, either directly or indirectly, from the revenues forecast. As a result, both the income statement and balance sheet grow with increases in revenues. The income statement reflects this growth concurrently. However, different balance sheet accounts reflect revenue growth in different ways. Some balance sheet accounts anticipate (or lead) revenue growth (inventories are one example). Some accounts reflect this growth concurrently (accounts receivable). And some accounts reflect revenue growth with a lag (for example, companies usually expand plant assets only after growth is deemed sustainable). Conversely, when revenues decline, so do the income statement and balance sheet, as the company shrinks to cope with adversity. Such actions include reduction of overhead costs and divestiture of excess assets. Exhibit 11.1 highlights crucial relations that are impacted by the revenues forecast for both the income statement and the balance sheet.

EXHIBIT 11.1 Income Statement and Balance Sheet Accounts Directly Impacted by the Revenues Forecast

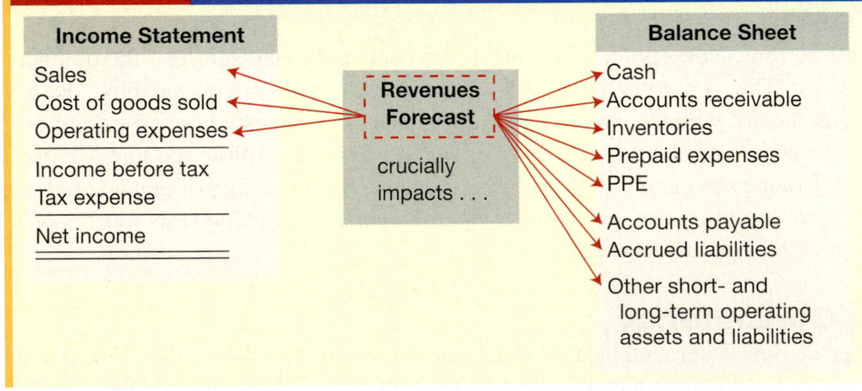

Dynamics of Income Statement (and Balance Sheet) Growth

The following accounts are impacted directly, and with a relatively short lead or lag time, by the revenues forecast (for convenience, *our discussion assumes an increase in revenues*):

- **Cost of goods sold** are impacted via increased inventory purchases, added manufacturing personnel, and greater depreciation from new manufacturing property, plant & equipment (PPE).

- **Operating expenses** increase concurrently with, or in anticipation of, increased revenues; these expenses include increased costs for buyers, higher advertising costs, payments to sales personnel, costs of after-sale customer support, logistics costs, and administrative costs.
- **Cash** increases and decreases directly with increases in revenues as receivables are collected and as payables and accruals are paid.
- **Accounts receivable** increase directly with increases in revenues as more products and services are sold on credit.
- **Inventories** normally increase in anticipation of higher sales volume to ensure a sufficient stock of inventory available for sale.
- **Prepaid expenses** increase with increases in advertising and other expenditures made in anticipation of higher sales.
- **PPE** assets are usually acquired once the revenues increase is deemed sustainable and the capacity constraint is reached; thus, PPE assets increase with increased revenue, but with a lag.
- **Accounts payable** increase as additional inventories are purchased on credit.
- **Accrued liabilities** increase concurrent with increases in revenue-driven operating expenses.
- **Other operating assets and liabilities** such as deferred revenues, deferred taxes, and pensions, increase and decrease concurrent with revenues.

Dynamics of Balance Sheet Growth

To understand the dynamics of growth in the balance sheet, it is useful to view it in three sections as depicted in Exhibit 11.2. Each of these sections experiences growth at different rates. As evident from Exhibit 11.1, most net operating assets grow roughly concurrently with increases in revenues. As net operating assets are normally positive, the asset side of the balance sheet grows faster than the liability side, in dollar terms. This creates an imbalance that must be managed by the company's finance and treasury departments.

EXHIBIT 11.2 Dynamics of Balance Sheet Growth

Marketable securities		Short-term debt	Buffer Zone (short and intermediate term)
Cash Accounts receivable Inventories PPE Other long-term operating assets		Accounts payable Accrued liabilities Long-term operating liabilities	Net Operating Assets plus Cash
		Long-term debt Common stock Additional paid-in capital Retained earnings Treasury stock	Financing Section (longer term)
Total assets	=	**Total liabilities and equity**	

The "buffer zone" represents that section of the balance sheet that responds to short- and intermediate-term imbalances. Cash declines as other operating assets increase, and companies typically finance that cash decline with short-term borrowings such as a seasonal line of credit from a bank. Conversely, companies typically invest excess cash in marketable securities (also titled short-term investments) to provide liquidity to meet future operating needs, investment opportunities, and similar near-term demands. Companies manage the "financing section" of the balance sheet on a long-term basis to provide funding for relatively permanent increases in net assets, such as PPE or even the acquisition of other companies. Further, income is reinvested in the business, long-term debt is borrowed, and equity securities are sold in proportions that are necessary to maintain the desired financial leverage for the company. Although the cash reinvestment decision is made continually, increases in long-term debt and equity occur relatively infrequently to meet longer-term funding needs. If the store of liquidity in the buffer zone is not needed for the foreseeable future, it can be used to retire long-term debt or to repurchase the company's outstanding shares.

Dynamics of Statement of Cash Flows Growth

The dynamics of the statement of cash flows mimic the dynamics of the income statement and balance sheet. This is because the statement of cash flows is prepared using both the income statement and balance sheet. Specifically, once we have forecasts of the income statement and balance sheet, we can compute the forecasted statement of cash flows just as we would its historical counterpart.

Identifying the Forecasting Steps

We apply the forecasting process in a four-step sequence:

1. **Forecast revenues.**
2. **Forecast operating and nonoperating expenses.** We assume a relation between revenue and each specific expense account.
3. **Forecast operating and nonoperating assets, liabilities and equity.** We assume a relation between revenue and each specific balance sheet account.
4. **Adjust short-term investments or short-term debt to balance the balance sheet.** We use marketable securities and short-term debt to balance the balance sheet. We then recompute net nonoperating expense (interest/dividend income or interest expense) to reflect any adjustments we make to nonoperating asset and liability account balances.

Forecasting Process: Procter & Gamble

We illustrate the forecasting process using the **Procter & Gamble** 10-K for the year ended June 30, 2013. First, we illustrate in detail, the type of forecasts that can be developed using publicly-available data only. Then we demonstrate the level of analysis that is performed by equity analysts with access to proprietary databases. The module includes an analysis report (together with the accompanying analysis spreadsheet) that has been provided to us by **Morgan Stanley**. That report was prepared in August 2013, shortly after P&G filed its fiscal 2013 10-K on August 8, 2013. We also benefitted from conversations with the Morgan Stanley analysts and we are grateful for the background information that they provided to us for the discussion of the forecasting process in this module.[1]

We begin our discussion by explaining the process of forecasting the income statement. P&G's reported income statement is reproduced in Exhibit 11.3 as a reference point.

STEP 1: FORECASTING REVENUES

LO2 Forecast revenues and the income statement.

Forecasting revenues is the most difficult and crucial step in the forecasting process. Further, many of the remaining income statement and balance sheet accounts are forecasted based on an assumed relation with forecasted revenues. We typically utilize both financial and nonfinancial information in developing forecasts. Each account must be separately analyzed using all relevant financial and nonfinancial information, including the insights gained from the first ten modules of this book.

To forecast revenues, then, we want to use all available, relevant information. But deciding what information is relevant and determining how to use the information varies across forecasters. As well, the level of information itself can vary across forecasters. For example, if we have access to inside information and we are developing forecasts as part of the strategic budgeting process for a company, we might have access to data regarding the competitive landscape, consumer trends and disposable income, new product introductions, production and marketing plans, and many other types of inside information. In this case, we can build our revenues forecast from the bottom up with unit sales and unit prices for each

[1] Copyright 2013 Morgan Stanley. Please note that materials that are referenced comprise excerpts from research reports and should not be relied on as investment advice. This material is only as current as the publication date of the underlying Morgan Stanley research. For important disclosures, stock price charts and equity rating histories regarding companies that are the subject of the underlying Morgan Stanley research, see www.morganstanley.com/researchdisclosures. Additionally, Morgan Stanley has provided their materials here as a courtesy. Therefore, Morgan Stanley and Cambridge Business Publishers do not undertake to advise you of changes in the opinions or information set forth in these materials.

EXHIBIT 11.3 Procter & Gamble Income Statement

Years Ended June 30 (In millions except per share amounts)	2013	2012	2011
Net sales	$84,167	$83,680	$81,104
Cost of products sold	42,428	42,391	39,859
Selling, general and administrative expense	26,950	26,421	25,750
Goodwill and indefinite-lived intangible asset impairment charges	308	1,576	—
Operating income	14,481	13,292	15,495
Interest expense	667	769	831
Interest income	87	77	62
Other nonoperating income, net	942	185	271
Earnings from continuing operations before income taxes	14,843	12,785	14,997
Income taxes on continuing operations	3,441	3,468	3,299
Net earnings from continuing operations	11,402	9,317	11,698
Net earnings from discontinued operations	—	1,587	229
Net earnings	11,402	10,904	11,927
Less: Net earnings attributable to noncontrolling interests	90	148	130
Net earnings attributable to Procter & Gamble	$11,312	$10,756	$11,797
Basic net earnings per common share	4.04	3.82	4.12
Diluted net earnings per common share	3.86	3.66	3.93
Dividends per common share	$2.29	$2.14	$1.97

product or service sold. However, if we are a company outsider, we have much less information. In this case, we must rely on public statements by company management in conference calls and meetings in addition to the information disclosed in the management discussion and analysis (MD&A) section of the 10-K and the growth of individual product lines from segment disclosures. We also use publicly available information from competitors, suppliers, and customers for additional insight into broader trends that can impact future revenues. Companies often provide "guidance" to outsiders to help refine forecasts, which is usually valuable as companies have a vested interest in correct forecasts so that their securities are accurately priced. Generally, the revenues forecast is obtained from the following formula:

$$\text{Forecasted revenues} = \text{Actual revenues} \times (1 + \text{Revenue growth rate in }\%)$$

The revenue growth rate can be either positive or negative depending on numerous company and economic factors, described above. The remainder of this section identifies and explains key factors that impact revenue growth and illustrates their application to Procter & Gamble.

Factors Impacting Revenue Growth

Forecasts are made within the broader context of the general economic environment and the competitive landscape in which the company operates. There are a number of specific factors that impact a company's revenue growth.

Impact of Acquisitions When one company acquires another, the revenues and expenses of the acquired company are consolidated but only from the date of acquisition onward (we discuss consolidation in Module 9). Acquisitions can greatly impact the acquirer's income statement, especially if the acquisition occurs toward the beginning of the acquirer's fiscal year. **Procter & Gamble**'s acquisition of Gillette in October 2005 provides an example. In its June 30, 2006, fiscal year-end income statement (ending eight months following the acquisition), P&G reported the following for sales:

Years ended June 30 ($ millions)	2006	2005	2004
Net sales	$68,222	$56,741	$51,407

These net sales amounts include Gillette product sales from October 2005 onward (for fiscal 2006), and none of Gillette's sales are reported in fiscal 2005 or fiscal 2004. P&G's 2006 sales growth of 20.2% ([$68,222/$56,741] − 1) was not P&G's organic growth, and we would have been remiss in forecasting a 20.2% increase for fiscal 2007.

Importantly, until all of the three annual income statements in the 10-K include the acquired company, the acquirer is required to disclose what revenue and net income would have been had the acquired company been consolidated for all three years reported in the current annual report. This "what if" disclosure is called *pro forma* disclosure. Procter & Gamble's pro forma disclosure in 2006 includes the following discussion and table:

The following table provides pro forma results of operations for the years ended June 30, 2006, 2005, and 2004, as if Gillette had been acquired as of the beginning of each fiscal year presented.

Pro forma results; Years ended June 30	2006	2005	2004
Net sales (in millions)	$71,005	$67,920	$61,112
Net earnings (in millions)	8,871	8,522	7,504
Diluted net earnings per common share	2.51	2.29	1.98

Using this disclosure, we would have been able to compute the growth rate in sales for 2006 as 4.5% ([$71,005/$67,920] − 1), and we would have used the pro forma net sales for 2006 as our forecasting base. That is, assuming a continuation of this 4.5% growth rate, we would have forecasted 2007 net sales as $74,200 (calculated as $71,005 × 1.045). P&G was careful to point out, however, that the pro forma earnings estimate must be viewed with caution:

Pro forma results do not include any anticipated cost savings or other effects of the planned integration of Gillette. Accordingly, such amounts are not necessarily indicative of the results if the acquisition had occurred on the dates indicated or that may result in the future.

Impact of Divestitures Companies are required to exclude sales and expenses of discontinued operations from the continuing operations portion of their income statements, and to present the net income and gain (loss) on sale of the divested entity, net of tax, below income from continuing operations (we discuss accounting for divestitures in Module 5 and Module 8). **Procter & Gamble**'s income statement in Exhibit 11.3 reports net earnings from discontinued operations of $1,587 million and $229 million for fiscal years 2012 and 2011, respectively. The following footnote from P&G's 2013 10-K provides information about these two discontinued operations:

Discontinued Operations In fiscal 2012, the Company completed the divestiture of our global snacks business to The Kellogg Company (Kellogg) for $2.7 billion of cash. . . The Company recorded an after-tax gain on the transaction of $1.4 billion, which is included in net earnings from discontinued operations in the Consolidated Statement of Earnings for the year ended June 30, 2012. The snacks business had historically been part of the Company's Snacks and Pet Care reportable segment. In accordance with the applicable accounting guidance for the disposal of long-lived assets, the results of the snacks business are presented as discontinued operations and, as such, have been excluded from both continuing operations and segment results for all years presented. Following is selected financial information included in net earnings from discontinued operations for the snacks business:

continued

($ millions)		Net Sales	Earnings from Discontinued Operations	Income Tax Expense	Gain on Sale of Discontinued Operations	Income Tax Benefit (Expense) on Sale	Net Earnings from Discontinued Operations
Snacks	2013	$ —	$ —	$ —	$ —	$ —	$ —
	2012	1,440	266	(96)	1,899	(482)	1,587
	2011	1,455	322	(93)	—	—	229

The revenues, expenses, and earnings for Procter & Gamble in fiscal years 2012 and 2011, as reported in its income statement, *exclude* the revenues, expenses, and earnings from its discontinued operations. The detail relating to the revenues, expenses, and earnings of discontinued operations (and their gain on sale) is reported in the footnote disclosure shown above. This additional information allows us to better evaluate the drivers of observed growth of revenues and earnings, and we would be remiss if we included the revenues and gains relating to discontinued operations in our forecasts.

Impact of Existing vs New Store Growth Retailers typically derive revenue growth from two sources: (1) from *existing* stores (organic growth), and (2) from *new* stores. We are interested in the breakdown between these two growth sources as the latter is obtained at considerably more cost. **Target Corporation** provides the following footnote disclosure to its 2012 10-K report.

				Percent Change	
Retail Segment Results (millions)	**2012**	**2011**	**2010**	**2012/2011**	**2011/2010**
Sales	**$71,960**	$68,466	$65,786	**5.1%**	4.1%
Cost of sales	**50,568**	47,860	45,725	**5.7**	4.7
Gross margin	**21,392**	20,606	20,061	**3.8**	2.7
SG&A expenses	**14,342**	13,774	13,367	**4.1**	3.0
EBITDA	**7,050**	6,832	6,694	**3.2**	2.1
Depreciation and amortization	**2,031**	2,067	2,065	**(1.8)**	0.1
EBIT	**$ 5,019**	$ 4,765	$ 4,629	**5.3%**	2.9%

Comparable-Store Sales	**2012**	**2011**	**2010**
Comparable-store sales change	**2.7%**	3.0%	2.1%
Drivers of changes in comparable-store sales:			
Number of transactions	**0.5%**	0.4%	2.0%
Average transaction amount	**2.3%**	2.6%	0.1%
Selling price per unit	**1.3%**	0.3%	(2.3)%
Units per transaction	**1.0%**	2.3%	2.5%

Our 2012 financial results in our U.S. Retail Segment reflect increased sales of 5.1 percent over the same period last year due to a 2.7 percent comparable-store increase, the contribution from new stores and the additional week in 2012.

At least three points in Target's footnote disclosure are noteworthy for forecasting purposes.

1. Retailers typically operate on a 52 or 53 week year, closing their books on a particular day of the week rather than on a constant date. Target has the following fiscal year-end policy:

Our fiscal year ends on the Saturday nearest January 31. Unless otherwise stated, references to years in this report relate to fiscal years, rather than to calendar years. Fiscal 2012 ended February 2, 2013, and consisted of 53 weeks. Fiscal 2011 ended January 28, 2012, and consisted of 52 weeks. Fiscal 2010 ended January 29, 2011, and consisted of 52 weeks. Fiscal 2013 will end February 1, 2014, and will consist of 52 weeks.

Target's fiscal year 2012 consists of 53 weeks while fiscal years 2011 and 2010 are only 52-weeks long. Target's 2012 income statement includes an extra week's sales, which makes it appear as if sales are growing at a higher rate than they are. To accurately forecast revenue growth, we must use numbers and rates that reflect a consistent 52-week year. To do this, we assume that sales are recorded evenly each week and we adjust revenues for the 53-week year by multiplying reported sales by 52/53. For fiscal year 2012, the adjusted sales for the U.S. Retail Segment are $71,960 × 52/53 = $70,602 and the adjusted growth rate for 2012 is 3.1% ([$70,602/$68,466] − 1) rather than the 5.1% reported in the table above.

2. More than 47% ([5.1% − 2.7%]/5.1% = 47.1%) of Target's 2012 sales growth is attributable to new store openings.
3. The average per store planned capital expenditure is about $47 million ($1,090 million reported CAPEX for new stores/23 new stores opened in 2012 as reported in the MD&A). Although acquired growth provides the organic growth of the future, it comes at considerable cost per store.

Impact of Unit Sales and Price Disclosures Forecasts that are built from anticipated unit sales and current prices are generally more informative, and accurate, than those derived from historical dollar sales. Most companies, however, do not provide unit sales data in their 10-Ks. **Apple Inc.**, is an exception, and the following footnote disclosure from its 2012 10-K provides useful information. Like Target, Apple operates on a 52- or 53-week fiscal year. To accommodate for the extra week in 2012, we added two columns (in dark maroon color) to the data provided by Apple; one that shows pro rated sales (2012 sales multiplied by 52/53) and a second that shows the recalculated change in sales.

Net Sales The Company's fiscal year is the 52- or 53-week period that ends on the last Saturday of September. The Company's fiscal years 2012, 2011 and 2010 ended on September 29, 2012, September 24, 2011, and September 25, 2010, respectively. Fiscal year 2012 spanned 53 weeks, with a 14th week included in the first quarter of 2012, as is done approximately every six years to realign the Company's fiscal quarters more closely to calendar quarters. . . . The following table shows . . . net sales and unit sales by product during 2012, 2011, and 2010 (dollars in millions and units in thousands):

	2012 (52 weeks)	Recalculated Change	2012	Change	2011	Change	2010
Net sales by product							
Desktops	$ 5,926	(8)%	$ 6,040	(6)%	$ 6,439	4%	$ 6,201
Portables	16,857	10%	17,181	12%	15,344	36%	11,278
Total Mac net sales	22,783	5%	23,221	7%	21,783	25%	17,479
iPod	5,509	(26)%	5,615	(25)%	7,453	(10)%	8,274
Other music related products and services	8,373	33%	8,534	35%	6,314	28%	4,948
iPhone and related products and services	78,959	68%	80,477	71%	47,057	87%	25,179
iPad and related products and services	31,812	56%	32,424	59%	20,358	311%	4,958
Peripherals and other hardware	2,726	17%	2,778	19%	2,330	28%	1,814
Software, service, and other sales	3,394	15%	3,459	17%	2,954	15%	2,573
Total net sales	$153,556	42%	$156,508	45%	$108,249	66%	$65,225
Unit sales by product							
Desktops	4,568	(2)%	4,656	0%	4,669	1%	4,627
Portables	13,247	10%	13,502	12%	12,066	34%	9,035
Total Mac unit sales	17,815	6%	18,158	9%	16,735	22%	13,662
iPod unit sales	34,502	(19)%	35,165	(17)%	42,620	(15)%	50,312
iPhone units sold	122,687	70%	125,046	73%	72,293	81%	39,989
iPad units sold	57,210	77%	58,310	80%	32,394	334%	7,458

Since Apple's fiscal year 2012 includes an extra week, we have added a column to multiply all the sales figures (units and dollars) by 52/53 and then recomputed the percentage changes.

From the adjusted figures above, we can form several insights useful for forecasting purposes:

1. On average, a Mac sold for $1,279 ($22,783,000/17,815) in 2012 and the per-unit selling price is about the same as it was two years ago ($17,479,000/13.662 = $1,279). However, unit sales have increased by 6% and 22% per year for the past two years.
2. The iPod unit sales have decreased over the past two years, probably reflecting increased competition from other MP3 players and market saturation.
3. The average sales price of iPods in 2012 is $160, about 9% less than the average sales price the year before.
4. iPhone unit sales are 122,687 thousand, up 70% from 2011 and 207% from 2010. iPhone (and related) dollar sales are $78,959 million in 2012, 68% higher than 2011 and 214% greater than in 2010.
5. iPad unit sales are 57,210 thousand in 2012, 77% greater than the prior year and 667% greater than 2010. As of 2012, iPad sales account for over one fifth of Apple's total sales.

Unit volume and price data provides useful information from which to develop the sales forecast. This is particularly evident in the forecast of Procter & Gamble's revenues which we illustrate below. P&G provides a substantial amount of price and volume data to better inform their revenue forecasts, and the approach that we take (as we will see, professional equity analysts take the same approach) is to build the sales forecast from more granular revenue forecasts for the company's products.

Detailed disclosures such as Apple's allow us to prepare more informed forecasts that consider both unit sales and selling prices.

Impact of Foreign Currency Fluctuations on Reported Sales As we discuss in Module 5, a change in the strength of the $US vis-à-vis foreign currencies has a direct effect on the $US equivalent for revenues, expenses, and income of the foreign subsidiary because revenues and expenses are translated at the average exchange rate for the period. When the $US weakens vis-à-vis other world currencies in which the company is conducting its business operations, revenues and expenses, which are reported in local currencies on the books of foreign subsidiaries, translate into more $US and, thus, reported revenues and expenses are higher than if the currencies had not fluctuated. On the other hand, when the $US strengthens, the subsidiary's revenues and expenses decrease in $US terms. Procter & Gamble discusses these foreign currency effects in the following excerpts from its 2013 10-K.

Financial Information about Foreign and Domestic Operations. Net sales in the United States account for approximately 36% of total net sales. No other individual country exceeds 10% of total net sales. . . Net sales . . . in the United States and internationally were as follows (in billions):

Net Sales (for the year ended June 30)	United States	International
2013	$30.3	$53.9
2012	$29.5	$54.2
2011	$29.9	$51.2

The primary factors driving year-over-year changes in net sales include overall market growth in the categories in which we compete, product initiatives, geographic expansion and acquisition and divestiture activity, all of which drive changes in our underlying unit volume, as well as pricing actions (which can also indirectly impact volume), changes in product and geographic mix and foreign currency impacts on sales outside the United States.

As we discuss below, P&G reports revenues by business segment and provides a detailed breakdown of the drivers of sales changes. That analysis reveals that the stronger $US resulted in a decrease in reported sales of 2% in 2013.

Forecasting Revenue Growth

To illustrate the forecasting process, we forecast revenue growth for P&G. Our information includes public disclosures by management in meetings and conference calls with analysts and the company's published financial reports including the management discussion and analysis (MD&A) section of the 10-K. We discuss the information in each of these sources.

Public Disclosures via Meetings and Calls P&G released its fourth quarter (4Q) results, together with guidance for fiscal 2014 on August 1, 2013, a week before the company released its fiscal 2013 financial statements. The presentation (publicly available on the "Investor Relations" section of P&G's Website) provides guidance in several areas that impact our forecasts and we include excerpts from that presentation in our discussion below.

Published Reports: Segment Disclosures and MD&A Companies are required to disclose summary financial results for each of their operating segments along with a discussion and analysis of each. (An operating segment is defined under GAAP as a component of the company for which financial information is available and disclosed to senior management.) P&G is organized into five operating segments as discussed in the following excerpt from its 2013 MD&A:

Global Business Units (GBU). Under U.S. GAAP, the GBUs are aggregated into five reportable segments: Beauty; Grooming; Health Care; Fabric Care and Home Care; and Baby Care and Family Care. The GBUs are responsible for developing overall brand strategy, new product upgrades and innovations and marketing plans. The following provides additional detail on our reportable segments and the key product categories and brand composition within each segment.

Reportable Segment	% of Net Sales*	% of Net Earnings*	GBUs (Categories)	Billion-Dollar Brands
Beauty	24%	21%	Beauty Care (Antiperspirant and Deodorant, Cosmetics, Personal Cleansing, Skin Care); Hair Care and Color; Prestige (SK-II, Fragrances); Salon Professional	Head & Shoulders, Olay, Pantene, SK-II, Wella
Grooming	9%	16%	Shave Care (Blades and Razors, Pre- and Post-Shave Products); Braun and Appliances	Fusion, Gillette, Mach3, Prestobarba
Health Care	15%	17%	Feminine Care (Feminine Care, Incontinence); Oral Care (Toothbrush, Toothpaste, Other Oral Care); Personal Health Care (Gastrointestinal, Rapid Diagnostics, Respiratory, Other Personal Health Care, Vitamins/Minerals/ Supplements)	Always, Crest, Oral-B, Vicks
Fabric Care and Home Care	32%	27%	Fabric Care (Bleach and Laundry Additives, Fabric Enhancers, Laundry Detergents); Home Care (Air Care, Dish Care, Surface Care); Personal Power (Batteries); Pet Care; Professional	Ace, Ariel, Dawn, Downy, Duracell, Febreze, Gain, Iams, Tide
Baby Care and Family Care	20%	19%	Baby Care (Baby Wipes, Diapers and Pants); Family Care (Paper Towels, Tissues, Toilet Paper)	Bounty, Charmin, Pampers

* Percent of net sales and net earnings from continuing operations for the year ended June 30, 2013 (excluding results held in Corporate).

P&G also reports a revenue history for each segment and its MD&A provides additional information relating to the breakdown of revenue increases for the current year into the portion relating to increases in unit volume sales, increases in prices, effects of foreign-currency translation, and changes in product mix. That disclosure and related discussion allow us to compile the following table:

Net Sales Change Drivers (2013 vs. 2012)	Volume with Acquisitions & Divestitures	Volume Excluding Acquisitions & Divestitures	Foreign Exchange	Price	Mix	Other	Net Sales Growth
Beauty	0%	0%	(2)%	2%	(1)%	(1)%	(2)%
Grooming	(1)%	0%	(4)%	2%	0%	(1)%	(4)%
Health Care	3%	3%	(3)%	1%	1%	1%	3%
Fabric Care and Home Care	3%	3%	(2)%	1%	(1)%	0%	1%
Baby Care and Family Care	4%	4%	(2)%	1%	(1)%	0%	2%
Total Company	2%	2%	(2)%	1%	0%	0%	1%

P&G's net sales (in dollars) increased by 1% in 2013 as a result of a 2% increase in units sold (although marked variation is evident across products) and a 1% increase in prices. Net sales declined, however, as a result of changes in product mix for the Beauty, the Fabric Care, and the Baby Care segments (more lower-priced products were sold), although the overall effect was negligible. This volume/price/mix analysis is potentially important because increased units sold is a stronger path to growth than price increases that might be unsustainable.

During 2013, the U.S. dollar strengthened vis-à-vis other world currencies in which P&G conduct its business. Thus, revenues denominated in foreign currencies decreased when translated into U.S. dollars. For P&G, foreign exchange fluctuations caused sales to fall by 2% (see Module 5 for a discussion of foreign exchange rate effects on sales). We must be aware of these foreign exchange fluctuations because they (and not quantity or price changes) might drive fluctuations in net sales.

Determining the Revenue Growth Forecast: Using Publicly-Available Information

Procter & Gamble issued its fourth quarter earnings release on August 1, 2013, as follows:

> CINCINNATI, Aug. 1, 2013 - The Procter & Gamble Company (NYSE:PG) reported fiscal year 2013 diluted net earnings per share from continuing operations of $3.86, up 24 percent versus the prior year. Core earnings per share were $4.05, an increase of five percent versus the prior year. Net sales were $84.2 billion, an increase of one percent including a negative two point impact from foreign exchange. Organic sales grew three percent for the fiscal year. . . Net sales increased one percent to $84.2 billion for fiscal 2013. Unit volume growth contributed two percent to sales growth, and pricing added one percent. Unfavorable foreign exchange reduced net sales by two percentage points. Organic sales increased three percent, with all segments growing organic sales.

In addition to the report of historical performance, P&G also provided guidance to analysts for 2014:

> **Fiscal Year 2014 Guidance.** For fiscal year 2014, P&G expects organic sales growth in the range of three percent to four percent compared to underlying global market growth of about 3.5 percent. All-in sales growth is forecast in the range of one percent to two percent, including a negative foreign exchange impact of approximately two percent.

The issuance of guidance to assist analysts in the preparation of their forecasts is common and it provides a useful starting point for our forecasts. P&G focuses its guidance on "organic sales growth" which it defines as follows in its 2013 10-K:

> **Organic Sales Growth.** Organic sales growth is a non-GAAP measure of sales growth excluding the impacts of acquisitions, divestitures and foreign exchange from year-over-year comparisons. We believe this provides investors with a more complete understanding of underlying sales trends by providing sales growth on a consistent basis.

Organic sales growth seeks to eliminate the effects of acquisitions and divestitures as well as the effects of foreign currency fluctuations which we discuss above. This measure of growth, therefore, focuses on sales changes resulting from changes in core (not acquired) unit volume, pricing and mix.

Analysts cannot blindly accept company guidance and must scrutinize it for reasonableness. P&G's historical organic growth has been in the range of 3% to 4% for the past four years as P&G reports in the following excerpt from its presentation to analysts at the *Barclays Back-to-School Conference* on September 4, 2013 (slides available on the investor relations section of P&G's Website):

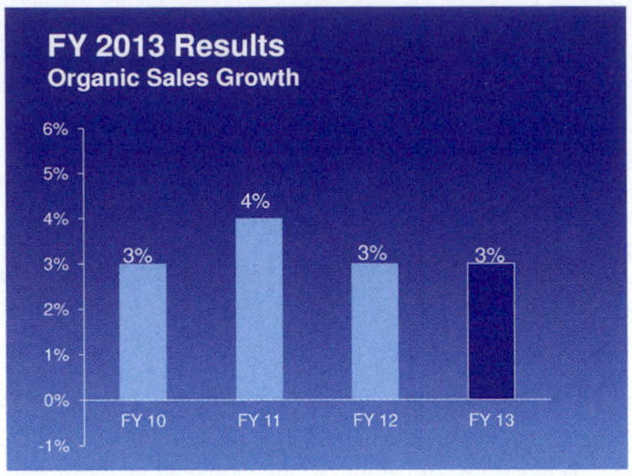

P&G also discloses that organic sales growth has been accelerating in the recent past as illustrated in the following slide from its 4Q (4th quarter) earnings release:

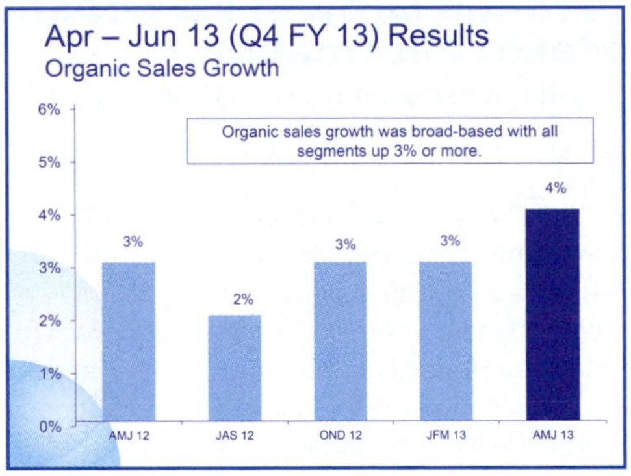

These slides lend some credence to an organic growth range of 3% to 4%. However, it is helpful to examine the components of organic growth (changes in unit volume, produce price changes, and changes in product mix). The following chart is prepared from data that P&G provides in its 10-K reports:

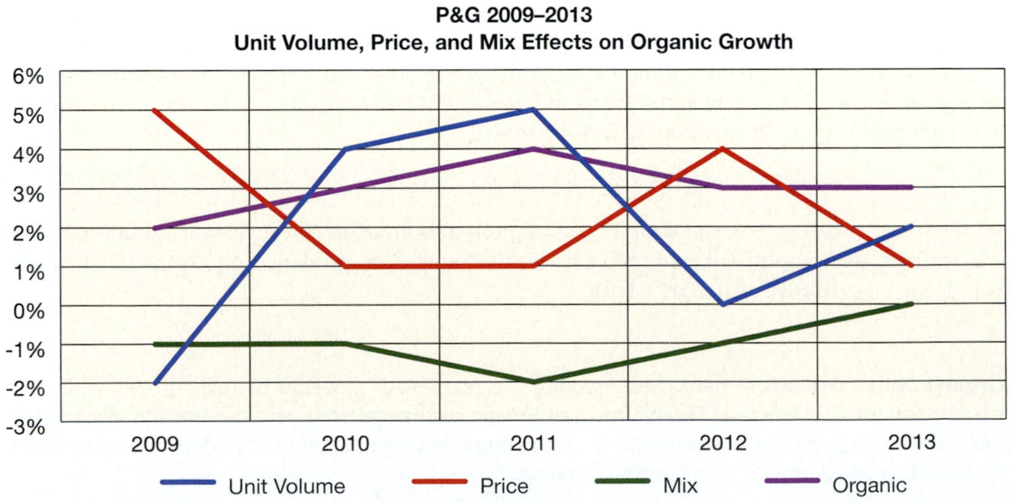

Unit volumes have fluctuated within a range of −2% to 5% over the past five years. More recently, unit volumes have increased by 0% and 2% for 2012 and 2013, respectively. Also during the past five years, increases in sales volume due to increases in product prices have ranged from 1% to 5%, with FY2013 at the low end. Finally, sales changes due to changes in the mix of products sold have been negative in the previous four years and were not a factor in the most recent year. On balance, an increase in unit volume of 2%, coupled with an increase in product prices of 1% to 2% does not seem unreasonable as the world economy continues to grow. This provides further support for the P&G guidance of 3% to 4% organic growth.

The sales that P&G will report in its FY2014 income statement, however, include the effects of foreign currency fluctuations, and P&G expects the $US to strengthen vis-à-vis other world currencies in which the company conducts its business:

FY 2014 Guidance
Organic Sales & EPS Growth

	FY'14
Organic Sales Growth	+3% to +4%
Currency	-2%
All-in Sales Growth	+1% to +2%
Core Earnings Per Share	+5% to +7%
All-in Earnings Per Share	+7% to +9%

The projected strengthening of the $US will result in a lower $US equivalent of foreign currency-denominated sales, yielding a net sales increase of 1% to 2%.

The bottom line is we forecast a sales growth for FY2014 of 1.5%, consisting of a 3.5% organic sales growth offset by a 2% decrease in sales resulting from a strengthening of the $US.

Determining Revenue Growth Forecast: Using Proprietary Databases

Banks and securities firms provide their equity analysts with a wealth of proprietary databases that are unavailable to the general public. The forecasting process can, as a result, employ a larger information set than the publicly-available data that we have utilized above. To illustrate the level of detail incorporated into forecasts by equity analysts, we focus on the forecast and related analyst report issued by **Morgan Stanley** (we provide the full report in the appendix to this module).

Following are a few observations that Morgan Stanley analysts conveyed to us about the way in which their sales forecasts are developed:

1. Each product forecast is built from the bottom up; that is, analysts use information about a product's market share and the forecasted growth rate for the market of each product within each country the product is sold. Development of such forecasts uses information about product market, pricing strategy, and competitive landscape. With this information, analysts forecast overall market growth, the market share for each product, changes in product pricing, and changes in the product sales mix. The total sales forecast is the sum of individual product forecasts for each product market.
2. P&G, like many companies, provides analysts with its own forecasts of sales growth by products, disaggregated into price and volume. Morgan Stanley analysts also have internally-developed databases of commodity-price indices, inflation indices, and other macroeconomic indices against which to evaluate the reasonableness of company-provided forecasts.
3. Sales forecasts are determined by quantity and price along with growth forecasts of the product markets, the company-provided future pricing strategy, and forecasts of price elasticity of demand. Analysts commonly consider, for example, the effects of a current discount pricing strategy to increase market share or to gain entrance into a new market, which are followed by price increases once volume levels and customer loyalty is solidified.

Morgan Stanley analysts forecast a 2.1% increase in sales for FY2014 that is built up from the following estimates:

Organic sales growth		3.7%
Volume	3.7%	
Pricing	0.2%	
Mix	(0.2)%	
Foreign exchange impact		(1.6)%
Acquisitions & divestitures		0.0%
Sales growth		2.1%

Morgan Stanley analysts forecast each of the organic sales growth components in the table above for each of P&G's segments to obtain an aggregate forecast of sales. To illustrate, following is an excerpt from the Morgan Stanley forecast spreadsheet for P&G's total sales and for its Beauty segment (the spreadsheet has similar forecasts for each segment).

	A B	AP	AU	AZ	BE	BF	BG	BH	BI	BJ	BK	BL	BM	BN	BO	BT
1	**Procter & Gamble Co (PG)**															
2	**Segment Breakdown**	FY2009	FY2010	FY2011	FY2012	Sep-12	Dec-12	Mar-13	Jun-13	FY2013	Sep-13E	Dec-13E	Mar-14E	Jun-14E	FY2014E	FY2015E
3	**Total Sales**	76,694.0	78,938.0	82,559.0	83,680.0	20,739.0	22,175.0	20,598.0	20,655.0	84,167.0	21,437.3	22,290.8	21,016.4	21,182.5	85,926.9	89,440.0
4	Organic Sales Growth	2.0%	4.0%	4.0%	3.7%	2.0%	3.0%	3.0%	4.0%	2.8%	5.2%	3.1%	4.0%	2.6%	3.7%	4.1%
5	Volume (Organic)	-2.0%	4.0%	5.2%	0.7%	0.0%	2.0%	2.0%	5.0%	2.0%	5.2%	3.1%	4.0%	2.5%	3.7%	3.7%
6	Pricing	5.0%	0.5%	0.4%	4.2%	2.0%	2.0%	1.0%	0.0%	1.4%	0.2%	0.2%	0.3%	0.2%	0.2%	0.4%
7	Mix	-1.0%	-1.1%	-1.6%	-1.2%	0.0%	-1.0%	0.0%	-1.0%	-0.5%	-0.2%	-0.2%	-0.2%	-0.2%	-0.2%	0.0%
8	FX Impact	-4.0%	-0.4%	0.2%	0.0%	-6.0%	-1.0%	-1.0%	-2.0%	-2.4%	-1.8%	-2.6%	-2.0%	0.0%	-1.6%	0.0%
9	Acq/Div	-0.8%	-0.1%	0.3%	-1.9%	0.0%	0.0%	0.0%	0.2%	0.0%	0.0%	0.0%	0.0%	0.0%	0.0%	0.0%
10	% Sales Growth	-2.8%	2.9%	4.6%	1.4%	-3.7%	2.0%	2.0%	2.2%	0.6%	3.4%	0.5%	2.0%	2.6%	2.1%	4.1%
11	**Beauty**															
12	**Beauty Care**	**18,924.0**	**19,491.0**	**20,157.0**	**20,318.0**	**4,940.0**	**5,403.0**	**4,763.0**	**4,850.0**	**19,956.0**	**5,135.6**	**5,310.3**	**4,897.3**	**4,874.3**	**20,217.4**	**21,228.3**
13	Organic Sales Growth	1.0%	3.2%	3.0%	2.0%	-2.0%	3.0%	-1.0%	3.0%	0.7%	5.5%	0.5%	4.5%	0.5%	2.7%	5.0%
14	Volume (Organic)	-1.0%	3.3%	4.5%	1.9%	-3.0%	0.0%	-1.0%	4.0%	-0.1%	6.0%	1.0%	5.0%	1.0%	3.2%	4.0%
15	Pricing	2.0%	0.9%	0.5%	3.5%	2.0%	3.0%	1.0%	0.0%	1.6%	0.0%	0.0%	0.0%	0.0%	0.0%	1.0%
16	Mix	0.0%	-0.4%	-2.0%	-3.4%	-1.0%	0.0%	-1.0%	-1.0%	-0.7%	-0.5%	-0.5%	-0.5%	-0.5%	-0.5%	0.0%
17	FX Impact	-4.0%	0.0%	1.2%	0.5%	-5.0%	0.0%	-1.0%	-2.0%	-2.0%	-1.5%	-2.2%	-1.7%	0.0%	-1.4%	0.0%
18	Acq/Div	-0.5%	-0.5%	-1.0%	-0.8%	0.0%	-1.0%	0.0%	0.0%	-0.3%	0.0%	0.0%	0.0%	0.0%	0.0%	0.0%
19	% Sales Growth	-3.7%	3.0%	3.4%	0.8%	-7.1%	0.9%	-1.7%	0.9%	-1.8%	4.0%	-1.7%	2.8%	0.5%	1.3%	5.0%
20	**Grooming**	**7,408.0**	**7,631.0**	**8,025.0**	**8,339.0**	**2,007.0**	**2,119.0**	**1,931.0**	**1,981.0**	**8,038.0**	**2,020.8**	**2,112.1**	**1,940.3**	**2,040.4**	**8,113.6**	**8,519.3**
21	Organic Sales Growth	-2.0%	3.0%	5.0%	1.5%	2.0%	2.0%	2.0%	4.0%	2.5%	3.0%	3.0%	3.0%	3.0%	3.0%	5.0%
22	Volume (Organic)	-5.0%	0.3%	3.3%	0.5%	-0.5%	0.0%	0.0%	2.0%	0.4%	2.0%	2.0%	2.0%	2.0%	2.0%	4.0%
23	Pricing	5.0%	3.7%	2.2%	2.0%	3.0%	2.0%	3.0%	2.0%	2.5%	1.0%	1.0%	1.0%	1.0%	1.0%	1.0%
24	Mix	-2.0%	-1.0%	-0.5%	-1.0%	-0.5%	0.0%	-1.0%	0.0%	-0.4%	0.0%	0.0%	0.0%	0.0%	0.0%	0.0%
25	FX Impact	-6.0%	0.0%	-0.1%	-0.4%	-8.0%	-3.0%	-1.0%	-3.0%	-3.8%	-2.3%	-3.3%	-2.5%	0.0%	-2.1%	0.0%
26	Acq/Div	-0.3%	0.2%	0.0%	0.0%	-1.0%	-1.0%	-3.0%	-2.0%	-1.7%	0.0%	0.0%	0.0%	0.0%	0.0%	0.0%
27	% Sales Growth	-8.6%	3.0%	5.2%	3.9%	-7.4%	-3.8%	-1.6%	-1.3%	-3.6%	0.7%	-0.3%	0.5%	3.0%	0.9%	5.0%

Analysts generate quarterly forecasts and the annual forecast is the sum of the four quarters. Each product in each business segment is separately forecast and the organic sales forecast is, essentially, built from the product level up. Further, each of these estimates is developed from sound underlying analysis and we touch on a few of the inputs in the following section.

Organic Sales Growth—Volume Analysts focus on the drivers of volume and develop their forecasts from forecasts of the drivers. For P&G, there is a strong association between the growth of global gross domestic product (GDP) and the growth of organic sales, more so than is the association between GDP growth and organic sales for P&G's peer companies, as indicated by the following statement and related charts from Morgan Stanley research (July 23, 2013 report on P&G):

> PG should benefit sequentially from rebounding U.S. consumer spending, given PG's outsized leverage to the U.S. (more than half of profit mix) and macro sensitivity. As evidence, since 2007, PG has the highest historical correlation between quarterly organic sales growth and weighted-average GDP growth (weighted by company geographic sales mix) among the large cap companies in our coverage at 55% (Exhibit 27). This is well above CL, PEP, and KO, which have had little relationship between these two metrics (Exhibit 28).

continued

Exhibit 27

Strong Correlation Between PG's Organic Sales Growth and Weighted-Average GDP Growth...

PG Y-o-Y Oranic Sales Growth (2007–Current)

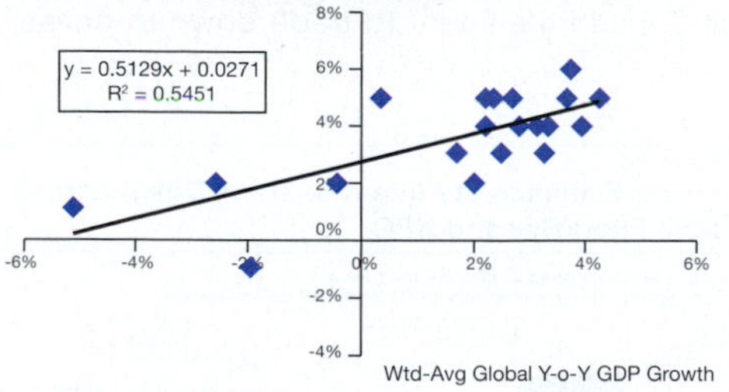

Source: Company data, Bloomberg, Morgan Stanley Research

Exhibit 28

PG is More Macro=Sensitive Than Staples Peers

Organic Sales Growth R-Squared Correlation to Geographic-Weighted Average GDP Growth (2007–Current)

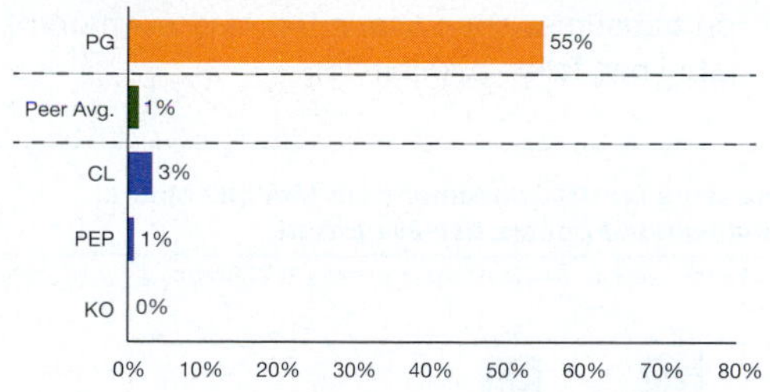

Source: Company data, Bloomberg, Morgan Stanley Research

Morgan Stanley, then, uses this association, together with its prediction of factors contributing to GDP growth, to justify its expectation of a stronger increase in unit volumes. They conclude:

US consumer spending was pressured in Q1, given higher payroll taxes, higher gas prices, and less favorable y-o-y weather (although we view these as temporary issues). However, we do think a longer-term US consumer spending recovery will likely transpire starting in the back half of the year, particularly given improving unemployment (Exhibit 21) and housing industry trends (Exhibit 22), and given consumer confidence is a five year high (Exhibit 23). Our US Economics team at Morgan Stanley, which recently increased its US GPD forecasts, while reducing its forecasted unemployment rate (Exhibit 24), gives credence to a recovery in consumer spending.

Exhibit 21

US Unemployment Rate Has Declined, While the Number Employed Has Accelerated

US Civilian Unemployment Rate and Total Employed

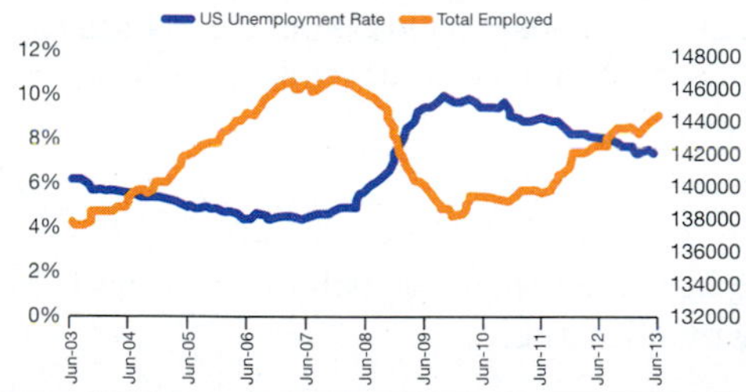

Source: Company data, Bloomberg, Morgan Stanley Research

Exhibit 22

US Home Sales Have Rebounded

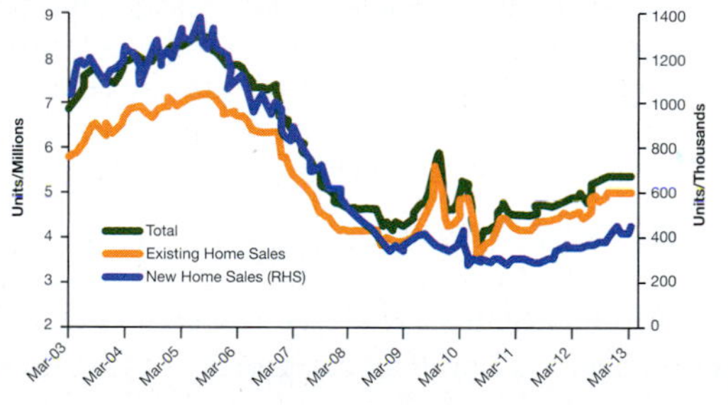

Source: Bloomberg, Morgan Stanley Research

Exhibit 23

US Consumer Confidence Is at 5-Year High

The Conference Board - Consumer Confidence Index

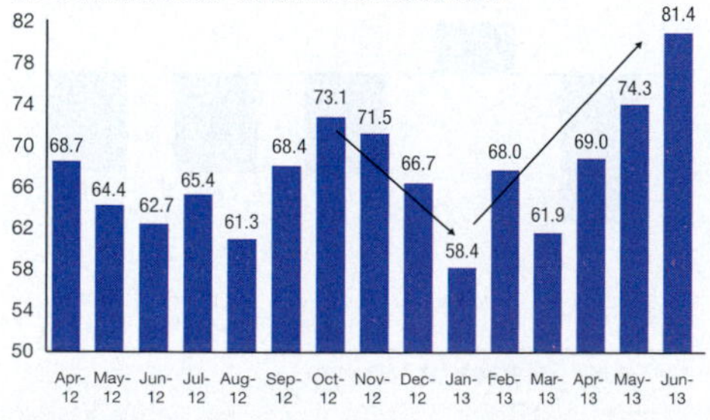

Source: Bloomberg, Morgan Stanley Research

Exhibit 24

MS Economics Team Has Increased Its US GDP Forecast and Lowering the Unemployment Rate

Morgan Stanley US GDP and Unemployment Rate Forecasts

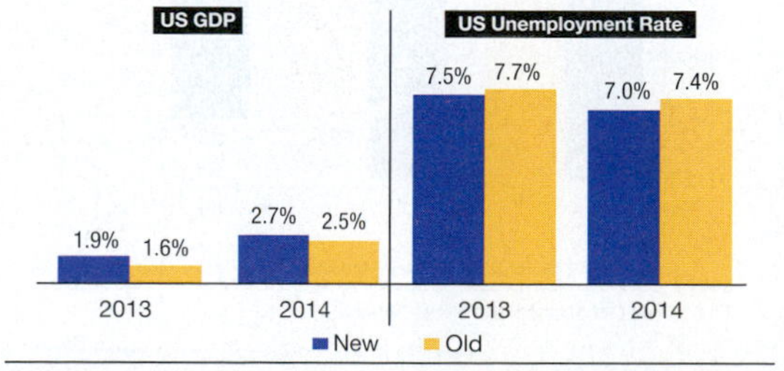

Source: Morgan Stanley Research

continued

continued from prior page

Furthermore, our recent AlphaWise consumer survey of 1,000 U.S. consumers in May 2013 indicates an improved outlook for the U.S. consumer, confirming macro trends. Compared to our 2011 results, our new survey finds that major economic headwinds will have a less measurable impact on consumer spending in the next six months (Exhibit 25) and the intent to trade down to private label has fallen (Exhibit 26).

Exhibit 25
Pressure on US Consumer from Multiple Macro Headwinds Appears to Have Eased

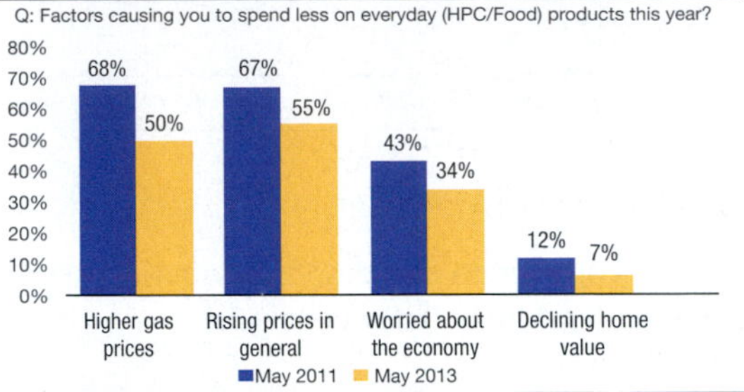

Source: AlphaWise, Morgan Stanley Research

Exhibit 26
Lower Evidence of / Intent to Trade Down Across both Food/Bev and HPC

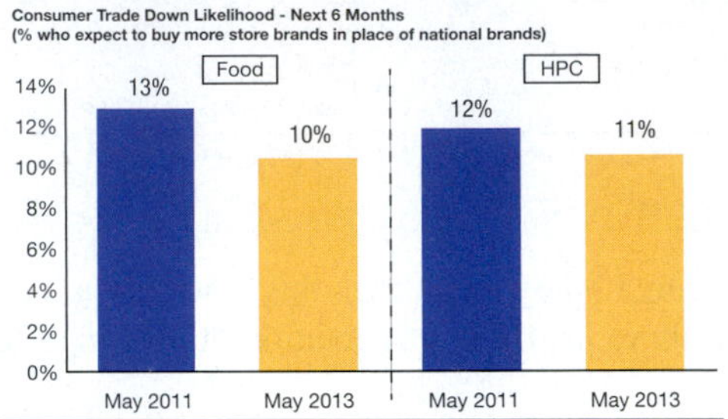

Source: AlphaWise, Morgan Stanley Research

Organic Sales Growth—Price While analysts forecast an increase in organic growth as a result of increases in unit volume as the world economy continues to grow, they are less optimistic about P&G's ability to raise prices and forecast only a 0.2% pricing effect that is likely to be offset by changes in product mix as consumers trade down in product categories (May 6, 2013 report on P&G):

PG's portfolio is at a disadvantage as it skews to the lower growth mass channel, which is losing share to the higher priced prestige channel as consumers trade up. However, within the lower priced mass channel, where the low-to-middle end consumer is still under pressure, PG skews to high-end. This has hurt results as consumers have moved to value-oriented products, particularly in color. While PG is making progress through innovation, changing the portfolio mix organically will take a long period of time given PG's large existing size.

The Morgan Stanley analysts' research cites a decline in market share, globally and in the U.S. and across nearly all product categories as the following charts illustrate:

Exhibit 12
PG Market Share Trends in the US and Globally Remain Down a Y-o-Y Basis

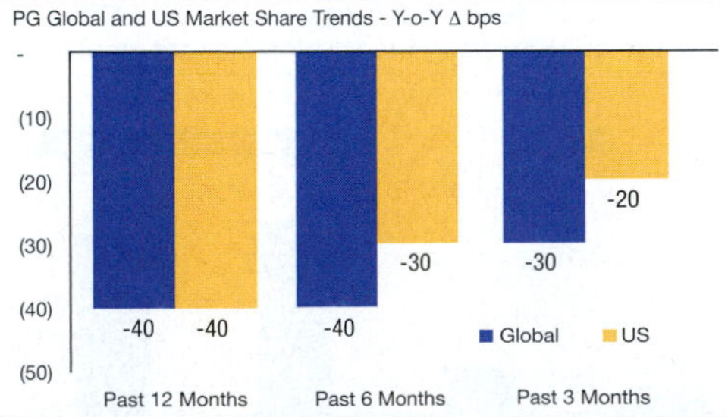

Source: Company Data, Morgan Stanley Research

Exhibit 13
PG Lost Market Share in Four out of Five Segments in the Most Recent Quarter

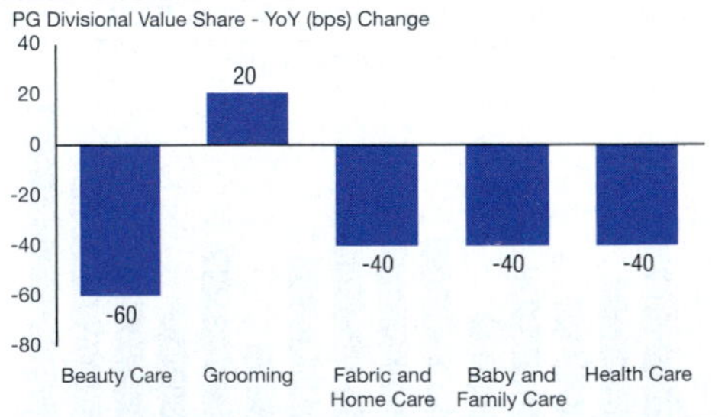

Source: Company Data, Morgan Stanley Research

This is especially important for the Beauty segment, in which market share losses have been more pronounced. The analysts conclude as follows:

> The competitive intensity in the beauty category has ramped up recently, given: a) the high growth and high margin channel is a long-term strategic priority for many companies, b) we believe many European companies (Unilever, L'Oreal) have targeted the high margin U.S. beauty category as a focus area given current European macro weakness, and c) a resurgent Unilever and Estée Lauder have successfully executed turnarounds under new CEOs over the last few years, making the competitive environment more difficult. Beauty category results have also slowed globally, particularly with a recent emerging markets slowdown.

Sales Forecast Summary Equity analysts have access to proprietary databases which provide them with more information than is available to individual investors. Their approach to the forecasting of top line growth is the same as that which we illustrate above; however, they build their forecasts from the product level up using estimates of unit volume and price to yield forecasted sales. Given the data available to professional analysts, they are able to forecast at a more granular level than we are able to using only publicly available data sources. As a result, their forecasts are able to incorporate analysis performed at a local (rather than global) level. On balance, our sales growth forecast of 1.5% is less optimistic than Morgan Stanley's 2.1% forecasted sales growth. Thus, we forecasted sales of $85,430 million for the full forecasted 2014 income statement.

STEP 2: FORECASTING EXPENSES

The next step in the forecasting process is to predict expenses; for our purposes this includes operating expenses and nonoperating revenues and expenses.

Forecasting Operating Expenses

Generally, we use the following formula to forecast individual operating expenses:

Forecasted operating expense = Forecasted revenues × Forecasted operating expense margin

The forecasted operating expense margin is the expense expressed as a percent of sales (the common-sized expense). We normally start with the prior year's margin and then adjust it based on our business analysis. One exception to this general formula is for income taxes where we apply the following:

Forecasted income taxes = Forecasted income before taxes × Forecasted effective tax rate

In this case, we begin with forecasted income before taxes, not with sales, and the current effective tax rate is often a reasonable predictor of the company's long-term effective tax rate, taking into consideration any transitory items reported in the effective tax rate reconciliation in the tax footnote.

Forecasting Nonoperating Expenses

Generally, forecasts of individual line items of nonoperating expenses are obtained from the following "no change" forecast model:

Forecasted nonoperating expense = Nonoperating expense for prior period

This assumes no change in nonoperating expenses, with an exception of a "zero forecast" for items related to discontinued operations. If we make balance sheet financing or investment adjustments in Step 4, we must adjust one or more nonoperating expenses.

Forecasting Expenses for P&G Using Public Information

Procter & Gamble's fourth quarter earnings release reported an increase in core earnings per share of 5%, due to both an increase in organic sales (discussed above) and a decrease in operating expenses, specifically cost of goods sold and SG&A expenses. The company describes the expense reduction as follows:

> Reported and core gross margin increased 30 basis points. Manufacturing and productivity savings improved gross margin by approximately 160 basis points, and pricing improved gross margin by 70 basis points. These benefits were largely offset by product and geographic mix and manufacturing start-up costs. Core SG&A costs increased 10 basis points. Overhead cost savings from the Company's productivity program of approximately 70 basis points and the benefit of sales leverage were more than offset by the impacts of foreign exchange, marketing investments, higher employment costs and merchandising spending. Including restructuring costs and other non-core impacts, reported SG&A increased 50 basis points.

In its meeting with analysts at the Barclays conference referenced above, P&G provided the following detail:

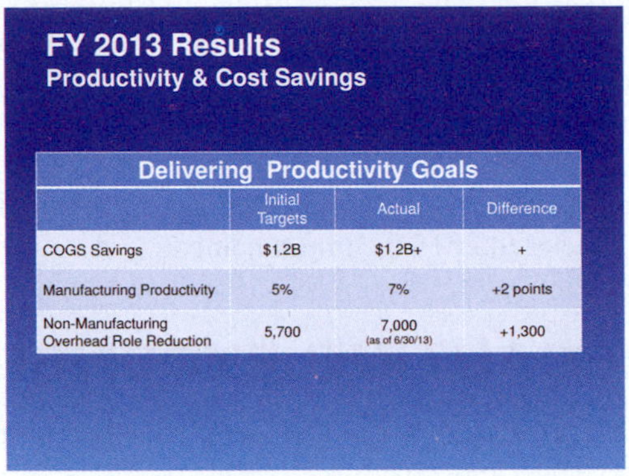

P&G's cost reduction initiatives have focused on cost of goods sold (COGS savings) and manufacturing productivity together with a substantial reduction in headcount. These initiatives have not only impacted FY2013, but will also impact our forecasts of FY2014 expenses. In its guidance to analysts, P&G cited three areas of emphasis:

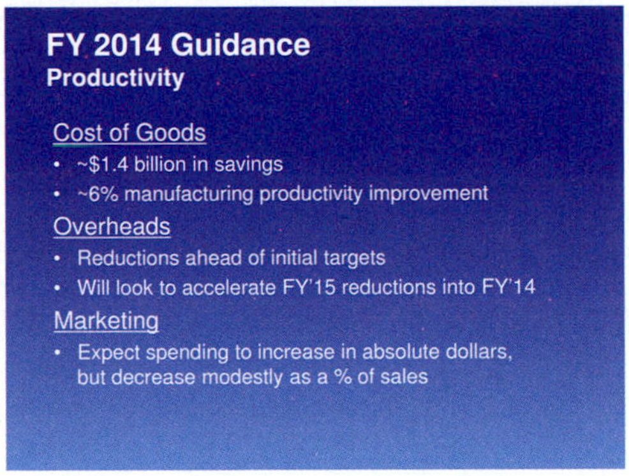

As a starting point in our forecast of operating expenses, we examine historical trends and, then, adjust those trends to incorporate additional information provided by P&G to the extent that we feel that information is reasonable.

To illustrate, take a closer look at P&G's 2013 income statement. P&G's biggest expenses are cost of products sold and selling, general and administrative expense. The income statement and the historical common-size numbers show that there is not an observable trend in these two expenses:

	Income Statement ($ millions)			Common-Size Income Statement		
Fiscal Year Ended	**2013**	**2012**	**2011**	**2013**	**2012**	**2011**
Net sales	$84,167	$83,680	$81,104	100.0%	100.0%	100.0%
Cost of products sold	$42,428	$42,391	$39,859	50.4%	50.7%	49.1%
Selling, general and administrative expense	$26,950	$26,421	$25,750	32.0%	31.5%	31.7%

We typically start with the prior year's margin and then adjust it based on our business analysis and company guidance. P&G's footnotes reveal that the company has been undergoing a restructuring that is expected to continue through 2016. This suggests that expenses (after the cost of the restructuring) will decrease in the future. Specifically, P&G confirms that the COGS percentage of sales is likely to trend lower in its guidance to analysts reproduced above. For FY2014, we forecast a further reduction in COGS as a percentage of sales from 50.4% to 50.1%.

SG&A expenses are expected to decrease as a percentage of sales. P&G reports that its FY2013 SG&A expenses were inflated by transitory items as disclosed in its 4Q earnings release:

	FY13	FY12
SG&A as a % net sales	**32.0%**	**31.5%**
Incremental restructuring	(0.4%)	(0.6%)
Venezuela balance sheet devaluation impacts	(0.4%)	—
Charges for European legal matters	(0.2%)	(0.1%)
Rounding	—	0.1%
Core SG&A as a % net sales	**31.0%**	**30.9%**
Basis point change	*10*	

We eliminate these transitory items from our SG&A forecast and project SG&A expense at the core level of 31% of sales.

As we discuss above, we do not assume any changes in nonoperating income and expense in this first iteration. We also assume a continuation of P&G's core effective tax rate of 23.2% as reported in its FY2013 10-K income tax footnote:

Years ended June 30	2013	2012	2011
U.S. federal statutory income tax rate	35.0%	35.0%	35.0%
Country mix impacts of foreign operations	(7.6)%	(8.1)%	(8.2)%
Change in uncertain tax positions	(1.8)%	(1.3)%	(3.6)%
Impairment adjustments	0.6%	3.7%	—%
Holding gain on joint venture buy-out	(1.4)%	—%	—%
Other	(1.6)%	(2.2)%	(1.2)%
Effective income tax rate	23.2%	27.1%	22.0%

Our general method to forecast income taxes is to predict little change, if any, in a company's effective (average) tax rate, *assuming* it is within reasonable limits. We might adjust the rate from its historical value if the company discloses substantial transitory items in the tax footnote or if we are aware of an anticipated tax-rate change. In fiscal 2013, P&G's effective rate is 23.2%, computed as $3,441 million tax expense divided by $14,843 million earnings before taxes. At that rate, tax expense for 2014 will be $3,830 million ($16,509 million income before tax × 23.2% effective tax rate—see Exhibit 11.4). It is important to remember that this is a preliminary estimate of tax expense. In Step 4 of our forecasting process, we adjust the nonoperating expenses and income, which will affect our forecasted pretax income number. This necessitates a recalculation of income tax expense; we will keep the rate the same (23.2%) and apply it to the adjusted pretax income amount. This core effective tax rate forecast of 23.2% is also consistent with P&G guidance to analysts in its 4Q earnings release that the rate will be "in-line with year ago."

These forecast assumptions result in the preliminary forecasted income statement for P&G in Exhibit 11.4. This initial forecast shows an increase in net profit from 13.4% of sales in FY2013 to 14.7% of sales in FY2014. This increase is consistent with P&G guidance in its 4Q earnings release:

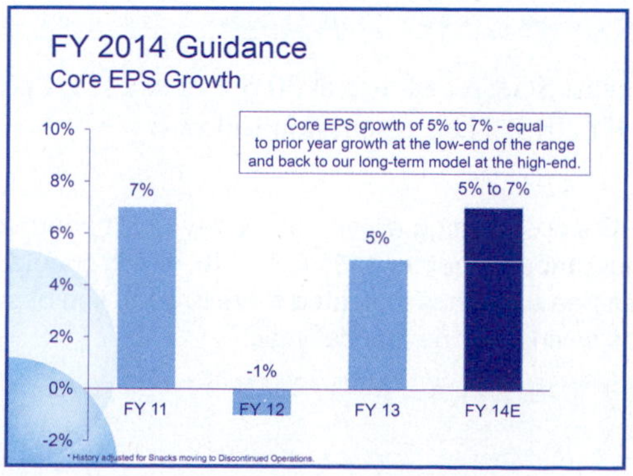

EXHIBIT 11.4 Initial Forecasted Income Statement for P&G

Years Ended June 30 ($ millions)	2013		Forecast Assumptions	2014 Est.	
Net sales	$84,167	100.0%	$84,167 × 1.015	$85,430	100.0%
Cost of products sold	42,428	50.4%	$85,430 × 50.1%	42,800	50.1%
Selling, general and administrative expense	26,950	32.0%	$85,430 × 31.0%	26,483	31.0%
Goodwill and indefinite-lived intangibles impairment charges	308	0.4%	assume $0	0	0.0%
Operating income	14,481	17.2%	subtotal	16,147	18.9%
Interest expense	667	0.8%	no change	667	0.8%
Interest income	87	0.1%	no change	87	0.1%
Other nonoperating income (expense), net	942	1.1%	no change	942	1.1%
Earnings before income taxes	14,843	17.6%	subtotal	16,509	19.3%
Income taxes on continuing operations	3,441	4.1%	$16,509 × 23.2%	3,830	4.5%
Net earnings	11,402	13.5%	subtotal	12,679	14.8%
Less: Net earnings attributable to noncontrolling interest	90	0.1%	no change	90	0.1%
Net earnings attributable to P&G	$11,312	13.4%	subtotal	$12,589	14.7%

As we discuss above, in this first iteration of our forecast, we assume interest expense and interest income do not change from 2013. In Step 4, as explained later in this module, we adjust interest-bearing accounts, such as marketable securities or debt, and we refine our estimates of interest expense and interest income at that time. These adjustments to interest expense and interest income affect earnings before income taxes, income tax expense, and net income. We illustrate those adjustments in Step 4.

Forecasting Expenses for P&G Using Proprietary Databases

Professional analysts build their COGS estimates from the product cost components of materials, labor and overhead. Analysis begins with an estimate of the component cost breakdown for each product. Materials and labor cost projections are based on proprietary databases of commodity and labor costs, weighted by their relative proportion of total product cost. This analysis is performed for each product and aggregated for all of the segments.

Cost of products sold as a percent of sales has remained above 50% for the past two years, about 1 percentage point higher than in 2011. Morgan Stanley analysts forecast a decrease in the COGS percentage by 40 bp (basis points, or 100ths of a percent) from 50.1% in 2012 to 49.7% in 2013. The 40bp decrease in COGS, and the resulting increase in the gross profit margin, is reasonable given PG's announced cost cutting measures over the past few years. The sales and COGS estimates by product are then aggregated into segment pretax income estimates. Following is an example for the Beauty segment from the Morgan Stanley analyst's spreadsheet:

	A	B	AP	AU	AZ	BE	BJ	BK	BL	BM	BN	BO	BT
1	Procter & Gamble Co (PG)												
5	Segment Breakdown		FY2009	FY2010	FY2011	FY2012	FY2013	Sep-13 E	Dec-13 E	Mar-14 E	Jun-14 E	FY2014E	FY2015E
69	Pretax income by segment												
72	Beauty Care		3,558.0	3,648.0	3,607.0	3,196.0	3,215.0	870.3	1,123.8	797.2	608.8	3,400.1	3,676.2
73	% Growth			2.5%	-1.1%	-11.4%	0.6%	2.2%	-1.2%	15.2%	14.2%	5.8%	8.1%
74	Grooming		1,900.0	2,007.0	2,183.0	2,395.0	2,458.0	626.2	692.7	617.2	574.5	2,510.7	2,678.8
75	% Growth			5.6%	8.8%	9.7%	2.6%	-1.2%	-0.3%	4.1%	7.2%	2.1%	6.7%

Morgan Stanley analysts forecast SG&A expense at 30.6% of sales, 1.4 percentage points less than the 32.0% reported by P&G for FY2013. Their discussion follows:

> As shown in Exhibit 30, PG's cost-cutting drove 15% y-o-y profit improvement in Q3, above ~8% in H1, and is expected to contribute another 11% in FY14e, which should help PG manage through weaker topline results than peers. PG has indicated there is good line of sight to at least $1.3 billion in additional cost of goods savings for next fiscal year.

continued

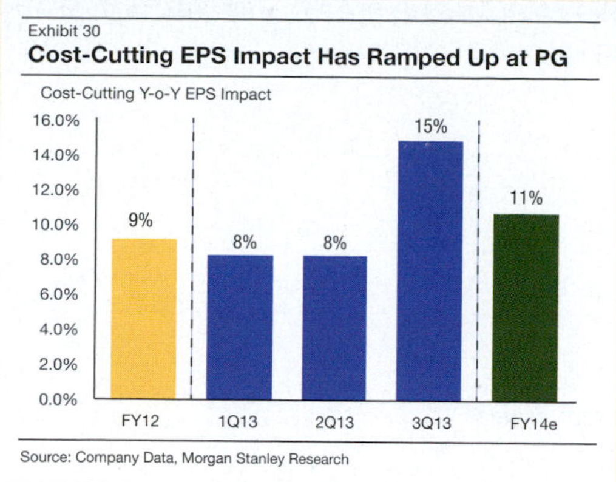

PG's core SG&A as a percentage of sales (excluding shipping and handling, ad spending, R&D expense, and stock option expense) of ~17% in FY12 was the highest in its large cap peer group despite PG's leading scale. As such, we believe PG has ample opportunity to pare back its SG&A spending, and also generate COGS cost savings/productivity. We also believe PG is more focused on cost cutting through simplifying the organization and streamlining bureaucracy, in order to better capitalize on its scale.

STEP 3: FORECASTING ASSETS, LIABILITIES AND EQUITY

LO3 Forecast the balance sheet.

Step 3 is to forecast balance sheet items, which consist of assets, liabilities, and equity. Special emphasis is on forecasts of operating assets and liabilities. We generally assume no change in nonoperating assets, liabilities, and equity (we discuss exceptions to this rule in this section and further adjustments to those accounts in Step 4). Step 3 proceeds with five steps as shown in Exhibit 11.5.

EXHIBIT 11.5 Process in Forecasting the Balance Sheet

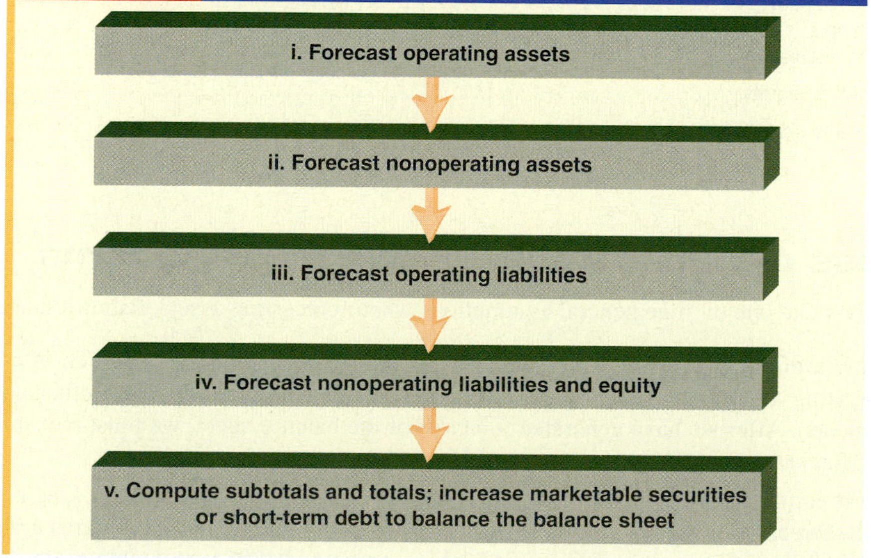

As a starting point, we begin with **Procter & Gamble**'s balance sheet for 2013 in Exhibit 11.6. We will refer to these statements throughout this section.

EXHIBIT 11.6 Procter & Gamble Balance Sheet

June 30, amounts in millions	2013	2012
Assets		
Current assets		
Cash and cash equivalents	$ 5,947	$ 4,436
Accounts receivable	6,508	6,068
Inventories		
Materials and supplies	1,704	1,740
Work in process	722	685
Finished goods	4,483	4,296
Total inventories	6,909	6,721
Deferred income taxes	948	1,001
Prepaid expenses and other current assets	3,678	3,684
Total current assets	23,990	21,910
Property, plant and equipment, net	21,666	20,377
Goodwill	55,188	53,773
Trademarks and other intangible assets, net	31,572	30,988
Other noncurrent assets	6,847	5,196
Total assets	$139,263	$132,244
Liabilities and shareholders' equity		
Current liabilities		
Accounts payable	$ 8,777	$ 7,920
Accrued and other liabilities	8,828	8,289
Debt due within one year	12,432	8,698
Total current liabilities	30,037	24,907
Long-term debt	19,111	21,080
Deferred income taxes	10,827	10,132
Other noncurrent liabilities	10,579	12,090
Total liabilities	70,554	68,209
Shareholders' equity		
Convertible Class A preferred stock	1,137	1,195
Non-voting Class B preferred stock	—	—
Common stock	4,009	4,008
Additional paid-in capital	63,538	63,181
Reserve for ESOP debt retirement	(1,352)	(1,357)
Accumulated other comprehensive income/(loss)	(7,499)	(9,333)
Treasury stock, at cost	(71,966)	(69,604)
Retained earnings	80,197	75,349
Noncontrolling interest	645	596
Total shareholders' equity	68,709	64,035
Total liabilities and shareholders' equity	$139,263	$132,244

Process of Forecasting Balance Sheet Items

We normally make one of three general assumptions when forecasting assets, liabilities, and equity.

1. **Forecast amounts with no change.** We can use a no-change forecast, which is common for nonoperating assets (investments in securities, discontinued operations, and other nonoperating investments). After we have generated forecasts of the balance sheet, we must reexamine the no-change forecasts to see if they are reasonable or if they require adjustment.
2. **Forecast contractual or specified amounts.** We can use contractual or other specified payment tables to forecast selected balance sheet items. For example, footnote disclosures contain scheduled maturities for long-term debt, capital leases, and mandatory redeemable preferred stock for a five-year period subsequent to the financial statement date. We can use those schedules and assume that the required payments are made as projected.

3. **Forecast amounts in relation to revenues.** We can use an item's relation to revenues to forecast that item. The underlying assumption is that, as revenues change, so does that item in some predictable manner. For example, in the case of operating assets, it is reasonable to assume that the required investment in receivables, inventories, and PPE is related, in some manner, to the level of revenues. Similarly, in the case of operating liabilities, it is reasonable to expect that accounts payable will grow with COGS (which grows with revenues), and accrued liabilities will grow with increases in payroll, utilities, advertising, and other expenses (which all grow with revenues).

When forecasting amounts in relation to revenues, the third forecasting assumption above, there are three common methods: (1) forecasts using the percent of revenues, (2) forecasts using turnover rates, and (3) forecasts using days outstanding ratios.

Forecasts Using Percent of Revenues Forecasts that use the percent of revenues build on the relation between revenues and the account being forecasted; this relation follows:

$$\textbf{Forecasted account balance} = \textbf{Forecasted revenues} \times \left(\frac{\textbf{Actual account balance}}{\textbf{Actual revenues}}\right)$$

For example, if the relation between the actual account balance to revenues is 10%, and forecasted revenues equal $100, then the forecasted account is $10, computed as $100 × 10%.

Forecasts Using Turnover Rates Turnover rates have the following general form: Turnover rate = Revenues (or COGS)/Average account balance. Using algebra to rearrange terms, we obtain: Average account balance = Revenues (or COGS)/Turnover rate. Substituting forecasted values we get:

Forecasted account balance = Forecasted revenues (or COGS)/Turnover rate

Consequently, if we have forecasted revenues (or COGS) and a forecasted turnover rate, we can forecast the account balance. However, there is a problem with this method if we use turnover rates as traditionally defined using average account balances; in this case the method would forecast the *average account balance*. Balance sheets report *ending account balances*. This issue is typically resolved in one of two ways:

1. Compute the turnover rate using ending balances rather than average balances; then, our forecast is for the ending account balance.
2. Multiply the forecasted average account balance by 2 and then subtract the beginning account balance; this yields the forecast for the ending account balance.

Forecasts Using Days Outstanding Days outstanding ratios have the following general form: Days outstanding = Account balance/Average daily revenues (or COGS), where Average daily revenues (or COGS) = Revenues (or COGS)/365. We can forecast the account balance by rearranging terms as follows:

Forecasted account balance = Days outstanding × [Forecasted revenues (or COGS)/365]

If days outstanding is computed using the ending balance of the account, the resulting forecast is for the ending balance of that account. However, some analysts prefer a shortcut method to compute days outstanding as 365/Turnover rate. Their justification is based on the mathematical equality where [365/Turnover rate] = [365/(Revenues/Account balance)] = [(Account balance × 365)/Revenues] = [Account balance/(Revenues/365)]. Importantly, however, if this turnover rate is computed in the conventional way using the *average* account balance, we would forecast the average account balance rather than the ending account balance. In this case, we must make one of the two adjustments explained in the previous section.

Equivalence of the Three Forecasting Methods If we compute the turnover rate and the days outstanding using ending account balances (meaning that we are properly forecasting the ending account balance), it does not matter which of these three forecasting methods we use. To illustrate, consider a company with current-period revenues of $1,000 and a forecasted revenue growth of 4% (or $1,040, computed as $1,000 × 1.04). Assume that the current accounts receivable ending balance is

$200 and that we want to forecast accounts receivable for next year. Using each of the three methods above, our forecasted accounts receivable is $208 and is computed as follows:

Forecast Method	Forecast	Forecast Computation
Percent of revenues	$208	$1,040 × ($200/$1,000)
Turnover rate	$208	$1,040/($1,000/$200)
Days outstanding	$208	{[($200 × 365)/$1,000] × $1,040}/365

Each of these forecasting methods yields the same result. Analysts commonly use either percent of sales or days outstanding. The choice between percent of sales and days outstanding depends on the audience. Percent of sales is simple and intuitive. Days outstanding is well suited for analyses that are used in discussions with operating managers, as most managers are familiar with days outstanding ratios and can identify with projected changes (for example, what is the effect of collecting our receivables two days faster?). The choice is a matter of personal preference as all three methods yield the same result.

We use the percent of sales in our forecasts of balance sheet accounts because (1) it appears to be the most commonly used method, (2) it is the method that P&G management uses in its meetings with analysts, and (3) it is the method used by many investment firms.

Forecasting Balance Sheet Items

We illustrate the forecasting of balance sheet items for **Procter & Gamble**.

Forecasting Operating Assets

This section describes the process of forecasting operating assets using the percent of revenues method.

Forecasting Accounts Receivable P&G's accounts receivable as a percentage of sales are 7.7% and 7.3% at year-end 2013 and 2012, respectively (an average of 7.5%). As the world economy continues to improve from the recessionary environment of 2007–2009, it is reasonable to expect a continued strengthening of the financial condition of P&G customers; meaning that some P&G customers are likely to pay more quickly and thus, P&G's accounts receivable balance would decrease relative to sales. A reasonable expectation is that collections return to this short-term average in 2014 and, thus, we use 7.5% in our forecast and arrive at accounts receivable of $6,407 million. The 7.5% ratio is equivalent to an average collection period of 27 days (0.075 × 365 days).

Forecasting Inventories P&G's inventories increased from 8.0% of sales in 2012 to 8.2% in 2013. In the MD&A section of its 10-K, P&G's management attributes the inventory cost increase to "higher commodity costs." This suggests that inventory prices and not quantities, are driving the balance sheet increase. While not immediately obvious, the company's ongoing restructuring efforts have a balance sheet (as well as an income statement) effect. The restructuring impact on cost control and efficiency will likely translate into lower inventory levels. We, therefore, assume that inventories will reduce to the 8.0% of sales that the company reported in the prior year. With forecasted sales of $85,430 million, we predict inventory to be $6,834 million. The 8.0% ratio is equivalent to an average inventory turnover period of 58.3 days (365/[$42,800/$6,834]), down slightly from 59.4 days at year-end 2013 (365/[$42,428/$6,909]).

Forecasting Deferred Income Tax Assets and Other Current Assets Deferred tax assets and liabilities arise because GAAP rules differ from those of the taxing authorities such as the Internal Revenue Service. (Module 5 describes the accounting for income taxes.) In fiscal 2013, P&G's deferred tax assets were 1.1% of sales ($948 million / $84,167 million). P&G's deferred tax footnote reveals that the largest deferred tax assets pertain to pension and postretirement benefits, stock-based compensation, and historical operating losses while the largest deferred tax liabilities relate to fixed assets and goodwill. With the exception of the operating losses (which expire if unused), we can expect deferred taxes to remain about the same in upcoming years. The historical operating losses account for about 10% of total deferred taxes on P&G's balance sheet (deferred tax assets net of the deferred tax liabilities). While the tax assets related to the losses will shrink in the coming years, the decrease will not occur entirely in 2014 and, thus, we predict no change in the relative size of either deferred tax assets or liabilities (forecasted later in this module). We forecast deferred tax assets as $940 million ($85,430 million × 1.1%).

Prepaid expenses and other current assets were 4.4% of sales in 2013 ($3,678 million/$84,167 million). Companies generally provide little information about these assets and, thus, we have no basis to forecast them as a different percentage of sales in 2014. Accordingly, we forecast prepaid expenses and other current assets to be $3,759 million ($85,430 million × 4.4%).

Forecasting Capital Expenditures, PPE, and Accumulated Depreciation In 2013, P&G reported capital expenditures (CAPEX) of $4,008 million or 4.8% of sales (see the investing section of P&G's statement of cash flow). In its guidance to analysts that it provides in the 4Q earnings release, P&G estimates 2014 CAPEX at 4% to 5% of sales:

FY 2014 Guidance
Cash Generation and Usage Assumptions

Free Cash Flow Productivity:	~ 90%
Capital Spending, % Sales:	4% to 5%
Dividends:	~$6.5B
Share Repurchase:	$5-7B

We use the average of the guidance range, 4.5%, in our forecast and apply this percentage for our forecasted sales to yield CAPEX of $3,844 million, computed as $85,430 million × 4.5%. If the company had not provided guidance, we would have used the historic ratio as a starting point and refined it for current economic conditions and any forward-looking information about investments from the latest SEC filing.

To estimate PPE, net, we first need an estimate of depreciation expense for 2014. This is typically estimated using the ratio of depreciation expense to prior year PPE. In particular, we compute the percentage of depreciation expense as a percentage of *beginning-year PPE, net.* P&G does not report depreciation expense as a separate line item on its income statement. The statement of cash flows, however, reports $2,982 million of depreciation *and* amortization expense (which includes amortization of intangible assets). The footnotes disclose that the increase in accumulated amortization during the year (a rough estimate of amortization expense for the year) is $355 million. We determine that 2013 depreciation expense is $2,627 million ($2,982 million − $355 million), or 12.9% of prior year (2012) PPE, net. Applying this percentage to the 2013 net PPE, yields estimated depreciation expense of $2,795 million ($21,666 million × 12.9%). Consequently, our forecast of FY2014 PPE, net, is $22,715 million as computed here:

Actual 2013 PPE, net	$21,666 million	
Add: 2014 CAPEX	3,844 million	($85,430 sales × 4.5%)
Less: 2014 Depreciation expense	(2,795) million	($21,666 × 12.9%)
Forecasted 2014 PPE, net	$22,715 million	

Forecasting Goodwill and Other Intangible Assets and Amortization Goodwill and other intangible assets arise mainly in connection with acquisitions of other companies. Unless an acquisition is pending at year-end, and we have sufficient information about its financial impact, we forecast no change for goodwill and other intangibles. Goodwill is not amortized, but some other intangible assets are (see Module 9). We assume that the 2014 amortization expense relates to trademarks and other intangible assets (discussed above) and will be the same as for 2013: $355 million. That yields a 2014 estimate for trademarks and other intangible assets of $31,217 million ($31,572 million − $355 million). This assumes that no new trademarks or other intangibles are acquired. We also assume that goodwill is not amortized; meaning that goodwill remains the same at $55,188 million.

Forecasting Other Noncurrent Assets Other noncurrent assets are assumed to be part of operating assets unless information suggests otherwise. For P&G, because we have no information to suggest otherwise, we forecast no change in other noncurrent assets.

Forecasting Nonoperating Assets

This section forecasts nonoperating assets for P&G. Generally, we use the no-change forecast model for nonoperating assets.

Forecasting Cash Our forecasting process assumes that the cash and cash equivalents on P&G's balance sheet reflect an economically appropriate amount. The 2013 fiscal year-end cash and cash equivalents balance is $5,947 million (7.1% of 2013 sales). We assume a similar proportion for the next fiscal year and forecast a cash and cash equivalents balance of $6,066 million ($85,430 million × 7.1%) for fiscal 2014.

Forecasting Investment Securities The no-change forecast model applies to marketable securities. P&G does not report marketable securities. We adjust the level of marketable securities or short-term debt in Step 4 when we balance the balance sheet.

BUSINESS INSIGHT **Does Separately Forecasting Cash and Securities Matter?**

Our forecasting process, and that of the Morgan Stanley analysts, is to forecast a cash balance and adjust the level of investment securities or short-term debt to balance the balance sheet. We assume that cash consists of cash equivalents and then forecast interest income on the cash balance at the same rate as that for investment securities. Both cash and marketable securities are treated as nonoperating assets. This means it makes no difference whether we assume a larger balance for cash and a correspondingly smaller balance for investment securities or whether we assume a smaller balance for cash and a larger balance for investment securities. However, we see in recent years that cash balances have ballooned as companies face economic uncertainty. Still, we are indifferent as to whether that excess liquidity is reported as cash or as investment securities as they are both nonoperating assets. We see in the next module that changes in both cash and securities increase or decrease the value of a company dollar-for-dollar. Our focus is on net operating assets (NOA), which impact company value to a much greater extent. Bottom line: do not focus on the mix between cash and securities.

Summary of Asset Forecasts To this point, we have forecasted all of P&G's operating and nonoperating assets. Following the forecast of liabilities and equity in the next section, we adjust the balance of investment securities or short-term debt to balance the balance sheet. This is Step 4.

Forecasting Operating Liabilities

This section describes the process of forecasting operating liabilities for P&G.

Forecasting Accounts Payable We forecast accounts payable as a percentage of sales and use the same percentage as for fiscal 2013 (10.4%) because there is no indication in the financial statement footnotes that the company anticipates a change in its payment policies. This yields a slightly greater forecasted balance of $8,885 million ($85,430 million × 10.4%). This balance implies an accounts payable days outstanding of 38 days (10.4% × 365).

Forecasting Accrued and Other Liabilities Footnotes reveal that P&G's accruals relate primarily to marketing and compensation expenses, although a large component is classified as "other," including restructuring accruals. The liability is 10.5% of sales in 2013. There is no reason in the financial statements or footnotes to believe that this liability will reduce in the coming year, especially given that P&G is continuing its restructuring efforts. Thus, we forecast a liability of $8,970 million ($85,430 million × 10.5%).

Forecasting Taxes Payable Because taxes payable relate directly to tax expense, we prefer to express taxes payable as a percentage of tax expense for forecasting purposes. P&G does not separately identify income taxes payable on its balance sheet. Hence, this account is not included in our forecasts directly, but is forecasted as part of another account. When we encounter a balance sheet with taxes payable as a line item, we suggest forecasting that account using the historical percentage of taxes payable to tax expense.

Forecasting Deferred Income Tax Liabilities Deferred tax assets and deferred tax liabilities generally relate to the level of business activity. Accordingly, we can make a case to forecast these accounts as a percentage of sales. Deferred income taxes are $10,827 million (12.9% of sales) as of

FY2013. As discussed above for deferred tax assets, we assume this percentage will not change during fiscal 2014, yielding an estimate of $11,020 million ($85,430 million × 12.9%). Indeed, Morgan Stanley follows this practice as well.

Forecasting Other Noncurrent Liabilities Other noncurrent liabilities for P&G primarily relate to pension and other post-retirement benefits. We reasonably assume that these obligations grow with the size of the business. For P&G, other noncurrent liabilities are $10,579 million (12.6% of sales) in 2013. Using this same percentage for 2014 yields a forecasted balance of $10,764 million ($85,430 million × 12.6%). Morgan Stanley also forecasts these liabilities as a constant percentage of sales.

Forecasting Nonoperating Liabilities and Equity

This section forecasts nonoperating liabilities and equity for P&G.

Forecasting Debt Due Within One Year P&G discloses the following table for its debt due within one year:

June 30, in millions	2013
Debt due within one year	
Current portion of long-term debt	$ 4,506
Commercial paper	7,642
Other	284
Total	$12,432

Of the $12,432 million total debt due within one year, $4,506 million represents contractual maturities of long-term debt and the $7,926 million remainder represents commercial paper and other short-term borrowings. We assume that all contractual maturities of long-term debt ($4,506 million) will be repaid in fiscal 2014 as planned. For the remainder ($7,926 million) we assume no-change (Step 4 revisits this assumption). Commercial paper is short-term unsecured debt that companies typically rollover at maturity (refinance with new commercial paper). Thus, we forecast $7,926 million as debt due within one year before any current portion of long-term debt. As we show below, the FY2015 current maturities of long-term debt are $3,798 million and, thus, we forecast total debt due within one year as $11,724 million ($7,926 million + $3,798 million).

Forecasting Long-Term Debt P&G's balance sheet reports long-term debt of $19,111 million, in 2013. We use the no-change method to forecast long-term debt (and potentially modify this with optional Step 4). Companies are required to disclose the maturities of long-term debt for each of the five years subsequent to the statement date. Following is the disclosure by P&G in its long-term debt footnote:

Long-term debt maturities during the next five years are as follows:

June 30 ($ millions)	2014	2015	2016	2017	2018
Debt maturities	$4,506	$3,798	$2,379	$1,085	$1,531

In our forecast for 2014, we classify the amount due in 2015, $3,798 million, as current maturities of long-term debt, and the remaining balance of $15,313 million ($19,111 million − $3,798 million) is forecasted as long-term debt. The $3,798 million current maturities of long-term debt are, then, added to short-term debt as we discuss in the preceding section.

Forecasting Equity Accounts Prior to Step 4, we forecast FY2014 equity items with no change, with a few exceptions. The first exception is retained earnings, which are increased by forecasted net income attributable to company stockholders and are reduced by forecasted dividends. There are three commonly used approaches to forecasting dividends:

1. Forecast dollar amount of dividends per share (based on historical dividends per share) and multiply by the forecasted number of shares outstanding (and not the average number of shares outstanding as reported in the EPS calculations), or

2. Forecast dollar amount of dividends per share (as a percent of sales) and multiply by the forecasted number of shares outstanding (and not the average number of shares outstanding as reported in the EPS calculations), or
3. Forecast a dividend payout ratio (dividends / net income) and multiply this dividend payout ratio by forecasted net income.

We utilize the first approach because it is more exact than the other two methods. In particular, dividend payout ratio can be affected by one-time gains or losses included in net income. Companies set dividend policy to provide a predictable dividend for shareholders. So, when available, the first approach is more exact. P&G's footnotes reports the following:

Quarter Ended	2012–2013	2011–2012
September 30	$0.5620	$0.5250
December 31	$0.5620	$0.5250
March 31	$0.5620	$0.5250
June 30	$0.6015	$0.5620

In the past two years, quarterly dividends appear to remain constant for the first three quarters and then P&G increases the dividend by about 4 cents. Following this pattern, we forecast 2014 dividends per share of $2.45 ([3 × $0.6015] + $0.6415). The statement of stockholders' equity reports 2,742,327,000 shares outstanding at year end. P&G reported in its 2013 10-K, planned stock repurchases of $5 to $7 billion in fiscal 2014. P&G's stock price was about $82 at year-end. Using the midpoint of $6 billion for stock repurchases and the $82 stock price, we predict the company will repurchase 73,170,732 shares during the year, which leaves 2,669,156,268 shares outstanding at June 31, 2014. Using the average shares outstanding during the year, we forecast 2014 dividends as $6,628 million ($2.45 dividends per share × [{2,742 million shares + 2,669 million shares}/2]). This is in line with P&G's FY2014 guidance of about $6.5B as follows:

FY 2014 Guidance
Cash Generation and Usage Assumptions

Free Cash Flow Productivity:	~ 90%
Capital Spending, % Sales:	4% to 5%
Dividends:	~$6.5B
Share Repurchase:	$5-7B

Our *initial* forecast for ending FY2014 retained earnings is $86,158 million, computed as follows:

$80,197 million beginning retained earnings
+ 12,589 million forecasted net income attributable to company stockholders
− 6,628 million forecasted dividends

$86,158 million ending retained earnings

This forecast will likely change in Step 4 once we forecast the income (expense) related to new investments (borrowing), thus affecting our estimate of net income.

The second exception concerns the noncontrolling interest. We add the net income attributable to noncontrolling interest on the income statement to the noncontrolling interest account on the balance sheet. For P&G, the income statement amount is $90 million, which brings the balance sheet account to $735 million ($645 + 90 million).

The third exception pertains to any share repurchases (treasury stock) that are announced or planned by a company. As discussed above, P&G indicates its intentions to repurchase about $5 to $7 billion worth of shares for treasury stock in 2014 fiscal year. This reflects continuation of P&G's share repurchase program that has resulted in the repurchase of $17 billion of treasury stock over the past three years. Consistent with P&G guidance, we forecast the purchase of treasury stock amounting to $6 billion in 2014.

STEP 4: ADJUST FORECASTED STATEMENTS

Our (initial) forecasted balance sheet yields total assets of $139,973 million and total liabilities and equity of $135,436 million. Because total assets exceed the total of liabilities and equity, additional financing is required and we assume an increase of $4,537 million of short-term debt to balance (another option would have been to reduce short-term investments, but P&G did not report short-term investments on its FY2013 balance sheet). In Step 4, we add the additional debt needed to balance the balance sheet and adjust interest expense for the additional interest bearing debt. There is some circularity here; meaning that the additional interest expense will reduce profitability and retained earnings, leading to a need for more debt, and so on. Given the number of estimates that are required in the forecasting process, we believe that only one iteration is needed in this step as the additional precision gained by further iterations is unnecessary. (However, Excel and other spreadsheets provide a routine to compute those iterative estimates.)[2]

Adjust Forecasted Income Statement: Nonoperating Expenses

Given our estimates of debt as a result of the "balancing" adjustment in Step 4, we can now finish our forecasts for the income statement (which we presented in Exhibit 11.4). Specifically, we can now forecast nonoperating expense (and revenue), compute pretax income, forecast tax expense, and compute net income. This section describes the process for forecasting those remaining items on the income statement.

Forecasting Interest Expense and "Other" To forecast interest expense we determine an average rate and apply that rate to our average forecasted debt levels during 2014. P&G's 2013 interest expense of $667 million implies a 2.2% interest rate based on average outstanding interest-bearing debt for that year of $30,661 million ([$8,698 million + $21,080 million + $12,432 million + $19,111 million]/2). We use the 2.2% rate to forecast interest expense for fiscal 2014. Our forecasted 2014 year-end debt is $31,574 million ($4,537 million + $11,724 million + $15,313 million) making the average debt outstanding during the year of $31,559 million ([$31,574 million + $31,543 million/2). Expected interest expense is $694 million, computed as $31,559 million × 2.2%. (We would have adjusted interest income in a similar fashion had we projected an increase in short-term investments.)

To forecast interest income we determine the average rate earned during 2013 and apply that rate to the average forecasted cash balance for fiscal 2014. Average cash during fiscal 2013 was $5,192 million computed as ($5,947 million + $4,436 million) /2). Interest income was $87 million or 1.7% of the average cash balance. We forecast an average 2014 cash balance of $6,007 million ([$5,947 million + $6,066 million]/2), which yields interest income of $102 million.

Other nonoperating income in 2013 of $942 million includes gains on divestitures of $881 million (per the financial statement footnotes). Since we are not forecasting any acquisitions or divestitures, we forecast other nonoperating income as the difference, $61 million, under the assumption that whatever nonoperating activities occurred in 2013 will continue at the same level in 2014.

Adjusting Income Taxes After reworking the nonoperating expense and income items, we obtain an adjusted pretax income of $15,616 million. Using the 23.2% rate (2013 effective rate), adjusted income tax expense is $3,623 million ($15,616 million × 23.2%).

Net Income The resulting forecasted consolidated net income is $11,993 million for 2014. Further, $11,903 million is attributable to P&G shareholders after an estimated $90 million is attributed to noncontrolling interests.

Adjust Forecasted Balance Sheet

The forecasted income statement and the revised forecasted balance sheet for Procter & Gamble are in Exhibits 11.8A and 11.8B. We show the FY2013 balance for each account and the computations required to obtain the forecasted FY2014 balance, including the updated retained earnings computation reflecting the net income computed.

[2] When adjusting the balance sheet to balance, we must take care to not inadvertently alter a company's financial leverage. Recall that companies seek to maintain optimal levels of debt and equity to achieve a desired credit rating for their debt, among other objectives. Thus, we must maintain the past debt-to-equity relation within reasonable limits when balancing the forecasted balance sheet. For example, if our decision is to retire debt or to repurchase common stock, we should do it so that the historical debt-to-equity relation is roughly maintained.

EXHIBIT 11.7A Revised Forecasted Income Statement for P&G

($ millions)	2013		Forecast Assumptions	Revised 2014 Est.	
Net sales	$84,167	100.0%	$84,167 × 1.015	$85,430	100.0%
Cost of products sold	42,428	50.4%	$85,430 × 50.1%	42,800	50.1%
Selling, general and administrative expense	26,950	32.0%	$85,430 × 31.0%	26,483	31.0%
Goodwill and indefinite-lived intangibles impairment charges	308	0.4%	assume $0	0	0.0%
Operating income	14,481	17.2%	subtotal	16,147	18.9%
Interest expense	667	0.8%	computed in step 4	694	0.8%
Interest income	87	0.1%	computed in step 4	102	0.1%
Other nonoperating income (expense), net	942	1.1%	computed in step 4	61	0.1%
Earnings before income taxes	14,843	17.6%	subtotal	15,616	18.3%
Income taxes on continuing operations	3,441	4.1%	$15,616 × 23.2%	3,623	4.2%
Net earnings	11,402	13.5%	subtotal	11,993	14.0%
Less: Net earnings attributable to noncontrolling interests	90	0.1%	no change	90	0.1%
Net earnings attributable to P&G	$11,312	13.4%	subtotal	$11,903	13.9%

EXHIBIT 11.7B Forecasted Balance Sheet for P&G

($ millions)	2013		Forecast Assumptions	2014 Est.
Current Assets				
Cash and cash equivalents	$ 5,947	7.1%	85,430 × 7.1%	$ 6,066
Accounts receivable	6,508	7.7%	85,430 × 7.5%	6,407
Inventories	6,909	8.2%	85,430 × 8.0%	6,834
Deferred income taxes	948	1.1%	85,430 × 1.1%	940
Prepaid expenses and other current assets	3,678	4.4%	85,430 × 4.4%	3,759
Total current assets	23,990	28.5%	subtotal	24,006
Net property, plant and equipment	21,666	25.7%	+ 3,844 − 2,795	22,715
Goodwill, net	55,188	65.6%	no change	55,188
Trademarks and other intangible assets, net	31,572	37.5%	− 355	31,217
Other noncurrent assets	6,847	8.1%	no change	6,847
Total assets	$139,263	165.5%	subtotal	$139,973
Current Liabilities				
Accounts payable	$ 8,777	10.4%	85,430 × 10.4%	$ 8,885
Accrued and other liabilities	8,828	10.5%	85,430 × 10.5%	8,970
Short-term debt		0.0%	plug	5,223
Debt due within one year	12,432	14.8%	− 4,506 + 3,798	11,724
Total current liabilities	30,037	35.7%	subtotal	34,802
Long-term debt	19,111	22.7%	− 3,798	15,313
Deferred income taxes	10,827	12.9%	85,430 × 12.9%	11,020
Other noncurrent liabilities	10,579	12.6%	85,430 × 12.6%	10,764
Total liabilities	70,554	83.8%	subtotal	71,899
Shareholders' equity		0.0%		
Preferred stock	1,137	1.4%	no change	1,137
Non-voting Class B preferred stock	0	0.0%	no change	0
Common stock, stated value $1 per share	4,009	4.8%	no change	4,009
Additional paid-in capital	63,538	75.5%	no change	63,538
Reserve for ESOP debt retirement	(1,352)	−1.6%	no change	(1,352)
Accumulated other comprehensive income (loss)	(7,499)	−8.9%	no change	(7,499)
Treasury stock	(71,966)	−85.5%	− 6,000	(77,966)
Retained earnings	80,197	95.3%	+ 11,903 − 6,628	85,472
Noncontrolling interest	645	0.8%	+ 90	735
Total shareholders' equity	68,709	81.6%	subtotal	68,074
Total liabilities and shareholders' equity	$139,263	165.5%	subtotal	$139,973

FORECASTING STATEMENT OF CASH FLOWS

LO4 Forecast the statement of cash flows.

We forecast the statement of cash flows using the forecasted income statement and forecasted balance sheet. We refer to the historical statement of cash flows mainly to check the reasonableness of our forecasts. We draw on the mechanics behind the preparation of the statement of cash flows, which we discuss in Modules 2 and 3 and Appendix B. Specifically, once we have forecasts of the balance sheet and income statement, we can compute the forecasted statement of cash flows just as we would its historical counterpart.

Process of Forecasting the Statement of Cash Flows

To illustrate the forecasting of the statement of cash flows we again turn to **Procter & Gamble**. Given its forecasted income statement in Exhibit 11.7A and its forecasted balance sheet in Exhibit 11.7B, we prepare its forecasted statement of cash flows using the procedures for preparing the statement of cash flows explained in Modules 2 and 3 and Appendix B. Our forecasted statement of cash flows is in Exhibit 11.8.

Forecasting Operating Activities We begin with the operating section and the forecasted net earnings of $11,993 million, which we compute above. We, then, adjust net earnings for operating expenses and revenues that do not impact cash, and for changes in current assets and liabilities. For the first category we have depreciation and amortization, which are in SG&A expense and are added back in the statement of cash flows because they do not use cash. (Computations for these expenses are explained in our discussion of forecasting capital expenditures and PPE, and forecasting goodwill and other intangibles.) Appendix 11A shows that Morgan Stanley also forecasts $352.9 million of compensation expense related to stock-based compensation as an add-back to net income, as it is a noncash expense; however, we are not privy to data that analysts had in making this estimate and do not include it in our forecasts.

For the second category we have four current assets and four current liabilities whose cash-flow effects we must consider. For example, the forecasted increase in accounts receivable reduces the available cash. We apply this logic to each of the other current assets and liabilities. Thus, net cash flow from operating activities is forecasted at $15,874 million for 2014.

Forecasting Investing Activities The forecasted investing section reports cash expenditures for short- and long-term investments as well as the purchase and sale of long-term operating assets. The only item for P&G is the forecasted $3,844 million outflow for capital expenditures (CAPEX). We discuss the computation of this amount in the section on forecasting capital expenditures and PPE, above. The remaining long-term assets are intangible and other nonoperating assets and we assumed no changes in those assets except for amortization of intangibles. Had we forecasted other changes in those assets, we would include the cash flow effects in the investing section.

Forecasting Financing Activities The forecasted financing section includes forecasted items that impact long-term nonoperating liabilities and equity. We forecast a reduction of long-term debt in the amount of $4,506 million relating to its contractual maturities. Those maturities are reported as part of debt due within one year on the 2013 balance sheet and we assume that all contractual obligations are paid as agreed.

This concludes our initial forecasts of the financial statements for Procter & Gamble. Appendix 11A reproduces an actual analyst forecast of P&G's financial statements from **Morgan Stanley**.

ADDITIONAL FORECASTING ISSUES

Reassessing Financial Statement Forecasts

After preparing the forecasted financial statements, it is useful to reassess whether they are reasonable in light of current economic and company conditions. This task is subjective and benefits from the forecaster's knowledge of company, industry, and economic factors. Many analysts and managers prepare "what-if" forecasted financial statements. Specifically, they change key assumptions, such as the forecasted sales growth or key cost ratios and then recompute the forecasted financial statements. These alternative forecasting scenarios indicate the sensitivity of a set of predicted outcomes to different assumptions about future economic conditions. Such sensitivity estimates can be useful for setting contingency plans and in identifying areas of vulnerability for company performance and condition.

EXHIBIT 11.8 Forecasted Statement of Cash Flows for P&G

($ millions)	Forecast Assumptions	2014 Est.
Operating activities		
Net income	via forecasted income stmt.	$11,993
Add: depreciation	21,666 × 12.9%	2,795
Add: amortization	no change	355
Change in accounts receivable	6,508 − 6,407	101
Change in inventories	6,909 − 6,834	75
Change in deferred income taxes (current)	948 − 940	8
Change in prepaid expenses and other current	3,678 − 3,759	(81)
Change in accounts payable	8,885 − 8,777	108
Change in accrued compensation and other liabilities	8,970 − 8,828	142
Change in deferred income taxes (non-current)	11,020 − 10,827	193
Change in other noncurrent liabilities	10,764 − 10,579	185
Net cash from operating activities	subtotal	15,874
Investing activities		
Capital expenditures	85,430 × 4.5%	(3,844)
Net cash from investing activities	subtotal	(3,844)
Financing activities		
Dividends	computed as dividends per share	(6,628)
Increase in short-term debt	plug in balance sheet above	5,223
Decrease in long-term debt	current maturities for FY2014	(4,506)
Purchase of treasury shares	assumed	(6,000)
Net cash from financing activities	subtotal	(11,911)
Net change in cash	subtotal	119
Beginning cash	from 2013 balance sheet	5,947
Ending cash	total	$ 6,066

Multiyear Forecasting of Financial Statements

LO5 Prepare multiyear forecasts of financial statements.

Many business decisions require forecasted financial statements for more than one year ahead. For example, managerial and capital budgeting, security valuation, and strategic analyses all benefit from reliable multiyear forecasts. Module 12 uses multiyear forecasts of financial results to estimate stock price for investment decisions.

Forecasting the Income Statement We forecast two years ahead using analysts' consensus growth estimates for sales and the remaining assumptions for our one-year-ahead forecasts, adjusting those assumptions as necessary. To illustrate, we forecast P&G's 2015 sales using analysts' consensus growth estimates of 4%, which reflect a continuing growth in the world economy and higher disposable income. Our 2015 sales estimate is $88,847 million, computed as our forecasted 2014 sales of $85,430 million × 1.04. Operating expenses are forecasted from this sales level using the methodology we describe earlier for one-year-ahead forecasts. As before, we begin with our prior estimate of nonoperating income and expense and adjust these amounts as required after we have computed our initial balance sheet. This yields a preliminary estimate for total net income of $12,488 million, of which $90 million is attributable to the noncontrolling interest (assume unchanged) and the remainder of $12,398 million is attributable to P&G stockholders.

Forecasting the Balance Sheet Assuming a continuation of the percent-of-revenues relation for current assets and liabilities, we can forecast current assets and current liabilities applying the same methodology used for one-year-ahead forecasts. For example, FY2015 accounts receivable are forecasted at $6,664 million, computed as $88,847 million × 7.5% (the same percentage we used to forecast 2014 receivables). Similarly, we forecast CAPEX at $3,998 million ($88,847 × 4.5%) and depreciation expense at $2,930 million ($22,715 in FY2014 PPE, net × 12.9% depreciation rate used previously). Forecasted net PPE is, then, equal to $23,783 million (computed as $22,715 million + $3,998 million − $2,930 million).

Operating liabilities are estimated using the same percent of estimated sales that we used in 2014. The long-term debt footnote (presented above) reveals that contractual maturities of long-term debt for FY2016 are $2,379 million, and we forecast long-term debt at $12,934 million ($15,313 million − current maturities for FY2016 of $2,379 million). As before, we assume that contractual maturities of long-term debt that were scheduled for FY2015 have been paid. Consequently, we forecast debt due within one year (which includes current maturities of long-term debt) at $10,305 million ($11,724 million for FY2014 − $3,798 million in prior-year current maturities + $2,379 million in FY2015 current maturities).

In the stockholders' equity section, we assume that the company will repurchase another $6 billion of common stock, the same amount as in 2013 because there is no indication in the footnotes or its 10-K or in its guidance to indicate that the company plans to increase their repurchases over 2014 levels. To forecast 2014 dividends, we assumed P&G paid $82 per share to repurchase shares; here we use $86, which is a 5% increase in stock price derived from the increase in net income from 2013 to 2014. This is a subjective evaluation that affects dividends, retained earnings, and short-term debt (our plugged figure). Retained earnings is updated for forecasted net income attributable to P&G stockholders of $12,398 million and decreased by forecasted dividends of $6,875 million, which results in forecasted 2015 year-end balance of $90,995 million. As before, we increase noncontrolling interest on the balance sheet by $90 million, which results in a balance of $825 million.

Adjust Forecasted Statements Our initial balance sheet yields estimated total assets of $141,646 million and total liabilities and equity of $132,151 million, indicating a *cumulative* financing need of $9,495 million (an additional $4,272 million in FY2015). Average interest bearing debt during FY2015 is $32,497 million ([$5,223 million + $11,724 million + $15,313 million + $9,495 million + $10,305 million + $12,934 million]/2), and our estimate of interest expense for FY2015, assuming a continuation of the 2.2% interest rate we used in the prior year, is $715 million ($32,497 million × 2.2%). Interest income, assuming a continuation of the 1.7% investment rate, is $105 million ([[$6,066 million + $6,308 million]/2] × 1.7%). We forecast other nonoperating income to remain unchanged ($61 million) from 2014.

Our forecasted income statement and balance sheet are presented in Exhibit 11.9 (FY2014 forecasts are shown in the first column). Given our forecasted nonoperating revenue (expense), we project pretax income at $16,243 million. Assuming a continuation of the 23.2% effective tax rate, we forecast tax expense of $3,768 million ($16,243 million × 23.2%) and net income of $12,475 million. Exhibit 11.9 also reports the two-year-ahead forecasted statement of cash flows which is prepared using the forecasted FY2014 and FY2015 balance sheets and our forecasted FY2015 income statement.

EXHIBIT 11.9 Forecasted Two-Year-Ahead Financial Statements for P&G

Income Statement ($ millions)	2014 Est.	Forecast Assumptions	2015 Est.
Net sales	$85,430	$85,430 × 1.04	$88,847
Cost of products sold	42,800	88,847 × 50.1%	44,512
Selling, general and administrative expense	26,483	88,847 × 31.0%	27,543
Goodwill and indefinite-lived intangibles impairment charges	0	no change	0
Operating income	16,147	subtotal	16,792
Interest expense	694	computed	715
Interest income	102	computed	105
Other nonoperating income (expense), net	61	computed	61
Earnings before income taxes	15,616	subtotal	16,243
Income taxes on continuing operations	3,623	16,243 × 23.2%	3,768
Net earnings	11,993	subtotal	12,475
Less: Net earnings attributable to noncontrolling interests	90	no change	90
Net earnings attributable to P&G	$11,903	subtotal	$12,385

continued

continued from prior page

Balance Sheet ($ millions)	2014 Est.	Forecast Assumptions	2015 Est.
Current assets			
Cash and cash equivalents	$ 6,066	88,847 × 7.1%	$ 6,308
Accounts receivable	6,407	88,847 × 7.5%	6,664
Inventories	6,834	88,847 × 8.0%	7,108
Deferred income taxes	940	88,847 × 1.1%	977
Prepaid expenses and other current assets	3,759	88,847 × 4.4%	3,909
Total current assets	24,006	subtotal	24,966
Net property, plant and equipment	22,715	3,998 − 2,930	23,783
Goodwill, net	55,188	no change	55,188
Trademarks and other intangible assets, net	31,217	− 355	30,862
Other noncurrent assets	6,847	no change	6,847
Total assets	$139,973		$141,646
Current liabilities			
Accounts payable	$ 8,885	88,847 × 10.4%	$ 9,240
Accrued and other liabilities	8,970	88,847 × 10.5%	9,329
Short-term debt	5,223	plug	9,508
Debt due within one year	11,724	− 3,798 + 2,379	10,305
Total current liabilities	34,802	subtotal	38,382
Long-term debt	15,313	− 2,379	12,934
Deferred income taxes	11,020	88,847 × 12.9%	11,461
Other noncurrent liabilities	10,764	88,847 × 12.6%	11,195
Total liabilities	71,899	subtotal	73,972
Shareholders' equity			
Preferred stock	1,137	no change	1,137
Common stock, stated value $1 per share	4,009	no change	4,009
Additional paid-in capital	63,538	no change	63,538
Reserve for ESOP debt retirement	(1,352)	no change	(1,352)
Accumulated other comprehensive income (loss)	(7,499)	no change	(7,499)
Treasury stock	(77,966)	− 6,000	(83,966)
Retained earnings	85,472	+ 12,385 − 6,875	90,982
Noncontrolling interest	735	+ 90	825
Total shareholders' equity	68,074	subtotal	67,674
Total liabilities and shareholders' equity	$139,973	subtotal	$141,646

Statement of Cash Flows	2014 Est.	Forecast Assumptions	2015 Est.
Operating activities			
Net income	$11,993	via forecasted income stmt.	$12,475
Add: depreciation	2,795	22,715 × 12.9%	2,930
Add: amortization	355		355
Change in accounts receivable	101	6,407 − 6,664	(257)
Change in inventories	75	6,834 − 7,108	(274)
Change in deferred income taxes (current)	8	940 − 977	(37)
Change in prepaid expenses and other current	(81)	3,759 − 3,909	(150)
Change in accounts payable	108	9,240 − 8,885	355
Change in accrued compensation and other liabilities	142	9,329 − 8,970	359
Change in deferred income taxes (noncurrent)	193	11,461 − 11,020	441
Change in other noncurrent liabilities	185	11,195 − 10,764	431
Net cash from operating activities	15,874	subtotal	16,628
Investing activities			
Capital expenditures	(3,844)	88,947 × 4.5%	(3,998)
Net cash from investing activities	(3,844)	subtotal	(3,998)
Financing activities			
Dividends	(6,628)	computed as dividends per share	(6,875)
Increase in short-term debt	5,223	plug	4,285
Decrease in long-term debt	(4,506)	current maturities via footnote	(3,798)
Purchase of treasury shares	(6,000)	assumed	(6,000)
Net cash from financing activities	(11,911)	subtotal	(12,388)
Net change in cash	119	subtotal	242
Beginning cash	5,947	from balance sheet	6,066
Ending cash	$ 6,066	subtotal	$ 6,308

MID-MODULE REVIEW

Following is financial statement information from **Colgate-Palmolive Company**.

Income Statement

For year ended December 31 ($ millions)	2012	2011
Net sales	$17,085	16,734
Cost of sales	7,153	7,144
Gross profit	9,932	9,590
Selling, general and administrative expenses	5,930	5,758
Other (income) expense, net	113	(9)
Operating profit	3,889	3,841
Interest expense, net	15	52
Income before income taxes	3,874	3,789
Provision for income taxes	1,243	1,235
Net income including noncontrolling interests	2,631	2,554
Less: Net income attributable to noncontrolling interests	159	123
Net income attributable to Colgate-Palmolive Company	$ 2,472	$ 2,431

Balance Sheet

As of December 31 ($ millions)	2012	2011
Assets		
Cash and cash equivalents	$ 884	$ 878
Receivables (net of allowances of $61 and $49, respectively)	1,668	1,675
Inventories	1,365	1,327
Other current assets	639	522
Total current assets	4,556	4,402
Property, plant and equipment, net	3,842	3,668
Goodwill, net	2,500	2,494
Other intangible assets, net	1,499	1,504
Deferred income taxes	92	115
Other assets	905	541
Total assets	$13,394	$12,724
Liabilities and Shareholders' Equity		
Notes and loans payable	$ 54	$ 34
Current portion of long-term debt	250	346
Accounts payable	1,290	1,244
Accrued income taxes	254	392
Other accruals	1,888	1,700
Total current liabilities	3,736	3,716
Long-term debt	4,926	4,430
Deferred income taxes	293	252
Other liabilities	2,049	1,785
Total liabilities	11,004	10,183
Shareholders' equity		
Common stock, $1 par value (2,000,000,000 shares authorized, 732,853,180 shares issued)	733	733
Additional paid-in-capital	1,551	1,336
Retained earnings	16,953	15,649
Accumulated other comprehensive income (loss)	(2,621)	(2,475)
Unearned compensation	(41)	(60)
Treasury stock, at cost	(14,386)	(12,808)
Total Colgate-Palmolive Company shareholders' equity	2,189	2,375
Noncontrolling interests	201	166
Total shareholders' equity	2,390	2,541
Total liabilities and shareholders' equity	$13,394	$12,724

Forecast the Colgate-Palmolive balance sheet, income statement, and statement of cash flows for 2013 using the following additional information; assume no change for all other accounts not listed below. All percentages, other than sales growth, are based on percent of revenues; assume all capital expenditures are purchases of PPE, and that depreciation and amortization are included as part of selling, general and administrative expenses.

Key Financial Relations and Measures ($ millions)	2012
Net sales growth [{$17,085/$16,734} − 1]	2%
Cost of sales/Net sales [$7,153/$17,085]	41.9%
Selling, general and administrative expenses/Net sales [$5,930/$17,085]	34.7%
Depreciation for 2013 [from its note 5]	$413
Amortization for 2013 [from its note 5]	$31
Other (income) expense, net [no change]	$113
Interest expense, net [no change]	$15
Provision for income taxes/Pretax income [$1,243/$3,874]	32.1%
Net income attributable to noncontrolling interests [no change]	$159
Cash and cash equivalents/Net sales [$884/$17,085]	5.2%
Receivables/Net sales [$1,668/$17,085]	9.8%
Inventories/Net sales [$1,365/$17,085]	8.0%
Other current assets/Net sales [$639/$17,085]	3.7%
Capital expenditures for 2013 [2012 CAPEX × Net sales growth %]	$576
Goodwill, net [no change]	$2,500
Other intangible assets, net [2012 Other intagible assets, net - 2013 Amortization]	$1,468
Deferred income tax assets [no change]	$92
Other assets/Net sales [$905/$17,085]	5.3%
Notes and loans payable [no change]	$54
Accounts payable/Net sales [$1,290/$17,085]	7.6%
Accrued income taxes/Provision for income taxes [$254/$1,243]	20.4%
Other accruals/Net sales [$1,888/$17,085]	11.1%
Deferred income tax liabilities/Net sales [$293/$17,085]	1.7%
Other liabilities/Net sales [$2,049/$17,085]	12.0%
Common stock [no change]	$733
Additional paid-in-capital [no change]	$1,551
Accumulated other comprehensive income (loss) [no change]	$(2,621)
Unearned compensation [no change]	$(41)
Treasury stock, at cost [no change]	$(14,386)
Noncontrolling interests [$201 + no change NCI of $159]	$360
Dividends/Net income attributable to Colgate-Palmolive stockholders [$1,277/$2,631]	49%
Long-term debt payments required in 2014 [from its note 6]	$887

The solution is on page 11-80.

PARSIMONIOUS MULTIYEAR FORECASTING

LO6 Implement a parsimonious method for multiyear forecasting of net operating profit and net operating assets.

The forecasting process described above uses a considerable amount of available information to derive accurate forecasts. We can, however, simplify the process by using less information. Stock valuation models commonly use more parsimonious methods to compute multiyear forecasts for an initial screening of prospective securities. For example, in Module 12 we introduce two stock valuation models that use parsimonious forecasting methods. One model utilizes forecasted free cash flows and the other uses forecasted net operating profits after tax (NOPAT) and net operating assets (NOA); see Module 4 for descriptions of these variables. Because free cash flows are equal to net operating profits after tax (NOPAT) less the change in net operating assets (NOA), we can accommodate both stock valuation models with forecasts of NOPAT and NOA.

Parsimonious Method for Forecasting

Our parsimonious approach to forecast NOPAT and NOA requires three crucial inputs:

1. Sales growth
2. Net operating profit margin (NOPM); defined in Module 4 as NOPAT divided by sales
3. Net operating asset turnover (NOAT); defined in Module 4 as sales divided by average NOA. For forecasting purposes, we define NOAT as sales divided by *year-end* NOA instead of average NOA because we want to forecast year-end values.

Multiyear Forecasting with Parsimonious Method

The remainder of this module describes and illustrates this parsimonious approach. To illustrate, we use **Procter & Gamble**'s 2013 income statement, from Exhibit 11.3, and its 2013 balance sheet, from Exhibit 11.6, to determine the following measures. We assume that P&G's statutory tax rate is 37% on nonoperating revenues and expenses.

($ millions)	2013
Sales	$84,167
Net operating profit after tax ($14,481 − {$3,441 + [($667 − $87 − $942) × 37%]}	$11,174
NOA (($139,263 − $5,947) − ($30,037 − $12,432) − $10,827 − $10,579)*	$94,305
NOPM ($11,174/$84,167)	13.3%
NOAT ($84,167/$94,305)*	0.89

*We use ending balance sheet amounts rather than average amounts because we forecast *ending* balance sheet amounts.

Using these inputs, we forecast P&G's sales, NOPAT, and NOA. Each year's forecasted sales is the prior year sales multiplied successively by (1 + Growth rate) and then rounded to whole digits. Consistent with our prior revenue growth rate assumptions for P&G, we define "1 + Growth rate" as 1.015 for 2014 and 4% for 2015 onward. NOPAT is computed using forecasted (and rounded) sales each year times the 2013 NOPM of 13.3%; and NOA is computed using forecasted (and rounded) sales divided by the 2013 NOAT of 0.89. Forecasted numbers for 2014 through 2017 are in Exhibit 11.10; supporting computations are in parentheses.

This forecasting process can be continued for any desired forecast horizon. Also, the forecast assumptions such as sales growth, NOPM, and NOAT can be varied by year, if desired. This alternative, parsimonious method is much simpler than the primary method illustrated in this module. However, its simplicity does forgo information that can impact forecast accuracy.

EXHIBIT 11.10 Procter & Gamble Multiyear Forecasts of Sales, NOPAT and NOA

	Reported	Forecast			
($ millions)	2013	2014 Est.	2015 Est.	2016 Est.	2017 Est.
Net sales growth		1.5%	4.0%	4.0%	4.0%
Net sales (unrounded)	$84,167	**$85,429.51** ($84,167 × 1.015)	**$88,846.69** ($85,429.51 × 1.04)	**$92,400.55** ($88,846.69 × 1.04)	**$96,096.57** ($92,400.55 × 1.04)
Net sales (rounded)	$84,167	**$85,430**	**$88,847**	**$92,401**	**$96,097**
NOPAT[1]	$11,174	**$11,362** ($85,430 × 0.133)	**$11,817** ($88,847 × 0.133)	**$12,289** ($92,401 × 0.133)	**$12,781** ($96,097 × 0.133)
NOA[2]	$94,305	**$95,989** ($85,430/0.89)	**$99,828** ($88,847/0.89)	**$103,821** ($92,401/0.89)	**$107,974** ($96,097/0.89)

[1] Forecasted NOPAT = Forecasted net sales (rounded) × 2013 NOPM
[2] Forecasted NOA = Forecasted net sales (rounded)/2013 NOAT

GLOBAL ACCOUNTING

There are no differences in forecasting financial statements prepared under IFRS versus U.S. GAAP. While factors influencing growth rates likely differ among countries across the globe, the method we use to assess growth is independent of the accounting principles applied. Similarly, the forecasting techniques and mechanics we describe in this module can be applied to any set of financial statements.

MODULE-END REVIEW

Johnson & Johnson (J&J) reports fiscal 2012 sales of $67,224 million, net operating profit after tax (NOPAT) of $10,809 million, and net operating assets (NOA) of $59,902 million. J&J's NOPM is computed as 16.1% ($10,809 million/$67,224 million) and its NOAT is computed as 1.12 ($67,224/$59,902).

Required

Use the parsimonious forecast model to project J&J's sales, NOPAT, and NOA for 2013 through 2016 assuming a sales growth rate of 3.4%.

The solution is on page 11-81.

APPENDIX 11A: Morgan Stanley's Forecast Report on Procter & Gamble

Morgan Stanley analysts developed their forecasts of P&G shortly after the release of P&G's 2013 10-K in August, 2013. We completed our analysis and developed our forecasts at about the same time. Thus, we have an opportunity to compare the analysis in this module with the Morgan Stanley analyst report. Following is the Morgan Stanley analysts' report on Procter & Gamble Co. that the firm issued on August 2, 2013 (Pages 9-15 of the report contain the customary disclosure information typical of analyst reports). *Please note that materials that are referenced comprise excerpts from research reports and should not be relied on as investment advice. This material is only as current as the publication date of the underlying Morgan Stanley research. For important disclosures, stock price charts, and equity rating histories regarding companies that are the subject of the underlying Morgan Stanley research, see www.morganstanley.com/researchdisclosures. Additionally, Morgan Stanley has provided their materials here as a courtesy. Therefore, Morgan Stanley and Cambridge Business Publishers do not undertake to advise you of changes in the opinions or information set forth in these materials.*

Morgan Stanley

MORGAN STANLEY RESEARCH
NORTH AMERICA

Morgan Stanley & Co. LLC

Dara Mohsenian, CFA
Dara.Mohsenian@morganstanley.com
+1 212 761 6575

Bob Doctor
Bob.Doctor@morganstanley.com
+1 212 761 7250

Victor Cruz
Victor.Cruz@morganstanley.com
+1 212 761 3210

August 2, 2013

Stock Rating
Equal-weight

Industry View
In-Line

Procter & Gamble Co.

EW; Progress, but Valuation Limits Upside

We remain EW PG. Positives are emerging, (a new CEO, organic sales growth improvement, cost-cuts, and a rebounding US consumer), but valuation already appears to be pricing in a recovery.

Q4 Beat: PG Q4 core EPS of $0.79 was +2c above consensus. +4% organic sales growth (~4.5% unrounded) was solid vs. 3.5-4.0% consensus, and driven by +5% volume, negative mix of -1% and flat pricing. Margins were disappointing (particularly with a lower than expected marketing increase), with gross margins -90 bps y-o-y (-90 bps vs. consensus) and operating margin -130bp y-o-y (-60bps vs. consensus).

Favorable FY14 Guide: PG expects core FY14 EPS growth of +5-7% including a -6% FX impact, (consensus +7%), which is better than the market (and we) expected. Low double-digit FX neutral EPS growth is clearly a signal that PG's cost-cutting is taking hold and driving EPS growth. Analytically, FY14 guidance looks aggressive given it is above peers, PG's recent trend, PG's HSD LT EPS growth guidance (despite topline being below LT guidance), and it is also H2 weighted. However, intuitively, we believe PG has taken a hard look at guidance under a new CEO, and thus we'll give PG the benefit of the doubt here, particularly with improved Q4 organic sales growth and FY14 cost-cuts worth ~12% of profit. Skeptics could quibble with weak margins in Q4, but given manufacturing variances, improving mix, and marketing spending increases should reverse, y-o-y margin trends should improve sequentially. Organic sales growth guidance in the range of +3-4% seems conservative given Q4 results.

EW: We continue to contend that positives are emerging at PG (a new CEO, organic sales growth improvement, cost-cutting (+320 bps in Q4), moderate commodities, and a rebounding US consumer). However, we remain EW as valuation preemptively appears to be pricing in a recovery (PG trades at only a 7% P/E discount to CL and 2% premium to KO despite lower LT topline growth).

Key Ratios and Statistics

Reuters: PG.N Bloomberg: PG US
Household & Personal Care / United States of America

Shr price, close (Aug 1, 2013)	$81.64
Mkt cap, curr (mm)	$238,895
52-Week Range	$82.54-63.25

Fiscal Year ending	06/11	06/12	06/13	06/14e
ModelWare EPS ($)	**3.95**	**3.85**	**4.05**	**4.30**
Prior ModelWare EPS ($)	**-**	**-**	**4.06**	**4.30**
P/E	**16.1**	**15.9**	**19.0**	**19.0**
Consensus EPS ($)§	**3.93**	**3.81**	**4.04**	**4.32**
Div yld (%)	3.1	3.4	3.0	3.0

Unless otherwise noted, all metrics are based on Morgan Stanley ModelWare framework (please see explanation later in this note).
§ = Consensus data is provided by Thomson Reuters Estimates.
e = Morgan Stanley Research estimates

Quarterly ModelWare EPS

Quarter	2012	2013 Prior	2013 Current	2014e Prior	2014e Current
Q1	1.01	-	1.06	1.13	1.07
Q2	1.09	-	1.22	1.29	1.25
Q3	0.94	-	0.99	1.03	1.09
Q4	0.82	-	0.79	0.85	0.89

e = Morgan Stanley Research estimates

Morgan Stanley does and seeks to do business with companies covered in Morgan Stanley Research. As a result, investors should be aware that the firm may have a conflict of interest that could affect the objectivity of Morgan Stanley Research. Investors should consider Morgan Stanley Research as only a single factor in making their investment decision.

For analyst certification and other important disclosures, refer to the Disclosure Section, located at the end of this report.

Morgan Stanley

MORGAN STANLEY RESEARCH

August 2, 2013
Procter & Gamble Co.

Procter & Gamble (PG, $81.64, Equal-weight)

Risk/Reward Not Compelling Despite Emerging Positives

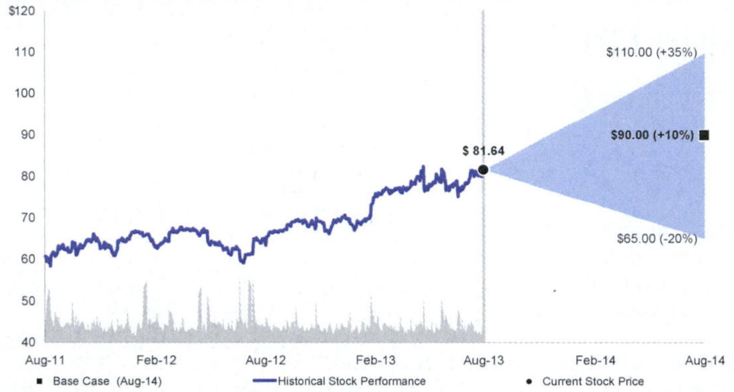

Source: Thomson Reuters, Morgan Stanley Research

Bull Case $110	24.0x Bull Case F2014e EPS of $4.57	**Topline rebounds to 4.5-5.0% organic sales growth.** Revenue upside as PG's marketing/innovation focus drives market share improvement, coupled with 50 bps of pricing upside. Cost cutting above our forecast trims 50 bps incrementally from SG&A. Valuation expands to 24.0x F2014e EPS (implies 16.8x EV/EBITDA).
Base Case $90	21.0x Base Case F2014e EPS of $4.30	**Muted sales growth, but cost-cutting drives margins.** Organic sales growth of ~4% as PG's premium portfolio that is skewed to developed markets limits growth given weak consumer spending. OM's expand by ~85 bps on cost savings. Valuation expands to 21.0x F2014e EPS (14.5x EV/EBITDA), above PG's 16x NTM P/E average over the past five years given a higher market multiple.
Bear Case $65	16.0x Bear Case F2014e EPS of $4.03	**Topline downside.** Pricing is 50 bps below our forecast due to a competitive environment and macros slow, hurting volume by 50 bps. Margins miss by 50 bps due to negative mix. Valuation contracts to 16.0x F2014e EPS (implies 11.2x EV/EBITDA).

Bear to Bull: Competitive Environment and Macros Are the Key Drivers

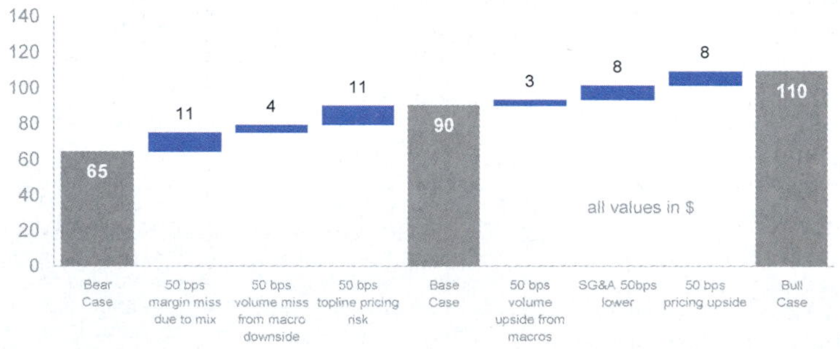

Source: Morgan Stanley Research, Thomson Reuters *Bull-to-Bear variable embed multiple de/re-rating

Why Equal-weight?

- **Positives Emerging:** We believe there are a number of emerging positives for PG, including a CEO change, potential macro-driven US consumer recovery, accelerating topline results, and cost-cutting cushion to EPS.
- **Muted Organic Sales Growth Expected to Improve:** PG's higher-price developed market skewed portfolio is still driving weaker topline growth than peers. However, we do expect PG's 4Q rebound to +4% organic sales growth to continue going forward given higher marketing spend from FY13, accelerating innovation, and better execution.
- **Limiting Geographic Skew:** PG over-indexes to slower-growth developed markets (nearly three-quarters of its profit mix) and has a premium-priced portfolio, which we believe will limit near-term topline growth results given soft consumer spending in developed markets.
- **Valuation Is Not Compelling:** Given PG is trading at only a 7% P/E discount to Colgate and 2% premium to KO, both of whom offer much greater long-term topline growth than PG, we do not view valuation as compelling

Morgan Stanley

MORGAN STANLEY RESEARCH

August 2, 2013
Procter & Gamble Co.

PG: Q4 EPS Beat (although profit miss), Better Than Expected FY14 Guidance

Strategy Changes Under Lafley

PG's CEO AG Lafley discussed tweaks in PG's strategy on his first conference call during his second stint as PG's CEO. Below we outline Lafley's key focus areas as CEO:

1) Deliver greater TSR, with focus at the business unit level: PG plans to bolster corporate results and shareholder returns by further emphasizing TSR, which includes sales growth, gross and operating margin improvement, and strong cash flow productivity. While the metrics under review remain largely the same, PG will likely be much more vigilant in monitoring performance, holding business unit leaders more accountable to such metrics, and placing a greater weight on them when determining compensation. Some units are already performing well, so the key here is to incentivize other units to improve performance through a focus on key metrics and establishing priorities.

2) Enhancing the value equation for consumers: PG will direct its efforts towards structurally more attractive product categories, regions, and channels. Specifically, there will be a heightened focus on enhancing PG's value proposition in core developed market businesses, chiefly in the US where more than half of PG's profit is sourced. In developing markets, investment will center around categories and countries with the "largest size of prize and the highest likelihood of winning", which appears inline with our view that PG will avoid "walled cities" of major competitors. We believe this strategy has a narrower focus than PG's prior "40, 20, 10" plan.

3) Strengthen and accelerate productivity: Lafley plans to deliver on the current $10B productivity initiative at an accelerated rate, as well as target new areas to extract incremental savings. Focus areas include: (i) redesigning and strengthening go-to-market operations in North America, (ii) scaling European operations across larger and fewer country clusters, (iii) continuing to localize production in developing markets, (iv) further reducing headcount via a leaner more flexible support staff, and (v) more efficient marketing spend via mix optimization and reduced non-ad spending. PG commented they have good line of sight to at least $1.4 billion in additional cost of goods savings in FY14, and in total represents ~12% of FY13 operating profit.

Exhibit 1

PG Has Accelerated Cost Cutting

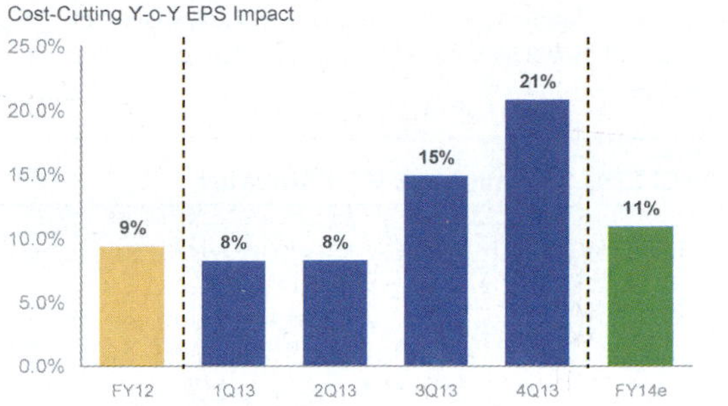

Source: Company Data, Morgan Stanley Research

3) Strategic investments behind innovation: PG plans to continue to invest selectively behind the most impactful innovation opportunities. Innovation is a key tenant under Lafley's value creation plan, as he expressed a willingness to invest behind PG's brands, albeit with more stringent ROI hurdles. PG commented that much of the FY14 innovation pipeline, while stronger than prior years, is still in the early stages of commercialization.

4) **Enhanced Execution**: Through improved operational discipline and enhanced execution, PG plans to win with both customers and consumers on a more consistent basis. PG is working to simplify and streamline current processes to create a more nimble organization, reduce lead-time in the decision making process across the organization, and enhance go-to-market capabilities. We believe Lafley efforts on this front will pertain primarily to the beauty business, where executional hiccups have resulted in significant share losses.

Long-term guidance targets: PG expects a long-term growth algorithm of organic sales growth slightly above category growth and high single digit EPS growth. PG eliminated quarterly guidance, although the company will likley provide some color for overall EPS results by quarter when its internal projections vary vs. consensus, as it did yesterday.

Morgan Stanley

MORGAN STANLEY RESEARCH

August 2, 2013
Procter & Gamble Co.

Q4 Detail

PG posted Q4 core EPS of $0.79, +2c above consensus (-1c below our estimate) and ahead of $0.69-$0.77 guidance. +4% organic sales growth (more like 4.5% unrounded) was solid in our minds vs. 3.5-4.0% consensus, driven by volumes of +5% partly offset by negative mix of -1% and flat pricing. Margins were disappointing, with gross margins –90 bps y-o-y (–90 bps vs. consensus) and operating margin -130bp y-o-y (-60bps vs. consensus) leading to 3.3% operating profit downside, but EPS was aided by below the line items which added ~$0.02 vs. our estimates.

Exhibit 2

4Q13 EPS Summary vs. MS Estimates

	MS Est. vs. Actual			Year-over-Year		
$ in millions, except EPS	MS Est. Jun-13 E	Actual Jun-13	+/-	Jun-12	Actual Jun-13	+/-
Sales	**$20,691**	**$20,655**	**-0.2%**	**$20,212**	**$20,655**	**2.2%**
% Growth	2.4%	2.2%		-3.1%	2.2%	
% Organic Growth	3.4%	4.0%		3.0%	4.0%	
Cost of Sales	**-10,627**	**-10,813**	**1.8%**	**-10,396**	**-10,813**	**0.0%**
% of Sales	51.4%	52.3%	99 bps	51.4%	52.3%	91 bps
% of Sales Bps Change	-07	91			91	
Gross Profit	**10,064**	**9,842**	**-2.2%**	**9,816**	**9,842**	**0.3%**
Gross Margin %	48.6%	47.7%	(99) bps	48.6%	47.7%	(91) bps
Gross Margin Bps Change	07	-91			-91	
SG&A Expense	**-6,844**	**-6,736**	**-1.6%**	**-6,511**	**-6,736**	**3.5%**
% of Sales	33.1%	32.6%	(46) bps	32.2%	32.6%	40 bps
% Growth	5.1%	3.5%			3.5%	
% of Sales Bps Change	86	40			40	
Operating Income	**3,220**	**3,106**	**-3.5%**	**3,306**	**3,106**	**-6.0%**
Operating Margin	15.6%	15.0%	(53) bps	16.4%	15.0%	(132) bps
% Growth	-2.6%	-6.0%			-6.0%	
Interest Expense	-$161	-$163	1.2%	-$182	-$163	-10.4%
Other Non-Operating Income, Net	$26	$41	n.m.f.	$24	$41	70.8%
Pretax Income	**3,086**	**2,984**	**-3.3%**	**3,148**	**2,984**	**-5.2%**
Taxes	**-708**	**-665**		**-705**	**-665**	**-10.4%**
Tax Rate	22.9%	22.3%		22.4%	22.3%	(10) bps
Minority Interests	-36.0	-7.0		-36.0	-7.0	
Net Income	**2,342**	**2,312**	**-1.3%**	**2,406**	**2,312**	**-3.9%**
EPS Diluted (Core)	**$0.80**	**$0.79**	**-1.6%**	**$0.82**	**$0.79**	**-4.2%**
EPS % Growth	-2.6%	-4.2%		-2.4%	-4.2%	
Diluted Shares	2,928.0	2,937.1	0.3%	2,930.0	2,937.1	0.2%

Source: Company data, Morgan Stanley Research

Improving topline results: Organic sales growth of +4% (more like 4.5% unrounded) came in ahead of consensus in the ~3.5-4.0% range and at the high end of PG's +3-4% guidance. On a two-year average basis, +3.5% organic growth in 4Q accelerated from +3.0% growth in 3Q and +3.2% an 1Q-3Q (see Exhibit 3). PG commented that global market share was flat y-o-y, improving sequentially throughout the quarter vs. y-o-y declines experienced throughout most of FY13.

Exhibit 3

4Q Organic Sales Growth Accelerated

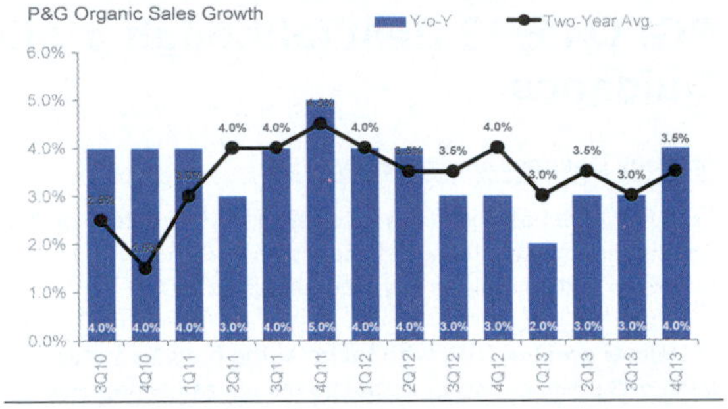

Source: Company Data, Morgan Stanley Research

By segment, strength in organic sales was broad based, with beats posted in Beauty (+3.0% vs. MS +2.5%), Fabric and Home Care (+5.0% vs. MS +2.5%), and Health Care (+7.0% vs. MS +4.0%), partially offset by slight downside in Grooming (+4.0% vs. MS +5.0%) and Baby and Family Care (+4.0% vs. MS +4.5%).

Exhibit 4

4Q13 Segment Results

	MS Est. vs. Actual			Year-over-Year		
$ in millions	MS Est. Jun-13 E	Actual Jun-13	+/-	Jun-12	Actual Jun-13	+/-
Total Sales	**$20,691**	**$20,655**	**-0.2%**	**$20,212**	**$20,655**	**2.2%**
Organic Sales Growth	3.4%	4.0%	64 bps	3.0%	4.0%	100bp
Volume (Organic)	3.1%	5.0%	194 bps	0.0%	5.0%	500bp
Pricing	0.9%	0.0%	(94) bps	4.0%	0.0%	-400bp
Mix	-0.6%	-1.0%	(39) bps	-1.0%	-1.0%	0bp
FX Impact	-1.0%	-2.0%	(97) bps	-4.0%	-2.0%	200bp
Beauty						
Beauty Care	**$4,884**	**$4,850**	**-0.7%**	**$4,806**	**$4,850**	**0.9%**
Organic Sales Growth	2.5%	3.0%	50bp	1.0%	3.0%	201bp
Pretax Profit	$550.4	$533.0	-3.2%	$544.0	$533.0	-2.0%
Grooming	**$2,081**	**$1,981**	**-4.8%**	**$2,007**	**$1,981**	**-1.3%**
Organic Sales Growth	5.0%	4.0%	-100bp	0.0%	4.0%	400bp
Pretax Profit	$572.4	$536.0	-6.4%	$534.0	$536.0	0.4%
Household Care						
Fabric and Home Care	**$6,643**	**$6,737**		**$6,551**	**$6,737**	
Organic Sales Growth	2.5%	5.0%	250bp	3.4%	5.0%	156bp
Pretax Profit	$889.9	$989.0	11.1%	$1,002.0	$989.0	-1.3%
Baby and Family Care	**$4,248**	**$4,192**	**-1.3%**	**$4,099**	**$4,192**	**2.3%**
Organic Sales Growth	4.5%	4.0%	-50bp	5.0%	4.0%	-99bp
Pretax Profit	$862.0	$816.0	-5.3%	$840.0	$816.0	-2.9%
Health & Well Being						
Health Care	**$3,014**	**$3,116**	**3.4%**	**$2,929**	**$3,116**	**6.4%**
Organic Sales Growth	4.0%	7.0%	300bp	3.4%	7.0%	360bp
Pretax Profit	$551.0	$547.0	-0.7%	$534.0	$547.0	2.4%

Source: Company Data, Morgan Stanley Research

Softer than anticipated margins: Margins were disappointing, with gross margins (down 90 bps y-o-y) negatively impacted by product mix (~200 bps), manufacturing and start up costs (~100 bps), and negative FX (~90 bps), partially offset by productivity (~250 bps) and topline leverage (~50bps). SG&A as a % of sales (up 40 bps y-o-y) was negatively impacted by increased marketing spend (~50 bps) and negative FX/increased investments (~60 bps), partially offset by productivity (~70 bps).

FY14 Guidance: PG expects core EPS growth for FY14 of +5-7%, which implies $4.25-4.33 in EPS vs. consensus heading into quarter at $4.32. Notably, FY14 EPS guidance includes a -6% impact from FX, implying low double-digit FX neutral EPS growth on an underlying basis. By quarter, PG expects EPS to be down modestly in Q1 on a y-o-y basis, up slightly in Q2, and than accelerate in F2H14. Other line item details include:

- **Sales:** +3-4% organic growth (FX -2% headwind)
- **Commodities:** slight headwind vs. FY13
- **Marketing spend:** a modest decrease as a % of sales
- **Tax rate:** in-line with FY13
- **Dividends:** ~$6.5 billion
- **Share repurchases:** $5-$7 billion
- **Cash flow productivity:** ~90%
- **Capex**: 4-5% as a % of sales:

Key Risks to Our Investment Thesis

Uncertain macro outlook. Given Procter & Gamble's skew to premium products, the company's organic sales growth prospects will be significantly influenced by consumer spending going forward. PG's volume is sensitive to macro conditions as evidenced by its 2% volume decline in FY09. We estimate that a 100-bp change in volume is worth 2% to our FY14 EPS estimate.

Vacillating pricing is a risk. If the industry environment was more competitive than we expect, we estimate that each 100 bps of pricing pressure would be worth 5% to FY13 EPS.

Cost-cutting. PG's core SG&A as a percentage of sales (excluding shipping and handling, ad spending, R&D expense, and stock option expense) of ~17% in FY12 was the highest in its large cap peer group despite PG's leading scale. As such, we believe PG has ample opportunity to pare back its SG&A spending, and also generate COGS cost savings/productivity. We also believe PG is more focused on cost cutting through simplifying the organization and streamlining bureaucracy, in order to better capitalize on its scale. Each 50 basis points change in core SG&A as a % of sales versus our forecast would be worth an estimated 2.5% to FY14 EPS.

Market share vacillates. There may be upside to PG's FY14 EPS if market share gains accelerate with PG ramping up investment behind the business and a strong innovation pipeline. On the other hand, market share could stall with weaker consumer spending given PG's premium portfolio. We estimate each 100 basis points of incremental volume would be worth 2% to FY14 EPS.

Currency movements. Nearly to-thirds of PG's sales are derived from outside the US. As such, fluctuation in currencies could materially impact our EPS estimates. We estimate that a 5% change in the USD versus PG's basket of currencies would have a 3% impact on EPS. PG is more insulated from FX risk than its peers given relatively less international exposure. In addition, PG's significant manufacturing footprint outside the US mitigates the potential transaction impact of FX.

Commodity cost volatility. While PG's diversified product portfolio spreads out its raw material exposure across a wide variety of input costs, volatile commodity costs could significantly impact EPS. We estimate that each 200 bps change in overall commodity costs would impact EPS by 3%.

Pershing's stake and potential activism. Pershing Square has confirmed the acquisition of a sizeable stake in P&G. An activist push by Pershing could drive upside in the stock if successful and/or well-received by investors, or a sale of Pershing's stake could drive downside.

Morgan Stanley

MORGAN STANLEY RESEARCH

August 2, 2013
Procter & Gamble Co.

Exhibit 5

PG Income Statement

Income Statement	FY2009	FY2010	FY2011	FY2012	Sep-12	Dec-12	Mar-13	Jun-13	FY2013	Sep-13 E	Dec-13 E	Mar-14 E	Jun-14 E	FY2014E
Sales	**76,694.0**	**78,938.0**	**82,559.0**	**83,680.0**	**20,739.0**	**22,175.0**	**20,598.0**	**20,655.0**	**84,167.0**	**21,437.3**	**22,290.8**	**21,016.4**	**21,182.5**	**85,926.9**
% Growth	-2.8%	2.9%	4.6%	1.4%	-3.7%	2.0%	2.0%	2.2%	0.6%	3.4%	0.5%	2.0%	2.6%	2.1%
% Organic Growth	2.0%	4.0%	4.0%	3.7%	2.0%	3.0%	3.0%	4.0%	2.8%	5.2%	3.1%	4.0%	2.6%	3.7%
Cost of Sales	-38,690.0	-37,919.0	-40,768.0	-42,318.1	-10,246.3	-10,826.0	-10,294.0	-10,812.7	-42,179.0	-10,677.1	-10,837.9	-10,313.9	-10,888.3	-42,717.2
% of Sales	50.4%	48.0%	49.4%	50.6%	49.4%	48.8%	50.0%	52.3%	50.1%	49.8%	48.6%	49.1%	51.4%	49.7%
% of Sales Bps Change		-241	134	119	-106	-144	-18	91	-46	40	-20	-90	-95	-40
Gross Profit	**38,004.0**	**41,019.0**	**41,791.0**	**41,361.9**	**10,492.7**	**11,349.0**	**10,304.0**	**9,842.3**	**41,988.0**	**10,760.2**	**11,452.8**	**10,702.4**	**10,294.2**	**43,209.7**
Gross Margin %	49.6%	52.0%	50.6%	49.4%	50.6%	51.2%	50.0%	47.7%	49.9%	50.2%	51.4%	50.9%	48.6%	50.3%
Gross Margin Bps Change		241	-134	-119	106	144	18	-91	46	-40	20	90	95	40
SG&A Expense (ex Incremental Restructuring)	**-22,240.0**	**-24,731.0**	**-25,668.0**	**-25,654.5**	**-6,230.6**	**-6,702.0**	**-6,435.0**	**-6,736.1**	**-26,103.7**	**-6,490.2**	**-6,550.3**	**-6,422.5**	**-6,803.7**	**-26,266.7**
% of Sales	29.0%	31.3%	31.1%	30.7%	30.0%	30.2%	31.2%	32.6%	31.0%	30.3%	29.4%	30.6%	32.1%	30.6%
% Growth		11.2%	3.8%	-0.1%	-2.3%	3.3%	2.4%	3.5%	1.8%	4.2%	-2.3%	-0.2%	1.0%	0.6%
% of Sales Bps Change		233	-24	-43	44	39	13	40	36	23	-84	-68	-49	-45
Operating Income (ex Incremental Restructuring	**15,764.0**	**16,288.0**	**16,123.0**	**15,707.4**	**4,262.1**	**4,647.0**	**3,869.0**	**3,106.2**	**15,884.3**	**4,270.0**	**4,902.6**	**4,279.9**	**3,490.5**	**16,943.0**
Operating Margin	20.6%	20.6%	19.5%	18.8%	20.6%	21.0%	18.8%	15.0%	18.9%	19.9%	22.0%	20.4%	16.5%	19.7%
% Growth	-5.2%	3.3%	-1.0%	-2.6%	-0.7%	7.4%	2.3%	-6.0%	1.1%	0.2%	5.5%	10.6%	12.4%	6.7%
Operating Margin Bps Change	20	8	-110	-76	63	105	5	-132	10	-63	104	158	144	85
OP Growth ex FX														
Interest Expense	-1,358.0	-946.0	-831.0	-769.0	-172.0	-169.0	-163.0	-163.0	-667.0	-157.7	-159.3	-157.4	-159.0	-633.4
Other Non-Operating Income, Net	397.0	-28.0	202.0	229.0	47.0	257.9	46.0	41.0	391.9	30.2	31.9	31.3	29.6	122.9
Pretax Income	**14,803.0**	**15,314.0**	**15,494.0**	**15,167.4**	**4,137.1**	**4,735.9**	**3,752.0**	**2,984.2**	**15,609.2**	**4,142.5**	**4,775.2**	**4,153.8**	**3,361.0**	**16,432.5**
Taxes	-3,834.0	-3,931.0	-3,644.0	-3,714.4	-1,003.2	-1,155.6	-832.9	-665.5	-3,657.2	-973.5	-1,122.2	-976.1	-789.8	-3,861.6
Tax Rate	25.9%	25.7%	23.5%	24.5%	24.3%	24.4%	22.2%	22.3%	23.4%	23.5%	23.5%	23.5%	23.5%	23.5%
Minority Interests	0.0	0.0	0.0	-115.0	-39.0	-19.0	-25.0	-7.0	-90.0	-39.0	-19.0	-25.0	-7.0	-90.0
Net Income	**10,969.0**	**11,383.0**	**11,850.0**	**11,338.0**	**3,095**	**3,561.3**	**2,894.1**	**2,311.8**	**11,862.0**	**3,130.0**	**3,634.0**	**3,152.7**	**2,564.2**	**12,480.9**
EPS Diluted (Core)	**$3.48**	**$3.67**	**$3.95**	**$3.85**	**$1.06**	**$1.22**	**$0.99**	**$0.79**	**$4.05**	**$1.07**	**$1.25**	**$1.09**	**$0.89**	**$4.30**
EPS % Growth	1.9%	5.6%	7.5%	-2.3%	4.4%	12.3%	5.6%	-4.2%	5.0%	1.6%	2.4%	10.2%	12.9%	6.2%
Basic Shares	2,952.0	2,896.2	2,804.0	2,751.4	2,748.6	2,735.2	2,735.2	2,738.0	2,739.2	2729.6	2718.6	2707.6	2696.6	2,713.1
Diluted Shares	3,154.1	3,100.2	3,001.9	2,941.2	2,931.7	2,919.1	2,930.7	2,937.1	2,930.6	2919.6	2908.6	2897.6	2886.6	2,903.1

Source: Company data, Morgan Stanley Research estimates

Morgan Stanley

MORGAN STANLEY RESEARCH

August 2, 2013
Procter & Gamble Co.

Exhibit 6

PG Balance Sheet

Balance Sheet	FY2009	FY2010	FY2011	FY2012	Sep-12	Dec-12	Mar-13	Jun-13	FY2013	Sep-13 E	Dec-13 E	Mar-14 E	Jun-14 E	FY2014E
Assets														
Surplus Cash	0.0	0.0	0.0	0.0	0.0	0.0	0.0	0.0	0.0	819.4	0.0	0.0	0.0	0.0
Cash & Equivalents	4,781.0	2,879.0	2,768.0	4,436.0	5,302.0	6,643.0	5,876.0	5,947.0	5,947.0	5,302.0	6,643.0	5,876.0	5,947.0	5,947.0
Investment Securities														
Receivables, Net	5,836.0	5,335.0	6,275.0	6,068.0	6,993.0	7,183.0	6,669.0	6,508.0	6,508.0	7,142.7	7,131.3	6,720.4	6,354.7	6,354.7
Inventories	6,880.0	6,384.0	7,379.0	6,721.0	7,332.0	7,219.0	7,240.0	6,909.0	6,909.0	7,554.8	7,140.3	7,171.5	6,881.4	6,881.4
Deferred Income Taxes	1,209.0	990.0	1,140.0	1,001.0	1,072.0	983.0	937.0	991.4	991.4	1,286.2	1,337.4	1,261.0	1,270.9	1,270.9
Prepaid Expenses and Other Current Assets	3,199.0	3,194.0	4,408.0	3,684.0	3,425.0	3,573.0	3,576.0	3,634.6	3,634.6	3,540.3	3,591.7	3,648.6	3,643.4	3,643.4
Total Current Assets	**21,905.0**	**18,782.0**	**21,970.0**	**21,910.0**	**24,124.0**	**25,601.0**	**24,298.0**	**23,990.0**	**23,990.0**	**25,645.5**	**25,843.7**	**24,677.5**	**24,097.5**	**24,097.5**
PP&E, Net	19,462.0	19,244.0	21,293.0	20,377.0	20,877.0	21,204.0	21,191.0	21,666.0	21,666.0	21,743.2	21,702.4	21,860.2	22,721.5	22,721.5
Goodwill, Net	56,512.0	54,012.0	57,562.0	52,943.0	54,332.0	55,687.0	55,067.0	55,067.0	55,067.0	55,067.0	55,067.0	55,067.0	55,067.0	55,067.0
Other Intangible Assets, Net	32,606.0	31,636.0	32,620.0	31,818.0	31,163.0	32,147.0	31,739.0	31,693.0	31,693.0	31,693.0	31,693.0	31,693.0	31,693.0	31,693.0
Other Assets	4,348.0	4,498.0	4,909.0	5,196.0	5,392.0	5,264.0	6,836.0	6,847.0	6,847.0	6,847.0	6,847.0	6,847.0	6,847.0	6,847.0
Total Assets	**134,833.0**	**128,172.0**	**138,354.0**	**132,244.0**	**135,888.0**	**139,903.0**	**139,131.0**	**139,263.0**	**139,263.0**	**140,995.7**	**141,153.1**	**140,144.7**	**140,426.0**	**140,426.0**
Liabilities														
Short-Term Debt	0.0	00.0	0.0	0.0	0.0	0.0	0.0	0.0	0.0	0.0	635.1	1,230.1	4,787.2	4,787.2
Notes and Loan Payable	0.0	0.0	0.0	0.0	0.0	0.0	0.0	0.0	0.0	0.0	0.0	0.0	0.0	0.0
Current Portion of Long-Term Debt	16,320.0	8,472.0	9,981.0	8,698.0	8,314.0	9,819.0	11,098.0	12,432.0	12,432.0	13,332.0	13,332.0	12,082.0	9,966.0	9,966.0
Accounts Payable	5,980.0	7,251.0	8,022.0	7,920.0	7,498.0	7,157.0	7,422.0	8,777.0	8,777.0	8,026.8	7,381.7	7,642.7	8,839.5	8,839.5
Accrued and Other Liabilities	8,601.0	8,559.0	9,290.0	8,289.0	9,086.0	9,254.0	8,892.0	8,828.0	8,828.0	9,306.2	9,213.2	8,862.4	8,517.5	8,517.5
Total Current Liabilities	**30,901.0**	**24,282.0**	**27,293.0**	**24,907.0**	**24,898.0**	**26,230.0**	**27,412.0**	**30,037.0**	**30,037.0**	**30,664.9**	**30,561.9**	**29,817.2**	**32,110.3**	**32,110.3**
Long-Term Debt	20,652.0	21,360.0	22,033.0	21,080.0	23,563.0	23,607.0	21,125.0	19,111.0	19,111.0	18,211.0	18,211.0	17,461.0	17,461.0	17,461.0
Deferred Income Taxes	10,752.0	10,902.0	11,070.0	10,132.0	10,164.0	10,567.0	10,725.0	10,354.1	10,354.1	10,484.8	10,599.9	10,921.8	10,597.3	10,597.3
Minority Interests	0.0	324.0	361.0	596.0	649.0	642.0	685.0	685.0	685.0	685.0	685.0	685.0	685.0	685.0
Other Liabilities	9,429.0	10,189.0	9,957.0	12,090.0	12,315.0	12,176.0	11,916.0	10,366.9	10,366.9	12,086.5	11,570.9	11,527.5	10,379.4	10,379.4
Total Liabilities	**71,734.0**	**67,057.0**	**70,714.0**	**68,805.0**	**71,589.0**	**73,222.0**	**71,863.0**	**70,554.0**	**70,554.0**	**72,132.3**	**71,628.6**	**70,412.6**	**71,233.0**	**71,233.0**
Shareholders' Equity														
Preferred Stock	1,324.0	1,277.0	1,234.0	1,195.0	1,170.0	1,156.0	1,143.0	1,143.0	1,143.0	1,143.0	1,143.0	1,143.0	1,143.0	1,143.0
Common Stock	4,007.0	4,008.0	4,008.0	4,008.0	4,009.0	4,009.0	4,009.0	4,009.0	4,009.0	4,009.0	4,009.0	4,009.0	4,009.0	4,009.0
Additional Paid-In Capital	61,118.0	61,697.0	62,405.0	63,181.0	63,166.0	63,204.0	63,358.0	63,358.0	63,358.0	63,358.0	63,358.0	63,358.0	63,358.0	63,358.0
Retained Earnings	57,309.0	64,614.0	70,682.0	75,349.0	76,574.0	79,045.0	80,035.0	80,624.8	80,624.8	81,998.6	83,883.1	85,292.9	85,955.8	85,955.8
Accumulated Other Comprehensive Income (Lo	-3,358.0	-7,822.0	-2,054.0	-9,333.0	-8,179.0	-7,694.0	-8,282.0	-6,415.8	-6,415.8	-6,135.2	-5,858.7	-5,560.8	-5,262.8	-5,262.8
Reserve for ESOP Debt Retirement	-1,340.0	-1,350.0	-1,357.0	-1,357.0	-1,355.0	-1,357.0	-1,351.0	-1,351.0	-1,351.0	-1,351.0	-1,351.0	-1,351.0	-1,351.0	-1,351.0
Treasury Stock	-55,961.0	-61,309.0	-67,278.0	-69,604.0	-71,086.0	-71,682.0	-71,644.0	-72,659.0	-72,659.0	-74,159.0	-75,659.0	-77,159.0	-78,659.0	-78,659.0
Total Shareholders' Equity	**63,099.0**	**61,115.0**	**67,640.0**	**63,439.0**	**64,299.0**	**66,681.0**	**67,268.0**	**68,709.0**	**68,709.0**	**68,863.4**	**69,524.4**	**69,732.1**	**69,193.0**	**69,193.0**
Total Liabilities & SE	**134,833.0**	**128,172.0**	**138,354.0**	**132,244.0**	**135,888.0**	**139,903.0**	**139,131.0**	**139,263.0**	**139,263.0**	**140,995.7**	**141,153.1**	**140,144.7**	**140,426.0**	**140,426.0**

Source: Company data, Morgan Stanley Research estimates

Morgan Stanley

MORGAN STANLEY RESEARCH

August 2, 2013
Procter & Gamble Co.

Exhibit 7

PG Cash Flow Statement

Cash Flow	FY2009	FY2010	FY2011	FY2012	Sep-12	Dec-12	Mar-13	Jun-13	FY2013	Sep-13 E	Dec-13 E	Mar-14 E	Jun-14 E	FY2014E
Net Income	10,969.0	11,383.0	11,850.0	11,338.0	3,094.8	3,561.3	2,894.1	2,311.8	11,862.0	3,130.0	3,634.0	3,152.7	2,564.2	12,480.9
Adjustments:														
Depreciation and Amortization	3,082.0	3,108.0	2838.0	3204.0	710.0	738.0	740.0	794.0	2982.0	754.9	768.6	757.4	833.3	3114.2
Stock-Based Compensation Expense	516.0	453.0	414.0	377.0	79.0	75.0	96.0	96.0	346.0	80.6	76.5	97.9	97.9	352.9
Deferred Income Taxes	596.0	36.0	128.0	-65.0	-18.0	36.0	57.0	-382.0	-307.0	-294.8	-51.2	76.5	-10.0	-279.5
Other	120.0	-1,121.0	-240.0	-964.0	-259.8	-427.3	-249.1	-131.8	-1068.0	225.0	63.8	265.0	-319.3	234.4
Changes in A/L														
Receivables	415.0	-14.0	-426.0	-427.0	-795.0	-119.0	410.0	89.0	-415.0	-634.7	11.4	411.0	365.6	153.3
Inventories	721.0	86.0	-501.0	77.0	-502.0	178.0	-168.0	267.0	-225.0	-645.8	414.6	-31.2	290.1	27.6
A/P, Accrued and Other Liabilities	-742.0	2446.0	358.0	-22.0	64.0	-352.0	204.0	1,337.0	1253.0	-272.1	-738.1	-89.7	852.0	-247.9
Other Operating Assets and Liabilities	-758.0	-305.0	-1190.0	-234.0	397.0	159.0	-122.0	11.0	445.0	1,719.6	-515.7	-43.3	-1,148.1	12.5
Cash Provided by Operations	**14,919.0**	**16,072.0**	**13,231.0**	**13,284.0**	**2,770.0**	**3,849.0**	**3,862.0**	**4,392.0**	**14,873.0**	**4,062.7**	**3,663.8**	**4,596.1**	**3,525.7**	**15,848.2**
Cash Flows from Investing Activities:														
Capital Expenditures	-3,238.0	-3,067.0	-3,306.0	-3,964.0	-805.0	-724.0	-897.0	-1,582.0	-4,008.0	-832.1	-727.8	-915.2	-1,694.6	-4,169.7
Proceeds from Asset Sales	1,087.0	3068.0	225.0	2893.0	66.0	408.0	85.0	25.0	584.0	0.0	0.0	0.0	0.0	0.0
Payment for Acquisitions	-368.0	-425.0	-474.0	-134.0	12.0	-1,135.0	-25.0	3.0	-1145.0	0.0	0.0	0.0	0.0	0.0
Other	166.0	-173.0	73.0	112.0	-12.0	-167.0	-1,481.0	-66.0	-1,726.0	0.0	0.0	0.0	0.0	0.0
Cash Used for Investing Activities	**-2,353.0**	**-597.0**	**-3,482.0**	**-1,093.0**	**-739.0**	**-1,618.0**	**-2,318.0**	**-1,620.0**	**-6,295.0**	**-832.1**	**-727.8**	**-915.2**	**-1694.6**	**-4,169.7**
Cash Flows from Financing Activites:														
Change in Short-Term Debt	-2,420.0	-1,798.0	151.0	-3,412.0	1033.0	3939.0	-820.0	-746.0	3,406.0	900.0	635.1	-655.0	1441.1	2321.2
Change in Long-Term Debt	2,339.0	-4,716.0	1,330.0	1,436.0	974.0	-2484.0	14.0	75.0	-1,421.0	-900.0	0.0	-750.0	0.0	-1650.0
Dividends Paid	-5,044.0	-5,458.0	-5,767.0	-6,139.0	-1605.0	-1601.0	-1591.0	-1722.0	-6,519.0	-1756.2	-1749.5	-1742.9	-1901.2	-7,149.8
Purchase of Treasury Shares	-6,370.0	-6,004.0	-7,039.0	-4,024.0	-2584.0	-1400.0	-1001.0	-1001.0	-5,986.0	-1500.0	-1500.0	-1500.0	-1500.0	-6,000.0
Proceeds From Stock Options, Other	681.0	721.0	1,302.0	1,729.0	951.0	711.0	1,068.0	719.0	3,449.0	200.0	200.0	200.0	200.0	800.0
Cash Used for Financing Activities	**-10,814.0**	**-17,255.0**	**-10,023.0**	**-10,410.0**	**-1,231.0**	**-835.0**	**-2,330.0**	**-2,675.0**	**-7,071.0**	**-3,056.2**	**-2,414.4**	**-4,447.9**	**-1,760.1**	**-11,678.5**
Cash Provided by Discontinued Operations	0.0	0.0	0.0	0.0	0.0	0.0	0.0	0.0	0.0	0.0	0.0	0.0	0.0	0.0
Exchange Rate Effect on Cash / Other	-284.0	-122.0	163.0	-113.0	66.0	-55.0	19.0	-26.0	4.0	0.0	0.0	0.0	0.0	0.0
Net Increase (Decrease) in Cash and Cash Equivs	1468.0	-1902.0	-111.0	1668.0	866.0	1341.0	-767.0	71.0	1511.0	174.4	521.6	-767.0	71.0	0.0
Cash and Cash Equivs, Beg	3,313.0	4,781.0	2,879.0	2,768.0	4,436.0	5,302.0	6,643.0	5,876.0	4,436.0	5,947.0	6,121.4	6,643.0	5,876.0	5,947.0
Cash and Cash Equivs, End	**4,781.0**	**2,879.0**	**2,768.0**	**4,436.0**	**5,302.0**	**6,643.0**	**5,876.0**	**5,947.0**	**5,947.0**	**6,121.4**	**6,643.0**	**5,876.0**	**5,947.0**	**5,947.0**

Source: Company data, Morgan Stanley Research estimates

Morgan Stanley

MORGAN STANLEY RESEARCH

August 2, 2013
Procter & Gamble Co.

Morgan Stanley

MORGAN STANLEY RESEARCH

August 2, 2013
Procter & Gamble Co.

MORGAN STANLEY ModelWare	**Morgan Stanley ModelWare is a proprietary analytic framework that helps clients uncover value, adjusting for distortions and ambiguities created by local accounting regulations.** For example, ModelWare EPS adjusts for one-time events, capitalizes operating leases (where their use is significant), and converts inventory from LIFO costing to a FIFO basis. ModelWare also emphasizes the separation of operating performance of a company from its financing for a more complete view of how a company generates earnings.

Disclosure Section

The information and opinions in Morgan Stanley Research were prepared by Morgan Stanley & Co. LLC, and/or Morgan Stanley C.T.V.M. S.A., and/or Morgan Stanley Mexico, Casa de Bolsa, S.A. de C.V. As used in this disclosure section, "Morgan Stanley" includes Morgan Stanley & Co. LLC, Morgan Stanley C.T.V.M. S.A., Morgan Stanley Mexico, Casa de Bolsa, S.A. de C.V. and their affiliates as necessary.
For important disclosures, stock price charts and equity rating histories regarding companies that are the subject of this report, please see the Morgan Stanley Research Disclosure Website at www.morganstanley.com/researchdisclosures, or contact your investment representative or Morgan Stanley Research at 1585 Broadway, (Attention: Research Management), New York, NY, 10036 USA.
For valuation methodology and risks associated with any price targets referenced in this research report, please email morganstanley.research@morganstanley.com with a request for valuation methodology and risks on a particular stock or contact your investment representative or Morgan Stanley Research at 1585 Broadway, (Attention: Research Management), New York, NY 10036 USA.

Analyst Certification

The following analysts hereby certify that their views about the companies and their securities discussed in this report are accurately expressed and that they have not received and will not receive direct or indirect compensation in exchange for expressing specific recommendations or views in this report: Dara Mohsenian.
Unless otherwise stated, the individuals listed on the cover page of this report are research analysts.

Global Research Conflict Management Policy

Morgan Stanley Research has been published in accordance with our conflict management policy, which is available at www.morganstanley.com/institutional/research/conflictpolicies.

Important US Regulatory Disclosures on Subject Companies

Within the last 12 months, Morgan Stanley managed or co-managed a public offering (or 144A offering) of securities of Clorox Co, Colgate-Palmolive Co, Coty Inc, **Procter & Gamble Co.**.
Within the last 12 months, Morgan Stanley has received compensation for investment banking services from Avon Products Inc., Clorox Co, Colgate-Palmolive Co, Coty Inc, Estee Lauder Companies Inc, **Procter & Gamble Co.**.
In the next 3 months, Morgan Stanley expects to receive or intends to seek compensation for investment banking services from Avon Products Inc., Church & Dwight Co., Inc., Clorox Co, Colgate-Palmolive Co, Coty Inc, Energizer Holdings Inc, Estee Lauder Companies Inc, Newell Rubbermaid Inc., **Procter & Gamble Co.**, Tupperware Brands Corp., Weight Watchers International.
Within the last 12 months, Morgan Stanley has received compensation for products and services other than investment banking services from Avon Products Inc., Church & Dwight Co., Inc., Clorox Co, Colgate-Palmolive Co, Coty Inc, Energizer Holdings Inc, Estee Lauder Companies Inc, **Procter & Gamble Co.**, Weight Watchers International.
Within the last 12 months, Morgan Stanley has provided or is providing investment banking services to, or has an investment banking client relationship with, the following company: Avon Products Inc., Church & Dwight Co., Inc., Clorox Co, Colgate-Palmolive Co, Coty Inc, Energizer Holdings Inc, Estee Lauder Companies Inc, Newell Rubbermaid Inc., **Procter & Gamble Co.**, Tupperware Brands Corp., Weight Watchers International.
Within the last 12 months, Morgan Stanley has either provided or is providing non-investment banking, securities-related services to and/or in the past has entered into an agreement to provide services or has a client relationship with the following company: Avon Products Inc., Church & Dwight Co., Inc., Clorox Co, Colgate-Palmolive Co, Coty Inc, Energizer Holdings Inc, Estee Lauder Companies Inc, Newell Rubbermaid Inc., **Procter & Gamble Co.**, Weight Watchers International.
An employee, director or consultant of Morgan Stanley is a director of Estee Lauder Companies Inc. This person is not a research analyst or a member of a research analyst's household.
Morgan Stanley & Co. LLC makes a market in the securities of Avon Products Inc., Church & Dwight Co., Inc., Clorox Co, Colgate-Palmolive Co, Coty Inc, Energizer Holdings Inc, Estee Lauder Companies Inc, Newell Rubbermaid Inc., **Procter & Gamble Co.**, Tupperware Brands Corp., Weight Watchers International.
The equity research analysts or strategists principally responsible for the preparation of Morgan Stanley Research have received compensation based upon various factors, including quality of research, investor client feedback, stock picking, competitive factors, firm revenues and overall investment banking revenues.
Morgan Stanley and its affiliates do business that relates to companies/instruments covered in Morgan Stanley Research, including market making, providing liquidity and specialized trading, risk arbitrage and other proprietary trading, fund management, commercial banking, extension of credit, investment services and investment banking. Morgan Stanley sells to and buys from customers the securities/instruments of companies covered in Morgan Stanley Research on a principal basis. Morgan Stanley may have a position in the debt of the Company or instruments discussed in this report.
Certain disclosures listed above are also for compliance with applicable regulations in non-US jurisdictions.

STOCK RATINGS

Morgan Stanley uses a relative rating system using terms such as Overweight, Equal-weight, Not-Rated or Underweight (see definitions below). Morgan Stanley does not assign ratings of Buy, Hold or Sell to the stocks we cover. Overweight, Equal-weight, Not-Rated and Underweight are not the equivalent of buy, hold and sell. Investors should carefully read the definitions of all ratings used in Morgan Stanley Research. In addition, since Morgan Stanley Research contains more complete information concerning the analyst's views, investors should carefully read Morgan Stanley Research, in its entirety, and not infer the contents from the rating alone. In any case, ratings (or research) should not be used or relied upon as investment advice. An investor's decision to buy or sell a stock should depend on individual circumstances (such as the investor's existing holdings) and other considerations.

Global Stock Ratings Distribution

(as of July 31, 2013)

For disclosure purposes only (in accordance with NASD and NYSE requirements), we include the category headings of Buy, Hold, and Sell alongside our ratings of Overweight, Equal-weight, Not-Rated and Underweight. Morgan Stanley does not assign ratings of Buy, Hold or Sell to the stocks we cover. Overweight, Equal-weight, Not-Rated and Underweight are not the equivalent of buy, hold, and sell but represent recommended relative weightings (see definitions below). To satisfy regulatory requirements, we correspond Overweight, our most positive stock rating, with a buy recommendation; we correspond Equal-weight and Not-Rated to hold and Underweight to sell recommendations, respectively.

Morgan Stanley

MORGAN STANLEY RESEARCH

August 2, 2013
Procter & Gamble Co.

	Coverage Universe		Investment Banking Clients (IBC)		
Stock Rating Category	Count	% of Total	Count	% of Total IBC	% of Rating Category
Overweight/Buy	**1009**	**35%**	**410**	**39%**	**41%**
Equal-weight/Hold	**1302**	**45%**	**496**	**47%**	**38%**
Not-Rated/Hold	**112**	**4%**	**27**	**3%**	**24%**
Underweight/Sell	**467**	**16%**	**123**	**12%**	**26%**
Total	**2,890**		**1056**		

Data include common stock and ADRs currently assigned ratings. An investor's decision to buy or sell a stock should depend on individual circumstances (such as the investor's existing holdings) and other considerations. Investment Banking Clients are companies from whom Morgan Stanley received investment banking compensation in the last 12 months.

Analyst Stock Ratings

Overweight (O). The stock's total return is expected to exceed the average total return of the analyst's industry (or industry team's) coverage universe, on a risk-adjusted basis, over the next 12-18 months.
Equal-weight (E). The stock's total return is expected to be in line with the average total return of the analyst's industry (or industry team's) coverage universe, on a risk-adjusted basis, over the next 12-18 months.
Not-Rated (NR). Currently the analyst does not have adequate conviction about the stock's total return relative to the average total return of the analyst's industry (or industry team's) coverage universe, on a risk-adjusted basis, over the next 12-18 months.
Underweight (U). The stock's total return is expected to be below the average total return of the analyst's industry (or industry team's) coverage universe, on a risk-adjusted basis, over the next 12-18 months.
Unless otherwise specified, the time frame for price targets included in Morgan Stanley Research is 12 to 18 months.

Analyst Industry Views

Attractive (A): The analyst expects the performance of his or her industry coverage universe over the next 12-18 months to be attractive vs. the relevant broad market benchmark, as indicated below.
In-Line (I): The analyst expects the performance of his or her industry coverage universe over the next 12-18 months to be in line with the relevant broad market benchmark, as indicated below.
Cautious (C): The analyst views the performance of his or her industry coverage universe over the next 12-18 months with caution vs. the relevant broad market benchmark, as indicated below.
Benchmarks for each region are as follows: North America - S&P 500; Latin America - relevant MSCI country index or MSCI Latin America Index; Europe - MSCI Europe; Japan - TOPIX; Asia - relevant MSCI country index.

Stock Price, Price Target and Rating History (See Rating Definitions)

Procter & Gamble Co. (PG.N) - As of 8/1/13 in USD
Industry : Household & Personal Care

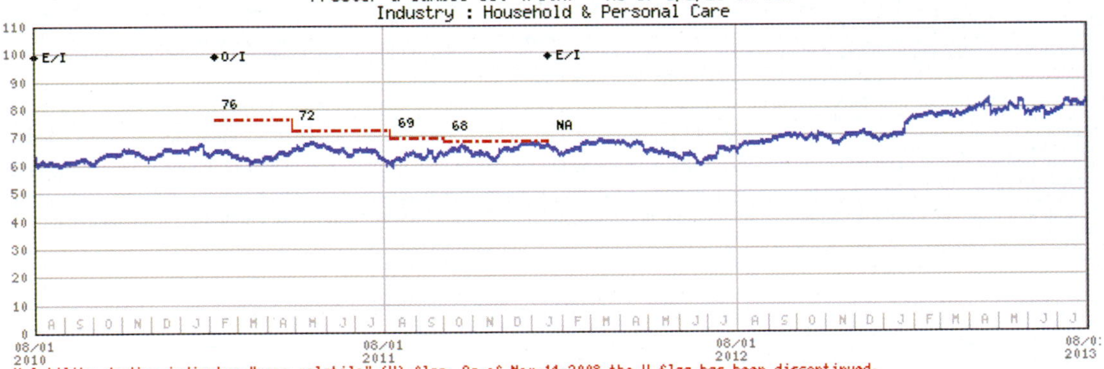

Volatility shading indicates "more volatile" (V) flag. As of Nov-14-2008 the V flag has been discontinued.

Stock Rating History: 8/1/10 : E/I; 2/7/11 : O/I; 1/20/12 : E/I
Price Target History: 7/15/10 : NA; 2/7/11 : 76; 4/28/11 : 72; 8/7/11 : 69; 10/3/11 : 68; 1/20/12 : NA

Source: Morgan Stanley Research Date Format : MM/DD/YY Price Target No Price Target Assigned (NA)
Stock Price (Not Covered by Current Analyst) Stock Price (Covered by Current Analyst)
Stock and Industry Ratings (abbreviations below) appear as ◆ Stock Rating/Industry View
Stock Ratings: Overweight (O) Equal-weight (E) Underweight (U) Not-Rated (NR) More Volatile (V) No Rating Available (NA)
Industry View: Attractive (A) In-line (I) Cautious (C) No Rating (NR)

Morgan Stanley

MORGAN STANLEY RESEARCH

August 2, 2013
Procter & Gamble Co.

Important Disclosures for Morgan Stanley Smith Barney LLC Customers

Citi Research publications may be available about the companies or topics that are the subject of Morgan Stanley Research. Ask your Financial Advisor or use Research Center to view any available Citi Research publications in addition to Morgan Stanley research reports.

Important disclosures regarding the relationship between the companies that are the subject of Morgan Stanley Research and Morgan Stanley Smith Barney LLC or Morgan Stanley or any of their affiliates, are available on the Morgan Stanley Wealth Management disclosure website at www.morganstanley.com/online/researchdisclosures.

For Morgan Stanley specific disclosures, you may refer to www.morganstanley.com/researchdisclosures.

Each Morgan Stanley Equity Research report is reviewed and approved on behalf of Morgan Stanley Smith Barney LLC. This review and approval is conducted by the same person who reviews the Equity Research report on behalf of Morgan Stanley. This could create a conflict of interest.

Other Important Disclosures

Morgan Stanley & Co. International PLC and its affiliates have a significant financial interest in the debt securities of Avon Products Inc., Clorox Co, Colgate-Palmolive Co, Coty Inc, Estee Lauder Companies Inc, Newell Rubbermaid Inc., **Procter & Gamble Co.**, Weight Watchers International.

Morgan Stanley is not acting as a municipal advisor and the opinions or views contained herein are not intended to be, and do not constitute, advice within the meaning of Section 975 of the Dodd-Frank Wall Street Reform and Consumer Protection Act.

Morgan Stanley produces an equity research product called a "Tactical Idea." Views contained in a "Tactical Idea" on a particular stock may be contrary to the recommendations or views expressed in research on the same stock. This may be the result of differing time horizons, methodologies, market events, or other factors. For all research available on a particular stock, please contact your sales representative or go to Client Link at www.morganstanley.com.

Morgan Stanley Research does not provide individually tailored investment advice. Morgan Stanley Research has been prepared without regard to the circumstances and objectives of those who receive it. Morgan Stanley recommends that investors independently evaluate particular investments and strategies, and encourages investors to seek the advice of a financial adviser. The appropriateness of an investment or strategy will depend on an investor's circumstances and objectives. The securities, instruments, or strategies discussed in Morgan Stanley Research may not be suitable for all investors, and certain investors may not be eligible to purchase or participate in some or all of them. Morgan Stanley Research is not an offer to buy or sell any security/instrument or to participate in any trading strategy. The value of and income from your investments may vary because of changes in interest rates, foreign exchange rates, default rates, prepayment rates, securities/instruments prices, market indexes, operational or financial conditions of companies or other factors. There may be time limitations on the exercise of options or other rights in securities/instruments transactions. Past performance is not necessarily a guide to future performance. Estimates of future performance are based on assumptions that may not be realized. If provided, and unless otherwise stated, the closing price on the cover page is that of the primary exchange for the subject company's securities/instruments.

The fixed income research analysts, strategists or economists principally responsible for the preparation of Morgan Stanley Research have received compensation based upon various factors, including quality, accuracy and value of research, firm profitability or revenues (which include fixed income trading and capital markets profitability or revenues), client feedback and competitive factors. Fixed Income Research analysts', strategists' or economists' compensation is not linked to investment banking or capital markets transactions performed by Morgan Stanley or the profitability or revenues of particular trading desks.

Morgan Stanley Research is not an offer to buy or sell or the solicitation of an offer to buy or sell any security/instrument or to participate in any particular trading strategy. The "Important US Regulatory Disclosures on Subject Companies" section in Morgan Stanley Research lists all companies mentioned where Morgan Stanley owns 1% or more of a class of common equity securities of the companies. For all other companies mentioned in Morgan Stanley Research, Morgan Stanley may have an investment of less than 1% in securities/instruments or derivatives of securities/instruments of companies and may trade them in ways different from those discussed in Morgan Stanley Research. Employees of Morgan Stanley not involved in the preparation of Morgan Stanley Research may have investments in securities/instruments or derivatives of securities/instruments of companies mentioned and may trade them in ways different from those discussed in Morgan Stanley Research. Derivatives may be issued by Morgan Stanley or associated persons.

With the exception of information regarding Morgan Stanley, Morgan Stanley Research is based on public information. Morgan Stanley makes every effort to use reliable, comprehensive information, but we make no representation that it is accurate or complete. We have no obligation to tell you when opinions or information in Morgan Stanley Research change apart from when we intend to discontinue equity research coverage of a subject company. Facts and views presented in Morgan Stanley Research have not been reviewed by, and may not reflect information known to, professionals in other Morgan Stanley business areas, including investment banking personnel.

Morgan Stanley Research personnel may participate in company events such as site visits and are generally prohibited from accepting payment by the company of associated expenses unless pre-approved by authorized members of Research management.

Morgan Stanley may make investment decisions or take proprietary positions that are inconsistent with the recommendations or views in this report.

To our readers in Taiwan: Information on securities/instruments that trade in Taiwan is distributed by Morgan Stanley Taiwan Limited ("MSTL"). Such information is for your reference only. The reader should independently evaluate the investment risks and is solely responsible for their investment decisions. Morgan Stanley Research may not be distributed to the public media or quoted or used by the public media without the express written consent of Morgan Stanley. Information on securities/instruments that do not trade in Taiwan is for informational purposes only and is not to be construed as a recommendation or a solicitation to trade in such securities/instruments. MSTL may not execute transactions for clients in these securities/instruments. To our readers in Hong Kong: Information is distributed in Hong Kong by and on behalf of, and is attributable to, Morgan Stanley Asia Limited as part of its regulated activities in Hong Kong. If you have any queries concerning Morgan Stanley Research, please contact our Hong Kong sales representatives.

Morgan Stanley is not incorporated under PRC law and the research in relation to this report is conducted outside the PRC. Morgan Stanley Research does not constitute an offer to sell or the solicitation of an offer to buy any securities in the PRC. PRC investors shall have the relevant qualifications to invest in such securities and shall be responsible for obtaining all relevant approvals, licenses, verifications and/or registrations from the relevant governmental authorities themselves.

Morgan Stanley Research is disseminated in Brazil by Morgan Stanley C.T.V.M. S.A.; in Japan by Morgan Stanley MUFG Securities Co., Ltd. and, for Commodities related research reports only, Morgan Stanley Capital Group Japan Co., Ltd; in Hong Kong by Morgan Stanley Asia Limited (which accepts responsibility for its contents); in Singapore by Morgan Stanley Asia (Singapore) Pte. (Registration number 199206298Z) and/or Morgan Stanley Asia (Singapore) Securities Pte Ltd (Registration number 200008434H), regulated by the Monetary Authority of Singapore (which accepts legal responsibility for its contents and should be contacted with respect to any matters arising from, or in connection with, Morgan Stanley Research); in Australia to "wholesale clients" within the meaning of the Australian Corporations Act by Morgan Stanley Australia Limited A.B.N. 67 003 734 576, holder of Australian financial services license No. 233742, which accepts responsibility for its contents; in Australia to "wholesale clients" and "retail clients" within the meaning of the Australian Corporations Act by Morgan Stanley Wealth Management Australia Pty Ltd (A.B.N. 19 009 145 555, holder of Australian financial services license No. 240813, which accepts responsibility for its contents; in Korea by Morgan Stanley & Co International plc, Seoul Branch; in India by Morgan Stanley India Company Private Limited; in Indonesia by PT Morgan Stanley Asia Indonesia; in Canada by Morgan Stanley Canada Limited, which has approved of and takes responsibility for its contents in Canada; in Germany by Morgan Stanley Bank AG, Frankfurt am Main and Morgan Stanley Private Wealth Management Limited, Niederlassung Deutschland, regulated by Bundesanstalt fuer Finanzdienstleistungsaufsicht (BaFin); in Spain by Morgan Stanley, S.V., S.A., a Morgan Stanley group company, which is supervised by the Spanish Securities Markets Commission (CNMV) and states that Morgan Stanley Research has been written and distributed in accordance with the rules of conduct applicable to financial research as established under Spanish regulations; in the US by Morgan Stanley & Co. LLC, which accepts responsibility for its contents. Morgan Stanley & Co. International plc, authorized by the Prudential Regulatory Authority and regulated by the Financial Conduct Authority and the Prudential Regulatory Authority, disseminates in the UK research that it has prepared, and approves solely for the purposes of section 21 of the Financial Services and Markets Act 2000, research which has been prepared by any of its affiliates. Morgan Stanley Private Wealth Management Limited, authorized by the Prudential Regulatory Authority and regulated by the Financial Conduct Authority and the Prudential Regulatory Authority, also disseminates Morgan Stanley Research in the UK. Private UK investors should obtain the advice of their Morgan Stanley & Co. International plc or Morgan Stanley Private Wealth Management representative about the investments concerned. RMB Morgan Stanley (Proprietary) Limited is a member of the JSE Limited and regulated by the Financial Services Board in South Africa. RMB Morgan Stanley (Proprietary) Limited is a joint venture owned equally by Morgan Stanley International Holdings Inc. and RMB Investment Advisory (Proprietary) Limited, which is wholly owned by FirstRand Limited.

The information in Morgan Stanley Research is being communicated by Morgan Stanley & Co. International plc (DIFC Branch), regulated by the Dubai Financial Services Authority (the DFSA), and is directed at Professional Clients only, as defined by the DFSA. The financial products or financial services to which this research relates will only be made available to a customer who we are satisfied meets the regulatory criteria to be a Professional Client.

The information in Morgan Stanley Research is being communicated by Morgan Stanley & Co. International plc (QFC Branch), regulated by the Qatar Financial Centre Regulatory Authority (the QFCRA), and is directed at business customers and market counterparties only and is not intended for Retail Customers as defined by the QFCRA.

Morgan Stanley

MORGAN STANLEY RESEARCH

August 2, 2013
Procter & Gamble Co.

As required by the Capital Markets Board of Turkey, investment information, comments and recommendations stated here, are not within the scope of investment advisory activity. Investment advisory service is provided in accordance with a contract of engagement on investment advisory concluded between brokerage houses, portfolio management companies, non-deposit banks and clients. Comments and recommendations stated here rely on the individual opinions of the ones providing these comments and recommendations. These opinions may not fit to your financial status, risk and return preferences. For this reason, to make an investment decision by relying solely to this information stated here may not bring about outcomes that fit your expectations.

The trademarks and service marks contained in Morgan Stanley Research are the property of their respective owners. Third-party data providers make no warranties or representations relating to the accuracy, completeness, or timeliness of the data they provide and shall not have liability for any damages relating to such data. The Global Industry Classification Standard (GICS) was developed by and is the exclusive property of MSCI and S&P. Morgan Stanley bases projections, opinions, forecasts and trading strategies regarding the MSCI Country Index Series solely on public information. MSCI has not reviewed, approved or endorsed these projections, opinions, forecasts and trading strategies. Morgan Stanley has no influence on or control over MSCI's index compilation decisions. Morgan Stanley Research or portions of it may not be reprinted, sold or redistributed without the written consent of Morgan Stanley. Morgan Stanley research is disseminated and available primarily electronically, and, in some cases, in printed form. Additional information on recommended securities/instruments is available on request.

Morgan Stanley Research, or any portion thereof may not be reprinted, sold or redistributed without the written consent of Morgan Stanley.

Morgan Stanley Research is disseminated and available primarily electronically, and, in some cases, in printed form.

Additional information on recommended securities/instruments is available on request.

Morgan Stanley

MORGAN STANLEY RESEARCH

The Americas
1585 Broadway
New York, NY 10036-8293
United States
Tel: +1 (1) 212 761 4000

Europe
20 Bank Street, Canary Wharf
London E14 4AD
United Kingdom
Tel: +44 (0) 20 7 425 8000

Japan
4-20-3 Ebisu, Shibuya-ku
Tokyo 150-6008
Japan
Tel: +81 (0) 3 5424 5000

Asia/Pacific
1 Austin Road West
Kowloon
Hong Kong
Tel: +852 2848 5200

Industry Coverage:Household & Personal Care

Company (Ticker)	Rating (as of)	Price* (08/01/2013)
Dara Mohsenian, CFA		
Avon Products Inc. (AVP.N)	E (10/04/2010)	$22.02
Church & Dwight Co., Inc. (CHD.N)	E (08/19/2009)	$65.04
Clorox Co (CLX.N)	E (07/15/2011)	$84.83
Colgate-Palmolive Co (CL.N)	E (03/15/2013)	$60.56
Coty Inc (COTY.N)	E (08/01/2013)	$17.27
Energizer Holdings Inc (ENR.N)	E (01/28/2013)	$102.31
Estee Lauder Companies Inc (EL.N)	O (12/03/2012)	$66.79
Newell Rubbermaid Inc. (NWL.N)	E (07/30/2012)	$27.73
Procter & Gamble Co. (PG.N)	E (01/20/2012)	$81.64
Tupperware Brands Corp. (TUP.N)	E (03/08/2013)	$86.31
Weight Watchers International (WTW.N)	E (02/18/2011)	$47.03

Stock Ratings are subject to change. Please see latest research for each company.
* Historical prices are not split adjusted.

DISCUSSION QUESTIONS

Q11-1. Identify at least two applications that use forecasted financial statements.

Q11-2. Forecasts of the income statement typically require estimates of cost of goods sold (gross profit) and operating and nonoperating expenses (revenues) as a percentage of revenues. Identify at least three financial statement adjustments that we discuss in previous modules that might affect our forecasts for gross profit margin and operating expense percentages.

Q11-3. Forecasts of the balance sheet commonly require estimates of the relative percentage of balance sheet accounts to revenues. Identify at least three financial statement adjustments to reported balance sheet items that can impact that item's relation to revenues. These can include adjustments to recognize assets and/or liabilities that are not recognized under GAAP.

Q11-4. What does the concept of financial statement articulation mean in the forecasting process?

Q11-5. Net operating assets typically move proportionately with revenues. How do the "buffer zone" and "financing" sections of the balance sheet offset some of these changes in net operating assets?

Q11-6. Identify and describe the four major steps in forecasting financial statements.

Q11-7. In addition to recent revenues trends, what other types and sources of information can we use to help us forecast revenues?

Q11-8. Describe the rationale for use of year-end balances in the computation of turnover rates (and other percentages) that are used to forecast selected balance sheet accounts.

Q11-9. What are "comparable store sales" for retailers and why are they important?

Q11-10. Capital expenditures are usually an important cash outflow for a company, and they figure prominently into forecasts of net operating assets. What are the sources of information about capital expenditures that we can draw upon?

Assignments with the ✓ logo in the margin are available in myBusinessCourse. See the Preface of the book for details.

MINI EXERCISES

✓ Abercrombie & Fitch Co. (ANF)

M11-11. Forecasting an Income Statement (LO2)

Abercrombie & Fitch Co. reports the following income statements.

Income Statement, For Fiscal Years Ended ($ thousands)	Feb. 2, 2013	Jan. 28, 2012	Jan. 29, 2011
Net sales	$4,510,805	$4,158,058	$3,468,777
Cost of goods sold	1,694,096	1,607,834	1,251,348
Gross profit	2,816,709	2,550,224	2,217,429
Stores and distribution expense	1,987,926	1,888,248	1,589,501
Marketing, general and administrative expense	473,883	437,120	400,804
Other operating expense (income), net	(19,333)	3,472	(10,056)
Operating income	374,233	221,384	237,180
Interest expense, net	7,288	3,577	3,362
Income from continuing operations before taxes	366,945	217,807	233,818
Tax expense from continuing operations	129,934	74,669	78,109
Net income from continuing operations	237,011	143,138	155,709
Income from discontinued operations, net of tax	—	796	—
Net Income	$ 237,011	$ 143,934	$ 155,709

Forecast Abercrombie & Fitch's fiscal 2014 income statement assuming the following income statement relations ($ in thousands). All percentages, other than sales growth and provision for income taxes, are based on percent of net sales.

Net sales growth	1.10
Cost of goods sold/Net sales	37%
Stores and distribution expense/Net sales	44%
Marketing, general and administrative expense/Net sales	11%
Other operating income, net	$(19,333)
Interest expense (income), net	$7,288
Tax expense from continuing operations (% of pretax income)	35%
Net loss from discontinued operations (net of taxes)	0

M11-12. Forecasting an Income Statement (LO2)

Macy's, Inc. reports the following income statements.

Macy's, Inc. (M)

Consolidated Statement of Operations Fiscal Years Ended (In millions)	February 2, 2013	January 28, 2012	January 29, 2011
Net sales	$27,686	$26,405	$25,003
Cost of sales	(16,538)	(15,738)	(14,824)
Gross margin	11,148	10,667	10,179
Selling, general and administrative expenses	(8,482)	(8,281)	(8,260)
Impairments, store closing costs, gain on sale of leases and division consolidation costs	(5)	25	(25)
Operating income	2,661	2,411	1,894
Interest expense	(425)	(447)	(513)
Premium on early retirement of debt	(137)	—	(66)
Interest income	3	4	5
Income before income taxes	2,102	1,968	1,320
Federal, state and local income tax benefit (expense)	(767)	(712)	(473)
Net income	$ 1,335	$ 1,256	$ 847

Forecast Macy's fiscal 2014 income statement assuming the following income statement relations ($ in millions). All percentages (other than revenue growth, and income tax expense) are based on percent of revenue.

Net sales growth	5%
Cost of sales/Net sales	60%
Selling, general and administrative expenses/Net sales	30%
Impairments, store closing costs and gain of leases	$0
Premium on early retirement of debt	$(137)
Interest income	$3
Interest expense	$(425)
Income tax expense (% of pretax income)	37%

M11-13. Forecasting an Income Statement (LO2)

General Mills, Inc. reports the following fiscal year income statements.

General Mills, Inc. (GIS)

Income Statement, Fiscal Year Ended ($ millions)	May 26, 2013	May 27, 2012	May 29, 2011
Net sales	**$17,774.1**	$16,657.9	$14,880.2
Cost of sales	**11,350.2**	10,613.2	8,926.7
Selling, general and administrative expenses	**3,552.3**	3,380.7	3,192.0
Divestitures (gain)	**—**	—	(17.4)
Restructuring, impairment, and other exit costs	**19.8**	101.6	4.4
Operating profit	**2,851.8**	2,562.4	2,774.5
Interest, net	**316.9**	351.9	346.3
Earnings before income taxes and after-tax earnings from joint ventures	**2,534.9**	2,210.5	2,428.2
Income taxes	**741.2**	709.6	721.1
After-tax earnings from joint ventures	**98.8**	88.2	96.4
Net earnings, including earnings attributable to redeemable and noncontrolling interests	**1,892.5**	1,589.1	1,803.5
Net earnings attributable to redeemable and noncontrolling interests	**37.3**	21.8	5.2
Net earnings attributable to General Mills	**$ 1,855.2**	$ 1,567.3	$ 1,798.3

Forecast General Mills' fiscal year 2014 income statement assuming the following income statement relations ($ in millions). All percentages (other than net sales growth, income taxes, and net earnings attributable to noncontrolling interests) are based on percent of sales.

Net sales growth	5%
Cost of sales/Net sales	63.9%
Selling, general, and administrative expenses/Net sales	20.0%
Divestiture (gain), net	$0.0
Restructuring, impairment, and other exit costs	$0.0
Interest, net	$316.9
Income taxes (% pretax income)	29.2%
After-tax earnings from joint ventures	$98.8
Net earnings attributable to noncontrolling interests (% net earnings before attribution)	2.0%

Harley-Davidson, Inc. (HOG)

M11-14. Analyzing, Forecasting, and Interpreting Working Capital Using Turnover Rates (LO3)

Harley-Davidson, Inc. reports 2012 net operating working capital of $1,888 million and 2012 long-term operating assets of $4,380 million.

a. Forecast Harley-Davidson's 2013 net operating working capital and 2013 long-term operating assets. Assume forecasted 2013 net revenue of $5,692 million, net operating working capital turnover of 2.95 times, and long-term operating asset turnover of 1.27 times. (Both turnover rates are computed here using year-end balances. Finance receivables and related debt are considered operating under the assumption that they are an integral part of Harley's operating activities.)

b. Most of Harley's receivables arise from its financing activities relating to purchases of motorcycles by consumers and dealers. What effect will these receivables have on Harley's operating working capital turnover rate?

Nike Inc. (NKE)

M11-15. Analyzing, Forecasting, and Interpreting Working Capital Using Turnover Rates (LO3)

Nike Inc. reports 2012 net operating working capital of $3,931 million and 2012 long-term operating assets of $2,666 million.

a. Forecast Nike's 2013 net operating working capital assuming forecasted sales of $25,819 million, net operating working capital turnover of 6.44 times, and long-term operating asset turnover of 9.49 times. (Both turnover rates are computed here using year-end balances.)

b. Nike's long-term operating asset turnover rate is comparatively high. Can you suggest a possible reason given Nike's business model? Explain.

General Mills, Inc. (GIS)

M11-16. Forecasting the Balance Sheet (LO3, 4)

Refer to the **General Mills, Inc.** information in M11-13. Assume the forecast of 2014 net sales is $18,662.8 million. Use the following financial statement relations to forecast General Mills' receivables, inventories, and accounts payable as of the end of May 2014.

	2014
Year-end receivables/Net sales	8.1%
Year-end inventories/Net sales	8.7%
Year-end accounts payable/Net sales	8.0%

Kraft Foods Group, Inc. (KRFT)

M11-17. Adjusting the Income Statement (LO2)

Kraft Foods Group, Inc., reports the following footnote to its 2012 10-K.

> **Pizza Divestiture** On March 1, 2010, we completed the sale of the assets of our North American frozen pizza business ("Frozen Pizza") to Nestlé USA, Inc. ("Nestlé") for $3.7 billion. Our Frozen Pizza business was a component of our Refrigerated Meals and International & Foodservice segments. The sale included the DiGiorno, Tombstone, and Jack's brands in the U.S., the Delissio brand in Canada and the California Pizza Kitchen trademark license. It also included two Wisconsin manufacturing facilities (Medford and Little Chute) and the leases for the pizza depots and delivery trucks. Approximately 3,600 of our employees transferred with the business to Nestlé. Accordingly, the results of our Frozen Pizza business have been reflected as discontinued operations on the consolidated statement of earnings for 2010. . . .

What adjustment(s) did Kraft have to consider before forecasting its 2011 income? How would you treat the cash proceeds realized on such a sale?

EXERCISES

E11-18. Analyzing, Forecasting, and Interpreting Income Statement and Balance Sheet (LO2, 3)
Following are the income statements and balance sheets of **Abercrombie & Fitch Co.**

Abercrombie & Fitch Co. (ANF)

Income Statement, For Fiscal Years Ended ($ thousands)	February 2, 2013	January 28, 2012	January 29, 2011
Net sales	$4,510,805	$4,158,058	$3,468,777
Cost of goods sold	1,694,096	1,607,834	1,251,348
Gross profit	2,816,709	2,550,224	2,217,429
Stores and distribution expense	1,987,926	1,888,248	1,589,501
Marketing, general and administrative expense	473,883	437,120	400,804
Other operating expense (income), net	(19,333)	3,472	(10,056)
Operating income	374,233	221,384	237,180
Interest expense, net	7,288	3,577	3,362
Income from continuing operations before taxes	366,945	217,807	233,818
Tax expense from continuing operations	129,934	74,669	78,109
Net income from continuing operations	237,011	143,138	155,709
Income from discontinued operations, net of tax	—	796	—
Net income	$ 237,011	$ 143,934	$ 155,709

Consolidated Balance Sheets

(Thousands, except par value amounts)	February 2, 2013	January 28, 2012
Current Assets		
Cash and equivalents	$ 643,505	$ 583,495
Marketable securities	—	84,650
Receivables	99,622	89,350
Inventories	426,962	679,935
Deferred income taxes	32,558	35,882
Other current assets	105,177	84,342
Total current assets	1,307,824	1,557,654
Property and equipment, net	1,308,232	1,197,271
Noncurrent marketable securities	—	14,858
Other assets	371,345	347,249
Total assets	$2,987,401	$3,117,032
Liabilities and stockholders' equity		
Current liabilities		
Accounts payable	$ 140,396	$ 211,368
Accrued expenses	395,734	369,073
Deferred lease credits	39,054	41,047
Income taxes payable	115,617	77,918
Total current liabilities	690,801	699,406
Long-term liabilities		
Deferred lease credits	168,397	183,022
Leasehold financing obligations	63,942	57,851
Other liabilities	245,993	245,418
Total long-term liabilities	478,332	486,291
Stockholders' equity:		
Class A common stock—$0.01 par value: 150,000 shares authorized and 103,300 shares issued at each of February 2, 2013 and January 28, 2012	1,033	1,033
Paid-in capital	403,271	369,171
Retained earnings	2,567,261	2,389,614
Accumulated other comprehensive (loss) income, net of tax	(13,288)	6,291
Treasury stock, at average cost—24,855 and 17,662 shares at February 2, 2013, and January 28, 2012, respectively	(1,140,009)	(834,774)
Total stockholders' equity	1,818,268	1,931,335
Total liabilities and stockholders' equity	$2,987,401	$3,117,032

a. Forecast Abercrombie & Fitch's fiscal 2014 income statement and balance sheet using the following relations ($ in thousands). Assume all capital expenditures are purchases of property and equipment.

Net sales growth	10%
Cost of goods sold/Net sales	37.6%
Stores and distribution expense/Net sales	44.1%
Marketing, general and administrative expense/Net sales	10.5%
Other operating income, net	$19,333
Interest expense, net	$7,288
Tax expense from continuing operations (% of pretax income)	35.4%
Net loss from discontinued operations (net of taxes)	$0
Cash and equivalents/Net sales	14.3%
Receivables/Net sales	2.2%
Inventories/Net sales	9.5%
Deferred income taxes/Net sales	0.7%
Other current assets/Net sales	2.3%
Other assets/Net sales	8.2%
Accounts payable/Net sales	3.1%
Accrued expenses/Net sales	8.8%
Deferred lease credits/Net sales	0.9%
Income taxes payable (% tax expense)	89.0%
Deferred lease credits/Net sales	3.7%
Capital expenditures (% of Sales)	7.5%
Depreciation & amortization	$224,245
Dividends (% net income)	24.3%
Current maturities of long-term debt	$0

b. What does the forecasted adjustment to balance the accounting equation from part *a* reveal to us about the forecasted financing needs of the company? Explain.

Abercrombie & Fitch Co. (ANF)

E11-19. Forecasting the Statement of Cash Flows (LO4)
Refer to the Abercrombie & Fitch Co. financial information in Exercise 11-18. Prepare a forecast of fiscal 2014 statement of cash flows.

Macy's, Inc. (M)

E11-20. Analyzing, Forecasting, and Interpreting Both Income Statement and Balance Sheet (LO2, 3)
Following are the income statements and balance sheets of Macy's, Inc.

Consolidated Statements of Income, Fiscal Years Ended ($ millions)	February 2, 2013	January 28, 2012	January 29, 2011
Net sales	$27,686	$26,405	$25,003
Cost of sales	(16,538)	(15,738)	(14,824)
Gross margin	11,148	10,667	10,179
Selling, general and administrative expenses	(8,482)	(8,281)	(8,260)
Impairments, store closing costs and gain on sale of leases	(5)	25	(25)
Operating income	2,661	2,411	1,894
Interest expense	(425)	(447)	(513)
Premium on early retirement of debt	(137)	—	(66)
Interest income	3	4	5
Income before income taxes	2,102	1,968	1,320
Federal, state and local income tax expense	(767)	(712)	(473)
Net income	$ 1,335	$ 1,256	$ 847

Consolidated Balance Sheets ($ millions)	February 2, 2013	January 28, 2012
Assets		
Current assets		
Cash and cash equivalents	$ 1,836	$ 2,827
Receivables	371	368
Merchandise inventories	5,308	5,117
Prepaid expenses and other current assets	361	465
Total current assets	7,876	8,777
Property and equipment—net accumulative depreciation 5,947 and 5,986	8,196	8,420
Goodwill	3,743	3,743
Other intangible assets—net	561	598
Other assets	615	557
Total assets	$20,991	$22,095
Liabilities and Shareholders' Equity		
Current liabilities		
Short-term debt	$ 124	$ 1,103
Merchandise accounts payable	1,579	1,593
Accounts payable and accrued liabilities	2,610	2,788
Income taxes	355	371
Deferred income taxes	407	408
Total current liabilities	5,075	6,263
Long-term debt	6,806	6,655
Deferred income taxes	1,238	1,141
Other liabilities	1,821	2,103
Shareholders' equity		
Common stock (387.7 and 414.2 shares outstanding)	4	5
Additional paid-in capital	3,872	5,408
Accumulated equity	5,108	4,015
Treasury stock	(2,002)	(2,434)
Accumulated other comprehensive loss	(931)	(1,061)
Total shareholders' equity	6,051	5,933
Total liabilities and shareholders' equity	$20,991	$22,095

a. Forecast Macy's fiscal 2014 income statement and balance sheet using the following relations ($ in millions). Assume that all capital expenditures are purchases of property and equipment.

Net sales growth	5%
Cost of sales/Net sales	59.7%
Selling, general and administrative expenses/Net sales	30.6%
Impairments, store closing costs and gain on sale of leases	$0
Interest expense	no change
Premium on early retirement of debt	$0
Interest income	no change
Income tax expense/Income before income taxes	36.5%
Cash and cash equivalents/Net sales	6.6%
Receivables/Net sales	1.3%
Merchandise inventories/Net sales	19.2%
Prepaid expenses and other current assets/Net sales	1.3%
CAPEX (Increase in gross Property and equipment)/Net sales	0.9%
Goodwill	no change
Other intangible assets	no change
Other assets/Net sales	2.2%
Merchandise accounts payable/Net sales	5.7%
Accounts payable and accrued liabilities/Net sales	9.4%
Income taxes/Net sales	1.3%
Current deferred income taxes/Net sales	1.5%
Noncurrent deferred income taxes/Net sales	4.5%
Other liabilities	6.6%
Depreciation expense/Prior year gross PPE	7.3%
Common stock and APIC	no change
Treasury stock	no change
Dividends/Net income	24.3%
Long-term debt payments required in fiscal 2014	$461
Long-term debt payments required in fiscal 2015	$481

b. What does the forecasted adjustment to balance the accounting equation from part *a* reveal to us about the forecasted financing needs of the company? Explain.

Macy's, Inc. (M)

E11-21. Forecasting the Statement of Cash Flows (LO4)
Refer to the Macy's, Inc. financial information from Exercise 11-20. Prepare a forecast of its fiscal year 2013 statement of cash flows.

General Mills, Inc. (GIS)

E11-22. Analyzing, Forecasting, and Interpreting Income Statement and Balance Sheet (LO2, 3)
Following are the income statements and balance sheets of General Mills, Inc.

Income Statement, Fiscal Years Ended (in millions)	May 26, 2013	May 27, 2012	May 29, 2011
Net sales	$17,774.1	$16,657.9	$14,880.2
Cost of sales	11,350.2	10,613.2	8,926.7
Selling, general and administrative expenses	3,552.3	3,380.7	3,192.0
Divestitures (gain)	—	—	(17.4)
Restructuring, impairment, and other exit costs	19.8	101.6	4.4
Operating profit	2,851.8	2,562.4	2,774.5
Interest, net	316.9	351.9	346.3
Earnings before income taxes and after-tax earnings from joint ventures	2,534.9	2,210.5	2,428.2
Income taxes	741.2	709.6	721.1
After-tax earnings from joint ventures	98.8	88.2	96.4
Net earnings, including earnings attributable to redeemable and noncontrolling interests	1,892.5	1,589.1	1,803.5
Net earnings attributable to redeemable and noncontrolling interests	37.3	21.8	5.2
Net earnings attributable to General Mills	$ 1,855.2	$ 1,567.3	$ 1,798.3

Balance Sheet (in millions expect per share data)	May 26, 2013	May 27, 2012
Assets		
Current assets		
Cash and cash equivalents	$ 741.4	$ 471.2
Receivables	1,446.4	1,323.6
Inventories	1,545.5	1,478.8
Deferred income taxes	128.0	59.7
Prepaid expenses and other current assets	437.6	358.1
Total current assets	4,298.9	3,691.4
Land, buildings, and equipment	3,878.1	3,652.7
Goodwill	8,622.2	8,182.5
Other intangible assets	5,015.1	4,704.9
Other assets	843.7	865.3
Total assets	$22,658.0	$21,096.8
Liabilities and equity		
Current liabilities		
Accounts payable	$ 1,423.2	$ 1,148.9
Current portion of long-term debt	1,443.3	741.2
Notes payable	599.7	526.5
Other current liabilities	1,827.7	1,426.6
Total current liabilities	5,293.9	3,843.2
Long-term debt	5,926.1	6,161.9
Deferred income taxes	1,389.1	1,171.4
Other liabilities	1,952.9	2,189.8
Total liabilities	14,562.0	13,366.3
Redeemable interest	967.5	847.8
Stockholders' equity		
Common stock, 754.6 shares issued, $0.10 par value	75.5	75.5
Additional paid-in capital	1,166.6	1,308.4
Retained earnings	10,702.6	9,958.5
Common stock in treasury, at cost, shares of 113.8 and 106.1	(3,687.2)	(3,177.0)
Accumulated other comprehensive loss	(1,585.3)	(1,743.7)
Total stockholders' equity	6,672.2	6,421.7
Noncontrolling interests	456.3	461.0
Total equity	7,128.5	6,882.7
Total liabilities and equity	$22,658.0	$21,096.8

a. Forecast General Mills' fiscal 2014 income statement and balance sheet using the following relations. Assume all capital expenditures are purchases of land, buildings and equipment, net, and that depreciation and amortization expense is included as part of selling, general and administrative expense ($ millions).

Net sales growth	5%
Cost of sales/Net sales	63.9%
Selling, general and administrative expenses/Net sales	20.0%
Divestiture (gain), net	$0.0
Restructuring, impairment, and other exit costs	$0.0
Interest, net	$316.9
Income taxes/Pretax income	29.2%
After-tax earnings from joint ventures	$98.8
Net earnings attributable to noncontrolling interests/Net earnings before attribution	2.0%
Cash/Net sales	4.2%
Receivables/Net sales	8.1%
Inventories/Net sales	8.7%
Deferred income taxes/Net sales	0.7%
Prepaid expenses and other current assets/Net sales	2.5%
Other intangible assets	$0 amortization
Other assets/Net sales	4.7%
Accounts payable/Net sales	8.0%
Other current liabilities/Net sales	10.3%
Current portion of long-term debt	$1,181.9
Deferred income taxes/Net sales	7.8%
Other liabilities/Net sales	11.0%
Capital expenditures/Net sales	3.5%
Depreciation/Prior year net PPE	16.1%
Dividends/Net earnings attributable to General Mills	46.8%

b. What does the forecasted adjustment to balance the accounting equation from part *a* reveal to us about the forecasted financing needs of the company? Explain.

E11-23. Forecasting the Statement of Cash Flows (LO4)

General Mills, Inc. (GIS)

Refer to the **General Mills, Inc.**, financial information from Exercise 11-22. Forecast General Mills' fiscal 2014 statement of cash flows. (Use net earnings, including earnings attributable to redeemable and noncontrolling interests to begin the statement of cash flows.)

E11-24. Adjusting the Balance Sheet for Operating Leases (LO1, 2, 3)

Delta Air Lines, Inc. (DAL)

Delta Air Lines, Inc. reports total net operating assets of $6,829 million, net nonoperating liabilities of $8,960 million, and equity of $(2,131) in its 2012 10-K. Footnotes reveal the existence of operating leases that have a present value of $6,475 million.

a. What balance sheet adjustment(s) might we consider relating to the leases before we forecast financial statements? (*Hint:* Consider the distinction between operating and nonoperating assets and liabilities.)

b. What income statement adjustment(s) might we consider? (*Hint:* Reflect on the operating and nonoperating distinction for lease-related expenses.)

E11-25. Adjusting the Balance Sheet for Equity Method Investments (LO3)

Abbott Laboratories (ABT)

TAP Pharmaceutical Products Inc.

Abbott Laboratories reports its 50% joint venture investment in **TAP Pharmaceutical Products Inc.** using the equity method of accounting in its 2007 10-K. The Abbott balance sheet reports an investment balance of $159 million. TAP has total assets of $1,354.2 million, liabilities of $1,036.7 million, and equity of $317.5 million. Abbott's investment balance is, thus, equal to its 50% interest in TAP's equity ($317.5 million × 50% = $158.75 million, rounded to $159 million). What adjustment(s) might we consider to Abbott's balance sheet before we forecast its financial statements? (*Hint:* Consider the distinction between operating and nonoperating assets and liabilities.) What risks might Abbott Laboratories face that are not revealed on the face of its balance sheet?

E11-26. Analyzing, Forecasting, and Interpreting Income Statement and Balance Sheet (LO2, 3)
Following are the income statement and balance sheet of **Whole Foods Market, Inc.**

Whole Foods Market, Inc. (WFM)

Income Statement, For Years Ended (in millions)	2013	2012	2011
Sales	$12,917	$11,699	$10,108
Cost of goods sold and occupancy costs	8,288	7,543	6,571
Gross profit	4,629	4,156	3,537
Direct store expenses	3,285	2,983	2,629
General and administrative expenses	397	372	311
Pre-opening expenses	52	47	41
Relocation, store closures and lease termination costs	12	10	8
Operating income	883	744	548
Interest expense	—	—	(4)
Investment and other income	11	8	8
Income before income taxes	894	752	552
Provision for income taxes	343	286	209
Net income	$ 551	$ 466	$ 343

Balance Sheet (in millions)	2013	2012
Assets		
Current assets		
Cash and cash equivalents	$ 290	$ 89
Short-term investments—available-for-sale securities	733	1,131
Restricted cash	111	103
Accounts receivable	188	197
Merchandise inventories	414	374
Prepaid expenses and other current assets	93	77
Deferred income taxes	151	132
Total current assets	1,980	2,103
Property and equipment, net of accumulated depreciation and amortization	2,428	2,193
Long-term investments—available-for-sale securities	302	221
Goodwill	679	663
Intangible assets, net of accumulated amortization	65	62
Deferred income taxes	72	43
Other assets	12	9
Total assets	$5,538	$5,294
Liabilities and Shareholders' Equity		
Current liabilities		
Current installments of capital lease obligations	$ 1	$ 1
Accounts payable	247	247
Accrued payroll, bonus and other benefits due team members	367	307
Dividends payable	37	26
Other current liabilities	436	396
Total current liabilities	1,088	977
Long-term capital lease obligations, less current installments	26	23
Deferred lease liabilities	500	441
Other long-term liabilities	46	51
Total liabilities	1,660	1,492
Shareholders' equity		
Common stock, no par value, 600.0 authorized; 375.7 and 371.6 shares issued; 372.4 and 370.9 share outstanding at 2013 and 2012, respectively	2,765	2,592
Common stock in treasury, at cost 3.3 and 0.7 shares at 2013 and 2012, respectively	(153)	(28)
Accumulated other comprehensive income	1	5
Retained earnings	1,265	1,233
Total shareholders' equity	3,878	3,802
Total liabilities and shareholders' equity	$5,538	$5,294

a. Forecast Whole Foods Market's 2014 income statement and balance sheet using the following relations ($ in millions).

Sales growth	10.0%
Cost of goods sold and occupancy costs/Sales	64.2%
Direct store expenses/Sales	25.4%
General and administrative expenses/Sales	3.1%
Pre-opening expenses/Sales	0.4%
Relocation, store closure and lease termination costs	$ 0
Interest expense	$ 0
Investment and other income	$ 11
Provision for income taxes/Income before income taxes	38.4%
Short-term investments—available-for-sale securities	$ 733
Cash and cash equivalents/Sales	2.2%
Restricted cash	$ 111
Accounts receivable/Sales	1.5%
Merchandise inventories/Sales	3.2%
Prepaid expenses and other current assets/Sales	0.7%
Current deferred income taxes	$ 151
Long-term investments—available-for-sale securities	$ 302
Goodwill	$ 679
Intangible assets, net of accumulated depreciation	$65
Noncurrent deferred income taxes	$72
Other assets/Sales	0.1%
Current installments of long-term debt and capital lease obligations	$ 3
Accounts payable/Sales	1.9%
Accrued payroll, bonus and other benefits due team members/Sales	2.8%
Dividends payable	$ 37
Other current liabilities/Sales	3.4%
Deferred lease liabilities	$ 500
Other long-term liabilities/Sales	0.4%
Common stock	$2,765
Treasury stock	$ (153)
Accumulated other comprehensive income (loss)	$ 1
Capital expenditures/Prior year net PPE	24.5%
Depreciation and amortization/Prior year net PPE	15.5%
Dividends/Net income	92.2%

b. What does the forecasted adjustment to balance the accounting equation from part *a* reveal to us about the forecasted financing needs of the company?

E11-27. Forecasting the Statement of Cash Flows (LO4)

Whole Foods Market, Inc. (WFM)

Refer to the **Whole Foods Market, Inc.**, financial information from Exercise 11-26. Prepare a forecast of its fiscal year 2014 statement of cash flows.

E11-28. Projecting NOPAT and NOA Using Parsimonious Forecasting Method (LO6)

Intel Corporation (INTC)

Following are **Intel Corporation**'s sales, net operating profit after tax (NOPAT), and net operating assets (NOA) for its year ended December 31, 2012 ($ millions).

Sales	$53,341
Net operating profit after tax (NOPAT)	10,857
Net operating assets (NOA)	42,065

Forecast Intel's sales, NOPAT and NOA for years 2013 through 2016 using the following assumptions:

Sales growth per year	10%
Net operating profit margin (NOPM)	20%
Net operating asset turnover (NOAT), based on NOA at December 31, 2012	1.3

E11-29. Projecting NOPAT and NOA Using Parsimonious Forecasting Method (LO6)
Following are **3M Company**'s sales, net operating profit after tax (NOPAT), and net operating assets (NOA) for its fiscal year ended 2012 ($ millions).

3M Company (MMM)

Sales	$29,904
Net operating profit after tax (NOPAT)	$ 4,594
Net operating assets (NOA)	$18,185

Forecast 3M's sales, NOPAT and NOA for fiscal years 2013 through 2016 using the following assumptions:

Sales growth per year	15%
Net operating profit margin (NOPM)	15%
Net operating asset turnover (NOAT), based on NOA at fiscal year-end	1.6

PROBLEMS

P11-30. Forecasting the Income Statement, Balance Sheet, and Statement of Cash Flows (LO2, 3, 4)
Following are fiscal year financial statements of **Cisco Systems, Inc.**

Cisco Systems, Inc. (CSCO)

Consolidated Statements of Operations Fiscal Years ended (in millions)	July 27, 2013	July 28, 2012
Revenue		
Product	$38,029	$36,326
Service	10,578	9,735
Total revenue	48,607	46,061
Cost of sales		
Product	15,541	14,505
Service	3,626	3,347
Total cost of sales	19,167	17,852
Gross margin	29,440	28,209
Operating expenses		
Research and development	5,942	5,488
Sales and marketing	9,538	9,647
General and administrative	2,264	2,322
Amortization of purchased intangible assets	395	383
Restructuring and other charges	105	304
Total operating expenses	18,244	18,144
Operating income	11,196	10,065
Interest income	654	650
Interest expense	(583)	(596)
Other income (loss), net	(40)	40
Interest and other income, net	31	94
Income before provision for income taxes	11,227	10,159
Provision for income taxes	1,244	2,118
Net income	$9,983	$8,041

Consolidated Balance Sheets May 31 (in millions, except par value)	July 27, 2013	July 28, 2012
Assets		
Current assets		
Cash and cash equivalents	$ 7,925	$ 9,799
Investments	42,685	38,917
Accounts receivable, net	5,470	4,369
Inventories	1,476	1,663
Financing receivables, net	4,037	3,661
Deferred tax assets	2,616	2,294
Other current assets	1,312	1,230
Total current assets	65,521	61,933
Property and equipment, net	3,322	3,402
Financing receivables, net	3,911	3,585
Goodwill	21,919	16,998
Purchased intangible assets, net	3,403	1,959
Other assets	3,115	3,882
Total assets	$101,191	$91,759
Liabilities and equity		
Current liabilities		
Short-term debt	$ 3,283	$ 31
Accounts payable	1,029	859
Income taxes payable	192	276
Accrued compensation	3,378	2,928
Deferred revenue	9,262	8,852
Other current liabilities	5,048	4,785
Total current liabilities	22,192	17,731
Long-term debt	12,928	16,297
Income taxes payable	1,748	1,844
Deferred revenue	4,161	4,028
Other long-term liabilities	1,034	558
Total liabilities	42,063	40,458
Equity		
Cisco shareholders' equity		
Preferred stock	—	—
Common stock and additional paid-in capital	42,297	39,271
Retained earnings	16,215	11,354
Accumulated other comprehensive income	608	661
Total Cisco shareholders' equity	59,120	51,286
Noncontrolling interests	8	15
Total equity	59,128	51,301
Total liabilities and equity	$101,191	$91,759

Required

Forecast Cisco's fiscal 2014 income statement, balance sheet, and statement of cash flows; round forecasts to $ millions. *Hint*: We forecast total revenues by projecting a continuation of year-over-year percentage growth rates for each revenue category that Cisco includes in its income statement (rounded to the nearest whole percent). (*Note*: Cisco's long-term debt footnote reports that current maturities of long-term debt are $3,260 million for fiscal year 2014 and $507 million for fiscal year 2015; Cisco includes the current maturities with "Short-term debt" on its balance sheet. Cisco reports capital expenditures of $1,160 million, dividends of $3,310 million, depreciation of $1,178 million, which it includes in G&A expense, and amortization of $395 million, which it reports separately. Identify all financial statement relations estimated and assumptions made; estimate forecasted income statement relations to 3 decimal places, for example, General and administrative/Total revenue is 4.7%. Assume no change for interest income and expense, goodwill, other long-term assets, amortization of purchased intangible assets, nonoperating income, common stock, accumulated other comprehensive income, and noncontrolling interests. What do the forecasts imply about the financing needs of Cisco?

P11-31. Forecasting the Income Statement, Balance Sheet, and Statement of Cash Flows (LO2, 3, 4)
Following are the financial statements of **Nike, Inc.**

Nike, Inc. (NKE)

Consolidated Statements of Income			
Year ended May 31 (in millions)	**2013**	**2012**	**2011**
Income from continuing operations:			
Revenues	$25,313	$23,331	$20,117
Cost of sales	14,279	13,183	10,915
Gross profit	11,034	10,148	9,202
Demand creation expense	2,745	2,607	2,344
Operating overhead expense	5,035	4,458	4,017
Total selling and administrative expense	7,780	7,065	6,361
Interest (income) expense, net	(3)	4	4
Other (income) expense, net	(15)	54	(25)
Income before income taxes	3,272	3,025	2,862
Income tax expense	808	756	690
Net income from continuing operations	2,464	2,269	2,172
Net income (loss) from discontinued operations	21	(46)	(39)
Net income	$ 2,485	$ 2,223	$ 2,133

Consolidated Balance Sheets		
May 31 (in millions)	**2013**	**2012**
Assets		
Cash and equivalents	$ 3,337	$ 2,317
Short-term investments	2,628	1,440
Accounts receivable, net	3,117	3,132
Inventories	3,434	3,222
Deferred income taxes	308	262
Prepaid expenses and other current assets	802	857
Assets of discontinued operations	—	615
Total current assets	13,626	11,845
Property, plant and equipment, net	2,452	2,209
Identifiable intangible assets, net	382	370
Goodwill	131	131
Deferred income taxes and other assets	993	910
Total assets	$17,584	$15,465
Liabilities and shareholders' equity		
Current liabilities:		
Current portion of long-term debt	$ 57	$ 49
Notes payable	121	108
Accounts payable	1,646	1,549
Accrued liabilities	1,986	1,941
Income taxes payable	98	65
Liabilities of discontinued operations	18	170
Total current liabilities	3,926	3,882
Long-term debt	1,210	228
Deferred income taxes and other liabilities	1,292	974
Commitments and contingencies	—	—
Redeemable preferred stock	—	—
Shareholders' equity		
Common stock at stated value		
Class A convertible — 178 and 180 shares outstanding	—	—
Class B — 716 and 736 shares outstanding	3	3
Capital in excess of stated value	5,184	4,641
Accumulated other comprehensive income	274	149
Retained earnings	5,695	5,588
Total shareholders' equity	11,156	10,381
Total liabilities and shareholders' equity	$17,584	$15,465

Required

Forecast Nike's fiscal year 2014 income statement, balance sheet, and statement of cash flows. Round the revenue growth rate to the nearest whole percent and round forecasts to $ millions. Identify all financial statement relations estimated and assumptions made; estimate forecasted income statement relations to 3 decimal places, for example, Inventories/Revenues is 13.6% (assume no change for: other expense or income, liabilities of discontinued operations, goodwill, notes payable, common stock, capital in excess of stated value, and accumulated other comprehensive income). Also assume no income/loss from discontinued operations for fiscal 2014. For fiscal 2013, capital expenditures are $636 million, depreciation expense is $438 million, amortization is $75 million, and dividends are $703 million. Footnotes reveal that the current portion of long-term debt due in 2015 is $46 million. What do the forecasts imply about Nike's financing needs for the upcoming year?

Home Depot, Inc. (HD)

P11-32. Forecasting the Income Statement, Balance Sheet and Statement of Cash Flows (LO2, 3, 4)
Following are the financial statements of **Home Depot, Inc.**

Consolidated Statements of Earnings

Amounts in millions	February 3, 2013	January 29, 2012	January 30, 2011
Net sales	$74,754	$70,395	$67,997
Cost of sales	48,912	46,133	44,693
Gross profit	25,842	24,262	23,304
Operating expenses			
Selling, general and administrative	16,508	16,028	15,849
Depreciation and amortization	1,568	1,573	1,616
Total operating expenses	18,076	17,601	17,465
Operating income	7,766	6,661	5,839
Interest and other (income) expense			
Interest and investment income	(20)	(13)	(15)
Interest expense	632	606	530
Other	(67)	—	51
Interest and other, net	545	593	566
Earnings before provision for income taxes	7,221	6,068	5,273
Provision for income taxes	2,686	2,185	1,935
Net earnings	$ 4,535	$ 3,883	$ 3,338

Consolidated Balance Sheets

Amounts in millions, except share and per share data	February 3, 2013	January 29, 2012
Assets		
Current assets:		
Cash and cash equivalents	$ 2,494	$ 1,987
Receivables, net	1,395	1,245
Merchandise inventories	10,710	10,325
Other current assets	773	963
Total current assets	15,372	14,520
Property and equipment, at cost	38,491	38,975
Less accumulated depreciation and amortization	14,422	14,527
Net property and equipment	24,069	24,448
Notes receivable	140	135
Goodwill	1,170	1,120
Other assets	333	295
Total assets	$41,084	$40,518

continued

Liabilities and stockholders' equity		
Current liabilities:		
Accounts payable	$ 5,376	$ 4,856
Accrued salaries and related expenses	1,414	1,372
Sales taxes payable	472	391
Deferred revenue	1,270	1,147
Income taxes payable	22	23
Current installments of long-term debt	1,321	30
Other accrued expenses	1,587	1,557
Total current liabilities	11,462	9,376
Long-term debt, excluding current installments	9,475	10,758
Other long-term liabilities	2,051	2,146
Deferred income taxes	319	340
Total liabilities	23,307	22,620
Stockholders' equity		
Common stock, par value $0.05; authorized: 10 billion shares; issued: 1.754 billion shares at February 3, 2013 and 1.733 billion shares at January 29, 2012; outstanding: 1.484 billion shares at February 3, 2013 and 1.537 billion shares at January 29, 2012	88	87
Paid-in-capital	7,948	6,966
Retained earnings	20,038	17,246
Accumulated other comprehensive income	397	293
Treasury stock, at cost, 270 million shares at February 3, 2013 and 196 million shares at January 29, 2012	(10,694)	(6,694)
Total stockholders' equity	17,777	17,898
Total liabilities and stockholders' equity	$41,084	$40,518

Required

Forecast Home Depot's fiscal year ended 2014 income statement, balance sheet, and statement of cash flows. Round the revenue growth rate to the nearest whole percent and forecasts to $ millions. Estimate forecasted income statement relations to 3 decimal places, for example, Accounts payable/Net sales is 7.2% (assume no change for: notes receivable, goodwill, interest income and expense, deferred income taxes, common stock and additional paid-in capital, treasury stock, and accumulated other comprehensive income). Capital expenditures were $1,312 million and dividends were $1,743 million for fiscal year ended 2013. Home Depot's long-term debt footnote indicates maturities of long-term debt of $32 million for 2014. What is our assessment of Home Depot's financial condition over the next year?

P11-33. Two-Year-Ahead Forecasting of Financial Statements **(LO5)**

Following are the financial statements of **Target Corp.**

Target Corp. (TGT)

Consolidated Statements of Operations

(millions, except per share data)	Feb. 2, 2013	Jan. 28, 2012	Jan. 29, 2011
Sales	$71,960	$68,466	$65,786
Credit card revenues	1,341	1,399	1,604
Total revenues	73,301	69,865	67,390
Cost of sales	50,568	47,860	45,725
Selling, general and administrative expenses	14,914	14,106	13,469
Credit card expenses	467	446	860
Depreciation and amortization	2,142	2,131	2,084
Gain on receivables held for sale	(161)	—	—
Earnings before interest expense and income taxes	5,371	5,322	5,252
Net interest expense	762	866	757
Earnings before income taxes	4,609	4,456	4,495
Provision for income taxes	1,610	1,527	1,575
Net earnings	$ 2,999	$ 2,929	$ 2,920
Basic earnings per share	$ 4.57	$ 4.31	$ 4.03
Diluted earnings per share	$ 4.52	$ 4.28	$ 4.00
Weighted average common shares outstanding			
Basic	656.7	679.1	723.6
Diluted	663.3	683.9	729.4

Consolidated Statements of Financial Position

(millions)	February 2, 2013	January 28, 2012
Assets		
Cash and cash equivalents, including short-term investments of $130 and $194	$ 784	$ 794
Credit card receivables, held for sale	5,841	—
Credit card receivables, net of allowance of $0 and $430	—	5,927
Inventory	7,903	7,918
Other current assets	1,860	1,810
Total current assets	16,388	16,449
Property and equipment		
Land	6,206	6,122
Buildings and improvements	28,653	26,837
Fixtures and equipment	5,362	5,141
Computer hardware and software	2,567	2,468
Construction-in-progress	1,176	963
Accumulated depreciation	(13,311)	(12,382)
Property and equipment, net	30,653	29,149
Other noncurrent assets	1,122	1,032
Total assets	$48,163	$46,630
Liabilities and shareholders' investment		
Accounts payable	$7,056	$6,857
Accrued and other current liabilities	3,981	3,644
Unsecured debt and other borrowings	1,494	3,036
Nonrecourse debt collateralized by credit card receivables	1,500	750
Total current liabilities	14,031	14,287
Unsecured debt and other borrowings	14,654	13,447
Nonrecourse debt collateralized by credit card receivables	—	250
Deferred income taxes	1,311	1,191
Other noncurrent liabilities	1,609	1,634
Total noncurrent liabilities	17,574	16,522

continued

Shareholders' investment		
Common stock	54	56
Additional paid-in-capital	3,925	3,487
Retained earnings	13,155	12,959
Accumulated other comprehensive loss		
Pension and other benefit liabilities	(532)	(624)
Currency translation adjustment and cash flow hedges	(44)	(57)
Total shareholders' investment	16,558	15,821
Total liabilities and shareholders' investment	$48,163	$46,630

Consolidated Statement of Cash Flows

(millions)	Feb. 2, 2013	Jan. 28, 2012	Jan. 29, 2011
Operating activities			
Net earnings	$2,999	$2,929	$2,920
Reconciliation to cash flow			
Depreciation and amortization	2,142	2,131	2,084
Share-based compensation expense	105	90	109
Deferred income taxes	(14)	371	445
Bad debt expense	206	154	528
Gain on receivables held for sale	(161)	—	—
Noncash (gains)/losses and other, net	14	22	(145)
Changes in operating accounts:			
Accounts receivable originated at Target	(217)	(187)	(78)
Inventory	15	(322)	(417)
Other current assets	(123)	(150)	(124)
Other noncurrent assets	(98)	43	(212)
Accounts payable	199	232	115
Accrued and other current liabilities	138	218	149
Other noncurrent liabilities	120	(97)	(103)
Cash flow provided by operations	5,325	5,434	5,271
Investing activities			
Expenditures for property and equipment	(3,277)	(4,368)	(2,129)
Proceeds from disposal of property and equipment	66	37	69
Change in accounts receivable originated at third parties	254	259	363
Other investments	102	(108)	(47)
Cash flow required for investing activities	(2,855)	(4,180)	(1,744)
Financing activities			
Change in commercial paper, net	970	—	—
Additions to short-term debt	—	1,500	—
Reductions of short-term debt	(1,500)	—	—
Additions to long-term debt	1,971	1,994	1,011
Reductions of long-term debt	(1,529)	(3,125)	(2,259)
Dividends paid	(869)	(750)	(609)
Repurchase of stock	(1,875)	(1,842)	(2,452)
Stock option exercises and related tax benefit	360	89	294
Other	(16)	(6)	—
Cash flow required for financing activities	(2,488)	(2,140)	(4,015)
Effect of exchange rate changes on cash and cash equivalents	8	(32)	—
Net decrease in cash and cash equivalents	(10)	(918)	(488)
Cash and cash equivalents at beginning of period	794	1,712	2,200
Cash and cash equivalents at end of period	$ 784	$ 794	$1,712
Supplemental information			
Interest paid, net of capitalized interest	$ 775	$ 816	$ 752
Income taxes paid	1,603	1,109	1,259
Noncash financing activities			
Property and equipment acquired through capital lease obligations	282	1,388	176

Required

Forecast Target's fiscal year ended 2014 and 2015 income statements, balance sheets, and statements of cash flows. Round revenue growth to the nearest whole percent and round forecasts to $ millions. Assume credit card revenue growth is the same as the sales revenue growth. Use the same forecasting assumptions for both years; estimate forecasted income statement relations to 3 decimal places, for example, Other current assets/Sales is 2.6% (assume no change for: interest expense, deferred tax liability, common stock, additional paid-in capital, and accumulated other comprehensive loss). Target's long-term debt footnote indicates maturities of $2,001 million in fiscal year ended 2014, $1,001 million in fiscal year ended 2015, and maturities of $27 million in fiscal year ended 2016. *Hint:* Nonrecourse debt is interest bearing debt. The outstanding debt of $1,500 million is included in the current maturities of $2,001 million for fiscal year ended 2014 (assume no additional debt will be acquired). The remaining $501 is unsecured debt and other borrowings. Assume a 1.5% rate for return on investments and a 4.3% rate for interest bearing debt. Also assume no gain on receivables in future years. What investment or financing assumptions are required for forecasting purposes? What is our assessment of Target's financial condition over the next two years?

IFRS

IFRS APPLICATIONS

Bombardier

I11-34. Projecting NOPAT and NOA Using Parsimonious Forecasting Method (LO6)

Following are **Bombardier**'s sales, net operating profit after tax (NOPAT) and net operating assets (NOA) for its fiscal year ended December 31, 2012 (in millions Canadian $):

Sales	$16,768
Net operating profit after tax (NOPAT)	$596
Net operating assets (NOA)	$3,138

Forecast Bombardier's sales, NOPAT, and NOA for fiscal years 2013 through 2016 assuming a sales growth rate of 2.5%.

Telstra Corporation Limited

I11-35. Forecasting the Income Statement, Balance Sheet, and Statement of Cash Flows (LO2, 3, 4)

Telstra Corporation Limited is an Australian telecommunications and media company that builds and provides land-based and mobile telecom services along with internet and pay television products. The company is Australia's largest 3G and 4G enabled mobile network covering 99.3 percent of the Australian population. Following are the financial statements for the 2012 year end, reported in Australian dollars.

TELSTRA CORPORATION LIMITED
Income Statement

($ millions)	2012	2011
Income		
Revenue (excluding finance income)	**$25,368**	$25,093
Other income	**135**	211
	25,503	25,304
Expenses		
Labour	**4,061**	3,924
Goods and services purchased	**6,179**	6,183
Other expenses	**5,029**	5,047
	15,269	15,154
Share of net (profit) from jointly controlled and associated entities	**—**	(1)
	15,269	15,153
Earnings before interest, income tax expense, depreciation and amortisation (EBITDA)	**10,234**	10,151
Depreciation and amortisation	**4,412**	4,459
Earnings before interest and income tax expense (EBIT)	**5,822**	5,692
Finance income	**134**	127
Finance costs	**1,022**	1,262
Net finance costs	**888**	1,135
Profit before income tax expense	**4,934**	4,557
Income tax expense	**1,510**	1,307
Profit for the year	**$ 3,424**	$ 3,250

TELSTRA CORPORATION LIMITED
Statement of Financial Position

($ millions)	2012	2011
Current assets		
Cash and cash equivalents	**$ 3,945**	$ 2,630
Trade and other receivables	**4,346**	4,137
Inventories	**260**	283
Derivative financial assets	**32**	83
Current tax receivables	**363**	4
Prepayments	**250**	275
Assets classified as held for sale	**754**	41
Total current assets	**9,950**	7,453
Non current assets		
Trade and other receivables	**851**	340
Inventories	**24**	22
Investments—accounted for using the equity method	**12**	2
Investments—other	**19**	1
Property, plant and equipment	**20,504**	21,790
Intangible assets	**7,421**	7,627
Derivative financial assets	**658**	285
Noncurrent tax receivables	**80**	382
Deferred tax assets	**6**	—
Defined benefit assets	**—**	11
Total noncurrent assets	**29,575**	30,460
Total assets	**39,525**	37,913
Current liabilities		
Trade and other payables	**4,131**	4,093
Provisions	**942**	846
Borrowings	**3,306**	1,990
Derivative financial liabilities	**299**	634
Current tax payables	**731**	404
Revenue received in advance	**1,170**	1,018
Liabilities classified as held for sale	**105**	5
Total current liabilities	**10,684**	8,990
Noncurrent liabilities		
Other payables	**174**	177
Provisions	**264**	244
Borrowings	**11,958**	12,178
Derivative financial liabilities	**2,349**	1,799
Deferred tax liabilities	**1,107**	1,730
Defined benefit liability	**831**	205
Revenue received in advance	**469**	298
Total noncurrent liabilities	**17,152**	16,631
Total liabilities	**27,836**	25,621
Net assets	**$11,689**	$12,292
Equity		
Share capital	**$ 5,635**	$5,610
Reserves	**(867)**	(843)
Retained profits	**6,712**	7,307
Equity available to Telstra Entity shareholders	**11,480**	12,074
Noncontrolling interests	**209**	218
Total equity	**$11,689**	$12,292

Required

Forecast Telstra's fiscal year 2013 income statement, balance sheet, and statement of cash flows. Round forecasts to the nearest whole dollar. Identify all financial statement relations estimated and assumptions made. Estimate forecasted income statement and balance sheet relations to one decimal place. Assume that revenue will increase by 3% in 2013. Calculate depreciation and amortisation expense as a percent of revenue. Assume no change for: other income, finance income and finance costs on the income statement. Assume no change for derivative financial assets, investments, current borrowings, derivative financial liabilities, share capital, reserves, and noncontrolling interests on the balance sheet. Assume that assets and liabilities classified as held for sale are eliminated in 2013. For fiscal 2013, capital expenditures are $4,001 million, and dividends are $3,475 million. Use the noncurrent borrowings as your plug account to balance the balance sheet. What do the forecasts imply about Telstra's financing needs for the upcoming year?

MANAGEMENT APPLICATIONS

MA11-36. Adjusting the Income Statement Prior to Forecasting (LO1, 2)

CBS Corporation (CBS)

Following is the income statement of CBS Corporation, along with an excerpt from its MD&A section.

Income Statement Year ended December 31 ($ millions)	2005	2004	2003
Revenues	$14,536.4	$14,547.3	$13,554.5
Expenses			
Operating	8,671.8	8,643.6	8,165.4
Selling, general and administrative	2,699.4	2,552.5	2,376.1
Impairment charges	9,484.4	17,997.1	—
Depreciation and amortization	498.7	508.6	501.7
Total expenses	21,354.3	29,701.8	11,043.2
Operating income (loss)	$ (6,817.9)	$(15,154.5)	$ 2,511.3

Operating Expenses: Table below presents consolidated operating expenses by type

Operating expenses by type Year ended December 31	2005	2004	Increase (Decrease) 2005 vs. 2004		2003	Increase (Decrease) 2004 vs. 2003	
Programming	$3,453.2	$3,441.8	$ 11.4	—%	$3,080.3	$361.5	12%
Production	2,453.5	2,584.7	(131.2)	(5)	2,661.9	(77.2)	(3)
Outdoor operations	1,134.2	1,102.7	31.5	3	1,012.6	90.1	9
Publishing operations	525.0	517.6	7.4	1	486.3	31.3	6
Parks operations	243.8	232.7	11.1	5	212.2	20.5	10
Other	862.1	764.1	98.0	13	712.1	52.0	7
Total operating expenses	$8,671.8	$8,643.6	$ 28.2	—%	$8,165.4	$478.2	6%

For 2005, operating expenses of $8.67 billion increased slightly over $8.64 billion in 2004. For 2004, operating expenses of $8.64 billion increased 6% over $8.17 billion in 2003. The major components and changes in operating expenses were as follows:

- Programming expenses represented approximately 40% of total operating expenses in 2005 and 2004 and 38% in 2003, and reflect the amortization of acquired rights of programs exhibited on the broadcast and cable networks, and television and radio stations. Programming expenses increased slightly to $3.45 billion in 2005 from $3.44 billion in 2004 principally reflecting higher costs for Showtime Networks theatrical titles. Programming expenses increased 12% to $3.44 billion in 2004 from $3.08 billion in 2003 reflecting higher program rights expenses for sports events and primetime series at the broadcast networks.
- Production expenses represented approximately 28% of total operating expenses in 2005, 30% in 2004, and 33% in 2003, and reflect the cost and amortization of internally developed television programs, including direct production costs, residuals and participation expenses, and production overhead, as well as television and radio costs

continued

including on-air talent and other production costs. Production expenses decreased 5% to $2.45 billion in 2005 from $2.58 billion in 2004 principally reflecting lower network costs due to the absence of *Frasier* partially offset by increased costs for new network series. Production expenses decreased 3% to $2.58 billion in 2004 from $2.66 billion in 2003 reflecting fewer network series produced in 2004 partially offset by higher news costs for political campaign coverage.

- Outdoor operations costs represented approximately 13% of total operating expenses in 2005 and 2004, and 12% in 2003, and reflect transit and billboard lease, maintenance, posting and rotation expenses. Outdoor operations expenses increased 3% to $1.13 billion in 2005 from $1.10 billion in 2004 principally reflecting higher billboard lease costs and maintenance costs associated with the impact of hurricanes in 2005. Outdoor operations costs increased 9% to $1.10 billion in 2004 from $1.01 billion in 2003 primarily reflecting higher transit and billboard lease costs.
- Publishing operations costs, which represented approximately 6% of total operating expenses in each of the years 2005, 2004 and 2003, reflect cost of book sales, royalties and other costs incurred with respect to publishing operations. Publishing operations expenses for 2005 increased 1% to $525.0 million and increased 6% to $517.6 million in 2004 from $486.3 million in 2003 primarily due to higher revenues.
- Parks operations costs, which represented approximately 3% of total operating expenses in each of the years 2005, 2004 and 2003, increased 5% to $243.8 million in 2005 from $232.7 million in 2004 principally reflecting the cost of fourth quarter 2005 winter events held at the parks and the impact of foreign currency translation. In 2004, Parks operations costs increased 10% to $232.7 million from $212.2 million in 2003 primarily from the impact of foreign currency translation.
- Other operating expenses, which represented approximately 10% of total operating expenses in 2005 and 9% in 2004 and 2003, primarily include distribution costs incurred with respect to television product, costs associated with digital media and compensation. Other operating expenses increased 13% to $862.1 million in 2005 from $764.1 million in 2004 primarily reflecting a 10% increase in distribution costs due to the DVD release of *Charmed* and increased costs associated with digital media from the inclusion of SportsLine.com, Inc. ("SportsLine.com") since its acquisition in December 2004. Other operating expenses for 2004 increased 7% to $764.1 million in 2004 from $712.1 million in 2003 principally reflecting 15% higher distribution costs due to additional volume of DVD releases of the *Star Trek* series and higher compensation.

Impairment Charges SFAS 142 requires the Company to perform an annual fair value-based impairment test of goodwill. The Company performed its annual impairment test as of October 31, 2005, concurrently with its annual budgeting process which begins in the fourth quarter each year. The first step of the test examines whether or not the book value of each of the Company's reporting units exceeds its fair value. If the book value for a reporting unit exceeds its fair value, the second step of the test is required to compare the implied fair value of that reporting unit's goodwill with the book value of the goodwill. The Company's reporting units are generally consistent with or one level below the operating segments underlying the reportable segments. As a result of the 2005 annual impairment test, the Company recorded an impairment charge of $9.48 billion in the fourth quarter of 2005. The $9.48 billion reflects charges to reduce the carrying value of goodwill at the CBS Television reporting unit of $6.44 billion and the Radio reporting unit of $3.05 billion. As a result of the annual impairment test performed for 2004, the Company recorded an impairment charge of $18.0 billion in the fourth quarter of 2004. The $18.0 billion reflects charges to reduce the carrying value of goodwill at the Radio reporting unit of $10.94 billion and the Outdoor reporting unit of $7.06 billion as well as the reduction of the carrying value of intangible assets of $27.8 million related to the FCC licenses at the Radio segment. Several factors led to a reduction in forecasted cash flows and long-term growth rates for both the Radio and Outdoor reporting units. Radio and Outdoor both fell short of budgeted revenue and operating income growth targets in 2004. Competition from other advertising media, including Internet advertising and cable and broadcast television reduced Radio and Outdoor growth rates. Also, the emergence of new competitors and technologies necessitated a shift in management's strategy for the Radio and Outdoor businesses, including changes in composition of the sales force and operating management as well as increased levels of investment in marketing and promotion.

Required

Identify and explain any income statement line items over the past three years that you believe should be considered for potential adjustment in preparation for forecasting the income statement of CBS.

ONGOING PROJECT

(This ongoing project began in Module 1 and continues through most of the book; even if previous segments were not completed, the requirements are still applicable to any business analysis.) This Module describes methods commonly used to forecast financial statements. The module shows how to forecast a complete set of financial statements (for one or more years). The module concludes with a parsimonious forecast of select balance sheet and income statement metrics. A project can include both types of forecasts. We can use the full set of financial statements to analyze the company's near-term future performance and position. We can then use the parsimonious forecast for longer-term forecasts as inputs for valuation models that estimate the company's stock price. Importantly, use a spreadsheet for the forecasting process. The SEC Website has "interactive data" for annual reports—these are spreadsheet-like arrays that can be copied into a spreadsheet. Also, many companies include on their investor relations page, an Excel version of their financial statements. Define as many cells as possible with formulas, and reference income statement totals to the related balance sheet accounts. To balance one's balance sheet, define a cell to be equal to the difference between forecasted assets and liabilities. Similarly, define each line on the forecasted statement of cash flows, as the difference between the current balance sheet (as reported by the company) and the forecasted balance sheet.

1. *Forecasting Preliminaries* Begin with the adjusted set of financial statements that reflect the company's net operating assets and its operating income that we expect to persist into the future. This requires that we exclude one-time items and adjust other items to reflect anticipated levels of ongoing activities. Next, adjust prior year balance sheets and income statements to ensure that we have comparable (apples-to-apples) numbers across periods. For example, look at inventory costing methods (adjust the balance sheet and income statement from LIFO to FIFO if needed; see Module 6) and for any omitted lease liabilities (see Module 10). The aim is to start with as clean a set of financial statements as possible.
2. *Model Assumptions and Inputs* The assumptions we use critically impact forecasted numbers. Be as thorough as possible in research and analysis in determining model inputs. The most critical assumption is sales growth. Before we begin, adjust any fiscal years to take care of the "13th week" (or 53rd week) problem. Then, use all of the reported years' sales numbers to compute historical growth numbers. Observe any trends. If the company reports segment sales, compute growth of each segment and compare it to total sales growth. We should forecast each segment separately if growth differs by segment. Read the company's MD&A, the footnotes, and any guidance the company voluntarily provides. Obtain an industry report and determine a consensus if possible about sales expectations and the cost environment. As discussed in the module, we assume that most costs (including COGS and SG&A) will not deviate from their historical percentages unless there is evidence to suggest otherwise. Again, scour the footnotes. In the end, use sound judgment and remember that forecasted numbers are subjective.
3. *Forecast the Income Statement* Use the sales growth assumption to forecast sales for the next fiscal year. Use cost level assumptions to forecast all of the operating expenses. At this first stage, we typically leave nonoperating expenses and revenues unchanged from prior year dollar levels. We return to fine tune these after we forecast the balance sheet. Forecast a preliminary tax expense and net income. We need those numbers to complete the balance sheet.
4. *Forecast the Balance Sheet* Use the percentage of sales approach to forecast each operating asset and liability and follow the method described in the module to forecast PPE and intangible assets. Certain operating assets and liabilities will be forecasted to remain unchanged year over year unless we learn otherwise from the financial statements. Forecast debt using the information about scheduled debt maturities. Pay careful attention to forecasting dividends and any stock repurchases or issuances. The "plug" figure will be either marketable securities or additional debt. Once the balance sheet balances, return to nonoperating expenses and adjust them for any additional debt or marketable securities. This will affect pretax income, tax expense, and retained earnings.
5. *Forecast the Statement of Cash Flows* We construct a statement of cash flows from the company's current balance sheet (from the Form 10-K or annual report) and the forecasted balance sheet. The net income number forecasted will also tie in. Remember that this statement is a mechanical operation, requiring no assumptions or new calculations.
6. *Prepare Forecasted Financial Statements or Parsimonious Forecasts* If estimates of the company's stock price are required, we need forecasts of accounting numbers. Start by determining the company's net operating assets (NOA) and NOPAT. Forecasting the financial statements is explained in Module 11. To implement a parsimonious model, see the Appendix to Module 11 (be careful with the rounding convention as one forecasts sales; use the ROUND function in Excel). If

we deviate from historical percentages for expense line items, we should also amend NOPM and/or NOAT. Use the forecasted percentages and not the historical ones for the parsimonious forecast.

SOLUTIONS TO REVIEW PROBLEMS

Mid-Module Review

Solution

Forecasted 2013 financial statements for Colgate-Palmolive follow.

Forecasted Income Statement

For year ended December 31 ($ millions)	2012	Forecast Assumptions	2013 Est.
Net sales	$17,085	17,085 × 1.02	$17,427
Cost of sales	7,153	$17,427 × 41.9%	7,302
Gross profit	9,932	subtotal	10,125
Selling, general and administrative expenses	5,930	$17,427 × 34.7%	6,047
Other (income) expense, net	113	no change	113
Operating profit	3,889	subtotal	3,965
Interest expense, net	15	no change	15
Income before income taxes	3,874	subtotal	3,950
Provision for income taxes	1,243	$3,950 × 32.1%	1,268
Net income including noncontrolling interests	2,631	subtotal	2,682
Less: Net income attributable to noncontrolling interests	159	no change	159
Net income attributable to Colgate-Palmolive Company	$ 2,472	subtotal	$ 2,523

Forecasted Balance Sheet

As of December 31 ($ millions)	2012	Forecast Assumptions	2013 Est.
Assets		computed	
Cash and cash equivalents	$ 884	17,427 × 5.2%	$ 906
Marketable securities		plug	1,078
Receivables (net of allowances of $61 and $49, respectively)	1,668	17,427 × 9.8%	1,708
Inventories	1,365	17,427 × 8.0%	1,394
Other current assets	639	17,427 × 3.7%	645
Total current assets	4,556	subtotal	5,731
Property, plant and equipment, net	3,842	+ 565 − 413	3,994
Goodwill, net	2,500	no change	2,500
Other intangible assets, net	1,499	− 31	1,468
Deferred income taxes	92	no change	92
Other assets	905	17,427 × 5.3%	924
Total assets	$13,394	subtotal	$14,720
Liabilities			
Notes and loans payable	$ 54	no change	$ 54
Current portion of long-term debt	250	footnote disclosure	887
Accounts payable	1,290	17,427 × 7.6%	1,324
Accrued income taxes	254	1,268 × 20.4%	259
Other accruals	1,888	17,427 × 11.1%	1,934
Total current liabilities	3,736	subtotal	4,458
Long-term debt	4,926	− 887	4,039
Deferred income taxes	293	17,427 × 1.7%	296
Other liabilities	2,049	17,427 × 12.0%	2,091
Total liabilities	11,004	subtotal	10,884

continued

continued from prior page

Shareholders' Equity			
Common stock, $1 par value (2,000,000,000 shares authorized, 732,853,180 shares issued)	733	no change	733
Additional paid-in-capital	1,551	no change	1,551
Retained earnings	16,953	+ 2,523 − 1,236	18,240
Accumulated other comprehensive income (loss)	(2,621)	no change	(2,621)
Unearned compensation	(41)	no change	(41)
Treasury stock, at cost	(14,386)	no change	(14,386)
Total Colgate-Palmolive Company shareholders' equity	2,189	subtotal	3,476
Noncontrolling interests	201	assumed	360
Total shareholders' equity	2,390	subtotal	3,826
Total liabilities and shareholders' equity	$13,394	subtotal	$14,720

Forecasted Statement of Cash Flows

($ millions)	Forecast Assumptions	2013 Est.
Net income including noncontrolling interests	via forecast income stmt.	$2,682
Add: Depreciation	given	413
Add: Amortization	given	31
Change in accounts receivable	$1,668 − $1,708	(40)
Change in Inventories	$1,365 − $1,394	(29)
Change in deferred income taxes	$639 − $645	(6)
Change in other current assets	$92 − $92	0
Change in other long-term assets	$905 − $924	(19)
Change in accounts payable	$1,324 − $1,290	34
Change in accrued income taxes	$259 − $254	5
Change in accrued liabilities	$1,934 − $1,888	46
Change in long-term deferred income taxes	$296 − $293	3
Change in other long-term liabilities	$2,091 − $2,049	42
Net cash from operating activities	subtotal	3,162
Capital expenditures	given	(576)
Increase in marketable securities	plug	(1,078)
Net cash from investing activities	subtotal	(1,654)
Dividends		(1,236)
Payments of long-term debt	prior-year current portion	(250)
Net cash from financing activities	subtotal	(1,486)
Net change in cash	subtotal	22
Beginning cash	via prior bal. sheet	884
Ending cash	subtotal	$ 906

Our forecasts yield liabilities in excess of assets of $1,078 million. In this example, we assume that marketable securities are increased by that amount. We might have also assumed repayment of debt and/or purchase of treasury stock, being careful to maintain the company's debt-to-equity ratio. One further adjustment we might make at this point would be to increase interest income assuming an investment return on the marketable securities.

Module-End Review

Solution

	2012	2013E	2014E	2015E	2016E
Sales growth		3.40%	3.40%	3.40%	3.40%
Sales (unrounded)	$67,224	**$69,509.62** ($67,224 × 1.034)	**$71,872.94** ($69,509.62 × 1.034)	**$74,316.62** ($71,872.94 × 1.034)	**$76,843.39** ($74,316.62 × 1.034)
Sales (rounded)	67,224	**$69,510**	**$71,873**	**$74,317**	**$76,843**
NOPAT	10,809	**$11,191** ($69,510 × 0.161)	**$11,572** ($71,873 × 0.161)	**$11,965** ($74,317 × 0.161)	**$12,372** ($76,843 × 0.161)
NOA	59,902	**$62,063** ($69,510/1.12)	**$64,172** ($71,873/1.12)	**$66,354** ($74,317/1.12)	**$68,610** ($76,843/1.12)

Module

12 Analyzing and Valuing Equity Securities

Learning Objectives

LO1 Identify equity valuation models and explain the information required to value equity securities. (p. 12-3)

LO2 Describe and apply the discounted free cash flow model to value equity securities. (p. 12-4)

LO3 Describe and apply the residual operating income model to value equity securities. (p. 12-7)

LO4 Explain how equity valuation models can inform managerial decisions. (p. 12-10)

Nike

Nike's mission is "Bring Inspiration and Innovation to Every Athlete in the World." And, as they say, "if you have a body, you are an athlete."

Bill Bowerman was a nationally respected track and field coach at the University of Oregon and constantly seeking ways to give his athletes a competitive advantage. He experimented with different track surfaces, rehydration drinks and—most importantly—innovations in running shoes. Phil Knight was a talented middle-distance runner from Portland, who enrolled at Oregon in the fall of 1955 and competed for Bowerman's track program. Knight made a cold-call on the Onitsuka Company in Kobe, Japan, manufacturer of Tiger shoes and persuaded the company to grant him rights to distribute Tiger running shoes in the United States. When the first sample shoes arrived, Knight sent several pairs to Bowerman, hoping to make a sale. Instead, Bowerman stunned Knight by offering to become his partner, and to provide his footwear design ideas to Tiger.

With a handshake, the two men formed Blue Ribbon Sports. With an initial contribution of $500 each they placed their first order of 300 pairs of shoes in January 1964. Knight sold the shoes out of the trunk of his green Plymouth Valiant. Bowerman began ripping apart Tiger shoes to see how he could make them lighter and better, and enlisted his University of Oregon runners to wear-test his creations. Bowerman and Knight then selected a brand mark today known internationally as the "Swoosh," which was created by a graphic design student at Portland State University named Carolyn Davidson. The new Nike line of footwear debuted in 1972, in time for the U.S. Track & Field Trials, which were held in Eugene, Oregon.

Today, Nike reports sales of over $25 billion. Its return on net operating assets (RNOA) has remained above 35% every year since 2008 and its free cash flow has tripled during this period. Nike's phenomenal operating performance has not been lost on investors who have pushed Nike's stock price from the low $20s in 2008 to over $60 today.

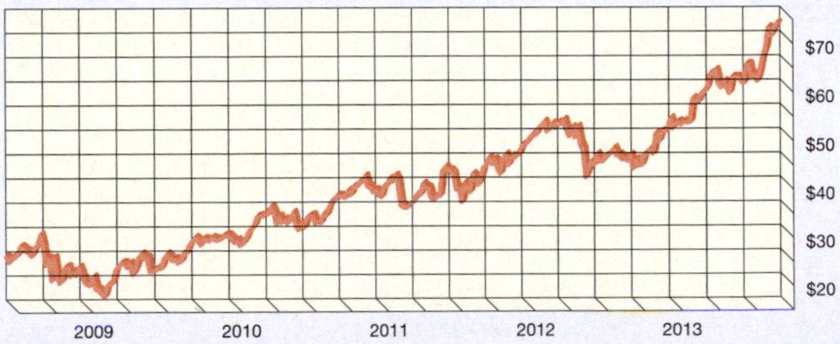

What is the relation between operating performance and stock price? Traditional finance theory posits that stock price is related to the company's generation of free cash flow (net cash flow from operating activities, net of interest expense, less capital expenditures). Nike's free cash flow (FCF) and its stock price over the past several years are illustrated in the following graphic. Nike's free cash flow exhibits an upward trend during the 2008-2013 period, as does its stock price. The relation between the two depicted

Courtesy of iStock

in this graph is not perfect, but a larger sample of companies would confirm a positive association. We examine the traditional finance theory of equity valuation in this module with a discussion of the discounted free cash flow (DCF) valuation model.

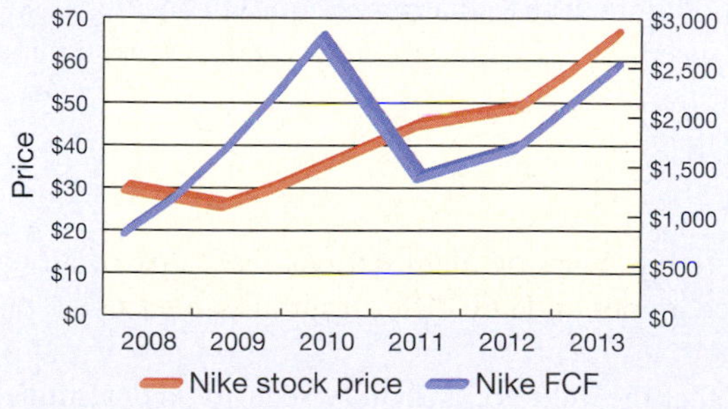

We know from earlier modules that the statement of cash flows is prepared from the income statement and comparative balance sheets. It should be the case, therefore, that there is a relation between free cash flows and the income statement and balance sheet numbers from which they are derived. We can express that relation as follows: Free cash flow = NOPAT − Increase in NOA. It is also true that stock price is related to RNOA as depicted in the following graphic for Nike.

We introduce a valuation model in this module drawing on the inputs of NOPAT and NOA, which is shown to yield the same result as the DCF valuation model. This model, called the residual operating income (ROPI) model, provides

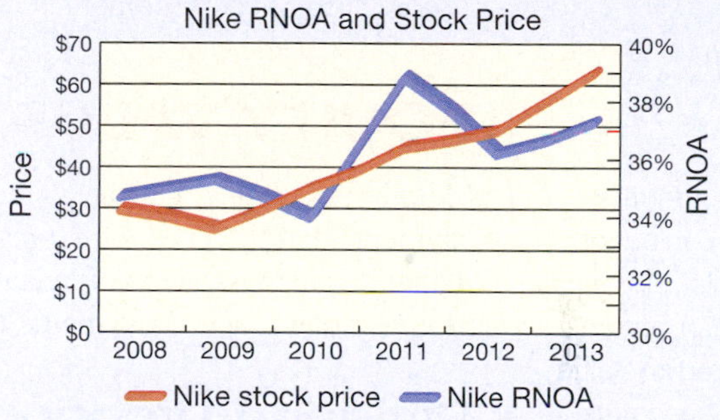

us with some important intuition for why NOPM and NOAT are value drivers and why, therefore, we should investigate them in our analysis of the company's financial statements. While the ROPI model has certain desirable properties, its real value lies in the analysis insights we gain from understanding its components and in the insights the model provides about how the company is being managed. Variants of the ROPI model are used extensively by equity analysts, management consulting companies, and designers of management compensation systems.

Nike President and CEO Mark Parker explains that "at NIKE, we run a complete offense, and it's based on a core commitment to innovation. That's how we stay opportunistic, serve the athlete, reward our shareholders, and continue to lead our industry." Nike has been a force in its industry and is likely to continue that trend provided it focuses on its valuation drivers.

Sources: *Nike* 10-Ks from 2008-2013, Nike Website.

MODULE ORGANIZATION

Analyzing and Valuing Equity Securities

Equity Valuation Models
- Dividend Discount Model
- Discounted Cash Flow Model
- Residual Operating Income Model

Discounted Cash Flow Model
- Model Structure
- Steps for Application
- Illustrating the Model

Residual Operating Income Model
- Model Structure
- Steps for Application
- Illustrating the Model

Insights into and Assessments of Valuation Models
- Focus on Firm Value
- Advantages and Disadvantages of Alternative Valuation Models

This module focuses on valuing equity securities (we explain the valuation of debt securities in Module 7). Specifically, we describe two approaches: the discounted free cash flow model (DCF) and residual operating income model (ROPI). We then conclude by discussing the management implications from an increased understanding of the factors that impact values of equity securities. It is important that we understand the determinants of equity value to make informed decisions. Employees at all levels of an organization, whether public or private, should understand the factors that create shareholder value so that they can work effectively toward that objective. For many senior managers, stock value serves as a scorecard. Successful managers are those who better understand the factors affecting that scorecard.

EQUITY VALUATION MODELS

LO1 Identify equity valuation models and explain the information required to value equity securities.

Module 7 explains that the value of a debt security is the present value of the interest and principal payments that the investor *expects* to receive in the future. The valuation of equity securities is similar in that it is also based on expectations. The difference lies in the increased uncertainty surrounding the timing and amount of payments from equity securities.

Dividend Discount Model

There are many equity valuation models in use today. Each of them defines the value of an equity security in terms of the present value of forecasted amounts. They differ primarily in terms of what is forecasted.

The basis of equity valuation is the premise that the value of an equity security is determined by the payments that the investor can expect to receive. Equity investments involve two types of payoffs: (1) dividends received during the holding period and (2) capital gains when the security is sold.[1] The value of an equity security is, then, based on the present value of expected dividends plus the present value of the security at the end of the forecasted holding period. This **dividend discount model** is appealing in its simplicity and its intuitive focus on dividend distribution. As a practical matter, however, the model is not always useful because many companies that have a positive stock price have never paid a dividend, and are not expected to pay a dividend in the foreseeable future.

Discounted Cash Flow Model

A more practical approach to valuing equity securities focuses on the company's operating and investing activities; that is, on the *generation* of cash rather than the *distribution* of cash. This approach is

[1] The future stock price is, itself, also assumed to be related to the expected dividends that the new investor expects to receive; as a result, the expected receipt of dividends is the sole driver of stock price under this type of valuation model.

called the **discounted cash flow (DCF)** model. The focus of the forecasting process for the DCF model is the company's expected *free cash flows to the firm*, which are defined as operating cash flows net of the expected new investments in net operating assets that are required to support the business.

Residual Operating Income Model

Another approach to equity valuation also focuses on operating and investing activities. It is known as the **residual operating income (ROPI)** model. This model uses both net operating profits after tax (NOPAT) and the net operating assets (NOA) to determine equity value; see Module 4 for complete descriptions of the NOPAT and NOA measures. This approach highlights the importance of return on net operating assets (RNOA), and the disaggregation of RNOA into net operating profit margin and NOA turnover. We discuss the implications of this insight for managers later in this module.

DISCOUNTED CASH FLOW (DCF) MODEL

LO2 Describe and apply the discounted free cash flow model to value equity securities.

The discounted cash flow (DCF) model defines firm value as follows:

Firm Value = Present Value of Expected Free Cash Flows to Firm

The expected free cash flows to the firm include cash flows arising from the operating side of the business; that is, cash generated from the firm's operating activities (but not from nonoperating activities such as interest paid on debt or dividends received on investments), and they do not include the cash flows from financing activities.

DCF Model Structure

Free cash flows to the firm (FCFF) equal net operating profit after tax that is not used to grow net operating assets. Using the terminology of Module 4 we can define FCFF as follows (see Business Insight box on next page for a more traditional definition):

FCFF = NOPAT − Increase in NOA

where

NOPAT = Net operating profit after tax
NOA = Net operating assets

Net operating profit after tax is normally positive and the net cash flows from increases in net operating assets are normally negative assuming that net operating assets increase each period. The sum of the two (positive or negative) represents the net cash flows available to creditors and shareholders. Positive FCFF imply that there are funds available for distribution to creditors and shareholders, either in the form of debt repayments, dividends, or stock repurchases (treasury stock). Negative FCFF imply that the firm requires additional funds from creditors and/or shareholders, in the form of new loans or equity investments, to support its business activities.

The DCF valuation model requires forecasts of *all* future free cash flows; that is, free cash flows for the remainder of the company's life. Generating an infinite stream of forecasts is not realistic. Consequently, analysts typically estimate FCFF over a horizon period, often 4 to 10 years, and then make simplifying assumptions about the FCFF subsequent to that horizon period.

MANAGERIAL DECISION **You Are the Chief Financial Officer**

Assume that you are the CFO of a company that has a large investment in plant assets and sells its products on credit. Identify steps you can take to increase your company's cash flow and, hence, your company's firm value. [Answer p. 12-18]

BUSINESS INSIGHT **Definitions of Free Cash Flow**

We often see free cash flows to the firm (unlevered free cash flow) defined as follows:

FCFF = Net cash flow from operating activities − Capital expenditures

Although somewhat similar to the definition in this book, NOPAT − Increase in NOA, there are important differences:

- Net cash flow from operating activities uses net income as the starting point; net income, of course, comingles both operating and nonoperating components (such as selling expense and interest expense). Analysts sometimes correct for this by adding back items such as after-tax net interest expense.
- Income tax expense (in net income) includes the effect of the interest tax shield (see Module 4); the usual NOPAT definition includes only the tax on operating income.
- Net cash flow from operating activities also includes nonoperating items in working capital, such as changes in interest payable and dividends payable, as well as inflows from securitization of receivables (see Module 10); NOA focuses only on operating activities.
- The FCFF definition in this box consists of net income, changes in working capital accounts, and capital expenditures; the usual NOA consists of changes in operating working capital accounts, capital expenditures, *and* changes in long-term operating liabilities.

We must be attentive to differences in definitions for free cash flow so that we understand the analytical choices we make and their implications to equity valuation. It also aids us in correctly interpreting analyst research reports that might apply different definitions of free cash flow.

Steps in Applying the DCF Model

Application of the DCF model to equity valuation involves five steps:

1. Forecast and discount FCFF for the **horizon period**.[2]
2. Forecast and discount FCFF for the post-horizon period, called **terminal period**.[3]
3. Sum the present values of the horizon and terminal periods to yield firm (enterprise) value.
4. Subtract net nonoperating obligations (NNO), along with any noncontrolling interest (NCI), from firm value to yield firm equity value. If NNO is positive, the usual case, we subtract it in step 4; if NNO is negative, we add it. (For many, but not all, companies, NNO is positive because nonoperating liabilities exceed nonoperating assets.)
5. Divide firm equity value by the number of shares outstanding to yield stock value per share.

Illustrating the DCF Model

To illustrate, we apply the DCF model to **Nike**. Nike's recent financial statements are reproduced in Appendix 12A. Forecasted financials for Nike (forecast horizon of 2014–2017 and terminal period of 2018) are in Exhibit 12.1.[4] The forecasts (in bold) are for sales, NOPAT, and NOA. Consistent with analysts' consensus estimates from July 2013, when the 2013 10-K became available, these forecasts assume an annual 9.0% sales growth during the horizon period, a terminal period sales

---

[2] When discounting FCFF, the appropriate discount rate (r_w) is the **weighted average cost of capital (WACC)**, where the weights are the relative percentages of debt (d) and equity (e) in the capital structure applied to the expected returns on debt (r_d) and equity (r_e), respectively: WACC $= r_w = (r_d \times \%$ of debt$) + (r_e \times \%$ of equity$)$; see footnote 7 for an example.

[3] For an assumed growth, g, the terminal period (T) present value of FCFF in perpetuity (beyond the horizon period) is given by, $\frac{FCFF_T}{r_w - g}$, where $FCFF_T$ is the free cash flow to the firm for the terminal period, r_w is WACC, and g is the assumed long-term growth rate of those cash flows. The resulting amount is then discounted back to the present using the horizon-end-period discount factor.

[4] We use a four-period horizon in the text and assignments to simplify the exposition and to reduce the computational burden. In practice, analysts use spreadsheets to forecast future cash flows and value the equity security, and typically have a forecast horizon of seven to ten periods.

growth of 2%, net operating profit margin (NOPM) of 10%, and a year-end net operating asset turnover (NOAT) of 4 (which is the 2013 turnover rate based on year-end NOA; year-end amounts are used because we are forecasting year-end account balances, not average balances).[5,6]

EXHIBIT 12.1 Application of Discounted Cash Flow Model

(In millions, except per share values and discount factors)	Reported 2013	Horizon Period 2014	2015	2016	2017	Terminal Period
Sales (unrounded)	$25,313	$27,591.17 (25,313 × 1.09)	$30,074.38 (27,591.17 × 1.09)	$32,781.07 (30,074.38 × 1.09)	$35,731.37 (32,781.07 × 1.09)	$36,445.99 (35,731.37 × 1.02)
Sales (rounded)		27,591	30,074	32,781	35,731	36,446
NOPAT*	2,462	2,759	3,007	3,278	3,573	3,645
NOA**	6,597	6,898	7,519	8,195	8,933	9,112
Increase in NOA		301	621	676	738	179
FCFF (NOPAT − Increase in NOA)		2,458	2,386	2,602	2,835	3,466
Discount factor $[1/(1 + r_w)^t]$‡		0.91575	0.83860	0.76795	0.70325	
Present value of horizon FCFF		2,251	2,001	1,998	1,994	
Cum present value of horizon FCFF	$ 8,244					
Present value of terminal FCFF	33,854					
Total firm value	42,098					
Less (plus): NNO†	(4,559)					
Less: NCI	0					
Firm equity value	$46,657					
Shares outstanding	716					
Stock value per share	$ 65.16					

*Assuming a combined federal and state statutory tax rate of 37.0%, NOPAT for 2013 is computed as follows ($ millions): ($11,034 − $7,780 + $15) − ($808 − [0.37 × $3]) = $2,462. A note on rounding: To forecast sales, we multiply prior year's unrounded sales by (1 + Growth rate); this is done for the horizon and terminal periods. Then, we round each year's forecasted sales to whole units and use rounded sales to compute NOPAT and NOA, where both are rounded to whole units. At each successive step, we round the number to whole units before proceeding to the next step.

**NOA computations for 2013 follow ($ millions): ($17,584 − $3,337 − $2,628) − ($1,646 + $1,986 + $98 + $1,292) = $6,597.

†NNO is the difference between NOA and total shareholders' equity; in this case NNO ($ millions) = $6,597 − $11,156 = $(4,559). Nike's NNO is negative because it carries substantial cash and securities that exceed its debt.

‡For simplification, present value computations use discount factors rounded to 5 decimal places.

The bottom line of Exhibit 12.1 is the estimated Nike equity value of $46,657 million, or a per share stock value of $65.16 (computed as $46,657/716 shares). The present value computations use a 9.2% WACC(r_w) as the discount rate.[7] Specifically, we obtain this stock valuation as follows:

1. **Compute present value of horizon period FCFF.** We compute the forecasted 2014 FCFF of $2,458 million from the forecasted 2014 NOPAT less the forecasted increase in 2014 NOA. The present value of this $2,458 million as of 2013 is $2,251 million, computed as $2,458 million × 0.91575 (the present value factor for one year at 9.2%). Similarly, the present value of 2015 FCFF (two years from the current date) is $2,001 million, computed as $2,386 million × 0.83860, and so on through 2017. The sum of these present values (*cumulative present value*) is $8,244 million.
2. **Compute present value of terminal period FCFF.** The present value of the terminal period FCFF is $33,854 million, computed as $\frac{\left(\frac{\$3{,}466 \text{ million}}{0.092 - 0.02}\right)}{(1.092)^4}$, or ($3,466/0.072) × 0.70325.

[5] **NOPAT** equals revenues less operating expenses such as cost of goods sold, selling, general, and administrative expenses, and taxes. NOPAT excludes any interest revenue and interest expense and any gains or losses from financial investments. NOPAT reflects the operating side of the firm as opposed to nonoperating activities such as borrowing and security investment activities. **NOA** equals operating assets less operating liabilities. (See Module 4.)

[6] NOPAT and NOA are typically forecasted using the detailed forecasting procedures discussed in Module 11. In this module we use the parsimonious method to multiyear forecasting (see Module 11) to focus attention on the valuation process.

[7] We use the 9.2% weighted average cost of capital for Nike provided by Bloomberg© as of July, 2013, the date that Nike's 10-K became available and the stock price estimate was performed. To learn more about the computation of the weighted average cost of capital (WACC), see finance-oriented books such as *Corporate Valuation: Theory, Evidence and Practice* by Holthausen and Zmijewski, 2014, Cambridge Business Publishers.

3. **Compute firm equity value.** Sum present values from the horizon and terminal period FCFF to get firm (enterprise) value of $42,098 million. Subtract the value of Nike's net nonoperating obligations of $(4,559) million to get firm equity value of $46,657. Nike has no noncontrolling interest on the balance sheet; if it did, we would subtract it, along with NNO, to get firm equity value. Dividing firm equity value by the 716 million shares outstanding yields the estimated per share valuation of $65.16.

We perform this valuation as of July 23, 2013, which is the SEC filing date for Nike's 10-K. Nike's stock closed at $63.19 on July 23, 2013. Our valuation estimate of $65.16 indicates that the stock is slightly undervalued as of that date. Analysts' mean price target was about $65 on that date.

BUSINESS INSIGHT **Analysts' Forecasts**

Earnings and cash-flow estimates are key to security valuation. Following are earnings estimates as of July 2013, for **Nike** from Yahoo!Finance. A total of 27 analysts provided earnings estimates. The median (consensus) EPS estimate for 2014 (current year) is $3.04 per share, with a high of $3.45 and a low of $2.95. This compares to an actual diluted EPS of $2.69 in 2013. For 2015 (slightly more than one year ahead), the consensus EPS estimate is $3.46. The average buy rating for Nike stock is 2.3 on a scale that runs from 1.0 (Strong BUY) to 5.0 (Strong SELL).

Estimate Period	Total Analysts	Ave. EPS Est.	High EPS Est.	Low EPS Est.
2014 Fiscal Year	27	$3.04	$3.45	$2.95
2015 Fiscal Year	26	$3.46	$3.65	$3.21
Average recommendation: 2.3 (1 = Strong Buy, 3 = Hold, 5 = Strong Sell)				

MID-MODULE REVIEW

Following are forecasts of **Procter & Gamble**'s sales, net operating profit after tax (NOPAT), and net operating assets (NOA). These are taken from Exhibit 11.10 in Module 11 and we assume a terminal growth rate of 4%.

(In millions)	Reported 2013	Horizon Period 2014	2015	2016	2017	Terminal Period
Sales growth.		1.5%	4.0%	4.0%	4.0%	4.0%
Sales (unrounded)	$84,167	**$85,429.51** ($84,167 × 1.015)	**$88,846.69** ($85,429.51 × 1.04)	**$92,400.56** ($88,846.69 × 1.04)	**$96,096.58** ($92,400.56 × 1.04)	**$99,940.44** ($96,096.58 × 1.04)
Sales (rounded)	$84,167	**$85,430**	**$88,847**	**$ 92,401**	**$ 96,097**	**$ 99,940**
NOPAT	$11,174	**$11,362**	**$11,817**	**$ 12,289**	**$ 12,781**	**$ 13,292**
NOA	$94,305	**$95,989**	**$99,828**	**$103,821**	**$107,974**	**$112,292**

Use the forecasts above to compute P&G's free cash flows to the firm (FCFF) and an estimate of its stock value using the DCF model. Make the following assumptions: discount rate (WACC) of 7% (Bloomberg estimate as of August, 2013), shares outstanding of 2,742.3 million, net nonoperating obligations (NNO) of $25,596 million, and noncontrolling interest (NCI) from the balance sheet of $645 million.

The solution is on page 12-33.

LO3 Describe and apply the residual operating income model to value equity securities.

RESIDUAL OPERATING INCOME (ROPI) MODEL

The residual operating income (ROPI) model focuses on net operating profit after tax (NOPAT) and net operating assets (NOA). This means it uses key measures from both the income statement and balance sheet in determining firm value.

ROPI Model Structure

The ROPI model defines firm value as the sum of two components:

Firm Value = NOA + Present Value of Expected ROPI

where

NOA = Net operating assets
ROPI = Residual operating income

Net operating assets (NOA) are the foundation of firm value under the ROPI model. This is potentially problematic because we measure NOA using the balance sheet, which is unlikely to fully and contemporaneously capture the true (or intrinsic) value of all of a firm's operating assets.[8] However, the ROPI model adds an adjustment that corrects for the undervaluation or overvaluation of NOA. This adjustment is the present value of expected residual operating income, and is defined as follows:

$$\text{ROPI} = \text{NOPAT} - \underbrace{(\text{NOA}_{Beg} \times r_w)}_{\text{Expected NOPAT}}$$

where

NOA_{Beg} = Net operating assets at beginning (***Beg***) of period
r_w = Weighted average cost of capital (WACC)

Residual operating income (ROPI) is the net operating profit a firm earns over and above the return that the operating assets are expected to earn given the firm's WACC. Shareholders expect the company to use NOA to generate, at least, a "hurdle" profit to cover the cost of capital (WACC). Companies that earn profits over and above that hurdle, create value for shareholders. This is the concept of residual income: that is, income earned over and above the minimum amount of return required by investors.

Understanding the ROPI model helps us reap the benefits from the disaggregation of return on net operating assets (RNOA) in Module 4. In addition, the ROPI model is the foundation for many internal and external performance evaluation and compensation systems marketed by management consulting and accounting services firms.[9]

Steps in Applying the ROPI Model

Application of the ROPI model to equity valuation involves five steps:

1. Forecast and discount ROPI for the horizon period.[10]
2. Forecast and discount ROPI for the terminal period.[11]
3. Sum the present values from both the horizon and terminal periods; then add this sum to current NOA to get firm (enterprise) value.

---

[8] If the assets earn more than expected, it could be because NOA does not capture all of the firms' assets. For example, R&D and advertising are not fully and contemporaneously reflected on the balance sheet as assets though they likely produce future cash inflows. Likewise, internally generated goodwill is not fully reflected on the balance sheet as an asset. Similarly, assets are generally not written up to reflect unrealized gains. Conversely, sometimes the balance sheet overstates the true value of NOA. For example, companies can delay the write-down of impaired assets and, thus, overstate their book values. These examples, and a host of others, can yield reported values of NOA that differ from the fair value of operating assets.

[9] Examples are economic value added (EVA™) from Stern Stewart & Company, the economic profit model from McKinsey & Co., the cash flow return on investment (CFROI™) from Holt Value Associates, the economic value management from KPMG, and the value builder from PricewaterhouseCoopers (PwC).

[10] The present value of expected ROPI uses the weighted average cost of capital (WACC) as its discount rate; same as with the DCF model.

[11] For an assumed growth, g, the present value of the perpetuity of ROPI beyond the horizon period is given by $\frac{\text{ROPI}_T}{r_w - g}$, where ROPI_T is the residual operating income for the terminal period, r_w is WACC for the firm, and g is the assumed growth rate of ROPI_T following the horizon period. The resulting amount is then discounted back to the present using the WACC, computed over the length of the horizon period.

4. Subtract net nonoperating obligations (NNO), along with any noncontrolling interest, from firm value to yield firm equity value.
5. Divide firm equity value by the number of shares outstanding to yield stock value per share.

Illustrating the ROPI Model

To illustrate application of the ROPI model, we again use **Nike**. Forecasted financials for Nike (forecast horizon of 2014–2017 and terminal period of 2018) are in Exhibit 12.2. The forecasts (in bold) are for sales, NOPAT, and NOA (the same forecasts from illustration of the DCF model). These forecasts assume an annual 9% sales growth for the horizon period, a terminal period sales growth of 2%, net operating profit margin (NOPM) of 10%, and a year-end net operating asset turnover (NOAT) of 4 (which is the 2013 turnover rate based on year-end NOA; year-end amounts are used because we are forecasting year-end account balances, not average balances).

EXHIBIT 12.2 Application of Residual Operating Income Model

(In millions, except per share values and discount factors)	Reported 2013	Horizon Period 2014	2015	2016	2017	Terminal Period
Sales (unrounded)	$25,313	**$27,591.17** (25,313 × 1.09)	**$30,074.38** (27,591.17 × 1.09)	**$32,781.07** (30,074.38 × 1.09)	**$35,731.37** (32,781.07 × 1.09)	**$36,445.99** (35,731.37 × 1.02)
Sales (rounded)		**27,591**	**30,074**	**32,781**	**35,731**	**36,446**
NOPAT*	2,462	**2,759**	**3,007**	**3,278**	**3,573**	**3,645**
NOA**	6,597	**6,898**	**7,519**	**8,195**	**8,933**	**9,112**
ROPI (NOPAT − [$NOA_{Beg} \times r_w$])		2,152	2,372	2,586	2,819	2,823
Discount factor [$1/(1 + r_w)^t$]‡		0.91575	0.83860	0.76795	0.70325	
Present value of horizon ROPI		1,971	1,989	1,986	1,982	
Cum present value of horizon ROPI	$ 7,928					
Present value of terminal ROPI	27,573					
NOA	6,597					
Total firm value	42,098					
Less (plus): NNO†	(4,559)					
Less: NCI	0					
Firm equity value	$46,657					
Shares outstanding	716					
Stock value per share	$ 65.16					

*Assuming a combined federal and state statutory tax rate of 37.0%, NOPAT for 2013 is computed as follows ($ millions): ($11,034 − $7,780 + $15) − ($808 − [0.37 × $3]) = $2,462. A note on rounding: To forecast sales, we multiply prior year's unrounded sales by (1 + Growth rate); this is done for the horizon and terminal periods. Then, we round each year's forecasted sales to whole units and use rounded sales to compute NOPAT and NOA, where both are rounded to whole units. At each successive step, we round the number to whole units before proceeding to the next step.

**NOA computations for 2013 follow ($ millions): ($17,584 − $3,337 − $2,628) − ($1,646 + $1,986 + $98 + $1,292) = $6,597.

†NNO is the difference between NOA and total shareholders' equity; in this case NNO ($ millions) = $6,597 − $11,156 = $(4,559). Nike's NNO is negative because it carries substantial cash and securities that exceed its debt.

‡For simplification, present value computations use discount factors rounded to 5 decimal places.

The bottom line of Exhibit 12.2 is the estimated Nike equity value of $46,657 million, or a per share stock value of $65.16. The present value computations use a 9.2% WACC as the discount rate. Specifically, we obtain this stock valuation as follows:

1. **Compute present value of horizon period ROPI.** The forecasted 2014 ROPI of $2,152 million is computed from the forecasted 2014 NOPAT ($2,759) less the product of beginning period NOA ($6,597) and WACC (0.092). The present value of this ROPI as of 2014 is $1,971 million, computed as $2,152 million × 0.91575 (the present value one year hence discounted at 9.2%). Similarly, the present value of 2015 ROPI (two years hence) is $1,989 million, computed as $2,372 million × 0.83860, and so on through 2017. The sum of these present values (*cumulative present value*) is $7,928 million.
2. **Compute present value of terminal period ROPI.** The present value of the terminal period ROPI is $27,573 million, computed as $\frac{\left(\frac{\$2{,}823 \text{ million}}{0.092 - 0.02}\right)}{(1.092)^4}$, or ($2,823/0.072) × 0.70325.

3. **Compute firm equity value.** We must sum the present values from the horizon period ($7,928 million) and terminal period ($27,573 million), plus NOA ($6,597 million), to get firm (enterprise) value of $42,098 million. We then subtract the value of net nonoperating obligations of $(4,559) million to get firm equity value of $46,657. Nike has no noncontrolling interest on the balance sheet; if it did, we would subtract it, along with NNO, to get firm equity value. Dividing firm equity value by the 716 million shares outstanding yields the estimated per share valuation of $65.16.

We perform this valuation as of July 23, 2013, which is the SEC filing date for Nike's 10-K. Nike's stock closed at $63.19 on July 23, 2013. Our valuation estimate of $65.16 suggests that Nike's stock is slightly undervalued as of that date. Analysts' average price target was about $65 on that date.

The ROPI model estimate is equal to that computed using the DCF model illustrated earlier in this module. This is the case so long as the firm is in a steady state, that is, NOPAT and NOA are growing at the same rate (for example, when RNOA is constant). When the steady-state condition is not met, for example, when a company has variable growth rates over time or when profit margins are changing from year to year, the two models yield different valuations. Analysts typically compute values from several models and use qualitative analysis to determine a final price estimate.

RESEARCH INSIGHT **Power of NOPAT Forecasts**

Discounted cash flow (DCF) and residual operating income (ROPI) models yield identical estimates when the expected payoffs are forecasted for an infinite horizon. For practical reasons, we must use horizon period forecasts and a terminal period forecast. This truncation of the forecast horizon is a main cause of any difference in value estimates for these models. Importantly, if we can forecast (GAAP-based) NOPAT and NOA more accurately than forecasts of cash inflows and outflows, we will obtain more accurate estimates of firm value given a finite horizon.

MANAGERIAL INSIGHTS FROM THE ROPI MODEL

LO4 Explain how equity valuation models can inform managerial decisions.

The ROPI model defines firm value as the sum of NOA and the present value of expected residual operating income as follows:

$$\text{Firm Value} = \text{NOA} + \text{Present Value of } \underbrace{[\text{NOPAT} - (\text{NOA}_{\text{Beg}} \times r_w)]}_{\text{ROPI}}$$

Increasing ROPI, therefore, increases firm value. Managers can increase ROPI in two ways:

1. Decrease the NOA required to generate a given level of NOPAT (improve efficiency)
2. Increase NOPAT with the same level of NOA investment (improve profitability)

These are two very important observations. It means that achieving better performance requires effective management of *both* the balance sheet and the income statement. Most operating managers are accustomed to working with income statements. Further, they are often evaluated on profitability measures, such as achieving desired levels of sales and gross profit or efficiently managing operating expenses. The ROPI model focuses management attention on the balance sheet as well.

The two points above highlight two paths to increase ROPI and, accordingly, firm value. First, let's consider how management can reduce the level of NOA while maintaining a given level of NOPAT. Many managers begin by implementing procedures that reduce net operating working capital, such as:

- Reducing receivables through:
  - Better assessment of customers' credit quality
  - Better controls to identify delinquencies and automated payment notices
  - More accurate and timely invoicing

- Reducing inventories through:
  - Use of less costly components (of equal quality) and production with lower wage rates
  - Elimination of product features not valued by customers
  - Outsourcing to reduce product cost
  - Just-in-time deliveries of raw materials
  - Elimination of manufacturing bottlenecks to reduce work-in-process inventories
  - Producing to order rather than to estimated demand
- Increasing payables through:
  - Extending the payment of low or no-cost payables (so long as the supplier relationships are unharmed)

Management would next look at its long-term operating assets for opportunities to reduce unnecessary operating assets, such as the:

- Sale of unnecessary property, plant or equipment
- Acquisition of production and administrative assets in partnership with other entities for greater throughput
- Acquisition of finished or semifinished goods from suppliers to reduce manufacturing assets

The second path to increase ROPI and, accordingly, firm value is to increase NOPAT with the same level of NOA investment. Management would look to strategies that maximize NOPAT, such as:

- Increasing gross profit dollars through:
  - Better pricing and mix of products sold
  - Reduction of raw material and labor cost without sacrificing product quality, perhaps by outsourcing, better design, or more efficient manufacturing
  - Increase of throughput to minimize overhead costs per unit (provided inventory does not build up)
- Reducing selling, general, and administrative expenses through:
  - Better management of personnel
  - Reduction of overhead
  - Use of derivatives to hedge commodity and interest costs
  - Minimization of tax expense

Before undertaking any of these actions, managers must consider both short- and long-run implications for the company. The ROPI model helps managers assess company performance (income statement) relative to the net operating assets committed (balance sheet).

MANAGERIAL DECISION **You Are the Chief Financial Officer**

The residual operating income (ROPI) model highlights the importance of increasing NOPAT and reducing net operating assets, which are the two major components of the return on net operating assets (RNOA). What specific steps can you take to improve RNOA through improvement of its components: net operating profit margin and net operating asset turnover? [Answer, p. 12-18]

ASSESSMENT OF VALUATION MODELS

Exhibit 12.3 provides a brief summary of the advantages and disadvantages of the DCF and ROPI models. Neither model dominates the other, and both are theoretically equivalent. Instead, professionals must choose the model that performs best under practical circumstances.

EXHIBIT 12.3 Advantages and Disadvantages of DCF and ROPI Valuation Models

Model	Advantages	Disadvantages	Performs Best
DCF	• Popular and widely accepted model • Cash flows are unaffected by accrual accounting • FCFF is intuitive	• Cash investments in plant assets are treated as cash outflows, even though they create shareholder value • Value not recognized unless evidenced by cash flows • Computing FCFF can be difficult as operating cash flows are affected by – Cutbacks on investments (receivables, inventories, plant assets); can yield short-run benefits at long-run cost – Securitization, which GAAP treats as an operating cash flow when many view it as a financing activity	• When the firm reports positive FCFF • When FCFF grows at a relatively constant rate
ROPI	• Focuses on value drivers such as profit margins and asset turnovers • Uses both balance sheet and income statement, including accrual accounting information • Reduces weight placed on terminal period value	• Financial statements do not reflect all company assets, especially for knowledge-based industries (for example, R&D assets and goodwill) • Requires some knowledge of accrual accounting	• When financial statements reflect more of the assets and liabilities; including those items often reported off-balance-sheet

There are numerous other equity valuation models in practice. Many require forecasting, but several others do not. A quick review of selected models follows:

The **method of comparables** (often called *multiples*) **model** predicts equity valuation or stock value using price multiples. Price multiples are defined as stock price divided by some key financial statement number. That financial number varies across investors but is usually one of the following: net income, net sales, book value of equity, total assets, or cash flow. The method then compares companies' multiples to those of their competitors to assign value.

The **net asset valuation model** draws on the financial reporting system to assign value. That is, equity is valued as reported assets less reported liabilities. Some investors adjust reported assets and liabilities for several perceived shortcomings in GAAP prior to computing net asset value. This method is commonly applied when valuing privately held companies.

The **dividend discount model** predicts that equity valuation or stock values equal the present value of expected cash dividends. This model is founded on the dividend discount formula and depends on the reliability of forecasted cash dividends.

There are additional models applied in practice that involve dividends, cash flows, research and development outlays, accounting rates of return, cash recovery rates, and real option models. Further, some practitioners, called *chartists* and *technicians,* chart price behavior over time and use it to predict equity value.

RESEARCH INSIGHT Using Models to Identify Mispriced Stocks

Implementation of the ROPI model can include parameters to capture differences in growth opportunities, persistence of ROPI, and the conservatism in accounting measures. Research finds differences in how such factors, across firms and over time, affect ROPI and changes in NOA. This research also hints that investors do not entirely understand the properties underlying these factors and, consequently, individual stocks can be mispriced for short periods of time. Other research contends that the apparent mispricing is due to an omitted valuation variable related to riskiness of the firm.

GLOBAL ACCOUNTING

There are no differences in the method or technique of valuing equity securities using IFRS financial statements. We can use the DCF or the ROPI method with IFRS data as inputs and determine intrinsic values. Regarding other inputs, it is important to note that WACC varies across countries. This is readily apparent when we recognize that the risk-free rate used to compute WACC is country specific; for example, following is the yield on 10-year government debt for several countries as of October 2013 (www.bloomberg.com/markets/rates-bonds). In comparison to countries such as Japan and Germany, the countries such as Greece and Brazil are riskier because of their debt levels and economic troubles. The higher the country risk, the higher the yield demanded on that country's debt.

Country	Yield to maturity
Japan	0.79%
Germany	1.66%
United States	2.71%
United Kingdom	2.40%
Australia	3.66%
Brazil	4.36%
Greece	9.69%

MODULE-END REVIEW

Following are forecasts of **Procter & Gamble**'s sales, net operating profit after tax (NOPAT), and net operating assets (NOA). These are taken from Exhibit 11.10 in Module 11 and we assume a terminal growth rate of 4%.

(In millions)	Reported 2013	Horizon Period 2014	2015	2016	2017	Terminal Period
Sales growth		1.5%	4.0%	4.0%	4.0%	4.0%
Sales (unrounded)	$84,167	**$85,429.51** ($84,167 × 1.015)	**$88,846.69** ($85,429.51 × 1.04)	**$92,400.55** ($88,846.69 × 1.04)	**$96,096.57** ($92,400.55 × 1.04)	**$99,940.44** ($96,096.57 × 1.04)
Sales (rounded)	84,167	**$85,430**	**$88,847**	**$ 92,401**	**$ 96,097**	**$ 99,940**
NOPAT	11,174	**$11,362**	**$11,817**	**$ 12,289**	**$ 12,781**	**$ 13,292**
NOA	94,305	**$95,989**	**$99,828**	**$103,821**	**$107,974**	**$112,292**

Use the forecasts above to compute P&G's free cash flows to the firm (FCFF) and an estimate of its stock value using the ROPI model. Make the following assumptions: discount rate (WACC) of 7% (Bloomberg estimate as of August, 2013), shares outstanding of 2,742.3 million, net nonoperating obligations (NNO) of $25,596 million, and noncontrolling interest (NCI) from the balance sheet of $645 million.

The solution is on page 12-34.

APPENDIX 12A: Nike Financial Statements

NIKE, INC. Balance Sheet May 31 (In millions)	2013	2012
Assets		
Cash and equivalents	$3,337	$2,317
Short-term investments	2,628	1,440
Accounts receivable, net	3,117	3,132
Inventories	3,434	3,222
Deferred income taxes	308	262
Prepaid expenses and other current assets	802	857
Assets of discontinued operations	—	615
Total current assets	13,626	11,845

continued

Property, plant and equipment, net	$ 2,452	$ 2,209
Identifiable intangible assets, net	382	370
Goodwill	131	131
Deferred income taxes and other assets	993	910
Total assets	$17,584	$15,465
Liabilities and shareholders' equity		
Current liabilities:		
Current portion of long-term debt	$ 57	$ 49
Notes payable	121	108
Accounts payable	1,646	1,549
Accrued liabilities	1,986	1,941
Income taxes payable	98	65
Liabilities of discontinued operations	18	170
Total current liabilities	3,926	3,882
Long-term debt	1,210	228
Deferred income taxes and other liabilities	1,292	974
Redeemable Preferred Stock	—	—
Shareholders' equity		
Common stock at stated value:		
Class A convertible — 178 and 180 shares outstanding	—	—
Class B — 716 and 736 shares outstanding	3	3
Capital in excess of stated value	5,184	4,641
Accumulated other comprehensive income	274	149
Retained earnings	5,695	5,588
Total shareholders' equity	11,156	10,381
Total liabilities and shareholders' equity	$17,584	$15,465

NIKE, INC.
Income Statement

For Fiscal Year Ended May 31 (In millions)	2013	2012	2011
Income from continuing operations			
Revenues	$25,313	$23,331	$20,117
Cost of sales	14,279	13,183	10,915
Gross profit	11,034	10,148	9,202
Demand creation expense	2,745	2,607	2,344
Operating overhead expense	5,035	4,458	4,017
Total selling and administrative expense	7,780	7,065	6,361
Interest (income) expense, net	(3)	4	4
Other (income) expense, net*	(15)	54	(25)
Income before income taxes	3,272	3,025	2,862
Income tax expense	808	756	690
Net income from continuing operations	2,464	2,269	2,172
Net income (loss) from discontinued operations	21	(46)	(39)
Net income	$ 2,485	$ 2,223	$ 2,133

* Notes indicate that "other (income) expense, net" relates to derivatives that Nike uses to hedge operating risks associated with global inventory purchases and manufacturing; thus, we classify this item as operating.

NIKE, INC. Statement of Cash Flows For Fiscal Year Ended May 31 ($ millions)	2013	2012	2011
Cash provided by operations			
Net income	$2,485	$2,223	$2,133
Income charges (credits) not affecting cash:			
Depreciation	438	373	335
Deferred income taxes	21	(60)	(76)
Stock-based compensation	174	130	105
Amortization and other	75	32	23
Net gain on divestitures	(124)	—	—
Changes in certain working capital components and other assets and liabilities:			
Decrease (increase) in accounts receivable	142	(323)	(273)
(Increase) in inventories	(197)	(805)	(551)
(Increase) in prepaid expenses and other current assets	(28)	(141)	(35)
Increase in accounts payable, accrued liabilities and income taxes payable	41	470	151
Cash provided by operations	3,027	1,899	1,812
Cash (used) provided by investing activities			
Purchases of short-term investments	(3,702)	(2,705)	(7,616)
Maturities of short-term investments	1,501	2,585	4,313
Sales of short-term investments	998	1,244	2,766
Additions to property, plant and equipment	(636)	(597)	(432)
Disposals of property, plant and equipment	14	2	1
Proceeds from divestitures	786	—	—
Increase in other assets, net of other liabilities	(28)	(37)	(30)
Settlement of net investment hedges	—	22	(23)
Cash (used) provided by investing activities	(1,067)	514	(1,021)
Cash used by financing activities			
Net proceeds from long-term debt issuance	986	—	—
Long-term debt payments, including current portion	(49)	(203)	(8)
Increase (decrease) in notes payable	15	(65)	41
Proceeds from exercise of stock options and other stock issuances	313	468	345
Excess tax benefits from share-based payment arrangements	72	115	64
Repurchase of common stock	(1,674)	(1,814)	(1,859)
Dividends — common and preferred	(703)	(619)	(555)
Cash used by financing activities	(1,040)	(2,118)	(1,972)
Effect of exchange rate changes	100	67	57
Net increase (decrease) in cash and equivalents	1,020	362	(1,124)
Cash and equivalents, beginning of year	2,317	1,955	3,079
Cash and equivalents, end of year	$3,337	$2,317	$1,955

APPENDIX 12B: RBC Capital Markets Valuation of Procter & Gamble

We explain the forecasting process in Module 11 and reproduce an analyst report on forecasted financial statements for **Procter & Gamble** in Appendix 11A. In this appendix, we extend that analysis and reproduce an analyst forecasted stock price for P&G. We include below, two excerpts from the **RBC Capital Markets** valuation report. The first excerpt provides a qualitative and quantitative analysis from RBC's report as of November 25, 2013 (*reproduced with permission*):

Investment summary We rate P&G Sector Perform. Its shares have performed well over the past two years and now trade at a valuation in line with its HPC peers despite lagging on both top-line and EBIT growth. While we continue to believe P&G has the inherent ability to deliver revenue, EPS, and cash flow growth above the sector average due to its stable of iconic brands and favorable geographic/category exposure, we wait on the sidelines until we get more clarity on: 1) any major changes that Mr. Lafley may make to the organizational design; 2) if the company's efforts to turn beauty will gain traction (not the case so far); and 3) if it can begin to close the overall growth gap between itself and its peers, with a healthy balance across categories and geographies.

continued

Target price/ base case In our DCF-driven base case, we value P&G shares at $91. Our assumptions include a top-line CAGR of 3% and peak EBIT margins of 23% by FY23. We expect P&G to grow organic sales in the low-single digits due to an elevated competitive environment and see the company expanding margins modestly behind ongoing cost savings. We assume a cost of capital in the long run of 7.7% and a terminal growth rate of 2.5%. Our $91 price target implies 18x our FY16 EPS estimate of $5.04.

Upside scenario In our DCF-driven upside case, we value P&G shares at $111. Our assumptions include a top-line CAGR of 4% and peak EBIT margins of 24% by FY23. In this scenario, we expect P&G to grow organic sales in the mid-single digits as it manages to turn around its struggling beauty business and executes on incremental cost-savings opportunities, driving margins higher. We assume a cost of capital in the long run of 7.7% and a terminal growth rate of 3%. Our $111 target implies 21x our FY16 EPS upside estimate of $5.27.

Downside scenario In our DCF-driven downside case, we value P&G shares at $70. Our assumptions include a top-line CAGR of 3% and peak EBIT margins of 21% by 2022. In this scenario, we see P&G's beauty and grooming businesses continuing to weigh on its top line and higher input costs limiting margin expansion. We assume a cost of capital in the long run of 7.7% and a terminal growth rate of 1.5%. Our $70 downside case implies 15x our FY16 downside EPS of $4.81.

Risks to our thesis 1) Economic and political instability in international markets, particularly in the euro zone, Middle East, Africa, Venezuela, and Argentina; 2) Volatility in input costs, particularly oil and resin; 3) Heightened promotional activity from competitors, including consumer preference for non-branded private-label products; and 4) Failure of new product launches, including Tide Pods, Simply Tide, and Bounty Basic.

Our second excerpt is a set of assumptions and computations developed by RBC analysts to forecast P&G's target stock price reported as of November 21, 2013 (*reproduced with permission*).

Procter & Gamble Multi-Stage Discounted Cash Flow Model

DCF Assumptions	Stage 1	Stable
Beta	0.80	0.80
Equity Risk Premium	6.0%	6.0%
10-year Treasury rate	3.0%	5.0%
Equity / Total Capital	70.0%	60.0%
Debt / Total Capital	30.0%	40.0%
Cost of Equity	7.8%	9.8%
Cost of Debt	6.0%	6.0%
Tax Rate	26.0%	26.0%
After-tax cost of debt	4.4%	4.4%
Adj. (Regulation Risk)	0.0%	0.0%
WACC	6.8%	7.7%
Terminal Growth:		**2.5%**

P&G	Value
Enterprise Value	$293,960
- Net Debt	28,658
Equity Value	$265,302
Shares Outstanding	2,924
Equity Value/Share	**$91**

Current Price	**$85**
Upside/Downside	**7%**
FY 16 EPS Estimate	$5.04
FY 16 P/E	**18x**
FY 16 EBITDA	$22,389
FY 16 EV/EBITDA	**13x**

			Stage 1		Stage 2 - Stable Period							
($MM)	**2012**	**2013**	**2014E**	**2015E**	**2016E**	**2017E**	**2018E**	**2019E**	**2020E**	**2021E**	**2022E**	**2023E**
Revenue	$83,680	$84,167	**$85,836**	**$88,579**	**$91,416**	**$94,352**	**$97,392**	**$100,541**	**$103,806**	**$107,190**	**$110,701**	**$114,343**
Y/Y Growth	2%	1%	*2%*	*3%*	*3%*	*3%*	*3%*	*3%*	*3%*	*3%*	*3%*	*3%*
EBIT	15,668	15,899	**16,973**	**17,937**	**18,733**	**19,663**	**20,642**	**21,671**	**22,753**	**23,889**	**25,084**	**26,338**
Y/Y Growth	48%	1%	*7%*	*6%*	*4%*	*5%*	*5%*	*5%*	*5%*	*5%*	*5%*	*5%*
EBIT Margin	19%	19%	*20%*	*20%*	*20%*	*21%*	*21%*	*22%*	*22%*	*22%*	*23%*	*23%*
Marginal Tax Rate	24%	23%	*25%*	*26%*	*26%*	*26%*	*26%*	*26%*	*26%*	*26%*	*26%*	*26%*
Tax-Affected EBIT	11,930	12,204	**12,796**	**13,273**	**13,862**	**14,551**	**15,275**	**16,037**	**16,837**	**17,678**	**18,562**	**19,490**
+ Depreciation	3,204	2,982	$3,356	$3,543	$3,657	$3,774	$3,896	$4,022	$4,152	$4,288	$4,428	$4,574
% of Sales	*4%*	*4%*	*3.9%*	*4%*	*4%*	*4%*	*4%*	*4%*	*4%*	*4%*	*4%*	*4%*
- CapEx	3,964	4,008	$3,310	$3,543	$3,657	$3,774	$3,896	$4,022	$4,152	$4,288	$4,428	$4,574
% of Sales	*5%*	*5%*	*4%*	*4%*	*4%*	*4%*	*4%*	*4%*	*4%*	*4%*	*4%*	*4%*
- Change in WC	-625	-827	-$646	-$430	-$360	-$251	-$134	-$139	-$144	-$149	-$154	-$160
			1	2	3	4	5	6	7	8	9	10
Free Cash Flow to Firm	11,795	12,005	**13,488**	**13,703**	**14,222**	**14,802**	**15,410**	**16,176**	**16,981**	**17,828**	**18,716**	**19,650**
Y/Y Growth		2%	*12%*	*2%*	*4%*	*4%*	*4%*	*5%*	*5%*	*5%*	*5%*	*5%*
Terminal Value												**$390,633**
Cost of Equity			8%	8%	10%	10%	10%	10%	10%	10%	10%	10%
Equity/Total Capital			70%	70%	60%	60%	60%	60%	60%	60%	60%	60%
After Tax Cost of Debt			4%	4%	4%	4%	4%	4%	4%	4%	4%	4%
Debt/Total Capital			30%	30%	40%	40%	40%	40%	40%	40%	40%	40%
Other Adjustments			0%	0%	0%	0%	0%	0%	0%	0%	0%	0%
WACC			**7%**	**7%**	**8%**	**8%**	**8%**	**8%**	**8%**	**8%**	**8%**	**8%**
PV of FCFF			**12,630**	**12,016**	**11,399**	**11,020**	**10,656**	**10,391**	**10,132**	**9,881**	**9,636**	**196,201**

Source: Company reports, RBC Capital Markets estimates. Note: Priced as of market close, November 21, 2013 ET.

continued

continued from prior page

		Weighted Average Cost of Capital				
		6.7%	7.2%	7.7%	8.2%	8.7%
Terminal Growth Rate	1.5%	$98	$88	$80	$73	$67
	2.0%	$106	$94	$85	$77	$70
	2.5%	$116	$102	$91	$82	$74
	3.0%	$128	$111	$98	$87	$79
	3.5%	$144	$123	$107	$94	$84

We make four observations on this analyst report regarding P&G's target stock price.

1. The analyst report defines free cash flow to the firm as follows:

	Earnings before interest and taxes (EBIT)
−	Taxes (EBIT × assumed tax rate)
+	Depreciation
−	Capital expenditures
−	Increase in working capital
=	Free cash flow to the Firm

2. This analyst report uses the same DCF computation we describe in this module. The analyst highlights the importance of the terminal period computation with a matrix that quantifies the impact on stock price of (1) growth rates subsequent to the forecasting horizon and (2) WACC. This type of sensitivity analysis is a useful way to identify crucial assumptions. We see that a 1 percentage point change in WACC results in a roughly 25% change in stock price estimate. Further, a 1 percentage point change in the terminal growth rate results in a roughly 15% change in stock price estimate.
3. The cost of equity capital is estimated using the capital asset pricing model (CAPM) as we describe in the module. The analyst's estimated WACC is 6.8% and 7.7% for the two period stages of the analysis, similar to the 7% WACC that we assumed in the module. It is not uncommon that model assumptions differ among analysts, which highlights the importance of sensitivity analyses that quantify the effects of varying model assumptions.
4. Bottom line: We see that this analyst's $91 stock price target is slightly higher than the $84.35 stock price estimate that we independently determined in this module. There are a number of differences between our forecast and that of the RBC analyst, including growth rates and margins. It is not uncommon for analyst reports to differ in their underlying assumptions.

APPENDIX 12C: Derivation of Free Cash Flow Formula

Derivation of the free cash flow formula follows; our thanks to Professor Jim Boatsman for this exposition:

Assets = Liabilities + Stockholders' Equity (SE)

NOA = NNO + SE

ΔNOA = ΔNNO + ΔSE [in change form, where Δ refers to change]

ΔNOA = ΔNNO + ΔContributed Capital (CC) + Net Income − Dividends (DIV)[substituting f

ΔNOA = ΔNNO + ΔCC + (NOPAT − NNE) − DIV [substituting for NI]

− NOPAT + ΔNOA = ΔNNO + ΔCC − NNE − DIV [rearranging terms]

NOPAT − ΔNOA = NNE − ΔNNO − ΔCC + DIV [multiplying by −1]

NOPAT − ΔNOA: Free cash flows to the firm (FCFF)

NNE − ΔNNO − ΔCC + DIV: Net payments to holders of net nonoperating obligations and stock

GUIDANCE ANSWERS

MANAGERIAL DECISION You Are the Chief Financial Officer

Cash flow can be increased by reducing assets. For example, receivables can be reduced by the following:

- Encouraging up-front payments or progress billings on long-term contracts
- Increasing credit standards to avoid slow-paying accounts before sales are made
- Monitoring account age and sending reminders to past-due customers
- Selling accounts receivable to a financial institution or special purpose entity

As another example of asset reduction, plant assets can be reduced by the following:

- Selling unused or excess plant assets
- Forming alliances with other companies to share specialized plant assets
- Owning assets in a special purpose entity with other companies
- Selling production facilities to a contract manufacturer and purchasing the output

MANAGERIAL DECISION You Are the Chief Financial Officer

RNOA can be disaggregated into its two key drivers: net operating profit margin and net operating asset turnover. Net operating profit margin can be increased by improving gross profit margins (better product pricing, lower-cost manufacturing, etc.) and closely monitoring and controlling operating expenses. Net operating asset turnover can be increased by reducing net operating working capital (better monitoring of receivables, better management of inventories, carefully extending payables, etc.) and making more effective use of plant assets (disposing of unused assets, forming corporate alliances to increase plant asset capacity, selling productive assets to contract producers and purchasing the output, etc.). The ROPI model effectively focuses managers on the balance sheet *and* income statement.

DISCUSSION QUESTIONS

Q12-1. Explain how information contained in financial statements is useful in pricing securities. Are there some components of earnings that are more useful than others in this regard? What nonfinancial information might also be useful?

Q12-2. In general, what role do expectations play in pricing equity securities? What is the relation between security prices and expected returns (the discount rate, or WACC, in this case)?

Q12-3. What are free cash flows to the firm (FCFF) and how are they used in the pricing of equity securities?

Q12-4. Define the weighted average cost of capital (WACC).

Q12-5. Define net operating profit after tax (NOPAT).

Q12-6. Define net operating assets (NOA).

Q12-7. Define the concept of residual operating income. How is residual operating income used in pricing equity securities?

Q12-8. What insight does disaggregation of RNOA into net operating profit margin and net operating asset turnover provide for managing a company?

Assignments with the ✔ logo in the margin are available in myBusinessCourse. See the Preface of the book for details.

MINI EXERCISES

M12-9. Interpreting Earnings Announcement Effects on Stock Prices (LO1, 2)

On October 30, 2013, **Starbucks Corp.** announced its 2013 earnings of $0.63 per share (up 17 cents per share over the prior year) and 3 cents higher than analysts' expectations. Starbucks' stock fell 3% in after-hours trading according to **CNBC**. Why do you believe that Starbucks' stock price fell despite the good news?

Starbucks Corp. (SBUX)

M12-10. Computing Residual Operating Income (ROPI) (LO3)

Halliburton Company reports net operating profit after tax (NOPAT) of $2,799 million in 2012. Its net operating assets at the beginning of 2012 are $15,338 million. Assuming a 10% weighted average cost of capital (WACC), what is Halliburton's residual operating income for 2012? Show computations.

Halliburton Company (HAL)

Halliburton Company (HAL)

M12-11. Computing Free Cash Flows to the Firm (FCFF) (LO2)
Halliburton Company reports net operating profit after tax (NOPAT) of $2,799 million in 2012. Its net operating assets at the beginning of 2012 are $15,338 million and are $18,126 million at the end of 2012. What are Halliburton's free cash flows to the firm (FCFF) for 2012? Show computations.

CVS Caremark Corp. (CVS)

M12-12. Computing, Analyzing and Interpreting Residual Operating Income (ROPI) (LO3)
In its 2012 fiscal year annual report, CVS Caremark Corp. reports net operating income after tax (NOPAT) of $4,452 million. As of the beginning of fiscal year 2012 it reports net operating assets of $46,152 million.

a. Did CVS earn positive residual operating income (ROPI) in 2012 if its weighted average cost of capital (WACC) is 7%? Explain.
b. At what level of WACC would CVS not report positive residual operating income for 2012? Explain.

Target Corporation (TGT)

M12-13. Estimating Share Value Using the DCF Model (LO1, 2)
Following are forecasts of Target Corporation's sales, net operating profit after tax (NOPAT), and net operating assets (NOA) as of February 2, 2013.

	Reported	Horizon Period				Terminal
(In millions)	2013	2014	2015	2016	2017	Period
Sales	$73,301	$76,893	$80,660	$84,613	$88,759	$89,646
NOPAT	3,479	3,614	3,791	3,977	4,172	4,213
NOA	27,581	28,907	30,323	31,809	33,368	33,702

Answer the following requirements assuming a terminal period growth rate of 1%, a discount rate (WACC) of 7%, common shares outstanding of 645 million, and net nonoperating obligations (NNO) of $11,023 million.

a. Estimate the value of a share of Target common stock using the discounted cash flow (DCF) model as of February 2, 2013.
b. Target Corporation (TGT) stock closed at $68.52 on March 20, 2013, the date the 10-K was filed with the SEC. How does your valuation estimate compare with this closing price? What do you believe are some reasons for the difference?

Target Corporation (TGT)

M12-14. Estimating Share Value Using the ROPI Model (LO3)
Refer to the information in M12-13 to answer the following requirements.

a. Estimate the value of a share of Target common stock using the residual operating income (ROPI) model as of February 2, 2013.
b. Target Corporation (TGT) stock closed at $68.52 on March 20, 2013, the date the 10-K was filed with the SEC. How does your valuation estimate compare with this closing price? What do you believe are some reasons for the difference?

EXERCISES

Abercrombie & Fitch Co. (ANF)

E12-15. Estimating Share Value Using the DCF Model (LO1, 2)
Following are forecasts of Abercrombie & Fitch Co.'s sales, net operating profit after tax (NOPAT), and net operating assets (NOA) as of February 2, 2013.

	Reported	Horizon Period				Terminal
(In millions)	2013	2014	2015	2016	2017	Period
Sales	$4,511	$4,872	$5,262	$5,683	$6,138	$6,261
NOPAT	242	261	282	305	329	336
NOA	1,446	1,562	1,687	1,821	1,967	2,007

Answer the following requirements assuming a discount rate (WACC) of 10%, a terminal period growth rate of 2%, common shares outstanding of 78.4 million, and net nonoperating obligations (NNO) of $(372) million (negative NNO reflects net nonoperating assets such as investments rather than net obligations).

a. Estimate the value of a share of Abercrombie & Fitch common stock using the discounted cash flow (DCF) model as of February 2, 2013.

b. Abercrombie & Fitch (ANF) stock closed at $45.46 on April 2, 2013, the date the 10-K was filed with the SEC. How does your valuation estimate compare with this closing price? What do you believe are some reasons for the difference?

E12-16. Estimating Share Value Using the ROPI Model (LO3)

Abercrombie & Fitch Co. (ANF)

Refer to the information in E12-15 to answer the following requirements.

a. Estimate the value of a share of Abercrombie & Fitch common stock using the residual operating income (ROPI) model as of February 2, 2013.

b. Abercrombie & Fitch stock closed at $45.46 on April 2, 2013, the date the 10-K was filed with the SEC. How does your valuation estimate compare with this closing price? What do you believe are some reasons for the difference?

E12-17. Estimating Share Value Using the DCF Model (LO1, 2)

Wal-Mart Stores, Inc. (WMT)

Following are forecasts of sales, net operating profit after tax (NOPAT), and net operating assets (NOA) as of January 31, 2013, for **Wal-Mart Stores, Inc.**

	Reported	Horizon Period				Terminal
(In millions)	2013	2014	2015	2016	2017	Period
Sales.	$469,162	$492,620	$517,251	$543,114	$570,269	$575,972
NOPAT	19,056	20,197	21,207	22,268	23,381	23,615
NOA	128,612	134,964	141,713	148,798	156,238	157,801

Answer the following requirements assuming a discount rate (WACC) of 7%, a terminal period growth rate of 1%, common shares outstanding of 3,314 million, net nonoperating obligations (NNO) of $46,874 million, and noncontrolling interest (NCI) on the balance sheet of $5,395 million.

a. Estimate the value of a share of Wal-Mart's common stock using the discounted cash flow (DCF) model as of January 31, 2013.

b. Wal-Mart (WMT) stock closed at $74.77 on March 26, 2013, the date the 10-K was filed with the SEC. How does your valuation estimate compare with this closing price? What do you believe are some reasons for the difference?

E12-18. Estimating Share Value Using the ROPI Model (LO3)

Wal-Mart Stores, Inc. (WMT)

Refer to the information in E12-17 to answer the following requirements.

a. Estimate the value of a share of Wal-Mart common stock using the residual operating income (ROPI) model as of January 31, 2013.

b. Wal-Mart (WMT) stock closed at $74.77 on March 26, 2013, the date the 10-K was filed with the SEC. How does your valuation estimate compare with this closing price? What do you believe are some reasons for the difference?

E12-19. Identifying and Computing Net Operating Assets (NOA) and Net Nonoperating Obligations (NNO) (LO1, 2)

Halliburton Company (HAL)

Following is the balance sheet for **Halliburton Company**.

HALLIBURTON COMPANY
Consolidated Balance Sheets

At December 31 (Millions of dollars and shares except per share data)	2012	2011
Assets		
Current assets:		
Cash and equivalents.	$ 2,484	$ 2,698
Receivables (less allowance for bad debts of $92 and $137)	5,787	5,084
Inventories	3,186	2,570
Current deferred income taxes.	351	321
Other current assets.	1,278	904
Total current assets	13,086	11,577
Property, plant, and equipment, net of accumulated depreciation of $8,056 and $7,096	10,257	8,492
Goodwill	2,135	1,776
Other assets.	1,932	1,832
Total assets.	$27,410	$23,677

continued

continued from prior page

Liabilities and shareholders' equity		
Current liabilities:		
Accounts payable	$ 2,041	$ 1,826
Accrued employee compensation and benefits	930	862
Deferred revenue	307	309
Other current liabilities	1,474	1,124
Total current liabilities	4,752	4,121
Long-term debt	4,820	4,820
Employee compensation and benefits	607	534
Other liabilities	1,441	986
Total liabilities	11,620	10,461
Shareholders' equity:		
Common shares, par value $2.50 per share – authorized 2,000 shares, issued 1,073 and 1,073 shares	2,682	2,683
Paid-in capital in excess of par value	486	455
Accumulated other comprehensive loss	(309)	(273)
Retained earnings	17,182	14,880
Treasury stock, at cost—144 and 152 shares	(4,276)	(4,547)
Company shareholders' equity	15,765	13,198
Noncontrolling interest in consolidated subsidiaries	25	18
Total shareholders' equity	15,790	13,216
Total liabilities and shareholders' equity	$27,410	$23,677

a. Compute net operating assets (NOA) and net nonoperating obligations (NNO) for 2012.

b. For 2012, show that: NOA = NNO + Stockholders' equity.

Halliburton Company (HAL)

E12-20. Identifying and Computing Net Operating Profit after Tax (NOPAT) and Net Nonoperating Expense (NNE) **(LO1, 2)**

Following is the income statement for **Halliburton Company**.

Consolidated Statements of Operations			
Year Ended December 31 (Millions of dollars)	**2012**	**2011**	**2010**
Revenue:			
Services	$22,196	$19,692	$13,779
Product sales	6,307	5,137	4,194
Total revenue	28,503	24,829	17,973
Operating costs and expenses:			
Cost of services	18,747	15,432	11,227
Cost of sales	5,322	4,379	3,508
General and administrative	275	281	229
Total operating costs and expenses	24,344	20,092	14,964
Operating income	4,159	4,737	3,009
Interest expense, net of interest income of $7, $5, and $11	(298)	(263)	(297)
Other, net	(39)	(25)	(57)
Income from continuing operations before income taxes	3,822	4,449	2,655
Provision for income taxes	(1,235)	(1,439)	(853)
Income from continuing operations	2,587	3,010	1,802
Income (loss) from discontinued operations, net of income tax (provision) benefit of $82, $(18), and $75	58	(166)	40
Net income	2,645	2,844	1,842
Noncontrolling interest in net income of subsidiaries	(10)	(5)	(7)
Net income attributable to company	$ 2,635	$ 2,839	$ 1,835
Amounts attributable to company shareholders:			
Income from continuing operations	$ 2,577	$ 3,005	$ 1,795
Income (loss) from discontinued operations, net	58	(166)	40
Net income attributable to company	$ 2,635	$ 2,839	$ 1,835

Compute net operating profit after tax (NOPAT) for 2012, assuming a federal and state statutory tax rate of 37%.

E12-21. Estimating Share Value Using the DCF Model (LO1, 2)

Following are forecasts of Halliburton Company's sales, net operating profit after tax (NOPAT), and net operating assets (NOA) as of December 31, 2012.

Halliburton Company (HAL)

(In millions)	Reported 2012	Horizon Period 2013	2014	2015	2016	Terminal Period
Sales.	$28,503	$32,778	$37,695	$43,349	$49,851	$51,845
NOPAT	2,799	3,219	3,702	4,257	4,895	5,091
NOA	18,126	20,878	24,010	27,611	31,752	33,022

Answer the following requirements assuming a discount rate (WACC) of 10%, a terminal period growth rate of 4%, common shares outstanding of 929 million, net nonoperating obligations (NNO) of $2,336 million, and noncontrolling interest (NCI) on the balance sheet of $25 million.

a. Estimate the value of a share of Halliburton's common stock using the discounted cash flow (DCF) model as of December 31, 2012.

b. Halliburton Company (HAL) stock closed at $40.87 on February 11, 2013, the date the Form 10-K was filed with the SEC. How does your valuation estimate compare with this closing price? What do you believe are some reasons for the difference?

E12-22. Estimating Share Value Using the ROPI Model (LO3)

Refer to the information in E12-21 to answer the following requirements.

Halliburton Company (HAL)

a. Estimate the value of a share of Halliburton Company common stock using the residual operating income (ROPI) model as of December 31, 2012.

b. Halliburton Company stock closed at $40.87 on February 11, 2013, the date the Form 10-K was filed with the SEC. How does your valuation estimate compare with this closing price? What do you believe are some reasons for the difference?

E12-23. Explaining the Equivalence of Valuation Models and the Relevance of Earnings (LO1, 2, 3)

This module focused on two different valuation models: the discounted cash flow (DCF) model and the residual operating income (ROPI) model. The models focus on free cash flows to the firm and on residual operating income, respectively. We stressed that these two models are theoretically equivalent.

a. What is the *intuition* for why these models are equivalent?

b. Some analysts focus on cash flows as they believe that companies manage earnings, which presumably makes earnings less relevant. Are earnings relevant? Explain.

E12-24. Applying and Interpreting Value Driver Components of RNOA (LO3)

The net operating profit margin and the net operating asset turnover components of return on net operating assets are often termed *value drivers,* which refers to their positive influence on stock value by virtue of their role as components of return on net operating assets (RNOA).

a. How do profit margins and asset turnover ratios influence stock values?

b. Assuming that profit margins and asset turnover ratios are value drivers, what insight does this give us about managing companies if the goal is to create shareholder value?

PROBLEMS

P12-25. Forecasting and Estimating Share Value Using the DCF Model (LO1, 2)

Following are the income statement and balance sheet for Intel Corporation.

Intel Corporation (INTC)

INTEL CORPORATION
Consolidated Statements of Income

Years Ended December (In Millions, Except Per Share Amounts)	2012	2011	2010
Net revenue	$53,341	$53,999	$43,623
Cost of sales	20,190	20,242	15,132
Gross margin	33,151	33,757	28,491
Research and development	10,148	8,350	6,576
Marketing, general and administrative	8,057	7,670	6,309
Amortization of acquisition-related intangibles	308	260	18
Operating expenses	18,513	16,280	12,903
Operating income	14,638	17,477	15,588
Gains (losses) on equity investments, net	141	112	348
Interest and other, net	94	192	109
Income before taxes	14,873	17,781	16,045
Provision for taxes	3,868	4,839	4,581
Net income	$11,005	$12,942	$11,464

INTEL CORPORATION
Consolidated Balance Sheets

As of Year Ended (In millions, except par value)	Dec. 29, 2012	Dec. 31, 2011
Assets		
Current assets		
Cash and cash equivalents	$ 8,478	$ 5,065
Short-term investments	3,999	5,181
Trading assets	5,685	4,591
Accounts receivable, net	3,833	3,650
Inventories	4,734	4,096
Deferred tax assets	2,117	1,700
Other current assets	2,512	1,589
Total current assets	31,358	25,872
Property, plant and equipment, net	27,983	23,627
Marketable equity securities	4,424	562
Other long-term investments[1]	493	889
Goodwill	9,710	9,254
Identified intangible assets, net	6,235	6,267
Other long-term assets	4,148	4,648
Total assets	$84,351	$71,119
Liabilities and stockholders' equity		
Current liabilities		
Short-term debt	$ 312	$ 247
Accounts payable	3,023	2,956
Accrued compensation and benefits	2,972	2,948
Accrued advertising	1,015	1,134
Deferred income	1,932	1,929
Other accrued liabilities	3,644	2,814
Total current liabilities	12,898	12,028
Long-term debt	13,136	7,084
Long-term deferred tax liabilities	3,412	2,617
Other long-term liabilities	3,702	3,479

continued

Stockholders' equity		
Preferred stock, $0.001 par value, 50 shares authorized; none issued	—	—
Common stock, $0.001 par value, 10,000 shares authorized; 4,944 issued and outstanding (5,000 issued and outstanding in 2011) and capital in excess of par value	19,464	17,036
Accumulated other comprehensive income (loss)	(399)	(781)
Retained earnings	32,138	29,656
Total stockholders' equity	51,203	45,911
Total liabilities and stockholders' equity	$84,351	$71,119

[1] These investments are operating assets as they relate to associated companies.

Required

a. Compute Intel's net operating assets (NOA) for year-end 2012.

b. Compute net operating profit after tax (NOPAT) for 2012, assuming a federal and state statutory tax rate of 37%.

c. Forecast Intel's sales, NOPAT, and NOA for years 2013 through 2016 using the following assumptions:

Sales growth	10%
Net operating profit margin (NOPM)	20.4%
Net operating asset turnover (NOAT) at year-end	1.27

Forecast the terminal period value assuming a 1% terminal period growth and using the NOPM and NOAT assumptions above.

d. Estimate the value of a share of Intel common stock using the discounted cash flow (DCF) model as of December 29, 2012; assume a discount rate (WACC) of 11%, common shares outstanding of 4,944 million, and net nonoperating obligations (NNO) of $(9,138) million (NNO is negative which means that Intel has net nonoperating investments).

e. Intel (INTC) stock closed at $21.09 on February 19, 2013, the date the Form 10-K was filed with the SEC. How does your valuation estimate compare with this closing price? What do you believe are some reasons for the difference? What investment decision is suggested from your results?

P12-26. Estimating Share Value Using the ROPI Model (LO3)

Intel Corporation (INTC)

Refer to the information in P12-25 to answer the following requirements.

Required

a. Estimate the value of a share of Intel common stock using the residual operating income (ROPI) model as of December 29, 2012.

b. Intel stock closed at $21.09 on February 19, 2013, the date the Form 10-K was filed with the SEC. How does your valuation estimate compare with this closing price? What do you believe are some reasons for the difference? What investment decision is suggested from your results?

P12-27. Forecasting and Estimating Share Value Using the DCF Model (LO1, 2)

CVS Caremark Corp. (CVS)

Following are the income statement and balance sheet for CVS Caremark Corp.

CVS CAREMARK CORP.
Balance Sheets

(In millions, except per share amounts)	Dec. 31, 2012	Dec. 31, 2011
Assets		
Cash and cash equivalents	$ 1,375	$ 1,413
Short-term investments	5	5
Accounts receivable, net	6,473	6,047
Inventories	10,759	10,046
Deferred income taxes	663	503
Other current assets	577	580
Total current assets	19,852	18,594
Property and equipment, net	8,632	8,467
Goodwill	26,395	26,458
Intangible assets, net	9,753	9,869
Other assets	1,280	1,155
Total assets	$65,912	$64,543

continued

continued from prior page

Liabilities		
Accounts payable	$ 5,070	$ 4,370
Claims and discounts payable	3,974	3,487
Accrued expenses	4,051	3,293
Short-term debt	690	750
Current portion of long-term debt	5	56
Total current liabilities	13,790	11,956
Long-term debt	9,133	9,208
Deferred income taxes	3,784	3,853
Other long-term liabilities	1,501	1,445
Redeemable noncontrolling interest	—	30
Shareholders' equity		
Preferred stock, par value $0.01: 0.1 shares authorized; none issued or outstanding		
Common stock, par value $0.01: 3,200 shares authorized; 1,667 shares issued and 1,231 shares outstanding at December 31, 2012 and 1,640 shares issued and 1,298 shares outstanding at December 31, 2011	17	16
Treasury stock, at cost: 435 shares at December 31, 2012 and 340 shares at December 31, 2011	(16,270)	(11,953)
Shares held in trust: 1 share at December 31, 2012 and 2 shares at December 31, 2011	(31)	(56)
Capital surplus	29,120	28,126
Retained earnings	25,049	22,090
Accumulated other comprehensive loss	(181)	(172)
Total shareholders' equity	37,704	38,051
Total liabilities and shareholders' equity	$65,912	$64,543

CVS CAREMARK, CORP.
Consolidated Statements of Income

(In millions)	Dec. 31, 2012	Dec. 31, 2011	Dec. 31, 2010
Net revenues	$123,133	$107,100	$95,778
Cost of revenues	100,627	86,539	75,559
Gross profit	22,506	20,561	20,219
Operating expenses	15,278	14,231	14,082
Operating profit	7,228	6,330	6,137
Interest expense, net	557	584	536
Loss on early extinguishment of debt	348	—	—
Income before income tax provision	6,323	5,746	5,601
Income tax provision	2,441	2,258	2,179
Income from continuing operations	3,882	3,488	3,422
Income (loss) from discontinued operations, net of tax	(7)	(31)	2
Net income	3,875	3,457	3,424
Net loss attributable to noncontrolling interest	2	4	3
Net income attributable to CVS Caremark	$ 3,877	$ 3,461	$ 3,427

Required

a. Compute net operating assets (NOA) as of December 31, 2012.

b. Compute net operating profit after tax (NOPAT) for fiscal year ended December 31, 2012, assuming a federal and state statutory tax rate of 37%.

c. Forecast CVS's sales, NOPAT, and NOA for 2013 through 2016 using the following assumptions:

Sales growth	10%
Net operating profit margin (NOPM)	3.6%
Net operating asset turnover (NOAT) at fiscal year-end	2.67

Forecast the terminal period value assuming a 1% terminal period growth and using the NOPM and NOAT assumptions above.

d. Estimate the value of a share of CVS common stock using the discounted cash flow (DCF) model as of December 31, 2012; assume a discount rate (WACC) of 7%, common shares outstanding of 1,231 million, and net nonoperating obligations (NNO) of $8,448 million.

e. CVS's stock closed at $51.12 on February 15, 2013, the date the Form 10-K was filed with the SEC. How does your valuation estimate compare with this closing price? What do you believe are some reasons for the difference?

P12-28. Estimating Share Value Using the ROPI Model (LO3)

Refer to the information in P12-27 to answer the following requirements.

CVS Caremark Corp. (CVS)

Required

a. Estimate the value of a share of CVS common stock using the residual operating income (ROPI) model as of December 31, 2012.

b. CVS stock closed at $51.12 on February 15, 2013, the date the Form 10-K was filed with the SEC. How does your valuation estimate compare with this closing price? What do you believe are some reasons for the difference? What investment decision is suggested from your results?

P12-29. Forecasting and Estimating Share Value Using the DCF Model (LO1, 2)

Following are the income statement and balance sheet for **Abbott Laboratories (ABT)**.

Abbott Laboratories (ABT)

ABBOTT LABORATORIES
Consolidated Balance Sheet

December 31 (dollars in thousands)	2012	2011	2010
Current Assets:			
Cash and cash equivalents	$10,802,163	$ 6,812,820	$ 3,648,371
Investments, primarily bank time deposits and U.S. treasury bills	4,371,821	1,284,539	1,803,079
Restricted funds, primarily U.S. treasury bills	—	—	1,872,490
Trade receivables, less allowances of — 2012: $405,921; 2011: $420,579; 2010: $388,564	7,612,860	7,683,920	7,184,034
Inventories:			
Finished products	2,345,455	2,220,527	2,058,735
Work in process	628,874	432,358	383,580
Materials	817,984	631,364	746,419
Total inventories	3,792,313	3,284,249	3,188,734
Deferred income taxes	2,986,216	2,700,540	3,076,051
Other prepaid expenses and receivables	1,757,210	2,002,706	1,544,770
Total current assets	31,322,583	23,768,774	22,317,529
Investments	273,595	378,225	302,049
Property and equipment, at cost:			
Land	604,462	633,917	648,988
Buildings	4,259,240	4,467,387	4,334,236
Equipment	13,110,833	12,216,388	11,813,618
Construction in progress	954,352	698,873	577,460
	18,928,887	18,016,565	17,374,302
Less: accumulated depreciation and amortization	10,865,840	10,142,610	9,403,346
Net property and equipment	8,063,047	7,873,955	7,970,956
Intangible assets, net of amortization	8,588,285	9,989,636	12,151,628
Goodwill	15,774,127	15,705,380	15,930,077
Deferred income taxes and other assets	3,213,307	2,560,923	1,901,613
	$67,234,944	$60,276,893	$60,573,852
Liabilities and shareholders' investment			
Current liabilities:			
Short-term borrowings	$ 2,081,839	$ 2,347,859	$ 4,349,796
Trade accounts payable	1,796,990	1,721,127	1,535,759
Salaries, wages and commissions	1,427,765	1,260,121	1,328,665
Other accrued liabilities	6,787,995	7,854,994	6,014,772
Dividends payable	221,340	754,284	680,749
Income taxes payable	655,424	514,947	1,307,723
Current portion of long-term debt	308,823	1,026,896	2,044,970
Total current liabilities	13,280,176	15,480,228	17,262,434
Long-term debt	18,085,302	12,039,822	12,523,517
Post-employment obligations and other long-term liabilities	9,056,234	8,230,698	8,022,770

continued

continued from prior page

Shareholders' investment:			
Preferred shares, one dollar par value authorized—1,000,000 shares, none issued	—	—	—
Common shares, without par value authorized—2,400,000,000 shares Issued at stated capital amount—Shares: 2012: 1,675,930,484; 2011: 1,638,870,201; 2010: 1,619,689,876	11,754,552	9,817,134	8,744,703
Common shares held in treasury, at cost—Shares: 2012: 99,262,992; 2011: 68,491,382; 2010: 72,705,928	(5,590,909)	(3,687,478)	(3,916,823)
Earnings employed in the business	24,150,996	20,907,362	19,215,768
Accumulated other comprehensive income (loss)	(3,593,678)	(2,597,185)	(1,366,846)
Total Abbott shareholders' investment	26,720,961	24,439,833	22,676,802
Noncontrolling interests in subsidiaries	92,271	86,312	88,329
Total shareholders' investment	26,813,232	24,526,145	22,765,131
	$67,234,944	$60,276,893	$60,573,852

ABBOTT LABORATORIES
Consolidated Statement of Earnings

For Year Ended December 31 (dollars in thousands)	2012	2011	2010
Net sales	$39,873,910	$38,851,259	$35,166,721
Cost of products sold	15,119,718	15,540,580	14,665,192
Research and development	4,322,182	4,129,414	3,724,424
Acquired in-process and collaborations research and development	288,000	672,500	313,200
Selling, general and administrative	12,059,495	12,756,817	10,376,324
Total operating cost and expenses	31,789,395	33,099,311	29,079,140
Operating earnings	8,084,515	5,751,948	6,087,581
Interest expense	592,403	530,141	553,135
Interest (income)	(79,225)	(85,196)	(105,453)
Net loss on extinguishment of debt	1,350,973	—	—
Net foreign exchange (gain) loss	(8,044)	(50,271)	(10,924)
Other (income) expense, net	(34,206)	158,632	(62,011)
Earnings before taxes	6,262,614	5,198,642	5,712,834
Taxes on earnings	299,694	470,193	1,086,662
Net earnings	$5,962,920	$4,728,449	$4,626,172

Required

a. Compute net operating assets (NOA) for year-end 2012.

b. Compute net operating profit after tax (NOPAT) for 2012 assuming a federal and state statutory tax rate of 37%.

c. Forecast Abbott Laboratories' sales, NOPAT, and NOA for 2013 through 2016 using the following assumptions:

Sales growth	3%
Net operating profit margin (NOPM)	15%
Net operating asset turnover (NOAT), year-end	1.2

Forecast the terminal period value assuming a 1% terminal period growth and using the NOPM and NOAT assumptions above. For simplicity, prepare your forecasts in $ millions.

d. Estimate the value of a share of Abbott Laboratories' common stock using the discounted cash flow (DCF) model as of December 31, 2012; assume a discount rate (WACC) of 7%, common shares outstanding of 1,577 million, net nonoperating obligations (NNO) of $5,250 million, and noncontrolling interest (NCI) from the balance sheet of $92 million.

e. Abbott Laboratories (ABT) stock closed at $35.08 on February 15, 2013, the date the Form 10-K was filed with the SEC. How does your valuation estimate compare with this closing price? What do you believe are some reasons for the difference? What investment decision is suggested from your results?

P12-30. Estimating Share Value Using the ROPI Model (LO3)
Refer to the information in P12-29 to answer the following requirements.

Abbott Laboratories (ABT)

Required

a. Estimate the value of a share of Abbott Laboratories common stock using the residual operating income (ROPI) model as of December 31, 2012. For simplicity, prepare your forecasts in $ millions.

b. Abbott Laboratories stock closed at $35.08 on February 15, 2013, the date the Form 10-K was filed with the SEC. How does your valuation estimate compare with this closing price? What do you believe are some reasons for the difference? What investment decision is suggested from your results?

P12-31. Forecasting and Estimating Share Value Using the DCF Model (LO1, 2)
Following are the income statement and balance sheet for Kellogg Company.

Kellogg Co. (K)

KELLOGG COMPANY Consolidated Statement of Income For Year Ended December 31 (in millions)	2012	2011	2010
Net sales	$14,197	$13,198	$12,397
Cost of goods sold	8,763	8,046	7,055
Selling, general and administrative expense	3,872	3,725	3,305
Operating profit	1,562	1,427	2,037
Interest expense	261	233	248
Other income (expense), net	24	(10)	1
Income before income taxes	1,325	1,184	1,790
Income taxes	363	320	510
Earnings (loss) from joint ventures	(1)	—	—
Net income	961	864	1,280
Net loss attributable to noncontrolling interests	—	(2)	(7)
Net income attributable to Kellogg Company	$ 961	$ 866	$ 1,287

KELLOGG COMPANY Consolidated Balance Sheet (millions, except share data)	2012	2011
Current assets		
Cash and cash equivalents	$ 281	$ 460
Accounts receivable, net	1,454	1,188
Inventories	1,365	1,174
Other current assets	280	247
Total current assets	3,380	3,069
Property, net	3,782	3,281
Goodwill	5,053	3,623
Other intangibles, net	2,359	1,454
Other assets	610	516
Total assets	$15,184	$11,943

continued

continued from prior page

Current liabilities		
Current maturities of long-term debt	$ 755	$ 761
Notes payable	1,065	234
Accounts payable	1,402	1,189
Other current liabilities	1,301	1,129
Total current liabilities	4,523	3,313
Long-term debt	6,082	5,037
Deferred income taxes	523	643
Pension liability	886	560
Other liabilities	690	592
Equity		
Common stock, $.25 par value, 1,000,000,000 shares authorized Issued: 419,718,217 shares in 2012 and 419,484,087 shares in 2011	105	105
Capital in excess of par value	573	522
Retained earnings	5,615	5,305
Treasury stock at cost:		
58,452,083 shares in 2012 and 62,182,500 shares in 2011	(2,943)	(3,130)
Accumulated other comprehensive income (loss)	(931)	(1,006)
Total Kellogg Company equity	2,419	1,796
Noncontrolling interests	61	2
Total equity	2,480	1,798
Total liabilities and equity	$15,184	$11,943

Required

a. Compute net operating assets (NOA) as of year-end 2012.

b. Compute net operating profit after tax (NOPAT) for 2012, assuming a federal and state statutory tax rate of 37%.

c. Forecast Kellogg's sales, NOPAT, and NOA for 2013 through 2016 using the following assumptions:

Sales growth	8%
Net operating profit margin (NOPM)	7.8%
Net operating asset turnover (NOAT), year-end	1.41

Forecast the terminal period value assuming a 1% terminal period growth and using the NOPM and NOAT assumptions above.

d. Estimate the value of a share of Kellogg common stock using the discounted cash flow (DCF) model; assume a discount rate (WACC) of 6%, common shares outstanding of 361.3 million, net nonoperating obligations (NNO) of $7,621 million, and noncontrolling interest (NCI) from the balance sheet of $61 million.

e. Kellogg's stock closed at $59.95 on February 26, 2013, the date the Form 10-K was filed with the SEC. How does your valuation estimate compare with this closing price? What do you believe are some reasons for the difference?

P12-32. Estimating Share Value Using the ROPI Model (LO3)

Kellogg Co. (K)

Refer to the information in P12-31 to answer the following requirements.

Required

a. Estimate the value of a share of Kellogg common stock using the residual operating income (ROPI) model.

b. Kellogg stock closed at $59.95 on February 26, 2013, the date the Form 10-K was filed with the SEC. How does your valuation estimate compare with this closing price? What do you believe are some reasons for the difference? What investment decision is suggested from your results?

IFRS APPLICATIONS

I12-33. Forecasting and Estimating Share Value Using the DCF Model (LO1, 2)
Following are the income statement and balance sheet for Shoppers' Drug Mart, a Canadian retail pharmacy chain. The company's financial statements are prepared in accordance with IFRS and are reported in thousands of Canadian dollars (CDN).

IFRS
Shoppers' Drug Mart (SC.TO)

SHOPPERS' DRUG MART CORPORATION
Income Statement

(in thousands of Canadian dollars, except per share amounts)	2012
Sales	$10,781,848
Cost of goods sold	(6,609,229)
Gross profit	4,172,619
Operating and administrative expenses	(3,291,698)
Operating income	880,921
Finance expenses	(57,595)
Earnings before income taxes	823,326
Income taxes	
Current	(235,791)
Deferred	20,946
	(214,845)
Net earnings	$ 608,481
Net earnings per common share	
Basic	$2.92
Diluted	$2.92
Weighted average common shares outstanding (millions)	
Basic	208.4
Diluted	208.5
Actual common shares outstanding (millions)	204.5

SHOPPERS' DRUG MART CORPORATION
Balance Sheet

(in thousands of Canadian dollars)	December 29, 2012
Current assets	
Cash	$ 104,529
Accounts receivable	469,683
Inventory	2,148,484
Prepaid expenses and deposits	42,301
Total current assets	2,764,997
Non-current assets	
Property and equipment	1,717,993
Investment property	16,379
Goodwill	2,572,707
Intangible assets	339,972
Other assets	22,824
Deferred tax assets	38,849
Total non-current assets	4,708,724
Total assets	$7,473,721

continued

continued from prior page

Liabilities	
Bank indebtedness	$ 170,927
Commercial paper	249,977
Accounts payable and accrued liabilities	1,206,748
Income taxes payable	17,994
Dividends payable	54,180
Current portion of long-term debt	449,798
Provisions	10,926
Associate interest	174,367
Total current liabilities	2,334,917
Long-term debt	247,009
Other long-term liabilities	517,323
Provisions	4,273
Deferred tax liabilities	46,872
Total long-term liabilities	815,477
Total liabilities	3,150,394
Shareholders' equity	
Share capital	1,431,315
Treasury shares	—
Contributed surplus	10,856
Accumulated other comprehensive loss	(35,192)
Retained earnings	2,916,348
Total shareholders' equity	4,323,327
Total liabilities and shareholders' equity	$7,473,721

Required

a. Compute net operating assets (NOA) as of year-end 2012.

b. Compute net operating profit after tax (NOPAT) for 2012, assuming a marginal tax rate of 25.6%.

c. Forecast Shoppers' Drug Mart sales, NOPAT, and NOA for 2013 through 2016 using the following assumptions:

Sales growth	5%
Net operating profit margin (NOPM)	6%
Net operating asset turnover (NOAT)	2.0

Estimate the terminal period value assuming a 2% terminal period growth and using the NOPM and NOAT assumptions, above. For simplicity, prepare your forecasts in millions of Canadian dollars.

d. Estimate the value of a share of Shoppers' Drug Mart's common stock (which trades on the Toronto Stock Exchange) using the discounted cash flow (DCF) model; assume a discount rate (WACC) of 7.5%, common shares outstanding of 204.5 million, and net nonoperating obligations (NNO) of CDN 1,051 million.

e. Shoppers' Drug Mart's stock price was CDN 43.17 on March 27, 2013, the date the annual report was filed with the Canadian Securities Administrators (CSA). How does your valuation estimate compare with this closing price? What do you believe are some reasons for the difference?

I12-34. Estimating Share Value Using the ROPI Model **(LO3)**

Refer to the information in I12-33 to answer the following requirements.

Required

a. Estimate the value of a share of Shoppers' Drug Mart's common stock (which trades on the Toronto Stock Exchange) using the residual operating income (ROPI) model.

b. Shoppers' Drug Mart's stock price was CDN 43.17 on March 27, 2013, the date the annual report was filed with the Canadian Securities Administrators (CSA). How does your valuation estimate compare with this closing price? What do you believe are some reasons for the difference? What investment decision do your results suggest?

MANAGEMENT APPLICATIONS

MA12-35. Management Application: Operating Improvement versus Financial Engineering **(LO4)**

Assume that you are the CEO of a small publicly traded company. The operating performance of your company has fallen below market expectations, which is reflected in a depressed stock price. At your direction, your CFO provides you with the following recommendations that are designed to increase your company's return on net operating assets (RNOA) and your operating cash flows, both of which will, presumably, result in improved financial performance and an increased stock price.

1. To improve net cash flow from operating activities, the CFO recommends that your company reduce inventories (raw material, work-in-progress, and finished goods) and receivables (through selective credit granting and increased emphasis on collection of past due accounts).
2. The CFO recommends that your company sell and lease back its office building. The lease will be structured so as to be classified as an operating lease under GAAP. The assets will, therefore, not be included in the computation of net operating assets (NOA), thus increasing RNOA.
3. The CFO recommends that your company lengthen the time taken to pay accounts payable (lean on the trade) to increase net cash flows from operating activities.
4. Because your company's operating performance is already depressed, the CFO recommends that you take a "big bath;" that is, write off all assets deemed to be impaired and accrue excessive liabilities for future contingencies. The higher current period expense will, then, result in higher future period income as the assets written off will not be depreciated and your company will have a liability account available to absorb future cash payments rather than recording them as expenses.
5. The CFO recommends that your company increase its estimate of expected return on pension investments. This will reduce pension expense and increase operating profit, a component of net operating profit after tax (NOPAT) and, thus, of RNOA.
6. The CFO recommends that your company share ownership of its outbound logistics (trucking division) with another company in a joint venture. This would have the effect of increasing throughput, thus spreading overhead over a larger volume base, and would remove the assets from your company's balance sheet since the joint venture would be accounted for as an equity method investment.

Evaluate each of the CFO's recommendations. In your evaluation, consider whether each recommendation will positively impact the operating performance of your company or whether it is cosmetic in nature.

ONGOING PROJECT

(This ongoing project began in Module 1 and continues through most of the book; even if previous segments were not completed, the requirements are still applicable to any business analysis.) Two common models used to estimate the value of company's equity are: the discounted cash flow (DCF) model and the residual operating income (ROPI) model. Estimate the value of equity and a stock price for the company(ies) under analysis. The aim is to determine an independent measure of value and assess whether the stock appears to be over or under-valued. Begin with the parsimonious forecasts prepared in Module 11. If such forecasts were not prepared, proceed to Module 11 and follow the forecasting steps outlined there.

1. *Model Assumptions and Inputs.* In addition to the assumptions used for the parsimonious model forecasts, we require several additional inputs.
   - Weighted average cost of capital (WACC) is required to discount future amounts to derive present values. We can find estimates at a number of Websites. Find the latest WACC at three or more sites and explore why they differ. One approach would be to use an average in the calculation and then perform sensitivity analysis for the high and the low in the range.
   - Net nonoperating obligations (NNO) is needed to determine the value of equity from total enterprise value.
   - Number of shares outstanding. Recall that shares outstanding is equal to shares issued less treasury shares. The balance sheet typically reports both numbers but if not, we can find the amounts in the statement of shareholders' equity or in a footnote.
2. *Model Estimation.* Use a spreadsheet and follow the method illustrated in Exhibits 12.1 and 12.2 to estimate the DCF and the ROPI models respectively. Here are some tips:
   - Pay close attention to the rounding conventions described in the footnotes in Exhibits 12.1 and 12.2. Use the spreadsheet rounding functions. Note: setting the format of a cell to "no decimals" is not the same as rounding the number; with the former, the decimals are still there, but they are not displayed.

- Make sure that NNO is subtracted from total enterprise value. In some cases, NNO is a negative number; this occurs when nonoperating assets such as cash and marketable securities exceed nonoperating liabilities. By subtracting this negative NNO, the value of equity will be greater than the enterprise value of the firm.
- The stock prices obtained are point estimates derived from a specific set of assumptions. To understand the impact of each assumption, compute alternative stock prices by varying the assumptions. The point is to determine a range of stock prices that derive from a reasonable set of assumptions. One approach is to increase and decrease each of the model assumptions by a reasonable amount such as +/– 10%. Use the spreadsheet functions to perform this sensitivity analysis. Identify which assumptions are most important or impactful.
- Determine the company's actual stock price. Compare the per share estimate to the actual stock price and form an opinion about the relative value. Is the stock over or under-valued according to the model?

3. *Interpretation.* The final step in the project is to evaluate the companies based on all the analysis performed in the ongoing project.
   - Revisit the conclusions made about the companies' performance (profit and margin analysis), asset efficiency, solvency, liquidity, off-balance-sheet financing, and future opportunities based on analysis of strengths, weaknesses, opportunities, and threats. Our goal is to assimilate the various components of analysis and to synthesize what we discovered and learned.
   - Access one or more analyst reports for each company. How do the other professionals see the firms? How does their view differ from ours?
   - Our analysis was based primarily on historical data from financial statements. What additional information would we like to have to refine our opinion? Is this missing information critical to our opinion?
   - Based on our analysis, would we consider investing in the company? Explain.

SOLUTIONS TO REVIEW PROBLEMS

Mid-Module Review

Solution

The following DCF results yield a P&G stock value estimate of $84.36 as of August, 2013. P&G's stock was valued at about $79 at that time. This estimate suggests that P&G's stock is undervalued on that date.

(In millions, except per share values and discount factors)	Reported 2013	Horizon Period 2014	2015	2016	2017	Terminal Period
Increase in NOA[a]		$1,684	$3,839	$3,993	$4,153	$4,318
FCFF (NOPAT − Increase in NOA)		9,678	7,978	8,296	8,628	8,974
Discount factor $[1/(1 + r_w)^t]$		0.93458	0.87344	0.81630	0.76290	
Present value of horizon FCFF		9,045	6,968	6,772	6,582	
Cum present value of horizon FCFF	$ 29,367					
Present value of terminal FCFF	228,209[b]					
Total firm value	257,576					
Less (plus): NNO	25,596					
Less: NCI	645					
Firm equity value	$231,335					
Shares outstanding	2,742.3					
Stock value per share	$ 84.36					

[a] NOA increases are viewed as a cash outflow.

[b] Computed as $\frac{\left(\frac{\$8{,}974\text{ million}}{0.07 - 0.04}\right)}{(1.07)^4}$, or ($8,974 million/0.03) × 0.76290, where 7% is WACC and 4% is the long-term (terminal period) growth rate.

Module-End Review

Solution

The following ROPI results yield a P&G stock value estimate of \$84.35 (small rounding difference from the DCF model) as of August, 2013. P&G's stock was valued at about \$79 at that time. This estimate suggests that P&G's stock is marginally undervalued on that date. The Morgan Stanley price estimate was \$90 as of this date (see Appendix 11A) and the mean analysts' consensus estimates, reported on Capital IQ, was \$86.53.

(In millions, except per share values and discount factors)	Reported 2013	Horizon Period 2014	2015	2016	2017	Terminal Period
ROPI (NOPAT − [$NOA_{Beg} \times r_w$])		\$4,761	\$5,098	\$5,301	\$5,514	\$5,734
Discount factor [$1/(1 + r_w)^t$]		0.93458	0.87344	0.81630	0.76290	
Present value of horizon ROPI		4,450	4,453	4,327	4,207	
Cum present value of horizon ROPI. . . .	\$ 17,437					
Present value of terminal ROPI	145,816[a]					
NOA	94,305					
Total firm value	257,558					
Less (plus): NNO	25,596					
Less: NCI	645					
Firm equity value	\$231,317					
Shares outstanding (millions)	2,742.3					
Stock value per share.	\$ 84.35					

[a]Computed as $\frac{\left(\frac{5{,}734 \text{ million}}{0.07 - 0.04}\right)}{(1.07)^4}$, or (\$5,734 million/0.03) × 0.76290.

The P&G stock price chart, extending from 2008 through 2013, follows.

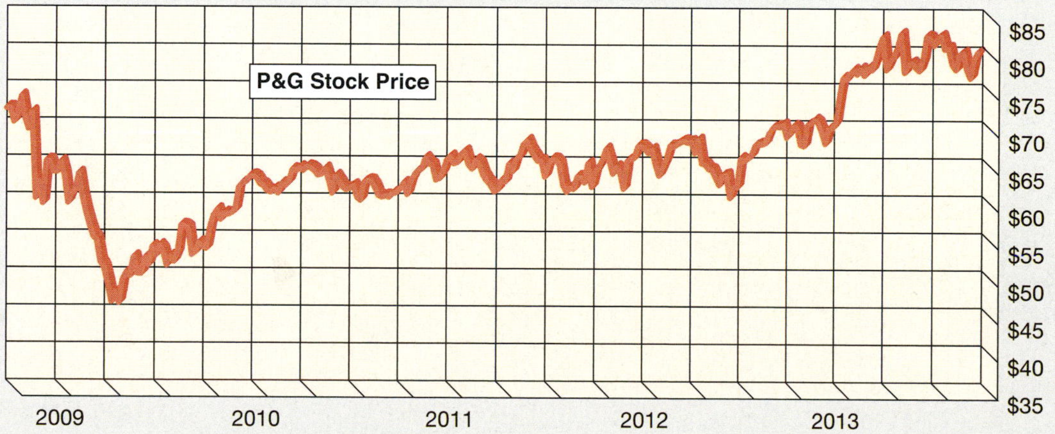

Appendix

A Compound Interest Tables

TABLE 1 Present Value of Single Amount $p = 1/(1 + i)^t$

Period	Interest Rate											
	0.01	0.02	0.03	0.04	0.05	0.06	0.07	0.08	0.09	0.10	0.11	0.12
1	0.99010	0.98039	0.97087	0.96154	0.95238	0.94340	0.93458	0.92593	0.91743	0.90909	0.90090	0.89286
2	0.98030	0.96117	0.94260	0.92456	0.90703	0.89000	0.87344	0.85734	0.84168	0.82645	0.81162	0.79719
3	0.97059	0.94232	0.91514	0.88900	0.86384	0.83962	0.81630	0.79383	0.77218	0.75131	0.73119	0.71178
4	0.96098	0.92385	0.88849	0.85480	0.82270	0.79209	0.76290	0.73503	0.70843	0.68301	0.65873	0.63552
5	0.95147	0.90573	0.86261	0.82193	0.78353	0.74726	0.71299	0.68058	0.64993	0.62092	0.59345	0.56743
6	0.94205	0.88797	0.83748	0.79031	0.74622	0.70496	0.66634	0.63017	0.59627	0.56447	0.53464	0.50663
7	0.93272	0.87056	0.81309	0.75992	0.71068	0.66506	0.62275	0.58349	0.54703	0.51316	0.48166	0.45235
8	0.92348	0.85349	0.78941	0.73069	0.67684	0.62741	0.58201	0.54027	0.50187	0.46651	0.43393	0.40388
9	0.91434	0.83676	0.76642	0.70259	0.64461	0.59190	0.54393	0.50025	0.46043	0.42410	0.39092	0.36061
10	0.90529	0.82035	0.74409	0.67556	0.61391	0.55839	0.50835	0.46319	0.42241	0.38554	0.35218	0.32197
11	0.89632	0.80426	0.72242	0.64958	0.58468	0.52679	0.47509	0.42888	0.38753	0.35049	0.31728	0.28748
12	0.88745	0.78849	0.70138	0.62460	0.55684	0.49697	0.44401	0.39711	0.35553	0.31863	0.28584	0.25668
13	0.87866	0.77303	0.68095	0.60057	0.53032	0.46884	0.41496	0.36770	0.32618	0.28966	0.25751	0.22917
14	0.86996	0.75788	0.66112	0.57748	0.50507	0.44230	0.38782	0.34046	0.29925	0.26333	0.23199	0.20462
15	0.86135	0.74301	0.64186	0.55526	0.48102	0.41727	0.36245	0.31524	0.27454	0.23939	0.20900	0.18270
16	0.85282	0.72845	0.62317	0.53391	0.45811	0.39365	0.33873	0.29189	0.25187	0.21763	0.18829	0.16312
17	0.84438	0.71416	0.60502	0.51337	0.43630	0.37136	0.31657	0.27027	0.23107	0.19784	0.16963	0.14564
18	0.83602	0.70016	0.58739	0.49363	0.41552	0.35034	0.29586	0.25025	0.21199	0.17986	0.15282	0.13004
19	0.82774	0.68643	0.57029	0.47464	0.39573	0.33051	0.27651	0.23171	0.19449	0.16351	0.13768	0.11611
20	0.81954	0.67297	0.55368	0.45639	0.37689	0.31180	0.25842	0.21455	0.17843	0.14864	0.12403	0.10367
21	0.81143	0.65978	0.53755	0.43883	0.35894	0.29416	0.24151	0.19866	0.16370	0.13513	0.11174	0.09256
22	0.80340	0.64684	0.52189	0.42196	0.34185	0.27751	0.22571	0.18394	0.15018	0.12285	0.10067	0.08264
23	0.79544	0.63416	0.50669	0.40573	0.32557	0.26180	0.21095	0.17032	0.13778	0.11168	0.09069	0.07379
24	0.78757	0.62172	0.49193	0.39012	0.31007	0.24698	0.19715	0.15770	0.12640	0.10153	0.08170	0.06588
25	0.77977	0.60953	0.47761	0.37512	0.29530	0.23300	0.18425	0.14602	0.11597	0.09230	0.07361	0.05882
30	0.74192	0.55207	0.41199	0.30832	0.23138	0.17411	0.13137	0.09938	0.07537	0.05731	0.04368	0.03338
35	0.70591	0.50003	0.35538	0.25342	0.18129	0.13011	0.09366	0.06763	0.04899	0.03558	0.02592	0.01894
40	0.67165	0.45289	0.30656	0.20829	0.14205	0.09722	0.06678	0.04603	0.03184	0.02209	0.01538	0.01075

TABLE 2 Present Value of Ordinary Annuity $p = \{1 - [1/(1 + i)^t]\}/i$

Period	Interest Rate											
	0.01	0.02	0.03	0.04	0.05	0.06	0.07	0.08	0.09	0.10	0.11	0.12
1	0.99010	0.98039	0.97087	0.96154	0.95238	0.94340	0.93458	0.92593	0.91743	0.90909	0.90090	0.89286
2	1.97040	1.94156	1.91347	1.88609	1.85941	1.83339	1.80802	1.78326	1.75911	1.73554	1.71252	1.69005
3	2.94099	2.88388	2.82861	2.77509	2.72325	2.67301	2.62432	2.57710	2.53129	2.48685	2.44371	2.40183
4	3.90197	3.80773	3.71710	3.62990	3.54595	3.46511	3.38721	3.31213	3.23972	3.16987	3.10245	3.03735
5	4.85343	4.71346	4.57971	4.45182	4.32948	4.21236	4.10020	3.99271	3.88965	3.79079	3.69590	3.60478
6	5.79548	5.60143	5.41719	5.24214	5.07569	4.91732	4.76654	4.62288	4.48592	4.35526	4.23054	4.11141
7	6.72819	6.47199	6.23028	6.00205	5.78637	5.58238	5.38929	5.20637	5.03295	4.86842	4.71220	4.56376
8	7.65168	7.32548	7.01969	6.73274	6.46321	6.20979	5.97130	5.74664	5.53482	5.33493	5.14612	4.96764
9	8.56602	8.16224	7.78611	7.43533	7.10782	6.80169	6.51523	6.24689	5.99525	5.75902	5.53705	5.32825
10	9.47130	8.98259	8.53020	8.11090	7.72173	7.36009	7.02358	6.71008	6.41766	6.14457	5.88923	5.65022
11	10.36763	9.78685	9.25262	8.76048	8.30641	7.88687	7.49867	7.13896	6.80519	6.49506	6.20652	5.93770
12	11.25508	10.57534	9.95400	9.38507	8.86325	8.38384	7.94269	7.53608	7.16073	6.81369	6.49236	6.19437
13	12.13374	11.34837	10.63496	9.98565	9.39357	8.85268	8.35765	7.90378	7.48690	7.10336	6.74987	6.42355
14	13.00370	12.10625	11.29607	10.56312	9.89864	9.29498	8.74547	8.24424	7.78615	7.36669	6.98187	6.62817
15	13.86505	12.84926	11.93794	11.11839	10.37966	9.71225	9.10791	8.55948	8.06069	7.60608	7.19087	6.81086
16	14.71787	13.57771	12.56110	11.65230	10.83777	10.10590	9.44665	8.85137	8.31256	7.82371	7.37916	6.97399
17	15.56225	14.29187	13.16612	12.16567	11.27407	10.47726	9.76322	9.12164	8.54363	8.02155	7.54879	7.11963
18	16.39827	14.99203	13.75351	12.65930	11.68959	10.82760	10.05909	9.37189	8.75563	8.20141	7.70162	7.24967
19	17.22601	15.67846	14.32380	13.13394	12.08532	11.15812	10.33560	9.60360	8.95011	8.36492	7.83929	7.36578
20	18.04555	16.35143	14.87747	13.59033	12.46221	11.46992	10.59401	9.81815	9.12855	8.51356	7.96333	7.46944
21	18.85698	17.01121	15.41502	14.02916	12.82115	11.76408	10.83553	10.01680	9.29224	8.64869	8.07507	7.56200
22	19.66038	17.65805	15.93692	14.45112	13.16300	12.04158	11.06124	10.20074	9.44243	8.77154	8.17574	7.64465
23	20.45582	18.29220	16.44361	14.85684	13.48857	12.30338	11.27219	10.37106	9.58021	8.88322	8.26643	7.71843
24	21.24339	18.91393	16.93554	15.24696	13.79864	12.55036	11.46933	10.52876	9.70661	8.98474	8.34814	7.78432
25	22.02316	19.52346	17.41315	15.62208	14.09394	12.78336	11.65358	10.67478	9.82258	9.07704	8.42174	7.84314
30	25.80771	22.39646	19.60044	17.29203	15.37245	13.76483	12.40904	11.25778	10.27365	9.42691	8.69379	8.05518
35	29.40858	24.99862	21.48722	18.66461	16.37419	14.49825	12.94767	11.65457	10.56682	9.64416	8.85524	8.17550
40	32.83469	27.35548	23.11477	19.79277	17.15909	15.04630	13.33171	11.92461	10.75736	9.77905	8.95105	8.24378

TABLE 3 Future Value of Single Amount

$f = (1 + i)^t$

						Interest Rate						
Period	**0.01**	**0.02**	**0.03**	**0.04**	**0.05**	**0.06**	**0.07**	**0.08**	**0.09**	**0.10**	**0.11**	**0.12**
1	1.01000	1.02000	1.03000	1.04000	1.05000	1.06000	1.07000	1.08000	1.09000	1.10000	1.11000	1.12000
2	1.02010	1.04040	1.06090	1.08160	1.10250	1.12360	1.14490	1.16640	1.18810	1.21000	1.23210	1.25440
3	1.03030	1.06121	1.09273	1.12486	1.15763	1.19102	1.22504	1.25971	1.29503	1.33100	1.36763	1.40493
4	1.04060	1.08243	1.12551	1.16986	1.21551	1.26248	1.31080	1.36049	1.41158	1.46410	1.51807	1.57352
5	1.05101	1.10408	1.15927	1.21665	1.27628	1.33823	1.40255	1.46933	1.53862	1.61051	1.68506	1.76234
6	1.06152	1.12616	1.19405	1.26532	1.34010	1.41852	1.50073	1.58687	1.67710	1.77156	1.87041	1.97382
7	1.07214	1.14869	1.22987	1.31593	1.40710	1.50363	1.60578	1.71382	1.82804	1.94872	2.07616	2.21068
8	1.08286	1.17166	1.26677	1.36857	1.47746	1.59385	1.71819	1.85093	1.99256	2.14359	2.30454	2.47596
9	1.09369	1.19509	1.30477	1.42331	1.55133	1.68948	1.83846	1.99900	2.17189	2.35795	2.55804	2.77308
10	1.10462	1.21899	1.34392	1.48024	1.62889	1.79085	1.96715	2.15892	2.36736	2.59374	2.83942	3.10585
11	1.11567	1.24337	1.38423	1.53945	1.71034	1.89830	2.10485	2.33164	2.58043	2.85312	3.15176	3.47855
12	1.12683	1.26824	1.42576	1.60103	1.79586	2.01220	2.25219	2.51817	2.81266	3.13843	3.49845	3.89598
13	1.13809	1.29361	1.46853	1.66507	1.88565	2.13293	2.40985	2.71962	3.06580	3.45227	3.88328	4.36349
14	1.14947	1.31948	1.51259	1.73168	1.97993	2.26090	2.57853	2.93719	3.34173	3.79750	4.31044	4.88711
15	1.16097	1.34587	1.55797	1.80094	2.07893	2.39656	2.75903	3.17217	3.64248	4.17725	4.78459	5.47357
16	1.17258	1.37279	1.60471	1.87298	2.18287	2.54035	2.95216	3.42594	3.97031	4.59497	5.31089	6.13039
17	1.18430	1.40024	1.65285	1.94790	2.29202	2.69277	3.15882	3.70002	4.32763	5.05447	5.89509	6.86604
18	1.19615	1.42825	1.70243	2.02582	2.40662	2.85434	3.37993	3.99602	4.71712	5.55992	6.54355	7.68997
19	1.20811	1.45681	1.75351	2.10685	2.52695	3.02560	3.61653	4.31570	5.14166	6.11591	7.26334	8.61276
20	1.22019	1.48595	1.80611	2.19112	2.65330	3.20714	3.86968	4.66096	5.60441	6.72750	8.06231	9.64629
21	1.23239	1.51567	1.86029	2.27877	2.78596	3.39956	4.14056	5.03383	6.10881	7.40025	8.94917	10.80385
22	1.24472	1.54598	1.91610	2.36992	2.92526	3.60354	4.43040	5.43654	6.65860	8.14027	9.93357	12.10031
23	1.25716	1.57690	1.97359	2.46472	3.07152	3.81975	4.74053	5.87146	7.25787	8.95430	11.02627	13.55235
24	1.26973	1.60844	2.03279	2.56330	3.22510	4.04893	5.07237	6.34118	7.91108	9.84973	12.23916	15.17863
25	1.28243	1.64061	2.09378	2.66584	3.38635	4.29187	5.42743	6.84848	8.62308	10.83471	13.58546	17.00006
30	1.34785	1.81136	2.42726	3.24340	4.32194	5.74349	7.61226	10.06266	13.26768	17.44940	22.89230	29.95992
35	1.41660	1.99989	2.81386	3.94609	5.51602	7.68609	10.67658	14.78534	20.41397	28.10244	38.57485	52.79962
40	1.48886	2.20804	3.26204	4.80102	7.03999	10.28572	14.97446	21.72452	31.40942	45.25926	65.00087	93.05097

TABLE 4 Future Value of an Ordinary Annuity

$f = [(1 + i)^t - 1]/i$

						Interest Rate						
Period	**0.01**	**0.02**	**0.03**	**0.04**	**0.05**	**0.06**	**0.07**	**0.08**	**0.09**	**0.10**	**0.11**	**0.12**
1	1.00000	1.00000	1.00000	1.00000	1.00000	1.00000	1.00000	1.00000	1.00000	1.00000	1.00000	1.00000
2	2.01000	2.02000	2.03000	2.04000	2.05000	2.06000	2.07000	2.08000	2.09000	2.10000	2.11000	2.12000
3	3.03010	3.06040	3.09090	3.12160	3.15250	3.18360	3.21490	3.24640	3.27810	3.31000	3.34210	3.37440
4	4.06040	4.12161	4.18363	4.24646	4.31013	4.37462	4.43994	4.50611	4.57313	4.64100	4.70973	4.77933
5	5.10101	5.20404	5.30914	5.41632	5.52563	5.63709	5.75074	5.86660	5.98471	6.10510	6.22780	6.35285
6	6.15202	6.30812	6.46841	6.63298	6.80191	6.97532	7.15329	7.33593	7.52333	7.71561	7.91286	8.11519
7	7.21354	7.43428	7.66246	7.89829	8.14201	8.39384	8.65402	8.92280	9.20043	9.48717	9.78327	10.08901
8	8.28567	8.58297	8.89234	9.21423	9.54911	9.89747	10.25980	10.63663	11.02847	11.43589	11.85943	12.29969
9	9.36853	9.75463	10.15911	10.58280	11.02656	11.49132	11.97799	12.48756	13.02104	13.57948	14.16397	14.77566
10	10.46221	10.94972	11.46388	12.00611	12.57789	13.18079	13.81645	14.48656	15.19293	15.93742	16.72201	17.54874
11	11.56683	12.16872	12.80780	13.48635	14.20679	14.97164	15.78360	16.64549	17.56029	18.53117	19.56143	20.65458
12	12.68250	13.41209	14.19203	15.02581	15.91713	16.86994	17.88845	18.97713	20.14072	21.38428	22.71319	24.13313
13	13.80933	14.68033	15.61779	16.62684	17.71298	18.88214	20.14064	21.49530	22.95338	24.52271	26.21164	28.02911
14	14.94742	15.97394	17.08632	18.29191	19.59863	21.01507	22.55049	24.21492	26.01919	27.97498	30.09492	32.39260
15	16.09690	17.29342	18.59891	20.02359	21.57856	23.27597	25.12902	27.15211	29.36092	31.77248	34.40536	37.27971
16	17.25786	18.63929	20.15688	21.82453	23.65749	25.67253	27.88805	30.32428	33.00340	35.94973	39.18995	42.75328
17	18.43044	20.01207	21.76159	23.69751	25.84037	28.21288	30.84022	33.75023	36.97370	40.54470	44.50084	48.88367
18	19.61475	21.41231	23.41444	25.64541	28.13238	30.90565	33.99903	37.45024	41.30134	45.59917	50.39594	55.74971
19	20.81090	22.84056	25.11687	27.67123	30.53900	33.75999	37.37896	41.44626	46.01846	51.15909	56.93949	63.43968
20	22.01900	24.29737	26.87037	29.77808	33.06595	36.78559	40.99549	45.76196	51.16012	57.27500	64.20283	72.05244
21	23.23919	25.78332	28.67649	31.96920	35.71925	39.99273	44.86518	50.42292	56.76453	64.00250	72.26514	81.69874
22	24.47159	27.29898	30.53678	34.24797	38.50521	43.39229	49.00574	55.45676	62.87334	71.40275	81.21431	92.50258
23	25.71630	28.84496	32.45288	36.61789	41.43048	46.99583	53.43614	60.89330	69.53194	79.54302	91.14788	104.60289
24	26.97346	30.42186	34.42647	39.08260	44.50200	50.81558	58.17667	66.76476	76.78981	88.49733	102.17415	118.15524
25	28.24320	32.03030	36.45926	41.64591	47.72710	54.86451	63.24904	73.10594	84.70090	98.34706	114.41331	133.33387
30	34.78489	40.56808	47.57542	56.08494	66.43885	79.05819	94.46079	113.28321	136.30754	164.49402	199.02088	241.33268
35	41.66028	49.99448	60.46208	73.65222	90.32031	111.43478	138.23688	172.31680	215.71075	271.02437	341.58955	431.66350
40	48.88637	60.40198	75.40126	95.02552	120.79977	154.76197	199.63511	259.05652	337.88245	442.59256	581.82607	767.09142

Appendix

B Constructing the Statement of Cash Flows

Learning Objectives

LO1 Define and describe the framework for the statement of cash flows. (p. B-5)

LO2 Define and explain net cash flows from operating activities. (p. B-8)

LO3 Define and explain net cash flows from investing activities. (p. B-13)

LO4 Define and explain net cash flows from financing activities. (p. B-14)

LO5 Describe and apply ratios based on operating cash flows. (p. B-22)

Starbucks

Starbucks Corporation is the leading retailer, roaster, and brander of specialty coffee. The company has broad geographic reach. At last count, Starbucks operated 11,457 stores in the U.S. and another 8,310 stores in scores of countries around the world. In 2012, the company reported strong operating results: net income of $1,384.7 million on revenue of $13.3 billion. Income is up for the third straight year, up by 46% compared to 2010.

The company was hard hit during the 2008–2009 recession when customers switched from "luxury" goods such as premium coffees to more economical items. The company recorded restructuring charges, made significant changes to its operations, and has not looked back. As Starbucks' income declined and then recovered, so too has the company's stock price as the following chart illustrates:

Over the 2007–2012 period, Starbucks' cash flows have been far less volatile than its net income, as the graphic below reveals. What is behind this relation? What does it mean? This appendix helps answer these and other questions. It begins by describing the process of constructing the statement of cash flows. Next, it explains how we use and interpret the statement of cash flows to aid both internal and external business decisions.

Sources: Starbucks 2012 10-K and Annual Report.

Starbucks' Net Income and Operating Cash Flow ($ millions)

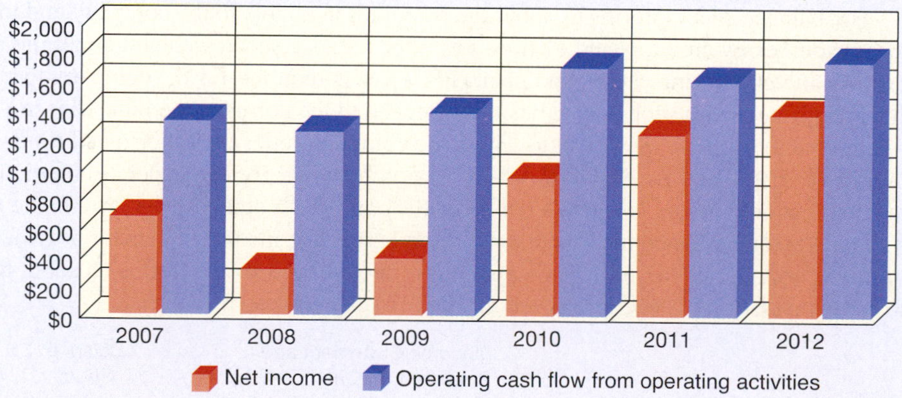

APPENDIX ORGANIZATION

Constructing the Statement of Cash Flows

Framework of the Statement of Cash Flows
- Operating Activities
- Investing Activities
- Financing Activities

Cash Flow from Operating Activities
- Steps to Compute Cash Flow from Operations
- Case Illustration

Cash Flows from Investing and Financing
- Case Illustration
- Analysis of Accounts
- Supplemental Disclosures

Appendix: Direct Method of Reporting
- Cash Flows from Operations
- Cash Flows from Investing and Financing
- Case Illustration

The **statement of cash flows** is a financial statement that summarizes information about the flow of cash into and out of a company. In this appendix, we discuss the preparation, analysis, and interpretation of the statement of cash flows. The statement of cash flows complements the balance sheet and the income statement. The balance sheet reports the company's financial position at a point in time (the end of each period) whereas the statement of cash flows explains the change in one of its components—cash—from one balance sheet date to the next. The income statement reveals the results of the company's operating activities for the period, and these operating activities are a major contributor to the change in cash as reported in the statement of cash flows.

Relation Among Financial Statements. Each of these three financial statements reveals a different view of the company, and a thorough financial analysis requires us to scrutinize the information contained in each. The income statement, for example, informs us about the degree to which consumers value the products and/or services offered by the company. How much does it cost to produce them, and can the company set prices that pass on these production costs to its customers? Is the company able to control labor costs, both for salaries and wages and for benefits offered to employees? Can the company effectively manage its overhead costs? How well is it insulated against fluctuations in interest rates, commodity prices, or foreign exchange rates? How well can it control its income tax obligations? These are but a few of the important questions that can be answered by our analysis of the income statement.

The balance sheet informs us about the resources available to the company and the claims against those resources by creditors and owners. From the balance sheet, we learn about the magnitude of investment in net working capital and plant (PPE) assets required for the company to conduct business. This is impacted by the company's business model and the norms of the industries in which it operates. We are able to estimate the extent to which the company relies upon borrowed funds, the structure of that indebtedness, and the degree to which the company has (or can generate) the liquidity required to meet its debt obligations. We also learn about the company's equity investors and the claims they have on the net assets and income of the company. Whereas the income statement provides us with insight into the economics of the company's operations, the balance sheet informs us about the resources that the company uses in its operations and the claims against those resources.

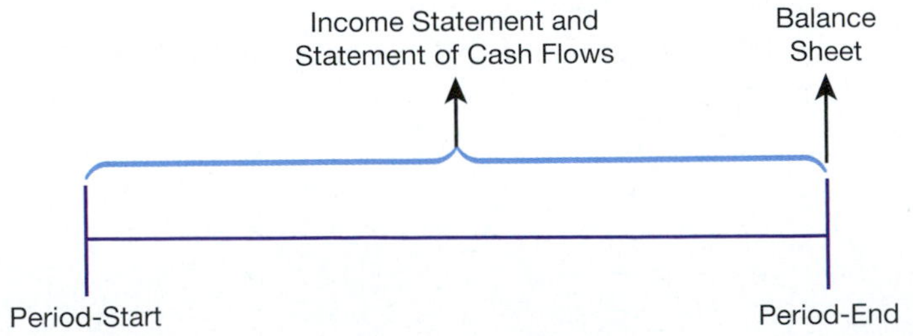

As we will learn in this module, the statement of cash flows is prepared from the company's income statement and comparative balance sheets. At first glance, it might appear that the information contained in the cash flow statement is redundant. (To that point, in Module 12 we define free cash flow as NOPAT less the increase in NOA and then value the company using NOPAT and NOA from the income statement and the balance sheet. Our valuation model did not use any information taken directly from the statement of cash flows.) However, to treat the statement of cash flows as a secondary statement would ignore potential information that can assist us in our analysis of the company.

The statement of cash flows is structured to highlight three primary activities of the company: operating activities, investing activities, and financing activities. Neither the income statement nor the balance sheet presents that perspective. Indeed, the FASB is considering a financial reporting model that will carry over this perspective to the income statement and the balance sheet, but we are not likely to see this new format soon because standard setters are currently grappling with issues that are perceived as more pressing.

The statement of cash flows emphasizes the role cash plays in the company's day-to-day operations; it is cash that pays employees, cash that pays debt, and cash that provides a return to equity holders in the form of dividends. Finance professionals often focus on free cash flow, and for good reason. Companies that fail typically do so because they lack the cash flow necessary to conduct their business. A focus solely on GAAP profit can obscure a deterioration of liquidity that can lead to company failure.

As an added benefit, the statement of cash flows highlights important operating items that are often not reported as separate line items in the income statement, such as depreciation on plant assets, impairments of tangible and intangible assets, the cost of stock-based compensation, the excess of reported equity income over dividends received from investee companies, the cash portion of income tax expense, and the gain or loss on the sales of assets. In addition, the statement of cash flows highlights items that are *not* reflected in the income statement, such as capital expenditures (CAPEX), dividend payments, and the repayment of the principle portion of company debt.

Finally, the statement of cash flows provides insight into the "quality" of company earnings. All profit must eventually be received in cash. So, when profit and operating cash flow diverge, we must investigate the reasons for the divergence because cash flow ultimately drives company value. If net income grows at a faster pace than operating cash flows, our analysis attempts to understand whether cash flow will increase in the future or whether income has been improperly recognized, only to be reversed in the future. Our assessment of the "quality" of company earnings is a difficult challenge, but one that is aided considerably by a thorough understanding of the statement of cash flows.

Key Performance Metrics and the Life Cycle. A product life-cycle framework can be helpful in interpreting cash flows. This framework proposes four stages for products or services: (1) introduction, (2) growth, (3) maturity, and (4) decline. The following figure plots the usual patterns for revenues, income, and cash flows at each of these four stages. For revenues, the "top line" number, we see the common pattern of growth over the first two stages, then a leveling out at maturity, then finally a decline. The length of time between introduction and decline depends on many of the factors considered by Porter's forces or a SWOT analysis. For example, products with short lives and those subject to fashion trends, technical innovation, or obsolescence will have a shorter life cycle and revenue will be at greater risk of fluctuation. Knowledge of product life cycles can help us assess the transitory or persistent nature of revenues.

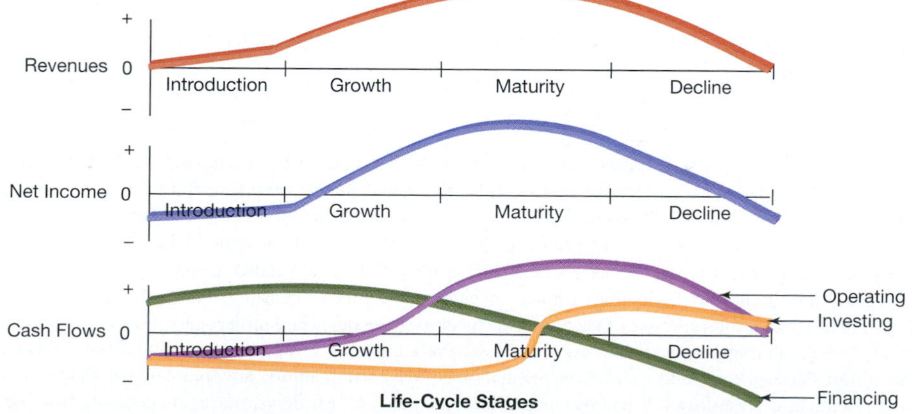

The second graph in the figure shows net income behavior over the four life-cycle stages. We commonly see losses in the introductory stage as companies struggle to recover startup costs and establish revenue streams. Accordingly, net income commonly peaks during the maturity stage before a gradual decrease in the decline stage. The third graph highlights cash flows from operating, investing, and financing over the product life cycle. Although we see variations due to product success, strategic planning, and cost controls, these trends for each cash flow are fairly descriptive.

In general, during the introductory stage revenues are limited, which results in low income and operating cash flows. The introductory stage also sees cash outflows for investing and cash inflows for financing. During the growth stage, revenues, income, and operating cash flows all increase, whereas both investing and financing cash flows increase or level out (each depending on predictions of future growth). The maturity stage sees peaks, and maybe some eventual decline, for revenues, income, and operating cash flows. This occurs as investing cash flows drop off, rendering additional financing cash inflows unnecessary. The decline stage brings large decreases in revenues, income, and operating cash flows. In decline, companies distribute cash flows for financing sources (repay debt, buy back stock, pay dividends) and realize some incoming investing cash flows as assets are gradually sold off. In summary, knowledge of product life cycles can help us understand the underlying economics, which will inform our business analysis. It can also help us interpret and possibly predict future streams of revenues, income, and cash flows.

FRAMEWORK FOR STATEMENT OF CASH FLOWS

LO1 Define and describe the framework for the statement of cash flows.

The statement of cash flows classifies cash receipts and cash payments into one of three categories:

- **Operating activities** Operating activities measure the net cash inflows and outflows as a result of the company's transactions with its customers. We generally prefer operating cash flows to be positive, although companies can report net cash outflows for operating activities in the short run during periods of growth (as outflows to increase working capital accounts outstrip inflows from profits).
- **Investing activities** Investing activities relate to net cash flows generally relating to long-term assets. Outflows occur when a company purchases long-term assets and inflows occur when long-term assets are sold.
- **Financing activities** Financing activities relate to long-term debt and stockholders' equity. Cash inflows result from borrowing money and issuing stock to investors. Outflows occur when a company repays debt, repurchases stock, or pays dividends to shareholders.

Classifying cash flows into these categories readily identifies the effects on cash from each of these three major activities of a company. The combined effects on cash of all three categories explain the net change in cash for that period.[1]

Preparation of the statement of cash flows draws mainly on information from the income statement and the balance sheet. Specifically, the three sections draw generally on the following information:

- **Net cash flows from operating activities** draws on the current asset and current liabilities sections of the balance sheet.
- **Net cash flows from investing activities** draws on the long-term assets section of the balance sheet.
- **Net cash flows from financing activities** draws on the long-term liabilities and stockholders' equity sections of the balance sheet.

These relations do not hold exactly, but they provide us a useful way to visualize the construction of the statement of cash flows.

[1] The statement of cash flows explains the change in a firm's cash *and* cash equivalents. **Cash equivalents** are short-term, highly liquid investments that are (1) easily convertible into a known cash amount and (2) close enough to maturity so that their market value is not sensitive to interest rate changes (generally, investments with initial maturities of three months or less). Treasury bills, commercial paper (short-term notes issued by corporations), and money market funds are typical examples of cash equivalents.

When preparing a statement of cash flows, the cash and cash equivalents are added together and treated as a single sum. This is done because the purchase and sale of investments in cash equivalents are considered to be part of a firm's overall management of cash rather than a source or use of cash. As statement users evaluate and project cash flows, for example, it should not matter whether the cash is readily available, deposited in a bank account, or invested in cash equivalents. Transfers back and forth between a firm's cash account and its investments in cash equivalents, therefore, are not treated as cash inflows and cash outflows in its statement of cash flows. When discussing the statement of cash flows, managers generally use the word *cash* rather than the term *cash and cash equivalents*. We follow the same practice in this appendix.

Exhibit B.1 reproduces Starbucks' statement of cash flows ($ millions). During 2012, Starbucks reported net income of $1,384.7 million and generated $1,750.3 million of cash from operating activities. The company used $(974.0) million of cash for investing activities and $(745.5) million of cash for financing activities. In sum, Starbucks increased its cash reserves by $40.5 million (after considering foreign exchange effects), from $1,148.1 million at the beginning of fiscal 2012 to $1,188.6 million at the end of fiscal 2012.

EXHIBIT B.1 Statement of Cash Flows for Starbucks

Year Ended (in millions)	Sept. 30, 2012	Oct. 2, 2011	Oct. 3, 2010
OPERATING ACTIVITIES:			
Net earnings including noncontrolling interests	$1,384.7	$1,248.0	$ 948.3
Adjustments to reconcile net earnings to net cash provided by operating activities:			
Depreciation and amortization	580.6	550.0	540.8
Gain on sale of properties	—	(30.2)	—
Deferred income taxes, net	61.1	106.2	(42.0)
Income earned from equity method investees, net of distributions	(49.3)	(32.9)	(17.2)
Gain resulting from acquisition of joint ventures	—	(55.2)	(23.1)
Stock-based compensation	153.6	145.2	113.6
Other	23.6	33.3	75.5
Cash provided/(used) by changes in operating assets and liabilities:			
Accounts receivable	(90.3)	(88.7)	(33.4)
Inventories	(273.3)	(422.3)	123.2
Accounts payable	(105.2)	227.5	(3.6)
Accrued liabilities and insurance reserves	23.7	(81.8)	(18.7)
Deferred revenue	60.8	35.8	24.2
Prepaid expenses, other current assets and other assets	(19.7)	(22.5)	17.3
Net cash provided by operating activities	1,750.3	1,612.4	1,704.9
INVESTING ACTIVITIES:			
Purchase of investments	(1,748.6)	(966.0)	(549.0)
Maturities and calls of investments	1,796.4	430.0	209.9
Acquisitions, net of cash acquired	(129.1)	(55.8)	(12.0)
Additions to property, plant and equipment	(856.2)	(531.9)	(445.8)
Cash proceeds from sale of property, plant and equipment	5.3	117.4	5.1
Other	(41.8)	(13.2)	2.3
Net cash used by investing activities	(974.0)	(1,019.5)	(789.5)
FINANCING ACTIVITIES:			
(Payments)/proceeds from short-term borrowings	(30.8)	30.8	—
Purchase of noncontrolling interest	—	(27.5)	(45.8)
Proceeds from issuance of common stock	236.6	250.4	132.8
Excess tax benefit from exercise of stock options	169.8	103.9	36.9
Cash dividends paid	(513.0)	(389.5)	(171.0)
Repurchase of common stock	(549.1)	(555.9)	(285.6)
Minimum tax withholdings on share-based awards	(58.5)	(15.0)	(4.9)
Other	(0.5)	(5.2)	(8.4)
Net cash used by financing activities	(745.5)	(608.0)	(346.0)
Effect of exchange rate changes on cash and cash equivalents	9.7	(0.8)	(5.2)
Net increase/(decrease) in cash and cash equivalents	40.5	(15.9)	564.2
CASH AND CASH EQUIVALENTS:			
Beginning of period	1,148.1	1,164.0	599.8
End of period	$1,188.6	$1,148.1	$1,164.0

Operating Activities

A company's income statement reflects primarily the transactions and events that constitute its operating activities. Generally, the cash effects of these operating transactions and events determine the net cash flow from operating activities. The usual focus of a firm's **operating activities** is on selling goods or rendering services, but the activities are defined broadly enough to include any cash receipts or payments that are not classified as investing or financing activities. For example, cash received from collection of receivables and cash payments to purchase inventories are treated as cash flows from operating activities. The following are examples of cash inflows and outflows relating to operating activities.

Operating Activities

Cash Inflows ↑	Cash Outflows ↓
■ Receipts from customers for sales made or services rendered.	■ Payments to employees or suppliers.
■ Receipts of interest and dividends.	■ Payments to purchase inventories.
■ Other receipts that are not related to investing or financing activities, such as lawsuit settlements and refunds received from suppliers.	■ Payments of interest to creditors.
	■ Payments of taxes to government.
	■ Other payments that are not related to investing or financing activities, such as contributions to charity.

Cash Flow from Operations Compared with Net Income. Transactions with the company's customers typically yield net income, which is a significant component of net cash inflows from operating activities. Net income and operating cash flows differ for a variety of reasons:

- Companies recognize revenues when they are earned, which does not necessarily coincide with cash receipts. Credit sales can be collected a month or two or more after revenue is recognized.
- Companies recognize expenses when they are incurred, which typically occurs in advance of the payment of cash.
- Companies report large noncash expenses, such as depreciation expense, stock compensation expense, and asset impairment expenses. These expenses involve no cash outflow, which causes net income to be much lower than operating cash flows.

On average, these three factors combine to yield operating cash flows that are greater than reported net income. Indeed, during fiscal 2012–2013, operating cash flows were nearly twice as big as net income for S&P500 companies. (We report detailed statistics about this later in the module.)

Investing Activities

A firm's transactions involving (1) the acquisition and disposal of property, plant, and equipment (PPE) assets and intangible assets, (2) the purchase and sale of stocks, bonds, and other securities (that are not cash equivalents), and (3) the lending and subsequent collection of money constitute the basic components of its **investing activities**. The related cash receipts and payments appear in the investing activities section of the statement of cash flows. Examples of these cash flows follow.

Investing Activities

Cash Inflows ↑	Cash Outflows ↓
■ Receipts from sales of property, plant, and equipment (PPE) assets and intangible assets.	■ Payments to purchase property, plant, and equipment (PPE) assets and intangible assets.
■ Receipts from sales of investments in stocks, bonds, and other securities (other than cash equivalents).	■ Payments to purchase stocks, bonds, and other securities (other than cash equivalents).
■ Receipts from repayments of loans by borrowers.	■ Payments made to lend money to borrowers.

Financing Activities

A firm engages in **financing activities** when it obtains resources from owners, returns resources to owners, borrows resources from creditors, and repays amounts borrowed. Cash flows related to these transactions are reported in the financing activities section of the statement of cash flows. Examples of these cash flows follow.

Financing Activities

Cash Inflows ▲	Cash Outflows ▼
■ Receipts from issuances of common stock and preferred stock and from sales of treasury stock.	■ Payments to acquire treasury stock.
■ Receipts from issuances of bonds payable, mortgage notes payable, and other notes payable.	■ Payments of dividends.
	■ Payments to settle outstanding bonds payable, mortgage notes payable, and other notes payable.

CASH FLOW FROM OPERATING ACTIVITIES

LO2 Define and explain net cash flows from operating activities.

The first section of a statement of cash flows presents a firm's net cash flow from operating activities. Two alternative formats are used to report the net cash flow from operating activities: the *indirect method* and the *direct method. Both methods report the same amount of net cash flow from operating activities.* (Net cash flows from investing and financing activities are prepared in the same manner under both the indirect and direct methods; only the format for cash flows from operating activities differs.)

The *indirect method* starts with net income and applies a series of adjustments to net income to convert it to a cash-basis income number, which is the net cash flow from operating activities. Accountants estimate that *more than 98% of companies preparing the statement of cash flows use the indirect method.* The indirect method is popular because (1) it is easier and less expensive to prepare than the direct method and (2) the direct method requires a supplemental disclosure showing the indirect method (thus, essentially reporting both methods).

The remainder of this appendix discusses the preparation of the statement of cash flows. The indirect method is presented in this section, and the direct method is presented in Appendix B1. (These discussions are independent of each other; both provide complete coverage of the preparation of the statement of cash flows.)

To prepare a statement of cash flows, we need a firm's income statement, comparative balance sheets, and some additional data taken from the accounting records. Exhibit B.2 presents this information for Java House. We use these data to prepare Java's 2013 statement of cash flows using the indirect method. Java's statement of cash flows explains the $25,000 increase in cash that occurred during 2013 (from $10,000 to $35,000) by classifying the firm's cash flows into operating, investing, and financing categories.

EXHIBIT B.2 Financial Data of Java House

JAVA HOUSE
Income Statement
For Year Ended December 31, 2013

Sales		$250,000
Cost of goods sold	$148,000	
Wages expense	52,000	
Insurance expense	5,000	
Depreciation expense	10,000	
Income tax expense	11,000	
Gain on sale of land	(8,000)	218,000
Net income		$ 32,000

Additional Data for 2013

1. Purchased the entirety of long-term stock investments for cash at year-end.
2. Sold land costing $20,000 for $28,000 cash.
3. Acquired $60,000 patent at year-end by issuing common stock at par.
4. All accounts payable relate to merchandise purchases.
5. Issued common stock at par for $10,000 cash.
6. Declared and paid cash dividends of $13,000.

JAVA HOUSE
Balance Sheet

	Dec. 31, 2013	Dec. 31, 2012
Assets		
Cash	$ 35,000	$ 10,000
Accounts receivable	39,000	34,000
Inventory	54,000	60,000
Prepaid insurance	17,000	4,000
Long-term investments	15,000	—
PPE assets	180,000	200,000
Accumulated depreciation	(50,000)	(40,000)
Patent	60,000	—
Total assets	$350,000	$268,000
Liabilities and Equity		
Accounts payable	$ 10,000	$ 19,000
Income tax payable	5,000	3,000
Common stock	260,000	190,000
Retained earnings	75,000	56,000
Total liabilities and equity	$350,000	$268,000

Steps to Compute Net Cash Flow from Operating Activities

The following four steps are applied to construct the net cash flows from operating activities section of the statement of cash flows:

1. **Begin with net income** The first line of the operating section of the statement of cash flows is net income, which is the bottom line from the income statement. This amount is recorded as a positive amount for net income and as a negative amount for a net loss.
2. **Adjust net income (loss) for *noncash* revenues, expenses, gains and losses**
   a. **Noncash revenues and expenses** The income statement often includes noncash expenses such as depreciation and amortization. These expenses are allocations of asset costs over their useful lives to match the revenues generated from those assets. The cash outflow normally occurs when the asset is acquired, which is reported in the *investing* section. Depreciation and amortization expenses do not entail cash outflows. Hence, we must eliminate them from the statement of cash flows by adding them back (to "zero them out" because they are negative amounts in the net income computation).
   b. **Gains and losses** Gains and losses on sales of assets are part of investing activities, not operating activities (unless the company is in the business of buying and selling assets). Thus, we must remove them from the operating section and record the net cash inflows or outflows in the investing section; namely, gains on sales are subtracted from income and losses on sales are added to income.
3. **Adjust net income (loss) for changes in current assets and current liabilities** Net income must be adjusted for changes in current assets and current liabilities (the operating section of the balance sheet). A decrease (from prior year to current year) in a noncash current asset is identified as a cash inflow and an increase is identified as a cash outflow. Conversely, an increase in a current liability is identified as a cash inflow and a decrease as a cash outflow. To make this computation, we use the following guide:

Balance Sheet Account	Cash flow increases from	Cash flow decreases from
Current assets (excluding cash). . .	Account decreases	Account increases
Current liabilities.	Account increases	Account decreases

4. **Sum the amounts from steps 1, 2 and 3 to get net cash flows from operating activities.**

Exhibit B.3 summarizes the adjustments to net income in determining operating cash flows. These are the adjustments applied under the indirect method of computing cash flow from operations.

EXHIBIT B.3 Converting Net Income to Net Cash Flow from Operating Activities

		Add (+) or Subtract (−) from Net Income
	Net income	$ #
Adjustments for noncash revenues, expenses, gains & losses	Add depreciation and amortization.	+
	Add (subtract): Losses (gains) on asset and liability dispositions	±
Adjustments for changes in noncash current assets and current liabilities	Adjust for changes in noncash current assets	
	Subtract increases in noncash current assets	−
	Add decreases in noncash current assets	+
	Adjust for changes in current liabilities	
	Add increases in current liabilities.	+
	Subtract decreases in current liabilities	−
	Net cash flow from operating activities	$ #

To better understand the adjustments for current assets and liabilities, the following table provides brief explanations of adjustments for receivables, inventories, payables and accruals.

	Change in account balance . . .	Means that . . .	Which requires this adjustment to net income to yield cash profit . . .
Receivables	Increase	Sales and net income increase, but cash is not yet received	Deduct increase in receivables from net income
	Decrease	More cash is received than is reported in sales and net income	Add decrease in receivables to net income
Inventories	Increase	Cash is paid for inventories that are not yet reflected in cost of goods sold	Deduct increase in inventories from net income
	Decrease	Cost of goods sold includes inventory costs that were paid for in a prior period	Add decrease in inventories to net income
Payables and accruals	Increase	More goods and services are acquired on credit, delaying cash payment	Add increase in payables and accruals to net income
	Decrease	More cash is paid than that reflected in cost of goods sold or operating expenses	Deduct decrease in payables and accruals from net income

Java House Case Illustration

We next explain and illustrate these adjustments with Java House's data from Exhibit B.2.

Depreciation and Amortization Expenses

Depreciation and amortization expenses represent write-offs of previously recorded assets; so-called noncash expenses. Because depreciation and amortization expenses are subtracted in computing net income, we add these expenses to net income as we convert it to a related net operating cash flow. Adding these expenses to net income eliminates them from the income statement and is a necessary adjustment to obtain cash income. Java House had $10,000 of 2013 depreciation expense, so this amount is added to Java's net income of $32,000.

Net income.	$32,000
Add: Depreciation.	**10,000**

Gains and Losses Related to Investing or Financing Activities

The income statement can contain gains and losses that relate to investing or financing activities. Gains and losses from the sale of investments, PPE assets, or intangible assets illustrate gains and losses from investing (not operating) activities. A gain or loss from the retirement of bonds payable is an example of a financing gain or loss. The full cash flow effect from these types of events is reported in the investing or financing sections of the statement of cash flows. Therefore, the related gains or losses must be eliminated as we convert net income to net cash flow from operating activities. To eliminate their impact on net income, gains are subtracted and losses are added to net income. Java House had an $8,000 gain from the sale of land in 2013. This gain relates to an investing activity, so it is subtracted from Java's net income.

Net income.	$32,000
Add: Depreciation.	10,000
Deduct: Gain on sale of land	**(8,000)**

Accounts Receivable Change

Credit sales increase accounts receivable; cash collections on account decrease accounts receivable. If, overall, accounts receivable decrease during a year, then cash collections from customers exceed credit sales revenue by the amount of the decrease. Because sales are added in computing net income, the decrease in accounts receivable is added to net income. In essence, this adjustment replaces the sales amount with the larger amount of cash collections from customers. If accounts receivable increase during a year, then sales revenue exceeds the cash collections from customers by the amount of the increase. Because sales are added in computing net income, the increase in accounts receivable is subtracted from net income as we convert it to a net cash flow from operating activities. In essence, this adjustment replaces the sales amount with the smaller amount of cash collections from customers. Java's accounts receivable increased $5,000 during 2013, so this increase is subtracted from net income under the indirect method.

Net income	$32,000
Add: Depreciation	10,000
Deduct: Gain on sale of land	(8,000)
Deduct: Accounts receivable increase	**(5,000)**

Inventory Change

The adjustment for an inventory change is one of two adjustments to net income that together cause the cost of goods sold expense to be replaced by an amount representing the cash paid during the period for merchandise purchased. The second adjustment, which we examine shortly, is for the change in accounts payable. The effect of the inventory adjustment alone is to adjust net income for the difference between the cost of goods sold and the cost of merchandise purchased during the period. The cost of merchandise purchased increases inventory; the cost of goods sold decreases inventory. An overall decrease in inventory during a period must mean, therefore, that the cost of merchandise purchased was less than the cost of goods sold by the amount of the decrease. Because cost of goods sold was subtracted in computing net income, the inventory decrease is added to net income. After this adjustment, the effect of the cost of goods sold on net income has been replaced by the smaller cost of merchandise purchased. Similarly, if inventory increased during a period, the cost of merchandise purchased is larger than the cost of goods sold by the amount of the increase. To replace the cost of goods sold with the cost of merchandise purchased, the inventory increase is subtracted from net income. Java's inventory decreased $6,000 during 2013, so this decrease is added to net income.

Net income	$32,000
Add: Depreciation	10,000
Deduct: Gain on sale of land	(8,000)
Deduct: Accounts receivable increase	(5,000)
Add: Inventory decrease	**6,000**

Prepaid Expenses Change

Cash prepayments of various expenses increase a firm's prepaid expenses. When the related expenses for the period are subsequently recorded, the prepaid expenses decrease. An overall decrease in prepaid expenses for a period means that the cash prepayments were less than the related expenses. Because the expenses were subtracted in determining net income, the indirect method adds the decrease in prepaid expenses to net income as it is converted to a cash flow amount. The effect of the addition is to replace the expense amount with the smaller cash payment amount. Similarly, an increase in prepaid expenses is subtracted from net income because an increase means that the cash prepayments during the year were more than the related expenses. Java's prepaid insurance increased $13,000 during 2013, so this increase is deducted from net income.

Net income	$32,000
Add: Depreciation	10,000
Deduct: Gain on sale of land	(8,000)
Deduct: Accounts receivable increase	(5,000)
Add: Inventory decrease	6,000
Deduct: Prepaid insurance increase	**(13,000)**

Accounts Payable Change

When merchandise is purchased on account, accounts payable increase by the cost of the goods purchased. Accounts payable decrease when cash payments are made to settle the accounts. An overall decrease in accounts payable during a year means that cash payments for purchases were more than the cost of the purchases. An accounts payable decrease, therefore, is subtracted from net income under the indirect method. The deduction, in effect, replaces the cost of merchandise purchased with the larger cash payments for merchandise purchased. (Recall that the earlier inventory adjustment replaced the cost of goods sold with the cost of merchandise purchased.) In contrast, an increase in accounts payable means that cash payments for purchases were less than the cost of purchases for the period. Thus, an accounts payable increase is added to net income as it is converted to a cash flow amount. Java House shows a $9,000 decrease in accounts payable during 2013. This decrease is subtracted from net income.

Net income	$32,000
Add: Depreciation	10,000
Deduct: Gain on sale of land	(8,000)
Deduct: Accounts receivable increase	(5,000)
Add: Inventory decrease	6,000
Deduct: Prepaid insurance increase	(13,000)
Deduct: Accounts payable decrease	**(9,000)**

Accrued Liabilities Change

Changes in accrued liabilities are interpreted the same way as changes in accounts payable. A decrease means that cash payments exceeded the related expense amounts; an increase means that cash payments were less than the related expenses. Decreases are subtracted from net income; increases are added to net income. Java has one accrued liability, income tax payable, and it increased by $2,000 during 2013. The $2,000 increase is added to net income.

Net income	$32,000
Add: Depreciation	10,000
Deduct: Gain on sale of land	(8,000)
Deduct: Accounts receivable increase	(5,000)
Add: Inventory decrease	6,000
Deduct: Prepaid insurance increase	(13,000)
Deduct: Accounts payable decrease	(9,000)
Add: Income tax payable increase	**2,000**

We have now identified the adjustments to convert Java's net income to its net cash flow from operating activities. The operating activities section of the statement of cash flows appears as follows under the indirect method:

Net income	$32,000
Add (deduct) items to convert net income to cash basis:	
Depreciation	10,000
Gain on sale of land	(8,000)
Accounts receivable increase	(5,000)
Inventory decrease	6,000
Prepaid insurance increase	(13,000)
Accounts payable decrease	(9,000)
Income tax payable increase	2,000
Net cash provided by operating activities	**$15,000**

To summarize, net cash flows from operating activities begins with net income (loss) and eliminates noncash expenses (such as depreciation) and any gains and losses that are properly reported in the investing and financing sections. Next, cash inflows (outflows) relating to changes in the level of current operating assets and liabilities are added (subtracted) to yield net cash flows from operating activities. During the period, Java earned cash operating profits of $34,000 ($32,000 + $10,000 − $8,000), but used $19,000 of cash (−$5,000 + $6,000 − $13,000 − $9,000 + $2,000) to increase net working capital. Cash outflows relating to the increase in net working capital are a common occurrence for growing companies, and this net asset increase must be financed just like the increase in PPE assets.

BUSINESS INSIGHT **Starbucks' Adjustments for Operating Cash Flow**

Starbucks reports $1,384.7 million of net income for 2012 and $1,750.3 million of operating cash inflows. The difference between these numbers is largely due to $580.6 million of depreciation and amortization expense that is included in net income. Depreciation is a noncash charge; it is an expense but Starbucks did not pay for it in cash. It is added back to net income in computing operating cash flows. Starbucks also reports an add-back of $61.1 million relating to deferred income tax expense (indicating that cash payments of taxes are less than tax expense reported in net income), a $49.3 million deduction to remove the noncash portion of income recognized on equity method investments (meaning that Starbucks received less in dividends from affiliated companies than it reported in equity income), and a $153.6 million add-back of noncash compensation expense in the form of stock-based compensation (because that compensation is paid in stock, not in cash). All of these are noncash items that must be removed from reported net income to yield net cash flow from operating activities.

MANAGERIAL DECISION **You Are the Securities Analyst**

You are analyzing a company's statement of cash flows. The company has two items relating to its accounts receivable. First, the company finances the sale of its products to some customers; the increase to notes receivable is classified as an investing activity. Second, the company sells its accounts receivable to a separate entity, such as a trust. As a result, sale of receivables is reported as an asset sale; this reduces receivables and yields a gain or loss on sale (in this case, the company is not required to consolidate the trust as a Primary Beneficiary of a Variable Interest Entity). This action increases its operating cash flows. How should you interpret this cash flow increase? [Answer, p. B-29]

CASH FLOWS FROM INVESTING ACTIVITIES

Analyze Remaining Noncash Assets

LO3 Define and explain net cash flows from investing activities.

Investing activities cause changes in asset accounts. Usually the accounts affected (other than cash) are noncurrent asset accounts such as property, plant and equipment assets and long-term investments, although short-term investment accounts can also be affected. To determine the cash flows from investing activities, *we analyze changes in all noncash asset accounts not used in computing net cash flow from operating activities.* Our objective is to identify any investing cash flows related to these changes.

As before, changes in long-term assets accounts (and investment accounts) are classified as cash inflows and cash outflows according to the following decision rule:

Balance Sheet Account	Cash flow increases from	Cash flow decreases from
Noncurrent assets	Account decreases	Account increases

Increases in long-term assets and investment accounts are identified as cash outflows. Decreases are identified as cash inflows.

Java House Case Illustration

Analyze Change in Long-Term Investments

Java's comparative balance sheets show that long-term investments increased $15,000 during 2013. The increase means that investments must have been purchased, and the additional data reported indicates that cash was spent to purchase long-term stock investments. Purchasing stock is an investing activity. Thus, a $15,000 purchase of stock investments is reported as a cash outflow from investing activities in the statement of cash flows.

Analyze Change in Property, Plant and Equipment Assets

Java's PPE assets decreased $20,000 during 2013. PPE assets decrease as the result of disposals, and the additional data for Java House indicate that land was sold for cash in 2013. Selling land is an investing activity. Thus, the sale of land for $28,000 is reported as a cash inflow from investing activities in the statement of cash flows. (Recall that the $8,000 gain on sale of land was deducted as a reconciling item in the operating section; see above.)

Analyze Change in Accumulated Depreciation

Java's accumulated depreciation increased $10,000 during 2013. Accumulated depreciation increases when depreciation expense is recorded. Java's 2013 depreciation expense was $10,000, so the total change in accumulated depreciation is the result of the recording of depreciation expense. As previously discussed, there is no cash flow related to the recording of depreciation expense, and we have previously adjusted for this expense in our computation of net cash flows from operating activities.

Analyze Change in Patent

We see from the comparative balance sheets that Java had an increase of $60,000 in a patent. The increase means that a patent was acquired, and the additional data indicate that common stock was issued to obtain a patent. This event is a noncash investing (acquiring a patent) and financing (issuing common stock) transaction that must be disclosed as supplementary information to the statement of cash flows.

BUSINESS INSIGHT **Starbucks' Investing Activities**

Starbucks used $974.0 million cash for investing activities in 2012. Two major investing activities involved "investments." Starbucks buys and sells marketable securities throughout the year as it invests its excess cash to generate interest, dividends, and capital gains. The company used cash of $1,748.6 million to purchase new securities and received cash of $1,796.4 from security sales. Starbucks also spent $129.1 million cash to acquire other companies. Note that this is the cash portion of the acquisitions. The company might also have issued debt and stock to finance its acquisition, which would be excluded from the investing section of the cash flow statement but would be specifically listed as a noncash investing activity in a footnote. Starbucks invested $856.2 million in property, plant, and equipment (PPE) and received cash of $5.3 million on sales of PPE during the year. These expenditures might have been for company-owned property or for leasehold improvements on leased property. It also spent $41.8 million on other, unspecified investments. Investing activities listed on the statement of cash flows can involve investments in operating assets (such as purchases of PPE or acquisitions of other companies) or investments in nonoperating assets (such as purchases and sales of marketable securities and other investments).

CASH FLOWS FROM FINANCING ACTIVITIES

Analyze Remaining Liabilities and Equity

LO4 Define and explain net cash flows from financing activities.

Financing activities cause changes in liability and stockholders' equity accounts. Usually the accounts affected are noncurrent accounts such as bonds payable and common stock, although a current liability such as short-term notes payable can also be affected. To determine the cash flows from financing activities, *we analyze changes in all liability and stockholders' equity accounts that were not used in computing net cash flow from operating activities.* Our objective is to identify any financing cash flows related to these changes.

As before, changes in long-term liability and equity accounts are classified as cash inflows and cash outflows according to the following decision rule:

Balance Sheet Account	Cash flow increases from	Cash flow decreases from
Noncurrent liabilities and equity. . . .	Account increases	Account decreases

Increases in long-term liabilities and equity accounts are identified as cash inflows. Decreases are identified as cash outflows.

Java House Case Illustration

Analyze Change in Common Stock

Java's common stock increased $70,000 during 2013. Common stock increases when shares of stock are issued. As noted in discussing the patent increase, common stock with a $60,000 par value was issued in exchange for a patent. This event is disclosed as a noncash investing and financing transaction. The other $10,000 increase in common stock, as noted in the additional data, resulted from an issuance of stock for cash. Issuing common stock is a financing activity, so a $10,000 cash inflow from a stock issuance appears as a financing activity in the statement of cash flows.

Analyze Change in Retained Earnings

Retained earnings grew from $56,000 to $75,000 during 2013—a $19,000 increase. This increase is the net result of Java's $32,000 of net income (which increased retained earnings) and a $13,000 cash dividend (which decreased retained earnings). Because every item in Java's income statement was considered in computing the net cash provided by operating activities, only the cash dividend remains to be considered. Paying a cash dividend is a financing activity. Thus, a $13,000 cash dividend appears as a cash outflow from financing activities in the statement of cash flows. We have now completed the analysis of all of Java's noncash balance sheet accounts and can prepare the 2013 statement of cash flows. Exhibit B.4 shows this statement.

If there are cash inflows and outflows from similar types of investing and financing activities, the inflows and outflows are reported separately (rather than reporting only the net difference). For example, proceeds from the sale of plant assets are reported separately from outlays made to acquire plant assets. Similarly, funds borrowed are reported separately from debt repayments, and proceeds from issuing stock are reported separately from outlays to acquire treasury stock.

BUSINESS INSIGHT **Starbucks' Financing Activities**

Starbucks realized cash outflows of $(312.5) million ($236.6 million − $549.1 million) from issuance of common stock, net of repurchases. Only stock issued for cash is reflected in the statement of cash flows. Stock issued in connection with acquisitions is not reflected because it does not involve cash. Issuance of stock is often related to the exercise of employee stock options, and companies frequently repurchase stock to offset the dilutive effect of granting the options and to have stock to sell to employees who exercise their options. Starbucks also reports a cash outflow of $(30.8) million from borrowings during the year. Starbucks used cash of $(513.0) million to pay dividends. The net effect is a decrease in cash of $(745.5) million from financing activities.

SUMMARY OF NET CASH FLOW REPORTING

Income statement accounts are all identified within the operating section of the statement of cash flows. Balance sheet items are classified as follows:

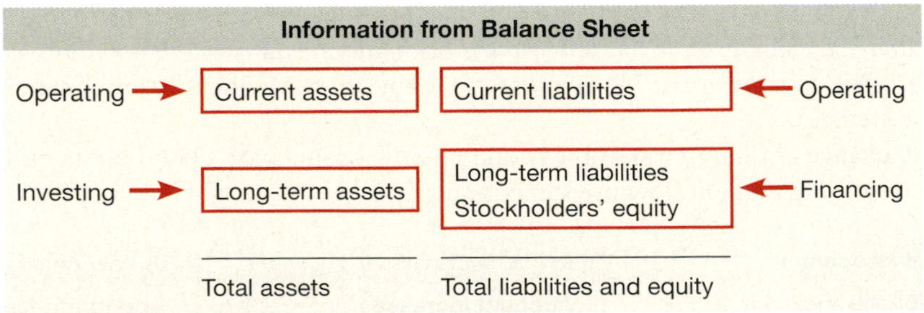

More specifically, and drawing on the Java House illustration, we can summarize the cash flow effects of the income statement and balance sheet information and categorize them into the operating, investing and financing classifications in the following table:

Account	Change	Source or Use	Cash flow effect	Classification on SCF
Current assets				
Accounts receivable	+5,000	Use	−5,000	Operating
Inventories	−6,000	Source	+6,000	Operating
Prepaid insurance	+13,000	Use	−13,000	Operating
Noncurrent assets				
PPE related				Investing
Accumulated depreciation	+10,000	Neither	+10,000	Operating
Sale of land				
Proceeds	+28,000	Source	+28,000	Investing
Gain	−8,000	Neither	−8,000	Operating
Investments	+15,000	Use	−15,000	Investing
Current liabilities				
Accounts payable	−9,000	Use	−9,000	Operating
Income tax payable	+2,000	Source	+2,000	Operating
Long-term liabilities				Financing
Stockholders' equity				
Common stock	+10,000	Source	+10,000	Financing
Retained earnings				
Net income	+32,000	Source	+32,000	Operating
Dividends	+13,000	Use	−13,000	Financing
Total (net cash flow)			+25,000	

The current year's cash balance increases by $25,000, from $10,000 to $35,000. Formal preparation of the statement of cash flows can proceed once we have addressed one final issue: required supplemental disclosures. We discuss that topic in the next section.

Supplemental Disclosures for Indirect Method

When the indirect method is used in the statement of cash flows, three separate disclosures are required: (1) two specific operating cash outflows—cash paid for interest and cash paid for income taxes, (2) a schedule or description of all noncash investing and financing transactions, and (3) the firm's policy for determining which highly liquid, short-term investments are treated as cash equivalents. Noncash investing and financing activities include the issuance of stocks, bonds, or leases in exchange for property, plant, and equipment (PPE) assets or intangible assets; the exchange of long-term assets for other long-term assets; and the conversion of long-term debt into common stock.

Java House Case Illustration

Java House incurred no interest cost during 2013. It did pay income taxes. Our discussion of the $2,000 change in income tax payable during 2013 revealed that the increase meant that cash tax payments were less than income tax expense by the amount of the increase. Income tax expense was $11,000, so the cash paid for income taxes was $2,000 less than $11,000, or $9,000.

Java House did have one noncash investing and financing event during 2013: the issuance of common stock to acquire a patent. This event, as well as the cash paid for income taxes, is disclosed as supplemental information to the statement of cash flows in Exhibit B.4.

EXHIBIT B.4 Statement of Cash Flows for Indirect Method with Supplemental Disclosures

JAVA HOUSE Statement of Cash Flows For Year Ended December 31, 2013		
Net cash flow from operating activities		
Net income	$32,000	
Add (deduct) items to convert net income to cash basis		
Depreciation	10,000	
Gain on sale of land	(8,000)	
Accounts receivable increase	(5,000)	
Inventory decrease	6,000	
Prepaid insurance increase	(13,000)	
Accounts payable decrease	(9,000)	
Income tax payable increase	2,000	
Net cash provided by operating activities		$15,000
Cash flows from investing activities		
Purchase of stock investments	(15,000)	
Sale of land	28,000	
Net cash provided by investing activities		13,000
Cash flows from financing activities		
Issuance of common stock	10,000	
Payment of dividends	(13,000)	
Net cash used by financing activities		(3,000)
Net increase in cash		25,000
Cash at beginning of year		10,000
Cash at end of year		$35,000
Supplemental cash flow disclosures		
Cash paid for income taxes	$ 9,000	
Schedule of noncash investing and financing activities		
Issuance of common stock to acquire patent	$60,000	

ANALYSIS OF CASH FLOW INFORMATION

Cash Flow Patterns

Typically, established companies have positive cash flow from operating activities. This cash flow provides most (if not all) of the total cash required to grow the business while maintaining appropriate levels of net working capital. On average, net cash flow from investing activities is negative as companies grow the PPE infrastructure needed to support the business. (Any excess cash invested in marketable securities typically generates cash flow, but this is small relative to the larger cash outflow for PPE and acquisitions.) Financing activities make up the difference between cash generated by operating activities and cash used by investing activities. Companies that generate more cash from operating activities than is required to support investing activities use that excess cash to pay down indebtedness, repurchase stock, or pay additional dividends. Companies that need cash for investing activities typically generate it from financing activities.

Exhibit B.5 presents various cash flow items as a percentage of total revenues for the S&P500 companies for the most recent year ending in fiscal 2012 and 2013. The median operating cash flow is 17% of total revenues. (The first and third quartiles are 10% and 26%, respectively, and only eight of the S&P500 companies reported negative operating cash flow.) Of the 17% of operating cash flows to revenue, net income explains 9 percentage points, and the add-backs for depreciation and stock based compensation explain 4 and 1 percentage points, respectively. The remaining 3 percentage points relate to cash inflows and outflows from net working capital accounts.

Investing activities typically represent an outflow of cash equal to 9% of revenues, with CAPEX comprising 44% of the total (4 percentage points out of 9). Other investing activities generally relate to investment of excess cash in marketable securities. The median S&P company generates more

RESEARCH INSIGHT **Net Income Versus Cash Flows**

By definition, GAAP net income consists of two components: cash and noncash items. Accountants call the noncash items "accruals" (defined as the difference between net income and cash from operations). Finance and accounting research investigates whether, and how, net earnings, operating cash flows, and accruals each predict (1) future earnings or future cash flows (this line of research is called predictability research), and (2) stock price (this line of research is called value-relevance research).

Although the statement of cash flows is very useful in a number of analysis situations, predictability research shows that it is net income and not current operating cash flow that better predicts future net income. Predictability research by Richard Sloan (*The Accounting Review*, 1996) found that the two components of net income (accruals and cash flows) have different impacts on future earnings; specifically, cash flows are more "persistent," meaning that they have longer-term implications for future earnings than accruals do. Later, work by Vuolteenaho (*Journal of Finance*, 2002) found that in addition to information about future earnings, the accruals and cash flows explain the riskiness of the firm. The interpretation is that because accruals are less persistent and they fluctuate more, they signal additional risk. One way to use this finding in our analysis is to compute the ratio of operating cash flow to net income: the higher that number, the lower the firm's operating risk.

Early value-relevance research from the late 1960s found that when firms announced that their earnings were higher (lower) than the prior year's earnings, stock price increased (decreased). This sparked much research into the relevance of accounting earnings for stock prices. With growth in the sources and speed of information, our current understanding is that although earnings are important for stock prices, most of the information conveyed by earnings is factored into stock price long before the company announces its official numbers. For example, Ball and Shivakumar (*Journal of Accounting Research*, 2008) find that earnings announcement events only account for 1% to 2% of the stock price movement each year. Later, value-relevance research investigated whether the stock market reacts differently to cash flow versus the accruals components of earnings. For example, Sloan's (1996) finding came to be known as the *accrual anomaly*—the fact that stock prices do not differentiate between accruals and cash flows—which causes mispricing because accruals fluctuate more wildly than cash flows. However, markets learn quickly from their mistakes and evidence of the accrual anomaly has decreased steadily since 1996. In sum, both of these research streams are ongoing and active areas as academics and analysts seek to understand how the various earnings components are related to future firm profitability as well as how the income statement, balance sheet, and statement of cash flows separately and collectively inform investors about firm value and riskiness.

operating cash flow than is required for investing activities, and reports negative cash flow of 4% of revenues for financing activities. These activities generally include the payment of dividends, the repayment of debt, and the repurchase of common stock.

EXHIBIT B.5 **Statement of Cash Flow Items as a Percentage of Total Revenues**

	Net Income	Depreciation and Amortization	Stock-Based Compensation	Cash from Operations	Cash from Investing	Capital Expenditure	Cash from Financing
Median	9%	4%	1%	17%	(9)%	(4)%	(4)%
Third Quartile . . .	15%	8%	1%	26%	(3)%	(7)%	1%
First Quartile. . . .	5%	3%	0%	10%	(22)%	(2)%	(9)%

During the fiscal years ending in 2012 and 2013, S&P companies are profitable (only 18 of the 500 companies report a net loss greater than 5% of revenues) and generate sizeable operating cash flows. It is common for large companies to generate more operating cash flow than is required for investing activities, thus permitting the payment of dividends, the retirement of debt, and the repurchase of common stock. We expect this profile for a healthy, mature company.

During extreme growth periods, however—for example, in the early part of a company's life cycle—operating cash flow may be negative because the company is not yet profitable but must use cash to grow inventories and provide credit to customers (accounts receivable delay cash collection). Debt and equity financing is required during that period. Ultimately, the company must generate positive operating cash flow because debt and equity financing options are not unlimited and investors are reluctant to finance operating losses beyond a few years.

Bed, Bath & Beyond (BBBY) is typical of most companies in the S&P500 sample, and its operating, investing, and financing activities for the last decade evince the typical pattern (see Exhibit B.6). BBBY's operating cash flow has grown throughout this period and provides sufficient cash to support the growth of net working capital and to partially finance the investment in PPE. Financing activities provide the remaining cash needed for investing activities. Notice how the investing and financing cash flows move in opposite directions, indicating greater financing inflows when cash outflows for investing activities increase, and vice versa. Most mature, healthy companies exhibit a similar cash flow profile.

EXHIBIT B.6 Bed, Bath & Beyond (BBBY) Operating, Investing, and Financing Cash Flows

Harley-Davidson (HOG) provides a good example of how a company can use financing activities to provide necessary cash during economic downturns (see Exhibit B.7). The economic downturn of 2008 markedly impacted the company, as it reports in the following section from its 2008 10-K (HDFS refers to Harley-Davidson Financial Services):

> The Company's 2008 results were impacted by the difficult economic environment including lower consumer confidence and significant disruptions in global capital markets. The Company's 2008 net revenue and net income were down 2.3% and 29.9%, respectively, compared to 2007. Operating income for the Motorcycles segment was down 21.5% while operating income for the Financial Services segment decreased 61.0%. . . During 2008, debt increased by $1.81 billion which was primarily driven by higher finance receivables outstanding as HDFS funded a greater percentage of its business through debt rather than through securitization transactions when compared to 2007.

As retail sales dried up, Harley was forced to finance its operations with additional debt. Lender financing was also required to support its finance receivables (notes and leases), as it became difficult to access the market in which Harley had previously sold (securitized) its receivables. Then, as operating cash flow recovered and securities markets stabilized in subsequent years, Harley was able to reduce its financing, as evidenced by the negative financing cash flows in 2010 through 2012.

EXHIBIT B.7 Harley-Davidson (HOG) Operating, Investing, and Financing Cash Flows

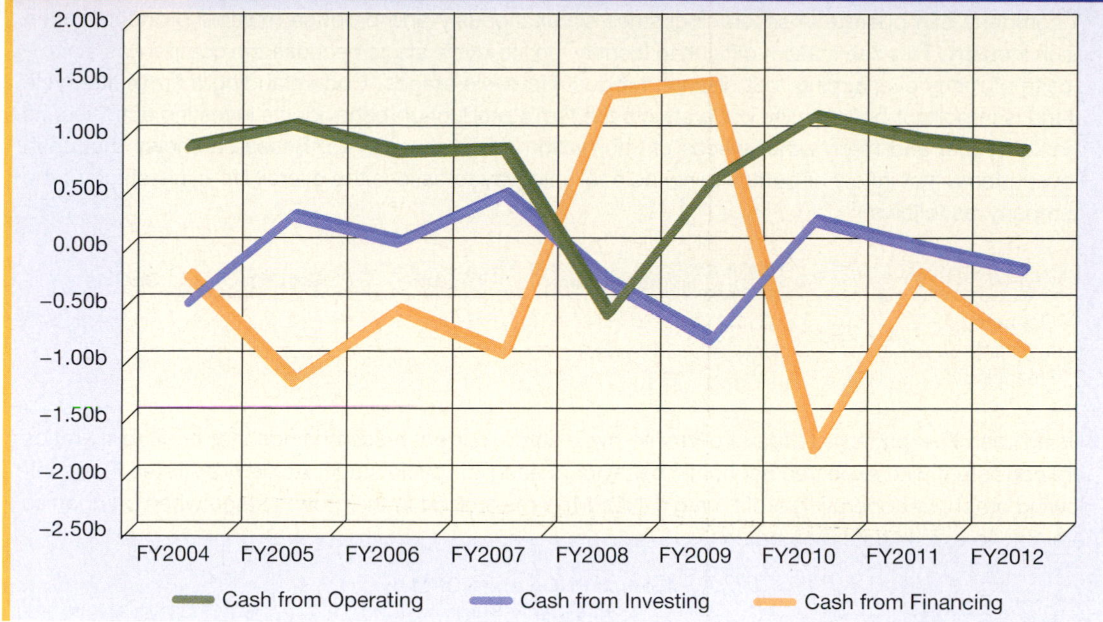

Finally, **Apple Inc. (AAPL)** presents the picture of health through fiscal 2012 (see Exhibit B.8). As its operating cash flows have soared, Apple has not required any external financing and has invested its excess cash in marketable securities. This presents a unique cash flow pattern. As of September 2012, Apple reported a staggering $110.5 billion in marketable securities in addition to $10.7 billion of cash and cash equivalents.

EXHIBIT B.8 Apple Inc. (AAPL) Operating, Investing, and Financing Cash Flows

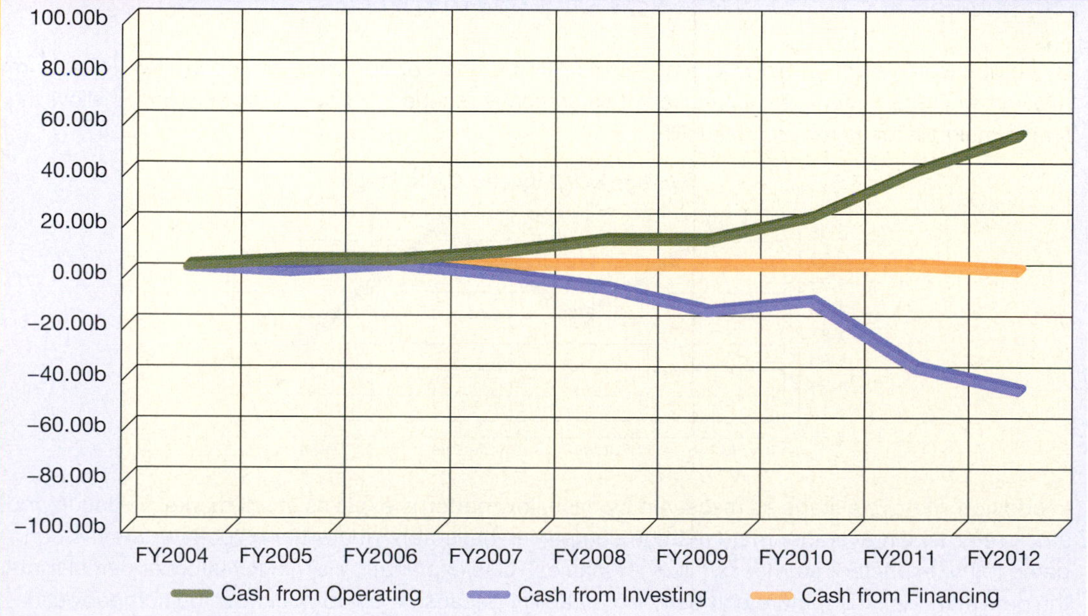

RESEARCH INSIGHT **Cash Flow Patterns as an Indicator of Firm Life Cycle**

A company can operate in several industries simultaneously and produce multiple products within each industry. This can make it difficult to identify the life-cycle stage because the company is a composite of many overlapping, but distinct, product life-cycle stages. Understanding a firm's life-cycle stage is important because life cycle affects the firm's production behavior, its investing activities, its market share, and many other pieces of information useful to analysis. Research shows that cash flow patterns (net inflow or outflow) provide a reliable way to assess the overall life-cycle stage of the company, as follows:

	Introduction	Growth	Maturity	Decline
Operating	−	+	+	−
Investing	−	−	−	+
Financing	+	+	−	+/−

Using cash flow patterns to identify firm life-cycle stage, current research finds that profitability ratios are consistent with expected economic behavior at each life-cycle stage. As demonstrated in the following graph, net operating profit margin (NOPM) is maximized in the growth stage when companies are able to differentiate their brands.

Average RNOA and NOPM by Life-Cycle Stage

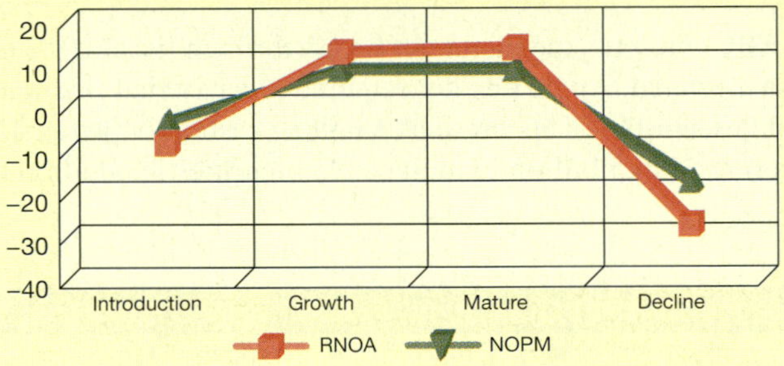

By comparison, return on net operating assets (RNOA) and net operating asset turnover (NOAT) are maximized in the maturity stage as market saturation is reached but operating efficiencies allow the firm to maintain (or increase) profitability.

Average NOAT by Life-Cycle Stage

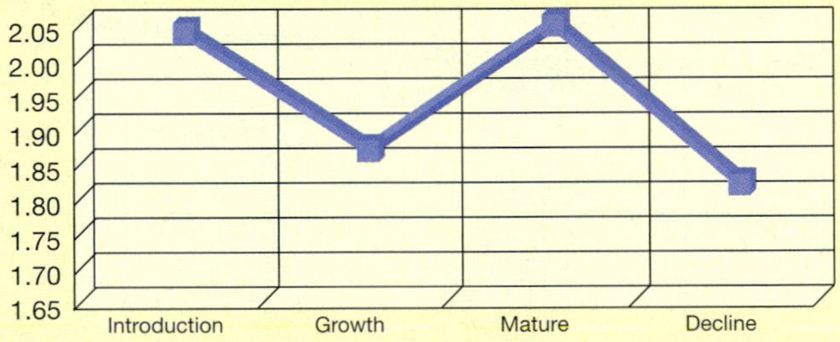

In addition, life-cycle stage as measured by cash flow patterns explains stock market valuation and stock returns. On average, mature-stage companies have abnormally high stock returns (as compared to the expected return for similar companies). One explanation is that investors underestimate the persistence of the mature company's profitability because they do not know the company's life-cycle stage and expect profits (and stock prices) to quickly revert to "normal" levels. (Source: Dickinson, Victoria, "Cash Flow Patterns as a Proxy for Firm Life Cycle," *The Accounting Review*, November 2011, 86(6): 1969–1994.)

BUSINESS INSIGHT **Objectivity of Cash**

Usefulness of financial statements is enhanced when the underlying data are objective and verifiable. Measuring cash and the changes in cash are among the most objective measurements that accountants make. Thus, the statement of cash flows is arguably the most objective financial statement. This characteristic of the statement of cash flows is welcomed by those investors and creditors interested in evaluating the quality of a firm's income.

Usefulness of the Statement of Cash Flows

A statement of cash flows shows the periodic cash effects of a firm's operating, investing, and financing activities. Distinguishing among these different categories of cash flows helps users compare, evaluate, and predict cash flows. With cash flow information, creditors and investors are better able to assess a firm's ability to settle its liabilities and pay its dividends. A firm's need for outside financing is also better evaluated when using cash flow data. Over time, the statement of cash flows permits users to observe and access management's investing and financing policies.

A statement of cash flows also provides information useful in evaluating a firm's financial flexibility. *Financial flexibility* is a firm's ability to generate sufficient amounts of cash to respond to unanticipated needs and opportunities. Information about past cash flows, particularly cash flows from operations, helps in assessing financial flexibility. An evaluation of a firm's ability to survive an unexpected drop in demand, for example, should include a review of its past cash flows from operations. The larger these cash flows, the greater is the firm's ability to withstand adverse changes in economic conditions. Other financial statements, particularly the balance sheet and its notes, also contain information useful for judging financial flexibility.

Some investors and creditors find the statement of cash flows useful in evaluating the quality of a firm's income. As we know, determining income under accrual accounting procedures requires many accruals, deferrals, allocations, and valuations. These adjustment and measurement procedures introduce more subjectivity into income determination than some financial statement users prefer. These users relate a more objective performance measure—cash flow from operations—to net income. To these users, the higher this ratio is, the higher is the quality of income.

In analyzing the statement of cash flows, we must not necessarily conclude that the company is better off if cash increases and worse off if cash decreases. It is not the cash change that is most important, but the sources of that change. For example, what are the sources of cash inflows? Are these sources transitory? Are these sources mainly from operating activities? We must also review the uses of cash. Has the company invested its cash in operating areas to strengthen its competitive position? Is it able to comfortably meet its debt obligations? Has it diverted cash to creditors or investors at the expense of the other? Such questions and answers are key to properly interpreting the statement of cash flows for business decisions.

Ratio Analyses of Cash Flows

LO5 Describe and apply ratios based on operating cash flows.

Data from the statement of cash flows enter into various financial ratios. Two such ratios are the operating cash flow to current liabilities ratio and the operating cash flow to capital expenditures ratio.

Operating Cash Flow to Current Liabilities Ratio

Two measures previously introduced—the current ratio and the quick ratio—emphasize the relation of current assets to current liabilities in an attempt to measure the ability of the firm to liquidate current liabilities when they become due. The **operating cash flow to current liabilities ratio** is another measure of the ability to liquidate current liabilities and is calculated as follows:

Operating Cash Flow to Current Liabilities = Cash Flow from Operating Activities/Average Current Liabilities

Net cash flow from operating activities is obtained from the statement of cash flows; it represents the excess amount of cash derived from operations during the year after deducting working capital needs and payments required on current liabilities. The denominator is the average of the beginning and ending current liabilities for the year.

To illustrate, the following amounts are taken from the 2012 financial statements for **Cisco Systems, Inc.**

Net cash flow from operating activities	$11,491 million
Current liabilities at beginning of the year	17,506 million
Current liabilities at end of the year	17,731 million

Its operating cash flow to current liabilities ratio of 0.65 is computed as follows:

$$\$11{,}491 \text{ million}/[(\$17{,}506 \text{ million} + \$17{,}731 \text{ million})/2] = 0.65$$

The higher this ratio, the stronger is a firm's ability to settle current liabilities as they come due. A ratio of 0.5 is considered a good ratio, so, Cisco's ratio of 0.65 is above average.

Operating Cash Flow to Capital Expenditures Ratio

To remain competitive, an entity must be able to replace, and expand when appropriate, its property, plant, and equipment. A ratio that helps assess a firm's ability to do this from internally generated cash flow is the **operating cash flow to capital expenditures ratio**, which is computed as follows:

$$\text{Operating Cash Flow to Capital Expenditures} = \frac{\text{Cash Flow from Operating Activities}}{\text{Annual Capital Expenditures}}$$

The numerator in this ratio comes from the first section of the statement of cash flows—the section reporting the net cash flow from operating activities. Information for the denominator can be found in one or more places in the financial statements and related disclosures. Data on capital expenditures are part of the required industry segment disclosures in notes to the financial statements. Capital expenditures are often also shown in the investing activities section of the statement of cash flows. Also, capital expenditures often appear in the comparative selected financial data presented as supplementary information to the financial statements. Finally, management's discussion and analysis of the statements commonly identify the annual capital expenditures.

A ratio in excess of 1.0 means that the firm's current operating activities are providing cash in excess of the amount needed to provide the desired level of plant capacity and would normally be considered a sign of financial strength. This ratio is also viewed as an indicator of long-term solvency—a ratio exceeding 1.0 means that there is operating cash flow in excess of capital needs that can then be used to repay outstanding long-term debt.

The interpretation of this ratio for a firm is influenced by its trend in recent years, the ratio size being achieved by other firms in the same industry, and the stage of the firm's life cycle. A firm in the early stages of its life cycle, when periods of rapid expansion occur, is expected to experience a lower ratio than a firm in the mature stage of its life cycle, when maintenance of plant capacity is more likely than expansion of capacity.

To illustrate the ratio's computation, **Cicso Systems** reported capital expenditures in 2012 of $1,126 million. Cisco's operating cash flow to capital expenditures ratio for that same year is 10.2, computed as $11,491 million/$1,126 million. Following are recent operating cash flow to capital expenditures ratios for several companies:

Colgate-Palmolive (consumer grocery products)	5.66
Lockheed Martin (aerospace)	1.66
Verizon Communications (telecommunications)	1.95
Harley-Davidson (motorcycle manufacturer)	4.24
Home Depot (home products)	5.32

APPENDIX-END REVIEW 1

Part A

1. Which of the following is not disclosed in a statement of cash flows?
   a. A transfer of cash to a cash equivalent investment
   b. The amount of cash at year-end
   c. Cash outflows from investing activities during the period
   d. Cash inflows from financing activities during the period
2. Which of the following events appears in the cash flows from investing activities section of the statement of cash flows?
   a. Cash received as interest
   b. Cash received from issuance of common stock
   c. Cash purchase of equipment
   d. Cash payment of dividends
3. Which of the following events appears in the cash flows from financing activities section of the statement of cash flows?
   a. Cash purchase of equipment
   b. Cash purchase of bonds issued by another company
   c. Cash received as repayment for funds loaned
   d. Cash purchase of treasury stock
4. Tyler Company has a net income of $49,000 and the following related items:

Depreciation expense.	$ 5,000
Accounts receivable increase.	2,000
Inventory decrease.	10,000
Accounts payable decrease.	4,000

   Using the indirect method, what is Tyler's net cash flow from operations?
   a. $42,000 *b.* $46,000 *c.* $58,000 *d.* $38,000

Part B

Expresso Royale's income statement and comparative balance sheets follow:

EXPRESSO ROYALE
Income Statement
For Year Ended December 31, 2013

Sales.		$385,000
Dividend income.		5,000
		390,000
Cost of goods sold.	$233,000	
Wages expense	82,000	
Advertising expense.	10,000	
Depreciation expense.	11,000	
Income tax expense.	17,000	
Loss on sale of investments.	2,000	355,000
Net income.		$ 35,000

EXPRESSO ROYALE Balance Sheets	Dec. 31, 2013	Dec. 31, 2012
Assets		
Cash	$ 8,000	$ 12,000
Accounts receivable	22,000	28,000
Inventory	94,000	66,000
Prepaid advertising	12,000	9,000
Long-term investments—Available-for-sale	30,000	41,000
Fair value adjustment to investments	—	(1,000)
Plant assets	178,000	130,000
Accumulated depreciation	(72,000)	(61,000)
Total assets	$272,000	$224,000
Liabilities and Equity		
Accounts payable	$ 27,000	$ 14,000
Wages payable	6,000	2,500
Income tax payable	3,000	4,500
Common stock	139,000	125,000
Retained earnings	97,000	79,000
Unrealized loss on investments	—	(1,000)
Total liabilities and equity	$272,000	$224,000

Cash dividends of $17,000 were declared and paid during 2013. Plant assets were purchased for cash in 2013, and, later in the year, additional common stock was issued for cash. Investments costing $11,000 were sold for cash at a $2,000 loss in 2013; an unrealized loss of $1,000 on these investments had been recorded in 2012 (at December 31, 2013, the cost and fair value of unsold investments are equal).

Required

a. Compute the change in cash that occurred during 2013.

b. Prepare a 2013 statement of cash flows using the indirect method.

The solution is on page B-48.

APPENDIX B1: Direct Method Reporting for the Statement of Cash Flows

To prepare a statement of cash flows, we need a firm's income statement, comparative balance sheets, and some additional data taken from the accounting records. Exhibit B.2 presents this information for Java House. We use these data to prepare Java's 2013 statement of cash flows using the direct method. Java's statement of cash flows explains the $25,000 increase in cash that occurred during 2013 (from $10,000 to $35,000) by classifying the firm's cash flows into operating, investing, and financing categories. To get the information to construct the statement, we do the following:

1. **Use the direct method to determine individual cash flows from operating activities.** We use changes that occurred during 2013 in various current asset and current liability accounts.
2. **Determine cash flows from investing activities.** We do this by analyzing changes in noncurrent asset accounts.
3. **Determine cash flows from financing activities.** We do this by analyzing changes in liability and stockholders' equity accounts.

The net cash flows from investing and financing are identical to those prepared using the indirect method. Only the format of the net cash flows from operating activities differs between the two methods, not the total amount of cash generated from operating activities.

Cash Flows from Operating Activities

The **direct method** presents net cash flow from operating activities by showing the major categories of operating cash receipts and payments. The operating cash receipts and payments are usually determined by converting the accrual revenues and expenses to corresponding cash amounts. It is efficient to do it this way because the accrual revenues and expenses are readily available in the income statement.

Converting Revenues and Expenses to Cash Flows

Exhibit B.9 summarizes the procedures for converting individual income statement items to corresponding cash flows from operating activities.

EXHIBIT B.9 Adjustments to Convert Income Statement Items to Operating Activity Cash Flows

Income Statement Item	Adjustment	Operating Activity Cash Flow
Sales	+ Decrease in accounts receivable *or* − Increase in accounts receivable **and** + Increase in deferred (unearned) revenue *or* − Decrease in deferred (unearned) revenue	= Receipts from customers
Cost of goods sold	+ Increase in inventory *or* − Decrease in inventory **and** + Decrease in accounts payable *or* − Increase in accounts payable	= Payments for merchandise
Operating expenses Interest expense Income tax expense (excluding items listed below)	+ Increase in related prepaid expense *or* − Decrease in related prepaid expense **and** + Decrease in related accrued liability *or* − Increase in related accrued liability	= Payments for expenses
Depreciation expense Depletion expense Amortization expense	+ Depreciation expense + Depletion expense + Amortization expense	= 0
Gains (investing and financing) Losses (investing and financing)	Exclude: Not related to cash from operating activities	= 0

Java House Case Illustration

We next explain and illustrate the process of converting Java House's 2013 revenues and expenses to corresponding cash flows from operating activities under the direct method.

Convert Sales to Cash Received from Customers

During 2013, accounts receivable increased $5,000. This increase means that during 2013, cash collections on account (which decrease accounts receivable) were less than credit sales (which increase accounts receivable). We compute cash received from customers as follows (this computation assumes that no accounts were written off as uncollectible during the period):

Sales	$250,000
− Increase in accounts receivable	(5,000)
= Cash received from customers	$245,000

Convert Cost of Goods Sold to Cash Paid for Merchandise Purchased

The conversion of cost of goods sold to cash paid for merchandise purchased is a two-step process. First, cost of goods sold is adjusted for the change in inventory to determine the amount of purchases during the year. Then the purchases amount is adjusted for the change in accounts payable to derive the cash paid for merchandise purchased. Inventory decreased from $60,000 to $54,000 during 2013. This $6,000 decrease indicates that the cost of goods sold exceeded the cost of goods purchased during the year. The year's purchases amount is computed as follows:

	Cost of goods sold	$148,000
−	Decrease in inventory	(6,000)
=	Purchases	$142,000

During 2013, accounts payable decreased $9,000. This decrease reflects the fact that cash payments for merchandise purchased on account (which decrease accounts payable) exceeded purchases on account (which increase accounts payable). The cash paid for merchandise purchased, therefore, is computed as follows:

	Purchases	$142,000
+	Decrease in accounts payable	9,000
=	Cash paid for merchandise purchased	$151,000

Convert Wages Expense to Cash Paid to Employees

No adjustment to wages expense is needed. The absence of any beginning or ending accrued liability for wages payable means that wages expense and cash paid to employees as wages are the same amount: $52,000.

Convert Insurance Expense to Cash Paid for Insurance

Prepaid insurance increased $13,000 during 2013. The $13,000 increase reflects the excess of cash paid for insurance during 2013 (which increases prepaid insurance) over the year's insurance expense (which decreases prepaid insurance). Starting with insurance expense the cash paid for insurance is computed as follows:

	Insurance expense	$ 5,000
+	Increase in prepaid insurance	13,000
=	Cash paid for insurance	$18,000

Eliminate Depreciation Expense and Other Noncash Operating Expenses

Depreciation expense is a noncash expense. Because it does not represent a cash payment, depreciation expense is eliminated (by adding it back) as we convert accrual expense amounts to the corresponding amounts of cash payments. If Java House had any amortization expense or depletion expense, it would eliminate them for the same reason. The amortization of an intangible asset and the depletion of a natural resource are noncash expenses.

Convert Income Tax Expense to Cash Paid for Income Taxes

The increase in income tax payable from $3,000 at December 31, 2012, to $5,000 at December 31, 2013, means that 2013's income tax expense (which increases income tax payable) was $2,000 more than 2013's tax payments (which decrease income tax payable). If we start with income tax expense, then we calculate cash paid for income taxes as follows:

	Income tax expense	$11,000
−	Increase in income tax payable	(2,000)
=	Cash paid for income taxes	$ 9,000

Omit Gains and Losses Related to Investing and Financing Activities

The income statement may contain gains and losses related to investing or financing activities. Examples include gains and losses from the sale of plant assets and gains and losses from the retirement of bonds payable. Because these gains and losses are not related to operating activities, we omit them as we convert income statement items to various cash flows from operating activities. The cash flows relating to these gains and losses are reported in the investing activities or financing activities sections of the statement of cash flows. Java House had an $8,000 gain from the sale of land in 2013. This gain is excluded; no related cash flow appears within the operating activities category.

We have now applied the adjustments to convert each accrual revenue and expense to the corresponding operating cash flow. We use these individual cash flows to prepare the operating activities section of the statement of cash flows; see Exhibit B.10

EXHIBIT B.10 Direct Method Operating Section of Statement of Cash Flows

Cash received from customers		$245,000
Cash paid for merchandise purchased	$151,000	
Cash paid to employees	52,000	
Cash paid for insurance	18,000	
Cash paid for income taxes	9,000	230,000
Net cash provided by operating activities		$ 15,000

Cash Flows from Investing and Financing

The reporting of investing and financing activities in the statement of cash flows is identical under the indirect and direct methods. Thus, we simply refer to the previous sections in this appendix for explanations.

Supplemental Disclosures

When the direct method is used for the statement of cash flows, three separate disclosures are required: (1) a reconciliation of net income to the net cash flow from operating activities, (2) a schedule or description of all noncash investing and financing transactions, and (3) the firm's policy for determining which highly liquid, short-term investments are treated as cash equivalents. The firm's policy regarding cash equivalents is placed in the financial statement notes. The other two separate disclosures are reported either in the notes or at the bottom of the statement of cash flows.

The required reconciliation is essentually the indirect method of computing cash flow from operating activities. *Thus, when the direct method is used in the statement of cash flows, the indirect method is a required separate disclosure.* We discussed the indirect method earlier in this appendix.

Java House did have one noncash investing and financing event during 2013: the issuance of common stock to acquire a patent. This event is disclosed as supplemental information to the statement of cash flows in Exhibit B.4.

APPENDIX-END REVIEW 2

Expresso Royale's income statement and comparative balance sheets follow:

EXPRESSO ROYALE
Income Statement
For Year Ended December 31, 2013

Sales		$385,000
Dividend income		5,000
		390,000
Cost of goods sold	$233,000	
Wages expense	82,000	
Advertising expense	10,000	
Depreciation expense	11,000	
Income tax expense	17,000	
Loss on sale of investments	2,000	355,000
Net income		$ 35,000

EXPRESSO ROYALE Balance Sheets	Dec. 31, 2013	Dec. 31, 2012
Assets		
Cash	$ 8,000	$ 12,000
Accounts receivable	22,000	28,000
Inventory	94,000	66,000
Prepaid advertising	12,000	9,000
Long-term investments—Available-for-sale	30,000	41,000
Fair value adjustment to investments	—	(1,000)
Plant assets	178,000	130,000
Accumulated depreciation	(72,000)	(61,000)
Total assets	$272,000	$224,000
Liabilities and Equity		
Accounts payable	$ 27,000	$ 14,000
Wages payable	6,000	2,500
Income tax payable	3,000	4,500
Common stock	139,000	125,000
Retained earnings	97,000	79,000
Unrealized loss on investments	—	(1,000)
Total liabilities and equity	$272,000	$224,000

Cash dividends of $17,000 were declared and paid during 2013. Plant assets were purchased for cash in 2013, and later in the year, additional common stock was issued for cash. Investments costing $11,000 were sold for cash at a $2,000 loss in 2013; an unrealized loss of $1,000 on these investments had been recorded in 2012 (at December 31, 2013, the cost and fair value of unsold investments are equal).

Required

a. Compute the change in cash that occurred during 2013.

b. Prepare a 2013 statement of cash flows using the direct method.

The solution is on page B-49.

GUIDANCE ANSWERS

MANAGERIAL DECISION You Are the Securities Analyst

Many companies, but not all, treat customers' notes receivable as an investing activity. In 2005, the SEC became concerned with this practice and issued letters to a number of companies objecting to this accounting classification. "Presenting cash receipts from receivables generated by the sale of inventory as investing activities in the company's consolidated statements of cash flows is not in accordance with GAAP," wrote the chief accountant for the SEC's division of corporation finance, in her letter to the companies ("Little Campus Lab Shakes Big Firms—Georgia Tech Crew's Report Spurs Change in Accounting for Operating Cash Flow," March 1, 2005, *The Wall Street Journal*). The SEC's position is that these notes receivable are an operating activity and analysts are certainly justified in treating them likewise. Concerning the sale of receivables, so long as the separate entity (a trust in this case) is properly structured, the transaction can be treated as a sale (rather than require consolidation) with a consequent reduction in receivables and a gain or loss on the sale recorded in the income statement. Many analysts treat this as a financing activity and argue that the cash inflow should not be regarded as an increase in operating cash flows. Bottom line: many argue that operating cash flows do not increase as a result of these two transactions and analysts should adjust the statement of cash flows to properly classify the financing of receivables as an operating activity and the sale of receivables as a financing activity.

Superscript B1 denotes assignments based on Appendix B1.

DISCUSSION QUESTIONS

Q B-1. What is the definition of *cash equivalents?* Give three examples of cash equivalents.

Q B-2. Why are cash equivalents included with cash in a statement of cash flows?

Q B-3. What are the three major types of activities classified on a statement of cash flows? Give an example of a cash inflow and a cash outflow in each classification.

Q B-4. In which of the three activity categories of a statement of cash flows would each of the following items appear? Indicate for each item whether it represents a cash inflow or a cash outflow:

a. Cash purchase of equipment.
b. Cash collection on loans receivable.
c. Cash dividends paid.
d. Cash dividends received.
e. Cash proceeds from issuing stock.
f. Cash receipts from customers.
g. Cash interest paid.
h. Cash interest received.

Q B-5. Traverse Company acquired a $3,000,000 building by issuing $3,000,000 worth of bonds payable. In terms of cash flow reporting, what type of transaction is this? What special disclosure requirements apply to a transaction of this type?

Q B-6. Why are noncash investing and financing transactions disclosed as supplemental information to a statement of cash flows?

Q B-7. Why is a statement of cash flows a useful financial statement?

Q B-8.[B1] What is the difference between the direct method and the indirect method of presenting net cash flow from operating activities?

Q B-9. In determining net cash flow from operating activities using the indirect method, why must we add depreciation back to net income? Give an example of another item that is added back to net income under the indirect method.

Q B-10. Vista Company sold for $98,000 cash land originally costing $70,000. The company recorded a gain on the sale of $28,000. How is this event reported in a statement of cash flows using the indirect method?

Q B-11. A firm uses the indirect method. Using the following information, what is its net cash flow from operating activities?

Net income	$88,000
Accounts receivable decrease	13,000
Inventory increase	9,000
Accounts payable decrease	3,500
Income tax payable increase	1,500
Depreciation expense	6,000

Q B-12. What separate disclosures are required for a company that reports a statement of cash flows using the indirect method?

Q B-13. If a business had a net loss for the year, under what circumstances would the statement of cash flows show a positive net cash flow from operating activities?

Q B-14.[B1] A firm is converting its accrual revenues to corresponding cash amounts using the direct method. Sales on the income statement are $925,000. Beginning and ending accounts receivable on the balance sheet are $58,000 and $44,000, respectively. What is the amount of cash received from customers?

Q B-15.[B1] A firm reports $86,000 wages expense in its income statement. If beginning and ending wages payable are $3,900 and $2,800, respectively, what is the amount of cash paid to employees?

Q B-16.[B1] A firm reports $43,000 advertising expense in its income statement. If beginning and ending prepaid advertising are $6,000 and $7,600, respectively, what is the amount of cash paid for advertising?

Q B-17.[B1] Rusk Company sold equipment for $5,100 cash that had cost $35,000 and had $29,000 of accumulated depreciation. How is this event reported in a statement of cash flows using the direct method?

Q B-18.[B1] What separate disclosures are required for a company that reports a statement of cash flows using the direct method?

Q B-19. How is the operating cash flow to current liabilities ratio calculated? Explain its use.

Q B-20. How is the operating cash flow to capital expenditures ratio calculated? Explain its use.

Q B-21. The statement of cash flows provides information that may be useful in predicting future cash flows, evaluating financial flexibility, assessing liquidity, and identifying financing needs. It is not, however, the best financial statement for learning about a firm's financial performance during a period; information about periodic financial performance is provided by the income statement. Two basic principles—the revenue recognition principle and the matching concept—work to distinguish the income statement from the statement of cash flows. (a) Define the revenue recognition principle and the matching concept. (b) Briefly explain how these two principles work to make the income statement a better report on periodic financial performance than the statement of cash flows.

Assignments with the ✔ logo in the margin are available in myBusinessCourse. See the Preface of the book for details.

MINI EXERCISES

M B-22. Classification of Cash Flows (LO1)

For each of the items below, indicate whether the cash flow relates to an operating activity, an investing activity, or a financing activity.

a. Cash receipts from customers for services rendered.
b. Sale of long-term investments for cash.
c. Acquisition of plant assets for cash.
d. Payment of income taxes.
e. Bonds payable issued for cash.
f. Payment of cash dividends declared in previous year.
g. Purchase of short-term investments (not cash equivalents) for cash.

M B-23. Classification of Cash Flows (LO1)

For each of the items below, indicate whether it is (1) a cash flow from an operating activity, (2) a cash flow from an investing activity, (3) a cash flow from a financing activity, (4) a noncash investing and financing activity, or (5) none of the above.

a. Paid cash to retire bonds payable at a loss.
b. Received cash as settlement of a lawsuit.
c. Acquired a patent in exchange for common stock.
d. Received advance payments from customers on orders for custom-made goods.
e. Gave large cash contribution to local university.
f. Invested cash in 60-day commercial paper (a cash equivalent).

M B-24. Net Cash Flow from Operating Activities (Indirect Method) (LO2)

The following information was obtained from Galena Company's comparative balance sheets. Assume that Galena Company's 2013 income statement showed depreciation expense of $9,000, a gain on sale of investments of $11,000, and a net income of $40,000. Calculate the net cash flow from operating activities using the indirect method.

	Dec. 31, 2013	Dec. 31, 2012
Cash	$ 19,000	$ 10,000
Accounts receivable	45,000	35,000
Inventory	55,000	49,000
Prepaid rent	6,000	7,000
Long-term investments	20,000	34,000
Plant assets	150,000	106,000
Accumulated depreciation	42,000	33,000
Accounts payable	25,000	20,000
Income tax payable	4,000	6,000
Common stock	121,000	92,000
Retained earnings	106,000	91,000

M B-25. Net Cash Flow from Operating Activities (Indirect Method) (LO2)
Cairo Company had a $19,000 net loss from operations for 2014. Depreciation expense for 2014 was $9,200 and a 2014 cash dividend of $6,000 was declared and paid. Balances of the current asset and current liability accounts at the beginning and end of 2014 follow. Did Cairo Company's 2014 operating activities provide or use cash? Use the indirect method to determine your answer.

	Ending	Beginning
Cash	$ 4,000	$ 8,000
Accounts receivable	16,000	25,000
Inventory	49,000	53,000
Prepaid expenses	6,000	10,000
Accounts payable	12,000	9,000
Accrued liabilities	5,500	7,600

M B-26.[B1] Operating Cash Flows (Direct Method) (LO2)
Calculate the cash flow for each of the following cases.

a. Cash paid for rent:

Rent expense	$65,000
Prepaid rent, beginning year	11,000
Prepaid rent, end of year	8,000

b. Cash received as interest:

Interest income	$15,500
Interest receivable, beginning year	3,000
Interest receivable, end of year	3,800

c. Cash paid for merchandise purchased:

Cost of goods sold	$87,000
Inventory, beginning year	19,000
Inventory, end of year	23,000
Accounts payable, beginning year	11,000
Accounts payable, end of year	8,000

M B-27.[B1] Operating Cash Flows (Direct Method) (LO2)
Howell Company's current year income statement reports the following:

Sales	$785,000
Cost of goods sold	450,000
Gross profit	$335,000

Howell's comparative balance sheets show the following (accounts payable relate to merchandise purchases):

	End of Year	Beginning of Year
Accounts receivable	$ 68,000	$60,000
Inventory	109,000	99,000
Prepaid expenses	2,000	8,000
Accounts payable	31,000	36,000

Compute Howell's current-year cash received from customers and cash paid for merchandise purchased.

EXERCISES

E B-28. Net Cash Flow from Operating Activities (Indirect Method) (LO2)
Lincoln Company owns no plant assets and reported the following income statement for the current year:

Sales		$700,000
Cost of goods sold	$425,000	
Wages expense	110,000	
Rent expense	38,000	
Insurance expense	15,000	588,000
Net income		$112,000

Additional balance sheet information about the company follows:

	End of Year	Beginning of Year
Accounts receivable	$56,000	$48,000
Inventory	60,000	66,000
Prepaid insurance	7,000	5,000
Accounts payable	22,000	18,000
Wages payable	11,000	15,000

Use the information to calculate the net cash flow from operating activities under the indirect method.

E B-29. Statement of Cash Flows (Indirect Method) (LO2, 3, 4)
Use the following information about Lund Corporation for 2013 to prepare a statement of cash flows under the indirect method.

Accounts payable increase	$ 9,000
Accounts receivable increase	4,000
Accrued liabilities decrease	3,000
Amortization expense	6,000
Cash balance, beginning of 2013	22,000
Cash balance, end of 2013	15,000
Cash paid as dividends	29,000
Cash paid to purchase land	90,000
Cash paid to retire bonds payable at par	60,000
Cash received from issuance of common stock	35,000
Cash received from sale of equipment	17,000
Depreciation expense	29,000
Gain on sale of equipment	4,000
Inventory decrease	13,000
Net income	76,000
Prepaid expenses increase	2,000

Nike, Inc. (NKE)

E B-30. Operating Section of Statement of Cash Flows (Indirect Method) (LO2)
Following are the income statement and balance sheet for Nike, Inc. for the year ended May 31, 2013, and a forecasted income statement and balance sheet for 2014.

Income Statement

($ millions)	2013 Actual	2014 Est.
Revenues	$25,313	$27,465
Cost of sales	14,279	15,490
Gross margin	11,034	11,975
Demand creation expense	2,745	2,966
Operating overhead expense	5,035	5,466
Interest expense (income), net	(3)	(3)
Other (income)	(15)	(19)
Income before income taxes	3,272	3,565
Income taxes	808	881
Net income	$ 2,464	$ 2,684

Balance Sheet

($ millions)	2013 Actual	2014 Est.
Cash and equivalents	$ 3,337	$ 3,625
Short-term investments	2,628	2,628
New investments	—	1,129
Accounts receivable, net	3,117	3,378
Inventories	3,434	3,735
Deferred income taxes	308	330
Prepaid expenses and other current assets	802	879
Total current assets	13,626	15,704
Property, plant and equipment, net	2,452	2,654
Identifiable intangible assets, net	382	304
Goodwill	131	131
Deferred income taxes and other assets	993	1,071
Total assets	$17,584	$19,864
Current portion of long-term debt	$ 57	$ 46
Notes payable	121	121
Accounts payable	1,646	1,785
Accrued liabilities	1,986	2,142
Income taxes payable	98	107
Liabilities of discontinued operations	18	18
Total current liabilities	3,926	4,219
Long-term debt	1,210	1,164
Deferred income taxes and other liabilities	1,292	1,401
Shareholders' equity:		
Common stock at stated value	3	3
Capital in excess of stated value	5,184	5,184
Accumulated other comprehensive income	274	274
Retained earnings	5,695	7,619
Total shareholders' equity	11,156	13,080
Total liabilities and shareholders' equity	$17,584	$19,864

Prepare the net cash flows from operating activities section of a forecasted statement of cash flows for 2014 using the indirect method. Treat current and noncurrent deferred tax assets and liabilities as operating. Operating expenses (Cost of sales) for 2014 include estimated depreciation expense of $485 million and amortization expense of $78 million.

E B-31. Operating Section of Statement of Cash Flows (Indirect Method) **(LO2)**
Following are the income statement and balance sheet for **General Mills, Inc.** for the year ended May 26, 2013, and a forecasted income statement and balance sheet for 2014.

General Mills, Inc. (GIS)

Income Statement

($ millions)	2013 Actual	2014 Est.
Net sales	$17,774.1	$18,662.8
Cost of sales	11,350.2	11,925.5
Selling, general, and administrative expenses	3,552.3	3,732.6
Restructuring, impairment, and other exit costs	19.8	0.0
Operating profit	2,851.8	3,004.7
Interest, net	316.9	316.9
Earnings before income taxes and after-tax earnings from joint ventures	2,534.9	2,687.8
Income taxes	741.2	784.8
After-tax earnings from joint ventures	98.8	98.8
Net earnings, including earnings attributable to noncontrolling interests	1,892.5	2,001.8
Net earnings attributable to noncontrolling interests	37.3	40.0
Net earnings attributable to General Mills	$ 1,855.2	$ 1,961.8

Balance Sheet

($ millions)	2013 Actual	2014 Est.
Cash and cash equivalents	$ 741.4	$ 783.8
Receivables	1,446.4	1,511.7
Inventories	1,545.5	1,623.7
Deferred income taxes	128.0	130.6
Prepaid expenses and other	437.6	466.6
Total current assets	4,298.9	4,516.4
Land, buildings, and equipment	3,878.1	3,906.9
Goodwill	8,622.2	8,622.2
Other intangible assets	5,015.1	5,015.1
Other assets	843.7	877.2
Total assets	$22,658.0	$22,937.8
Current liabilities:		
Accounts payable	$ 1,423.2	$ 1,493.0
Short-term debt	—	1,275.9
Current portion of long-term debt	1,443.3	1,181.9
Notes payable	599.7	599.7
Other current liabilities	1,827.7	1,922.3
Total current liabilities	5,293.9	6,472.8
Total long-term debt	5,926.1	4,744.2
Deferred income taxes	1,389.1	1,455.7
Other liabilities	1,952.9	2,052.9
Total liabilities	14,562.0	14,725.6
Redeemable interest	967.5	—
Stockholders' equity:		
Common stock	75.5	75.5
Additional paid-in capital	1,166.6	1,166.6
Retained earnings	10,702.6	11,746.3
Common stock in treasury	(3,687.2)	(3,687.2)
Accumulated other comprehensive loss	(1,585.3)	(1,585.3)
Total stockholders' equity	6,672.2	7,715.9
Noncontrolling interests	456.3	496.3
Total equity	7,128.5	8,212.2
Total liabilities and equity	$22,658.0	$22,937.8

Prepare the net cash flows from operating activities section of a forecasted statement of cash flows for 2014 using the indirect method. Operating expenses (such as Cost of sales and Selling, general and administrative expenses) for 2014 include estimated depreciation expense of $624.4 million. Estimated 2014 retained earnings includes dividends of $918.1 million.

E B-32.[B1] Operating Cash Flows (Direct Method) (LO2)
Calculate the cash flow for each of the following cases.
a. Cash paid for advertising:

Advertising expense	$62,000
Prepaid advertising, beginning of year	11,000
Prepaid advertising, end of year	15,000

b. Cash paid for income taxes:

Income tax expense	$29,000
Income tax payable, beginning of year	7,100
Income tax payable, end of year	4,900

c. Cash paid for merchandise purchased:

Cost of goods sold	$180,000
Inventory, beginning of year	30,000
Inventory, end of year	25,000
Accounts payable, beginning of year	10,000
Accounts payable, end of year	12,000

E B-33.[B1] Statement of Cash Flows (Direct Method) (LO2, 3, 4)
Use the following information about the 2013 cash flows of Mason Corporation to prepare a statement of cash flows under the direct method.

Cash balance, end of 2013	$ 12,000
Cash paid to employees and suppliers	148,000
Cash received from sale of land	40,000
Cash paid to acquire treasury stock	10,000
Cash balance, beginning of 2013	16,000
Cash received as interest	6,000
Cash paid as income taxes	11,000
Cash paid to purchase equipment	89,000
Cash received from customers	194,000
Cash received from issuing bonds payable	30,000
Cash paid as dividends	16,000

E B-34.[B1] Operating Cash Flows (Direct Method) (LO2)
Refer to the information in Exercise B-28. Calculate the net cash flow from operating activities using the direct method. Show a related cash flow for each revenue and expense.

E B-35. Investing and Financing Cash Flows (LO3, 4)
During 2014, Paxon Corporation's long-term investments account (at cost) increased $15,000, which was the net result of purchasing stocks costing $80,000 and selling stocks costing $65,000 at a $6,000 loss. Also, its bonds payable account decreased $40,000, the net result of issuing $100,000 of bonds at $103,000 and retiring bonds with a face value (and book value) of $140,000 at a $9,000 gain. What items and amounts appear in the (a) cash flows from investing activities and (b) cash flows from financing activities sections of its 2014 statement of cash flows?

PROBLEMS

P B-36. Statement of Cash Flows (Indirect Method) (LO2, 3, 4)
Wolff Company's income statement and comparative balance sheets follow.

WOLFF COMPANY Income Statement For Year Ended December 31, 2013		
Sales		$635,000
Cost of goods sold	$430,000	
Wages expense	86,000	
Insurance expense	8,000	
Depreciation expense	17,000	
Interest expense	9,000	
Income tax expense	29,000	579,000
Net income		$ 56,000

WOLFF COMPANY Balance Sheet	Dec. 31, 2013	Dec. 31, 2012
Assets		
Cash	$ 11,000	$ 5,000
Accounts receivable	41,000	32,000
Inventory	90,000	60,000
Prepaid insurance	5,000	7,000
Plant assets	250,000	195,000
Accumulated depreciation	(68,000)	(51,000)
Total assets	$329,000	$248,000
Liabilities and Stockholders' Equity		
Accounts payable	$ 7,000	$ 10,000
Wages payable	9,000	6,000
Income tax payable	7,000	8,000
Bonds payable	130,000	75,000
Common stock	90,000	90,000
Retained earnings	86,000	59,000
Total liabilities and equity	$329,000	$248,000

Cash dividends of $29,000 were declared and paid during 2013. Also in 2013, plant assets were purchased for cash, and bonds payable were issued for cash. Bond interest is paid semiannually on June 30 and December 31. Accounts payable relate to merchandise purchases.

Required

a. Compute the change in cash that occurred during 2013.

b. Prepare a 2013 statement of cash flows using the indirect method.

Macy's, Inc. (M)

P B-37. Statement of Cash Flows (Indirect Method) (LO2, 3, 4)

Following are the income statement and balance sheet for **Macy's, Inc.** for the year ended February 2, 2013, and a forecasted income statement and balance sheet for 2014.

Income Statement ($ millions)	2013	2014 Est.
Net sales	$27,686	$29,070
Cost of sales	16,538	17,355
Gross margin	11,148	11,715
Selling, general and administrative expenses	8,482	8,895
Impairments, store closing costs and gain on sale of leases	(5)	(0)
Operating income	2,661	2,820
Interest expense	(425)	(425)
Premium on early retirement of debt	(137)	0
Interest income	3	3
Earnings before income tax expense	2,102	2,398
Income tax expense	(767)	(875)
Net income	$ 1,335	$ 1,523

Balance Sheet ($ millions)	2013	2014 Est.
Cash and cash equivalents	$ 1,836	$ 1,919
Short-term investments		1,478
Receivables	371	378
Merchandise inventories	5,308	5,581
Prepaid expenses and other current assets	361	378
Total current assets	7,876	9,734
Property and equipment, net	8,196	7,426
Goodwill	3,743	3,743
Other intangible assets, net	561	561
Other assets	615	640
Total assets	$20,991	$22,104
Current liabilities		
Short-term debt	$ 124	$ 144
Merchandise accounts payable	1,579	1,657
Accounts payable and accrued liabilities	2,610	2,733
Income taxes	355	378
Deferred income taxes	407	436
Total current liabilities	5,075	5,348
Long-term debt	6,806	6,325
Deferred income taxes	1,238	1,308
Other liabilities	1,821	1,919
Shareholders' equity		
Common stock	4	4
Additional paid-in capital	3,872	3,872
Accumulated equity	5,108	6,261
Treasury stock	(2,002)	(2,002)
Accumulated other comprehensive income	(931)	(931)
Total shareholders' equity	6,051	7,204
Total liabilities and equity	$20,991	$22,104

Required

Prepare a forecasted statement of cash flows for 2014 using the indirect method. Operating expenses for 2014 (such as Cost of goods sold and General and administrative expenses) include capital expenditures of $262, estimated depreciation and amortization expense of $1,032 million; and estimated retained earnings assume the payment of $370 million in dividends.

P B-38. Statement of Cash Flows (Indirect Method) (LO2, 3, 4)
Arctic Company's income statement and comparative balance sheets follow.

ARCTIC COMPANY
Income Statement
For Year Ended December 31, 2013

Sales		$728,000
Cost of goods sold	$534,000	
Wages expense	190,000	
Advertising expense	31,000	
Depreciation expense	22,000	
Interest expense	18,000	
Gain on sale of land	(25,000)	770,000
Net loss		$ (42,000)

ARCTIC COMPANY
Balance Sheet

	Dec. 31, 2013	Dec. 31, 2012
Assets		
Cash	$ 49,000	$ 28,000
Accounts receivable	42,000	50,000
Inventory	107,000	113,000
Prepaid advertising	10,000	13,000
Plant assets	360,000	222,000
Accumulated depreciation	(78,000)	(56,000)
Total assets	$490,000	$370,000
Liabilities and Stockholders' Equity		
Accounts payable	$ 17,000	$ 31,000
Interest payable	6,000	—
Bonds payable	200,000	—
Common stock	245,000	245,000
Retained earnings	52,000	94,000
Treasury stock	(30,000)	—
Total liabilities and equity	$490,000	$370,000

During 2013, Arctic sold land for $70,000 cash that had originally cost $45,000. Arctic also purchased equipment for cash, acquired treasury stock for cash, and issued bonds payable for cash in 2013. Accounts payable relate to merchandise purchases.

Required

a. Compute the change in cash that occurred during 2013.

b. Prepare a 2013 statement of cash flows using the indirect method.

P B-39. Statement of Cash Flows (Indirect Method) (LO2, 3, 4)
Dair Company's income statement and comparative balance sheets follow.

DAIR COMPANY
Income Statement
For Year Ended December 31, 2013

Sales		$700,000
Cost of goods sold	$440,000	
Wages and other operating expenses	95,000	
Depreciation expense	22,000	
Amortization expense	7,000	
Interest expense	10,000	
Income tax expense	36,000	
Loss on bond retirement	5,000	615,000
Net income		$ 85,000

DAIR COMPANY
Balance Sheet

	Dec. 31, 2013	Dec. 31, 2012
Assets		
Cash	$ 27,000	$ 18,000
Accounts receivable	53,000	48,000
Inventory	103,000	109,000
Prepaid expenses	12,000	10,000
Plant assets	360,000	336,000
Accumulated depreciation	(87,000)	(84,000)
Intangible assets	43,000	50,000
Total assets	$511,000	$487,000
Liabilities and Stockholders' Equity		
Accounts payable	$ 32,000	$ 26,000
Interest payable	4,000	7,000
Income tax payable	6,000	8,000
Bonds payable	60,000	120,000
Common stock	252,000	228,000
Retained earnings	157,000	98,000
Total liabilities and equity	$511,000	$487,000

During 2013, the company sold for $17,000 cash old equipment that had cost $36,000 and had $19,000 accumulated depreciation. Also in 2013, new equipment worth $60,000 was acquired in exchange for $60,000 of bonds payable, and bonds payable of $120,000 were retired for cash at a loss. A $26,000 cash dividend was declared and paid in 2013. Any stock issuances were for cash.

Required

a. Compute the change in cash that occurred in 2013.
b. Prepare a 2013 statement of cash flows using the indirect method.
c. Prepare separate schedules showing (1) cash paid for interest and for income taxes and (2) noncash investing and financing transactions.

Whole Foods Market, Inc. (WFM)

P B-40. Statement of Cash Flows (Indirect Method) **(LO2, 3, 4)**
Following are the income statement and balance sheet for **Whole Foods Market, Inc.**, for the year ended September 29, 2013, and a forecasted income statement and balance sheet for 2014.

Balance Sheet		
($ millions)	**2013 Actual**	**2014 Est.**
Current assets:		
Cash and cash equivalents	$ 290	$ 313
Short-term investments—available-for-sale securities	733	733
Restricted cash	111	111
Accounts receivable	188	213
Merchandise inventories	414	455
Prepaid expenses and other current assets	93	99
Deferred income taxes	151	151
Total current assets	1,980	2,075
Property and equipment, net of accumulated depreciation and amortization	2,428	2,647
Long-term investments—available-for-sale securities	302	302
Goodwill	679	679
Intangible assets, net of accumulated amortization	65	65
Deferred income taxes	72	72
Other assets	12	14
Total assets	$ 5,538	$ 5,854
Liabilities and shareholders' equity		
Current liabilities:		
Current installments of capital lease obligations	$ 1	$ 3
Accounts payable	247	270
Short-term debt	—	157
Accrued payroll, bonus and other benefits due team members	367	398
Dividends payable	37	37
Other current liabilities	436	483
Total current liabilities	1,088	1,348
Long-term capital lease obligations, less current installments	26	23
Deferred lease liabilities	500	500
Other long-term liabilities	46	57
Total liabilities	1,660	1,928
Commitments and contingencies		
Shareholders' equity:		
Common stock, no par value, 600.0 shares authorized; 375.7 and 371.6 shares issued; 372.4 and 370.9 shares outstanding at 2013 and 2012, respectively	2,765	2,765
Common stock in treasury, at cost, 3.3 and 0.7 shares at 2013 and 2012, respectively	(153)	(153)
Accumulated other comprehensive income	1	1
Retained earnings	1,265	1,313
Total shareholders' equity	3,878	3,926
Total liabilities and shareholders' equity	$ 5,538	$ 5,854

Income Statement ($ millions)	2013 Actual	2014 Est.
Sales	$12,917	$14,209
Cost of goods sold and occupancy costs	8,288	9,122
Gross profit	4,629	5,087
Direct store expenses	3,285	3,609
General and administrative expenses	397	440
Pre-opening expenses	52	57
Relocation, store closure and lease termination costs	12	—
Operating income	883	981
Interest expense	—	—
Investment and other income	11	11
Income before income taxes	894	992
Provision for income taxes	343	381
Net income	$ 551	$ 611

Required

Prepare a forecasted statement of cash flows for 2014 using the indirect method. Assume the following:

- Operating expenses for 2014 (such as General and administrative) include depreciation and amortization expense of $376 million.
- The company did not dispose of or write-down any long-term assets during the year.
- The company paid dividends of $563 million in 2014.

P B-41. Statement of Cash Flows (Indirect Method) **(LO2, 3, 4)**

Rainbow Company's income statement and comparative balance sheets follow.

RAINBOW COMPANY Income Statement For Year Ended December 31, 2013		
Sales		$750,000
Dividend income		15,000
		765,000
Cost of goods sold	$440,000	
Wages and other operating expenses	130,000	
Depreciation expense	39,000	
Patent amortization expense	7,000	
Interest expense	13,000	
Income tax expense	44,000	
Loss on sale of equipment	5,000	
Gain on sale of investments	(10,000)	668,000
Net income		$ 97,000

RAINBOW COMPANY Balance Sheet	Dec. 31, 2013	Dec. 31, 2012
Assets		
Cash and cash equivalents	$ 19,000	$ 25,000
Accounts receivable	40,000	30,000
Inventory	103,000	77,000
Prepaid expenses	10,000	6,000
Long-term investments—Available-for-sale	—	50,000
Fair value adjustment to investments	—	7,000
Land	190,000	100,000
Buildings	445,000	350,000
Accumulated depreciation—Buildings	(91,000)	(75,000)
Equipment	179,000	225,000
Accumulated depreciation—Equipment	(42,000)	(46,000)
Patents	50,000	32,000
Total assets	$903,000	$781,000
Liabilities and Stockholders' Equity		
Accounts payable	$ 20,000	$ 16,000
Interest payable	6,000	5,000
Income tax payable	8,000	10,000
Bonds payable	155,000	125,000
Preferred stock ($100 par value)	100,000	75,000
Common stock ($5 par value)	379,000	364,000
Paid-in capital in excess of par value—Common	133,000	124,000
Retained earnings	102,000	55,000
Unrealized gain on investments	—	7,000
Total liabilities and equity	$903,000	$781,000

During 2013, the following transactions and events occurred in addition to the company's usual business activities:

1. Sold long-term investments costing $50,000 for $60,000 cash. Unrealized gains totaling $7,000 related to these investments had been recorded in earlier years. At year-end, the fair value adjustment and unrealized gain account balances were eliminated.
2. Purchased land for cash.
3. Capitalized an expenditure made to improve the building.
4. Sold equipment for $14,000 cash that originally cost $46,000 and had $27,000 accumulated depreciation.
5. Issued bonds payable at face value for cash.
6. Acquired a patent with a fair value of $25,000 by issuing 250 shares of preferred stock at par value.
7. Declared and paid a $50,000 cash dividend.
8. Issued 3,000 shares of common stock for cash at $8 per share.
9. Recorded depreciation of $16,000 on buildings and $23,000 on equipment.

Required

a. Compute the change in cash and cash equivalents that occurred during 2013.
b. Prepare a 2013 statement of cash flows using the indirect method.
c. Prepare separate schedules showing (1) cash paid for interest and for income taxes and (2) noncash investing and financing transactions.

P B-42.[B1] Statement of Cash Flows (Direct Method) **(LO2, 3, 4)**
Refer to the data for Wolff Company in Problem B-36.

Required

a. Compute the change in cash that occurred during 2013.
b. Prepare a 2013 statement of cash flows using the direct method.

P B-43.[B1] Statement of Cash Flows (Direct Method) **(LO2, 3, 4)**
Refer to the data for Arctic Company in Problem B-38.

Required

a. Compute the change in cash that occurred during 2013.
b. Prepare a 2013 statement of cash flows using the direct method.

P B-44.[B1] Statement of Cash Flows (Direct Method) **(LO2, 3, 4)**
Refer to the data for Dair Company in Problem B-39.

Required

a. Compute the change in cash that occurred in 2013.
b. Prepare a 2013 statement of cash flows using the direct method. Use one cash outflow for "cash paid for wages and other operating expenses." Accounts payable relate to inventory purchases only.
c. Prepare separate schedules showing (1) a reconciliation of net income to net cash flow from operating activities (see Exhibit B.3) and (2) noncash investing and financing transactions.

P B-45.[B1] Statement of Cash Flows (Direct Method) **(LO2, 3, 4)**
Refer to the data for Rainbow Company in Problem B-41.

Required

a. Compute the change in cash that occurred in 2013.
b. Prepare a 2013 statement of cash flows using the direct method. Use one cash outflow for "cash paid for wages and other operating expenses." Accounts payable relate to inventory purchases only.
c. Prepare separate schedules showing (1) a reconciliation of net income to net cash flow from operating activities (see Exhibit B.3) and (2) noncash investing and financing transactions.

Amgen Inc. (AMGN)

P B-46. Interpreting the Statement of Cash Flows (LO1, 5)
Following is the statement of cash flows of Amgen Inc.

Year Ended December 31 (In millions)	2012	2011	2010
Cash flows from operating activities:			
Net income	$ 4,345	$3,683	$ 4,627
Depreciation and amortization	1,088	1,060	1,017
Stock-based compensation expense	362	341	353
Deferred income taxes	28	(328)	(151)
Property, plant and equipment impairments	178	6	118
Other items, net	(74)	63	140
Changes in operating assets and liabilities, net of acquisitions:			
Trade receivables, net	348	(557)	(210)
Inventories	(150)	(383)	153
Other assets	124	(204)	20
Accounts payable	161	(95)	142
Accrued income taxes	87	(20)	(656)
Legal reserve	(780)	780	—
Other liabilities	165	773	234
Net cash provided by operating activities	5,882	5,119	5,787
Cash flows from investing activities:			
Purchases of property, plant and equipment	(689)	(567)	(580)
Cash paid for acquisitions, net of cash acquired	(2,390)	(701)	—
Purchases of marketable securities	(26,241)	(21,183)	(14,602)
Proceeds from sales of marketable securities	17,372	20,871	10,485
Proceeds from maturities of marketable securities	1,994	749	642
Other	(36)	45	(97)
Net cash used in investing activities	(9,990)	(786)	(4,152)
Cash flows from financing activities:			
Net proceeds from issuance of debt	4,933	10,387	2,471
Repayment of debt	(123)	(2,500)	—
Net proceeds from issuance of commercial paper	—	762	—
Repayments of commercial paper	—	(762)	—
Repurchases of common stock	(4,607)	(8,315)	(3,786)
Dividends paid	(1,118)	(500)	—
Net proceeds from issuance of common stock in connection with the Company's equity award programs	1,288	242	80
Other	46	12	3
Net cash provided by (used in) financing activities	419	(674)	(1,232)
Increase (decrease) in cash and cash equivalents	(3,689)	3,659	403
Cash and cash equivalents at beginning of period	6,946	3,287	2,884
Cash and cash equivalents at end of period	$ 3,257	$ 6,946	$ 3,287

Required

a. Amgen reports that it generated $5,882 million in net cash from operating activities in 2012. Yet, its net income for the year amounted to only $4,345 million. Much of this difference is the result of depreciation. Why is Amgen adding depreciation to net income in the computation of operating cash flows?

b. In determining cash provided by operating activities, Amgen adds $362 million relating to stock-based compensation expense in 2012. What is the purpose of this addition?

c. Amgen reports $348 million relating to trade receivables. What does the sign (positive or negative) on this amount signify about the change in receivables during the year compared with the sign on the amount for 2011?

d. Amgen reports $178 relating to property, plant and equipment impairments. Explain why this amount is on the statement of cash flows.

e. Calculate and compare operating cash flow to current liabilities and operating cash flow to capital expenditures for 2012 and 2011. Current liabilities were $8,191 million, $5,754 million, and $6,570 million at 2012, 2011 and 2010, respectively.

f. Does the composition of Amgen's cash flow present a "healthy" picture for 2012? Explain.

P B-47. Interpreting the Statement of Cash Flows (LO1, 5)
Following is the statement of cash flows of Staples, Inc.

Staples, Inc. (SPLS)

For Year Ended, In thousands	February 2, 2013
Operating activities:	
Consolidated net (loss) income, including (loss) income from the noncontrolling interests	$ (210,825)
Adjustments to reconcile net (loss) income to net cash provided by operating activities:	
Depreciation	408,413
Amortization of intangible assets	78,900
Impairment of goodwill and long-lived assets	810,996
Stock-based compensation	117,813
Excess tax benefits from stock-based compensation arrangements	(185)
Deferred income tax expense	112,148
Loss on early extinguishment of debt	56,958
Loss related to equity method investment	26,211
Other	7,208
Change in assets and liabilities:	
Decrease (increase) in receivables	122,628
Decrease (increase) in merchandise inventories	87,246
(Increase) decrease in prepaid expenses and other assets	(48,145)
(Decrease) increase in accounts payable	(260,263)
Decrease in accrued expenses and other liabilities	(111,246)
Increase in other long-term obligations	21,331
Net cash provided by operating activities	1,219,188
Investing activities:	
Acquisition of property and equipment	(349,574)
Proceeds from the sale of property and equipment	9,500
Acquisition of businesses, net of cash acquired	(1,941)
Net cash used in investing activities	(342,015)
Financing activities:	
Proceeds from the exercise of stock options and the sale of stock under employee stock purchase plans	49,993
Proceeds from borrowings	1,087,843
Payments on borrowings	(485,554)
Early settlement of debt	(689,740)
Purchase of noncontrolling interest	(7,910)
Cash dividends paid	(294,147)
Excess tax benefits from stock-based compensation arrangements	185
Repurchase of common stock	(472,935)
Net cash used in financing activities	(812,265)
Effect of exchange rate changes on cash and cash equivalents	5,245
Net increase (decrease) in cash and cash equivalents	70,153
Cash and cash equivalents at beginning of period	1,264,149
Cash and cash equivalents at end of period	$1,334,302

Required

a. Staples reports net loss of $210,825 thousand and net cash inflows from operating activities of $1,219,188 thousand. Part of the difference relates to depreciation and amortization of $487,313 thousand. Why does Staples add this amount in the computation of operating cash flows?

b. Staples reports a positive amount of $117,813 thousand relating to stock-based compensation. What does this positive amount signify?

c. Staples reports a cash outflow of $349,574 thousand relating to the acquisition of property, plant and equipment. Is this cash outflow a cause for concern? Explain.

d. Staples' net cash flows from financing activities is $(812,265) thousand. For what purposes is Staples using this cash?

e. Calculate operating cash flow to current liabilities and operating cash flow to capital expenditures. Current liabilities were $4,418,625 thousand at February 2, 2013 and $4,074,278 thousand at January 28, 2012, respectively. What do these ratios measure?

f. Staples' cash balance increased by $70,153 thousand during the year. Does Staples present a "healthy" cash flow picture for the year? Explain.

IFRS APPLICATIONS

I B-48. Interpreting the Statement of Cash Flows (LO1, 5)

Following is the statement of cash flows for Roger's Communications, a Canadian company operating in the telecom and media industry.

CONSOLIDATED STATEMENTS OF CASH FLOWS Years ended December 31 (in millions of Canadian dollars)	2012	2011
Cash provided by (used in):		
Operating activities:		
Net income for the year	$1,700	$1,563
Adjustments to reconcile net income to net cash flows from operating activities:		
Depreciation and amortization	1,819	1,743
Impairment of assets	80	—
Program rights amortization	73	83
Finance costs	664	738
Income tax expense	610	535
Pension contributions, net of expense	(36)	(41)
Settlement of pension obligations	—	11
Stock-based compensation expense	77	64
Share of the income of associates and joint ventures	(235)	(7)
Other	(23)	9
	4,729	4,698
Change in non-cash operating working capital items	(248)	(169)
	4,481	4,529
Income taxes paid	(380)	(99)
Interest paid	(680)	(639)
Cash provided by operating activities	3,421	3,791
Investing activities:		
Additions to property, plant and equipment	(2,142)	(2,127)
Change in non-cash working capital items related to PP&E	136	(89)
Acquisitions, net of cash and cash equivalents acquired	—	(532)
Investments	(707)	—
Additions to program rights	(90)	(56)
Other	(31)	(27)
Cash used in investing activities	(2,834)	(2,831)
Financing activities:		
Issuance of long-term debt	2,090	4,100
Repayment of long-term debt	(1,240)	(2,802)
Premium on repayment of long-term debt	—	(76)
Payment on settlement of cross-currency interest rate exchange agreement and forward contracts	—	(1,208)
Proceeds on settlement of cross-currency interest rate exchange agreement and forward contracts	—	878
Transaction costs incurred related to long-term debt	(14)	(10)
Repurchase of Class B Non-Voting shares	(350)	(1,099)
Proceeds received on exercise of stock options	—	3
Dividends paid	(803)	(758)
Cash used in financing activities	(317)	(972)
Change in cash and cash equivalents	270	(12)
Cash and cash equivalents, beginning of year	(57)	(45)
Cash and cash equivalents, end of year	$ 213	$ (57)

continued

The change in non-cash operating working capital items is as follows:		
Accounts receivable	$ 15	$ (86)
Other current assets	(131)	(33)
Accounts payable and accrued liabilities	(140)	(46)
Unearned revenue	8	(4)
	$ (248)	$ (169)
Supplemental cash flow disclosure:		
Non-cash acquisition of spectrum licenses	$ 360	$ —

Cash and cash equivalents (bank advances) are defined as cash and short-term deposits, which have an original maturity of less than 90 days, less bank advances.

Required

a. Roger's reports net income of $1,700 million and net cash inflows from operating activities of $3,421 million. Part of the difference relates to depreciation and amortization of $1,819 million. Why does Roger's add this amount in the computation of operating cash flows?

b. Roger's reports a positive amount of $77 million relating to stock-based compensation. What does this positive amount signify?

c. Roger's reports a cash outflow of $2,142 million relating to the acquisition of property, plant and equipment. Is this cash outflow a cause for concern? Explain.

d. Roger's net cash outflow used for financing activities is $317 million. What did Roger's use this cash for?

e. The statement reports changes in non-cash operating working capital items. Explain the positive amount for accounts receivable and the negative amount for accounts payable and accrued liabilities.

SOLUTIONS TO REVIEW PROBLEMS

Appendix-End Review 1

Part A: Solution

1. *a* 2. *c* 3. *d* 4. *c*

Part B: Solution

a. $8,000 ending balance − $12,000 beginning balance = $4,000 decrease in cash

b. (1) Use the indirect method to determine the net cash flow from operating activities.

- Adjustments to convert Expresso Royale's net income of $35,000 to a net cash provided by operating activities of $38,000 are shown in the following statement of cash flows.

(2) Analyze changes in remaining noncash asset (and contra asset) accounts to determine cash flows from investing activities.

- Long-Term Investments: $11,000 decrease resulted from sale of investments for cash at a $2,000 loss. Cash received from sale of investments = $9,000 ($11,000 cost − $2,000 loss).
- Fair Value Adjustment to Investments: $1,000 decrease resulted from the elimination of this account balance (and the Unrealized Loss on Investments) at the end of 2013. No cash flow effect.
- Plant Assets: $48,000 increase resulted from purchase of plant assets for cash. Cash paid to purchase plant assets = $48,000.
- Accumulated Depreciation: $11,000 increase resulted from the recording of 2013 depreciation. No cash flow effect.

(3) Analyze changes in remaining liability and stockholders' equity accounts to determine cash flows from financing activities.

- Common Stock: $14,000 increase resulted from the issuance of stock for cash. Cash received from issuance of common stock = $14,000.
- Retained Earnings: $18,000 increase resulted from net income of $35,000 and dividend declaration of $17,000. Cash dividends paid = $17,000.
- Unrealized Loss on Investments: $1,000 decrease resulted from the elimination of this account balance (and the Fair Value Adjustment to Investments) at the end of 2013. No cash flow effect.

The statement of cash flows follows:

EXPRESSO ROYALE Statement of Cash Flows For Year Ended December 31, 2013		
Net cash flow from operating activities		
Net income	$35,000	
Add (deduct) items to convert net income to cash basis		
Depreciation	11,000	
Loss on sale of investments	2,000	
Accounts receivable decrease	6,000	
Inventory increase	(28,000)	
Prepaid advertising increase	(3,000)	
Accounts payable increase	13,000	
Wages payable increase	3,500	
Income tax payable decrease	(1,500)	
Net cash provided by operating activities		$38,000
Cash flows from investing activities		
Sale of investments	9,000	
Purchase of plant assets	(48,000)	
Net cash used by investing activities		(39,000)
Cash flows from financing activities		
Issuance of common stock	14,000	
Payment of dividends	(17,000)	
Net cash used by financing activities		(3,000)
Net decrease in cash		(4,000)
Cash at beginning of year		12,000
Cash at end of year		$ 8,000

Appendix-End Review 2

Solution

a. \$8,000 ending balance − \$12,000 beginning balance = \$4,000 decrease in cash

b. (1) Use the direct method to determine the individual cash flows from operating activities.

- \$385,000 sales + \$6,000 accounts receivable decrease = \$391,000 cash received from customers
- \$5,000 dividend income = \$5,000 cash received as dividends
- \$233,000 cost of goods sold + \$28,000 inventory increase − \$13,000 accounts payable increase = \$248,000 cash paid for merchandise purchased
- \$82,000 wages expense − \$3,500 wages payable increase = \$78,500 cash paid to employees
- \$10,000 advertising expense + \$3,000 prepaid advertising increase = \$13,000 cash paid for advertising
- \$17,000 income tax expense + \$1,500 income tax payable decrease = \$18,500 cash paid for income taxes

(2) Analyze changes in remaining noncash asset (and contra asset) accounts to determine cash flows from investing activities.

- Long-term investments: \$11,000 decrease resulted from sale of investments for cash at a \$2,000 loss. Cash received from sale of investments = \$9,000 (\$11,000 cost − \$2,000 loss).
- Fair value adjustment to investments: \$1,000 decrease resulted from the elimination of this account balance (and the unrealized loss on investments) at the end of 2013. No cash flow effect.
- Plant assets: \$48,000 increase resulted from purchase of plant assets for cash. Cash paid to purchase plant assets = \$48,000.
- Accumulated depreciation: \$11,000 increase resulted from the recording of 2013 depreciation. No cash flow effect.

(3) Analyze changes in remaining liability and stockholders' equity accounts to determine cash flows from financing activities.

- Common stock: $14,000 increase resulted from the issuance of stock for cash. Cash received from issuance of common stock = $14,000.
- Retained earnings: $18,000 increase resulted from net income of $35,000 and dividend declaration of $17,000. Cash dividends paid = $17,000.
- Unrealized loss on investments: $1,000 decrease resulted from the elimination of this account balance (and the fair value adjustment to investments) at the end of 2013. No cash flow effect.

The statement of cash flows under the direct method follows:

EXPRESSO ROYALE Statement of Cash Flows For Year Ended December 31, 2013		
Cash flows from operating activities		
Cash received from customers	$391,000	
Cash received as dividends	5,000	
Cash paid for merchandise purchased	(248,000)	
Cash paid to employees	(78,500)	
Cash paid for advertising	(13,000)	
Cash paid for income taxes	(18,500)	
Net cash provided by operating activities		$ 38,000
Cash flows from investing activities		
Sale of investments	9,000	
Purchase of plant assets	(48,000)	
Net cash used by investing activities		(39,000)
Cash flows from financing activities		
Issuance of common stock	14,000	
Payment of dividends	(17,000)	
Net cash used by financing activities		(3,000)
Net decrease in cash		(4,000)
Cash at beginning of year		12,000
Cash at end of year		$ 8,000

Appendix C

Comprehensive Case

Learning Objectives

LO1 Explain and illustrate a review of financial statements and their components. (p. C-4)

LO2 Assess company profitability and creditworthiness. (p. C-27)

LO3 Forecast financial statements. (p. C-29)

LO4 Describe and illustrate the valuation of firm equity. (p. C-32)

Kimberly-Clark

The past decade has seen a shift in the competitive landscape for consumer products companies. Gone are numerous competitors. Many were gobbled up in the industry's consolidation trend. Also gone is media control. Now, hundreds of different media outlets and venues compete for promotion space and scarce consumer time.

Another development is in-store branding. Companies such as **Costco**, with its Kirkland Signature brand on everything from candy to apparel, threaten the powerhouse brands from **Kimberly-Clark**, **Procter & Gamble**, **Colgate-Palmolive**, and other consumer products companies.

Ten years ago, when Thomas J. Falk assumed the top spot at Kimberly-Clark, the nation's largest disposable diaper producer, he inherited some extra baggage: a company in the throes of an identity crisis, a decades-long rivalry with consumer-products behemoth Procter & Gamble, and a group of investors short on patience following a series of earnings misses.

In a move aimed at boosting its stock price and its return on equity, Kimberly-Clark spun off its paper and pulp businesses in 2004, and began a strategic investment and streamlining initiative in 2005. Under Falk's leadership, the company has steadily improved its focus on its health and hygiene segments.

Kimberly-Clark has also moved to shore up its brand images across its immense product line. With sales of more than $21 billion, the company manufactures such well-recognized brands as Huggies and Pull-Ups disposable diapers, Kleenex facial tissue, Viva paper towels, and Scott bathroom tissue.

Despite formidable competitors like Procter & Gamble, Kimberly-Clark's financial performance has been steady, as

Courtesy of Getty Images

has been its stock price rise over the past five years (see the stock price chart below). Moreover, Kimberly-Clark's earnings performance is consistent, and its financial position is solid. Kimberly-Clark's RNOA for 2012 was 18.0%, and its nonoperating return increased RNOA to yield a robust 34.2% in return on equity. It also reported $19.9 billion in assets, 41% of which is concentrated in plant, property, and equipment, and another 18% in intangible assets.

This module presents a financial accounting analysis and interpretation of Kimberly-Clark. It is intended to illustrate the key financial reporting topics covered in the book. We begin with a detailed review of Kimberly-Clark's financial statements and notes, followed by the forecasting of key accounts that we use to value its common stock.

Source: *Kimberly-Clark* 2012 10-K Filings and Annual Report to Shareholders.

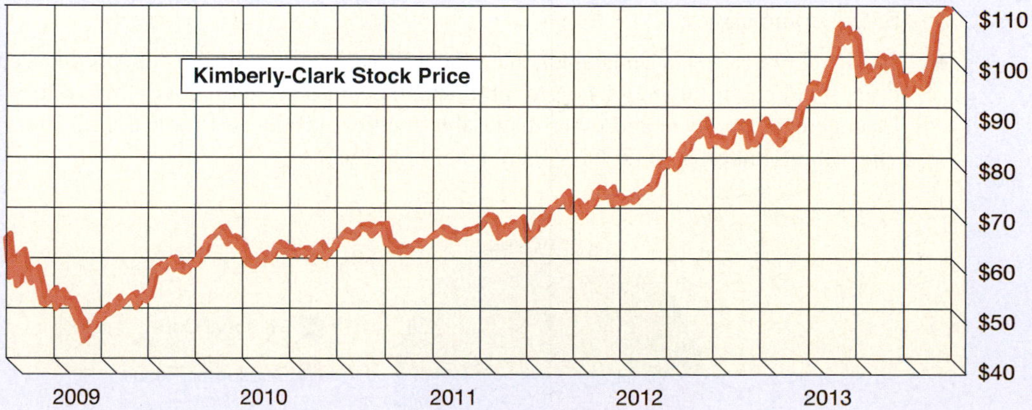

APPENDIX ORGANIZATION

Comprehensive Case

Reviewing the Financial Statements
- Income Statement
- Balance Sheet
- Off-Balance-Sheet
- Statement of Cash Flows
- Audit Opinion

Assessing Profitability and Creditworthiness
- ROE Disaggregation
- RNOA Disaggregation
- Disaggregation of Margin and Turnover
- Credit Analysis

Forecasting Accounting Numbers
- Forecasting Assumptions
- Forecasting Financial Statements

Valuing Equity Securities
- Discounted Cash Flow Valuation
- Residual Operating Income Valuation

INTRODUCTION

Kimberly-Clark is one of the largest consumer products companies in the world. It is organized into four general business segments (percentages are for 2012):

- **Personal Care** (45% of sales), which manufactures and markets disposable diapers, training and youth pants, swim pants, baby wipes, feminine and incontinence care products, and related products. Products in this segment are primarily for household use and are sold under a variety of brand names, including Huggies, Pull-Ups, Little Swimmers, GoodNites, Kotex, Depend, Poise and other brand names.
- **Consumer Tissue** (31% of sales), which manufactures and markets facial and bathroom tissue, paper towels, napkins and related products for household use. Products in this segment are sold under the Kleenex, Scott, Cottonelle, Viva, Andrex, Scottex, Hakle, Page and other brand names.
- **Professional & Other** (16% of sales), which manufactures and markets facial and bathroom tissue, paper towels, napkins, wipes and a range of safety products for the away-from-home marketplace. Products in this segment are sold under the Kleenex, Scott, WypAll, Kimtech and Jackson Safety brand names.
- **Health Care** (8% of sales), which manufactures and markets health care products such as surgical drapes and gowns, infection control products, face masks, exam gloves, respiratory products, pain management products and other disposable medical products. Products in this segment are sold under the Kimberly-Clark, ON-Q and other brand names.

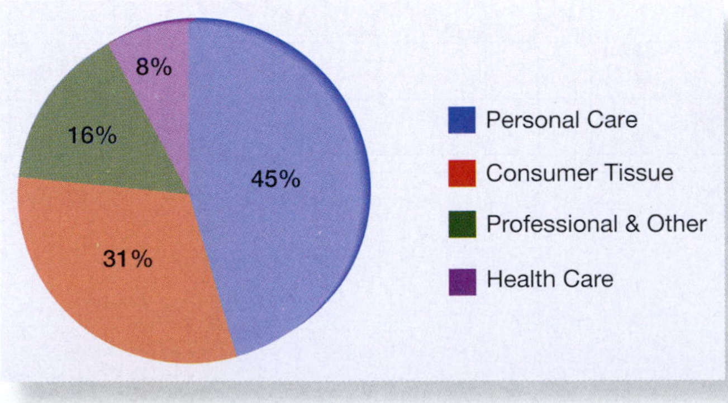

Approximately 49% of Kimberly-Clark's sales are in North America, 15% in Europe and 36% in Asia, Latin America, and other areas. In addition, approximately 12% of Kimberly-Clark's sales are made to **Walmart**, primarily in the personal care and consumer tissue businesses (source: Kimberly-Clark 2012 10-K).

In the MD&A section of its 10-K, Kimberly-Clark describes its competitive environment as follows:

> We compete in highly competitive markets against well-known, branded products and low-cost or private label products both domestically and internationally. Inherent risks in our competitive strategy include uncertainties concerning trade and consumer acceptance, the effects of consolidation within retailer and distribution channels, and competitive actions. Our competitors for these markets include not only our traditional competitors but also private label manufacturers, low-cost manufacturers and rapidly expanding international manufacturers. Some of these competitors may have better access to financial resources and greater market penetration, which enable them to offer a wider variety of products and services at more competitive prices. Alternatively, some of these competitors may have significantly lower product development and manufacturing costs, allowing them to offer products at a lower price. The actions of these competitors could adversely affect our financial results. It may be necessary for us to lower prices on our products and increase spending on advertising and promotions, each of which could adversely affect our financial results. In addition, we compete in highly competitive regional markets, such as Latin America, Europe, Africa and Asia. Intense competition in these areas may slow our sales growth and earnings potential, as well as adversely impact our margins.
>
> Our ability to develop new products is affected by whether we can successfully anticipate consumer needs and preferences, develop and fund technological innovations, and receive and maintain necessary patent and trademark protection. In addition, we incur substantial development and marketing costs in introducing new and improved products and technologies. The introduction of a new consumer product (whether improved or newly developed) usually requires substantial expenditures for advertising and marketing to gain recognition in the marketplace. If a product gains consumer acceptance, it normally requires continued advertising and promotional support to maintain its relative market position. Some of our competitors may spend more aggressively on advertising and promotional activities, introduce competing products more quickly and respond more effectively to changing business and economic conditions.

Beyond the competitive business risks described above, Kimberly-Clark faces fluctuating prices for cellulose fiber, the company's principle raw material, uncertain energy costs for manufacturing operations, foreign currency translation risks, and risks resulting from fluctuating interest rates.

Given this background, we begin the accounting analysis of Kimberly-Clark with a discussion of its financial statements.

REVIEWING THE FINANCIAL STATEMENTS

This section reviews and analyzes the financial statements of Kimberly-Clark.

LO1 Explain and illustrate a review of financial statements and their components.

Income Statement Reporting and Analysis

Kimberly-Clark's income statement is reproduced in Exhibit C.1. The remainder of this section provides a brief review and analysis for Kimberly-Clark's income statement line items.

EXHIBIT C.1 Kimberly-Clark Income Statement

KIMBERLY-CLARK CORPORATION AND SUBSIDIARIES
Consolidated Income Statement

Year Ended December 31 (Millions of dollars, except per share amounts)	2012	2011	2010
Net sales	**$21,063**	$20,846	$19,746
Cost of products sold	**14,314**	14,694	13,196
Gross profit	**6,749**	6,152	6,550
Marketing, research and general expenses	**4,069**	3,761	3,673
Other (income) and expense, net	**(6)**	(51)	104
Operating profit	**2,686**	2,442	2,773
Interest income	**18**	18	20
Interest expense	**(284)**	(277)	(243)
Income before income taxes and equity interests	**2,420**	2,183	2,550
Provision for income taxes	**(768)**	(660)	(788)
Income before equity interests	**1,652**	1,523	1,762
Share of net income of equity companies	**176**	161	181
Net income	**1,828**	1,684	1,943
Net income attributable to noncontrolling interests	**(78)**	(93)	(100)
Net income attributable to Kimberly-Clark Corporation	**$ 1,750**	$ 1,591	$ 1,843
Per share basis			
Net income attributable to Kimberly-Clark Corporation			
Basic	**$ 4.45**	$ 4.02	$ 4.47
Diluted	**$ 4.42**	$ 3.99	$ 4.45

Net Sales

Exhibit C.1 reveals that sales increased 1.04% in 2012 to $21,063 million, following a 5.57% sales increase in the prior year. In its 2012 MD&A report, management attributes the increase equally to volume, price and mix effects.

Kimberly-Clark describes its revenue recognition policy as follows:

> Sales revenue is recognized at the time of product shipment or delivery, depending on when title passes, to unaffiliated customers, and when all of the following have occurred: a firm sales agreement is in place, pricing is fixed or determinable, and collection is reasonably assured. Sales are reported net of returns, consumer and trade promotions, rebates and freight allowed. Taxes imposed by governmental authorities on our revenue-producing activities with customers, such as sales taxes and value-added taxes, are excluded from net sales.

Its revenue recognition conditions are taken directly from GAAP and SEC guidelines, which recognize revenues when "earned and realizable." For Kimberly-Clark, *earned* means when title to the goods passes to the customer, and *realizable* means an account receivable whose collection is reasonably assured.

Sales for retailers and manufacturers are straightforward: revenue is recognized when the product is transferred to the buyer, an obligation for payment exists and collection of that payment is reasonably assured. In that case, the revenue is deemed to have been "earned." The primary issue for retailers and manufacturers relates to sales return allowances. These allowances pertain to product return or sales discounts (sometimes called *mark-downs*). Companies can only report sales when earned, that is, past the return allowance period. Further, companies can only report *net* sales as revenue (i.e., gross sales less any sales discounts, including volume discounts). K-C's footnotes provide the following table relating to sales allowances:

December 31, 2012 ($ millions)	Balance at Beginning of Period	Additions: Charged to Costs and Expenses	Additions: Charged to Other Accounts	Deductions: Write-Offs and Reclassifications	Balance at End of Period
Allowances for sales discounts	$21	$280	—	$281	$20

K-C's balance sheet includes a contra-asset related to sales discounts. The table indicates that the company had $21 million in sales discounts accrued at the start of the year that relate to sales in the prior year. During 2012, K-C granted its customers $280 million in additional sales discounts, $281 million of which had been taken by the customers by the end of the year. The remaining amount of $20 million, relates to discounts granted, but not yet taken, and is held over to the following year. These year-end amounts typically relate to discounts given toward the end of the year that are ultimately taken in the first quarter of the following year.

The sales discount process affects net sales and, thus, profit. This allowance works just like any other allowance. If K-C underestimated the sales discount allowance, net sales and profit in the current year would be increased. Overestimation of the sales discount allowance would have the opposite effect: current sales and profit would be depressed. K-C's allowance has not changed appreciably in 2012 and is, therefore, not of concern.

Revenue recognition in service industries and those industries that have multiple-element sales contracts can be problematic. Often, determining when a particular element of the contract has been "earned" can be difficult and revenue can easily be mis-estimated, either intentionally or not. For example, Hewlett Packard acquired Autonomy in 2011 and later claimed that serious accounting improprieties on the part of Autonomy forced HP to take an $8.8 billion charge to income. HP CEO, Meg Whitman, asserted that Autonomy accelerated revenue recognition and misconstrued lower-margin hardware sales as higher-margin software business. Prior to the deal, Autonomy's accounts were audited by HP's public accountants, who arguably missed the revenue recognition errors on the multiple-element sales at Autonomy.

Cost of Products Sold and Gross Profit

Kimberly-Clark's 2012 gross profit margin is 32% ($6,749/$21,063), which is about one percentage point less than what it was in 2010 (33.2%). As a benchmark, **Procter & Gamble**, the company's principle competitor, recently reported sales of $84.2 billion, over four times the level of K-C's sales, and a gross profit margin of 49.6%. This comparison highlights the intense competition that K-C faces from its much larger rival.

The choice of inventory costing method affects cost of goods sold. K-C uses the LIFO method to cost its inventory. In 2012, the company's LIFO reserve decreased by $49 million (see inventory discussion later in this Appendix). This decreased cost of goods sold and improved gross profit by $49 million.

Marketing, Research and General Expenses

Kimberly-Clark's marketing, research and general expenses have increased to 19.3% of sales from 18.0% in the prior year. This increase resulted from general cost inflation as well as from the company's restructuring efforts designed to improve long-run manufacturing and operating costs. K-C reports 2012 net operating profit after taxes (NOPAT) of $1,996 million [($2,686 million + $176 million) − ($768 million + {$284 million − $18 million} × 37%)] or $1,828 million + [($284 million − $18 million) × (1 − 37%)] and a net operating profit margin (NOPM) of 9.48% ($1,996 million/$21,063 million) of sales.[1] P&G, by contrast, is able to use its higher gross profit margin to fund a higher level of advertising and other SGA expenditures, resulting in a NOPM of 13.3%, computed as $11,174 million/$84,167 million.

[1] We include equity income of $176 million (labeled as "share of net income of equity companies" in K-C's income statement) as operating because it relates to investments in paper-related companies and it, therefore, aligns with K-C's primary operating activities. This amount is reported by K-C net of tax, and therefore, no tax adjustment is necessary when computing NOPAT.

Pension Costs. Kimberly-Clark's marketing, research and general expenses include $122 million of pension expense. This is reported in the following table in the pension footnote:

Components of Net Periodic Benefit Cost

Year Ended December 31 (Millions of dollars)	Pension Benefits 2012	Pension Benefits 2011	Pension Benefits 2010	Other Benefits 2012	Other Benefits 2011	Other Benefits 2010
Service cost	$ 45	$ 57	$ 56	$15	$14	$14
Interest cost	279	307	309	36	41	44
Expected return on plan assets[a]	(329)	(345)	(336)	—	—	—
Amortization of prior service cost and transition amount	(4)	6	5	(1)	1	3
Recognized net actuarial loss	111	94	99	1	—	1
Settlements	20	—	—	—	—	—
Net periodic benefit cost	$122	$119	$133	$51	$56	$62

[a] The expected return on plan assets is determined by multiplying the fair value of plan assets at the remeasurement date, typically the prior year-end (adjusted for estimated current year cash benefit payments and contributions), by the expected long-term rate of return.

For 2012, the expected return on pension investments ($329 million) provides an offset to the company's pension service and interest costs ($45 million and $279 million, respectively). Footnotes reveal that Kimberly-Clark's pension investments realized an *actual* return of $556 million in 2012 (from the pension footnote in its 10-K report). So, for 2012, use of the expected return results in an unrecognized *gain* that is deferred, along with other unrecognized gains and losses, in the computation of reported profit.

Kimberly-Clark describes how it determines the expected return in its footnotes. It is instructive to review the company's rationale and, thus, the footnote follows:

> Strategic asset allocation decisions are made considering several risk factors, including plan participants' retirement benefit security, the estimated payments of the associated liabilities, the plan funded status, and Kimberly-Clark's financial condition. The resulting strategic asset allocation is a diversified blend of equity and fixed income investments. Equity investments are typically diversified across geographies and market capitalization. Fixed income investments are diversified across multiple sectors including government issues and corporate debt instruments with a portfolio duration that is consistent with the estimated payment of the associated liability. Actual asset allocation is regularly reviewed and periodically rebalanced to the strategic allocation when considered appropriate. The expected long-term rate of return is evaluated on an annual basis. In setting this assumption, we consider a number of factors including projected future returns by asset class relative to the current asset allocation. The weighted-average expected long-term rate of return on pension fund assets used to calculate pension expense for the Principal Plans was 6.68 percent in 2012 compared with 7.35 percent in 2011 and will be 6.43 percent in 2013.

The expected return on pension assets offsets service and interest costs, and serves to reduce pension expense. In general, increasing (decreasing) the expected return on pension assets, increases (decreases) profit. In 2012, K-C reduced its expected return from 7.14% to 6.49% (65 basis points). The discount rate (used to compute the interest cost component of pension expense) declined by 64 basis points (5.51% to 4.87%).

Transitory versus Persistent Line Items

Expenses relating to restructuring activities have become increasingly common in the past two decades. In its MD&A section of its 2012 10-K, Kimberly-Clark announced the following restructuring plan ($ in millions):

> On October 23, 2012, we approved strategic changes related to our Western and Central European consumer and professional businesses to focus our resources and investments on stronger market positions and growth opportunities. We will be exiting the diaper category in that region, with the

continued

exception of the Italian market, and divesting or exiting some lower-margin businesses, mostly in consumer tissue, in certain markets . . . The businesses that will be exited or divested generate annual net sales of approximately $500 and negligible operating profit. Restructuring actions related to the strategic changes will involve the sale or closure of five of our European manufacturing facilities and a streamlining of our administrative organization. In total, these actions will result in reducing our European workforce by approximately 1,300 to 1,500 positions. The restructuring actions commenced in the fourth quarter of 2012 and are expected to be completed by December 31, 2014. The restructuring is expected to result in cumulative charges of approximately $250 to $350 after tax ($300 to $400 pre-tax) over that period. Cash costs related to severance and other expenses are expected to account for approximately 50 to 60 percent of the charges. Noncash charges will consist primarily of asset impairment charges and incremental depreciation.

These initiatives are designed to further improve the company's competitive position by accelerating investments in targeted growth opportunities and strategic cost reductions to streamline manufacturing and administrative operations.

Classification of these charges as transitory or persistent is a judgment call. In K-C's case, these charges relate to a multi-year program that is expected to continue through 2014. Therefore, we classify these expenses as persistent. Our review of the financial statements did not identify any other transitory items and thus, we classified all other activity as persistent.

Earnings per Share

Net income attributable to Kimberly-Clark has increased from $1,591 million in 2011 to $1,750 million in 2012. Basic (diluted) earnings per share increased from $4.02 ($3.99) to $4.45 ($4.42). Following is Kimberly-Clark's computation of earnings per share:

Earnings Per Share A reconciliation of the average number of common shares outstanding used in the basic and diluted EPS computations follows:

Average Common Shares Outstanding (Millions)	2012	2011	2010
Average shares outstanding.	**393.0**	395.4	411.3
Participating securities.	**—**	0.3	1.1
Basic.	**393.0**	395.7	412.4
Dilutive effect of stock options.	**1.8**	1.6	1.1
Dilutive effect of restricted share unit awards	**1.3**	1.3	0.9
Diluted	**396.1**	398.6	414.4

Options outstanding that were not included in the computation of diluted EPS mainly because their exercise price was greater than the average market price of the common shares are summarized below:

Description	2012	2011	2010
Average number of share equivalents (millions).	**1.1**	3.6	13.9
Weighted-average exercise price.	**$78.54**	$71.49	$66.00
Options outstanding at year-end (millions).	**1.7**	3.0	14.7

The number of common shares outstanding as of December 31, 2012, 2011 and 2010 was 389.3 million, 395.7 million and 406.9 million, respectively.

Most of the difference between basic and diluted earnings per share usually arises from the dilutive effects of employee stock options. (We should note that if stock options are *under water*, meaning that K-C's stock price is lower than the exercise price of the options, they are considered *antidilutive*, meaning that including them would increase EPS. Accordingly, they are excluded in the diluted EPS computation, but remain potentially dilutive if K-C's stock price subsequently rises above the exercise price of the options.) Although not present for Kimberly-Clark, convertible debt and preferred shares are also potentially dilutive for many companies.

Income Taxes

Kimberly-Clark's net income has been negatively affected over the past three years by an increase in its effective tax rate from 30.9% to 31.7% as K-C describes in the following footnote:

Year Ended December 31	2012	2011	2010
Tax at U.S. statutory rate applied to income before income taxes	35.0%	35.0%	35.0%
State income taxes, net of federal tax benefit	1.7	1.8	1.8
Statutory rates other than U.S. statutory rate	(2.8)	(2.3)	(3.0)
Other—net[(a)]	(2.2)	(4.3)	(2.9)
Effective income tax rate	31.7%	30.2%	30.9%

[(a)] Other—net is comprised of numerous items, none of which is greater than 1.75 percent of income before income taxes.

Common-Size Income Statement

It is useful for analysis purposes to prepare common-size statements. Exhibit C.2 shows Kimberly-Clark's common-size income statement covering the two most recent years.

EXHIBIT C.2 Kimberly-Clark Common-Size Income Statement

Year Ended December 31	2012*	2011*
Net sales	**100.0%**	100.0%
Cost of products sold	**68.0**	70.5
Gross profit	**32.0**	29.5
Marketing, research and general expenses	**19.3**	18.0
Other (income) and expense, net	**0.0**	(0.2)
Operating profit	**12.8**	11.7
Interest income	**0.1**	0.1
Interest expense	**(1.3)**	(1.3)
Income before income taxes and equity interests	**11.5**	10.5
Provision for income taxes	**(3.6)**	(3.2)
Income before equity interests	**7.8**	7.3
Share of net income of equity companies	**0.8**	0.8
Net income	**8.7**	8.1
Net income attributable to noncontrolling interests	**(0.4)**	(0.4)
Net income attributable to Kimberly-Clark Corporation	**8.3%**	7.6%

* All percentages are computed by dividing each income statement line item by that year's net sales.

The gross profit margin increased from 29.5% in 2011 to 32.0% in 2012. This increase, while seemingly minor, is significant given the competitive environment in which K-C operates. The increased gross profit was partially offset by an increase in marketing, research and general expense from 18% of sales in 2011 to 19.3% in 2012. Accordingly, 2012 income before taxes increased by 1.0 percentage point relative to 2011, from 10.5% of sales to 11.5%. Finally, net income as a percentage of sales increased by 0.6 percentage points from 8.1% of sales to 8.7%, and net income attributable to K-C shareholders increased from 7.6% of sales in 2011 to 8.3% in 2012.

Management Discussion and Analysis

The Management Discussion and Analysis section of a 10-K is usually informative for interpreting company financial statements and for additional insights into company operations. To illustrate, Kimberly-Clark provides the following analysis of its operating results in the MD&A section of its 2012 10-K:

Overview of 2012 Results

- Net sales increased 1 percent due to increases in net selling prices and volumes, partially offset by unfavorable currency effects.
- Operating profit and net income attributable to Kimberly-Clark Corporation each increased 10 percent and diluted earnings per share increased 11 percent.
- Results in 2012 include pre-tax charges of $299, $242 after tax, related to the strategic changes in Western and Central Europe. Additionally, comparisons are impacted by $135 in pre-tax charges, $86 after tax, for the pulp and tissue restructuring actions in 2012 versus $415 in pre-tax charges, $289 after tax, in 2011.
- Cash provided by operations was $3.3 billion compared to $2.3 billion last year, with the increase primarily due to higher earnings, improved working capital and lower defined benefit pension contributions ($110 in 2012 versus $679 in 2011).

Results of Operations and Related Information *2012 versus 2011*

- Personal care net sales in North America increased 2 percent. Net selling prices rose 3 percent, driven by improved revenue realization for Huggies diapers and baby wipes. Overall volumes were down 1 percent as infant care volumes decreased mid-single digits, primarily reflecting category declines. This decrease was mostly offset by improvements in adult care volumes of mid-single digits and feminine care of low-single digits, primarily due to innovations in Depend and U by Kotex brands.

  In KCI, personal care net sales increased 8 percent despite a 5 percent decrease from unfavorable changes in currency rates. Sales volumes were up 9 percent, with high-single digit to low-double digit growth in each major region. Volume performance was strong in a number of markets, including Brazil, China, Russia, South Africa, South Korea, Vietnam and Venezuela. Overall net selling prices improved 3 percent compared to the year-ago period, driven by increases in Latin America.

  In Europe, personal care net sales increased 2 percent, despite an unfavorable currency impact of 6 percent. Sales volumes rose 10 percent, mostly due to growth in non-branded offerings, Huggies baby wipes and child care offerings.
- Consumer tissue net sales in North America were down 3 percent compared to the prior year, including a 5 percent decrease from lost sales in conjunction with pulp and tissue restructuring actions. Organic sales volumes (i.e., sales volume impacts other than lost sales from restructuring actions) were essentially flat with 2011, as gains in paper towels were offset by lower volumes in facial tissue. Overall net selling prices increased 3 percent and changes in product mix reduced net sales 1 percent.

  Consumer tissue net sales decreased 1 percent in KCI. Currency rates were unfavorable by 4 percent and lost sales in conjunction with pulp and tissue restructuring actions reduced sales volumes by 1 percent. Net selling prices increased 3 percent and changes in product mix increased net sales by 1 percent. These benefits were partially offset by decreases in organic sales volumes of 1 percent.

  In Europe, consumer tissue net sales decreased 8 percent, including an unfavorable currency impact of 5 percent. Changes in product mix, net selling prices and volumes each decreased net sales by 1 percent.
- Net sales of KCP products in North America were essentially even with the prior year. Although washroom product volumes increased, these gains were offset by lower volumes in other areas, including safety products and wipers.

  KCP net sales increased 5 percent in KCI, despite a 4 percent decrease from unfavorable changes in currency rates. Sales volumes increased 6 percent, driven by double-digit growth in Latin America, and net selling prices rose 3 percent.

  In Europe, KCP net sales decreased 9 percent. Currency rates were unfavorable by 6 percent and lost sales in conjunction with pulp and tissue restructuring actions reduced sales volumes by 4 percent. Organic sales volumes were essentially flat with 2011 and net selling prices increased 1 percent.

  Net sales of health care products increased 1 percent as sales volumes increased 2 percent and unfavorable currency effects reduced net sales by 1 percent. Medical device volumes increased 3 percent and surgical and infection prevention volumes increased 2 percent.

Business Segments

Generally accepted accounting principles require that companies disclose the composition of their operating profit by business segment. Segments are investment centers (those having both income statement and balance sheet data) that the company routinely evaluates at the chief executive level.

We outlined and discussed Kimberly-Clark's business segments at the beginning of the appendix: personal care, consumer tissue, professional & other, and health care. Following are its GAAP disclosures for each of its business segments:

Consolidated Operations by Business Segment

(Millions of dollars)	Personal Care	Consumer Tissue	Professional & Other	Health Care	Corporate & Other	Consolidated Total
Net sales						
2012	**$9,576**	**$6,527**	**$3,283**	**$1,622**	**$ 55**	**$21,063**
2011	9,128	6,770	3,294	1,606	48	20,846
2010	8,670	6,497	3,110	1,460	9	19,746
Operating profit						
2012	**1,660**	**887**	**545**	**229**	**(635)**	**2,686**
2011	1,526	775	487	219	(565)	2,442
2010	1,764	660	468	174	(293)	2,773
Depreciation and amortization						
2012	**315**	**331**	**141**	**59**	**11**	**857**
2011	296	541	187	55	12	1,091
2010	277	329	142	56	9	813
Assets						
2012	**7,014**	**5,531**	**2,739**	**2,531**	**2,058**	**19,873**
2011	6,582	5,685	2,783	2,529	1,794	19,373
2010	6,316	6,106	2,962	2,410	2,070	19,864
Capital spending						
2012	**551**	**352**	**116**	**42**	**32**	**1,093**
2011	543	255	114	53	3	968
2010	436	331	156	40	1	964

Given these data, it is possible for us to perform a rudimentary return analysis for each segment. This analysis provides insight into a company's dependence on any one segment. Following is a brief summary analysis of K-C's segment return disaggregation for 2012:

(Millions of dollars)	Personal Care	Consumer Tissue	Professional & Other	Health Care
Net sales	**$9,576**	**$6,527**	**$3,283**	**$1,622**
Operating profit	**1,660**	**887**	**545**	**229**
Assets	**7,014**	**5,531**	**2,739**	**2,531**
Operating profit margin	17.3%	13.6%	16.6%	14.1%
Year-end asset turnover	1.37	1.18	1.20	0.64
Operating profit divided by year-end assets	23.7%	16.0%	19.9%	9.0%

The intensely competitive nature and capital intensity of the health care market is evident in its low return on year-end assets (9.0%), driven primarily by its low asset turnover rate (0.64). K-C relies, to a great extent, on its personal care segment to generate income.

Balance Sheet Reporting and Analysis

Kimberly-Clark's balance sheet is reproduced in Exhibit C.3.

EXHIBIT C.3 Kimberly-Clark Balance Sheet

KIMBERLY-CLARK CORPORATION AND SUBSIDIARIES
Consolidated Balance Sheet

December 31 (Millions of dollars)	2012	2011
ASSETS		
Current assets		
Cash and cash equivalents	**$ 1,106**	$ 764
Accounts receivable, net	**2,642**	2,602
Inventories	**2,348**	2,356
Other current assets	**493**	561
Total current assets	**6,589**	6,283
Property, plant and equipment, net	**8,095**	8,049
Investments in equity companies	**355**	338
Goodwill	**3,337**	3,340
Other intangible assets	**246**	265
Long-term note receivable	**395**	394
Other assets	**856**	704
Total assets	**$19,873**	$19,373
LIABILITIES AND STOCKHOLDERS' EQUITY		
Current liabilities		
Debt payable within one year	**$ 1,115**	$ 706
Trade accounts payable	**2,443**	2,388
Accrued expenses	**2,244**	2,026
Dividends payable	**289**	277
Total current liabilities	**6,091**	5,397
Long-term debt	**5,070**	5,426
Noncurrent employee benefits	**1,992**	1,460
Other liabilities	**884**	1,014
Redeemable preferred and common securities of subsidiaries	**549**	547
Stockholders' Equity		
Kimberly-Clark Corporation stockholders' equity		
Preferred stock—no par value—authorized 20.0 million shares, none issued	**—**	—
Common stock—$1.25 par value—authorized 1.2 billion shares; issued 428.6 million shares at December 31, 2012 and 2011	**536**	536
Additional paid-in capital	**481**	440
Common stock held in treasury, at cost—39.3 million and 32.9 million shares at December 31, 2012 and 2011	**(2,796)**	(2,105)
Retained earnings	**8,823**	8,244
Accumulated other comprehensive income (loss)	**(2,059)**	(1,866)
Total Kimberly-Clark Corporation stockholders' equity	**4,985**	5,249
Noncontrolling interests	**302**	280
Total stockholders' equity	**5,287**	5,529
Total liabilities and stockholders' equity	**$19,873**	$19,373

Kimberly-Clark reports total assets of $19,873 million in 2012. Although 2012 current ratio is 1.08, the company is relatively illiquid because a large proportion of current assets consists of accounts receivable and inventories. Cash is 5.6% ($1,106 million/$19,873 million) of total assets at year-end 2012, up from 3.9% in 2011 but the company reports no marketable securities that can serve as another source of liquidity, if needed. The lack of liquidity is usually worrisome, but is not a serious concern in this case given Kimberly-Clark's moderate financial leverage and high level of free cash flow (see later discussion in this section).

Following is a brief review and analysis for each of Kimberly-Clark's balance sheet line items.

Accounts Receivable

Kimberly-Clark reports $2,642 million in net accounts receivable at year-end 2012. This represents 13.3% ($2,642 million/$19,873 million) of total assets, down from 13.4% in the previous year. Footnotes reveal the following additional information:

Summary of Accounts Receivable, Net ($ millions), December 31	2012	2011
Accounts receivable		
From customers	**$2,346**	$2,352
Other	**376**	328
Less allowance for doubtful accounts and sales discounts	**(80)**	(78)
Total	**$2,642**	$2,602

Most accounts receivables are from customers. This means we must consider the following two issues:

1. **Magnitude**—Receivables are generally non-interest-bearing and, therefore, do not earn a return. Further, the company incurs costs to finance them. Accordingly, a company wants to optimize its level of investment in receivables—that is, keep them as low as possible while still meeting industry specific credit policies to meet customer demands.
2. **Collectibility**—Receivables represent unsecured loans to customers. It is critical therefore, to understand the creditworthiness of these borrowers. Receivables are reported at net realizable value, that is, net of the allowance for doubtful accounts. Kimberly-Clark reports an allowance of $80 million, which includes an allowance for sales discounts. In addition, the footnotes reveal the following history of the company's allowance versus its write-offs:

		Additions		Deductions	
Description (December 31, 2012)	Balance at Beginning of Period	Charged to Costs and Expenses	Charged to Other Accounts	Write-Offs and Reclassifications	Balance at End of Period
Allowance for doubtful accounts	$57	$9	—	$6	$60

The company reported a balance in the allowance for doubtful accounts of $57 million at the beginning of 2012, which is 2.1% of gross receivables [$57 million/($2,602 million + $57 million)]. During 2012, it increased this allowance account by $9 million. This is the amount of bad debt expense that is reported in the income statement. Write-offs and reclassifications of uncollectible accounts amounted to $6 million during the year, yielding a $60 million balance at year-end, which is 2.2% of gross receivables [$60 million/($2,642 million + $60 million)]. It appears, therefore, that the company's receivables were of slightly higher quality at the start of the year relative to year end, but the difference is not great.

The allowance for doubtful accounts should always reflect the company's best estimate of the potential loss in its accounts receivable. This amount should not be overly conservative (which would understate profit), and it should not be inadequate (which would overstate profit). K-C's estimate of its potential losses results from its own (unaudited) review of the age of its receivables (older receivables are at greater risk of uncollectibility).

Inventories

Kimberly-Clark reports $2,348 million in inventories as of 2012. Footnote disclosures reveal the following inventory costing policy:

Inventories and Distribution Costs For financial reporting purposes, most U.S. inventories are valued at the lower of cost, using the Last-In, First-Out (LIFO) method, or market. The balance of the U.S. inventories and inventories of consolidated operations outside the U.S. are valued at the lower of cost, using either the First-In, First-Out (FIFO) or weighted-average cost methods, or market. Distribution costs are classified as cost of products sold.

Most of its U.S. inventories are reported on a LIFO basis. Some of its U.S. inventories, as well as those outside of the U.S., are valued at FIFO or weighted-average. The use of multiple inventory costing methods for different pools of inventories is common and acceptable under GAAP.

Kimberly-Clark provides the following footnote disclosure relating to the composition of its inventories:

Summary of Inventories ($ millions), December 31	2012 LIFO	2012 Non-LIFO	2012 Total	2011 LIFO	2011 Non-LIFO	2011 Total
Inventories by major class:						
At the lower of cost determined on the FIFO or weighted-average cost methods or market:						
Raw materials	$ 148	$ 346	$ 494	$ 163	$ 334	$ 497
Work in process	194	135	329	245	126	371
Finished goods	656	786	1,442	708	760	1,468
Supplies and other	—	314	314	—	300	300
	998	1,581	2,579	1,116	1,520	2,636
Excess of FIFO or weighted-average cost over LIFO cost	(231)	—	(231)	(280)	—	(280)
Total	$ 767	$1,581	$2,348	$ 836	$1,520	$2,356

Companies aim to optimize their investment in inventories because inventory is a non-income-producing asset until sold. Inventories must also be financed, stored, moved, and insured at some cost. Kimberly-Clark reports $494 million of raw materials, which is 19% of the total of $2,579 million FIFO inventories (see table above). Work-in-process inventories amount to another $329 million, and supplies and other amount to $314 million. The bulk of its inventories, or $1,442 million (56% of total inventories), is in finished goods.

Kimberly-Clark reports its total inventory cost *at FIFO* is $2,579 million then subtracts $231 million from this amount (the *LIFO reserve*) to yield the inventories balance of $2,348 million at LIFO as reported on the balance sheet. This means that, over time, Kimberly-Clark has reduced gross profit and pretax operating profit by a cumulative amount of $231 million. This has also reduced pretax income and saved federal income tax, and generated cash flow, of approximately $85.5 million (assuming a 37% marginal tax rate and computed as $231 million × 37%). During 2012, its LIFO reserve decreased by $49 million, resulting in a $49 million increase in gross profit and pretax operating profit, and an $18.1 million ($49 million × 37%) *decrease* in cash flow from increased federal income taxes.

Property, Plant, and Equipment

Kimberly-Clark reports Property, Plant, and Equipment (PPE), net, of $8,095 million at year-end 2012:

Summary of Property, Plant and Equipment, Net, December 31	2012	2011
Property, plant and equipment:		
Land	$ 199	$ 193
Buildings	2,732	2,858
Machinery and equipment	13,993	14,676
Construction in progress	732	513
	$17,656	18,240
Less accumulated depreciation	(9,561)	(10,191)
Total	$ 8,095	$ 8,049

PPE makes up 40.7% of total assets and is the largest single asset category. Given the cost of depreciable assets of $16,725 (calculated as $13,993 million in machinery and equipment and $2,732 in buildings) million and accumulated depreciation of $9,561 million (not reported here), PPE is 57.2% depreciated assuming straight-line depreciation ($9,561 million/$16,725 million) as of 2012. This suggests these assets are older than the average age that we would expect assuming a regular replacement policy. Footnotes reveal a useful life range of 40 years for buildings and 16 to 20 years for machinery as follows:

> **Property and Depreciation** For financial reporting purposes, property, plant and equipment are stated at cost and are depreciated on the straight-line method. Buildings are depreciated over their estimated useful lives, primarily 40 years. Machinery and equipment are depreciated over their estimated useful lives, primarily ranging from 16 to 20 years. Purchases of computer software, including external costs and certain internal costs (including payroll and payroll-related costs of employees) directly associated with developing significant computer software applications for internal use, are capitalized. Computer software costs are amortized on the straight-line method over the estimated useful life of the software, which generally does not exceed five years . . . The cost of major maintenance performed on manufacturing facilities, composed of labor, materials and other incremental costs, is charged to operations as incurred. Start-up costs for new or expanded facilities are expensed as incurred.

Again, assuming straight-line depreciation, Kimberly-Clark's 2012 depreciation expense of $828 million ($857 depreciation and amortization expense reported in its statement of cash flows, Exhibit C.5, less $29 million reported as amortization expense in footnotes not reproduced in the text, but equal to the difference in accumulated amortization) reveals that its long-term depreciable assets, as a whole, are being depreciated over an average useful life of about 20.2 years, computed as depreciable assets of $16,725 million divided by $828 million depreciation expense.

Each year, Kimberly-Clark tests PPE for impairment and records a write-down to net realizable value if the PPE is deemed to be impaired. Following is Kimberly-Clark's discussion relating to its impairment testing:

> Estimated useful lives are periodically reviewed and, when warranted, changes are made to them. Long-lived assets are reviewed for impairment whenever events or changes in circumstances indicate that their carrying amount may not be recoverable. An impairment loss would be indicated when estimated undiscounted future cash flows from the use and eventual disposition of an asset group, which are identifiable and largely independent of the cash flows of other asset groups, are less than the carrying amount of the asset group. Measurement of an impairment loss would be based on the excess of the carrying amount of the asset over its fair value. Fair value is measured using discounted cash flows or independent appraisals, as appropriate. When property is sold or retired, the cost of the property and the related accumulated depreciation are removed from the Consolidated Balance Sheet and any gain or loss on the transaction is included in income.

Other (income) and expense, net for 2012 includes $19 million in asset impairment charges.

If present, impairment losses should be treated as a transitory item. Further, we must consider the effects of such losses on current and future income statements. An impairment loss depresses current period income. Further, depreciation expense in future years is decreased because it is computed based on the asset's lower net book value (cost less accumulated depreciation) following the write-down. This will increase future period profitability. The net effect of an impairment charge, therefore, is to shift profit from the current period into future periods. However, we choose not to adjust for Kimberly-Clark's 2012 impairment charge because it is a very small amount (immaterial).

Investments in Equity Companies

K-C's balance sheet reports equity investments of $355 million at year-end 2012. This amount represents the book value of its investments in affiliated companies over which Kimberly-Clark can exert significant influence, but not control. Footnotes reveal investments in the following companies:

> **Investments in Equity Companies** Investments in companies which the Corporation does not control but over which we have the ability to exercise significant influence and that, in general, are at least 20 percent-owned by us, are stated at cost plus equity in undistributed net income. These investments are evaluated for impairment when warranted. An impairment loss would be recorded whenever a decline in value of an equity investment below its carrying amount is determined to be other than temporary. In judging "other than temporary," we would consider the length of time and extent to which the fair value of the equity company investment has been less than the carrying amount, the near-term and longer-term operating and financial prospects of the equity company, and our longer-term intent of retaining the investment in the equity company.

Consolidation is not required unless the affiliate is "controlled." Generally, control is presumed at an ownership level of more than 50%. By this rule, Kimberly-Clark does not control any of these companies. Thus, the company uses the equity method to account for these investments. This means that only the net equity owned of these companies is reported on the balance sheet. We further discuss these investments in the section on off-balance-sheet financing.

Goodwill and Other Intangible Assets

Kimberly-Clark reports $3,337 million of goodwill and $246 million of other intangible assets at year-end 2012. This amount represents the excess of the purchase price for acquired companies over the fair market value of the acquired tangible and identifiable intangible assets (net of liabilities assumed). Under GAAP, goodwill is not systematically amortized, but is annually tested for impairment. K-C reports that the estimated useful lives for its other intangible assets range from 2 to 30 years for trademarks, 5 to 17 years for patents and developed technologies, and 5 to 16 years for other intangible assets. These other intangible assets are also tested annually for impairment and are written down to fair value if found to be impaired.

Other Assets

Kimberly-Clark reports $856 million as "other assets." There is no table detailing what assets are included in this total, but footnotes reveal the following: $224 million of time deposits, and $127 million of long-term investments and assets related to derivative financial instruments. No information is given on the remaining $505 million of other assets, but K-C likely includes part of its deferred tax assets in this line item.

Kimberly-Clark provides the following disclosure relating to deferred tax assets. Later in this appendix we discuss deferred tax liabilities.

December 31 (Millions of dollars)	2012	2011
Deferred tax assets:		
Pension and other postretirement benefits	$ 972	$ 756
Tax credits and loss carryforwards	729	812
Property, plant and equipment, net	110	128
Other	492	562
	2,303	2,258
Valuation allowance	(215)	(229)
Total deferred assets	2,088	2,029
Deferred tax liabilities:		
Pension and other postretirement benefits	269	206
Property, plant and equipment, net	1,228	1,305
Installment sales	120	119
Unremitted earnings	108	58
Other	385	365
Total deferred tax liablilities	2,110	2,053
Net deferred tax liablilities	$ 22	$ 24

Most of this deferred tax asset (benefit) results from pension costs recognized for tax purposes, but not yet recognized in financial statements and from tax loss carryforwards. The IRS allows companies to carry forward losses to offset future taxable income, thereby reducing future tax expense. This benefit can only be realized if the company expects taxable income in the specific entity that generated the tax losses before the carryforwards expire. If the company deems it more likely than not that the carryforwards will *not* be realized, a valuation allowance for the unrealizable portion is required (this is similar to establishing an allowance for uncollectible accounts receivable). As of 2012, Kimberly-Clark has such a valuation allowance (of $215 million). Following is its discussion relating to this allowance:

> Valuation allowances decreased $14 and $58 in 2012 and 2011, respectively, of which $3 and $36 impacted 2012 and 2011 earnings, respectively. Valuation allowances at the end of 2012 primarily relate to tax credits and income tax loss carryforwards of $1.1 billion. If these items are not utilized against taxable income, $491 of the loss carryforwards will expire from 2013 through 2032. The

continued

remaining $638 have no expiration date. Realization of income tax loss carryforwards is dependent on generating sufficient taxable income prior to expiration of these carryforwards. Although realization is not assured, we believe it is more likely than not that all of the deferred tax assets, net of applicable valuation allowances, will be realized. The amount of the deferred tax assets considered realizable could be reduced or increased due to changes in the tax environment or if estimates of future taxable income change during the carryforward period.

Tax loss carryforwards reduce income tax expense in the year they are recognized, similar to tax loss carry-backs. However, companies commonly establish both the loss carryforward and the valuation allowance concurrently. The net effect is to leave tax expense (and net income) unchanged. In future years, however, a reduction of the deferred tax asset valuation account, in anticipation of utilization of the tax carryforwards (and not as a result of their expiration), reduces tax expense and increases net income. This is a transitory increase in profit and should not be factored into projections.

Long-term Note Receivable

Kimberly-Clark holds a note receivable received from the 2012 sale of certain nonstrategic assets. The note receivable is backed by standby letters of credit, which means that there is relatively no risk associated with this note. The note receivable matures on September 30, 2014, and earns interest at LIBOR plus 75 bps. This represents a nonoperating asset (like an investment).

Current Liabilities

Kimberly-Clark reports current liabilities of $6,091 million on its year-end balance sheet for 2012 ($5,397 million in 2011), which consists of the following:

Current Liabilities ($ millions), December 31	2012	2011
Debt payable within one year	**$1,115**	$ 706
Trade accounts payable	**2,443**	2,388
Accrued expenses	**2,244**	2,026
Dividends payable	**289**	277
Total current liabilities	**$6,091**	$5,397

Regarding K-C's current liabilities, $1,404 of this amount relates to financial items, such as maturing long-term debt ($1,115 million), and dividends payable ($289 million). The remaining items in current liabilities arise from common external transactions, such as trade accounts payable and accrued expenses. These transactions are less prone to management reporting bias. We must, however, determine the presence of excessive "leaning on the trade" as a means to boost operating cash flow. K-C's trade accounts payable have not increased as a percentage of total assets (12.3%) and have only slightly increased as a percentage of sales (11.5% to 11.6%). This increase is not of concern.

The possibility of management reporting bias is typically greater for accrued liabilities, which are often estimated (and difficult to audit), involve no external transaction, and can markedly impact reported balance sheet and income statement amounts. One of Kimberly-Clark's accrued liabilities involves promotions and rebates, reported at $340 million in the footnotes as of 2012. Following is the description of its accrual policy in this area:

Sales Incentives and Trade Promotion Allowances Among those factors affecting the accruals for promotions are estimates of the number of consumer coupons that will be redeemed and the type and number of activities within promotional programs between us and our trade customers. Generally, the estimates for consumer coupon costs are based on historical patterns of coupon redemption, influenced by judgments about current market conditions such as competitive activity in specific product categories. Estimates of trade promotion liabilities for promotional program costs incurred, but unpaid, are generally based on estimates of the quantity of customer sales, timing of promotional activities and forecasted costs for activities within the promotional programs. Trade promotion programs include introductory marketing funds such as slotting fees, cooperative marketing programs, temporary price reductions, favorable end-of-aisle or in-store product displays

continued

and other activities conducted by our customers to promote our products. Promotion accruals as of December 31, 2012 and 2011 were $319 and $339, respectively. Rebate accruals are based on estimates of the quantity of products expected to be sold to specific customers, and were $340 and $344 at December 31, 2012 and 2011, respectively.

All accruals have similar effects on the financial statements: when the accrual is established the company recognizes both an expense in the income statement and a liability on the balance sheet. The company subsequently reduces the liability as payments are made. Companies can (and do) use accruals to shift income from one period to another, say by over-accruing in one period to intentionally depress current period profits, and later reducing the liability account, rather than recording an expense, to increase future period profits. Accruals are sometimes referred to as "pads." They represent a cost that has previously been charged to the income statement. They also represent an account that can absorb future costs. We need to monitor accrual accounts carefully for evidence of earnings management.

Long-Term Debt

Kimberly-Clark reports $5,826 million of long-term debt as of 2012. Footnotes reveal the following:

Long-term debt is composed of the following:

($ millions)	Weighted-Average Interest Rate	Maturities	December 31 2012	December 31 2011
Notes and debentures	5.53%	2013–2046	**$4,857**	$4,984
Dealer remarketable securities	4.22%	2013–2016	**200**	200
Industrial development revenue bonds	0.24%	2015–2034	**261**	280
Bank loans and other financings in various currencies	2.57%	2013–2047	**508**	581
Total long-term debt			**5,826**	6,045
Less current portion			**756**	619
Long-term portion			**$5,070**	$5,426

Most of its long-term financing is in the form of notes and debentures, specifically $4,857 million in 2012, which mature over the next 34 years. GAAP requires disclosure of scheduled maturities for each of the five years subsequent to the balance sheet date. Kimberly-Clark's five-year maturity schedule follows:

Scheduled maturities of long-term debt for the next five years are $756 in 2013, $523 in 2014, $343 in 2015, $46 in 2016 and $957 in 2017.

Our concern with debt maturity dates is whether or not a company is able to repay debt as it comes due. Alternatively, a company can refinance the debt. If a company is unable or unwilling to repay or refinance its debt, it must approach creditors for a modification of debt terms for those issuances coming due. Creditors are often willing to oblige but will likely increase interest rates or impose additional debt covenants and restrictions. However, if creditors deny default waivers, the company might face the prospect of bankruptcy. This highlights the importance of long-term debt maturity disclosures.

We have little concern about Kimberly-Clark's debt maturity schedule as the company has strong cash flows. It is worth noting that **Standard & Poor's** (S&P) debt rating for K-C is A. This rating is solid (described as "upper-medium grade" debt).

Noncurrent Employee Benefits and Other Obligations

Kimberly-Clark reports a (negative) funded status of its pension plan of $(1,215) million at year-end 2012 (disclosed in footnotes). This means that the company's pension plans are underfunded by that amount. This underfunding is computed as the difference between the pension benefit obligation (PBO) of $6,590 million and the fair value of the company's pension plan assets of $5,375 million (these amounts are also reported in the pension footnote not reproduced here).

The central issue with respect to pensions and other post-employment obligations, which K-C calls post-retirement obligations, is the potential demand they present on operating cash flows. Companies can tap cash from two sources to pay pension and other post-employment obligations: from the returns on plan assets (i.e., the cumulative contributions and investment returns that have not yet been paid out to beneficiaries) and/or from operating cash flow. To the extent that plan assets are insufficient to meet retirement obligations, companies must divert operating cash flows from other investment activities, potentially reducing the dollar amount of capital projects that can be funded.

We can gain insight into potential cash flow issues by comparing expected future benefit payments to the funds available to make those payments. Companies must provide these disclosures in a schedule to the pension footnotes. K-C provides the following schedule of expected payments in the footnotes to its 10-K:

Estimated Future Benefit Payments Over the next ten years, we expect that the following gross benefit payments will occur:

(Millions of dollars)	Pension Benefits	Other Benefits
2013	$ 352	$ 58
2014	354	57
2015	357	56
2016	357	57
2017	365	58
2018–2022	1,915	300

The schedule shows that K-C expects to pay out $352 million in benefits to pension beneficiaries and $58 million in health care and other post-employment benefits (OPEB) to its former employees in 2013. The schedule also reveals that the company expects these amounts to increase slightly over the next five years.

K-C also reports the following table relating to its pension and other post-employment benefit plans' assets:

Change in Plan Assets Year Ended December 31 (Millions of dollars)	Pension Benefits 2012	Pension Benefits 2011	Other Benefits 2012	Other Benefits 2011
Fair value of plan assets at beginning of year	**$5,214**	$4,600	—	—
Actual return on plan assets	**556**	309	—	—
Employer contributions	**110**	679	—	—
Currency and other	**60**	(15)	—	—
Benefit payments	**(478)**	(359)	—	—
Settlements	**(87)**	—	—	—
Fair value of plan assets at end of year	**$5,375**	$5,214	—	—

In 2012, K-C contributed $110 million to its pension plan. That amount, when combined with investment returns of $556 million, was more than sufficient to cover 2012 benefit payments of $478 million. Should pension assets decline markedly as a result of severe underfunding or investment losses, K-C will need to divert operating cash flows from other investment activities into pension contributions, or to borrow funds to meet its pension obligations. Although K-C's pension obligations are under-funded (as represented by the negative funded status), its current contribution levels and investment returns are sufficient to meet its anticipated pension obligations, at least in the near future.

Other post-employment benefit obligations (future health care payments) present a different picture. Because federal law does not require minimum funding of these plans, and companies do not receive a tax deduction for such contributions, companies rarely fund OPEB plans. All of the OPEB payments to beneficiaries, therefore, must be funded by concurrent company contributions. These payments amounted to $55 million in 2012. Given K-C's $3.3 billion in operating cash flow for 2012, the $55 million cash requirement is not material. However, OPEB funding requirements have been a burden for many companies, most notably General Motors prior to its bankruptcy.

Other Liabilities

Kimberly-Clark reports the catch-all category of Other Liabilities that includes deferred income tax liabilities. The financial statement footnote is displayed above, in the deferred tax asset discussion.

Most of the noncurrent deferred tax liability ($1,228 million) arises from K-C's use of straight-line depreciation for GAAP reporting and accelerated depreciation for tax reporting. As a result, tax depreciation expense is higher in the early years of the assets' lives. This will reverse in later years for individual assets, resulting in higher taxable income and tax liability. The deferred tax liability account reflects this future expected tax expense.

Although accelerated depreciation expense for an individual asset declines over time, thus increasing taxable income and tax liability, if K-C adds new assets at a sufficient rate, the additional first-year depreciation on those assets will more than offset the reduction of depreciation expense on older assets, resulting in a long-term reduction of tax liability. That is, the deferred tax liability is unlikely to reverse in the aggregate. For this reason, some analysts treat the deferred tax liability as a "quasi-equity" account.

Still, while deferred taxes can be postponed, they cannot be eliminated. If the company's asset growth slows markedly, it will realize higher taxable income and tax liability. We need to be mindful of the potential for a "real" tax liability (requiring cash payment) when companies begin to downsize.

Redeemable Preferred and Common Securities of Subsidiary

These securities represent the sale of stock by a subsidiary of Kimberly-Clark to outside interests. Because these securities are redeemable, the subsidiary must repurchase the securities at some future point. This makes them somewhat like a liability and consequently they are not reported in K-C's stockholders' equity but, instead, are reported between liabilities and equity.

Stockholders' Equity

Kimberly-Clark reports the following statement of stockholders' equity for 2012:

Dollars in million, shares in thousands	Common Stock Issued		Additional Paid-in Capital	Treasury Stock		Retained Earnings	Accumulated Other Comprehensive Income (Loss)	Noncontrolling Interests
	Shares	Amount		Shares	Amount			
Balance at Dec. 31, 2011	428,597	$536	$440	32,937	$(2,105)	$8,244	$(1,866)	$280
Net income in stockholders' equity	—	—	—	—	—	1,750	—	47
Other comprehensive income:								
Unrealized translation	—	—	—	—	—	—	195	20
Employee postretirement benefits, net of tax	—	—	—	—	—	—	(372)	(5)
Other	—	—	—	—	—	—	(16)	—
Stock-based awards exercised or vested	—	—	(78)	(10,492)	643	—	—	—
Income tax benefits on stock-based compensation	—	—	43	—	—	—	—	—
Shares repurchased	—	—	—	16,877	(1,333)	—	—	—
Recognition of stock-based compensation	—	—	67	—	—	—	—	—
Dividends declared ($2.96 per share)	—	—	—	—	—	(1,163)	—	(38)
Other	—	—	9	—	(1)	(8)	—	(2)
Balance at Dec. 31, 2012	428,597	$536	$481	39,322	$(2,796)	$8,823	$(2,059)	$302

K-C has issued 428,597,000 shares of its $1.25 par value common stock. The common stock account is, therefore, equal to $536 million, computed as 428,597,000 shares × $1.25. The additional paid-in capital (APIC) represents the excess of proceeds from stock issuance over par value. It includes adjustments relating to the recognition of stock-based compensation and the exercise of stock-based awards and other minor adjustments.

Kimberly-Clark's stockholders' equity is reduced by $2,796 million relating to repurchases of common stock. These treasury shares are the result of a stock purchase plan approved by K-C's board of directors, and evidences K-C's conviction that its stock is undervalued by the marketplace. The repurchased shares are held in treasury and reduce stockholders' equity by the purchase price until such time as they are reissued, perhaps to fund an acquisition or to compensate employees under a stock purchase or stock option plan (treasury shares can also be retired). During 2012, the company repurchased an additional $1,333 million of shares and issued stock amounting to $643 million for share-based compensation.

K-C compensates employees via restricted stock in addition to other forms of compensation. Under its restricted stock plan, eligible employees are issued stock, which is restricted as to sale until fully vested (owned). When issued, the market value of the restricted stock is deducted from stockholders' equity. As the employees gain ownership of the shares (that is, the restricted stock vests), a portion of this account is transferred to the income statement as compensation expense. The consequent reduction in retained earnings offsets the reduction (and increase in equity) of the restricted stock account. Stockholders' equity is, therefore, unaffected in total, although its components change.

Retained earnings increased by $1,750 million due to net income and decreased by $1,163 million due to the declaration of dividends. Accumulated other comprehensive income (AOCI), which is often aggregated with retained earnings for analysis purposes, began 2012 with a balance of $(1,866) million; this negative balance reduces stockholders' equity. During the period, this AOCI account increased (became less negative) by $195 million relating to the increase in the $US value of net assets of foreign subsidiaries. This increase in net asset value resulted from a weakened $US vis-à-vis other currencies in which the company conducts its operations in 2012. In addition, the AOCI account was decreased by $372 million relating to employee post-employment benefits adjustments and decreased (made more negative) by $16 million for activities designated as "other."

Noncontrolling Interests in Subsidiaries

K-C reports $302 million for the equity interests of noncontrolling shareholders in subsidiaries. Noncontrolling interests are shareholder claims against the net assets and cash flows of subsidiaries of the company (after all senior claims are settled). Consequently, we treat noncontrolling interest as a component of stockholders' equity.

Common-Size Balance Sheet

Similar to our analysis of the income statement, it is useful to compute common-size balance sheets. Such statements can reveal changes or relations masked by other analyses. Kimberly-Clark's common-size balance sheet covering its recent two years is shown in Exhibit C.4.

Total current assets increased from 32.4% of total assets in 2011 to 33.2% in 2012. This increase was due to an increase in cash and equivalents (from 3.9% to 5.6% of total assets) that offset declines in accounts receivable (13.4% to 13.3%) and inventories (12.2% to 11.8%). The company has reduced its operating assets, which saves working capital holding costs and decreases NOA. Net PPE decreased as a percent of total assets, from 41.5% in 2011 to 40.7% in 2012. K-C also reported reductions in goodwill and other intangible assets and a slight increase in other assets.

On the liability side, current liabilities increased as a percent of the total from 27.9% in 2011 to 30.6% in 2012. This was largely due to an increase in accrued expenses (from 10.5% to 11.3%) and debt payable within one year (3.6% to 5.6%). On balance, K-C became somewhat more financially leveraged in 2012 as stockholders' equity decreased from 28.5% of the total in 2011 to 26.6%. The relative proportions of debt and equity do not appear out of line as the ratio is less than 3 to 1.

Off-Balance-Sheet Reporting and Analysis

There are numerous assets and liabilities that do not appear on the balance sheet. Some are excluded because managers and accounting professionals only report what they can reliably measure. Others are

EXHIBIT C.4 Kimberly-Clark Common-Size Balance Sheet

December 31	2012*	2011*
Current assets		
Cash and cash equivalents	5.6%	3.9%
Accounts receivable, net	13.3	13.4
Inventories	11.8	12.2
Other current assets	2.5	2.9
Total current assets	33.2	32.4
Property, plant and equipment, net	40.7	41.5
Investments in equity companies	1.8	1.7
Goodwill	16.8	17.2
Other intangible assets	1.2	1.4
Long-term notes receivable	2.0	2.0
Other assets	4.3	3.6
Total assets	100.0%	100.0%
Current liabilities		
Debt payable within one year	5.6%	3.6%
Trade accounts payable	12.3	12.3
Accrued expenses	11.3	10.5
Dividends payable	1.5	1.4
Total current liabilities	30.6	27.9
Long-term debt	25.5	28.0
Noncurrent employee benefits	10.0	7.5
Other liabilities	4.4	5.2
Redeemable preferred and common securities of subsidiaries	2.8	2.8
Stockholders' equity		
Preferred stock—no par value		
Common stock—$1.25 par value	2.7	2.8
Additional paid-in capital	2.4	2.3
Common stock held in treasury, at cost	(14.1)	(10.9)
Retained earnings	44.4	42.6
Accumulated other comprehensive income (loss)	(10.4)	(9.6)
Total Kimberly-Clark Corporation stockholders' equity	25.1	27.1
Stockholders' equity attributable to noncontrolling interest	1.5	1.4
Total stockholders' equity	26.6	28.5
Liabilities and stockholders' equity, total	100.0%	100.0%

* Percentages are computed by dividing each balance sheet line item by that year's total assets.

excluded because of the rigidity of accounting standards. Following are some areas we might consider in our evaluation and adjustment of the Kimberly-Clark balance sheet.

Internally Developed Intangible Assets

Many brands and their corresponding values are excluded from the balance sheet. For example, consider the brand "Kleenex." Many individuals actually refer to facial tissues as Kleenex—that is successful branding! So, is the Kleenex brand reported and valued on Kimberly-Clark's balance sheet? No. That brand value cannot be reliably measured and, hence, is not included on K-C's balance sheet.

Likewise, other valuable assets are excluded from the company's balance sheet. Examples are the value of a competent management team, high employee morale, innovative production know-how, a superior supply chain, customer satisfaction, and a host of other assets.

R&D activities often create internally generated intangible assets that are mostly excluded from the balance sheet. Footnotes reveal that Kimberly-Clark spends over $356 million (1.7% of sales) on R&D to remain competitive—and, this is for an admittedly non-high-tech company. Further, K-C reveals that it spends $810 million (3.8% of sales) on advertising. Both R&D and advertising costs are expensed under GAAP as opposed to being capitalized on the balance sheet as tangible assets. These unrecognized intangible assets often represent a substantial part of a company's market value.

Equity Method Investments

Kimberly-Clark reports equity investments of $355 million at year-end 2012. These are unconsolidated affiliates over which K-C can exert significant influence (but not control) and, hence, are accounted for using the equity method. The amount reported on the balance sheet represents the initial cost of the investment, plus (minus) the percentage share of investee earnings (losses), and minus any cash dividends received. Consequently, the investment balance equals the percentage owned of the affiliates' stockholders' equity (plus any unamortized excess purchase price).

Footnotes reveal that, in sum, these K-C affiliates have total assets of $2,122 million, liabilities of $1,549 million, and stockholders' equity of $573 million. K-C's reported investment balance of $355 million in the balance sheet does not reveal the extent of the investment (assets) required to manage these companies, nor the level of potential liability exposure. For instance, if one of these affiliates falters financially, K-C might have to invest additional cash to support it rather than let it fail. Failure of an important affiliate might affect K-C's ability to finance another such venture in the future.

These investments are reported at cost, not at fair market value as are passive investments. This means that unrecognized gains and losses can be buried in such investment accounts. For example, K-C footnotes reveal the following:

> Kimberly-Clark de Mexico, S.A.B. de C.V. is partially owned by the public and its stock is publicly traded in Mexico. At December 31, 2012, our investment in this equity company was $252 million, and the estimated fair value of the investment was $3.8 billion based on the market price of publicly traded shares.

Thus, for at least one of its investments, there is an unrecognized gain of $3,548 million ($3,800 million − $252 million).

Operating Leases

Kimberly-Clark has leases classified as "operating" for financial reporting purposes. As a result, neither the lease asset nor the lease obligation are reported on its balance sheet. For example, K-C reports the following disclosure relating to its operating leases:

> **Leases** We have entered into operating leases for certain warehouse facilities, automobiles and equipment. The future minimum obligations under operating leases having a noncancelable term in excess of one year are as follows:

Year Ending December 31	(Millions of dollars)
2013	$174
2014	141
2015	109
2016	89
2017	64
Thereafter	124
Future minimum obligations	$701

These leases represent an unreported asset and an unreported liability; both amounting to $622 million. This amount is computed as follows and assumes a 4% discount rate ($ millions):

Year	Operating Lease Payment	Discount Factor (i = 0.04)	Present Value
1	$174	0.96154	$167
2	141	0.92456	130
3	109	0.88900	97
4	89	0.85480	76
5	64	0.82193	53
>5	124 [$64 for ~1.938 years]	1.88609* × 0.82193	99**
			$622

Remaining life = $124/$64 = 1.938 or 2 years
*The annuity factor for 2 years at 4% is 1.88609 (alternatively, one could compute the annuity factor using 1.938 years).
**1.88609 × 0.82193 × $64 = $99

The classification of leases as operating for financial reporting purposes often involves a rigid application of accounting rules that depend solely on the structure of the lease. A large amount of assets and liabilities is excluded from many companies' balance sheets because leases are structured as operating leases. For K-C, these excluded assets amount to $622 million. The valuation of K-C common stock (shown later) uses net operating assets (NOA) as one of its inputs. Our adjustment to the K-C balance sheet, then, would entail the addition of these assets to NOA and the inclusion of $622 million in *non*operating liabilities.

Pensions

Kimberly-Clark's pension plan is underfunded as explained earlier. Total pension obligations are $6,590 million and pension assets have a market value of $5,375 million at year-end 2012. Neither of these amounts appears on the balance sheet, but are reported in the footnotes. Only the net amount of $(1,215) appears on the balance sheet via three component amounts as identified in the following footnote disclosure:

Amounts Recognized in the Balance Sheet	
Noncurrent asset—Prepaid benefit cost	$ 8
Current liability—Accrued benefit cost.	(12)
Noncurrent liability—Accrued benefit cost.	(1,211)
Net amount recognized	$(1,215)

Variable Interest Entities

Footnotes reveal that Kimberly-Clark owns investments in entities that are considered to be a variable interest entity (VIE) under GAAP. These entities are typically non-stock entities, such as joint ventures, partnerships and trusts, and the accounting for these entities depends upon whether the investor is deemed to be the primary beneficiary. If so, the investor must consolidate the VIE. If not, the investor accounts for its investment using the equity method. K-C's footnote disclosure relating to these investments reports that all such VIE investments are consolidated; and thus, no adjustment is required:

> At December 31, 2012, we have a minority voting interest in a financing entity used to monetize a note receivable received from the sale of nonstrategic timberlands and related assets to a nonaffiliated buyer. We are the primary beneficiary of the entity and, accordingly, consolidate the entity in our Consolidated Financial Statements.

Derivatives

Kimberly-Clark is exposed to a number of market risks as outlined in the following footnote to its 10-K:

> As a multinational enterprise, we are exposed to risks such as changes in foreign currency exchange rates, interest rates and commodity prices. A variety of practices are employed to manage these risks, including operating and financing activities and, where deemed appropriate, the use of derivative instruments. Derivative instruments are used only for risk management purposes and not for speculation. All foreign currency derivative instruments are entered into with major financial institutions. Our credit exposure under these arrangements is limited to agreements with a positive fair value at the reporting date. Credit risk with respect to the counterparties is actively monitored but is not considered significant since these transactions are executed with a diversified group of financial institutions.

The company hedges these risks using derivatives, including forwards, options, and swap contracts. This hedging process transfers risk from K-C to another entity (called the counterparty), which assumes that risk for a fee.

The accounting for derivatives is summarized in an appendix to Module 9. In brief, the derivative contracts, and the assets or liabilities to which they relate, are reported on the balance sheet at fair market value. Any unrealized gains and losses are ultimately reflected in net income, although they can be accumulated in AOCI for a short time. To the extent that a company's hedging activities are effective, the market values of the derivatives and the assets or liabilities to which they relate are largely offsetting, as are the net gains or losses on the hedging activities. As a result, the effect of derivative activities is generally minimal on both income and equity. (It is generally only when companies use derivatives for speculative purposes that these investments markedly affect income and equity. The aim of the derivatives standard was to highlight these speculative activities and we need to read risk footnotes carefully to assess whether companies are hedging or speculating with derivatives.)

Statement of Cash Flows Reporting and Analysis

The statement of cash flows for **Kimberly-Clark** is shown in Exhibit C.5.

In 2012, K-C generated $3,288 million of operating cash flow, primarily from income (net income plus the depreciation add-back equals $2,685 million). This amount is well in excess of K-C's capital expenditures of $1,093 million. K-C used excess cash to pay $1,151 million in dividends to shareholders.

Kimberly-Clark offers the following commentary regarding its 2012 operating cash flow:

> Cash provided by operations was $3.3 billion compared to $2.3 billion last year, with the increase primarily due to higher earnings, improved working capital and lower defined benefit pension contributions ($110 in 2012 versus $679 in 2011).

Overall, the cash flow picture for Kimberly-Clark is strong: operating cash flows are more than sufficient to cover capital expenditures and acquisitions, leaving excess cash that is being returned to the shareholders in the form of dividends and share repurchases. The strength of its operating cash flows mitigates any concerns we might have regarding its relative lack of liquidity on the balance sheet.

EXHIBIT C.5 Kimberly-Clark Statement of Cash Flows

KIMBERLY-CLARK CORPORATION AND SUBSIDIARIES
Consolidated Cash Flow Statement

Year Ended December 31 (Millions of dollars)	2012	2011	2010
Operating Activities			
Net income	**$ 1,828**	$ 1,684	$ 1,943
Depreciation and amortization	**857**	1,091	813
Asset impairments	**171**	58	—
Stock-based compensation	**67**	48	52
Deferred income taxes	**224**	274	(12)
Net losses (gains) on asset dispositions	**35**	(6)	26
Equity companies' earnings in excess of dividends paid	**(27)**	(23)	(48)
Decrease (increase) in operating working capital	**119**	(262)	24
Postretirement benefits	**7**	(574)	(125)
Other	**7**	(2)	71
Cash provided by operations	**3,288**	2,288	2,744
Investing Activities			
Capital spending	**(1,093)**	(968)	(964)
Proceeds from maturity of note receivable	**—**	220	—
Proceeds from sales of investments	**23**	28	47
Investments in time deposits	**(212)**	(158)	(131)
Maturities of time deposits	**95**	141	248
Proceeds from disposition of property	**9**	51	9
Other	**(6)**	5	10
Cash used for investing	**(1,184)**	(681)	(781)
Financing Activities			
Cash dividends paid	**(1,151)**	(1,099)	(1,066)
Net increase (decrease) in short-term debt	**271**	13	(28)
Proceeds from issuance of long-term debt	**315**	839	515
Repayments of long-term debt	**(492)**	(107)	(506)
Redemption of redeemable preferred securities of subsidiary	**—**	(500)	—
Cash paid on redeemable preferred securities of subsidiary	**(28)**	(57)	(54)
Proceeds from exercise of stock options	**565**	435	131
Acquisitions of common stock for the treasury	**(1,284)**	(1,246)	(803)
Other	**2**	(19)	(48)
Cash used for financing	**(1,802)**	(1,741)	(1,859)
Effect of exchange rate changes on cash and cash equivalents	**40**	22	(26)
Increase (decrease) in cash and cash equivalents	**342**	(112)	78
Cash and cash equivalents, beginning of year	**764**	876	798
Cash and cash equivalents, end of year	**$ 1,106**	$ 764	$ 876

Independent Audit Opinion

Kimberly-Clark is subject to various audit requirements. Its independent auditor is **Deloitte & Touche LLP**, which issued the following clean opinion on K-C's 2012 financial statements:

REPORT OF INDEPENDENT REGISTERED PUBLIC ACCOUNTING FIRM

To the Board of Directors and Stockholders of Kimberly-Clark Corporation:

We have audited the accompanying consolidated balance sheets of Kimberly-Clark Corporation and subsidiaries (the "Corporation") as of December 31, 2012 and 2011, and the related consolidated statements of income, comprehensive income, stockholders' equity, and cash flows for each of the

continued

continued from prior page

three years in the period ended December 31, 2012. Our audits also included the financial statement schedule listed in the Index at Item 15. These financial statements and financial statement schedule are the responsibility of the Corporation's management. Our responsibility is to express an opinion on the financial statements and financial statement schedule based on our audits.

We conducted our audits in accordance with the standards of the Public Company Accounting Oversight Board (United States). Those standards require that we plan and perform the audit to obtain reasonable assurance about whether the financial statements are free of material misstatement. An audit includes examining, on a test basis, evidence supporting the amounts and disclosures in the financial statements. An audit also includes assessing the accounting principles used and significant estimates made by management, as well as evaluating the overall financial statement presentation. We believe that our audits provide a reasonable basis for our opinion.

In our opinion, such consolidated financial statements present fairly, in all material respects, the financial position of Kimberly-Clark Corporation and subsidiaries as of December 31, 2012 and 2011, and the results of their operations and their cash flows for each of the three years in the period ended December 31, 2012, in conformity with accounting principles generally accepted in the United States of America. Also, in our opinion, such financial statement schedule, when considered in relation to the basic consolidated financial statements taken as a whole, presents fairly, in all material respects, the information set forth therein.

We have also audited, in accordance with the standards of the Public Company Accounting Oversight Board (United States), the Corporation's internal control over financial reporting as of December 31, 2012, based on the criteria established in *Internal Control—Integrated Framework* issued by the Committee of Sponsoring Organizations of the Treadway Commission and our report dated February 22, 2013, expressed an unqualified opinion on the Corporation's internal control over financial reporting.

Deloitte & Touche LLP
Dallas, Texas
February 22, 2013

Although this report is a routine disclosure, it should not be taken for granted. Exceptions to a clean audit report must be scrutinized. Also, any disagreements between management and the independent auditor must be documented in an SEC filing. If this occurs, it is a "red flag" that must be investigated. Management activities and reports that cannot meet usual audit standards raise serious concerns about integrity and credibility. At a minimum, the riskiness of investments and relationships with such a company markedly increases.

ASSESSING PROFITABILITY AND CREDITWORTHINESS

LO2 Assess company profitability and creditworthiness.

This section reports a profitability analysis of **Kimberly-Clark**. We begin by computing several key measures that are used in the ROE disaggregation, which is the overriding focus of this section. The ROE disaggregation process is defined in Module 4, and a listing of the ratio acronyms and definitions is in the review section at the end of the book.

K-C's 2012 net operating profit after taxes, or NOPAT, is $1,996 million, computed as ($2,686 million + $176 million) − ($768 million + [{$284 million − $18 million} × 37%]). In 2012, K-C's net operating assets, or NOA, total $10,809 million, computed as $19,873 − $1,106 − $395 − ($6,091 − $1,115 − $289) − $1,992 − $884 ($ millions). For 2011, NOA totals $11,327 million.

ROE Disaggregation

Our first step is to compute the ROE and, then, disaggregate it into its operating (return on net operating assets or RNOA) and nonoperating components. Using the computations in the previous section, the 2012 disaggregation analysis of ROE for Kimberly-Clark follows. (Many of these ratios require computation of averages, such as average assets. If we wanted to compute ratios for years prior to 2012, then we would obtain information from prior 10-Ks to compute the necessary averages for these ratios.)

ROE	=	RNOA	+	Nonoperating return
34.20%	=	**18.03%**	+	**16.17%**

where

ROE = $1,750 million /[($4,985 million + $5,249 million)/2]*
RNOA = $1,996 million/[$10,809 million + $11,327 million)/2]

*We use net income and stockholders' equity attributed to K-C shareholders.

RNOA accounts for 53% (18.03%/34.20%) of K-C's ROE. K-C successfully uses its nonoperating activities to increase its 18.03% RNOA to produce a 34.20% ROE.

Disaggregation of RNOA—Margin and Turnover

The next level analysis of ROE focuses on RNOA disaggregation. Kimberly-Clark's net operating profit margin (NOPM) and net operating asset turnover (NOAT) are as follows:

RNOA	=	NOPAT/Average Net Operating Assets	=	NOPAT/Sales	×	Sales/Average Net Operating Assets
				NOPM		**NOAT**
		18.03%	=	**9.48%**	×	**1.903** (0.001 rounding difference)

where

NOPM = $1,996 million/$21,063 million
NOAT = $21,063 million/[($10,809 million + $11,327 million)/2]

Kimberly-Clark's RNOA of 18.03% consists of a net operating profit margin of 9.47% and a net operating asset turnover of 1.903 times.

Disaggregation of Margin and Turnover

This section focuses on the disaggregation of profit margin and asset turnover to better understand the drivers of RNOA. Again, understanding the drivers of financial performance (RNOA) is key to predicting future company performance. Our analysis of the drivers of operating profit margin and asset turnover for Kimberly-Clark follows (all $ in millions):

Disaggregation of NOPM	
Gross profit margin (GPM) ($6,749 million/$21,063 million)	32.0%
Marketing, research and general expense, to sales ($4,069 million/$21,063 million)	19.3%
Disaggregation of NOAT	
Accounts receivable turnover (ART) {$21,063 million/[($2,642 million + $2,602 million)/2]}	8.0
Inventory turnover (INVT) {$14,314 million/[($2,348 million + $2,356 million)/2]}	6.1
PPE turnover (PPET) {$21,063 million/[($8,095 million + $8,049 million)/2]}	2.6
Accounts payable turnover (APT) {$14,314 million/[($2,443 million + $2,388 million)/2]}	5.9
Related turnover measures	
Average collection period [$2,642 million/($21,063 million/365 days)]	45.8 days
Average inventory days outstanding [$2,348 million/($14,314 million/365 days)]	59.9 days
Average payable days outstanding [$2,443 million/($14,314 million/365 days)]	62.3 days

First, let's look at the disaggregation of NOPM. K-C reports an increase in its gross profit margin from 29.5% in 2011 to 32.0% in 2012. This increase is impressive. As K-C points out in the excerpt from its MD&A that we reproduce on page C-4, the company operates in a very competitive market that makes gross profit margins difficult to maintain. Offsetting the increase in gross profit margins, was an increase in marketing, research and general expenses as a percentage of sales from 18.0% to 19.3%, which included "higher strategic marketing spending" as K-C explains in its MD&A. Further, K-C's "administrative and research spending also increased, in part to build further capabilities and support future growth."

Next, we consider the disaggregation of NOAT. K-C's receivables turnover rate of 8.0 times corresponds to an average collection period of 45.8 days, which is reasonable considering normal credit terms. However, the more important issue here is asset productivity (turnover) instead of credit quality. This is because most of K-C's sales are to large retailers; for example, 12% of Kimberly-Clark's sales are to Walmart.

Inventories turn over 6.1 times a year, resulting in an average inventory days outstanding of 59.9 days in 2012. Inventories are an important (and large) asset for companies like Kimberly-Clark. Improved turnover is always a goal so long as the company maintains sufficient inventories to meet market demand.

K-C's property, plant, and equipment are turning over 2.6 times a year, which is about average for publicly traded companies. The issue with respect to PPET is throughput, and K-C does not discuss this aspect of its business in its financial filings.

K-C's trade accounts payable turnover is 5.9, resulting in an average payable days outstanding of 62.3 days. Because payables represent a low-cost source of financing, we would prefer to see its days payable lengthened so long as K-C is not endangering its relationships with suppliers.

Credit Analysis

Credit analysis is an important part of a complete company analysis. Following is a selected set of measures for 2012 that can help us gauge the relative credit standing of Kimberly-Clark ($ millions):

Current ratio ($6,589/$6,091)	1.08
Quick ratio ([$1,106 + $2,642]/$6,091)	0.62
Total liabilities/Equity* ([$19,873 − $5,287]/$5,287)	2.76
Long-term debt/Equity ([$5,070 + $1,115]/$5,287)	1.17
Earnings before interest and taxes/Interest expense ([$2,420 + $284]/$284)	9.52
Net operating cash flows/Total liabilities ($3,288/[$19,873 − $5,287])	0.23

*Includes noncontrolling interest as equity as we analyze the company from the perspective of all equity holders; if we prefer to examine the company from the perspective of the company's equity holders only, then we would exclude noncontrolling interest.

K-C's current and quick ratios are not particularly high, and both have decreased slightly over the past two years (not shown here). These ratios do not imply any excess liquidity, and probably do not suggest any room for a further decrease in liquidity.

K-C's financial leverage, as reflected in both the liability-to-equity and long-term-debt-to-equity ratios, is slightly above the median for all publicly traded companies. Normally, this is cause for some concern. However, Kimberly-Clark has strong operating and free cash flows that mitigate this concern.

K-C's times interest earned ratio of 9.52 is healthy, indicating a sufficient buffer to protect creditors if earnings decline. It also has relatively little off-balance-sheet exposure. Thus, we do not have any serious concerns about K-C's ability to repay its maturing debt obligations.

Summarizing Profitability and Creditworthiness

An increasingly competitive environment has diminished Kimberly-Clark's gross profit margin. Operating expense reductions have not offset this decline and its NOPAT has declined slightly as a result. Its level of net operating asset turnover is acceptable, although not stellar. K-C does not provide sufficient information for us to further assess the throughput performance of its operating assets. Finally, its leverage, although higher than average, is not of great concern given K-C's strong cash flows.

FORECASTING FINANCIAL STATEMENT NUMBERS

LO3 Forecast financial statements.

The valuation of K-C's common stock requires forecasts of NOPAT and NOA over a forecast horizon period and a forecast terminal period. Our approach is to project individual income statement and balance sheet items using the methodology we discuss in Module 11. K-C presented its 4Q results and

2013 guidance to analysts on January 25, 2013, and provided the following slide relative to its expectations for 2013 (posted on the K-C investor relations Website).

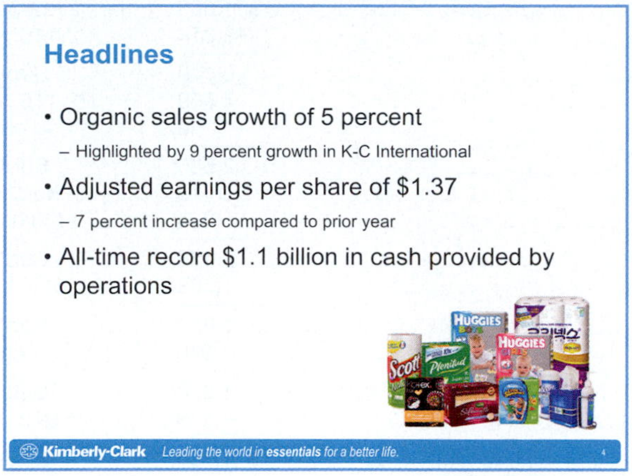

We use K-C's sales growth prediction of 5% in our forecast of the company's sales for 2013. We also make the following additional forecast assumptions:

1. We assume that operating expenses retain their 2012 relation to sales and that all operating assets and liabilities also retain their 2012 relation to sales, except as noted below.
2. We assume that the dollar value of interest income and share of net income of equity companies will remain at 2012 levels.
3. We assume that net income attributable to noncontrolling interests will be the same proportion of consolidated net income as for 2012.
4. The effective tax rate has been in the range of 30% to 32%. We use 31% in our forecast.
5. In 2012, the capital spending (CAPEX) was 5.2% of sales. We use that percentage applied to forecasted sales to estimate 2013 CAPEX.
6. Depreciation as a percentage of prior-year PPE, net was 10.3%. We use that percentage applied to prior year PPE, net to estimate 2013 depreciation expense. We assume there is no depreciation expense on the 2013 CAPEX.
7. Share repurchases have been at $1,500 million per year under a program with a cap (approved by the Board of Directors) of $3 billion. We use $1,500 million per year in our forecast for the next two years.
8. The dividend payout ratio (dividends as a percentage of net income attributable to K-C stockholders) was 65.8%. We use that dividend payout percentage applied to forecasted net income attributable to K-C stockholders. We assume that dividends payable account is related to dividends declared in the same proportion as for 2012.
9. We forecast "no change" for the following balance sheet items: investments in equity companies, goodwill, long-term notes receivable, redeemable preferred securities, common stock, APIC, and AOCI.

Our initial forecast results in total assets of $20,523 million and total liabilities and equity of $18,389 million. K-C does not hold marketable securities, thus, we do not adjust assets, but instead, we assume that the difference between forecasted assets and liabilities ($2,134 million) is made up through additional short-term financing. K-C's bond rating is "A" and we assume that the new borrowing will be at the current pre-tax bond rate of 3%. We assume that the $2,134 million in additional financing is borrowed evenly over the year. This means that interest expense is expected to increase by $32 million ([$2,134 million / 2] × 3%), from $284 million to $316 million. The increase to interest expense impacts the income statement, including taxes and net income, and then impacts the balance sheet line via retained earnings (because of the income revision). The resulting forecasts of the K-C income statement and balance sheet for 2013, reflecting these assumptions and subsequent changes, are in Exhibit C.6.

EXHIBIT C.6 Forecasts of Income Statement and Balance Sheet of Kimberly-Clark

Consolidated Income Statement ($ millions)	2012	Forecast Assumptions	2013 Est.
Net sales	$21,063	21,063 × 1.05	$22,116
Cost of products sold	14,314	22,116 × 68.0%	15,039
Gross profit	6,749	Subtotal	7,077
Marketing, research and general expenses	4,069	22,116 × 19.3%	4,268
Other (income) and expense, net	(6)	no change	(6)
Operating profit	2,686	Subtotal	2,815
Interest income	18	no change	18
Interest expense	(284)	(284) − 32*	(316)
Income before income taxes and equity interests	2,420	Subtotal	2,517
Provision for income taxes	(768)	2,517 × 31.0%	(780)
Income before equity interests	1,652	Subtotal	1,737
Share of net income of equity companies	176	no change	176
Net income	1,828	Subtotal	1,913
Net income attributable to noncontrolling interests	(78)	1,913 × 4.3%	(82)
Net income attributable to Kimberly-Clark Corporation	$ 1,750	Subtotal	$ 1,831

* See text discussion

Consolidated Balance Sheet ($ millions)	2012	Forecast Assumptions	2013 Est.
Current assets			
Cash and cash equivalents	$ 1,106	22,116 × 5.3%	$ 1,172
Accounts receivable, net	2,642	22,116 × 12.5%	2,765
Inventories	2,348	22,116 × 11.1%	2,455
Other current assets	493	22,116 × 2.3%	509
Total current assets	6,589	Subtotal	6,901
Property, plant and equipment, net	8,095	8,095 + 1,150 − 834	8,411
Investments in equity companies	355	no change	355
Goodwill	3,337	no change	3,337
Other intangible assets	246	246 − 29	217
Long-term notes receivable	395	no change	395
Other assets	856	22,116 × 4.1%	907
Total assets	$19,873	Subtotal	$20,523
Current Liabilities			
New financing		plug	$ 2,146
Debt payable within one year	$ 1,115	from debt footnote	756
Trade accounts payable	2,443	22,116 × 11.6%	2,565
Accrued expenses	2,244	22,116 × 10.7%	2,366
Dividends payable	289	1,205 × 25.1%	302
Total current liabilities	6,091	Subtotal	8,135
Long-term debt	5,070	5,070 − 756	4,314
Noncurrent employee benefits	1,992	22,116 × 9.5%	2,101
Other liabilities	884	22,116 × 4.2%	929
Redeemable preferred and common securities of subsidiaries	549	no change	549
Stockholders' equity			
Preferred stock, no par value, authorized 20.0 million shares, none issued	0	no change	0
Common stock, $1.25 par value, authorized 1.2 billion shares; issued 428.6 million shares at December 31, 2012 and 2011	536	no change	536
Additional paid-in capital	481	no change	481
Common stock held in treasury, at cost: 39.3 million and 32.9 million shares at December 31, 2012 and 2011	(2,796)	(2,796) − 1,500	(4,296)
Retained earnings	8,823	8,823 + 1,831 − 1,205	9,449
Accumulated other comprehensive income (loss)	(2,059)	no change	(2,059)
Total Kimberly-Clark Corporation stockholders' equity	4,985	Subtotal	4,111
Noncontrolling interests	302	302 + 82	384
Total stockholders' equity	5,287	Subtotal	4,495
Liabilities and stockholders' equity, total	$19,873	Subtotal	$20,523

The forecasted statement of cash flows is in Exhibit C.7. This forecasted statement utilizes the forecasted income statement and comparative balance sheets as presented in Exhibit C.6 and is prepared as explained in Module 11. We forecast that K-C will generate $2,886 million in cash from operating activities in 2013. Given projected CAPEX of $1,150 million, dividends of $1,203 million, and stock repurchases of $1,500 million, we forecast that K-C will require external financing of $2,146 million. The forecasted year-end cash balance of $1,172 million is equal to 5.3% of estimated sales, the same relation to sales that the company reported in 2012.

EXHIBIT C.7 Forecast of Statement of Cash Flows for Kimberly-Clark

$ millions	Forecast Assumptions	2013 Est.
Operating activities		
Net income including noncontrolling interests	via forecasted income statement	$1,913
Add: Depreciation	8,095 × 10.3%	834
Add: Amortization	no change	29
Change in accounts receivable	2,642 − 2,765	(123)
Change in inventories	2,348 − 2,455	(107)
Change in other current assets	493 − 509	(16)
Change in other long-term assets	856 − 907	(51)
Change in accounts payable	2,565 − 2,443	122
Change in accrued expenses	2,366 − 2,244	122
Change in dividends payable	302 − 289	13
Change in noncurrent employee benefits	2,101 − 1,992	109
Change in other liabilities	929 − 884	45
Net cash from operating activities	subtotal	2,890
Investing activities		
Capital expenditures	22,116 × 5.2%	(1,150)
Net cash from investing activities	subtotal	(1,150)
Financing activities		
Dividends	1,831 × 0.658	(1,205)
Stock purchase	company guidance	(1,500)
Payments of long-term debt	2012 current maturities of LTD	(1,115)
New financing	plug	2,146
Net cash from financing activities	subtotal	(1,674)
Net change in cash	subtotal	66
Beginning cash	from balance sheet	1,106
Ending cash	subtotal	$1,172

VALUING EQUITY SECURITIES

This section estimates the values of Kimberly-Clark's equity and common stock per share.

LO4 Describe and illustrate the valuation of firm equity.

Parsimonious Forecast

For valuation purposes we must forecast the financial statements for more than one year ahead. In particular, we need NOPAT and NOA for the forecast horizon and for the terminal period. Exhibit C.8 displays the parsimonious forecast for Kimberly Clark. The methods used in this forecasting process follow those described in the module on forecasting.

We assume a sales growth of 5%, consistent with our detailed forecast above and for the terminal year, we assume a sales growth of 1%. We use the year-end NOPM (9.48%) and year-end NOAT (1.95) to forecast the following:

EXHIBIT C.8 Kimberly-Clark Multiyear Forecasts of Sales, NOPAT and NOA

($ millions)	Reported 2012	Horizon Period 2013	2014	2015	2016	Terminal Period 2017
Net sales growth.		5.0%	5.0%	5.0%	5.0%	1.0%
Net sales (unrounded) . .	$21,063	**$22,116.15** ($21,063 × 1.05)	**$23,221.96** ($22,116.15 × 1.05)	**$24,383.06** ($23,221.96 × 1.05)	**$25,602.21** ($24,383.06 × 1.05)	**$25,858.23** ($25,602.21 × 1.01)
Net sales (rounded)	$21,063	**$22,116**	**$23,222**	**$24,383**	**$25,602**	**$25,858**
NOPAT[1].	$1,996	**$2,097** ($22,116 × 0.0948)	**$2,201** ($23,222 × 0.0948)	**$2,312** ($24,383 × 0.0948)	**$2,427** ($25,602 × 0.0948)	**$2,451** ($25,858 × 0.0948)
NOA[2].	$10,809	**$11,342** ($22,116/1.95)	**$11,909** ($23,222/1.95)	**$12,504** ($24,383/1.95)	**$13,129** ($25,602/1.95)	**$13,261** ($25,858/1.95)

[1] Forecasted NOPAT = Forecasted net sales (rounded) × 2012 NOPM
[2] Forecasted NOA = Forecasted net sales (rounded)/2012 NOAT

Discounted Cash Flow Valuation

Exhibit C.9 shows the discounted cash (DCF) model results. In addition to the forecasted NOPAT and NOA from Exhibit C.8, we assume a discount rate (WACC) of 5.8%, which we obtained from Bloomberg. We use shares outstanding of 389.3 million (from the balance sheet), net nonoperating obligations (NNO) of $5,522 million calculated as: $1,115 + $289 + $5,070 + $549 − $1,106 − $395, and noncontrolling interest of $302 (all in $ millions).

EXHIBIT C.9 Kimberly-Clark Discounted Cash Flow (DCF) Valuation

(In millions, except per share values and discount factors)	Reported 2012	Horizon Period 2013	2014	2015	2016	Terminal Period
NOPAT		$2,097	$2,201	$2,312	$2,427	$2,451
Increase in NOA		533	567	595	625	132
FCFF (NOPAT − Increase in NOA)		1,564	1,634	1,717	1,802	2,319
Discount factor $[1/(1+r_w)^t]$		0.94518	0.89336	0.84439	0.79810	
Present value of horizon FCFF		1,478	1,460	1,450	1,438	
Cum present value of horizon FCFF.	$ 5,826					
Cum present value of terminal FCFF	38,558[a]					
Total firm value	44,384					
Less: NNO	5,522					
Less: NCI	302					
Firm equity value	38,560					
Shares outstanding	389.3					
Stock value per share.	$ 99.05					

[a] Computed as $\frac{\left(\frac{\$2{,}319 \text{ million}}{0.058 - 0.01}\right)}{(1.058)^4}$

The DCF valuation model yields a stock price estimate of $99.05 per share. The mean price target for 18 analysts who publicly reported their forecasts, is $100.50 with a high of $115.00 and a low of $86.00. Our estimate is within that range. The average analyst's buy-sell recommendation is 3.1 on a scale of 1.0–5.0, indicating a hold recommendation, which we can infer to mean that K-C's stock price was fairly priced that day.

Residual Operating Income Valuation

Exhibit C.10 reports estimates of the values of Kimberly-Clark's equity and common stock per share using the residual operating income (ROPI) model. All of the assumptions remain the same as for the DCF model, above.

EXHIBIT C.10 Kimberly-Clark Residual Operating Income (ROPI) Valuation

(In millions, except per share values and discount factors)	2012	Horizon Period 2013	2014	2015	2016	Terminal Period
NOPAT		$2,097	$2,201	$2,312	$2,427	$2,451
NOA		11,342	11,909	12,504	13,129	13,261
ROPI (NOPAT − [$NOA_{Beg} \times r_w$])		1,470	1,543	1,621	1,702	1,690
Discount factor [$1/(1 + r_w)^t$]		0.94518	0.89336	0.84439	0.79810	
Present value of horizon ROPI		1,389	1,378	1,369	1,358	
Cum present value of horizon ROPI	$ 5,494					
Present value of terminal ROPI	28,100[a]					
NOA	10,809					
Total firm value	44,403					
Less: NNO	5,522					
Less: NCI	302					
Firm equity value	38,579					
Shares outstanding	389.30					
Stock value per share	$ 99.10	($0.05 difference from DCF due to rounding)				

[a] Computed as $\dfrac{\left(\dfrac{\$1{,}690 \text{ million}}{0.058 - 0.01}\right)}{(1.058)^4}$

Sensitivity Analysis of Valuation Parameters

We estimate Kimberly-Clark's equity value at $38,579 million as of December 2012, which implies a per share value estimate of $99.10. As expected, equity value estimates are identical (minor difference due to rounding) for both models (because K-C is assumed to be in a steady state, that is, NOPAT and NOA growing at the same rate and, therefore, RNOA is constant).

Our stock price estimate uses only one set of assumptions and derives only one stock price. We illustrate the sensitivity of our stock price estimate to changes in input assumptions for WACC and terminal growth rate in the following table. We can expand this sensitivity analysis to any assumption or estimate we use in our financial statement adjusting, forecasting, and valuing process.

		Terminal Growth Rate				
		0.0%	0.5%	1.0%	1.5%	2.0%
WACC	4.8%	$108.03	$117.88	$130.32	$146.59	$168.67
	5.3%	$95.86	$103.48	$112.86	$124.78	$140.30
	5.8%	$85.79	$91.80	$99.05	$108.04	$119.40
	6.3%	$77.33	$82.14	$87.85	$94.80	$103.37
	6.8%	$70.13	$74.03	$78.60	$84.07	$90.69

Assessment of the Valuation Estimate

The closing stock price on December 31, 2012, for Kimberly-Clark (KMB) was $84.43 per share. Our model's estimates, therefore, suggest that K-C stock is undervalued as of that date. As it turns out, this valuation proved prophetic as its stock price increased to the low $90s subsequent to that date as shown in the following graph:

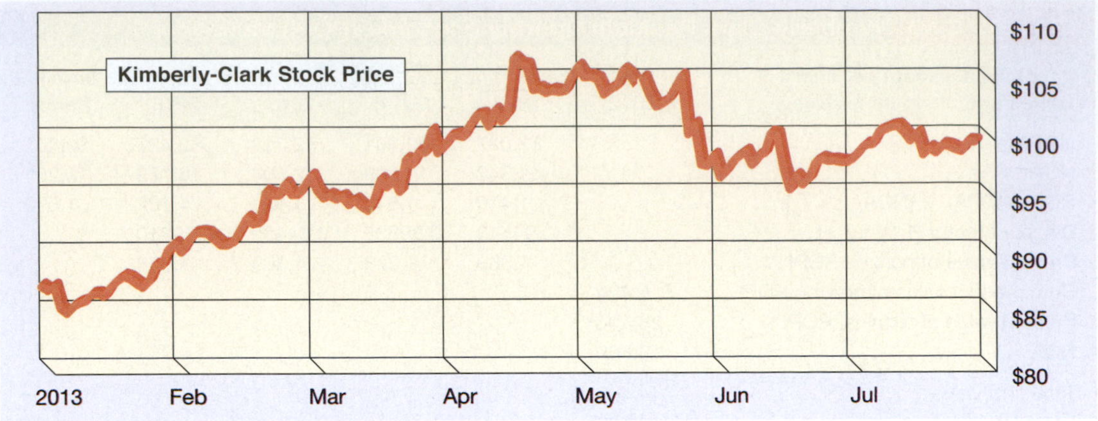

Summary Observations

Overall, this appendix presents a financial accounting analysis and interpretation of Kimberly-Clark's performance and position. It illustrates many of the key financial reporting topics covered in the book. We review the company's financial statements and notes, forecast key accounts, and conclude with estimates of K-C's equity value.

The Kimberly-Clark case provides an opportunity for us to apply many of the procedures conveyed in the book in a comprehensive manner. With analyses of additional companies, we become more comfortable with, and knowledgeable of, variations in financial reporting, which enhances our analysis and business decision-making skills. Our analysis of a company must go beyond the accounting numbers to include competitor and economic factors, and we must appreciate that estimation and judgment are key ingredients in financial accounting.

Appendix

D Chart of Accounts with Acronyms

Assets

Cash	Cash
MS	Marketable securities
AR	Accounts receivable
AU	Allowance for uncollectible accounts
INV	Inventory (or Inventories)
SUP	Supplies
PPD	Prepaid expenses
PPDA	Prepaid advertising
PPRNT	Prepaid rent
PPI	Prepaid insurance
PPE	Property, plant and equipment (PPE)
AD	Accumulated depreciation
INT	Intangible assets
DTA	Deferred tax assets
OA	Other assets
EMI	Equity method investments

Liabilities

NP	Notes payable
AP	Accounts payable
ACC	Accrued expenses
WP	Wages payable
SP	Salaries payable
RNTP	Rent payable
RSL	Restructuring liability
UP	Utilities payable
TP	Taxes payable
WRP	Warranty payable
IP	Interest payable
CMLTD	Current maturities of long-term debt
UR	Unearned (or deferred) revenues
DP	Dividends payable
LTD	Long-term debt
CLO	Capital lease obligations
DTL	Deferred tax liabilities
OL	Other liabilities

Equity

EC	Earned capital
CS	Common stock
APIC	Additional paid-in capital
RE	Retained earnings
DIV	Dividends
TS	Treasury stock
AOCI	Accumulated other comprehensive income
DC	Deferred compensation expense
NCI	Noncontrolling interest
EQ	Total stockholders' equity
CI	Equity attributable to controlling interest

Revenues and Expenses

Sales	Sales
REV	Revenues
COGS	Cost of goods sold (or Cost of sales)
OE	Operating expenses
WE	Wages expense
SE	Salaries expense
AE	Advertising expense
BDE	Bad debts expense
UTE	Utilities expense
DE	Depreciation expense
RDE	Research and development expense
RNTE	Rent expense
RSE	Restructuring expense
WRE	Warranty expense
AIE	Asset impairment expense
INSE	Insurance expense
SUPE	Supplies expense
GN (LS)	Gain (loss)–operating
TE	Tax expense
ONI (E)	Other nonoperating income (expense)
IE	Interest expense
UG (UL)	Unrealized gain (loss)
DI	Dividend income (or revenue)
EI	Equity income (or revenue)
GN (LS)	Gain (loss)–nonoperating

Closing Account

IS	Income summary

Glossary

A

accelerated cost recovery system (ACRS, MACRS) A system of accelerated depreciation for tax purposes introduced in 1981 (ACRS) and modified starting in 1987 (MACRS); it prescribes depreciation rates by asset classification for assets acquired after 1980

accelerated depreciation method Any depreciation method under which the amounts of depreciation expense taken in the early years of an asset's life are larger than the amounts expensed in the later years; includes the double-declining balance method

access control matrix A computerized file that lists the type of access that each computer user is entitled to have to each file and program in the computer system

account A record of the additions, deductions, and balances of individual assets, liabilities, equity, revenues, and expenses

accounting The process of measuring the economic activity of an entity in money terms and communicating the results to interested parties; the purpose is to provide financial information that is useful in making economic decisions

accounting adjustments (adjusting entries) Entries made at the end of an accounting period under accrual accounting to ensure the proper recording of expenses incurred and revenues earned for the period

accounting cycle A series of basic steps followed to process accounting information during a fiscal year

accounting entity An economic unit that has identifiable boundaries and that is the focus for the accumulation and reporting of financial information

accounting equation An expression of the equivalency of the economic resources and the claims upon those resources of a specific entity; often stated as Assets = Liabilities + Owners' Equity

accounting period The time period, typically one year (or quarter), for which periodic accounting reports are prepared

accounting system The structured collection of policies, procedures, equipment, files, and records that a company uses to collect, record, classify, process, store, report, and interpret financial data

accounts payable turnover The ratio obtained by dividing cost of goods sold by average accounts payable

accounts receivable A current asset that is created by a sale on a credit basis; it represents the amount owed the company by the customer

accounts receivable aging method A procedure that uses an aging schedule to determine the year-end balance needed in the allowance for uncollectible accounts

accounts receivable turnover Annual net sales divided by average accounts receivable (net)

accrual accounting Accounting procedures whereby revenues are recorded when they are earned and realized and expenses are recorded in the period in which they help to generate revenues

accruals Adjustments that reflect revenues earned but not received or recorded and expenses incurred but not paid or recorded

accrued expense An expense incurred but not yet paid; recognized with an accounting adjustment

accrued revenue Revenue earned but not yet billed or received; recognized with an accounting adjustment

accumulated depreciation The sum of all depreciation expense recorded to date; it is subtracted from the cost of the asset in order to derive the asset's net book value

accumulated other comprehensive income (AOCI) Current accumulation of all prior periods' other comprehensive income; *see* definition for *other comprehensive income*

adjusted trial balance A list of general ledger accounts and their balances taken after accounting adjustments have been made

adjusting The process of adjusting the historical financial statements prior to the projection of future results; also called recasting and reformulating

aging schedule An analysis that shows how long customers' accounts receivable balances have remained unpaid

allowance for uncollectible accounts A contra asset account with a normal credit balance shown on the balance sheet as a deduction from accounts receivable to reflect the expected realizable amount of accounts receivable

allowance method An accounting procedure whereby the amount of uncollectible accounts expense is estimated and recorded in the period in which the related credit sales occur

Altman's Z-score A predictor of potential bankruptcy based on multiple ratios

amortization The periodic writing off of an account balance to expense; similar to depreciation and usually refers to the periodic writing off of an intangible asset

annuity A pattern of cash flows in which equal amounts are spaced equally over a number of periods

articles of incorporation A document prepared by persons organizing a corporation in the United States that sets forth the structure and purpose of the corporation and specifics regarding the stock to be issued

articulation The linkage of financial statements within and across time

asset turnover Net income divided by average total assets

asset write-downs Adjustment of carrying value of assets down to their current fair value

assets The economic resources of an entity that are owned or controlled will provide future benefits and can be reliably measured

audit An examination of a company's financial statements by a firm of independent certified public accountants

audit report A report issued by independent auditors that includes the final version of the financial statements, accompanying notes, and the auditor's opinion on the financial statements

authorized stock The maximum number of shares in a class of stock that a corporation may issue

available-for-sale securities Investments in securities that management intends to hold for capital gains and dividend income; although it may sell them if the price is right

average cash conversion cycle Average collection period + average inventory days outstanding − average payable days outstanding

average collection period Determined by dividing accounts receivable by average daily sales, sometimes referred to as days sales outstanding or DSO

average inventory days outstanding (AIDO) An indication of how long, on average, inventories are on the shelves, computed as inventory divided by average daily cost of goods sold

B

balance sheet A financial statement showing an entity's assets, liabilities, and owners' equity at a specific date; sometimes called a statement of financial position

bearer One of the terms that may be used to designate the payee on a promissory note; means whoever holds the note

bond A long-term debt instrument that promises to pay interest periodically and a principal amount at maturity, usually issued by the borrower to a group of lenders; bonds may incorporate a wide variety of provisions relating to security for the debt involved, methods of paying the periodic interest, retirement provisions, and conversion options

book value The dollar amount carried in the accounts for a particular item; the book value of a depreciable asset is cost less accumulated depreciation; the book value of an entity is assets less liabilities

book value per share The dollar amount of net assets represented by one share of stock; computed by dividing the amount of stockholders' equity associated with a class of stock by the outstanding shares of that class of stock

borrows at a discount When the face amount of the note is reduced by a calculated cash discount to determine the cash proceeds

C

calendar year A fiscal year that ends on December 31

call provision A bond feature that allows the borrower to retire (call in) the bonds after a stated date

capital expenditures Expenditures that increase the book value of long-term assets; sometimes abbreviated as CAPEX

capital lease A lease that transfers to the lessee substantially all of the benefits and risks related to ownership of the property; the lessee records the leased property as an asset and establishes a liability for the lease obligation

capital markets Financing sources, which are formalized when companies issue securities that are traded on organized exchanges; they are informal when companies are funded by private sources

capitalization The recording of a cost as an asset on the balance sheet rather than as an expense on the income statement; these costs are transferred to expense as the asset is used up

capitalization of interest A process that adds interest to an asset's initial cost if a period of time is required to prepare the asset for use

cash An asset category representing the amount of a firm's available cash and funds on deposit at a bank in checking accounts and savings accounts

cash and cash equivalents The sum of cash plus short-term, highly liquid investments such as treasury bills and money market funds; includes marketable securities maturing within 90 days of the financial statement date

cash discount An amount that a purchaser of merchandise may deduct from the purchase price for paying within the discount period

cash-basis accounting Accounting procedures whereby revenues are recorded when cash is received and expenses are recorded when cash payments are made

cash (operating) conversion cycle The period of time (typically measured in days) from when cash is invested in inventories until inventory is sold and receivables are collected

certificate of deposit (CD) An investment security available at financial institutions generally offering a fixed rate of return for a specified period of time

change in accounting estimate Modification to a previous estimate of an uncertain future event, such as the useful life of a depreciable asset, uncollectible accounts receivable, and warranty expenses; applied currently and prospectively only

changes in accounting principles Modification of accounting methods (such as depreciation or inventory costing methods)

chart of accounts A list of all the general ledger account titles and their numerical code

clean surplus accounting Income that explains successive equity balances

closing procedures A step in the accounting cycle in which the balances of all temporary accounts are transferred to the retained earnings account, leaving the temporary accounts with zero balances

commitments A contractual arrangement by which both parties to the contract still have acts to perform

common stock The basic ownership class of corporate capital stock, carrying the rights to vote, share in earnings, participate in future stock issues, and share in any liquidation proceeds after prior claims have been settled

common-size financial statement A financial statement in which each item is presented as a percentage of a key figure such as sales or total assets

comparative financial statements A form of horizontal analysis involving comparison of two or more periods' financial statements showing dollar and/or percentage changes

compensating balance A minimum amount that a financial institution requires a firm to maintain in its account as part of a borrowing arrangement complex capital structure

comprehensive income The total change in stockholders' equity other than those arising from capital (stock) transactions; computed as net income plus other comprehensive income (OCI); typical OCI components are unrealized gains (losses) on available-for-sale securities and derivatives, minimum pension liability adjustment, and foreign currency translation adjustments

conceptual framework A cohesive set of interrelated objectives and fundamentals for external financial reporting developed by the FASB

conservatism An accounting principle stating that judgmental determinations should tend toward understatement rather than overstatement of net assets and income

consistency An accounting principle stating that, unless otherwise disclosed, accounting reports should be prepared on a basis consistent with the preceding period

consolidated financial statements Financial statements reflecting a parent company and one or more subsidiary companies and/or a variable interest entity (VIE) and its primary beneficiary

contingent liabilities A potential obligation, the eventual occurrence of which usually depends on some future event beyond the control of the firm; contingent liabilities may originate with such events as lawsuits, credit guarantees, and environmental damages

contra account An account related to, and deducted from, another account when financial statements are prepared or when book values are computed

contract rate The rate of interest stated on a bond certificate

contributed capital The net funding that a company receives from issuing and acquiring its equity shares

convertible bond A bond incorporating the holder's right to convert the bond to capital stock under prescribed terms

convertible securities Debt and equity securities that provide the holder with an option to convert those securities into other securities

copyright An exclusive right that protects an owner against the unauthorized reproduction of a specific written work or artwork

core income A company's income from its usual business activities that is expected to continue (persist) into the future

corporation A legal entity created by the granting of a charter from an appropriate governmental authority and owned by stockholders who have limited liability for corporate debt

cost of goods sold The total cost of merchandise sold to customers during the accounting period

cost of goods sold percentage The ratio of cost of goods sold divided by net sales

cost method An investment is reported at its historical cost, and any cash dividends and interest received are recognized in current income

cost principle An accounting principle stating that asset measures are based on the prices paid to acquire the assets

coupon bond A bond with coupons for interest payable to bearer attached to the bond for each interest period; whenever interest is due, the bondholder detaches a coupon and deposits it with his or her bank for collection

coupon (contract or stated) rate The coupon rate of interest is stated in the bond contract; it is used to compute the dollar amount of (semiannual) interest payments that are paid to bondholder during the life of the bond issue

covenants Contractual requirements put into loan or bond agreements by lenders

credit (entry) An entry on the right side (or in the credit column) of any account

credit card fee A fee charged retailers for credit card services provided by financial institutions; the fee is usually stated as a percentage of credit card sales

credit guarantee A guarantee of another company's debt by cosigning a note payable; a guarantor's contingent liability that is usually disclosed in a balance sheet footnote

credit memo A document prepared by a seller to inform the purchaser that the seller has reduced the amount owed by the purchaser due to a return or an allowance

credit period The maximum amount of time, usually stated in days, that the purchaser of merchandise has to pay the seller

credit rating An opinion formed by a credit-rating agency (such as Standard & Poor's, Moody's or Fitch) concerning the creditworthiness of a borrower (a corporation or a government) based on an assessment of the borrower's likelihood of default

credit terms The prescribed payment period for purchases on credit with discount specified for early payment

cumulative (preferred stock) A feature associated with preferred stock whereby any dividends in arrears must be paid before dividends may be paid on common stock

cumulative effect of a change in principle The cumulative effect on net income to the date of a change in accounting principle

cumulative translation adjustment The amount recorded in the equity section as necessary to balance the accounting equation when assets and liabilities of foreign subsidiaries are translated into $US at the rate of exchange prevailing at the statement date

current assets Cash and other assets that will be converted to cash or used up during the normal operating cycle of the business or one year, whichever is longer

current liabilities Obligations that will require within the coming year or operating cycle, whichever is longer, (1) the use of existing current assets or (2) the creation of other current liabilities

current rate method Method of translating foreign currency transactions under which balance sheet amounts are translated using exchange rates in effect at the period-end consolidation date and income statement amounts using the average exchange rate for the period

current ratio Current assets divided by current liabilities

D

days' sales in inventory Inventories divided by average cost of goods sold

debenture bond A bond that has no specific property pledged as security for the repayment of funds borrowed

debit (entry) An entry on the left side (or in the debit column) of any account

debt-to-equity ratio A firm's total liabilities divided by its total owners' equity

declining-balance method An accelerated depreciation method that allocates depreciation expense to each year by applying a constant percentage to the declining book value of the asset

default The nonpayment of interest and principal and/or the failure to adhere to the various terms and conditions of the bond indenture

deferrals Adjustments that allocate various assets and revenues received in advance to the proper accounting periods as expenses and revenues

deferred revenue A liability representing revenues received in advance; also called unearned revenue

deferred tax liability A liability representing the estimated future income taxes payable resulting from an existing temporary difference between an asset's book value and its tax basis

deferred tax valuation allowance Reduction in a reported deferred tax asset to adjust for the amount that is not likely to be realized

defined benefit plan A type of retirement plan under which the company promises to make periodic payments to the employee after retirement

defined contribution plan A retirement plan under which the company makes cash contribution into an employee's account (usually with a third-party trustee like a bank) either solely or as a matching contribution

depletion The allocation of the cost of natural resources to the units extracted and sold or, in the case of timberland, the board feet of timber cut

depreciation The decline in economic potential (using up) of plant assets originating from wear, deterioration, and obsolescence

depreciation accounting The process of allocating the cost of equipment, vehicles, and buildings (not land) to expense over the time period benefiting from their use

depreciation base The acquisition cost of an asset less estimated salvage value

depreciation rate An estimate of how the asset will be used up over its useful life—evenly over its useful life, more heavily in the early years, or in proportion to its actual usage

derivatives Financial instruments such as futures, options, and swaps that are commonly used to hedge (mitigate) some external risk, such as commodity price risk, interest rate risk, or risks relating to foreign currency fluctuations

diluted earnings per share The earnings per share computation taking into consideration the effects of dilutive securities

dilutive securities Securities that can be exchanged for shares of common stock and, thereby, increase the number of common shares outstanding

discontinued operations Net income or loss from business segments that are up for sale or have been sold in the current period

discount bond A bond that is sold for less than its par (face) value

discount on notes payable A contra account that is subtracted from the Notes Payable amount on the balance sheet; as the life of the note elapses, the discount is reduced and charged to interest expense

discount period The maximum amount of time, usually stated in days, that the purchaser of merchandise has to pay the seller if the purchaser wants to claim the cash discount

discounted cash flow (DCF) model The value of a security is equal to the present value of the expected free cash flows to the firm, discounted at the weighted average cost of capital (WACC)

discounting The exchanging of notes receivable for cash at a financial institution at an amount that is less than the face value of the notes

dividends account A temporary equity account used to accumulate owner dividends from the business

dividend discount model The value of a security today is equal to the present value of that security's expected dividends, discounted at the weighted average cost of capital

dividend payout ratio Annual dividends per share divided by the earnings per share or by net income

dividend yield Annual dividends per share divided by the market price per share

double-entry accounting system A method of accounting that recognizes the duality of a transaction such that the analysis results in a recording of equal amounts of debits and credits

E

earned When referring to revenue, the seller's execution of its duties under the terms of the agreement, with the resultant passing of title to the buyer with no right of return or other contingencies

earned capital The cumulative net income (losses) retained by the company (not paid out to shareholders as dividends)

earnings per share (EPS) Net income less preferred stock dividends divided by the weighted average common shares outstanding for the period

earnings quality The degree to which reported earnings represent how well the firm has performed from an economic standpoint

earnings smoothing Earnings management with a goal to provide an earnings stream with less variability

EBIT Earnings before interest and taxes

EBITDA Earnings before interest, taxes, depreciation and amortization

economic profit The number of inventory units sold multiplied by the difference between the sales price and the replacement cost of the inventories (approximated by the cost of the most recently purchased inventories)

economic value added (EVA) Net operating profits after tax less a charge for the use of capital equal to beginning capital utilized in the business multiplied by the weighted average cost of capital (EVA = NOPAT − [r_w × Net operating assets])

effective interest method A method of amortizing bond premium or discount that results in a constant rate of interest each period and varying amounts of premium or discount amortized each period

effective interest rate The rate determined by dividing the total discount amount by the cash proceeds on a note payable when the borrower borrowed at a discount

effective rate The current rate of interest in the market for a bond or other debt instrument; when issued, a bond is priced to yield the market (effective) rate of interest at the date of issuance

efficient markets hypothesis Capital markets are said to be efficient if at any given time, current equity (stock) prices reflect all relevant information that determines those equity prices

employee severance costs Accrued (estimated) costs for termination of employees as part of a restructuring program

employee stock options A form of compensation that grants a select group of employees the right to purchase a fixed number of company shares at a fixed price for a predetermined time period

equity carve out A corporate divestiture of operating units

equity method The prescribed method of accounting for investments in which the investor company has a significant influence over the investee company (usually taken to be ownership between 20-50% of the outstanding common stock of the investee company)

ethics An area of inquiry dealing with the values, rules, and justifications that governs one's way of life

executory contract A contract where a party has a material unperformed obligation that, if not performed, will result in a breach of contract

expenses Decreases in owners' equity incurred by a firm in the process of earning revenues

extraordinary items Revenues and expenses that are both unusual and infrequent and are, therefore, excluded from income from continuing operations

F

face amount The principal amount of a bond or note to be repaid at maturity

factoring Selling an account receivable to another company, typically a finance company or a financial institution, for less than its face value

fair value Value that an asset could be sold for (or an obligation discharged) in an orderly market, between willing buyers and sellers; often, but not always, is current market value

fair value method Method of accounting that records on the balance sheet, the asset or liabilities fair value, and records on the income statement, changes in the fair value

financial accounting The area of accounting activities dealing with the preparation of financial statements showing an entity's results of operations, financial position, and cash flows

Financial Accounting Standards Board (FASB) The organization currently responsible for setting accounting standards for reporting financial information by U.S. entities

financial assets Normally consist of excess resources held for future expansion or unexpected needs; they are usually invested in the form of other companies' stock, corporate or government bonds, and real estate

financial leverage The proportionate use of borrowed funds in the capital structure, computed as net nonoperating obligations (NNO) divided by average equity

financial reporting objectives A component of the conceptual framework that specifies that financial statements should provide information (1) useful for investment and credit decisions, (2) helpful in assessing an entity's ability to generate future cash flows, and (3) about an entity's resources, claims to those resources, and the effects of events causing changes in these items

financial statement elements A part of the conceptual framework that identifies the significant components—such as assets, liabilities, owners' equity, revenues, and expenses—used to put financial statements together

financing activities Methods that companies use to raise the funds to pay for resources such as land, buildings, and equipment

finished goods inventory The dollar amount of inventory that has completed the production process and is awaiting sale

first-in, first-out (FIFO) method One of the prescribed methods of inventory costing; FIFO assumes that the first costs incurred for the purchase or production of inventory are the first costs relieved from inventory when goods are sold

fiscal year The annual accounting period used by a business firm

five forces of competitive intensity Industry competition, bargaining power of buyers, bargaining power of suppliers, threat of substitution, threat of entry

fixed assets An alternate label for long-term assets; may also be called property, plant, and equipment (PPE)

fixed costs Costs that do not change with changes in sales volume (over a reasonable range)

forecast The projection of financial results over the forecast horizon and terminal periods

foreign currency transaction The $US equivalent of an asset or liability denominated in a foreign currency

foreign exchange gain or loss The gain (loss) recognized in the income statement relating to the change in the $US equivalent of an asset or liability denominated in a foreign currency

forward earnings Earnings expected to be reported in the next period

franchise Generally, an exclusive right to operate or sell a specific brand of products in a given geographic area

free cash flow This excess cash flow (above that required to manage its growth and development) from which dividends can be paid; computed as NOPAT − Increase in NOA

full disclosure principle An accounting principle stipulating the disclosure of all facts necessary to make financial statements useful to readers

fully diluted earnings per share *See* diluted earnings per share

functional currency The currency representing the primary currency in which a business unit conducts its operations

fundamental analysis Uses financial information to predict future valuation and, hence, buy-sell stock strategies

funded status The difference between the pension obligation and the fair value of the pension investments

future value The amount a specified investment (or series of investments) will be worth at a future date if invested at a given rate of compound interest

G

general journal A journal with enough flexibility so that any type of business transaction can be recorded in it

general ledger A grouping of all of an entity's accounts that are used to prepare the basic financial statements

generally accepted accounting principles (GAAP) A set of standards and procedures that guide the preparation of financial statements

going concern concept An accounting principle that assumes that, in the absence of evidence to the contrary, a business entity will have an indefinite life

goodwill The value that derives from a firm's ability to earn more than a normal rate of return on the fair market value of its specific, identifiable net assets; computed as the residual of the purchase price less the fair market value of the net tangible and intangible assets acquired

gross margin The difference between net sales and cost of goods sold; also called gross profit

gross profit on sales The difference between net sales and cost of goods sold; also called gross margin

gross profit margin (GPM) (percentage) The ratio of gross profit on sales divided by net sales

H

held-to-maturity securities The designation given to a portfolio of bond investments that are expected to be held until they mature

historical cost Original acquisition or issuance costs

holding company The parent company of a subsidiary

holding gain The increase in replacement cost since the inventories were acquired, which equals the number of units sold multiplied by the difference between the current replacement cost and the original acquisition cost

horizon period The forecast period for which detailed estimates are made, typically 5-10 years

horizontal analysis Analysis of a firm's financial statements that covers two or more years

I

IASB International Accounting Standards Board, independent, privately funded accounting standard-setter based in London, responsible for developing IFRS and promoting the use and application of these standards

IFRS International Financial Reporting Standards, a body of accounting standards developed by the International Accounting Standards Board and used for financial reports across much of the world

impairment A reduction in value from that presently recorded

impairment loss A loss recognized on an impaired asset equal to the difference between its book value and current fair value

income statement A financial statement reporting an entity's revenues and expenses for a period of time

indirect method A presentation format for the statement of cash flows that refers to the operating section only; that section begins with net income and converts it to cash flows from operations

intangible assets A term applied to a group of long-term assets, including patents, copyrights, franchises, trademarks, and goodwill, that benefit an entity but do not have physical substance

interest cost (pensions) The increase in the pension obligation due to the accrual of an additional year of interest

internal auditing A company function that provides independent appraisals of the company's financial statements, its internal controls, and its operations

internal controls The measures undertaken by a company to ensure the reliability of its accounting data, protect its assets from theft or unauthorized use, make sure that employees are following the company's policies and procedures, and evaluate the performance of employees, departments, divisions, and the company as a whole

inventory carrying costs Costs of holding inventories, including warehousing, logistics, insurance, financing, and the risk of loss due to theft, damage, or technological or fashion change

inventory shrinkage The cost associated with an inventory shortage; the amount by which the perpetual inventory exceeds the physical inventory

inventory turnover Cost of goods sold divided by average inventory

investing activities The acquiring and disposing of resources (assets) that a company uses to acquire and sell its products and services

investing creditors Those who primarily finance investing activities

investment returns The increase in pension investments resulting from interest, dividends, and capital gains on the investment portfolio

invoice A document that the seller sends to the purchaser to request payment for items that the seller shipped to the purchaser

invoice price The price that a seller charges the purchaser for merchandise

IOU A slang term for a receivable

IRS Internal Revenue Service, the U.S. taxing authority

issued stock Shares of stock that have been sold and issued to stockholders; issued stock may be either outstanding or in the treasury

J

journal A tabular record in which business transactions are analyzed in debit and credit terms and recorded in chronological order

just-in-time (JIT) inventory Receive inventory from suppliers into the production process just at the point it is needed

L

land improvements Improvements with limited lives made to land sites, such as paved parking lots and driveways

last-in, first-out (LIFO) method One of the prescribed methods of inventory costing; LIFO assumes that the last costs incurred for the purchase or production of inventory are the first costs relieved from inventory when goods are sold

lease A contract between a lessor (owner) and lessee (tenant) for the rental of property

leasehold The rights transferred from the lessor to the lessee by a lease

leasehold improvements Expenditures made by a lessee to alter or improve leased property

lessee The party acquiring the right to the use of property by a lease

lessor The owner of property who transfers the right to use the property to another party by a lease

leveraging The use of borrowed funds in the capital structure of a firm; the expectation is that the funds will earn a return higher than the rate of interest on the borrowed funds

liabilities The obligations, or debts, that an entity must pay in money or services at some time in the future because of past transactions or events

LIFO conformity rule IRS requirement to cost inventories using LIFO for tax purposes if they are costed using LIFO for financial reporting purposes

LIFO liquidation The reduction in inventory quantities when LIFO costing is used; LIFO liquidation yields an increase in gross profit and income when prices are rising

LIFO reserve The difference between the cost of inventories using FIFO and the cost using LIFO

liquidation value per share The amount that would be received by a holder of a share of stock if the corporation liquidated

liquidity How much cash the company has, how much is expected, and how much can be raised on short notice

list price The suggested price or reference price of merchandise in a catalog or price list

long-term liabilities Debt obligations not due to be settled within the normal operating cycle or one year, whichever is longer

lower of cost or market (LCM) GAAP requirement to write down the carrying amount of inventories on the balance sheet if the reported cost (using FIFO, for example) exceeds market value (determined by current replacement cost)

M

maker The signer of a promissory note

management discussion and anaysis (MD&A) The section of the 10-K report in which a company provides a detailed discussion of its business activities

managerial accounting The accounting activities carried out by a firm's accounting staff primarily to furnish management with accounting data for decisions related to the firm's operations

manufacturers Companies that convert raw materials and components into finished products through the application of skilled labor and machine operations

manufacturing costs The costs of direct materials, direct labor, and manufacturing overhead incurred in the manufacture of a product

market cap Market capitalization of the firm, or value as perceived by investors; computed as market value per share multiplied by shares outstanding

market (yield) rate This is the interest rate that investors expect to earn on the investment in this debt security; this rate is used to price the bond issue

market value The published price (as listed on a stock exchange)

market value per share The current price at which shares of stock may be bought or sold

matching principle An accounting guideline that states that income is determined by relating expenses, to the extent feasible, with revenues that have been recorded

materiality An accounting guideline that states that transactions so insignificant that they would not affect a user's actions or perception of the company may be recorded in the most expedient manner

materials inventory The physical component of inventory; the other components of manufactured inventory are labor costs and overhead costs

maturity date The date on which a note or bond matures

measuring unit concept An accounting guideline noting that the accounting unit of measure is the basic unit of money

merchandise inventory A stock of products that a company buys from another company and makes available for sale to its customers

merchandising firm A company that buys finished products, stores the products for varying periods of time, and then resells the products

method of comparables model Equity valuation or stock values are predicted using price multiples, which are defined as stock price divided by some key financial statement number such as net income, net sales, book value of equity, total assets, or cash flow; companies are then compared with their competitors

minority interest *See* noncontrolling interest

modified accelerated cost recovery system (MACRS) *See* accelerated cost recovery system

multiple element arrangements Sales (revenue) arrangements containing multiple deliverables and, in some cases, multiple cash-flow streams

N

natural resources Assets occurring in a natural state, such as timber, petroleum, natural gas, coal, and other mineral deposits

net asset based valuation model Equity is valued as reported assets less reported liabilities

net assets The difference between an entity's assets and liabilities; net assets are equal to owners' equity

net book value (NBV) The cost of the asset less accumulated depreciation; also called carrying value

net income The excess of a firm's revenues over its expenses

net loss The excess of a firm's expenses over its revenues

net nonoperating expense (NNE) Nonoperating expenses and losses (plus any net income attributable to noncontrolling interest) less nonoperating revenues and gains, all measured after-tax

net nonoperating expense percentage (NNEP) Net nonoperating expense divided by net nonoperating obligations (NNO)

net nonoperating obligations (NNO) All nonoperating obligations (plus any noncontrolling interest) less nonoperating assets

net operating asset turnover (NOAT) Ratio obtained by dividing sales by net operating assets

net operating assets (NOA) Current and long-term operating assets less current and long-term operating liabilities; or net operating working capital plus long-term net operating assets

net operating profit after tax (NOPAT) Operating revenues less operating expenses (including taxes)

net operating profit margin (NOPM) Ratio obtained by dividing net operating profit after tax (NOPAT) by sales

net operating working capital (NOWC) Current operating assets less current operating liabilities

net realizable value The value at which an asset can be sold, net of any costs of disposition

net sales The total revenue generated by a company through merchandise sales less the revenue given up through sales returns and allowances and sales discounts

net working capital Current assets less current liabilities

nominal rate The rate of interest stated on a bond certificate or other debt instrument

noncash investing and financing activities Significant business activities during the period that do not impact cash inflows or cash outflows

noncontrolling interest The portion of equity (net assets) in a subsidiary not attributable, directly or indirectly, to a parent. A noncontrolling interest (formerly called minority interest) typically represents the ownership interest of shareholders other than those of the parent company.

noncurrent liabilities Obligations not due to be paid within one year or the operating cycle, whichever is longer

nonoperating expenses Expenses that relate to the company's financing activities and include interest income and interest expense, gains and losses on sales of securities, and income or loss on discontinued operations

no-par stock Stock that does not have a par value

NOPAT Net operating profit after tax

normal operating cycle For a particular business, the average period of time between the use of cash in its typical operating activity and the subsequent collection of cash from customers

note receivable A promissory note held by the note's payee

notes to financial statements Footnotes in which companies discuss their accounting policies and estimates used in preparing the statements

not-sufficient-funds check A check from an individual or company that had an insufficient cash balance in the bank when the holder of the check presented it to the bank for payment

O

objectivity principle An accounting principle requiring that, whenever possible, accounting entries are based on objectively determined evidence

off-balance-sheet financing The structuring of a financing arrangement so that no liability shows on the borrower's balance sheet

operating activities Using resources to research, develop, produce, purchase, market, and distribute company products and services

operating cash flow to capital expenditures ratio A firm's net cash flow from operating activities divided by its annual capital expenditures

operating cash flow to current liabilities ratio A firm's net cash flow from operating activities divided by its average current liabilities

operating creditors Those who primarily finance operating activities

operating cycle The time between paying cash for goods or employee services and receiving cash from customers

operating expense margin (OEM) The ratio obtained by dividing any operating expense category by sales

operating expenses The usual and customary costs that a company incurs to support its main business activities; these include cost of goods sold, selling expenses, depreciation expense, amortization expense, research and development expense, and taxes on operating profits

operating lease A lease by which the lessor retains the usual risks and rewards of owning the property

operating profit margin The ratio obtained by dividing NOPAT by sales

operational audit An evaluation of activities, systems, and internal controls within a company to determine their efficiency, effectiveness, and economy

organization costs Expenditures incurred in launching a business (usually a corporation), including attorney's fees and various fees paid to the state

other comprehensive income (OCI) Current period change in stockholders' equity *other than* those arising from capital (stock) transactions and those included in net income; typical OCI components are unrealized gains (losses) on available-for-sale securities and derivatives, minimum pension liability adjustment, and foreign currency translation adjustments

outstanding checks Checks issued by a firm that have not yet been presented to its bank for payment

outstanding stock Shares of stock that are currently owned by stockholders (excludes treasury stock)

owners' equity The interest of owners in the assets of an entity; equal to the difference between the entity's assets and liabilities

P

packing list A document that lists the items of merchandise contained in a carton and the quantity of each item; the packing list is usually attached to the outside of the carton

paid-in capital The amount of capital contributed to a corporation by various transactions; the primary source of paid-in capital is from the issuance of shares of stock

par (bonds) Face value of the bond

par value (stock) An amount specified in the corporate charter for each share of stock and imprinted on the face of each stock certificate, often determines the legal capital of the corporation

parent company A company owning one or more subsidiary companies

parsimonious method to multiyear forecasting Forecasting multiple years using only sales growth, net operating profit margin (NOPM), and the turnover of net operating assets (NOAT)

partnership A voluntary association of two or more persons for the purpose of conducting a business

password A string of characters that a computer user enters into a computer terminal to prove to the computer that the person using the computer is truly the person named in the user identification code

patent An exclusive privilege granted for 20 years to an inventor that gives the patent holder the right to exclude others from making, using, or selling the invention

payee The company or individual to whom a promissory note is made payable

payment approval form A document that authorizes the payment of an invoice

pension plan A plan to pay benefits to employees after they retire from the company; the plan may be a defined contribution plan or a defined benefit plan

percentage-of-completion method Recognition of revenue by determining the costs incurred per the contract as compared to its total expected costs

percentage of net sales method A procedure that determines the uncollectible accounts expense for the year by multiplying net credit sales by the estimated uncollectible percentage

performance obligation A promise in a contract with a customer to transfer a good or service to the customer; includes promises that are implied by business practices, published policies, or explicit statements if those promises create an expectation of the customer that the entity will perform

period statement A financial statement accumulating information for a specific period of time; examples are the income statement, the statement of owners' equity, and the statement of cash flows

permanent account An account used to prepare the balance sheet; that is, asset, liability, and equity capital (capital stock and retained earnings) accounts; any balance in a permanent account at the end of an accounting period is carried forward to the next period

physical inventory A year-end procedure that involves counting the quantity of each inventory item, determining the unit cost of each item, multiplying the unit cost times quantity, and summing the costs of all the items to determine the total inventory at cost

plant assets Land, buildings, equipment, vehicles, furniture, and fixtures that a firm uses in its operations; sometimes referred to by the acronym PPE

pooling of interests method A method of accounting for business combinations under which the acquired company is recorded on the acquirer's balance sheet at its book value, rather than market value; this method is no longer acceptable under GAAP for acquisitions occurring after 2001

position statement A financial statement, such as the balance sheet, that presents information as of a particular date

post-closing trial balance A list of general ledger accounts and their balances after closing entries have been recorded and posted

postdated check A check from another person or company with a date that is later than the current date; a postdated check does not become cash until the date of the check

preemptive right The right of a stockholder to maintain his or her proportionate interest in a corporation by having the right to purchase an appropriate share of any new stock issue

preferred stock A class of corporate capital stock typically receiving priority over common stock in dividend payments and distribution of assets should the corporation be liquidated

premium bond A bond that is sold for more than its par (face) value

present value The current worth of amounts to be paid (or received) in the future; computed by discounting the future payments (or receipts) at a specified interest rate

price-earnings ratio Current market price per common share divided by earnings per share

pro forma income A computation of income that begins with the GAAP income from continuing operations (that excludes discontinued operations, extraordinary items and changes in accounting principle), but then excludes other transitory items (most notably, restructuring charges), and some additional items such as expenses arising from acquisitions (goodwill amortization and other acquisition costs), compensation expense in the form of stock options, and research and development expenditures; pro forma income is not GAAP

promissory note A written promise to pay a certain sum of money on demand or at a determinable future time

purchase method The prescribed method of accounting for business combinations; under the purchase method, assets and liabilities of the acquired company are recorded at fair market value, together with identifiable intangible assets; the balance is ascribed to goodwill

purchase order A document that formally requests a supplier to sell and deliver specific quantities of particular items of merchandise at specified prices

purchase requisition An internal document that requests that the purchasing department order particular items of merchandise

Q

qualitative characteristics of accounting information The characteristics of accounting information that contribute to decision usefulness; the primary qualities are relevance and reliability

quarterly data Selected quarterly financial information that is reported in annual reports to stockholders

quick ratio Quick assets (that is, cash and cash equivalents, short-term investments, and current receivables) divided by current liabilities

R

realized (or realizable) When referring to revenue, the receipt of an asset or satisfaction of a liability or performance obligation as a result of a transaction or event

recognition criteria The criteria that must be met before a financial statement element may be recorded in the accounts; essentially, the item must meet the definition of an element and must be measurable

registered bond A bond for which the issuer (or the trustee) maintains a record of owners and, at the appropriate times, mails out interest payments

relevance A qualitative characteristic of accounting information; relevant information contributes to the predictive and evaluative decisions made by financial statement users

reliability A qualitative characteristic of accounting information; reliable information contains no bias or error and faithfully portrays what it intends to represent

remeasurement The computation of gain or loss in the translation of subsidiaries denominated in a foreign currency into $US when the temporal method is used

residual operating income Net operating profits after tax (NOPAT) less the product of net operating assets (NOA) at the beginning of the period multiplied by the weighted average cost of capital (WACC)

residual operating income (ROPI) model An equity valuation approach that equates the firm's value to the sum of its net operating assets (NOA) and the present value of its residual operating income (ROPI)

retailers Companies that buy products from wholesale distributors and sell the products to individual customers, the general public

retained earnings Earned capital, the cumulative net income and loss, of the company (from its inception) that has not been paid to shareholders as dividends

retained earnings reconciliation The reconciliation of retained earnings from the beginning to the end of the year; the change in retained earnings includes, at a minimum, the net income (loss) for the period and dividends paid, if any, but may include other components as well; also called statement of retained earnings

return The amount earned on an investment; also called yield

return on assets (ROA) A financial ratio computed as net income divided by average total assets

return on common stockholders' equity (ROCE) A financial ratio computed as net income less preferred stock dividends divided by average common stockholders' equity

return on equity (ROE) The ultimate measure of performance from the shareholders' perspective; computed as net income divided by average equity

return on investment The ratio obtained by dividing income by average investment; sometimes referred to by the acronym ROI

return on net operating assets (RNOA) The ratio obtained by dividing NOPAT by average net operating assets

return on sales (ROS) The ratio obtained by dividing net income by net sales

revenue recognition principle An accounting principle requiring that revenue be recognized when earned and realized (or realizable)

revenues Increases in owners' equity a firm earns by providing goods or services for its customers

S

sale on account A sale of merchandise made on a credit basis

salvage value The expected net recovery when a plant asset is sold or removed from service; also called residual value

secured bond A bond that pledges specific property as security for meeting the terms of the bond agreement

Securities and Exchange Commission (SEC) The commission, created by the 1934 Securities Act, that has broad powers to regulate the issuance and trading of securities, and the financial reporting of companies issuing securities to the public

segments Subdivisions of a firm for which supplemental financial information is disclosed

serial bond A bond issue that staggers the bond maturity dates over a series of years

service cost (pensions) The increase in the pension obligation due to employees working another year for the employer

share-based payment Payment for a good or service using the entity's equity securities; an example is restricted stock used to compensate employees

significant influence The ability of the investor to affect the financing or operating policies of the investee

sinking fund provision A bond feature that requires the borrower to retire a portion of the bonds each year or, in some cases, to make payments each year to a trustee who is responsible for managing the resources needed to retire the bonds at maturity

solvency The ability to meet obligations, especially to creditors

source document Any written document or computer record evidencing an accounting transaction, such as a bank check or deposit slip, sales invoice, or cash register tape

special purpose entity *See* variable interest entity

spin-off A form of equity carve out in which divestiture is accomplished by distribution of a company's shares in a subsidiary to the company's shareholders who then own the shares in the subsidiary directly rather than through the parent company

split-off A form of equity carve out in which divestiture is accomplished by the parent company's exchange of stock in the subsidiary in return for shares in the parent owned by its shareholders

spread The difference between the return on net operating activities (RNOA) and the net nonoperating expense percentage (NNEP)

stated value A nominal amount that may be assigned to each share of no-par stock and accounted for much as if it were a par value

statement of cash flows A financial statement showing a firm's cash inflows and outflows for a specific period, classified into operating, investing, and financing categories

statement of equity *See* statement of stockholders' equity

statement of financial position A financial statement showing a firm's assets, liabilities, and owners' equity at a specific date; also called a balance sheet

statement of owners' equity A financial statement presenting information on the events causing a change in owners' equity during a period; the statement presents the beginning balance, additions to, deductions from, and the ending balance of owners' equity for the period

statement of retained earnings *See* retained earnings reconciliation

statement of stockholders' equity The financial statement that reconciles all of the components of stockholders' equity

stock dividends The payment of dividends in shares of stock

stock split Additional shares of its own stock issued by a corporation to its current stockholders in proportion to their current ownership interests without changing the balances in the related stockholders' equity accounts; a formal stock split increases the number of shares outstanding and reduces proportionately the stock's per share par value

straight-line depreciation A depreciation procedure that allocates uniform amounts of depreciation expense to each full period of a depreciable asset's useful life

subsequent events Events occurring shortly after a fiscal year-end that will be reported as supplemental information to the financial statements of the year just ended

subsidiaries Companies that are owned by the parent company

subsidiary ledger A set of accounts or records that contains detailed information about the items included in the balance of one general ledger account

summary of significant accounting policies A financial statement disclosure, usually the initial note to the statements, which identifies the major accounting policies and procedures used by the firm

sum-of-the-years'-digits method An accelerated depreciation method that allocates depreciation expense to each year in a fractional proportion, the denominator of which is the sum of the years' digits in the useful life of the asset and the numerator of which is the remaining useful life of the asset at the beginning of the current depreciation period

T

T account An abbreviated form of the formal account in the shape of a T; use is usually limited to illustrations of accounting techniques and analysis

temporary account An account used to gather information for an accounting period; at the end of the period, the balance is transferred to a permanent owners' equity account; revenue, expense, and dividends accounts are temporary accounts

term loan A long-term borrowing, evidenced by a note payable, which is contracted with a single lender

terminal period The forecast period following the horizon period

times interest earned ratio Income before interest expense and income taxes divided by interest expense

total compensation cost The sum of gross pay, payroll taxes, and fringe benefits paid by the employer

trade credit Inventories purchased on credit from other companies

trade discount An amount, usually based on quantity of merchandise purchased, that the seller subtracts from the list price of merchandise to determine the invoice price

trade name An exclusive and continuing right to use a certain term or name to identify a brand or family of products

trade receivables Another name for accounts receivable from customers

trademark An exclusive and continuing right to use a certain symbol to identify a brand or family of products

trading on the equity The use of borrowed funds in the capital structure of a firm; the expectation is that the funds will earn a return higher than the rate of interest on the borrowed funds

trading securities Investments in securities that management intends to actively trade (buy and sell) for trading profits as market prices fluctuate

trailing earnings Earnings reported in the prior period

transitory items Transactions or events that are not likely to recur

translation adjustment The change in the value of the net assets of a subsidiary whose assets and liabilities are denominated in a foreign currency

treasury stock Shares of outstanding stock that have been acquired (and not retired) by the issuing corporation; treasury stock is recorded at cost and deducted from stockholders' equity in the balance sheet

trend percentages A comparison of the same financial item over two or more years stated as a percentage of a base-year amount

trial balance A list of the account titles in the general ledger, their respective debit or credit balances, and the totals of the debit and credit amounts

U

unadjusted trial balance A list of general ledger accounts and their balances taken before accounting adjustments have been made

uncollectible accounts expense The expense stemming from the inability of a business to collect an amount previously recorded as a receivable; sometimes called bad debts expense; normally classified as a selling or administrative expense

unearned revenue A liability representing revenues received in advance; also called deferred revenue

units-of-production method A depreciation method that allocates depreciation expense to each operating period in proportion to the amount of the asset's expected total production capacity used each period

useful life The period of time an asset is used by an entity in its operating activities, running from date of acquisition to date of disposal (or removal from service)

V

variable costs Those costs that change in proportion to changes in sales volume

variable interest entity (VIE) Any form of business organization (such as corporation, partnership, trust) that is established by a sponsoring company and provides benefits to that company in the form of asset securitization or project financing; VIEs were formerly known as special purpose entities (SPEs)

vertical analysis Analysis of a firm's financial statements that focuses on the statements of a single year

voucher Another name for the payment approval form

W

warranties Guarantees against product defects for a designated period of time after sale

wasting assets Another name for natural resources; *see* natural resources

weighted average cost of capital (WACC) The discount rate where the weights are the relative percentages of debt and equity in the capital structure and are applied to the expected returns on debt and equity respectively

work in process inventory The cost of inventories that are in the manufacturing process and have not yet reached completion

working capital The difference between current assets and current liabilities

Z

z-score The outcome of the Altman Z-score bankruptcy prediction model

zero coupon bond A bond that offers no periodic interest payments but that is issued at a substantial discount from its face value

Index

Note: The letter "e" refers to an exhibit on the stated page, and the letter "n" indicates that the information is included in a footnote on the given page. For example, 15n7 means footnote 7 on page 15.

G

H

I

J

K

L

M

N

O

P

Q

R

S